Lecture Notes in Computer Science 2690

Edited by G. Goos, J. Hartmanis, and J. van Leeuwen

Springer-Verlag Berlin Heidelberg GmbH

Jiming Liu   Yiuming Cheung
Hujun Yin (Eds.)

Intelligent
Data Engineering and
Automated Learning

4th International Conference, IDEAL 2003
Hong Kong, China, March 21-23, 2003
Revised Papers

 Springer

Series Editors

Gerhard Goos, Karlsruhe University, Germany
Juris Hartmanis, Cornell University, NY, USA
Jan van Leeuwen, Utrecht University, The Netherlands

Volume Editors

Jiming Liu
Yiuming Cheung
Hong Kong Baptist University
Department of Computer Science
7/F, Sir Run Run Shaw Building, Hong Kong
E-mail: {jiming/ymc}@comp.hkbu.edu.hk

Hujun Yin
University of Manchester Institute of Science and Technology
Department of Electrical Engineering and Electronics
Manchester, M60 1QD, UK
E-mail: H.Yin@umist.ac.uk

Cataloging-in-Publication Data applied for

A catalog record for this book is available from the Library of Congress.

Bibliographic information published by Die Deutsche Bibliothek
Die Deutsche Bibliothek lists this publication in the Deutsche Nationalbibliografie;
detailed bibliographic data is available in the Internet at <http://dnb.ddb.de>.

CR Subject Classification (1998): H.2.8, F.2.2, I.2, F.4, K.4.4, H.3, H.4

ISSN 0302-9743
ISBN 978-3-540-40550-4   ISBN 978-3-540-45080-1 (eBook)
DOI 10.1007/978-3-540-45080-1

http://www.springer.de

© Springer-Verlag Berlin Heidelberg, 2003
Originally published by Springer-Verlag Berlin Heidelberg New York in 2003

Printed on acid-free paper   SPIN: 10927861   06/3142   5 4 3 2 1 0

Preface

Intelligent Data Engineering and Automated Learning (IDEAL) was initially a biennial forum dedicated to emerging and challenging topics in intelligent data analysis, knowledge discovery, and statistical and computational learning. The huge success of recent IDEAL conferences and the continuous growth of the field have compelled it to become an annual conference after 2003. It is now a major international, interdisciplinary event covering subjects from data mining, information retrieval and management, autonomous learning, and agents to financial engineering, neural networks, emerging learning paradigms and systems, bioinformatics, and pattern recognition. Data analysis and processing has become a common theme and plays a crucial role in many disciplines, especially in finance, biology, engineering, and information technology. Demand for intelligent methodologies and tools is immense. The multidisciplinary nature of current research is pushing the traditional boundaries and bringing new ideas and solutions, and it is the way forward.

This volume contains 164 refereed and finally accepted papers presented at the 4th International Conference on Intelligent Data Engineering and Automated Learning (IDEAL 2003), held in Hong Kong, March 21–23, 2003. IDEAL 2003 received a record level of submissions, 321 in total, from all over the world. They were subsequently peer-reviewed by the Program Committee. The conference was held together with the 2003 IEEE International Conference on Computational Intelligence for Financial Engineering at the modern and magnificent Hong Kong Convention and Exhibition Centre. Both conferences shared their technical sessions and stimulating discussions, and attendees enjoyed the tutorials given by leading experts, Amir Atiya, John Moody and Halbert White, and the keynote talks by distinguished guest speakers, Yaser Abu-Mostafa, Tim Bollerslev, Michael Dempster, and Stephen Figlewski.

We would like to thank the International Advisory Committee and the Steering Committee for their guidance and advice. We would also like to thank the Program Committee members for their rigorous and efficient reviewing of the contributed papers, and the Organizing Committee for their enormous efforts and excellent work. In addition, we are especially grateful to Hong Kong Baptist University, IEEE Neural Networks Society, and Springer-Verlag for their support and continued collaborations.

April 2003

Jiming Liu
Yiu-ming Cheung
Hong Kong Baptist University, Hong Kong

Hujun Yin
University of Manchester, Institute of Science and Technology, UK

Organization

IDEAL 2003 was sponsored by Hong Kong Baptist University (HKBU), and organized by the Computer Science Department of HKBU.

IDEAL Advisory Committee

Lei Xu (Chair)	CUHK (Chinese University of Hong Kong), Hong Kong
Yaser Abu-Mostafa	Caltech, USA
Shun-ichi Amari	RIKEN, Japan
Michael Dempster	Cambridge, UK
Lalit M. Patnaik	IIS, India
Erkki Oja	Helsinki University, Finland

IDEAL Steering Committee

Lai-wan Chan (Chair)	Hong Kong
Hujun Yin (Co-chair)	UK
Nigel Allinson	UK
Yiu-ming Cheung	Hong Kong
Marc M. Van Hulle	Belgium
John Keane	UK
Jimmy Lee	Hong Kong
Malik Magdon-Ismail	USA
Ning Zhong	Japan

IDEAL 2003 Organization

General Co-chairs

Nigel Allinson	UK
Lai-wan Chan	Hong Kong
Tao Tang	Hong Kong

Program Committee

Jiming Liu (Chair)(Hong Kong)
Hujun Yin (Co-chair)(UK)
Sherlock Au (Hong Kong)
Jim Austin (UK)

Keith Chan (Hong Kong)
Lai-wan Chan (Hong Kong)
Ming-Syan Chen (Taiwan)
Yiu-ming Cheung (Hong Kong)

Sungzoon Cho (Korea)
Carlos Coello (Mexico)
David Corne (UK)
Kalyanmoy Deb (USA)
Colin Fyfe (UK)
Ling Feng (The Netherlands)
Joydeep Ghosh (USA)
Howard Hamilton (Canada)
Markus Hegland (Australia)
Charlotte Hemelrijk (Switzerland)
Howard Ho (USA)
Joshua Zhexue Huang (Hong Kong)
Marc M. Van Hulle (Belgium)
Tony Holden (UK)
Xiaolong Jin (Hong Kong)
Hiroyuki Kawano (Japan)
Samuel Kaski (Finland)
John Keane (UK)
Martin Kersten (The Netherlands)
Irwin King (Hong Kong)
Kevin B. Korb (Australia)
Doheon Lee (Korea)
Jimmy Lee (Hong Kong)
Loo Hay Lee (Singapore)
Hong Va Leong (Hong Kong)
Bing Liu (Singapore)
Huan Liu (USA)
Malik Magdon-Ismail (USA)

Luc Moreau (UK)
Akira Namatame (Japan)
Michael Ng (Hong Kong)
Ichiro Nishizaki (Japan)
Omers F. Rana (UK)
V.J. Rayward-Smith (UK)
Guenter Rudolph (Germany)
Marc Schoenauer (France)
Bernhard Sendhoff (Germany)
Kyuseok Shim (Korea)
Jennie Si (USA)
Il-Yeol Song (USA)
Hideyuki Takagi (Japan)
Atsuhiro Takasu (Japan)
Ah-Hwee Tan (Singapore)
Bhavani Thuraisingham (USA)
Kwok-ching Tsui (Hong Kong)
Ke Wang (Canada)
Lipo Wang (Singapore)
Xin Yao (UK)
Ikuo Yoshihara (Japan)
Clement Yu (USA)
Jeffrey Yu (Hong Kong)
Mohammed Zaki (USA)
Ali M.S. Zalzala (UK)
Byoung-Tak Zhang (Korea)
Frank Wang (UK)

Organizing Committee

Yiu-Ming Cheung (Chair)	Hong Kong
Sherlock Au	Hong Kong
Man-Chung Chan	Hong Kong
Rongbo Huang	China
Xiaolong Jin	Hong Kong
Lap-Tak Law	Hong Kong
Kwok-Ching Tsui	Hong Kong
Kelvin Ka-Kui Wan	Hong Kong
Kelvin CK Wong	Hong Kong

Table of Contents

Agents

Automated Learning

Bioinformatics

Data Mining

Financial Engineering

Multimedia Information

A Two-Stage Bayesian Network for Effective Development of Conversational Agent

Jin-Hyuk Hong and Sung-Bae Cho

Dept. of Computer Science, Yonsei University,
134 Shinchon-dong, Sudaemoon-ku, Seoul 120-749, Korea
hjinh@candy.yonsei.ac.kr, sbcho@cs.yonsei.ac.kr

Abstract. Conversational agent is a system that provides user with proper information and maintains the context of dialogue based on natural language. When experts design the network for conversational agent of a domain, the network is usually very complicated and is hard to be understood. So the simplification of network by separating variables in the domain is helpful to design the conversational agent more efficiently. Composing Bayesian network as two stages, we aim to design conversational agent easily and analyze user's query in detail. Also, by using previous information of dialogue, it is possible to maintain the context of conversation. Actually implementing it for a guide of web pages, we can confirm the usefulness of the proposed architecture for conversational agent.

1 Introduction

In the age of information, we need to learn a way for finding proper information. Since information providers do not supply a common method or protocol, users cannot help learning several ways [1]. In many publications, it is well known that dialogue is very useful to exchange information and to understand speaker's intention [2]. Conversational agent provides a familiar interface as it does not use keywords or menu but uses natural language dialogue [3]. In order to interpret user's query, conversational agent has to analyze and infer user's intention. There are various techniques for it, and Bayesian network is distinguished one among them [4,5].

If the design of application domain is complex and many variables are mixed in it, inference of user's intention becomes very difficult. It is because designing the network for conversational agent is very complicated in those domains. In this paper, we propose an architecture of conversational agent using Bayesian network in two stages, with which the design of domain is easier than conventional methods and it is possible to infer user's intention in more detail.

2 Conversational Agent

Conversational agent is a system that exchanges information between user and agent using natural language dialogue [6,7]. It understands user's intention through conversation and helps user by executing an appropriate action [4,8]. Contrary to conventional ways based on menu and keyword, dialogue which is a medium of interaction between human and computer makes it possible to interact more naturally and to include more complicated information than a usual keyword [2]. Therefore

J. Liu et al. (Eds.): IDEAL 2003, LNCS 2690, pp. 1–9, 2003.

conversational agent can be an effective user interface in complex system [3]. Table 1 shows the technologies for developing analysis component of conversational agent.

Table 1. Technologies used in designing analysis component

Technology	Example Task	Task Complexity	
Simple pattern matching	Web search engine	Simple query answering	Easy
Canned script-based model	Game	Simple answer selection	
Finite state model	Long-distance dialing	Restrict flexibility based on changing state	⇕
Frame-based model	Train reservation	Information collection based on simple pattern matching	
Plan-based model	Kitchen design consultant	Dynamic topic changing	Hard

Most approaches except plan-based model are general to design conversational agent. They are designed based on simple conversation, so it can be done without much difficulty. For simple task, they are very simple and work well enough because they are based on static process which predefines all possible types and matches one of them. But they do not manage more realistic conversation, such as dynamic topic changing or proceeding dialogue to solve some problems. Sometimes they are easy to make dialogue needlessly long and to repeat same sentence. Also the size of database increases to analyze a complicated query, and information is apt to be duplicated unnecessarily, thereby the performance of the system decreases rapidly if the domain becomes more complex.

Plan-based model is different from previous approaches in considering user's plan and deciding actions to achieve it. Every time partial information is gathered from each queries, and agent predicts user's intention gradually. So it needs dynamic process to deal with it, and it keeps up dialogue until it collects enough information. Plan-based model usually gets better performance than previous approaches, but it costs too much to implement and maintain the system.

With these techniques, conversational agent has been implemented as a guider for web pages [6] and program [4], buying commodity [3], touring [9] and so forth. There are several commercial products such as Nicole of NativeMinds, SmartBot of Artificial Life, Verbot of Virtual Personalities, and so on.

In this paper, we present a plan-based model for designing analysis component of conversational agent to make it more flexible and powerful. Especially we use a modified Bayesian network as an inference engine of analysis component to deal with a dynamic process which is necessary to understand user's intention in query.

3 Two-Stage Bayesian Network

3.1 Inference with Bayesian Network

The environment of real application of conversational agent is very uncertain [10]. Because users usually do not describe their problems exactly and cannot select one correct sentence for it, in addition, query includes much uncertainty: ellipsis, useless words or duplicated information. Instead, they use several queries, each of which has only a piece of information about user's goal. In spite of these difficulties, conversational agent has to collect information and to decide the meaning of sentence.

Bayesian probabilistic inference is one of the famous models for inference and representation of the environment with insufficient information. The node of Bayesian network represents random variable, while the arc represents the dependency between variables [11, 12]. In order to infer the network, the structure must be designed and the probability distribution must be specified. Usually the structure is designed by expert while the probability distribution is calculated by expert or collected data from the domain. By observing evidence, the probability of each node is computed without excessive computation by Bayesian inference algorithm based on the conditional probability table and independence assumption.

3.2 Bayesian Network Architecture

We can extract two kinds of information, topic and sentence pattern from query [6]. Topic is related with words, while the sentence pattern is related with sequence of words. We adopt them as evidences of Bayesian network. If agent is designed by one Bayesian network using words and sentence pattern of query, the network becomes very complicated. Especially dividing them into two-stage Bayesian network, we can accomplish in-depth analysis of query and avoid the complexity occurred in designing the network for large domain. Fig. 1 shows the overall structure of the proposed architecture of conversational agent.

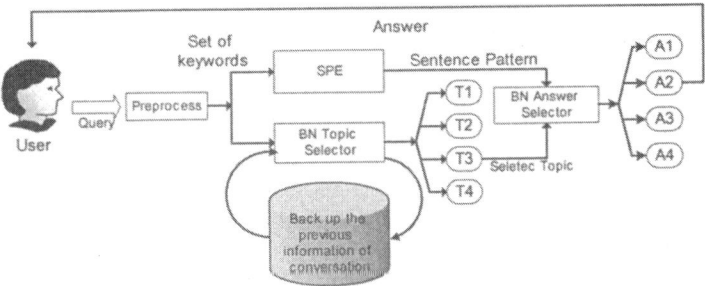

Fig. 1. Structure of the proposed architecture of conversational agent

The proposed system consists of two-stage Bayesian network, BN (Bayesian network) topic selector and BN answer selector, and SPE (Sentence Pattern Extractor) which generates sentence pattern. After user gives a query to conversational agent, it performs preprocessing step to extract predefined keywords. With these extracted keywords BN topic selector executes to infer the topic of the query, and once a topic is selected, BN answer selector corresponding to it obtains a correct answer with sentence pattern generated by SPE. Finally it selects the best answer satisfying the topic and the sentence pattern of query.

3.2.1 BN Topic Selector
In this stage we divide the domain into topics that consist of three hierarchical levels by its role, keyword, top-topic and sub-topic. First level is for the keywords used in the domain, and the individuals and attributes of the domain form top-topics. Sub-topic represents the individual that has determined its attributes. This hierarchical modeling helps to have the conversation to understand a detailed user's intention [13]. Limiting the scope of common knowledge between human and agent into unit topics, it classifies the intention specifically, and minimizes the uncertainty in each

hierarchical stage when topic is changed in conversation [13, 14]. It avoids misleading which can be happened by inferring the intention at once, and reduces the uncertainty of inference by progressing hierarchically [9, 10]. Moreover, it gives easy facility of understanding concepts of the domain in designing the network.

When some keywords are included in query, they are used as the evidence of BN topic selector. After inference, we get the highest probability sub-topic as the topic of the query. Fig. 2 shows the process of inference in BN topic selector.

Step 1 : Set the probability of keyword node as 1, whose keyword is included in user's query, and not-included one's as 0.

Step 2 : Execute Bayesian inference algorithm.

Step 3 : Select the highest probability sub_topic node, above threshold1. If there is no selected node, then go to Step 5.

Step 4 : Select the topic of user's query, and finish the BN topic selector.

Step 5 : Check the top_topic node whose probability is over threshold2 If there is no node selected, then give up giving an answer. Finish the BN topic selector.

Step 6 : Give an answer of top_topic to collect more information.

Fig. 2. The process of inference of BN topic selector

Usually people do not give just one query to express their intention, and they produce a query based on previous conversation [15,16]. Each sentence has a piece of information, so that a query is not sufficient to analyze the topic. By accumulating information through conversation, we get sufficient information to infer the intention. Then we use Bayesian network chain as dynamic knowledge-base to deal with the maintenance of context through conversation. When BN topic selector infers the topic, it considers network of the last query. By weighing the probability of nodes with previous one, agent uses the piece of information of previous query.

3.2.2 BN Answer Selector

Once the topic is selected, BN answer selector corresponding to the selected topic performs to choose an answer that is suitable to the sentence pattern. It uses sentence pattern and detailed keywords of input query as evidences. In this paper, we construct SPE with a set of classifying automata [6]. Sentence patterns can be categorized as shown in Table 2. Classifying automata is designed for each sentence pattern with a set of keywords and sequences, and Fig. 3 shows one for "WhatIf" question.

Table 2. Sentence Pattern

Query Classification	Sentence Pattern
Question	Can, Who, WhatIf, Method, Location, Reason, Should, Time, Description, Fact
Statement	Message, Act, Is, Have, Want, Fact

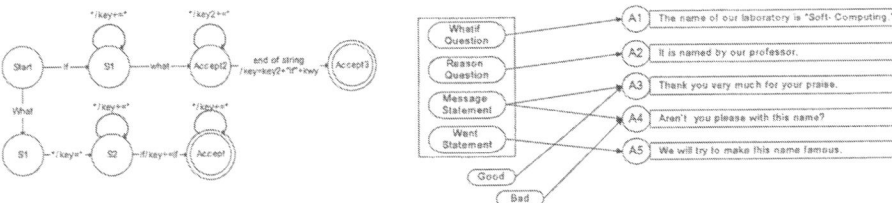

Fig. 3. Automaton for classification of "WhatIf" question

Fig. 4. The structure of BN Answer Selector for "The name of laboratory"

With this sentence pattern generated, BN answer selector selects a proper answer. Each BN answer selector has a set of answers of the topic based on sentence patterns and some detailed keywords. The detailed keywords used in this stage are different from those used in BN topic selector in detailed level. Fig. 4 shows the structure of BN answer selector for topic, "The name of laboratory."

4 Illustration

In this paper, a query is divided into three types: 1) Enough-information, 2) use-previous-information, and 3) need-more-information. That is because in common conversation an ellipsis is frequently happened, and usually speaker uses background knowledge. The proposed conversational agent can deal with these types of queries.

4.1 Enough-Information Type

If user's query contains all the information to estimate user's intention, agent gives a proper answer obtained by the inference of the system. Dialogue 1 is an example for this case.

User :   What is the name of your laboratory?
            Keyword (name, laboratory)
BN topic selector (sub-topic: The name of laboratory)
            Sentence pattern (Question, Whatif)
            BN answer selector (Question of the name of laboratory)
ChatBot : The name of our laboratory is soft-computing.

User :   The name of your laboratory is very good.
            Keyword (name, laboratory)
              BN topic selector (sub-topic: The name of laboratory)
            Sentence pattern (Statement, Is)
            Detail keyword (good)
            BN answer selector (praise for the name of laboratory)
ChatBot : Thanks very much.

Dialogue 1. Enough-information type and differentiation by sentence pattern

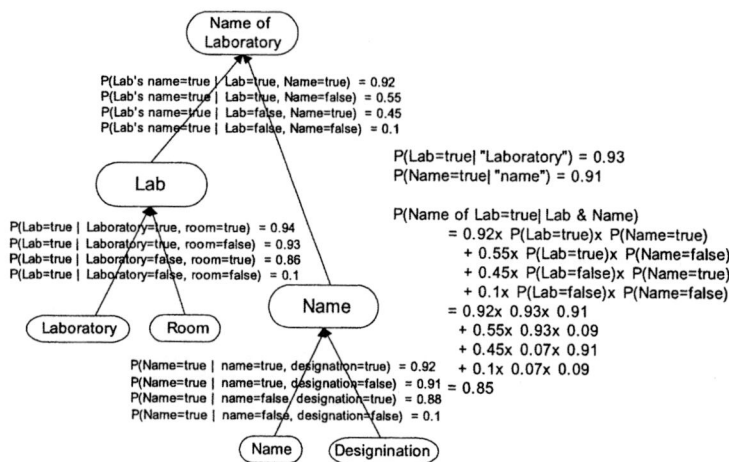

Fig. 5. Simple Bayesian network to show the course for inference of "Name of Lab"

In the preprocessing step, the words "laboratory" and "name" are extracted, they are passed as inputs of BN topic selector. BN topic selector executes the inference with them as evidences, picks up the best suitable topic for user's query. Fig. 5 shows the minimum Bayesian network for selecting the topic, "Name of Lab." First, the probability of node for extracted keyword is set as 1 and the others are set as 0. With Bayesian inference algorithm, the values of node "Name" and "Lab" become 0.91 and 0.93, respectively. The probability of sub-topic "Name of Lab" becomes 0.85 which exceeds the threshold of 0.75, and is selected as the topic of user's query. Usually the others are not selected because they may not go beyond the threshold, otherwise the highest one is selected among them. Consequently BN answer selector for "Name of Lab" is activated. With the WhatIf-question type obtained by SPE, it understands that user wants to know the name of laboratory and answers about that. It is possible that the real meaning of the queries is different while the topics of queries are same, because of sentence patterns. That is as shown in lower part of Dialogue 1.

4.2   Use-Previous-Information Type: Maintain the Context of Conversation

Through the conversation between human and agent, user may change the topic of what he or she wants to know. In this case, agent has to maintain the context of conversation [16]. Because most of topic changed is based on previous dialogue, the content of previous dialogue provides the information to analyze the current dialogue. Dialogue 2 is the example dialogue for this case.

4.3   Need-More-Information Type: Active Conversation

In many cases user has background knowledge in addition to the contents of conversation, so that it frequently happens that the query does not include all the information for the inference of user's intention. It is because the knowledge bases for user and agent are different. The agent manages to infer the topic of user's query roughly, and the supplementary information must be supplied. Agent gets this supplementary information by requesting to user. When the agent asks to user, it bases a top-topic that is roughly inferred. Dialogue 3 is the example of active conversation of agent.

User : What is your professor's telephone number? 　　　　Keyword (number, telephone, professor) 　　　　BN topic selector (sub-topic: Professor's phone number) 　　　　Sentence pattern (Question, Whatif) 　　　　BN answer selector (Question of professor's phone number) **ChatBot** :　　　Our professor's phone number is 2123-2720. **User** : What about you? 　　　　Keyword (you) 　　　　High probability nodes (phone-number, professor) 　　　　BN topic selector (sub-topic: The phone number of Agent) 　　　　Sentence pattern (Question, Whatif) 　　　　BN answer selector (Question of the phone number of Agent) **ChatBot** :　　　I'm sorry, I don't have any phone. **User** : Hmm, so what about email address? 　　　　Keyword (email, address) 　　　　High probability nodes (phone-number, Agent) 　　　　BN topic selector (sub-topic: The email address of Agent) 　　　　Sentence pattern (Question, Whatif) 　　　　BN answer selector (Question of the email address of Agent) **ChatBot** :　　　My email address is chatbot@candy.yonsei.ac.kr.

Dialogue 2. Use-previous-information Type

User : What is the phone number? 　　　　Keyword (number, phone) 　　　　BN topic selector (top-topic: phone-number) 　　　　➔ Not enough information for inference **ChatBot** :Whose telephone number do you want to know? 　　　　Laboratory's or professor's? **User** : I would like to know the professor's 　　　　Keyword (professor) 　　　　Sentence pattern (Question, Whatif) 　　　　BN topic selector ➔ Add more information 　　　　(sub-topic: The phone number of professor) 　　　　BN answer selector (Question of the phone number of professor) **ChatBot** :　　　Our professor's phone number is 2123-2720.

Dialogue 3. Need-more-information Type

5 Concluding Remarks

Conversation is one of the most representative communication methods to express one's knowledge and intention. However it has uncertainty, such as implication and ellipsis, and it usually uses one's background knowledge. So there are limits with conventional approaches like simple pattern matching to manage them. Moreover if the domain becomes larger, it becomes very hard to design each pattern or network.

In this paper, we model conversational agent using two-stage Bayesian network, with which it gets to be more flexible and detailed to infer the intention. Besides, the task of designing network becomes easier and more comprehensible by one's intuition. We analyze the conversation on the types of queries to induce more active conversation. If some information is insufficient to infer, agent can ask user more information. Using sentence pattern, more suitable type of answer is offered. Bayesian network chain is useful to maintain the context of conversation.

Analysis of domain and design of network is prerequisite to develop conversational agent. They are dependent on human's hand, so that it is very expensive. As the application domain changes, the network must be changed. The research on automatic construction of network is left for future work, in order to let the human design abstract network and construct detailed networks automatically. Some problems commonly occurred in conversation, such as social interaction and insertion sequence, will be solved out with future work.

Acknowledgements. This paper was supported by Biometrics Engineering Research Center, and Brain Science and Engineering Research Program sponsored by Korean Ministry of Science and Technology.

References

1. Y. Yang, L. Chien and L. Lee, "Speaker intention modeling for large vocabulary mandarin spoken dialogues," Proc. of the 4th Int. Conf. on Spoken Language, pp. 713–716, 1996.
2. J. Allen, D. Byron, M. Dzikovska, G. Ferguson, L. Galescu and A. Stent, "Towards conversational human-computer interaction," AI Magazine, 22(4), pp. 27–37, 2001.
3. J. Chai, V. Horvath, N. Nicolov, M. Budzikowska, N. Kambhatla, and W. Zadrozny, "Natural language sales assistant: A web-based dialog system for online sales," Proc. of the 13th Annual Conf. on Innovative Applications of Artificial Intelligence, pp.19–26, 2001.
4. E. Horvitz, J. Breese, D. Heckerman, D. Hovel and K. Rommelse, "The lumiere project: Bayesian user modeling for inferring the goals and needs of software users," Proc. of the 14th Conf. Uncertainty in Artificial Intelligence, pp. 256–265, 1998.
5. D. Albrecht, I. Zukerman, A. Nicholcon and A. Bud, "Towards a Bayesian model for keyhole plan recognition in large domains," Proc. of the 6th Int. Conf. on User Modeling, pp. 365–376, 1997.
6. S.-I. Lee, C. Sung and S.-B. Cho, "An effective conversational agent with user modeling based on Bayesian network," Lecture Notes in Computer Science, 2198, pp. 428–432, 2001.
7. S. Macskassy and S. Stevenson, "A conversational agent," Master Essay, Rutgers University, 1996.
8. D. Heckerman and E. Horvitz, "Inferring informational goals from free-text queries: A Bayesian approach," Proc. of the 14th Conf. on Uncertainty in Artificial Intelligence, pp.230–237, 1998.
9. G. Ferguson, J. Allen and B. Miller, "TRAINS-95: Towards a mixed-initiative planning assistant," Proc. of the 3rd Conf. on Artificial Intelligence Planning Systems, pp.70–77, 1996.
10. T. Paek and E. Horvitz, "Conversation as action under uncertainty," Proc. of the 16th Conf. on Uncertainty in Artificial Intelligence, pp.455–464, 2000.
11. E. Charniak, "Bayesian networks without tears," AI Magazine, 12(4), pp.50–63, 1991.

12. T. Stephenson, "An introduction to Bayesian network theory and usage," IDIAP-RR00-03, 2000.
13. E. Horvitz and T. Paek, "A computational architecture for conversation," Proc. of the 7th Int. Conf. on User Modeling, pp.201–210, 1999.
14. J. Allen, G. Ferguson and A. Stent, "An architecture for more realistic conversational systems," Proc. of Intelligent User Interfaces, pp.1–8, 2001.
15. J. Allen, "Mixed Initiative Interaction," IEEE Intelligent Systems, 14(6), pp.14–23, 1999.
16. X. Wu, F.Zheng and M. Xu, "TOPIC Forest: A plan-based dialog management structure," Int. Conf. on Acoustics, Speech and Signal Processing, pp.617–620, 2001.

Intelligent Agent Technology in E-commerce

Ong Sing Goh[1] and Chun Che Fung[2]

[1]Faculty of Information and Communication Technology,
National Technical College University of Malaysia, Malaysia.
goh@kutkm.edu.my
[2]School of Information Technology, Murdoch University,
Murdoch WA 6150, Australia.
L.Fung@murdoch.edu.au

Abstract. Use of Internet has surged at an exponential rate in recent years. In particular, it has led to many new and innovative applications in the area of E-Commerce. In this paper, we introduce an intelligent agent termed AINI, the Artificial Intelligent Solution Humanoid. We also show how current e-commerce technological trends can be enhanced by using AINI. AINI is a chatterbot integrated with 3D animated agent character, Speech Technology and Artificial Intelligence Markup Language (AIML) is utilised. This agent technology is mainly used to improve customer services and to reduce customer reliance on human operators. By using artificial intelligence techniques, AINI is able to provide appropriate answers to service inquiries. In this paper, issues on Intelligent Agents Technology, Speech Technology, AIML and the use of 3D animated character in E-Commerce are discussed.

1   Introduction

In this cyber age, business-to-client (B2C) transactions such as online shopping and online banking have huge social, economic and commercial implications. For example, online shopping or banking offer both convenience and many choices. They eliminate the need for travel and one operates within the comfort of the home or office. Goods and services may be obtained without the need to negotiate queues, crowds, traffic and of course, the unexpected natural elements such as weather [1]. However, it is recognized that such facility is not necessarily user friendly and convenient as one may think. In particular, when a retailer is far away and e-mail messages are not instantly responded. Users are frustrated in dealing with uncertain and unreliable unknown systems. According to the technology research firm, Forrester Research, one of the comments on today's web services is "DUMB, BORING, and DUSTY" [2]. On the other hand, the Internet is changing the way companies interact with customers. The high-speed Internet is supplanting yesterday's "brick and mortar" businesses with web sites offering products and services on a 24x7 basis [3]. With the new era underway, companies must prepare to utilize Internet-based communication to the best of their benefits and be ready to face the perils of a new competitive landscape. To many businesses, one of the main challenges is to improve customer services on general enquiries, sales and supports. In addition, it is necessary to increase the productivity and efficiency in these important business

J. Liu et al. (Eds.): IDEAL 2003, LNCS 2690, pp. 10–17, 2003.
© Springer-Verlag Berlin Heidelberg 2003

operations. Typical areas with much rooms to improve are: to engage in application or problem specific conversations, to boost the learning capability on new vocabulary and terminologies, to increase the accuracy on word and speech recognition, to enhance the portability of the core technologies and to widen the application areas.

Research by Datamonitor has stated that *"U.S. businesses lost more than $6.1 billion (US$) in potential Internet sales in 1999 because of poor online customer service, and estimated that an industry-wide failure to resolve the problem could lead to at least $173 billion in lost revenues through 2004."* In addition, Datamonitor also reported that 7.8 percent of online transactions initiated by consumers are abandoned because of poor customer service. It is definite that more and more companies have realized that live interaction is required to promote customer loyalty [4]. These studies have indicated that customers prefer having Intelligent Agent and with speech-enabled to answer their queries and needs.

In this paper, we report the development of an intelligent Agent technology using AINI chatterbot deployed by using Artificial Intelligence Markup Language (AIML). The main application is in e-commerce in order to enable web businesses to be more interactive. In this social interaction model, the agent offers to help the customers with information it has already acquired. The new breed of agent is highly customizable, allowing e-tailers to brand them as they wish. The "agents" also aim to assist and reassure the customers by displaying appropriate emotion. For example, if an agent cannot answer a particular question, it expresses disappointment and tries again. Alternatively, it may prompt the user toward another channel of service. If the customer expresses interest in a particular product, the agent will suggest related items. If a transaction is completed, the agent will thank the customer and invites him or her to re-visit. The following sections describe the objective and various features of the intelligent agent.

1.1   Objective

The objective of this project is to create a chatterbot namely AINI, which is, adopted from the previous ELIZA and ALICE chatter bots. AINI chatterbot is different because it has facial expressions and emotion represented by a 3D animated character called "eBee". The technology has been initiated and created by research teams at the Multimedia University, Malaysia. We have included voice recognition technology in the human computer interfaces which enhances the trust factor in the E-Commerce web sites by humanizing the interface design. This also makes the process of buying and selling more interesting. eBee is able to guide the user in the transaction and to motivate the user by presenting an engaging manner. This results in a longer interaction time and a high quality E-Commerce web site.

In this system, Customer Relationship Management (CRM) is emphasized which aims to help and respond to the customer needs. Building a strong relationship with the customers is an important element of e-commerce. AINI is unique because it helps customers in a similar way to a human sales person. AINI provides customers with quick answers as if they were conversing with a human online. This improves customer interaction on the web, hence build strong and loyal relationships. AINI also adds a "human" element of personality represented by the eBee agent character.

1.2   Use of BOTS in E-commerce

Intelligent Agent or Bots are important companions in E-Commerce. Apart from making the transaction more interesting, they can be used to help users by providing expert advices and assist the users in their decisions on what to buy. Intelligent Agents could help to reduce information overload, increase productivity and to achieve competitive advantages. Intelligent agents however do not necessarily to be present upfront on the Internet. They can perform equally well at the background. However, the Internet is where the intelligent agents have spawned much interest and imagination from the public. The Net also offers great opportunities for the deployment of intelligent agents. Currently, there are already a few e-commerce web portals using chatterbots such as Archangelis, CGIsupport.com, Coolware, Inc, Artificial-Life.com and Botizen.com.

Many businesses today are seeking to increase the service level and the ease of use of their web sites. "Chatter bots" programs that interact with users in natural language are great advances in customer services. A chatter bot often presents a human-like image, and allows a user to type questions in daily languages which are responded to the best of the bot's knowledge. Chatter bots can be programmed to converse on any subject including products and services that are on offer. Chatter bots can assist in e-commerce in a number of ways. Bots represented by a 3D Animated Character will assist the users according to their specifications and returns with recommendations on the products which meet the requirements. The "salesperson" could also provide product or service information and sales advice. In addition, they can help "troubleshoot" if problems occur. [5]

In order to run the Intelligent Agent Technology, we have developed AgentValley as a prototype of online shopping website. AgentValley plays an important role in E-commerce online shopping. AgentValley is created with an aim to reduce customer reliance on live agents by providing more appropriate answers to service inquiries. The convergence of Intelligent Agent system and Internet technologies offers the customer the freedom of choice while interacting with the web site. The exciting new possibilities for customer interaction include online shops, chats and collaborative browsing. The Internet browsers of both the agent and the customer are linked and could be controlled by either party. In addition, voice technology and 3D animated agent character or avatars are also incorporated.

BOTizen.com, launch by VQ Interactive Sdn Bhd and it is a well known MSC Status company in Malaysia, states that "The AI technology provides BOTizen with the expertise to communicate with users in Natural language, text or speech. Throughout the discussion, a customer can be guided and consulted, BOTizen is able to display the appropriate web pages, answer questions and even make relevant recommendations." [6] As for Artificial-Life.com, launch by Artificial Life, Inc. one of the listed companies in Nasdaq, announced the introduction of a new class of e-commerce software that answers online customer needs. Unlike shopping bots that merely compare prices, Artificial Life's new e-commerce application will allow online customers to interface with virtual assistant robots that the customer then sends on missions to help them make smarter purchases [7]. They also announced results for the second quarter year to date 2000 revenues are $4,343,318 compared to same period revenues in 1999 of $1,324,551, an increase of $3,018,767 or 227.91%.

2 The Technology

There are a number of chatterbots currently being used in e-commerce, e-learning, e-government and similar environemtns. AINI performs with improved and enhanced services. The agents communicate using AIML that facilitate high-level corporation and interoperation among the agents. Architecture of AINI is illustrated in Figure 1 below.

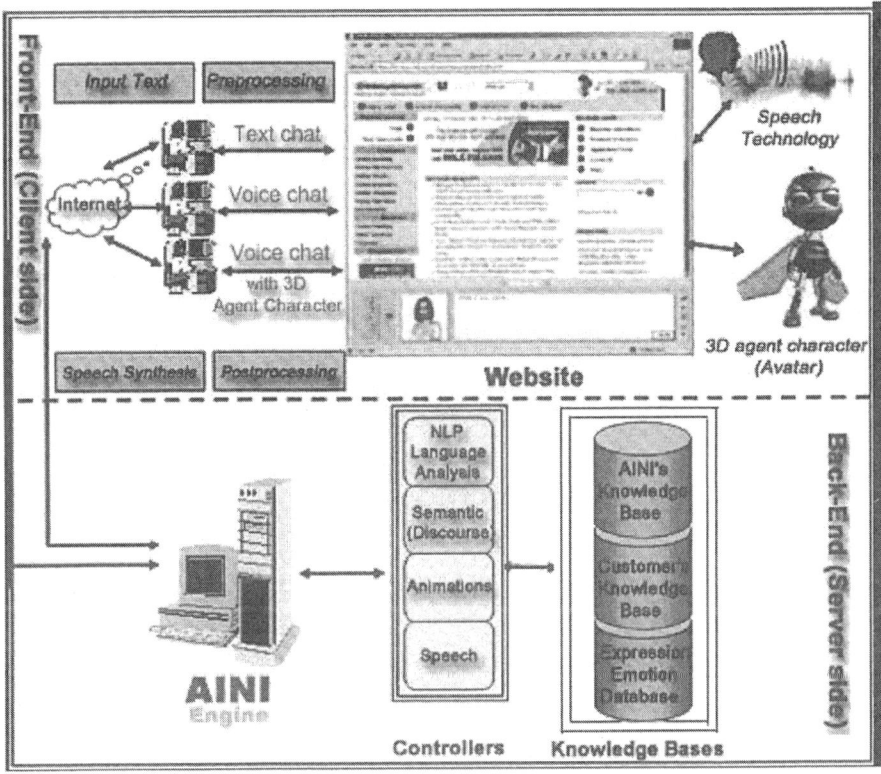

Fig. 1. Architecture of AINI

The backbone of AgentValley system is a unique intelligent agent framework that is the AINI Intelligent Agent with an AIML-based engine, which processes AIML tags. Moreover, it is a natural language artificial intelligence chatterbot able to deal with an understanding of textual language for the system. Case Based Reasoning (CBR) technique is used because it maps well onto the AINI algorithm. The CBR uses an explicit database of problem solutions (cases) to address new problem-solving situations. The CBR "cases" are the categories in AIML. The bot will attempt to match the input query of the user with relevant information that is available in its knowledge base.

AINI searches the application's knowledge base as well as other enterprise data sources connected to the system. It aims to return appropriate responses to the inquiries. The knowledge represented in the patterns is represented in the AIML specifications of XML. The goal of AINI is a totally integrated solution by incorporating existing database server domains in the Internet

AIML is an XML language extension with specifications for programming chatterbots. The emphasis in the language design is minimalism. The simplicity of AIML makes it easy for developers who have prior knowledge of HTML to implement chatterbots. The categories in AIML are comparable to the rules of grammar. The algorithm finds the best matching pattern for each input. The category connects the stimulus pattern directly to the response template.

Natural Language Processing (NLP), language analysis, Semantic Template Matching, Animation engine and Speech Control are utilized. They are used in response to dialogue output requests and to generate the animated motion, speech and sound effects necessary to communicate with the user. For this subsystem, the goal is to create a convincing visual and aural representation of a character which carries out the user's requests. We have however chosen to forego the flexibility of a general text-to-speech system because such systems currently lack the naturalness and expressiveness that are required by the agent. The system consists of three types of interface called Text-chat, Voice-chat and Voice with 3D Animated Characters. These features will give the user a choice for their preferred response. This is illustrated in Fig. 2 below.

Multilanguage support with 3 interfaces
(Text-chat, Voice-chat and 3D Animated Avatar)

Fig. 2.   Three types of Interface: Text, Chat and Animated Avatar

The knowledge base is contained in the AIML knowledge base consisting of the Customer Service knowledge base, the Speech and Animation Database, and, the Action Templates Database. Every chatterbot contains a domain independent and reusable standard AIML libraries (the AIML knowledge base), animation and action templates. AIML provides a powerful tool to deal with sentences that contain redundant information which are words that are not essential to the understanding of the global meaning of the question. These libraries are mainly used to transform different user inputs that have similar meanings into a standard sentence. This standardized sentence is then passed onto the relevant domain specific library. The libraries containing over 30,000 categories. With the collection of categories, it is relatively easy to create a new bot with unique features applicable to specific applciations. Any number of expert agents can be added to the system from third parties by adding customer service knowledge base.

Text-To-Speech (TTS) and Voice Recognition enable the computer responds to user-spoken commands and provide the user with verbal feedback. Voice recognition technology applied to E-commerce web sites will help to encourage the users in buying, selling or browsing through the product details. As the trends of technology are moving towards wider utilization of voice recognition technologies, the feature will provide the users with easier accessibility.

3 Features of AINI

Because non-verbal signs are integral parts of the communicative process, Microsoft Agent is used to integrate gesture, intonation, and facial expression into multi-modal human figure animation. Appropriate speech, intonation, facial expression and gesture are generated by rules from a semantic representation that originates in AIML. The output of the dialogue generation is used to drive a graphical animation of a conversation. For embodied conversational agents, non-verbal behaviors related to the process of conversation called envelope feedback, is much more important than other form of feedback, such as emotional expression for the customer service. In order to interact socially with a human, an agent must convey intentionality, that is, the human must believe that the agent has beliefs, desires, and intentions. The developed bot is an agent which exploits natural human social tendencies to convey intentionality through motor actions and facial expressions.

The chatterbot allows users to quickly find a keyword or phrase in any of the conversation logs collected in the knowledge base. For example, a user wants to find a keyword "Car", the chatterbot will ask which search engine that the user wishes to display the results. It also allows the user to display only part of the conversations that belong to a certain topic or knowledge base. Or, certain parts that contain only keywords or phrases can be displayed. This permits the user to locate specific information from the conversations.

Collaborative filtering tools compare personal preferences and transaction patterns between individuals with similar profiles and buying behaviors. This technique is based on a form of referential surveying, which is a complex statistical algorithm that makes product recommendations based on purchasing patterns. The resulting germane content is presented to the customer. The collaboration comes from individual customers in essence making recommendations to others.

This inferential method of collecting personal data is done by posing questions to potential customers at various touch points. The resulting data is used to create an ever-increasing targeted dialogue. Customers are asked questions about their interests and buying habits that can be used to personalize their records.

The system also has the added feature of being able to generate valuable reports and statistics. The system will include facilities which provide utilities to run reports and statistics to the user. These reports can be used to understand and study on the type of conversations users are having on your web site. The information provided allows an administrator to customize his/her bots knowledge base to cover any information.

The system provides the administrators with a powerful tool for market research by allowing them to analyze log files of anonymous user conversations and most importantly, increase the traffic on their web-site. Another feature is that this system will track a history of interactions that a user has performed with the agents, allowing the advisor agent to keep track of services. The user profiles are created and used to associate with the customer's interaction. The log files created for bot conversations as well as e-mail questions and responses are saved in the profiling database. These files provide an invaluable source of information. Examples of the reports are shown in Fig. 3.

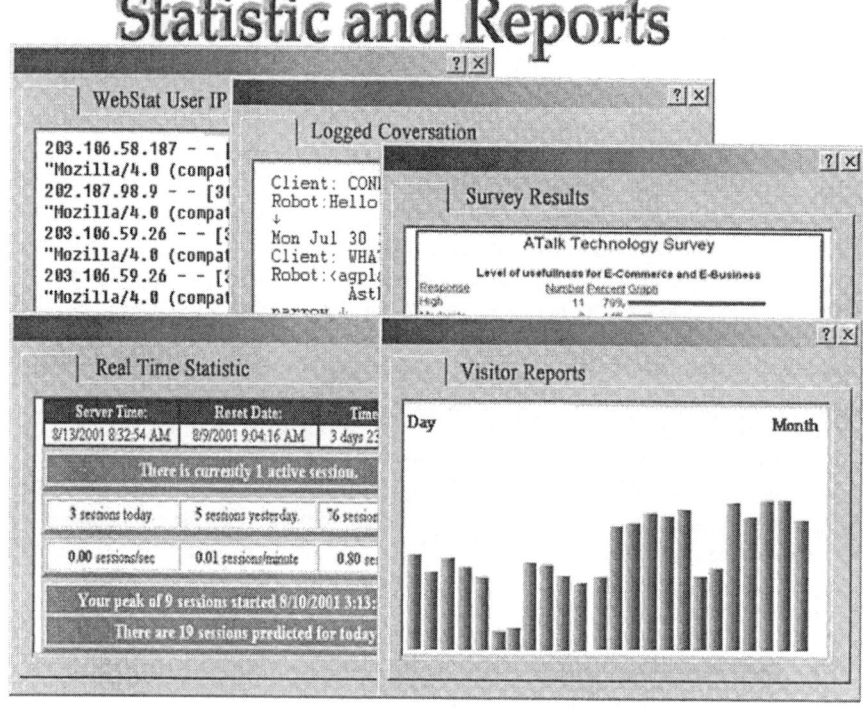

Fig. 3. Displays of Statistical information and Reports

An AIML knowledge base can be constructed in multiple languages such as English (British or US), French, Japanese, Korean, Italian, German, Malay and etc. This system can translate into 5 languages such as Italian, German, Japanese, French and Spanish by using Systran™ machine translation system. We also integrated Online Dictionary, Online Database (connect directly to any existing company database) and online Search Engines such as Yahoo, Google, altavista.

4 Conclusion

Intelligent Agent and Speech Recognition technologies including Agent Characters are viable solutions to many current problems in today's complex E-Commerce web sites. The present problems are mainly due to the fact that many current E-Commerce technologies are not as user-friendly as it seems. Users prefer to have "someone" to guide them on online activities. In addition, the use of keyboard is not as natural as interaction with voice and speech. The use of intelligent agent is capable to implement a companion or a virtual salesperson on the web site. The agent is capable to guide the user in the buying/selling process. In this paper, the use of Intelligent Agent, Voice Recognition and Agent Characters are presented as the essential components in the AINI system to enhance the E-commerce operation. Further works are carried out to evaluate the effectiveness of the system in practical systems.

References

1. Online shopping advice from the Office of Fair Trading (OFT) at
http://www.oft.gov.uk/html/shopping/
2. Scarlet Pruitt (2001) "Forrester Research says the web will die" available at
http://iwsun4.infoworld.com/articles/hn/xml/01/05/17/010517hnxinternet.xml
3. Forrester Research and InformationWeek, "Changes in Customer Contact" White paper.
4. Jon Weisman, (2001) "Is Live Interaction Ready for Prime Time?",
EcommerceTimes.com, available at. http://www.crmdaily.com/perl/story/4558.html
5. A.L.I.C.E. AI Foundation: Promoting the adoption and development of AliceBot and AIML Free Software, Article on "Why You Don't Need Proprietary Bot Software" by Noel Bush Available online at
http://alicebot.org/articles/bush/wallaceconversation.html
6. An online personality to assist customers Published in: Computimes (News Straits Times) Thursday October 12, 2000 available online at
http://www.botizen.com/press9.html
7. First E-Commerce Application Based on Software Robots to be Released available online at http://www.artificial-life.com/default_luci.asp?pContent=http://www.artificial-life.com/press_alife/1999_03_30_3.asp

Connected Replicator Dynamics and Their Control in a Learning Multi-agent System

Masaaki Kunigami and Takao Terano

GSSM Tsukuba University
3-29 Otsuka Bunkyo-ku Tokyo, JAPAN
mkunigami@nifty.ne.jp, terano@gssm.otsuka.tsukuba.ac.jp

Abstract. This paper analyzes complex behaviors of a multi-agent system, which consists of interacting agents with evolutionally learning capabilities. The interaction and learning of agents are modeled using Connected Replicator Dynamics expanded from the evolutional game theory. The dynamic systems show various behavioral and decision changes the including bifurcation of chaos in physics. The main contributions of this paper are as follows: (1) In the multi-agent system, the emergence of chaotic behaviors is general and essential, although each agent does not have chaotic properties; (2) However, simple controlling agent with the KISS (Keep-It-Simple-Stupid) principle or a sheepdog agent domesticates the complex behavior.

1 Introduction

In a social or economic multi-agent system, Equilibrium of a spontaneous cooperation or a self-organization usually emerges. However, since the chaotic behavior is also common in complex adaptive systems, such permanent unstable motion of a multi-agent system should be investigated as failure of self-organization or as a meaningful state in itself.

Expressing the agent's functions by the expanded Replicator Dynamics first, this paper shows that such a state instability will universally emerge from the agents' interaction. Second, it demonstrates a simple controlling agent based on the Keep-It-Simple-Stupid principle [1] or a sheepdog agent works well for such chaotic and unpredictable multi-agent system. Here, we propose an improved technique of conventional chaos control mechanisms.

In a multi-agent system, each agent is not always optimized in a static environment independently. Since agents interact each other, the environment and the internal landscape of each agent changes simultaneously. Therefore, the interaction among agents and their reaction speed over the environment are often more critical to their behaviors than their rationality or optimality.

There are static and dynamic approaches to study such interacting agents' behaviors. The static approach analytically derives the equilibrium of the rational agents. On the

J. Liu et al. (Eds.): IDEAL 2003, LNCS 2690, pp. 18–26, 2003.

other hand, the dynamic finds the path-dependence of multiple equilibria or observes the permanent states such as long-lived transients [2]. Based on the bounded rational agents' micro behaviors, the macro state changes must be described dynamically particularly as a hetero-critical cycle or a strange attractor.

In the literature, Hogg and Hurberman [3][4] have studied on the chaos and its stabilization in a multi-agent system, in which agents use multiple resources competitively with time delay and incomplete information. Since, in the Hogg-Hurberman system, the uncertainty and the time delay are represented explicitly, it is difficult to generally illustrate the emergence of chaos in an agents system.

Kunigami and Terano [5] have shown that the chaotic motion emerges from a mutually learning agents system by connecting two Replicator Dynamics. In that paper, they have suggested the effectiveness of the chaos control for multi-agent system. Independently, Sato and Crutchfield [6] have studied on Coupled Replicator Dynamics. They have investigated the relation of the game structure and bifurcation to the chaos.

Based on the researches, this paper will numerically investigate the following three propositions.

- In the multi-agent system, emergence of the chaos is common phenomenon.
- The interaction between agents is essential for the emergence.
- A chaos control technique is applicable and has preferable natures for multi-agent system control.

To verify the above, we will adopt the following strategies:

- For the first proposition, agents are modeled as simple as possible with the minimum characteristic as agent, according to Axelrod's KISS principle [1].
- For the second, each agent does not have any chaotic properties, and the bifurcation parameters to chaos are only characterized by the interaction among agents.
- For the third, a control agent adaptively determines its essential control parameters from only observation of the external state of agents.

2   A Multi-agent System Representation by the Connected Replicator Dynamics

In this section, we will extend Replicator Dynamics to represent a mutually learning agent system.

Replicator Dynamics (RD) has been introduced as a population dynamics in the evolutionary game theory, and is usually described as follows. [7]

$$\frac{1}{x_i}\frac{dx_i}{dt} = c \cdot \left((\mathbf{Ax})_i - \mathbf{xAx} \right), \quad \sum_{i=1}^{N} x_i = 1 \tag{1}$$

$$\mathbf{x} = (x_1, x_2, \cdots, x_N), \quad \mathbf{A} \in \mathbf{M}_{N \times N}$$

In the evolutionary game theory, the state variable x_i means the population ratio of the individual who chooses the i-th alternative of N kinds of pure strategies. The matrix A= {a_{ij}} represents a pay-off, when an individual taking the i-th strategy plays a game against another taking the j-th one. At each moment, some individuals are picked randomly, play games, and take payoff. The RD (1) describes that a population ratio of i-th strategy player is changing in proportion to the relative fitness that is defined as difference between the expected pay-off from i-th strategy and the group mean pay-off.

So far, the characteristics of this dynamics have been studied, which include the uniqueness of equilibrium, the evolutionary stability, and equivalence to the Lotka-Volterra system [7]. In the field of the evolutionary game theory, Skyrms has discussed the chaotic behavior of single Replicator Dynamics. [8]

However, for the agent's decisions based on the internal belief, such polymorphism interpretation from the evolutionary game is insufficient, as x_i means the ratio of population, which chooses the pure strategy i. There, x_i should be interpreted as the inner resource allocation (or mixed strategy) of an agent. We assume that the evaluation (i.e. a_i $(x_i|x)$) to the choice i in the resource allocation x is given with an linear function (i.e. a_i $(x_i|x) = (Ax)_i$). In this viewpoint, the matrix A is considered as internal model of agent to evaluate its own choice, and RD(1) describes the changing decisions based on this internal model. The change ratio of x is driven by the difference (satisfaction or regret) from the expectation (i.e. $x \cdot Ax$).

Next, RD (1) should be extended to the observation of the environment. We assume that variable y states the external world, and that the state of the observed external world is evaluated by linear function $\gamma A_0 y$.

$$\frac{dx_i}{dt} = c \cdot x_i \left((Ax)_i + \gamma \cdot (A_0 y)_i - xAx - \gamma \cdot xA_0 y \right), \quad \sum_{i=1} x_i = 1 \qquad (2)$$

Connecting of these equations (2), the Connected Replicator Dynamics minimally represents agents with the internal evaluation and the mutual interaction.

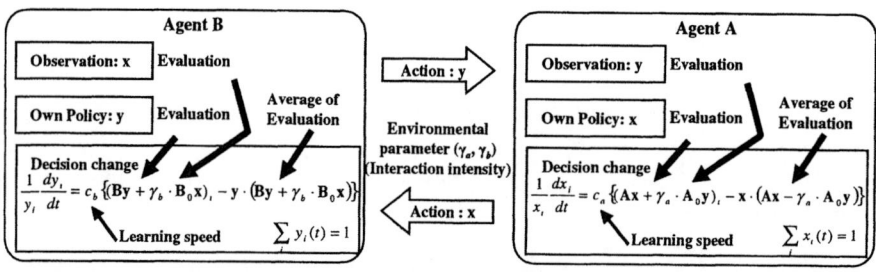

For example, such an agent's interaction is found out in the game of flaunting consumption. Each agent evaluates the utility from its consumption by the internal model represented by matrices A and B. Furthermore, they observe and evaluate consumption of other's by the internal model expressed by matrices A_0 and B_0, in which γ_a and γ_b are sensitivity constants. Therefore, this dynamics expresses the "bandwagon effect" (to follow others) and the "snob effect" (to be pretense) in the consumption behavior.

3 Emergence of Chaos

In this section, the emergence of chaos is numerically observed on the "connected Replicator Dynamics" described in the previous section. Here, evaluation matrices ($\mathbf{A}$, $\mathbf{A_0}$, $\mathbf{B}$, $\mathbf{B_0}$) and time constants of learning (c_a, c_b) are set up as follows, and the interaction coefficients γ_a and γ_b are changed as the bifurcation parameters.

- At first, in the no-interaction case (i.e. gamma = 0), both agents in the system converge to steady state independently. Periodicity comes to be observed if gamma becomes to some extent large. As gammas grow large enough, the system reaches unpredictable behavior through a quasi-periodic motion. (Fig.1). The positive maximum Lyapunov exponent (= 0.17) observed along the attractor proves the chaos [9]. A typical bifurcation pattern to the chaos can be found in this system. (Fig.2).
- The system shown above is an interaction between two 3-dimensional continuous dynamics. Since each dynamics has one constraint, the independent degrees of freedom are 2 each. Thus, from the Poincaré-Bendixson's theorem, any agents do not generate chaos independently (gamma= 0).
- For this reason, the chaos of this multi-agent system is essentially caused by the mutual interaction of agents who are not chaotic.

In this minimally constructed example, the bifurcation to chaos is caused by the changes of the interaction intensity parameter (gamma). Such interaction intensity between agents correspond to the spatial distance or the social relation. It suggests the importance of control and/or the stabilization of a chaotic behavior that even in the individually stable agents, some changes of their interaction intensity or reaction speed will cause chaotic behavior in a whole system.

4 A Control Agent for Chaos in the Multi-agent System

This section discusses the control and the stabilization for chaos of the agent system.
In the multi-agent system control, the institutional design through micro-macro link is realized by changing macroscopic system parameters [10]. In the field of chaos control, this corresponds to tuning of the bifurcation parameter (e.g. OGY method [11]) with knowledge on dynamics.

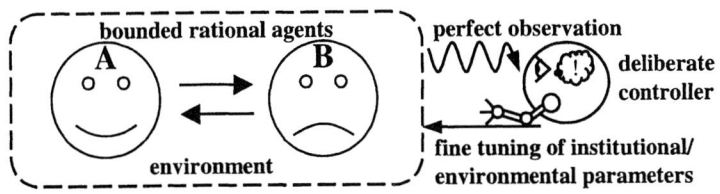

Such deliberate control often requires the omniscience and the omnipotence. Even the design of an indirect control, it is not realistic that the controller has the perfect knowledge over individual agent's internal models (utility and preference) or over the

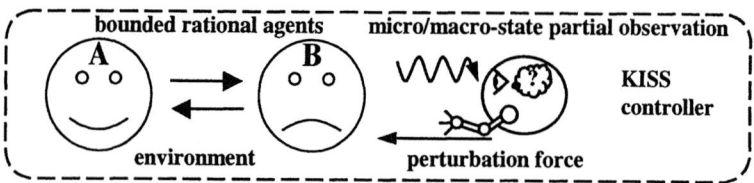

system equation. For the stabilization of autonomous distributed agents, KISS control agent like a "sheepdog" will become effective. The following part illustrates that such simple and stupid "sheepdog" can work effectively based on the partial observation and the partial control.

Among various methods (including OGY) for controlling chaos, this research improves Pyragas' method [12], since it is a continuous and simple control method, which does not require the prior knowledge on the system. The following figure shows the outline of Pyragas' method, which determines the feedback force by the difference between delayed output and current one, and stabilizes a chaotic orbit into a periodic orbit.

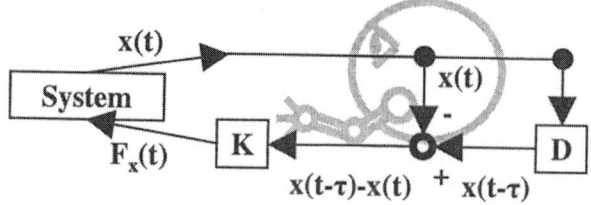

Compared with the other methods, this method has the following preferable features as a KISS control agent. First, neither the prior knowledge nor the system and system identification are required. Next, this method is relatively robust against noises. On the other hand, there exist chaotic systems that cannot be stabilized by this method. In addition, the essential parameter τ cannot be determined adaptively.

As a method of determining delay-time autonomously from observed data, Kittel-Pyragas [13] has proposed self-adapting delay-time control. However, this method tends to expand small high frequency fluctuation as delay time, so that the system sometimes becomes more unstable. Therefore, this research improves stability by making feedback of high frequency components reduced like the following formula.

The improved example of feedback stabilization is shown in Fig. 3. Although stabilization fails after a while since it has partial observation and partial control, after that, stabilization is restarted with new cycle adapted autonomously.

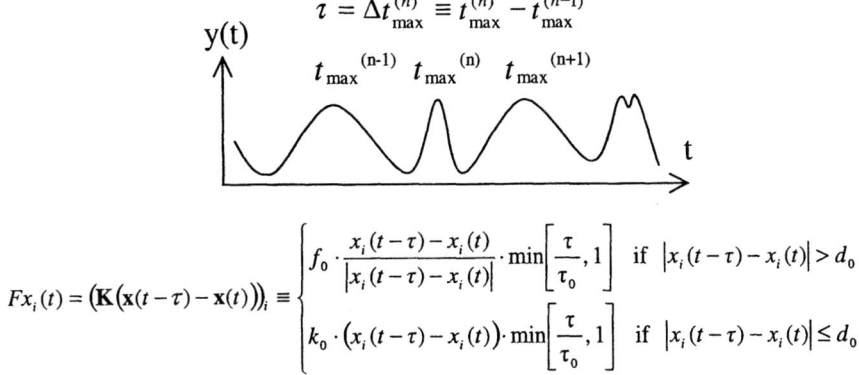

$$Fx_i(t) = \left(\mathbf{K}\left(\mathbf{x}(t-\tau)-\mathbf{x}(t)\right)\right)_i \equiv \begin{cases} f_0 \cdot \dfrac{x_i(t-\tau)-x_i(t)}{\left|x_i(t-\tau)-x_i(t)\right|} \cdot \min\left[\dfrac{\tau}{\tau_0},1\right] & \text{if } \left|x_i(t-\tau)-x_i(t)\right| > d_0 \\[4mm] k_0 \cdot \left(x_i(t-\tau)-x_i(t)\right) \cdot \min\left[\dfrac{\tau}{\tau_0},1\right] & \text{if } \left|x_i(t-\tau)-x_i(t)\right| \le d_0 \end{cases}$$

5   Concluding Remarks and Future Directions

This paper has illustrated the emergence of chaos and its control in 2-agents system. This section considers on the generalization beyond 2-agents system, and on possible directions future research. Since independent degree of freedom will also increase if the number of agents increases, chaos will be observed more easily. However, unlike 2-agents case, the behavior of the multi-agent system strongly depends on the graph structure of interaction.

Examples in typical behaviors observed are shown in Fig.4.1-4.3 about three different typical structure of the interaction. From these, state instability (chaos) is probably universal and potentially essential in agent society.

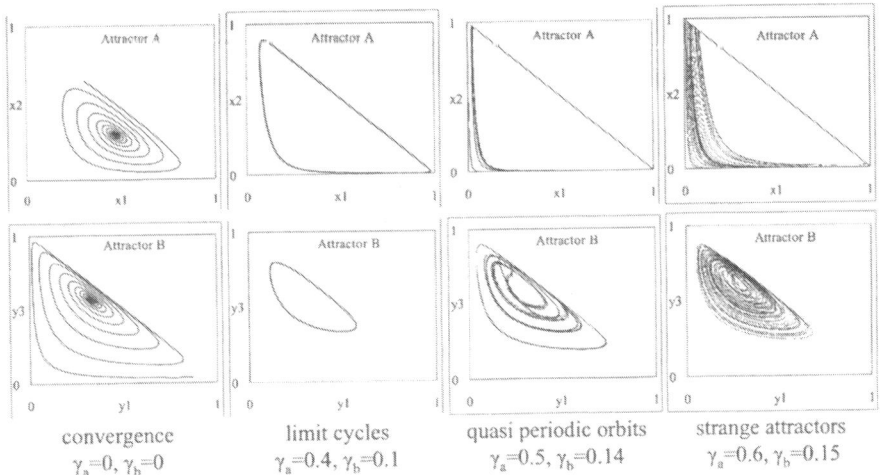

convergence
$\gamma_a=0$, $\gamma_b=0$

limit cycles
$\gamma_a=0.4$, $\gamma_b=0.1$

quasi periodic orbits
$\gamma_a=0.5$, $\gamma_b=0.14$

strange attractors
$\gamma_a=0.6$, $\gamma_b=0.15$

Fig. 1. Phase diagrams of emergence of chaotic behavior in the 2-agents system.

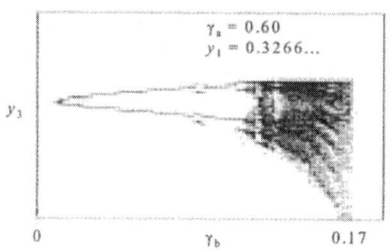

Fig. 2. Bifurcation diagram in the 2-agents system for $\gamma_b - y_3$.

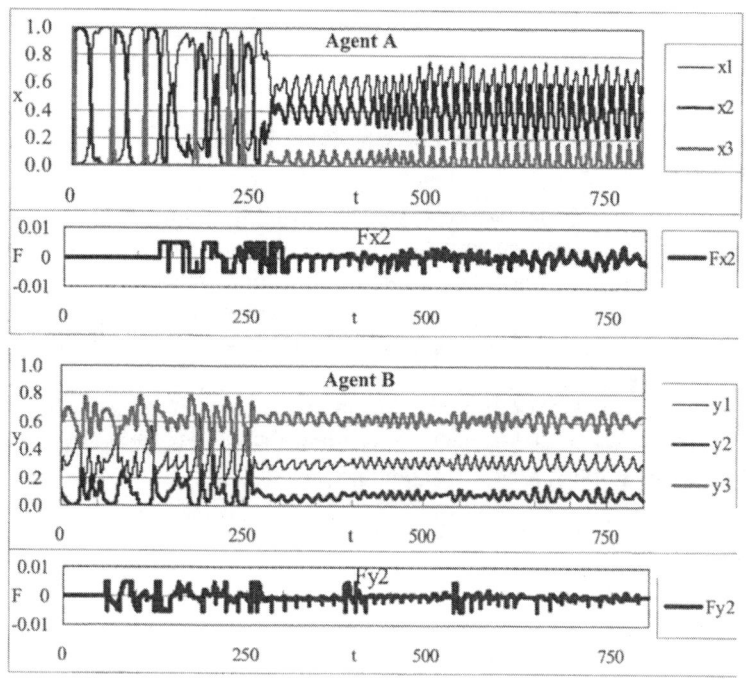

Fig. 3. Time series of agents with Self-Adapted Delayed feedback (controls start from t=50).

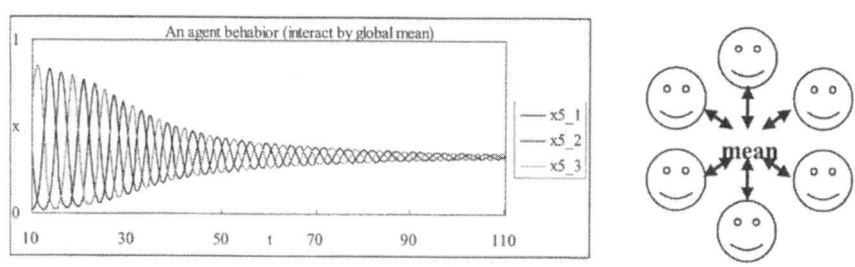

Fig. 4-1. Time series of an agent group when 6 homogeneous agents interact by global mean field

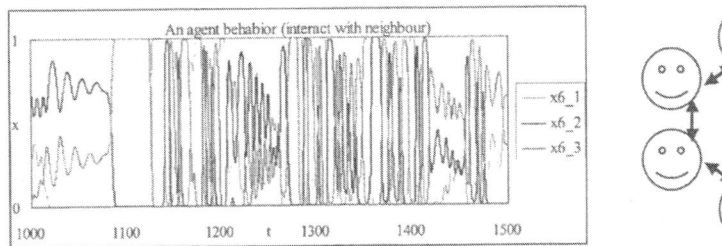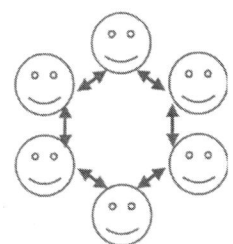

Fig. 4-2. Time series of an agent group when 6 homogeneous agents interact with neighbors (local mean)

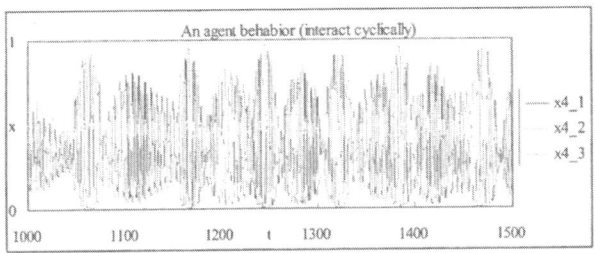

Fig. 4-3. Time series of an agent group when 6 homogeneous agents interact cyclically (hyper-cycle)

References

1. R. Axelrod, The Complexity of Cooperation, pp.5, Princeton, 1997.
2. R.L. Axtell, "Why Agents? On The Varied Motivations for Agent Computing in the Social Sciences", working paper No.17, Center on Social and Economic Dynamics, The Brookings Inst., 2000.
3. T. Hogg, B. Huberman, Controlling Chaos in Distributed Systems, IEEE Transactions on Systems, Man, and Cybernetics, Vol.21 No.6, pp.1325–1332, 1991.
4. T. Ushio, T. Imamori, T. Yamasagi, Controlling Chaos in Discrete-Time Computational Ecosystem, in Controlling Chaos and Bifurcations in Engineering Systems, Chen(eds.), pp.625–644, CRC Press, 2000.
5. M. Kunigami, T. Terano, "Behavior and Control in Replicator Dynamics as an Agents System " (in Japanese), proceedings of Multi Agent and Cooperative Computation '01 (MACC2001), 2001,
    www-kasm.nii.ac.jp/macc2001-proceedings/ MACC2001-24.pdf.
6. Y. Sato, J.P. Crutchfield, "Coupled Replicator Equations for the Dynamics of Learning in Multiagent Systems", working paper of Santa Fe Institute, April, 2002,
    www.santafe.edu/sfi/publications/ Working-Papers/02-04-017.pdf

7. J. Hofbauer, K. Sigmund, Evolutionary Games and Population Dynamics, Cambridge Univ. Press, 1998

8. B. Skyrms, Chaos and the explanatory significance of equilibrium: Strange attractors in evolutionary game dynamics, in The Dynamics of Norms, C. Bicchieri et al.(eds.) pp.199–222, Cambridge univ. press, 1997.

9. W-H. Steeb, The Nonlinear Workbook, pp.85-86 World Scientific Pub.,Singapore, 1999.

10. H. Deguchi, Norm Game and Indirect Regulation of Multi agents Society, Computational Analysis of social and Organizational Systems: CASOS Conf. 2000, pp92-95, Carnegie Mellon, 2000.

11. E. Ott, C. Grebogi, J.A. Yorke, Controlling Chaos, Physical Review Letters, vol.64, pp.1196–1199, 1990.

12. K. Pyragas, "Continuous control of chaos by selfcontrolling feedback", Physics Letters A, Vol.170 No.6, pp.421–428, 1992.

13. A. Kittel, J. Parisi, K. Pyragas, "Delayed feedback control of chaos by self-adapting delay time", Physics Letters A, Vol.198, pp.433–436, 1995.

Agent-Based Modeling of Efficient Markets

Sze Wah Lim, Kwok Yee Michael Wong, and Peixun Luo

Department of Physics, Hong Kong University of Science and Technology
Clear Water Bay, Hong Kong, China
{swlim,phkywong,physlpx}@ust.hk

Abstract. We consider the Minority Game which models the collective behavior of agents simultaneously and adaptively competing in a market, or distributively performing load balancing tasks. The variance of the buy-sell decisions is a measure of market inefficiency. When the initial condition of the strategies picked by the agents are the same, the market is inefficient in the regime of low agent complexity, caused by the maladaptive behavior of the agents. However, the market becomes increasingly efficient when the randomness in the initial condition increases. Implications to the occurence of maladaptation, the prediction of market trend and the search for optimal load balancing are discussed.

1 Introduction

In recent years, there is an increasing interest in the use of multi-agent systems in distributed tasks and control. In contrast with the conventional centralized control method, multi-agent systems reduce the computational and communication load of the central controller, and share the load among the community of agents, with the objectives that an optimal performance and a high adaptability to potential environmental changes can be attained. Instead of dictating the actions of the individual agents, the collaboration of the agents is achieved by assigning appropriate payoff functions to individuals, with the objective that useful self-organizing behavior can emerge. A popular approach is to let the agents compute the optimum points corresponding to Nash equilibria, and act accordingly [1].

However, multi-agent systems are dynamical systems, with agents interacting with each other and the environment. Hence it is not clear whether the performance optimum can be approached, even if it can be computed precisely by an agent. Instead, it is possible that the system evolves periodically or even chaotically around the optimum, or gets trapped in suboptimal attractors. It is therefore important to study the collective dynamical behavior of multi-agent systems.

In this paper, we consider the Minority Game (MG) which models the collective behavior of interacting agents simultaneously and adaptively competing for limited resources, or to be in a minority [2]. The model may be applied to biology, social sciences, engineering or economics. For examples, it may correspond to predators searching for hunting grounds with fewer competitors, rush-hour

J. Liu et al. (Eds.): IDEAL 2003, LNCS 2690, pp. 27–34, 2003.

drivers looking for the least congested highway, network routers trying to find the path with least delay, or traders in a financial market trying to buy stocks at a low price when most other traders are trying to sell (or vice versa).

In the context of this conference, we consider MG to be a model in engineering or economics. Macroscopically, we are interested in whether the entire system performs efficiently. For example, if the MG corresponds to the distribution of resources among a network of load balancers, then the system is said to be efficient if the load is uniformly distributed among the agents. Similarly, if the MG corresponds to trading agents in a stock market, then the system is said to be efficient if the fractions of winners and losers are the same.

Previous work [3] showed that when the complexity of the agents' strategies is too high, the agents cannot collectively explore the strategy space thoroughly, thus limiting the market efficiency. On the other hand, when the complexity of the agents' strategies is too low, the market efficiency suffers from the existence of maladaptive behavior of the agents, meaning that they prematurely rush to adapt to market changes in bursts. Hence there is an intermediate complexity at which the market efficiency is optimal. This picture has been confirmed in several variants of MG [4,5].

The contribution of this paper is to show that this optimum of market efficiency is in fact sensitive to the initial condition of the agents. Indeed, the conventional initial condition that all agents share a common preference to all strategies cannot lead to the best market efficiency. In a market, it is more natural to expect that the agents enter the market with their own preferences. A diversity of the initial virtual points among the agents allows the market dynamics to explore a larger phase space, hence leading to a better market efficiency.

2   The Minority Game

The Minority Game (MG) involves a group of agents repeatedly competing to be in the minority group in an environment of limited resources [2]. In the market, each of the N agents can choose to be a buyer or seller at each time step, N being odd. Each agent makes her decision independently according to her own finite set of "strategies" which will be defined later. After all agents have made their choices, both the numbers of buyers and sellers are counted. If there are fewer buyers than sellers, the buyers win and we denote the outcome by 1; otherwise, the sellers win and the outcome is 0. The time series of 1's and 0's is called "history", and is made available to all agents as the only global information for their next choices.

At each time step, the agents make their decisions based on the most recent m bits in the history, hence m is known as the memory size. So for the agents there are 2^m possible histories. A strategy is then a function which maps each of the 2^m histories to buy (1) or sell (0) decisions. Therefore there exist 2^{2^m} different strategies for a given m. The whole set of possible strategies form the strategy pool of the game.

Before the game starts, each agent randomly picks s strategies from the pool, with repetitions allowed. Each agent holds her strategy set throughout the whole game. At each time step, the agents choose, out of the s strategies she has, the most successful one and make decisions accordingly. The success of a strategy is measured by its virtual point, which is initialized to zero before the game starts, and increases by 1 if it indicates the winning decision at a time step, irrespective of whether it is chosen at that time step by an agent or not. The availability of multiple strategies provides an agent with adaptivity, such that she may use an alternative strategy when the one she chooses does not work well. Though we only consider random strategies instead of organized ones, we expect that the model is sufficient to capture the main features of the macroscopic collective behavior of many agents with diverse strategies.

In this paper, we modify the homogeneous initial condition in the original version of MG, by randomly assigning R points to the s strategies of each agent before the game starts, R being an integer. Hence the initial virtual point of each strategy obeys a multinomial distribution with mean R/s and variance $R(s-1)/s^2$. R can thus be considered as a parameter of randomness. The game then proceeds as in the original version.

3   Features of the Original MG

To understand the effects of initial conditions, we first summarize in this section the features of MG with zero initial virtual points for all strategies. Let $N_1(t)$ and $N_0(t)$ be the population of buyers and sellers at the t-th time step respectively, and $N_1(t) + N_0(t) = N$. As shown in the insets of Fig. 1, the time series of $N_1(t)$ flucutate around the mean value of $N/2$. The fluctuation of $N_1(t)$ is smaller when $m = 6$ than $m = 4$ for $N = 257$, reflecting a more efficient market, in the sense that (i) the agents take a lower risk, and (ii) there is a smaller waste of the resources. Extensive simulations show that the variance σ^2 of the buyer population scales as the *complexity* $2^m/N$, as shown in Fig. 1 [3]. When m is small, agents with increasing memory m create time series of decreasing fluctuations. However, the variance does not decrease with m monotonically. Instead, there is a minimum at $2^m/N = 0.5$, after which it increases gradually to a so-called coin-toss limit, as if they were making their decisions randomly, with $\sigma^2/N = 0.25$.

The existence of a minimum variance lower than the coin-toss limit shows that the agents are able to cooperate to improve the market efficiency, despite the fact that the agents are selfish and making independent decisions. Savit *et al* [3] identified that as m changes across the minimum value m_c, the system undergoes a phase transition. In the high complexity phase, the agents cannot coordinate to explore the strategy space effectively. This is because the coordination of the agents' strategies depends on the availability of information of the population's responses to 2^m different strings. When $N \ll 2^m$, the number sN of strategies possessed by the population is much less than the number 2^m of input states

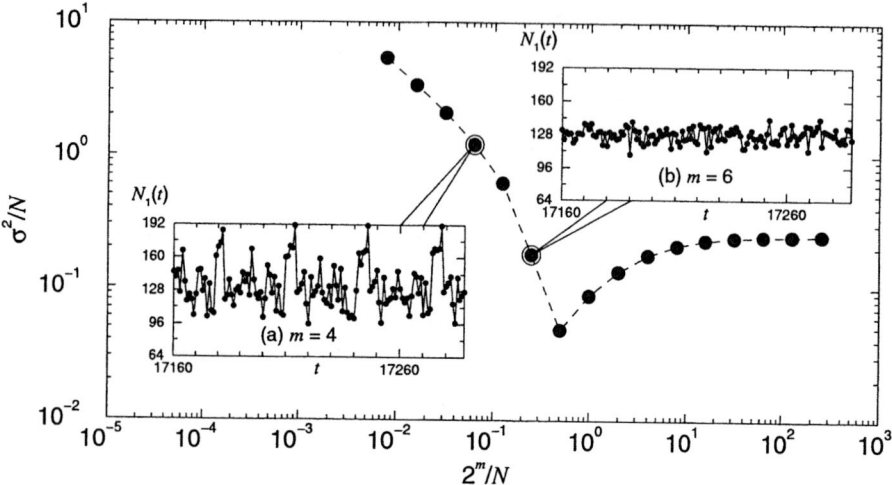

Fig. 1. The dependence of the variance on the complexity for the original MG at $s = 2$ and $N = 257$, averaged over 128 samples at each data point. Insets: typical time series of the buyer population for (a) $m = 4$ and (b) $m = 6$. The periodic component is evident in (a).

of the strategies. This makes the coordination of agents difficult, limiting the market efficiency.

On the other hand, the dynamics is dominated by periodic components in the low complexity phase [3,6,7]. This periodicity is caused by the existence of some agents who, on losing the game, switch their strategies in an attempt to win at the next occurence of the same game history. However, their switch turns out to tip the balance of the strategy distribution, and the previously winning bit (which used to be the minority bit) becomes at the next occurence a losing bit (which newly becomes the majority bit). This switching can go on back and forth indefinitely, resulting in the periodic dynamics. In other words, the market is undesirably influenced by agents who are maladaptive to the environment. This causes the very large volatility of the market, which becomes larger than that of the random market in most of the low complexity phase.

4   Effects of Random Initial Conditions

In the original version of MG, the initial virtual points of all strategies adopted by all agents are the same. This leads to the further simplification that the virtual points of a strategy appears the same to all agents subsequently. This has been utilised conveniently to simplify the analysis such as that in the crowd-anticrowd theory [8].

However, this assumption needs to be re-examined for two reasons. First, if the MG is used as a model of financial markets, it is not natural to expect that all agents have the same preference of a strategy at all instants of the game. Second, if the MG is used as a model of distributed load balancing, it becomes natural to investigate whether the artificially created maladaptive behavior has prevented an efficient exploration of the phase space, thus hindering the attainment of optimal system efficiency.

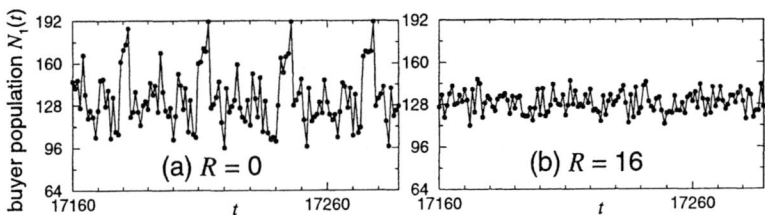

Fig. 2. Typical time series of the buyer population for $R = 0$ and $R = 16$ at $m = 4$, $s = 2$ and $N = 257$. The time series of $R = 0$ has been shown in Fig. 1 inset (a).

Figure 2(b) shows the buyer population as a function of time at the steady state. Compared with the case of the homogeneous initial condition in Fig. 2(a), its fluctuation and periodic behavior is much reduced. The variance is plotted in Fig. 3, showing that it decreases significantly with randomness in the low complexity phase, although it remains unaffected in the high complexity phase. Furthermore, we note that for a randomness of $R = 100 \cdot 2^m$, the optimal variance shifts from $\sigma^2/N = 0.048$ for homogeneous initial conditions to $\sigma^2/N = 0.017$ for random initial conditions, indicating that the market is much more efficient. The optimal complexity also shifts from $2^m/N = 0.50$ to $2^m/N = 0.031$. The simulation also shows that the phase transition at the optimal complexity, where a kink is present in the variance curve, is now replaced by a smooth curve for random initial conditions. This indicates that the original phase transition may not be very relevant in the broader context of arbitrary initial conditions.

Figure 3 also illustrates the scaling of the variance with respect to complexity and randomness. When both m and N vary, we find that the data points collpase together for the same values of $R/2^m$ and $2^m/N$. This means that randomness affects the system behavior in mulitples of 2^m. To illustrate the physical picture, we consider the fraction of agents switching strategies at low values of m. In this case, there are relatively few pairs of possible strategies. Hence for a strategy pair, the virtual point distribution can be described by a multinomial with standard deviation scaling as $\sqrt{R}$. At each time step, the fraction of agents switching strategies is determined by those whose strategies have equal virtual points. Hence this fraction scales as $1/\sqrt{R}$, leading to a variance of $\sigma^2/N \sim N/R = (N/2^m)(2^m/R)$. For a given complexity $2^m/N$, $\sigma^2/N \sim 2^m/R$. Qualitatively, with random initial conditions, there is now a diversity of agents having different preferences of strategies. At each time step, only those with weak

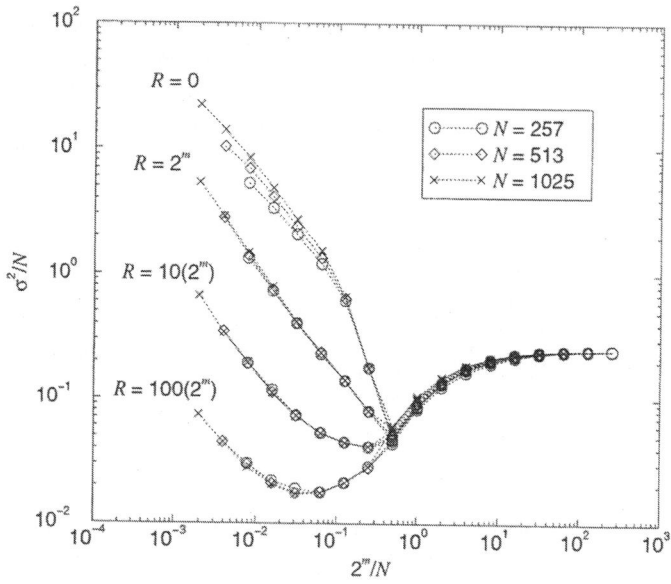

Fig. 3. The dependence of the variance on the complexity at $s = 2$ and averaged over 128 samples for each data point. The randomness are 0, 2^m, $10 \cdot 2^m$, $100 \cdot 2^m$. The population sizes N are 257 (circle), 513 (diamond) and 1025 (cross). The data set at $N = 257$ and $R = 0$ has been shown in Fig. 1.

preferences switch strategies. This greatly reduces the maladaptive behavior and the population variance.

It is instructive to consider how the distribution of wealth or resources changes with the market condition. We measure the wealth or resource acquired by an individual agent in terms of the fraction of time steps that she makes a winning decision. Figure 4 shows the individual wealth of the agents, ranked from left to right in descending order for games with various randomness. For $R = 0$, the market is relatively inefficient, since even the most successful agents cannot reach a winning probability of 0.5. When the randomness increases, there is an increasing fraction of agents with a maximal winning probability. It is interesting to note that the individual wealth of the agents has a maximum winning probability of essentially 0.5 in all cases with randomness, indicating the tendency of the game to distribute resource evenly. The collective wealth acquired by the market, or the overall resource utilization, is measured by the area under the curve of individual wealth, which again increases with randomness.

5   Conclusion

We have studied the effects of initial conditions on the Minority Game, which is a multi-agent system applicable to the modeling of financial markets, or dis-

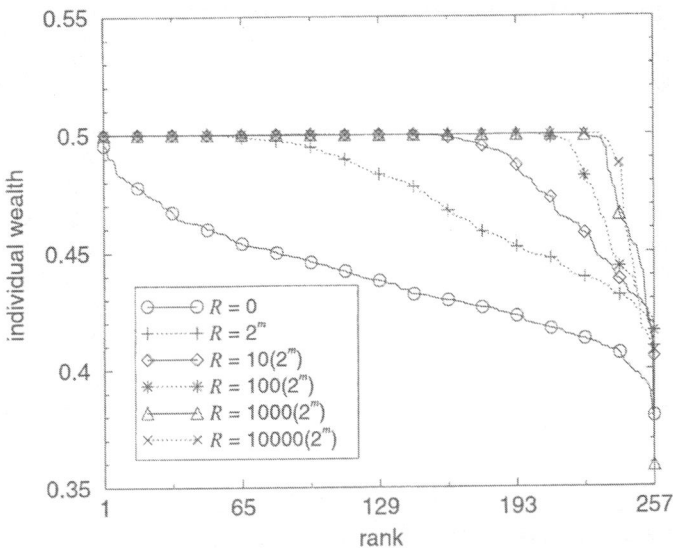

Fig. 4. The individual wealth of all agents (in descending order) for six different games with $m = 4$, $s = 2$ and $N = 257$, averaged over 1024 or 256 samples.

tributed control of load balancing. We find that a diversity of the initial preference of strategies lead to an increase in the system efficiency, and a reduction of the required complexity for optimal efficiency. Scaling studies show that the efficiency depends on the randomness scaled by the number of strategy inputs. The variance in the low complexity phase decreases, showing that the maladaptive behavior is reduced.

The dependence on initial conditions was also noted in MG models with exogenous information (that is, models in which the economic state is determined by external information, rather than its own temporal history) [5,9]. The model of [5] can be described by the ground state of a Hamiltonian, which becomes degenerate in the low complexity phase. Same as the present model, dependence on initial conditions and periodic motions were expected. In the model of [9], senesitivity to initial conditions was also observed in the low complexity phase, and the efficiency can be better than that of the random market. However, to the best of our knowledge, no detailed studies on the effects of initial conditions have so far been reported.

The sensitivity of the steady state to the initial conditions has several implications. First, when the MG is used as a model of financial markets, it shows that the maladaptive behavior is, to a large extent, an artifact of the homogeneous initial condition. In practice, when agents enter the market with diverse views on the values of the strategies, the corresponding initial condition should be randomized. The agents' views are still correlated, so that maladaptation still exists, but to a lesser extent. Due to the agents' diversity, the market efficiency can be better than that of a random market in most of the low complexity phase, and the optimal complexity may shift.

The second implication concerns the interest in MG as a model for economic prediction. For homogeneous initial conditions, the dynamics has a very strong periodic component in the low complexity phase, and is thus very predictable. In practice, for more general initial conditions, the periodic structure diminishes. The entropy of the attractor state, to be presented elsewhere, also increases with randomness. Contrary to previous expectations, it is possible that the low complexity phase is as difficult to predict as the high complexity phase.

Third, when the MG is used as a model of distributed load balancing, the present study illustrates the importance to explore general initial conditions in order to attain the optimal system efficiency. Even when the complexity of the agents is low, they nevertheless can collaborate to achieve a state of low output fluctuations, provided that their initial preferences of the strategies are sufficiently diverse.

This work is supported by the research grant HKUST6153/01P from the Research Grant Council of Hong Kong.

References

1. M. Kearns, Computational Game Theory: A Tutorial, http://www.cis.upenn.edu/~mkearns/nips02tutorial (2002).
2. D. Challet and Y. C. Zhang, Emergence of cooperation and organization in an evolutionary game, Physica A **246**, pp. 407–418 (1997).
3. R. Savit, R. Manuca, and R. Riolo, Adaptive competition, market efficiency, and phase transitions, Phys. Rev. E **82**, pp. 2203–2206 (1999).
4. A. Cavagna, J. P. Garrahan, I. Giardina, and D. Sherrington, Thermal model for adaptive competition in a market, Phy. Rev. E **83**, pp. 4429–4432 (1999).
5. D. Challet, M. Marsili, and R. Zecchina, Statistical mechanics of systems with heterogeneous agents: minority games, Phys. Rev. E **84**, pp. 1824–1827 (2000).
6. D. Zheng and B. H. Wang, Statistical properties of the attendance time series in the minority game, Physica A **301**, pp. 560–566 (2001).
7. C. Y. Lee, Is memory in the minority game relevant? Phys. Rev. E **64**, 015102(R) (2001).
8. M. Hart, P. Jefferies, P. M. Hui, and N. F. Johnson, Crowd-anticrowd theory of multi-agent market games, Eur. Phys. J. B **20**, pp. 547–550 (2001).
9. J. P. Garrahan, E. Moro, and D. Sherrington, Continuous time dynamics of the thermal minority game, Phys. Rev. E **62**, pp. R9–R12 (2000).

Agent Compromises in Distributed Problem Solving

Yi Tang[1,2], Jiming Liu[3], and Xiaolong Jin[3]

[1] Department of Mathematics, Zhongshan University, Guangzhou, China
[2] Department of Mathematics, Guangzhou University, Guangzhou, China
tyi@guangztc.edu.cn,
[3] Department of Computer Science, Hong Kong Baptist University
Kowloon Tong, Hong Kong
{jiming, jxl}@comp.hkbu.edu.hk

Abstract. ERA is a multi-agent oriented method for solving constraint satisfaction problems [5]. In this method, agents make decisions based on the information obtained from their environments in the process of solving a problem. Each agent has three basic behaviors: *least-move*, *better-move*, and *random-move*. The *random-move* is the unique behavior that may help the multi-agent system escape from a local minimum. Although *random-move* is effective, it is not efficient. In this paper, we introduce the notion of agent compromise into ERA and evaluate its effectiveness and efficiency through solving some benchmark Graph Coloring Problems (GCPs). When solving a GCP by ERA, the edges are transformed into two types of constraints: local constraints and neighbor constraints. When the system gets stuck in a local minimum, a compromise of two neighboring agents that have common violated neighbor constraints may be made. The compromise can eliminate the original violated neighbor constraints and make the two agents act as a single agent. Our experimental results show that agent compromise is an effective and efficient technique for guiding a multi-agent system to escape from a local minimum.

Keywords: Agent Compromises, Distributed Constraint Satisfaction Problem, Graph Coloring Problem, Distributed GCP Solving

1 Introduction

A distributed constraint satisfaction problem (distributed CSP) is a constraint satisfaction problem where variables and constraints are distributed to multiple agents. Several multi-agent system based problem solving methods have been proposed for solving distributed CSPs [5] [9]. In these methods, each agent deals with a subproblem that is specified by some variables and related constraints of the given problem.

ERA (Environment, Reactive rules, and Agents) is an example of this kind of methods [5]. In ERA, each agent represents several variables and stays in a lattice-like environment corresponding to the Cartesian product of the variable

J. Liu et al. (Eds.): IDEAL 2003, LNCS 2690, pp. 35–42, 2003.
© Springer-Verlag Berlin Heidelberg 2003

domains. The agent tries to move to a certain lattice so as to make as many as possible constraints satisfied. To do so, at each step, it will select one of the basic reactive behaviors: *better-move*, *least-move*, and *random-move*.

Graph Coloring Problem (GCP) is a class of CSPs. In this paper, we will introduce the notion of agent compromise into ERA for solving GCPs. In solving a GCP by ERA , each agent represents a group of vertices in the given GCP and decides the colors of these vertices. The edges in the GCP are transformed into two types of constraints: local constraints and neighbor constraints. The agent needs to minimize the number of unsatisfied neighbor constraints in order to solve the GCP. When the system gets stuck in a local minimum, we will adopt not only the technique of *random-move* but also agent compromise to lead the system to escape from the local minimum. An agent compromise is made by two neighboring agents that have common violated neighbor constraints. It aims at eliminating the original violated neighbor constraints. When an agent compromise is made, the corresponding two agents will act as a single agent (we call it *compromise agent*) to make their decisions, i.e., decide their common local behaviors. The compromise will be abandoned after a reaction is finished.

The rest of the paper is organized as follows. In Section 2, we describe the background of the paper. In Section 3, we introduce the notion of agent compromise and integrate the agent compromise strategy to ERA. In section 4, we present our experimental results and discussions. Section 5 is the conclusion of the paper.

2   Background

2.1   Graph Coloring Problems

Graph Coloring Problems (GCPs) are NP-hard. Many practical problems can be transformed into GCPs [4]. There are several types of GCPs [10]. One of them is as follows:

Given an undirected graph $G = (V, E)$ where V is a set of vertices and E is a set of pairs of vertices called edges, and a set of available colors $S = \{1, 2, ..., k\}$. The problem is to find a mapping C: $V \rightarrow S$ such that $C(u) \neq C(v)$ if $(u, v) \in E$.

In short, a GCP is to determine whether or not it is feasible to color a graph with a certain number of colors. Fig. 1 shows a simple GCP instance. This graph contains 6 vertices and 7 edges. It can be colored with 3 colors.

2.2   Definitions

Assume that the vertices in a GCP have been divided into n groups [1]: $\{V_1, V_2, ..., V_n\}$, where $V_i \cap V_j = \phi$ and $\cup_{i=1}^{n} V_i = V$. We further assume that a set of agents: $\{agent_1, agent_2, ..., agent_n\}$ is used to represent vertex groups. Specifically, $agent_i$ represents the vertices in V_i.

---

[1] Each vertex can be regarded as a variable whose domain is the color set.

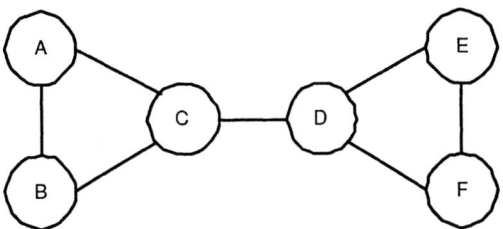

Fig. 1. A 3 colorable graph.

Definition 1. *(Local constraints, neighbor constraints, and local color vector)*

1. *Local constraints of $agent_i$ are the edges among vertices in V_i;*
2. *Neighbor constraints of $agent_i$ are the edges between vertices in V_i and those in $V - V_i$.*
3. *A local color vector of $agent_i$ is a tuple of color assignments of all vertices in V_i that satisfied all local constraints of $agent_i$.*

Definition 2. *(Agent environment)*
    The environment of $agent_i$ is composed of lattices corresponding to all local color vectors of $agent_i$. The size of $agent_i$'s environment is m, if and only if $agent_i$ has m local color vectors.

An agent always stays in one of lattices in its environment. An agent stays at a lattice indicates its vertices are assigned colors corresponding to the local color vector.

For example, in Fig. 1, we can divide the vertices into two groups: {A, B, C} and {D, E, F}. Two agents, $agent_1$ and $agent_2$, are used to represent them respectively. Edges AB, BC and AC are local constraints of $agent_1$, and edge CD is its neighbor constraint with $agent_2$. If S = {1, 2, 3} is the color set, (1, 2, 3) is a local color vector of $agent_1$ which means A, B, and C are colored with colors 1, 2, and 3, respectively. The local color vectors of $agent_1$ are (1, 2, 3), (1, 3, 2), (2, 1, 3), (2, 3, 1), (3, 1, 2), and (3, 2, 1). The size of $agent_1$'s environment is 6.

Note that based on the above definitions, the local constraints of $agent_i$ are always satisfied in any states.

3   Distributed GCP Solving by ERA with Agent Compromises

3.1   Reactive Behaviors of Agents

In order to solve a given GCP, at each step, an agent will probabilistically select the following three predefined local reactive behaviors to decide which lattice it will move to [5]:

- *least-move*: the agent moves to a lattice where it has the minimum number of violated neighbor constraints;
- *better-move*: the agent moves to a random lattice where the number of violated neighbor constraints caused is fewer than that at its current lattice;
- *random-move*: the agent randomly moves to a lattice.

When an agent selects a *least-move* or a *better-move*, it may not move to a new lattice because at its current lattice this agent has already a minimum number of violated neighbor constraints or it is in a *zero-position* [5]. When none of the agents can move by a *least-move* or a *better-move*, it means the system gets stuck in a local minimum. The *random-move* behavior is the unique reactive behavior that an agent can use to escape from a local minimum. Different *random-move* ratios, namely, the probability ratios of $P_{random\_move} : P_{least\_move} : P_{better\_move}$, may yield different performances. In order to explore the optimal *random-move* ratio, we conduct a set of experiments on an instance, *myciel7.col*, with different *random-move* ratios by 64 agents. . The results in Tab. 1 show that a relative small ratio is better than others. $5 : 1000 : 1000$ is the optimal one.

Table 1. Comparisons among different *random-move* ratios. The results are obtained by solving an instance, *myciel7.col*, with 64 agents. This instance, downloaded from [10], contains 191 vertices and 2,360 edges. It can be colored with 8 colors. We run the ERA algorithm 100 times in each case and calculate the average results.

random-move Ratio	Num. of Movements
2 : 1000 : 1000	235
3 : 1000 : 1000	252
5 : 1000 : 1000	**222**
8 : 1000 : 1000	250
10: 1000 : 1000	235
20: 1000 : 1000	259

The *random-move* behavior is simple and effective, but it is not efficient. Although we can select a suitable *random-move* ratio, we cannot slide over that the results are broken away by the randomness caused by *random-move*. The reason that we need randomness during a problem solving is that it can lead the multi-agent system to escape from a local minimum. There are other techniques to provide the function that lead the system out of a local minimum [7] [8]. In the following, we will propose a new technique for helping agents escape from a local minimum in a distGCP solving.

3.2   Agent Compromises

Why do there exist local minima when solving a given problem? An intuitional explanation is that there is a set of *primary* variables. It is hard to find suitable values for these variables in a few steps, which satisfy all the related constraints. After assigned values for these *primary* variables, the values of other variables will be easily determined [1]. In the case of distGCP, since each vertex is represented by a certain agent, the characteristic of *primary* variables is partially demonstrated by the *hard* neighbor constraints between agents. If we can make them satisfied as early as possible, we might improve the solving. Motivated by this view, we propose an agent compromise strategy for agents. We equip the agents with the behavior of *make-compromise.*

The compromise of agents is made by two neighboring agents (i.e. the two agents have at least one common neighbor constraint) in the distGCP solving. It can be viewed as a virtual agent whose variables and constraints are inherited from the original two agents. We call the two agents as *component agents* and the virtual agent as *compromise agent*. The local constraints of *compromise agent* are not only inherited from the local constraints of the two agents, but also from the neighbor constraints between them. Once a compromise has been made, a *compromise agent* is activated and the two *component agents* are deactivated. The environment of the *compromise agent* is composed of those of the two *component agents*. The same as an agent in a distGCP solving, when the *compromise agent* stays in its environment, its local constraints are satisfied. Furthermore, the *compromise agent* will inherit some reactive behaviors of the two component agents and determine its local reactive behavior based on its local environment. This implicitly makes the two component agents moving in coherence. The compromise will be abandoned after the above reaction is finished. At the same time, the two *component agents* are recovered and they inherit the moving results of the *compromise agent*. This means that all neighbor constraints between these two *component agents* are satisfied.

3.3   The Process of a Make-Compromise

When solving a given GCP, if an agent wants to make a compromise with other neighbor agents, it will start the procedure of a *make-compromise*. And, we will call this agent *master.*

The *master* will choose one of its neighbors, called *slave*, to form a compromise agent based on a criterion that the number of violated neighbor constraints between the *master* and the *slave* is the largest. If several *masters* select the same *slave*, the one that has the largest number of violated neighbor constraints with the *slave* will win the competition and form a compromise agent with the *slave* finally. The reactive behaviors of the *compromise agent* can be *least-move*, *better-move*, and *random-move*. After finishing a selected behavior, the compromise is abandoned. The values of the variables in the compromise are returned to the *master* or the *slave*. The neighbor constraints between the *master* and the *slave* are satisfied. The state of the multi-agent system is then updated and the system will continue running from the updated state.

4   Experimental Results and Discussions

4.1   Experiments and Results

In the following experiments, we classify reactive behaviors into two types: *random* and *non-random*, and set the probability ratio of these two types behaviors as 5:2000. We set *better-move* and *least-move* with the same probability. We further introduce the *make-compromise* ratio, denoted by the probability ratio, $p_{make\_compromise} : p_{non\_random}$. For example, if this ratio is 5:100, it means that the probability ratio of the four reactive behaviors $p_{random\_move} : p_{make\_compromise} : p_{least\_move} : p_{better\_move}$ is 5:100:950:950. The vertices in each GCP instance are equally partitioned into groups according to the label sequence. A corresponding number of agents will be used to represent these vertex groups.

In the experiments, the asynchronous operations of distributed agents are simulated by means of sequentially dispatching agents and allowing them to sense the current state of their environments. All agents are dispatched randomly and are given the same *random-move* ratio. For simplicity, we assume *least-move* is the unique reactive behavior of a *compromise agent*.

1. Comparisons between different *make-compromises* ratios

    In this set of experiments, we show what is the optimal *make-compromises* ratio by solving an instance, *myciel7.col*, in [10]. Tab. 2 shows the results of the experiments. It shows that if choosing the ratio between 5 and 10, the performance is better.

Table 2. Comparisons between different *make-compromises* ratios. The results are obtained by solving an instance, *myciel7.col*, with 64 agents. The instance is from [10] and contains 191 vertices and 2,360 edges. It can be colored with 8 colors. We run the solver 100 times in each case and calculate the average number of movements and that of compromises.

make-compromise Ratio $p_{make\_compromise} : p_{non\_random}$	Num. of Movements	Num. of Compromises
-	222	-
1 : 100	182	8
2 : 100	169	13
5 : 100	**141**	**23**
8 : 100	**142**	**33**
10 : 100	**139**	**33**
15 : 100	152	59
30 : 100	146	88
40 : 100	155	110

2. Comparisons between the performances with/without *make-compromises*

We select 8 instances from [10] to compare the performances of ERA without/with agent compromises. We run each instances in each case 100 times. In each run with compromises, we set the *make-compromise* ratio as 5:100. Tab. 3 shows the experimental results. It shows that ERA can reduce the number of movements on average 26% (ranging from 14% to 44%) if adopting *make-compromise*.

Table 3. Comparisons between different distributed GCP solving with/without *make-compromises*. The results are obtained by solving 8 instances from [10]. We run the ERA algorithm 100 times in each cases. The number of movements(with/without compromises) are on average and the reduction(%) is the percents of the movements reduced after introducing agent compromise.

Instance ID (vertices, edges, colors)	Num. of Agents	Num. of Movements (with/without compromises)	Reduction (%)
anna.col (138, 493, 11)	46	187 / 334	44
jean.col (80, 254, 10)	27	43 / 51	16
miles250.col (128, 387, 8)	43	169 / 296	43
queen5_5.col (25, 160, 5)	8	38 / 44	14
queen6_6.col (36, 290, 7)	12	1,960 / 2,291	14
queen7_7.col (49, 476, 7)	16	2,363 / 2,834	17
myciel6.col (95, 755, 7)	32	51 / 71	28
myciel7.col (191, 2360, 7)	64	141 / 222	36

4.2 Discussions

In order to help agents escape from a local minimum, we endue each agent with the behavior of *make-compromise*. An agent compromise is made by two neighboring agents that have common unsatisfied constraints. It can eliminate these constraints. Behind the introduction of agent compromise is the existence of the *primary* variables. Since these variables are *hard* to set a suitable values that satisfy all related constraints, it is one of the main reasons why the agents get stuck in local minima. The compromise between two agents gives the multi-agent system more chances to set these variables with suitable values. As compared with the *random-move* behavior, the *make-compromise* behavior is addressed the structure of a problem. This is based on that the *hard* constraints are often associated with the *primary* variables, especially when the system has been running a few time steps.

On the other hand, the behavior of a *compromise agent* can be viewed as a partially global behavior, because it is a temporary union of two neighboring agents and the corresponding two *component agents* can make decisions in coherence. According to the results of our experiments, the employment of this kind of global behavior can improve the performance of ERA in solving a GCP.

However, we cannot exempt the agents from the behavior of *random-move*. Although a *compromise agent* can make the violated neighbor constraints satisfied, the variables changed might not belong to the *primary* variables. This may lead to the different reduction of agent movements. We need further study on the structure of a problem.

5   Conclusion

In this paper, we introduce the notion of agent compromise to the ERA method in distributed GCP solving. When solving a given GCP with ERA, we equip each agent with the behavior of *make-compromise*. This behavior provides another ability for agents to escape from a local minimum. As compared with the *random-move* behavior, this behavior integrates two neighboring agents and makes them. moving in coherence. We have examined the compromise strategy in distributed GCP solving. The experimental results show an obvious improvement of ERA with agent compromises in solving some benchmark GCPs.

Acknowledgements. This project is supported in part by a HKBU FRG grant and conducted at the Computer Science Department of HKBU.

References

1. Gomes, C. P., Selman, B., Crato, N., Kautz, H.: Heavy-tailed phenomena in satisfiability and constraint satisfaction problems, Journal of automated reasoning, **24**, (2000), 67–100.
2. Gu, J.: Efficient local search for very large-scale satisfiability problem, SIGART Bulletin, **3**, (1992), 8–12.
3. Hoos, H.H., Stutzle, T.: Systematic vs. Local Search for SAT, Proc. of KI-99, LNAI 1701, Springer, (1999), 289–293.
4. Leighton, F.: A graph coloring algorithm for large scheduling problems, Journal of Research of the National Bureau of Standards, **84**, (1979), 489–503
5. Liu, J., Jing, H., Tang, Y.Y.: Multi-agent oriented constraint satisfaction, Artificial Intelligence. **138**, (2002) 101–144.
6. Nareyek, A.: Using global constraints for local search, Constraint Programming and Large Scale Discrete Optimization, DIMACS, **57**, (2001) 9–28.
7. Schuurmans, D., Southey, F., Holte, R. C.: In Proceedings of the 17th International Joint Conference On Artificial Intelligence (IJCAI-01), (2001) 334–341.
8. Shang, Y., Wah,B.W.: A discrete Lagrangian-based global-search method for solving satisfiability problems, Journal of global optimization. **12(1)**, (1998) 61–99.
9. Yokoo, M., Durfee, E.H., Ishida, T., Kuwabara, K.: The distributed constraint satisfaction problem: Formalization and algorithms, IEEE Transaction on Knowledge and Data Engineering. **10(5)**, (1998) 673–685.
10. http://mat.gsia.cmu.edu/COLOR02

A Multi-agent System for Emergency Decision Support

Martin Molina and Gemma Blasco

Department of Artificial Intelligence, Universidad Politécnica de Madrid,
Campus de Montegancedo S/N 28660 Boadilla del Monte, Madrid, Spain
mmolina@fi.upm.es, gblasco@isys.dia.fi.upm.es

Abstract. This paper describes the multi-agent organization of a computer system that was designed to assist operators in decision making in the presence of emergencies. The application was developed for the case of emergencies caused by river floods. It operates on real-time receiving data recorded by sensors (rainfall, water levels, flows, etc.) and applies multi-agent techniques to interpret the data, predict the future behavior and recommend control actions. The system includes an advanced knowledge based architecture with multiple symbolic representation with uncertainty models (bayesian networks). This system has been applied and validated at two particular sites in Spain (the Jucar basin and the South basin).

1 Introduction

In Spain, the SAIH National Programme (Spanish acronym for Automatic System Information in Hydrology) was initiated with the goal of installing sensor devices and telecommunications networks in the main river basins to get on real time in a control center the information on rainfall, water levels and flows in river channels. One of the main goals of this type of control centers is to help to react in the presence emergency situations as a consequence of river floods.

This task may be facilitated with the help of a computer system conceived as an *intelligent assistant* [1]. The development of such a system presents certain difficulties such as: (1) the system has to include a model to automatically provide on real time answers about future hypotheses of behavior, (2) the system has to explain and justify its conclusions given that the operator must take the final responsibility of decisions, and (3), since the SAIH Programme develops several of realizations of such systems for different river basins, it is also important to consider the reusability of the software architecture.

In this paper we describe the multi-agent organization of a decision support computer system, called SAIDA, for flood emergency management in the context of the SAIH Programme. The paper describes first the functional model, describing the main tasks: evaluation, prediction and recommendation. Then, the paper describes how these tasks are simulated in a distributed manner according to a multiagent architecture. Finally, the last section presents how the system was implemented with the help of a knowledge engineering tool.

J. Liu et al. (Eds.): IDEAL 2003, LNCS 2690, pp. 43–51, 2003.

2 The Functional Model for Decision Support

In order to develop the SAIDA system, we formulated a knowledge model based on the tasks that operators perform during flood emergency situations. For each task we selected an appropriate problem solving method that help to construct the computational version [2]. According to this, the resulting knowledge model for SAIDA includes three main tasks: evaluation, prediction and recommendation. The goal of the *evaluation task* is to identify potential emergency situations by interpreting sensor data about the current state of the river basin, based on certain patterns of scenarios about rain, water levels, flows and reservoir states. This corresponds to a typical classification task that selects a category (a type of problem) within a prefixed set, based on a set of observations (sensor data). In this case, this task can be solved by an adaptation of the *heuristic classification* method [3] with two steps: (1) *abstract* to abstract data from sensors, and (2) *match* to find patterns of problems that match the current information from sensors.

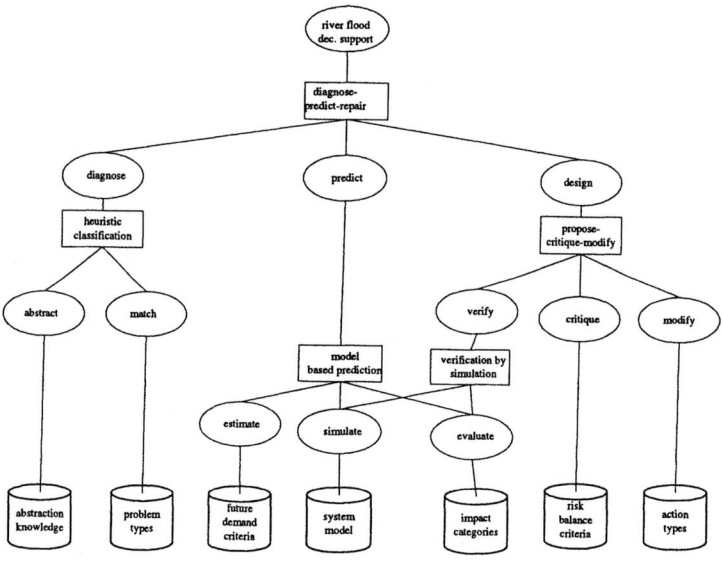

Fig. 1. A functional view of the model for decision support in the field of emergency management during floods. Legend: circle (task), square (method), cylinder (knowledge base).

The goal of the *prediction task* is to predict the future behavior and estimate potential damages. This task can be carried out by a method that performs the following steps: (1) *estimate future rain* to generate hypotheses of future rain for the next H hours (e.g. H = 8 hours), based on a heuristic model about the river basin and the global weather forecast received as input, (2) *simulate the river behavior* that uses a model of the river basin based on causal relations following a bayesian approach in order to provide the range of potential behaviors using statistical measures, and (3) *estimate potential damages* to estimate the impact of the flows in terms of potential damages by using empirical knowledge that relates water levels and flows with qualitative ranges of severity for each particular critical location.

The goal of the *recommendation task* is to suggest possible control actions as an answer to the detected problem. This distinguishes between two possibilities: (a) *hydraulic actions*, that establish discharge policies at the dams to avoid undesirable impacts and (b) *defensive actions*, such as population alert, evacuation procedures, etc. involving different organizations like traffic police, health services, fire brigades, army, etc. The first case can be performed by a method that explores a search space of potential hydraulic actions using a heuristic approach. The basic idea is that the method evaluates the current situation and, based on empirical knowledge, proposes a set of hydraulic actions that potentially can solve the problem. Then, these actions are tested by simulation and, if the result of the test is not satisfactory, empirical knowledge is used again to modify the hydraulic actions. These steps are performed in a loop until a satisfactory set of control actions is found. In the artificial intelligence literature, this method receives the name of *propose-critique-modify* [4][5]. The set of defensive actions is found by using a classification method supported by a model that relates types of problems with types of defensive actions (for the shake of simplicity, this method is not included in the figure corresponding to the complete model).

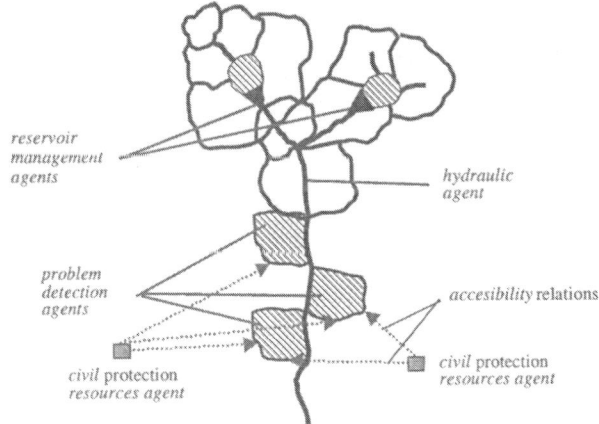

Fig. 2. Types of agents

3   The Multi-agent Organization

In order to cope with the knowledge complexity, we followed the concept of multi-agent system to complement the previous knowledge model. To develop the multi-agent approach we followed the distributed nature of the decisions and the geographical distribution. We identified four types of agents: (1) *hydraulic agents* to give answers about the behavior of the physical process, (2) *problem detection agents*, to evaluate the flood risk in a particular geographical area, (3) *reservoir management agents*, with criteria for exploitation strategy for each reservoir, and (4) *civil protection agents,* responsible to provide with resources of different types according to the demands of the problem detection agents.

3.1   Domain Knowledge Distribution between Agents

Figure 3 shows how we distributed the different knowledge bases between agents. There is an agent for each specific decision point at certain location in the river basin depending on its nature (problem area, reservoir, river channel or protection). For each agent, there is a set of types of knowledge bases, each one with its particular language representation. For example, problem detection agents include a total of six knowledge bases that provide the necessary domain criteria for the agent's tasks. Some of the types of knowledge bases for problem detection agents are the same for reservoir management agents. They have the same representation and role in the reasoning process but the content is different for each agent.

A model for a particular river basin is constructed formulating this set of knowledge bases. Figure 3 shows a summary of a complete model for the case of a river basin in Spain (the Júcar river basin). This includes a total of 23 agents, one for each specific decision point at certain location in the river basin depending on its nature (problem area, reservoir, river channel or protection). For each agent, there is a set of types of knowledge bases, each one with its particular language representation, with a total of 143 knowledge bases.

Agents	N. of agents	Knowledge Bases	Knowledge Representation	N. of KBs
Problem detection agents	15	Abstraction	Functional + temporal represent.	15
		Problem types	Frames with uncertainty degrees	15
		Future Demand	Rules	15
		Impact categories	Bayesian network	15
		Risk balance criteria	Rules	1
		Action types: agent relations	Horn Logic Clauses	15
Reservoir management agents	4	Abstraction	Functional + temporal represent.	4
		Problem types	Frames with uncertainty degrees	4
		Future Demand	Rules	4
		Impact categories	Bayesian nets	4
		Risk balance criteria	Rules	1
		Action types: discharge strategies	Rules	1
Hydraulic agents	2	Abstraction	Functional + temporal represent.	2
		System model: influence diagram	Temporal causal network	2
		System model: infiltration	Bayesian network	12
		System model: discharge	Bayesian network	12
		System model: reservoir discharge	Bayesian network	4
		System model: junction	Bayesian network	11
Protection agents	2	Action types: transport network	Rules	2
		Action types: population	Rules	2
		Action types: constructions	Rules	2
TOTAL	23 Ag.		TOTAL	143 KBs

Fig. 3. Summary of knowledge bases corresponding to a particular model

3.2 Task Distribution between Agents

According to the multi-agent organization, the previous three tasks (evaluation, prediction and recommendation) are distributed among the different agents, in such a way that they communicate partial results to complete general goals. For example, the evaluation task is distributed among problem detection agents, in such a way that each one includes local knowledge to determine whether in its local geographical area there is a significant risk of floods according to the current state of the river basin. For this purpose they consult data from sensors and classify the situation according to the method for evaluation described in the previous section.

When a particular problem detection agent identifies a potential dangerous scenario, it asks for a prediction of behavior to the corresponding hydraulic agents and, then, it interprets this information to conclude the level of severity of the future problem. In order to predict the behavior of the river, the hydraulic agent is specialized in simulating the local physical phenomena (rainfall, runoff, etc.) of a particular river, by using local river models based on bayesian networks.

The last of the three tasks (the recommendation task) is carried out by a method that simulates how the agents with potential problems ask other agents to help them in decreasing their risk level by performing a kind of cooperation. For this purpose, we designed a multi-agent version of the centralized knowledge-based method called *propose-critique-modify*. Based on this method, we consider the following steps (figure 4): (1) *propose,* a new state of the river basin is proposed by simulation (using bayesian networks) considering the effect of a current control action, (2) *critique* the current proposal of hydraulic actions, (2) *modify* the current proposal of hydraulic action based on the previous critiques and following certain heuristic rules.

```
1. PROPOSE STEP
1.1  Hydraulic agents propagate the effect of the current control actions by simulation.

2. CRITIQUE STEP
2.1  Every agent (problem detection and reservoir management) evaluates its risk level.
2.2  IF the maximum risk condition and the risk balance condition are satisfied THEN end.

3. MODIFY STEP
3.1  Aᵢ is the agent with the worst risk level.
3.2  Aᵢ looks for a friend agent Aⱼ.
3.3  IF Aⱼ is found THEN an Aᵢ and Aⱼ interact to modify the current control action.
3.4  Go to 1.
```

Fig. 4. Multi-agent version of the propose-critique-modify method

In order to perform the critique step, the model uses the concept of *risk level.* The risk level is a discrete value that goes from 1 to 10 and represents globally the severity of the situation at certain location. For the case of *problem detection agents* the risk level is evaluated based on the sort-term prediction of the flow in the problem area. For this purpose, a bayesian network is defined for each location in such a way that low (high) values of flow are related with low (high) values of risk. The bayesian representation provides the required freedom to calibrate each particular case according to the specific physical structure. The risk level is computed for every future time step so that the final risk level is the maximum value of the values of risk level for each time step. For the case of *reservoir management agents* the risk level is computed based on the sort-term prediction of the reservoir storage. For this purpose a parameter S (*safe factor*) is computed with $S = 100 \, (C - V_0) / (V_{max} - V_0)$ where C is the capacity of the reservoir, V_0 is the current storage of the reservoir and V_{max} is the maximum storage corresponding to the sort-term prediction. Then, the risk level is determined using conditional heuristic relations in form of production rules in such a way that low levels of safe factor and high values of current storage are related with high values of risk levels.

Taking into account that the goal is to minimize the maximum risk level, the critique step uses a social rule expressed with two conditions that determines when the current hydraulic control is acceptable:

- *Maximum risk condition:* Every agent must present a risk level lower than a threshold (e.g., lower than 5).

- *Risk balance condition:* The different between the highest and lowest risk levels must be lower than a threshold (e.g., lower than 3).

During the modify step, the goal is to find a new proposal of control actions by considering how to decrease the highest risk level. This step considers the social rule that the agent A_i with the *highest risk level* is in charge of finding a new proposal. Since the reduction of a risk level for a particular agent usually implies to increase the risk level of others, A_i looks for another agent A_j, called the *friend agent*, that could help by increasing its own risk level. A_j is considered a *friend* of A_i when:

- A_i is a reservoir management agent, A_j is a downstream agent of A_i, there are not river confluences between A_i and A_j, A_j presents a low risk level, or

- A_i is an agent (reservoir management or problem detection), A_j is an upstream reservoir management agent, A_j is not closed, there are not closed reservoirs between A_i and A_j, A_j presents a low risk level.

If the friend agent is found, an interaction between both agents is performed based on local heuristic rules to find a control action. For instance, this interaction is based on the idea that an agent A_i (e.g., problem detection agent) asks to the other A_j (e.g., reservoir agent) to decrease the discharge in order to decrease its own risk level one point. For this purpose A_i computes locally the desired risk level to determine the flow decrease and A_j computes locally the flow decrease to determine the new storage objective. As a result of the interaction, one of the agents, A_i or A_j, proposes a modification of the control in form of a new storage objective for a particular reservoir. Then, the effect of this control action is simulated and the process continues in an iterative loop until a satisfactory solution is found.

4 Implementation

To implement the SAIDA system we used a knowledge engineering tool called KSM [6]. With this tool it is possible to formulate an abstract knowledge model as a structured collection of knowledge bases and problem-solvers, supported by a library of primitives of representation (software components that implement each type of knowledge representation and inference). Then, this abstract structure can be instantiated in different ways, using specific domain knowledge, to produce different knowledge systems.

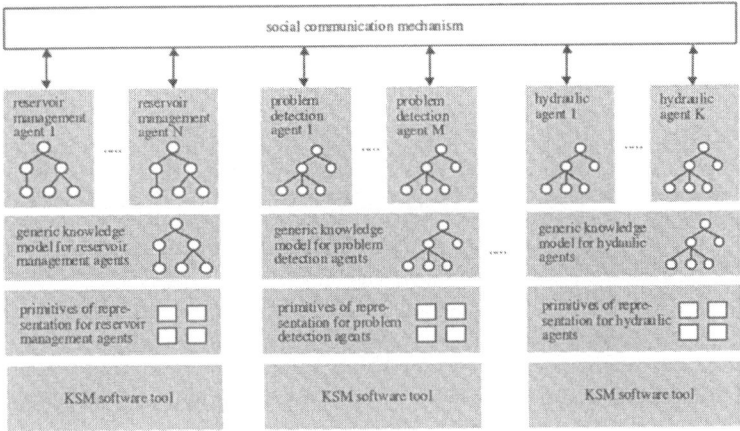

Fig. 5. Software architecture to support the multi-agent organization.

We followed this idea to define an abstract knowledge organization for each type of agent (reservoir management agent, problem detection agent, etc.) as a structured collection of classes of tasks, knowledge bases, symbolic representation, etc. Then, each specific agent (e.g., the Forata reservoir management agent) is built as particularization of the abstract structure providing domain knowledge (specific domain rules, etc.)[7]. Thus, different copies of KSM, one for each family with the same generic structure, support the complete society of agents (Figure 5). Therefore, KSM provided a solution to build general knowledge structures that are shared by different instances of agents, giving the required freedom to write the particular adaptations of each agent in their particular knowledge bases.

On the other hand, to facilitate the model construction and maintenance for each particular river basin, we built a software tool called CAM-Hidro that assists developers and end-users providing guidance and assistance for consistency checking and complementary views (abstract views, dependence relations, etc.) of the model.

5 Conclusions

In summary, the application presented in this paper, SAIDA, corresponds to an innovative multi-agent based solution for a system with complex and heterogeneous agents. Each type of agent was designed as a knowledge-based system with multiple representation (rules, bayesian networks, logic clauses, etc.) and different tasks. The multi-agent approach was very useful to organize in a modular and natural structure the different components of the whole knowledge model.

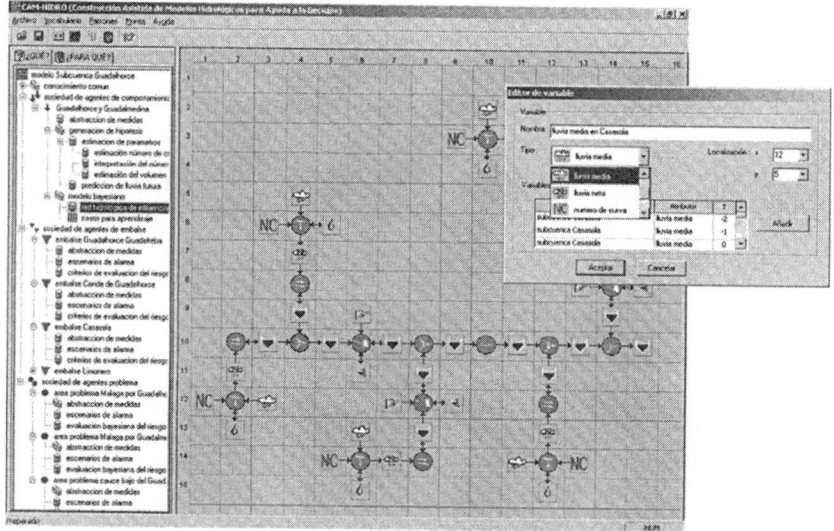

Fig. 6. Example of screen presented by the user interface of the CAM-Hidro tool.

We developed two realizations of this system for two different river basins in Spain. For instance, the Júcar River Basin included 23 agents with a total of 143 knowledge bases. For the implementation, the KSM tool provided enough flexibility and efficiency to operate on real time and the CAM-Hidro tool were useful to facilitate the process of construction and maintenance of knowledge models.

Acknowledgements. The development of the SAIDA system was supported by the Ministry of Environment of Spain (*Dir. General de Obras Hidráulicas y Calidad de las Aguas*) with the participation of local public organizations from river basins (*Conf. Hidrográfica del Júcar* and *Conf. Hidrográfica del Sur de España.*). The development of the CAM-Hidro tool was supported by the Ministry of Science and Technology of Spain within the RIADA project.

References

1. Boy, G., Gruber T.R.: "Intelligent Assistant Systems: Support for Integrated Human-Machine Systems" Proc. of 1990 AAAI Spring Symposium on *Knowledge-Based Human-Computer Communication*, March 1990, Stanford University.
2. Molina M., Ossowski S.: "Knowledge Modelling in Multiagent Systems: The Case of the Management of a National Network" in "Intelligence in Service and Networks. Paving the Way for an Open Service Market" *Lecture Notes in Computer Science 1597*, Springer, 1999.

3. W. Clancey: "Heuristic Classification". *Artificial Intelligence 27*, 1985.
4. Brown D., Chandrasekaran B.: *Design Problem-solving: Knowledge Structures and Control Strategies*, Morgan Kaufman, 1989.
5. Marcus S., McDermott J.: "SALT: A knowledge acquisition language for propose-and-revise systems". Artificial Intelligence, 39(1) 1–38, 1989.
6. J. Cuena, M. Molina: "The Role of Knowledge Modeling Techniques in Software Development: A General Approach Based on a Knowledge Management Tool". *International Journal of Human-Computer Studies* (2000) 52, 385–421.
7. Molina M., Cuena J.: Using Knowledge Modelling Tools for Agent-based Systems: The Experience of KSM. In J.Cuena et al. (eds.) "Knowledge Engineering and Agent Technology" IOS Press, Ámsterdam, in press (2003).

The Artificial Ecosystem: A Multiagent Architecture

Maurizio Miozzo, Antonio Sgorbissa, and Renato Zaccaria

DIST – University of Genoa, Via Opera Pia 13, Tel +39 010 3532801
{maurizio.miozzo,antonio.sgorbissa, renato.zaccaria}@unige.it

Abstract. We propose a multiagent, distributed approach to autonomous mobile robotics which is an alternative to most existing systems in literature: robots are thought of as mobile units within an intelligent environment where they coexist and co-operate with fixed, intelligent devices that are assigned different roles: helping the robot to localize itself, controlling automated doors and elevators, detecting emergency situations, etc. To achieve this, intelligent sensors and actuators (i.e. physical agents) are distributed both onboard the robot and throughout the environment, and they are handled by Real-Time software agents which exchange information on a distributed message board. The paper describes the approach and shows the details of its implementation, by outlining the benefits in terms of efficiency and Real-Time responsiveness.

1 Introduction

In the last twenty years, many approaches were proposed in order to implement fully autonomous mobile robots. In most cases, the main focus of discussion has been the importance to be given to reactive and deliberative activities to govern the robot's actions: see for example the contraposition between behavior-based architectures (like Subsumption Architecture [1], ALLIANCE [2]) and hybrid approaches (like AuRA [3], ATLANTIS [4]). However, in spite of their differences, almost all the existing systems share a philosophical choice (partially due to efficiency reasons) which unavoidably lead to a centralized design. We call it the *autarchic robot design*; it can be summarized in the following two points:

- robots must be fully autonomous: i.e., they are often asked to co-operate with humans or other robots but they mainly relies on their own sensors, actuators, and decision processes in order to carry out their tasks.
- robots must be able to operate in non structured environments (i.e. environments which have not been purposely modified to help robots to perform their tasks).

Up to now, this approach has not been very successful. No robot (or team of robots) has proven yet to be really "autonomous" in a generic, "non structured" environment, i.e. able to work continuously, for a long period of time, carrying out its tasks with no performance degradation or human intervention. On the opposite, the few examples of robots which are closer to be considered autonomous (in the sense which has been just given) were designed to work in a specific –even if unstructured- environment: see for example the museum tour-guide robot Rhino [5], which heavily relied on the building's ceiling lights to periodically correct its position in the environment.

Having learnt the lesson, we face all the problem related to autonomy in a full multiagent perspective; robots are thought of as mobile physical agents within an

J. Liu et al. (Eds.): IDEAL 2003, LNCS 2690, pp. 52–59, 2003.

intelligent environment (we metaphorically call it an "Artificial Ecosystem - AE") where they coexist and cooperate with fixed physical agents, i.e. intelligent sensing/actuating devices that are assigned different roles: devices which provide the robots with clues about their position in the environment, devices that control automated doors and elevators, devices for detecting emergency situations such as fires or liquid leaks, cameras for surveillance, etc. Both robots and intelligent devices are handled by software agents, which can communicate through a distributed message board and are given a high level of autonomy. According to this definition, autonomy (and intelligence) is not just a characteristic attribute to robots, but it is distributed throughout the building (Fig. 1 on the left): we say that robots are *autonomous* but not *autarchic*. Next, we extend the concept of intelligent devices to the sensors and actuators on board the robot: analogously to fixed, intelligent devices distributed throughout the building, onboard sensors and actuators are implemented as autonomous devices, i.e. they are handled by software agents which can communicate with other agents through the distributed message board and are given a high level of autonomy in taking decisions. Thus, intelligent control on the robot is performed at two different levels (Fig. 1 on the right): on the lower level a higher reactivity is reached through simple reactive agents which control sensors and actuators; on a higher level, sensorial inputs are collected by agents running on the onboard computer and performing more sophisticate computations before issuing control to actuators. This increases the tolerance of the system to failures: the coupling of intelligent sensors and actuators is able to produce an emergency behavior even in case of a failure in the onboard software.

In Section 2 we show the overall architecture of the system, by outlining implementation details; in Section 3 we show how the AE approach can help to simplify problems related to autonomous navigation and localization. In Section 4 some experimental results are given.

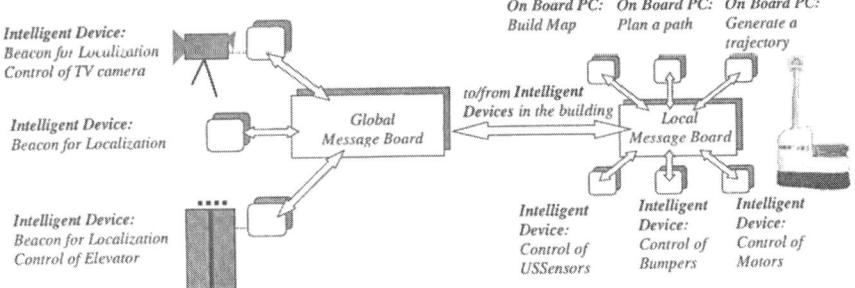

Fig. 1. The Artificial Ecosystem – Left: agents in the building; Right: agents on the robot.

2 Agent Architecture

Three different types of software agents are devised in the AE architecture (agents are classified according to Russel and Norvig's definition [6]):

- type 1: *simple reflex agents*, i.e. agents with no internal state governed by condition-action rules. These agents are used for purely reactive behaviors, e.g.

stopping the motors to avoid a collision (a task fundamental for mobile robots) or opening an automated door upon request (a task usually assigned to fixed devices).

- type 2: *agents that keep track of the world*, i.e. agents which maintain an internal state and/or representation in order to choose which action to perform. These agents are used for more complex tasks, e.g. avoiding obstacles on the basis of a continuously updated local map of the environment (a task for mobile robots) or controlling an elevator dealing with multiple requests (a task for fixed devices).
- type 3: *goal-based agents*, i.e. agents which handle goals and find action sequences to achieve this goals. These agents are used for high-level planning tasks, e.g. finding a sequence of STRIPS-like rules to reach a target location (a task for mobile robots).

Notice that the agents in the system are requested to run on different hardware platform and operating systems: agents controlling intelligent devices are scheduled by dedicated low cost microprocessors with small computational power and memory storage (no type 3 - goal-based agents run on fixed devices), while agents for high-level control of the robot are executed on a standard PC platform with the Linux OS: for sake of simplicity, we will refer to them as ID agents and PC agents. In spite of differences in their internal model and their implementation, ID and PC agents have some common requirements in terms of *Communication* and *Scheduling*:

Communication: agents are not omniscient: at any given time, they have only partial knowledge of the state of the world and the system. To share information, all agents can communicate on the basis of a publish/subscribe protocol. This allow to dynamically add/remove agents in the system without other agents being aware of that, thus increasing the versatility/reconfigurability of the system. In particular, we need to implement a two-level message board (Fig. 1), composed of 1) a global message-board, which contains information of general interest and to which all agents in the system can publish/subscribe 2) many local message-boards, which contain information which are relevant only within a single subset of agents, and to which only these agents can publish/subscribe (i.e. only the agents running on a robot need to know the trajectory to be followed to avoid an obstacle).

Scheduling: agents have different requirements in terms of computational resource and timing constraints. Since we want the system to operate in the real world and to deal with an uncertain and dynamic environment, the system architecture must have Real-Time characteristics in order to guarantee a predictable and safe behavior of the system when computational resources are limited.

In particular, in order to build intelligent devices (sensors/actuators both in the building and on board the robot) and implement ID agents, we refer to fieldbus technology for distributed control (in particular Echelon LonWorks, a standard for building automation). Communication and scheduling are thus handled as follows:

Communication (ID): the message board and the publish/subscribe communication protocol are implemented by connecting all the control nodes on a common communication bus (as usual in fieldbus systems). ID agents are thus allowed to exchange information by sharing "network variables", i.e. strongly typified data which are propagated on the bus and delivered to all agents in the system which have subscribed to that kind of information ("network variables" abstraction is provided by the Application Layer of the LonWorks communication protocol). Notice that all the control nodes in the system (i.e. sensors/actuators both on board the robot and distributed in the building) are connected to the same bus (we adopt an infrared channel for the communication between robot's devices and the building network).

Scheduling (ID): Echelon's microprocessors allow fast response to inputs and fast communication between network's nodes, but they do not allow to explicitly set hard Real-Time constraints. Thus, ID agents computational load must always be lower than the computational resources available on the intelligent device microprocessor, if we want to guarantee a response in Real-Time. However, ID agents can be easily programmed by means of an event based programming language: "when" clauses allow to produce a behavior either periodically (i.e., upon the expiration of a timer) or as a consequence of a particular event (i.e., upon the reception of a subscribed message or a particular I/O signal: see Fig. 2 on the left). This allows us to easily implement ID agents of type 1 and 2 which quickly react to environmental changes.

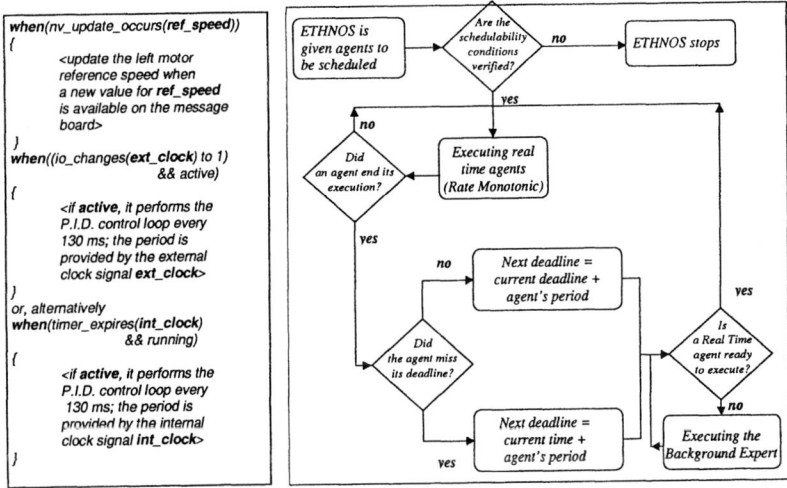

Fig. 2. Left: An ID agent controlling a motor. Right: ETHNOS Real-Time scheduling policy.

To implement PC agents, we refer to ETHNOS (Expert Tribe in a Hybrid Network Operating System), an operating system and programming environment for distributed robotics application which has been described in details in [7]. Communication and scheduling requirements are handled as follows:

Communication (PC): ETHNOS allows PC agents to post/read messages from the global/local message board to which all agents can publish/subscribe (both PC and ID agents). In particular, agents must specify –when publishing a message- if they want to post it to the global message board or the local one; they can make the decision in run-time, by calling the appropriate communication primitive. Finally, some PC agents work as a bridge between the fieldbus (which connects ID agents) and the standard TCP/IP network (which connect PC agents in ETHNOS), thus making inter-agent communication totally transparent.

Scheduling (ID): ETHNOS can schedule three different kind of agents: 1) periodic agents, i.e. executing at a fixed rate (mostly dealing with type 1 and 2 activities, such as piloting actuators, reading sensors, etc.), 2) sporadic agents, i.e. executing in subordination to specific conditions (mostly type 1 and 2 activities, such as purely reactive behaviours, emergency recovery procedures, etc.), 3) background agents, i.e.

non Real-Time agents which execute when the scheduler has no pending requests coming from periodic and sporadic agents to satisfy (mostly type 3 deliberative activities, whose computational time and frequency cannot be predicted or upper bounded and whose execution is not critical for the system). Fig. 2 on the right shows ETHNOS scheduling policy in details.

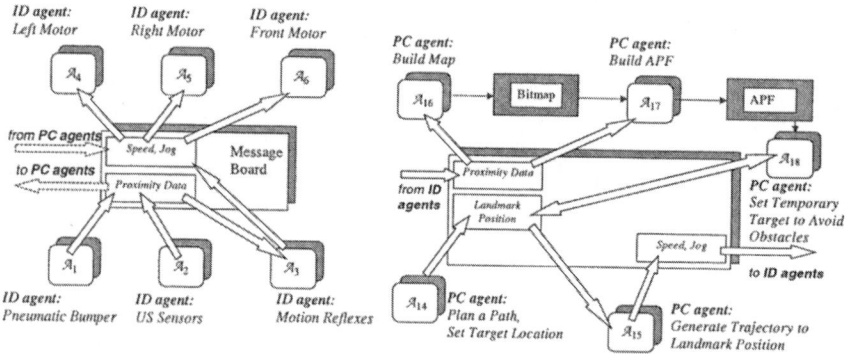

Fig. 3. Left: ID agents - emergency behavior. Right: PC agents - trajectory generation.

3   A Case Study: An Artificial Ecosystem at Gaslini Hospital

The AE approach is being tested at the Gaslini Hospital of Genova: the experimental set-up is composed of the mobile robot Staffetta and a set of intelligent devices distributed in the building, which are given the primary purpose of controlling active beacons for localization and elevators. The robot simulates transportation tasks, i.e. it is able to execute concurrently the following activities: 1) plan paths to the target 2) localize itself 3) generate smooth trajectories and finally 4) follow the trajectory while avoiding unpredicted obstacles in the environment.

All ID agents are type 1 and 2 agents   (in Section 2 classification); i.e., simple reflex agents and agents with internal state (no goal-based agents).

ID agents on board the robot: $\mathcal{A}_1$ controls a pneumatic bumper which is able to detect collisions on different areas of the robot chassis; $\mathcal{A}_2$ controls sixteen ultrasonic sensors; $\mathcal{A}_3$ generates motion reflexes to avoid detected obstacles; $\mathcal{A}_4$, $\mathcal{A}_5$, and $\mathcal{A}_6$ control the two rear motors and the front steering wheel; $\mathcal{A}_7$ controls the DLPS (the onboard rotating laser and the infrared communication device, which are part of the beacon-based localization systems); $\mathcal{A}_8$ monitors the batteries' state; $\mathcal{A}_9$ is directly connected to the motors and works as a watchdog, by periodically communicating with the onboard PC and disabling the motors whenever this communication fails; $\mathcal{A}_{10}$ computes inverse kinematics and odometrical reconstruction; $\mathcal{A}_{11}$ takes control of the motors in case of a system crash, in order to move the robot to a safe location. Finally, one agent handles the communication between the ID and the PC agents.

ID agents in the building: a varying number of agents $\mathcal{A}_{12}^{i}$, each controlling a beacon i for localization, two agents $\mathcal{A}_{13}$ which control the elevator.

Notice that ID agents, in spite of their internal simplicity, are able to produce interesting behaviours. For example, they guarantee safe motion even when agents on the onboard PC are no more able to correctly control the robot's motion, either because of some bug in the software or even because of a crash of the operating system. Fig. 3 on the left shows how interacting ID agents can increase the reactivity of the system to obstacles which suddenly appear in the environment (as long as they are detected by the ultrasonic sensors or the pneumatic bumper). The sensorial data collected by $\mathcal{A}_1$ (pneumatic bumper) and $\mathcal{A}_2$ (US sensors) are posted to the local message board (message type *Proximity Data*), thus being available to PC agents for map building, trajectory generation, localization, etc. However, *Proximity Data* are also available to the ID agent $\mathcal{A}_3$, which is able to generate simple motion reflexes: when required, $\mathcal{A}_3$ produces a message *Speed, Jog* containing speed and jog values which allow to avoid an imminent collision (for example, speed=jog=0) and posts it to the message board. Finally $\mathcal{A}_4$, $\mathcal{A}_5$, and $\mathcal{A}_6$, which control the two rear motors and the front steering wheel, read speed and jog values on the message board and consequently stop the motors before waiting for a command from PC agents (which require a higher computational time and are therefore more critical).

PC agents can be agents of type 1, 2, and 3; i.e., simple reflex agents, agents with internal state, and goal-based agents (see Fig. 3 on the right). Agent $\mathcal{A}_{14}$ is a type 3 goal-based agent responsible of plan selection and adaptation, allowing the robot to execute high-level navigation tasks such as "go into office A". These tasks, depending on the current robot context, may be decomposed into many, possibly concurrent, sub-tasks such as "localise, go to the door, open door, etc..." and eventually into primitive actions such as "go to position (x,y,θ)". In the Figure, $\mathcal{A}_{14}$ plans a path to a target as a sequence of landmarks positions, and posts to the message board the location of the next landmark to be visited (message type *Landmark Position*). Agent $\mathcal{A}_{15}$ is a type 1 agent which subscribes to *Landmark Position* and is capable of executing smooth trajectories from the robot current position to the landmark specified, relying on a non linear law of motion. It produces speed and jog values which are made available to ID agents $\mathcal{A}_4$, $\mathcal{A}_5$, and $\mathcal{A}_6$ to control motors: however, $\mathcal{A}_{15}$ cannot deal with obstacles in the robot path. In the figure two shared representations (indicated as grey rectangles) can be observed: the bitmap, an ecocentrical statistical dynamic description of the environment the robot moves in, and the APF - Abstract Potential Field, based on the bitmap and on direct sensorial information. These representations are handled and continuously updated to maintain consistency with the real world based on sensor data by two agents of type 2: $\mathcal{A}_{16}$ (for the bitmap) and $\mathcal{A}_{17}$ (for the APF); the details of these agents is beyond the scope of this paper but can be found in [8]). During normal navigation, agents $\mathcal{A}_{16}$ and $\mathcal{A}_{17}$, together with $\mathcal{A}_{15}$ and $\mathcal{A}_{18}$, are responsible of smooth obstacle avoidance: should a collision become imminent, ID simple reactive agents would take control by stopping the motors to deal with the emergency (as we already explained).

Consider now both ID and PC agents on board the robot: the agents in the architecture communicate using messages conveying the type of information or command to be executed at the appropriate level (i.e. *Landmark Position, Speed and Jog*, etc). However, all agents operate concurrently and the architecture is only partially hierarchical, thus implying a dynamic competition on the allocation of "resources". For example, both PC agent $\mathcal{A}_{15}$ (which generates a smooth trajectory) and ID agent $\mathcal{A}_3$ (which produces motion reflexes) publish *Speed, Jog* messages, thus competing with each other; ID agents $\mathcal{A}_4$, $\mathcal{A}_5$, and $\mathcal{A}_6$ need a way to choose which speed and jog commands should be issued to actuators. The conflict is solved using an authority-based protocol. Each agent is assigned a specific *authority* (possibly varying in time) with which it issues command messages. The receiving agent stores the command associated authority and begins its execution (for example speed = 2 cm/s). If the action, as in the given example, continues indefinitely or requires some time to be executed, the agent continues its execution until a contrasting message with a similar or higher authority is received. On the other hand, messages with lower authorities are not considered. For example, in the architecture, $\mathcal{A}_3$ has a higher authority than $\mathcal{A}_{15}$, thus overriding any command from the latter in case of an emergency.

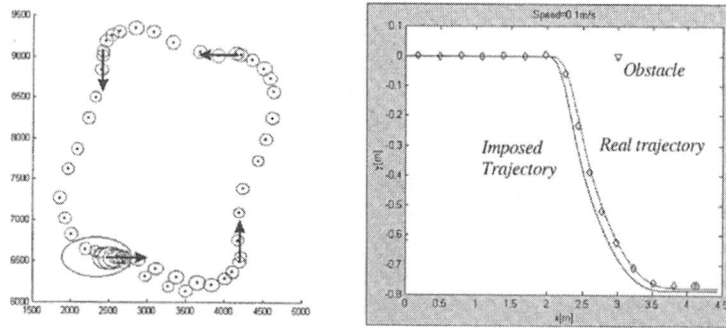

Fig. 4. Left: Localization through beacons. Right: Avoiding an unpredicted obstacle.

4   Experimental Results

The whole system has been tested in Gaslini Hospital of Genoa and during many public exhibitions. During the experiments, all the PC and ID agents described in the previous Section are running: thus, the robot performs concurrently goal-oriented navigation, map making, smooth trajectory generation, obstacle avoidance, localization, etc. Finally, the environment is intrinsically dynamic because of the presence of people. However, in spite of the complexity of the environment, the system keeps working with no performance degradation: during the Tmed exposition (*Magazzini Del Cotone, Porto Antico di Genova, October 2001*), the system was running from opening to closing hours, meeting a lot people and interacting with them (i.e., saying sentences in particular situations). We were sometimes forced to stop the robot for battery recharge, but never because the robot got lost in the environment: thanks to the intelligent devices (beacons) distributed in the building, computing the robot's position becomes a straightforward problem through the interaction of ID agents $\mathcal{A}_{12}{}^{i}$ and $\mathcal{A}_7$ and PC agent $\mathcal{A}_{20}$ (not described here) Fig. 4 on the left shows the estimated position of the robot (dots) together with the estimated uncertainty (ellipses) as it varies in time. Notice that the initial uncertainty (when the robot is in 2500,6500) drastically decreases as more beacons are detected and the position is corrected by $\mathcal{A}_{20}$ through an Extended Kalman Filter. Finally, experiments show that distributing control increases the robustness of the system. For example, we test the reactivity of the system to the presence of an unknown obstacle quickly approaching the robot. When the robot detects a very close obstacle by means of ultrasonic readings (Fig. 4 on the right), the reflex behavior generated by $\mathcal{A}_3$ temporarily takes the control of $\mathcal{A}_4$, $\mathcal{A}_5$, and $\mathcal{A}_6$ and computes speed and jog values in order to safely avoid a collision (thus inhibiting $\mathcal{A}_{15}$'s output). Next, it releases the control and the robot moves again towards its target.

5 Conclusions

In this paper we describe the "Artificial Ecosystem", a novel multiagent approach to intelligent robotics: we claim that, given the current technological state in sensors and actuators, mobile robots will have a lot of difficulties in substituting humans in a generic, human inhabited environment, even for the simplest navigation task. Thus, on one side, we continue pursuing the final target of a fully autonomous artificial being which can adapt to "live" in the same environment where biological being live; on the other side, we think that modifying the environment to fit the robot's requirements can be a temporary solution to obtain significant results given the current technological state. To achieve this, we distribute sensors and actuators not only onboard the robot, but also in the building. As a consequence, intelligence is not only a characteristic of each single robot; instead, robots are considered as the mobile units within a "forest" of intelligent fixed devices, which are handled by cooperating software agents with a high level of autonomy in taking decisions. The experiments performed in different real world environments seem to validate the approach.

References

1. Brooks, R. (1986). A Robust Layered Control System for a mobile robot, IEEE J. of Robotics and Automation, RA-2 1
2. Parker, L. E. (1998) ALLIANCE: An Architecture for Fault Tolerant Multi-Robot Cooperation, IEEE Transactions on Robotics and Automation, 14 (2)
3. Arkin, R. C. (1990). Motor Schema-Based Mobile Robot Navigation, International Journal of Robotics Research.
4. Gat, E. (1992) Integrating Planning and Reacting in a Heterogeneous Asynchronous Architecture for Controlling Real-World Mobile Robots, Proceedings of the National Conference on Artificial Intelligence (AAAI).
5. Burgard, W., Cremers, A.B., Fox, D., Hähnel, D., Lakemeyer, G., Schulz, D., Steiner, W., and Thrun., S. (2000). Experiences with an interactive museum tour-guide robot, Artificial Intelligence (AI), 114 (1–2),
6. Russell, S. and Norvig, P. Artificial Intelligence: A Modern Approach. Prentice Hall, Englewood Cliffs, NJ, 1995.
7. Piaggio, M., Sgorbissa, A., Zaccaria, R. (2000). Pre-emptive Versus Non Pre-emptive Real Time Scheduling in Intelligent Mobile Robotics. Journal of Experimental and Theoretical Artificial Intelligence, (12)2.
8. Piaggio, M., Zaccaria, R. (1997), An Autonomous System for a Vehicle Navigating in a Partially or Totally Unknown Environment, Proc. Int. Workshop on Mechatronical Computer Systems for Perception and Action MCPA, Pisa, Italy.

Noise Correction in Genomic Data*

Choh Man Teng

Institute for Human and Machine Cognition
University of West Florida
40 South Alcaniz Street, Pensacola FL 32501, USA
cmteng@ai.uwf.edu

Abstract. *Osteogenesis Imperfecta* (OI) is a genetic collagenous disease caused by mutations in one or both of the genes COLIA1 and COLIA2. There are at least four known phenotypes of OI, of which type II is the severest and often lethal. We applied a noise correction mechanism called *polishing* to a data set of amino acid sequences and associated information of point mutations of COLIA1. Polishing makes use of the inter-relationship between attribute and class values in the data set to identify and selectively correct components that are noisy. Preliminary results suggest that polishing is a viable mechanism for improving data quality, resulting in a more accurate classification of the lethal OI phenotype.

1 Approaches to Noise Handling

Imperfections in data can arise from many sources, for instance, faulty measuring devices, transcription errors, and transmission irregularities. Except in the most structured and synthetic environment, it is almost inevitable that there is some noise in any data we have collected. Data quality is a prime concern for many tasks in learning and induction. The utility of a procedure is limited by the quality of the data we have access to. For a classification task, for instance, a classifier built from a noisy training set might be less accurate and less compact than one built from the noise-free version of the same data set using an identical algorithm.

Imperfections in a data set can be dealt with in three broad ways. We may leave the noise in, filter it out, or correct it. On the first approach, the data set is taken as is, with the noisy instances left in place. Algorithms that make use of the data are designed to be *robust*; that is, they can tolerate a certain amount of noise in the data. Robustness is typically accomplished by avoiding overfitting, so that the resulting classifier is not overly specialized to account for the noise. This approach is taken by, for example, c4.5 [Quinlan, 1987] and CN2 [Clark and Niblett, 1989].

On the second approach, the data is *filtered* before being used. Instances that are suspected of being noisy according to certain evaluation criteria are

---

* This work was supported by NASA NCC2-1239 and ONR N00014-03-1-0516.

J. Liu et al. (Eds.): IDEAL 2003, LNCS 2690, pp. 60–67, 2003.

discarded [John, 1995,Gamberger et al., 1996,Brodley and Friedl, 1999]. A classifier is then built using only the retained instances in the smaller but cleaner data set. Similar ideas can be found in robust regression and outlier detection techniques in statistics [Rousseeuw and Leroy, 1987].

On the first approach, robust algorithms do not require preprocessing of the data, but each algorithm has to institute its own noise handling routine, duplicating the effort required even if the same data set is used in each case. In addition, the noise in the data may interfere with the mechanism, and a classifier built from a noisy data set may be less accurate and its representation may be less compact than it could have been if the data were not noisy. On the second approach, by filtering out the noisy instances from the data, there is a tradeoff between the amount of information available for building the classifier and the amount of noise retained in the data set. Filtering is not information-efficient; the more noisy instances we discard, the less data remains.

On the third approach, the noisy instances are identified, but instead of tossing these instances out, they are repaired by replacing the corrupted values with more appropriate ones. These corrected instances are then reintroduced into the data set. Noise correction has been shown to give better results than simply removing the noise from the data set in some cases [Drastal, 1991,Teng, 2001].

We have developed a data correction method called *polishing* [Teng, 1999]. Data polishing, when carried out correctly, would preserve the maximal information available in the data set, approximating the noise-free ideal situation. A classifier built from this corrected data should have a higher predictive power and a more streamlined representation. Polishing has been shown to improve the performance of classifiers in a number of situations [Teng, 1999,Teng, 2000]. In this paper we study the effects of applying polishing to a data set in the biomedical domain.

2 Polishing

Machine learning methods such as the naive Bayes classifier typically assume that different components of a data set are (conditionally) independent. It has often been pointed out that this assumption is a gross oversimplification of the actual relationship between the attributes; hence the word "naive" [Mitchell, 1997, for example]. Extensions to the naive Bayes classifier have been introduced to loosen the independence criterion [Kononenko, 1991,Langley et al., 1992], but some have also investigated alternative explanations for the success of this classifier [Domingos and Pazzani, 1996].

Controversy aside, most will agree that in many cases there is a definite relationship within the data; otherwise any effort to mine knowledge or patterns from the data would be ill-advised. Polishing takes advantage of this interdependency between the components of a data set to identify the noisy elements and suggest appropriate replacements. Rather than utilizing the features only to predict the target concept, we can just as well turn the process around and utilize the target together with selected features to predict the value of another feature. This provides a means to identify noisy elements together with their correct values. Note that except for totally irrelevant elements, each feature would be at least related to some extent to the target concept, even if not to any other features.

The basic algorithm of polishing consists of two phases: prediction and adjustment. In the *prediction* phase, elements in the data that are suspected of being noisy are identified together with nominated replacement values. In the adjustment phase, we selectively incorporate the nominated changes into the data set. In the first phase, the predictions are carried out by systematically swapping the target and particular features of the data set, and performing a ten-fold classification using a chosen classification algorithm for the prediction of the feature values. If the predicted value of a feature in an instance is different from the stated value in the data set, the location of the discrepancy is flagged and recorded together with the predicted value. This information is passed on to the next phase, where we institute the actual adjustments.

Since the polishing process itself is based on imperfect data, the predictions obtained in the first phase can contain errors as well. We should not indiscriminately incorporate all the nominated changes. Rather, in the second phase, the *adjustment* phase, we selectively adopt appropriate changes from those predicted in the first phase. A number of strategies are used to identify the best combination of changes that would improve the fitness of a datum, and a set of changes is acceptable if it leads to a correct prediction of the target concept by the classifiers obtained from the prediction phase.

Further details of polishing can be found in [Teng, 1999, Teng, 2000].

3   Osteogenesis Imperfecta

Osteogenesis Imperfecta (OI), commonly known as brittle bone disease, is a genetic disorder characterized by bones that fracture easily for little or no reason. This disorder is caused by mutations in one or both of the genes, COLIA1 and COLIA2, which are associated with the production of peptides of type I collagen. Type I collagen is a protein found in the connective tissues in the body. A mutation in COLIA1 or COLIA2 may lead to a change in the structure and expression of the type I collagen molecules produced, which in turn affects the bone structure.

There are at least four known phenotypes of *osteogenesis imperfecta*, namely, types I, II, III, and IV. Of these four type II is the severest form of OI and is often lethal. At least 70 different kinds of point mutations in COLIA1 and COLIA2 have been found to be associated with OI, and of these approximately half of the mutations are related to type II, the lethal form of OI [Hunter and Klein, 1993].

While OI may be diagnosed with collagenous or DNA tests, the relevant structure and the relationship between the point mutations and the types of OI are still under investigation [Klein and Wong, 1992, Mooney et al., 2001, for example].

3.1   Data Description

Below we will describe a data set consisting of information on sequences of amino acids, each with a point mutation in COLIA1. The sequences are divided into lethal (type II) and non-lethal (types I, III, and IV) forms of OI. The objective is to generate a classification scheme that will help us understand and differentiate between lethal and non-lethal forms of OI.

Each instance in the data set contains the following attributes.

$A_1, \ldots, A_{29}$: a sequence of 29 amino acids.

These are the amino acids at and around the site of the mutation. The mutated residue is centered at A_{15}, with 14 amino acids on each side in the sequence. Each attribute A_i can take on one of 21 values: each of the 20 regular amino acids (A, R, N, D, C, Q, E, G, H, I, L, K, M, F, P, S, T, W, Y, V), and hydroxyproline (O), a modified proline (P) which can be found in collagen molecules.

Four attributes provide supplementary information regarding hydrogen bonds in the molecules.

S-W : number of solute hydrogen bonds wild type;
S-M : number of solute hydrogen bonds mutated type;
SS-W : number of solute-solvent hydrogen bonds wild type;
SS-M : number of solute-solvent hydrogen bonds mutated type.

These are the number of hydrogen bonds of the specified types that are present in the wild (un-mutated) and mutated protein molecules more than 80% of the time.

The class of each instance can be one of two values.

y : lethal OI (type II);
n : non-lethal OI (types I, III, or IV).

Thus, each instance contains 33 attributes and a binary class.

3.2   Data Characteristics

A number of characteristics of the data suggest that this data set is an appropriate candidate for polishing. First of all, the amino acid sequence and associated information are prone to noise arising from the clinical procedures. Thus, there is a need for an effective measure for noise handling.

The number of possible values for many of the attributes is fairly large, resulting in a data set that is sparse with little redundancy. This makes it undesirable to use an information-inefficient mechanism such as filtering for noise handling, since discarding any data is likely to lose some information that is not duplicated in the remaining portion of the data set.

While the precise relationship between the different amino acid blocks is not clear, we do know that they interact, and this inter-relationship between amino acids in a sequence can be exploited to generate replacement values for

Table 1. Average classification accuracy and size of the decision trees constructed from the unpolished and polished data. The difference between the classification accuracies is significant at the 0.05 level.

	Accuracy ± Std Deviation	Tree Size
Unpolished	60.0 ± 11.8%	11.6
Polished	66.0 ± 15.0%	11.4

the attributes using the polishing mechanism. In addition, the conformation of collagen molecules is exceptionally linear, and thus we can expect that each attribute may be predicted to a certain extent by considering only the values of the neighboring attributes in the sequence.

4   Experiments

We used the decision tree builder c4.5 [Quinlan, 1993] to provide our basic classifiers, and performed ten-fold cross-validation on the OI data set described in the previous section.

In each trial, nine parts of the data were used for training and a tenth part was reserved for testing. The training data was polished and the polished data was then used to construct a decision tree. The unseen (and unpolished) instances in the test data set were classified according to this tree. For each trial a tree was also constructed from the original unpolished training data for comparison purposes.

We analyzed a number of aspects of the results obtained from the experiments, including classifier characteristics (accuracy and size), the list of relevant attributes selected by the classifiers, as well as the amount of change induced by the polishing mechanism.

4.1   Classifier Characteristics

The average classification accuracy and size of the decision trees (with pruning) constructed from the unpolished and polished data are reported in Table 1.

The difference between the classification accuracies of the trees constructed from the unpolished and polished data is statistically significant at the 0.05 level, using a one-tailed paired t-test. This suggests that polishing was effective in improving the quality of the training data such that more accurate classifiers could be built.

Even though previously we have found that polishing led to a decrease in tree size [Teng, 1999, Teng, 2000], in this study the tree sizes resulting from the two approaches do not differ much.

Table 2. Relevant attributes, in decreasing order of the average percentage of occurrence in the decision trees.

Unpolished		Polished	
Attribute	% of Occurrence	Attribute	% of Occurrence
S-M	33.3%	A_{15}	50.0%
S-W	16.7%	A_{11}, A_{14}	25.0%
A_{15}, A_{20}, A_{22}	16.7%		

4.2   Relevant Attributes

We are interested in identifying the relevant features contributing to the lethal phenotype of OI and the relationship between these features. We looked at the attributes used in constructing the unpolished and polished trees, as these attributes were the ones that were considered predictive of the phenotype in the decision tree setting.

We used the number of trees involving a particular attribute as an indicator of the relevance of that attribute. Table 2 gives the normalized percentages of occurrence of the attributes, averaged over the cross validation trials, obtained from the trees constructed using the unpolished and polished data sets respectively.

While there are 33 attributes altogether in each instance, the number of attributes used in building the decision trees is relatively low, as indicated by both the number of relevant attributes in Table 2 as well as the small tree size reported in Table 1. This suggests that a small number of attributes determine the classification generated.

We expected A_{15}, the attribute denoting the mutated amino acid in the molecule, to play a significant role in the classification of OI disease types. This was supported by the findings in Table 2. We also noted that A_{15} was used more frequently in the decision trees constructed from the polished data than in those constructed from the unpolished data (16.7% versus 50.0%). The stronger emphasis placed on this attribute may account for the increase in the classification accuracy resulting from polishing.

The other attributes that were picked out as being relevant from using the unpolished and polished data were dissimilar. Domain expertise is needed to further interpret the implications of these results.

4.3   Estimated Adjustment Level

By comparing the unpolished and polished data, we can quantify the amount of change that has occurred during polishing. Conservatively speaking, this amount tells us how much difference has been imposed on the data by the polishing mechanism.

Table 3. Average percentage of instances and attributes that have been adjusted during polishing.

Unit of Adjustment	% Adjustment
Attributes	7.1%
Instances	73.5%

We tallied the adjustments made to the data during polishing. The average percentages of instances and attributes that have been adjusted are reported in Table 3.

An attribute is counted as having been adjusted if its value in the polished data differs from the value in the original data. An instance is counted as having been adjusted if at least one of its attributes has been adjusted. We observed that although a fairly high percentage of instances (73.5%) were polished, the percentage of attributes adjusted in each such instance is considerably lower (7.1%). This again suggests that only a small number of attributes are relevant to the classification task and thus polishing can be effective even when concentrating on only a select few of the attributes.

By making the assumption that polishing did locate and correct the errors in the data set, we can take the above percentages as estimates of the noise level in the original data. Arguably this is a very strong assumption. External evidence and expert knowledge is needed before we can obtain an accurate estimate of the true level of noise.

5   Remarks

The scientific objective of this research is to understand the structure of and the relationship between the features characterizing the genetic disease *osteogenesis imperfecta*. The work described in this paper is exploratory research on applying novel machine learning techniques to realistic problems in the biomedical domain.

The findings reported here are encouraging although preliminary. The experimental results suggested that polishing is a viable mechanism for improving data quality by making corrections to the noisy data. The classifiers built from the polished data were more accurate than those built from the unpolished data. We in addition analyzed the results from a number of other aspects of interest.

Future work includes examining, with the help of domain experts, the classifier structure as well as the polished attributes and values for biomedical significance, and re-engineering the data and polishing mechanism to take into account amino acid groupings that can reduce the potential number of values taken by each attribute.

References

[Brodley and Friedl, 1999] Carla E. Brodley and Mark A. Friedl. Identifying mislabeled training data. *Journal of Artificial Intelligence Research*, 11:131–167, 1999.

[Clark and Niblett, 1989] P. Clark and T. Niblett. The CN2 induction algorithm. *Machine Learning*, 3(4):261–283, 1989.

[Domingos and Pazzani, 1996] Pedro Domingos and Michael Pazzani. Beyond independence: Conditions for the optimality of the simple Bayesian classifier. In *Proceedings of the Thirteenth International Conference on Machine Learning*, pages 105–112, 1996.

[Drastal, 1991] George Drastal. Informed pruning in constructive induction. In *Proceedings of the Eighth International Workshop on Machine Learning*, pages 132–136, 1991.

[Gamberger et al., 1996] Dragan Gamberger, Nada Lavrač, and Sašo Džeroski. Noise elimination in inductive concept learning: A case study in medical diagnosis. In *Proceedings of the Seventh International Workshop on Algorithmic Learning Theory*, pages 199–212, 1996.

[Hunter and Klein, 1993] Lawrence Hunter and Teri E. Klein. Finding relevant biomolecular features. In *Proceedings of the International Conference on Intelligent Systems for Molecular Biology*, pages 190–197, 1993.

[John, 1995] George H. John. Robust decision trees: Removing outliers from databases. In *Proceedings of the First International Conference on Knowledge Discovery and Data Mining*, pages 174–179, 1995.

[Klein and Wong, 1992] Teri E. Klein and E. Wong. Neural networks applied to the collagenous disease osteogenesis imperfecta. In *Proceedings of the Hawaii International Conference on System Sciences*, volume I, pages 697–705, 1992.

[Kononenko, 1991] Igor Kononenko. Semi-naive Bayesian classifier. In *Proceedings of the Sixth European Working Session on Learning*, pages 206–219, 1991.

[Langley et al., 1992] P. Langley, W. Iba, and K. Thompson. An analysis of Bayesian classifiers. In *Proceedings of the Tenth National Conference on Artificial Intelligence*, pages 223–228, 1992.

[Mitchell, 1997] Tom M. Mitchell. *Machine Learning*. McGraw-Hill, 1997.

[Mooney et al., 2001] Sean D. Mooney, Conrad C. Huang, Peter A. Kollman, and Teri E. Klein. Computed free energy differences between point mutations in a collagen-like peptide. *Biopolymers*, 58:347–353, 2001.

[Quinlan, 1987] J. Ross Quinlan. Simplifying decision trees. *International Journal of Man-Machine Studies*, 27(3):221–234, 1987.

[Quinlan, 1993] J. Ross Quinlan. *C4.5: Programs for Machine Learning*. Morgan Kaufmann, 1993.

[Rousseeuw and Leroy, 1987] Peter J. Rousseeuw and Annick M. Leroy. *Robust Regression and Outlier Detection*. John Wiley & Sons, 1987.

[Teng, 1999] Choh Man Teng. Correcting noisy data. In *Proceedings of the Sixteenth International Conference on Machine Learning*, pages 239–248, 1999.

[Teng, 2000] Choh Man Teng. Evaluating noise correction. In *Lecture Notes in Artificial Intelligence: Proceedings of the Sixth Pacific Rim International Conference on Artificial Intelligence*. Springer-Verlag, 2000.

[Teng, 2001] Choh Man Teng. A comparison of noise handling techniques. In *Proceedings of the Fourteenth International Florida Artificial Intelligence Research Society Conference*, pages 269–273, 2001.

Gradient Based Method for Symmetric and Asymmetric Multiagent Reinforcement Learning

Ville Könönen

Neural Networks Research Centre
Helsinki University of Technology
P.O. Box 5400, FIN-02015 HUT, Finland
ville.kononen@hut.fi

Abstract. A gradient based method for both symmetric and asymmetric multiagent reinforcement learning is introduced in this paper. Symmetric multiagent reinforcement learning addresses the problem with agents involved in the learning task having equal information states. Respectively, in asymmetric multiagent reinforcement learning, the information states are not equal, i.e. some agents (leaders) try to encourage agents with less information (followers) to select actions that lead to improved overall utility value for the leaders. In both cases, there is a huge number of parameters to learn and we thus need to use some parametric function approximation methods to represent the value functions of the agents. The method proposed in this paper is based on the VAPS framework that is extended to utilize the theory of Markov games, i.e. a natural basis of multiagent reinforcement learning.

1 Introduction

Reinforcement learning methods have received lots of attention in recent years. Although these methods and procedures were considered to be too ambitious and to lack a firm foundation in the early years, they have now been established as practical methods for solving Markov decision processes (MDPs). However, the requirement for reinforcement learning methods to work is that the problem domain in which the methods are applied obeys the Markov property. In many real-world problems this property is not fully satisfied but reinforcement learning methods can still handle these situations relatively well. Especially, in the case of two or more decision makers in the same system, the Markovian property does not hold and more advanced methods should be applied. One possible solution is to use competitive Markov decision processes since a suitable theoretical framework for these processes exists and some learning methods have also been proposed.

We begin the paper by introducing the background and basic solution concepts of mathematical games. Then we go briefly through the theory behind Markov games and introduce some learning methods used with multiagent reinforcement learning. Finally, we introduce the VAPS framework and our extensions for the multiagent case.

J. Liu et al. (Eds.): IDEAL 2003, LNCS 2690, pp. 68–75, 2003.

2 Game Theory

This section is mainly concerned with the basic problem setting and definitions of game theory. We start with some preliminary information about mathematical games and then proceed to their solution concepts which are essential for the rest of the paper.

2.1 Basic Concepts

Mathematical games can be represented in different forms. The most important forms are the *extensive* form and the *strategic* form. Although the extensive form is the most richly structured way to describe game situations, the strategic form is conceptually simpler and it can be derived from the extensive form. In this paper, we use games in strategic form for making decisions at each time step.

Games in strategic form are usually referred to as *matrix games* and, particularly, in the case of two players if the payoff matrices for both players are separated, as *bimatrix games*. In general, a N-person matrix game is defined as follows:

Definition 1. *A* matrix game *is a tuple $\Gamma = (A^1, \ldots, A^N, r^1, \ldots, r^N)$, where N is the number of players, A^i is the strategy space for the player i and $r^i : A^1 \times A^2 \times \ldots \times A^N \to \mathbb{R}$ is the payoff function for the player i.*

In a matrix game, each player i simultaneously chooses a strategy $a^i \in A^i$. In this paper, we restrict our inspection only to pure strategies, i.e. strategies chosen by probability one.

2.2 Equilibrium Concepts

In decision problems with only one decision maker, it is adequate to maximize the expected utility of the decision maker. However, in games there are many players and we need to define more elaborate solution concepts. Next we will shortly present two relevant solution concepts of matrix games.

Definition 2. *If N is the number of players, the strategies $a_*^1, \ldots, a_*^N$ constitute a* Nash equilibrium *solution of the game if the following inequality holds for all $a^i \in A^i$ and for all i:*

$$r^i(a_*^1, \ldots, a_*^{i-1}, a^i, a_*^{i+1}, \ldots, a_*^N) \le r^i(a_*^1, \ldots, a_*^N)$$

The idea behind the Nash equilibrium solution is that the strategy choice of each player is a best response to his opponents' play and therefore there is no need for deviation from this equilibrium point for any player alone. Thus, the concept of Nash equilibrium solution provides a reasonable solution concept for a matrix game when the roles of the players are symmetric. However, there are decision problems in which one of the players has the ability to enforce his strategy to other players. For solving this kind of optimization problems, we have to use a hierarchical equilibrium solution concept, e.g. the two-player *Stackelberg equilibrium* concept, where one player is acting as the leader (player 1) and the another as the follower (player 2). The leader enforces his strategy to the opponent and the follower reacts rationally to this strategy.

The basic idea is that the leader announces his strategy so that it enforces the opponent to select the response that leads to the optimal response for the leader. Algorithmically, in the case of finite bimatrix games when the player 1 is the leader and the player 2 is the follower, obtaining a Stackelberg solution $(a_s^1, a_s^2(a^1))$ can be seen as the following two-step algorithm:

1. $a_s^2(a^1) = \arg\max_{a^2 \in A^2} r^2(a^1, a^2)$
2. $a_s^1 = \arg\max_{a^1 \in A^1} r^1(a^1, a_s^2(a^1))$

In the step 1, follower's strategy is expressed as a function of the leader's strategy. In the step 2, the leader maximizes his own utility. The only requirement is that the follower's response is unique; if this is not the case, some additional restrictions must be set.

3 Multiagent Reinforcement Learning

In this section, we briefly introduce mathematical theory of competitive Markov decision processes. Moreover, the connections of this theory to game theory and multiagent reinforcement learning are also discussed.

3.1 Markov Games

With two or more agents in the environment, the fundamental problem of using single-agent MDPs is that the approach treats other agents as a part of the environment and thus ignores the fact that decisions of these agents may influence the state of the environment.

One possible solution to this problem is to use *competitive Markov decision processes*, *Markov games*. In a Markov game, the process changes its state according to the action choices of all agents and it can thus be seen as a multicontroller Markov decision process. Formally, we define a Markov game as follows:

Definition 3. *A* Markov game *(stochastic game) is defined as a tuple* $< S, A^1, \ldots, A^N, p, r^1, \ldots, r^N >$, *where N is the number of agents, S is the set of all states, A^i is the set of all actions for each agent $i \in [1, N]$, $p : S \times A^1 \times \ldots \times A^N \to \Delta(S)$ is the state transition function, $r^i : S \times A^1 \times \ldots \times A^N \to \mathbb{R}$ is the reward function for the agent i. $\Delta(S)$ is the set of probability distributions over the set S.*

As in the case of single-agent MDP, we need a *policy* π^i, i.e. a rule determining what to do, given the knowledge of the current state of the environment, for each agent i:

$$\pi^i : S \rightarrow A^i, \forall i \in [1, N]. \tag{1}$$

In (1), the policy π^i is assumed to be stationary, i.e. there are no time dependents in the policy. The expected discounted utility of the agent i is the following:

$$
\begin{aligned}
V^i_{\pi^1,\dots,\pi^N}(s) &= E_{\pi^1,\dots,\pi^N}[R^i|s_0 = s] \\
&= E_{\pi^1,\dots,\pi^N}\left[\sum_{t=0}^{\infty} \gamma^t r^i_{t+1}|s_0 = s\right],
\end{aligned} \tag{2}
$$

where r^i_t is the immediate reward at time step t for the agent i and γ is a discount factor. Moreover, the value for each state-actions tuple is

$$
\begin{aligned}
Q^i_{\pi^1,\dots,\pi^N}&(s,a^1,\dots,a^N) \\
&= E_{\pi^1,\dots,\pi^N}[R^i|s_0 = s, a_0^1 = a^1,\dots,a_0^N = a^N] \\
&= r^i(s,a^1,\dots,a^N) + \gamma\sum_{s'} p(s'|s,a^1,\dots,a^N)V^i_{\pi^1,\dots,\pi^N}(s'),
\end{aligned} \tag{3}
$$

where $r^i(s,a^1,\dots,a^N)$ is the immediate reward for the agent i when actions $a^1,\dots,a^N$ are selected in the state s. A thorough treatment of Markov games is given in [3].

3.2 Symmetric Multiagent Reinforcement Learning

In the case of symmetric multiagent reinforcement learning, it is not sufficient to maximize the expected utility of individual agents. Instead, our goal is to find an equilibrium policy π^i_*, i.e. a Nash equilibrium policy defined as follows:

Definition 4. *If N is the number of agents and Π^i is the policy space for the agent i, the policies $\pi^1_*,\dots,\pi^N_*$ constitute a Nash equilibrium solution of the game if in every state s the following inequality holds for all $\pi^i \in \Pi^i$ and for all i:*

$$V^i_{\pi^1_*,\dots,\pi^i,\dots,\pi^N_*}(s) \leq V^i_{\pi^1_*,\dots,\pi^N_*}(s)$$

It is noteworthy that Definition 4 coincides with Definition 2 when individual strategies are replaced with policies. We refer to methods built on Markov games with the Nash equilibrium solution concept as *symmetric multiagent reinforcement learning methods*.

A Markov game can be seen as a set of matrix games associated with each state $s \in S$. In these matrix games, payoffs for each player i are equal to the function $Q^i_{\pi^i,\dots,\pi^N}$.

As in the case of single-agent reinforcement learning, equilibrium Q-values can be learned from the observations using some iterative algorithm. For example, in the two-agent case, if we use Q-learning, the update rule for the agent 1 is [4]:

$$Q^1_{t+1}(s_t, a^1_t, a^2_t) = (1 - \alpha_t)Q^1_t(s_t, a^1_t, a^2_t) \\ + \alpha_t[r^1_{t+1} + \gamma \mathrm{Nash}\{Q^1_t(s_{t+1})\}], \tag{4}$$

where $\mathrm{Nash}\{Q^1_t(s_{t+1})\}$ is the Nash equilibrium outcome of the bimatrix game defined by the payoff function $Q^1_t(s_{t+1})$ for the agent 1. The update rule for the agent 2 is symmetric.

3.3   Asymmetric Multiagent Reinforcement Learning

As stated earlier in this paper, a Markov game can be seen as a set of matrix games associated with each state $s \in S$. One possible way to obtain an asymmetric solution of the Markov game is to solve the matrix game associated with each state s using the Stackelberg equilibrium solution concept. In the following three stage protocol (two agents, the agent 1 is the leader and the agent 2 is the follower), this is done so that it also takes into account the actual, possible stochastic, action selection scheme used by the agents:

1. Determination of the cooperation strategies $a^c = (a^{1c}, a^{2c})$ by finding the maximum element of the matrix game $Q^1_{\pi_1,\pi_2}$ in the state s:

$$\arg \max_{\substack{a^1 \in A^1 \\ a^2 \in A^2}} Q^1_{\pi^1,\pi^2}(s, a^1, a^2). \tag{5}$$

2. Determination of the leader's announcement (and action, $a^1_s = g(s, a^c)$):

$$g(s, a^c) = \arg \min_{a^1 \in A^1} \|E[f(Q^2_{\pi^1,\pi^2}(s, a^1, a^2))], a^{2c}\|. \tag{6}$$

3. Determination of the follower's response a^2_s:

$$a^2_s = \arg \max_{a^2 \in A^2} Q^2_{\pi^1,\pi^2}(s, g(s, a^c), a^2). \tag{7}$$

In the protocol, $\|a, a^c\|, a \in A^2$ is a distance measure, defined in the Q-value space of the leader, measuring the distance between the Q-value corresponding a particular action and the Q-value associated to the cooperation strategies (maximal possible payoff for the leader). The function f is used to select actions by the player 2; e.g. in the case of of greedy action selection $f = \arg \max_{a^2 \in A^2}$. For the cases where f includes randomness, e.g. *softmax* action selection is used, there is an expectation operator E (over the action space of the follower) in Eq. (6). In practical implementations of the protocol, the minimization in the step 2 can be replaced with the *softmin* function and the maximization in the step 3 with the function f for ensuring the proper exploration of the state-action space.

4   VAPS for Multiagent Reinforcement Learning

In this section we go through a class of stochastic gradient descent algorithms for multiagent reinforcement learning. This class of algorithms is called VAPS (*Value And Policy Search*) and was originally proposed by Baird and Moore in [1]. Unlike direct gradient descent methods, the VAPS is guaranteed to converge with arbitrary function approximators even when exploration policy changes during learning. In this section, we extend the VAPS framework for the multiagent case with two agents.

4.1   VAPS

The main idea of the VAPS is to minimize the expected total error of the policy, i.e. minimize the error E:

$$E = \sum_{t=0}^{\infty} \sum_{h_t \in H_t} P(h_t) e(h_t), \tag{8}$$

where $e(\cdot)$ is the immediate error function. $h_t \in H_t$ is the history (sequence) containing all states, actions and rewards generated by the policy until the time instance t and $P(h_t)$ is the probability of the history h_t.

4.2   Symmetric Case

We start with the symmetric case by including the action performed by the opponent in the game history. Let us define the action pair (a_t^{1*}, a_t^{2*}) to be the Nash equilibrium point of the matrix game associated with the state at the time step t. We get following definitions of the game histories for agents 1 and 2:

$$\begin{aligned} h_t^1 &= \{s_0, a_0^1, a_0^{2*}, r_1^1, s_1, u_1^1, u_1^{2*}, r_2^1, \ldots, s_{t-1}, a_{t-1}^1, a_{t-1}^{2*}, r_t^1\}, \\ h_t^2 &= \{s_0, a_0^{1*}, a_0^2, r_1^2, s_1, a_1^{1*}, a_1^2, r_2^2, \ldots, s_{t-1}, a_{t-1}^{1*}, a_{t-1}^2, r_t^2\}. \end{aligned} \tag{9}$$

When the error function of the agent 1, E^1, is derived with respect to the parameter vector $\boldsymbol{\theta}^1$ of the agent 1, we get:

$$\frac{\partial E^1}{\partial \boldsymbol{\theta}^1} = \sum_{t=1}^{\infty} \sum_{h_t^1 \in H_t^1} P(h_t^1) \left[\frac{\partial e(h_t^1)}{\partial \boldsymbol{\theta}^1} + e(h_t^1) \sum_{i=0}^{t-1} \frac{\partial}{\partial \boldsymbol{\theta}^1} \ln P(a_i^1 | s_i, a_i^{2*}) \right]. \tag{10}$$

The immediate error function of the agent 1 based on Eq. (4) is as follows:

$$\begin{aligned} e(h_t^1) = \frac{1}{2} \sum_{s_t} P(s_t | s_{t-1}, a_{t-1}^1, a_{t-1}^{2*}) [r_t^1 + \gamma \mathrm{Nash}\{Q_{t-1}^1(s_t)\} \\ - Q_{t-1}^1(s_{t-1}, a_{t-1}^1, a_{t-1}^{2*})]^2. \end{aligned} \tag{11}$$

The determination of the Nash equilibrium point and the corresponding Nash equilibrium outcome of the bimatrix game determined by Q_t^1 and Q_t^2 can be done e.g. using the *Lemke-Howson* algorithm [2].

4.3 Asymmetric Case

In the asymmetric case, the leader (agent 1) is capable to calculate the Stackelberg equilibrium point (a_t^{1s}, a_t^{2s}) alone. However, the follower (agent 2) makes his decision based on the leader's announcement $g(s_t, a_t^c)$ at the time instant t. Formally, histories for both agents are:

$$
\begin{aligned}
h_t^1 &= \{s_0, a_0^1, a_0^{2s}, r_1^1, s_1, a_1^1, a_1^{2s}, r_2^1, \ldots, s_{t-1}, a_{t-1}^1, a_{t-1}^{2s}, r_t^1\}, \\
h_t^2 &= \{s_0, g(s_0, a_0^c), a_0^2, r_1^2, s_1, g(s_1, a_1^c), a_1^2, r_2^2, \ldots, s_{t-1}, g(s_{t-1}, a_{t-1}^c), a_{t-1}^2, r_t^2\}.
\end{aligned}
\tag{12}
$$

Also in this case, we can write the derivative of the follower's history probability $\partial P(h_t^2)/\partial \theta^2$ with the help of the probability $P(h_t^2)$ itself and thus get the derivative of the global error:

$$
\frac{\partial E^2}{\partial \theta^2} = \sum_{t=1}^{\infty} \sum_{h_t^2 \in H_t^2} P(h_t^2) \left[\frac{\partial e(h_t^2)}{\partial \theta^2} + e(h_t^2) \sum_{i=0}^{t-1} \frac{\partial}{\partial \theta^2} \ln P(a_i^2 | s_i, g(s_i, a_i^c)) \right]. \tag{13}
$$

For the follower's immediate error function in the case of Q-learning we get the following equation:

$$
\begin{aligned}
e(h_t^2) = \frac{1}{2} \sum_{s_t} P(s_t | s_{t-1}, g(s_{t-1}, a_{t-1}^c), a_{t-1}^2) \\
[r_t^2 + \gamma \max_{b \in A^2} Q_{t-1}^2(s_t, g(s_t, a_t^c), b) \\
- Q_{t-1}^2(s_{t-1}, g(s_{t-1}, a_{t-1}^c), a_{t-1}^2)]^2.
\end{aligned}
\tag{14}
$$

In (13) and (14), the announcement $g(\cdot)$ is determined by Eq. (6).

5   Example Application

In this section we solve a simple example problem, the grid world problem, which is used for testing reinforcement learning algorithms in many sources. Our test case is the same as in [4], where the problem was solved using a tabular version of the symmetric multiagent reinforcement algorithm. In this example (the leftmost part in Fig. 1), we have a grid world containing nine cells, two agents and two goal cells. The agents are starting from lower corners 1 and 2 and they are capable to move to adjacent (4-neighborhood) cells of the current cell. A large positive payoff is levied when the agent reaches the goal cell. If the agents collide, both agents are returned back to their original cells.

In the asymmetric model, the agent 1 is acting as the leader and the agent 2 as the follower. A small negative payoff is levied only to the leader when the agents are moving into the same cell and the leader is thus enforcing his action so that he tries to avoid the collision. In the symmetric model, a small negative payoff is levied to both agents. The problem is solved by fixing VAPS to Q-learning algorithm (discount factor $\gamma = 0.99$). The state space of the problem

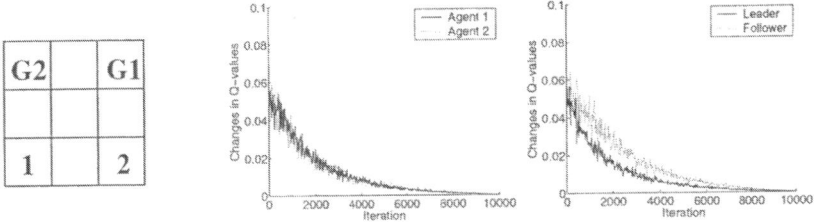

Fig. 1. Left: the game board used in the example, Center: convergence of the symmetric model, Right: convergence of the asymmetric model

consists of joint positions of the agents and the value function is approximated with the linear approximator (one parameter for each state-actions tuple). The results shown in Fig. 1 are averages of 50 test runs.

In both symmetric and asymmetric models, the algorithms converge with an equal pace. In the symmetric model, Fig. 1 (center), both agents are learning at the same pace. In the asymmetric model, Fig. 1 (right), the follower is learning at the lower pace than the leader due to leader's enforcements.

6   Conclusions and Future Research

A gradient based method for symmetric and asymmetric multiagent reinforcement learning is presented in this paper. The method is based on the VAPS framework, which is extended to use Markov games as the underlying mathematical theory. Additionally, a small example problem is solved using the method.

In the future, other learning algorithms are tested with VAPS framework. In addition, the method will be tested with real-world applications.

References

1. L. Baird and A. Moore. Gradient descent for general reinforcement learning. In M. Kearns, S. Solla, and D. Cohn, editors, *Advances in Neural Information Processing Systems*, volume 11, Cambridge, MA, USA, 1999. MIT Press.
2. R. W. Cottle, R. E. Stone, and J.-S. Pang. *The Linear Complementarity Problem.* Academic Press, New York, USA, 1992.
3. J. A. Filar and K. Vrieze. *Competitive Markov Decision Processes.* Springer-Verlag, New York, NY, USA, 1997.
4. J. Hu and M. P. Wellman. Multiagent reinforcement learning: Theoretical framework and an algorithm. In *Proceedings of the Fifteenth International Conference on Machine Learning (ICML'98)*, Madison, Wisconsin, USA, July 1998. Morgan Kaufmann Publishers.

Revocable Anonymity of Undeniable Signature Scheme

Winson K.Y. Yeung[1] and Song Han[2]

[1] Department of Computer Science, City University of Hong Kong
83 Tat Chee Avenue, Kowloon, Hong Kong
kyyeung@cs.cityu.edu.hk
[2] Department of Mathematics, Peking University, Beijing 100871, P. R. China
hanust@math.pku.edu.cn

Abstract. We present a new *revocable* anonymous protocol for the undeniable signatures. Our scheme allows some designated entity for example the government to revoke the anonymity of some signer who has done illegal actions in the group. Our scheme improves the signing algorithm of the traditional undeniable signatures such that the signing algorithm is more efficiency referring to the time and space cost.

1 Introduction

The model of the undeniable signature schemes was first proposed by Chaum and van Antwerpen [3] in CRYPTO'89. Since then many researchers have done some works in this field, for example [7], [8] and [4]. Undeniable signatures are like ordinary digital signatures, except that testing validity of a signature requires interacting with the signer. With the confirmation and denial protocols, recipient of an undeniable signature can challenge its signer and the signer cannot falsely deny a valid signature. Galbraith and Mao [6] first introduced the anonymity property of the undeniable signature schemes recently. They also gave a precise definition for anonymity and provided some practical and efficient schemes with this security property. However, they just described the perfect anonymity, i.e., the scheme always preserve the anonymity of the signers in any case and the signers have perfect privacy, not *revocable* privacy. So when some emergence cases appear, we are unable to revoke the original signer. Therefore, we describe a new model, i.e., the *revocable anonymity* of the undeniable signature schemes that improve Galbraith and Mao's scheme [6] to achieve *revocable anonymity*.

It is known that the main ingredient impacting on the efficiency of one protocol in cryptography is the "on-line" computation in the underlying cryptographic protocol. Moreover, in most cases, the "off-line" computation or the pre-computation will contribute to the efficiency of the underlying protocol. Consequently, in our scheme the trusted agency center is treated as the entity who can do some pre-computations before the signing algorithm is executed by the signer. Thus, the actions of the trusted agency center will contribute to the efficiency of our scheme. Our work also improves the signing algorithm of [6] such that the signing algorithm of our scheme requites less time and space cost.

J. Liu et al. (Eds.): IDEAL 2003, LNCS 2690, pp. 76–83, 2003.

Examples of application of our undeniable signature scheme would be some digital transaction protocols including bid auction, stock exchange and digital cash. Suppose there are several banks generating digital cash by signing on the digital banknote for users to use. Users can confirm the validity of the signed digital cash by interacting with the banks through the confirmation protocol while other banks can deny having generated the digital cash by running the denial protocol. Of course those banks are all anonymous from users. In case of a dispute, a designated trusted entity, e.g. the government, can revoke the anonymity to reveal the original signing bank.

The rest of this paper is organized as follows. The next section presents some related works and our definition for *revocable anonymity*. Section 3 describes the details of our new signature scheme. The security and *revocable anonymity* properties are proved in Section 4. Finally, we conclude our paper in Section 5.

2 Related Works

The idea of anonymous for an undeniable signature scheme was first introduced by Galbraith and Mao [6]. If we let {**Gen, Sign, Confirm, Deny**} be an undeniable signature scheme. then a **distinguisher D** can be viewed as an adversary under a chosen message attack with the input of (pk_0, pk_1) where (pk_0, pk_1) are two public keys of two key pairs (pk_0, sk_0) and (pk_1, sk_1) generated by **Gen** on input a security parameter 1^k. The distinguisher **D** is permitted to interact with the hash function oracles, to obtain signatures on messages and to run signature **Confirm** and **Deny** protocols (with the signer) corresponding to both of these public keys. At some time **D** constructs a message m and requests a challenge signature s through $\mathbf{Sign}_{sk_b}(m)$ where the bit $b \in \{0, 1\}$ is hidden from **D**. The restriction for **D** is that **Confirm** and **Deny** protocols cannot be executed on the challenge message-signature pair (m, s). The output of **D** is a guess b' for the hidden bit b. A distinguisher **D** with output b' is said to be successful with advantage $\epsilon(k)$ where advantage $= \left|\Pr(\text{D's guess of } b' = b) - \frac{1}{2}\right|$, if with probability at least $\frac{1}{2} + \epsilon(k)$, $b' = b$. We say that an undeniable signature scheme has the anonymity property if there is no distinguisher who runs in polynomial time and has a non-negligible advantage.

Galbraith and Mao [6] proposed an undeniable signature scheme that extends Gennaro, Krawczyk, and Rabin's [8] undeniable/confirmer signature scheme based on RSA so as to provide the anonymity property. However, the above model for the anonymity of the undeniable signature scheme is sometimes too strong and not reasonable since such undeniable signature has perfect anonymity. Therefore, we design a new model for the undeniable signature scheme:

Definition 1. (Revocable Anonymity) *A new undeniable signature system consists of { one trusted agency center, signers, designated verifiers}–participants and {**Gen, Sign, Confirm, Deny, DelAnonymity**}–algorithms. One **distinguisher** to the scheme as defined above. Such undeniable signature scheme has the* revocable anonymity *if there is no **distinguisher** who runs in polynomial time and has a non-negligible advantage, except that the trusted agency center is able to revoke the anonymity when some emergence appears.*

3   New Undeniable Signature Scheme

3.1   Restriction for Trusted Agency Center

To realize the *revocable anonymity* of the undeniable signature scheme, we should restrict the actions of the trusted agency center. We know that some righteous restrictions apply for some participants are permitted in cryptography [2].

We assume that the new undeniable signature scheme has one trusted agency center and N signers. After the trusted agency center creates the database by running the **Gen** algorithm, she is "away from the protocol", i.e., she is not allowed to run the **Sign** algorithm, the **Confirm** algorithm and the **Deny** algorithm. Because we are working in the situation of the undeniable signature scheme, only the signer is able to run the **Sign** algorithm herself, run the **Confirm** algorithm and the **Deny** algorithm interactively with the verifier, so it is righteous to restrict the actions of the trusted agency center. As soon as some emergence cases appear, the trusted agency center will be "on-line". She will run the **DelAnonymity** algorithm and revoke the anonymity of the corresponding signer from the undeniable signature scheme.

3.2   The Scheme

There is a security parameter of fixed bit-length k such that all n_i, $1 \leq i \leq N$, are at most k bits long. There is also a soundness bound B as in [7].

Gen algorithm:

1. The trusted agency center chooses N pairs of prime numbers $\{p_i, q_i\}$, $1 \leq i \leq N$ such that $p_i \equiv q_i \equiv 3 \pmod{4}$, and all prime factors of $(p_i - 1)/2$ and $(q_i - 1)/2$ are greater than B.
2. She computes the product $n_i = p_i q_i$.
3. She chooses e_i, d_i from $Z_{n_i}^*$ randomly such that $e_i d_i \equiv 1 \pmod{\varphi(n_i)}$, where $\varphi(\cdot)$ is Euler phi function.
4. And $\{(n_i, p_i, q_i, e_i, d_i) | 1 \leq i \leq N\}$ forms the database of the trusted agency center, then she sends n_i and the ciphertext of $\{e_i, d_i\}$ to the *signer$_i$* for $1 \leq i \leq N$; here the trusted agency center uses the Cramer-Shoup public key encryption system [5], which is provably secure against adaptive chosen ciphertext attack, to encrypt $\{e_i, d_i\}$.
5. For any $1 \leq i \leq N$, the *signer$_i$* gets the ciphertext of $\{e_i, d_i\}$ from the trusted agency center, and then decrypts it.
6. She chooses $x_i \in Z_{n_i}^*$ randomly, computes $g_i = x_i^2 \pmod{n_i}$ and $h_i = g_i^{e_i} \pmod{n_i}$.
7. Then she preserves $\{e_i, d_i, x_i\}$ as the private key and publishes $\{n_i, g_i, h_i\}$ as the public key for the undeniable signature scheme.

After generating the public and private keys, any *signer$_i$*, for $1 \leq i \leq N$, can sign a message m as follows:

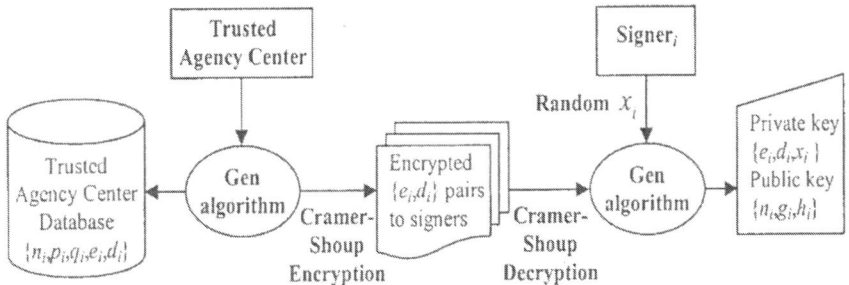

Fig. 1. The **Gen** algorithm for trusted agency center to set up the database and signers to generate their public and private keys.

Sign algorithm:

1. The $signer_i$ chooses $r \in Z_{n_i}^*$ randomly and constructs the randomized padding value $H(m\|r)$. Then she computes $s = x_i H(m\|r)^{d_i}$ $(\bmod\ n_i)$.
2. The $signer_i$ enlarges s to a bit-string s' of length at most k by adding a suitable random multiple of n_i. That is $s' = s + t n_i$ where t is chosen such that $|s'| \leq k$. Thereupon, the undeniable signature on m is the pair $\{H(m\|r), s'\}$.

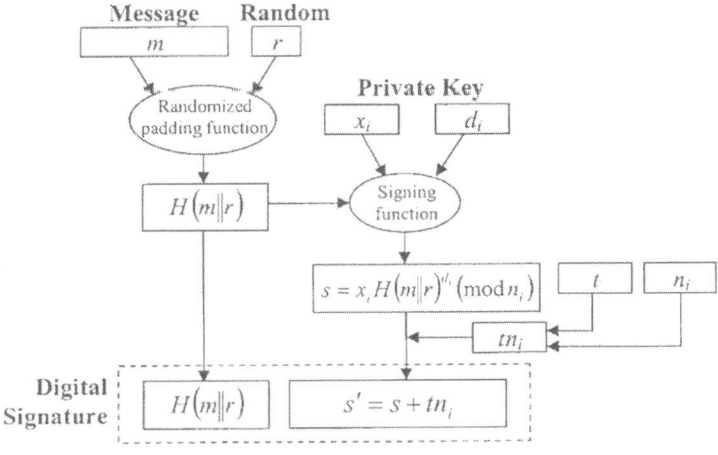

Fig. 2. The **Sign** algorithm uses to create an undeniable signature.

Remark 1. To prevent the Jacobi symbols attack, Galbraith and Mao's scheme [6] define signatures by $s = \xi H(m)^d$ $(\bmod\ N)$ where ξ is a randomly chosen square root of 1 in Z_N^* by the signer. However, it is impractical in our scheme as this time the signer knows only the value of n_i but not p_i and q_i, it is computationally hard for the signer to determine the values of ξ in $Z_{n_i}^*$. So we modify the signature by replacing ξ with x_i chosen by the $signer_i$ herself. Since the probability that the Jacobi symbol of x_i equals 1 is about $\frac{1}{2}$, so there is no longer any relationship between $\left(\frac{H(m\|r)}{n_i}\right)$ and $\left(\frac{s}{n_i}\right)$. Now an adversary cannot eliminate some candidate signers by checking if these values are equal and increase the probability of guessing who the actual signer is.

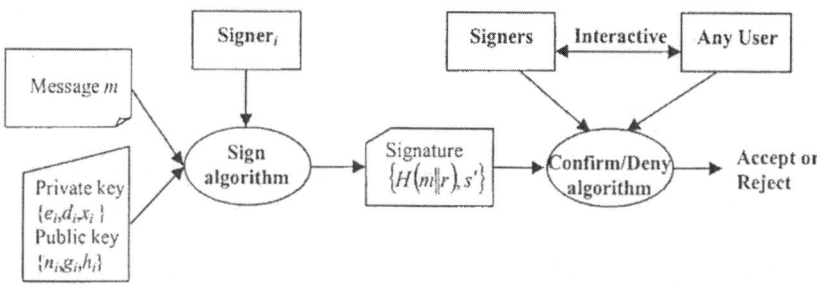

Fig. 3. The **Sign** algorithm and **Confirm or Deny** algorithms.

Any user can check the validity of the signature by interacting with the corresponding signer or any other signer can deny having generated the signature as follows:

Confirm or Deny algorithms:

They are the interactive algorithms between the signers and the verifiers. To confirm or deny an alleged undeniable signature $\{H(m\|r), s'\}$, the $signer_i$ executes the non-interactive, designated verifier versions of the proofs (as in [7] which prove the relationships $g_i \equiv h_i^{d_i} \pmod{n_i}$ and $s' \pmod{n_i}^{2e_i} \equiv h_i H(m\|r)^2 \pmod{n_i}$.

In case of a dispute, trusted agency center will execute the following algorithm:

DelAnonymity algorithm:

This is an algorithm that only the trusted agency center is able to run. Whenever some emergence case appears, the trusted agency center will quickly be "on-line" and search her database. For $j = 1$ to N, the trusted agency center checks whether $(s' \pmod{n_j})^{2e_j} \equiv h_j H(m\|r)^2 \pmod{n_j}$. If there exists an I such that $(s' \pmod{n_I})^{2e_I} \equiv h_I H(m\|r)^2 \pmod{n_I}$, then the trusted agency center will tell us that it is just the $signer_I$ who has signed the signature $\{H(m\|r), s'\}$.

Remark 2. We should note that although the anonymity of the *signer$_I$* is revoked by the trusted agency center, that is the case only in this stage. It does not damage the signature of *signer$_I$* before and after this stage.

Remark 3. From the first view of the actions of the trusted agency center, we probably think that the protocol is inefficient as its computation is proportional to the number of signers N. It needs about $\frac{N}{2}$ computation time to revoke the original signer and so requires a long time when N is large. However, we should realize that such action is just an abnormal case, i.e., this action only performs when there is a signer who has done some illegal action or there is a dispute, so such irregular computation will not affect the normal operation very much.

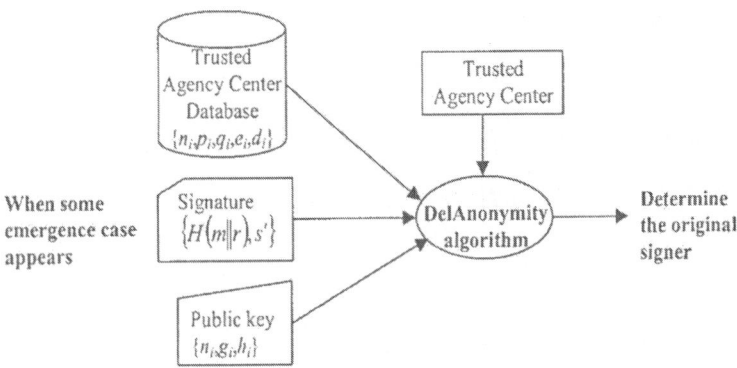

Fig. 4. The **DelAnonymity** algorithm uses to determine the original signer.

4 Security and Fair Anonymity of the Undeniable Signature

4.1 Security Analysis

We note that our scheme is improved on the construction of [6]. Therefore, the new scheme has the properties of secure undeniable signatures.

Lemma 1. *The confirmation and denial protocols have the properties of completeness, soundness and simulatability (see [7] and [8] for the details).*

Theorem 1. *Our undeniable signature scheme is secure against chosen messages attack under the condition that the underlying regular RSA signature is unforgeable against the adaptive chosen messages attack.*

Proof. We first look at the plain RSA signature:

$$\text{Message: } m$$
$$\text{Signature: } s = m^d \pmod{n}.$$

It is well known that the plain RSA signature is not unforgeable against the adaptive chosen messages attack. Hence, some researchers for example Bellare and Rogaway [1] suggest using the padding scheme for the plain RSA signature in order to make it unforgeable against the adaptive chosen messages attack.

Therefore, the regular RSA signature is one of the following formulas:

$$\text{Message:}\quad m$$
$$\text{Signature: } s = E(m)^d \quad (\text{mod } n).$$

In the above regular signature, $E(m)$ is the encryption of the message m. For example m can be hashed by a padding scheme $H(m\|r)$, where $H(\cdot)$ is a collision-free hash function, and r is a random element chosen from Z_n^* . From the proof of [1], the regular RSA signature is unforgeable against chosen messages attack.

Now let us return to our undeniable signature: Suppose $\{H(m\|r), s\}$ is a valid signature for a message m; then

$$s = x_i H(m\|r)^{d_i} \quad (\text{mod } n_i). \tag{1}$$

We will transform the form of s as follows:

$$s = x_i H(m\|r)^{d_i} \quad (\text{mod } n_i) \tag{2}$$
$$= \left(x_i^{\frac{1}{d_i}}\right)^{d_i} H(m\|r)^{d_i} \quad (\text{mod } n_i) \tag{3}$$
$$= (x_i^{e_i} H(m\|r))^{d_i} \quad (\text{mod } n_i) \quad . \tag{4}$$

By the underlying scheme, only the signer knows the values of e_i and x_i. Naturally we can view $x_i^{e_i} H(m\|r)$ as the encryption of the message m, so the new undeniable signature is equivalent to its underlying regular RSA signature. However, the regular RSA signature is secure against chosen messages attack [1]. Hence, our undeniable signature is secure against chosen message attack.   □

4.2   Revocable Anonymity

Now we discuss how to realize the *revocable anonymity* of the undeniable signature scheme. We first explain why it has the anonymity property, and then demonstrate that its anonymity can be revoked by the trusted agency center when some emergence cases appear.

Lemma 2. *In the random oracle model the above new undeniable signature scheme has the anonymity property under the assumption that the special composite decision Diffie-Hellman problem is hard and the trusted agency center is trusted belonging to the assumption.*

Proof. The proof is omitted here as it is similar to the Theorem 3 in [6].   □

Lemma 3. *The trusted agency center is able to revoke the anonymity of the signers from the undeniable signature scheme if there are some emergence cases.*

Proof. By the construction of the new scheme we know the trusted agency center has a database $\{(n_i, p_i, q_i, e_i, d_i) | 1 \leq i \leq N\}$. If some emergence cases appear, for example some $signer_i$ does not use the scheme legally and there is a dispute, then the trusted agency center can run the **DelAnonymity** algorithm to revoke the anonymity of $signer_i$. In order to realize this property, the trusted agency center will search her database. For $j = 1$ to N, she checks whether

$$(s' \pmod{n_j})^{2e_j} \equiv h_j H(m\|r)^2 \pmod{n_j}. \tag{5}$$

If there exists an I such that $(s' \pmod{n_I})^{2e_I} \equiv h_I H(m\|r)^2 \pmod{n_I}$, then the trusted agency center will tell us that it is just the $signer_i$ who has signed the signature. Therefore, the trusted agency center is able to delete the anonymity of the signer from the undeniable signature scheme. □

Theorem 2. *The new undeniable signature scheme based on Steven D. Galbraith and Wenbo Mao's construction has the* revocable anonymity *property.*

Proof. By Lemma 2 and Lemma 3, we prove the correctness of the theorem. □

5 Conclusion

This paper describes a new model for the undeniable signature scheme, i.e. the *revocable anonymity* of the undeniable signature scheme. At the same time, we prove our new undeniable signature scheme secure against chosen message attack and has the *revocable* property.

References

1 Bellare, M., Rogaway, P.: The Exact Security of Digital Signature–How to sign with RSA and Rabin. EUROCRYPT 1996, LNCS 1070, Springer, (1996) 399–416
2. Camenisch, J., Micheal, M.: Confirmer Signature Schemes Secure Against Adaptive Adversaries. EUROCRYPT 2000, LNCS 1807, Springer, (2000) 243–258
3. Chaum, D., van Antwerpen, H.: Undeniable Signatures. CRYPTO 1989, LNCS 435, Springer, (1990) 212–216
4. Chaum, D.: Zero-Knowledge Undeniable Signatures. EUROCRYPT 1990, LNCS 473, Springer, (1991) 458–464
5. Cramer, R., Shoup, V.: A Practical Public Key Cryptosystem Provably Secure Against Adaptive Chosen Ciphertext Attack. CRYPTO 1998, LNCS 1462, Springer, (1998) 13–25
6. Galbraith, S.D., Mao, W.: Anonymity and Denial of Undeniable and Confirmer Signatures. HP Labs technical report HPL, (2001) 303
7. Galbraith, S.D., Mao, W., Paterson, K.G.: RSA-Based Undeniable Signatures for General Moduli. CT-RSA 2002. LNCS 2271, Springer, (2002) 200–217
8. Gennaro, R., Krawczyk, H., Rabin T.: RSA-Based Undeniable Signatures. CRYPTO 1997. LNCS 1294, Springer, (1997) 132–149. Also in Journal of Cryptology **13** (2000) 397–416

Learning Classifier System for Generating Various Types of Dialogues in Conversational Agent

Eun-Kyung Yun and Sung-Bae Cho

Department of Computer Science, Yonsei University,
134 Shinchon-dong, Sudaemoon-ku, Seoul 120-749, Korea
ekfree@candy.yonsei.ac.kr, sbcho@cs.yonsei.ac.kr

Abstract. Most of the conversational agents respond to the users in an unsatisfactory way because of using the simple sequential pattern matching. In this paper, we propose a conversational agent that can respond with various sentences for improving the user's familiarity. The agent identifies the user's intention using DA (Dialogue Acts) and increases the intelligence and the variety of the conversation using LCS (Learning Classifier System). We apply this agent to the introduction of a web site. The results show that the conversational agent has the ability to present more adequate and friendly response to user's query.

1 Introduction

One of the first conversational agents, ELIZA, was contrived for the research on natural language processing. This agent uses simple pattern matching technique [1]. ALICE is written in a language called AIML that is based on XML (http://alicebot.org). However, it has shortcomings of not being able to respond to users reflecting their intentions because of simple sequential pattern matching based on keywords. Tackling this problem requires much time and effort in constructing the response database. Most of the conversational agents respond with the fixed answer sentences that are stored in the response database in advance. Therefore, the user may be easily bored as time passes and feel less familiarity to the site. This paper proposes a conversational agent that is able to communicate with the user in various sentences through learning with Learning Classifier Systems (LCS) [2].

2 Learning Classifier Systems

LCS is a kind of methods of genetic-based machine learning [3, 4], and it uses genetic algorithm with a classifier system. Classifier systems, associated with rule-based systems, spend much cost of constructing rules, and it is impossible to work in a changing environment [5]. LCS is appropriate to that case. Classifier system consists of rules (classifiers): one classifier has one or more condition parts that consist of ternary elements {0, 1, #} and one action part that consists of {0, 1}. The character '#' can take either '0' or '1.' LCS is composed of three modules as shown in Fig. 1.

➢ Classifier system: The system compares input messages with the condition part of all classifiers and performs matching. The matching classifiers enter

J. Liu et al. (Eds.): IDEAL 2003, LNCS 2690, pp. 84–88, 2003.

> competition for posting their output messages, and only the winner of the competition actually posts messages. The measure of each classifier is the value of bid as follows:

$$bid = c \times specificit \, y \times strength$$

where c: constant less than 1, *specificity*: condition's length minus number of '#' symbols, and *strength*: the measure of confidence in a classifier.

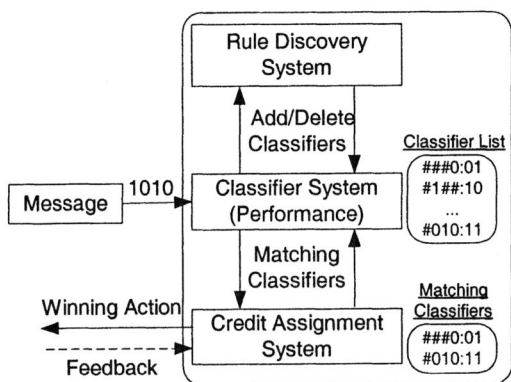

Fig. 1. Structure of LCS

> Credit assignment system [6]: When the rewards from the environment transmit, it causes the strength of the classifiers to change to reflect their relevance to the system performance. This is to classify rules according to their usefulness. The conventional algorithm used for this purpose is the bucket brigade algorithm.

> Rule discovery system: The process of rule discovery in the classifier systems utilizes genetic algorithm. The GA selects the classifiers with greater strength to reproduce, generating new individuals by their recombination and mutation. The new classifiers generated take the places of the weaker ones, modifying the classifier set of the system.

3 A Conversational Agent Based on LCS

Fig. 2 shows the structure of conversational agent in this paper. The key techniques in this system are as follows. First, it classifies input sentences through a dialogue act categorization [7]. It can figure out user's intention roughly and find a response close to user's intention by dialogue act categorization [8]. Then it matches the most appropriate response in the script database for user to get the appropriate response to that query. In this point, we introduce LCS for giving not static answer sentences but dynamic ones.

In dialogue act categorization, queries are classified into two general categories, question and statement, which are subcategorized into primary or secondary. Automata that are constructed on keywords and their sequential information implement the dialogue act categorization module.

In order to respond, the agent accesses the script database. The script consists of a list of classifiers, and topic is the primary component that represents a classifier list.

For all the topics, the conditional part of a topic is compared with the query, dialogue acts, and the keywords extracted during dialogue act categorization. This returns the scores of all the topics as a result. The topic with the highest score is selected and then the agent begins to read the classifier list file of that topic.

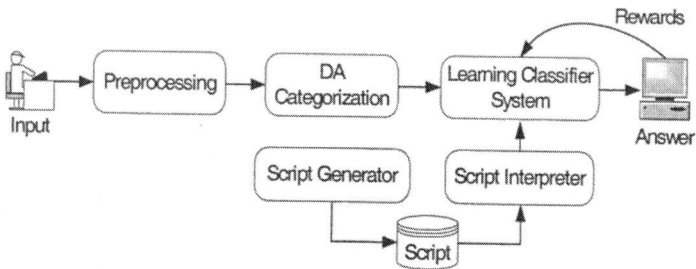

Fig. 2. System overview

Fig. 3 shows the structure of one classifier. The condition part consists of the bits to specify dialogue acts and two bits to specify the structure of sentences, which can determine the structure of answer sentences. In other words, the last two bits represent a complete sentence, a sentence only with keywords, and a sentence with modifiers. The current implementation does not have the two bits that will be very useful information to improve the agent for future system based on user modeling. The action part consists of subject, keywords, and predicates that answer sentence contains.

Condition Part (n-bits)					
Dialogue Act 1	Dialogue Act 2	......	Dialogue Act n-2	n-1	n

(a) Condition part

Action Part (m-bits)		
Subject Part	Keyword Part	Predicate Part

(b) Action part

Fig. 3. Condition and action parts

After selecting the appropriate topic and reading classifier list, the agent finds matching classifiers. If there is any matching one, corresponding answer sentence posts; otherwise new sentence is created randomly and is added to the classifier list (See Fig. 4). At the same time, new classifiers are created by GA operators, crossover and mutation, and added to the classifier list. Fitness evaluation is performed using strength value that is controlled by user's feedback (evaluation score). In other words, user scores the agent's answer sentence from -2 to +2 and the strength is recomputed.

4   Experimental Results

To show the conversational capabilities of the agent, we apply it to introduction of a certain research laboratory. Each classifier list has the same number of classifiers with manual initialization.

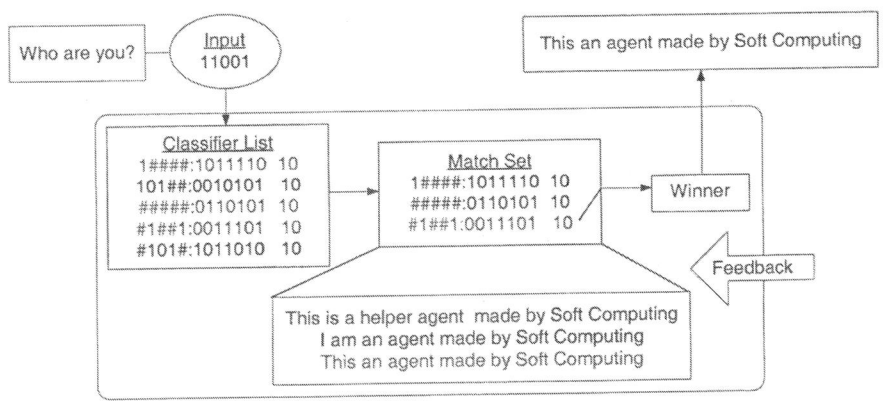

Fig. 4. Structure of the conversational agent

Table 1 shows a stream of conversations about "laboratory location." In conversation 1, new answer sentence was created in spite of the same question. In conversation 2, there was no matching classifier in the beginning. In this case, the agent responded by creating classifiers randomly but there was no predicate in answer sentence. After user's feedback, it responded as a complete sentence.

Table 1. An example of conversation

[Conversation 1] **User**: Where is your laboratory? **Agent**: It is located at the 3rd engineering building in Yonsei university **User**: Where is your laboratory? **Agent**: It is located at 529, the 3rd engineering building in Yonsei university
[Conversation 2] **User**: Tell me where your laboratory is. **Agent**: 529, the 3rd engineering building, 134, Yonsei university, Shinchon-dong, Seodaemoon-gu, Seoul **User**: Tell me where your laboratory is **Agent**: It is located at 529, the 3rd engineering building, 134, Yonsei university, Shinchon-dong, Seodaemoon-gu, Seoul

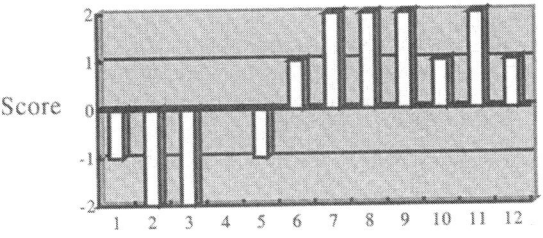

Conversation iterations

Fig. 5. User evaluation score against the response sentences

In addition, we have generated various types of sentences through several conversations. After repeated learning, the agent responded using only complete sentences that had been received higher scores. Fig. 5 shows the user evaluation scores against the response sentences about the topic "agent." Because the agent can generate various types of sentences by itself, not only it makes the designer spend less time to write scripts but also the familiarity on the agent increases.

5   Conclusions

As the conversational agents respond with fixed sentences, they tend to lack the flexibility and variety. In this paper, we have proposed a conversational agent based on LCS that can give various types of answer sentences to user's queries in natural language. By generating new sentences, it increases the variety and flexibility of conversations. However, this agent does not have knowledge enough to understand the structures of sentences and meanings. The reason is that the sentence is constructed simply by mixing the given phrases. Therefore, we will make the agent by itself to generate the correct sentences through the investigation of grammar.

Acknowledgements. This work was supported by Brain Science and Engineering Research Program sponsored by Korean Ministry of Science and Technology and Biometrics Engineering Research Center.

References

1. J. Weizenbaun, "ELIZA - A Computer Program for the Study of Natural Language Communication between Man and Machine," *Communications of the ACM*, vol. 9, no. 1, pp. 36–45, 1965.
2. L. B. Booker, D. E. Goldberg, and J. H. Holland, "Classifier Systems and Genetic Algorithms," *Artificial Intelligence*, vol. 40, pp. 235–282, 1989.
3. D. Katagami and S. Yamada, "Interactive Classifier System for Real Robot Learning," *Proceedings of the 2000 IEEE International Workshop on Robot and Human Interactive Communication*, pp.258–263, 2000.
4. D. E. Goldberg, *Genetic Algorithms in Search, Optimization, and Machine Learning*, Addison-Wesley: Reading, MA, 1989.
5. A. D. McAulay, and J. C. Oh, "Improving Learning of Genetic Rule-Based Classifier Systems," *IEEE Transactions on Systems, Man, and Cybernetics*, vol. 24, no.1, pp.152–159, 1994.
6. D. Haung, "A Framework for the Credit-Apportionment Process in Rule-Based Systems," *IEEE Transactions on Systems, Man, and Cybernetics*, vol. 19, no.3, pp.489–498, 1989.
7. M. G. Core, and J. F. Allen, "Coding Dialogs with the DAMSL Annotation Scheme," *Working Notes of the AAAI Fall Symposium on Communicative Action in Humans and Machines*, pp. 28–35, 1997.
8. S.-I. Lee and S.-B. Cho, "An Intelligent agent with structured pattern matching for a virtual representative," *Intelligent Agent Technology*, pp. 305–309, Maebashi, Japan, Oct. 2001.

An Enhanced Security Model for Mobile Agent System

Li Feng[1], Feng Shan[1], and Wei Ying[2]

[1] Department of Control Science and Engineering,
Huazhong University of Science and Technology,China
FengLee_Jeff@hotmail.com
[2] Department of Systems Engineering and Engineering Management,
Chinese University of Hong Kong,Hong Kong
ywei@se.cuhk.edu.hk

Abstract. The obvious disadvantage of using mobile agent based applications is the concern that they will introduce vulnerability into the network. Since conventional security techniques did not address those security threats caused, an urgent need is to modify standard security models. This paper presents an enhanced security model in an attempt to more efficiently utilize its new mechanism to guarantee an acceptable security level of the mobile agent based applications, the model based system can react actively to attacks without disturbing the running mobile agent applications. The proposed model equipped with the function that can also bewilder attackers though redirecting and spreading network flows to avoid someone to reach target.

1 Introduction

Mobile agents(MAs) offer a new paradigm for distributed computation, but their potential benefits must be weighted against the very real security threats they pose.

Threats to the security of mobile agent system(MAS) generally fall into four comprehensive classes: disclosure of information, denial of service, corruption of information, and interference or nuisance. It is important to note that many of the threats that are discussed have counterparts in classical client-server systems and have always existed in some form in the past. MAS simply offer a greater opportunity for abuse and misuse, broadening the scale of threats significantly. New threats arising from the MAs paradigm are due to the fact that threats originate not just in malicious agents but in malicious agent platform as well.

2 Overview

So far, some traditional countermeasures for MAS basically share the common idea that all of them focus on protecting mobile agent system itself. They try best to consummate themselves(agent and agent platform) to obstruct attackers,

J. Liu et al. (Eds.): IDEAL 2003, LNCS 2690, pp. 89–93, 2003.

namely passive recovery policy. This policy has limited ability to keep away attack, once breakthrough or pass by security defense, it has no ability to deal with the attack problem.

The proposed model for MAS also focuses on these essential passive recovery policies, however, more attentions are paid to actively detection and response to the attack attempts. For example, the system will respond to the illegal activity detected, by re- programming firewall to disallow network traffic from a suspected hostile source. In proposed model, a sub-system of special light intrusion detection and response is embedded in MAs platform. Another sub-system works parallelly to bewilder attackers by redirecting and spreading the data flow to several ports, just like a special simply proxy serverfirewall.

3   The Proposed Model

The proposed model is made up of three sub-systems: the special light intrusion detection and response system, the fast encrypting system, and the special simply proxy server/firewall. All packets incoming and outgoing are processed by these three sub-systems in serials. Firstly, the special light intrusion detection and response system will capture all packets from system kernel stacks, reject and log the suspect packets, filter the packets the MAS generated. Secondly, after verifying the integrality, the packets the MAS generated will be decrypted or encrypted depended on the direction of flow. And then, the packets incoming from several ports will be converged into the port that the ongoing MAS communicate with; the packets outgoing from the port of the ongoing MAS will be redirected to several ports randomly. At last, the packets will be restored to kernel stacks. Since we work on kernel stacks, the ongoing MAS will handle packets from kernel stacks later without a little awareness.

Figure 1 presents the architecture(layered model) for the proposed system. The layers are numbered, starting from the Special Light Intrusion Detection and Response System(layer 1), and each layer represents a group of specific tasks performed by agents specialized in the functions of that layer. In addition, Layer N uses the services of layer N-1, performs its tasks and provides services to layer N+1.

3.1   Special Light Intrusion Detection and Response Sub-system

Although firewall and IDRS well deployed deny most attack attempt, they can't detect the attack aimed at the MAS. It is due to the layer where they work-network and transport layer that they can't identify automatically the occurrence of anomalous behavior on the application layer. As a result, an application-oriented light intrusion detection and response system is needed to protect MAS.

This sub-system is made up of Monitoring Agents, Decision-Making Agents, Notifying Agents, Reaction Agents, and the architecture presented as figure 1. Each agent is a simple entity that carries out a specific activity and cooperates with other agents as efficiently as possible. When an agent considers an activity

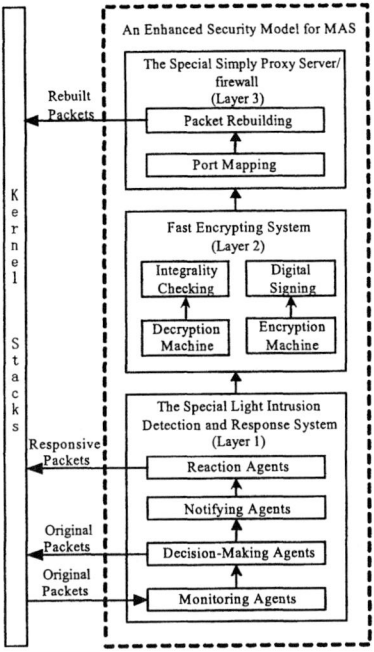

Fig. 1. Layer modeling for the proposed system

suspect, it immediately advises other agents of the system of the suspected intrusion. At that moment, an agent with a higher level of specialization for that type of suspected intrusion is activated.

Based on packets captured from kernel stacks by Monitoring Agents, Decision-Making Agents go into action, analyzing and identifying possible intrusions. If these agents consider a packet suspect, they activate Notification Agents, which then either notify the network manager or activate the agents of the upper level. On the last, top level are Reaction Agents, which automatically counter-attack any possible intrusion based on the information they receive from the notifying agents. Those packets filtered unsuspected will be parsed, if packets belongs to MAS, it will be transfer to the next layer; others will be restored to kernel stack unchanged.

Monitoring Agents. Monitoring Agents are responsible for capturing packets from operation system kernel stacks. We register hook subroutines in system hook chains. Therefore, we can capture and process each incoming packet before processed by operation system and application, and each outgoing packet before sent out by net interface.

Decision-Making Agents. This layer consists of the agents that perform the system's decision-making functions. An agent in this layer receives packet from the Monitoring Agents and, based on analysis of this packet, it either identifies an intrusion (or attempted intrusion) at the moment it occurs or filter the packets generated by other applications. In order to minimize the degree of bothering system, these agents identify an anomaly or improper use simply by matching the packet obtained with well-defined patterns of attack (attack signatures). Decision-Making Agents will activate the agents of the Notifying Agent to log the information of anomalous behavior.

Notifying Agents. These agents are responsible for notifying the network manager and for activating the agents of Reaction Agents, based on message received from Decision-Making Agents. Network manager can define new attacking pattern based on characteristics mined from log database, which can be done using the modern techniques of data mining, artificial intelligence.

Reaction Agents. Among the functions of these agents are the blocking a connection, dropping a packet, rejecting a service request, denying an IP address. As a reaction example, the Reaction Agents can build and send a packet with RST flag on to block a connection. Furthermore, the Reaction Agents exercise an interaction with the firewall or the IDRS requesting to deny that malicious host.

3.2   Fast Encrypting Sub-system

A fundamental technique for guarding MAS is signing code or other objects with a digital signature. Digital signature serves as means of confirming the authenticity of an object, its origin, and its integrity. Typically the code signer is either the creator of the agent, the user of the agent, or some entity that has reviewed the agent. In the model proposed, encryption and digital signature is deployed in layer 2 as figure 1 described.

We encrypt every packet MAS generated to counter those threats of disclosure or corruption with sniffer tools. And, the module of identity authentication is responsible to verify the integrity and repudiation of transmitted information.

We also log information of packets that failed to pass the integrity verification. If evidences indicate the occurrence of attack, IP Spoofing, Packet Faking, etc., we will cooperate with the firewall or IDRS to blockade that connection.

3.3   Special Simply Proxy Server/Firewall

One inherent weakness in modern MAS is due to their distributed nature. For example, if one attack MAs host though the known communication ports using SYN Flooding tools, application resources, even system resources of the MAs host will be exhausted, and the service will be halted. However, MAS has to exchange information through network, and IP address with Port is necessary to communicating in environment of Ethernet.

The objective of our work is to enable information exchange between hosts while bewilder attacker with dynamic communication channels. Our interesting is in making MAS resisting denial of service attacks that disable MAS nodes.

In our proposed model, we redirect packets flow to several virtual communication channels (several ports predefined), and choose one of these channels to communicate randomly. If attackers can't trap and decrypt all the packets in right sequence, they can't grasp the correct information. Furthermore, since we sign our connection request, all connection requests for the virtual ports will be suspected as attack attempts. At last, we will restore packet to kernel stack, waiting for ongoing MAS processing.

4   Conclusion

The area of mobile agent security is in a state of immaturity, but rapidly improving. The traditional orientation toward passive recovery techniques persists and, therefore, available protection mechanisms tend to focus on protecting the mobile agent system itself. Emphasis is beginning to move toward developing techniques that are oriented toward actively detecting and reacting to attack behavior, a much more difficult problem.

This paper presents an architecture and model for exploring a security MAS. This architecture aims to integrate a special light intrusion and response system, a special simply proxy server/firewall (port mapping and packet filter) into MAS.

References

1. Young, A.,Yung, M.:Sliding Encryption:A Cryptographic Tool for Mobile Agents. Proceedings of the 4th International Workshop on Fast Software Encryption, FSE'97.
2. Sander,T., Tschudin,C.,Vinga, G.(ed.):Protecting Mobile Agents Against Malicious Hosts. Mobile Agents and Security, Springer-Verlag, Lecture Notes in Computer Science,Vol. 1419. (1998) 44–60
3. Hohl, F.,Vinga, G.(ed.):Time Limited Blackbox Security: Protecting Mobile Agents from Malicious Hosts. Mobile Agents and Security, Springer-Verlag, Lecture Notes in Computer Science,Vol. 1419. (1998) 92–113
4. Helmer,G.:Intelligent agents for intrusion detection. Proceedings of IEEE Information Technology Conference, (1998) 121–124

A Ring-Based Architectural Model for Middle Agents in Agent-Based System

Chunsheng Li[1], Chengqi Zhang[1], and Zili Zhang[2]

[1] Faculty of Information Technology, University of Technology, Sydney
PO Box 123, BROADWAY, NSW 2007, AUSTRALIA
{csli, chengqi}@it.uts.edu.au
[2] Department of Computer Science, Southwest China Normal University
Chongqing 400715, China
zzhang@deakin.edu.au

Abstract. In agent-based systems, the performance of middle agents not only relies on the matchmaking algorithms employed by them, but also the architecture that organizes them with suitable organizational structure and coordination mechanism. In this paper, we contribute a framework and develop a couple of middle agents with logical ring organizational structure to match requester agents with service provider agents. The middle agent is of the features of proliferation and self-cancellation according to the sensory input from its environment. The token-based coordination mechanism of middle agents is designed. Two kinds of middle agents, namely, host and duplicate, are designed for promoting the scalability and robustness of agent-based systems. We demonstrate the potentials of the architecture by case study.

1 Introduction

In agent-based systems, different types of middle agents are usually employed for solving the matchmaking problem between service provider agents and requester agents. How to organize those middle agents efficiently and unfailingly in agent-based systems is an open problem. In this paper, we contribute a self-organizing ring-based architectural model to organize the middle agents in agent-based system. The ring-based architectural model is based on logical ring organizational structure and token-based coordination mechanism. About the organizational structure, the middle agents are divided into hosts and duplicates according to their roles in the system. About the coordination mechanism, elected coordinator mechanism is employed to build the logical ring, manage token, and proliferate or cancel middle agents based on agent group concept. For verifying the performance of the ring-based architectural model, an application-based information-gathering system from WWW is designed. We develop a couple of middle agents (matchmakers) with ring-based architectural model to match requester agent with information retrieval middleware agents. The matchmaker is of the features of proliferation and self-cancellation according to the sensory input from its environment. Two kinds of matchmakers (host and duplicate) are implemented for promoting the scalability and robustness of the system.

J. Liu et al. (Eds.): IDEAL 2003, LNCS 2690, pp. 94–98, 2003.

The remaining sections of this paper are organized as follows: Section 2 chiefly presents the related work about this research. Section 3 introduces the methodology of ring-based architectural model for middle agents. Section 4 describes the agent-based information-gathering system as a case study. Section 5 concludes the paper.

2 Review of Related Work

How to design architecture is very important issue in agent-based system construction. Lee and Kim researched architecture modeling and evaluation for generic agent-based system. They proposed seven valid architectural models for agent-based system by combining three organization structures (Peer-to-Peer, Grouping with facilitator, and Tree) [1,2,4] and four coordination mechanisms (Direct search, Matchmaker, Broker, and Contact-net) [2,4]. The idea of this research is very important for designing agent-based systems. However, the models are not enough to cover the gamut of work on agent-based system construction, especially, on the scalability and robustness of agent-based system. Tewissen, et al. presented a software toolkit 'matchmaker' allowed for synchronizing already existing software applications by plugging in transparent event listener mechanisms that distribute information via a central server to other remote applications. The token passing approach to organizing multiagent decision aggregation in complex system is proposed [5]. A virtual decision making agent ring was constructed. However, how to dynamically construct the ring is a problem. All above work somewhat promoted our research.

3 Methodology

Ring-based architectural model is powerful for promoting the scalability and robustness of the middle agents in agent-based system. The ring-based architectural model is based on logical ring organizational structure and token-based coordination mechanism. The logical ring organizational structure is showed in Figure 1.

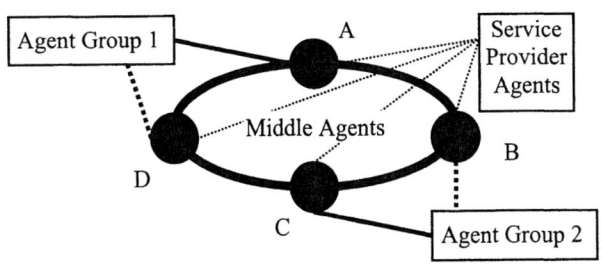

Fig. 1. Ring organizational structure

The middle agent A, B, C, and D serve for requester agents of two applications, that is, Agent Group 1 and Agent Group 2. Each agent group includes a set of requester agents that are of similar feature or close cooperate to achieve a chief goal, which can be regarded as an application-based system. The requester agents in an agent group may be organized as peer-to-peer or tree structure. A requester agent in an agent group cannot directly contact with one in another agent group. However, a requester agent can belong to more than one agent group. All information of service provider agents is stored in every middle agent by coordination mechanism. The service provider agent advertises its information to the coordinator of the ring. The information is transmitted to all middle agents by token-based coordination mechanism. Each middle agent stores meta necessary information about its supervised child agents.

The middle agents are organized as logical ring structure. That is, middle agent A can only contact directly with B and D, but C. If A wants to contact with C, the message must be transmitted by B or D. For simplifying control mechanism, the logical ring is designed to be of the feature of one way in transmitting message. The middle agents are divided into two categories, namely, host and duplicate, according to their roles in the system. The host middle agents, for example A and C, are the superior agents of agent group 1 and agent group 2, respectively, in normal case. If the host middle agent A or C crashed, the ring would be automatically reorganized. At the same time, its duplicate middle agent D or B will act as a host and automatically proliferate a new duplicate. The meta information in host middle agent and its duplicate must be synchronized in time.

The token-based coordination mechanism consists of two algorithms, namely, logical ring establishing algorithm and token control algorithm. For efficiently establishing the logical ring of middle agents, there is a coordinator among them at any time to establish a logical ring (system beginning, token lost or the ring broken down). In general, it does not matter which middle agent takes on this special responsibility, but one of them has to do it. For selecting a middle agent as coordinator, each middle agent is assigned a unique number (0 to 255). In general, election algorithm attempts to locate the middle agent with the highest number and designate it as coordinator. Furthermore, it is assumed that every middle agent knows the number of every other middle agent. What the middle agents do not know is which ones are currently up and which ones are currently down. The goal of election algorithm is to ensure that when an election starts, it concludes with all middle agents agreeing on who the new coordinator is to be. In our research, we employed ring election algorithm [3]. This algorithm is based on the use of a ring, but without a token. It is assumed that the middle agents are logically ordered, so that each middle agent knows whom its successor is. When any middle agent notices that the coordinator is not functioning (the token interval is overtime), it builds an ELECTION message containing its own number and sends the message to its successor. If the successor is down, the sender skips over the successor and goes to the next member along the ring, or the one after that, until a running middle agent is located. At each step, the sender adds its own number to the list in the message. Eventually, the message gets back to the middle agent that started it all. That middle agent recognizes this event when it receives an incoming message containing its own number. At that point, the message type is changed to COORDINATOR and circulated once again, this time to inform everyone else who the coordinator is (the list member with the highest number) and who the members of the new ring are.

When this message has circulated once, it is removed and coordinator starts to manage the ring. The coordinator is in charge of managing the token, receiving service provider agent's advertisement, receiving new application (agent group) request for proliferating a pair of new middle agents (host and its duplicate), receiving an application removing request for canceling the related middle agents (host and its duplicate) and removing them from the ring, maintaining he logical ring (control to proliferate new middle agents or remove old ones), etc.

When the ring is initialized, the coordinator will produce a token. The token circulates around the ring. It is passed from middle agent k to k+1 (modulo the ring size, 256) in point-to-point messages. When a middle agent acquires the token from its neighbor, it has three aspects of tasks to do. Firstly, it checks the token if there is a service provider agent that has just advertised it to the coordinator. If yes, it registers service provider agent information. Secondly, if there is any maintaining message (new application information, canceled application information, applied middle agent numbers, etc.) on the token, the middle agent updates related items or state. Thirdly, if the middle agent is a host, it checks if its duplicate is normal (If not, it proliferates a duplicate and makes it on the ring). If the middle agent is a duplicate, it checks if its host is normal (If not, it acts as the host, proliferates a duplicate and makes it on the ring). When the coordinator holds the token, it will clear the token and reload it again according to the environment.

4   Case Study

The middle agents with ring-based architectural model are applied in the application-based information gathering system from WWW. In this system, we developed a middleware agent with legacy software wrapping view to retrieve relevant documents from a website based on the keywords or expression. The middleware agent is run in the same server with a specific website. From agent point of view, the middleware agent is a wrapper of a specific website, which makes the website exhibit the agent characteristics in agent-based environment. The middle agents play the role of matchmaker in the system. A pair of matchmakers (host and it duplicate) is corresponding with an application that deals with a specialized category information gathering. There are not direct interactions between those applications. The interactions are implied in the retrieved data in data file server.

The system consists of three parts, that is, application-based information-gathering agents, ring-based matchmakers, and middleware agents with their websites. Ring-based matchmakers are placed in the middle between the information-gathering agents of all applications and middleware agents of the websites. We designed two independent information-gathering systems (one for petroleum information gathering and another for financial investment information gathering). Each information-gathering system consists of Query Preprocessing Agent (QPA$_i$), Information Filtering Agent (IFA$_i$), and File Operating Agent (FOA). Where i equals 1 or 2, which indicates Application1 and Application2. Because both applications operate the same file server, they share the only FOA to operate documents (query statements, category-based training documents, and retrieved documents from websites) in file server. The part of middleware agents includes websites and middleware agents which of each middleware agent only directly operates a specific website.

We are interesting in locating some information about 'what information is available on petroleum exploration in the South Atlantic' that is stored on 4 websites, which contain more than 500 documents on various aspects of petroleum as an experiment. Certainly, the system has been trained by categorized petroleum information before the query. The result is that 307 documents are retrieved and 29 articles are got after filtering, but one out of 29 articles was non-relevant. The precision and recall rate of the filtering algorithm are about 97% and 9%, respectively. However, the results very depend on the training documents and the articles on the websites.

Along with more and more information gathering applications are created, there will be more and more middle agents on the ring. In consequence token will need more time in a cycle. However, this does not affect matching performance because each information gathering application has its own matchmaker. The performance of ring-based middle agents will change with creating or canceling an information gathering application.

5 Conclusions

To promote the scalability and robustness of middle agents in agent-based systems, we introduced a ring-based architectural model. This model enriches the architecture of middle agents that are the distillation of most agent-based systems. In considering a sampling of existing agent-oriented architectures, we point to the need for a scalable and robust architecture capable of dealing with the many facets of agent-based systems. Accordingly, we specified a generic ring-based architecture that is intended to satisfy the practical applications.

The result of this research shows that the ring-based architectural model can be used to organize middle agents for matching task agent and middleware agent; furthermore, the ring-based architectural model can be used as a basis for the agent-based systems that need to use middle agents. The performance of the system will abate to the lowest point while the coordinator is elected and the ring is initialized.

References

1. Lander, S.E., Issues in multiagent design systems, IEEE Expert, 12(2), 1997, 18–26.
2. Lejter, M. and Dean, T., A framework for the development of multiagent architectures, IEEE Expert, 11(6), 1996, 47–59.
3. Tanenbaum, S. Distributed operating systems, Prentice-Hall, Inc. New Jersey, USA, 1995.
4. Wooldridge, M. An introduction to multiagent systems, John Wilery & Sons, Ltd. England, 2002.
5. Zhang, Z. An Agent-based hybrid framework for decision making on complex problems, Ph. D. Thesis, Deakin University, Australia, 2001.

Belief Revision for Adaptive Recommender Agents in E-commerce

Raymond Y.K. Lau

Centre for Information Technology Innovation
Queensland University of Technology
GPO Box 2434, Brisbane, Qld 4001, Australia
r.lau@qut.edu.au

Abstract. Recommender systems are a well-known technology for E-commerce. This paper illustrates a novel recommender agent model which combines the inductive power brought by text mining methods with the non-monotonic reasoning capability offered by a belief revision system to improve the agents' prediction effectiveness, learning autonomy, and explanatory capabilities.

1 Introduction

Figure 1 depicts the system architecture of the belief revision based adaptive recommender agent system. The *inference module* of an adaptive recommender agent compares the logical representation d of each incoming product description (i.e., a document) with the representation K of a recommendation context (e.g., a user's product preferences). If there is a sufficiently close match between d and K, the product details together with the agent ID are transferred to the output database. At each learning cycle (e.g. after n product descriptions are viewed by a consumer), the *learning module* of a recommender agent is activated to analyse the consumer's explicit or implicit feedback stored in the output database. The resulting statistical data is used to induce the agent's beliefs about a consumer's product preferences. These beliefs are then revised into the corresponding agent's knowledge base via the belief revision mechanism. Moreover, an off-line process is invoked regularly to mine the term association rules [1] representing a recommendation context. In particular, a symbolic framework offers sufficient expressive power to capture a *recommendation context* (e.g., the associations between products, correlation between consumers, background of specific consumers, etc.). As less direct feedback is required to train the recommender agents, the *learning autonomy* of these agents is enhanced. A symbolic framework can improve recommender agents' explanatory power as the agents can explain their decisions based on appropriate recommendation contexts (e.g., the association rules).

2 The Rapid Maxi-Adjustment Method

For a computer-based implementation of the AGM belief revision framework [2], the *finite partial entrenchment ranking* **B** which ranks a finite subset of beliefs with the minimum possible degree of entrenchment ($\leqslant_{\mathbf{B}}$) was developed by

J. Liu et al. (Eds.): IDEAL 2003, LNCS 2690, pp. 99–103, 2003.

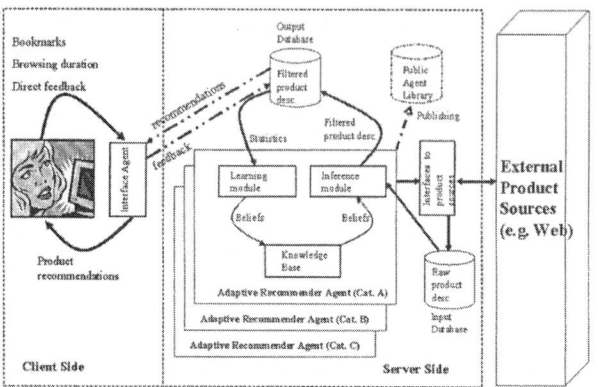

Fig. 1. Belief-Based Adaptive Recommender Agents

Williams [5,6]. In addition, several transmutation methods were developed to implement iterated belief revision based on finite partial entrenchment rankings. One of them is the Maxi-adjustment transmutation method [6]. A finite partial entrenchment ranking is a function **B** that maps a finite subset of sentences in a classical language $\mathcal{L}$ into the interval $[0, 1]$ such that the following conditions are satisfied for all $\alpha \in dom(\mathbf{B})$: (PER1) $\{\beta \in dom(\mathbf{B}) : \mathbf{B}(\alpha) < \mathbf{B}(\beta)\} \nvdash \alpha$; (PER2) If $\vdash \neg\alpha$ then $\mathbf{B}(\alpha) = 0$; (PER3) $\mathbf{B}(\alpha) = 1$ if and only if $\vdash \alpha$.

Definition 1. *Let $\alpha \in \mathcal{L}$ be a contingent sentence. Let* **B** *be a finite partial entrenchment ranking and $\beta \in exp(\mathbf{B})$. The degree of acceptance of an implicit belief α is defined by:*

$$degree(\mathbf{B}, \alpha) = \begin{cases} sup\{\mathbf{B}(\beta) \in ran(\mathbf{B}) : cut_{\leqslant}(\beta) \vdash \alpha\} \\ \qquad if \ \alpha \in content(\mathbf{B}) \\ 0 \qquad\qquad otherwise \end{cases}$$

The *sup* operator returns the maximal degree of acceptance from a set of ordinals in the *range* of **B**. The $cut_{\leqslant}(\beta)$ operation extracts a set of explicit beliefs which is at least as entrenched as β from an epistemic entrenchment ordering $\leqslant$ generated based on a finite partial entrenchment ranking **B**. $\vdash$ is the classical inference relation. In the proposed recommender agent model, a recommendation context (i.e., a consumer's product preferences and the background information about the consumers and the products) is represented by a set of beliefs. When a user's needs change, the entrenchment degrees of the corresponding beliefs are raised or lowered in the agent's knowledge base. Raising or lowering the entrenchment degree of a belief is conducted via a Rapid Maxi-adjustment (RAM) operation $\mathbf{B}^{\star}(\alpha, i)$ where α is a belief and i is the new entrenchment degree. One of the contributions of this paper is the development of an efficient transmutation method called Rapid Maxi-Adjustment (RAM) to implement the AGM belief functions.

Definition 2. *Let α be a contingent sentence, $j = degree(\mathbf{B}, \alpha)$ and $0 \leqslant i < 1$. The (α, i) Rapid Maxi-adjustment of* **B** *is $\mathbf{B}^{\star}(\alpha, i)$ defined by:*

$$\mathbf{B}^{\star}(\alpha, i) = \begin{cases} \mathbf{B}^{-}(\alpha, i) & \text{if } i < j \\ (\mathbf{B}^{-}(\neg\alpha, 0))^{+}(\alpha, i) & \text{if } i > j \\ \mathbf{B}^{+}(\alpha, i) & \text{if } i = j > 0 \text{ and} \\ & \alpha \notin exp(\mathbf{B}) \\ \mathbf{B} & \text{otherwise} \end{cases}$$

where for all $\beta \in dom(\mathbf{B})$, $\mathbf{B}^{-}(\alpha, i)$ is defined as follows:

1. For β with $\mathbf{B}(\beta) > j$, $\mathbf{B}^{-}(\alpha, i)(\beta) = \mathbf{B}(\beta)$.
2. For β with $i < \mathbf{B}(\beta) \leqslant j$,

$$\mathbf{B}^{-}(\alpha, i)(\beta) = \begin{cases} i & \text{if } \{\gamma : \mathbf{B}^{-}(\alpha, i)(\gamma) > \mathbf{B}(\beta)\} \cup \\ & \{\delta : \mathbf{B}^{-}(\alpha, i)(\delta) = \mathbf{B}(\beta) \wedge \\ & Seq(\delta) \leq Seq(\beta)\} \vdash \alpha \\ \mathbf{B}(\beta) & \text{otherwise} \end{cases}$$

3. For β with $\mathbf{B}(\beta) \leqslant i$, $\mathbf{B}^{-}(\alpha, i)(\beta) = \mathbf{B}(\beta)$.

For all $\beta \in dom(\mathbf{B}) \cup \{\alpha\}$, $\mathbf{B}^{+}(\alpha, i)$ is defined as follows:

1. For β with $\mathbf{B}(\beta) \geqslant i$ $\mathbf{B}^{+}(\alpha, i)(\beta) = \mathbf{B}(\beta)$.
2. For β with $j \leqslant \mathbf{B}(\beta) < i$,

$$\mathbf{B}^{+}(\alpha, i)(\beta) = \begin{cases} i & \text{if } i < degree(\mathbf{B}, \alpha \rightarrow \beta) \\ degree(\mathbf{B}, \alpha \rightarrow \beta) & \text{otherwise} \end{cases}$$

3. For β with $\mathbf{B}(\beta) < j$ $\mathbf{B}^{+}(\alpha, i)(\beta) = \mathbf{B}(\beta)$.

The intuition of the RAM method is that if the new entrenchment degree i of a sentence α is less than its existing degree j, a contraction operation (i.e., lowering its entrenchment degree) is invoked. If the new degree of α is higher than its existing degree, a revision operation will be initiated. Hence, $\neg\alpha$ must first be assigned the lowest entrenchment degree (i.e., contracting it from the theory). Then, the degree of α is raised to the new degree i. During raising or lowering the entrenchment degree of α, the degrees of other sentences are adjusted in a *minimal* way such that PER1, PER2, and PER3 are always maintained. If a finite partial entrenchment ranking $\mathbf{B}$ has x natural partitions, it only requires $\log_2 x$ classical satisfiability checks [3]. Therefore, given the propositional Horn logic $\mathcal{L}_{Horn}$ as the representation language, the RAM method only involves polynomial time complexity, and so it can scale up for real-life applications.

3 Mining Contextual Knowledge

The *unsupervised* text mining method employed in the recommender agent system is based on the Apriori algorithm which was originally developed to mine transactional databases [1]. A database (i.e., a document collection for text mining) contains a set of transactions (i.e., documents) with each transaction t containing a subset of *items* (i.e., tokens) from a finite set of items

$\mathcal{I} = \{k_1, k_2, \ldots, k_n\}$. The Apriori algorithm successively finds *large item sets* L_k which satisfy the minimal *support*. Then, association rules are constructed based on each element $Z \in L_k$ which satisfies the minimal *confidence*. An association rule is an implication of the form $X \to Y$, where $X \subset Z$, $Y \subset Z$, and $X \cap Y = \emptyset$. Rule support is the priori probability $Pr(Z) = \frac{\text{No. trans. containing } z}{\text{Total no. of trans.}}$, and rule confidence is the conditional probability $Pr(Z|X) = \frac{\text{No. trans. containing } z}{\text{No. of trans. containing } x}$. Since our prototype agent system employs propositional Horn logic $\mathcal{L}_{Horn}$ as its representation language, the consequent Y must be a single item. To convert the term association rules to beliefs in an agent's knowledge base, an entrenchment degree is derived by multiplying the rule support s and rule confidence c by an adjustment factor ϵ.

4   Learning and Recommendation

Table 1 depicts the results before/after the agent learns a belief via a Rapid Maxi-adjustment operation $\mathbf{B}^\star(\text{camry}, 0.427)$. A RAM operation ensures that the representation of the recommendation context (i.e., the agent's knowledge base depicted in table 1) is revised in a *minimal* and *consistent* way. Through such a learning process, the agent can automatically deduce that the consumer may also be interested in "car", "automobile", but not interested in "boat". Therefore, the *learning autonomy* of the agent is enhanced. The upper section of Table 1 lists all explicit beliefs. Moreover, some implicit beliefs relevant for our discussion are listed in the lower section of table 1. The entrenchment degrees of the implicit beliefs are computed according to Definition 1. A belief with zero entrenchment degree means that it is not in the agent's knowledge base K. *Similarity measures* are often used to develop document rankings in IR [4]. An *entrenchment-based* similarity measure $Sim(\mathbf{B}, d)$ Eq.(1) is developed to approximate the *semantic correspondence* $Sim(Ctx, Prod)$ between a recommendation context Ctx and an item $Prod$.

$$Sim(\mathbf{B}, d) = \sum_{\alpha \in d} degree(\mathbf{B}, \alpha) - \sum_{\alpha \in d} degree(\mathbf{B}, \neg\alpha) \tag{1}$$

If the following three product descriptions: $d_1 = \{camry, car, automobile\}$, $d_2 = \{camry, car, helicopter\}$, and $d_3 = \{helicopter, automobile, boat\}$ are inspected by the agent, the resulting item ranking will be: $Prod_1 \preceq Prod_2 \preceq Prod_3$, where $Prod_i \preceq Prod_j$ means that item $Prod_i$ is at least as preferred as item $Prod_j$ with respect to a consumer's preferences. If a threshold t is used, binary recommendation can also be made.

$Sim(\mathbf{B}, d_1) = (0.427 + 0.427 + 0.427) - 0.000 = 1.281$
$Sim(\mathbf{B}, d_2) = (0.427 + 0.427) - 0.000 = 0.854$
$Sim(\mathbf{B}, d_3) = 0.427 - 0.214 = 0.213$

Table 1. Learning and Adaptation in Recommender Agent

Belief:α	$\mathbf{B}(\alpha)$ Before	$\mathbf{B}(\alpha)$ After
$car \leftrightarrow automobile$	0.713	0.713
$camry \rightarrow car$	0.427	0.427
$automobile \rightarrow camry$	0.427	0.427
$automobile \rightarrow \neg boat$	0.214	0.214
$camry$	**0.000**	**0.427**
car	**0.000**	**0.427**
$automobile$	**0.000**	**0.427**
$\neg boat$	**0.000**	**0.214**

5   Conclusions and Future Work

The Rapid Maxi-Adjustment method provides an efficient way of implementing the learning functions in adaptive recommender agents. The induction power brought by text mining is complementary to the nonmonotonic reasoning capability of a belief revision system. More effective text mining methods will be examined to improve recommender agents' prediction effectiveness in future research.

References

1. R. Agrawal and R. Srikant. Fast algorithms for mining association rules in large databases. In Jorge B. Bocca, Matthias Jarke, and Carlo Zaniolo, editors, *VLDB'94, Proceedings of 20th International Conference on Very Large Data Bases*, pages 487–499, Santiago de Chile, Chile, September 12–15 1994. Morgan Kaufmann Publishers.
2. C.E. Alchourrón, P. Gärdenfors, and D. Makinson. On the logic of theory change: partial meet contraction and revision functions. *Journal of Symbolic Logic*, 50:510–530, 1985.
3. J. Lang. Possibilistic Logic: Algorithms and Complexity. In J. Kohlas and S. Moral, editors, *Handbook of Algorithms for Uncertainty and Defeasible Reasoning*. Kluwer Academic Publishers, Norwell, Massachusetts, 1997.
4. G. Salton and M.J. McGill. *Introduction to Modern Information Retrieval*. McGraw-Hill, New York, New York, 1983.
5. M.-A. Williams. Iterated theory base change: A computational model. In Chris S. Mellish, editor, *Proceedings of the Fourteenth International Joint Conference on Artificial Intelligence*, pages 1541–1547, Montréal, Canada, August 20–25, 1995. Morgan Kaufmann Publishers.
6. M.-A. Williams. Anytime belief revision. In Martha E. Pollack, editor, *Proceedings of the Fifteenth International Joint Conference on Artificial Intelligence*, pages 74–79, Nagoya, Japan, August 23–29, 1997. Morgan Kaufmann Publishers.

Managing Fault Tolerance Information
in Multi-agents Based Distributed Systems[1]

Dae Won Lee[1], Kwang Sik Chung[2], Hwa Min Lee[1],
Sungbin Park[1], Young Jun Lee[3], Heon Chang Yu[1], and Won Gyu Lee[1]

[1] Department of Computer Science Education, Korea University
1, 5-Ka, Anam-dong, Sungbuk-ku, Seoul
{daelee, zelkova, yjlee, yuhc, lee}@comedu.korea.ac.kr
http://comedu.korea.ac.kr
[2] Department of Computer Science, University College
London Gower Street, London, WCIE 6BT
k.chung@cs.ucl.ac.uk
[3] Department of Computer Education, Korea National University of Education
yjlee@knue.ac.kr

Abstract. In a fault tolerant system using rollback-recovery protocols, the performance of the system is degraded because of the increment of saved fault tolerance information. To avoid degrading its performance, we propose novel multi-agents based garbage-collection technique that deletes useless fault tolerance information. We define and design a garbage-collection agent for garbage-collection of fault tolerance information, a information agent for management of fault tolerant information, and a facilitator agent for communication between agents. And we propose the garbage-collection algorithm(GCA) using these agents. Our rollback recovery method is based on independent checkpointing protocol and sender based pessimistic message logging protocol. To prove the correctness of the garbage-collection algorithm, we introduce failure injection during operation and compare the domain knowledge of the proposed system using GCA with the domain knowledge of another system without GCA.

1 Introduction

The development of distributed computing systems enables a task to be executed on several processors that are connected by network. Since distributed computing systems are sensitive to failures, many rollback-recovery techniques have been developed. The rollback-recovery techniques are classified into checkpoint-based protocols and log-based protocols. For rollback-recovery, fault tolerance information such as checkpoints and message logs, is saved in a stable storage. When a process failure occurs, fault tolerance information is used to recover the states of the system. The management of fault tolerance information is a very important issue. Because the increment of

---

[1] This work was supported by grant No. R01-2001-000-00354-0 from the Korea Science & Engineering Foundation.

saved fault tolerance information makes storage overflow, the performance of the system is degraded. To avoid performance degradation, distributed computing systems need garbage-collection protocols[1]. The garbage-collection protocol finds useless fault tolerance information and decides garbage-collection point, when garbage-collection condition is satisfied. Checkpoint-based protocols that solely rely on check-pointing for restoring the states of system[1]. The target of garbage collection is checkpoint and all checkpoints taken before a consistent global checkpoint are deleted. In log-based protocols, useless message log is identified as garbage information. Because the selection is based on log order, the exchange of additional message is required for garbage collection of message content logs.

In previous works, there was an approach for garbage-collection without sending additional messages[2]. In this paper we propose multi-agents based garbage-collection protocol in multi-agent system. Proposed multi-agent system consists of garbage-collection, information, and facilitator agent. It's based on independent checkpointing protocol and sender based pessimistic message logging protocol.

This paper is organized as follows: In section 2 we present a system model and garbage-collection method. In section 3 we show the garbage-collection algorithm using agents. The implementation and simulation result of the multi-agent system using Java and CORBA is shown in section 4. Finally this paper concludes in section 5.

2 Multi-agent Based Garbage-Collection System

2.1 System Model

Many researches have been interested in an agent that is a component of communication software. The agent consists of a task engine, domain knowledge, and a communication module.

Our proposed system model is based on the distributed multi-agent system environment that consists of a process that runs a application program, a garbage-collection agent for garbage collection, an information agent that manages fault tolerance information, a facilitator agent that manages communication between agents, and a communication channel. Our system model has been developed under following assumptions: a network partition doesn't occur, processes communicate via messages sent through reliable first-in-first-out(FIFO) channels, according to the fail-stop model, and following Lamport's happened before relation[8].

In this paper, for communication between agents, we use KQML and for inner language, we use KIF. In this paper, for communication among garbage-collection agents, information agents, and facilitator agents, we define ontology for garbage-collection protocol, and KIF for domain knowledge and define KQML.

2.2 Garbage-Collection for Fault Tolerance Information

In existing garbage-collection techniques of fault tolerance information, useless-rollbacks may be occurred due to the lost messages during recovery. As the previous algorithms such as [2] use a checkpoint interval, a lost message doesn't occur. In this paper, to avoid rollback propagation, we send a message with last checkpoint number and thus find a garbage-collection point. The message MSG is defined in [Definition 1].

[Definition 1] a message MSG that a process p_k sends :
$$\text{MSG } p_k \stackrel{def}{=} \{content_m, m.ssn, p_{id}, last\_chpt\_num\}$$

When a process p_i sends a message m to p_j through a reliable channel, garbage-collection of fault tolerance information is performed if [Condition 1] is satisfied.

[Condition 1] Conditions for garbage-collection

i) $\exists$ chpt$^{p-1}_i$, chpt$^{p-1}_i \rightarrow$ received$_i$(m) and,

ii) $\exists$ chpt^p_i, received$_i$(m) $\rightarrow$ chpt^p_i

3 GCA : Garbage-Collection Algorithm

Our proposed garbage-collection algorithm consists of two parts; (1) agent's registration phase, the agents are created with a process. An information agent(IA) and a garbage-collection agent(GA), then, are registered to a facilitator agent(FA). (2) garbage-collection phase, when a process receives a system message_call, the GA finds useless fault tolerance information that [condition 1] is satisfied and decides them as a garbage. And the GA runs garbage-collection protocol.

```
Function GAServer() {
   GA_i is created with process p_i;
   GA_i sends register message to FA_i;
   GA_i receives ack message from FA_i;}
Function GAImpl() {
   if GA_i receives system message_call from FA_i then {
      GA_i requests eventlist to IA_i;
      GA_i waits eventlist from IA_i;}
   if GA_i receives eventlist from IA_i then {
      for(eventlist_i(chpt_x, log, c^e_{jx}) relating to p_j in p_i) {
         if (c^m_{jy} > c^e_{jx}) and (m.ssn^m > m.ssn^e) then {
            declare the eventlist as a garbage; }}
   GA_i requests garbage collection to IA_i;}}
```

Fig. 1. A garbage-collection agent's operation

Data structures used in GCA are as follows:
- register message: sending message from GA/IA to FA for registration
- system message_call: call for receiving a new message
- last_chpt: the last checkpoint that process takes during execution
- eventlist$_i$ (chpt$_k$, log, c$^e_{jk}$): the happened event list after process takes the last checkpoint. It consists of checkpoint, log and receiving chpt_num

As shown in the above, the GA selects fault tolerance information and sets garbage collection point. Two more agents are involved in a garbage collection process.

One is an IA that manages fault tolerance information on a process. The IA translates fault tolerance information that includes a checkpoint, a message log, last_chpt_num from a received message, and m.ssn to KIF and they are saved in the domain knowledge base. To decide the target of garbage-collection, the GA requests the IA to send eventlist. And by request from the GA, the IA deletes useless fault tolerance information. The other is a FA that manages communication between agents, and monitors events on a process. If the FA detects new event on a process, it sends information about event to the IA and sends system message_call to the GA. For garbage-collection, it helps communication between a GA and an IA.

4   Garbage-Collection Agent System Experiment and Result

In this paper, we use CORBA(VisiBroker for Java 4.5.1) for communication between agents, and implement components in Java(JDK 1.3.1). Our proposed multi-agent system, which consists of three nodes, is based on distributed computing environment. For each node, we use P-III 933 and MS windows 2000. Only one process is executed at each node, and each process has a GA, an IA, and a FA.

Assumptions for implementation are 1) communication between processes is based on message passing 2) agents communicate through a facilitator agent 3) every process starts at the same time 4) agent's failure doesn't occur.

To prove the correctness, we implement two kinds of prototype systems that execute same operations; one with GCA and the other without GCA. Then, we involve failure injection during normal operation. After rollback recovery, we check whether their domain knowledge is same. The rollback recovery technique in the experiment is based on the existing research[3]. In Fig. 2, there is sample system where horizontal lines represent the execution of each process, and arrows between processes represent messages.

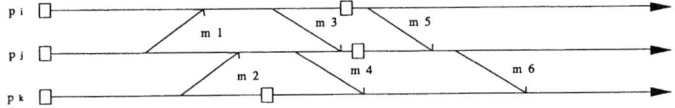

Fig. 2. An example of a message-passing system with three processes

And we implement a garbage-collection technique using agents, analyze results, and show the novel property of this implementation. By simulation result, every event on process is saved on domain knowledge in sequence. And we compare two kinds of prototype systems: one without garbage-collection and the other with garbage-collection. Comparing their domain knowledge, we can see that useless fault tolerance information is deleted.

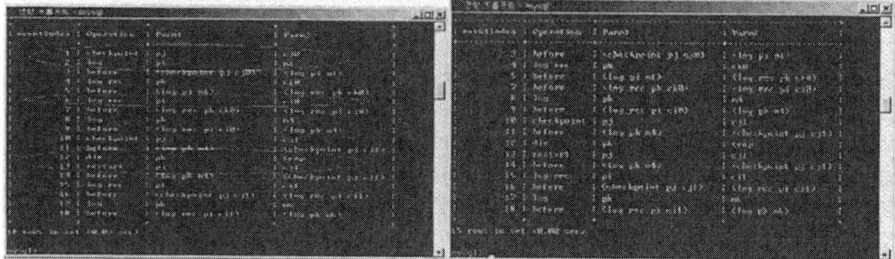

Fig. 3. Process p_j's domain knowledge without GCA and with GCA

For proof of correctness, we involve failure injection during operation and compare the system using GCA with the other system without GCA. Fig. 3 shows domain knowledge of a process p_j without GCA and with GCA. We can see that useless fault tolerance information is deleted and they show same order after rollback-recovery.

As shown in the implementation result, information agents have correctly constructed the domain knowledge by using the process' event information through facilitator agent. This paper shows that a garbage-collection agent correctly performs garbage-collection procedure through cooperating with an information agent, and our proposed system guarantees correct execution.

5   Conclusion

In this paper, we proposed new garbage-collection technique based on multi-agent system that is independent of OS. The garbage-collection agent created with a process, deletes useless fault tolerance information through cooperation with an information agent that manages fault tolerance information using sending/receiving messages. And we implemented garbage-collection technique that interacts among agents. Our proposed garbage-collection technique using agents is independent of operating system. Also, We complemented previous fault tolerance protocol using agent in previous work[3]. [3] isn't concerned about garbage collection, there might be storage overflow as failure.

References

1. M. V. Sreenivas, Subhash Bhalla, "Garbage Collection in Message Passing Distributed Systems," *Proceeding of International Symposium on Parallel Algorithms/Architecture Synthesis, IEEE Computer Society Press,* (March 1995) 213–218
2. Kwang Sik Chung, Heon-Chang Yu, Maeng-Soon Baik, Jin Gon Shon, Jong-Sun Hwang, "A Garbage Collection of Message logs without Additional Message on Causal Message Logging Protocol", *Journal of KISS : Computer System and Theory ,* Vol. 28, Num 7–8, (Aug. 2001)
3. Hwa-Min Lee, Kwang-Sik Chung, Sang-Chul Shin, Dae-Won Lee, Won-Gyu Lee, and Heon-Chang Yu, "A Recovery Technique Using Multi-agent in Distributed Computing Systems", Lecture Notes in Computer Science 2315, (2002) 236–249

Agent-Based Layered Intelligent Information Integration System Using Ontology and Metadata Registry

Jeong-Oog Lee[1] and Yo-Han Choi[2]

[1] Dept. of Computer Science, Konkuk University,
322 Danwol-dong, Chungju-si, Chungcheongbuk-do, 380-701, Korea
ljo@kku.ac.kr
[2] Dept. of Computer Science & Engineering, Korea University,
1, 5-ka, Anam-dong, Sungbuk-gu, Seoul, 136-701, Korea
dino9612@software.korea.ac.kr

Abstract. To share and exchange information, especially in the multi-database environments, each component database must know the meanings and the representations of the information of other sources. And users who are searching integrated information on the Web have limitation to obtain schema information for the underlying component databases. To solve these problems, in this paper, we present an Agent-based Layered Intelligent Information Integration System (ALI3S) using metadata registry(MDR) and ontology.[1] The purpose of the proposed architecture is to define an information integration model, which combines characteristics of both standard specification of MDRs and functionality of ontology for the concepts and relations. Adopting agent technology to the proposed model plays a key role to support the hierarchical and independent information integration architecture.

1 Introduction

In conventional database systems, information was created, stored, and used independently to meet specific requirements. As the amount of information grew rapidly, it became harder to manage it efficiently in one database system. Also, in large knowledge base such as Web, many questions often can be answered using integrated information than using single source. Therefore the need for integrating disjoint databases became increasingly. However, making it possible for two or more databases to interoperate effectively has many unresolved problems. The most basic and fundamental problem is heterogeneity. It can be categorized into platform heterogeneity and semantic heterogeneity[1][2].

While there is a significant amount of researches discussing platform heterogeneity, work on semantic heterogeneity is insufficient. Early researches on semantic heterogeneity focused on procedures to merge individual component

---

[1] This work was supported by the Faculty Research Fund of Konkuk University in 2002.

J. Liu et al. (Eds.): IDEAL 2003, LNCS 2690, pp. 109–113, 2003.

databases schemas into a single global schema[3][4]. The disadvantage of this approach is that a user must re-engineer the global schema whenever any of the sources change or when new sources are added. Multidatabase language approach eliminates problems of creating and maintaining the global schema, but presents a more complex global interface to the user[5]. In several researches[6][7][8], an information mediator has been developed for integrating of information in dynamic and open environments. A common assumption of these approaches is that users know pre-existing domain knowledge for integrating information, which might be a burden to the users.

In this paper, using metadata registries, ontology, and agent technology, we suggest an Agent-based Layered Intelligent Information Integration System(ALI3S), which frees users from the tremendous tasks of acquiring domain knowledge and schema information of each database and allows new databases to join in the system easily.

A metadata registry(MDR) is a place to keep facts about characteristics of data that are necessary for data sharing and exchange in a specific domain[9]. However, when there are multiple MDRs, there exists the problem of semantic heterogeneity among MDRs as in the case of multiple databases. An ontology defines concepts and relations among concepts[10][11][12][13]. Through conceptualization of data elements in MDRs and management of relations, ontology can be used to resolve schema heterogeneity among concepts of data elements. Data heterogeneity which is due to the differences of representation such as format, size, unit, and etc. among data elements can be resolved by constructing knowledge base. In order to provide semantic mappings between data elements using ontology and knowledge base, the system needs autonomous and intelligent agents. For flexible extensibility, the system has been constructed in terms of layered architecture, which enables each agent to act independently when new databases are added to the system.

The rest of this paper is organized as follows. In section 2, we suggest agent-based layered intelligent information integration system using metadata registries and ontology. Also we explain agent architecture for the system. Section 3 offers our conclusions.

2   ALI3S Architecture

2.1   Overview of System

We have constructed an Agent-based Layered Intelligent Information Integration System(ALI3S) using ontology and metadata registries. Basis of information integration has been established by constructing semantic network using ontology and by using information sharability and standardization of metadata registries. The main components of the system are ontology, value mapper, metadata mapper, and so forth, as in figure 1. The development of the system is on the hierarchical structure, which can manage independability of the system components so that it provides flexibility of change to the system. For independability of the system components, agents with intelligent are needed[14].

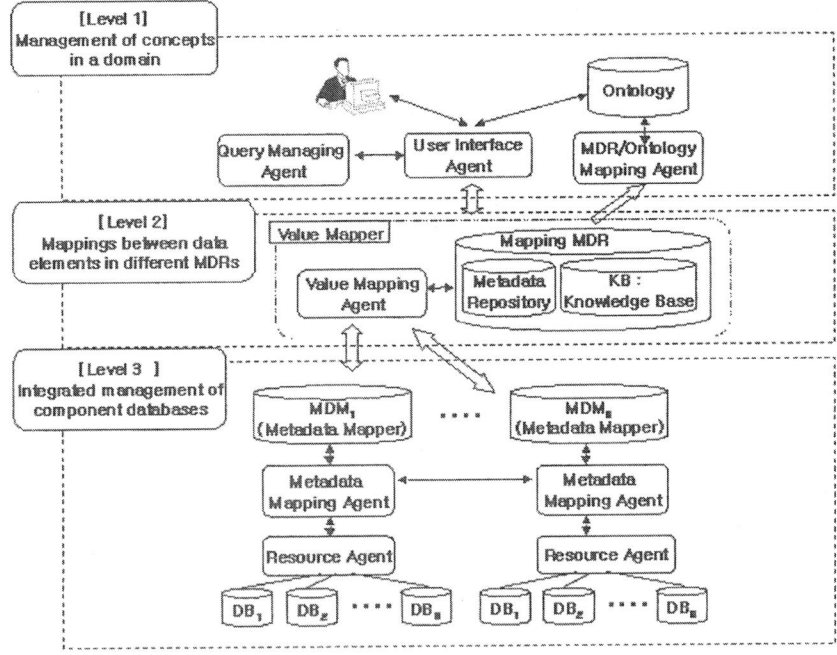

Fig. 1. An architecture of ALI3S

The descriptions of main system components and agents in each level are as follows.

2.2   Level 1 – Management of Concepts in a Domain

Level 1 manages concepts of a domain of interest and processes user's queries.

- User Interface Agent(UIA)
  UIA parses user's query, extracts concepts in the query using concepts and relations in ontology, requests query processing, and displays the processed results to the user.
- Query Managing Agent(QMA)
  QMA manages creation, tracing, termination of tasks which are originated by multiple queries, using threads.
- MDR/Ontology Mapping Agent(MOMA)
  MOMA is an agent which conducts new mappings between ontology and MDR, when new data element concepts must be added to the MDR because of new databases being added to the system.

2.3   Level 2 – Mappings between Data Elements in Different MDRs

Level 2 undertakes mappings between data elements in different MDRs using concepts and relations in ontology. Value Mapper consists of Metadata Repository, Knowledge Base, and Value Mapping Agent.

- Metadata Repository(MR)
  MR manages mappings between data elements which are identified seman-tically related or equivalent according to the concepts and relations in on-tology.
- Knowledge Base(KB)
  KB defines the rules of transformation and stores the transformed data for re-solving data heterogeneity originated from representations of data elements.
- Value Mapping Agent(VMA)
  VMA has two roles. One is that VMA stores mapping information between data elements into Metadata Repository. And the second is that VMA cre-ates sub-queries for each MDR which are processed by Metadata Mapper in Level 3. In the process of creating sub-queries, VMA resolves value hetero-geneity between data elements identified as equivalent concept using Meta-data Repository and Knowledge Base.

2.4   Level 3 – Integrated Management of Component Databases

Level 3 undertakes responsibility for integrated management of component databases.

- Metadata Mapping Agent(MDMA)
  MDMA is located in between MDM and RA. It creates mappings between metadata and schema information of each component database, and provides VMA with changed information, if any.
- Resource Agent(RA)
  RA is an agent which resides in each component database. It re-formulates the sub-query received from VMA according to the schema information of the database in which it resides, executes the sub-query, and sends the results to MDM.
- Metadata Mapper(MDM)
  There are standardized data elements in each MDR. Schema information of each component database mapped to these data elements needs to be iden-tified. MDM stores and manages mappings between data elements in MDR and schema information provided from RA in each component database.

3   Conclusions

This paper has suggested an agent-based layered intelligent information integra-tion system which merges the characteristics of the MDR-based information inte-gration systems and the ontology-based information integration systems. When a user who does not have domain knowledge issues a query in a semantic query language using his/her own concepts, ontology provides semantic network for analyzing concepts in the query and mapping these concepts to the data ele-ments in a metadata registry. A metadata registry plays an important role in resolving semantic heterogeneity and integrating component databases through management of standard data elements. The level-independent characteristic of ALI3S has been needed for dynamic extensibility of the system, which is the reason for adopting intelligent agents. One of the advantages of ALI3S is that it enables users not knowing schema information of all the component databases to integrate desired information. Also, ALI3S provides flexibility in adding new databases using agent systems.

More efforts must be devoted to the researches on mapping types and mapping rules among values for Value Mapper, so that more reliable knowledge base can be constructed. Also, in further research, we will develop an automatic reconstructable ontology, which enables users to add new concepts to the ontology with ease.

References

1. Won Kim and Jungyun Seo, "Classifying Schematic and Data Heterogeneity in Multidatabase Systems", IEEE Computer, 1991.
2. Jeong-Oog Lee, Doo-Kwon Baik, "SemQL: A Semantic Query Language for Multidatabase Systems", In Proceedings of the 8th International Conference on Information and Knowledge Management, 1999.
3. R. Ahmed, P. De Smedt, W. Du, W. Kent, M. A. Ketabchi, W. A. Litwin, A. Rafli, and M. C. Shan, "The Pegasus heterogenous multidatabase system", IEEE Computer, 1991.
4. C. Collet, M. Huhns, W. Shen "Resource Integration Using a Large Knowledge Base in Carnot", IEEE Computer, 1991.
5. V. Dayal, H. Hwang, "View Definition ad Generalization for Database Integration in a Multidatabase System", IEEE Transaction on Software Engineering, 1984.
6. C. A. Knoblock et al., "Modeling Web Sources for Information Integration", In Proceedings of 11th Nat'l Conference on Artificial Intelligence, 1998.
7. S. Adali, K. S. Candan, Y. Papakonstantinou, and V. S. Subrahmanian, "Query caching and optimization in distributed mediator systems", In Proceedings of the ACM SIGMOD International Conference on Management of Data, 1996.
8. Marian Nodine, Jerry Fowler, Brad Perry, "An Overview of Active Information Gathering in InfoSleuth", InfoSlueth Group, 1998.
9. ISO/IEC, "ISO/IEC FDIS 11179 : Information technology- Specification and standardization of data elements", 1999.
10. Mike Uschold and Michael Gruninger,"Ontologies: Principles, Methods and Applications", Knowledge Engineering Review, 1996.
11. Thomas R.Gruber, "Toward Principles for the Design of Ontologies Used for Knowledge Sharing", International Journal of Human-Computer Studies, 1995.
12. Maurizio Panti, Luca Spalazzi, Alberto Giretti, "A Case-Based Approach to Information Integration" , Proceedings of the 26th VLDB conference, 2000.
13. J. Hammer, H. H. Garcia-Molina, K. Ireland, Y. Papakonstantinou, J. Ullman, J. Widom, "Information translation, mediation, and mosaic-based browsing in the tsimmis system", In Proceedings of the ACM SIGMOD International Conference on Management of Data, 1995.
14. Joseph P. Bigus, Jennifer Bigus, 'Constructing Intelligent agents with Java', Wiley Computer Publishing, 1998.

Fluctuation in Multi-agent System of Supermarket Chain Network

Kwok Yip Szeto and Chiwah Kong

Department of Physics, Hong Kong University of Science and Technology
Clear Water Bay, Hong Kong SAR, China
phszeto@ust.hk,

Abstract. Resource allocation on a supermarket chain network in shopping malls is modeled by a Multi-Agent System describing competition and cooperation between branches of companies. Shops are occupied by one of two companies, B (black) or W (white) and they compete with each other for domination. Fluctuation in the market share is measured as a function of noise, which is a result of advertisement and discount between competing agents. Existence of a critical value of noise level where competition drives large fluctuation in the market share is demonstrated by results in Monte Carlo simulation.

1 Introduction

Competition of chain stores in a city is an interesting problem in which the tools of statistical analysis within Multi-agent systems can be employed. A simple model describing the competition of companies for market share is based on the competition for occupancy of the shopping mall. In recent papers, soap froth model [1-3] has been used as a basis of discussion for the competition and collaborations among companies in a two-dimensional point pattern. In soap froth, the evolving topology simulates the evolution of agents in the system. In this paradigm, each point, here representing a particular shopping mall, defines a Voronoi cell, or, in the soap froth case, a two-dimensional bubble. The point pattern of shopping mall in a city map becomes a cellular pattern of regions of loyal customers. If the company is a supermarket, its location in a shopping mall becomes a problem of occupancy of cells in the two-dimensional cellular pattern. Each shopping mall can be associated with a specific company labeled by a particular color. The area of a given cell i is interpreted as the resource of the particular agent i, while the perimeter of the cell measures the set of customers opened for competition between agent i and its neighbors. Each cell i is initially assigned one of two colors for two competing companies. The agents collaborate when two cells are the same color and compete otherwise. In [1-3], we only use Voronoi patterns; here we consider real soap froth. Soap froth is a well-controlled experimental system for studying evolving network topologies [4-11]. Gas diffusion across membranes of bubbles is the driving mechanism for evolution in soap froth [12]. This is similar to customer diffusion in a city from one shopping mall to another. These

J. Liu et al. (Eds.): IDEAL 2003, LNCS 2690, pp. 114–118, 2003.

physical laws on soap froth provide some guidance for the more complex problem of the evolution of color patterns on a *changing* cellular network. The statistical properties of the color pattern can be modeled with the Ising model in physics.

Fig. 1. Multi-agent system with 3000 agents.

2 Model

We consider the competition between two large chains of supermarkets (B and W) in a city map, which we model with a soap froth cellular pattern in the steady state from an experiment in physics. An example of a multi-agent system containing 3000 agents (cells) is shown in Fig.1. If we assume that the center of each cell in Fig.1 denotes a shopping mall accommodating one supermarket, then we color the cell white if the supermarket belongs to chain W and black if it belongs to chain B. For customers living inside a particular cellular area in the network, they will save travel expense if they make their purchase in the supermarket located in the mall at the center of that cell. If there is a sale in the neighboring mall, customers may like to travel longer distance to shop there. Thus, neighboring malls will try different advertising and discounting to attract customers. Among all those customers living in neighboring cells, those who live right at the boundary between two cells can choose either cell in which to shop, depending on the marketing strategy of the two companies. We assume that the two chains contain almost the same resources, so that initially about half of the cells (and 50 percent of the area) are black.

3 Switching Dynamics

Let interaction strength J_{ij} between color i bubble and color j bubble ($i,j \in \{W,B\}$), assume only three values: J_{BB}, J_{WW}, and $J_{WB} = J_{BW}$. In a recent paper[13], we have shown that when the n-sided cell initially is white, and $\varepsilon_{same} = J_{WW} = J_{BB}$ and $\varepsilon_{diff} = -J_{BW} = -J_{WB}$, the change in energy of the configuration is given by

$$\Delta E\big|_{\text{Cell is initially white}} = (m_{diff} - m_{same})(\varepsilon_{diff} + \varepsilon_{same}) = -\Delta E\big|_{\text{Cell is initially black}}. \tag{1}$$

Here m_{same} and m_{diff} are the number of neighboring cells with the same and different colors, respectively. The concept of energy borrowed from physics is here interpreted as benefits for the customers, so that the problem of minimizing energy in physics corresponds here to the maximization of benefits for customers. When energy is decreased (benefits increase), the probability of switching color is unity. If energy is increased after switching, (ΔE is positive), there should be a finite probability $e^{-\beta \Delta E}$ that the switching is still active due to noise (such as advertisement and discounts). Thus, the probability of agent j to switch color is given by $\min\left(1, e^{-\beta \Delta E}\right)$ after one cycle of evolution. The system evolves up to 40000 cycles in the simulation with β in the range of 10^{-7} to 10^{2}; then the patterns are recorded. For analysis, we study only the subset of systems whose bubbles are enclosed in the region shown Fig.1 to avoid boundary effects. Our simulation is repeated over 20 random seeds.

4 Results

4.1 Interior Bubble Distribution

An interior agent (or bubble) is an agent (a bubble) surrounded by neighbors all with the same color as itself. At high noise level ($\beta \sim 10^{-7}$), our system after 5000 MC steps of evolutions is totally randomized. The number of interior agents is very small. Since formation of interior agent implies certain group behavior, which is hard to achieve when there is a large temptation to betray your fellow agents at noise level. If β is increased to around 10, i.e., at a low noise level, agents belonging to the same group would form cluster and the number of interior bubbles increase greatly, forming clustered pattern. Agents now find that by teaming together, the energy can be minimized (the cost is minimized by forming a cluster, allowing for better collaboration). This is possible when there is little temptation for the agent to betray his fellow agents, and agents prefer solidarity in a cluster to compete with the enemy. In Fig.2, we plot the number of interior bubbles as a function of the logarithm of β. The number of interior bubbles for small β, high noise level, is small; while at large β, low noise, it is high due to the appearance of clusters.

4.2 Color Fluctuation

An interesting feature of the color evolution can be observed from the fluctuation of color, as measured by the variance

$$V_{Color} = \left\langle \left(m - \langle m \rangle\right)^2 \right\rangle. \tag{2}$$

The variable m is the magnetization and it measures the difference between the two colors. In Fig.3, we plot the magnetic susceptibility $\chi = N\beta V_{Color}$ as a function of inverse noise factor for N cells system. At small noise, the fluctuation is large, but it decreases rapidly as noise increases beyond a critical value. Heuristically, for high noise, when the number of interior bubble is small so that a bubble is likely to be surrounded by bubbles of both colors, the fluctuation in color is approximately constant. However, at low noise level, cluster formation begins. When color switches, it is more probable to have a large domain of color following the switch, resulting in larger fluctuation. In application, the critical level of noise associated with the sudden increase in fluctuation can be used to decide the level of advertisement.

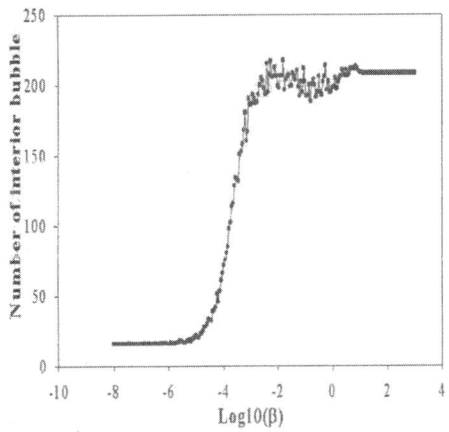

Fig. 2. Interior bubbles as a function of the logarithm of inverse temperature.

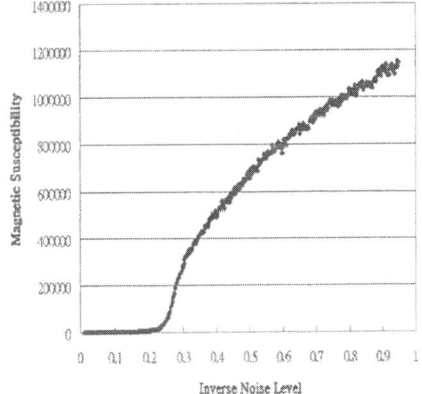

Fig. 3. Fluctuation of Color as a function of inverse noise level

5 Discussion

Our simulation results indicate that there are only two qualitatively distinct states: clustered state at small noise and randomized states at high noise. We address the average lifetime of an agent and the average color neighborhood of those long living agents elsewhere [14-16]. K.Y. Szeto acknowledges support from RGC grant no. HKUST6144/00P and HKUST6157/01P.

References

1. K.F. Lor and K.Y. Szeto, Existence of Minority in Multi-Agent Systems using Voronoi Tessellation, Lecture Notes in Computer Sciences Series, V.1983, Ed. K.S. Leung, L.W. Chan, and H. Meng, Spriger-Verlag, Heidelberg, 2000, IDEAL 2000, p.320–325.
2. W.K.F. Lor and K.Y. Szeto, Switching Dynamics of Multi-Agent Systems: Soap Froth Paradigm, International Joint Conference on Neural Networks 2000, Neural Computing: New Challenges and Perspectives for the New Millennium, IJCNN IEEE-INNS-ENNS Volume VI, pp. 625–628, 2000.
3. Ming Jiang, Yupin Luo, K.Y. Szeto, Shiyuan Yang; Dynamics of Negotiating Agent in a Soap Froth World; Proceeding of ICONIP'2001, Shanghai. 2001, Vol.1 pp154–159.
4. K.Y. Szeto; *Shell Model of Soap Froth.* Invited talk in the Proceedings of the Inauguration conference of the Asia-Pacific Center of Theoretical Physics, Current Topics in Physics, Ed. Y.M. Cho, J.B. Hong, and C.N. Yang. 4–10, June, 1996. World Scientific. Vol.1, 361–375, (1998).
5. K.Y. Szeto and W.Y. Tam; *Universal Topological Properties of Layers in Soap Froth,* Phys.Rev. E53, 4213–4216, (1996)
6. K.Y. Szeto , T. Aste, and W.Y. Tam; *Topological Correlations in Soap Froth.* Phys.Rev.E58,2656–2659(1998);
7. T.Aste, K.Y. Szeto, and W.Y. Tam ; Statistical properties and Shell analysis in random cellular structures; Phys. Rev. E54, 5482–5492(1996)
8. K.Y. Szeto and W.Y. Tam; Evolution of Soap Froth from an Initial Bubble Crystal State to the Scaling State, Invited talk at the APCTP conference on Biophysics, July 1999, published by AIP, 1999.
9. Stavans, J., Domany, E., and Mukamel, D., "Universality and Pattern Selection in Two-Dimensional Cellular Structures", Europhysics Letters, 15 (5), 1991, pp. 479–484.
10. Szeto, K.Y., and Tam, W.Y., "Edge Scaling of Soap Froth", Physica A,254, 1998, p248.
11. B. Dubertret, K.Y. Szeto and W.Y. Tam;*T1-correlations in soap froths*; (Europhysics Letter, Vol.45, p.143–148(1999)
12. Von Neumann, J., "Discussion", Metal Interfaces(American Society for Metals, Cleveland), 1952, pp. 108–110.
13. K.Y. Szeto and Kong Chiwah, Computational Economics Accepted for publication.
14. W.Y. Tam, K.M. Cheung and K.Y. Szeto; Ancestors of soap froth; Phys.Rev.E57, 7354–7357(1998).
15. K.Y. Szeto, Xiujun Fu, and Wing Yim Tam; Universal Topological Properties of Two-dimensional Cellular Patterns, Phys.Rev. Lett. 138302-1–138302-3, 2002
16. K.Y. Szeto, unpublished.

A Self-Organizing Channel Assignment Algorithm: A Cellular Learning Automata Approach

Hamid Beigy and Mohammad Reza Meybodi*

Soft Computing Laboratory
Computer Engineering Department
Amirkabir University of Technology
Tehran, Iran
{beigy, meybodi}@ce.aut.ac.ir

Abstract. Introduction of micro-cellular networks offer a potential increase in capacity of cellular networks, but they create problems in management of the cellular networks. A solution to these problems is self-organizing channel assignment algorithm with distributed control. In this paper, we first introduce the model of cellular learning automata in which learning automata are used to adjust the state transition probabilities of cellular automata. Then a cellular learning automata based self-organizing channel assignment algorithm is introduced. The simulation results show that the micro-cellular network can self-organize by using simple channel assignment algorithm as the network operates.

1 Introduction

With increasing popularity of mobile computing, demand for channels is on the rise. Since the number of channels allocated to the cellular network is limited, efficient management and sharing of channels among numerous users become an important issue. The limited number of channels means that channels have to be reused as much as possible in order to support the many thousands of simultaneously calls that may arise in any typical mobile communication environment. In order to support wireless communication for mobile hosts, geographical area covered by mobile network is divided into smaller regions called *cells*. Each cell has a fixed server computer called *base station* (BS), which is located at its center. A number of BSs are linked to a fixed computer called *mobile switching center* (MSC) which also acts as a gateway of the mobile network to the existing wired-line networks. The BSs are connected to the wired-line network and communicate with mobile hosts through wireless links and with MSCs through wired-line links. A mobile host communicates with any other node in the network, fixed or mobile, only through the BS of its cell using wireless communication. If a channel is used concurrently by more than one communication sessions in the same

---

* This work is partially supported by Iranian Telecommunication Research Center (ITRC), Tehran, Iran.

J. Liu et al. (Eds.): IDEAL 2003, LNCS 2690, pp. 119–126, 2003.

cell or in the neighboring cells, the signal of communicating units will interfere with others. Such interference is called *co-channel interference*. However, the same channel can be used in geographically separated cells such that their signal do not interfere with each other. The minimum distance at which co-channel can be reused with acceptable interference is called *co-channel reuse distance*. The set of all neighboring cells that are in co-channel interference range of each other form a *cluster*. At any time, a channel can be used to support at most one communication session in each cluster. The problem of assigning channels to communication sessions is called *channel assignment problem*. There are several schemes for assigning channels to communication sessions, which can be divided into a number of different categories depending on the comparison basis. For example, when channel assignment algorithms are compared based on the manner in which co-channels are separated, they can be classified as *fixed channel assignment* (FCA), *dynamic channel assignment* (DCA), and *hybrid channel assignment* (HCA) schemes [1]. In FCA schemes, a set of channels are permanently allocated to each cell, which can be reused in another cell, at sufficiently distance, such that interference is tolerable. FCA are formulated as generalized graph coloring problem and belongs to class of NP-Hard problems [2]. In DCA schemes, there is a global pool of channels from where channels are assigned on demand and the set of channels assigned to a cell varies with time. After a call is completed, the assigned channel is returned to the global pool. In HCA schemes, channels are divided into *fixed* and *dynamic* sets. Fixed set contains a number of channels that are assigned to cells as in the FCA schemes. The fixed channels of a particular cell are assigned only for calls initiated in that cell. Dynamic set of channels is shared between all users in network to increase flexibility. When a request for service is received by a base station, if there is a free channel in fixed set then the base station assigns a channel from fixed set and if all channels in the fixed set are busy, then a channel is allocated from dynamic set. Any DCA strategies can be used for assigning channels from dynamic set.

In this paper, we first introduce cellular learning automata (CLA) model. The basic idea of CLA is to use learning automata (LA) to adjust the state transition probability of cellular automata (CA). Then we propose a self-organizing channel assignment algorithm based on the CLA. The proposed algorithm reduces the time needed by the algorithms that use exhaustive search for finding optimal solution of FCA. In order to show the feasibility of the proposed algorithm, computer simulations are conducted. The simulation results show that the cellular network can self-organize the assignment of channels by using simple channel assignment algorithm as network operates.

The rest of this paper is organized as follows. In section 2, a brief review of learning automata is given and in section 3, the cellular learning automata is presented. Sections 4 and 5 presents the proposed algorithm and numerical example, respectively and section 6 concludes the paper.

2   Learning Automata

The automata approach to learning involves determination of an optimal action from a set of allowable actions. An automaton can be regarded as an abstract object that has finite number of actions. It selects an action from its finite set of actions and applies to a random environment. The random environment evaluates the applied action and emits a response. This response is used by automaton to select its next action. By continuing this process, the automaton learns to select the action with the best response. The learning algorithm used by automaton to determine the selection of next action from the response of environment. An automaton acting in an unknown random environment and improves its performance in some specified manner, is referred to as *learning automaton*. LA can be classified into two main families: *fixed structure LA* and *variable structure LA* [3]. Variable structure LA are represented by triple $<\beta, \alpha, T>$, where β is a set of inputs, α is a set of actions, and T is learning algorithm. The learning algorithm is a recurrence relation and is used to modify action probabilities (p) of the automaton. It is evident that the crucial factor affecting the performance of the variable structure LA, is learning algorithm for updating the action probabilities. Various learning algorithms have been reported in the literature. In what follows, two learning algorithms for updating the action probability vector are given. Let α_i be the action chosen at time k as a sample realization from probability distribution $p(k)$. In linear reward-ϵpenalty algorithm $(L_{R-\epsilon P})$ scheme the recurrence equation for updating p is defined as

$$p_j(k+1) = \begin{cases} p_j(k) + a \times [1 - p_j(k)] & \text{if } i = j \\ p_j(k) - a \times p_j(k) & \text{if } i \neq j \end{cases} \quad (1)$$

when $\beta(k) = 0$ and

$$p_j(k+1) = \begin{cases} p_j(k) \times (1 - b) & \text{if } i = j \\ \frac{b}{r-1} + p_j(k)(1 - b) & \text{if } i \neq j \end{cases} \quad (2)$$

when $\beta(k) = 1$. Parameters $0 < b \ll a < 1$ represent *step lengths* and r is the number of actions for LA. The $a(b)$ determines the amount of increase(decreases) of the action probabilities. If $a = b$, then the recurrence equations (1) and (2) is called *linear reward penalty*(L_{R-P}) algorithm and if $b = 0$, then the recurrence equations (1) and (2) is called *linear reward inaction*(L_{R-I}) algorithm. LA have been used successfully in many applications such as telephone and data network routing [4], solving NP-Complete problems [5], capacity assignment [6] and neural network engineering [7,8] to mention a few.

3   Cellular Learning Automata

Cellular automata are mathematical models for systems consisting of large numbers of simple identical components with local interactions. The simple components act together to produce complicated patterns of behavior. CA perform complex computation with high degree of efficiency and robustness [9]. CA are non-linear dynamical systems in which space and time are discrete. A CA consists of a finite dimensional lattice of cells whose states are restricted to a finite set of integers $\phi = \{0, 1, \cdots, k-1\}$. The state of each cell at any time instant is determined by a rule from states of neighboring cells at the previous time instant. Given a finite set ϕ and a finite dimension d, CA can be considered as a d-dimensional lattice Z^d in which every point has a label from set ϕ.

A *cellular learning automata* (CLA) is a CA in which an LA (or multiple LA) is assigned to its every cell. The LA residing in a particular cell determines its state on the basis of its action probability vector. Like CA, there is a rule that CLA operate under it. The rule of CLA and state of neighboring cells of any particular cell determine the reinforcement signal to the LA residing in that cell. In CLA, the neighboring cells of any particular cell constitute the environment for that cell. Because the neighboring cells produce the reinforcement signal to the LA residing in that cell. The operation of CLA could be described as follows: At the first step, the internal state of every cell is specified. The internal state of every cell is determined on the basis of action probability vectors of LA residing in that cell. The initial value of the action probability vectors may be chosen on the basis of past experience or at random. In the second step, the rule of CLA determines the reinforcement signal for each LA. Finally, each LA updates its action probability vector on the basis of supplied reinforcement signal and the action chosen by the cell. This process continues until the desired state reached. The CLA can be classified into *synchronous* and *asynchronous* CLA. In synchronous CLA, all cells are synchronized with a global clock and executed at the same time.

In [10], an asynchronous CLA is proposed and used as an adaptive controller. In his model, the state space of the environment(system under control) is uniformly discretized into cells, and each cell contain a number of LA. The actions of each LA corresponds to discritized values of the corresponding control variable. Based on the state of system (S_0) one cell in CLA is activated. Every LA of the activated cell chooses an action based on its action probability vector. These actions are applied to the system and the system changes its state from S_0 to S_1. The environment then passes a reinforcement signal to the LA of the activated cell. Depending on the reinforcement signal, LA in activated cell and its neighboring cells update their action probability vectors. This process continues until termination state is reached. In [11], a model of synchronous CLA has been proposed in which each cell can hold one LA. This model of CLA have been used in several applications such as image processing and rumor diffusion, to mention a few. In what follows, we extend the idea given in [11].

A CLA, as shown in figure 1, consists of following major components: neighboring cells, local rule, and a set of LA. The operation of CLA can be described as follows: Without loss of generality assume that an automaton is assigned to every cell. At instant n, the LA A associated to a particular cell u selects one of its actions, say $\alpha(n)$ based on its action probability vector. The reinforcement signal $\beta(n)$ is produced by a local rule R from the state of neighborhood cells.

Every LA updates its action probability vector based on the reinforcement signal $\beta(n)$, and selected action $\alpha(n)$. This process continues until the average received penalty is minimized.

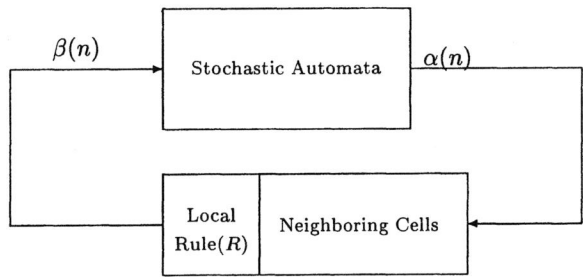

Fig. 1. Block diagram of one cell of CLA

Definition 1. A CLA mathematically can be described by a tuple $\{d, \Phi, N, A, R\}$, where

1. d is a positive integer indicating the dimension of CLA. When d equals to one (two) the CLA is referred to as *one-(two-)dimensional CLA*.
2. $\Phi = \{\phi_1, \cdots, \phi_k\}$ is the set of internal state, where $\phi_i \in \{0, 1, \ldots, L-1\}$ and L is an integer.
3. N is a neighborhood vector $N = (x_1, x_2, \cdots, x_m)$ of different elements in Z^d, which determines the relative position of neighboring sites from any given site u in the lattice Z^d. The neighbors of cell u are cells $\{u + \bar{x}_i | i = 1, 2, \cdots, m\}$. There is a neighborhood function $\bar{N}(u) = (u + \bar{x}_1, u + \bar{x}_2, \cdots, u + x_m)$ that maps a site u to set of its neighbors. For the sake of simplicity, we assume that the first element of neighborhood vector (i.e. $\bar{x}_1$) is equals to d-tuple $(0, 0, \cdots, 0)$. $\bar{N}(u)$ satisfies in the two following conditions:
   - $u \in \bar{N}(u)$ for all $u \in Z^d$.
   - $u_1 \in \bar{N}(u_2) \Longleftrightarrow u_2 \in \bar{N}(u_1)$ for all $u_1, u_2 \in Z^d$.
4. A is a set of LA associated to a particular cell.
5. $R : \Phi^m \to \beta$ is the local rule of the CLA, which produces the reinforcement signal $\beta(n)$ from the state of neighboring cells.

4   The Proposed Channel Assignment Algorithm

In this section, we introduce a self-organizing channel assignment algorithm based on the CLA introduced in the previous section. In this algorithm, at first a CLA is build from the cellular network with neighborhood function $\bar{N}(.)$ and then channels are assigned to the cells according to the algorithm given in figure 2. The neighborhood function $\bar{N}(u)$ represents the set of cells in the reuse distance of cell u; i.e. the set of cells in a cluster with center u. In the proposed algorithm, a set of LA $\underline{A} = \{A_1, \ldots, A_\sigma\}$ each with two actions are associated to each cell, where σ denotes the number of channels assigned to the network. In this algorithm, the automaton A_i is used for allocation of channel i. The action α_1 of automaton A_i represents that the channel i is a candidate for assignment to that cell and the action α_2 of automaton A_i represents that the channel i isn't a candidate for assignment to that cell. The state of each cell, Φ, is a set with σ elements $\Phi = \{\phi_1, \ldots, \phi_\sigma\}$, where the element $\phi_i \in \{0, 1\}$ (for $i = 1, \ldots, \sigma$) represents whether the suggested allocation of channel i for that cell is feasible or not. When $\phi_i = 0$ ($\phi_i = 1$), it means that the suggested assignment of channel i is feasible (infeasible) for that cell. The local rule of CLA determines whether the given channel is assigned to any cell in the cluster or not. For example the used rule is: if channel i is assigned to any cell in the cluster and it isn't assigned to cell u, then the result of the rule is 0; otherwise the result of the rule is 1.

Algorithm
1.   Build a CLA and initialize it.
2.   **for** $k = 1$ **to** N **do in parallel**
3.   **for** $i = 1$ **to** σ **do in parallel**
4.   Select action of automaton A_i and denote it as α^i
5.   **if** $\alpha^i = \alpha_1$ **then**
6.   **if** channel i is used in the cluster **then**
7.   Penalize action α_1.
8.   **else**
9.   Reward action α_1.
10.   **end if**
11.   **else**
12.   **if** channel i is used in the cluster **then**
13.   Reward action α_2.
14.   **else**
15.   Penalize action α_2.
16.   **end if**
17.   **end if**
18.   **end for**
19.   **end for**
    end Algorithm

Fig. 2. The CLA based self-organizing channel assignment algorithm.

The description of the proposed algorithm for M cells one dimensional cellular network is shown algorithmically in figure 2, which can be described as follows. At first a CLA is build and initialized based on the topology of the cellular network. Then each cell do the following operation for each automaton A_i (for $i = 1, \ldots, \sigma$) associated to it. Automaton A_i (for $i = 1, \ldots, \sigma$) selects its action and then updates its action probability vector based on the result of local

Table 1. The simulation results of self-organizing channel Assignment algorithm.

Run	Cell 1	Cell 2	Cell 3	Cell 4	Cell 5	Cell 6	Cell 7	Cell 8	Cell 9	Cell 10
1	1	2	1	2	1	2	1	2	1	2
2	2	1	2	1	2	1	2	1	2	1
3	1	2	1	2	1	2	1	2	1	2
4	2	1	2	1	2	1	2	1	2	1
5	1	2	1	2	2	1	2	1	2	1
6	1	2	1	2	1	2	1	2	1	2
7	1	2	1	2	1	2	1	2	1	2
8	1	2	1	2	1	2	1	2	1	2
9	2	1	2	1	2	1	2	1	2	1
10	1	2	1	2	1	2	1	2	1	2

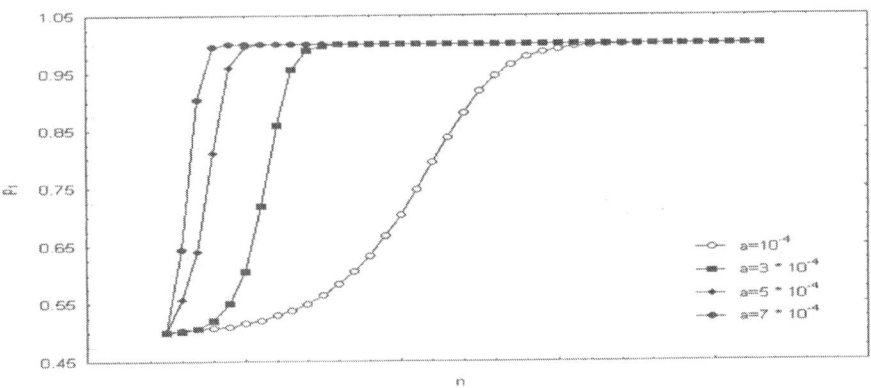

Fig. 3. The speed of convergence of a typical LA in the CLA.

rule. The local rule is evaluated as follows: if the selected action is (isn't) the assignment of channel i to the cell, then the cell checks for assignment of this channel in the cluster. If channel i is assigned to at least one cell in the cluster; then the result of local rule is to penalize (reward) the selected action; otherwise the selected action is rewarded (penalized).

5   Numerical Example

In what follows, we give the results of simulation for the proposed self-organizing channel assignment algorithm. In this simulation, we have 10 cells organized in a linear array and 2 channels with reuse distance of 2; i.e. the same channel cannot be used in the neighboring cells. Thus in each cell, we have two LA each with two actions. The LA used in each cell use L_{R-I} algorithm. The results of simulation are given in table 1. Each row of this table shows the result of a typical run. By carefully inspecting of this table, it is evident that the proposed channel assignment algorithm is self-organizing and converges to the optimal assignment. For more simulation results, the reader may refer to [12].

Figure 3 shows the convergence behavior of a typical LA in a cell for a typical run for different values of learning parameter, a. This figure shows that increasing the learning parameter, a, increases the speed of convergence of CLA.

6   Conclusions

In this paper, cellular learning automata is introduced. The cellular learning automata is a model in which learning automata are used to adjust the state transition probabilities of cellular automata. Then as application of cellular learning automata, a self-organizing channel assignment algorithm based on cellular learning automata is given. In order to show the power of the proposed method, the computer simulations are conducted.

References

1. I. Katzela and M. Naghshineh, "Channel Assignment Schemes for Cellular Mobile Telecommunication Systems: A Comprehensive Survey," *IEEE Personal Communications*, pp. 10–31, June 1996.
2. W. K. Hale, "Frequence Assignment:Theory and Applications," *Proceedings of IEEE*, vol. 68, pp. 1497–1514, Dec. 1980.
3. K. S. Narendra and K. S. Thathachar, *Learning Automata: An Introduction*. New York: Printice-Hall, 1989.
4. P. R. Srikantakumar and K. S. Narendra, "A Learning Model for Routing in Telephone Networks," *SIAM Journal of Control and Optimization*, vol. 20, pp. 34–57, Jan. 1982.
5. B. J. Oommen and E. V. de St. Croix, "Graph Partitioning Using Learning Automata," *IEEE Transactions on Commputers*, vol. 45, pp. 195–208, Feb. 1996.
6. B. J. Oommen and T. D. Roberts, "Continuous Learning Automata Solutions to the Capacity Assignment Problem," *IEEE Transactions on Commputers*, vol. 49, pp. 608–620, June 2000.
7. M. R. Meybodi and H. Beigy, "A Note on Learning Automata Based Schemes for Adaptation of BP Parameters ," *Journal of Neuro Computing*, vol. 48, pp. 957–974, Nov. 2002.
8. M. R. Meybodi and H. Beigy, "New Learning Automata Based Algorithms for Adaptation of Backpropagation Algorithm Parameters," *International Journal of Neural Systems*, vol. 12, pp. 45–68, Feb. 2002.
9. N. H. Packard and S. Wolfram, "Two-Dimensional Cellular Automata," *Journal of Statistical Physics*, vol. 38, pp. 901–946, 1985.
10. K. Krishna, "Cellular Learning Automata: A Stochastic Model for Adaptive Controllers," Master's thesis, Department of Electrical Engineering, Indian Institue of Science, Banglore, India, June 1993.
11. M. R. Meybodi, H. Beigy, and M. Taherkhani, "Cellular Learning Automata and its Applications," *Accepted for Publication in Journal of Sharif*.
12. H. Beigy and M. R. Meybodi, "Cellular Learning Automata Based Self-Organizing Channel Assignment Algorithms," Tech. Rep. TR-CE-2002-008, Computer Engineering Department, Amirkabir University of Technology, Tehran, Iran, 2002.

Learning from Average Experience

James Bergin[1] and Dan Bernhardt[2]

[1] Department of Economics, Queen's University, Kingston,
Ontario K7L 3N6, CANADA
[2] Department of Economics, University of Illinois, Champaign, IL 61820, USA

Abstract. We study repeated interaction over time and explore long-run behavior when individuals imitate successful past performers, selecting actions that yielded better average historical performance. For a class of environments (such as the oligopoly environment) it is known that such behavior results in very inefficient outcomes. Increasing ones own payoff comes partly at the expense of others and the dynamics generated by imitative behavior lead to low welfare in the long run. We show that this conclusion rests on the assumption that individuals have short memories. The situation differs sharply if agents have longer memories and evaluate actions according to average performance. In that case, it turns out that highly cooperative or collusive arise. In particular, with sufficiently long memory the unique stochastically stable outcome is the maximally collusive outcome.

1 Introduction

In strategic environments, agents may have little faith in their ability to predict the behavior of others and may have limited ability to determine what constitutes a "good decision". In such circumstances, the levels of rationality and knowledge mandated by traditional game theoretic models seem implausible — pre-supposing that individuals have full knowledge of the environment, have the ability to anticipate how others will behave, and are capable of making difficult computations.

In many environments, it has been shown that imitative behavior leads to low welfare in the long run (Vega-Redondo [3]). We show that this conclusion rests on the assumption that individuals have short memories, recalling just *one* period. Outcomes are sharply different if agents have longer memories. In competitive environments where an increase in the payoff of one comes at the expense of others, individuals come to recognize the destructive consequences of short-term improvement; they recognize the consequent matching behavior of other players leads to a downward spiral in overall welfare. The impact is dramatic: if individuals' memories are sufficiently good, then the unique stochastically stable outcome is the maximally collusive outcome. Even if memory is quite short, long-run outcomes feature substantial collusion. Thus, with sufficient memory, selection of "best-performers" leads to outcomes that differ dramatically from those that obtain when only the immediate past can be recalled.

J. Liu et al. (Eds.): IDEAL 2003, LNCS 2690, pp. 127–134, 2003.

The canonical example where these features arise is the Cournot oligopoly. There, when a firm raises output the impact is to lower the payoffs of others, whatever the impact on own payoff. Thus, in that case, from a point where firms make a common choice, an increase in the output of one makes that firms profit greater that others and the incentive to imitate arises — even though it is detrimental to all.

2   The Framework

In each period, each of n identical agents chooses an action from a common finite set of actions, $X = \{x_0, x_1, ... x_z\}$. Actions are ordered with $x_k < x_{k+1}$. Let x denote a representative element by x. Agent i's payoff function is $\pi^i(x^i, x^{-i})$, where x^i is the choice by agent i and x^{-i} is the $n-1$ vector of choices by the other agents. At a symmetric point where $x^i = x^j = x$, write $\pi^*(x) = \pi_i(x, x, \ldots, x)$. Since agents are identical, $\pi^*(x)$ is independent of i. Given a vector $(x^1, x^2, \ldots x^i, \ldots x^n)$, to highlight the impact of i's action on a player j's payoff, we emphasize the ith position or choice of i by writing $(x^1, x^2, \ldots [x^i]^i, \ldots x^n)$.

Denote by x_c the symmetric Nash equilibrium, and write x_m for the most collusive (or monopoly) choice: x_m solves $\max_x \pi^*(x)$. Finally, let x_w denote the equilibrium in relative payoffs: for $x^i \neq x_w$, $\pi^i(x_w, \ldots, [x^i]^i, \ldots, x_w) < \pi^j(x_w, \ldots, [x^i]^i, \ldots, x_w)$. At x_w, no individual can raise his payoff vis-a-vis other players. In an oligopoly setting, x_m corresponds to the equal ($\frac{1}{n}$th) share of the monopoly output, while x_w corresponds to the Walrasian output level. We assume that $\pi^*(x)$ is strictly increasing for $x < x_m$ and strictly decreasing for $x > x_m$. We further assume that

$$\text{If } x < x_c, \text{ for } x < \tilde{x}^i \leq x_c, \text{ then } \pi^i(x, x, \ldots, [\tilde{x}^i]^i, x, \ldots, x) > \pi^*(x). \quad (1)$$

$$\text{If } x \geq x_c, \text{ for } x_c \leq \tilde{x}^i < x, \text{ then } \pi^i(x, x, \ldots, [\tilde{x}^i]^i, x, \ldots, x) > \pi^*(x). \quad (2)$$

This assumption ensures that there is a unique symmetric Nash equilibrium. At a common choice below x_c, a small increase in agent i's action raises his payoff; while at a common choice above x_c, small reductions in action raise payoffs. We assume that x_m, x_c and x_w are in the action set X. Abusing notation slightly, we let x_{m+1} be the smallest feasible action exceeding x_m, and so on.

We consider those environments in which actions are either substitutes or complements. Actions are *substitutes* if, (a) actions are strategic substitutes (monotone decreasing best response functions), and (b) an action increase by some agent lowers the payoff of other agents:

$$\text{If } j \neq i, x^j > 0, \text{ and } \tilde{x}^i > x^i \text{ then}$$
$$\pi^j(x^1, \ldots, [\tilde{x}^i]^i, \ldots, x^n) < \pi^j(x^1, \ldots, [x^i]^i, \ldots, x^n). \quad (3)$$

Similarly, actions are *complements* if, (a) actions are strategic complements, and (b) an increased action choice by some agent raises the payoff of other agents:

$$\text{If } j \neq i, x^j > 0, \text{ and } \tilde{x}^i > x^i \text{ then}$$
$$\pi^j(x^1, \ldots, [\tilde{x}^i]^i, \ldots, x^n) > \pi^j(x^1, \ldots, [x^i]^i, \ldots, x^n) \quad (4)$$

If actions are substitutes, then $x_m < x_c$; while if actions are complements, $x_m > x_c$. Environments in which actions are substitutes include: (i) oligopoly production games in which firm outputs are perfect or imperfect substitutes; (ii) the tragedy of the commons, where an increase in grazing by one farmer lowers the payoffs of other farmers; and (iii) pollution games, where an increase in output by one firm raises production costs for other firms, and firms are competitive price-takers. Environments in which actions are complements include: (i) private provision of public goods; and (ii) R&D games with spillovers.

2.1 Experience-Based Choices

Agents can observe the actions taken by other agents and the associated payoffs. At the beginning of each date $t + 1$, an agent can recall the actions and payoffs for the past $l + 1$ periods, $t, t - 1, \ldots, t - l$. Since actions uniquely determine payoffs, we conserve on notation and write the state or history of the economy as a $n \times (l+1)$ vector of choices made by agents in the previous $l+1$ periods.[1] At the beginning of date $t + 1$, the state is given by $s = \mathbf{x}(t) = (x_{t-l}, \ldots, x_{t-1}, x_t)$, where $x_\tau \in X^n$ is an n vector of choices by agents, $t - l \leq \tau \leq t$. Given a state $s = \mathbf{x}(t)$, let $X(s) = \{x \in X \mid \exists i, \ t - l \leq \tau \leq t, \ x = x_\tau^i\}$, so that $x' \in X(s)$ if at state s some player in the history identified by s chose x'.

At date t, given the state $\mathbf{x}(t)$, we consider the average historical performance of each choice. Given $x \in X(\mathbf{x}(t))$, one can determine the number of periods in which x was chosen. Let $T_t(x \mid \mathbf{x}(t)) = \{\tau \mid t - l \leq \tau \leq t, \ \exists j, \ x_\tau^j = x\}$ be the set of times at which x was chosen by at least one agent. In any period where agents made the same choice, they received the same payoff.

Write $\bar\pi[x : s]$ to denote the average payoff from the choice x at state s, averaged over those periods in which x was chosen and can be recalled. At each $t' \in T_t(x \mid \mathbf{x}(t))$, let $k(x, t')$ be an arbitrary agent who played x at that date, so that $\pi^{k(x,t')}(x, x_t^{-k(x,t')})$ is the payoff to those agents, including $k(x, t')$, who chose x at time t'. The average payoff from action x is

$$\bar\pi[x : s] = \frac{1}{\#T_t(x \mid \mathbf{x}(t))} \sum_{t' \in T_t(x|\mathbf{x}(t))} \pi^{k(x,t')}(x, x_t^{-k(x,t')}). \tag{5}$$

If $x, x' \in X(s)$, then both are in the memory frame and may be compared by all agents. Results are unchanged if we average over agents as well as time periods since in any period agents taking the same action receive the same payoff.

Agents select choices based on average historical performance: in a stationary environment, lessons learned from one period are no more or less valuable than those learned in other periods. It therefore seems appropriate to weight experience from different periods equally. The most demanding choice criterion is that agents select from those choices that yielded the highest average performance; a less demanding criterion is that agents select from those actions with a better

---

[1] Specifically, individuals observe the choices made and the rewards received; but they may not know how choices determine payoffs — the payoff functions.

than average historical performance. A minimal requirement for reasonable behavior is that agents not choose the worst outcome whenever there is a better
alternative. The worst performing choice solves: $\min_{x' \in X(\mathbf{x}(t))} \bar{\pi}[x'; x(t)]$. Let

$$S(\mathbf{x}(t)) = \{x \in X(\mathbf{x}(t)) | \bar{\pi}(x; \mathbf{x}(t)] > \min_{x' \in X(\mathbf{x}(t))} \bar{\pi}[x'; \mathbf{x}(t)]\}. \tag{6}$$

be the set of actions with average payoffs that strictly exceed the minimum.
If $S(\mathbf{x}(t))$ is non-empty, let $B(\mathbf{x}(t))$ be any non-empty subset of $S(\mathbf{x}(t))$; and
if $S(\mathbf{x}(t))$ is empty (because every action that can be recalled yielded the same
historical average performance), then let $B(\mathbf{x}(t))$ correspond to the set of actions
that have been played in the last $l+1$ periods: $B(\mathbf{x}(t)) = \{x \in X(\mathbf{x}(t))\}$. Write $\mathcal{B}$
for the class of B's that satisfy these conditions. With this notation we postulate
the following form of agent behavior — that an agent does not select a worst
performer, when one exists:

Definition Agent i *optimizes imitatively* according to imitation criterion $B \in \mathcal{B}$
if at every state $s = \mathbf{x}(t)$, his choice of action for period $t + 1$ is drawn from a
probability distribution $\gamma^i(s)$ with support $B(\mathbf{x}(t))$.

Theorem 1 below only requires that the mapping B not pick the worst performer
— so the result is robust to a *large* range of alternative behavior specifications. A
more conventional requirement is that agents pick from best performers, rather
than just avoid the worst ones. Denote the rule defined this way as B^*:

$$B^*(\mathbf{x}(t)) = \{x \in X(\mathbf{q}(t)) \mid \bar{\pi}[x; \mathbf{x}(t)] \geq \max_{x' \in X(\mathbf{x}(t))} \bar{\pi}[x'; \mathbf{x}(t)]\}. \tag{7}$$

For generic payoff functions, the mapping B^* is single valued, and we assume
this in what follows; alternatively, we could adopt a tie-breaking rule. Theorem
2 shows that only the maximally-collusive action, *e.g.* the monopoly output,
corresponds to a stochastically stable state. The intuition for this result is given
in remark 2.

Following Kandori, Mailath and Rob [2] and Young [4], we introduce a small
probability that an agent may select an action not drawn from the support
$B(\mathbf{x}(t))$. That is, with probability $1 - \epsilon$ an agent optimizes imitatively, and
with small probability ϵ, the next choice for agent i is drawn from the set of
feasible actions. Following a mutation, i is equally likely to choose each action,
and 'mutation' probabilities are independently and identically distributed across
agents, states and dates.

3   Results

We show that long memory supports cooperative behavior — and only cooperative behavior (under the criterion of stochastic stability). This theme is
developed in two results. Theorem 1 asserts that relative to the non-cooperative
outcome, x_c, long-run memory drives actions to the "collusive side". This is true

for a very large class of imitative rules. Under the specific rule of selecting best historical performer, theorem 2 establishes that the most collusive outcome is the unique stochastically stable outcome. One can show that in the region between monopoly and Cournot output, states have a degree of "stickiness" — in the sense that single mutations do not move the system to a new state. This is in contrast to the states associated with the region above the Cournot level where single downward mutations move the system down. Thus, starting above the Cournot level, one expects relatively quick movement down toward Cournot output and slower movement downward to monopoly output from within the monopoly-Cournot region.

Theorem 1 asserts that if agents have long memories, then in the long-run substantial cooperation is sustained — a lower bound on long-run payoffs is the Nash equilibrium payoffs. This contrasts with short-sighted imitation which, in the case of oligopoly, leads to the zero-profit Walrasian outcome. The intuition for the result is relatively simple, but the proof is involved and appears in Bergin and Bernhardt [1].

Theorem 1. *Suppose that l is large, and agents optimize imitatively according to some $B \in \mathcal{B}$. Then if actions are substitutes, the set of stochastically stable states is a subset of $\{x_m, x_{m+1}, \ldots, x_c\}$. If actions are complements the set of stochastically stable states is a subset of $\{x_c, x_{c+1}, \ldots, x_m\}$.*

Remark 1. To see the motivation for this result, consider a homogeneous oligopoly and suppose that the system is at rest at some output level between Cournot and Walrasian. Now consider the impact of a perturbation in the output of some firm — in the first instance say a small increase in the output by firm i. Relative to the initial quantity, i's profit is below the status quo profit, since the status quo output exceeded Cournot. In the period following the perturbation, i's profit exceeds that of other firms whose profit was depressed by the increase in i's output. But when this lower profit of the other firms is averaged over all periods in which the status quo output was chosen, the single period has a small impact on the average. In contrast, i's profit has fallen relative to the average. Hence, this upward perturbation in output is not adopted. Now suppose i's output drops a small amount. Then, i's profit rises, and the profit of the other firms from playing the status quo, averaged over those periods in which the status quo was played, is approximately unchanged. Hence, the average profit from the lower output exceeds the profit from the status quo output. As a result, all firms adopt this lower output level. This further raises the profit obtained from output reduction, so this lower output persists.

Theorem 1 establishes that when the history is sufficiently long, all stochastically stable outcomes lie between the Cournot-Nash level and the maximally collusive level. (The appendix provides some additional discussion on the structure of transition probabilities with mutations.) Theorem 1 only required that the mapping B not pick the worst performer — so the result is robust to a *large* range of alternative behavior specifications. A more conventional requirement is that agents pick from best performers, rather than just avoid the worst ones. Denote the rule defined this way as B^*:

$$B^*(\mathbf{x}(t)) = \{x \in X(\mathbf{q}(t)) \mid \bar{\pi}[x; \mathbf{x}(t)] \geq \max_{x' \in X(\mathbf{x}(t))} \bar{\pi}[x'; \mathbf{x}(t)]\}. \qquad (8)$$

For generic payoff functions, the mapping B^* is single valued, and we assume this in what follows; alternatively, we could adopt a tie-breaking rule. Theorem 2 shows that only the maximally-collusive action, $e.g.$ the monopoly output, corresponds to a stochastically stable state. The intuition for this result is given in remark 2.

Theorem 2. *Suppose that l is large, agents optimize imitatively according to imitation criterion B^*, and that actions are either substitutes or complements. Then the unique stochastically stable state is x_m.*

Remark 2. The proof of theorem 2 is lengthy (see Bergin and Bernhardt [1]). However, some motivating intuition for theorem 2 can be given. Suppose that multiple agents' choices are perturbed at the same time, starting from a common action x between the Nash and monopoly level. Either the status quo action, x, is best, or some action, $\tilde{x} \neq x$, gives the highest payoff. In the latter case, suppose that $\tilde{x} > x$. Once $\tilde{x}$ is adopted, the per-period performance is below that of x. Therefore, if $\tilde{x}$ is chosen for sufficiently many periods, it will generate an average below that achieved by x prior to the mutation. As a result, with sufficient memory, choices above x cannot be sustained without their poor performance being revealed. More generally, with mutations occurring over time, take any pattern of n mutations over a period of fixed length. In the case where all mutations exceed the status quo, which, in turn, exceeds x_m, each mutation can be chosen only for a fixed period before its average falls below the initial status quo. Once every mutation is "tested" in this manner, individuals revert to x. In the case where not every mutation is above the initial status quo, any point can be played for a most a fixed period before its payoff relative to the status quo is determined. The only points that can survive over the history are those with higher average performance than the status quo (if any such point is present in the mutation profile.) Thus, the system drops to a more profitable constant choice or reverts to the status quo.

In contrast, some downward mutations will be sustained. In particular, suppose that each agent mutates down to a common action x', where $x_m \leq x' < x$, a positive probability event. Immediately, this new choice is adopted — since the average exceeds that from x, and x is permanently replaced. Thus, there is positive probability (at least ϵ^n) of transition to a more collusive state, and relatively smaller probability (at most ϵ^{n+1}) of a transition to a less collusive state.

4   Other Environments

Although the discussion has been restricted to the class of models described in the framework outlined earlier, the insights apply more generally. Consider the following prisoner's dilemma game:

$$
\begin{array}{cc}
 & \begin{array}{cc} C & D \end{array} \\
\begin{array}{c} C \\ D \end{array} & \left(\begin{array}{cc} (3,3) & (0,4) \\ (4,0) & (1,1) \end{array} \right)
\end{array}
$$

With just two players, a history consists of $l+1$ pairs, $[(c_{t-l}^1, c_{t-l}^2), \ldots, (c_t^1, c_t^2)]$, where c_τ^i is the choice if i in period t. Under imitative dynamics only monomorphic states (where agents take the same action over time) can be stable, so it is sufficient to restrict attention to such states. Consider a history of the form $[(C,C), \ldots, (C,C), (C,C)]$ after which a mutation flips player 2's choice to D — so that next period's history is $[(C,C), \ldots, (C,C), (C,D)]$. The average payoff to C is $\frac{l}{l+1}3 + \frac{1}{l+1}0 = \frac{l}{l+1}3$, and the average payoff to D is 4. Imitation leads player 1 to switch to D, leading to the history, $[(C,C), \ldots, (C,C), (C,D), (D,D)]$. At this point, with l observations on C the average payoff to C is $\frac{l-1}{l}3 + \frac{1}{l}0 = \frac{l-1}{l}3$ and the average payoff to D is $\frac{1}{2}4 + \frac{1}{2}1 = \frac{5}{2}$. Hence, the average performance of C is better than D if $\frac{l-1}{l}3 > \frac{5}{2}$ or $l > 6$. If two players mutate simultaneously, yielding history $[(C,C), \ldots, (C,C), (D,D)]$, reversion to C is immediate. If two mutations occur, one after the other, history $[(C,C), \ldots, (C,C), (C,D), (D,C)]$ can arise (where C and D are matched twice), and without further mutation both now play D. Two periods later, the history becomes $[(C,C), \ldots, (C,C), (C,D), (D,C), (D,D), (D,D)]$. The average payoff from C is $\frac{l-3}{l-1}3 + \frac{2}{l-1}0 = \frac{l-3}{l-1}3$, and the payoff from D is $\frac{1}{4}(4 + 4 + 1 + 1) = \frac{5}{2}$. Reversion by both players to C occurs if $\frac{l-3}{l-1}3 > \frac{5}{2}$ or $l > 13$.

Now consider the constant defection history, $[(D,D), \ldots, (D,D), (D,D)]$. A mutation to C by one player leads to $[(D,D), \ldots, (D,D), (D,C)]$ followed by reversion to $[(D,D), \ldots, (D,D), (D,D)]$, since C produces a lower average payoff than D, reversion to D occurs. However, if mutations for both occur, the history becomes $[(D,D), \ldots, (D,D), (C,C)]$, the average from C is higher and both play C thereafter. Thus, with memory of at least length 14, the stochastically stable outcome has both players choose C.

5   Conclusion

This paper shows that the critical role of memory and evaluation of historical performance of choices in the study of imitative behavior. When memory is very short, destructive competition arises simply because agents cannot see the destructive nature of competitively improving one's position. When agents take a longer view and evaluate the performance of actions in terms of average payoff, such matters come into focus. Taking a longer view in evaluating actions has dramatic impact on both individual behavior and long-run equilibrium, leading to very collusive outcomes in the long run.

References

1. Bergin, J. and D. Bernhardt (2002): "Imitative Learning", *mimeo*, Queen's University.
2. Kandori, M., G. Mailath, and R. Rob (1993): "Learning, Mutations and Long-Run Equilibria in Games", *Econometrica*, 61, 29–56.
3. Vega-Redondo, F. (1997): "The Evolution of Walrasian Behavior", *Econometrica*, 65, 375–384.
4. Young, P. (1993): "The Evolution of Conventions", *Econometrica*, 61, 57–84.

The Inductive Inverse Kinematics Algorithm for Manipulating the Posture of an Articulated Body

Jin Ok Kim[1], Bum Ro Lee[2], and Chin Hyun Chung[2]

[1] School of Information and Communication Engineering, Sungkyunkwan University,
300, Chunchun-dong, Jangan-gu, Suwon, Kyunggi-do, 440-746, KOREA
`jinny@ece.skku.ac.kr`
[2] Department of Information and Control Engineering, Kwangwoon University,
447-1, Wolgye-dong, Nowon-gu, Seoul, 139-701, KOREA
`chung@daisy.kwangwoon.ac.kr`

Abstract. Inverse kinematics is a very useful method for controlling the posture of an articulated body. In most inverse kinematics processes, the major matter of concern is not the posture of an articulated body itself, but the position and direction of the end effector. In some applications such as 3D character animation, however, it is more important to generate an overall natural posture for the character rather than to place the end effector in the exact position. Indeed, when an animator wants to modify the posture of a human-like 3D character with many physical constraints, he has to undergo considerable trial-and-error to generate a realistic posture for the character. In this paper, the Inductive Inverse Kinematics (IIK) algorithm using a Uniform Posture Map (UPM) is proposed to control the posture of a human-like 3D character. The proposed algorithm quantizes human behaviors without distortion to generate a UPM, and then generates a natural posture by searching the UPM. If necessary, the resulting posture could be compensated with a traditional Cyclic Coordinate Descent (CCD). The proposed method could be applied to produce 3D-character animation based on the key frame method, 3D games and virtual reality.

1 Introduction

In traditional animation production, huge amounts of time are spent drawing each frame manually. With the aid of computer graphics, the tedious processes have been automated to make the overall production process more efficient. Key frame animation is a very useful method for producing successive frames automatically in character animation. If an animator sets several key frames, the computer system automatically generates intermediate frames among the key frames. Therefore, it is very important for an animator to set the key frames properly [1] [2] [3]. Many animators use the inverse kinematics algorithm to control the posture of a 3D character [4] [5]. Inverse kinematics technique adopted

J. Liu et al. (Eds.): IDEAL 2003, LNCS 2690, pp. 135–142, 2003.

from robotics has the potential to relieve the animator from deciding the specification of every motion parameter within a frame. It calculates the angles of each joint of the limbs when the end effector points to a specific place. Thus, an animator can control the posture of the limbs by dragging the end effector. In character animation that uses motion capture, the inverse kinematics algorithms are also available to correct the motion capture error by improving false posture that does not observe physical laws. If an animator wants to control the 3D character with many physical constraints, he actually has to undergo considerable trial-and-error to generate a realistic posture. The Cyclic Coordinate Descent (CCD) algorithm [6] [7] is a heuristic inverse kinematics algorithm, that is suitable for interactive control of an articulated body. Like other inverse kinematics algorithms, it can generate many different resulting postures in accordance with the initial posture. However, it is very difficult to choose a feasible posture among many resulting postures. To reform these problems, the Inductive Inverse Kinematics (IIK) algorithm using a Uniform Posture Map (UPM) is proposed in this paper to control the posture of human-like characters. The UPM is organized through the quantization of various postures with an unsupervised learning algorithm, and the learning algorithm prevents the generating of invalid output neurons. This guarantees that the postures generated by the UPM are realistic postures which observe physical constraints. Therefore, it is possible to get a natural posture by finding a posture whose forward kinematics point is closest to its desired position. Because most animators are concerned about the desired natural posture itself rather than the exact position and direction of end effector, the IIK using UPM contributes to the production of character animation efficiently. The IIK algorithm consists of three phases. First, we generate a UPM that reflects the motion tendency of an articulated body and find a proper inverse kinematics solution in generating the UPM. Then, if necessary, we compensate the solution by using the CCD algorithm. This method can be applied to produce 3D-character animation based on the key frame method, 3D games and virtual reality.

2   The Inductive Inverse Kinematics Algorithm

2.1   The Inverse Kinematics Algorithm

Most industrial robotic systems have an end effector at the end of the kinematics chains. To control the position and direction of the end effector, the controller has to calculate the proper angles of each joint. To calculate the proper angle set, the inverse kinematics has been researched according to various points of view. As a natural consequence, the major matter of concern is not the posture itself of an articulated body, but the position and direction of the end effector in most inverse kinematics processes. Indeed, inverse kinematics algorithms using the Jacobian matrix [8] and energy constraints [9] focus on calculating the position of the end effector [10] [11] [12]. In some applications, such as 3D-character animation, however, it could be more important to generate a natural and realistic posture rather than the exact position and direction of the end effector [13] [14] [15]. Because most 3D animation producing tools adopt the traditional inverse kinematics algorithm, when an animator wants to control the 3D character with physical constraints using tools, he actually has to undergo considerable trial-and-error to generate a realistic posture. For these reasons, it is necessary to develop the special inverse kinematics algorithm to control the posture of human-like configurations. For these practical needs, the inductive inverse kinematics algorithm using a Uniform Posture Map (UPM) is proposed, and compared with a traditional inverse kinematics algorithm of a Cyclic Coordinate Descent (CCD).

2.2   The Inductive Inverse Kinematics Algorithm

It is difficult to control the posture of a human-like articulated body using physical constraints through general inverse kinematics, because its major objective is to locate the end effector at the desired point with the desired direction. Except for the case of obstacle avoidance, most inverse kinematics algorithms have been developed from this point of view. If the control target is not an industrial robotic system but the arm or leg of a human-like 3D character, the natural posture itself could be the major purpose of the inverse kinematics. In such applications, many animators have used the traditional inverse kinematics to generate a natural posture through trial-and-error or multiple applications to a partial joint. Therefore it is necessary to research the inverse kinematics algorithm from a different viewpoint than that of the robot control. In this paper, we propose the Inductive Inverse Kinematics (IIK) algorithm using a UPM. This algorithm consists of two phases and one optional phase. First we generated a uniform posture map which reflected the motion tendency of a human-like articulated body. In this phase, a pre-calculated forward kinematics table is recommended. The forward kinematics table contains the forward kinematics values of each output neuron and it contributes to the reduction of the computational cost in a run-time. In the second phase, we searched the forward kinematics table to find the point with the smallest distance from the desired point, and to choose the posture vector Q associated with the point. In most cases, the posture vector Q has a realistic nature, and its end effector is close enough to the desired point. If an animator wants to make the current end point approach desired point more closely, he could use the traditional CCD algorithm in an optional phase. In the optional phase, we compensated for the solution using the CCD algorithm with constraints according to the DOF range table. The DOF table contains the ranges of each DOF acquired from an experiment and it constrains the degree of rotation of joint through the traditional CCD algorithm. In each step, we checked the calculated rotation angle ϑ whether the resulting angle beyond the limit specified in DOF range table. If the rotation angle ϑ made the DOF exceed its DOF range, we substituted ϑ with $\vartheta/2$, and checked again. This step was repeated until we could find ϑ observing the constraint, or the number of repetition reaching the repetitional limit. If we could find a satisfactory ϑ, we rotated the joint by ϑ; otherwise we processed the next joint. We repeated such entire iteration until the end effector is close enough to the desired position. Algorithm 1 describes the inductive inverse kinematics algorithm.

Algorithm 1: The Inductive Inverse Kinematics Algorithm

Data   : φ (initial angles of joints)

Result : Ψ (the angle set that makes the end effector direct the desired point)

begin

   | initialization

         $\psi \longleftarrow$ the posture vector

         $N \longleftarrow$ the number of links

         $C \longleftarrow$ a watchdog counter

         $\varepsilon \longleftarrow$ a permissible error

         $\eta \longleftarrow$ a permissible count

1   Generate a uniform posture map and build a DOF range table and a forward kinematics table.

2   Search the forward kinematics table to find the point with smallest distance from the desired point.

3   Calculate ϑ of the angle between the vector $\overrightarrow{RE}$ and the vector $\overrightarrow{RD}$ by the dot product of two vectors. $\overrightarrow{RE}$ is the distance from R to E of the current end-effector position and $\overrightarrow{RD}$ is the distance from R to D of the desired endpoint.

4   Calculate $\overrightarrow{P} = \overrightarrow{RD} \times \overrightarrow{RE}$. The vector $\overrightarrow{P}$ is used as the pivot to rotate Nth bone.

5   **if** *the angle ϑ makes the DOF out of its DOF range* **then**

      | $\vartheta = \vartheta/2$.

      | $C = C + 1$.

      | **if** $C < \eta$ **then**

         | Go to Step 5.

      | **else**

         | Go to Step 6.

    else

      | Rotate the bone by ϑ on the $\overrightarrow{P}$.

6   Decrease N.

7   **if** $N \neq 0$ **then**

    | Go to Step 2.

    else

      | Compute D that is the distance between the desired position and the location of the current end effector.

      | **if** $|D < \varepsilon|$ **then**

         | **return** Ψ.

      | **else**

         | Go to Step 2.

end

If the proposed algorithm is applied to control a human-like 3D character, it is possible to get the available posture vector. In robot application, it could be important to get an exact position and direction of the end effector in a 3D space. On the other hand, 3D-character animation production does not require calculations for an exact position and directions of the end effector, but the control of the posture of the character following common behavior patterns. Therefore it is not absolutely necessary to compensate for the resulting posture with the optional posture-compensation process.

3   Experiment and Result

The inductive inverse kinematics algorithm consists of three separate processes: the UPM leaning process, the posture extraction using the UPM, and the optional compensation for the posture using the traditional CCD algorithm. In the UPM leaning process, we used the actual human motion capture data which was acquired with the optical motion-capture system. The right leg of the applied human character was chosen as a testing limb out of the entire skeletal hierarchy, consisting of 3 joints. Then we set a map topology with 9 input neurons, trained the posture map and generated $1,608$ output neurons. After generating a UPM, we calculated the distance between the desired position and all positions of the end effector associated with each output neuron, and selected an output neuron with a minimum distance. If the minimum distance exceeded the predefined acceptable range, we compensate for the resulting posture using the traditional CCD.

Figure 1 shows the variation of the right leg, while the desired point is moved from the point $(20, -60, -70)$ to the point $(20, -45, -50)$. The result proves that the right leg preserves its physical characteristics despite of the movement of the end effector.

Figure 2 shows different results from the CCD and IIK. Figures 2(a) and 2(b) have a desired point $(20, -40, 10)$ and 2(c) and 2(d) have a desired point $(65, -30, 0)$, and 2(e) and 2(f) have a desired point $(-4, -50, -65)$. Figures 2(a), 2(c) and 2(e) are results from the CCD algorithm and 2(b), 2(d) and 2(f) are results from the IIK algorithm. In Fig. 2, a small pink ball (upper ball) specifies the root of the right leg and the cyan ball (bottom ball) specifies the desired position. Three gray balls attached to the end of each links specify the joint. The third link from its root is the foot link. Figures 2(b), 2(d) and 2(f) show that the IIK algorithm observes the physical constraints, and preserves the nature of posture. On the other hand, Figures 2(a), 2(c) and 2(e) show that the CCD algorithm does not consider the nature of posture.

4   Conclusion

The inverse kinematics method is used to control the posture of an articulated body in key frame animation production, but has some common problems in spite of its convenience. A common problem is that most inverse kinematics

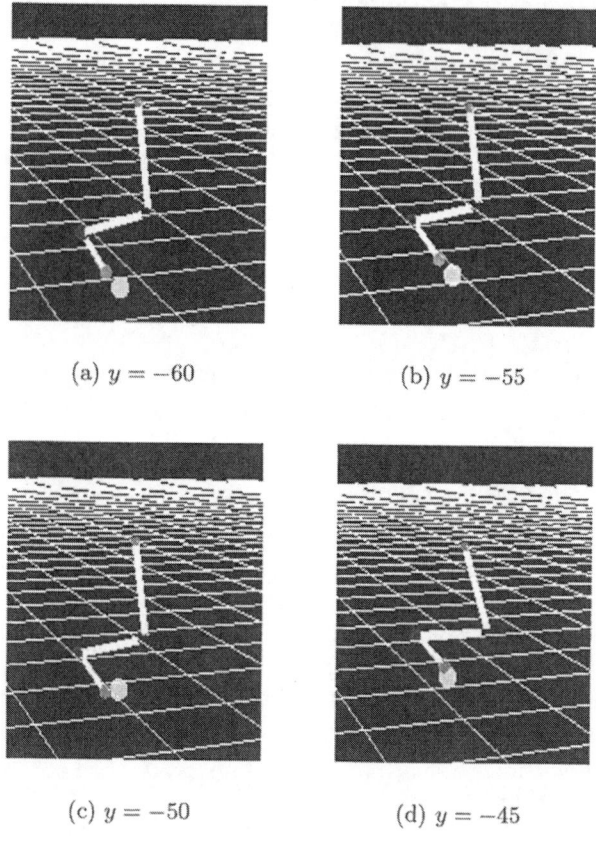

(a) $y = -60$ (b) $y = -55$

(c) $y = -50$ (d) $y = -45$

Fig. 1. Results of applying IIK according to variations of the axis y.

algorithms have multiple solutions for a desired point. If an articulated body has many physical constraints like the human body, the multiple solutions can be divided into two classes: some solutions represent existing posture; others represent unreal posture. With the traditional key-frame method, this problem is solved by repetitious trials and errors by applying inverse kinematics algorithms to each joint separately. However, this requires considerable cost and time. In this paper, the inductive inverse kinematics algorithm is proposed to solve this problem, and we prove that the inductive inverse kinematics can place the end effector on a desired position at a specific time, and that the resulting posture observes physical constraints. Inductive inverse kinematics algorithm increases efficiency to produce the desired key-frame in the animation production and reduces production costs and time. The inductive inverse kinematics algorithm can be applied to various fields such as 3D-character animation, 3D games, and virtual reality.

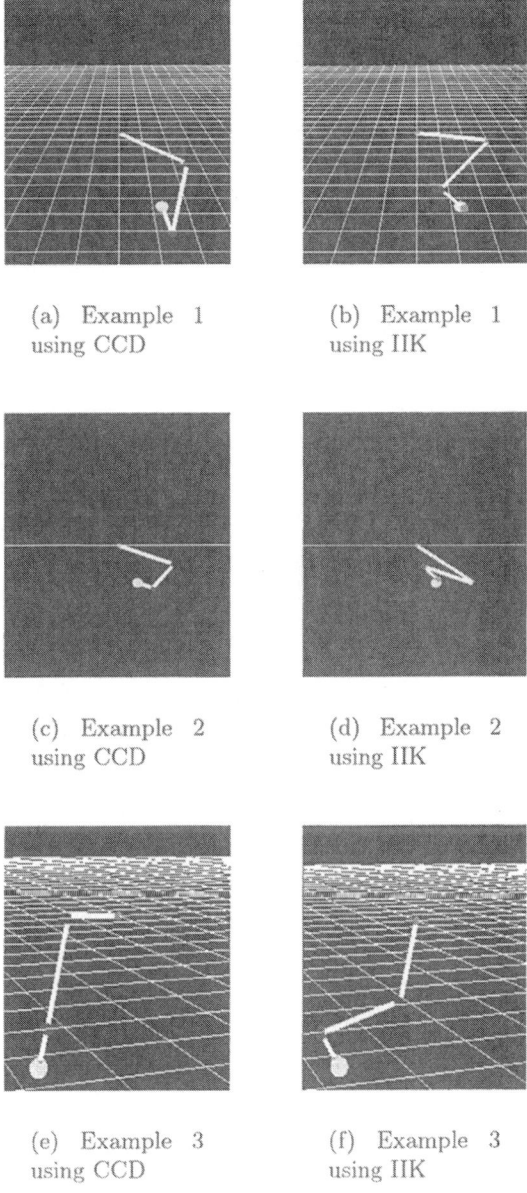

(a) Example 1
using CCD

(b) Example 1
using IIK

(c) Example 2
using CCD

(d) Example 2
using IIK

(e) Example 3
using CCD

(f) Example 3
using IIK

Fig. 2. Comparison of result.

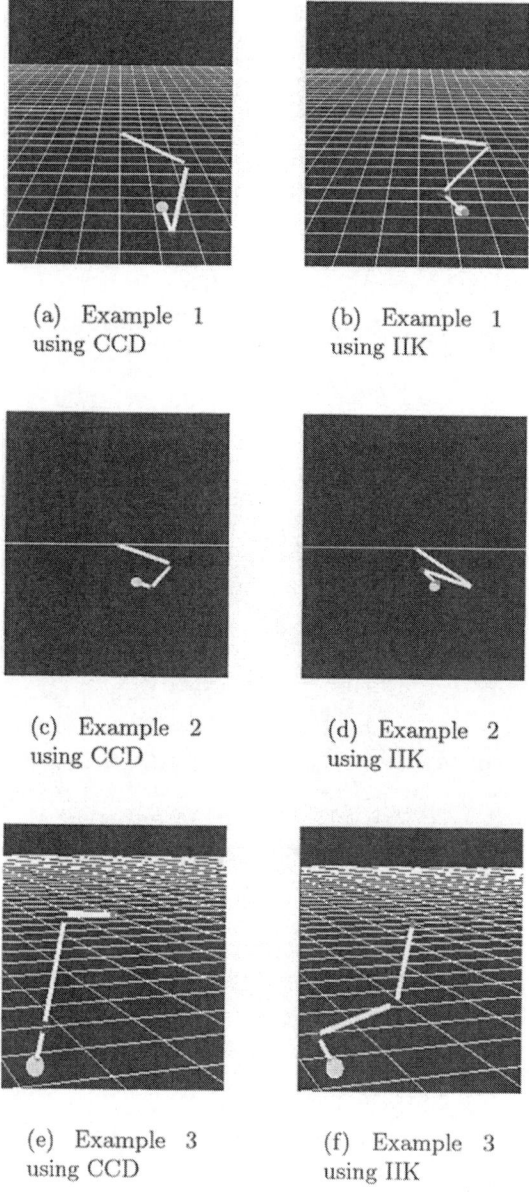

(a) Example 1
using CCD

(b) Example 1
using IIK

(c) Example 2
using CCD

(d) Example 2
using IIK

(e) Example 3
using CCD

(f) Example 3
using IIK

Fig. 2. Comparison of result.

A Fast Implementation of Radial Basis Function Networks with Application to Time Series Forecasting

Rong-bo Huang[1] and Yiu-ming Cheung[2]

[1] Department of Mathematics
Zhong Shan University
Guangzhou, PRC
hrongbo@163.net

[2] Department of Computer Science
Hong Kong Baptist University
Hong Kong, PRC
ymc@comp.hkbu.edu.hk

Abstract. This paper presents a new divide-and-conquer learning approach to radial basis function networks (DCRBF). The DCRBF network is a hybrid system consisting of several sub-RBF networks, each of which takes a sub-input space as its input. Since this system divides a high-dimensional modeling problem into several low-dimensional ones, it can considerably reduce the structural complexity of a RBF network, whereby the net's learning becomes much faster. We have empirically shown its outstanding learning performance on forecasting two real time series as well as synthetic data in comparison with a conventional RBF one.

1 Introduction

In the literature, RBF nets have been intensively studied with a lot of applications, e.g. in data mining [9], pattern recognition [11], and time series forecasting [5,10]. In general, the structural complexity of a RBF network depends on the number of the hidden nodes. Often, the node number increases along with the increase of the net's input dimension. Hence, effective dimension reduction of the net's input space can considerably decrease the network structural complexity, whereby the network's performance converges faster. Traditionally, principle component analysis (PCA) is a prevalent statistical tool for input dimension reduction. Since the PCA technique only uses second-order statistics information to select the first several principal components to be the new representation, some useful information in the non-principal components may be discarded as well during the dimension reduction process. Consequently, the performance of the RBF network may become worse after PCA preprocess [6].

Recently, independent component analysis (ICA) has been widely studied in the fields of neural networks and signal processing. It uses high-order statistics to

J. Liu et al. (Eds.): IDEAL 2003, LNCS 2690, pp. 143–150, 2003.

extract independent components from the inputs. In the literature, it has been shown that ICA outperforms PCA in extracting the hidden feature information and structures from the observations [1,2,7,14]. Actually, our recent paper [6] has successfully applied ICA to reduce the input dimension of a RBF network without deteriorating the net's generalization ability. However, ICA generally does not assign a specific principle order to the extracted components. To our best knowledge, selecting first several principle independent components is still an open problem.

In our recent paper [4], a dual structural radial basis function network has been presented to deal with a recursive RBF. In this dual system, the input is divided into two parts with each modelled by a sub-network. The preliminary studies have shown its success on recursive function estimation. In this paper, we further extend its concept and give out a divide-and-conquer approach to radial basis function (DCRBF) network, in which the original large input space has been decomposed into a direct sum of sub-input spaces. This DCRBF is a hybrid system consisting of several sub-RBF networks that individually take a sub-input as its input. Subsequently, the whole output of the DCRBF is a linear combination of the outputs of these sub-RBF networks. We give out an algorithm to learn the combination coefficients together with the parameters in each sub-network. The experiments on time series forecasting have shown its fast learning speed with a slight improved generalization capabilities in comparison with a conventional RBF network.

2   DCRBF Network

2.1   Architecture

The structure of the DCRBF network is shown in Figure 1. We decompose a RBF network into q sub-networks denoted as RBF_r, $r = 1, 2, \ldots, q$. Let k_r represent the number of hidden units in RBF_r. In the DCRBF, the input separator divides the input space into q sub-ones by a direct sum decomposition. That is, the input of the RBF_r is

$$\mathbf{x}_t(r) = [x_t^{(i_{1,r})}, x_t^{(i_{2,r})}, \ldots, x_t^{(i_{d_r,r})}] \in \mathbf{V}_r \tag{1}$$

where $\{i_{1,r}, i_{2,r}, \ldots, i_{d_r,r}\} \subseteq \{1, 2, \ldots, d\}$. the d_r-dimension $\mathbf{V}_r$ is the rth direct sum subspace of $\mathbf{V}$ such that

$$\mathbf{V}_1 \oplus \mathbf{V}_2 \oplus \ldots \oplus \mathbf{V}_q = \mathbf{V} \tag{2}$$

and

$$\sum_{r=1}^{q} d_r = d. \tag{3}$$

where $\oplus$ means for any $\mathbf{v} \in \mathbf{V}$, there exists a unique $\mathbf{v}_i \in \mathbf{V}_i$, $i = 1, 2, \dots, q$, such that $\mathbf{v} = [\mathbf{v}_1^T, \mathbf{v}_2^T, \dots, \mathbf{v}_q^T]^T$. We let the actual output of the DCRBF network

$$\hat{\mathbf{y}}_t = \sum_{r=1}^{q} c_r \mathbf{z}_t(r), \tag{4}$$

as the estimate of the desired output $\mathbf{y}_t$ at time step t, where $\mathbf{z}_t(r)$ is the RBF_r's output, and c_r is the linear combination coefficient.

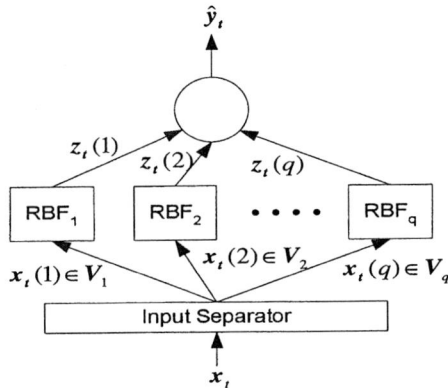

Fig. 1. The DCRBF network model.

2.2 Learning Algorithm

Given the desired output $\mathbf{y}_t$ at time step t, we calculate the output residual

$$\hat{\mathbf{e}}_t = \mathbf{y}_t - \hat{\mathbf{y}}_t. \tag{5}$$

Consequently, we can learn the combination coefficients c_r in Eq. (4) as well as the parameters of each RBF_r's by minimizing the cost function

$$J(\Theta) = \frac{1}{N} \sum_{t=1}^{N} (\mathbf{y}_t - \hat{\mathbf{y}}_t)^T (\mathbf{y}_t - \hat{\mathbf{y}}_t) \tag{6}$$

where N is the number of inputs, $\Theta = \mathbf{C} \bigcup \Theta_1 \bigcup \Theta_2 \bigcup \dots \bigcup \Theta_q$ with $\mathbf{C} = \{c_1, c_2, \dots, c_q\}$, and Θ_r being the parameters of the RBF_r. In implementation, at each step time t, we adaptively tune Θ with a little small step along the descent direction of minimizing $(\mathbf{y}_t - \hat{\mathbf{y}}_t)^T (\mathbf{y}_t - \hat{\mathbf{y}}_t)$. That is, we adjust Θ by

$$c_r^{new} = c_r^{old} + \eta \hat{\mathbf{e}}_t^T \mathbf{z}_t(r), r = 1, 2, \dots, q \tag{7}$$

$$\Theta_r^{new} = \Theta_r^{old} - \eta \frac{\partial J(\Theta)}{\partial \Theta_r} |_{\Theta_r^{old}} \tag{8}$$

where the positive constant η is the learning rate.

The detailed steps in Eq. (8) depend on the implementation of each RBF_r, $r = 1, 2, \ldots, q$ which can be realized by a variety of RBF network models. In this paper, we adopt the Extended Normalized RBF (ENRBF) network proposed in [12]. The general architecture of an ENRBF network is shown in Figure 2. The net's output is

$$\mathbf{z}_t = \sum_{j=1}^{k} (\mathbf{W}_j \mathbf{x}_t + \boldsymbol{\beta}_j) O_j(\mathbf{x}_t) \tag{9}$$

where $\mathbf{z}_t = [z_t^{(1)}, z_t^{(2)}, \ldots, z_t^{(n)}]^T$, $\mathbf{x}_t = [x_t^{(1)}, x_t^{(2)}, \ldots, x_t^{(d)}]^T$ is an input, $\mathbf{W}_j$ is an $n \times d$ matrix and $\boldsymbol{\beta}_j$ is an $n \times 1$ vector. $O_j(\mathbf{x}_t)$ is the output of unit j in the hidden layer with

$$O_j(\mathbf{x}_t) = \frac{\phi[(\mathbf{x}_t - \mathbf{m}_j)^T \Sigma_j^{-1} (\mathbf{x}_t - \mathbf{m}_j)]}{\sum_{i=1}^{k} \phi[(\mathbf{x}_t - \mathbf{m}_i)^T \Sigma_i^{-1} (\mathbf{x}_t - \mathbf{m}_i)]} \tag{10}$$

where $\mathbf{m}_j$ is the center vector, and Σ_j is the receptive field of the basis function $\phi(.)$. In common, the Gaussian function $\phi(s) = exp(-0.5s^2)$ is chosen. Consequently, Eq. (9) becomes

$$\mathbf{z}_t = \sum_{j=1}^{k} (\mathbf{W}_j \mathbf{x}_t + \boldsymbol{\beta}_j) \frac{exp[-0.5(\mathbf{x}_t - \mathbf{m}_j)^T \Sigma_j^{-1} (\mathbf{x}_t - \mathbf{m}_j)]}{\sum_{i=1}^{k} exp[-0.5(\mathbf{x}_t - \mathbf{m}_i)^T \Sigma_i^{-1} (\mathbf{x}_t - \mathbf{m}_i)]}. \tag{11}$$

In the above equation, two parameter sets should be learned. One is $\{\mathbf{m}_j, \Sigma_j | j = 1, 2, \ldots, k\}$ in the hidden layer, and the other is $\{\mathbf{W}_j, \boldsymbol{\beta}_j | j = 1, 2, \ldots, k\}$ in the output layer. In the paper [12], these parameters learning has been connected with the mixture-of-experts model, whereby an expectation-maximization (EM) based single-step learning algorithm is proposed. Here, for simplicity, we prefer to learn the two parameter sets in the same way as the traditional approaches with the two separate steps:

Step 1: Learn $\{\mathbf{m}_j, \Sigma_j | j = 1, 2, \ldots, k\}$ in the hidden layer via a clustering algorithm such as k-means [8], RPCL [13], or RPCCL [3];

Step 2: Learn $\{\mathbf{W}_j, \boldsymbol{\beta}_j | j = 1, 2, \ldots, k\}$ in the output layer under the least mean square criterion. That is, we learn them as well as $\mathbf{C}$ by minimizing Eq. (6). Consequently, the detailed implementations of Step 2 are given as follows:

Step 2.1: Given $\mathbf{x}_t$ and $\mathbf{y}_t$, we calculate $\hat{\mathbf{y}}_t$ by Eq. (4).

Step 2.2: We update

$$\mathbf{W}_j^{new}(r) = \mathbf{W}_j^{old}(r) + \eta \triangle \mathbf{W}_j(r) \tag{12}$$

$$\beta_j^{new}(r) = \beta_j^{old}(r) + \eta \triangle \beta_j(r) \tag{13}$$

with

$$\triangle \mathbf{W}_j(r) = c_r^{old} O_j(\mathbf{x}_t(r)) \hat{\mathbf{e}}_t \mathbf{x}_t(r)^T \tag{14}$$

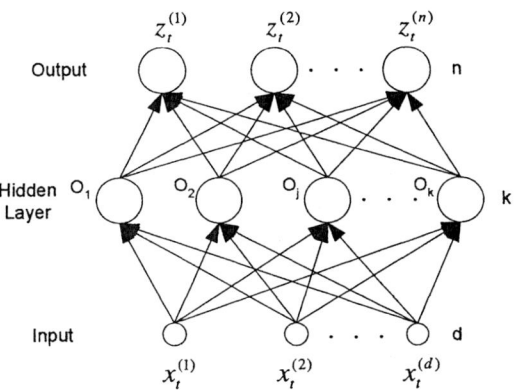

Fig. 2. ENRBF network model.

$$\triangle \beta_j(r) = c_r^{old} O_j(\mathbf{x}_t(r)) \hat{\mathbf{e}}_t \tag{15}$$

where $\{\mathbf{W}_j(r), \beta_j(r) | j = 1, 2, \ldots, k_r, \ r = 1, 2, \ldots, q\}$ is the RBF_r parameter set.

The iterations of Step 2.1 and 2.2 do not stop until the parameters converge.

3   Experimental Results

3.1   Experiment 1

We investigated the performance of the DCRBF network in time series forecasting. We generated 5,100 data points of a time series data with the time-lag order 9 as follows:

$$u(t) = 0.08u^2(t-1) - 0.33u(t-2) + \sin(u(t-3)) + 0.08u(t-4)$$
$$+ 0.2u(t-5) + 0.064u^2(t-6)u(t-7) - 0.6u(t-8)u(t-9). \tag{16}$$

Let,

$$\mathbf{x}_t = [x_t^{(1)}, x_t^{(2)}, \ldots, x_t^{(9)}]$$
$$= [u(t-1), u(t-2), \ldots, u(t-9)]$$

be the input of the RBF network and $y_t = u(t)$ be the output. We let the first 5,000 data points be the training set, and the remaining 100 data points be the testing set. The input space of RBF network was decomposed into three subspaces with the input dimension $d_1 = 2, d_2 = 3, d_3 = 4$ respectively. Meanwhile, the RBF network was decomposed into three sub-networks with the size of hidden nodes $k_1 = 2, k_2 = 2, k_3 = 2$ respectively. Let the size of hidden units in the conventional ENRBF network be $k = 6$. In the experiment, we fixed the learning rate $\eta = 0.0001$. The performance on the testing set of ENRBF and DCRBF under the MSE criterion is shown in Figure 3. We found that the DCRBF network converges much faster than the ENRBF network.

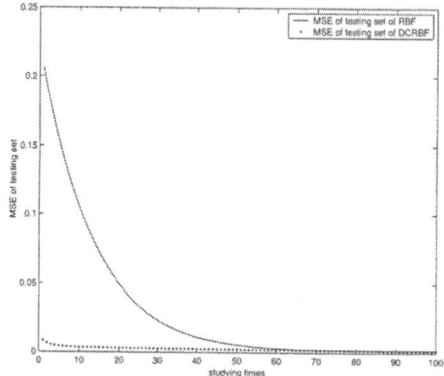

Fig. 3. The comparison between the performance of ENRBF network and DCRBF network on the synthetic time-series data.

3.2 Experiment 2

We performed an experiment on the benchmark data getting from the famous Rob Hyndman's Time Series Data Library. We used the FOREX daily foreign exchange rates of 9 countries from 31st December, 1979 to 31st December, 1998 with the 4,774 data points in total. We let the first 4,674 data be the training set, and the remaining 100 data be the testing set. Also, we set the dimension of input space of ENRBF network at $d = 9$, which was further decomposed into three subspaces with the input dimension $d_1 = 2, d_2 = 3, d_3 = 4$ respectively. We let the number of hidden units in the ENRBF network be $k = 8$, while the number of hidden units in the three sub-networks of the DCRBF be $k_1 = 2, k_2 = 3, k_3 = 3$ respectively. The experimental result is shown in Figure 4. It can be seen again that the DCRBF network converges much faster than the ENRBF with a slight improvement of net's generalization ability.

3.3 Experiment 3

We applied the DCRBF in the famous time series of annual average number of the sunspot from year 1700 to 1979 observed by Rudolph Wolf. We used the first 250 data to be the training set, and the remaining 30 to be the testing set. The number of hidden units of the ENRBF network was $k = 8$, while the hidden units of the three sub-networks in the DCRBF were $k_1 = 2, k_2 = 3, k_3 = 3$. We let the input dimension of the ENRBF be $d = 9$, and the input dimension of three decomposed sub-network in DCRBF be $d_1 = 3, d_2 = 3, d_3 = 3$. The experimental results are shown in Figure 5. Once again, we found that the DCRBF converges much faster than the ENRBF with a slight better generalization ability.

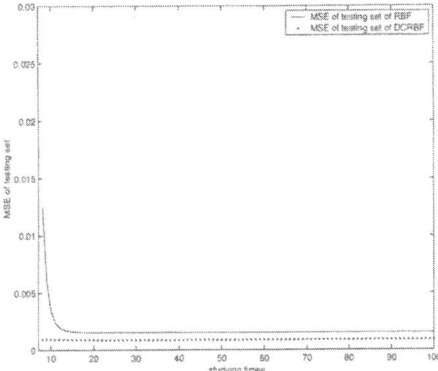

Fig. 4. The comparison between the performance of RBF network and DCRBF network on FOREX daily foreign exchange data.

4 Concluding Remarks

We have presented a divide-and-conquer learning approach for RBF network (DCRBF), which is a hybrid system consisting of several sub-RBF networks. Since this system divides a high-dimensional modelling problem into several low-dimensional ones, its structural complexity is generally simpler than a conventional RBF network. The experiments have shown that the proposed approach has a much faster learning speed with a slight better generalization ability. In this paper, we decompose the input space into sub-input spaces heuristically without the guidance of a general rule. Further studies are therefore still desired.

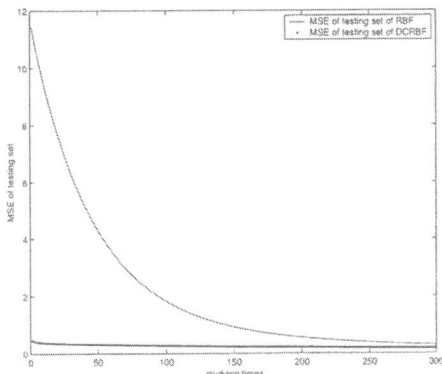

Fig. 5. The comparison between the performance of the ENRBF and the DCRBF networks on sunspot data.

Acknowledgment. The work described in this paper was supported by a Faculty Research Grant of Hong Kong Baptist University with the project code: FRG/02-03/II-40.

References

1. A. D. Back, A. S. Weigend, "A First Application of Independent Component Analysis to Extracting Structure from Stock Returns," *International Journal of Neural System*, Vol. 8(4), pp. 473–484, 1997.
2. M. S. Bartlett, H. M. Lades, T. J. Sejnowski, "Independent Component Representations for Face Recognition," *Proceedings of the SPIE Symposium on Electronic Imaging: Science and Technology; Conference on Human Vision and Electronic Imaging III*, pp. 528–539, 1998.
3. Y. M. Cheung, "Rival Penalization Controlled Competitive Learning for Data Clustering with Unknown Cluster Number", *Proceedings of 9th International Conference on Neural Information Processing* (Paper ID: 1983 in CD-ROM Proceeding), Singapore, November 18–22, 2002
4. Y. M. Cheung, L. Xu, "A Dual Structure Radial Basis Function Network for Recursive Function Estimation," *Proceedings of International Conference on Neural Information Processing (ICONIP'2001)*, Vol. 2, pp. 1903–1097, 2001.
5. N. Davey, S. P. Hunt, R. J. Frank, "Time Series Prediction and Neural Networks," *Journal of Intelligent and Robotic Systems*, Vol. 31, pp. 91–103, 2001.
6. R. B. Huang, L. T. Law, Y. M. Cheung, "An Experimental Study: On Reducing RBF Input Dimension by ICA and PCA," *Proceedings of 1st International Conference on Machine Learning and Cybernetics 2002 (ICMLC'02)*, Vol. 4, pp. 1941–1946, Beijing, Novermber 4–5, 2002.
7. G. J. Jang, T. W. Lee, Y. H. Oh, "Learning Statistically Efficient Features for Speaker Recognition," *Proceedings of IEEE International Conference on Acoustics, Speech and Signal Processing*, Salt Lake City, Utah, May, 2001.
8. J. MacQueen, "Some Methods for Classification and Analysis of Multivariate Observations," *Proceedings of the Fifth Berkeley Symposium on Mathematical statistics and probability, Berkeley, University of California Press*, Vol. 1, pp. 281–297, 1967.
9. K. J. McGarry, S. Wermter, J. MacIntyre, "Knowledge Extraction from Radial Basis Function Networks and Multilayer Perceptrons," *Proceeding of International Joint Conference on Neural Networks*, Vol. 4, pp. 2494–2497, 1999.
10. A. Saranli, B. Baykal, "Chaotic time-series prediction and the relocating LMS (RLMS) algorithm for radial basis function networks," *European Signal Processing Conference (EUSIPCO)*, Vol. 2, pp. 1247–1250, September 1996.
11. B. Verma, "Handwritten Hindi Character Recognition using RBF and MLP Neural Networks," *IEEE International Conference on Neural Networks (ICNN)*, Perth, pp. 86–92, 1995.
12. L. Xu, "RBF Nets, Mixture Experts, and Bayesian Ying-Yang Learning," *Neurocomputing*, Vol. 19, No. 1–3,pp. 223–257, 1998.
13. L. Xu, "Rival Penalized Competitive Learning, Finite Mixture, and Multisets Clustering," *Proceedings International Joint Conference on Neural Networks*, May 5–9, 1998, Anchorage, Alaska, Vol. II, pp. 2525–2530, 1998.
14. A. Ziehe, G. Nolte, T. Sander, K. R. Muller, G. Curio, "A Comparison of ICA-based Artifact Redction Methods for MEG," *12th International Conference on Biomagnetism*, Helsinki University of Technology, Finland, 2000.

On the Effects of Outliers on Evolutionary Optimization

Dirk V. Arnold and Hans-Georg Beyer

Department of Computer Science XI
University of Dortmund
44221 Dortmund, Germany
{dirk.arnold,hans-georg.beyer}@cs.uni-dortmund.de

Abstract. Most studies concerned with the effects of noise on evolutionary computation have assumed a Gaussian noise model. However, practical optimization strategies frequently face situations where the noise is not Gaussian, and sometimes it does not even have a finite variance. In particular, outliers may be present. In this paper, Cauchy distributed noise is used for modeling such situations. A performance law that describes how the progress of an evolution strategy using intermediate recombination scales in the presence of such noise is derived. Implications of that law are studied numerically, and comparisons with the case of Gaussian noise are drawn.

1 Introduction

In studies of optimization strategies, it is frequently assumed that the objective function value of a candidate solution can be determined exactly. However, given the noisy nature of many real-world optimization problems, that assumption often is an idealization. Noise can stem from sources as different as — and not restricted to — measurement limitations, the use of randomized algorithms, incomplete sampling of large spaces, and human computer interaction. Understanding how noise impacts the performance of optimization strategies is important for choosing appropriate strategy variants, for the sizing of strategy parameters, and for the design of new, more noise resistant algorithms.

A number of studies have dealt with the effects of noise on the performance of genetic algorithms. Fitzpatrick and Grefenstette [11] have explored the tradeoff between averaging over multiple fitness evaluations versus increasing the population size. Rattray and Shapiro [13] have studied finite population effects in the presence of additive Gaussian noise. Miller and Goldberg [12] have investigated the effect of Gaussian noise on different selection mechanisms. A more extensive overview of related work can be found in [8].

In the realm of evolution strategies, we have studied the effects of noise on the local performance of the algorithms by considering a noisy version of the sphere model. A comprehensive summary of the work can be found in [2]. In [5], the performance of the $(1 + 1)$-ES has been studied. It was found that the overvaluation of the fitness of candidate solutions that results from the use

J. Liu et al. (Eds.): IDEAL 2003, LNCS 2690, pp. 151–160, 2003.

of plus-selection severely affects both the local performance of the strategy and the functioning of success probability based step length adaptation mechanisms. In [4], a performance law has been derived for the $(\mu/\mu, \lambda)$-ES with intermediate recombination. In [3], that performance law has been used to address the issue of resampling in order to reduce the amount of noise present. It was found that in contrast to results obtained for the $(1, \lambda)$-ES, for the $(\mu/\mu, \lambda)$-ES, increasing the population size is preferable to averaging over multiple samples if the truncation ratio μ/λ is chosen appropriately. This is an encouraging result as it shows that the evolution strategy is able to handle the noise more effectively than by blind averaging. The influence of finite search space dimensionalities has been explored in [6]. Finally, in [7], the performance of evolution strategies in the presence of noise has been compared with that of other direct search algorithms.

All of the aforementioned studies as well as many other investigations of the effects of noise on the performance of optimization strategies have in common that either Gaussian noise or at least noise of a finite variance is assumed. However, it is doubtful whether Gaussian noise satisfactorily models all variants of noise that occur in practical applications. There is a possibility that the results that have been obtained may qualitatively depend on that assumption.

Beyer, Olhofer, and Sendhoff [9] have considered particular situations involving non-Gaussian noise. Their approach is to apply transformations that make the noise nearly Gaussian and to then use the results obtained for the case of Gaussian noise. While proceeding as such extends significantly the realm of situations that can be considered, there are situations where a transformation that makes the noise nearly Gaussian is not possible. In particular, in practice, optimization strategies frequently face outliers. In order to model such situations, noise distributions with tails much longer than those of a normal distribution need to be considered. One such distribution is the Cauchy distribution that has impacted the optimization literature in the past not as a noise model but as a mutation strategy. Szu and Hartley [17] have suggested to use Cauchy distributed mutations in simulated annealing in order to better be able to escape local optima by occasional long jumps. Rudolph [15] has studied the effects of Cauchy distributed mutations in evolution strategy optimization.

In the present paper, we investigate the effects that outliers have on the performance of the $(\mu/\mu, \lambda)$-ES by considering Cauchy distributed noise. The choice of strategy is motivated both by the fact that it is relatively amenable to mathematical analysis and by its proven good performance. In Sect. 2, the strategy as well as the fitness environment considered are introduced. As outliers need to be modeled, a transformation to normality of the noise is not possible. Also, as the Cauchy distribution does not have finite moments, an approach using expansions of probability distributions in terms of their moments is excluded. In Sect. 3, the expected average of concomitants of selected Cauchy order statistics is computed. As a result of the calculations, numerical comparisons of the effects of Cauchy noise with those of Gaussian noise can be performed in Sect. 4. We conclude with a brief discussion of the results and suggest directions for future research.

2 Preliminaries

The $(\mu/\mu, \lambda)$-ES in every time step generates $\lambda > \mu$ offspring candidate solutions from a population of μ parents and subsequently replaces the parental population by the μ best of the offspring. Using isotropic normal mutations, for real-valued objective functions $f : I\!R^N \to I\!R$, generation of an offspring candidate solution consists of adding a vector $\sigma\mathbf{z}$, where $\mathbf{z}$ consists of independent, standard normally distributed components, to the centroid of the parental population. The standard deviation σ of the components of vector $\sigma\mathbf{z}$ is referred to as the mutation strength, vector $\mathbf{z}$ as a mutation vector. The average of those mutation vectors that correspond to offspring candidate solutions that are selected to form the population of the next time step is the progress vector $\langle\mathbf{z}\rangle$.

Since the early work of Rechenberg [14], the local performance of evolution strategies has commonly been studied on a class of functions known as the sphere model. The sphere model is the set of all functions $f : I\!R^N \to I\!R$ with

$$f(\mathbf{x}) = g(\|\hat{\mathbf{x}} - \mathbf{x}\|),$$

where $g : I\!R \to I\!R$ is a strictly monotonic function of the distance $R = \|\mathbf{R}\| = \|\hat{\mathbf{x}} - \mathbf{x}\|$ of a candidate solution $\mathbf{x}$ from the optimizer $\hat{\mathbf{x}}$. It has frequently served as a model for fitness landscapes at a stage where the population of candidate solutions is in relatively close proximity to the optimizer and is most often studied in the limit of very high search space dimensionality. In this paper, it is assumed that there is noise present in the process of evaluating the objective function in that evaluating a candidate solution $\mathbf{x}$ does not yield the candidate solution's true fitness $f(\mathbf{x})$, but a noisy fitness

$$f_\epsilon(\mathbf{x}) = f(\mathbf{x}) + \sigma_\epsilon Z, \tag{1}$$

where Z is a random variable. While in our previous work, we had always assumed that the distribution of Z is standard normal, in the present paper, the case that Z is drawn from a Cauchy distribution is investigated.

A commonly used measure for the performance of evolution strategies on the sphere model is the progress rate

$$\varphi^{(t)} = \mathrm{E}\left[\langle R\rangle^{(t)} - \langle R\rangle^{(t+1)}\right]$$

that is defined as the expectation of the decrease in the distance between the population centroid and the optimizer in a single time step. The commonly used approach to computing the progress rate relies on a decomposition of vectors that is illustrated in Fig. 1. A vector $\mathbf{z}$ originating at search space location $\mathbf{x}$ can be written as the sum of two vectors $\mathbf{z}_A$ and $\mathbf{z}_B$, where $\mathbf{z}_A$ is parallel to $\mathbf{R} = \hat{\mathbf{x}} - \mathbf{x}$ and $\mathbf{z}_B$ is in the hyperplane perpendicular to that. In the present context, $\mathbf{z}$ can be either a mutation vector or a progress vector. The vectors $\mathbf{z}_A$ and $\mathbf{z}_B$ are referred to as the central and lateral components of vector $\mathbf{z}$, respectively. The signed length z_A of the central component of vector $\mathbf{z}$ is defined to equal $\|\mathbf{z}_A\|$ if $\mathbf{z}_A$ points towards the optimizer and to equal $-\|\mathbf{z}_A\|$ if it points away from it.

In what follows, we make use of a number of simplifications that hold exactly in the limit $N \to \infty$, but that have been seen to provide good approximations for

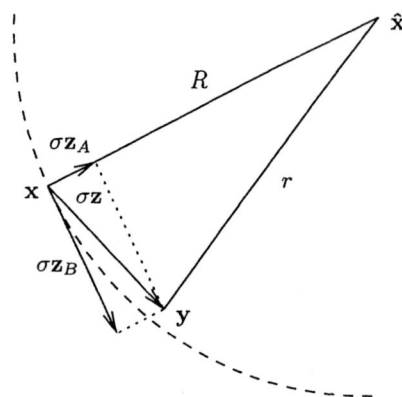

Fig. 1. *Decomposition of a vector* $\mathbf{z}$ *into central component* $\mathbf{z}_A$ *and lateral component* $\mathbf{z}_B$. *Vector* $\mathbf{z}_A$ *is parallel to* $\hat{\mathbf{x}} - \mathbf{x}$, *vector* $\mathbf{z}_B$ *is in the hyperplane perpendicular to that. The starting and end points,* $\mathbf{x}$ *and* $\mathbf{y} = \mathbf{x} + \sigma\mathbf{z}$, *of vector* $\sigma\mathbf{z}$ *are at distances* R *and* r *from the optimizer* $\hat{\mathbf{x}}$, *respectively.*

moderately large values of N already. A more complete justification of the argument that follows and that remains somewhat sketchy due to space limitations can be found in [4].

The $(\mu/\mu, \lambda)$-ES applies all mutations to a single point — the population centroid. Selection of candidate solutions is on the basis of their (noisy) fitness. The lateral components of all mutation vectors contribute equally to the fitness of the offspring candidate solutions they generate. They are thus selectively neutral. The contribution of the central components of the mutation vectors to the fitness of the offspring candidate solutions is asymptotically normal. Introducing normalizations

$$\sigma^* = \sigma\frac{N}{\langle R \rangle}, \quad \sigma_\epsilon^* = \sigma_\epsilon\frac{N}{\langle R \rangle g'(\langle R \rangle)}, \quad \text{and} \quad \varphi^* = \varphi\frac{N}{\langle R \rangle},$$

and defining the noise-to-signal ratio $\vartheta = \sigma_\epsilon^*/\sigma^*$, the performance law

$$\varphi^* = \sigma^* M_{\mu/\mu, \lambda}(\vartheta) - \frac{\sigma^{*2}}{2\mu} \tag{2}$$

has been derived in [4]. The first term on the right hand side of the equation is due to the central component of the progress vector, the second term is due to its lateral component. The factor μ in the denominator of the second term is a result of the independence of the lateral components of the mutation vectors and signifies the presence of genetic repair. The term $M_{\mu/\mu, \lambda}(\vartheta)$ is frequently referred to as the progress coefficient and results from the (noisy) selection of μ of the λ offspring candidate solutions that have been generated. It is to be defined more formally and computed for the case of Cauchy noise in the next section.

3 Determining the Progress Coefficient

Let Y be a standard normally distributed random variable corresponding to the standardized contributions of the central components of the mutation vectors to the true fitness of the offspring candidate solutions they generate. Letting Z be the noise variate from Eq. (1), random variable X is defined as

$$X = Y + \vartheta Z \qquad (3)$$

and reflects the standardized noisy fitness of an offspring candidate solution. We generate λ bivariate observations $(X_1, Y_1), \ldots, (X_\lambda, Y_\lambda)$ by λ times independently sampling Y and Z and using Eq. (3). We then order the observations by their X variates. The order statistics of X are denoted as usual by $X_{i:\lambda}$, $1 \leq i \leq \lambda$. That is, $X_{1:\lambda} \leq X_{2:\lambda} \leq \cdots \leq X_{\lambda:\lambda}$. The Y variate associated with $X_{i:\lambda}$ is called the concomitant of the ith order statistic and is denoted by $Y_{i:\lambda}$. The term $M_{\mu/\mu,\lambda}(\vartheta)$ from Sect. 2 is the expectation of the average of the concomitants of the μ largest order statistics

$$M_{\mu/\mu,\lambda}(\vartheta) = \mathrm{E}\left[\frac{1}{\mu}\sum_{i=1}^{\mu} Y_{\lambda-i+1;\lambda}\right]. \qquad (4)$$

For the case of Gaussian noise, $M_{\mu/\mu,\lambda}(\vartheta)$ has been computed in [4]. The derivation that follows assumes a general noise distribution and closely parallels the aforementioned one. The specialization to the case of Cauchy noise will be presented in Sect. 4. The reader not interested in the particulars of the calculations may safely skip the following paragraphs and jump to Eq. (6) for the result.

Let $P(y) = \Phi(y)$ denote the cumulative distribution function (cdf) of the standardized normal distribution, and let $p(y) = \mathrm{d}\Phi/\mathrm{d}y = \exp(-y^2/2)/\sqrt{2\pi}$ denote the corresponding probability density function (pdf). Furthermore, let $P_\epsilon(z)$ and $p_\epsilon(z)$ denote the cdf and the pdf, respectively, of the ϑZ variate. The distribution of the X variate is the convolution of those of the other two variates and thus has pdf

$$q(x) = \int_{-\infty}^{\infty} p(y)p_\epsilon(x-y)\mathrm{d}y. \qquad (5)$$

The corresponding cdf $Q(x)$ can be obtained by integration.

According to David and Nagaraja [10], the pdf of the concomitant of the ith order statistic is

$$p_{i;\lambda}(y) = \frac{\lambda!}{(\lambda-i)!(i-1)!}p(y)\int_{-\infty}^{\infty} p_\epsilon(x-y)[1-Q(x)]^{\lambda-i}[Q(x)]^{i-1}\mathrm{d}x.$$

Using this pdf in Eq. (4) and swapping the order of the integration and summation, the expectation of the average of the μ selected concomitants is

$$M_{\mu/\mu,\lambda}(\vartheta) = \frac{1}{\mu}\sum_{i=1}^{\mu}\int_{-\infty}^{\infty} y p_{\lambda-i+1;\lambda}(y)\mathrm{d}y$$

$$= \frac{\lambda!}{\mu}\int_{-\infty}^{\infty} y p(y)\int_{-\infty}^{\infty} p_\epsilon(x-y)\sum_{i=1}^{\mu}\frac{[Q(x)]^{\lambda-i}[1-Q(x)]^{i-1}}{(\lambda-i)!(i-1)!}\mathrm{d}x\mathrm{d}y.$$

Using the identity (compare Abramowitz and Stegun [1], Eqs. **6.6.4** and **26.5.1**)

$$\sum_{i=1}^{\mu} \frac{Q^{\lambda-i}[1-Q]^{i-1}}{(\lambda-i)!(i-1)!} = \frac{1}{(\lambda-\mu-1)!(\mu-1)!} \int_0^Q z^{\lambda-\mu-1}[1-z]^{\mu-1}dz,$$

it follows

$$M_{\mu/\mu,\lambda}(\vartheta) = (\lambda-\mu)\binom{\lambda}{\mu}\int_{-\infty}^{\infty} yp(y)\int_{-\infty}^{\infty} p_\epsilon(x-y)$$
$$\int_0^{Q(x)} z^{\lambda-\mu-1}[1-z]^{\mu-1}dzdxdy.$$

Substituting $z = Q(w)$ yields

$$M_{\mu/\mu,\lambda}(\vartheta) = (\lambda-\mu)\binom{\lambda}{\mu}\int_{-\infty}^{\infty} yp(y)\int_{-\infty}^{\infty} p_\epsilon(x-y)$$
$$\int_{-\infty}^{x} q(w)[Q(w)]^{\lambda-\mu-1}[1-Q(w)]^{\mu-1}dwdxdy.$$

Changing the order of the integrations results in

$$M_{\mu/\mu,\lambda}(\vartheta) = (\lambda-\mu)\binom{\lambda}{\mu}\int_{-\infty}^{\infty} q(w)[Q(w)]^{\lambda-\mu-1}[1-Q(w)]^{\mu-1}I(w)dw,$$

where, using the fact that the mean of the standardized normal distribution is zero,

$$I(w) = \int_{-\infty}^{\infty} yp(y)\int_{w}^{\infty} p_\epsilon(x-y)dxdy$$
$$= \int_{-\infty}^{\infty} yp(y)[1-P_\epsilon(w-y)]dy$$
$$= \int_{-\infty}^{\infty} [-yp(y)]P_\epsilon(w-y)dy.$$

As $dp/dy = -yp(y)$, partial integration yields

$$I(w) = p(y)P_\epsilon(w-y)\Big|_{-\infty}^{\infty} + \int_{-\infty}^{\infty} p(y)p_\epsilon(w-y)dy.$$

The first of the two terms on the right hand side equals zero. Comparison of the second term with Eq. (5) shows that $I(w) = q(w)$ and therefore that

$$M_{\mu/\mu,\lambda}(\vartheta) = (\lambda-\mu)\binom{\lambda}{\mu}\int_{-\infty}^{\infty} [q(w)]^2[Q(w)]^{\lambda-\mu-1}[1-Q(w)]^{\mu-1}dw. \quad (6)$$

The remaining integral generally cannot be solved in closed form but needs to be evaluated numerically.

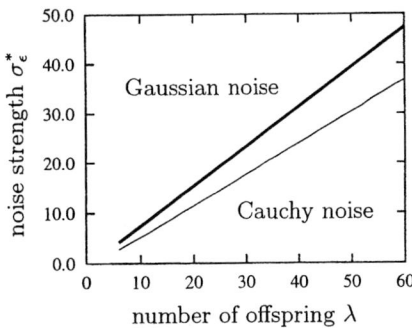

Fig. 2. *The normalized noise strength σ_ϵ^* up to which nonzero progress is possible as a function of the number of offspring λ generated per time step. The truncation ratio μ/λ is chosen to be optimal. The bold line represents the result for Gaussian noise, the thin line that for Cauchy noise.*

4   Gaussian Noise versus Cauchy Noise

In case the distribution of the noise is Gaussian, the distribution of the X variates is the convolution of two normal variates and is thus itself normal. More specifically, the cdf of the X variate is $Q(w) = \Phi(w/\sqrt{1+\vartheta^2})$. Using the substitution $x = w/\sqrt{1+\vartheta^2}$ in Eq. (6), it follows

$$M_{\mu/\mu,\lambda}^{(\text{Gauss})}(\vartheta) = \frac{c_{\mu/\mu,\lambda}}{\sqrt{1+\vartheta^2}} \tag{7}$$

for the progress coefficient, where

$$c_{\mu/\mu,\lambda} = \frac{\lambda-\mu}{2\pi}\binom{\lambda}{\mu}\int_{-\infty}^{\infty}e^{-x^2}[\Phi(x)]^{\lambda-\mu-1}[1-\Phi(x)]^{\mu-1}dx$$

is independent of the noise level ϑ and depends on the population size parameters μ and λ only. The result agrees with that from [4]. In that reference, it has been seen that the strong performance of the $(\mu/\mu,\lambda)$-ES in the presence of Gaussian noise is due to the presence of genetic repair. The factor μ in the denominator of the fraction in Eq. (2) not only reduces the term that makes a negative contribution to the progress rate, but it also has the effect that the search space can be explored at higher mutation strengths. Those increased mutation strengths decrease the noise-to-signal ratio $\vartheta = \sigma_\epsilon^*/\sigma^*$ that the strategy operates under and make the $(\mu/\mu,\lambda)$-ES vastly more efficient than other types of evolution strategy on the noisy sphere.

In the case of Cauchy noise, separating the influence of ϑ from that of μ and λ is not possible. The cdf and the pdf of the noise term are $P_\epsilon(z) = 1/2 + \arctan(z/\vartheta)/\pi$ and $p_\epsilon(z) = \vartheta/(\pi(\vartheta^2 + z^2))$, respectively. In order to numerically evaluate the integral in Eq. (6), both the pdf and the cdf of the X variate need to be determined. For that purpose, either Eq. (5) can be used or an approach based on characteristic functions can be employed. The characteristic function of the Y variates is $\phi(t) = \exp(-t^2/2)$, that of the noise term in Eq. (3) is $\exp(-\vartheta|t|)$. The characteristic function of the convolution is the product of the two. According to Stuart and Ord [16], the pdf of the X variates can be obtained from that characteristic function and be written as

$$q(x) = \frac{1}{\pi}e^{\vartheta^2/2}\int_0^{\infty}\cos(tx)\exp\left(-\frac{1}{2}(t+\vartheta)^2\right)dt.$$

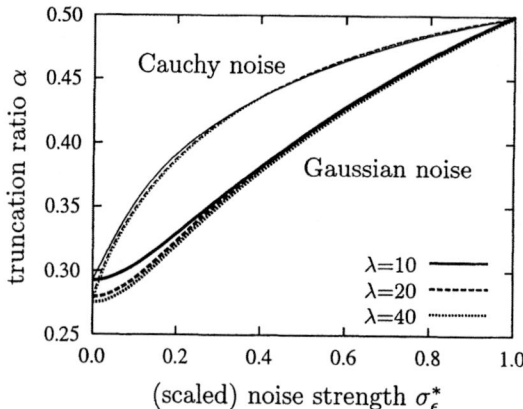

Fig. 3. *The optimal truncation ratio as a function of the normalized noise strength σ_ϵ^*. The normalized noise strengths on the horizontal axis have been scaled by division by the maximum normalized noise strength for which nonzero progress is possible. The bold lines represent results for Gaussian noise, the thin lines those for Cauchy noise.*

The corresponding cdf can be obtained by integration and be written as

$$Q(x) = \frac{1}{2} + \frac{1}{\pi} e^{\vartheta^2/2} \int_0^\infty \frac{\sin(tx)}{t} \exp\left(-\frac{1}{2}(t+\vartheta)^2\right) dt.$$

Using those relationships in the numerical evaluation of Eq. (6) yields results that make it possible to compare the performance of the $(\mu/\mu, \lambda)$-ES in the presence of Cauchy noise with that in the presence of Gaussian noise. It is important to keep in mind, however, that a naive quantitative comparison is problematic due to the basic incomparability of the parameter ϑ for the two types of distribution. While in the case of Gaussian noise ϑ is the standard deviation, in the case of Cauchy noise ϑ is simply a scale parameter the choice of which is somewhat arbitrary. Nonetheless, keeping that caveat in mind and proceeding with care, meaningful comparisons can be made.

One of the main results of the analysis in [4] is that in the presence of Gaussian noise, the $(\mu/\mu, \lambda)$-ES is capable of nonzero progress up to a normalized noise strength σ_ϵ^* that is proportional to the number of offspring λ generated per time step. As a consequence, by sufficiently increasing the population size, positive progress on the noisy sphere can be achieved for any noise strength. Increased population sizes make it possible to use larger mutation strengths that in turn reduce the noise-to-signal ratio ϑ. Figure 2 has been obtained by numerically evaluating Eq. (6) and suggests that that benefit of genetic repair is enjoyed also in the presence of Cauchy noise. As for Gaussian noise, the noise strength up to which progress is possible appears to be linear in λ.

A second important insight gained in [3] is that the $(\mu/\mu, \lambda)$-ES can partially compensate for a lack of reliable information by using the noisy information provided by a larger number of parents than it would optimally use in the absence of noise. While in the absence of noise, the $(\mu/\mu, \lambda)$-ES ideally operates

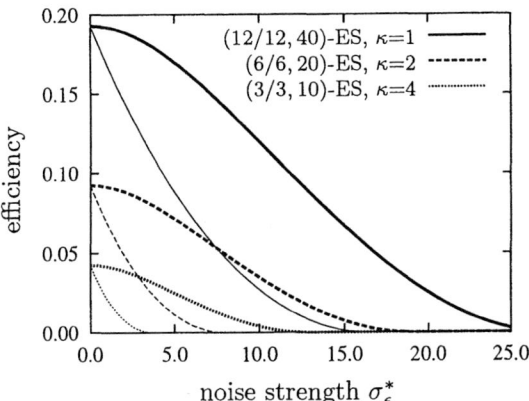

Fig. 4. *The efficiencies (defined as the normalized maximum progress rate per evaluation of the objective function) of various $(\mu/\mu, \lambda)$-ES that average κ objective function measurements as functions of the normalized noise strength σ_ϵ^*. The bold lines represent results for Gaussian noise, the thin lines those for Cauchy noise. Note that direct comparisons between curves corresponding to different noise models are relatively meaningless as explained in the text.*

with a truncation ratio $\alpha = \mu/\lambda$ in the vicinity of 0.27, that value gradually increases to 0.5 at the point where nonzero progress ceases to be possible. Figure 3 demonstrates that the same is true in the presence of Cauchy noise.

Finally, it has been seen in [3] that in the presence of Gaussian noise, larger population sizes are preferable to averaging over multiple evaluations of candidate solutions. The averaging in search space that is implicit in the recombination procedure of the $(\mu/\mu, \lambda)$-ES is more powerful than the explicit averaging of $\kappa > 1$ objective function values in fitness space. In the presence of Gaussian noise, averaging κ samples reduces the variance of the noise by a factor of κ. For Cauchy noise, the average of κ independent samples has the same distribution as the individual samples, rendering resampling entirely useless. Figure 4 confirms that by showing that while all of the strategies in that figure use the same number of objective function evaluations per time step, those that do not resample but rather rely on larger population sizes have the highest efficiencies.

To conclude, the differences between the effects that Gaussian noise and Cauchy noise have on the performance of the $(\mu/\mu, \lambda)$-ES are merely quantitative. Outliers that are frequent in the case of Cauchy noise do not lead to qualitatively new effects. The important conclusions with respect to the choice of population size parameters and to the use of resampling that were drawn for the case of Gaussian noise in previous studies remain valid in the case of Cauchy noise. It is important, however, to note that that result cannot be expected to hold for strategies in which candidate solutions can survive for several time steps and are not reevaluated periodically. The investigation of the behavior of such strategies as well as the analysis of the influence of finite search space dimensionalities along the lines of [6] remain as challenges for future research.

Acknowledgments. This work was supported by the Deutsche Forschungsgemeinschaft (DFG) under grant Be 1578/6-3 as well as through the Collaborative Research Center SFB531.

References

1. M. Abramowitz and I. A. Stegun. *Handbook of Mathematical Functions.* Dover, New York, 1965.
2. D. V. Arnold. *Noisy Optimization with Evolution Strategies.* Genetic Algorithms and Evolutionary Computation Series. Kluwer Academic Publishers, Norwell, MA, 2002.
3. D. V. Arnold and H.-G. Beyer. Efficiency and self-adaptation of the $(\mu/\mu_I, \lambda)$-ES in a noisy environment. In M. Schoenauer et al., editor, *Parallel Problem Solving from Nature — PPSN VI,* pages 39–48. Springer Verlag, Berlin, 2000.
4. D. V. Arnold and H.-G. Beyer. Local performance of the $(\mu/\mu_I, \lambda)$-ES in a noisy environment. In W. N. Martin and W. M. Spears, editors, *Foundations of Genetic Algorithms 6,* pages 127–141. Morgan Kaufmann, San Francisco, 2001.
5. D. V. Arnold and H.-G. Beyer. Local performance of the $(1 + 1)$-ES in a noisy environment. *IEEE Transactions on Evolutionary Computation,* 6(1):30–41, 2002.
6. D. V. Arnold and H.-G. Beyer. Performance analysis of evolution strategies with multi-recombination in high-dimensional $I\!R^N$-search spaces disturbed by noise. *Theoretical Computer Science,* 289(1):629–647, 2002.
7. D. V. Arnold and H.-G. Beyer. A comparison of evolution strategies with other direct search methods in the presence of noise. *Computational Optimization and Applications,* 24(1):135–159, 2003.
8. H.-G. Beyer. Evolutionary algorithms in noisy environments: Theoretical issues and guidelines for practice. *Computer Methods in Mechanics and Applied Engineering,* 186:239–267, 2000.
9. H.-G. Beyer, M. Olhofer, and B. Sendhoff. On the behavior of $(\mu/\mu_I, \lambda)$-ES optimizing functions disturbed by generalized noise. In J. Rowe et al., editor, *Foundations of Genetic Algorithms 7.* Morgan Kaufmann, San Francisco, 2003. In press.
10. H. A. David and H. N. Nagaraja. Concomitants of order statistics. In N. Balakrishnan and C. R. Rao, editors, *Handbook of Statistics,* volume 16, pages 487–513. Elsevier, Amsterdam, 1998.
11. J. M. Fitzpatrick and J. J. Grefenstette. Genetic algorithms in noisy environments. *Machine Learning,* 3:101–120, 1988.
12. B. L. Miller and D. E. Goldberg. Genetic algorithms, selection schemes, and the varying effects of noise. *Evolutionary Computation,* 4(2):113–131, 1997.
13. M. Rattray and J. Shapiro. Noisy fitness evaluation in genetic algorithms and the dynamics of learning. In R. K. Belew and M. D. Vose, editors, *Foundations of Genetic Algorithms 4,* pages 117–139. Morgan Kaufmann, San Francisco, 1997.
14. I. Rechenberg. *Evolutionsstrategie: Optimierung technischer Systeme nach den Prinzipien der biologischen Evolution.* Frommann-Holzboog, Stuttgart, 1973.
15. G. Rudolph. Local convergence rates of simple evolutionary algorithms with Cauchy mutations. *IEEE Transactions on Evolutionary Computation,* 1(4):249–258, 1997.
16. A. Stuart and J. K. Ord. *Kendall's Advanced Theory of Statistics. Volume 1: Distribution Theory.* Edward Arnold, London, sixth edition, 1994.
17. H. Szu and R. Hartley. Fast simulated annealing. *Physics Letters A,* 122:157–162, 1987.

Initialising Self-Organising Maps

Emilio Corchado and Colin Fyfe

School of Information and Communication Technologies,
The University of Paisley,
Scotland.

Abstract. We review a technique for creating Self-Organising Maps (SOMs) in a Feature space which is nonlinearly related to the original data space. We show that convergence is remarkably fast for this method. By considering the linear feature space, we show that it is the interaction between the overcomplete basis in which learning takes place and the mixture of one-shot and incremental learning which comprises the method that gives the method its power. We illustrate the method on real and artificial data sets.

1 Introduction

The Self-organising Map (SOM) is one of the most widely used unsupervised learning techniques in the field of artificial neural networks [1]. Yet it has major problems with convergence: one of the major difficulties with learning occurs when the initial conditions and early samples from the data set are such that twists occur in the formation of the map meaning that an incorrect topography has been learned. Such twists can take very many iterations to unwind. In this paper, we show a new initialisation method which seems to obviate this difficulty.

The paper is structured as follows: in section 2, we review K Means clustering in feature spaces; in section 3, we review the Kernel Self Organising Map and then analyse the linear version to uncover why it converges so quickly. We show how it can be used as an initialisation method for the standard SOM and investigate its ability to quantise real data sets.

2 Kernel K-Means Clustering

We will follow the derivation of [4] who have shown that the k means algorithm can be performed in Kernel space. The aim is to find k means, $\mathbf{m}_\mu$ so that each point is close to one of the means. Now as with KPCA, each mean may be described as lying in the manifold spanned by the observations, $\phi(\mathbf{x}_i)$ i.e. $\mathbf{m}_\mu = \sum_i w_{\mu i} \phi(\mathbf{x}_i)$. Now the k means algorithm choses the means, $\mathbf{m}_\mu$, to minimise the Euclidean distance between the points and the closest mean

$$||\phi(\mathbf{x}) - \mathbf{m}_\mu||^2$$
$$= ||\phi(\mathbf{x}) - \sum_i w_{\mu i} \phi(\mathbf{x}_i)||^2$$

J. Liu et al. (Eds.): IDEAL 2003, LNCS 2690, pp. 161–168, 2003.

$$= k(\mathbf{x}, \mathbf{x}) - 2 \sum_i w_{\mu i} k(\mathbf{x}, \mathbf{x}_i)$$

$$+ \sum_{i,j} w_{\mu i} w_{\mu j} k(\mathbf{x}_i, \mathbf{x}_j)$$

i.e. the distance calculation can be accompished in Kernel space by means of the K matrix alone.

Let $M_{i\mu}$ be the cluster assignment variable. i.e. $M_{i\mu} = 1$ if $\phi(\mathbf{x}_i)$ is in the μth cluster and is 0 otherwise. [4] initialise the means to the first training patterns and then each new training point, $\phi(\mathbf{x}_{t+1}), t+1 > k$, is assigned to the closest mean and its cluster assignment variable calculated using

$$M_{t+1,\alpha} = \begin{cases} 1 & \text{if } \|\phi(\mathbf{x}_{t+1}) - \mathbf{m}_\alpha\| \\ & < \|\phi(\mathbf{x}_{t+1}) - \mathbf{m}_\mu\|, \forall \mu \neq \alpha \\ 0 & \text{otherwise} \end{cases} \tag{1}$$

In terms of the kernel function (noting that $k(\mathbf{x}, \mathbf{x})$ is common to all calculations) we have

$$M_{t+1,\alpha} = \begin{cases} 1 & \text{if } \sum_{i,j} w_{\alpha i} w_{\alpha j} k(\mathbf{x}_i, \mathbf{x}_j) \\ & -2 \sum_i w_{\alpha i} k(\mathbf{x}, \mathbf{x}_i) \\ & < \sum_{i,j} w_{\mu i} w_{\mu j} k(\mathbf{x}_i, \mathbf{x}_j) \\ & -2 \sum_i w_{\mu i} k(\mathbf{x}, \mathbf{x}_i), \forall \mu \neq \alpha \\ 0 & \text{otherwise} \end{cases} \tag{2}$$

We must then update the mean, $\mathbf{m}_\alpha$ to take account of the $(t+1)^{th}$ data point

$$\mathbf{m}_\alpha^{t+1} = \mathbf{m}_\alpha^t + \zeta(\phi(\mathbf{x}_{t+1}) - \mathbf{m}_\alpha^t) \tag{3}$$

where we have used the term $\mathbf{m}_\alpha^{t+1}$ to designate the updated mean which takes into account the new data point and

$$\zeta = \frac{M_{t+1,\alpha}}{\sum_{i=1}^{t+1} M_{i,\alpha}} \tag{4}$$

Now (3) may be written as

$$\sum_i w_{\alpha i}^{t+1} \phi(\mathbf{x}_i) = \sum_i w_{\alpha i}^t \phi(\mathbf{x}_i)$$

$$+ \zeta(\phi(\mathbf{x}_{t+1}) - \sum_i w_{\alpha i}^t \phi(\mathbf{x}_i))$$

which leads to an update equation of

$$w_{\alpha i}^{t+1} = \begin{cases} w_{\alpha i}^t (1 - \zeta) & \text{for } i \neq t+1 \\ \zeta & \text{for } i = t+1 \end{cases} \tag{5}$$

3   The Kernel Self Organising Map

We have previously used the above analysis to derive a Self Organising Map [2] in Kernel space. The SOM algorithm is a k means algorithm with an attempt to distribute the means in an organised manner and so the first change to the above algorithm is to update the closest neuron's weights and those of its neighbours. Thus we find the winning neuron (the closest in feature space) as above but now instead of (2), we use

$$M_{t+1,\mu} = \Lambda(\alpha, \mu), \forall \mu \tag{6}$$

where α is the identifier of the closest neuron and $\Lambda(\alpha, \mu)$ is a neighbourhood function which in the experiments reported herein was a gaussian. Thus the winning neuron has a value of M=1 while the value of M for other neurons decreases monotonically with distance (in neuron space) away from the winning neuron. For the experiments reported in this paper, we used a one dimensional vector of output neurons numbered 1 to 20 or 30. The remainder of the algorithm is exactly as reported in the previous section.

The Kernel SOM was reported in [2] to have very fast convergence and results in that paper were based on Gaussian kernels. We now report that equally fast convergence can be found with linear kernels and so use these to investigate the reasons for this speed of convergence.

3.1   The Linear Map

In this section we will consider the linear Kernel SOM in order to investigate its very fast convergence. Note that the learning

$$w_{\alpha i}^{t+1} = \begin{cases} w_{\alpha i}^t (1 - \zeta) & \text{for } i \neq t + 1 \\ \zeta & \text{for } i = t + 1 \end{cases} \tag{7}$$

has two modes:

1. The first mode is one shot learning for the current input; the weights from all outputs to the current input are set to the exponential of the negative squared distance in output space of the output neurons from the winning neuron.
2. The second mode is decay from the values set in the first mode; note that we need only consider this decay subsequent to the one shot learning because the one shot learning removes any previously learned values and the algorithm ensures that each node is selected exactly once for the one shot learning.

The second thing to emphasise is that while we are working in the space of input variables we are using an unusual basis in treating every data point as the end point of a basis vector. This will typically give us a very overcomplete representation.

Let the first time neuron α wins a competition be the competition for the ith input, $\mathbf{x}_i$. Then the weight $w_{\alpha i}$ is set to $\frac{e^0}{e^0} = 1$ where the denominator is the history to date of its winnings to date. For the time being, we will ignore the interaction with other neurons in the environment of α. Let the neuron α now win the competition for the input, $\mathbf{x}_j$. Then the weight $w_{\alpha j}$ is set to $\frac{e^0}{\sum_{i,j} e^0} = \frac{1}{2}$.

Also the weight $w_{\alpha i}$ decays to $w_{\alpha i} * (1 - \frac{1}{2})$, so that now the neuron's centre is the mean of the two data points for which it has won the competition. Similarly if the same neuron wins the competition to represent $\mathbf{x}_k$, the weight $w_{\alpha k}$ is set to $\frac{e^0}{\sum_{i,j,k} e^0} = \frac{1}{3}$, and the weights $w_{\alpha i}$ and $w_{\alpha j}$ decay to $\frac{1}{3}$, which again means the centre of the neuron is the mean of the three data points for which it has won the competition. A recursive argument shows that this will always be the case.

Now consider the effect of these three competitions on a neuron, μ in the neighbourhood of α. When neuron α wins the competition be for the ith input, $\mathbf{x}_i$, the weight, $w_{\mu i}$ is set to $\frac{\Lambda(\alpha,\mu)}{\Lambda(\alpha,\mu)} = 1$. When neuron α wins the competition for the input, $\mathbf{x}_j$, the weight, $w_{\mu j}$ is set to $\frac{\Lambda(\alpha,\mu)}{\sum_{i,j} \Lambda(\alpha,\mu)} = \frac{1}{2}$ and the weight $w_{\mu i}$ decays to $\frac{1}{2}$. Note the strength of the effect of the neighbourhood function which explains the strong grouping effect of the method.

Thus initially all neurons will respond to the first inputs met during training. But the above argument ignores the interaction between different responses. Consider the effect on neuron α's weight vector when neuron μ wins the competition for the lth, input, $\mathbf{x}_l$. Now

$$\zeta_\mu = \frac{\Lambda(\mu,\alpha)}{\Lambda(\mu,\alpha) + \sum_{i,j,k} e^0} = \frac{\Lambda(\mu,\alpha)}{\Lambda(\mu,\alpha) + 3} \tag{8}$$

where we have used ζ_μ to designate that part of the ζ vector devoted to μ. For μ sufficiently far from α, this will be rather small and both of the learning effects will be negligible as a response to this input. Note that quite the opposite effect happens at μ and vectors close to it. Their previous history has given very small values of $\sum \Lambda(\alpha, \mu)$ and so now a value of $\Lambda(\mu, \mu) = 1$ will easily dominate the learning of these neurons and a type of phase change will take place as these neurons respond to a new input region due to the one-shot learning.

The effect of this learning on artificial data is illustrated in Figure 1 in which we show the weights learned after the each of the first five data points are presented. In Figure 2, we show the weights after all 90 data points were presented. The converged weights can be translated back into the data space, of course, by simply using the weights found and multiplying by the respective data points. A converged map is shown in Figure 3.

3.2   An Initialisation Method

Since the proposed method has elements similar to the BatchSOM, we might ask how these methods compare. We carried out 100 simulations on our standatd data set, 90 samples from the uniform distribution in [0,1]*[0,1] with both the BatchSOM and our new method. We found that in 67 cases out of 100, the

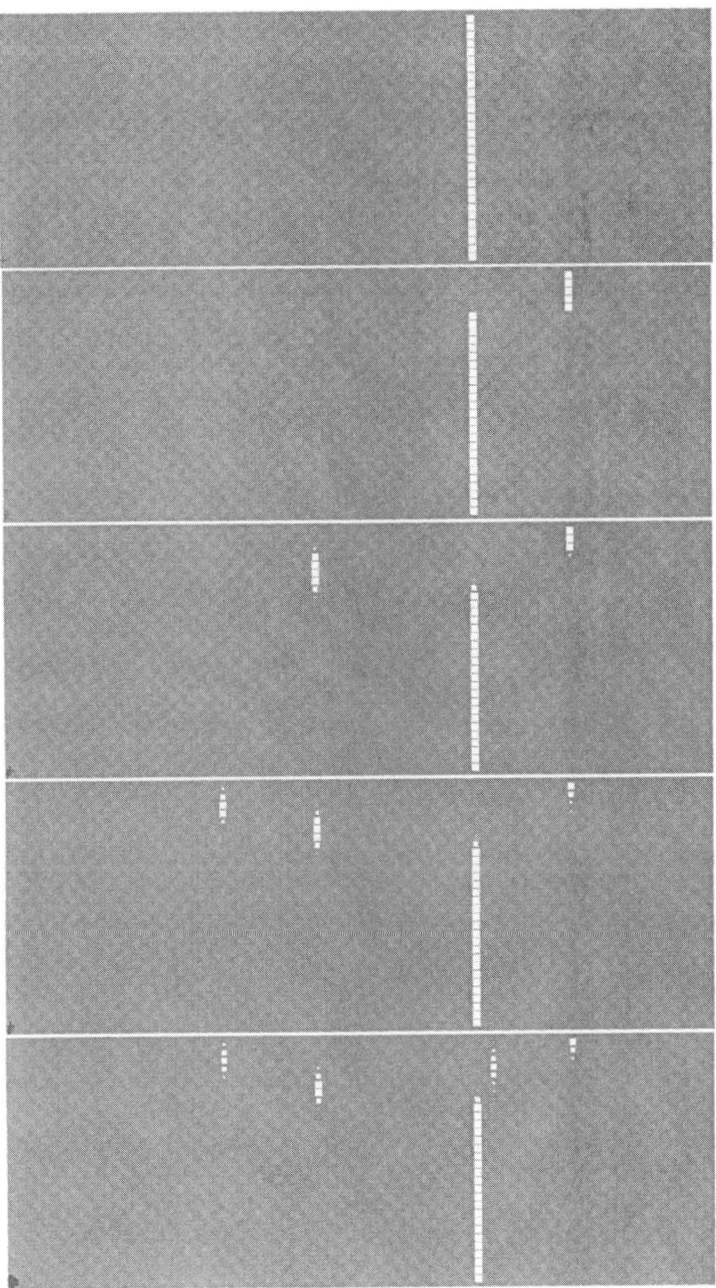

Fig. 1. Each diagram is 90 by 30 which is the number of data points by the number of centres. The top diagram shows that all centres respond totally to the first presented data point; the second shows a group of centres changing (one-shot) to a second data point; the third shows a second group of centres responding to a third data point. This is continued with the fourth and fifth data point presentation.

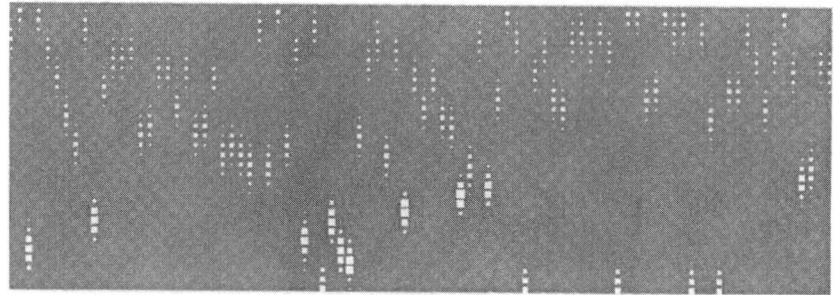

Fig. 2. The map of the previous figure after all 90 data points have been presented.

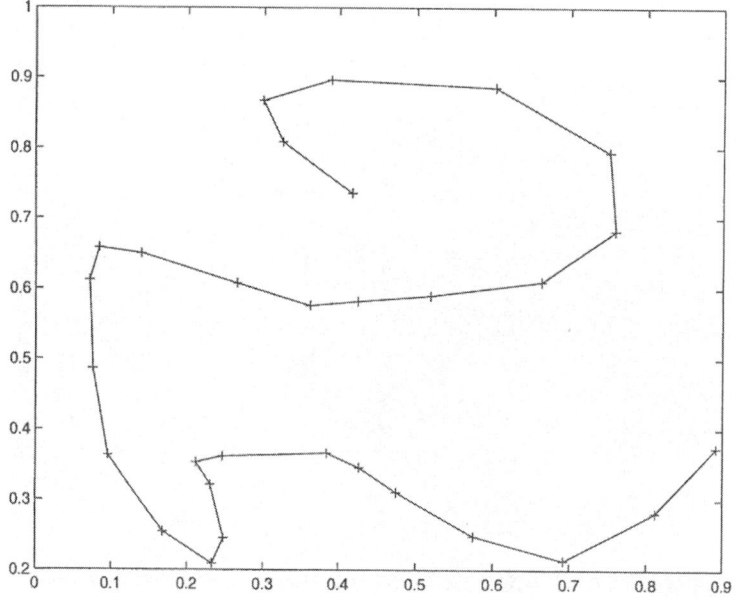

Fig. 3. The converged weights of the SOM found by the new training algorithm on one pass through artificial data drawn uniformly from [0,1]*[0,1].

BatchSOM had twists or overlaps early in training; some of these were minor and would easily be straightened out during subsequent training while some were major and could have taken many epochs before unravelling. In no cases (out of 100 simulations) did we see any twists or overlaps with the method proposed in this paper.

3.3   Real Data Sets

Of course, we used the proposed method on the ubiquitous Iris data set (e.g. [3]). This data set comprises 50 samples of each of three varieties of iris each of which is measured in 4 ways.

Results of the classification are shown in Figure 4; the three types of iris are clearly identifia ble.

Fig. 4. The three classes of iris are clearly seen in this clustering of the iris data set.

The second data set we investigated was from a scientific study of various forms of algae some of which have been manually identified. Each sample is recorded as a 18 dimensional vector representing the magnitudes of various pigments. Some algae have been identified as belonging to specific classes which are numbered 1 to 9. Others are as yet unclassified and these are labelled 0; it may be that some of these are actually members of the classes 1 to 9 while others are members of new classes.

Results are shown in Figure 5. We see the strong structure to the left of the diagram which comprises samples which the marine biologists had already classified into one of the nine groups. The samples to the right were those labelled 0 - they may be members of the classes 1 to 9 but the biologists are not sure as yet with each individual sample. The weights show why the human classification may be in some difficulty but also suggest which samples may actually be classifiable as one of the specified 9 groups.

Fig. 5. The clustering of the algae data set shows the clear divisions in the alrea, classified groups (to the left of the figure) and also suggests that why the mar biologists did not clearly classify the algae to the right of the figure.

4   Conclusion

We have reviewed the Kernel Self-organising Map and investigated why it converges so unreasonably quickly. We conclude that it is the interaction between working in the basis defined by the data points (in almost all cases this will be an overcomplete basis) and the mixture of batch and incremental learning which gives the method its power to converge quickly.

We have shown on artificial data sets that the method can be used as an initialisation method for the standard online SOM; the centres found are often very good starting points for the standard SOM. We have shown how the method can be used as a quantisation method on real data.

Future work will consider different topologies and dimensionalities of maps. In particular we are interested in whether the method can be extended to automatically determine the optimal dimensionality of a SOM at least locally.

References

1. Tuevo Kohonen. *Self-Organising Maps.* Springer, 1995.
2. D. MacDonald and C. Fyfe. The kernel self-organising map. In R.J. Howlett and L. C. Jain, editors, *Fourth International Conference on Knowledge-based Intelligent Engineering Systems and Allied Technologies, KES2000*, 2000.
3. D. Michie, D. J. Spiegelhalter, and C. C. Taylor, editors. *Machine learning, neural and statistical classification.* Ellis Horwood, 1994.
4. B. Scholkopf, A. Smola, and K.-R. Muller. Nonlinear component analysis as a kernel eigenvalue problem. *Neural Computation*, 10:1299–1319, 1998.

On the Comparisons between RLSA and CLA for Solving Arbitrary Linear Simultaneous Equations[1]

De-Shuang Huang

Institute of Intelligent Machines, Chinese Academy of Sciences
P.O.Box 1130, Hefei, Anhui 230031, China
huangdeshuang@yahoo.com

Abstract. This paper compares the performance by using constrained learning algorithm (CLA) and recursive least square algorithm (RLSA) to solve linear simultaneous equations. It was found in experiments that the convergent speed for this CLA is much faster than the recursive least square back propagation (RLS-BP) algorithm. Finally, related experimental results are presented.

1 Introduction

Feedforward neural network (FNN) is a very important model structure among many neural network models. It has been widely applied in many fields including pattern recognition, image processing, adaptive filtering, speech processing, etc. [1]. Furthermore, FNN's can be also used to do neural computations in linear algebra issues such as inversion of matrix [2], factorization of polynomials with several elements [3], finding real roots of polynomials [4], etc. These successful applications show that FNN's are indeed of many utilities.

In fact, neural networks can solve more practical problems if the corresponding efficient and effective training algorithms could be sought. In other words, the reason why neural networks could not be used to solve more problems is that those more efficient and effective training algorithms have been not found so far. For instance, the conventional back propagation algorithm (BPA) with a gradient descent type [5] can indeed address the training problems of multiple layers of networks, but the training speed for some problems are much so slow that ones can not endure [1-3]. Therefore, to extend neural networks to solve more real problems, ones have to develop some new and efficient training algorithms.

In 1992, Jiguni et.al proposed a fast learning algorithm based on the extended Kalman filtering [6], which is indeed faster than the BPA. After that, Huang extended this result to a linear case, and resulted in a recursive least square algorithm (RLSA) [7]. It can be used to solve many linear problems or nonlinear ones that can be approximated into linear ones. But they could not still avoid the local minima on the error surface.

---

[1] This work was supported by NSF of China and the Grant of "Hundred Talents Program" of Chinese Academy of Sciences of China.

In 1995, Perantonis *et al* proposed imposing the *a priori* information from problems into the conventional BP algorithm to construct the constrained learning algorithm (CLA) to train FNN's [8]. The results show that the CLA not only exhibits rapid convergence, but also renders accurate computation values. Specifically, it was observed in experiments that when the *a priori* information from the issues can be fully used, there might have no local minima on the error surface. Inspired by this training approach, we have applied this CLA to finding (real or complex) roots of polynomials [9]. Some computer simulation results showed that this CLA is indeed efficient and feasible.

In this paper, we further extend this CLA to solving the linear simultaneous equations by regarding the sets of equations as constraint conditions. Specifically, to compare, we also use RLSA to do the same problem. Finally, related simulation results will be reported.

This paper is organized as follows. Section 2 presents the general principle of FNN based approach for solving the linear simultaneous equations. Section 3 introduces and discusses the complex version of CLA for solving the linear simultaneous equations. In Section 4, some experimental results are reported and discussed. Finally, Section 5 gives several concluding remarks.

2   Neural Network Model for Solving Linear Simultaneous Equations

2.1 n Order Linear Simultaneous Equations Problem

Assume that a given n order linear simultaneous equation:

$$\begin{cases} a_{11}x_1 + a_{12}x_2 + \cdots + a_{1n}x_n = b_1 \\ a_{21}x_1 + a_{22}x_2 + \cdots + a_{2n}x_n = b_2 \\ \vdots \\ a_{n1}x_1 + a_{n2}x_2 + \cdots + a_{nn}x_n = b_n \end{cases} \tag{1}$$

which can be simplified into $Ax = b$,and

$$A = \begin{bmatrix} a_{11}, a_{12}, \cdots, a_{1n} \\ a_{21}, a_{22}, \cdots, a_{2n} \\ \vdots \quad \vdots \quad \vdots \\ a_{n1}, a_{n2}, \cdots, a_{nn} \end{bmatrix} \quad \text{and} \quad b = \begin{bmatrix} b_1 \\ b_2 \\ \vdots \\ b_n \end{bmatrix} \tag{2}$$

If we write A in form of the row vectors, then there have:

$$A = \begin{bmatrix} a_1 \\ a_2 \\ \vdots \\ a_n \end{bmatrix} \quad \text{and} \quad a_i = [a_{i1}, a_{i2}, \cdots, a_{in}] \tag{3}$$

As a result, eqn.(1) can be rewritten as:

$$a_i x = b_i \quad (i = 1, 2, \cdots, n) \tag{4}$$

where $x = [x_1, x_2, \cdots, x_n]^T$ with T denoting the transpose of a vector or matrix.

In the past, one uses generally iterating methods to solve this problem. Here, we consider using FNN technique to obtain the solutions. Assume that we construct an FNN to map this problem of solving linear simultaneous equations into it, then the n approximate solutions w_i ($i = 1, 2, \cdots, n$) are estimated from the involved network. As a result, we can rewrite eqn (1) into

$$Aw \approx b \tag{5}$$

where $w = [w_1, w_2, \cdots, w_n]^T$ is the neural network weights, also referred to as the approximate solutions of eqn.(1).

From the above analyses, we wish to design a neural network to solve the linear simultaneous equations. In the following subsection, we will present the neural network model structure for solving the linear simultaneous equations.

2.2 Neural Network Model for Solving Linear Simultaneous Equations

For an n order linear simultaneous equation $Ax = b$, the idea for solving the linear simultaneous equation by neural networks is to use an FNN to represent (or approximate) this equation so that those weights in the network try to represent or approximate the corresponding solutions. Assume that a one-layered linear FNN model, as shown in Fig. 1, is configured to perform solving the mentioned above linear simultaneous equations. Obviously, this network is of the size of n -1 with a structure of n input neurons and one output neuron. Moreover, all neurons in the network are linear. There have n input neurons in the network corresponding to the terms of x_1, x_2, $\cdots$ and x_n. They are weighted by the network weight w_1, w_2, $\cdots$ and w_n, respectively, then through the one output neuron to output the result.

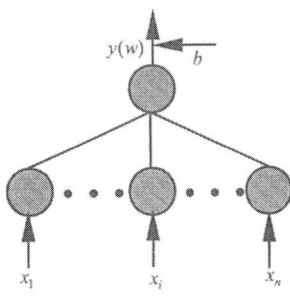

Fig. 1. The FNN model architecture for solving the linear simultaneous equations

From the above analyses, in mathematical terminology, for the ith row input pattern from the input matrix A, the output of the network can be written as:

$$y_i(w) = a_i w \quad (i = 1, 2, \cdots, n) \tag{6}$$

where w_i $(i = 1, 2, \cdots, n)$ are the input-to-output layer weights of the network , i.e., the solutions of the linear simultaneous equation. Obviously, the outer-supervised (target) signal defined at the output of this network model is b.

3 Complex Constrained Learning Algorithm

For the linear simultaneous equation defined in eqn.(1), we can describe it into the approximate problem of n linear equations defined in eqn.(4) or (6). Consequently, an error cost function can be defined at the output of the network:

$$E(w) = \frac{1}{2P} \sum_{p=1}^{P} |e_p(w)|^2 = \frac{1}{2P} \sum_{p=1}^{P} |o_p - y_p|^2 \tag{7}$$

where $p = 1, 2, \cdots, n$ is an index labeling the training patterns; the target (outer-supervised) signal is $o_p = b_p$ and the actual output $y_p(w) = a_p w$.

Below, we present the complex CLA proposed by Perantonis et.al in order to solve an arbitrary linear simultaneous equation. Here the additional information available is the constraint relations defined in eqns.(4) or (6). We can uniformly write them as follows $\Phi = 0$, where $\Phi = [\Phi_1, \Phi_2, \cdots, \Phi_m]^T$ $(m \leq n)$ is a vector composed of the constraint conditions.

Likewise, we give another constraint condition as $\sum_{i=1}^{n} |dw_i|^2 = (\delta P)^2$. Before proceeding to the complex CLA, assume $d\Phi$ to be equal to a predetermined vector quantity δQ , designed to bring Φ closer to its target (zero). In addition, we introduce a vector $V = [v_1, v_2, \cdots, v_m]^T$ of Lagrange multipliers for the constraints in $\Phi = 0$ and another Lagrange multiplier μ for $\sum_{i=1}^{n} |dw_i|^2 = (\delta P)^2$. To ensure the maximum possible change in $|dE(w)|$ at each epoch, we introduce a function. Consequently, $d\varepsilon$ is defined as follows:

$$d\varepsilon = dE(w) + (\delta Q^H - d\Phi^H)V + \mu \left[(\delta P)^2 - \sum_{i=1}^{n} |dw_i|^2 \right] \tag{8}$$

where the superscript H denotes the conjugate transpose of a vector or matrix.

By expanding the terms on the right hand side of eqn (9), we easily obtain:

$$d\varepsilon = \sum_{i=1}^{n} J_i dw_i + (\delta Q^H - \sum_{i=1}^{n} dw_i F_i^H)V + \mu \left[(\delta P)^2 - \sum_{i=1}^{n} |dw_i|^2 \right] \tag{9}$$

where $F_i = [F_i^{(1)}, F_i^{(2)}, \cdots, F_i^{(m)}]^T$, $F_i^{(j)} = \dfrac{\partial \Phi_j}{\partial w_i}$ ($i = 1,2,\cdots,n, j = 1,2,\cdots,m$), and for solving the linear simultaneous equations, J_i can be expressed as $J_i = \dfrac{\partial E(w)}{\partial w_i} = -\dfrac{1}{n}\sum_{p=1}^{n} a_{pi}(b_p - a_p w)$

Similar to the derivation of [8], we can derive the following relation:

$$dw_i = \frac{J_i}{2\mu} - \frac{F_i^H V}{2\mu} \tag{10}$$

Eqn.(10) forms the new weight update rule called as complex CLA instead of the conventional steepest gradient descent algorithm.

Furthermore, the values of Lagrange multipliers μ and V in eqn.(10) can be readily evaluated $\mu = -\dfrac{1}{2}\left[\dfrac{I_{JJ} - I_{JF}^H I_{FF}^{-1} I_{JF}}{(\delta P)^2 - \delta Q^H I_{FF}^{-1}\delta Q}\right]^{1/2}$ and $V = -2\mu I_{FF}^{-1}\delta Q + I_{FF}^{-1} I_{JF}$, where

$I_{JJ} = \sum_{i=1}^{n}|J_i|^2$ is a scalar, I_{JF} is a vector whose components are defined by

$I_{JF}^{(j)} = \sum_{i=1}^{n} J_i F_i^{(j)}$,($j = 1,2,\cdots,m$). Specifically, I_{FF} is a matrix, whose elements are

defined by $I_{FF}^{jk} = \sum_{i=1}^{n} F_i^{(j)} F_i^{(k)*}$ ($j,k = 1,2,\cdots,m$), where $*$ denotes the complex conjugate.

Generally, the parameter δP is often selected as a fixed value. However, the vector parameters $\delta Q_j (j = 1,2,\cdots,m)$ are often selected as proportional to Φ_j , i.e., $\delta Q_j = -k\Phi_j$ ($j = 1,2,\cdots,m$, $k > 0$), which ensures that the constraints Φ move towards zero at an exponential rate as the training progresses.

From μ , we note that k should satisfy $k \le \delta P(\Phi^H I_{FF}^{-1}\Phi)^{-1/2}$. In fact, the simplest choice for k is $k = \eta\delta P / \sqrt{\Phi^H I_{FF}^{-1}\Phi}$, where $0 < \eta < 1$ is another free parameter of the algorithm apart from δP . In fact, as introduced in [9], we can adaptively choose the parameters δP as $\delta P(t) = \delta P_0(1 - e^{-\frac{\theta_p}{t}})$, where δP_0 is the initial value for δP , which is usually chosen as a larger value; t is the time index for training, θ_p is the scale coefficient of time t , which is usually set as $\theta_p > 1$.

4   Experimental Results

To verify the efficiency and feasibility of our approach, an example $Ax = b$ is given, where

$$A = \begin{bmatrix} 1+2.1i & 4-3.1i & 2.2+1.9i & 3.4i & 1.7-0.9i \\ 2.03+1.56i & 0.45i & 3.49-5.1i & 3+3i & 6.3-0.98i \\ 0.24-3.45i & 1.23+3.56i & 6.5 & 4.78i & 0.78-3.12i \\ 0.9i & 1.23-8.34i & 0.78-1.05i & 4.67+2.3i & 0.98i \\ 1.6-3.56i & 2.34+4.56i & 3.4+4.5i & 2.17+2.9i & 3.49-7.13i \end{bmatrix} \quad \text{and} \quad b = \begin{bmatrix} 1.3 \\ 3.4i \\ 5.6+0.9i \\ 1.13-2.34i \\ 3 \end{bmatrix}$$

Assume that a 5-1 structured one layered linear FNN is designed to solve this LSE. For the CLA, the three learning parameters are respectively set as $\delta P_0 = 10.0, \eta = 0.6, \theta_p = 8.0$, the termination error $e_r = 1.0 \times 10^{-13}$; for RLSA, $\lambda = 0.99$. Consequently, after 438 and 2899 iterations, the network converges. Figs.2 and 3 respectively shows the two learning error curves and the 10 learning solution curves for the CLA and the RLSA. The two figures show that the CLA is obviously faster than the RLSA. Table 1 lists the estimated averaged solutions of the LSE for two training algorithms after 20 repeated trials. In addition, we also obtain the real solutions by Matlab 6.0 (shown in Table 1). From Table 1 it can also be observed that the CLA is of higher accuracy than the RLSA (where σ denotes the estimated variance).

Table 1. The performance comparison between the CLA and the RLSA

Indices	x_1	x_2	x_3	x_4	x_5	Iterating Numbers
True	-0.1513+ 1.5182i	-0.0399 + 0.7617i	-0.4105+ 0.3756i	-0.6118- 0.9727i	0.1788+ 0.3328i	
CLA	-0.1513+ 1.5182i	-0.03993+ 0.7617i	-0.4105+ 0.3756i	-0.6118- 0.9727i	0.1788+ 0.3328i	543
σ	3.4090E-5	2.7349E-5	3.5604E-5	2.1457E-5	3.1347E-5	
RLSA	-0.15134+ 1.5182i	-0.03993+ 0.7617i	-0.4105+ 0.3756i	-0.6118- 0.9727i	0.1788+ 0.3328i	3142
σ	3.5034E-4	5.6721E-4	2.7868E-4	3.2102E-4	2.1303E-4	

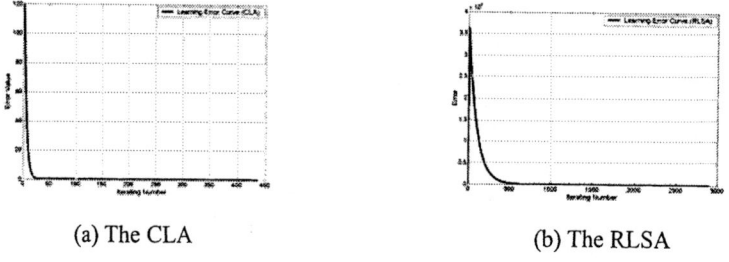

(a) The CLA   (b) The RLSA

Fig. 2. The Learning error curves for the CLA and the RLSA

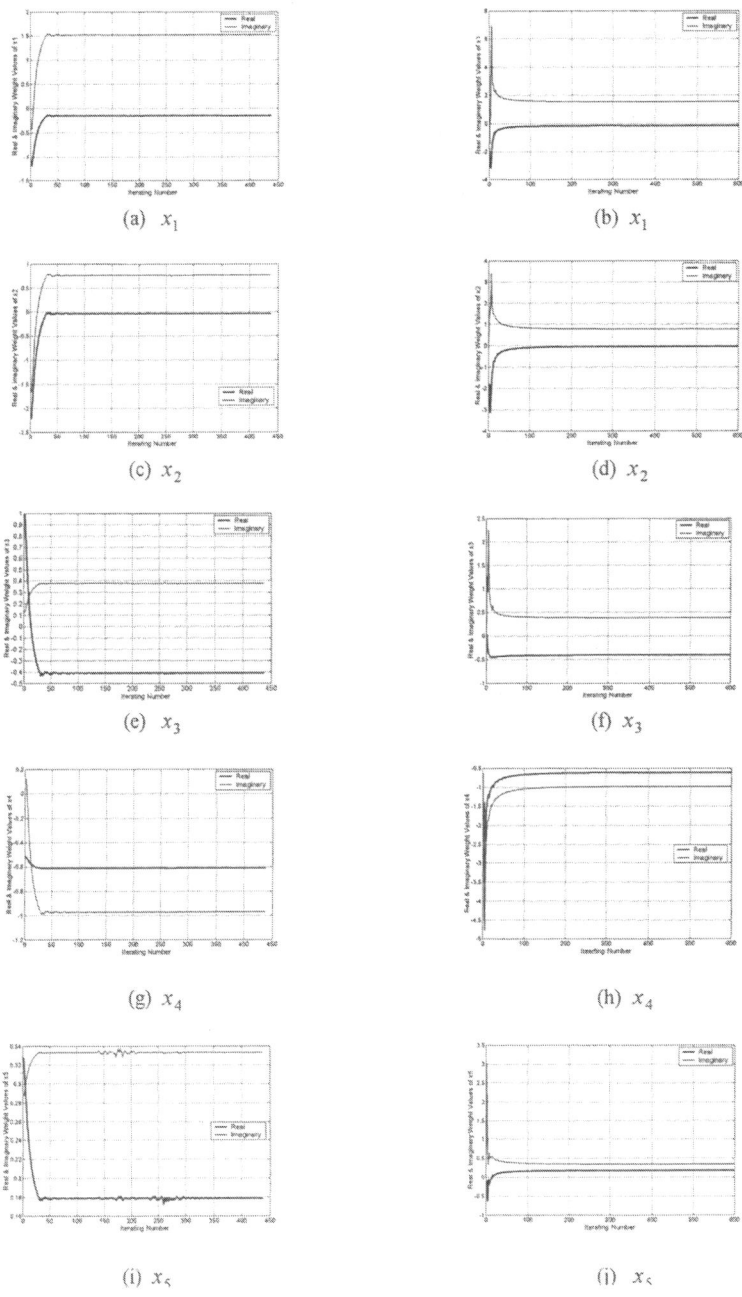

(a) x_1

(b) x_1

(c) x_2

(d) x_2

(e) x_3

(f) x_3

(g) x_4

(h) x_4

(i) x_5

(j) x_5

Fig. 3. The 10 sets of learning solution curves for the CLA and the RLSA. The CLA: (a), (c), (e), (g) and (i); The RLSA: (b), (d), (f), (h) and (j)

5   Conclusions

The proposed approach of constrained learning technique based neural networks for solving linear simultaneous equations is shown by experiments to be very effective and feasible method. The fast training speed and high accuracy are the most important advantages for this method. In addition, the simulation parts also compare the performance of this CLA with the RLSA. The experimental results show that the CLA is obviously faster than the RLSA.

References

1.   D.S.Huang: Systematic Theory of Neural Network for Pattern Recognition. Publishing House of Electronic Industry, Beijing, China (1996)
2.   D. S. Huang: One-Layer Linear Perceptron for the Inversion of Nonsingular Matrix. IC On ROVPIA'96, Nov. 28 ~ 30, Ipoh, Malaysia (1996) 639–643
3.   D.S. Huang, M.S. Zhao: A Neural Network Based Factorization Model for Polynomials in Several Elements. 2000 5th International Conference on Signal Processing Proceedings (WCC2000-ICSP2000), Aug.21–25, Beijing, China (2000) 1617–1622
4.   D.S. Huang. Application of neural networks to finding real roots of polynomials in one element. ICONIP-2000 Proceedings, Taejon, Korea, Nov.14–17, Vol.II (2000) 1108–1113
5.   D.E. Rumelhart, G.E. Hinton, and R.J. Williams: Learning Representations by Backpropagating Errors. Nature, Vol.323 (1986) 533–536
6.   Y.Jiguni, H.Sakai and H.Tokumaru: A Real-Time Learning Algorithm for a Multilayered Neural Network Based on the Extended Kalman Filter. IEEE Trans. SP, 40(4) (1992) 959–966.
7.   D.S.Huang, X.X.Lv, K.P.Yuan: A Study of Backpropagation Learning Algorithm of Multilayer Perceptron Networks Based on Recursive Least Squares. Proc. of the 6th Japan-China International Conference on Computer Applications, Sept. 16–18, Sapporo, Japan (1994), 169–172 (J–4)
8.   D.A. Karras and S.J. Perantonis: An Efficient Constrained Training Algorithm for Feedforward Networks.. IEEE Trans. Neural Networks, Vol.6 (1995), 1420–1434
9.   D.S.Huang, Zheru Chi: Finding Complex Roots of Polynomials by Feedforward Neural Networks. 2001 Int. Joint Conf. On Neural Networks (IJCNN2001), Washington, DC, Vol. Addendum, 13–18, July 15–19, 2001

Exploiting Heterogeneous Features for Classification Learning*

Yiqiu Han and Wai Lam

Department of Systems Engineering and Engineering Management,
The Chinese University of Hong Kong,
Shatin,
Hong Kong
{yqhan,wlam}@se.cuhk.edu.hk

Abstract. This paper proposes a framework for handling heterogeneous features containing hierarchical values and texts under Bayesian learning. To exploit hierarchical features, we make use of a statistical technique called shrinkage. We also explore an approach for utilizing text data to improve classification performance. We have evaluated our framework using a yeast gene data set which contain hierarchical features as well as text data.

Keywords: hierarchical features, Bayesian learning, parameter estimation

1 Introduction

Some data sets may contain features whose domain values are organized in a hierarchical structure. A hierarchy, in fact, reveals knowledge about interrelationships and differences in different levels. If utilized properly, these background knowledge can help deal with problems related to hierarchical features including data sparseness. McCallum et al. [4] applied shrinkage [3,6] technique in a hierarchy of classes and showed some improvements on text classifications. The hierarchy they used is composed of classes and their model does not utilize children or siblings. Segal and Koller [5] introduced a general probabilistic framework for clustering data into a hierarchy. Hierarchical classes are considered in their work, but little work has been done in features with hierarchical domain values. Domingos and Pazzani [2] explained why good predictive performance can be achieved by Naive Bayes on classification problems even it requires independence assumption which may be invalid in the data set. Under Maximum A Posteriori Principle, the independence assumption does not degrade the classification much.

This paper investigates Bayesian learning model in classification problems with hierarchical features. Inspired by the statistical technique called *shrinkage*,

---

* The work described in this paper was partially supported by grants from the Research Grant Council of the Hong Kong Special Administrative Region, China (Project Nos: CUHK 4385/99E and CUHK 4187/01E).

we introduce a framework for exploiting the hierarchical structure of domain values of a particular feature.

Apart from ordinary features such as nominal or numeric attributes, many data sets may also have texts associated with each record. Texts may come from questionnaire or document articles collected together with other features. Tan et al. [7] developed a technique for extracting information from hybrid fixed-format and free-text fields of service center call records. The result supports the fact that incorporating free-form texts could potentially induce better classification models. We are interested in developing a model that can incorporate text features during the classification learning process.

We present experimental results for our framework using a yeast gene data set obtained from KDD Cup 2002 Task 2. The results show that our framework can improve the classification performance in comparison with classical Bayesian learning model in this sparse data set.

2   Classical Bayesian Learning

Consider a feature with categorical values organized in a hierarchical structure. In this paper, we call it *hierarchical feature*. The hierarchical structure is basically a tree and each node on the tree corresponds to a distinct domain value of this particular feature. The value represented by a parent node denotes a more general concept with respect to the value represented by a child node. For instance, in the gene data set of KDD Cup 2002 Task 2, there are three hierarchical features and each of them is associated with a pre-defined hierarchy.

We investigate the learning problem by considering a parametric model. The training data is used to estimate the model parameters. After training, the model equipped with the model parameters can be used for predicting the class label or calculating the membership likelihood for a certain class. One issue we need to deal with is the handling of hierarchical features. To facilitate the discussion, we first provide some definitions.

Definition We define *raw frequency*, denoted by $R(n)$, of a node n in a hierarchy as the number of training instances having the same feature value represented by the node n. We define *raw hit frequency*, denoted by $R(C, n)$, of a node n in a hierarchy as the number of training instances having class label C and the same feature value represented by the node n. $\diamond$

Let the new instance be represented by a set of features $F = (f_1, \ldots, f_m)$ where f_i denotes the values of the feature F_i for this instance. For a hierarchical feature, its possible values corresponding f_i's is associated with a node in the domain value hierarchy. To obtain the membership likelihood of a new instance belonging to the class C, we can make use of Bayes' theorem as follows:

$$P(C|F) = \frac{P(C)P(F|C)}{P(F)} \tag{1}$$

Given the assumption that the features are conditionally independent of each other, Equation 1 can be expressed as:

$$P(C|F) = \frac{P(C) \prod_i^m P(F_i = f_i|C)}{P(F)} = \frac{P(C)^{1-m} \prod_{i=1}^m P(C \wedge F_i = f_i)}{P(F)}$$

$$= \frac{P(C)^{1-m} \prod_{i=1}^m P(F_i = f_i)}{P(F)} \prod_{i=1}^m P(C|F_i = f_i) \qquad (2)$$

In many real-world classification problems, the goal is a ranked list of the likelihood of instances belonging to one specific class C. Let $\bar{C}$ denote the fact that an instance does not belong to C. Equation 2 becomes:

$$P(C|F) = \frac{P(C)^{1-m} \prod_{i=1}^m P(C \wedge F_i = f_i)}{P(C)P(F|C) + P(\bar{C})P(F|\bar{C})} = \frac{1}{1 + \frac{P(\bar{C})^{1-m} \prod_{i=1}^m P(\bar{C} \wedge F_i=f_i)}{P(C)^{1-m} \prod_{i=1}^m P(C \wedge F_i=f_i)}} \qquad (3)$$

Since $\frac{1}{1+x}$ is monotonic increasing with $\frac{1}{x}$ when $x > 0$, we only need to consider the following:

$$\frac{P(C)^{1-m} \prod_{i=1}^m P(C \wedge F_i = f_i)}{P(\bar{C})^{1-m} \prod_{i=1}^m P(\bar{C} \wedge F_i = f_i)} = \frac{P(C)^{1-m}}{P(\bar{C})^{1-m}} \prod_{i=1}^m \frac{P(C \wedge F_i = f_i)}{P(\bar{C} \wedge F_i = f_i)} \qquad (4)$$

In fact, $\frac{P(C)^{1-m}}{P(\bar{C})^{1-m}}$ can be ignored because it is a constant for all instances in binary classification and will not affect the ranking of the instances. The posterior part can also be simplified to $\prod_{i=1}^m P(C \wedge F_i = f_i)/P(F_i = f_i)$ because $\frac{x}{1+x}$ is monotonic increasing with x when $x > 0$. $\hat{P}(C|F)$ can be estimated by:

$$\hat{P}(C|F) = \prod_{i=1}^m \frac{\Theta(C, f_i)}{\Theta(f_i)} \qquad (5)$$

$\Theta(C, f_i)$ and $\Theta(f_i)$ are two model parameters estimated from the training instances. A common technique is to employ the maximum likelihood estimates. Then, $\Theta(C, f_i)$ and $\Theta(f_i)$ are given by raw hit frequency $R(C, f_i)$ and raw frequency $R(f_i)$ respectively. Suppose we are given a set of new instances. If we are interested in a ranked list of these instances belonging to the class C, we can compute a score function, $L(C|F)$, by:

$$L(C|F) = \frac{\prod_i^m R(C, f_i)}{\prod_i^m R(f_i)} \qquad (6)$$

In the next section, we will discuss how to improve the classification performance under this Bayesian learning framework by exploiting hierarchical feature values and utilizing relaxed conditional probability estimations.

3 Exploiting the Hierarchical Structure

One observation about data sets with hierarchical features is that they tend to suffer from the problem of sparse data. One reason is due to the large number of possible domain values. For example, the gene data set of the KDD Cup 2002 Task 2 is very sparse for those hierarchical features. If we directly apply the standard classical Bayesian learning, the maximum likelihood estimates are very unreliable and thus resulting in poor classification performance.

3.1   Shrinkage-Based Approach

To cope with the problem commonly found in hierarchical features, we propose a framework for conducting Bayesian learning by exploiting the hierarchical structure of the domain values. The main idea is inspired by a statistical technique called *shrinkage* which provides a way for improving parameter estimation coping with limited amount of training data [3,6].

Another characteristic of a hierarchical feature is that it contains data distributed among all the nodes in the hierarchy. This kind of hierarchy is quite common. In these hierarchies, a non-leaf node is not just a "virtual" category, instead it can be viewed as a cluster which contains its own instances.

We investigate a model under Bayesian learning which attempts to exploit the hierarchy to help probabilistic parameter estimation. It is a shrinkage-based Bayesian learning algorithm called SHA. To facilitate the discussion, we provide some definitions as follows:

Definition We define *tree frequency*, denoted by $T(n)$, of a node n in a hierarchy as the number of training instances having feature values represented by the node n or any nodes in the sub-tree rooted by n. The relationship of $T(n)$ and $R(n)$ can be expressed as follows:

$$T(n) = \sum_{i \in \Upsilon(n)} R(i)$$

where $\Upsilon(n)$ represents the set of all the nodes in the sub-tree rooted at n. ◇

Definition Let C denote a class. We define *tree hit frequency*, denoted by $T(C,n)$, of a node n in a hierarchy as the number of training instances having class label C and the same feature values represented by the node n or any nodes in the sub-tree rooted by n. The relationship of $T(C,n)$ and $R(C,n)$ can be expressed as follows:

$$T(C,n) = \sum_{i \in \Upsilon(n)} R(C,i)$$

◇

As mentioned in Section 2, we need to estimate $\Theta(C, f_i)$ and $\Theta(f_i)$ in Equation 5 during the Bayesian learning process. The shrinkage model is used for replacing parameter estimation of a node with one of its ancestors. In our SHA model, the ancestor refers to the minimum subtree containing the specific node because it is more general than just using the parent node especially when every node represents a corresponding nominal domain value with its own instances.

We attempt to further explore the hierarchy. It can be observed that the data located at a parent node basically share more common characteristics of the data located in the sub-tree. The data distribution of the parent node is similar to the data distribution of its sub-tree. Hence, we can use distributional parameter estimation of the sub-tree to replace the parameter estimation of the parent node. When the sample size of the parent node is very small. More robust result can be achieved in this way.

Conversely, when we need to estimate the parameter of a sub-tree, it should be helpful to use the parameter estimation of the parent node to get more accurate result when the sample size of the parent node is insufficient. If we perform these two replacements guided by the sample size, the error can be controlled and the precision can be improved. Based on the above idea, we develop a shrinkage-based Bayesian learning algorithm called SHA. The details of SHA is depicted in Figure 1.

```
1   If R(f_i) > ξ
2       Θ̂(C, f_i) = R(C, f_i);
3       Θ̂(f_i) = R(f_i);
4   Else
    {
5       Let τ equal to the node corresponding to f_i
6       while (R(Υ(τ)) < ξ
7           τ = Parent(τ);
8       If (R(τ)) > ξ       //Use the root of the tree instead
9           Θ̂(C, f_i) = R(C, τ);
10          Θ̂(f_i) = R(τ);
11      Else     //Use the tree directly
12          Θ̂(C, f_i) = T(C, Υ(τ));
13          Θ̂(f_i) = T(Υ(τ));
    }
```

Fig. 1. Shrinkage-Based Bayesian Learning (SHA) Algorithm

4   Utilizing Text Data

We attempt to utilize text data to improve the classification performance. Instead of treating text data an ordinary feature and applying text classification, we explore a technique for extracting feature values from text data. Blaschke and Valencia [1] developed a system called SUISEKI that can analyze sentences that have co-occurrence of two entities indicating a relationship between them.

We attempt to develop an automatic method to process text. Suppose the text data contains information about some attributions of the problem domain, particularly, descriptions concerned with some features in the data set. By analyzing the co-occurrence of terms related to feature values and instances. It is possible to extract some useful evidence about the association of feature values for certain instances. For example, in the yeast gene data set, if the names of two genes appear together is a sentence, it is very likely they interact with each other.

We mainly focus on extracting from texts the nominal feature values. Text data will be pre-processed before extraction. Typically, a lexicon containing all possible values of a feature can be prepared. Tokenization breaks the texts into tokens. Stemming technique is also used to resolve tokens to the word stem.

---

1   For every piece of text
2   Preprocess the text
3   Scan with fix sized sliding window W
4   If W contains name of instance i
5   Search feature values in W
6   If W contains feature value j
7   sum the weight D_1 of lexical unit delimiter between i and j
8   sum the weight D_2 of keywords between i and j
9   calculate the likelihood $L(i, j) = \frac{D_2}{D_1}$
10 For every instance i
11   assign feature value j to i if $L(i, j) = max(L(i, *))$

Fig. 2. The Algorithm for Mining Feature Values From Texts

Figure 2 depicts the framework of our algorithm for mining feature values from texts. Instead of breaking text into sentences, we use a sliding window to sequentially scan through the text. Once token i is detected to be related to an instance, we will search in the sliding window to locate token j that relates to feature values.

The distance between i and j in the sliding window will be used to estimate the likelihood of assigning j to be feature value of instance i. Tokens that are likely delimiters of lexical units such as sentence boundary will be penalized in the distance calculation. Some useful keywords can be trained to help calculate the distance function. These trained keywords will shorten the distance. The weight of the keywords can be trained using the term frequency and inverse document frequency statistics commonly found in information retrieval techniques. The weight is defined as the number of co-occurrence in a sliding window with some i and j over its frequency. To improve the efficiency, only top ranking keywords will be used to help estimate the likelihood.

5   Experimental Results

The data set used in our experiment is a yeast gene data set obtained from KDD Cup 2002 Task 2[1]. Each instance is represented by a set of features listed as follows:

- The *interaction* of the gene-coded protein. This feature is organized as a pair list.

---

[1] The detail can be found at http://www.biostat.wisc.edu/~craven/kddcup/faqs.html

- The sub-cellular *localization* of the gene-coded protein. This is a hierarchical feature whose domain values are organized in a hierarchy.
- The *protein class* of the gene-coded protein. This is a hierarchical feature whose domain values are organized in a hierarchy.
- The *functional class* of the gene-coded protein. This is a hierarchical feature whose domain values are organized in a hierarchy.
- *Abstracts* drawn from the MEDLINE articles in free text form.

The data set is very sparse and noisy, reflecting existing knowledge of the yeast genes. There are missing feature values, aliases and typographical errors.

The objective is to return a ranked list of genes in the testing set in the order of their likelihood of belonging to an interested category. The first category is called "narrow" classification whose aim is to predict the class "change". The second category is called "broad" classification whose aim is to predict the union of the classes "change" and "control".

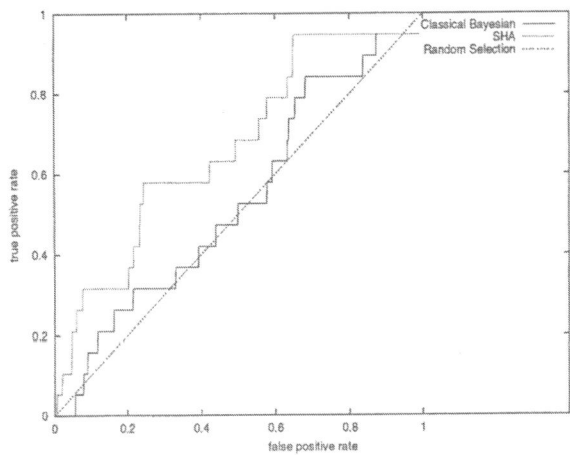

Fig. 3. The classification performance measured by ROC curve for the gene data set

The evaluation metric used to measure the classification performance is based on Receiver Operating Characteristic (ROC) score offered by the KDD Cup 2002 Task 2.

Figure 3 depicts the classification performance of classical Bayesian and SHA algorithm for the "narrow" classification problem. The ROC curve is not smooth because the gene data only has less than twenty positive instances out of thousands of testing instances. It shows that the classical Bayesian learning cannot handle the data sparseness problem in this gene data set. The ROC curve is similar to the random prediction. SHA shows significant improvements on the classical Bayesian model. It demonstrates that our framework can handle learning from extremely sparse data and offer a more reliable result in comparison with classical Bayesian learning.

This data set also contains text data in the form of abstracts corresponding to different genes. We have conducted another experiment with our SHA model integrated with text data. Table 1 shows the results after incorporating text data. The results demonstrate that the classification performance can be improved after considering text data. We have also conducted 3-fold cross validation and the result is similar. As for reference, in the KDD Cup 2002 Task 2, the ROC score of the winner for the "broad" classification task was 0.684. The ROC score of another winner for the "narrow" classification task was 0.678^2.

Table 1. Classification performance measured by ROC score for the gene data set

	Classical Bayesian	SHA	SHA w/texts
Broad	0.512	0.700	0.712
Narrow	0.520	0.640	0.684

6   Conclusions and Future Work

In this paper we have developed a framework exploiting the feature hierarchy for improving classification performance under Bayesian learning. We have also investigated the incorporation of the text features to improve classification performance. We have conducted experiments on a real-world data set about yeast genes. The results demonstrate the effectiveness of our method.

References

1. C. Blaschke and A. Valencia. The frame-based module of the SUISEKI information extraction system. *IEEE Intelligent Systems*, 17(2):14–19, 2002.
2. P. Domingos and M. Pazzani. Beyond independence: Conditions for the optimality of the simple Bayesian classifier. *Machine Learning*, 29:103–130, 1997.
3. W. James and C. Stein. Estimation with quadratic loss. In *Proceedings of the Fourth Berkeley Symposim on Mathematical Statistics and Probability 1*, pages 361–379, 1961.
4. A. McCallum, R. Rosenfeld, T. Mitchell, and A. Y. Ng. Improving text classification by shrinkage in a hierarchy of classes. In *Proceedings of the Fourteenth International Conference on Machine Learning ICML*, pages 359–367, 1998.
5. E. Segal and D. Koller. Probabilistic hierarchical clustering for biological data. In *Annual Conference on Research in Computational Molecular Biology*, pages 273–280, 2002.
6. C. Stein. Inadmissibility of the usual estimator for the mean of a multivariate normal distribution. In *Proceedings of the Third Berkley Symposim on Mathematical Statistics and Probability 1*, pages 197–206, 1955.
7. P. N. Tan, H.Blau, S.Harp, and R. Goldman. Textual data mining of service center call records. In *Proceedings of ACM SIGKDD International Conference on Knowledge Discovery and Data Mining*, pages 417–422, 2000.

---

[2] The distribution of submitted results is available at
http://www.biostat.wisc.edu/~ craven/kddcup/test.html

Locally Balanced Incremental Hierarchical Discriminant Regression[*]

Xiao Huang[1], Juyang Weng[1], and Roger Calantone[2]

[1] Department of Computer Science and Engineering
Michigan State University
East Lansing, MI 48824, USA
{huangxi4, weng}@cse.msu.edu
[2] The Eli Broad College of Business
Michigan State University
East Lansing, MI 48824, USA
{rogercal}@msu.edu

Abstract. Incremental hierarchical discriminant regression faces several challenging issues: (a) a large input space with a small output space and (b) nonstationary statistics of data sequences. In the first case (a), there maybe few distinct labels in the output space while the input data distribute in a high dimensional space. In the second case (b), a tree has to be grown when only a limited data sequence has been observed. In this paper, we present the Locally Balanced Incremental Hierarchical Discriminant Regression (LBIHDR) algorithm. A novel node self-organization and spawning strategy is proposed to generate a more discriminant subspace by forming multiple clusters for one class. The algorithm was successfully applied to different kinds of data set.

1 Introduction

Decision trees (class labels as outputs) and regression trees (numerical vectors as outputs) organize the data in a hierarchy so that retrieval time can be logarithmic, which is essential for a real-time, online learning systems like real-time content-based retrieval and vision-based navigation. Traditionally, classification and regression trees use a univariate split at each internal node, such as in CART [1], C5.0, [8] and many others [5]. This means that the partition of input space by each node uses a hyper-plane that is orthogonal to an axis in the input space X. OC1 [6] and SHOSLIF tree [10] are two methods for constructing oblique trees. OC1 uses iterative search to find a split. SHOSLIF uses the principal component analysis (PCA) and the linear discriminant analysis (LDA) to directly compute splits. The Hierarchical Discriminating Regression (HDR) algorithm [3] casts both classification problems and regression problems into a unified regression

---

[*] The work is supported in part by National Science Foundation under grant No. IIS 9815191, DARPA ETO under contract No. DAAN02-98-C-4025, and DARPA ITO under grant No. DABT63-99-1-0014.

J. Liu et al. (Eds.): IDEAL 2003, LNCS 2690, pp. 185–194, 2003.

problem. Virtual labels in the output space provide membership information for forming clusters in the input space.

With the demand of online, real-time, incremental, multi-modality learning with high dimensional sensing by an autonomously learning image-classifier or a mobile robot agent, we require a general purpose regression technique that satisfies all of the following challenging requirements: (a) It must take high-dimensional inputs with very complex correlation between components in the input vector. (b) It must perform one-instance learning. (c) It must dynamically adapt to increasing complexity. (d) It must deal with the local minima problem. (e) It must be incremental. (f) It must be able to retain most of the information in long-term memory. (g) It must have a very low time complexity. The incremental hierarchical discriminant regression (IHDR) by Hwang and Weng [4] grows the regression tree incrementally with the above requirements as the designed goal.

However, IHDR face several challenging problems. First, some data sets have high dimensional data in the input space while there are only few distinct labels in the output space. Some financial and marketing data only have two labels. In this case, the dimension of discriminant subspace of IHDR is only one, which is not enough to partition a high-dimensional input space. Second, in real-time learning, a segment of sensory stream is not stationary, but is typically very biased. Consider vision-based navigation as an example, if the robot learns by trying first in a straight corridor, almost all incoming samples are associated with one control signal ("Go straight"). A node must spawn children if the number of stored prototypes in it hits a certain limitation. Otherwise, the retrieval time increases linearly. This situation of biased statistics is true with human mental developmental [12] by which our line of work is motivated. The above problems are very challenging and have not been addressed by the existing literature. We proposed a novel node self-organization and spawning strategy which generates more discriminant subspace by forming multiple clusters for one class and balancing the number of samples in each cluster. The requirements for real-time and incremental learning are satisfied too.

2   Locally Balanced Incremental Hierarchical Discriminant Regression

2.1   Incremental Hierarchical Discriminant Regression

Many problems like content-based retrieval, vision-based navigation and intelligent data engineering can be formulated as a complicated function which maps high dimensional input and the current state to low-dimensional output signals. We use a regression tree to approximate this function. In order to build such a tree, two types of clusters are incrementally updated at each node of the IHDR algorithm — y-clusters and x-clusters [3]. The y-clusters are clusters in the output space $\mathcal{Y}$ and x-clusters are those in the input space $\mathcal{X}$. There are a maximum of q clusters of each type at each node. The idea is that each node models a region of the input space using q Gaussians.

For each new sample (x, y), y finds the nearest y-cluster in Euclidean distance and updates the center of the y-cluster. This y-cluster indicates which corresponding x-cluster the input (x, y) belongs to. Then, the x part of (x, y) is used to update the statistics of the x-cluster (the mean vector and the covariance matrix). Each node keeps up to q x-clusters. The centers of these q x-clusters are denoted by $C = \{c_1, c_2, ..., c_q \mid c_i \in \mathcal{X}, i = 1, 2, ..., q\}$.

In online-learning, the algorithm updates the tree's statistics incrementally for each new training example. The average of n input examples $x_1, x_2, ..., x_n$ can be recursively computed from the current input data x_n and the previous average $\bar{x}^{(n-1)}$ by equation (1):

$$\bar{x}^{(n+1)} = \frac{n-l}{n+1}\bar{x}^{(n)} + \frac{1+l}{n+1}x_{n+1} \tag{1}$$

where l is a parameter. If $l > 0$, the new input gets more weight than old inputs. We called this implementation the amnesic average. The covariance matrix can be updated incrementally by using the amnesic average too. A more detailed description of the algorithm can be found in [4].

2.2   Locally Balanced Tree and Time Smoothing

However, IHDR faces several challenging problems. First, many applications in intelligent data engineering only have two distinct labels in the output space, for example, whether a customer switches from one company to another one or not. As shown in Fig. 1(a), there are two classes whose samples are specified by "+" and "-". The dimension of input space is three. m_1 and m_2 are two vectors describing the centers of the two classes. The Fisher's linear discriminant vector D_1 for two classes [2] is determined by Eq. (2).

$$D_1 = S_w^{-1}(m_1 - m_2) \tag{2}$$

D_1 is a vector along the most discriminating 1-D subspace. According to the IHDR algorithm described above, the discriminant subspace is also one-dimensional. This low dimension of space limits the power of discrimination. In Fig. 1(a), one of these two classes is not unimodel. Thus, the Gaussian distribution assumption of two-class Fisher's LDA does not apply. The one-dimensional discriminating subspace meets a big problem: the two classes are not separable in the subspace. As shown in Fig. 1(a), the separator (the thicker line) based on D_1 can not totally partition these two classes.

The second challenging problem is caused by the nonstationary statistics of a segment of sensory stream. Given vision-based navigation as an example, when the robot navigates in a straight corridor, almost all incoming images are paired with the same control signal ("Go straight"). In order to make sure that the learning is conducted in real-time, a node must spawn children if the number of stored prototypes in it hits a certain limitation. Nonstationary statistics causes the following problems: (a) A segment of output contains only few values, which is similar to the first case. (b) The performance of a tree cannot degrade after spawning children from a node. It is challenging for new children to maintain the performance realized earlier by the experienced parent. (c) Spawning children requires distribution of micro-prototypes, which could slow down the system response without a carefully designed spawning strategy. In order to tackle these problems, we proposed a new node self-organization and spawning strategy.

Suppose there are two classes, say c_1 ("+"), c_2 ("-"), as shown in Fig. 1(b). The number of micro-prototypes of each class is N_i, $i = 1, 2$. The number of clusters in

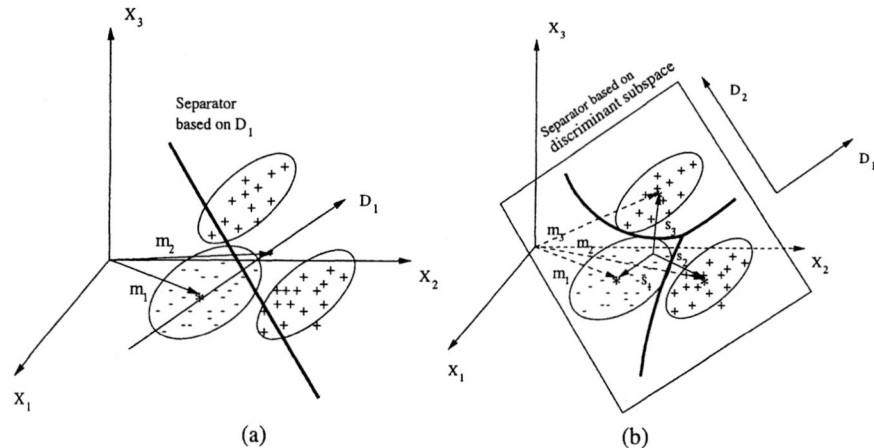

Fig. 1. (a) A one-dimensional discriminant subspace is formed for two classes. (b) Locally balanced node. Two clusters are generated for class 1. A more discriminant subspace is formed.

a node is q. If $q > 2$ (say $q = 3$), we try to allocate some micro-prototypes of c_1 to those clusters that are not in use. Each class in the old tree could be mapped to multiple clusters in the balanced tree. For the ith class, the algorithm will generate q_i' clusters in the new node.

$$q_i' = q \frac{N_i}{N_t} \qquad (3)$$

where N_t = total number of micro-prototypes in this leaf node. In Eq. 3, the q_i' could be float. Eq. 4 converts it to an integer.

$$q_i' = [\sum_{j=1}^{i} q_j'] - \sum_{j=1}^{i} \bar{q}_j' \qquad (4)$$

where $i = 1, 2, ..., N_y$, N_y is the number of classes of training samples. $\bar{q}_i'$ is defined as: $\bar{q}_i' = \max\{1, q_i'\}$, which guarantees that at least one cluster is generated for each old class.

Fig. 1(b) shows the balanced node. Originally, there were 2 classes. Now, there are 3 clusters. Two clusters are formed for c_1. A two-dimensional subspace passes the head tips of the three center vectors: m_1, m_2 and m_3. The scatter vectors are defined by the following equation:

$$s_i = m_i - \bar{m} \qquad (5)$$

where $i = 1, 2, 3$, $\bar{m}$ is the mean of all center vectors. Let S be the set that contains these scatter vectors: $S = \{s_i | i = 1, 2, 3\}$. The discriminant subspace spanned by S, denoted by span(S), consists of all the possible linear combinations from vectors in S. By applying Gram-Schmidt Orthogonalization (GSO), we can get two orthogonalized discriminant vectors D_1 and D_2. Now the separators (the thicker arcs) based on D_1 and D_2 can partition these two classes. We should note that the algorithm only balances the micro-prototypes in each node, while the entire tree may not be strictly balanced. So this is a local balancing method.

After the node is balanced, the statistics of the new structure must be generated. However, in real-time navigation, the updating frequency is around 10Hz. If the robot calculates the statistical information in one time slot, it will get stuck in the road, which is not allowed. In order to smooth the updating time for each new sample, the algorithm keeps two sets of statistics. The old statistic is used to build the tree. At the same time, the new balanced statistic is updated incrementally after the old statistic is half-mature (the number of micro-prototypes in the node hits half of the limitation). When the new statistics is mature, the old one is thrown away and micro-prototypes are redistributed and updated based on the new structure.

2.3   Algorithm

Procedure 1 Update-tree: *Given the root of the tree and sample* (x, y), *update the tree using* (x, y).

1. *From the root of the tree, update the node by calling* Update-node *and get active clusters. For every active cluster received, check if it points to a child node. If it does, explore the child node by calling* Update-node.
2. *Do the above step until all active leaf nodes are reached.*
3. *Each leaf node keeps micro-prototypes* $(\hat{x}_i, \hat{y}_i)$ *that belong to it. If y is not given, the output is* $\hat{y}_i$ *if* $\hat{x}_i$ *is the nearest neighbor among these micro-prototypes.*
4. *If y is given, do the following: If* $||x - \hat{x}_i||$ *is less than certain threshold,* (x, y) *updates* $(\hat{x}_i, \hat{y}_i)$ *only. Otherwise,* (x, y) *is a new sample to keep in the leaf.*
5. *If the leaf node is half-mature, call* Balance-node.
6. *If the number of micro-prototypes hits the limitation required for estimating statistics in the new children, the leaf node spawns q children and is frozen. The micro-prototypes are redistributed through multiple steps.*

Procedure 2 Update-node: *Given a node N and* (x, y), *update the node N using* (x, y) *incrementally.*

1. *Find the top matched x-cluster in the following way. If y is given, do (a) and (b); otherwise do (b).*
   a) *Update the mean of the y-cluster nearest y in Euclidean distance. Incrementally update the mean and the covariance matrix of the x-cluster corresponding to the y-cluster.*
   b) *Find the nearest x-cluster according to the probability-based distances. Update the x-cluster if it has not been updated in (a). Mark this central x-cluster as active.*
2. *Return the chosen x-cluster as active cluster.*

Procedure 3 Balance-node: *When the total number of micro-prototypes in this leaf is equal to half of the limitation, balance the micro-prototypes of each cluster.* N_y *is the number of classes in the old node.*

1. *For each y, if $q \leq N_y$, do y-space clustering. Otherwise, $(q > N_y)$, sort X-clusters according to the number of micro-prototypes (increasing).*
2. *Calculate the number of clusters for each old class.*
3. *Conduct K-mean algorithm   [2] to generate new clusters. Reallocate micro-prototypes to each new cluster.*
4. *Calculate new statistics for the balanced node.*

3   The Experimental Results

In order to show the effectiveness of the new algorithm, we applied our method to three kinds of problem: marketing data engineering, face recognition and vision-based navigation.

3.1   Experiments Using Marketing Data

Two kinds of marketing data were used to test the algorithm (Tab. 1). Two thirds of each data set were used for training respectively while the remaining samples were used to for testing. In dataset 1 managers rated 16 different project scenarios as to the ability of the product to successfully enter a market [9]. The input dimension is 12. In dataset 2 customers of a transportation system evaluated the system based on their usage experiences and indicated their satisfaction based on the choice of using that transportation mode again. Only two types of outcomes are provided: satisfied or not based on 18 input dimensions.

Table 1. Marketing data sets

Data set	Training samples	Testing samples	Input dimensions	Classes
Data1	9306	3098	12	16
Data2	1768	590	18	2

We compared the error rate of the proposed LBIHDR algorithm with HDR, IHDR and other methods. As we can see from Tab. 2, if the number of classes is larger (data set 1), then the LBIHDR has the same performance as that of IHDR. However, data set 2 shows that the new algorithm improves the recognition rate. In this experiment, $q = 6$ and $N_t = 100$. The dimension of the discriminant space is five while that of the original IHDR is only one. A more discriminant subspace is formed and the error rate reduces from 12.92% to 8.22%. For these two datasets, some additional traditional marketing research methods were used to test the discrimination of the variables. Linear discriminant analysis was used and achieved a misclassification rate of 46% for dataset 1 while obtaining a misclassification of 23.02% for dataset 2. Next logistic regression was used and misclassification of 43.1% obtained for dataset 1 and 24.14% for dataset 2. The LBIHDR approach outperforms other methods.

Table 2. Error rates of different approaches

Method	Data1	Data2
LDA	46%	23.02%
LR	43%	24.11%
HDR	13.37%	13.57%
IHDR	12.98%	12.92%
LBIHDR	12.98%	8.22%

Fig. 2. The demonstration of the image normalization process. (a): The original images from the FERET data set. (b): The normalized images. (c): The masked images.

3.2 Experiments Using Face Data

Because our goal is to apply the algorithm to high dimensional data, we tested the new algorithm with appearance-based face image retrieval tasks. We performed the experiment using the FERET face data set [7]. The input dimension is 5632! Thirty four human subjects were involved in this experiment. Each person had three face images for the purpose of training. The other face images were used for testing. In order to reduce the effect of background and non-facial areas, a face normalization program was used to translate, scale, and rotate each face image into a canonical image of 88 rows and 64 columns so that eyes are located at the prespecified positions as shown in Fig. 2.

A summary of the performance comparison with some existing major tree classifiers is listed in Table 3. We plugged in the result of major tree algorithms from [11]. The result shows that LBIHDR is really better than some other decision tree methods when the input dimension is very high. Because other methods generate univariate trees, that is, each internal node used only one input component to partition the samples, we cannot expect this type of tree to work well in a high dimensional space.

3.3 Experiments Using Navigation Image Data

We applied the LBIHDR algorithm to vision-based indoor navigation on our SAIL robot. The robot is trained online on second floor in the Engineering building of our University. In the training phase, at each time interval, the robot accepts a pair of stereo images and a control signal, incrementally updates its context which contains past sensory inputs and actions, and then updates the statistics of the regression tree. In the testing phase, a pair of input images is used to retrieve the best match. The associated control signal of the match is the output.

Table 3. The performance of decision tree for FERET test

Method	Error rate		Time (sec)	
	Training	Testing	Training	Testing
CART	10%	53%	2108.00	0.029
C5.0	1%	41%	21.00	0.030
OC1	6%	56%	2206.00	0.047
LBIHDR	0%	0%	8.92	0.027

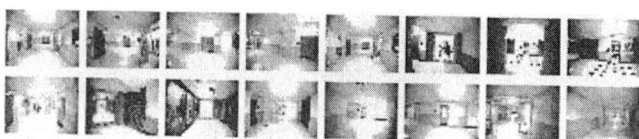

Fig. 3. A subset of images which were inputs to guide the robot turn.

Some of the example input images are shown in Fig 3. A total of 5443 color stereo images with the corresponding heading directions were used for training (one trip). The resolution of each image is 30 by 40. The input dimension is $30 \times 40 \times 3 \times 2 = 7200$, where 3 is the length of context, 2 stands for two eyes. We used the other 5764 (another trip) stereo images to test the performance of the trained system. There are three kinds of output control signals: "Go Straight", "Left", "Right".

We performed both resubstitution and disjoint tests with different rejection measurements. The parameters are defined as follows: $q = 8$, the limitation of the number of samples in each node is 200. The performance is improved significantly compared with the existing IHDR [4]. As shown in Tab. 4, in the resubstitution test, the recognition rate of LBIHDR can reach 100%. In the disjoint test, the recognition rates of LBIHDR is 94% while IHDR can only reach 87%. The retrieval time is also less because the new algorithm balances the distribution of samples in each node. The result testifies that LBIHDR works very well for nonstationary data like visual images in navigation.

Table 4. Comparison of IHDR and LBIHDR

Method	Resubstitution test	Disjoint test	Testing time (ms)
IHDR	92.72%	87.35%	28.6
LBIHDR	100%	94.28%	15.7

In order to guarantee that IHDR can be implemented in real time, we applied the time smoothing algorithm. Fig. 4 records the updating time for each sample in different steps. Here only shows the time profile of 715 samples. The first row shows the total learning time of each sample. The second row shows the updating time except doing local

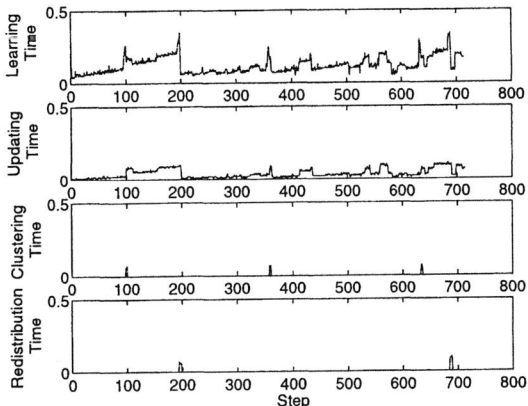

Fig. 4. The timing recording for learning a set of 715 images.

clustering and redistribution. Time records of calculating new statistics (local clustering) and redistribution are shown in third and fourth rows respectively. When the node is half mature (i.e, the node already has 100 micro-prototypes), the new statistics are computed through multiple steps; when the node is mature (i.e, the node has 200 micro-prototypes), micro-prototypes are redistributed. At these moments, the learning time reaches peaks. However, with the time smoothing algorithm, the updating rate still could reach about 3-4Hz, which is extreme important for online learning.

4 Conclusions

In order to solve the major problems due to the nonstationary nature of input-output experience and few distinct labels in the output space with a high-dimensional input space, a new node self-organization and spawning strategy is proposed. Partition of the input space is carried out without relying on a sufficient number of output clusters. Multiple clusters could be generated for one class. The number of samples in each cluster is balanced. Thus, more discriminant subspace can be formed. The performance of the tree is stable before and after children spawn. The presented method for distribution of computational load over time during spawning avoids a slow down of the system response to satisfy the real-time requirement. The experimental results showed that the LBIHDR technique worked well in different applications.

References

1. L. Breiman, J. Friedman, R. Olshen, and C. Stone. *Classification and Regression Trees*. Chapman & Hall, New York, 1993.
2. R. Duda, P. Hart, and D. Stork. *Pattern Classification*. Wiley, New York, NY, 2001.
3. W. Hwang and J.Weng. Hierarchical discriminant regression. *IEEE Trans. Pattern Analysis and Machine Intelligence*, 22(11):1277–1293, 2000.

4. W. Hwang and J. Weng. Incremental hierarchical discriminant regression for indoor visual navigation. In *Int'l Conf. on Image Processing*, Thessaloniki, Greece, October 2001.
5. S. Murthy. Automatic construction of decision trees from data: A multidisciplinary survey. *Data Mining and Knowledge Discovery*, 1998.
6. S. Murthy, S. Kasit, and S. Salzberg. A system for induction of oblique decision trees. *Journal of Artificial Intelligence*, 2:1–33, Aug. 1994.
7. P. Phillips, H. Moon, S. Rizvi, and P. Rauss. The FERET evaluation methodology for facere-cognition algorithms. *pami*, 22:1090–1103, 2000.
8. J. Quinlan. *C4.5: Programs for Machine Learning*. Morgan Kaufmann, San Mateo, CA, 1993.
9. R. Roger, Di. Benedetto, and J. Schmidt. Using the analytic hiearchy process in new product screening. *The jouranl of Product Innovation Management*, 16:1:65–76, 1999.
10. D. L. Swets and J.Weng. Hierarchical discriminant analysis for image retreival. *IEEE Trans. Pattern Analysis and Machine Intelligence*, 1997. under 2nd-round review.
11. J. Weng and W. Hwang. An incremental learning algorithm with automatically derived dis-criminating features. In *Asian Conference on Computer Vision*, pages 426–431, Taipei, Tai-wan, Jan 2000.
12. J. Weng, J. McClelland, A. Pentland, O. Sporns, I. StockMan, M. Sur, and E. Thelen. Au-tonomous mental development by robots and animals. *Science*, 291:599–600, 2000.

A Comparative Study of Several Cluster Number Selection Criteria

Xuelei Hu and Lei Xu

Department of Computer Science and Engineering,
The Chinese University of Hong Kong, Shatin, NT, Hong Kong
{xlhu, lxu}@cse.cuhk.edu.hk

Abstract. The selection of the number of clusters is an important and challenging issue in cluster analysis. In this paper we perform an experimental comparison of several criteria for determining the number of clusters based on Gaussian mixture model. The criteria that we consider include Akaike's information criterion (AIC), the consistent Akaike's information criterion (CAIC), the minimum description length (MDL) criterion which formally coincides with the Bayesian inference criterion (BIC), and two model selection methods driven from Bayesian Ying-Yang (BYY) harmony learning: harmony empirical learning criterion (BYY-HEC) and harmony data smoothing criterion (BYY-HDS). We investigate these methods on synthetic data sets of different sample size and the iris data set. The results of experiments illustrate that BYY-HDS has the best overall success rate and obviously outperforms other methods for small sample size. CAIC and MDL tend to underestimate the number of clusters, while AIC and BYY-HEC tend to overestimate the number of clusters especially in the case of small sample size.

1 Introduction

Cluster analysis is a generic term for a variety of methods for finding groups or clusters in multivariate data. One important issue in cluster analysis is the selection of the number of clusters. In past decades, many efforts have been made to estimate the number of clusters based on mixture models [1][2][3].

In this paper we concentrate on the two-phase style methods. The methods in this class usually obtain a set of candidate models for a range of values of the number of clusters via some parameter learning in the first phase, and then select the number of clusters according to some model selection criterion in the second phase. Typical examples of model selection criteria include Akaike's information criterion (AIC) [4], its extension Bozdogan's consistent Akaike's information criterion (CAIC) [5], and Rissanen's minimum description length (MDL) criterion [6][7] which formally coincides with Schwarz's Bayesian inference criterion (BIC) [8]. These model selection criteria are based on the maximum likelihood (ML) estimators of model parameters. The standard algorithm to implement the maximum likelihood learning is the expectation-maximization (EM) algorithm [9].

J. Liu et al. (Eds.): IDEAL 2003, LNCS 2690, pp. 195–202, 2003.

More recently a series of cluster number selection criteria and clustering algorithms driven from the Bayesian Ying-Yang (BYY) harmony learning have been proposed in [10][3]. We consider two model selection criteria among them in this study. One is BYY harmony empirical learning criterion (BYY-HEC), first proposed in [10] and further developed in [3]. It also can be used based on the ML estimators of mixture parameters obtained by EM algorithm. Another is BYY harmony data smoothing learning criterion (BYY-HDS) that was newly proposed in [3]. Being different from above approaches, in first phase we estimate competing model parameters by a smoothed EM algorithm that implements the regularized ML learning by data smoothing techniques [11][12][13].

The purpose of this study is to compare above model selection methods: AIC, CAIC, MDL, BYY-HEC, and BYY-HDS on selecting the number of clusters in Gaussian mixture based clustering by experiments with respect to sample size. We investigate these methods on synthetic data sets of different sample size for both spherical clustering and elliptic clustering. We also give a real data example of the well known Iris data set. The most remarkable result of our study is that BYY-HDS method has the best overall success rates and obviously outperforms other methods for small sample size. CAIC and MDL tend to underestimate the number of clusters, while AIC and BYY-HEC have higher overestimating rates especially in the case of small sample size. BYY-HDS has no obviously tendency to overestimate or underestimate.

The remainder of this paper is organized as follows. In Section 2, we review the methods for the selection of the number of clusters considered in our study. In Section 3 we describe the design of the experimental study, illustrate the results, and analyze the results. Finally we draw a conclusion in Section 4.

2   Several Cluster Number Selection Methods

The probability density function of Gaussian mixture distribution with k components can be written as

$$p(x) = \sum_{l=1}^{k} \alpha_l G(x|m_l, \Sigma_l) \tag{1}$$

with $\alpha_l \geq 0, l = 1, ..., k$, and $\sum_{l=1}^{k} \alpha_l = 1$, where and throughout this paper, $G(x|m, \Sigma)$ denotes a Gaussian density with mean vector m and covariance matrix Σ. We let $\theta_k = \{m_1, ..., m_k, \Sigma_1, ..., \Sigma_k, \alpha_1, ..., \alpha_k\}$ being the set of parameters of the mixture with k components.

By using Gaussian mixture densities as models for cluster analysis, the clustering problem becomes that of estimating the parameters and the number of components of the assumed mixture based on a finite number of observations $x_1, x_2, ..., x_n$. Given the number of components k, we can estimate the parameters θ_k according to

$$\hat{\theta}_k = \arg\max_{\theta_k} C(\theta_k), \tag{2}$$

where $C(\theta_k)$ is some cost function according to some learning principle. For the ML learning, $C(\theta_k)$ is equal to the log likelihood function $L(\theta_k)$ denoted by

$$L(\theta_k) = \ln \prod_{i=1}^{n} p(x_i) = \sum_{i=1}^{n} \ln \sum_{l=1}^{k} \alpha_l G(x_i|m_l, \Sigma_l). \tag{3}$$

The ML learning can be effectively implemented by the expectation-maximization (EM) algorithm [9]. It alternatingly applying two steps:

E-Step Calculate the posterior probability $\hat{P}(l|x_i) = \frac{\hat{\alpha}_l G(x_i|\hat{m}_l, \hat{\Sigma}_l)}{\sum_{l=1}^{k} \hat{\alpha}_l G(x_i|\hat{m}_l, \hat{\Sigma}_l)}$

for $l = 1, ..., k$ and $i = 1, ..., n$.

M-Step Update parameters by $\hat{\alpha}_l = \frac{1}{n} \sum_{i=1}^{n} \hat{P}(l|x_i)$, $\hat{m}_l = \frac{1}{n\hat{\alpha}_l} \sum_{i=1}^{n} \hat{P}(l|x_i)x_i$, and $\hat{\Sigma}_l = \frac{1}{n\hat{\alpha}_l} \sum_{i=1}^{n} \hat{P}(l|x_i)(x_i - \hat{m}_l)(x_i - \hat{m}_l)^T$ for $l = 1, ..., k$.

The problem that remains in clustering is how to select the number of components. The two-phase style cluster number selection procedure can be described as follows. In the first phase, we define a range of values of k from k_{min} to k_{max} which is assumed to contain the optimal k. At each specific k, we estimate the parameters θ_k according to some learning principle. In the second phase, with the results $\hat{\theta}_k, k = k_{min}, ..., k_{max}$ obtained in the first phase, we obtain the estimate of the number of clusters $\hat{k}$ from k_{min} to k_{max} according to

$$\hat{k} = \arg\min_{k}\{J(\hat{\theta}_k, k), k = k_{min}, ..., k_{max}\}, \tag{4}$$

where $J(\hat{\theta}_k, k)$ is some model selection criterion.

2.1   Three Popular Model Selection Criteria

Next we introduce several frequently used model selection criteria: AIC, CAIC, and MDL. These criteria are based on the maximum likelihood (ML) estimators of model parameters. Generally, these three model selection criteria take the form [14]

$$J(\hat{\theta}_k, k) = -2L(\hat{\theta}_k) + A(n)D(k) \tag{5}$$

where $L(\hat{\theta}_k)$ is the log likelihood Eq. 3 based on the ML estimates of mixture parameters, $D(k)$ is the number of independent parameters in k-component mixture, $A(n)$ is a function with respect to the number of observations. According to [2], for arbitrary means and covariances $D(k) = (k-1) + k(d+d(d+1)/2)$ where d is the dimension of x. If a different and spherical covariances are assumed then $D(k) = (k-1) + k(d+1)$. Different approaches lead to different choices of $A(n)$. $A(n) = 2$ for Akaike's information criterion (AIC) [4], $A(n) = \ln n + 1$ for Bozdogan's consistent Akaike's information criterion (CAIC) [5], and $A(n) = \ln n$ for Rissanen's minimum description length (MDL) criterion [6] that formally coincides with Schwarz's Bayesian inference criterion (BIC) [8].

These criteria are derived from different theories. One possible interpretation is that the first term is a measure of lack of fit when the maximum likelihood estimators of the mixture parameters are used, the second term is a measure of model complexity that penalizes the first term due to the unreliability of the first term.

2.2   Two BYY Harmony Learning Criteria

A series of clustering methods have been developed based on the Bayesian Ying-Yang (BYY) harmony leaning [3][13]. Here we only outline some results related to this study, for details please refer to [3][13]. The BYY harmony empirical learning model selection criterion (BYY-HEC) [10][3] for Gaussian mixture based clustering takes the form

$$J_{BYY-HEC}(\hat{\theta}_k, k) = 0.5 \sum_{l=1}^{k} \hat{\alpha}_l \ln |\hat{\Sigma}_l| - \sum_{l=1}^{k} \hat{\alpha}_l \ln \hat{\alpha}_l, \tag{6}$$

where $\hat{\theta}_k$ are the ML estimates of parameters that can be obtained by the EM algorithm.

The BYY harmony data smoothing model selection criterion(BYY-HDS), driven from BYY data smoothing regularization technique [11][12][13], can be described as [3]

$$J_{BYY-HDS}(\hat{\theta}_k^h, k) = \sum_{l=1}^{k} \hat{\alpha}_l(0.5 \ln |\hat{\Sigma}_l| + 0.5\hat{h}^2 Tr[\hat{\Sigma}_l^{-1}] - \ln \hat{\alpha}_l), \tag{7}$$

We denote θ_k^h as parameters consist model parameters θ_k and smoothing parameter h. Note that $\hat{\theta}_k^h$ are the data smoothing regularized ML estimates of parameters [3]. A smoothed EM algorithm was given in [3][13] to automatically learn the θ_k^h. The iteration of the smoothed EM algorithm also consists two steps: E-Step and M-Step. In the E-Step we calculate the posterior probability in the same way as the EM algorithm. In the M-Step, first we fix the smoothing parameter h, and update model parameters θ_k. We update mixture priors and means in the same way as the EM algorithm. For covariances, we estimate them by $\hat{\Sigma}_l = \frac{1}{n\hat{\alpha}_l} \sum_{i=1}^{n} \hat{P}(l|x_i)(x_i - \hat{m}_l)(x_i - \hat{m}_l)^T + \hat{h}^2 I$. Second, with θ_k fixed we update the smoothing parameter h as described in [13]. This algorithm not only prevents the covariance matrices from being singular which usually occurs in the EM algorithm but also provides a new way to update the smoothing parameter.

3   Experiments

In this section, we illustrate the experimental performances of the model selection criteria: AIC, CAIC, MDL, BYY-HEC, and BYY-HDS on two group of synthetic data sets with different sample size and the well known Iris data set. In experiments, we estimated the number of clusters according to the two-phase procedure described above. In the first phase, we used the EM algorithm to estimate the mixture parameters for AIC, CAIC, MDL, and BYY-HEC methods, and we used the smoothed EM algorithm to estimate both model parameters and smoothing parameter for BYY-HDS. The initial parameter estimates for the EM algorithm and smoothed EM algorithm were obtained by randomly allocating observations to subpopulations and computing the prior, sample means and covariance matrices of these initial components. Of the five random starts, the one which gave the largest value of the resulting log-likelihood was used as the solution. The smoothing parameter h for the smoothed EM algorithm was initialized by $h^2 = \frac{1}{dn^3} \sum_{i=1}^{n} \sum_{j=1}^{n} \|x_i - x_j\|^2$. Other initialization strategies are also possible.

3.1   A Spherical Clustering Example

In the first example the data sets of size 80, 200, and 400 were randomly generated from a 4-component bivariate Gaussian mixture distribution with equal mixture priors, mean vectors located at $[-0.1, -0.2]^T$, $[-0.2, 0.2]^T$, $[0.2, -0.2]^T$, and $[0.2, 0.2]^T$, and equal spherical covariance matrices $0.01I$. We used a Gaussian mixture model with different spherical covariance matrices and specified $k_{min} = 2$ and $k_{max} = 6$. Since there is some uncertainty due to different simulations and initializations, we repeated the experiment 100 times. We randomly generated 100 data sets with each sample size, and examined all the methods on very data set. The rates of underestimating, success, and overestimating of each methods are shown in Tab. 1. In experiments, we observe that BYY-HDS had better performance than BYY-HEC for small sample size and had similar performance with BYY-HEC for large sample size. With the number of observations increasing the smoothing parameter h decreased.

3.2   An Elliptic Clustering Example

In the second example, we considered a more general case of Gaussian mixtures with arbitrate different covariance matrices. We randomly generated data sets of size 100, 250, and 500 from a 5-component bivariate Gaussian mixture. Fig. 1(a) shows the data sets in one simulation of each size. We used a Gaussian mixture with arbitrate different covariance matrices and specified $k_{min} = 3$ and $k_{max} = 7$. Fig. 1(b) shows the normalized value of $J(\hat{\theta}_k, k)$ of the methods: BYY-HDS, AIC, CAIC, and MDL on the corresponding data sets shown in Fig. 1(a). The normalized value of $J(\hat{\theta}_k, k)$, denoted by $J_{norm}(k)$, was obtained by $J_{norm}(k) = \frac{J(\hat{\theta}_k,k)-J_{min}}{J_{max}-J_{min}}$ where J_{min} and J_{max} are the minimum and maximum value of $J(\hat{\theta}_k, k), k = k_{min}, ..., k_{max}$. From Fig. 1 we find that BYY-HDS always selected the right number for varying sample sizes. For small sample size CAIC, MDL underestimated the number, while AIC overestimated the number. On the data set with largest sample size, MDL and CAIC got the correct results. Tab. 1 illustrates the rates of underestimating, success, and overestimating of each methods in 100 replications. From Tab. 1, we observe that BYY-HDS has the highest total success rate and obviously outperforms other methods when sample size is small.

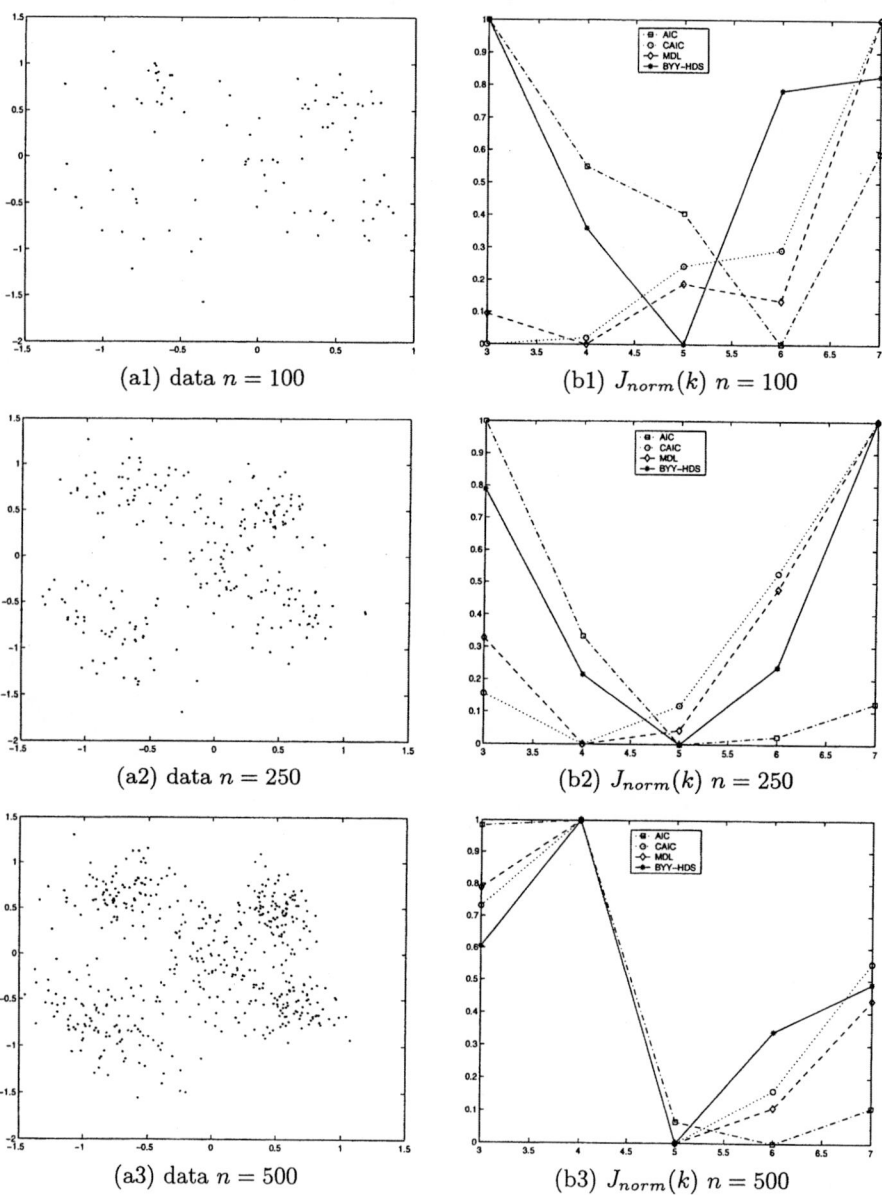

Fig. 1. The curves of normalized value of $J(\hat{\theta}_k, k)$ of the criteria BYY-HDS, AIC, CAIC, and MDL on the data sets of 5 Elliptic Gaussians with different sample size. (a) shows the data points, (b) shows corresponding results. AIC (dashdot line with square), CAIC (dotted line with circle), MDL (dashed line with diamond), and BYY-HDS (solid line with star)

Table 1. Rates of underestimating (U), success (S), and overestimating (O) by each criteria on the simulation data sets of two type Gaussian mixtures in 100 replications for varying sample sizes

Example	Sample size	AIC			CAIC			MDL			BYY-HEC			BYY-HDS		
		U	S	O	U	S	O	U	S	O	U	S	O	U	S	O
Spherical	$n = 80$	0	26	74	69	31	0	48	52	0	0	20	80	11	76	13
	$n = 200$	0	48	52	16	79	5	12	85	3	0	57	43	6	84	10
	$n = 400$	0	43	57	12	87	1	8	90	2	0	64	36	5	88	7
Elliptic	$n = 100$	0	21	79	87	13	0	82	18	0	0	13	87	16	61	23
	$n = 250$	0	34	66	69	31	0	57	43	0	1	25	74	14	59	27
	$n = 500$	0	23	77	41	59	0	37	62	1	9	61	30	12	69	19
	Overall	0	32.5	67.5	49.0	50.0	1.0	40.7	58.3	1.0	1.7	40.0	58.3	10.7	72.8	16.5

3.3 Iris Data Set

Next we consider the well-known Iris data set which contains 150 four-dimensional points from three classes, 50 per class. We used a Gaussian mixture with arbitrary covariance matrices and chose $k_{min} = 1$ and $k_{max} = 5$. AIC chose the number five, CAIC selected the number two, MDL chose the number two, BYY-HEC selected the number five, and BYY-HDS chose the number three which is the correct number.

3.4 Summary of Results

In this section we summarize some most important results of our experimental study. Firstly, we measure the performance of the various model selection criteria by their overall success rates. BYY-HDS criterion has the best overall success rate, followed by MDL, BYY-HEC, CAIC, and AIC. Second we discuss the properties of these methods with respect to the sample size. BYY-HDS obviously outperforms the other methods for small sample size. It is reasonable because BYY-HDS uses the data smoothing technique which is a regularization technique that aims to deal with the small sample problem [13]. While the other methods are usually derived from the assumption of large-scale sample size. We also observe that BYY-HDS tend to coincide the results of BYY-HEC when the sample size increasing due to that the estimate of parameter h becomes smaller with the sample size increasing. Third we investigate the property of underestimating and overestimating. AIC and BYY-HEC have high rate of overestimating, while MDL and CAIC have high risk of underestimating the number of clusters. BYY-HDS has no obvious tendency of overestimating or underestimating. A final note is made about the computational complexity. Since every iteration in the smoothed EM algorithm involves $O(n^2)$ calculation of Gaussian, so the smoothed EM algorithm takes a larger computational cost than EM algorithm.

4   Conclusion

We have made an experimental comparison of several cluster number selection criteria based on Gaussian mixture model. The considered criteria include three typical model selection criteria: AIC, CAIC, and MDL/BIC, and two model selection criteria driven from BYY harmony learning theory: BYY-HEC and BYY-HDS. We could say that the harmony data smoothing learning criterion (BYY-HDS) outperforms the other methods especially for small sample size.

References

1. Jain, A.K., Duin, R.P.W., Mao, J.: Statistical pattern recognition: A review. IEEE Transactions on Pattern Analysis and Machine Intelligence **22** (2000) 4–37
2. Bozdogan, H.: Mixture-model cluster analysis using model selection criteria and a new informational measure of complexity. In Bozdogan, H., ed.: Proceedings of the First US/Japan Conference on the Frontiers of Statistical Modeling: An Informational Approach. Volume 2., Dordrecht, the Netherlands, Kluwer Academic Publishers (1994) 69–113
3. Xu, L.: Byy harmony learning, structural rpcl, and topological self-organizing on mixture models. Neural Networks **15** (2002) 1125–1151
4. Akaik, H.: A new look at statistical model identification. IEEE Transactions on Automatic Control **19** (1974) 716–723
5. Bozdogan, H.: Model selection and akaike's information criterion (aic): the general theory and its analytical extensions. Psychometrika **52** (1987) 345–370
6. Rissanen, J.: Modeling by shortest data description. Automatica **14** (1978) 465–471
7. Barron, A., Rissanen, J.: The minimum description length principle in coding and modeling. IEEE Trans. Information Theory **44** (1998) 2743–2760
8. Schwarz, G.: Estimating the dimension of a model. The Annals of Statistics **6** (1978) 461–464
9. Dempster, A., Laird, N., D.Rubin: Maximum likelihood estimation from incomplete data via the em algorithm. J. Royal Statistical Soc. B **39** (1977) 1–38
10. Xu, L.: Bayesian ying-yang machine, clustering and number of clusters. Pattern Recognition Letters **18** (1997) 1167–1178
11. Xu, L.: Bayesian ying-yang system and theory as a unified statistical learning approach: (i) unsupervised and semi-unsupervised learning. In Amari, S., Kassabov, N., eds.: Brain-like Computing and Learning, Springer-Verlag (1997) 241–274
12. Xu, L.: Byy harmony learning, independent state space, and generalized apt financial analyses. IEEE Tansactions on Neural Networks **12** (2001) 822–849
13. Xu, L.: Data smoothing regularization, multi-sets-learning, and problem solving stategies. in press, Neural Networks (2003)
14. Sclove, S.L.: Some aspects of model-selection criteria. In Bozdogan, H., ed.: Proceedings of the First US/Japan Conference on the Frontiers of Statistical Modeling: An Informational Approach. Volume 2., Dordrecht, the Netherlands, Kluwer Academic Publishers (1994) 37–67

Automating Stock Prediction with Neural Network and Evolutionary Computation

Sio Iong Ao

Systems Engineering and Engineering Management,
The Chinese University of Hong Kong, Shatin, Hong Kong
siao@se.cuhk.edu.hk

Abstract. In the previous studies [1, 2, 3], it has been found that there is strong correlation between the US market and the Asian markets in the long run. The VAR analysis shows that the US indices lead the Asian ones. But, such correlation is time-dependent and affects the performance of using the historical US data to predict the Asian markets by neural network. Here, a simplified automated system is outlined to overcome this difficulty by employing the evolutionary computation to simulate the markets interactive dynamics. The aim is to supplement the previous studies like [4, 5], which have focused more or less solely on the local stock market's historical data, with additional information from other leading markets' movements.

1 Introduction

Many experts in the stock markets have employed the technical analysis for better prediction for a long time. Generally speaking, the technical analysis derives the stock movement from the stock's own historical value. The historical data can be used directly to form the support level and the resistance or they can be plugged into many technical indicators for further investigation.

It has been tried incorporated other markets' historical data into the prediction of the index movement. Previous econometric study has shown that such lead-lag relationship does exist [2, 3]. In the paper [1, 6, 7], the neural network has been employed to incorporate other leading markets into the prediction of the lagging markets. The result has been found to be positive in general. But, it is also found that such correlation is time-dependent and experts' opinion or current correlation magnitude is needed to determine whether at a particular time, such a correlation is strong or weak and which model is to be adopted. Here, a system with the neural network working together with the evolutionary computation is built to see if such a process can be automated.

J. Liu et al. (Eds.): IDEAL 2003, LNCS 2690, pp. 203–210, 2003.

1.1 Overview of the Econometric Analysis of the Lead-Lag Relationship of Stock Markets

The Vector Autoregression (VAR) method is mainly used to investigate the relationship between different variables. Its advantage is that multiple variables can be investigated at the same time and the interdependence can be tested automatically with the sophisticated statistically significance level. The results [1, 6] are summarized as followed (the dependence is tested with 5% significance level):

(1) HK depends on its past price, JP, Nasdaq, S&P and DJ;
(2) AU depends on its past price, S&P and DJ;
(3) SG depends on its past price, HK, Nasdaq, S&P and DJ;
(4) JP depends on its past price, Nasdaq, S&P and DJ;
(5) Nasdaq depends on its past price only;
(6) DJ depends on its past price and Nasdaq;
(7) S&P depends on its past price and Nasdaq;

The results from the VAR modeling suggest that, for the Asian markets, the relevant information are its own historical value as well as the stock movements from the US markets. It is also positive to know the extent and time-dependant nature of the markets' dynamics when we draw the correlation diagram of the local market with the US markets. For example, Fig. 1 shows the changes of Hong Kong's correlation with S&P over the recent ten years. It can be observed that the correlation is time-dependent. Further investigation can tell us that, at the time of low correlation like the late 90's of the Asian Financial crisis, the Hong Kong market (and similarly other Asian markets) are dominated by the local events like the currency problems. At other periods, the local markets are greatly correlated with the US markets.

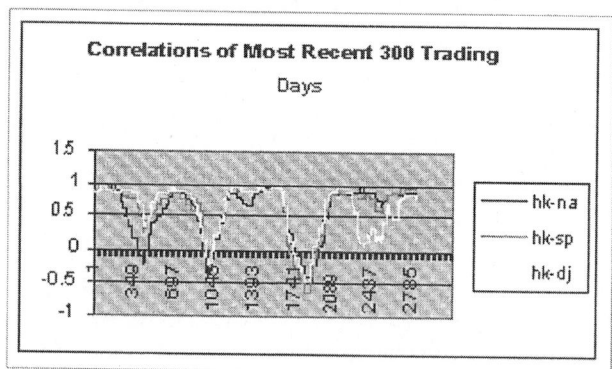

Fig. 1. Correlation of Hong Kong index with US's S&P, using the correlation formulas of 300-trading days

1.2 Previous Results of Employing the Stand-Alone Neural Network

In the neural network, the three-layer architecture is usually employed. The layers are the input layer, the hidden layer and the output layer as shown in Fig. 2. The inspiring idea for this structure is to mimic the working of our brain. The above layers correspond to the axons for inputs, synapses, soma, and axons for outputs [8, 9].

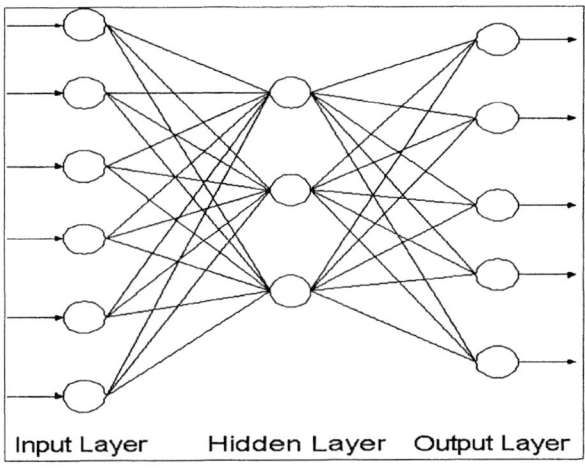

Fig. 2. The three-layer architecture structure of a typical neural network design employed

The previous results of the prediction with neural network are as followed in Table 1 of two periods 1 and 2 respectively. It can be observed that for different periods, the prediction made with both HK and S&P inputs can outperform that with HK inputs only at the period 1, which is with high correlation between these two markets. At the time of low correlation, the situation is reverse and it underperforms. As we can't obtain the current correlation data before the prediction is made, it is not possible to automate the process to decide which model will be employed. Human expert's opinion is needed to make the decision. Here, the evolutionary computation is employed to simulate this process.

Table 1. Prediction of the Hong Kong stock market by NN for different time periods

Prediction	HK_SP_1	HK_1	HK_SP_2	HK_2
Mean Abs. Error	46.24	96.11	737.47	314.59
Mean Index Value	3656.96	3656.96	14904.71	14904.71
Percentage Error	1.26%	2.63%	4.95%	2.11%

1.3 Brief Description of the Evolutionary Computation

The objective here is to develop a system that can take over the task of an expert for the above model selection process. The system is expected to have the capability to learn which model should be employed at different periods. Previous studies [10] have recognized the close relationships between the economic learning models and models of evolutionary computation. The tactic employed here is the genetic algorithm learning (GA) of the evolutionary computation.

The goal of the GA is to let the strategy with higher payoff to remain while that with lower payoff more likely to disappear. This methodology is suitable for our evolutionary purpose. We can image that there exists many experts, who favor the different models dynamically as time passes. The evolutionary process come into play, as these imaginary experts with better prediction should survive more likely than the one with poor records.

GA can be considered as a stochastic process [11] to search for a heuristic solution that best suits for the problem. The solutions set for the problem can be represented as the population of GA. Then, each solution can be regarded as a chromosome of the population. The genes inside the chromosome characterize the chromosome. The genes of the fitter chromosome are more likely to survive in each evolutionary cycle. In the evolutionary cycle, there are four main steps:

(1) **Selection**, which is to let the fittest to survive in the enlarged population;
(2) **Crossover**, which is to produce child chromosome of genes from parent chromosomes;
(3) **Mutation**, which is to make stochastic changes to the chromosomes;
(4) **Reproduction**, which is to increase the population size by the above crossover and mutation process.

The encoding and decoding of the problems set for the study here will be discussed in the Sect. 3.

2 Data Descriptions

The stock data covers the stock markets in US and East Asia region, namely HK, JP, AU, SG, NASA100, PSCOMP and DJINDUS. The data is in daily formal from 3rd May 1990 to 3rd May 2002, available from the DataStream and Reuters.

3 Working Mechanism of the Hybrid VAR-NN-EC

The hybrid Vector Autoregression, neural network and evolutionary computation (VAR-NN-EC) can supplement its separate stand-alone components. The aim of the system here is to automate the decision process of prediction. The methodology of the VAR-NN-EC is shown as followed:

(1) **VAR analysis**, which is to search for the correlated and leading indicators by the VAR method automatically;
(2) **Neural network** prediction, which is to make forecasting from the relevant inputs decided by the VAR analysis;
(3) **Evolutionary process**, which is to evaluate each forecasting series by the neural network and select the fittest to survive.

Generally speaking, this methodology can work for inputs data like indices of the regional countries and influential countries. Input data, like the trade volume, economic growth rate and currency exchange rate, etc., can also be tested in the VAR analysis. For the input variables with significance level below a pre-defined level, they can be served as the input variable for the neural network. The prediction made by the neural network with these input variable may be time-dependent. In some periods, some input variables may be fitter for the prediction, while, in other periods, they may be poorer in fact. These neural network predictors with different inputs can be regards as experts of different opinions of the relevant economical factors. Their prediction may vary with time, as said. The selection and evaluation of these expert predictors can be made in the evolutionary cycle. Experts with higher forecasting accuracy in each cycle are going to be weight more heavily in the coming round. This process is achieved in step (3) of the evolutionary process. Fig. 3 is the scheme diagram of how this mechanism works.

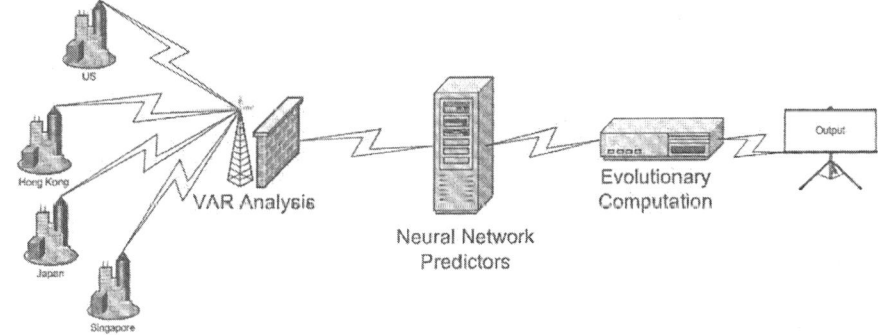

Fig. 3. The scheme diagram of how this mechanism works

In this study, this methodology has been demonstrated with the regional index data as well as that from the US markets. The VAR analysis has shown that, as an example, Hong Kong's markets are influences by its most recent price changes and that from the US. Then, it is to be followed by employing the neural network to make predictions with different input combinations. These predictions can be regarded as the population of experts of different weighting to the input variables. The different experts are going to be encoded as the chromosomes in evolutionary process. Fitter chromosome means the one with better prediction. The corresponding weightings of the input variables by each expert serve as the genes of the chromosome. For example, Fig. 4 shows us an example of an expert of the weighting of input S&P, Nasdaq and

HK data as 2:1:1 in the chromosome parent 1. In parent 2, the ratio of the opinion of importance is 1:1:2. The child 1 is reproduced from the crossover of parent 1 and parent 2, by inheriting the first half of genes from parent 1 and the second half from parent 2. The child 2 is formed from the mutation process, by stochastically selecting the third and forth genes of parent 1 to change to other values. This mutation is to ensure that the population will be able to cover all possible opinions and has a globally suitable solution.

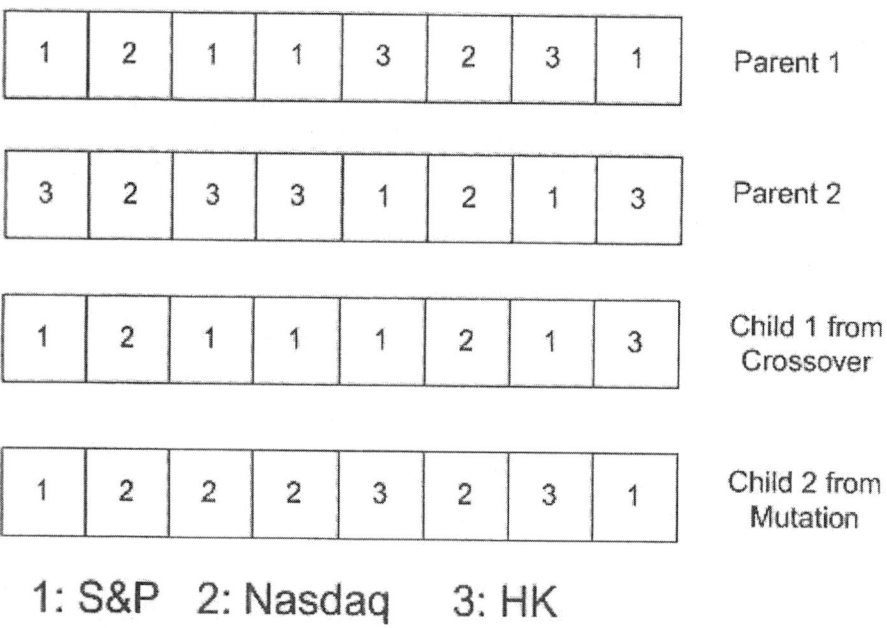

Fig. 4. An example of how to form the chromosome with genes, representing the stock experts

4   Comparing Results from the VAR-NN-EC System

The simplified evolutionary computation is carried to demonstrate how the GA works here. The population is consisted of 11 chromosomes (experts of different opinions). The initial opinions of the experts distribute evenly between 0% and 100% of the weighting of the variable S&P. That is 0%, 10%, 20%, 30%, and up to 100%. For the case of an expert of 20% of the confidence of the HK_SP model, the genes of this chromosome will be assigned a probability of 20% being this model while 80% probability being the other model. This is to introduce the stochastic nature of the initial chromosomes.

The results HK_SP_2 and HK_2 (the second testing period), where the 1651st to 1850th dates have been used for training and then the next 100 dates for the prediction validation, are used here for the investigation. When setting the mutation and crossover rate to zero, the mean absolute error is 514.49. That for the HK_SP model is 737.47 and that for HK model is 314.59. It can be observed that the simplified GA model is better than the poor model, while not as accurate as the good model. The advantage of this model is that we do not need the human expert to determine the nature of the interaction of S&P and Hong Kong (to what extent the correlation is at a particular period). The rate of the mutation and the crossover process in the GA model can be varied. Using different rates determines the stochastic search nature of the GA for the fittest solution, for example, how fast it is to reproduce and how much genes it is to exchange. In order to bring more accurate result in the real-life applications, the structure is needed to decide to suit the particular environment involved.

5   Conclusion

Technical analysis has traditionally focused on the historical prices and the trading volume of the market studied. The experts in the field can recognize different patterns of the market and make their prediction with this information. Neural network has been known for its capability for pattern recognition and has played a more and more active role in the forecasting field. For the experts in the financial economics, they have employed various econometric tests for the analysis of the interdependence of multivariate factors in the stock markets. One of the most common methods is the VAR analysis. The hybrid VAR-NN system has been employed here to study the dynamics of the markets as a whole. While taking different weighting of the input variables can make predictions of various accuracies, it is desirable to employ the most suitable expert at its fittest time. This task is achieved by the evolutionary computation here. Combing these three procedures together, the hybrid VAR-NN-EC system for the prediction is designed to automate the process of selecting input variables, expert predictions and the evaluations of various predictions.

Acknowledges. The author would like to thank Professor K. P. Lam for his advice and comment on my research and for his encouragement to me to publish my research results. His works in the genetic algorithm [12] has inspired my interest in the evolutionary computation.

References

1. S. I. Ao, Analysis of the Interaction of Asian Pacific Indices and Forecasting Opening Prices by Hybrid VAR and Neural Network Procedures, *Proc. International Conf. on Computational Intelligence for Modelling, Control and Automation 2003, Vienna, Austria*, Feb 2003.
2. Ling T. He, Time variation paths of international transmission of stock volatility-US vs Hong Kong and South Korea, *Global Finance Journal*, 12, 2001, 79–93.

3. Arie Dekker, Kunal Sen, Martin R. Young, Equity market linkages in the Asia Pacific region A comparison of the orthogonalised and generalized VAR approaches, *Global Finance Journal*, 12, 2001, 1–33.

4. J. W. Baek, S. Z. C, An up-trend detection using an auto-associative neural network: KOSPI 200 futures, *Proc. Intelligent Data Engineering and Automated Learning 2002, Hong Kong.*

5. B. R. Oscar, S. R. Simon, F. R. Fernando, Non-Linear forecasting methods: some applications to the analysis of financial series, *Progress in Economics Research II* (Nova Science, 2002, P77-96).

6. S. I. Ao, Incorporating Correlated Markets' Prices into Stock Modeling with Neural Network, *Proc. IASTED International Conf. on Modelling and Simulation 2003, Palm Springs, USA,* Feb 2003, 353–358.

7. S. I. Ao, Econometric and Intelligent Analysis of the Interdependence of Asian Pacific Indices and their Standard Deviations, *Proc. Workshop of International Conf. on Computational Intelligence for Financial Engineering 2003: Soft Computing for Financial Analysis,* Hong Kong, March 2003.

8. Nikola K. Kasabov, *Foundations of neural networks, fuzzy systems, and knowledge engineering* (The MIT Press, 1997).

9. Larry R. Medstker, *Hybrid Intelligent Systems* (Kluwer Academic Publishers, 1995).

10. S. H. Chen, *Evolutionary computation in economics and finance* (Physica-Verlag, 2002, p47–57).

11. P. P. Angelov, *Evolving rule-based models* (Physica-Verlag, 2002, p49–63).

12. Y. H. Fu, K. P. Lam, A subset ARIMA approach for intraday prediction with genetic algorithm, *Proc. Workshop of International Conf. on Computational Intelligence for Financial Engineering 2003: Soft Computing for Financial Analysis,* Hong Kong, March 2003.

Estimation of Diffusion Parameters by a Nonparametric Drift Function Model

Isao Shoji

Institute of Policy and Planning Sciences, University of Tsukuba,
Tsukuba Ibaraki, 305-8573, Japan
shoji@sk.tsukuba.ac.jp

Abstract. The paper presents a method to estimate diffusion parameters without specifying drift functions of one dimensional stochastic differential equations. We study finite sample properties of the estimator by numerical experiments at several observation time intervals with total time interval fixed. The results show the estimator is getting efficient as observation time interval becomes smaller. By comparing with the quadratic variation method which is proven to have consistency, the proposed method produces almost the same finite sample properties as that.

1 Introduction

It is essential for modeling time series by a regression method to set up a regression function. This is also true for modeling by diffusion processes in a continuous time context where we must choose an appropriate drift function. This choice, however, is very difficult without specific knowledge about time series of interest. Instead of specifying a regression function in discrete time series, some nonparametric methods are used to form the conditional mean which is equivalent to the regression function.

There have been many nonparametric methods for discrete time series, [2] proposed an autoregressive model with functional coefficients. Although the model implies many families of time series models, it is not easy to specify the functional forms of the coefficients. For a more systematic approach kernel estimators of a conditional expectation, e.g. [11] are known. These are considered as examples of a local polynomial model which is fully discussed in [4]. Local polynomial models have been extensively studied in recent literatures and consequently had a wide variety of the models. See for example, [3], [5], [7] and [8].

Since these methods can work for discrete time processes, we can not directly apply them to continuous time ones, ie diffusion processes. In fact, the dynamics of a diffusion process, X_t, is formulated by the following stochastic differential equation (SDE),

$$dX_t = f(X_t)dt + \sigma dB_t,$$

where B_t is a Brownian motion. Suppose that we are interested in estimating a drift function, f, in a nonparameteric way. It can be easily seen that the

J. Liu et al. (Eds.): IDEAL 2003, LNCS 2690, pp. 211–217, 2003.

above nonparametric methods for discrete time series are inapplicable because f is formulated in a differential form. Of course, we may use some discretization techniques to derive a difference equation to which we want to apply the nonparametric methods for discrete time series. This approach, however, is not promising because the regression function of a discretized process is very different from f except for such a simple discretization as the Euler method which is inefficient unless discrete time interval is fairly short. The nonparametric methods as above are basically methods to estimate a regression function of the discretized process but not to estimate f itself. Even if discretizing a SDE, we hardly get information about f. So an alternative approach is required.

In the first place the Taylor's expansion tells us that f can be approximated by a polynomial function as accurately as we wish. Thus a polynomial approximation of f is a straightforward way. As indicated by [4] and [3], fitting a polynomial model is unattractive because of numerical difficulty and inaccuracy in estimating coefficients of the polynomial, particularly of higher order. This numerical intractability is the same even when applying a local polynomial model of higher order because coefficients of the polynomial must be locally estimated. Here recalling coefficients produced by the Taylor's expansion, they are characterized by derivatives of f. Specifically using the expansion at X_t, its i-th coefficient is characterized by $f^{(i)}(X_t)$ which represents the i-th derivative of f at X_t. By the implication of a local polynomial model, $f^{(i)}$ is locally constant but varies globally. As this idea goes further, we consider $f^{(i)}(X_t)$ as a stochastic variable, i.e. a stochastic process, which is unobservable. Combining the variables of the derivatives with the original observable process, we set up a state vector of certain dimension which is determined by what order of polynomial expansion we may apply. Then we want to estimate the state vector from the observable process. To this end we can use the Kalman filter algorithm by which observable and unobservable states of the processes can be easily estimated.

This approach can nonparametrically give estimates of unobservable states, especially states of unknown f and its derivatives; see [9]. And besides it can also give an estimate of a diffusion parameter σ. This paper focuses on this additional feature of the method and studies the finite sample properties of the estimator by numerical experiments. We investigate how the estimator behaves when observation time interval changes from large to small with total time interval fixed and compare its statistical properties with the quadratic variation method.

2   Nonparametric Estimation Method

We consider a one-dimensional diffusion process, X_t, which satisfies the following SDE,

$$dX_t = f(X_t)dt + \sigma dB_t, \tag{1}$$

where B_t is a standard Brownian motion and σ is constant. We assume f to be a smooth function. Suppose that discrete time series of X_t, $\{X_{t_k}\}_{0 \le k \le n}$, which are observed at discrete times with equal time interval. In the first place we apply the Taylor's expansion up to $(m+1)$ to f, which gives,

$$f(x) = f(x_0) + f^{(1)}(x_0)(x - x_0) + \cdots + \frac{f^{(m)}(x_0)}{m!}(x - x_0)^m$$
$$+ \frac{f^{(m+1)}(x_\eta)}{(m+1)!}(x - x_0)^{(m+1)},$$

where $f^{(i)}$ is an i-th derivative of f and $x_\eta = \eta x + (1 - \eta)x_0$ for some $\eta \in [0,1]$. We approximate f by its m-th truncated function f_m defined as,

$$f_m(x) = f_m(x_0) + f_m^{(1)}(x_0)(x - x_0) + \cdots + \frac{f_m^{(m)}(x_0)}{m!}(x - x_0)^m. \tag{2}$$

Letting $x = X_t$ and $x_0 = X_s$ with $s \leq t$, repeated application of the Ito's formula gives,

$$Y_t^{(0)} - Y_s^{(0)} = \int_s^t Y_u^{(1)} dX_u + \frac{\sigma^2}{2} \int_s^t Y_u^{(2)} du,$$

$$Y_t^{(1)} - Y_s^{(1)} = \int_s^t Y_u^{(2)} dX_u + \frac{\sigma^2}{2} \int_s^t Y_u^{(3)} du,$$

$$\vdots$$

$$Y_t^{(m-1)} - Y_s^{(m-1)} = \int_s^t Y_u^{(m)} dX_u,$$

$$Y_t^{(m)} - Y_s^{(m)} = 0,$$

where $Y_t^{(i)} = f_m^{(i)}(X_t)$ $(0 \leq i \leq m)$ and $Y_t^{(0)} = f_m(X_t)$. To discretize the process at discrete times, $\{t_k\}_{0 \leq k \leq n}$, we use a usual assumption on which each integrand, $Y_u^{(i)}$, is a constant, $Y_{t_k}^{(i)}$, over the time interval, $[t_k, t_{k+1})$. Since having no knowledge about a functional form of f, we estimate $Y_{t_k}^{(i)}$ from discrete observation, $\{X_{t_k}\}_{0 \leq k \leq n}$. To this end, we replace $Y_{t_k}^{(i)}$ with $E[Y_{t_k}^{(i)}|\{X_{t_j}\}_{0 \leq j \leq k}] = Y_{t_k|t_k}^{(i)}$. This replacement is used for the formulation of the extended Kalman filter algorithm. Furthermore, the last equality implies that $Y_t^{(m)}$ is a constant. We estimate this constant, θ, as a nuisance parameter from data. Under the above setting, we obtain the following linear discrete time model,

$$Y_{t_{k+1}}^{(0)} - Y_{t_k}^{(0)} = Y_{t_k|t_k}^{(1)}(X_{t_{k+1}} - X_{t_k}) + \frac{\sigma^2}{2}Y_{t_k|t_k}^{(2)}\Delta t, \tag{3}$$

$$Y_{t_{k+1}}^{(1)} - Y_{t_k}^{(1)} = Y_{t_k|t_k}^{(2)}(X_{t_{k+1}} - X_{t_k}) + \frac{\sigma^2}{2}Y_{t_k|t_k}^{(3)}\Delta t,$$

$$\vdots$$

$$Y_{t_{k+1}}^{(m-1)} - Y_{t_k}^{(m-1)} = \theta(X_{t_{k+1}} - X_{t_k}).$$

As [10], substituting f in (1) for f_m together with $Y_t^{(0)} - Y_s^{(0)} = Y_{s|s}^{(1)}(X_t - X_s) + \frac{\sigma^2}{2}Y_{s|s}^{(2)}(t - s)$, we get,

$$X_{t_{k+1}} = X_{t_k} + (Y_{t_k|t_k}^{(1)})^{-1}\left\{\exp\left(Y_{t_k|t_k}^{(1)}\Delta t\right) - 1\right\}Y_{t_k}^{(0)} \tag{4}$$

$$+(Y_{t_k|t_k}^{(1)})^{-2}\left\{\exp\left(Y_{t_k|t_k}^{(1)}\Delta t\right)-1-Y_{t_k|t_k}^{(1)}\Delta t\right\}\frac{\sigma^2}{2}Y_{t_k|t_k}^{(2)}$$

$$+\int_{t_k}^{t_{k+1}}\exp\left\{Y_{t_k|t_k}^{(1)}(t_{k+1}-u)\right\}\sigma dB_u.$$

The last integral follows the normal distribution with mean zero and variance,

$$\frac{\sigma^2\left\{\exp\left(2Y_{t_k|t_k}^{(1)}\Delta t\right)-1\right\}}{2Y_{t_k|t_k}^{(1)}(\Delta t)}.\tag{5}$$

Here we define $(m+1)$-dimensional state vector ξ_k as $(X_{t_k}, Y_{t_k}^{(0)}, \cdots, Y_{t_k}^{(m-1)})^T$ whose first component is an observable state and others are unobservable ones. Consequently the following linear state space model in discrete time is obtained. Hereafter we call the model a nonparametric model of order m:

$$\xi_{k+1} = F_k\xi_k + G_kb_k + G_k\epsilon_{k+1},\tag{6}$$
$$X_{t_k} = H\xi_k.$$

where,

$$F_k = G_kA_k,$$

$$A_k = \begin{pmatrix} 1 & \left(Y_{t_k|t_k}^{(1)}\right)^{-1}\left\{\exp(Y_{t_k|t_k}^{(1)}\Delta t)-1\right\} & \cdots & 0 \\ -Y_{t_k|t_k}^{(1)} & 1 & & \cdots & 0 \\ \vdots & & \ddots & \vdots \\ -\theta & & & \cdots & 1 \end{pmatrix},$$

$$G_k = \begin{pmatrix} 1 & 0 & \cdots & 0 \\ Y_{t_k|t_k}^{(1)} & 1 & \cdots & 0 \\ \vdots & & \ddots & \vdots \\ \theta & & \cdots & 1 \end{pmatrix},$$

$$b_k = \begin{pmatrix} \left(Y_{t_k|t_k}^{(1)}\right)^{-2}\left\{\exp(Y_{t_k|t_k}^{(1)}\Delta t)-1-Y_{t_k|t_k}^{(1)}\Delta t\right\}\frac{\sigma^2}{2}Y_{t_k|t_k}^{(2)} \\ \frac{\sigma^2}{2}Y_{t_k|t_k}^{(2)}\Delta t \\ \vdots \\ 0 \end{pmatrix},$$

$$\epsilon_t = \begin{pmatrix} \sigma\int_{t_k}^{t_{k+1}}\exp\left\{Y_{t_k|t_k}^{(1)}(t_{k+1}-u)\right\}dB_u \\ 0 \\ \vdots \\ 0 \end{pmatrix},$$

$$H = \begin{pmatrix} 1 & 0 & \cdots & 0 \end{pmatrix}.$$

Thanks to the Kalman filter algorithm, the prediction and filtering update equations are formulated as follows. See for example [1].

$$\xi_{k+1|k} = F_k \xi_{k|k} + G_k b_k,$$
$$\Sigma_{k+1|k} = F_k \Sigma_{k|k} F_k^T + G_k Q_k G_k^T,$$
$$K_k = \Sigma_{k|k-1} H^T (H \Sigma_{k|k-1} H^T)^{-1},$$
$$\xi_{k|k} = \xi_{k|k-1} + K_k (X_{t_k} - H \xi_{k|k-1}),$$
$$\Sigma_{k|k} = (I - K_k H) \Sigma_{k|k-1},$$

where,

$$\Sigma_{k+1|k} = E\left[(\xi_{k+1} - \xi_{k+1|k})(\xi_{k+1} - \xi_{k+1|k})^T \left| \{X_{t_j}\}_{0 \le j \le k}\right.\right],$$
$$\Sigma_{k|k} = E\left[(\xi_k - \xi_{k|k})(\xi_k - \xi_{k|k})^T \left| \{X_{t_j}\}_{0 \le j \le k}\right.\right],$$
$$Q_k = E\left[\epsilon_k \epsilon_k^T \left| \{X_{t_j}\}_{0 \le j \le k}\right.\right].$$

The diffusion paramete σ and the nuisance parameter θ can be estimated by the maximum likelihood method by using the following likelihood function of $\{X_{t_k}\}_{0 \le k \le n}$:

$$p(X_{t_0}, \cdots, X_{t_n}) = p(X_{t_0}) \prod_{k=1}^{n} (2\pi H \Sigma_{k|k-1} H^T)^{-1/2} \exp\left\{-\frac{(X_{t_k} - H\xi_{k|k-1})^2}{2H\Sigma_{k|k-1}H^T}\right\}.$$

(7)

3   Numerical Experiments

In the first place we consider the following nonlinear SDE with $\sigma = 0.1$.

$$dX_t = -\frac{X_t(X_t^2 - 0.25)}{1 + X_t + X_t^2} dt + \sigma dB_t$$

where $X_0 = 0$. Applying the nonparametric model of order 7 to a discrete sample path of observation time interval Δt, the diffusion parameter σ is estimated by the maximum likelihood estimation by using $(X_{t_0}, -X_{t_0}, -0.001, 0)^T$ and the identity matrix as the initial states $\xi_{0|0}$ and $\Sigma_{0|0}$, respectively. Here the number of discrete observations of the sample path, N, depends on Δt; because the total time interval is fixed at one hundred, N is given as $N = 100/\Delta t$. In the experiment we take 0.2, 0.1, 0.05 and 0.025 for Δt. Data are generated by the discretized process of the SDE by the Euler method with discrete time interval $1/80$.

For each Δt the estimation is conducted repeatedly five hundred times and the distribution of estimates is obtained. The resulting distributions of estimates of σ are all displayed in the upper of figure 1. It can be easily seen that the estimator is getting efficient as Δt becomes smaller. And besides the bias of estimation seems very small, and so the estimator seems to have consistency.

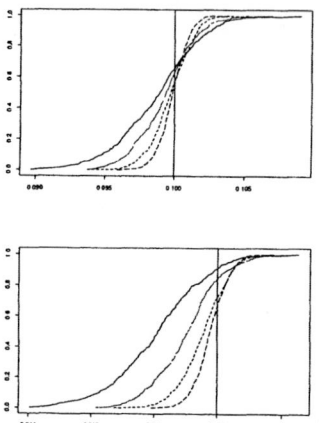

Fig. 1. Distributions of estimates of σ for different observation time interval Δt: the example 1 (upper) and the example 2 (lower)

That also holds for the next example.

$$dX_t = \left[\sum_{i=1}^{3} m_i (X_t - c_i) \exp \left\{ -\frac{(X_t - c_i)^2}{b^2} \right\} \right] dt + \sigma dB_t$$

where $X_0 = 0$, $m_i = (-1)^i$, $(c_1, c_2, c_3) = (-0.2, 0, 0.2)$, $b = 0.2$, and $\sigma = 0.05$. After application of the nonparametric model of order 9, the resulting distributions of estimates are displayed in the lower of figure 1. Unlike the first example this case shows somewhat bias, particularly for large Δt. But the bias is getting improved as Δt becomes smaller.

If we confine ourselves only to estimation of diffusion parameter, we can use the quadratic variation method. Here the quadratic variation method is to estimate σ nonparmetrically by,

$$\hat{\sigma} = \sqrt{\frac{1}{N\Delta t} \sum_{1 \leq k \leq N} (X_{t_k} - X_{t_{k-1}})^2}$$

This estimator is proven to have consistency by [6]. Table 1 presents the summary statistics of the two estimators and show that the two estimators have almost the same finite sample properties. Although from numerical viewpoints, this also suggests that the proposed estimator has consistency.

Table 1. BIAS= $\frac{1}{M}\sum(\hat{\sigma}_k - \sigma)$ and RMSE= $\frac{1}{M}\sum(\hat{\sigma}_k - \sigma)^2$, where $M(= 500)$ stands for the number of experiments.

		Δt			
		0.2	0.1	0.05	0.025
(1st example)					
Nonpara					
	BIAS	-0.0013	-0.0007	-0.0003	-0.0001
	RMSE	0.0033	0.0022	0.0015	0.0011
Quadratic					
	BIAS	-0.0014	-0.0008	-0.0003	-0.0001
	RMSE	0.0034	0.0022	0.0016	0.0011
(2nd example)					
Nonpara					
	BIAS	-0.0019	-0.0010	-0.0005	-0.0002
	RMSE	0.0024	0.0014	0.0009	0.0006
Quadratic					
	BIAS	-0.0020	-0.0010	-0.0005	-0.0002
	RMSE	0.0024	0.0014	0.0009	0.0006

References

1. Anderson, B. D. O. & Moore, J. B. (1979). *Optimal Filtering*. New Jersey: Prentice-Hall.
2. Chen, R. & Tsay, R. S. (1993). Functional-coefficient autoregressive models. *J. Am. Statist. Assoc.* **88**. 298–308.
3. Cheng, M., Hall, P., & Turlach, B. A. (1999). High-derivative parametric enhancements of nonparametric curve estimation. *Biometrika* **86**. 417–28.
4. Fan, J. & Gijbels, I. (1996). *Local Polynomial Modelling and Its Applications*. London : Chapman and Hall.
5. Fan, J., Hall, P., Martin, M. A., & Patil, P. (1996). On local smoothing of nonparametric curve estimators. *J. Am. Statist. Assoc.* **91**. 258–66.
6. Florens-Zmirou, D. (1989). Approximate discrete-time schemes for statistics of diffusion processes. *Statistics* **20**. 547–557.
7. Linton, O. B. (1997). Efficient estimation of additive nonparametric regression models. *Biometrika* **84**. 469–73.
8. Linton, O. B., Chen, R., Wang, N., & Härdle, W. (1997). An analysis of transformations for additive nonparametric regression. *J. Am. Statist. Assoc.* **92**. 1512–21.
9. Shoji, I. (1998). Nonparametric state estimation of diffusion processes. *Biometrika* **89**. 451–6.
10. Shoji, I. & Ozaki, T. (1998). A statistical method of estimation and simulation for systems of stochastic differential equations. *Biometrika* **85**. 240–3.
11. Tjøsthaim, D. & Auestad, B. H. (1994). Nonparametric identification of nonlinear time series: projections. *J. Am. Statist. Assoc.* **89**. 258–66.

Temporal Difference Coding in Reinforcement Learning

Kazunori Iwata and Kazushi Ikeda

Department of Systems Science, Graduate School of Informatics, Kyoto University
Yoshida-Honmachi, Sakyo-ku, Kyoto 606-8501, Japan
{kiwata,kazushi}@sys.i.kyoto-u.ac.jp

Abstract. In this paper, we regard the sequence of returns as outputs from a parametric compound source. The coding rate of the source shows the amount of information on the return, so the information gain concerning future information is given by the sum of the discounted coding rates. We accordingly formulate a temporal difference learning for estimating the expected information gain, and give a convergence proof of the information gain under certain conditions. As an example of applications, we propose the ratio w of return loss to information gain to be used in probabilistic action selection strategies. We found in experiments that our w-based strategy performs well compared with the conventional Q-based strategy.

1 Introduction

Reinforcement learning [1] is an effective framework to describe a general process that consists of interactions between an agent and an environment. This concerns the adaptive optimization of systems governed by a Markov decision process (MDP) when the state transition probabilities are not known. It is of increasing interest in the fields of task-scheduling, online clustering, and financial engineering [2,3,4], for example.

We often try to know how much taking an action contributes for estimating expected return. An effective and viable method is to work out the coding rate of the return which corresponds to the mean of the codeword length when the observed return is encoded, since the coding rate is written as the sum of the essential uncertainty (entropy rate) and the distance between the true and the estimated distributions (redundancy). In other words, the coding rate shows the amount of information on the return, so the "information gain" concerning future information is given by the sum of the discounted coding rates. We accordingly formulate a temporal difference (TD) learning for estimating the expected information gain, and prove the convergence of the information gain under certain conditions. As an example of applications, we propose the ratio w of return loss to information gain to be used in probabilistic action selection strategies. We apply it to a typical probabilistic strategy, and show in experiments that our w-based strategy performs well compared with the conventional Q-based strategy.

The organization of this paper is as follows. We begin with the estimation of the information gain by the TD learning in Section 2. In Section 3, we apply the proposed criterion w to the softmax method, and show the experimental results comparing the w-based strategy with the conventional Q-based strategy. Finally, we give some conclusions in Section 4.

J. Liu et al. (Eds.): IDEAL 2003, LNCS 2690, pp. 218–227, 2003.
© Springer-Verlag Berlin Heidelberg 2003

2 TD Learning for Information Gain Estimation

We first review the framework of discrete-time reinforcement learning with discrete states and actions. Let $\mathcal{T} = \{t \mid t = 0, 1, 2, \dots\}$ denote the set of time steps. Let $\mathcal{S}$ be the finite set of states of the environment, $\mathcal{A}$ be the finite set of actions, and $\Re$ be the set of real numbers. At each step t, an agent senses a current state $s_t \in \mathcal{S}$, and chooses an action $a_t \in \mathcal{A}(s_t)$, where $\mathcal{A}(s_t)$ denotes the set of actions available in the state s_t. The selected action a_t changes the current state s_t to a subsequent state $s_{t+1} \in \mathcal{S}$. The environment yields a scalar reward $r_{t+1} \in \Re$ according to the state transition. The interaction between the agent and the environment produces a sequence of states, actions, and rewards, $s_1, a_1, r_2, s_2, a_2, r_3, \dots$ The goal of the agent is to learn the optimal policy $\pi^* : \mathcal{S} \to \mathcal{A}$, that maximizes the "return" over time,

$$x(s_t, a_t) = r_{t+1} + \gamma r_{t+2} + \gamma^2 r_{t+3} + \cdots = \sum_{i=0}^{\infty} \gamma^i r_{t+i+1}, \tag{1}$$

where r_{t+1} is called an immediate reward, whereas $r_{t+2}, r_{t+3}, \dots$ are called delayed rewards. The parameter γ is the discount factor that balances the immediate reward and the delayed rewards.

2.1 Return Source

Assume that the agent chooses an action $a \in \mathcal{A}$ at a state $s \in \mathcal{S}$ n or more times in the experience. Let $x_i(s, a)$ be the return given by (1) in the ith trial for "fixed" state-action pair (s, a). We regard the returns in n trials as a sequence of length n and denote the "return sequence" by

$$x^n(s, a) = x_1(s, a), x_2(s, a), \dots, x_n(s, a). \tag{2}$$

We will make the following three assumptions regarding return sources. First, the return source $\mathbf{X} = \{X_i(s, a) \mid (s, a) \in \mathcal{S} \times \mathcal{A}, i = 1, 2, \dots\}$ is i.i.d. (independently and identically distributed) and determined by a parametric probability distribution,

$$p_{\theta(s,a)}(x_i(s, a)) = \Pr(X_i(s, a) = x_i(s, a) \mid (s, a) \in \mathcal{S} \times \mathcal{A}), \tag{3}$$

where $\theta(s, a) = (\theta_1(s, a), \theta_2(s, a), \dots, \theta_k(s, a))$ denotes the k-dimensional parameter vector of the distribution $p_{\theta(s,a)}$ in a compact set $\Theta \subset \Re^k$. Second, the model set of probability distributions $\mathcal{M}_k = \{p_{\theta(s,a)} \mid \theta(s, a) \in \Theta\}$ includes the true probability distribution. Third, the return source satisfies the ergodic theorem due to Birkhoff [5]. This means that it is possible to estimate the true parameter from a large number of trials. Otherwise we can not gather sufficient information to identify the parameter no matter how many returns are observed. For notational simplicity, we omit (s, a) henceforth, for example we use x, X, and θ.

2.2 ℓ-Learning

Consider a coding algorithm for the return source $\mathbf{X}$, so that we obtain the coding rate that means the amount of information on the return. In order for the algorithm to apply to the framework of reinforcement learning, it should work on-line, and its coding rate should asymptotically converge to the entropy rate. We accordingly employ Rissanen's predictive coding [6] for calculating the coding rate, and give a TD learning for estimating the information gain given by the sum of the discounted coding rates.

The predictive coding algorithm sequentially encodes a sequence x^n for any fixed state-action (s, a). For $i \geq 1$, the algorithm finds the maximum likelihood estimate $\hat{\theta}^{(i-1)}$ from the observed sequence x^{i-1}, and calculates the conditional probability distribution,

$$p_{\hat{\theta}^{(i-1)}}(x_i \mid x^{i-1}) = \frac{p_{\hat{\theta}^{(i-1)}}(x^i)}{p_{\hat{\theta}^{(i-1)}}(x^{i-1})}. \tag{4}$$

Since the return source is i.i.d. the distribution is rewritten as

$$p_{\hat{\theta}^{(i-1)}}(x_i \mid x^{i-1}) = p_{\hat{\theta}^{(i-1)}}(x_i). \tag{5}$$

The codeword length of the ith return x_i is then

$$l(x_i) = -\log_2 p_{\hat{\theta}^{(i-1)}}(x_i). \tag{6}$$

Therefore, the total codeword length of the sequence x^n is written as $l(x^n) = \sum_{i=1}^{n} l(x_i)$. By taking its expectation, we have $L(X^n) = \sum_{i=1}^{n} E[l(X_i)]$. Under the assumptions in Section 2.1, the total codeword length is asymptotically equal to what is called the stochastic complexity given by

$$L(X^n) = \mathcal{H}(X^n) + \frac{k}{2} \log_2 n + o(1), \tag{7}$$

where $\mathcal{H}(\cdot)$ denotes the entropy. For the proof, see [7, pp. 231–233]. Note that the coding rate $L(X^n)/n$ converges to the entropy rate of the return source as $n \to \infty$.

Using the above predictive coding idea, let us formulate TD learning algorithm, called "ℓ-learning" in this paper, for the purpose of approximating the mean of the information gain. Since we can not directly observe the return x in practice, we encode the return estimate $\hat{x}$ instead of x. The parameter estimate $\hat{\theta}$ is also calculated using TD methods. Let the integer $n(s, a)$ denote the number of times that the state-action pair (s, a) has been tried. Let γ_Q be the discount factor for the value of Q and γ_ℓ be the discount factor for the value of the information gain ℓ. We describe the ℓ-learning algorithm under the one-step versions of Q-learning [8]. The ℓ-learning algorithm takes a similar approach to the Q-learning. The algorithm can be readily extended to 2-step or more versions.

ℓ-learning under Q-learning: For each step t, given a one-step episode $(s_t, a_t, r_{t+1}, s_{t+1})$, Q-learning has the update form,

$$Q(s_t, a_t) \leftarrow Q(s_t, a_t) + \alpha_{n(s_t, a_t)} \delta Q_t, \tag{8}$$

where the learning rate $\alpha_{n(s_t, a_t)}$ is set within $[0, 1]$ and

$$\delta Q_t = r_{t+1} + \gamma_Q \max_{a' \in \mathcal{A}(s_{t+1})} Q(s_{t+1}, a') - Q(s_t, a_t). \tag{9}$$

With the estimate $\hat{\theta}_t = \hat{\theta}(s_t, a_t)$ of the parameter vector at time step t, the information gain is updated according to the rule,

$$\ell(s_t, a_t) \leftarrow \ell(s_t, a_t) + \alpha_{n(s_t, a_t)} \delta\ell_t, \tag{10}$$

where

$$\delta\ell_t = -\log_2 p_{\hat{\theta}_t}(\hat{x}(s_t, a_t)) + \gamma_\ell \max_{a' \in \mathcal{A}(s_{t+1})} \ell(s_{t+1}, a') - \ell(s_t, a_t), \tag{11}$$

$$\hat{x}(s_t, a_t) = r_{t+1} + \gamma_Q \max_{a' \in \mathcal{A}(s_{t+1})} Q(s_{t+1}, a'). \tag{12}$$

Under some conditions of ℓ and the convergence conditions of Q-learning, the value of ℓ converges to the expected value (see Appendix A). If $\hat{\theta}$ is the true parameter and $\gamma_\ell = 0$, then the information gain converges to the entropy rate of the return source. Notice that when $\gamma_\ell > 0$ the information gain ℓ expresses the amount of information,

$$\ell(s_t, a_t) = -\sum_{i=0}^{\infty} \gamma_\ell^i \log_2 p_{\hat{\theta}_{t+i}}(\hat{x}(s_{t+i}, a_{t+i})), \tag{13}$$

that can be expected in the future.

2.3   Asymptotic Behavior of ℓ-Learning under Q-Learning

The behavior of the information gain ℓ is not simple, since for any state-action pair (s, a) the time evolution of the sequence $\{\ell_t(s, a) \mid t \in \mathcal{T}\}$ depends on the time evolution $\{\hat{\theta}_t(s, a) \mid t \in \mathcal{T}\}$ of the parameter vector estimate. However if the learning rate of the parameter is small, the parameter changes slowly, roughly speaking, we can assume that the parameter is almost constant. We hence introduce the fixed-θ process in order to study an asymptotic behavior of the information gain.

For simplicity of notation, let Q^* be the expected return and θ be the fixed parameter vector hereafter. Let $\mathcal{P}^a_{s,s'}$ denote the transition probability that taking action a in state s produces a subsequent state s'. Define

$$\ell^*(s, a) \stackrel{\text{def}}{=} l^*(s, a) + \gamma_\ell \sum_{s' \in \mathcal{S}} \mathcal{P}^a_{s,s'} \max_{a' \in \mathcal{A}(s')} \ell^*(s', a'), \tag{14}$$

where

$$l^*(s, a) = -E[\log_2 p_\theta(r_{t+1} + \gamma_Q \max_{a' \in \mathcal{A}(s_{t+1})} Q^*(s_{t+1}, a')) \mid s_t = s, a_t = a]. \tag{15}$$

For fixed θ, define the expectations, which are conditioned on the minimal σ-algebra $\mathcal{F}_t$ created by the set $\{s_i, a_i, s_t \mid i = 0, 1, \dots, t-1\}$, by

$$\mathrm{T}(\hat{x}(s_t, a_t)) \stackrel{\text{def}}{=} E[r_{t+1} + \gamma_Q \max_{a' \in \mathcal{A}(s_{t+1})} Q(s_{t+1}, a') \mid \mathcal{F}_t, a_t] \tag{16}$$

and

$$T(\ell(s_t, a_t)) \stackrel{\text{def}}{=} E[-\log_2 p_\theta(r_{t+1} + \gamma_Q \max_{a' \in \mathcal{A}(s_{t+1})} Q(s_{t+1}, a'))$$

$$+ \gamma_\ell \max_{a' \in \mathcal{A}(s_{t+1})} \ell(s_{t+1}, a') \mid \mathcal{F}_t, a_t]. \qquad (17)$$

By the Markovian property, we can rewrite this as

$$T(\hat{x}(s_t, a_t)) = E[r_{t+1} \mid s_t, a_t] + \gamma_Q \sum_{s' \in \mathcal{S}} \mathcal{P}^{a_t}_{s_t, s'} \max_{a' \in \mathcal{A}(s')} Q(s', a') \qquad (18)$$

and

$$T(\ell(s_t, a_t)) = -E[\log_2 p_\theta(r_{t+1} + \gamma_Q \max_{a' \in \mathcal{A}(s_{t+1})} Q(s_{t+1}, a')) \mid s_t, a_t]$$

$$+ \gamma_\ell \sum_{s' \in \mathcal{S}} \mathcal{P}^{a_t}_{s_t, s'} \max_{a' \in \mathcal{A}(s')} \ell(s', a'), \qquad (19)$$

respectively. Define the noise of $\hat{x}$ by

$$\delta M_t(\hat{x}(s_t, a_t)) \stackrel{\text{def}}{=} \hat{x}(s_t, a_t) - T(\hat{x}(s_t, a_t)). \qquad (20)$$

With the definition of the noise term

$$\delta M_t(\ell(s_t, a_t)) \stackrel{\text{def}}{=} -\log_2 p_\theta(T(\hat{x}(s_t, a_t)) + \delta M_t(\hat{x}(s_t, a_t)))$$

$$+ \gamma_\ell \max_{a' \in \mathcal{A}(s_{t+1})} \ell(s_{t+1}, a') - T(\ell(s_t, a_t)), \qquad (21)$$

(11) is rewritten as

$$\delta \ell_t = T(\ell(s_t, a_t)) + \delta M_t(\ell(s_t, a_t)) - \ell(s_t, a_t). \qquad (22)$$

Note that $\delta M_t(\cdot)$ is the martingale difference and the conditioned variance is bounded uniformly in t, namely, $E[\delta M_t(\cdot) \mid \mathcal{F}_t, a_t] = 0$ and $E[(\delta M_t)^2(\cdot) \mid \mathcal{F}_t, a_t] < \infty$. As written in [9, chapter 2], the map T is a Lipschitz continuous contraction with respect to the supremum norm and ℓ^* is a unique fixed point. Under the convergence conditions of the above and Q-learning, for every pair (s, a) the value of $\ell(s, a)$ converges to the value of $\ell^*(s, a)$ with probability one, as will be seen in Appendix A.

There is also a value of $d_{s,a}$ lying in the interval $[1/\bar{u}_{s,a}, 1]$, where the value of $\bar{u}_{s,a}$ bounds the time interval between occurrences of the pair (s, a). For any pair (s, a), the mean ordinary differential equation that characterizes the limit point is given by

$$\dot{\ell}(s, a) = d_{s,a}(T(\ell(s, a)) - \ell(s, a)) + z_{s,a}, \qquad (23)$$

where $z_{s,a}$ works only to hold $|\dot{\ell}(s, a)| \leq B$ for a large B.

3   New Criterion for Probabilistic Action Selection Strategies

In this section, we consider a new criterion for probabilistic action selection strategies using the information gain.

3.1   Ratio of Return Loss to Information Gain

Typical "Q-based" selections refer only to the estimates of the expected return (Q-value). For example, the softmax method widely used in many cases has the form,

$$\pi(s, a) \overset{\text{def}}{=} \frac{g(Q(s, a)/\tau)}{\sum_{a' \in \mathcal{A}(s)} g(Q(s, a')/\tau)}, \tag{24}$$

where $\pi(s, a)$ is the probability that an action a takes place in a state s. This is called the Q-based "Boltzmann selection" when $g(\cdot) = \exp(\cdot)$. To promote a strategy of exploitation the parameter τ is gradually decreased over time. In practice, it is difficult to tune the temperature parameter without any prior knowledge of the values of Q.

Although the estimate is an experience-intensive value for exploitative strategies, but not for exploratory strategies. This is one reason why controlling the exploration-exploitation dilemma [1, Section 1.1] is a difficult problem. Recall that we can get the information gain concerning future information using the ℓ-learning algorithm as described. We then find the optimal policy via a strategy based on the ratio of return loss to information gain, for any state-action pair,

$$w(s, a) \overset{\text{def}}{=} \frac{\text{loss}(s, a)}{\ell(s, a)}, \tag{25}$$

where the loss function is

$$\text{loss}(s, a) \overset{\text{def}}{=} \max_{a' \in \mathcal{A}(s)} Q(s, a') - Q(s, a). \tag{26}$$

Note that $w(s, a) = 0$ for action $a = \arg\max_{a' \in \mathcal{A}(s)} Q(s, a')$. The smaller the criterion $w(s, a)$ is, the better the state-action pair (s, a) is in both exploration and exploitation. By setting a large value as the initial value of ℓ, during early stages the information gain ℓ is large compared to the loss function loss since the estimated parameter is far from the true parameter, that is, the redundancy of the coding rate is large. Hence, taking action $a \neq \arg\max_{a' \in \mathcal{A}(s)} Q(s, a')$ that exhibits the smaller value of $w(s, a)$ (where $w(s, a) > 0$) is a more efficient exploration so that we get a larger amount of information for estimating the expected return. As the estimated parameter tends to the true parameter the information gain ℓ tends to a constant value, and the value of w is determined mainly by the loss function loss. Therefore, taking action a that shows the smaller value of $w(s, a)$ is better because it yields a smaller loss, in other words, a higher return. We can see that for any state the action which gives the minimum value $w(s, a) = 0$ is consistent with $a = \arg\max_{a' \in \mathcal{A}(s)} Q(s, a')$. Accordingly, by assigning higher probabilities to actions with the smaller value of w we do an efficient exploration in early stages and a good exploitation in later stages of learning.

Now taking the minus value of w and then applying it to the form of the softmax method, we have

$$\pi(s, a) \overset{\text{def}}{=} \frac{g(-w(s, a)/\tau)}{\sum_{a' \in \mathcal{A}(s)} g(-w(s, a')/\tau)}. \tag{27}$$

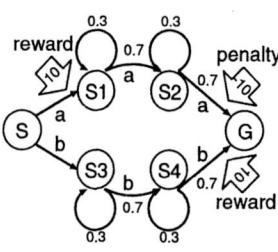

Fig. 1. Misleading Domain

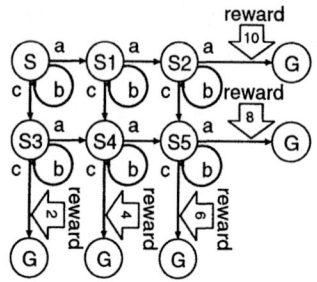

Fig. 2. Deterministic Domain

Notice that smaller values of w assign higher probabilities to actions. We call this the w-based "Boltzmann selection" when $\mathrm{g}(\cdot) = \exp(\cdot)$. Since the values of w are automatically tuned during the learning process, this alleviates some of trouble associated with tuning τ.

3.2 Experiments

We have examined the performance of the Q-based and the w-based Boltzmann selections. For simplicity, we tested them on two domains governed by an MDP (see Figures 1 and 2).

In these figures, the circle and the narrow arrow are the state of the environment and the state transition, respectively. The number accompanied with each narrow arrow represents the probability of the state transition, and the alphabets "a", "b", and "c" denote the actions available in each state. The wide arrow represents a scalar reward or a penalty. During each episode, the agent begins at the initial state "S," and is allowed to perform actions until it reaches the goal state "G." For every state-action pair (s, a), we used the normal distribution $p_{\theta(s,a)}$ with the parameter $\theta(s, a) = (Q(s, a), v(s, a))^T$ where $Q(s, a)$ and $v(s, a)$ denote the mean return and its variance, respectively, and initialized as $\theta(s, a) = (0, 1)^T$. The agent learned Q, v, and ℓ by the tabular versions of the one-step Q-learning, variance-learning [10], and ℓ-learning, respectively. The learning rate of these algorithms was decreased as $\alpha_{n(s,a)} = 20/(100 + n(s, a))$ and the discount factors, γ_Q and γ_ℓ, were set to 0.95. For every state-action pair (s, a), the initial information gain was set as $\ell(s, a) = 50$ to prevent from dividing by zero in the calculation of $w(s, a)$ during early phases of the learning process[1]. We applied the function $\mathrm{g}(\cdot) = \exp(\cdot)$ to each softmax method, namely, we used the Boltzmann selection. Let $n(s) = \sum_{a \in A(s)} n(s, a)$. In order to shift the strategy from exploration to exploitation, the temperature of each strategy was decreased as $\tau_{n(s)} = m \times 100/(n(s) + 1)^2$ where the parameter m was tuned as appropriately for each domain as possible. The values of m are shown in Table 1.

The domain in Figure 1 is a misleading domain composed of five states, two actions for state S, and one goal. This has a suboptimal policy that the agent tends to accept.

---

[1] Of course, any large value can be set as the initial value.

Table 1. Parameters m in each domain

Table 2. Total return per trial (mean and standard deviation)

Strategy	Misleading	Deterministic
Q-based Boltz.	$m = 50$	$m = 30$
w-based Boltz.	$m = 1$	$m = 1$

Strategy	Misleading		Deterministic	
	mean	s.d.	mean	s.d.
Q-based Boltz.	769.46	37.38	753.26	99.23
w-based Boltz.	791.59	31.84	759.8	64.07

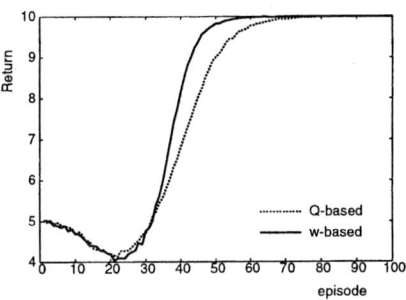

Fig. 3. Return in misleading domain

Fig. 4. Return in deterministic domain

At first sight choosing action "a" looks better because of the reward at the start of the episode, but the reward is finally offset by the penalty. The point is to avoid the suboptimal policy as soon as possible, so that the optimal policy taking "b" is encouraged. Next, the domain in Figure 2 is a deterministic domain where state transitions are deterministic. This consists of six states, three actions for each state, and five goals each with a different reward. Here the problem is that the agent attempts to select the best of the goals without performing sufficient exploration. The optimal policy is to select action "a" everywhere. There are several ways for measuring the learning performance of a particular strategy. To measure the efficiency of a strategy during a fixed number of episodes, we evaluate the learning performance by three measures, collected total return per trial, its standard deviation, and return per episode. The return per episode yields an analysis of how the efficiency of each strategy changes as the number of episodes increases.

The total return and the standard deviation are shown in Table 2. Figures 3 and 4 show the results of the return per episode measure. These results are averaged over 10000 trials and each trial consists of 100 episodes. From the total return results, we find that the w-based strategy is better than the conventional Q-based strategy in terms of policy optimization. The results of the standard deviation, especially in deterministic domain, show that the w-based strategy also has a superiority in stability. From the results of the return per episode, we see that the w-based strategy is more efficient without leading to a suboptimal policy. Furthermore, in Table 1 we confirm that some trouble regarding turning is alleviated because the values of m in the w-based strategy are constant regardless of the value of return given in each domain. Thus, the proposed criterion w is a good criterion for strategies of a probabilistic action selection, yet it is simple.

4 Conclusions

In this paper, we regarded the sequence of returns as outputs given by a parametric compound source. We then described the ℓ-learning algorithms based on the predictive coding idea for estimating the expected information gain and gave the convergence proof. As an example of applications, we proposed the ratio w of return loss to information gain as a new criterion for action selection, and applied it to the softmax strategy. In experimental results, we found our w-based strategy performs well compared with the conventional Q-based strategy.

Acknowledgments. We would like to thank Prof. Hideaki Sakai at the Graduate School of Informatics, Kyoto University for his fruitful comments on the earlier draft of the paper. This research was supported in part by a grant for Scientific Research (No.14003714) from the Ministry of Education, Culture, Sports, Science, and Technology of Japan.

References

[1] Sutton, R.S., Barto, A.G.: Reinforcement Learning : An Introduction. Adaptive Computation and Machine Learning. MIT Press, Cambridge, MA (1998)

[2] Zhang, W., Dietterich, T.G.: A reinforcement learning approach to job-stop scheduling. In Mellish, C.S., ed.: Proceedings of the 14th International Joint Conference on Artificial Intelligence, Montreal, Canada, Morgan Kaufmann, San Mateo, CA (1995) 1114–1120

[3] Likas, A.: A reinforcement learning approach to on-line clustering. Neural Computation **11** (1999) 1915–1932

[4] Sato, M., Kobayashi, S.: Variance-penalized reinforcement learning for risk-averse asset allocation. In Leung, K.S., Chan, L.W., Meng, H., eds.: Proceedings of the 2nd International Conference on Intelligent Data Engineering and Automated Learning. Volume 1983 of Lecture Notes in Computer Science., Hong Kong, China, Springer-Verlag, Berlin (2000) 244–249

[5] Billingsley, P.: Probability and Measure. 3rd edn. Wiley Series in Probability and Mathematical Statistics. John Wiley & Sons, New York (1995)

[6] Rissanen, J.: Stochastic complexity and modeling. The Annals of Statistics **14** (1986) 1080–1100

[7] Han, T.S., Kobayashi, K.: Mathematics of Information and Coding. Volume 203 of Translations of Mathematical Monographs. American Mathematical Society, Providence, RI (2002) Translated by Joe Suzuki.

[8] Watkins, C.J.C.H., Dayan, P.: Technical note : Q-learning. Machine Learning **8** (1992) 279–292

[9] Kushner, H.J., Yin, G.G.: Stochastic Approximation Algorithms and Applications. Volume 35 of Apprications of Mathematics. Springer-Verlag, New York (1997)

[10] Sato, M., Kobayashi, S.: Average-reward reinforcement learning for variance penalized markov decision problems. In Brodley, C.E., Danyluk, A.P., eds.: Proceedings of the 18th International Conference on Machine Learning, Williams College, Morgan Kaufmann Publishers, San Francisco, CA (2001) 473–480

A   Rough Proof of Information Gain Convergence

The proof that we discuss below is based on the manner due to Kushner and Yin [9, chapter 12]. Let us show the convergence by describing that the theorem [9, chapter 12, theorem 3.5] that all $\ell(s, a)$ converge to the limit point $\ell^*(s, a)$ holds under the following conditions. The other conditions that we do not write are either obvious or not applicable for the convergence theorem.

We deal with a practical constrained algorithm in which the value of ℓ is truncated at $H = [-B, +B]$ for large B, and assume a constant learning rate for simplicity of development. The proof for a decreasing learning rate is virtually the same. Define $C = \max_{(s,a) \in \mathcal{S} \times \mathcal{A}} \ell(s, a)$, and let $B > C/(1 - \gamma_\ell)$. For any (s, a) we use $\ell_t(s, a)$ to denote the information gain $\ell(s, a)$ at time step t. The dimension of the problem is determined by the number d of state-action pairs and $\{\ell_t(s, a) \mid t \in \mathcal{T}\}$ existing in H^d.

Let α be a small real constant and $I_t(s, a)$ be the event indicator function that the pair (s, a) is observed at time step t. Recall that ℓ-learning algorithm with truncation has the form,

$$\ell_{t+1}(s, a) \leftarrow \Pi_H[\ell_t(s, a) + \alpha \delta \ell_t I_t(s, a)], \tag{28}$$

where $\delta \ell_t$ is given by (22) and $\Pi_H[\cdot]$ denotes the truncation which brings $\cdot$ to the closest point in H if $\cdot$ goes out of H. Suppose that the state transition process is reducible with probability one. Let $t_{s,a}(n + 1)$ be the time step that the $(n + 1)$st update for the pair (s, a) is done, and let $\tau_{s,a}(n)$ denote the time interval between the nth and the $(n + 1)$st occurrences of the pair (s, a). Define the expectation of the time interval, $u_{s,a}(n + 1) = E[\tau_{s,a}(n + 1) \mid \mathcal{F}_{t_{s,a}(n+1)}]$. Suppose that for any n $u_{s,a}(n)$ is uniformly bounded by a real number $\bar{u}_{s,a} \geq 1$ and that the time evolution $\{\tau_{s,a}(n) \mid n, (s, a) \in \mathcal{A} \times \mathcal{S}\}$ is uniformly integrable. Let $\ell(s, a, \cdot)$ denote the piecewise constant interpolation [9, chapter 4] of $\{\ell_t(s, a) \mid t \in \mathcal{T}, (s, a) \in \mathcal{S} \times \mathcal{A}\}$ with interpolation intervals α in "scaled real" time. Under the given conditions, $\{\ell(s, a, T_\alpha + \cdot) \mid (s, a) \in \mathcal{S} \times \mathcal{A}, T_\alpha \in \Re\}$ is tight [9, chapter 7] for any sequence of real numbers T_α, so under Q-learning convergence conditions [8] we can show that if T_α tends to infinity, then as α tends to zero it exhibits a weak convergence to the process with constant value defined by (14). The process is written as the ordinary differential equation given by (23). We will show that all solutions of (23) tend to the unique limit point given by (14). Suppose that $\ell(s, a, t) = B$ for some t and pair (s, a). By the lower bound B,

$$\sup_{\ell = B}[\mathrm{T}(\ell(s, a)) - \ell(s, a)] \leq C + \gamma_\ell \sum_{s' \in \mathcal{S}} \mathcal{P}^a_{s, s'} B - B = C - (1 - \gamma)B < 0. \tag{29}$$

This means

$$\begin{cases} \dot{\ell}(s, a, t) < 0 & \text{if } \ell(s, a, t) = B \\ \dot{\ell}(s, a, t) > 0 & \text{if } \ell(s, a, t) = -B \end{cases} \tag{30}$$

Hence, the boundary of H^d is not accessible by a trajectory of the ordinary differential equation given by (23) from any interior point. From the contraction property of T and by neglecting $z_{s,a}$, for every (s, a) $\ell^*(s, a)$ is the unique limit point of (23). Taking into account that (23) is the limit mean ordinary differential equation, all the conditions for the proof is satisfied. Accordingly, the convergence proof is complete.   ∎

Combination of Linear and General Regression Neural Network for Robust Short Term Financial Prediction

Tony Jan

Department of Computer Systems,
University of Technology, Sydney,
P.O. Box 123, Broadway, NSW, 2007, Australia

Abstract. In business applications, robust short term prediction is important for survival. Artificial neural network (ANN) have shown excellent potential however it needs better extrapolation capacity in order to provide reliable short term prediction. In this paper, a combination of linear regression model in parallel with general regression neural network is introduced for short term financial prediction. The experiment shows that the proposed model achieves comparable prediction performance to other conventional prediction models.

1 Introduction

Robust short term financial prediction is of great practical interest for many financial institutes such as bank, insurance and government agencies. Recent advances in powerful computers and wide availability of information have instigated many new exciting developments in financial predictions.

Among many, the prediction based on Artificial Neural Networks (ANN) is gaining strong interests from diverse communities due to its ability to identify the patterns that are not readily observable. Recent survey shows that Portfolio management systems using neural networks [1] reported good results as well as the Lucid Captical Networks on future market prediction [2]. Lowe reports of an analog multilayer perceptron network for portfolio management [3]. However despite recent successes, ANN based prediction is still deemed unreliable. The reason is that; though ANNs have shown to provide accurate estimates of the outputs for the range of sample inputs by accurately interpolating between available sample input/output pairs, but when an unusual inputs which differ from their training data emerges, the ANN output is usually unreliable. In order for the ANN to be useful in prediction applications, it needs to provide accurate and continuous estimates of the outputs for the inputs that are different from the training sample inputs. It is essential that some degree of extrapolation capacity must be incorporated in the ANN based predictor.

In this paper, a model is introduced which combines a simple linear regression model in parallel with a general regression neural network for short term financial

J. Liu et al. (Eds.): IDEAL 2003, LNCS 2690, pp. 228–235, 2003.

prediction. The paper shows that combination of pure linear and ANN model can perform better than either the single linear or ANN model alone.

The proposed prediction model is as accurate as it can be based on the available training data with the linear part providing useful underlying coarse-scale information for generalization and short term prediction. The experiment shows that the proposed model achieves superior prediction performance compared to the conventional prediction methods such as the Volterra series based predictor or popular MultiLayer Perceptron (MLP) based prediction models.

2   Method

The proposed model defines a multivariate scalar function over the whole data space. It can always be tuned to produce the best approximation in the region of sample data. The idea is that, in void of sample data, it is best to extrapolate using combination of the best linear prediction and the best nonlinear (residual) prediction generated by the neural network.

The model is a linear regression model connected with MPNN in parallel as shown in Figure 1, and described in equations 1 and 2.

$$\hat{y}(X) = [w_o + \underline{W}\,\underline{x}] + \left[\frac{\sum Z_i y_{N_i} f_i(\underline{x} - \underline{c}_i, \sigma)}{\sum Z_i f_i(\underline{x} - \underline{c}_i, \sigma)} \right] \tag{1}$$

where

$$y_{N_i} = y_i(\underline{x}_i) - [w_o + W_i \underline{x}_i] \tag{2}$$

and

$\underline{x}=$ input vector,

$\underline{x}_i=$ training input vector,

$y_t =$ scalar training output,

$y_{N_i}=$ difference between the linear approximation and the training output,

$\underline{c}_i =$ center vector for class i in the input space,

$Z_i=$ no. of vectors $\underline{x}_i$ associated with each $\underline{c}_i$,

$w_o=$ initial offset,

$W_i=$ weights of the linear model.

The piecewise linear regression model is firstly approximated by using all available training data in a simple regression fitting analysis. Then the MPNN is constructed to compensate for the higher ordered characteristics of the problem. This is explained in section 2.2.

2.1   Introduction to MPNN

The MPNN was initially introduced by Specht in 1991. It is closely related to Specht's GRNN and his previous work, Probabilistic Neural Network (PNN) [4]. The basic MPNN and GRNN methods have similarities with the method of Moody and Darken [5], [6]; the method of RBF's [7], [8]; the CMAC [9]; and

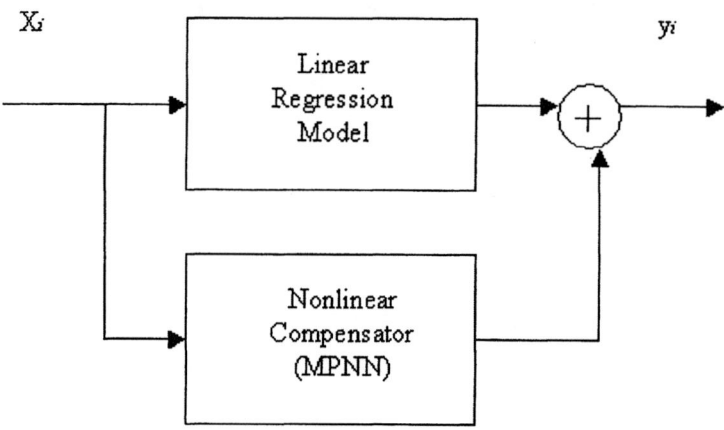

Fig. 1. Combination of Linear Regression Model with MPNN as Nonlinear Regression Model

a number of other nonparametric kernel-based regression techniques stemming from the work of Nadaraya and Watson [10].

The general algorithm for the MPNN is:

$$\widehat{y}(\underline{x}) = \frac{\sum_{i=o}^{M} Z_i y_i f_i(\underline{x})}{\sum_{i=0}^{M} Z_i f_i(\underline{x})} \tag{3}$$

with

$$f_i(\underline{x}) = exp\frac{-(\underline{x} - \underline{c}_i)^T (\underline{x} - \underline{c}_i)}{2\sigma^2} \tag{4}$$

$\underline{x}$ = input vector,
y_i = scalar training output,
$\underline{c}_i$ = center vector for class i in the input space,
Z_i = no. of vectors $\underline{x}_i$ associated with each $\underline{c}_i$
M = number of unique centers $\underline{c}_i$

A Gaussian function is often used for $f_i(\underline{x})$ as defined in equation 4. However any adequate Radial Basis Function (RBF) can be used as $f_i(\underline{x})$. Tuning of the MPNN simply involves finding the optimal σ giving the minimum mean squared error (mse) between the MPNN output and the desired output using a representative set of known sample vector pairs by a convergent optimization algorithm. The MPNN can be effectively implemented by utilizing its inherent parallelism.

2.2 Compensator

Linear regression based prediction offers many advantages such as stability, analysability and fast adaptation. However for many real life applications, nonlinear regression based prediction is required for acceptable accuracy, however their adaptation, computation time and complexity makes it difficult for real time realization [11]. A practical solution to this problem is to retain the linear part of the modeling and then replacing the second and higher terms with a simpler model algorithm such as MPNN.

The MPNN part will only model higher ordered complexities which have been defined by the difference between the linear model and the training data. Any data which is outside this training data will produce a minimal residual effect from the MPNN/GRNN and the linear model will dominate for reliable short term prediction. The linear modeling can be achieved using the standard least mean square error rule. The MPNN adaptation can be achieved as described in subsection 2.1.

The advantage of this model are:

1. There is a strong underlying simpler regression influence for reliable short term prediction.
2. The MPNN embodies only higher term function approximation.
3. The MPNN can be more efficient than high-order Volterra realizations.
4. The system is quick and easy to use for arbitrary nonlinear modeling.

3 Experiment

Figure 2 shows the New York Stock Exchange (NYSE) values for the period of 410 days between 1st of July 1999 to 14th of August 2000. The sample data represents 'share price index' which are influenced by several economic factors. The share price index and the various economic factors share an intimate relationship however they are hard to be observed. In this paper, an ANN is used to identify the hidden relationship from available finite sample data.

In order to compare the prediction performance of the proposed model, a number of different prediction models were also tested. Each prediction model was trained with the data from first 320 days, and then was tested to perform extrapolation (prediction) for next 20 days. The 20 day period was rather a short period for testing prediction; however we believe that the short term prediction is used more frequently in practice, hence we limited our prediction testing to short term only. Also there are some other hidden factors to be considered such as the seasonal variations. The experiment was performed under the assumption that the seasonal variations was known a prior which is true for most practical financial analysis. The experiment compares the prediction performance of the proposed model and the conventional popular prediction models such as the Volterra (polynomial) models and MLP neural network.

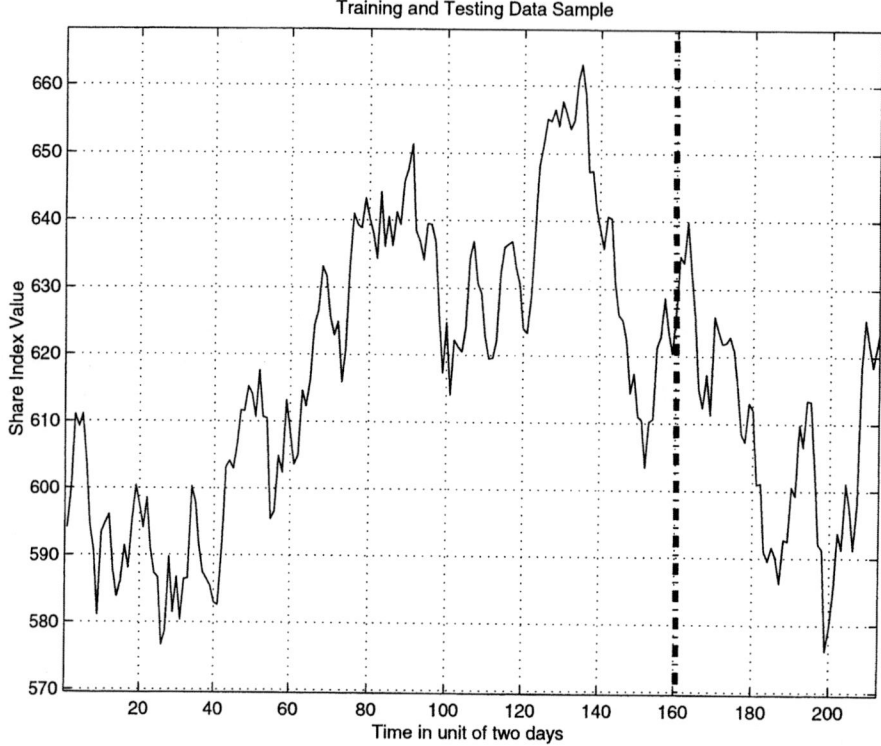

Fig. 2. The training sample are from values 1 to 160; the extrapolation testing set are values from 161 to 200 inclusive

4   Results and Analysis

A few conventional nonlinear modelling techniques were used for prediction and their performance are compared on the basis of four sets of measurements, namely, the mean square error (MSE) between the prediction output and the desired sample output, network training time, testing time, and the overall effectiveness as a predictor.

4.1   Single Volterra Model for Prediction

Volterra models for nonlinear prediction are frequently used in various fields such as signal processing, communication and image processing [12]. In many practical problems, Volterra models of higher order than three are seldom used due to very large computations and slow convergence. We used the third order Volterra model to predict for the problem given in figure 2.

The MSE from the network using a Volterra model was - 4 dB. The prediction performance was not acceptable and the training and testing time was very long, making its implementation in practical applications difficult.

Table 1. The performance of Volterra filter as a nonlinear compensator

MSE	Training Time	Testing Time
-4 dB	119 seconds	91 seconds

4.2   Single MLP for Prediction

MultiLayer Perceptron (MLP) is a well recognised nonlinear modeling technique. MLP has proven successful in speech recognition and etc [13]. For our experiment, the MLP architecture was chosen empirically as a 20-5-1 network (1 input layer with 20 neurons, 1 hidden layer with 5 hidden neurons, and 1 output layer with 1 neuron). It is possible to achieve better nonlinear modeling performance using more number of neurons however it increases computational complexity exponentially. The training was performed using popular backpropagation algorithms [13].

Table 2. The performance of MLP as a nonlinear compensator

MSE	Training Time	Testing Time
-14 dB	91 seconds	14 seconds

The MSE for the network of a linear regression model and a MLP was -14 dB. The prediction performance was not very good. MLP did not prove to be an effective predictor since the MLP produced an unpredictable output for the inputs outside the training sample sets.

4.3   Single MPNN for Prediction

In our experiment, MPNN used Gaussian function as a radial basis function. Refer section 2.1 for details on MPNN.

Table 3. The performance of MPNN as a nonlinear compensator

MSE	Training Time	Testing Time
-24 dB	12 seconds	6 seconds

The MSE of the MPNN was -24 dB. The prediction performance was better than any of single Volterra model or MLP. MPNN proved be a better predictor by effectively interpolating between the given sample pairs of input/outputs. However the prediction performance was still not good enough for reliable implementation. The training and testing time were acceptable for the given tasks.

4.4   Combination of Linear Model and MLP for Prediction

A combination of a linear model and MLP was used to perform prediction. The MLP architecture was chosen empirically as a 20-5-1 network (1 input layer with 20 neurons, 1 hidden layer with 5 hidden neurons, and 1 output layer with 1 neuron). As again, the training was performed using backpropagation algorithms.

Table 4. The performance of MLP as a nonlinear compensator

MSE	Training Time	Testing Time
-19 dB	91 seconds	14 seconds

The MSE for the network of a linear regression model and a MLP was -19 dB. The prediction performance was improved over the performance of a single MLP. However MLP did not prove to be an effective nonlinear compensator due to its unpredictable output for the inputs which are outside the training set. The output from MLP was required to reduce close to zero for extrapolation, leaving linear model to provide its best linear fit, however MLP produced an unpredictable output for the inputs outside of the training region, degrading overall performance of the combined model.

4.5   Combination of Linear Model and MPNN for Prediction

A combination of linear model and MPNN was used for prediction. The MPNN used Gaussian radial basis functions. For details of the architecture, refer section 2.

Table 5. The performance of MPNN as a nonlinear compensator

MSE	Training Time	Testing Time
-32 dB	12 seconds	6 seconds

The MSE of the network of a linear regression model and a MPNN was -32 dB. The prediction performance was improved over any other models. Also, MPNN proved be a better nonlinear compensator by effectively reducing the MPNN output to zero for the inputs outside the training samples, allowing the linear regression model to provide the best fit. As more data becomes available, MPNN and linear model adjusts its parameter in order to cater for new knowledge adaptively. The training and testing time were acceptable for the given tasks.

5   Conclusion and Future Work

This paper identified the effectiveness and utility of combining a linear regression model with the MPNN. Although the methods presented in the paper includes a simple linear model, it is possible to substitute the linear model for any other justifiable analytic model such as simple Hidden Markov Model and etc. for an appropriate class of problems.

References

[1]   C. L. Wilson, Self-organising neural networks for trading common stocks, in *Proc. IEEE World Congr. Neural Networks*, Orlando, FL, pp. 3657–3661, 1994.

[2]   J. Konstenius, Mirrored Markets, in *Proc. IEEE World Congress on Neural Network*, pp. 3671–3675, Orlando, Florida, 1994.

[3]   D. Lowe, Novel exploitation of neural network methods in financial markets, in *Proc. IEEE World Congr. Neural Networks*, pp. 3623–3627, Orlando, FL., 1994.

[4]   D. F. Specht, Probabilistic Neural Networks, *Int. Neural Network Soc., Neural Networks*, vol. 3, p 109–118, 1990.

[5]   J. Moody & C. Darken, Fast learning in networks of locally tuned processing units, *Neural Comput.*, vol. 1, no. 2, pp. 281–294, Sept. 1989.

[6]   J. Moody & C. Darken, Learning localized receptive fields, in *Proc. 1988 Connectionist Models Summer Sch.*, Touretzky, Hinton, and Sejnowski, Eds. San Francisco, CA: Morgan-Kaufmann, pp. 133–143, 1988.

[7]   M. J. D. Powell, Radial basis functions for multivariate interpolation: A review, Tech. *Rept. DAMPT 1985/NA 12 Dept. Appl. Math. Theoretical Phys.* Cambridge, MA, Nov. 1974.

[8]   D. S. Broomhead & D. Lowe, Radial basis functions, multi-variable functional interpolation and adaptive networks, *Royal Signals Radar Est. Memo. 4248*, Mar. 28, 1988.

[0]   J. S. Albus, A new approach to manipulator control: The cerebellar model articulation controller (CMAC), *J. Dyn. Syst. Meas. Contr.*, pp. 220–227, Sept. 1975.

[10] E. A. Nadaraya, On estimating regression, *Theory Probab. Appl.*, Vol. 9, pp. 141–142, 1964.

[11] M. H. Hayes, *Statistical Digital Signal Processing and Modeling*, John Wiley & Sons, Inc. 1996.

[12] D. J. Krusienski, & K. Jenkins, Comparative analysis of neural network filters and adaptive Volterra filters, *Proceedings of the 44th IEEE 2001 Midwest Symposium on*, Vol., 1, page(s): 49–52, vol. 1, 2001.

[13] S. Haykin, em Neural Networks: comprehensive foundations, Prentice Hall, Upper Saddle River, New Jersey, 1996.

[14] T. Jan & A. Zaknich, Adjustable model from linear to nonlinear regression, *Proceedings of IEEE Conference on International Joint Conference on Neural Networks*, Washington DC, USA, Paper No. 635, 10th-16th July 1999.

[15] X. Huang, X. Ma, X. Li, Y. Fu & J. Lu, Study on recognition of speech based on HMM/MLP hybrid network, *Signal Processing Proceedings, 2000, WCCC-ICSP 2000, 5th International Conference on*, vol. 2, page(s): 718–721, vol. 2, 2000.

[16] W. T. Miller, F. H. Glantz & L. G. Kraft, CMAC: An association neural network alternative to backpropagation, *Proc. IEEE*, vol. 78, pp. 1561–1567, Oct. 1990.

Generating Explicit Self-Organizing Maps by Information Maximization

Ryotaro Kamimura[1] and Haruhiko Takeuchi[2]

[1] Information Science Laboratory
and Future Science and Technology Joint Research Center, Tokai University,
1117 Kitakaname Hiratsuka Kanagawa 259-1292, Japan
ryo@cc.u-tokai.ac.jp
[2] Human-Computer Interaction Group,
Institute for Human Science and Biomedical Engineering,
National Institute of Advanced Industrial Science and Technology,
1-1-1 Higashi, Tsukuba 305-8566, Japan
takeuchi.h@aist.go.jp

Abstract. In this paper, we propose a new information theoretic method for self-organizing maps. In realizing competition, neither the winner-all-take algorithm nor lateral inhibition is used. Instead, the new method is based upon mutual information maximization between input patterns and competitive units. Thus, competition processes are flexibly controlled to produce explicit self-organizing maps. We applied our method to a road classification problem. Experimental results confirmed that the new method could produce more explicit self-organizing maps than conventional self-organizing methods.

1 Introduction

In this paper, we propose a new information theoretic method for producing self-organizing maps. The new approach is considerably different from conventional SOM in that competition is realized by maximizing information.

Information theoretic approaches have been used in various aspects of neural computing. For example, Linsker [1] proposed a principle of maximum information preservation in information processing systems. In this framework, networks self-organize to preserve maximum information in each processing layer. Then, the principle was applied to self-organizing maps by maximizing mutual information. The algorithm developed by Linkser [2] is rather complex, and we have had some difficulty in applying it to actual problems. On the other hand, Kohonen's self-organizing map is one of the most successful methods for self-organizing maps, because the method is simple and easy to be implemented by neural networks. Self-organizing maps are produced by updating neighboring neurons so as to make them as similar as possible. However, final activation patterns do not necessarily produce coherent patterns, and sometimes it is difficult to interpret final representations. Thus, many attempts to enhance interpretations of self-organizing maps have been made[3].

J. Liu et al. (Eds.): IDEAL 2003, LNCS 2690, pp. 236–245, 2003.

To overcome these problems of the previous self-organizing maps methods, we propose an information theoretic method to produce explicit self-organizing maps. In our new method, competition is realized by maximizing mutual information between input patterns and competitive units[4]. In addition, our method makes neighboring neurons as similar as possible. By controlling information content, different types of self-organizing maps are easily generated. Especially, when information is sufficiently maximized, self-organizing maps are explicit, and we can easily interpret the meaning of self-organizing maps.

2 Self-Organization

2.1 Competitive Processes

Self-organizing processes are produced by controlling information content in competitive units. We consider information content stored in competitive unit activation patterns. For this purpose, let us define information to be stored in a neural system. Information stored in a system is represented by decrease in uncertainty [5]. Uncertainty decrease, that is, information I, is defined by

$$I = -\sum_{\forall j} p(j) \log p(j) + \sum_{\forall s} \sum_{\forall j} p(s) p(j \mid s) \log p(j \mid s), \qquad (1)$$

where $p(j)$, $p(s)$ and $p(j|s)$ denote the probability of the jth unit, the probability of the sth input pattern and the conditional probability of the jth unit, given the sth input pattern, respectively.

Let us present update rules to maximize information content. As shown in Figure 1, a network is composed of input units x_k^s and competitive units v_j^s. We used as the output function the inverse of the Euclidean distance between

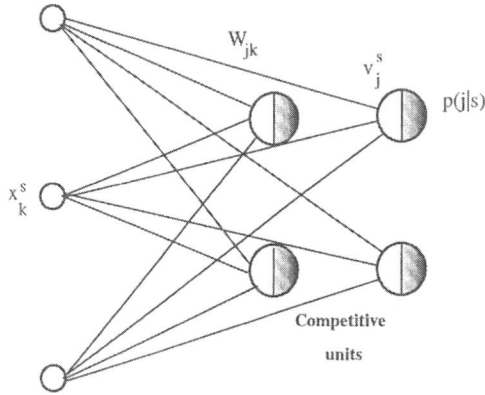

Input units

Fig. 1. A network architecture for information maximization.

connections weights and outputs. Thus, an output from the jth competitive unit can be computed by

$$v_j^s = \frac{1}{\sum_{k=1}^{L}(x_k^s - w_{jk})^2},\tag{2}$$

where L is the number of input units, and w_{jk} denote connections from the kth input unit to the jth competitive unit. The output is increased as connection weights are closer to input patterns.

The conditional probability $p(j \mid s)$ is computed by

$$p(j \mid s) = \frac{v_j^s}{\sum_{m=1}^{M} v_m^s},\tag{3}$$

where M denotes the number of competitive units. Since input patterns are supposed to be uniformly given to networks, the probability of the jth competitive unit is computed by

$$p(j) = \frac{1}{S}\sum_{s=1}^{S} p(j \mid s).\tag{4}$$

Information I is computed by

$$I = -\sum_{j=1}^{M} p(j) \log p(j) + \frac{1}{S}\sum_{s=1}^{S}\sum_{j=1}^{M} p(j \mid s) \log p(j \mid s).\tag{5}$$

Differentiating information with respect to input-competitive connections w_{jk}, we have

$$\Delta w_{jk} = -\beta \sum_{s=1}^{S}\left(\log p(j) - \sum_{m=1}^{M} p(m \mid s) \log p(m)\right) Q_{jk}^s\tag{6}$$

$$+\beta \sum_{s=1}^{S}\left(\log p(j \mid s) - \sum_{m=1}^{M} p(m \mid s) \log p(m \mid s)\right) Q_{jk}^s,$$

where β is the learning parameter, and

$$Q_{jk}^s = \frac{2(x_k^s - w_{jk})}{S\sum_{m=1}^{M} v_m^s \left(\sum_{k=1}^{L}(x_k^s - w_{jk})^2\right)^2}.\tag{7}$$

Let us explain how information maximization realizes competitive processes. The mutual information is composed of first order entropy $-\sum_j p(j) \log p(j)$ and second order entropy $-1/S\sum_s\sum_j P(j \mid s) \log p(j \mid s)$. In maximizing mutual information, first order entropy should be increased as much as possible, while second order entropy should be minimized. When second order entropy is minimized, a neuron tends to responds to a specific input pattern. Thus, the second order entropy minimization may realize competition processes. However, it happens that one neuron always respond to the specific input patterns. All other neurons do not always respond to any input patterns. These can be called *dead neurons*. In mutual information maximization, the first order entropy is simultaneously maximized. This means that all neurons must equally be used. Thus, as mutual information is increased, all neurons tend to respond to different input patterns. When the number of the competitive units is restricted to a smaller number of units, then the competitive unit tends to classify input patterns into the corresponding groups. As can be inferred from the equation of the information, each competitive unit tends to respond to the same number of input patterns. This is actually done by using traditional competitive learning.

2.2   Cooperative Processes

Let us introduce cooperative processes to produce self-organizing maps. To realize cooperative processes, neurons must behave similarly to neighboring neurons. Following Kohonen [6], we introduce lateral distance d_{jm} between the jth and mth neurons as follows:

$$d_{jm} = \| \mathbf{r}_j - \mathbf{r}_m \|, \tag{8}$$

where the discrete vector $\mathbf{r}_j$ denotes the jth neuron position in the two dimensional lattice. By using this distance function, we define the topological neighborhood function:

$$\Phi_{jm} = p(m) \exp \left(-\frac{d_{jm}^2}{2\sigma^2} \right), \tag{9}$$

where σ denotes a parameter, representing the effective width of the topological neighborhood. If a neuron fires very strongly, it surely affects the firing of its neighboring neurons. Thus, the probability $p(m)$ is introduced to incorporate this effect. One of the principal characteristics of cooperative processes is that neighboring neurons must behave similarly to each other. Many methods to incorporate this behavior are possible. By extensive experiments, we have chosen a method to update connections so that connections to neighboring neurons are as similar as possible. Thus, we have the following rule G:

$$G_{jk} = \sum_{m=1}^{M} \Phi_{jm} \left(w_{mk} - w_{jk} \right). \tag{10}$$

This equation shows that as the jth neuron is closer to the mth neuron, connections into the jth and mth neurons are made as similar as possible, as shown in Figure 2.

Differentiating information with respect to input-competitive connections w_{jk} and adding the equation G, we have

$$\Delta w_{jk} = -\frac{\beta}{S} \sum_{s=1}^{S} \left(\log p(j) - \sum_{m=1}^{M} p(m \mid s) \log p(m) \right) Q_{jk}^s \tag{11}$$

$$+\frac{\beta}{S}\sum_{s=1}^{S}\left(\log p(j \mid s) - \sum_{m=1}^{M} p(m \mid s)\log p(m \mid s)\right)Q_{jk}^{s}$$

$$+\gamma\sum_{m=1}^{M}\Phi_{jm}\left(w_{mk}-w_{jk}\right), \tag{12}$$

where β and γ are the learning parameters.

For actual experiments, we change the parameters for cooperative processes following the method by M.M Van Hulle [7]. Now, let $\Phi_{jm}(t)$ denote the topological neighborhood function at the time t. Then, the function is defined by

$$\Phi_{jm}(t) = p(m;t)\exp\left(-\frac{d_{jm}^{2}}{2\sigma^{2}(t)}\right), \tag{13}$$

where $p(m;t)$ represents the firing rate of the jth competitive unit at the tth epoch, and $\sigma(t)$ is defined by

$$\sigma(t) = \sigma(0)\exp\left(-2\sigma(0)\frac{t}{t_{max}}\right), \tag{14}$$

where $\sigma(0)$ is the half of the linear dimension of the lattice, and t_{max} is the maximum number of epochs.

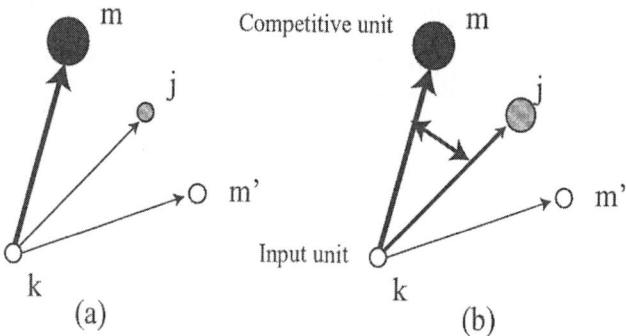

Fig. 2.   Concept of cooperative processes.

3   Road Scene Classification

We here present experimental results on a road classification problem. In this problem, networks must infer whether a driver drives in a mixed traffic road or a motor road. In the experiments, we prepared 49 road photographs taken from the drivers' viewpoint. Figure 3 shows some examples of photos from the total of

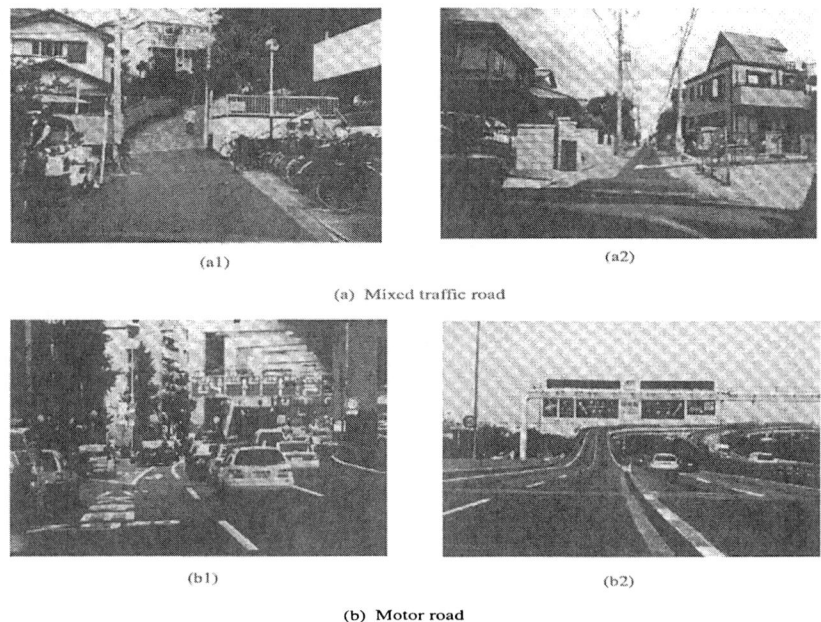

(a1)   (a2)

(a) Mixed traffic road

(b1)   (b2)

(b) Motor road

Fig. 3.   Four photos used in our experiments.

49 photos. Of the 49 photos, 23 photos are classified as mixed traffic roads that are relatively narrow, as the examples shown in Figure 3(a1) and (a2) illustrate. On the other hand, the remaining 26 photos are those of relatively wide motor roads, as the samples shown in Figure 3(b1) and (b2) illustrate. We carefully examined these photos and made a linguistic check list composed of 36 features, for example, *walkers*, *bicycles*, *houses*, *road signs* and so on. For the experiment, we examine whether the networks can classify those photos into appropriate classes, and try to see what kinds of features can be extracted by the neural networks. Figure 4 shows a network architecture in which the number of competitive units is 100 (10×10) units. As the number of competitive units is larger, clearer patterns can be seen. We decided the number of the competitive units, considering the computational time. Figure 5 shows information as a function of the number of epochs. We have seen that as the cooperation time is longer, more clear maps can be obtained. As can be seen in the figure, no information increase can be observed until the number of epochs is about 7,000 epochs. Then, information is rapidly increased up to about 87 percent of maximum information content, and reaches its steady state.

Figure 6 shows the firing rates $p(j)$ of neurons when information is 0.2, 0.4, 0.6 and 0.8. The magnitude of the squares in the figures represents the strength of neuron firing rates, and the label number in the figures shows maximally fired neurons. Figure 6(a) shows the firing rates when information is 0.2. Some neurons on the lower left hand side fire more strongly than neighboring neurons. These neurons correspond to the photos of mixed traffic roads. In addition, some

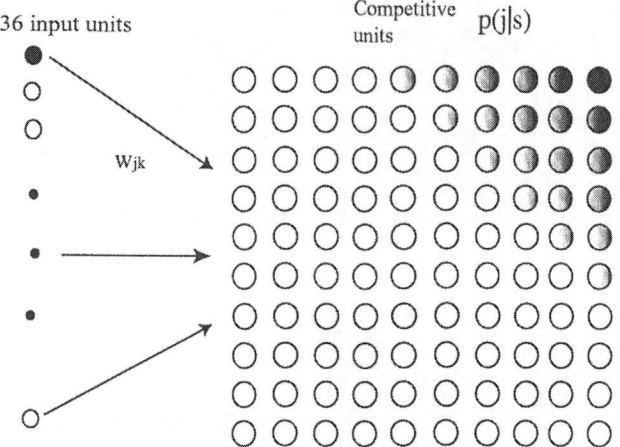

Fig. 4. A network architecture for the road scene classification.

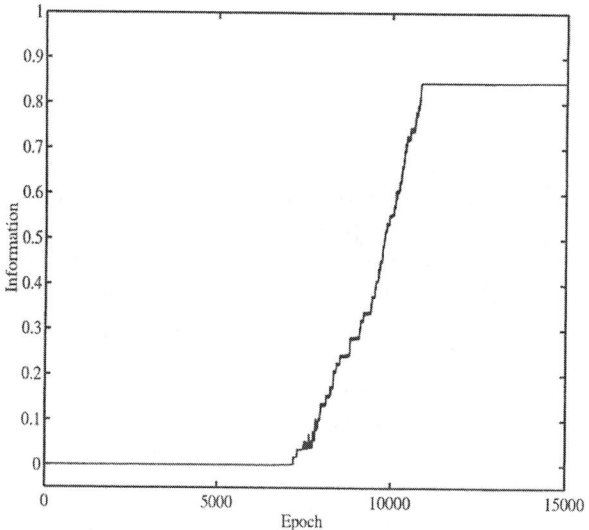

Fig. 5. Information as a function of the number of epochs.

other neurons on the upper right hand side fire more strongly than neighboring neurons. These neurons correspond to motor roads. When information is increased to 0.4, neurons on the lower left hand side and the upper right hand side fire more clearly, and a boundary between two groups moved downward slightly. When information is increased to 0.6 and 0.8 (Figure 6(c) and (d)), the same firing rates can be seen. That is, different neurons tend to fire for different input patterns. In addition, it is easy to see a boundary between two groups, because in the boundary region few neurons fire strongly.

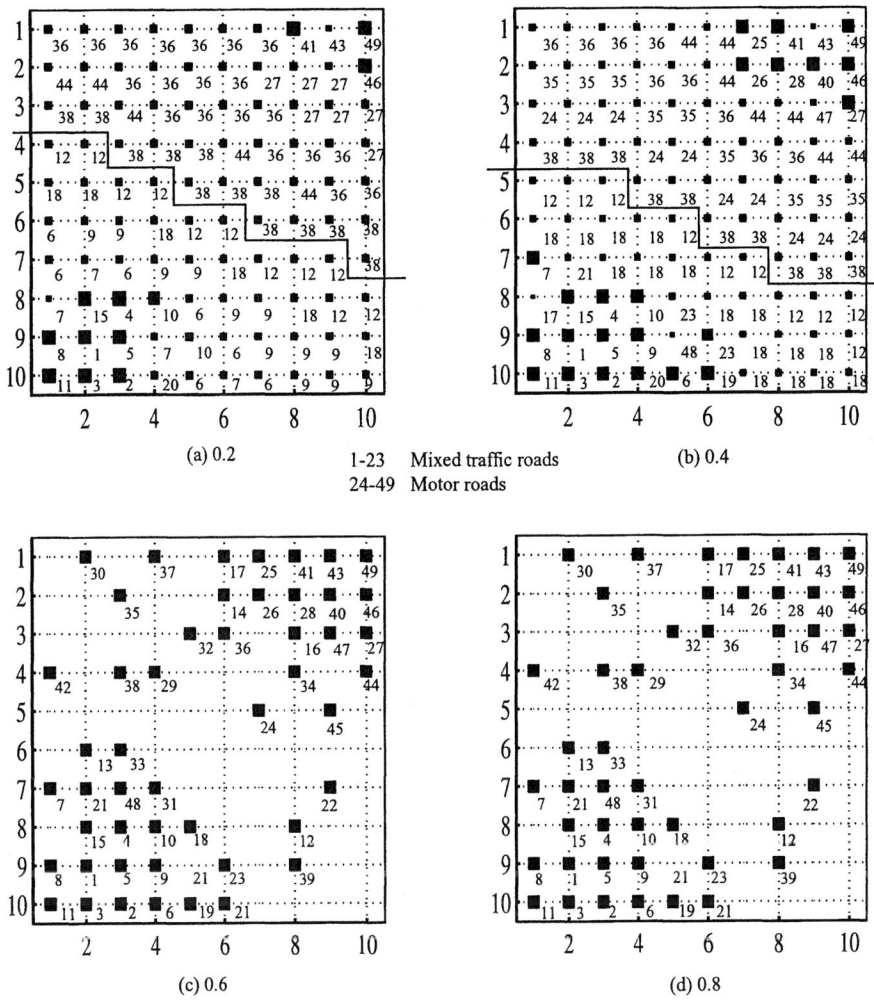

Fig. 6. Neuron firing rates $p(j)$ for the road classification problem. The label numbers for neurons shows maximally fired neurons.

For comparison, we computed the firing rates by using the conventional SOM[1]. However, almost uniform firing rates could be obtained. Thus, instead of the firing rate, we computed the number of maximally fired neurons for input patterns. We also computed the U-matrices, because the U-matrix is one of the most popular visualization methods. Figure 7(a) shows the firing rates by the standard SOM. As can be seen in the figure, less clear representations can be obtained. Though slightly clearer representations can be obtained by the batch

---

[1] Experiments were performed by using Matlab neural network package and SOM toolbox for Matlab with all default values for easy comparison.

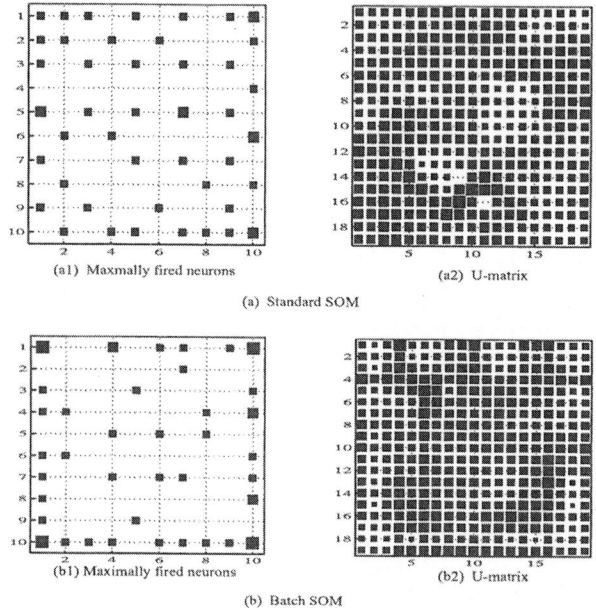

(a1) Maxmally fired neurons

(a2) U-matrix

(a) Standard SOM

(b1) Maximally fired neurons

(b2) U-matrix

(b) Batch SOM

Fig. 7. The number of maximally fired neurons for input patterns and U-matrices by (a) the standard SOM and (b) the batch SOM.

SOM, still representations are less clear than those obtained by the information theoretic method.

4   Conclusion

In this paper, we have proposed a new information theoretic method for self-organizing maps. In the method, mutual information maximization is used for neurons to compete with each other. Thus, competition processes are flexibly controlled. In addition, the method makes neighboring neurons behave as similar as possible. We applied our method to a road classification problem. Experimental results confirmed that the new method could produce more explicit self-organizing maps than conventional self-organizing methods.

For further development of our method, we should mention three points to consider. First, to compute information, networks need extra computation time. Thus, we should develop some methods to accelerate learning. Second, our cooperative process adopted in this paper is only one of the many possible ways. Thus, we should examine what kinds of cooperative processes are appropriate. Third, final representations obtained by our method are clear enough for easy interpretation. However, we need more sophisticated ways to visualize final representations. Though some improvement is needed, we think that this method certainly opens up a new perspective in self-organizing maps.

References

1. R. Linsker, "Self-organization in a perceptual network," *Computer*, vol. 21, pp. 105–117, 1988.
2. R. Linsker, "How to generate ordered maps by maximizing the mutual information between input and output," *Neural Computation*, vol. 1, pp. 402–411, 1989.
3. S. Kaski, J. Nikkila, and T. Kohonen, "Methods for interpreting a self-organized map in data analysis," in *Proceedings of European Symposium on Artificial Neural Networks*, (Bruges, Belgium), 1998.
4. R. Kamimura, T. Kamimura, and H. Takeuchi, "Greedy information acquisition algorithm: A new information theoretic approach to dynamic information acquisition in neural networks," *Connection Science*, 2002.
5. L. L. Gatlin, *Information Theory and Living Systems*. Columbia University Press, 1972.
6. T. Kohonen, *Self-Organization Maps*. Springer-Verlag, 1995.
7. M. Marc and M. V. Hulle, *Faithful representations and topographic maps*. New York: John Wiley and Sons, Inc, 2000.

A Clustering Approach to the Vision-Based Interface for Interactive Computer Games

Hyun Kang[1], Chang Woo Lee[1], Keechul Jung[2], and Hang Joon Kim[1]

[1]Dept. of Computer Engineering, Kyungpook National Univ.,
Daegu, South Korea
{hkang, cwlee, kimhj}@ailab.knu.ac.kr
[2]School of Media, College of Information Science, Soongsil Univ.
Seoul, South Korea
kcjung@ssu.ac.kr

Abstract. In interactive computer games, vision can be a powerful interface between humans and computers. In this paper, we propose a vision-based interface for 3D action games. We make dynamic gestures to input of the interface and represent a user's gesture as an ordered sequence of a user's poses. To estimate a human poses, we classify whole frames using K-Means clustering. For recognizing a gesture, each symbols from input sequence is matched with templates composed of ordered pose symbol sequences that indicate the specific gestures. Our interface recognizes ten gesture commands with a single commercial camera and no markers. Experimental results with 50 humans show an average recognition rate of 93.72 % per a gesture command.

1 Introduction

Vision can be a powerful interface between human and computer. Vision-based interaction makes machine interaction more enjoyable, engaging, and perhaps safer. In interactive games, developing the vision-based interface is challenging. As game technologies glow up, game developers should supply more complicated interaction for more variable abilities. Thus, the vision-based interface is a new alternative for game industries. Many systems that use computer vision techniques have been developed, and a commercial vision-based system has also been developed [1-3].

Vision-based game interface pose particular challenges; the response time of interaction should be fast, computer vision algorithms should be reliable, and the interface system has economic constraints [1].

We propose a vision-based interface for tracking and interpreting upper-body motion in image sequences using a single commercial camera in interactive computer games. For interactive graphics applications, Freeman has introduced and demonstrated several efficient computer vision algorithms [1, 2]. Additionally, Bradski has shown his game interface using CAMSHIFT [3]. These systems were limited to object tracking and simple recognition for action. Our interface recognizes 10 gestures from video sequence without losses in functionality of system.

J. Liu et al. (Eds.): IDEAL 2003, LNCS 2690, pp. 246–253, 2003.
© Springer-Verlag Berlin Heidelberg 2003

In our interface, a dynamic gesture of a user is recognized as an input of interactive games. Gesture commands are composed of an ordered sequence of human poses, which can be estimated from the position of human body parts: a head and two hands. To classify human poses from image sequences we used unsupervised learning. In each frame of the interface, human body parts are detected, tracked, and used for estimating a human pose in the frame.

The rest of this paper is organized as follows. In section 2, an overall structure of the proposed interface is described. In section 3, clustering techniques used in our system and clusters that are assumed to be human pose are introduced. Next, we show the dynamic gestures and our recognition method for these in section 4. In section 5, image processing techniques used to estimate the human pose are presented. Some experimental results are presented in section 6 followed by concluding remarks.

2   System Overview

In this section, we describe the structure of the proposed interface, the functionality of each process in this structure, and the commands to be recognized. The gesture of a user is recognized as an input of interactive games through our interface. Our interface consists of three processes: Body part detections, Pose estimations, and Recognition. With a single commercial camera and no markers, we detect a user's body parts in each frame, we estimate human pose from clusters to make symbols, and recognize a symbol sequence in the gesture of users. An illustration of our interface is shown in figure 1.

Fig. 1. An illustration of the proposed interface: the user gestures the commands 'hold the move and keep the duck in the position of avatar'.

First, body part detection process detects body parts in each frame. It consists of four steps that are usually used in image processing techniques. The first step is skin color detection, the second step is morphological operation, the third step is connected component, and the last step is heuristic rules for labeling the connected component as body parts: a head and hands.

In the next process, pose estimation decides on the pose symbol using the position of the body parts. A clustering technique such as K-Means is used for pose estimation. The last process, gesture recognition, is based on pose symbol sequences and decides on a command using dynamic programming. These processes are also shown in Figure 2.

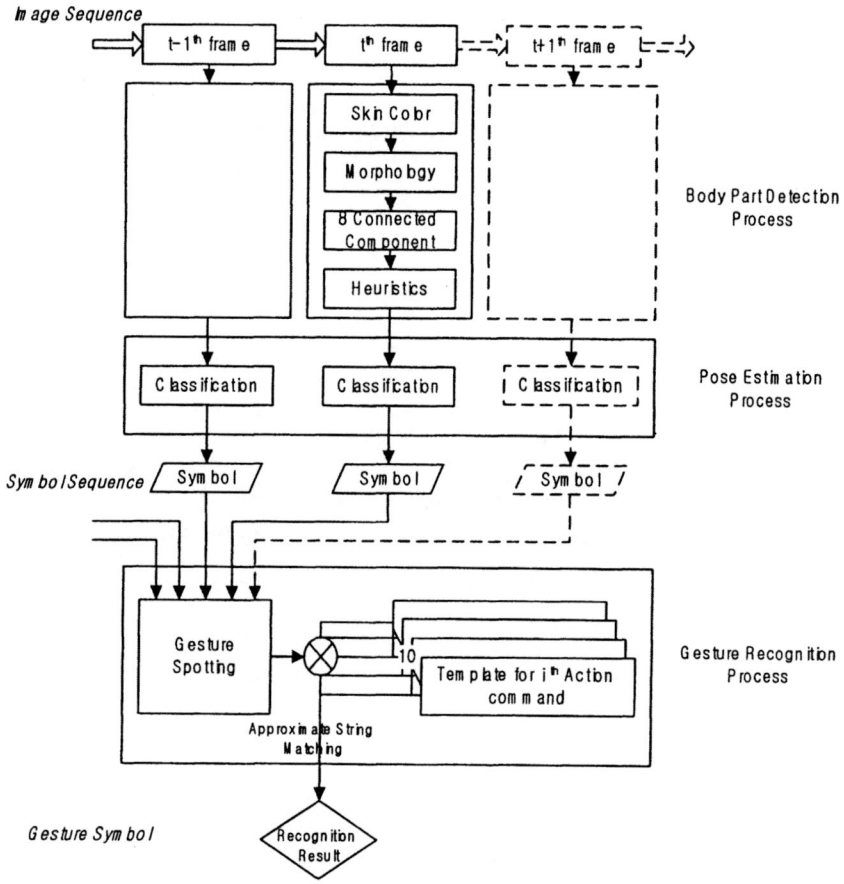

Fig. 2. An overall structure of the proposed system: the name of each stage are named on the right side. Texts on the left side of this figure are intermediate data.

We strive to detect a small number of body parts with a single camera and passive sensing. We define commands of a user as input of the proposed interface, and show detailed descriptions of these commands in table 1. Table 1 has 10 kinds of gesture descriptions and 1 command by mouse. In shooting a gun, it is more natural to mouse-click than to make any gesture.

Table 1. The user commands are used as an input of the interfaces.The first 10 commands are user's gestures. The last command is a simple direct interaction with wireless mouse.

Control commands	Description
System Setting Action	Unfold your arms in three seconds, and fold them in three seconds.
Stop System	Cross your arms.
Gun Left Move	Bring your hands together, and move your hands to your left.
Gun Right Move	Join both hands, and move your hands to your right.
Body Left Move	Keep your hands together, and move your upper body to left.
Body Right Move	Keep your hands together, and move your upper body to right.
Walk	Shake your right hands in forward direction.
Duck	Raise your right hand.
Move Stop	Put your hands on the desk.
Run	Shake your hands when running.
Shot/Weapon Change	Wireless mouse left/right click.

3   Clustering

In our work, a user's gesture is represented as an ordered sequence of poses. Our interface is based on this representation and classifies each frame to estimate a human pose. Because manual data labeling is costly, an automatic clustering method is chosen to classify sample data. The clustering algorithm in the interface is K-Means clustering.

K-Means is probably the most popular clustering algorithm. It requires one to specify the number of classes K, where each class corresponds to a pose of the user in our interface. It automatically generates clusters by minimizing the sum of squared errors from all patterns in a cluster to the center of the cluster. The pattern samples are constructed using the position values of 3 upper body parts. A main assumption of K-Means is that clusters are hyper-ellipsoidal [4].

In our interface system, clustering has two different stages: a training phase and a lookup phase. During the training phase, users generate different gestures in several times while capturing the training image sequence with a single camera. It constructs clusters that correspond to poses of users. During the lookup phase, the interface estimates a user's poses by comparing the best matches of body parts in a frame and clusters of poses.

For good results in the next recognition process, we examine clustering performance. Thus, we should determine three options: 1) the representation of sample data, 2) K, cluster's number, and 3) distance measure, metric. Sample data have a 6-tuple vector representation that consists of head, left hand, and right hand position. The representation of sample data is important because clusters should be invariant to the transformations that are inherent in our problem [4]. Table 2 shows the representations of sample data. First, the data representation tested is simple absolute positions of 3 body parts and the second representation is absolute position of the head and relative position of the left/right hand to the head position.

Table 2. The Representations of samples

	Head	Left and Right hand
A	Absolute positions	Absolute positions
B	Absolute positions	Positions relative to heads

We then determine the second option of clustering, K. We experiment with K set to 20~50, and we can find pertinent K value. Lastly, we determine metric. We experiment clustering with 2 metrics: general Minkowski metric q=1 and q=2. We can get good metric in our problem. Table 3 shows for these two metrics.

Table 3. The metrics: the functions of the general Minkowski metric q=1 and q=2 are shown, where d is the dimension of vector **x**.

Metrics	Functions
Minkowski metric q=1: Manhattan distance	$d(\mathbf{x}, \mathbf{x}') = \sum_{k=1}^{d} \left| x_k - x'_k \right|$
Minkowski metric q=2: Euclidean distance	$d(\mathbf{x}, \mathbf{x}') = \left(\sum_{k=1}^{d} \left| x_k - x'_k \right|^2 \right)^{1/2}$

4 Gesture Recognition

Given a pose symbol sequence, gesture recognition process makes a decision which a specific gesture is the sequence. Usually, HMM, DTW, and finite state machines are chosen for gesture recognition [5]. In this study, upper body motion is regarded as a sequence of symbols that identify some pose. Thus, we use dynamic programming to determine gestures between the gesture templates. It is important to define the recursive property in dynamic programming. In our matching algorithm, the recursive property is then:

$$dist_{i,j} = cost(i, j) + \min\{dist_{i-1,j}, dist_{i-1,j-1}, dist_{i,j-1}\} \tag{1}$$

where $dist_{i,j}$ is the minimum matching value between i-th symbol and j-th symbol, and cost(i, j) is the function that returns distance between i-th symbol and j-th symbol. This cost function uses Euclidean distance between the center of the i-th cluster and the center of the j-th cluster.

Gesture templates are manually made using training samples data. When developing continuous gesture recognition, one must be thought of a gesture spotting. In our interface, a sequence consists of discrete symbols, and every action in a gesture input is terminated in 0.5sec ~ 1sec (7~11 frames). Thus, we easily solve this gesture spotting by applying some heuristics.

5 Image Processing

In our interface, the image processing step detects a small object that might be the head or hands of user. Our interface uses a commercial camera that produces low quality of image. Roughly speaking, small object detection and tracking in a vision-based interface is a difficult problem for satisfactory performance and detection quality.

In the total system, the inputs of the image processing process are frame sequences. Image processing executes each frame in times and produce positions of body parts in the image. The process consists of four steps. The first step is a skin color detection, the second step is a morphological operation, the third step is a connection component connection and the last step are heuristic rules for labeling the connected components as body parts; head and hands.

Detecting pixels with the skin color provides a reliable method for detecting body parts. Since a RGB representation obtained by most video cameras includes brightness, this color space is not necessarily the best color representation for detecting pixels with skin color. The brightness may be removed by dividing the three components of a color pixel according to the intensity. The color distribution of human skin is clustered in a small area of chromatic color space and can be approximated by a 2D-Gaussian distribution [6].

In the morphological operation step, a closing operation is used to eliminate noise in skin detected binary image. The connected component step produces box-list data in the binary image that was processed in previous step. The last step discriminates body parts in a box-list in output of the previous step. Table 4 shows that heuristic rules are used in this step.

Table 4. The heuristic rules for discriminating body parts

Rules
Box(es) in size < m should be thrown.
The biggest box might be head.
Right hand might be right side, and left hand might be left side.
Only one box in the list might be merged head and hands
When two boxes are in the list, upper box might be head and lower box might be hands

6 Experimental Results

In order to validate the clustering and gesture recognition method, we have collected data of human poses and the gesture templates of 5 persons, and data of the experimental input of 50 persons. We construct symbols about human poses by K-Means clustering as described in section 3, and we construct the template of gesture for approximate string matching method in recognition process as described in section 4. The vision-based game interface is performed with visual C++ and runs on a 1.3GHz standard PC at about 10Hz from a commercial USB camera that has 24bit RGB colors and a 320x240 resolution.

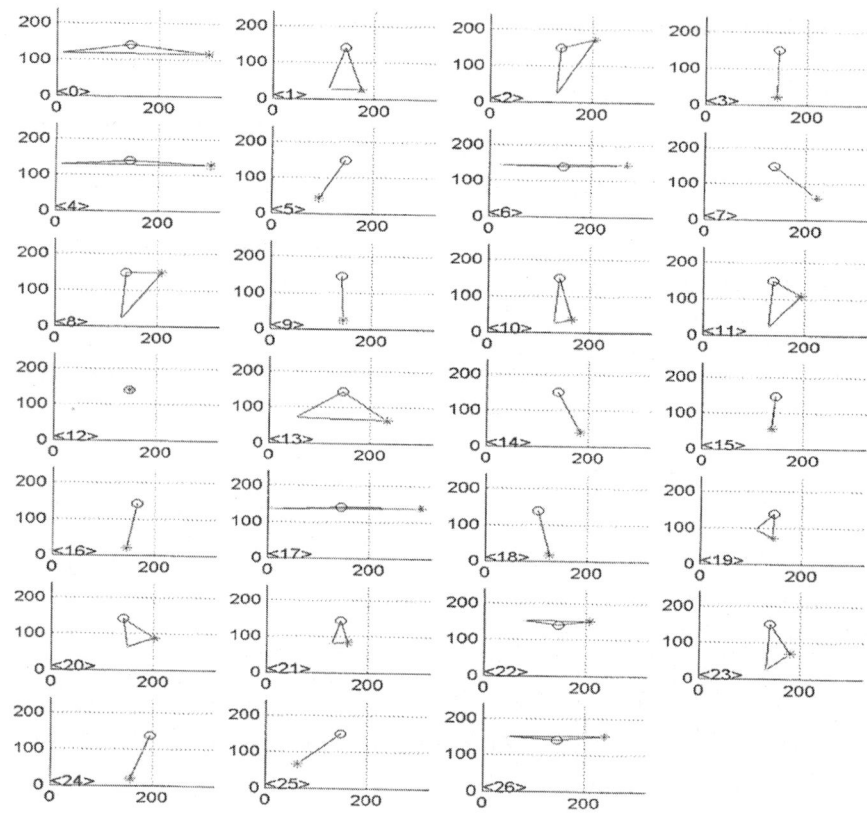

Fig. 3. A View about centers of clusters: each chart has x and y axes that they are correspond to x and y of image, respectively. The circle, star ('*'), and dot ('.') in the charts are head, right hand, and left hand, respectively.

A visual view of our clustering results is shown in figure 3. To evaluate the performance of the interface, each of the control commands was repeatedly issued 10 times per one man to test the vision-based game interface. The total average recognition rate was 93.72% in table 5.

Table 5. Experimental results of the proposed interface.

Control commands	Recognition rate	Control commands	Recognition rate
System Setting Action	478/500	Body Right Move	488/500
Stop System	464/500	Walk	453/500
Gun Left Move	477/500	Duck	413/500
Gun Right Move	489/500	Move Stop	446/500
Body Left Move	491/500	Run	487/500

7   Conclusion

In this paper, we have proposed a clustering approach to estimate human poses and to apply a vision-based interface to interactive computer games. Therefore, we have obtained good experimental results with our proposed interface. These results lead to the conclusion that gestures of the user in the interface for games are composed of sequences of poses that can be recognized by the proposed approach.

Presently, we are looking at ways to make robust gesture spotting techniques in complex situation involving unintentional movements of a user. Our research can be extended to robust and reliable interface for interactive computer games.

Acknowledgement. This work was supported by the Soongsil University Research Fund.

References

1. Freeman, William T., Anderson, David B., Beardsley, Paul A., Dodge, Chris N., Roth, Michal, Weissman, Craig D., Yerazunis, William S.: Computer Vision for Interactive Computer Graphics. IEEE Computer Graphic and Application, Vol. 18. (1998) 42–53
2. Freeman, William T., Tanaka, K., Ohta, J., Kyuma, K.: Computer vision for computer games, IEEE Proceedings of the Second International Conference on Automatic Face and Gesture Recognition, 14-16 Oct, (1996) 100–105
3. Bradski, Gary R.: Computer Vision Face Tracking For Use in a Perceptual User Interface, Intel Technology Journal Q2 (1998) 1–15
4. Duda, Richard O., Hart, Peter E., Strok, David G.: Pattern Classification (2nd ed.). A Wiley Interscience Publication (2000)
5. Pavlovic, V. I., Sharma, R., Huang, T. S., 1997. Visual interpretation of hand gestures fro human-computer interaction: a review, IEEE Trans. Pattern Anal. Mach. Intell. 19 (7), 677–695.
6. Lee, C.W., Lee,Y.C., Park, S.Y., Kim, H.J.: Real-Time Face Detection and Tracking Using PCA and NN. Lecture Notes in Artificial Intelligence, Vol. 2417. Springer-Verlag, Berlin Heidelberg New York (2002) 615–625

Evolution at Learning: How to Promote Generalization?

Ibrahim Kuschchu

GSIM, International University of Japan
Yamato-machi, Minami Uonuma-gun
Niigata 949-7277 JAPAN
ik@iuj.ac.jp

Abstract. This paper introduces generalisation concept from machine learning research and attempts to relate it to the evolutionary research. Fundamental concepts related to computational learning and the issue of genaralisation are presented. Then some evolutionary experiments are evaluated according to how well they relate to these established concepts in traditional learning. The paper concludes with emphasizing the importance of generalisation in evolutionary learning practices.

Keywords: Machine Learning, Evolutionary Learning and Generalisation

1 Introduction

Investigation of learning in artificial intelligence (AI) has developed in parallel with major paradigms of AI such as symbolic, connectionist and evolutionary methods. A careful examination of research in learning would clearly reveal a significant gap between conventional learning methods (i.e., connectionist or symbolic) and evolutionary methods. This may be due to the fact that evolutionary methods have a shorter history than conventional methods. The course of research related to conventional methods reflect comparatively well established theoretical and practical approaches to many aspects of developing artificial learning systems.

One of the important aspects of learning systems is concerned with the performance assessment of a learner. Among few alternative performance assessment methods, measuring the *generalisation* performance of the learner is an important and arguably one of the most widely used. Most of the common practices of conventional methods use a learning process, which is carried out in two stages: training and testing. Conventional learning methods have already established some effective principles and methods in designing learning systems and measuring the generalisation performance. Evolutionary methods, however, are a relative newcomer. Recently some research [26,25,24,1,19,6] sometimes directly but sometimes indirectly have promoted importance of understanding and using the concept of generalisation from machine learning. This has resulted in

J. Liu et al. (Eds.): IDEAL 2003, LNCS 2690, pp. 254–261, 2003.

improved practices in the areas of evolutionary learning (see section 3). However, still a big gap may exist between research in evolutionary methods and conventional methods with regard to developing effective learning systems. One major contribution to the investigation of learning might come from bridging the gap between conventional learning and evolutionary methods and promoting a beneficial interaction between them.

This paper is another attempt to promote the interaction between traditional learning and evolutionary learning research. It presents some examples of evolutionary learning experiments according to how good they practice generalisation. Finally, the paper concludes with a discussion of the importance of evolutionary generalisation.

2   Some Examples of Evolutionary Learning Implementations

This section focuses on learning research in classififer systems and Genetic Programming (GP). One interesting area of evolutionary learning which is not covered here is related to evolution of artificial neural networks (see [29] for a recent example of work in this area).

2.1   Examples from Learning Classifier Systems

A classifier system (CS) is a machine learning system that learns using simple condition-action rules which are called classifiers [18,13,38]. By the help of genetic algorithms, the CS constructs the rules needed to perform as desired in the environment. It can be seen as a learning system applicable to diverse environments and problems. It may be able to learn with incomplete information. One of the techniques employed in CS is that it can classify the environment into hierarchies by constructing simple to more general classifiers.

In [39,9], the issue of generalisation in a XCS is viewed somewhat differently than what it would be in traditional machine learning. While machine learning researchers are interested in systems which perform according to the method of induction discussed under PAC Learning framework, for a classifier system, however, generalisation is used as a way of succesfully *reducing a large instance space to a compact set of classifiers*. Here, the instance space corresponds to those messages presented to the system. In other words, since there are no distinctive training and testing data sets, there is no concept of 'generalisation over the testing data'. What is expected from XCS is to *compress* the instance space presented to it by capturing the regularities of the instance space. A large instance space is compressed by creating some general rules. A *limited* form of induction carried out by a XCS is the capability of a particular classifier to predict correctly as many instances as possible. Thus, a set of classifiers has the power to generalise *within* the instance space presented. In other words, XCS has more power to "treat as equivalent those situations which seems different but have equivalent consequences for the system" [39,9]. For example, in the same paper Wilson states that generalisation in XCS is achieved by using "internal structure of significantly less complexity than the raw environment". In this way those messages requiring the same action but having different condition parts can be merged into a single classifier or a small set of classifiers (through evolution) that generalise over the differences. In fact, the measure of generalisation in his experiments was the number of classifiers evolved. Generalisation would be considered as greater for a smaller number of classifiers. Obviously, *developing artificial learning systems with such an attitude to generalisation may result in systems lacking predictive accuracy since a decrease in the number of the classifier is an insufficient measure of generalisation.* Since there are no training and testing data sets to evaluate the generalisation performance, only compression is promoted but not generalisation to some unseen test data.

Recently, increasing number of researchers (see for example [8,9,5,2,3,4] examined the generalisation issue in XCS. A recent survey of the current state of the research on XCS can be found in [10].

Most of these studies consistently follow the original experimental set-up (i.e. the multiplexer problem or the maze environment where all the input space is presented to the classifier system). They anlyse the performance of the XCS in producing maximally general accurate classifiers [2,3,4]. Through successive sudies Kovacs has shown how XCS can produce optimal set of such classifiers, which is defined under optimality hypothesis [2] as an extension of Wilson's generalisation hypothesis[8].

In one of the studies [6] the issue of generalisation is examined under partially observable environments in which case the classifier system must have some sort of memory to hold the knowledge of the previously seen characteristics of the environment and required action. It is observed XCS may not be able to produce optimally general behaviors applicable to all the positions in the environment due to XCSs simple exploration strategies.

One of the important consideration of generalisation within the machine learning framework comes from a recent study by Kovacs [1]. In this study Kovacs questions the type of the solution learned by the XCS within both the previous efforts in XCS literature and the machine learning literature. The study starts with explaining how Wilson's explore/exploit scheme [8] is appropriate for single-step tasks and how this may be inefficient for for multi-step problem formulations. He explicitly states that use of different testing and training sets is the norm in machine learning but the studies on learning the boolean function do not use separate training and testing sets and the system is trained on the complete set of possible instances.

Later, the study continues by enumerating 4 properties of rule sets relaxant to learning in classifier systems: (1) completeness where the rule set covers each possible input, (2)correctness where the each input is mapped to a correct action, (3) minimality where the rule set contains minimal number of rules and (4) lack of overlaps where an input should not be matched by two rules having the same action pattern. In a previous work [2] these properties have been presented as the optimal rule set.

It is discussed that some of these properties may have both desirable and undesirable aspects. Correctness can only make sense only if all of the inputs defining a problem is presented to the user. However in the case of real world situations such as data mining where the set of possible inputs may not be know beforehand, this property may result in over-fitting. Similarly, minimality is in many cases is very advantageous and have been the major goal of some of the work in classifier systems [2,8,9]. However, in cases where a learning system is not evaluated based on unseen cases minimal and non-overlapping rule sets may disadvantageous in that the system is restricted to generating hypothesis (i.e.input/output mappings) which are good only for the seen cases. This limits the likelihood of success of a classifier system generalising to input sets on which it is not trained.

Apart from the above work, two recent studies [11,7] evaluates the generalisation performance of XCS within the framework of machine learning. In these studies, XCS is used to find solutions to input output mappings with separate training and test sets. These are the situations where the real measure of generalisation ability of XCS can be observed. The results of these studies have shown that in simple problems such as Monk1 nad Monk3 the performance of the XCS is comparable to other learning methods. In a more difficult cases, XCS presents concerns of over-fitting with reduced performance in the testing phases of both Monk2 [7] and Wisconsin Breast Cancer Data Sets [11]. The research above constitute recent evidences that evolutionary learning and generalisation are being considered in the context of traditional machine learning framework.

2.2   Examples from Genetic Programming

GP has been proposed as a machine learning method [23] and solutions to various learning problems are sought by means of an evolutionary process of program discovery. These learning problems, in general, can be classified into two kinds according to the way in which a problem is defined: some problems use a data set such as input/output mappings of supervised learning problems and other problems deal with real or simulated robot behaviours in an environment. Recently, growing numbers of researchers [12,20,34,32] report that solutions to learning problems may result in non-robust or brittle programs. Robustness of a solution is defined as the desired successful performance of the solution when it is applied to an environment similar to the one it is evolved for. In [12] several approaches used by GP researchers to promote robustness are discussed. The authors identify three major ways of dealing with brittle solutions: modifying fitness function (i.e., producing shorter solutions), improving on the selection of fitness cases and using co-evolution.

A broader review of issue of generalisation in genetic programming is presented elsewhere [26]. Common to most of the learning research in GP are the problems with obtaining generalisation and the attempts to overcome these problems. Unfortunately, almost all of these attempts seems to be far from being generic and in some cases are ad hoc approaches to generalisation. These issues can be summarised as follows:

- The conventional approach to solving learning problems involves only a training process and does not encourage use of a testing process. In this way, solutions are found to rely on pure compression (i.e., the complete set of instances of a problem is used in the computation of the fitness) [23,17].
- Only recently training and testing phases have been used. In order to promote generalisation in supervised learning problems, changing training instances from one generation to another and evaluation based on subsets of training instances are suggested. For the simulation methods, changing the initial condition of the robot, introducing noise, using more than one fitness cases and modifying the fitness function are proposed [20,34].
- There seems to be a lack of formal methods to determine how the training and testing processes should be conducted and the generalisation performance should be measured. Most experiments involve ad hoc solutions and experimental set-ups to deal with this problem. For example, some experiments use test cases to compute the fitness of the individual [16]. Some use a generational evaluation of test performances [32]. Others change the initial starting conditions of the robot/environment without following a certain formal approach [34].

In [19] extensions to GP in terms of Bagging (BagGP) and Boosting (BoostGP) is presented. Bagging and Boosting are two important data manipulation methods of traditional machine learning. These systems are applied to discovery of trigonometric identities, prediction of chaotic time series and 6-bit multiplexer problems (for multiplexer problem, training cases were used as testing cases). When these systems were compared with standard GP, for the first two experiments both systems found lower mean square errors and for the multiplexer problem successful solution were found during earlier generations. This research represents one of the good examples of bridging the gap between machine learning and GP approaches to learning.

Another set of experiments (for more details please refer to [25]) employ a constructive induction, which is a method that improves on both representational and procedural bias. In this framework, GP is used to evolve a set of additional attributes of supervised learning problems (i.e. change in the representational bias) which results in increased generalisation performance (i.e. improved procedural bias) of the back-propagation learning algorithm.

A good example of experiments attempting to reduce brittleness of the programs generated by GP is presented in [32]. The system in this paper evolves optimised manoeuvres for the pursuer/evader problem. The results of this study suggest that use of a fixed set of training cases may result in brittle solutions due to the fact that such fixed fitness cases may not be representative of possible situations that the agent may encounter. It is shown that use of randomly generated fitness cases at the end of each generation can reduce the brittleness of the solutions when tested against a set of large representative situations after the evolution. A more recent work [27] suggest a different method for improving generalisation of solutions produced for the artificial ant problem. Rather than using training and testing approaches proposed in [24], the research suggest that the limitations of the solutions may stem from the limitations in the problem definition.

Another good approach to promoting robustness by means of co-evolution is presented in [35]. The paper presents a simple competitive co-evolution method to produce robust controllers for artificial ants. The controllers are evolved simultaneously with the fitness cases resulting in robust behaviours in comparison with a "hand-coded controller" or a "test-evolved controller". Although, co-evolutionary approach to promoting robustness seems to be very promising, it requires further investigation in assessing the difficulty and the cost of co-evolving both solutions and fitness cases for more complex and larger problems.

3   Conclusions

The power of learning lies in the fact that learning systems can extract implicit relationships that may exist in the input-output mapping or the interaction of the learner with the environment. Learning such an implicit relationship only during the training phases may not be sufficient and a generalisation of learned task or behaviour may be essential for several reasons.

When designing a learning system certain characteristics of the environment or examples of the input-output mappings may not be known or available or too cumbersome to be provided to the learner. Promoting generalisation ability of the learning system increases the likelihood of the success of the system when the new facts about the problem are known or available. This should prevent a costly process of adapting or changing the learning system to the new situation.

Also the environments change constantly over time and learning systems should be built so that they can adapt reasonably to the changes in the environment rather than they are re-designed over and over again.

A generalisation oriented attitude in developing learning systems can result in a process which brings economies of scale in the design and performance of the learning systems when they are faced with new examples or situations in the environment.

In this paper, through examining some of the research in learning classifier systems and in genetic programming, it is shown that increasing number of researchers are turning into borrowing methodology from traditional learning in order produce better artificial learning systems with better generalisation ability.

References

1. Tim Kovacs. What should classifier system learn. In *Proc. of the 2001 Congress on Evolutionary Computation*, pages 775–782, IEEE, 2001.
2. Tim Kovacs. Evolving optimal populations with XCS classifier systems. Technical Report CSRP-96-17, 1996.
3. Tim Kovacs. XCS Classifier System Reliably Evolves Accurate, Complete, and Minimal Representations for Boolean Functions. In Roy, Chawdhry, and Pant, editors, *Soft Computing in Engineering Design and Manufacturing*, pages 59–68. Springer-Verlag, London, 1997.

4. Tim Kovacs. Strength or accuracy? fitness calculation in learning classifier systems. In *Learning Classifier Systems*, pages 143–160, 1999.
5. Pier Luca Lanzi. A Study of the Generalization Capabilities of XCS. In *In T. Baeck, ed., Proceedings of the Seventh International Conference on Genetic Algorithms (ICGA97)*, pages 418–425. Morgan Kaufmann, 1997.
6. Pier Luca Lanzi. Adding Memory to XCS. In *Proceedings of the IEEE Conference on Evolutionary Computation (ICEC98)*. IEEE Press, 1998.
7. S. Saxon and A. Barry. Xcs and the monk's problem, 1999.
8. Stewart W. Wilson. Classifier fitness based on accuracy. *Evolutionary Computation*, 3(2):149–175, 1995.
9. Stewart W. Wilson. Generalization in the XCS classifier system. In *In Proceedings of the Third Annual Genetic Programming Conference, J. Koza et al (eds.)*, pages 665–674. Morgan Kaufmann, 1998.
10. Stewart W. Wilson. State of XCS classifier system research. In *Learning Classifier Systems*, pages 63–82, 1999.
11. Stewart W. Wilson. Mining oblique data with XCS. In *IWLCS*, pages 158–176, 2000.
12. Tommaso F. Bersano-Begey and Jason M. Daida. A discussion on generality and robustness and a framework for fitness set construction in genetic programming to promote robustness. In John R. Koza, editor, *Late Breaking Papers at the 1997 Genetic Programming Conference*, pages 11–18, Stanford University, CA, USA, 13–16 July 1997. Stanford Bookstore.
13. Lashon B. Booker. Classifier systems that learn internal world models. *Machine Learning*, 3(2/3):161–192, October 1988.
14. G. Carbonell, Jaime. *Machine Learning: paradigms and methods*. The MIT Press, London, 1990.
15. T. G. Dietterich and E. B. Kong. Machine learning bias, statistical bias, and statistical variance of decision tree algorithms. Technical report, Department of Computer Science, Oregon State University, Corvallis, OR, 1995.
16. Frank D. Francone, Peter Nordin, and Wolfgang Banzhaf. Benchmarking the generalization capabilities of a compiling genetic programming system using sparse data sets. In John R. Koza, David E. Goldberg, David B. Fogel, and Rick L. Riolo, editors, *Genetic Programming 1996: Proceedings of the First Annual Conference*, pages 72–80, Stanford University, CA, USA, July 1996. MIT Press.
17. D. Goldberg. *Genetic Algorithms in Search, Optimization and Machine Learning*. Addison-Wesley, Massachusettes, 1989.
18. J. Holland. *Adaptation in Natural and Artificial Systems*. University of Michigan Press, Ann Arbor, MI, USA, 1975.
19. Hitoshi Iba. Bagging, boosting, and bloating in genetic programming. In Wolfgang Banzhaf, Jason Daida, Agoston E. Eiben, Max H. Garzon, Vasant Honavar, Mark Jakiela, and Robert E. Smith, editors, *Proceedings of the Genetic and Evolutionary Computation Conference*, volume 2, pages 1053–1060, Orlando, Florida, USA, 13–17 July 1999. Morgan Kaufmann.
20. Takuya Ito, Hitoshi Iba, and Masayuki Kimura. Robustness of robot programs generated by genetic programming. In John R. Koza, David E. Goldberg, David B. Fogel, and Rick L. Riolo, editors, *Genetic Programming 1996: Proceedings of the First Annual Conference*, Stanford University, CA, USA, 28–31 July 1996. MIT Press. 321–326.
21. M. Kearns. *The Computational Complexity of Machine Learning*. The MIT Press, 1990.

22. M. Kearns and U. Vazirani. *An Introduction to Computational Learning Theory.* MIT Press, Cambridge, Massachussets, USA, 1994.
23. John Koza. *Genetic Programming:On the programming of computers by means of natural selection.* MIT Press, Cambridge, MA, 1992.
24. Ibrahim Kuscu. Evolving a generalised behavior: Artificial ant problem revisited. In V. William Porto, editor, *Seventh Annual Conference on Evolutionary Programming*, Mission Valley Marriott, San Diego, California, USA, 1998. Springer-Verlag.
25. Ibrahim Kuscu. A genetic constructive induction model. In Peter J. Angeline, Zbyszek Michalewicz, Marc Schoenauer, Xin Yao, and Ali Zalzala, editors, *International Congress on Evolutionary Computation*, pages 212–217. IEEE press, 1999.
26. Ibrahim Kushchu. Genetic programming and evolutionary generalisation. *IEEE Transactions on Evolutionary Computation*, 6(5):431–442, October, 2002.
27. Parks D. J., R. K. Vail, E. M. Harpel, and F. W. Moore. The evolution of general intelligent behavior. In *Eleventh Midwest Artificial Intelligence and Cognitive Science Conference*, 2000.
28. Pat Langley. *Elements of Machine Learning.* Morgan Kauffmann, San Fransisco, 1996.
29. Y. Liu, X.Yao, and T. Higuchi. Evolutionary ensembles with negative correlation learning. *IEEE Transactions on Evolutionary Computation*, 4(4):380–387, 2000.
30. R. S. Michalski, J. G. Carbonell, and T. M. Mitchell. *Machine Learning an Artificial Intelligence Approach.* Morgan-Kaufmann, 1983.
31. R. S. Michalski, J. G. Carbonell, and T. M. Mitchell. *Machine Learning an Artificial Intelligence Approach Vol II.* Morgan-Kaufmann, 1986.
32. F. W. Moore and O. N. Garcia. New methodology for reducing brittleness in genetic programming. In E. Pohl, editor, *Proceedings of the National Aerospace and Electronics 1997 Conference (NAECON-97).* IEEE Press, 1997.
33. J. R. Quinlan. Induction of decision trees. *Machine Learning*, 1(1):81–106, 1986.
34. Craig W. Reynolds. An evolved, vision-based behavioral model of obstacle avoidance behaviour. In Christopher G. Langton, editor, *Artificial Life III*, volume XVII of *SFI Studies in the Sciences of Complexity*, pages 327–346. Addison-Wesley, Santa Fe Institute, New Mexico, USA, 15–19 June 1992 1994.
35. Andreas Ronge and Mats G. Nordahl. Genetic programs and co-evolution developing robust general purpose controllers using local mating in two dimensional populations. In Hans-Michael Voigt, Werner Ebeling, Ingo Rechenberg, and Hans-Paul Schwefel, editors, *Parallel Problem Solving from Nature IV, Proceedings of the International Conference on Evolutionary Computation*, volume 1141 of *LNCS*, pages 81–90, Berlin, Germany, 22–26 September 1996. Springer Verlag.
36. Jude Shavlik, W. and G. Dietterich, Thomas. *Readings in Machine Learning.* Morgan Kaufmann, San Mateo, California, USA, 1992.
37. L.G. Valiant. A theory of the learnable. *Communications of ACM*, 27:1134–1142, 1984.
38. Stewart W. Wilson. Classifier systems and the animat problem. *Machine Learning*, 2(3):199–228, November 1987.
39. Stewart W. Wilson. Generalisation in XCS. In Terry Fogarty and Gilles Venturini, editors, *ICML Workshop on Evolutionary Computing and Machine Learning*, 1996.

Automatic Extraction of Moving Objects Using Distributed Genetic Algorithms

Eun Yi Kim[1] and Se Hyun Park[2*]

[1]College of Internet and Media, Konkuk Univ.,
1 Hwayang-dong, Gwangjin-gu, Seoul, Korea
eykim@kkucc.konkuk.ac.kr
[2]Division of Computer Engineering, College of Electronic and Information, Chosun Univ.,
375 Susuk-dong, Dong-gu, Gwangju, Korea
sehyun@chosun.ac.kr

Abstract. This paper proposes an automatic segmentation method using genetic algorithms that can automatically extract the moving objects and track them. Each frame of the video sequence is decomposed into the objects forming the scene, which are tracked through a whole video sequence. The proposed method is evaluated on a number of different input data and is applied for car detection and people detection in the video surveillance system. The obtained results have confirmed the validity of the proposed method.

1 Introduction

Video segmentation has been the subject of intensive research due to its importance in a variety of applications, including vision systems, pattern recognition, and object based coding standard such as MPEG-4 and MPEG-7 [1-4].

Until now, various techniques and algorithms have been proposed for video segmentation. These methods can be categorized into three basic approaches according to the information they use for segmentation: spatial segmentation; motion segmentation; spatiotemporal segmentation. The first approach uses only spatial information, such as intensity, color, or optical flow, and can detect precise object boundaries. However, this type of method fails to produce a meaningful partition, as objects in a video sequence are not normally characterized by just spatial information. To overcome this problem, motion information has recently been used in many segmentation techniques, as the most important characteristic for identifying objects in a scene. However, the methods based on motion information have a major drawback: regions with coherent motion can also contain multiple objects and therefore require further segmentation for object extraction. As a result, the third approach, which uses both spatial and temporal information (i.e., color and motion), has become a recent focus of intensive research and would seem to produce a more meaningful segmentation.

Accordingly, this paper presents a segmentation method that uses the information from both spatial and temporal domain. The proposed method is described in Fig. 1.

The problem of object extraction is formulated here as the separation of moving objects from a stationary background. To obtain meaningful partitions of a video sequence and accurate objects boundaries, the proposed extraction method is composed

---

* The corresponding author: Tel. +82-62-230-7021; Fax: +82-62-230-7021.

J. Liu et al. (Eds.): IDEAL 2003, LNCS 2690, pp. 262–269, 2003.

of two major modules, spatial segmentation and temporal segmentation. The spatial segmentation divides each frame in a video sequence into regions with accurate boundaries, and the temporal segmentation produces a change detection mask (CDM) that dictates the foreground and background. VOPs for each frame are then produced by combining the spatial segmentation result and the change detection mask.

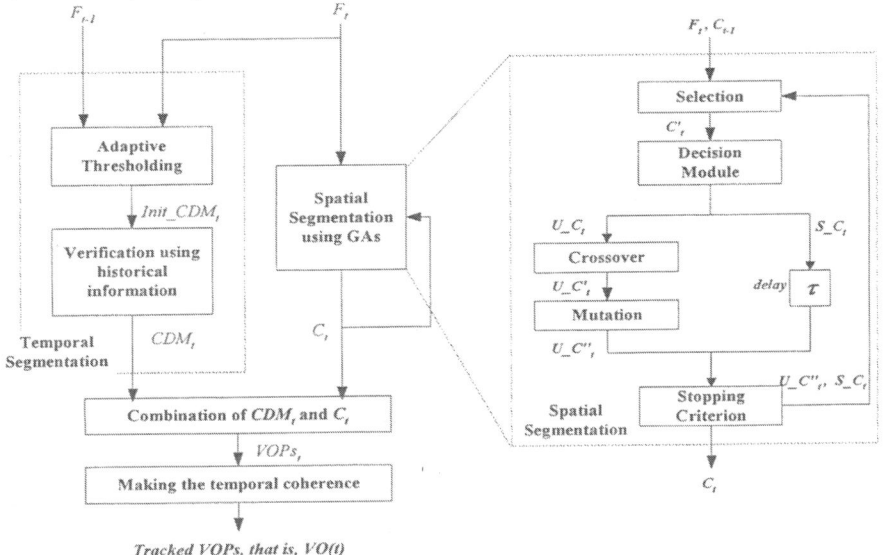

Fig. 1. Outline of the proposed spatiotemporal segmentation method

To make the temporal correspondence of the same objects between the successive frames, the object tracking modules is performed. The proposed method is able to deal with scenes that include multiple objects, and keep track of objects even when they stop moving for an arbitrarily long time.

2 Spatial Segmentation Using Genetic Algorithms

In our method, the spatial segmentation is carried out by chromosomes that evolve using DGAs. A chromosome consists of a label and a feature vector, which are described in [3]. Its fitness is defined as the Euclidean distance of the estimated feature vector and the observed feature vector. A set of chromosomes is called a population and represents a segmentation result. The process of spatial segmentation is described in Fig. 1

The segmentation of the frames in a sequence is successively obtained. For the first frame, the chromosomes are initiated with random values, whereas, for later frames they are started from the segmentation of the previous frame. The segmentation for the starting frame is determined using conventional DGAs [5]. Thereafter, the remaining frames are segmented using the modified DGAs.

The modified DGAs have two distinct features compared to the conventional DGAs. The first initializes the chromosomes using the segmentation results from the previous frame to segment subsequent frames. The second provides some chromosomes corresponding to moving object parts more opportunity to be evolved by crossover and mutation. The role of the mating operators in DGAs is to generate an improved new population from the existing population: crossover controls the size of the solution space that can be explored, while mutation creates new chromosomes that may be useful. When considered from the viewpoint of video segmentation, these operators enable the chromosomes initialized by the segmentation results of the previous frame to track the information that changed between the successive frames. Therefore, it is reasonable that the operators are first applied to the chromosomes allocated to actually moving object parts. Consequently, the new mechanisms introduced in the current work facilitate the effective exploitation and exploration of the search space, thereby improving the performance of the proposed method in terms of speed and segmentation quality. The details are described in [3].

3   Localization and Extraction of Moving Objects

Temporal information helps to separate the moving objects from the background. In our work, it is performed by two steps: detection by adaptive thresholding and use of historical information. Firstly, initial CDM is produced by adaptive thresholding [4]. Second, the resulting CDM is modified by history information. Here, the *history information* of a pixel means whether or not the pixel belongs to the moving object parts in the previous frame. If it belongs to part of a moving object in the previous frame and its label is the same as one of the corresponding pixel in the previous frame, the pixel is marked as the foreground area in the current frame.

After spatial segmentation and temporal segmentation are performed, both results are combined to yield video object planes. This combination is very simple. If the majority part of a region belongs to the foreground part of the CDM_t, the region is marked as a foreground region, i.e., the parts of moving objects. Thereafter, the adjacent foreground regions are merged into a moving component (MC). If a foreground region is not sufficiently large, it is merged into the adjacent foreground regions, thereby moving components are obtained. We assume a moving component to be corresponding to a physical object.

4   Establishment of Temporal Coherence

An overview of the proposed object-tracking method is given in Fig. 2 and it consists of three steps: natural correspondence, modification of erroneous parts, and disappearance or appearance of video objects. In the proposed method, a VOP in the current segmentation, $Q \in VOP(t)$ is called a child, while the previously detected VOP $P \in VOP(t-1)$ is referred to as a parent. The parents have a distinctive object number. As such, if child Q is identified and put into correspondence with father P, the VOP is temporally tracked. That is, it has the same object number with the corresponding parents. The first step of the proposed method involves the VOPs in the current segmentation that have obvious relationships with previously detected objects by natural correspondence. In natural correspondence, VOPs in the current frame corresponds to previously detected VOPs with similar label distribution. If the first step does not identify all the objects in the current spatiotemporal segmentation, the second or third step is applied. If only the parents or children do not correspond in the first step, the proposed object-tracking method jumps to the third step; otherwise the second step is carried out. The second step aims at fixing those situations. If child Q and parent P are located close to each other, and their size is homogeneous, a temporal correspondence is established between the two VOPs. Finally, the third step gathers information from the first and second steps. As a result, it determines whether new video objects have appeared or whether video objects have disappeared. Hence the final correspondence information permits the tracking of video objects at time t.

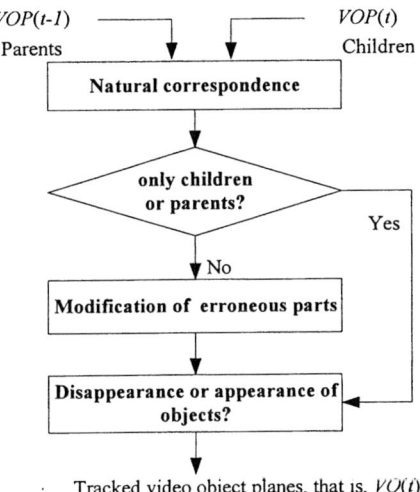

Fig. 2. Overview of the proposed object-tracking method.

5 Segmentation Results

The parameters used for experiments were fixed as follows: the label size at 64, the window size at 5×5, mutation rate as 0.005 and crossover rate as 0.1.

Fig. 3 shows the segmentation results from the natural scene. Fig. 3(a) shows the original frames at time 63, 64, and 65. Then, the corresponding spatial segmentation results and temporal segmentation results are shown in Figs. 3(b) and (c), respectively. As you can see in Fig. 3 (d), the boundary of VOPs was correctly extracted by the proposed method.

To fully demonstrate the validity of the proposed methods for object extraction and tracking, they were applied to a video sequence with more than two objects. Fig. 4 shows a succession of certain frames from a traffic monitoring sequence. Then, the succession of spatial segmentation results is shown in Fig. 5, and the corresponding CDMs are shown in Fig. 6. The extracted VOPs from the sequence are shown in Figs. 7 – 10. The tracking of the vehicles was also correct when using the proposed method, in spite of the fast motion of the vehicles and their relatively small sizes.

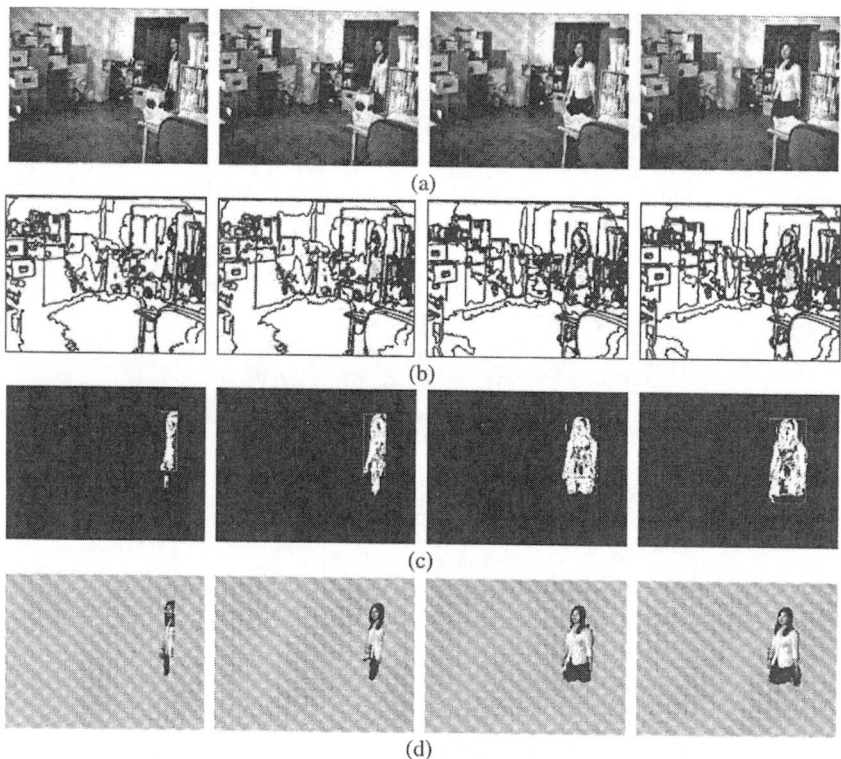

Fig. 3. Extraction of video objects from indoor surveillance sequence. (a) Original frames, (b) spatial segmentation results, (c) change detection masks, (d) VOPs for people in the respective frames.

As shown in Fig. 3-10, the proposed method can produce meaningful partitions from video sequences where no priori information is not known such as the number of objects and the background.

Fig. 4. Succession of frames from the traffic monitoring sequence.

Fig. 5. Succession of spatial segmentation results corresponding to Fig. 4.

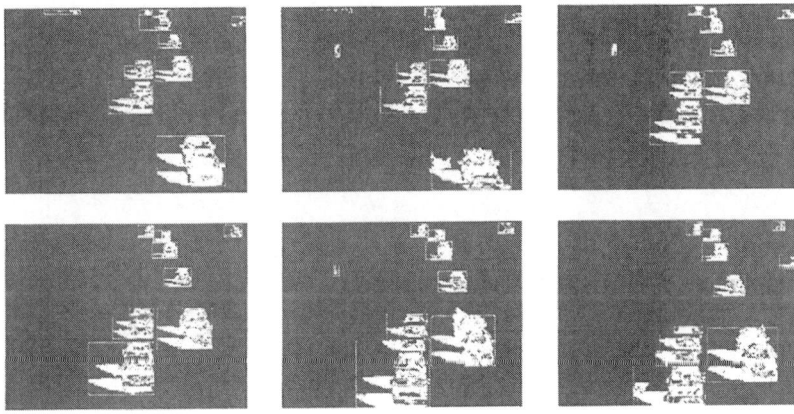

Fig. 6 Succession of change detection masks corresponding to Fig. 4.

Fig. 7 Extraction of the first vehicle from the traffic monitoring sequence.

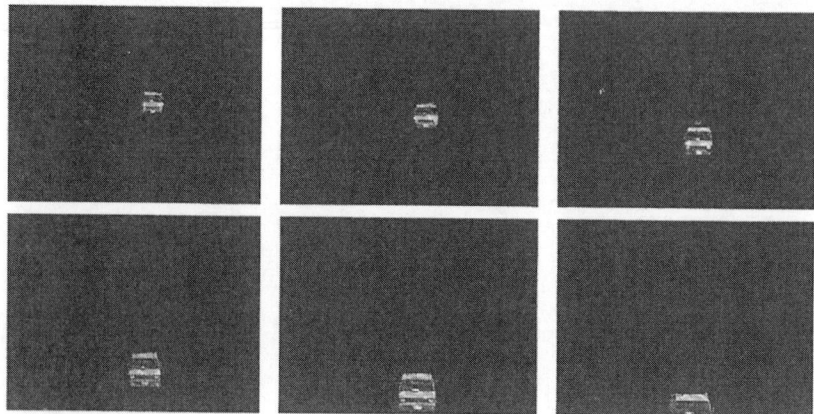

Fig. 8. Extraction of the second vehicle from the traffic monitoring sequence.

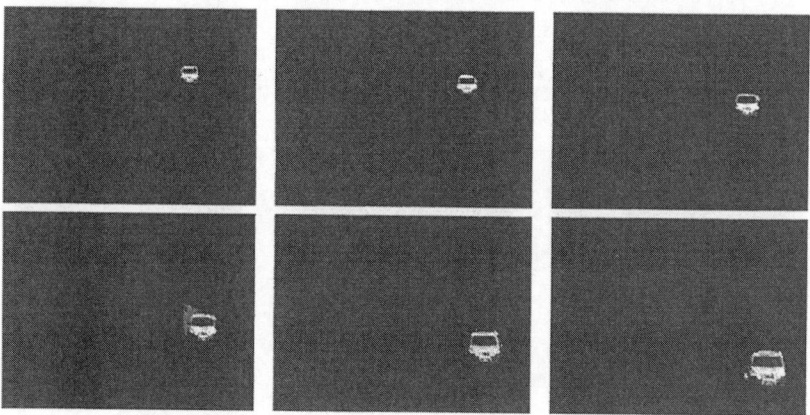

Fig. 9. Extraction of the third vehicle from the traffic monitoring sequence.

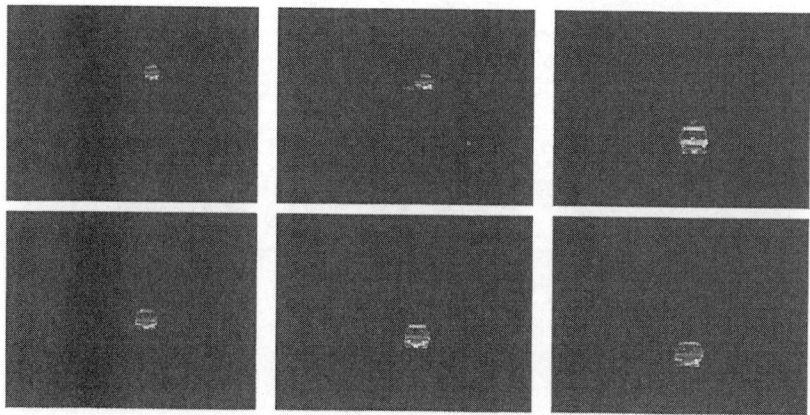

Fig. 10. Extraction of the forth vehicle from the traffic monitoring sequence.

6 Conclusion

This paper presented a new unsupervised video segmentation method using GAs, which exploits both spatial and temporal information for obtaining meaningful partitions with accurate boundaries. The proposed method was performed in four steps: spatial segmentation, temporal segmentation, object extraction and tracking. The spatial segmentation was performed by chromosomes that evolve using distributed genetic algorithms (DGAs). Temporal segmentation produced the change detection mask that dictates the foreground and background. Moving objects are extracted through combination of two segmentation results. Finally, the extracted objects are tracked using the proposed tracking algorithm. The experimental results tested with several real video sequences showed that the proposed method can be applicable to the real multimedia systems.

Acknowledgement. This work was supported by research funds from Chosun university, 2002.

References

1. ISO/IEC JTC1/SC29/WG11, MPEG-4 Visual Final Committee Draft, Dubin, Ireland, July, 1998.
2. Sikora, T.: The MPEG-4 video standard verification model. IEEE Trans. Circuits Syst. Video Technol. 7-1 (1997) 1, 19–31.
3. Kim, E. Y., S. W. Hwang, S. H. Park and H. J. Kim: A genetic algorithm based segmentation of Markov random field images. IEEE Signal Processing Letters. 7-11 (2000) 301–303.
4. Habili, N., A. Moini, and N. Burgess: Automatic thresholding for change detection in digital video. Proc. SPIE. 4067(2000) 133–142.
5. Pal, S. K. and Wang, P.: Genetic Algorithms for Pattern Recognition. CRC press. (1996).

The Approach for Data Warehouse to Answering Spatial OLAP Queries

Ying Li, Ying Chen, and Fangyan Rao

IBM China Research Lab. Beijing,
10085, P.R.China
{lying,yingch,raofy}@cn.ibm.com

Abstract. Spatial data are pervasive in traditional business applications like the customer address and store location. With the advance in mobile computing and digital earth, much more spatial data have been collected, stored and integrated into the business system. Analyzing these spatial data, to understand the relationships among them, and the relationships between spatial data and non-spatial data, would help companies gain deeper geographical insight into their business and customers, and explore more other potential business value. However, neither the design of data warehouse takes the spatial dimension of data into consideration, nor the data warehousing tools (e.g., ETL) support spatial data in the preprocessing stages. Consequently, the deployed data warehouses without spatial aware can not support spatial analysis. Research in spatial data warehousing and OLAP is an necessary to exploit the information and knowledge hidden in the spatial dimension and spatial relationships during the processing of data warehousing. This paper proposes a novel approach for data warehouses to be spatially aware and to provide certain spatial analysis capabilities. A spatial transformation builder is developed and deployed as an ETL tool to extract facts including complex spatial relationships from spatial data sources according to business requirements. The facts capturing the spatial relationships from original sources are presented by non-spatial relation model and stored in the data warehouse, where some kinds of spatial OLAP queries could be issued.

1 Introduction

It is claimed that 80% of the overall information collected by human being is geo-spatial related, either explicitly or implicitly [3]. Currently a large amount of spatial data, for example, location data of mobile users, have been collected and stored into the business information systems. The huge amount of spatial data should be analyzed efficiently since spatial analysis is important for decision-support systems, especially in those application areas that spatial is one of the primary factors, for example, traffic control, mobile network optimization, etc. Analyzing these spatial data, to understand the relationship among them, and the relationship between spatial data and non-spatial data, would help companies gain deeper geographical insight into their business and customers, and explore

J. Liu et al. (Eds.): IDEAL 2003, LNCS 2690, pp. 270–277, 2003.

more precise potential business value. Data warehousing and on-line analytical processing (OLAP) are important tools for decision making in corporations and other organizations. The data in the warehouse are often modeled as a multidimensional cube, which allows the data to be organized around natural business concepts, namely measures and dimensions, to facilitate the OLAP query engine, where queries typically aggregate data across many dimensions in order to detect trends and anomalies.

This paper provides a feasible and efficient approach for traditional data warehouse to answering spatial OLAP queries. Furthermore, a spatial transformation builder is implemented to facilitate the spatial ETL while building spatial data warehouses.

2   Motivating Example

To explain the role of spatial relationships in the spatial OLAP queries, the Traffic Control for Medical Emergency Rescue is taken as an example in this paper. We formulate a data warehouse for analyzing traffic data based on the road network of Beijing (see the road network in the window of Fig. 2).

Table 1. Station Table   **Table 2.** Detector Table   **Table 3.** Volume Table

id	road	location
S1	Chang An Jie	
S2	Han Dian Nan Lu	
S3	Zhong Guan Cun	
S4	Dong Da Jie	

id	station	lane
D1	S1	L1
D2	S2	L1
D3	S2	L2
D4	S2	L3

time	detector	volume
2002112014:00	D1	30
2002112014:05	D2	20
2002112014:10	D3	15
2002112014:10	D4	20

There are three basic tables for traffic data. The station table stores the geographical location and some related attributes for each road where a detection station is deployed. The detector table stores the belonging relationship between detector and station. The volume table records the traffic volume collected by each detector at a predefined interval, for example, five minutes. In fact, those traffic data are usually integrated and applied in other applications to support decision making, for example, the Medical Emergency Rescue. We build a data warehouse model illustrated in Fig. 1(a) that integrates the traffic data with hospital information. In the data warehouse EMS_warehouse, the fact table *volume_fact_table* is defined with four *dimensions*, *road,lane*, *hospital* and *time*[1], and one measure, *volume*. The *road* dimension and *hospital* dimension

---

[1] We assume that each station corresponds to each road, and each detector corresponds to each lane. So we directly consider the road and the lane other than station and detector.

are defined as spatial dimensions since they have the explicit spatial attributes[2]. Spatial OLAP queries will use those four dimensions as selection dimensions or

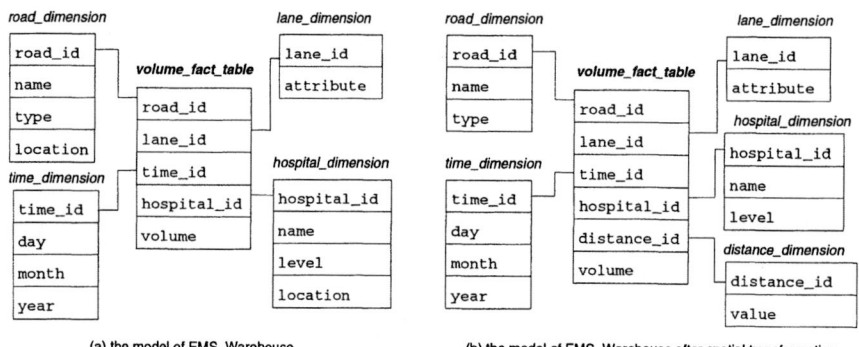

(a) the model of EMS_Warehouse   (b) the model of EMS_Warehouse after spatial transformation

Fig. 1. The model of data warehouse EMS_warehouse

output dimensions. In terms of SQL statements, those dimensions are attributes in GROUPBY clause and WHERE clause. A more complex spatial OLAP query based on the EMS_warehouse is:

Q1: *What is the total traffic volume of roads within 2 km of FirstHosptial and SecondHospital between January and March?*

In this query, output dimensions are *road*, *detector* and *volume*, while selection dimensions are *hospital*, *time* and *road*. Since all queries take the *volume* as output, we do not specifically define the *volume* attribute in the following representation of the query. We define Q1 as F(hospital,road, time)O(road, lane), F specifies the selection or GROUPBY dimensions, while O specifies the output dimensions of the query. The order of dimensions in F and O is unimportant.

3   Representation of Spatial Relationship in the Spatial OLAP Queries

The selection dimension set in the traditional OLAP queries could be value, range or arbitrary subset of domains. The spatial OLAP queries extend the traditional OLAP queries, that is, the selection dimension set can be dimensions that satisfy the spatial relationship with other dimensions. For example, the selection dimension set of Q1 includes the road dimension that satisfies the spatial relationship (within 2 km of) with hospital dimension.

Based on the conceptual model proposed in [1], we give the representation of a spatial OLAP queries as follows:

---

[2] Relative to implicit spatial attribute that is represented by text address such as No 7, 5th Street , the explicit spatial attribute means to be represented by geometry such as point, line and polygon on the map

Definition 1. A cell of a k-dimensional data cube with attributes $A_1, A_2, \ldots, A_k$ with cardinalities $d_1, d_2, \ldots, d_k$ respectively is the smallest full-dimensional cube seated at a point $P = (x_1, x_2, \ldots, x_k)$, where $x_i \in [1..d_i]$.

Definition 2. A spatial OLAP query SQ is an aggregate operation performed on the cells of a k-dimensional data cube, $SQ = F(A_1, A_2, ..., A_r)O(A_1, A_2, ..., A_t)$, where $A_X \in \{A_1, A_2, \ldots, A_k\}$, r is the number of selection dimensions, and t is the number of output dimensions. $F(A_1, A_2, ..., A_r)$ is a tuple of the form $F = (s_{i_1}, s_{i_2}, \ldots, s_{i_r})$, where $i_x \in \{1, \ldots, k\}$, $1 \leq x \leq r$. Each selection s_{i_j} can be one of the following. Let $i_j = w$:

1. A partial selection, $\{t_1, t_2, \ldots, t_r\}, 2 \leq r \leq d_w$, $t_i \in \{1, 2, , d_w\}$, specifying any subset of domain values for dimension i_j.
2. A range selection $[a, b]$, specifying a continual range in the domains of some of the attributes, $[a, b] \subset [1..d_w]$
3. A singleton value a, $a \in [1..d_w]$.
4. A selection set satisfying spatial relationship $SR(s_{i_j}, s_{k_m})$, $t_i \mid |t_i \in \{1, 2, \ldots d_w\} \wedge SR(t_i, s_{k_m})$ specifying the subset of domain values for dimension i_j that is satisfy the spatial relationship $SR(s_{i_j}, s_{k_m})$ with the selection s_{k_m}, where s_{k_m} can be one of three above selection

So Q1 in section 2 can be written as Q1 = F(hospital, road, time)O(road, lane) = (First-Hospital, Second-Hospital, [January, March], road i| |i ∈ $\{allroad\} \wedge$ distance(i,FirstHospital, Second-Hospital)$\leq$ 2k))O(lane,road). Based on the fact table and dimension tables of the EMS_warehouse in Fig. 1(a), the SQL statement for Q1 is:

```
SELECT f.road_id, SUM(f.volume)
FROM volume_fact_table f, hosptial_dimension h
    road_dimension r, time_dimension t
WHERE t.month between January and March AND t.time_id = f.time_id
AND h.name in (First-Hospital,Second-Hospital)
AND distance(r.location, h.location) ≤ 2km AND r.road_id = f.road_id
GROUP by f.road_id
```

Notes that the above SQL statement accesses two spatial dimension tables since it needs to compute the distance from hospital to road.

We analyze the above query statement, and find that the Q1 can be rewritten as Q1 = F (time, hospital, F (road, hospital) O(road))O(road, lane). That is, we can handle the selection with spatial relationship before the other normal selection dimensions are computed. So the SQL statement could also be rewritten in a nested format:

```
SELECT f.road_id, SUM(f.volume)
FROM volume_fact_table f, hosptial_dimension h
    road_dimension r, time_dimension t
WHERE t.month between January and March AND t.time_id = f.time_id
AND h.name in (First-Hospital,Second-Hospital)
```

```
AND f.road_id IN
    (SELECT r.road_id
    FROM road_dimension r
    WHERE distance(r.location, h.location) ≤ 2km
GROUP by f.road_id
```

4   Preprocess of Spatial Relationship

As section 3 mentioned, the spatial relationship can be preprocessed before the normal aggregation. While actually, in many applications there may exist some default or predefined spatial relationships that group the spatial objects. for example, there may be grouping of the city roads based on the emergency service area of hospitals (the predefined spatial relationship is that roads within 2 km of hospital), and another grouping for the areas that are covered by each fire station (the predefined spatial relationship is roads within 10 km of each fire station). Such cases implicitly indicates that such predefined spatial relationships can be preprocessed while building the spatial data warehouses.

Considering EMS_warehouse again, the spatial relationships between roads and hospitals can be computed in advance during the preprocessing or transformation [2] process. The pairs of road and hospital that satisfy the predefined spatial relationships (for example, the distance less than 2 km or 4 km) will be extracted, and load into the EMS_warehouse, while other non spatial dimensions such as time are load as usual. Then the EMS_warehouse can answer spatial OLAP queries just like Q1.

The procedure of building data warehouse and solving the example spatial OLAP query consists of three steps:

(1) Select pairs of road and hospital satisfying the predefined spatial relationships by using spatial SQL statements provided by spatial database, such as DB2 spatial extender.

(2) Load the pairs into the EMS_warehouse. In this step, the distances from roads to hospitals are also recorded in a dimension table called distance_dimension. Those distances are not arbitrary numeric of real distance, actually, they are the range or comparison value specified in the predefined spatial relationships. For example, the predefined spatial relationship may focus on the roads whose distance from hospitals less than 2 km, so we distinguishingly select those two hospitalroad pairs, and then set 2km for the corresponding record, other than their actual distance such as 1.23km. The model of the data warehouse after spatial transformation is depicted in Fig. 1(b).

(3) Build the data cubes based on the model where the interested spatial relationships are reserved. Since there are no explicit spatial attributes in this warehouse, the traditional OLAP server could aggregate on the data cubes and answer the spatial OLAP queries focusing on the spatial relationships.

Step 1 above plays an important role in the spatial transformation in the sense that it extracts the interested spatial relationships from spatial data sources. The spatial SQL statements employed in the step is, in most cases, so complex that it is hard to write by data warehouse developer. We developed Spatial Transformation Builder, a GUI tool facilitating the warehouse developers to do spatial transformation, especially task in step 1. With the tool, the developers do not have to know detail knowledge about spatial, but just point and draw on the map, then the transformation model will be built and the corresponding complex spatial SQL statements will be generated.

5   Spatial Transformation Builder

The interface of Spatial Transformation Builder is depicted in Fig. 2 . The main functions provided by Spatial Transformation Builders are:

. Modeling the spatial relationships by providing several visual spatial operators
. Generating the spatial SQL statement based on the modeled spatial relationship
. Issuing the SQL to underlying database to extract these data and load them into target tables of data warehouse

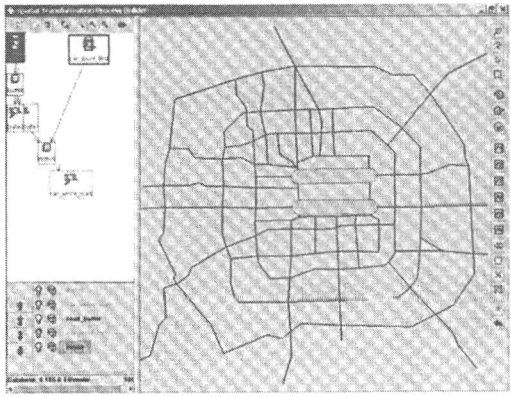

Fig. 2. Spatial Transformation Builder

To facilitate developer to understand the complex spatial relationships, a process model is employed in the upper right panel of the GUI. In this model, a process is composed of a series of steps to represent the sequence of transformations for the data. A step specifies how the spatial data are to be selected and transformed from the sources to the targets. A spatial transformation process is built based on following specifications:

. One or more source spatial objects (stored in corresponding tables). Those spatial objects can be selected on the map displayed on the right panel of the GUI. For example, The roads and hospitals are the basic source spatial objects upon which other spatial objects are built via steps.

. In each step, source spatial objects are input to an visual spatial operator to generate a target spatial objects. The visual spatial operator, for example, intersection, within or distance, can be specified by selecting and clicking the corresponding buttons on the right panel of the GUI. For some visual operators, a pop-up window would be pop up to allow the user to define the operator-specific parameters, such as distance less than 2 km. The visual spatial operator is easily translated to function or predicate supported by spatial SQL. Basically, a SQL statement is generated for each step. The target object generated in one step could be source to another step for further transformation. For example, After hospitals that within 4 km of the city center are selected, the roads within 2 km of each hospital need to be selected, and so on.

. If all steps of a process have been defined, the target table is created according to the complex SQL statement derived from the process model.

The Spatial Transformation Builder is implemented using Java and based on IBM DB2 UDB, spatial extender. The usage of the Spatial Transformation Builder is consistent with the Process Model of DB2 Data Warehouse Center, and developed as UDP (User Defined Program) of DB2 Data Warehouse Center. It could be easily integrated into the DB2 UDB and provides the data warehouse developer an uniform interface for data warehousing of spatial and non-spatial.

6   Related Work

Although advances in data warehousing technology have led to a proliferation of business information and decision support systems, the use of data warehouse technology to analyze spatial information has only recently become a topic of active research.

The paper [4] was the first one to propose a framework for spatial data warehouses. It proposed an extension of the star-schema with spatial dimensions and measures and a method for selecting spatial objects for materialization. It focuses on the spatial measures while in this paper we concentrate on the spatial relationship among spatial dimensions, which we think is more meaningful and ubiquitous in the real applications.

Several approaches were proposed to represent spatial data into data warehouse. [5]presented a set-based model for the data warehouse other than traditional star schema and quad tree for spatial dimension representation in order to facilitates a single representation for both well-structured and spatial data in data warehouses. Then the special set-based query evaluation algorithm can be applied to the spatial dimension. [7] proposed to build a spatial index on the objects of the finer granularity in the spatial dimension. All those approaches modified the classical star schema in the existing data warehouses, but the approach presented by this paper reserved the star schema while representing the spatial.

The pre-aggregation, the prior materialization of aggregate queries for later use, is a technique for ensuring efficiency of data warehousing. [7] presented methods to process arbitrary aggregation on the spatial dimension. The aggregated results were stored in the index. [6] extended previous works on pre-aggregation for irregular data structures to also cover special spatial issues such as partially overlapping areas. As [4], it focused on spatial measures.

7   Conclusion and Future Work

Motivated by the increasing amount of spatial data in the business information system, this paper investigated the use of data warehouse technology to analyze spatial data, in order to support decision for spatial applications. This paper improved the data warehouse in several ways. First, the spatial relationship in the spatial OLAP query was analyzed, and it was shown why traditional data warehouse did not work. Second, this knowledge was used to extend the preprocessing stage of data warehousing to handle the spatial relationship. Furthermore, a GUI-based Spatial Transformation Builder was provided to facilitate the data warehouse developer for spatial data warehousing.

In the future work, several research directions are interesting. First, exploring how to make the spatial data warehouse and OLAP answer the spatial OLAP queries with ad-hoc spatial relationship is the next step to be taken. Second, experiments with using the technique for large real-world spatial data sets will be carried out and analyzed to identify the value of the technique.

References

1. Lixin Fu, Joachim Hammer: CubiST: A New Algorithm for Improving the Performance of Ad-hoc OLAP Queries. Proceedings of the ACM Third International Workshop on Data Warehousing and OLAP, Washington, DC (2000)
2. OMG: Common Warehouse Metamodel Specification Version 1.0.2. http://www.omg.org(2001)
3. Daratech: Geographic Information Systems Markets and Opportunities. Daratech, Inc.(2000)
4. Jiawei Han, Nebojsa Stefanovic, and Krzysztof Koperski: Selective Materialization: An Efficient Method for Spatial Data Cube Construction. Proc. Pacific-Asia Conf. on Knowledge Discovery and Data Mining (PAKDD'98),Melbourne, Australia(1998)144–158
5. A. Rauber, P. Tomich, and H. Riedel: Integrating Geo-spatial Data into OLAP Systems using a Set-based Quad-tree Representation. Proceedings of the 4th IEEE / IFIP International Conference on Information Technology for BALANCED AUTOMATION SYSTEMS in Production and Transportation (BASYS2000),Kluwer Academic Publishers, Berlin, Germany(2000)
6. T.B. Pedersen and N. Tryfona: Pre-aggregation in Spatial Data Warehouses. Proceedings of the Seventh International Symposium on Spatial and Temporal Databases, Redondo Beach, California, USA(2001) 460–478
7. D. Papadias, P. Kalnis, Jun Zhang and Yufei Tao: Efficient OLAP Operations in Spatial Data Warehouses. Proceedings of the 7th International Symposium on Spatial and Temporal Databases, (SSTD), LA, California, Spinger Verlag, LNCS(2001) 443–459

A Hybrid Search Algorithm of Ant Colony Optimization and Genetic Algorithm Applied to Weapon-Target Assignment Problems

Zne-Jung Lee[1] and Wen-Li Lee[2]

[1]Kang-Ning Junior College of Nursing
137, Lane75, Sec. 3, Kang-Ning Rd. Nei-Hu, Taipei, Taiwan, R.O.C.
johnlee@mis.knjc.edu.tw
[2]Kang-Ning Junior College of Nursing
137, Lane75, Sec. 3, Kang-Ning Rd. Nei-Hu, Taipei, Taiwan, R.O.C.
wesleyli@mis.knjc.edu.tw

Abstract. Weapon-Target Assignment (WTA) problems are to find a proper assignment of weapons to targets with the objective of minimizing the expected damage of own-force asset. In this paper, a novel hybrid algorithm of ant colony optimization (ACO) and genetic algorithm is proposed to solve WTA problems. The proposed algorithm is to enhance the search performance of genetic algorithms by embedded ACO so as to have locally optimal offspring. This algorithm is successfully applied to WTA problems. From our simulations for those tested problems, the proposed algorithm has the best performance when compared to other existing search algorithms.

1 Introduction

Weapon-Target Assignment (WTA) problems, known as NP-Complete problems, are to find the proper assignment of weapons to targets with the objective of minimizing the expected damage of own-force assets. [1][2]. Traditional methods for solving WTA problems result in exponential computational complexities. Then, it is difficult to solve this type of problems directly while the number of targets or weapons are large [3][4]. Recently, genetic algorithms (GAs) and ant colony optimization (ACO) have widely been used as search algorithms in various applications and have also demonstrated satisfactory performances [5][6]. In our previous work [7][8], we have employed GA and ACO to solve WTA problems. Even though those approaches could find the best solution in those simulated cases, the search efficiency seemed not good enough. In this paper, we propose a hybrid algorithm, in which a genetic algorithm with ant colony optimization for WTA problems is introduced.

GAs use a population of solutions, from which, using crossover, mutation and selection operators, better and better solutions can be produced. GAs can handle any kind of objective functions and constraints without much mathematical requirements about the optimization problems. However, GAs may cause certain degeneracy in search performance if their operators are not carefully designed [9,10]. ACO is a class of algorithms using artificial ants with the capability of mimicking the behavior of

J. Liu et al. (Eds.): IDEAL 2003, LNCS 2690, pp. 278–285, 2003.

real ants [6]. Ants are capable of exploring and exploiting pheromone information, which have been left on the traversed ground. Ants then can choose paths based on the amount of pheromone. With such concept, a multi-agent algorithm called ACO has been widely employed as a cooperative search algorithm for solving optimization problems [6,11,12]. In our research, the ACO is embedded into GA to improve the local search efficiency.

The paper is organized as follows. In section 2, a mathematical formulation of WTA problems is introduced. The general GA and ACO for WTA problems are described in section 3. The proposed algorithm is presented and discussed in section 4. In section 5, the results of employing the proposed algorithm to solve general WTA problems are presented. Finally, section 6 concludes the paper.

2 The Formulation of WTA Problems

For the formulation of WTA problems, we consider that there are W weapons and T targets. Two assumptions are made for WTA problems. The first one is that all weapons must be assigned to targets. The second one is that the individual probability of killing (K_{ij}) by assigning the i-th target to the j-th weapon is known for all i and j. This probability defines the effectiveness of the j-th weapon to destroy the i-th target. The overall probability of killing (PK) value for a target (i) to damage the asset is computed as:

$$PK(i) = 1 - \prod_{j=1}^{W}(1 - K_{ij})^{X_{ij}}$$

(1)

where X_{ij} is a Boolean value indicating whether the j-th weapon is assigned to the i-th target. $X_{ij} = 1$ indicates that the j-th weapon is assigned to the i-th target. The considered WTA problems are to minimize the following cost function [13,14]:

$$C(\pi) = \sum_{i=1}^{T} EDV(i) * PK(i)$$

(2)

subject to the assumption that all weapons must be assigned to targets; that is,

$$\sum_{i=1}^{T} X_{ij} = 1, j = 1, 2, \ldots, W$$

(3)

Here $EDV(i)$ is the expected damage value of the i-th target to the asset. π is a feasible weapon-target assignment list, and $\pi(j) = i$ indicates weapon j is assigned to target i.

3 The Algorithms of ACO and GA

The algorithms of ACO and GA maintain a population of structure as key elements in the design and implementation of problem solving algorithms. Each individual in the population is evaluated according to its cost value. These algorithms are sufficiently complex to provide powerful adaptive search approaches, and usually can be embedded together to speed up their search performances for specific problems. The basics of ACO and GA are described latter.

3.1 Ant Colony Optimization (ACO)

Recently, many search activities have been devoted to artificial ants, which are agents with the capability of mimicking the behavior of real ants. Agents are capable of exploring and exploiting pheromone information, which have been left on the ground when they traversed. They then can choose routes based on the amount of pheromone. While building the solutions, each agent collects pheromone information on the problem characteristics and uses this information to modify the representation of the problem, as seen by the other agents. The larger amount of pheromone lefts on a route, the greater is the probability of selecting the route by agents. With such concepts, a multi-agent (population-based) algorithm called Ant Colony Optimization (ACO) has been widely used as a new cooperative search algorithm in optimization problems [6]. In the algorithm, agents find solutions starting from a start node and moving to feasible neighbor nodes in the process of ants_generation_and_activity. During the process, information collected by agents is stored in the so-called pheromone trails. In the process, agents can release pheromone while building the solution (online step-by-step) or while the solution is built (online delayed). An ant-decision rule, made up of the pheromone and heuristic information, governs agents' search toward neighbor nodes stochastically. Pheromone_evaporation is a process of decreasing the intensities of pheromone trails over time. This process is used to avoid locally convergence and to explore more search space. Daemon actions are optional for ACO, and they are often used to collect useful global information by depositing additional pheromone.

3.2 Genetic Algorithm (GA)

When applying to optimization problems, genetic algorithms provide the advantages to perform global search and hybridize with domain-dependent heuristics for specific problems [15]. Genetic algorithms start with a set of randomly selected chromosomes as the initial population that encodes a set of possible solutions. In GAs, variables of a problem are represented as genes in a chromosome, and the chromosomes are evaluated according to their cost values using some measures of profit or utility that we want to optimize. Recombination typically involves two genetic operators: crossover and mutation. The genetic operators alter the composition of genes to create new chromosomes called offspring. The selection operator is an artificial version of natural selection, a Darwinian survival of the fittest among populations, to create populations from generation to generation, and chromosomes with better cost have higher probabilities of being selected in the next generation. After several generations, GA can converge to the best solution. Let $P(t)$ and $C(t)$ are parents and offspring in generation t. A usual form of general GA is shown in [15,16]. Basically, the one cut point crossover, inversion mutation and $(u+\lambda)$–ES (evolution strategy) survival [17], where u is the population size and λ is the number of offspring created, are employed as the operators of GAs for WTA problems. However, these operations are not carefully designed for general WTA problems, the search in the solution space might become inefficient or even random.

4 The Proposed Algorithm

Recently, genetic algorithms with local search have also been considered as good alternatives for solving optimization problems. The flow chart of the GA with local search is shown as follows [18,19].
Procedure: GA with local search
   Begin

   $t \leftarrow 0$;
   Initialize $P(t)$;
   Evaluate $P(t)$;
   While (not matched for the termination conditions) do

      Apply crossover on $P(t)$ to generate $c_1(t)$;

      Apply local search on $c_1(t)$ to yield $c_2(t)$;

      Apply mutation on $c_2(t)$ to yield $c_3(t)$;

      Apply local search on $c_3(t)$ to yield $c_4(t)$;

      Evaluate $C(t) = \{ c_1(t), c_2(t), c_3(t), c_4(t) \}$;

      Select $P(t+1)$ from $P(t)$ and $C(t)$;

      $t \leftarrow t+1$;

   End;
   End;
It is noted that the GA with local search becomes a general GA if the local search is omitted. Local search can explore the neighborhood in an attempt to enhance the cost of the solution in a local manner. Traditionally, general local search and simulated annealing are used for local search [17~20,23].

   In this paper, we propose the algorithm of using ACO, as local search, embedded into GA to enhance the local search performance. The proposed algorithm first use the best solution of each generation founded by GA to update the pheromone trail as described in Equation (4). When the best solution has been found, the pheromone trail update rule is performed as:

$$\tau_{ij}(t+1) = (1-\rho)\, \tau_{ij}(t) + \rho\, \Delta\tau_{ij}(t) \tag{4}$$

where $0 < \rho \leq 1$ is a parameter governing the pheromone decay process, $\Delta\tau_{ij}(t) = 1/C^{best}$, and C^{best} is the cost of the best solution. Then, a weapon is randomly chosen in the assignment list, and ant successively assigns targets to weapons until weapons have been completely assigned. In the ant's generation and activities of ACO, the ant-decision table for ant k assigning target i to weapon j is governed by:

$$
\pi(j) = \begin{cases} \arg\{ \max_{i=allowed_k(t)} [\tau_{ij}(t) \cdot \eta_{ij}^{\beta}] \} & when(q \leq q_0) \\ S & otherwise \end{cases}
\tag{5}
$$

where η_{ij} is the heuristic information and is set as the highest value of $K_{ij}*EDV(i)$. and β is a parameter representing the importance of heuristic information, q is a random number uniformly distributed in [0,1], q_0 is a pre-specified parameter $(0 \leq q_0 \leq 1)$, $allowed_k(t)$ is the set of feasible nodes currently not assigned by ant k at time t, and S is an index of node selected from $allowed_k(t)$ according to the probability distribution given by

$$
P_{rs}^k(t) = \begin{cases} \dfrac{\tau_{rs}(t)\eta_{rs}^{\beta}}{\displaystyle\sum_{u \in allowed_k(t)} \tau_{ru}(t)\eta_{ru}^{\beta}} & if\ s \in allowed_k(t) \\ 0, & otherwise; \end{cases}
\tag{6}
$$

In finding feasible solutions, ants perform online step-by-step pheromone updates as:

$$
\tau_{ij}(t+1) \longleftarrow (1-\psi)\,\tau_{ij}(t) + \psi\,\Delta\tau_k
\tag{7}
$$

where $0 < \psi \leq 1$ is a constant, $\Delta\tau_k$ is the cost found by the k-th ant. In Equation (7), pheromone update rule has the effects of making the visited paths less and less attractive if ants do not visit those paths again.

In the proposed algorithm, we also propose an elite preserving crossover (GEX) operator for WTA problems. The concept of GEX is to construct offspring with possibly good genes from parents. GEX is modified from CX (also called UX) in [17]. In the CX operator, the information contained in both parents is preserved. GEX also adopts the similar concept, except preserves only those genes supposed to be good. Here, a gene is good if it is an assignment of the jth weapon to the target with the highest $K_{ij}*EDV(i)$ among all i. The GEX operation is described as follows:

Step 1: Find genes with the same values i in both parents.
Step 2: Inherit good genes from both parents.
Step 3: Randomly select two genes that are not inherited from parents.
Step 4: Exchange the selected genes in both parents to generate offspring.
Step 5: Go to *Step 1* until a stop criterion is satisfied.
Step 6: Return the solution.

These steps are repeated until a stop criterion is satisfied. The used criterion is simply that the process is repeated M_c times, which is randomly generated and $M_c < W$.

Table 1. The simulation results for randomized data of W=10 and T=10. Results are averaged over 10 trials.

Algorithm	Operator	Best cost	Percentage of convergence	CPU time (sec)
General GA	OCP	92.7668	10 %	N/A
	CX	75.9367	20%	N/A
	GEX	69.3263	40 %	N/A
GA with ACO	OCP	58.4774	100%	78.19
	CX	58.4774	100%	52.29
	GEX	**58.4774**	**100%**	**21.05**

N/A-Not Available

Table 2. Compare the best cost of randomized scenarios obtained by various search algorithms. Results are averaged over 10 trials.

Algorithm	W=50 T=50	W=80 T=80	W=100 T=80	W=120 T=80
General GA	282.6500 (47.6715)	351.7641 (52.9217)	279.558 (50.4279)	140.1381 (38.2817)
GA with general local search	226.335 (30.7316)	348.4352 (60.7415)	197.8655 (37.1495)	106.4778 (12.9815)
GA with SA as local search	230.5209 (27.981)	347.1698 (55.215)	203.586 (30.9173)	105.5135 (14.517)
ACO with general local search	193.0035 (10.2913)	277.2656 (15.8872)	169.6705 (9.0167)	70.2907 (6.2714)
ACO with SA as local search	148.5712 (6.8915)	204.2938 (7.9671)	103.8276 (5.8216)	63.8636 (5.3581)
The proposed algorithm	**131.3853** (5.872)	**182.8294** (6.721)	**91.6631** (5.791)	**48.3589** (4.672)

5 Simulation and Results

In the following simulations, the default following values are used: the size of the initial population for GAs is the same as the maximum number of targets or weapons considered, the crossover probability P_c=0.8 and the mutation probability P_m=0.1, ρ=0.1, ψ=0.1, q_0=0.8, β=2, ant number is set as the maximum number of weapons or targets, and γ=0.5 for SA. In this paper, first scenario is to test the performance for crossover operators. It consists of randomized data for 10 targets and weapons. All algorithms consistently use the same initial population when they are randomly generated. In this study, the effects for crossover operator of one-cut-point (OCP), CX, and GEX are studied. The maximum generation is 500, and experiments were run on PCs with Pentium 1GHz processor. The simulation is conducted for 10 trials and the average results are reported here. The simulation results are listed in Table 1. From Table 1, it is evident that the GEX operator can have the best performances among all operators in both general GA, and the proposed algorithm. Since the GEX operator can result in better performance, in the following simulations GEX is used as the crossover operator.

Several scenarios are considered to compare the performances of existing algorithms. These algorithms include GA with general local search, GA with SA as local search, and the proposed algorithm. Since those algorithms are search algorithms, it is not easy to stop their search in a fair basis from the algorithm itself. In our comparison, we simply stopped these algorithms after a fixed time of running. Experiments were also run on PCs with Pentium 1GHz processor, and were stopped after two hours of running. The results with standard deviation in parentheses are listed in Table 2. From Table 2, it is easy to see that algorithms with local search have better performance than algorithms without them. It also shows that the proposed algorithm can always find the best solution among these algorithms; meanwhile other algorithms may not find the best solution all the time.

6 Conclusions

In this paper, we presented a hybrid search algorithm of ACO and GA by including specific designed GEX operator for solving WTA problems. From simulations, it can be found that the proposed algorithm can indeed have best search efficiency among existing genetic algorithms with local search.

References

1. Lloyd, S. P. and Witsenhausen, H. S.: IEEE Summer Simulation Conference. Weapon allocation is NP-Complete, Reno, Nevada (1986)
2. William, Meter, and Preston, F. L.: A Suite of Weapon Assignment Algorithms for a SDI Mid-Course battle Manager, AT&T Bell Laboratories (1990)
3. Hammer, P. L., Hansen, P., and Simeone, B.: Mathematical Programming. Roof duality, complementation and persistency in quadratic 0-1 optimization, Vol. 28 (1984) 121–155

4. Ibarraki, T. and Katoh, N.: Resource allocation Problems. The MIT Press: Cambridge, Massachusetts (1988)
5. Dorigo, M. and Caro, G. D.: Proceedings of the 1999 Congress on Evolutionary Computation. Ant colony optimization: A new meta-heuristic, Vol. 2 (1999) 1470–1477
6. Bonabeau, E. Dorigo, M. and Theraulaz, G.: Swarm Intelligence From Natural to Artificial Systems, Oxford University Press (1999)
7. Lee, Zne-Jung Su, Shun-Feng and Lee, Chou-Yuan: Journal of the Chinese Institute of Engineers. A Genetic Algorithm with Domain Knowledge for Weapon-Target Assignment Problems, Vol. 25 no. 3, (2002) 287–295
8. Lee, Zne-Jung Su, Shun-Feng and Lee, Chou-Yuan: Applied Soft Computing. An Immunity Based Ant Colony Optimization Algorithm for Solving Weapon-Target Assignment Problem, Vol. 2 (2002) 39–47
9. Reeves, C. R.: Modern Heuristic Techniques for Combinatorial Problems, Blackwell Scientific Publications, Oxford (1993)
10. Merz, P. and Freisleben, B.: Proceedings of the 1999 Congress on Evolutionary Computation, A comparison of memetic algorithms, tabu search, and ant colonies for the quadratic assignment problem, Vol. 3 (1999) 2063–2070
11. Maniezzo, V. and Colorni, A.: IEEE Transactions on Knowledge and Data Engineering. The ant system applied to the quadratic assignment problem, Vol. 11, (1999) 769–778
12. Stützle, T. and Hoos, H.: IEEE International Conference on Evolutionary Computation. MAX-MIN ant system and local search for the traveling salesman problem (1997) 299–314
13. Pepyne, D. L. et al.: Proceedings of 1997 IEEE International Conference on Evolutionary Computation (ICEC '97). A decision aid for theater missile defense (1997)
14. Bjorndal, A. M. H. et al.: European Journal of Operational Research. Some thoughts on combinatorial optimization (1995) 253–270
15. Gen, M. and Cheng, R.: Genetic Algorithms and Engineering Design, John Wiley & Sons Inc. (1997)
16. Aarts, E. H. L and Lenstra, J. K.: Local Search in Combinatorial Optimization, John Wiley & Sons Inc. (1997)
17. Merz, P. and Freisleben, B.: IEEE Trans. On Evolutionary Computation. Fitness landscape analysis and memetic algorithms for quadratic assignment problem, Vol. 4, no. 4 (2000) 337–352
18. Burke, E. K. and Smith, A. J.: IEEE Trans. On Power Systems. Hybrid evolutionary techniques for the maintenance scheduling problem, Vol. 15 (2000) 122–128
19. Miller, J., Potter, W., Gandham, R. and Lapena, C.: IEEE Trans. On Systems, Man and Cybernetics. An evaluation of local improvement operators for genetic algorithms, Vol. 23, no. 5 (1993) 1340–1341
20. Aarts, E. H. L and Korst, J.: Simulated Annealing and Boltzmann Machines, John Wiley & Sons Inc. (1989)

Detecting Distributed Denial of Service (DDoS) Attacks through Inductive Learning[*]

Sanguk Noh[1], Cheolho Lee[2], Kyunghee Choi[2], and Gihyun Jung[3]

[1]School of Computer Science and information Engineering,
The Catholic University of Korea, Bucheon, Korea
sunoh@catholic.ac.kr
[2]Graduate School of Information and Communication,
Ajou University, Suwon, Korea
cheolholee@cesys.ajou.ac.kr, khchoi@madang.ajou.ac.kr
[3]Division of Electronics Engineering,
Ajou University, Suwon, Korea
khchung@madang.ajou.ac.kr

Abstract. As the complexity of Internet is scaled up, it is likely for the Internet resources to be exposed to Distributed Denial of Service (DDoS) flooding attacks on TCP-based Web servers. There has been a lot of related work which focuses on analyzing the pattern of the DDoS attacks to protect users from them. However, none of these studies takes all the flags within TCP header into account, nor do they analyze relationship between the flags and the TCP packets. To analyze the features of the DDoS attacks, therefore, this paper presents a network traffic analysis mechanism which computes the ratio of the number of TCP flags to the total number of TCP packets. Based upon the calculation of TCP flag rates, we compile a pair of the TCP flag rates and the presence (or absence) of the DDoS attack into state-action rules using machine learning algorithms. We endow alarming agents with a tapestry of the compiled rules. The agents can then detect network flooding attacks against a Web server. We validate our framework with experimental results in a simulated TCP-based network setting. The experimental results show a distinctive and predictive pattern of the DDoS attacks, and our alarming agents can successfully detect various DDoS attacks.

1 Introduction

As the complexity of Internet is scaled up, it is likely for the Internet resources to be exposed to Distributed Denial of Service (DDoS) attacks [2], [6], [10]. There has been a lot of related work [3], [7], [15] which focus on analyzing the pattern of the DDoS

---

[*] This work has been supported by the Korea Research Foundation under grant KRF-2002-041-D00465, by the KISTEP under National Research Laboratory program, and by the Catholic University of Korea research fund granted in the program year of 2003.

J. Liu et al. (Eds.): IDEAL 2003, LNCS 2690, pp. 286–295, 2003.

attacks to protect users from them. Most of related work keeps track of source Internet Protocol (IP) addresses and checks the distribution of the IP addresses, whether or not the DDoS attacks occur. If the randomness of the source IP addresses is getting higher than usual one, their approaches set alarms upon the detection of the DDoS attacks. However, these approaches are useless when attackers reduce the level of randomness of the source IP addresses or when the attackers use the actual IP address instead of the spoofed IP address. To be more generally applicable in realistic settings, therefore, this paper presents a network traffic analysis mechanism of the DDoS attacks using all of the flags, i.e., SYN, FIN, RST, ACK, etc., within Transmission Control Protocol (TCP) header and taking into account relationship between the flags and the network packets. Based upon our analysis mechanism of the DDoS attacks, further, our paper addresses the question of how to detect the DDoS attacks on Web Servers.

To understand the features of DDoS attacks, we introduce the analysis mechanism of the DDoS attacks in two settings: the normal Web server without any attack and the Web server with the DDoS attacks. In these settings, we measure TCP flag rates, which are expressed in terms of the ratio of the number of TCP flags to the total number of TCP packets. For example, the number of SYNs drastically increases in case of SYN flooding attacks which is the most common DDoS attacks. In consequence, the increasing number of SYNs indicates the possibility of the DDoS attacks. Our analysis mechanism calculates the TCP flag rates and provides the basis of the DDoS attacks detection in a TCP-based network environment.

We also propose a DDoS attacks detection mechanism using inductive learning algorithms [1], [13] and Bayesian classifier [4]. To identify the DDoS attacks, we endow an alarming agent with a tapestry of reactive rules. The reactive tools [11] are constructed by compiling the results of TCP flag rates and presence (or absence) of flooding attacks into state-action rules. The compilation process exploits the regularities of the DDoS attacks, if any, and enables our alarming agents to detect them. The rules can be obtained from machine learning algorithms which use the results of TCP flag rates performed offline as their inputs. Further, it is desirable that each of the compilation methods be assigned a measure of performance that compares it to the benchmark. The various compilations available constitute a spectrum of approaches to making detections under various attacks on Web sites.

In the following section of this paper we discuss related approaches to our analysis and detection mechanism. Section 3 describes the details of our framework, and Section 4 describes a simulated, TCP-based network setting to test our approach. We validate our framework empirically, and discuss the experimental results. In conclusion, we summarize our results and further research issues.

2 Related Work

Regarding the analysis and detection of DDoS network flooding attacks, many researchers have investigated the randomness and distribution of source IP addresses. From this perspective, if the randomness of the source IP addresses is getting higher than usual one, they issue alarms based upon the detection of the DDoS attacks.

Gil and Poletto [3] examine flows in one direction vs. flows in the opposite direction over IP packets by using their own data-structure, MULTOPS. Their network monitoring device using the MULTOPS detects flooding attacks by "the difference between packet rates going to and coming from the attacker." Their assumption for the detection is based on the disproportional difference between the packet rates, which is caused by randomness of 'malicious' packets. Kulkarni et al. [7] trace the source IP addresses and construct Kolmogorov Complexity Metrics [9] for identifying their randomness. The Kolmogorov Complexity Metrics change according to the degree of randomness of spoofed source IP addresses. Actually, the randomness of source IP addresses is very low without any DDoS attack; otherwise, it is very high under DDoS attacks with randomly distributed source IP addresses. However, these approaches are not applicable when attackers reduce the level of randomness of the source IP addresses or when the attackers use the actual IP address instead of the spoofed IP address.

In another approach to detection mechanism, Wang et al. [15] examine the protocol behavior of TCP SYN-FIN (RST) pairs. If there are no DDoS attacks against a TCP-based server, the rate of SYN flag for TCP connection establishment and the rate of FIN flag for TCP connection termination will be the same value, or rarely different in case of retransmission. Otherwise, the rate of SYN, for example, in SYN Flooding attacks, clearly differs from the one of FIN. The metric of SYN-FIN (RST) pairs could be useful to detect SYN Flooding attacks against Web servers. This approach is somewhat similar to our approach in that both of them take into account TCP flags to detect DDoS flooding attacks. However, their method can be applicable only to SYN Flooding attacks. On the other hand, our approach is more general so that our mechanism can be applicable to all types of DDoS attacks, i.e., SYN Flooding attacks, UDP Flooding attacks, ICMP Flooding attacks, and so on. Further, to our best knowledge, applying machine learning algorithms to the flooding detection mechanism is a pretty new approach in this field of research.

3   Network Traffic Analysis and DDoS Attacks Detection

We rely on the dynamics of differences between the rates of TCP flag to analyze the features of DDoS attacks. Due to the burstiness of TCP flags, the ratio of the number of a specific TCP flag within TCP header, for example, SYN, FIN, RST, ACK, etc., to the total number of TCP packets, during normal operations on Web servers, clearly differs from the ones under the DDoS attacks.

3.1   Traffic Rate Analysis

We present a network traffic analysis mechanism, Traffic Rate Analysis (TRA). This mechanism calculates two measuring factors: TCP flag rate and protocol rate. The traffic rate analysis uses the traffic flowing into a victim (a host) as inbound, and the traffic flowing from the victim as outbound. A packet collecting agent captures IP packets and classifies them into *TCP, UDP,* or *ICMP* packets. In case of the TCP packet, further, the classification procedure separates the packet into TCP header and payload. From the TCP header containing *SYN, FIN, RST, ACK, PSH,* and *URG* flags, the flags are tested to determine whether or not they are set. If any flag of six TCP flags turns on, the agent counts it and sums it up. The packet collecting agents also count the total number of TCP packets during a specific observation period t_d (sec). Our alarming agents then compute two metrics TCP flag rates and protocol rates. A flag rate is expressed in terms of the ratio of the number of a TCP flag to the total number of TCP packets as follows:

$$R_{td}[Fi] = \frac{total\ number\ of\ a\ flag\ (F)\ in\ a\ TCP\ header}{total\ number\ of\ TCP\ packets}\ (inbound)$$

$$R_{td}[Fo] = \frac{total\ number\ of\ a\ flag\ (F)\ in\ a\ TCP\ header}{total\ number\ of\ TCP\ packets}\ (outbound)$$

$$(1)$$

Here, t_d means the sampling period. In the equation 1, K stands for one of six flags: *SIN, FIN, RST, ACK, PSH,* and *URG* flags, denoted as *S, F, R, A, P,* and *U,* for either inbound (i) or outbound (o) network traffic. For example, $R_1[Ai]$ represents the *ACK* flag rate of inbound traffic when the sampling period is one second.

A protocol rate is also defined by the ratio of the number of *TCP, UDP,* or *ICMP* packets to the total number of IP packets. Similarly, for example, $R_2[UDPo]$ stands for the UDP protocol rate of outbound network traffic during the sampling period two seconds.

The traffic rate analysis can be applicable even to scaled-up network settings because the mechanism utilizes a rate scheme. This enables us to examine the various traffic patterns and to identify the features of DDoS attacks in various network environments.

3.2 Detecting DDoS Attacks Using Machine Learning Algorithms

We propose a brokering agent architecture, as consisting of a packet collecting agent and an adaptive reasoning agent - an alarming agent - that analyze network traffic, detect DDoS network flooding attacks upon the traffic rate, and finally issue an alarm in case of DDoS attacks. Let S be the set of traffic states that the adaptive reasoning agent can discriminate among. Let L be the set of compilation methods (learning algorithms) that the agent employs.

Given a learning method $l \in L$, a compilation procedure of an adaptive reasoning agent implements a function ρ_l: $S \rightarrow \{attacks,\ no\ attacks\}$, representing whether a flooding attack occurs in the state $s \in S$. Thus, various machine learning algorithms compile the models of network traffic into different functions ρ_l. We generate the training examples for these learning algorithms from a TCP-based network environment.

4   Simulations and Results

We have implemented a simulated network environment using SPECweb99 [14], Tribe Flood Network 2000 (TFN2K) [12], and libpcap [8]. In the simulated, Web-based setting, the SPECweb99 located in Web clients generates web traffic, the TFN2K on DDS attackers simulates DDoS attacks, and the libpcap used by a packet collecting agent captures the stream of network traffic. While the Web clients request of the Web server that they should be serviced, the DDoS attackers make various flooding attacks towards the Web server.

We construct the simulated network environment on LINUX machines, which consist of Web server using Apache, Web clients, DDoS attackers, a network monitoring device including a packet collecting agent and an alarming agent (700 MHz Pentium III, 256 MB memory), and the network bandwidth of 100 Mbps. Figure 1 presents the simulated network setting, and our agents working on the network monitoring device.

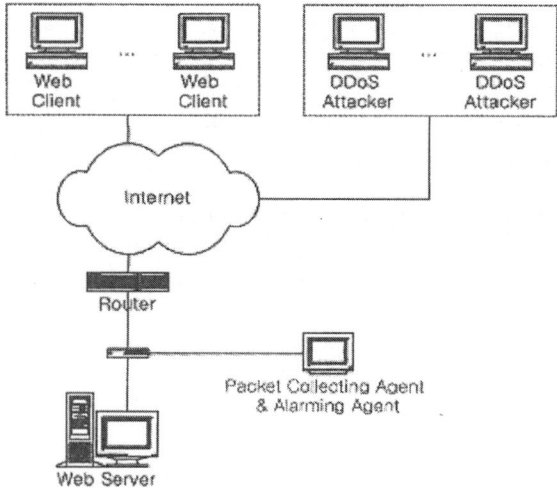

Fig. 1. A simulated Network Environment which consists of Web clients, DDoS attackers, Web Server (Victim), and our agents.

We tested our framework in the simulated network environment, as depicted in Figure 1, and measured TCP flag rates. The network traffic models were generated in two settings: the normal Web server without any attack and the Web server with DDoS attacks. For each network traffic setting, we changed two factors Simultaneous Connections (SC) and Requests per Connection (R/C) to get various Web traffic patterns. The SC indicates the number of HTTP connections at a given time, which approximates the number of users. The R/C represents the number of requests to be issued in a HTTP connection. In the experiment, we used 5, 10, 50, 100, 150, and 200 for SC and 1, 2, 5, and 10 for R/C. The sampling time t_d (sec) to compute TCP flag rates was 1 second.

4.1 Normal Web Server without Any Attack

The experimental results of normal Web traffic are illustrated in Figure 2. Even if SC ranges from 5 to 200, the results of TCP flag rates are almost identical.

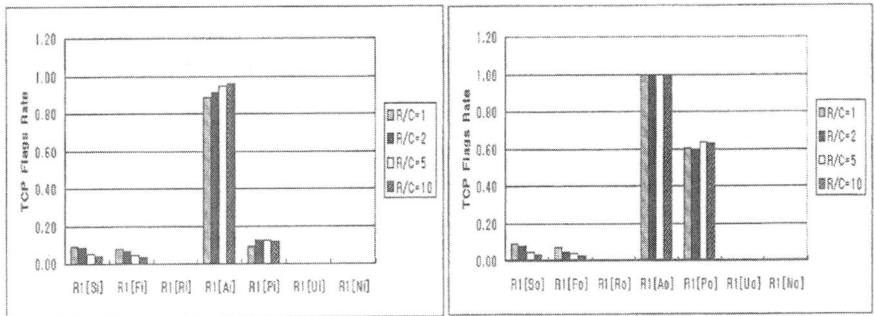

Fig. 2. TCP flag rates in the normal Web when SC=200.

We measured TCP flag rates for inbound and outbound network traffic, respectively. In both of inbound and outbound TCP flag rates, the rates of SYN and FIN were less than 0.1. On the other hand, the rate of an ACK flag was close to 1.0. This revealed the fact that most of the TCP packets set an ACK flag bit in their header for the purpose of sending an acknowledgement as a notification of receipt.

4.2 Web Server with DDoS Attacks

Figure 3 presents the inbound and outbound TCP flag rates when SYN flooding attacks occur.

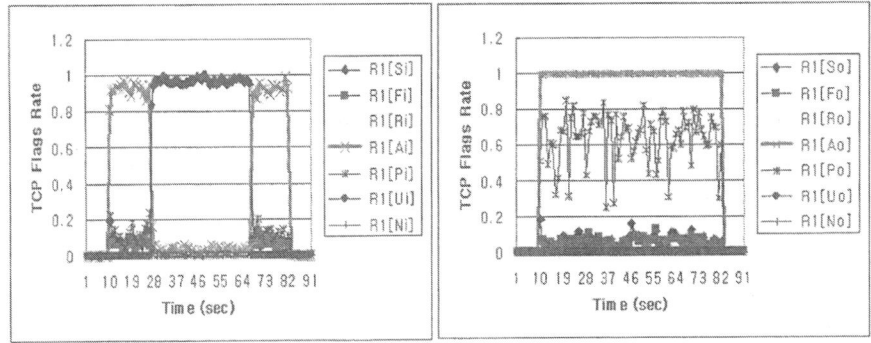

Fig. 3. TCP flag rates in the Web with SYN flooding attacks. The TFN2K was used to simulate SYN flooding attacks from 30 to 70 seconds.

$R_i[Ai]$ went down to about 0.0, due to the SYN's burst during the attack. This indicates that web traffic flow was blocked by enormous amount of SYN packets. On the other hand, $R_i[Si]$ and $R_i[Ui]$ in the inbound flag rates drastically changed and went up to almost 1.0. The outbound TCP flag rates except $R_i[So]$ were not affected by the attack at all. Since a victim followed the TCP three-way handshaking protocol, it replied to all SYN packets with SYN flags, if the SYN flooding attack was made on open ports. That's the reason why $R_i[So]$ increased.

4.3 Learning Results

To construct compiled rules for our alarming agents, we used three machine learning algorithms: C4.5 [13], CN2 [1], and Bayesian classifier [4]. C4.5 represents its output as a decision tree, and the output of CN2 is an ordered set of if-then rules. For the Bayesian classifier, the results are represented as rules specifying the probability of occurrence of each attribute value given a class [1], in our case "attacks" and "no attacks."

In our traffic rate analysis mechanism, under the SYN flooding attack, the attributes of situations that the alarming agents could sense were the SYN flag rate for inbound traffic $R_i[Si]$ and the ACK flag rate for inbound traffic $R_i[Ai]$. For the benchmark, we also computed the rate of SYN-FIN pair, which is a core of Wang's SYN flooding detection mechanism [15].

Using the three learning algorithms [5] and the training examples as inputs, we could get the compiled rules as described in Figure 4 and Figure 5.

```
MaxTrain: 719, MinTest: 0
C4.5 Trees:
      R[Si] <= 0.4 : WEB (361.0/1.0)
   R[Si] > 0.4 : SYN (359.0)
Errors = 1/720
CN2 Decision List:
   IF    "R[Si]" > 0.48
   THEN  class = "SYN"  [0 359]
   ...
     ELSE
   (DEFAULT) class = "SYN"  [0 1]
Errors = 0/720
Bayes Classifier:
 P(class=WEB) = 0.500000
   P(R[Si]|class=WEB) = G(0.071971,0.051441)
   P(R[Ai]|class=WEB) = G(0.928013,0.051446)
 P(class=SYN) = 0.500000
   P(R[Si]|class=SYN) = G(0.982168,0.067275)
   P(R[Ai]|class=SYN) = G(0.017831,0.067275)
Errors = 1/720
```

Fig. 4. Learning results by TRA.

For the TRA, C4.5 indicated that the SYN flooding attacks occurred if $R_i[Si]$ was greater than 0.4. The rules obtained by CN2, as shown in Figure 4, was similar to the ones of C4.5 but the resulting value of the SYN flag rate was 0.48. The Bayesian classifier showed that the average of $R_l[Si]$ was 0.98 given the class of "attacks." The learning results for Wang's work, as shown in Figure 5, were generated over the SYN-FIN pair, $R_l[Fi]/R_l[Si]$.

```
MaxTrain: 719, MinTest: 0
C4.5 Trees:
   R[Fi]/R[Si] <= 0.038656 : SYN (360.0/2.0)
   R[Fi]/R[Si] > 0.038656 : WEB (360.0/2.0)
   Errors = 4/720
CN2 Decision List:
   IF   "R[Fi]/R[Si]" > 0.83
   THEN  class = "WEB"  [263 0]
   ...
   ELSE
   (DEFAULT) class = "WEB"  [1 1]
   Errors = 3/720
Bayes Classifier:
P(class=WEB) = 0.500000
   P(R[Fi]/R[Si]|class=WEB) = G(0.965380,0.402598)
P(class=SYN) = 0.500000
   P(R[Fi]/R[Si]|class=SYN) = G(0.003586,0.044161)
   Errors = 8/720
```

Fig. 5. Learning results by Wang's work [15].

To evaluate the quality of various rule sets generated by different learning algorithms the performance obtained was expressed in terms of the ratio of {total number of alarms − (number of false alarms + number of missed alarms)} to the total number of alarms. The false alarm is defined as the alert turns on when the DDoS attack does not occur, and the missed alarm is defined as the alert does not turn on when the DDoS attack does occur.

To find a meaningful size of the training set which could guarantee the soundness of the learning hypothesis, we generated several sets of training examples whose size was 48, 96, 144, 192, 240, 480, 720, 960, 1200, and 1440 tuples, respectively. The resulting performances (%) and the sizes of training examples are shown in Figure 6. In the traffic rate analysis, the best performance was achieved by the rules compiled using Bayesian classifier, as depicted in Figure 6 (a), when the training instances were 720. In the learning curve of the Wang's work, as depicted in Figure 6 (b), since the performances obtained by C4.5 and Bayes algorithms were almost identical, the rules compiled using C4.5 with 1440 training instances were chosen.

By using the compiled rules, we tested the performances of the two network traffic analysis mechanisms (TRA and Wang's work) on new sets of network flow patterns. The testing network flows were generated during 100 seconds. In the testing network environment, the Simultaneous Connections (SC) were 7, 15, 40, 70, 130 and 160, the Requests per Connection (R/C) were 4, 12, 18, and 24, and the DDoS flooding attacks were made using three different time slots, i.e., four 10 seconds, two 10 seconds, and one 30 seconds ranging from 30 to 60 seconds. These combinations, thus, lead to eventually 72 different Web traffics including the DDoS attacks.

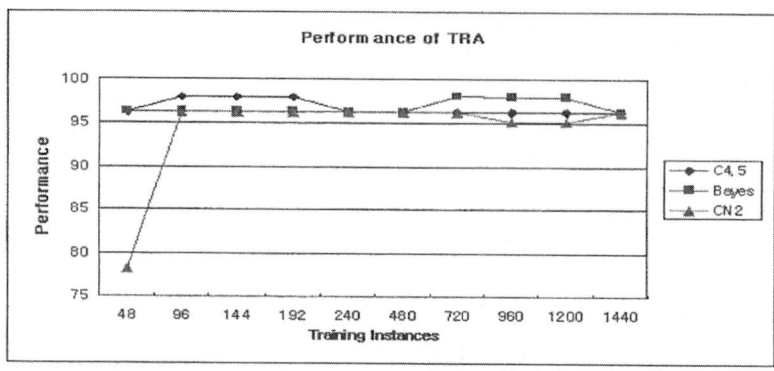

(a)   Detection performance using the compiled rules in TRA

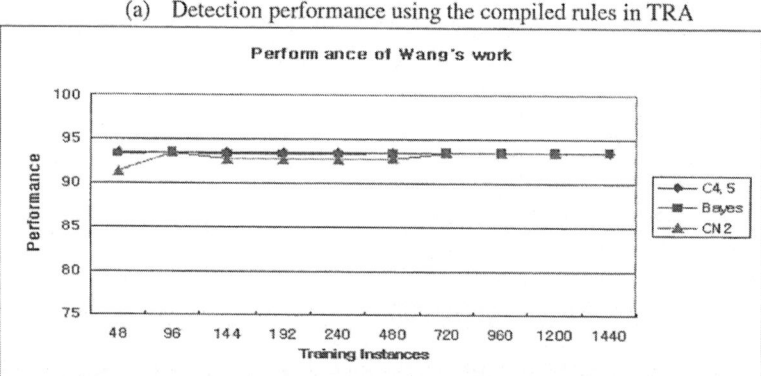

(b) Detection performance using the compiled rules in Wang's work

Fig. 6. The DDoS attacks detection performances using the resulting rules compiled by C4.5, Bayes, and CN2 learning algorithms in TRA and Wang's work.

We analyzed the performance results in Table 1 using the standard analysis of variance (ANOVA) method.

Table 1. Performances in TRA and Wang's work

Methods	Performances (%)
TRA	99.881321 +/- 0.316758
Wang's work	97.022569 +/- 1.791220
ANOVA	$f = 178.015076$

Since the computed value of $f = 178.015076$ in ANOVA exceeds 6.63 (= $f_{.01,1,142}$), we know that the two mechanisms were not all equally effective at the 0.01 level of significance, i.e., the differences in their performance were not due to chance with probability of 0.99. In the experiment, missed alarms didn't happen and all the errors measured were caused by false alarms. Our alarming agent's performance using the TRA mechanism was better than that of Wang's SYN flooding detection mechanism. This result indicates that $R_i[Ai]$ was more crucial than $R_i[Fi]$ in case of the SYN flooding attacks detection.

5 Conclusions

We investigated the traffic rate analysis (TRA) as a traffic flow analysis mechanism and, using our TRA mechanism, analyzed TCP-based network flows under DDoS attacks. Further, we detected the DDoS network flooding attacks using the state-action rules compiled by machine learning algorithms, and compared our detection performance to the benchmark. The combination of traffic rate analysis and flooding attacks detection mechanism enables Internet resources to be safe and stable from the ongoing flooding attacks. In our future research, to determine the reliability of our method, we will continuously test our framework in different network settings, for example, SMTP and FTP servers.

References

1. Clark, P. and Niblett, T.: The CN2 Induction Algorithm. *Machine Learning Journal 3(4)* (1989) 261–283
2. Garber, L.: Denial-of-Service Attacks Rip the Internet, *IEEE Computer, vol. 33(4)* (2000) 12–17
3. Gil, T.M, and Poletto, M.: MULTOPS: a data-structure for bandwidth attack detection, In *Proceedings of the 10th USENIX Security Symposium* (2001) 23–38
4. Hanson, R., Stutz, J., and Cheeseman, P.: Bayesian Classification Theory. *Technical Report FIA-90-12-7-01*, NASA Ames Research Center, AI Branch (1991)
5. Holder, L.: ML v2.0: Machine Learning Program Evaluator, available on-line: http://www-cse.uta.edu/~holder/ftp/ml2.0.tar.gz
6. Houle, J.K., and Weaver, M.G.: Trends in Denial of Service Attack Technology, CERT Coordination Center (2001)
7. Kulkarni, A.B., Bush, S.F., and Evans, S.C.: Detecting Distributed Denial-of-Service Attacks Using Kolmogorov Complexity Metrics. TR1/6, GE Research Center (2001)
8. Lawrence Berkeley National Labs Network Research Group.: libpcap, available on-line: http://ftp.ee.lbl.gov
9. Li, M., and Vitanyi, P.: An Introduction to Kolmogorov Complexity and Its Applications, *Springer-Verlag* (1997)
10. Moore, D., Voelker, G.M., and Savage, S.: Inferring Internet Denial-of-Service Activity. In *Proceedings of the 10th USENIX Symposium* (2001) 9–22
11. Noh, S. and Gmytrasiewicz, P. J.: Towards Flexible Multi-Agent Decision-Making Under Time Pressure. In Proceedings of *IJCAI* (1999) 492–498
12. Packet Storm.: *Tribe Flood Network 2000 (TFN2K) DDoS tool*, available on-line: http://packetstormsecurity.org/distributed/TFN2k_Analysis-1.3.txt
13. Quinlan, J.R.: *C4.5: Programs for Machine Learning.* Morgan Kaufmann Publishers (1993)
14. Standard Performance Evaluation Corporation.: *SPECweb99 Benchmark,* available on-line: http://www.spec.org/osg/web99
15. Wang, H., Zhang, D., and Shin, K.G.: Detecting SYN Flooding Attacks. In *Proceedings of IEEE INFOCOM, vol. 21(1)* (2002) 1530–1539

Dynamic Construction of Category Hierarchy Using Fuzzy Relational Products

Bumghi Choi[1], Ju-Hong Lee[2], and Sun Park[2]

[1] Quark Co., Ltd. Seoul, Korea
bumghichoi@yahoo.co.kr
[2] School of Computer Science and Engineering, Inha University, Incheon, Korea
juhong@inha.ac.kr,sunpark@datamining.inha.ac.kr

Abstract. Overwhelming search results often daunt web surfers on the web search engine. There have been many systems to try to solve this problem by constructing more specific search methods. Auto categorization and clustering have been presented. However, an efficient way of constructing the hierarchy of generated or pre-existing categories has not been suggested. We provide a dynamic category hierarchy structuring algorithm to reinforce the categorization and the clustering with using the fuzzy relational products. In this paper, we also propose a novel search method using this algorithm to complement the conventional directory search or category browsing and enhance the efficiency of search. Results from our evaluation show that our method helps users find categories more quickly and easily than conventional directory searching methods.

1 Introduction

Traditional information retrieval systems usually adopt index terms (keywords) to index and retrieve documents. IR depends on various models. One of them is vector model [1,2]. But in this model, a lot of the semantics in a document or user request is lost when we replace its text as a set of words. To be more related to the real semantic contents of the respective documents and queries, a fuzzy set model has been proposed by Ogawa, Morita, and Kobayashi [8]. In this model, using keyword connection matrix, a fuzzy set associated to each keyword is defined. Besides that, alternative algebraic models like the latent semantic indexing models [6] are to approach more semantically, avoiding the simple keyword matching model.

Despite of doing such efforts, there still may be a limit of semantic approach hard to overcome, with only keyword-based documents retrieval models. Recent works have been focused more on categorization and clustering. The categorization means that system automatically classifies the input documents according to pre-existing categories as classifiers. The clustering groups documents that satisfy a set of common properties and labels them as categories. Although there are many models for them, they seem to be a kind of variations or incorporations depending on the latent semantic indexing using Singular-Value Decomposition and transforming document vectors

J. Liu et al. (Eds.): IDEAL 2003, LNCS 2690, pp. 296–302, 2003.

into more semantically compressed and encoded form through learning using Neural Networks or alike [11].

The importance of category hierarchy comes from category browsing or directory search. Yahoo! [12] organizes Web pages into a hierarchy consisting of thousands of category labels. Topical category hierarchies give an overview to a large set of document collections. Shneiderman [10] advocates an interaction model in which user begins with an overview of the information. However, Yahoo! does not give a compact overview restructured according to the subjects given by users.

With this motive, we propose an algorithm in which categories are restructured automatically and semantically according to search subjects. We introduce a fuzzy category set whose elements are keywords. It is quite a different from a fuzzy set model of keyword-based document retrieval [8]. In the fuzzy set model, the main target is to draw information about the semantically extended relevancy of keyword and document with given keyword-keyword correlations. But the main target of our proposed model is to dynamically construct the hierarchical relation between categories with given keyword-category association. Once the fuzzy category sets are constructed, we can compute the hierarchical relation between two fuzzy category sets by using the fuzzy relational products.

We propose a novel automatic directory-searching method by using the proposed algorithm. To do so, we need a premise that categories indexed by keywords already exist in the system and each category associates with documents or subcategories. Actually, we extract necessary information from Yahoo! directory pages and construct a category-keyword association matrix using directory pages linked to categories.

The proposed method in this paper has the following advantages: First, it creates a dynamic category hierarchy, not a fixed one, providing the hierarchy with multi-inheritable sharing and flexibility of levels, thus dynamically showing the results of category retrieval according to the search subjects. Second, it can enhance the recall rate of directory search.

This paper is organized as follows. In Section 2, we review the fuzzy relational products. In Section 3, the algorithm of dynamic restructuring of category hierarchy is described and we propose a search method using this algorithm. Section 4, some experimental results are presented to show the efficiency of the proposed method comparing with the conventional directory search. Finally, conclusions are made in Section 5.

2 The Fuzzy Relational Products

In this section, we give a brief introduction to the Fuzzy Relational Products that is used in this paper [7].

Definition 1. α-cut of a fuzzy set A, denoted by A_α, is a set that contains all elements whose membership degrees are equal to or greater than α. $A_\alpha = \{ x \in X \mid \mu_A(x) \geq \alpha \}$.

A fuzzy implication operator is an extended crisp implication operator to be applied in the fuzzy theory. A crisp implication operator is defined as $\{0,1\} \times \{0,1\} \rightarrow \{0,1\}$, while a fuzzy implication operator is defined as $[0,1] \times [0,1] \rightarrow [0,1]$ to be extended in multi-valued logic. We use the implication operator defined as follows [4].

$$a \rightarrow b = (1 - a) \vee b = \max(1 - a, b), \; a = 0 \sim 1, b = 0 \sim 1 \tag{1}$$

Definition 2. Let U_1, U_2, U_3 be finite sets, R be a fuzzy relation from U_1 to U_2, S be a fuzzy relation from U_2 to U_3. That is, R is a fuzzy subset of $U_1 \times U_2$ and S is a fuzzy sub-set of $U_2 \times U_3$. Fuzzy relational products are fuzzy operators that represent the degree of fuzzy relation from a to c for a $\in U_1$, c $\in U_3$. The fuzzy triangle product as a fuzzy relation from U_1 to U_2, $\triangleleft$ is defined as follows

$$(R \triangleleft S)_{ik} = \frac{1}{N_j} \sum_j (R_{ij} \rightarrow S_{jk})$$

This is called Fuzzy Relational Products.

Definition 3. The fuzzy implication operators vary in the environments of given prob-lems. The afterset aR for a $\in U_1$ is a fuzzy subset of U_2 such that y is related to a, for y $\in U_2$. Its membership function is denoted by $\mu_{aR}(y) = \mu_R(a,y)$. The foreset Sc for c $\in U_3$ is a fuzzy subset of U_2 such that y is related to c, for y $\in U_2$. Its membership function is denoted by $\mu_{Sc}(y) = \mu_S(y,c)$ for y $\in U_2$. The mean degree that aR is a subset of Sc is meant by the mean degree such that the membership degree of y $\in aR$ implies the membership degree of y $\in Sc$, so it is defined as follows:

$$\pi_m(aR \subseteq Sc) = \frac{1}{N_{U_2}} \sum_{y \in U_2} (\mu_{aR}(y) \rightarrow \mu_{Sc}(y)) \tag{2}$$

Here, π_m is a function to calculate the mean degree ♦

The above mean degree denoted by $R \triangleleft S$ can be regarded as the mean degree of relation from a to c [5].

3 Dynamic Restructuring of the Hierarchy of Searched Categories

In this paper, the relationship between keywords and categories can be decided by normalized term frequency values between 0 and 1 (meaning a fuzzy degree of mem-bership). That is, a category can be regarded as a fuzzy set comprising the keywords appearing in the documents pertaining to the corresponding category. To check the similarity of two categories, we may have to use a more sophisticated method rather than the similarity check method based on the vector models. Actually, in the domain of categories, we must consider the hierarchical inclusion between categories as well as the similarity between categories. That is why we rely on the fuzzy relational products, which is able to describe the inclusive relation of two objects. The relationship of two categories can be decided by calculating the average degree of inclusion of a fuzzy set to another one using the fuzzy implication operator. An average degree of fuzzy set inclusion can be used for making a similarity relationship between two categories. By using this, similarity relations of categories can be obtained dynamically.

By applying the fuzzy implication operator of the formula (1) to the fuzzy relational products of the formula (2), we can get the average degree of fuzzy sets inclusion for categories, $\pi_m(C_i \subseteq C_j)$. We interpret this degree as the *similarity relationship degree* of C_i to C_j, it is the degree to which C_i is similar to C_j, or we interpret it as the *fuzzy hierarchical degree* of C_i to C_j , it is the degree to which C_j can be a subcategory of C_i. An attention is required from the fact that the hierarchical ordering is reverse to the concept of set inclusion in that C_j is the superset of C_i, but C_j is the hierarchical subcategory of C_i. Intuitively, it is conjectured that the category comprising many keywords likely inherits the properties from super-class categories. However, $\pi_m(C_i \subseteq C_j)$ have some problems representing the fuzzy hierarchical degree of C_i to C_j. That is, if C_i had many element x's of which membership degrees, $\mu_{Ci}(x)$, are small, we could have a problem in which the fuzzy relational products tend to be converged to 1 regardless of the real degree of fuzzy sets inclusion of $C_i \subseteq C_j$. Thus, we define *Restricted Fuzzy Relational Products* as follows to calculate the real degree of fuzzy sets inclusion of two categories, $\pi_{m,\beta}(C_i \subseteq C_j)$.

$$\pi_{m,\beta}(C_i \subseteq C_j) = (R^T \triangleleft_\beta R)_{ij} = \frac{1}{|C_{i\beta}|} \sum_{K_k \in C_{i\beta}} (R^T_{ik} \to R_{kj}) \qquad (3)$$

Here, K_k is the k'th category, and C_i, C_j are the i'th and the j'th category respectively, $C_{i,\beta}$ is C_i's β-restriction, that is, $\{x \mid \mu_{C_i}(x) \geq \beta\}$, $|C_{i,\beta}|$ is the number of elements in $C_{i,\beta}$, R is $m \times n$ matrix such that R_{ij} is $\mu_{C_j}(K_i)$,that is, the membership degree of $K_i \in C_j$. R^T is the transposed matrix of R such that $R_{ij} = R'_{ji}$. The following example is derived from formula (3).

Example 1. When $\beta = 0.9$, $\pi_{m,\beta}(C_2 \subseteq C_3)$ denoted by $(R^T \triangleleft_\beta R)_{23} = 0.96$, and $\pi_{m,\beta}(C_5 \subseteq C_4)$ denoted by $(R^T \triangleleft_\beta R)_{54} = 0.62$. *Fuzzy hierarchical* relations of any two categories are implemented by *Restricted Fuzzy Relational Products* (3) as shown in the tables 1.

Table 1. *Restricted Fuzzy Relational Products* of categories and keywords

	C_1	C_2	C_3	C_4	C_5
K_1	0.9	0.0	1.0	0.0	0.0
K_2	1.0	1.0	0.8	0.0	1.0
K_3	1.0	0.1	0.0	1.0	1.0
K_4	1.0	0.1	1.0	0.0	0.8
K_5	1.0	1.0	1.0	0.1	1.0

(a) R

	C_1	C_2	C_3	C_4	C_5
C_1	0.98	0.46	0.76	0.24	0.78
C_2	1.00	1.00	0.96	0.62	1.00
C_3	0.98	0.64	1.00	0.42	0.76
C_4	1.00	0.82	0.80	1.00	1.00
C_5	1.00	0.82	0.76	0.62	1.00

(b) $(R^T \triangleleft_\beta R)$

We transform values of $(R^T \triangleleft_\beta R)$ to crisp values using α-cut. (a) of table 2 is the final output of $(R^T \triangleleft_\beta R)$ using $\alpha = 0.82$. That is, the ones lower than 0.82 are discarded as 0, the ones greater than or equal to 0.82 are regarded as 1. (b) of table 2 is the final output using $\alpha = 0.76$.

Figure 1 shows the relation diagram (this is called Hasse diagram [13]) of categories as the final results obtained from table 2. Figure 1 (a) shows the diagram regarding the fuzzy hierarchical relations of categories in the case of $\alpha = 0.82$, the category C_1 is a subcategory of all categories presented, C_3 and C_5 are subcategories of C_2, C_4 respectively. Figure 1 (b) shows the diagram in the case of $\alpha = 0.76$, C_4 is located at the highest of the hierarchy, while C_1 and C_3 are at the lowest. It can be indicated that the case in (b) has a broader diagram than the case of (a), including all relations in the case of (a).

Table 2. the final output of $(R^T \triangleleft_\beta R)$ using α-cut.

	C_1	C_2	C_3	C_4	C_5
C_1	1	0	0	0	0
C_2	1	1	1	0	1
C_3	1	0	1	0	0
C_4	1	1	0	1	1
C_5	1	1	0	0	1

(a) $\alpha = 0.82$

	C_1	C_2	C_3	C_4	C_5
C_1	1	0	1	0	1
C_2	1	1	1	0	1
C_3	1	0	1	0	1
C_4	1	1	1	1	1
C_5	1	1	1	0	1

(b) $\alpha = 0.76$

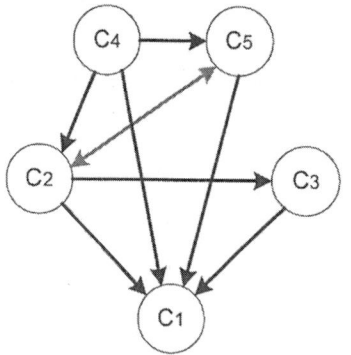

(a) Fuzzy hierarchy in case of $\alpha = 0.82$

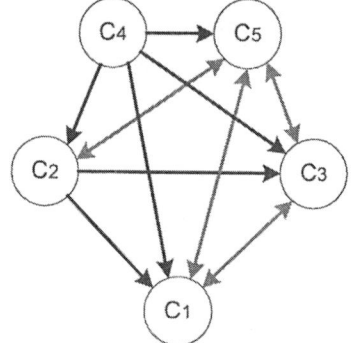

(b) Fuzzy hierarchy in case of $\alpha = 0.76$

Fig. 1. Fuzzy hierarchy as final results

The fuzzy hierarchy relations of categories are created dynamically as Figure 1 shows. It can be used for directory search on Web. That is, we can extend the selected category to several similar subcategories in case we are not satisfied with the results obtained from the directory search, even if the category may be a leaf. This is called the similarity expansion.

4   Experimental Results

For exact comparisons, we implemented the web search engine named Pandora [9]. The keyword-category association table based on frequency from the categories and their hierarchical structure copied from Yahoo! Korea has to be prepared before the search is activated. Once the collecting robot and keyword extraction process have done this, we can continue to use this table for search without any change. Pandora automatically browsed categories structured by TreeView. It also have the capability of expanding the selected category even if it may be a leaf in the tree structure by using *Restricted Fuzzy Relational Products* proposed in this paper. We assert that Pandora will show better recall rate than Yahoo! Korea [13].

Experiment. 100 university freshmen took part in this experiment. The students are divided into two groups. The students of one group are supposed to search by the directory search of Yahoo! Korea. The students of the other group are supposed to search by Pandora. We start with 5 subjects. Each subject has a keyword representing the subject best. And each subject has a set of the most frequently appeared words in the article titled by the subject's keyword in Donga encyclopedia in order of appearing frequency. The students check whether the retrieved documents are relevant or not through comparing the 10 most frequently words appeared in the retrieve document with the set of words with respect to the corresponding subject. If more than 5 words are matched, then we regard the document as relevant. Table 3 shows that the students have retrieved more relevant documents in Pandora than in Yahoo! Korea. This means that the proposed method is better than the directory search of Yahoo! Korea in recall rate

Table 3. The comparison of recall rate between Yahoo! Korea and Pandora

Subjects	Whale		Carnival		City bank		Inha univ.		Incheon	
Search Eng.	Y	P	Y	P	Y	P	Y	P	Y	P
The number of retrieved relevant document	19	25	12	19	1	1	70	109	659	826

Y:YAHOO! KOREA, P:PANDORA

5   Conclusions

We have proposed a new search algorithm and method to improve the efficiency of document retrieval by using *Restricted Fuzzy Relation Products*. We can substantiate the following beneficial characteristics from the actually implemented system and an experiment.

- The system makes web searching easy for the keywords of vague meaning by providing automatic categories retrieval and dynamic restructuring of category hierarchy.
- Due to our some evaluation, it has been substantiated that the proposed automatic directory searching method. That is, automatic category retrieval gives a much easier and effective way of searching than conventional manual directory search.

We will leave the research on the methods of more robust construction of the fuzzy implication operator and saving time for creating dynamic subcategories for future work.

References

1. Alrashid, T. M., Barker, J. A., Christian, B. S., Cox, S.C., Rabne, M. W., Slotta E. A., Upthegrove, L. R., : Safeguarding Copyrighted Contents, Digital Libraries and Intellectual Property Management, CWRU's Rights Management System. D-Lib Magazine, April 1998. http://www.dlib.org/dlib/april98/04barker.html.
2. AltaVista: Main page. http://www.altavista.com (1996)
3. Baeza-Yates, R., Ribeiro-Neto, B. : Modern Information Retrieval. Addison Wesley (1999)
4. Bandler, W., Kohout, L. : Fuzzy Power Sets and Fuzzy Implication Operations. Fuzzy Set and Systems, Vol.4, No.1 (1980) 13–30
5. Bandler, W., Kohout, L. : Semantics of Implication Operators and Fuzzy Relational Products. International Journal of Man-Machine Studies. Vol. 12 (1980) 89–116
6. Furnas, G. W., Deerwester, S., Dumais, S. T., Landauer, T. K., Harshman, R. A., Streeter, L. A., Lochbaum, K. E. : Information retrieval using a singular value decomposition model of latent semantic structure. In Proceedings of the 11th Annual International ACM SIGIR Conference on Research and Development in Information Retrieval (1988) 465–480
7. Lee, K. H., Oh, G. L. : Fuzzy Theory and Application Volume I : Theory. HongReung Science Publishing Co. (1991)
8. Ogawa, Y., Morita, T., Kobayashi, K. : A fuzzy document retrieval system using the keyword connection matrix and a learning method. Fuzzy Sets and System (1991) 163–179
9. Quark. : http://www.quark.co.kr/maindemo_frame.htm, data extracted from "YAHOO Korea" (2002)
10. Shneiderman, B. : The eyes have it: A task by data type taxonomy. In Proceedings of IEEE Symposium. Visual Languages, Boulder, CO, USA (1996) 336–346.
11. Syu, I., Lang, S. D., Deo, N. : Incorporating Latent Semantic Indexing into a Neural Network Model for Information Retrival. In Proceedings of the 5th Annual International ACM SIGIR Conference on Research and Development in Information Retrieval (1996) 145–153
12. Yahoo!: Main page. http://www.yahoo.com (1995)
13. Yahoo! KOREA: Main page. http://kr.yahoo.com (1997)

Evolution Strategies with a Fourier Series Auxiliary Function for Difficult Function Optimization

Kwong-Sak Leung and Yong Liang

Department of Computer Science & Engineering,
The Chinese University of Hong Kong, Shatin, N.T., Hong Kong
{ksleung, yliang}@cse.cuhk.edu.hk

Abstract. Through identifying the main causes of low efficiency of the currently known evolutionary algorithms for difficult function optimization problem, the complementary efficiency speed-up strategy—Fourier series auxiliary function technique is suggested, analyzed, and partially explored. The Fourier series auxiliary function could guide an algorithm to search for optima with small attraction basins efficiently. Incorporation of this technique with any known evolutionary algorithm leads to an accelerated version of the algorithm for the difficult function optimization. As a case study, the developed technique has been incorporated with evolution strategies (ES), yielding accelerated Fourier series auxiliary function evolution strategies: the FES. The experiments demonstrate that the FES consistently outperforms the standard ES in efficiency and solution quality.

1   Introduction

Evolutionary algorithms (EAs) are global search procedures based on the evolution of a set of solutions viewed as a population of interacting individuals, and have broad applications and successes as tools for search and optimization. But for solving large scale and complex optimization problems, EAs have not demonstrated itself to be very efficient as expected [4]. We believe the main factor which causes low efficiency of the current EAs is the convergence toward an undesired attractor. This phenomenon occurs when the objective function has some local optima with large attraction basins or its global optimum is located in a small attraction basin in a minimization case. We call these functions as difficult function optimization problems.

In this paper, we propose a Fourier series auxiliary function, a complementary efficient and practical technique to establish an accelerated EAs for solving a difficult functions optimization problem. It can enlarge the small attraction basins of the optima and flatten the large attraction basins. Moreover, the algorithm can be guided to search the optima with small attraction basins more efficient, and these optima are difficult to find in the objective function by EAs. In the case study, the developed technique is incorporated with evolution strategies (ES) [3], yielding an accelerated Fourier series auxiliary function evolution

J. Liu et al. (Eds.): IDEAL 2003, LNCS 2690, pp. 303–312, 2003.

strategies algorithm: the FES. Simulation examples demonstrate that the new ES consistently outperforms the previous ES in efficiency and solution quality for the difficult function optimization problems.

The paper in organized as follows: we will explain the a Fourier series auxiliary function technique for EAs implementation in Sections 2, and present the accelerated version of ES for difficult function optimization—the ES with Fourier series auxiliary function (FES) in Section 3. The FES is then experimentally examined, analyzed and compared with difficult function optimization problems in Section 4. The paper concludes in Section 5 with some useful remarks on future research related to the present work.

2   A Fourier Series Auxiliary Function

Fourier series arise from the practical task of representing a given objective function $f(x)$ in terms of cosine and sine functions. These series are trigonometric series whose coefficients are determined from $f(x)$ by certain formulas. Here we take an example in a one dimension space. Let us assume that $f(x)$ is subject to a feasible solution space $[u, v]$ that can be represented by a trigonometric series

$$f(x) = a_0 + \sum_{n=1}^{\infty} (a_n \cos \frac{2n\pi}{u-v}x + b_n \sin \frac{2n\pi}{u-v}x); \quad where$$

$$a_n = \frac{1}{u-v} \int_u^v f(x) \cos \frac{2n\pi}{v-u} x dx; \quad b_n = \frac{1}{u-v} \int_u^v f(x) \sin \frac{2n\pi}{v-u} x dx.$$

These $n = 0, 1, 2, \cdots$ and a_n, b_n are called the Fourier coefficients of $f(x)$.

At first, we introduce the convergence of the Fourier series.

Lemma 1: If an objective function $f(x)$ is piecewise continuous and has a left-hand derivative and a right-hand derivative at each point of that interval, then the Fourier series of $f(x)$ is convergent. Its sum is $f(x)$, except at a point x_0 at which $f(x)$ is discontinuous and the sum of the series is the average of the left- and right-hand limits of $f(x)$ at x_0.([2])

Lemma 1 explains the convergence of the Fourier series when the series is infinite. Now we mainly analyze a finite partial sum of the Fourier series. For the convenience of the theoretical presentation, we define the finite partial sum of the Fourier series called $F_\ell^k(x) = \sum_{n=\ell}^{k} (a_n \cos \frac{2n\pi}{u-v}x + b_n \sin \frac{2n\pi}{u-v}x)$.

Lemma 2: The Fourier coefficients a_n and b_n all tend to zero as $n \to \infty$.([1])

The infinite Fourier series $F_1^\infty(x)$ converges to $f(x)$ at any point, but the convergent speed of the finite partial sum $F_1^\ell(x)(\ell < \infty)$ is different at each point. For numerical function optimization, if x^* is the optimum with a small attraction basin in $f(x)$, the finite partial sum $F_1^\ell(x^*)(\ell < \infty)$ converges to $f(x^*)$ much slower than that where x^* is the optimum with a large attraction basin. This indicates the partial sum $|F_\ell^\infty(x^*)| = |f(x^*) - F_1^\ell(x^*)|$ at x^* with a small attraction basin is larger than at x^* with a large attraction basin. According to the lemma 2, when an integer $k \to \infty$, the coefficients of the kth Fourier series term a_k and $b_k \to 0$, the infinite partial sum $F_k^\infty(x) \to 0$. So we consider the finite partial sum $F_\ell^k(x)(\ell < k)$ instead of $F_\ell^\infty(x)$. Suppose x^* is the optimum with small attraction basin and x' is the optimum with lager attraction basin respectively, the proposition $|F_\ell^\infty(x^*)| > |F_\ell^\infty(x')|$ equals to $|F_\ell^k(x^*)| > |F_\ell^k(x')|(\ell < k)$.

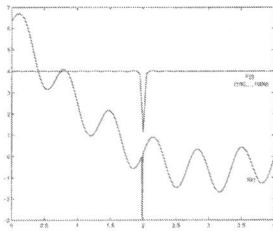

Fig. 1. A schematic illustration for the feature of the Fourier series finite partial sum $F_\ell^k(\ell = 100, k = 1000)$.

The features of the finite partial sum $F_\ell^k(x)(\ell < k)$ include enlarging small attraction basins, and flatting large attraction basins of $f(x)$, schematically shown in Fig.1. Using evolutionary algorithms to search $F_\ell^k(x)$ we could easily find the optima with small attraction basins, which are difficult to find in the objective function $f(x)$.

Region Partition Strategy. Now we consider whether $F_\ell^k(x)$ could represent all optima with small attraction basins in objective function $f(x)$. In Fig.2-(a), the two attraction basins are in the same region, and there is a 10-time difference between them. Here the width of the smaller attraction basin is 10^{-14}, and the other is 10^{-13}. The finite partial sum $F_{100}^{200}(x)$ represents these two optima at the same time and enlarges the lengths of both attraction basins to 10^{-3} (c.f. Fig.2-(b)). However, as shown in Fig.2-(c), the width of the larger basin is 1 and the other is 10^{-3}. The finite partial sum $F_{100}^{1000}(x)$ could not represent the smaller one, as shown in Fig.2-(d). The reason is that the coefficients of the Fourier series a_n and b_n are determined by an integral in the whole feasible solution space, and if the difference between the widths of the attraction basins is large, the partial sum $F_\ell^k(x)$ will give prior converge to the optimum with comparatively larger attraction basin. In such a case, to represent the small attraction basins, $F_\ell^k(x)$ needs more higher terms. This will lead to more complex computation.

To search the optima with comparatively small attraction basins, our strategy is to bisect the whole feasible solution space into two subregions at the currently located optimum point, usually with a comparatively larger attraction basin. Thus, the finite partial sum $F_\ell^k(x)$ with less terms could represent all the optima in each subregion, where the coefficients a_n and b_n of the partial sum $F_\ell^k(x)$ are determined by an integral in the subregion. In a process of the algorithm, after finding the optimum x^* in $F_\ell^k(x)$, the region $[u, v]$ is divided into two subregions $[u, x^*]$ and $[x^*, v]$ at this optimum. Then the $F_\ell^k(x)$ could represent more optima with a relatively small attraction basin. Through the region partition strategy, all the optima with small attraction basins are gradually represented by the finite partial sum $F_\ell^k(x)$ with a small number of terms. In the experiment, we set the parameters $\ell = 100$ and $k = 200$ in the finite partial sum $F_\ell^k(x)$.

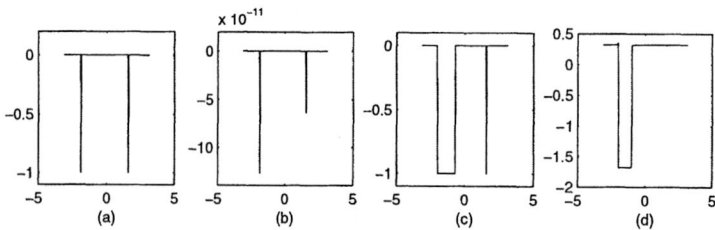

Fig. 2. A schematic illustration that the difference between lengths of attraction basins affect the representation of Fourier series finite partial sum F_l^k. (a) shows the lengths of two attraction basins are 10^{-13} and 10^{-14} respectively; (b) shows the representation of (a) by Fourier series finite partial sum $F_\ell^k(x)$, $(\ell = 100, k = 200)$; (c) shows the lengths of two attraction basins are 1 and 10^{-3}, respectively; (d) shows the representations of (c) by $F_\ell^k(x)$, $(\ell = 100, k = 1000)$.

One Element Strategy. In an n dimensional optimization, the Fourier cosine and sine trigonometric system has many elements $(\cos m_1 x_1 \cos m_2 x_2 \cdots \cos m_n x_n; \cdots\cdots; \sin m_1 x_1 \sin m_2 x_2 \cdots \sin m_n x_n)$, where each row is an element of the Fourier trigonometric system. The number of these elements is 2^n. We propose a strategy called one element strategy to decrease the number of the elements to 1 for constructing the finite partial sum $F_\ell^k(x)$ to significantly reduce the computational complexity.

Here we take an example in a two dimension space. Figs.3-(a) and (b) show the original function $f(x)$ and its Fourier series finite partial sum $F_{100}^{200}(x)$ of the complete trigonometric system, respectively. We call Fig.3-(b) a complete Fourier representation of $f(x)$. The optimal point $(-2, -2)$ of $f(x)$ is represented as a sharp point in its complete Fourier representation. Each sub-figure in the Fig.4 is a Fourier series finite partial sum of the one trigonometric element of $f(x)$, which is called a one element Fourier representation. The sum of these one element Fourier representations is the complete Fourier representation. As shown in Fig.4, one element Fourier representation could also represent the optimum of $f(x)$ at point $(-2, -2)$. However in the feasible solution space of $f(x)$, there also exist the symmetric points $(2, 2)$, $(2, -2)$ and $(-2, 2)$ of the real optimal point $(-2, -2)$ representing by the sharp points of the one element Fourier representation, called dummy optima. We will explain that the one element Fourier representation could take the place of the complete Fourier representation. Firstly, we will prove that one element Fourier representation can represent the optimum of $f(x)$. Let us assume if the center of the feasible solution space of $f(x)$ is the coordinate origin, $f(x)$ is not symmetric with respect to any axis and the coordinate origin. Since if $f(x)$ is an even function, we could directly use the Fourier cosine series to construct the finite partial sum $F_\ell^k(x)$ and all the coefficients of the Fourier sine series of $f(x)$ are zero.

Theorem 1: Assuming $x = (x_1, x_2, \cdots, x_n)$ is the optimum of $f(x)$ in R^n, if the complete Fourier representation can be used to locate the optimum x, then the one element Fourier representation can also be used to locate the optimum x.

Proof : Assume the optima (the heights of peaks) of the 4 one element Fourier representations are z_1, z_2, z_3, and z_4 respectively in the 2-D case as shown in the Figs.4-(a), (b), (c) and (d).

As shown in Fig.3-(b), the real optimum is a sharp point at $(-2, -2)$ and the complete Fourier representation is the sum of the 4 one element Fourier representations. We obtain $z_1 + z_2 + z_3 + z_4 \neq 0$.

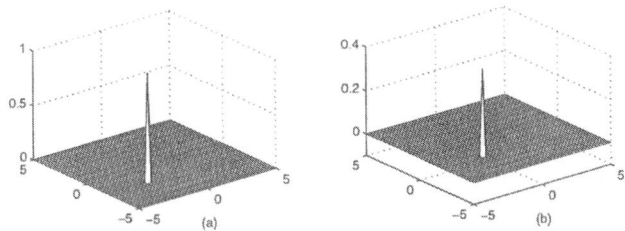

Fig. 3. Two dimensional plot of the representation of the Fourier complete trigonometric system. (a) shows original function $f(x)$ and (b) shows the partial sum $F_l^k(x)$ by the Fourier complete system representation of $f(x)$.

While at the smooth flat symmetric points $(2, 2)$, $(2, -2)$ and $(-2, 2)$ of the real optimum, we could obtain the homogeneous linear system of equations below.(c.f. Fig.3-(b) and Figs.4-(a), (b), (c), (d))

$$\begin{cases} z_1 + z_2 - z_3 - z_4 = 0 \\ z_1 - z_2 - z_3 + z_4 = 0 \\ z_1 - z_2 + z_3 - z_4 = 0 \end{cases}$$

Suppose $z_1 = 0$, this linear system of equations only have a trivial solution $z_k = 0$, $(k = 2, 3, 4)$. This contradicts $z_1 + z_2 + z_3 + z_4 \neq 0$, so $z_k \neq 0$, $(k = 1, 2, 3, 4)$.

The homogeneous linear system of equations only has a trivial solution because the $cos(x)cos(y)$, $cos(x)sin(y)$, $sin(x)cos(y)$, $sin(x)sin(y)$ terms are linearly independent in the two dimension function space. The high dimension trigonometric bases also are independent in high dimension function space, so this proof and the theorem are applicable in high dimension space.

Consequently, we could construct the auxiliary function $g(x)$ using the finite partial sum of the one element of the Fourier trigonometric system, $g(x) = \sum_{m=\ell}^{k} a_m \times \prod_{i=1}^{n} \cos m x_i$, where $a_m = \frac{1}{u-v} \int_u^v f(x) \cos \frac{2m\pi}{v-u} x \, dx$. to locate the optima of the original function $f(x)$.

Double Integral Region Strategy. When we construct the auxiliary function $g(x)$ using the finite partial sum of the one Fourier trigonometric element, according to the implicit symmetry of each element of the Fourier trigonometric system like $cos(x)cos(y)$, many dummy optima will be generated at the symmetry points of the real optimum in $g(x)$(c.f. Fig.5-(b)). So we design the double integral region strategy to expand the dummy optima out of the original region of $f(x)$. Suppose the original region of $f(x)$ is $[u, v]$, we could enlarge the region to $[u, 2v]$ and assume $f(x)$ is a constant at the expanded regions to calculate the parameter a_m of $g(x)$, $a_m = \frac{1}{u-2v} \int_u^{2v} f(x) \cos \frac{2m\pi}{2v-u} x dx$.

As shown in Fig.5-(c), the dummy optima in $g(x)$ are located outside the original region $[u, v]$. Hence, we will only have the real optimum to deal with if we only work on the original region after the expansion and the original position of the optimum remains unchanged.

3   FES: The Evolution Strategies with a Fourier Series Auxiliary Function

In this section, we will particularly embedded the new technique into ES as an example to yield new versions of the algorithms to solve the difficult optimization problems, called the FES. The incorporation of the developed technique with other known evolutionary algorithms might be straightforward, and could be done similarly as that in the example presented below.

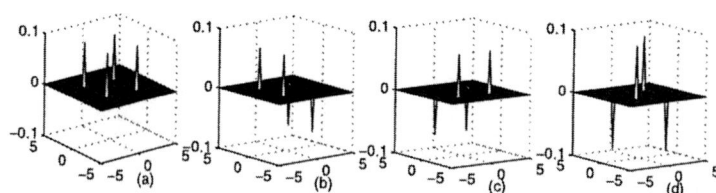

Fig. 4. Two dimensional plot of the representation of the one element Fourier trigonometric system. (a), (b), (c) and (d) show the representations by one Fourier trigonometric element $\cos(x)\cos(y)$, $\cos(x)\sin(y)$, $\sin(x)\cos(y)$ and $\sin(x)\sin(y)$, respectively.

The FES algorithm is given as follows:

I. Initialization Step Initialize all the ES parameters including: $k-$ the number iteration; $N-$ the population size; $M-$ the maximum generations of ES evolution in each iteration.

II. Iteration Step

II.1. *ES Search in the auxiliary function $g(x)$:*

   (a) randomly select N individuals to form an initial population;

   (b) perform M generations of ES, yielding the currently best minimum $g_{best}^{(k)}$;

   (c) If generation = 1, put these points into population of ES for $f(x)$; if generation > 1, compare the fitness of $f(x)$ at these points with the current optimum of $f(x)$, and only put the points which values of $f(x)$ smaller than the current optimum of $f(x)$.

II.2. *ES Search in the objective function $f(x)$:*

   (a) use the fixed points by step II.1 and some random selected points to form initial population;

   (b) perform M generations of ES, yielding the currently best minimum $f_{best}^{(k)}$;

   (c) let $f_{best}^{(k)} \leftarrow \min\{f_{best}^{(k)}, f_{best}^{(k-1)}\}$.

III. Termination Test Step

The Fourier series auxiliary function technique could be applied to the continuous or merely piecewise continuous function (continuous except for finitely many finite jumps in the feasible solution space). The reason is that these discontinuous points of $f(x)$ are represented by large attraction basins in $g(x)$, like the optimum point with a small attraction basin of $f(x)$. We could find these discontinuous points in $g(x)$, and delete or keep them in $f(x)$ through comparing their fitness in $f(x)$ with the current optimum of $f(x)$. Adopting this comparison criterion could efficiently eliminate interference caused by other kinds of points (like discontinuous points).

4 Simulations and Comparisons

We experimentally evaluate the performance of the FES, and compare it with the standard evolution strategies (SES). The FES has been implemented with the population size $N = 100$, and the maximal generations M of the ES evolution was taken uniformly to be 500 at each iteration on $g(x)$ and $f(x)$ respectively. All these parameters and schemes were kept invariant unless noted otherwise. For fairness of comparison, we have also implemented the SES with the same parameter settings and the same initial population. All experiments were run for ten times with random initial populations, and the averages of the ten runs were taken as the final results. The test suite used in our experiments include those minimization problems listed in Table 1.

We designed the test function based on benchmark multimodal functions $f_i, i = 1, 2, 3$. Three optima with small attraction basins are generated randomly in the feasible solution space of $f(x)$ and they have the following properties respectively: $(-0.5, 10^{-3})$, $(-0.5, 10^{-3})$ and $(-1, 10^{-5})$, representing the value

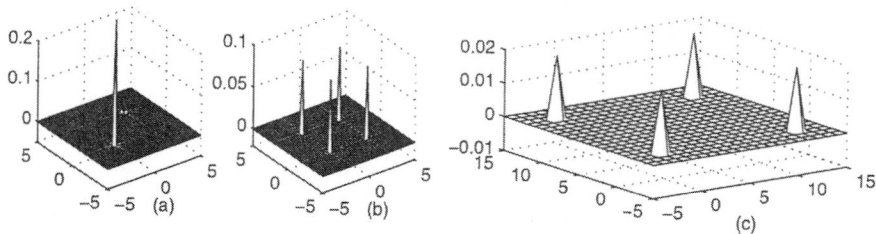

Fig. 5. A graphical illustration of the dummy points of $g(x)$, the parameters of which are determined by $[u, 2v]$. (a) shows the complete Fourier system representation; (b) shows one element Fourier representation with parameters determined by $[u, v]$; (c) shows one element Fourier representation with parameters are determined by $[u, 2v]$.

Table 1. The test suite (only 3 out of 6 examples shown)difficult functions used

$f_1 = x_2^2 + 2x_1^2 - 0.3cos(3\pi x_2) - 0.4cos(3\pi x_1) + 0.7, n = 2, x \in [-5.12, 5.12]$;

$f_2 = \sum_{i=1}^{n/4} 3[\exp(x_{4i-3} - x_{4i-2})^2 + 100(x_{4i-2} - x_{4i-1})^6 + [tan(x_{4i-1} - x_{4i})^4 + x_{4i-3}^8], n = 40, x \in [-4, 4]$;

$f_3 = \frac{1}{4000} \sum_{i=1}^{n} x_i^2 - \prod_{i=1}^{n} cos(\frac{x_i}{\sqrt{i}}) + 1, n = 40, x \in [-600, 600]$;

of the optimum and the width of its attraction basin in the bracket, respectively. The locations of these optima are decided in random.

The first part of experiments aims to exhibit the evolution processes of the FES in detail, and to demonstrate the features of the Fourier series auxiliary function. Fig.6-(a) shows random version of f_1. Figs.6-(b) and (c) show the results of the FES within the first and second iterations respectively, the points $*$ are obtained from the FES in the search in $g(x)$. The Fig.6-(b) demonstrates that the FES can find the two optima $(-0.5, 10^{-3})$ in the first iteration step, however the optimum $(-1, 10^{-5})$ is not represented in $g(x)$ at this time. In the second iteration, after bisecting the whole space between these two optima $(-0.5, 10^{-3})$, the optimum $(-1, 10^{-5})$ is represented by $g(x)$ and identified by the FES(c.f. Fig.6-(c)). These results confirm that the FES can find these three optima with small attraction basins in $g(x)$. On the other hand, to assess the effectiveness and efficiency of the FES, its performance is compared with the standard ES (SES). Figs.6-(c) and (d) present the solution quality comparison results when the FES and SES are applied to the random version of f_1. We can observe that while the FES consistently find the global optima (1) for the test function through 2 iterations (2000 generations), SES is converged to the optimum $f_1(0,0) = 0$ after 10000 generations, which is the global optimum of the original function f_1. However, this point is not the global optimum of random version of f_1. We have also tested the FES on 6 benchmark function optimization problems and

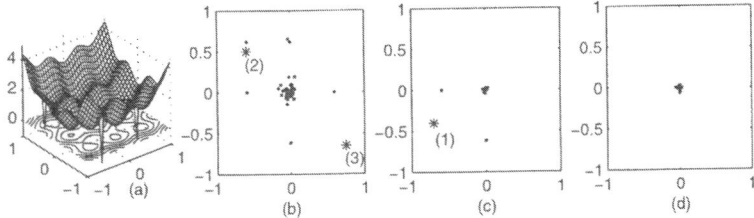

Fig. 6. A schematic illustration that the FES and SES to search on f_1. (a) shows random version of f_1; (b) show the results of FES search after a first and second iteration (generations=1000); (c) show the results of FES search after a second iteration (generations=2000); (d) show the results of SES search after 10000 generations. The points (1), (2) and (3) show the optima $(-1, 10^{-5})$, $(-0.5, 10^{-3})$ and $(-0.5, 10^{-3})$, respectively.

the FES consistently outperforms the SES in efficiency and solution quality for difficult function optimization (See the 2 examples given in Tables 1 and 2).

Table 2. The results of the FES and SES when applied to test functions

Function	Iterations	The running time (minute)		The solution precision attained	
		SES	FES	SES	FES
f_1	2	3.4	1.1	10^{-5}	10^{-8}
f_2	5	21.6	15.8	10^{-3}	10^{-8}
f_3	9	56.8	29.1	10^{-3}	10^{-8}

5   Conclusion

To overcome deficiency of EAs, the complementary Fourier series auxiliary function technique has been proposed. According to the features of the Fourier series theory, we construct the Fourier series auxiliary function $g(x)$ by one element trigonometric representation. This auxiliary function $g(x)$ could enlarge the small attraction basins and flatten the large attraction basins in objective function $f(x)$. Therefore, EAs could find these optima with small attraction basins in $g(x)$ more easily than that in $f(x)$.

As an example, we have endowed evolution strategies with the technique, yielding an accelerated evolution strategies for difficult function optimization problem—the FES. The FES has been experimentally tested with a difficult test problem consisted of complex multimodal function example with small attraction basins, and is compared against the standard evolution strategies (SES). The experimental results have demonstrated that the FES consistently outperforms the SES in efficiency and solution quality, particularly in finding the optima with small attraction basins.

Acknowledgment. This research was partially supported by RGC Earmarked Grant 4212/01E of Hong Kong SAR and RGC Direct Grant for Research of the Chinese University of Hong Kong.

References

1. Gerald B. Folland, Fourier Analysis and its Applications, *Wadsworth & Brooks/Cole Advanced Book & Software*,1998.
2. R.E.Edwards, Fourier Series, Second Edition, *Springer-Verlag New York Heidelberg Berlin*, 1999
3. Schwefel, H.-P. & Rudolph.G, Contemparary Evolution Strategies. *In F.Morana, A Moreno, J.J.Merelo, and P.Chaon (Eds), Adavances in Artificial Life*, Third ECAL Proceedings, Berlin, Springer-Verlag, 1995 pp.893–907
4. Xin Yao, Evolutionary computation : theory and applications, Singapore ;*New Jersey : World Scientific*, 1999

AD+Tree: A Compact Adaptation of Dynamic AD-Trees for Efficient Machine Learning on Large Data Sets

Jorge Moraleda and Teresa Miller

Aerospace Robotics Lab, Stanford University, Stanford, CA, 94305,
{moraleda,tgmiller}@sun-valley.stanford.edu

Abstract. This paper introduces the AD+tree, a data structure for quickly counting the number of records that match conjunctive queries in a data set. The structure is useful for machine learning on large data sets. The AD+tree is an adaptation of the Dynamic AD-tree data structure [1].
We analyze the performance of AD+trees, comparing them to static AD-trees and Dynamic AD-trees. We show AD+trees maintain a very compact cache that enables them to handle queries on massively large data sets very efficiently even under complex, unstructured query patterns.

1 Introduction

The AD–tree (All–Dimensions tree) is a data structure for caching counting statistics for a categorical data set introduced in [2] and [3]. This data structure is referred to here as static AD-tree to distinguish it from the Dynamic AD-tree introduced by [1].

Sect. 2.1 contains a very brief introduction to the static AD-tree data structure. Sect. 2.2 is a terse description of the Dynamic AD-tree, a "lazy and incremental" implementation of the static AD tree. Throughout the paper a small-scale example is used to illustrate the basic properties of the data structures described.

In Sect. 3, the AD+tree data structure is described, including its construction and usage. In Sect. 4, the AD+tree data structure is analyzed. It is shown that AD+trees can be several times smaller than Dynamic AD-trees when the learning process requires unstructured queries. AD+trees continue to provide the same advantages as Dynamic AD-trees [1] when compared with static AD-trees [2]. These advantages are: (1) the new structure scales better with the number of attributes in the data set; (2) it adaptively caches only statistics relevant to the current task; and (3) it can be used incrementally in cases where new data is frequently being appended to the data set.

We conclude that AD+trees are thus a very appropriate structure to cache sufficient statistics in machine learning. This is especially true in domains where the learning process requires unstructured queries such as Bayesian Network structure learning [4], or data driven rule induction[5].

J. Liu et al. (Eds.): IDEAL 2003, LNCS 2690, pp. 313–320, 2003.

2   Previous Work

The AD–tree (All–Dimensions tree) is a data structure for caching counting statistics for a categorical data set introduced in [2] and [3].

Static AD-trees are completely built before any query can be made of them. Komarek et alt. [1] remark that in many practical cases the majority of the AD-tree is not needed to answer the queries of interest, and moreover the entire AD-tree would be too large to fit in main memory . They introduce the Dynamic AD-tree as a "lazy and incremental" implementation of the AD-tree structure.

2.1   Static AD-Trees

Table 1 shows a very small data set with $M = 3$ symbolic (i.e., categorical) attributes (the columns a_1, a_2, a_3), and $R = 63$ records (the rows). This dataset will be used through the paper to illustrate the data-structures. Identical records have been grouped for sparsity in the paper representation. The "count" column indicates the number of identical records that match the given pattern. Attribute a_1 ranges between 0 and 1, while attributes a_2 and a_3 range between 0 and 2. In all figures the values of the attributes are assumed to increase from left to right.

Table 1. A sample data set with $M = 3$ attributes and $R = 63$ records

a_1 a_2 a_3	COUNT[1]
0 0 0	1
0 0 1	2
0 2 1	4
1 0 1	8
1 1 1	16
1 2 0	32

A query is a request to count the number of records matching the query. The AD-tree corresponding to the data set in Table 1 is shown in Fig. 1.

The answer to any counting query can be read directly from the AD-tree in time proportional to the number of attributes in the query. E.g. The emphasized AD-node in Fig. 1 answers the query "How many records exist with $a_2 = 0$ and $a_3 = 1$". The answer is 10.

An AD-tree constructed in this way would still be enormous for all but the most trivial data sets. One of the most notable contributions in [2] is that the AD-tree can be significantly pruned by removing all subtrees rooted at an AD-node that has the largest count of all the AD-nodes sharing the same Vary node

---

[1] The fact that the count column in the sample data set of Table 1 contains powers of two has no influence on the algorithm. Because any number has a unique decomposition as a sum of powers of two, this choice may help the reader follow later explanations more clearly.

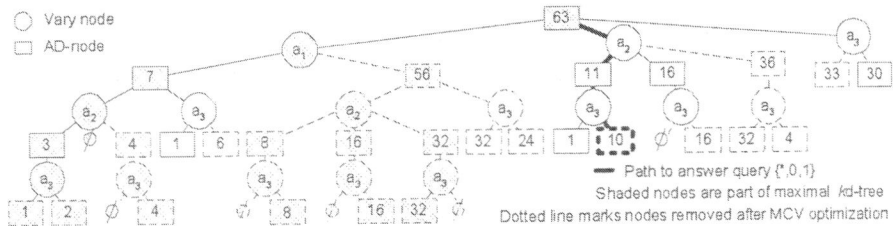

Fig. 1. Sample static AD-tree for data set in Table 1.

parent. An AD-node with this property is called an MCV node (Most-Common-Value). Dotted nodes in Fig. 1 can be removed using this optimization.

The paper goes on to show that any counting query, not merely those that have not been pruned, can still be answered very efficiently and they provide a recursive algorithm for doing so.

2.2   Dynamic AD-Trees

Dynamic AD-tree are a build on demand implementation of the AD-tree structure [1]. Dynamic AD-trees start with only a root node, and they are expanded on demand as queries arrive. Every AD-node maintains an *inst list* of all the records in the database that match the query that the AD-node answers. Thus when the AD-node needs to be expanded to refine its query, only those records need to be queried.

The Dynamic AD-tree is a fast data structure, maintaining all the desirable properties of static AD-trees while avoiding the cost of building large unused portions, and also enabling dynamic updates. However the *inst lists* quickly become enormous, much larger than the AD-tree itself. Thus it is proposed that each list maintains an associated time stamp [1], implementing a least frequency used deletion scheme every time memory becomes low.

This scheme works best for learning algorithms that successively refine queries and thus explore the AD-tree in a structured manner. Some algorithms follow a more stochastic pattern, such as bayesian network structure learning [4], or data driven rule induction [5]. In these cases many queries arrive when the necessary *inst lists* have been deleted and need to be recomputed by traversing the entire data set. This slows down the query answering process significantly.

3   AD+Trees

The AD+tree is a variation on the Dynamic AD-tree presented above, which maintains all its beneficial properties, but address stochastic queries in a more effective manner. It accomplishes this by maintaining significantly smaller *inst lists*.

The AD+tree is initialized by pre-building its maximal kd-tree. This is a subsection of the full static AD-tree (without MCV optimization) that contains sufficient statistics for the entire data set. The AD+tree substitutes the Dynamic AD-tree *inst lists* pointers to the original records for pointers to nodes in the maximal kd-tree. In Sect. 3.2 it will be shown that significantly fewer pointers need to be kept, and yet the desired answer can be computed in an amount of time that in the worst case is linear with the time Dynamic AD-tree takes, but is often much shorter.

3.1 Maximal Kd-Tree Construction

A kd-tree splits the data in only one dimension at each level [6]. The maximal kd-tree embedded in an static AD-tree (without MCV optimization) splits the data in all dimensions in order. The maximal kd-tree is grayed out in Fig. 1 for easy visualization, and it is shown by itself in the right hand side of Fig. 2.

The maximal kd-tree contains all the information stored in the initial data set. Thus if the maximal kd-tree is pre-built when initializing the AD-tree, the original data set may be discarded as all the information required to build the rest of the AD-tree is contained in the pre-built part.

3.2 Maximal Kd-Tree Usage

The maximal kd-tree is used to build the AD+tree by providing counts to queries that are not yet cached. When a query $\{Q\}$ arrives whose count is not cached, the kd-tree is traversed, and the counts of all the AD-nodes that satisfy the query are added to provide the answer C. The bound on the number of nodes that satisfy this query is defined by the following equation:

$$|\mathcal{N}| \le \min(\prod_{\substack{i=1 \\ a_i \notin S}}^{i=l} |a_i|, \mathcal{C}) \tag{1}$$

Variables in the above equation are defined in Table 2.

The two terms of this minimum can be explained as follows: For the first term, if a_i is not specified ($a_i \notin S$) then a search must continue down all of a_i's branches, resulting in additional matching nodes. For example, examine the query of Example 2 in Table 2. As the query is $\{*, *, 1\}$, no value for a_1 is specified so the results $(0, \ldots)$ and $(1, \ldots)$ are possible paths en route to matching nodes. A value for a_2 is also not specified so $(0, 0, \ldots)$, $(1, 0, \ldots)$, $(0, 1, \ldots)$, $(1, 1, \ldots)$, $(0, 2, \ldots)$, and $(1, 2, \ldots)$ are all possible paths to matching nodes. Therefore, a total of 6 is the value of the first part of the minimum.

The second half of the minimum, $\mathcal{C}$, pertains to the absence of repeated records. In the maximal kd-tree nodes are not included for counts of zero. This decreases the number of possible nodes in the AD+tree to $\mathcal{C}$. For example, examine Example 2 of Table 2 again. No records exist that would satisfy the queries

Table 2. Variables and examples related to Equation 1

VARIABLE	DEFINITION	EXAMPLE 1	EXAMPLE 2
$\{Q\}$	Query	$\{*,0,1\}$	$\{*,*,1\}$
C	Number of matches to $\{Q\}$	10	30
C	Number of distinct matches	2	4
$\mathcal{N}$	Set of matching nodes	$\boxed{2},\ \overset{8}{\boxed{[1]}}$	$\boxed{2},\ \overset{4}{\boxed{[1]}},\ \overset{8}{\boxed{[1]}},\ \overset{16}{\boxed{[1]}}$
S	Set of specific attributes	a_2, a_3	a_3
l	Index of last specified attribute	3	3
$|a_i|$	Arity of attribute a_i	$|a_1| = 2,\ |a_2| = 3,\ |a_3| = 2$	
R	Number of total records	63	63
$\mathcal{R}$	Number of distinct records	6	6
$|\mathcal{N}|$	Upper bound on number of nodes that satisfy the query	$\min(|a_1| = 2, 2) = 2$	$\min(|a_1| \cdot |a_2|, 4) = 4$

$\{0, 1, 1\}$ and $\{1, 2, 1\}$, so no nodes are included for them. This makes the value of this section of the minimum 4.

Notice that the set $\mathcal{N}$ can be found in time linear with $\min(\prod_{\substack{i=1 \\ a_i \notin S}}^{i=l} |a_i|, \mathcal{R})$ by traversing the kd-tree.

The bound on $|\mathcal{N}|$ above can be significantly improved by not starting the search at the root of the kd-tree for every query. Instead *inst lists* can be cached at every AD-node in the AD-tree. These lists point to the nodes in the maximal kd-tree such that all the records underneath satisfy the query that the AD-node answers. The set of those records is thus $\mathcal{N}$ [2]

Figure 2 shows the sequence of AD+trees and the maximal kd-tree for the data set in Table 1, when $\{*, 0, 1\}$ is the first query. Compare in particular the sizes of the cached lists with the sizes of the cached lists in the equivalent Dynamic AD-tree. For example the *inst list* in the root node of the AD+tree has size 1, whereas the root node of the dynamic AD-tree has an *inst list* with size 63.

4   Performance and Size of AD+Tree

In this section the performance and size requirements of AD+trees is analyzed and compared with the performance and size requirements of Dynamic AD-trees. The fundamental results shown are:

- Setup time is linear with the size of the database in both Dynamic AD-trees and AD+trees, however the constant factor is larger in AD+trees. (The size of a database is defined as the number of records times number of attributes.)

---

[2] Remark: The lists of the AD-nodes that belong to the maximal kd-tree consist of a single pointer to the node itself.

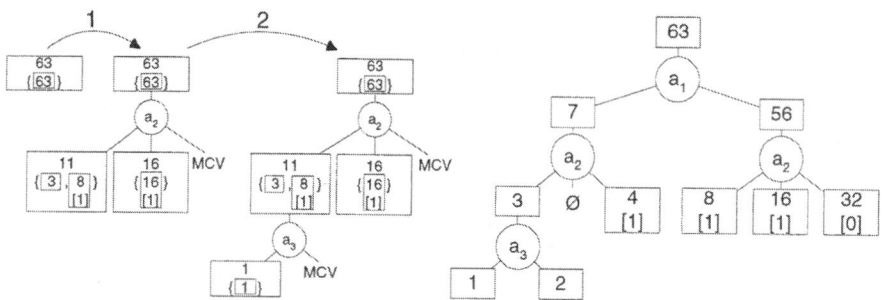

Fig. 2. Left: Sequence of AD+trees for the query of Example 1 in Table 2. The *inst lists* contain pointers to AD-nodes in the maximal kd-tree (Right).

- The amount of time required to answer an uncached query grows linearly with the number of records that match the query when using Dynamic AD-trees. In AD+trees this time only grows linearly with the number of *distinct* records that match the query.
- A large fraction of the size of AD-trees is cache. The ratio of cache sizes in AD+trees to cache sizes in Dynamic AD-trees is at most equal to the ratio of *distinct* records in the database ($\mathcal{R}$) to the total number of records (R), and can be significantly smaller if the number of records is sufficiently large.

4.1 Size of Row Caches in AD-Nodes

The cache sizes in AD-nodes are analyzed in this section. For this analysis the cache size of an AD-node is the number of pointers that the AD-node maintains. Also, an analysis will be done, not of individual AD-node cache sizes, but instead of the total cache sizes of all children of a Vary node. This analysis is simpler but still gives a clear indication of the cache size savings of AD+trees.

The combined sizes of all AD-nodes that answer queries that specify the same set of attributes $\mathcal{S}$, where l is the index of the last attribute specified in $\mathcal{S}$ is bounded by:

$$\min(\prod_{j=1}^{l} |a_j|, k^{*|\mathcal{S}|}\mathcal{R}) \tag{2}$$

The first term of the minimization is an upper bound on the number of nodes in the maximal kd-tree at level l. This bound is achieved only if none of the affected nodes in the maximal kd-tree has a count of zero.

The second term of the minimization expresses the expected number of distinct records that can be in the given caches. Note that at each level, a savings factor of k^* occurs due to MCV Node savings (where k^* is an average value).

Thus for low indices the first term of the minimum dominates. If the number of distinct records is sufficiently small ($k^*\mathcal{R} < \prod_{j=1}^{M} |a_j|$) then the second term of the minimization dominates for indices greater than $l^*_{|\mathcal{S}|}$. This transition point is defined such that $\prod_{j=1}^{l^*_{|S|}} |a_j| \simeq k^{*|S|}\mathcal{R}$. The ratio of cache size in first AD-nodes to cache size in Dynamic AD-tree AD-nodes as a function of the node index is shown in Fig. 3.

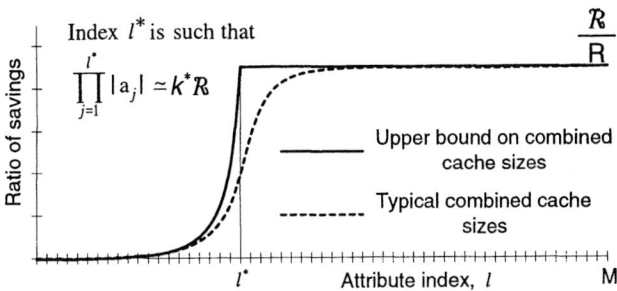

Fig. 3. Ratio of cache sizes between first level AD-nodes in an AD+tree and cache sizes in equivalent AD-nodes in a Dynamic AD-tree as a function of the node index.

An useful simplification is that the cache size for AD-nodes is 0 if the last index specified in a query is smaller than $l^*_{|S|}$, and equal to $\mathcal{R}/R$ otherwise. Note that this simplification is actually on the unfavorable side since $l^*_{|S|}$ is always less than or equal to l^*). Note that in a Dynamic AD-tree the sums of all equivalent caches sizes are $k^{*|S|}R$.

Assuming a uniform distribution of attributes among queries where $|S|$ attributes are specified, it is evident that the probability that the index of the of the last attribute specified is smaller than l^* is $(l^*/M)^{|S|}$.

Thus it is easily seen that the expected savings in $|S|$ level AD-node caches of AD+trees compared to Dynamic AD-trees is approximately:

$$(1 - \frac{l^*}{M})^{|S|} \frac{\mathcal{R}}{R} \tag{3}$$

4.2   Performance

Dynamic AD-trees and AD+trees have very similar performance in terms of speed, with Dynamic AD-trees having shorter setup time. In AD+trees this is compensated by faster query refinement when repeated records exist.

Dynamic AD-trees have virtually zero setup time, as they only require loading the data set in RAM. AD+trees have to build the maximal kd-tree as well, which can be done in log-linear time with the number of records.

The amount of time required to answer a query that is cached in the AD-tree is identical in Dynamic AD-trees and AD+trees, as they perform the same operations.

The amount of time required to obtain the answer to a refined query that is not present in Dynamic AD-trees grows linearly with the number of records that match the unrefined query, C. This is because it is necessary traverse the cache lists in the AD-node corresponding to the unrefined query. The amount of time required when using AD+tree's caches grows linearly only with the number of distinct records that match the unrefined query, C. In this case it is necessary to traverse that number of AD-nodes in the maximal kd-tree to refine the query.

5   Conclusion

This paper describes the AD+tree: A new structure for caching sufficient statistics in machine learning applications with large data sets.

An AD+tree is a modified Dynamic AD-tree. It has been modified by pre-building its maximal kd-tree, and substituting pointers to the original data (as in Dynamic AD-trees) for pointers to AD-nodes in the maximal kd-tree.

It has been shown that the new data structure can be significantly smaller than the equivalent Dynamic AD-tree by reducing significantly the sizes of the caches necessary to grow on demand in an efficient manner.

The benefits of the new data structure are most apparent in applications where stochastic queries occur such in Bayesian Network structural learning, or data driven rule induction. In these application the new caches are significantly smaller and thus many more of them can be maintained simultaneously. The new structure also offers benefits both in size and speed for applications where repeated records abound, which is frequently the case in a variety of domains.

Acknowledgements. The authors want to acknowledge the personnel of the Stanford Aerospace Robotics Laboratory, and of DecisionQ Corporation for their helpful discussions and support. MacGregor Belniak deserves a special mention for his constructive comments and reviews. Author Teresa Miller is a Stanford Gabilan Fellow.

References

1. Komarek, P., Moore, A.W.: A dynamic adaptation of ad-trees for efficient machine learning on large data sets. In: Proceedings of the 17th International Conference on Machine Learning. (2000)
2. Moore, A.W., Lee, M.S.: Cached sufficient statistics for efficient machine learning with large datasets. Journal of Artificial Intelligence Research **8** (1998)
3. Anderson, B., Moore, A.W.: Rich probabilistic models for gene expression. In: Proceedings of the 4th International Conference on Knowledge Discovery and Data Mining, AAAI. (1998) 134–138
4. Heckerman, D. In: A tutorial for learning in bayesian networks. Kluwer Academic Publishers, Dordrecht, The Netherlands (1998) 301–354
5. Dzeroski, S., N. Lavrac, e.: Relational Data Mining. Springer-Verlag (2001)
6. Gaede, V., Günther, O.: Multidimensional access methods. In: ACM Computing Surveys. Volume 30(2). (1998) 170–231

Evolvable Hardware Using Genetic Programming

Nadia Nedjah and Luiza de Macedo Mourelle

Department of Systems Engineering and Computation, Faculty of Engineering,
State University of Rio de Janeiro,
Rio de Janeiro, Brazil
{nadia, ldmm}@eng.uerj.br
http://www.eng.uerj.br/~ldmm

Abstract. In this paper, we propose a methodology based on genetic programming to automatically generate data-flow based specifications for hardware designs of combinational digital circuits. We aim at allowing automatic generation of *balanced* hardware specifications for a given input/output behaviour. It minimises space while maintaining reasonable response time.

1 Introduction

The problem of interest consists of designing efficient and creative circuits that implement a given input/output behaviour without much designing effort. The obtained circuits are expected to be *minimal* both in terms of space and time requirements: The circuits must be *compact* i.e. use a reduced number of gates and *efficient*, i.e. produce the output in a short response time. The response time of a circuit depends on the number and the complexity of the gates forming the longest path in it. The complexity of a gate depends solely on the number of its inputs. Furthermore, the design should take advantage of the all the kind of gates available on reconfigurable chip of field programmable gate array (FPGAs).

Evolutionary hardware is a hardware that is yield using simulated evolution as an alternative to conventional-based electronic circuit design. *Genetic evolution* is a process that evolves a set of individuals, which constitutes the *population*, producing a new population. Here, individuals are hardware designs. The more the design obeys the constraints, the more it is used in the reproduction process. The design constraints could be expressed in terms of hardware area and/or response time requirements. The freshly produced population is yield using some *genetic operators* such as *crossover* and *mutation* that attempt to simulate the natural breeding process in the hope of generating new design that are *fitter* i.e. respect more the design constraints. Genetic evolution is usually implemented using *genetic algorithms*.

In this work, we design innovative and efficient evolutionary digital circuits. Circuit evaluation is based on their possible implementation using *CMOS* technology [4], [9]. The produced circuits are *balanced* i.e. use a reduced number of gate equivalent and propagate result signals in a reduced response time such that the factor *area×performance* is minimised. We do so using *genetic programming*.

J. Liu et al. (Eds.): IDEAL 2003, LNCS 2690, pp. 321–328, 2003.

The remainder of this paper is divided in five sections. In Section 2, we describe the principles of genetic programming. In Section 3, we describe the methodology we employ to evolve new compact and fast hardware for a given input/output behaviour. In Section 4, we compare the discovered hardware against existing most popular ones. Finally, we draw some conclusions.

2   Genetic Programming

Genetic programming [6] is an extension of genetic algorithms. The chromosomes are computer programs and the genes are instructions. In general, genetic programming offers a mechanism to get a computer to provide a solution of problem without being told exactly how to do it. In short, it allows one to automatically create a program. It does so based on a high level statement of the constraints the yielded program should obey to. The input/output behaviour of the expected program is generally considered as an omnipresent constraint. Furthermore, the generated program should use a minimal number of instructions and have an optimal execution time.

Starting form random set of computer programs, which is generally called *initial population*, genetic programming breeds a population of programs through a series of steps, called *generations*, using the Darwinian principle of natural *selection*, recombination also called *crossover*, and *mutation*. Individuals are selected based on how much they adhere to the specified constraints. Each program is assigned a value, generally called its *fitness*, which mirrors how *good* it is in solving the program. Genetic programming [6] proceeds by first, randomly creating an initial population of computer programs; then, iteratively performing a generation, which consists of going through two main steps, as far as the constraints are not met. The first step in a generation assigns for each computer program in the current population a fitness value that measures its adherence to the constraints while the second step creates a new population by applying the three genetic operators, which are *reproduction*, *crossover* and *mutation* to some selected individuals. *Selection* is done with on the basis of the individual fitness. The fitter the program is, the more probable it is selected to contribute to the formation of the new generation. *Reproduction* simply copies the selected individual from the current population to the new one. *Crossover* recombines two chosen computer programs to create two new programs using single-point crossover or two-points crossover as shown in Figure 1. Mutation yields a new individual by changing some randomly chosen instruction in the selected computer program. The number of genes to be mutated is called *mutation degree* and how many individuals should suffer mutation is called *mutation rate*.

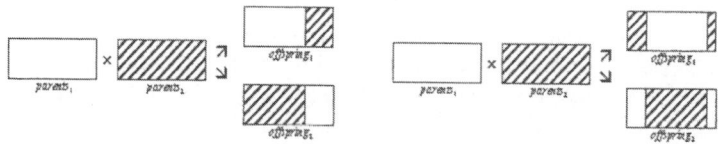

Fig. 1. *Single-point and double-point crossover techniques*

3 Evolving Hardware for Combinational Digital Circuits

There three main aspects in implementation of genetic programming [6], [7]: *(i)* program encoding; *(ii)* crossover and mutation of programs; *(iii)* program fitness. In this section, we explain how we treat these three aspects in our implementation.

3.1 Circuit Specification Encoding

Encoding of individuals is one of the implementation decisions one has to take in order to use evolutionary computation. It depends highly on the nature of the problem to be solved. There are several representations that have been used with success: *binary encoding* which is the most common mainly because it was used in the first works on genetic algorithms, represents an individual as a string of bits; *permutation encoding* mainly used in ordering problem, encodes an individual as a sequence of integer; *value encoding* represents an individual as a sequence of values that are some evaluation of some aspect of the problem; and *tree encoding* represents an individual as tree. Generally, the tree coincides with the *concrete tree* as opposed to *abstract tree* [1] of the computer program, considering the grammar of the programming language used.

   Here a design is specified using register transfer level equations. Each instruction in the specification is an output signal assignment. A signal is assigned the result of an expression wherein the operators are those that represent basic gates in CMOS technology of VLSI circuit implementation and the operands are the input signals of the design. Note that all gates introduce a minimal propagation delay as the number of input signal is minimal, which is 2.

   A NOT gate inverts the input signal, an and-gate propagates a 1-signal when both input signals are 1 and 0-signal otherwise and an or-gate propagates a 0-signal when both input signals are 0 and 1-signal otherwise. An AND gate inverts the signal propagated by a NAND gate while an OR gate inverts that propagated by a NOR gate. Note that, in CMOS technology, an and-gate is a NAND gate coupled with a NOT gate and an OR gate is a nor-gate followed by a not-gate and not the inverse [4]. The XOR gate is a CMOS basic gate that has the behaviour of sum of products $x\bar{y}+\bar{x}y$ wherein x and y are the input signals. However, a XOR gate is not implemented using 2 AND gates, 2 NOT gates and an OR gate. A 2to1-multiplexer MUX is also a CMOS basic gate and implements the sum of products $x\bar{s}+ys$ wherein x and y are the first and the second input signals and s is the control signal. It is clear that a XOR and MUX gates are of the same complexity [4], [9].

   For instance, a 2-bit multiplier has 4-bit result signal so an evolved register transfer level specification is as follows, wherein the input operands are $X=<x_1x_0>$ and $Y=<y_1y_0>$ and the output is the product $P=<p_3p_2\ p_1p_0>$. The schematic of the digital circuit implementing the above specification is given in Figure 2.

$$p_3 \ \Leftarrow \ (x_0 \text{ AND } y_0) \text{ AND } (x_1 \text{ AND } y_1)$$
$$p_2 \ \Leftarrow \ (x_0 \text{ NAND } y_0) \text{ AND } (x_1 \text{ AND } y_1)$$
$$p_1 \ \Leftarrow \ (x_1 \text{ NAND } y_0) \text{ XOR } (x_0 \text{ NAND } y_1)$$
$$p_0 \ \Leftarrow \ (y_0 \text{ AND } x_0) \text{ OR } y_0$$

We encode specifications using an array of concrete trees corresponding to its signal assignments. The *i*th tree represents the evaluation tree of the expression on the left-hand side of the *i*th signal assignment. Leaf nodes are labelled with a literal representing a single bit of an input signal while the others are labelled with an operand. The individual corresponding to above specification is shown in Figure 3.

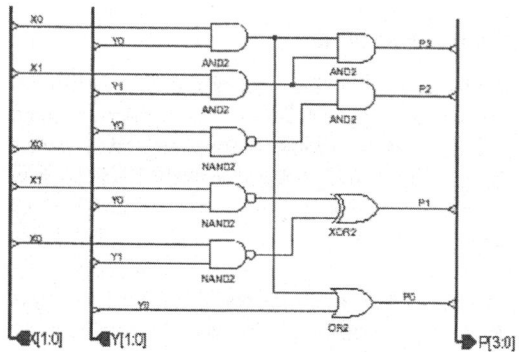

Fig. 2. *Evolved 2-bit multiplier*

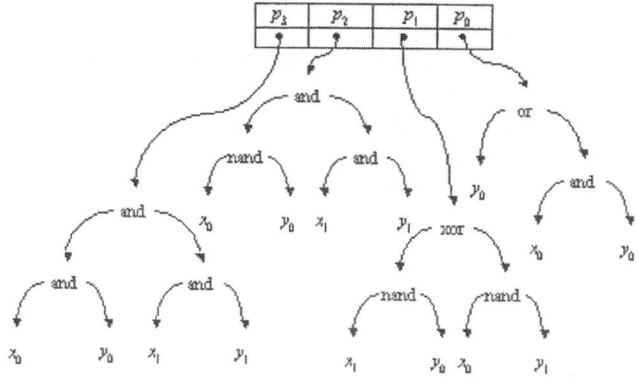

Fig. 3. *Chromosome for the evolved 2-bit multiplier*

3.2   Circuit Specification Reproduction

Crossover of circuit specification is implemented using a double-point crossover as described in Figure 1. One of the important and complicated operators for genetic programming is the *mutation*. It consists of changing a gene of a selected individual. The number of individuals that should suffer mutation is defined by the *mutation rate* while how many genes should be altered within a chosen individual is given by the *mutation degree*.

Here, a gene is the tree of the expression on the left hand side of a signal assignment. Altering an expression can be done in two different ways depending the node that was randomised and so must be mutated. A node represents either an operand or operator. In the former case, the operand, which is a literal representing a bit in the input signal, is substituted with either a literal or *simple* expression. The decision is random. In the case in which the operand has to be changed by another operand, the literal representing the bit of lesser significance in the binary notation of the input signal or that representing its most significant bit is used. This is performed as indicated by function $mutate_1$ below, wherein $X = <x_{n-1}x_{n-2} \ldots x_1x_0>$ is the signal obtained by the concatenation of all input signals:

$$mutate_1(x_i) = \begin{cases} x_{n-1} & i = 0 \\ x_{i-1} & \text{otherwise} \end{cases}$$

In the case of mutating an operand node to an operator node, we proceed as follows: First let x_i be the operand being mutated. We choose randomly an operator among those available. Let OP be this operator. Its first operand is x_i. So if the chosen operator is NOT then the operand node is mutated to NOT x_i. When the selected operator is binary, a new literal is generated using $mutate_1(x_i)$. Thus, in this case, x_i is mutated to either x_i OP $mutate(x_i)$, wherein OP is an available binary operator. If the chosen operator is MUX, then a third operand is generated using $mutate_1(mutate_1(x_i))$. Last but not least, when the selected operator is quaternary a fourth literal is generated in the same way, i.e. using $mutate_1(mutate_1(mutate_1(x_i)))$. This mutation procedure is implemented by function $mutate_2$ below wherein the notation $mutate_1^{[i]}(x)$ represents the i times application of $mutate_1$ and $\#OP$ represents the arity of operator OP:

$$mutate_2(x_i) = \begin{cases} NOT\ x_i & \#OP = 1 \\ x_i\ OP\ mutate_1^{[1]}(x_i) & \#OP = 2 \\ MUX\ x_i\ mutate_1^{[1]}(x_i)\ mutate_1^{[2]}(x_i) & \#OP = 3 \\ x_i\ mutate_1^{[1]}(x_i)\ OP\ mutate_1^{[2]}(x_i)\ mutate_1^{[3]}(x_i) & \#OP = 4 \end{cases}$$

So far we explained how an operand node is mutated. Now, we describe the mutation process of an operator node. Let OP be the operator being changed. An operator node can be mutated to another operator node or to an operand node. In the latter case, a literal is randomised and used to substitute the operator node. In the former case, however, things become a little more complicated depending on the relation between the arity OP and that of the operator selected to substitute it, say OP'. So we mutate OP to OP'. When $\#OP = \#OP'$ we leave the operands unchanged. Note that this case happens only for binary and quaternary operators. When $\#OP >$

#OP', we use only a random subset of OP's operands. Finally, i.e. when #OP < #OP', we generate a random set of literals using function mutate₁ repetitively as in function mutate₂ above. Note that, the last case can occur for NOT, MUX and binary operators but not for quaternary operators.

3.3 Circuit Specification Evaluation

Another important aspect of genetic programming is to provide a way to evaluate the adherence of evolved computer programs to the imposed constraints. In our case, these constraints are of three kinds. First of all, the evolved specification must obey the input/output behaviour, which is given in a tabular form of expected results given the inputs. This is the truth table of the expected circuit. Second, the circuit must have a reduced size. This constraint allows us to yield compact digital circuits. Thirdly, the circuit must also reduce the signal propagation delay. This allows us to reduce the response time and so discover efficient circuits. In order to take into account both area and response time, we evaluate circuits using the *area×performance* factor. We evolve *balanced* digital circuits that implement a given behaviour that require a reduced hardware area and produce the result in a reduced time such that *area×performance* factor is minimal.

We estimate the necessary area for a given circuit using the concept of *gate equivalent*. This is the basic unit of measure for digital circuit complexity [4], [9]. It is based upon the number of logic gates that should be interconnected to perform the same input/output behaviour. This measure is more accurate that the simple number of gates [4].

Let *C* be a digital circuit that uses a subset (or the complete set) of the gates. Let *Gates(C)* be a function that returns the set of all gates of circuit *C* and *Levels(C)* be a function that returns the set of all the gates of *C* grouped by level. For instance, applied to the circuit of Figure 2, it returns the set of sets {{AND, AND, NAND, NAND, NAND}, {AND, AND, XOR, OR}}. Notice that the number of levels of a circuit coincides with the cardinality of the set expected from function *Levels*. On the other hand, let *Value(T)* be the Boolean value that the considered circuit *C* propagates for the input Boolean vector *T* assuming that the size of *T* coincides with the number of input signal required for circuit *C*. The fitness function, which allows us to determine how much an evolved circuit adheres to the specified constraints, is given as follows, wherein *In* represents the input values of the input signals while *Out* represents the expected output values of the output signals of circuit *C*, *n* denotes the number of output signals that circuit *C* has and function *Delay* returns the propagation delay of a given gate as shown in [4].

$$Fitness(C) = \sum_{j=1}^{n} \left(\sum_{i \mid Value(In[i]) \neq Out[i,j]} Penalty \right) + \sum_{g \in Gates(C)} GateEquivalent(g) * \sum_{L \in Levels(C)} MaxDelay(g)$$

Note that for a correct circuit the first term in the definition of function *Fitness* is zero and so the value returned by this function is the factor *area*×performance of the evaluated circuit.

4 Evolutionary vs. Conventional Designs

In this section, we compare the evolutionary circuits yield by our genetic programming based evolution to those designed by a human as well as to those evolved by Coelho's genetic algorithm [2].

The convergence graphs of our evolutionary process for the examples are shown in Figure 4. The best circuits for the 1st, 2nd and 3rd examples were obtained in 100, 280 and 320 generations.

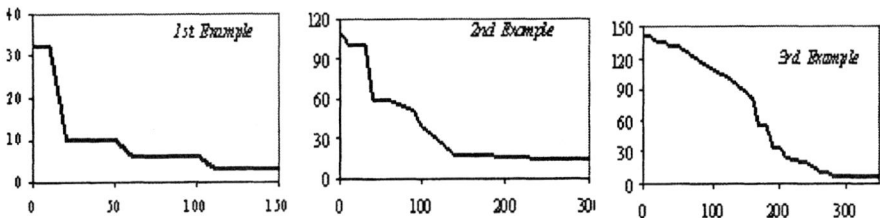

Fig. 4. *Convergence graphs for the evolution of the circuits of the three examples*

In order to evolve the circuits for all of the examples we used a population of 100 individuals. The double-point crossover was used with mutation rate of 0.5 and a mutation degree of 1.

Table 1 shows a comparison between the fittest circuits engineered by a human designer, Coelho's genetic algorithm and our genetic algorithm, which is based on genetic programming. For each proposed example, the required hardware area, the necessary propagation delay and the product *area*×performance are detailed. The graphical representation of these figures is shown in the chart of Figure 5.

Table 1. *Numerical comparison of the area×delay for the three methods*

	area			delay			area×performance		
	Our's	Coelho's	Human's	Our's	Coelho's	Human's	Our's	Coelho's	Human's
1st	8	9	12	0.424	0.637	0.637	3.392	5.733	7.644
2nd	15	16	20	0.973	0.918	0.702	14.595	14.696	14.050
3rd	9	15	20	0.639	0.699	0.912	5.751	10.492	18.250
4th	16	16	24	0.425	0.842	0.853	6.800	13.472	20.472
5th	22	21	34	0.799	1.065	0.703	17.589	22.365	23.919

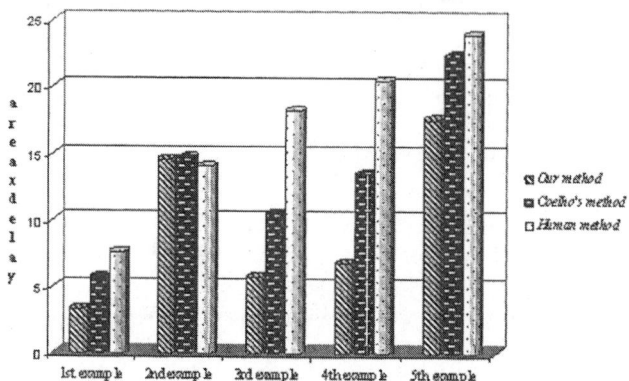

Fig. 5. *Graphical comparison of the area×delay factor for the three methods*

5 Conclusions

In this paper, we described an evolutionary technique to engineer compact, efficient and creative digital combinational circuit given the expected input/output behaviour. We explored the use of genetic programming and changing from the binary representation of circuits to a tree representation. An advantage of using genetic programming consists of the readability of the evolved circuit for synthesis using synthesis tools.

Our evolutionary process is multi-objective as it allows one to yield balanced i.e. compact and efficient digital circuits. The proposed fitness function evaluates a given circuit with respect to correctness, required hardware area and necessary propagation delay of output signals. It does so using the well-agreed-upon factor *area×performance* as a measure to appreciate the complexity of a digital circuit.

We evolved a better circuit for every example used by Coelho et al. [2] compared to both human designs and evolved circuit that only consider the number of required gates to evaluate an evolved solution.

References

1. A.V. Aho, S. Ravi and J.D. Ullman, *Compilers: principles, techniques and tools*, Addison-Wesley, 1986.
2. A.A.C. Coelho, A.D. Christiansen and A.H. Aguirre, *Towards Automated Evolutionary Design of Combinational Circuits*, Comput. Electr. Eng., **27**, pp. 1–28, 2001
3. M.D. Ercegovac, T. Lang and J.H. Moreno, *Introduction to digital systems*, John Wiley, 1999.
4. J. R. Koza, *Genetic Programming*. MIT Press, 1992.
5. J.F. Miller and D. Job, *Principles in the evolutionary design of digital circuits*
6. V.T. Rhyne, *Fundamentals of digital systems design*, F.F. Kuo Ed. Prentice-Hall Electrical Engineering Series, 1973.

Minimal Addition-Subtraction Sequences for Efficient Pre-processing in Large Window-Based Modular Exponentiation Using Genetic Algorithms

Nadia Nedjah and Luiza de Macedo Mourelle

Department of Systems Engineering and Computation, Faculty of Engineering,
State University of Rio de Janeiro,
Rio de Janeiro, Brazil
{nadia, ldmm}@eng.uerj.br
http://www.eng.uerj.br/~ldmm

Abstract. This paper introduces a novel application of genetic algorithms for evolving optimal addition-subtraction sequences that allow one to perform pre-computations necessary in the window-based modular exponentiation methods. When the window size is large, the pre-processing step becomes very expensive. Evolved addition/addition-subtraction sequences are of minimal size so they allow one to perform exponentiation with a minimal number of multiplication and/or divisions and hence implementing efficiently the exponentiation operation.

1 Introduction

Public-key cryptographic systems (such as the RSA encryption scheme [7], [13]) often involve raising large elements of some groups fields (such as GF(2^n) or elliptic curves [10]) to large powers. The performance and practicality of such cryptosystems is primarily determined by the implementation efficiency of the modular exponentiation. As the operands (the plain text of a message or the cipher (possibly a partially ciphered) are usually large (i.e. 1024 bits or more), and in order to improve time requirements of the encryption/decryption operations, it is essential to attempt to minimise the number of modular multiplications performed.

A simple procedure to compute $C = T^E$ mod M based on the paper-and-pencil method is described in Algorithm 1. This method requires $E-1$ modular multiplications. It computes all powers of T: $T \to T^2 \to T^3 \to \dots \to T^{E-1} \to T^E$.

Algorithm 1. *simpleExponentiationMethod*(T, M, E)
```
    1: C = T;
    2: for i = 1 to E-1 do C = (C × T) mod M;
    3: return C
end algorithm.
```

The paper-and-pencil method computes more multiplications than necessary. For instance, to compute T^{31}, it needs 30 multiplications. However, T^{31} can be computed using only 7 multiplications: $T \to T^2 \to T^3 \to T^6 \to T^{10} \to T^{11} \to T^{21} \to T^{31}$. But if division is allowed, T^{31} can be computed using only 5 multiplications and one division: $T \to T^2 \to T^4 \to T^8 \to T^{16} \to T^{32} \to^- T^{31}$, where $\to^-$ denotes a division.

J. Liu et al. (Eds.): IDEAL 2003, LNCS 2690, pp. 329–336, 2003.

Recently, several cryptosystems based on the Abelian group defined over elliptic curves are proposed. In these crypotosystems, the inverse of element is easily obtained. Hence for such groups one can compute exponentiations by an interleaved sequence of multiplications and divisions.

The basic question is: what is the fewest number of multiplications to compute T^E, given that the only operation allowed is multiplying two already computed powers of T? Answering the above question is NP-hard, but there are several efficient algorithms that can find a near optimal ones [12]. However, these algorithms need some pre-computations that if not performed efficiently can deteriorate the algorithm overall performance. The pre-computations are themselves an ensemble of exponentiations and so it is also NP-hard to perform them optimally. In this paper, we concentrate on this problem and engineer a minimal addition-subtraction chain perform the necessary pre-computations very efficiently. We do so using evolutionary computation. We compare our results with those obtained using the Brun's algorithm [1]. Note, however, that the latter yields only addition chains. We use it as a reference because, as far as we know, no work has been done to generate addition-subtraction sequences.

Evolutionary algorithms are computer-based solving systems, which use evolutionary computational models as key element in their design and implementation. A variety of evolutionary algorithms have been proposed. The most popular ones are *genetic algorithms* [3], [5]. They have a conceptual base of simulating the evolution of individual structures via the Darwinian natural selection process. The process depends on the performance of the individual structures as defined by its environment. Genetic algorithms are well suited to provide an efficient solution of NP-hard problems [3], [5], [12].

This paper will be structured as follows: in Section 2, we present the sliding window-based methods; in Section 3, we explain how these concepts can be used to compute a minimal addition-subtraction chain to perform efficiently necessary pre-computations in the window methods; in Section 4, we apply genetic algorithms concepts to solve the addition-subtraction sequence minimisation problem. In Section 5, we present some useful results. Finally, we conclude in Section 6.

2 The Sliding Window-Based Methods

Generally speaking, the window methods for exponentiation [6] may be thought of as partitioning in k-bits windows the binary representation of the exponent E, pre-computing the powers in each window one by one, squaring them k times to shift them over, and then multiplying by the power in the next window.

There are several partitioning strategies. The window size may be constant or variable. For the m-ary methods, the window size is constant and the windows are next to each other. On the other hand, for the sliding window methods the window size may be of variable length. It is clear that zero-windows, i.e. those that contain only zeros, do not introduce any extra computation. So a good strategy for the sliding window methods is one that attempts to maximise the number of zero-windows.

For the sliding window methods the window size may be of variable length and hence the partitioning may be performed so that the number of zero-windows is as large as possible, hence reducing the number of modular multiplication necessary in the squaring and multiplication phases. Furthermore, as all possible partitions have to start (i.e. in the right side) with digit 1, the pre-processing step needs to be performed for odd values only. The sliding method algorithm is presented in Algorithm 2, wherein d denotes the number of digits in the largest possible partition and L_i the length of partition P_i.

Algorithm 2. `slidingWindowMethod`(T, M, E)
```
  1: Partition E using the given strategy;
  2: for i = 2 to 2^d -1 step 2 Compute T^i mod M;

  3: C = T^{P_{p-1}}  mod M;
  4: for i = p-2 downto 0

  5:    C = T^{2^{L_i}} mod M;

  6:    if V_i≠0 then C = C×T^{V_i}  mod M;
  return C;
end algorithm.
```

In adaptive methods [8] the computation depends on the input data, such as the exponent E. M-ary methods and window methods compute all possible partitions, knowing that the partitions of the actual exponent may or may not include all possible partitions. Thus, the number of modular multiplication in the pre-processing step can be reduced if partitions of E do not contain all possible windows.

Let $\wp(E)$ be the list of partitions obtained from the binary representation of E. Assume that the list of partition is non-redundant and ordered according to the ascending value of the partitions contained in the expansion of E. As before let p be the number of the partition of E and recall that V_i and L_i are the decimal value and the number of digits of partition P_i. The generic algorithm for describing the computation of T^E mod M using the window methods is given in Algorithm 3.

Algorithm 3. `AdaptiveWindowMethod`(T, M, E)
```
  Partition E using the given strategy;

  1: for each partition in \wp(E) Compute T^{V_i} mod M;

  2: C = T^{V_{b-1}} mod M;
  3: for i = p-2 downto 0

  4:    C = T^{2^{L_i}} mod M;

  5:    if V_i ≠ 0 then   C = C×T^{V_i} mod M;
  7: return C;
end algorithm.
```

Algorithm 3 does not suggest how to compute the powers needed to use the adaptive window methods. Finding the best way to compute them is a *NP*-hard problem [4], [8].

3   Addition-Subtraction Sequences

An *addition-subtraction chain* of length l for an positive integer N is a list of positive integers $(a_0, a_1, a_2, ..., a_l)$ such that $a_0 = 1$, $a_l = N$ and $a_k = a_i \pm a_j$, $0 \le i \le j < k \le l$.

Finding a minimal addition-subtraction chain for a given positive integer is an *NP*-hard problem. It is clear that a short addition-subtraction chain for exponent E yields a fast algorithm to compute T^E mod M as we have if $a_k = a_i + a_j$ then $T^{a_k} = T^{a_i} \times T^{a_j}$ and if $a_k = a_i - a_j$ then $T^{a_k} = T^{a_i} / T^{a_j}$. The adaptive window methods described earlier use a near optimal addition-subtraction chain to compute T^E mod M. However these methods do not prescribe how to perform the pre-processing step (line 1 of Algorithm 3). In the following we give show how to perform this step with minimal number of modular multiplications.

There is a generalisation of the concept of addition-subtraction chains, which can be used to formalise the problem of finding a minimal sequence of powers that should be computed in the pre-processing step of the adaptive window method.

An *addition-subtraction sequence* for the list of positive integers $V_0, V_1, \ldots, V_p$ such that $V_0 > V_1 > \ldots > V_p$ is an addition-subtraction chain for integer V_p, which includes all the remaining integers $V_0, V_1, \ldots, V_p$ of the list. The length of an addition-subtraction sequence is the numbers of integers that constitute the chain. An addition-subtraction sequence for a list of positive integers $V_0, V_1, \ldots, V_p$ will be denoted by $S(V_0, V_1, \ldots, V_p)$.

Hence, to optimise the number of modular multiplications needed in the pre-processing step of the adaptive window methods for computing T^E mod M, we need to find an addition-subtraction sequence of minimal length (or simply minimal addition-subtraction sequence) for the values of the partitions included in the non-redundant ordered list $\wp(E)$. This is an *NP*-hard problem and we use genetic algorithm to solve it. General principles of genetic algorithms are explained in the next section.

4   Addition-Subtraction Sequence Minimisation Problem

It is perfectly clear that the shorter the addition-subtraction sequence is, the faster Algorithm 3. We propose a novel idea based on genetic algorithm to solve this minimisation problem. The addition-subtraction sequence minimisation problem consists of finding a sequence of numbers that constitutes an addition-subtraction sequence for a given ordered list of n positive integers, say V_i for $1 \le i \le n-1$. The addition-subtraction sequence should be of a minimal length.

4.1   Individual Encoding

Encoding of individuals is one of the implementation decisions one has to take in order to use genetic algorithms. It very depends on the nature of the problem to solve. There are several representations that have been used with success: *binary encoding* which is the most common mainly because it was used in the first works on genetic algorithms, represents an individual as a string of bits; *permutation encoding* mainly used in ordering problem, encodes an individual as a sequence of integer; *value encoding* represents an individual as a sequence of values that are some evaluation of some aspect of the problem [9], [11].

In our implementation, an individual represents an addition sequence. We use the binary encoding wherein 1 implies that the entry number is a member of the addition sequence and 0 otherwise. Let $V_1 = 3$, $V_2 = 7$ and $V_3 = 13$, be the exponent, the encoding of Fig. 1 represents the addition-subtraction chain $(1, 2, 4, 6)$:

1	2	3	4	5	6	7	8	9	10	11	12	13	14
1	1	1	1	0	0	1	0	0	0	0	0	1	1

Fig. 1. Addition-subtraction sequence encoding

4.2 The Genetic Operators

The main genetic operators are the *selection, mutation* and *crossover* operators as well as the *fitness* evaluation function. The implementations of these operators are described in the following.

Selection. The selection function as described in Algorithm 4, returns two populations: one represents the population of first parents, which is *parents*[1][] and the other consists of the population of second parents, which is *parents*[2][].

Algorithm 4. `select(population pop):population[]`
```
  1: population[] parents[2];
  2: for i = 1 to popSize
  3:    n1 = random(0,1); n2 = random(0,1);
  4:    for j = 1 to popSize do
  5:       parents[1][i]= parents[2][i]= parents[popSize];
  6:       if SP[j] ≥ n1 then parents[1][i] = pop[j]
  8:          else if SP[j] ≥ n2 then parents[2][i]=pop[j];
 10: return parents;
end algorithm.
```

The selection proceeds like this: whenever no individual that attends to the selection criteria is encountered, one of the last individuals of the population is then chosen, i.e. one of the fitter individuals of population. Note that the population from which the parents are selected is sorted in decreasing order with respect to the fitness of individuals, which will be described later on. The array *SP* consists of *selection probabilities* is set up at initialisation step and privileges fitter individuals.

Crossover. There are many ways how to perform crossover such as *single-point crossover, double-points crossover, uniform crossover* and *arithmetic crossover*. The use of these depends on the individual encoding used [9].

The single point and two points crossover use randomly selected crossover points to allow variation in the generated offspring and to avoid premature convergence on a local optimum [2], [9]. In our implementation, we tested all four-crossover strategies.

Mutation. Mutation consists of changing some genes of some individuals of the current population. The number of individuals that should be mutated is given by the parameter *mutation rate* (*mr*) while the parameter *mutation degree* (*md*) states how many genes of a selected individual should be altered.

The mutation parameters have to be chosen carefully as if mutation occurs very often then the genetic algorithm would in fact change to *random search* [2]. Algorithm 5 describes the mutation procedure used in our genetic algorithm.

When either of *mr* or *md* is null, the population is then kept unchanged, i.e. the population obtained from the crossover procedure represents actually the next generation population.

Algorithm 5. `mutate(population pop, int md, int mr):population;`
```
1: if(mr ≠ 0)and(md ≠ 0)then
2:    for a = 1 to PopSize do
3:       n = random(0,1);
4:       if n ≤ mr then
5:          for i = 1 to md do
6:             gene = random(2, n-1);
7:             pop[a][gene] = (pop[a][gene]+1) mod 2;
8: return pop;
end algorithm.
```

Fitness. This step of the genetic algorithm allows us to classify the population so that fitter individuals are selected more often to contribute in the constitution of a new population.

The fitness evaluation of addition-subtraction chain is done with respect to two aspects: *(i)* how much a given addition-subtraction chain adheres to the Definition 1, i.e. how many members of the addition-subtraction chain cannot be obtained summing up two previous members of the chain; *(ii)* how far the addition-subtraction chain is reduced, i.e. what is the length of the addition-subtraction chain. Algorithm 6 describes the evaluation of fitness used in our genetic algorithm.

For a valid addition sequence, the fitness function returns its length, which is smaller than the last integer V_n. The evolutionary process attempts to minimise the number of ones in a valid addition sequence and so minimise the corresponding length. Individuals with fitness larger or equal to V_n are invalid addition-subtraction chains. The constant *Penalty* should be larger than V_n. With well-chosen parameters, the genetic algorithm deals only with valid addition sequences.

Algorithm 6. `int evaluate(individual s)`
```
1: int fitness = 0;
2: for i = 2 to n-1 do
3:    if s[i] == 1 then fitness = fitness + 1;
5:    if i == Vᵢ & s[i]≠1 then fitness = fitness + Penalty;
7:    if ∄ j,k s.t. 1≤j,k≤i & i=j+k|i=j-k & s[i]=s[k]=1 then
8:       fitness = fitness + Penalty;
9: return fitness;
end algorithm.
```

5 Implementation Results

In applications of genetic algorithms to a practical problem, it is difficult to predict a priori what combination of settings will produce the best result for the problem in a relatively short time. The settings consist of the population size, the crossover type, the mutation rate and the mutation degree. We investigated the impact of different values of these parameters in order to choose the more adequate ones to use. We found out that the ideal parameters are: a population of at most 50 individuals; the double-points crossover; a mutation rate between 0.4 and 0.7 and a mutation degree of about 1% of the value of the last value in sequence V.

The Brun's algorithm [1] yields (1, 2, 4, 6, 7, 8, 15, 17, 30, 47, 94, 109, 117, 234, 343) and the genetic algorithm yield the same addition sequence as well as (1, 2, 4, 8, 10, 11, 18, 36, 47, 55, 91, 109, 117, 226, 343). Both addition sequences have the same length. Using these addition sequences to perform the pre-computation step requires 14 modular multiplications. The fittest addition-subtraction chain evolved by our genetic algorithm for the list partition values 47, 117 and 343 was (1, 2, 3, 5, 7, 12, 24, 48, 47, 43, 86, 129, 117, 172, 344, 343). It requires 11 multiplications and 4 divisions.

Finding the best addition-subtraction sequence is impractical. However, we can find near-optimal ones. Our genetic algorithm always finds addition sequences far shorter than those used by the m-ary method and the sliding windows independently of the value of m and the partition strategy used respectively, and as short as the addition sequence yield by the Brun's algorithm. Concerning the addition-subtraction chains, we do not know of any previous results to compare ours with.

A comparison of the performance of the m-ary, sliding window and the Brun's method vs. the genetic algorithm is shown in Fig. 2. A satisfactory addition sequence can be obtained in a 7 seconds to 2 minutes using a Pentium III with a 256 MB of RAM.

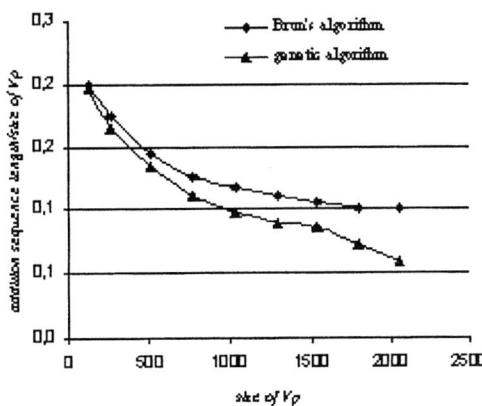

Fig. 2. Ratio for the addition sequences yield by the GA vs. Brun's methods.

6 Conclusions

In this paper, we presented an application of genetic algorithms to minimisation of addition sequences. We first explained how individuals are encoded. Then we described the necessary algorithmic solution. Then we presented some empirical observations about the performance of the genetic algorithm implementation.

This application of genetic algorithms to the minimisation problem proved to be very useful and effective technique. Shorter addition sequences compared with those obtained by the m-ary methods, those obtained for the sliding window methods as well as those obtained using Brun's algorithm can be obtained with a little computational effort.

References

1.   Begeron, R. Berstel, J, Brlek, S. and Duboc, C., *Addition chains using continued fractions*, Journal of Algorithms, no. 10, pp. 403–412, 1989.
2.   DeJong, K. and Spears, W.M., *An analysis of the interacting roles of the population size and crossover type in genetic algorithms*, In Parallel problem solving from nature, pp. 38–47, Springer-Verlag, 1990.
3.   DeJong, K. and Spears, W.M., *Using genetic algorithms to solve NP-complete problems*, Proceedings of the Third International Conference on Genetic Algorithms, pp. 124–132, Morgan Kaufmann, 1989.
4.   Erdös, P., *Remarks on number theory III: On addition chain*, Acta Arithmetica, pp 77–81, 1960.
5.   Haupt, R.L. and Haupt, S.E., *Practical genetic algorithms*, John Wiley and Sons, New York, 1998.
6.   Knuth, D.E., *The Art of Programming: Seminumerical Algorithms*, vol. 2. Reading, MA: Addison_Wesley, Second edition, 1981.
7.   Koç, Ç.K., *High-speed RSA Implementation*, Technical report, RSA Laboratories, Redwood City, califirnia, USA, November 1994.
8.   Kunihiro, N. and Yamamoto, H., *New methods for generating short addition chain*, IEICE Transactions, vol. E83-A, no. 1, pp. 60–67, January 2000.
9.   Michalewics, Z., *Genetic algorithms + data structures = evolution program*, Springer-Verlag, USA, third edition, 1996.
10. Menezes, A.J., *Elliptic curve public key cryptosystems*, Kluwer Academic, 1993.
11. Neves, J., Rocha, M., Rodrigues, Biscaia, M. and Alves, J., *Adaptive strategies and the design evolutionary applications*, Proceedings of the Genetic and the Design of Evolutionary Computation Conference, Orlando, Florida, USA, 1999.
12. Nedjah, N. and Mourelle, L.M., *Minimal addition chains using genetic algorithms*, Proceedings of the Fifteenth International Conference on Industrial & Engineering Applications of Artificial Intelligence & Expert Systems, Cairns, Australia, (to appear in Lecture Notes in Computer Science, Springer-Verlag), 2002.
13. Rivest, R.L., Shamir, A. and Adleman, L., *A method for obtaining digital signature and public-key cryptosystems*, Communication of ACM, vol. 21, no.2, pp. 120–126, 1978.

Hybrid Recommendation: Combining Content-Based Prediction and Collaborative Filtering

Ekkawut Rojsattarat and Nuanwan Soonthornphisaj

Department of Computer Science
Faculty of Science, Kasetsart University
Bangkok, Thailand
{g4464024, fscinws}@ku.ac.th

Abstract. Recommender systems improve access to relevant products and information by making personalized suggestions based on historical data of user's likes and dislikes. They have become fundamental application in electronic commerce and information access, provide suggestions that effective prune large information spaces so that users are directed toward those item that best meet their needs and preferences. Collaborative filtering and content-based recommending are two fundamental techniques that have been proposed for performing recommendation. Both techniques have their own advantages however they cannot perform well in many situations. To improve performance, various hybrid techniques have been considered. This paper proposes a framework to improve the recommendation performance by combining content-based prediction based on Support Vector Machines and conventional collaborative filtering. The experimental results show that SVMs can improve the performance of the recommender system.

1 Introduction

The original motivation of a recommender system is to solve the information overload problem. The system aims to filter out insignificant materials but provides to the user with more important information. Nowadays, the recommender system also play important role in the business sector. Many e-commerce web sites are already using recommender systems to help their customers find product to purchase. Recommender systems employ historical data on users' preferences to predict items that fit the users. There are two traditional approaches to construct recommender systems: collaborative filtering and content-based recommending. Collaborative Filtering or Social Filtering uses explicit user feedback in the form of rating for item in given domain and utilize similarities and differences among profiles of several users in determining how to recommend an item. On the other hand, Content-Based Recommending learns individualized profile from descriptions of examples and provides recommendation by comparing representations of content contained in an item to representations of content that interest the user. As a result, content-based

J. Liu et al. (Eds.): IDEAL 2003, LNCS 2690, pp. 337–344, 2003.

methods can uniquely make recommendations without having to match their interest to the others.

Content-based recommending and collaborative filtering have been implemented in various domains. Both methods have their own advantages but they cannot perform well in many situations. For example, collaborative filtering cannot provide an efficient recommend if the rating matrix is sparse or have many items that have not been rated by users. Moreover, the content-based recommending lacks of the ability to provide serendipitous recommendations from learned user preference from descriptions of rated item and recommend items that have contents close to user preference. Our hypothesis is that the combination of both techniques should be able to enhance the accuracy of the recommendation.

In this paper, we propose an alternative technique for combining content-based prediction using Support Vector Machines and collaborative filtering based on neighborhood-based algorithm.

2   Background and Related Work

In this section we briefly review some of the previous works related to our work.

2.1 Collaborative Filtering (CF)

CF is the most familiar, most widely implemented and most mature of the recommender system technology. CF aggregates ratings or recommendations of items, recognizes commonalities between users on the basis of their ratings, and generate new recommendations based on inter-user comparison. A variety of collaborative filtering algorithms have designed and deployed. Tapestry [1] is one of earliest implementations of collaborative filtering. GroupLens [2, 21] applied collaborative filtering to email and Usenet news. Ringo [3] and Video Recommender [4] used collaborative filtering to recommend music and movies. Herlocker, et al. presents an analysis of exist collaborative filtering algorithms [19].

The goal of the collaborative filtering is to predict the users' preference, referred to as the active user, based on the preference of a group of users. Collaborative filtering works by collecting human judgment (known as rating) for items in a given domain and matching with people who share the same information need or the same tastes. The problem space of the collaborative filtering can be formulated as a matrix of users versus items, with each cell representing a user's rating on specific item. Under this formulation, the problem is to predict the values of the specific empty cell.

2.2 Neighborhood-Based Algorithm

In neighborhood-based algorithm, a subset of users is chosen based on their similarities to the active user, and a weighted aggregate of their ratings is used to generate predictions for the active user. The neighborhood-based algorithm consists of three steps.

Step 1 Weight all users with respect to similarity of the active user. The similarities between users are measured using the Pearson correlation between their rating vectors as shown in equation 1.

$$P_{a,u} = \frac{\sum_{i=1}^{m}\left(r_{a,i} - \bar{r}_a\right) \times \left(r_{u,i} - \bar{r}_u\right)}{\sqrt{\sum_{i=1}^{m}\left(r_{a,i} - \bar{r}_a\right)^2 \times \sum_{i=1}^{m}\left(r_{u,i} - \bar{r}_u\right)^2}}$$

(1)

where $r_{a,i}$ is the rating given to items i by user a; and $\bar{r}_a$ is the mean rating given by user a; and m is the total number of items.

Step 2 Select n users that have the highest similarity to the active user. These users form the neighborhood.

Step 3 Compute a prediction from a weight combination of the selected neighbor's ratings. (See equation 2)

$$p_{a,i} = \bar{r}_a + \frac{\sum_{u=1}^{n}\left(r_{u,i} - \bar{r}_u\right) \times P_{a,u}}{\sum_{u=1}^{n} P_{a,u}}$$

(2)

where $p_{a,i}$ is the prediction for the active user a for item i; $P_{a,u}$ is the similarity between active users a and u; and n is the number of user in neighborhood.

Neighborhood-based algorithms have been used successfully to build recommender system in various domains. However they suffered from two fundamental problems.

The Sparse Matrix Problem is a problem that most users do not rate most items and hence the rate matrix is typically very sparse. Therefore, the probability of finding a set of users with significant similar rating is usually low. This is often the case when systems have very high item-to-user ratio this problem is highly affected when the system is in the initial stage of use.

Another problem of neighborhood-based algorithm is *The First-rater Problem*. In the neighborhood-based technique, the recommendation scores of each item are the weighted combination of the neighbor's rating. An item cannot be recommended unless a user has rated it before. This problem will occur when we apply new item into the system.

2.3 Content-Based Recommending (CB)

CB is an outgrowth and continuation of information filtering research [5]. In the content-based system, the objects of interest are defined by their associated features. For example, the newsgroup filtering system NewsWeeder [6] uses the words of their text as features. CB learns a profile of the user's interests based on the features that present in items the user has rated. For that reason, it can make recommendations without having to match their interest to someone else's.

CB has been applied to build recommender systems in various domains. LIBRA [11] is content-based book recommender system which applies automated text categorization method, naive Bayes classifier, by using a database of book information extracted from web pages at Amazon.com. Syskill&Webert [10] suggest web pages that might interest the user.

The drawback of CB is lacking of "cross-genre" or "outside the box" recommendation ability from learned user preference from descriptions of rated item and recommended items that have contents close to user preference.

2.4 Support Vector Machines (SVMs)

Support Vector Machines is a new binary classification technique which based on the principle of the structural risk minimization [7]. The approach aims to minimize the upper bound of the generalization error through maximizing the margin between the separating hyperplane and data.

In the basic form, SVMs learn linear decision rules $h(x) = sign\{w \cdot x + b\}$ described by a weight vector w and a threshold b. Input is a sample of n training example $S_n = ((x_1, y_1), \ldots, (x_n, y_n))$, $x_i \in \Re^N$, $y_i \in \{-1, +1\}$. For linearly separable S_n, SVMs find the optimal margin hyperplane with maximum Euclidian distance to the closet training examples by solving an optimization problem [15].

$$\text{minimize} \quad 1/2 \|w\|^2$$
$$\text{subject to the constraints:} \quad (1) \quad y_i(w \cdot x_i + b) \geq 1 \quad, i = 1, \ldots, l \tag{3}$$

The main problem with the optimal margin hyperplane is that it always produces perfectly a consistent hypothesis, which is a hypothesis with no training error. Now we introduce the soft margin hyperplane which allow us to construct the maximum margin hyperplane with some training error. By adding a penalty term (the sum of deviations ξ_i) to the minimization problem [13].

$$\text{minimize} \quad 1/2 \|w\|^2 + C \sum_{i=1}^{l} \xi_i$$
$$\text{subject to the constraints:} \quad (1) \quad y_i(w \cdot x_i + b) \geq 1 - \xi_i \quad, i = 1, \ldots, l \tag{4}$$
$$(2) \quad \xi_i \geq 0, \forall_i.$$

where C is the weight of penalty term for misclassifying training examples. Selecting large value of C spend more computation time since it requires more exhaustive search to minimize the number of misclassified examples.

For a multi-class classification problem, SVMs treats the problem as a collection of binary classification problems. In this subsection, we discuss two multi-class classification approaches for SVMs.

The one-against-the-rest approach is approach works by constructing a set of k binary classifiers. The ith classifier is trained with all of the examples in the ith class with positive labels, and all other example with negative labels. The final output is the class that corresponds to the classifier with the highest output value [15].

The one-against-one approach constructs all possible two-class classifiers from a training set of k classes. Each classifier is trained on only two out of k classes. Thus, there will be $k(k-1)/2$ classifiers. Thubthong and Kijsirikul employs two algorithms, Max Wins algorithm and Decision Directed Acyclic Graph, to evaluate the final output

Max Wins algorithm. A test set is classified by all classifiers each classifier provides one vote for its preferred class and the majority vote is used to make the final output [16]. However, if there is more than one class giving the highest score, a class will be randomly select as the final output.

Decision Directed Acyclic Graph [14] uses a rooted binary direct acyclic graph with k leaves labeled by the classes where each of the $k(k-1)/2$ internal nodes is labeled with an element of Boolean function. The nodes are arranged in triangle with the single root node at the top, two nodes in the second layer and so on until the final layer of k leaves. The ith node in layer $j<k$ is connected to the ith and $(i+1)^{th}$ nodes in the $(j+1)^{th}$ layer. To evaluate a Decision Directed Acyclic Graph, start at the root node, the binary function at a node is evaluated. The node is then exited via the left edge, if the binary function is -1; or the right edge, if the binary function is 1. The next node's binary function is then evaluated. The value of the decision function is the value associated with the final leaf node.

3   Our Approach

In our approach, we try to improve the performance of the recommendation process by unifying the content-based recommending and the collaborative filtering. In pure collaborative filtering, recommendation scores are the combination of ratings that given by n users who are chosen based on the Pearson correlation [19]. The sparsity of rating matrix becomes the difficulty in finding the way to choose n users in neighborhood. However, we can apply a useful property of content-based methods to defeat this problem. Accordingly, in our hybrid technique, we try to predict the rating of items that has not rated by the user using Support Vector Machines and perform neighborhood-based collaborative filtering on the dense rating matrix.

4   Experiment

4.1 Data Collection and Data Preprocessing

We utilize the EachMovie data set which provided by the GroupLens Research Project at the University of Minnesota as the data set. It consists of 943 users, 1682 movies in 18 genres (movies can be in several genres at once.) and 100,000 ratings (1-5). For each user has rated at least 20 movies. The content for each movie will be collected from the Internet Movie Database (IMDb). By crawling follow the IMDb hyperlinks provided for every movie in EachMovie data set and collecting information from various links of the main URL. We download contents such as director, cast, user comment, tagline, award, plot key-word and plot summary. For the preprocessing step, we eliminated stop words and other non-informative parts and modify several forms of name to unique token form (First name_Last name). The TF-IDF [17] is applied to weight each term in feature vector. Finally, we put them into a vector of words (one vector for each movie)

4.2 Content-Based Prediction

We treat user ratings 1-5 as one of five class labels and utilize the content of the movies in each class as training data. We apply both naive Bayes text classifier [12] and SVMs to construct a pseudo user-ratings vector for every user. The pseudo user-ratings vector, v_u consists of the item rating provided by user u, where available, and those predicted by the content-based predictor otherwise. The pseudo user-rating of all user put together give the dense pseudo rating matrix

4.3 Similarity Weighting

We now perform the collaborative filtering using dense rating matrix from the content-based prediction. The similarity between an active user, a, and another user, u, is computed using the Pearson correlation coefficient. Since the significant of similarities depends on the accuracy of content-based prediction, thus we multiply the similarities between the active user a and another u by hybrid correlation weight $hw_{a,u}$ [18].

$$hw_{a,u} = hm_{a,u} + sg_{a,u} \tag{5}$$

The $sg_{a,u}$ is the significant weighting factor. If two users have less than 50 co-rated items, $sg_{a,u}$ is $n/50$, where n is the number of co-rated items. If the number of overlapping items is greater than 50, then $sg_{a,u}$ is 1. $hw_{a,u}$ is the harmonic mean weighting factor computed by Equation 6.

$$hm_{a,u} = \frac{2m_a m_u}{m_a + m_u} \quad , \qquad m = \begin{cases} n/50 : \text{if } n < 50 \\ 1 \ : \text{otherwise} \end{cases} \tag{6}$$

4.4 Producing Prediction

The prediction of the combination is computed as follows:

$$P_{a,i} = \overline{v}_a + \frac{sw_a(c_{a,i} - \overline{v}_a) + \sum_{u=1}^{n} hw_{a,u} P_{a,u}(v_{u,i} - \overline{v}_u)}{sw_a + \sum_{u=1}^{n} hw_{a,u} P_{a,u}} \tag{7}$$

In Equation 9, $c_{a,i}$ corresponds to the content-based prediction for the active user, a, and item i. $v_{u,i}$ is the pseudo rating for user u and item i and sw_a is self weighting factor for content-based prediction in the final prediction.

5   Results

We compare the performance of our approach to hybrid technique using naive Bayes Classifier, pure content-based methods and pure collaborative filtering. MAE (Mean Absolute Error) and ROC (Receiver Operating Characteristic) [19] are applied for the evaluation metrics. After we ran the experiment five times using 5-fold cross validation [12], the results of the experiment are summarized in table 1.

Table 1. Summary of experimental results

Algorithm	MAE	ROC-4
Pure content-based using NB	0.9113	0.6279
Pure content-based using SVMs	0.8840	0.6448
Pure collaborative filtering	0.9236	0.6517
Hybrid approach using NB	0.8604	0.6782
Hybrid approach using SVMs	0.8312	0.6947

The results show that our hybrid approach present better performances than the other algorithms on both metrics. On the MAE metric, our approach performs 6.6% better than pure content-based using NB, 3.7% better than pure content-based using SVMs, 7.8% better than pure CF, 2.2% better than hybrid approach using NB.

On the ROC-4 metric, our approach performs 10.6% better than pure content-based using NB, 7.7% better than pure content-based using SVMs, 6.6% better than pure CF, 2.4% better than hybrid approach using NB. This means that our approach has higher ability to recommend high quality items than other algorithms.

6   Conclusion and Future Work

We found that the combination of content-based prediction and collaborative filtering obtains better performance than either content-based methods or collaborative filtering. The content-based prediction part of our approach can solve the sparse matrix and the first-rater problem of pure CF by predicted ratings of unrated items using prior knowledge about user preference from rated items. Moreover, hybrid technique also has "cross genre" recommendation ability which is the constraint of pure CB. Since the performance of the hybrid approach usually depends on the accuracy of the content-based prediction, the experimental results show that Support Vector Machines contributes to a better performance than the naive Bayes classifier in content-based prediction tasks. This leads to the performance enhancement of the hybrid recommendation.

Although, our hybrid approach improves the performance of recommendation, but the difference is not very large. We are currently attempting to improve the performance of hybrid technique by applying Transductive Support Vector Machines [20], to enhance the accuracy of content-based prediction. Besides, we also plan to test the performance of hybrid approach with other collaborative filtering algorithms in the future.

References

1.   Goldberg, D., Nichols, D., Oki, B. M., Terry, D.: Using Collaborative Filtering to Weave an Information Tapestry. Communications of the ACM 35(12). (1992) 61–70

2.   Resnick, P., Iacovou N., Suchak M., Bergstorm P., Riedl J.: GroupLens: An open architecture for collaborative filtering of netnews. In Proceedings of 1994 Conference on Computer Supported Collaborative Work. (1994) 175–186

3.   Shardanand, U., Maes P.: Social information filtering: Algorithms for automating "Word of Mouth". In Proceeding of ACM CHI'95. (1995) 210–217

4. Hill, W., Stead, L., Rosenstein, M., Riedl, J.: Recommending and Evaluating Choice in a Virtual Community of Use. In Proceedings of CHI'95. (1995) 194–201
5. Belkin, N. J., Croft, W. B.: Information Filtering and Information Retrieval: Two Sides of the Same Coin? Communications of ACM 35(12). (1992) 29–38
6. Lang, K.: Newsweeder: Learning to Filter News. In Proceeding of the 12th International Conference on Machine Learning, Lake Tohoe, CA, (1995) 331–339.
7. Burges, C.: A tutorial on Support Vector Machines for pattern recognition. Data Mining and Knowledge Discovery 2(2) (1998) 121–167
8. EachMovie dataset. http://research.compaq.com/SRC/eachmovie.
9. Internet Movie Database. http://www.imdb.com.
10. Pazzani M., Muramatsu J., Billsus D.: Syskill & Webert: Identifying interesting web sites. In Proceedings of the Thirteenth National Conference on Artificial Intelligence. (1996) 54–61
11. Mooney, R. J., Roy L.: Content-based book recommending using learning for text categorization. In Proceedings of the Fifth ACM Conference on Digital Libraries. (2000) 195–204
12. Mitchell, T. M.: Machine Learning. Mc Graw Hill. (1997)
13. Cristianini, N., Taylor J.S.: An introduction to Support Vector Machines and other kernel-based learning methods. Cambridge University Press. (2000)
14. Thubthong, N., Kijsirikul B.: Support Vector Machines for Thai phoneme recognition. International Journal of Uncertainty, Fuzziness and Knowledge-Based Systems. (2001)
15. Vapnik, V.: Statistical Learning Theory. Wiley. (1998)
16. Friedman, J. H.: Another approach to polychotomous classification. Technical report, Department of Statistics, Standford. (1996)
17. Salton, G.: Automatic text processing: The transformation, analysis, and retrieval of information by Computer. Wesley. (1989)
18. Melville, P., Mooney R. J., Nagarajan R. Content-boosted collaborative filtering. In Proceeding of the SIGIR-2001 Workshop on Recommender Systems. (2001)
19. Herlocker, J., Konstan J., Borchers A., Riedl J.: An algorithmic framework for performing collaborative filtering. In Proceedings of the 1999 Conference on Research and Development in Information Retrieval. (1999)
20. Joachims, T. Transductive inference for text classification using Support Vector Machines. In Proceeding of 16th International Conference on Machine Learning. (1999)
21. Konstan, J. A., Miller B. N., Maltz D., Herlocker J. L., Gordon L. R., Riedl J.: GroupLens: Applying collaborative filtering to Usenet news. Communication of the ACM 40(3). (1997) 77–87

A Tolerance Concept in Data Clustering

Fu-Shing Sun and Chun-Hung Tzeng

Computer Science Department
Ball State University
Muncie, IN 47306
{fsun, tzeng}@cs.bsu.edu

Abstract. This paper introduces the concept of tolerance space as an abstract model of data clustering. The similarity in the model is represented by a relation with both reflexivity and symmetry, called a tolerance relation. Three types of clusterings based on a tolerance relation are introduced: maximal complete similarity clustering, representative clustering, and closure clustering. This paper also discusses experiments on unsupervised learning, in which Hamming distance is used to define a family of tolerance relations.

1 Introduction

This paper reports some preliminary results of a study of tolerance space as a mathematical data-clustering model. The task of data clustering is to group *similar* data together [4]. Numerical (continuous) data has inherent property of similarity. For example, an Euclidean distance function can be used to measure similarity. For non-numerical (e.g., boolean or categorical) data, the concept of such similarity is vague and sometimes intuitive. Many metrics have been used to measure such similarity (or dissimilarity) such as simple matching coefficient, Jaccard coefficient, and category utility functions [3,4,5].

This paper uses a *reflexive* and *symmetric* binary relation to postulate a similarity. That is, an object is always similar to itself. And if an object x is similar to another object y, then y should also be similar to x. Preciseness among similarities is defined by comparing related binary relations. A set of elements with such a relation is called a *tolerance space* and the relation is called a *tolerance relation* [6]. In a tolerance space, three types of clustering based on the given similarity are introduced: maximal complete similarity (MCS) clustering, representative clustering, and closure clustering. Except the closure clustering, the clusterings in a tolerance space are in general not partitions. That is, two clusters may have non-empty intersection, which is common in many real-world problems. Both MCS and representative clusterings depend on data input order. However, each closure clustering is always insensitive to input order.

This paper provides a different view in the study of data clustering, where clusters are derived from the data similarity. To demonstrate the use of tolerance space, this paper introduces experiments on a machine learning task. The example is learning by observation and does not use the predefined classes in data

J. Liu et al. (Eds.): IDEAL 2003, LNCS 2690, pp. 345–352, 2003.
© Springer-Verlag Berlin Heidelberg 2003

clustering [4]. As a result, relative to a certain tolerance relation, the predefined classes are re-discovered.

The rest of the paper is organized as follows. Section 2 is the introduction of tolerance space. Section 3 introduces the three types of data clustering. Experimental results are discussed in Section 4. Conclusion and future work are in Section 5.

2   Tolerance Relations

Let Ω be a finite set. A binary relation ξ on Ω is a subset of the Cartesian product: $\xi \subset \Omega \times \Omega$.

Definition 2.1 A *tolerance relation* ξ on Ω is a binary relation with the following conditions

1. $(x, x) \in \xi$ for any $x \in \Omega$ (reflexivity), and
2. $(x, y) \in \xi \Rightarrow (y, x) \in \xi$ (symmetry).

The pair (Ω, ξ) is called a *tolerance space*.

We also use ξ as the predicate: $\xi(x, y)$ if and only if $(x, y) \in \xi$. If $\xi(x, y)$, we say that x is ξ-*similar* to y. We use *similar* directly if there is no ambiguity. On each metric space (M, d) (including Hamming distance), we may define a set of tolerance relations. For each positive real number $\varepsilon > 0$, the relation d_ε defined in the following is a tolerance relation: for $x, y \in M$, $d_\varepsilon(x, y)$ if $d(x, y) < \varepsilon$. That is, x is d_ε-*similar* to y if the metric between x and y is less than ε.

Any undirected graph can be treated as a tolerance space (and vice versa), where Ω is the set of all vertices, and two vertices are similar if they are the same vertex or they are adjacent (e.g., Figure 1). Any equivalent relation ξ of a space Ω is a special tolerance relation which has the transitive property: $\xi(x, y)$ and $\xi(y, z) \Rightarrow \xi(x, z)$. We define preciseness among tolerance relations as follows. Let ξ and η be two tolerance relations on a space Ω.

Definition 2.2 The tolerance relation ξ is *more precise* than η or η is *less precise* than ξ if $\xi \subset \eta$, denoted by $\xi \leq \eta$. That is,

$$\xi \leq \eta \text{ if } \xi(x, y) \Rightarrow \eta(x, y) \text{ for any } x, y \in \Omega.$$

It is always $\xi \leq \xi$. If $\xi \leq \eta$, then any ξ-similar elements are also η-similar. For a metric space (M, d), we always have that $d_{\varepsilon_1} \leq d_{\varepsilon_2}$ if $\varepsilon_1 \leq \varepsilon_2$.

On the space Ω, the *most precise* tolerance relation, denoted by Ω^0, is the relation in which each element x is similar only to x itself. We call Ω^0 the *discrete tolerance relation*. On the other hand, the *least precise* tolerance relation, denoted by Ω^∞, is the relation in which all elements are similar. We call Ω^∞ the *trivial tolerance relation*.

From a tolerance space (Ω, ξ), we define a sequence of related tolerance relations. We say that an element x can reach an element y in k ($k \geq 1$) steps if there are $k - 1$ elements $w_1, w_2, ..., w_{k-1}$, so that the following pairs are similar: $(x, w_1), (w_1, w_2), ..., (w_{k-1}, y)$. Suppose Ω has n elements. If y is reachable from x, then x can always reach y in less than n steps because a path consisting of more than n vertices has an unnecessary cycle. Such reachability defines following tolerance relations.

Definition 2.3 The $k-extended$ *tolerance relation* ξ^k is the relation such that $\xi^k(x,y)$ if x can reach y in no more than k steps.

Note that $\xi^1 = \xi$. Let ξ^∞ be the union of all ξ^k's; that is, $\xi^\infty(x,y)$ if and only if x can reach y eventually. Actually, ξ^∞ is the transitive closure of ξ and is an equivalent relation. We call ξ^∞ the *closure* of ξ. The extended tolerance relation ξ^k becomes the closure ξ^∞ when k is large enough (e.g., $k \geq n$). All ξ^k's form an increasing sequence: $\Omega^0 \leq \xi^1(= \xi) \leq \xi^2 \leq ... \leq \xi^{n-2} \leq \xi^{n-1} = \xi^\infty \leq \Omega^\infty$. Note that the data reachability in [1,4] is the concept of this extended tolerance relation. The extended tolerance relations can be represented by the following matrix.

Definition 2.4 The *similarity matrix* S_ξ of the tolerance space (Ω, ξ) is a function on $\Omega \times \Omega$ with the following properties.

1. $S_\xi(x,x) = 0$ for any $x \in \Omega$,
2. $S_\xi(x,y) = k$ if $\xi^k(x,y)$ but not $\xi^{k-1}(x,y)$,
3. $S_\xi(x,y) = \infty$ for other cases.

If we label the elements of Ω by 1, 2, ..., and n (n is the number of elements in Ω), then S_ξ is a symmetric $n \times n$ matrix, in which all values on the diagonal are zeros. For the discrete relation Ω^0, $S_{\Omega^0}(x,y) = \infty$ for any $x \neq y$. For the trivial relation Ω^∞, $S_{\Omega^\infty}(x,y) = 1$ for any $x \neq y$. Consider (Ω, ξ) as an undirected graph and the length of each edge is 1. Then $S_\xi(x,y)$ is the shortest distance from x to y, which can be computed by Dijkstra's shortest-path algorithm.

For example, the similarity matrix of the tolerance space in Figure 1 is as follows.

Table 1. The similarity matrix of Figure 1.

	1	2	3	4	5	6	7
1	0	1	1	2	3	∞	∞
2	1	0	1	2	3	∞	∞
3	1	1	0	1	2	∞	∞
4	2	2	1	0	1	∞	∞
5	3	3	2	1	0	∞	∞
6	∞	∞	∞	∞	∞	0	1
7	∞	∞	∞	∞	∞	1	0

From the matrix S_ξ, the extended tolerance relation can be derived by as follows. Let $x, y \in \Omega$.

1. $\xi^k(x,y)$ if and only if $S_\xi(x,y) \leq k$.
2. $\xi^\infty(x,y)$ if and only if $S_\xi(x,y) \neq \infty$.

This matrix is useful in computing clusters studied in this paper.

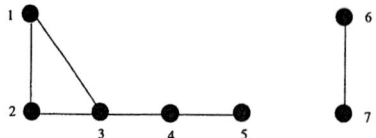

Fig. 1. A tolerance space.

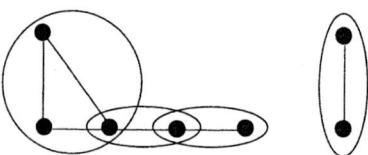

Fig. 2. All MCS clusters.

3   Data Clusterings of a Tolerance Space

In this section, we study meaningful clusters based on a tolerance relation. Let (Ω, ξ) be a tolerance space. First consider subspaces in which all elements are similar to each other. Such a subspace is called a *complete similarity* set. For example, each singleton is a complete similarity set. Any two similar elements also form a complete similarity set.

Definition 3.1 A *maximal complete similarity cluster* (an MCS cluster) M of ξ is a maximal subset of Ω having the following property: $x, y \in M \Rightarrow \xi(x, y)$. M_ξ is the set of all MCS clusters.

For any element $x \in \Omega$, the complete similarity set $\{x\}$ is always contained in an MCS cluster, which is not necessarily unique in general. For example, all MCS clusters of Figure 1 are shown on Figure 2, in which the vertex 3 is contained in two MCS clusters $\{1, 2, 3\}$ and $\{3, 4\}$.

Second, we consider clusters representable by single elements.
Definition 3.2 For an element $x \in \Omega$ and an integer $k \geq 1$, the *representative cluster* of order k at x is the set $\xi^k(x) = \{y \in \Omega : \xi^k(x, y)\}$, and x is called the *representative*. $\mathbf{R}_\xi^k$ is the set of all representative clusters of order k.

The cluster $\xi^k(x)$, uniquely determined by x, consists of all elements reachable from x in no more than k steps. For example, all representative clusters of order 1 of Figure 1 are shown in Figure 3.

Last, we consider the transitive closure ξ^∞. Since ξ^∞ is an equivalent relation, both the MCS clusters and the representative clusters degenerate into the partition of the equivalent relation. The member of the partition containing x is $\xi^\infty(x) = \{y \in \Omega : \xi^k(x, y)$ for an integer $k \geq 1\}$. The set $\xi^\infty(x)$ is called the *closure cluster* at x. And the corresponding partition of ξ^∞ is called the *closure partition* of ξ (e.g., Figure 6): $\mathbf{R}_\xi^\infty = \{\xi^\infty(x) : x \in \Omega\}$. Elements from different closure clusters can never reach to each other through the tolerance relation ξ.

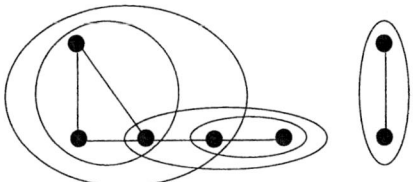

Fig. 3. All representative clusters of order 1.

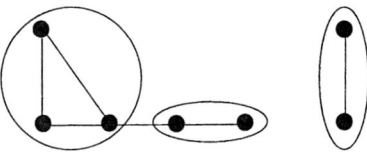

Fig. 4. An MCS clustering.

A *clustering* of a space Ω is a family of subspaces $\mathbf{C} = \{C_i : 1 \leq i \leq k\}$ such that Ω is the union of the subspaces:

$$\bigcup_{i=1}^{k} C_i = \Omega,$$

and any proper subfamily does not have this property; that is, we cannot remove any C_i away from $\mathbf{C}$. Each C_i is called a *cluster*. Each partition of Ω is always a clustering. But in our definition, a clustering is in general not a partition and two clusters may have a non-empty intersection.

Let (Ω, ξ) be a tolerance space. From the families of clusters $\mathbf{M}_\xi$, $\mathbf{R}_\xi^k$, and $\mathbf{R}_\xi^\infty$, we define the following clusterings.

Definition 3.3 A clustering of the tolerance space is called a *maximal complete similarity clustering* (MCS clustering) if each cluster is an MCS cluster. A clustering is called a *representative clustering* of order k ($k \geq 1$) if each cluster is a representative cluster of order k. The closure partition $\mathbf{R}_\xi^\infty$, being a clustering, is also called the *closure clustering*.

The tolerance space has in general different MCS clusterings and representative clusterings, which depend on data input order in computation. However, the closure clustering $\mathbf{R}_\xi^\infty$ is always unique; that is, $\mathbf{R}_\xi^\infty$ is insensitive to data input order. Each MCS cluster is in a closure cluster and so are representative clusters. Therefore, all MCS clusterings and representative clusterings have at least as many clusters as $\mathbf{R}_\xi^\infty$ has. For example, Figure 4 is an MCS clustering, Figure 5 is a representative clustering of order 1, and Figure 6 is the closure clustering.

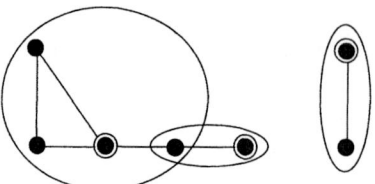

Fig. 5. A representative clustering of order 1.

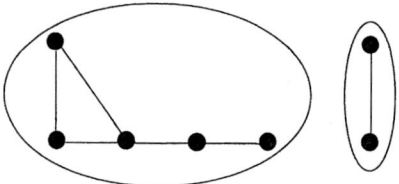

Fig. 6. The Closure clustering.

4   Experiments

In this section, we show some initial results of our experiments on the popular
soybean disease dataset from UC Irvine machine learning data repository [7].
We use the smaller soybean dataset, denoted by Ω, which consists of 47 records
with 35 attributes (denoted by A_k , $1 \leq k \leq 35$) and in 4 diagnosis classes: $D1$,
$D2$, $D3$, and $D4$ (as the 36th attribute, denoted by A_{36}). All the 35 attributes
are in categorical values [2]. The dataset is split into two subsets: the learning
set (31 records), denoted by Ω_l, and the testing set (16 records), denoted by Ω_t.

As an example of learning by observation [4], the experiments do not use the
given diagnosis classes (i.e., A_{36}) in clustering the data set Ω (47 records). And
each attribute A_k ($1 \leq k \leq 35$) is equally weighted in the tolerance relations
defined by Hamming distance.

Each record is a vector of the 35 attributes. Let $H(x, y)$ be the Hamming
distance between x and y, which is the number of attributes A_k's ($1 \leq k \leq
35$) on which x and y have different values. For an integer $\varepsilon > 0$, consider
the tolerance relation: $H_\varepsilon(x, y)$ if $H(x, y) < \varepsilon$. The relation H_1 is the discrete
tolerance relation: $H(x, y) \geq 1$ for any different records x and y. On the other
hand, H_{20} is the trivial tolerance relation: $H(x, y) < 20$ for any two records x
and y. In the experiment, several ε's have been chosen. For each ε, we compute a
representative clustering of order k starting from $k = 1$ until the closure partition
is found. A summary of the experiment is shown on Table 2.

For fixed ε and k, a representative clustering is not a partition in general.
Furthermore, the clusterings depend on the input order. However, the closure
partitions are insensitive to the input order. For the discrete relation H_1, each
record forms a cluster of order 1; therefore, there are 47 clusters, which already
form the closure partition. For $\varepsilon = 3$, the representative clustering of order 1
has 39 clusters. The closure partition is found when the clustering of order 2

Table 2. A summary of experiments.

ε	no_of_clusters of order 1	no_of_clusters of order 2	no_of_clusters of order 3	no_of_clusters of order 4	diagnosis family of closure partition
1	**47** (closure)				47 singletons
3	39	35	**34** (closure)		34 singletons
4	27	20	20	**17** (closure)	17 singletons
5	17	10	**7** (closure)		7 singletons
6	12	5	**4** (closure)		$((D1)(D2)(D3)(D4))$
7	7	4	4	**3** (closure)	$((D1)(D2)(D3\ D4))$
9	5	3	**3** (closure)		$((D1)(D2)(D3\ D4))$
10	5	3	**2** (closure)		$((D2)(D1\ D3\ D4))$
15	2	**1** (closure)			$((D1\ D2\ D3\ D4))$
17	**1** (closure)				$((D1\ D2\ D3\ D4))$

has been computed. When ε is increased, the number of clusters decreases. For example, all H_ε's for $\varepsilon = 7, 8, 9$ have the same closure partition, which has only three clusters. Finally, both H_{15} and H_{17} has only one closure cluster: the whole space of the 47 records.

For interpretation of the clusterings, we study Attribute 36. We assemble all diagnoses of each cluster into a list, called the *diagnosis set* of the cluster. The *diagnosis family* of a clustering is the list of all diagnosis sets. The diagnosis families of the closure partitions for $\varepsilon \geq 6$ are explicitly shown on Table 2. If all records in a cluster have the same diagnosis, then its diagnosis set is a singleton. All diagnosis sets are singletons for $\varepsilon \leq 6$. If a cluster consists of records of different diagnoses, the diagnosis set becomes a list of the different diagnoses. For the significance of the clusterings, we consider the clusters in terms of the disease diagnoses first. If two records are in the same cluster, we would like them to have the same diagnosis. Under this consideration, H_ε is a well-defined similarity for $\varepsilon \leq 6$ but not for $\varepsilon \geq 7$. Next, we consider the number of clusters in each clustering. From a practical point of view a reasonable number of clusters is usually desired. Under this consideration, the similarities H_1, H_3 and H_4 are not favorable because they induce too many clusters. Note that the closure clustering relative to H_6 is exactly the same as the given diagnosis classes.

5   Conclusion

This paper introduces tolerance space as a mathematical model of similarity in data-clustering tasks. Although this paper uses a heuristic Hamming function to measure similarity for a machine learning problem, more measure methods are still necessary for different types of problems. Our current effort is focusing on the mathematical theory of tolerance space and the conceptual clustering domain. In the future, we plan to extend the model with other features such as uncertainty reasoning and inference.

References

1. Ester, M., Kriegel, H.-P., Sander, J., and Xu, X. A Density-Based Algorithm for Discovering Clusters in Large Spatial Databases with Noise, *Proceedings of the 2nd International Conference on Knowledge Discovery and Data Mining*, pages 226–231, Portland, OR, USA, 1996.
2. Fisher, D. Knowledge Acquisition Via Incremental Concept Clustering, *Machine Learning*, 2, pages 139–172, 1987.
3. Goodall, D. W. A New Similarity Index Based on Probability, *Biometrics*, 22, pages 882–907, 1966.
4. Han, J. and Kamber, M. *Data Mining: Concepts and Techniques*, Morgan Kaufmann, 2001.
5. Mirkin, B. Reinterpreting the Category Utility Function, *Machine Learning*, 45, pages 219–228, 2001.
6. Tzeng, C.-H. and Tzeng, O. Tolerance Spaces and Almost Periodic Functions, *Bulletin of The Institute of Mathematics Academia Sinica*, (6), pages 159–173, 1978.
7. University of California at Irvine, Machine Learning Repository. http://www.ics.uci.edu/~mlearn/MLRepository.html

Power Control and Evolutionary Computation in CDMA Cellular Radio Networks

Won Jay Song[1], Sun Jin Kim[1], Won Hee Kim[2],
Byung Ha Ahn[3], Munkee Choi[1], and Bo Gwan Kim[2]

[1] Optical Internet Research Center and Grid Middleware Research Center,
Information and Communications University, 305-732, Republic of Korea
songwonjay@ieee.org & {kimsj,mkchoi}@icu.ac.kr
[2] VLSI and CAD Labs, Department of Electronics Engineering,
Chungnam National University, 305-764, Republic of Korea
kimwonhee@ieee.org & bgkim@cnu.ac.kr
[3] Systems Control and Management Labs, Department of Mechatronics,
KwangJu Institute of Science and Technology, 500-712, Republic of Korea
bayhay@kjist.ac.kr

Abstract. This paper has proposed the distributed power control (PC) algorithms that employ two evolutionary computation (EC) or genetic algorithm (GA) techniques in order to solve linear systems of equations for power update in CDMA cellular radio systems. The proposed algorithms are modeled on applying evolutionary computation algorithms with the phenotypic and genotypic views to the CDMA power control problem. The major gain from the applied evolutionary computation algorithms is more rapid optimization on linear systems of equations compared with the simple genetic algorithm (SGA). Employing the distributed constrained power control (DCPC) and bang-bang (BB) algorithms as the basic reference algorithms, we have designed and implemented computational experiments on the DS-CDMA system. The simulation results indicate that the proposed EC-DCPC phenotypic and GA-DCPC genotypic algorithms significantly decrease the mobile terminal power consumption compared with the DCPC and BB algorithms, respectively.

1 Introduction

Effectively centralized and distributed transmitter power controls in network levels should be essential and important for high-capacity cellular radio communication systems [3][4]. In special, the power control (PC) should be one direct solution for the near-far problem existing in a direct sequence (DS) code division multiple access (CDMA) system. In recent, many researchers have investigated a wide variety of power control algorithms from different viewpoints [1]-[14].

The optimization and calculation speed of power control algorithms are one of the most important role in a given power control algorithm. A preferable power control algorithm should quickly and distributively converge to the state of solutions, where the feasible system supports as many users as possible [15]. Modeling and designing such the feasible power control algorithms using genetic algorithms are the topic of this research paper [16][20]-[23].

J. Liu et al. (Eds.): IDEAL 2003, LNCS 2690, pp. 353–360, 2003.
© Springer-Verlag Berlin Heidelberg 2003

2   Cellular CDMA Distributed and Constrained Power Control System Models

2.1   Distributed Power Control Model

We have only considered an uplink (i.e., reverse link) of a cellular CDMA system [12][17]. The mobile terminals of M are active status in the system. We should only consider the snapshot analysis at a time instant. It means that the link gain between every base station of i and every mobile terminal of j is stationary and is given by the link gain matrix component of G_{ij}.

The received interference plus noise power is I_i at the receiver of i as follows

$$I_i = \sum_{i=1, i \neq j}^{M} C_{ij} G_{ij} P_{ij} + N_i \tag{1}$$

where N_i is the thermal noise at the receiver of i, P_j is the transmission power at the mobile terminal of j, and C_{ij} is the normalized cross-correlation factor between the signals from the transmitters of i and j at the receiver of i [15]. The factor is $C_{ij} = 1$ for $i \neq j$ and $C_{ij} = 0$ for $i = j$. We assume that each mobile should achieve a received signal-to-interference-plus-noise ratio (SINR) or carrier-to-interference ratio (CIR) of R_i as follows

$$R_i = \frac{G_{ii} P_i}{I_i} \geq T_i \tag{2}$$

where $i = 1, 2, 3, \cdots, M$. The above Eq. (2) means a minimum requirement for the mobile terminal of i in order to success communications such that R_i should be not less than T_i, where T_i is a minimum target SINR or CIR ratio. In order to make useful and mathematical equations using matrix and vector notations, we also define H_{ij} and B_i as follows

$$H_{ij} = \frac{R_i C_{ij} G_{ij}}{G_{ii}} \tag{3}$$

and

$$B_i = \frac{R_i N_i}{G_{ii}}. \tag{4}$$

Then, we have the power control problem $\mathbf{AP} = \mathbf{B}$, where $\mathbf{A} = \mathbf{I} - \mathbf{H}$, $\mathbf{H} = [H_{ij}]$, $\mathbf{B} = [B_i]$, and $\mathbf{P} = [P_i]$ denotes the power level vector [15]. In this paper, we focus on the case in which the above power control problem has a unique solution of a positive power level vector $\mathbf{P}^*$.

2.2   Constrained Power Control Model

Since the transmission power of a mobile terminal of i has the limited power levels such as $P_i^{min} \leq P_i \leq P_i^{max}$ and the power levels has discrete-value characteristics in the practical mobile terminal systems, we should consider the constraint condition on the transmission power of P_i as follows

$$P_i \in \{P_i^1, P_i^2, \cdots, P_i^{k-1}, P_i^k\} \tag{5}$$

where P_i has the power levels of k and P_i^1 and P_i^k describe the minimum and maximum transmission power levels of the mobile terminal of i, respectively [9][15].

2.3   IS-95 and W-CDMA Systems Power Control Model

The bang-bang (BB) algorithm in the IS-95 and W-CDMA systems is used as a reference algorithm [15][17][19]. In this algorithm power is updated as follows

$$P_i^{n+1} = \min \left[\frac{T_i}{R_i^n} P_i^n, P_i^m \right] \quad \text{for} \quad n = 0, 1, 2, \cdots \tag{6}$$

where R_i^n denotes the received SINR of the mobile terminal of i at the iteration of n, T_i is the minimum target SINR as shown in Eq. (2), and P_i^m describes the maximum power of the mobile terminal of i in Eq. (5).

3   Proposed Power Control Algorithms Using Evolutionary Computation

3.1   Phenotypic View

The theoretical roots of most of all power control algorithms, including our proposed algorithm, can be found in numerical analysis based on linear algebra [15]. Therefore, we can also consider the power control problem as linear systems of equations $\mathbf{AP} = \mathbf{B}$ derived from the signal-to-interference-plus-noise ratio (SINR) constraint on mobile terminals. The goal of finding and searching the power level vector $\mathbf{P}$ would be very similar to minimize the norm $||\mathbf{B} - \mathbf{AP}||$ [16][23]. The most basic scheme starts with an arbitrary initial power level vector $\mathbf{P_i}$ and varies it systematically until an feasible solution $\mathbf{P_f}$ is discovered using evolutionary computation (EC) algorithms [16][23].

We have only used a genetic mutation operator in order to generate offsprings, whose operator can be simultaneously employed to certain components of an power level vector $\mathbf{P}$ [21][23]. The mutation operator is related to a monotone function of the distance between the true solution and the candidate vector [16]. The optimum probability of mutation is $1/M$, where M is mobile terminals. Several different means for adjusting components of a candidate power level vector $\mathbf{P}$ are offered [16], the amount O_i^{EC} by which P_i at the mobile terminal of i is altered or changed being determined as follows

$$O_i^{EC} = \frac{Z_i^{EC}}{M} ||\mathbf{B} - \mathbf{AP}|| \tag{7}$$

where Z_i^{EC} is a uniform random number between 0 to 1. The mutation operator of O_i^{EC} of EC algorithms has changed and updated a component of power level vector $\mathbf{P}$, without any GA coding process, whose component is P_i.

The proposed phenotypic algorithm includes the simultaneous mutation of every gene in a candidate solution of power levels. Computational experiments indicate that a change in perspective to a phenotypic view [16], where all the genes change at once, can lead to more rapid optimization on linear systems of equations in order to solve distributed power control problems in CDMA cellular radio systems.

3.2   Genotypic View

A power level value is an individual as a potential solution for the power control problem. A set of these power level values should become a population. In order to represent a power level value of a user as an individual with a specific gene, we should transform or code all power level values into binary numbers or strings [20][22], while the values should also satisfy the constraint condition of Eq. (5). Each mobile terminal updates iteratively and distributively its power level within the discrete power levels of k as shown in Eq. (5). The power levels of each mobile terminal of i constitute one population of P_i. Therefore, if the number of mobiles is M, there are M groups of population.

The evaluation function of F_i^{GA} determines the fitness of potential solutions. The following evaluation function about the mobile terminal of i is used in order to support systems as many mobiles as possible. The value of D_i^{GA} means an absolute difference between T_i and R_i, where $D_i^{GA} = |R_i - T_i|$ is calculated from the both sides of Eq. (2). The better individual has the lowest fitness value, because the lowest fitness is imposed as D_i^{GA} or the power level becomes smaller. In order to search for various and good individuals efficiently, the evaluation function with three slopes or inclines should be used as follows

$$
F_i^{GA} = \begin{cases} P_i + [D_i^{GA}] & \text{for} \quad D_i^{GA} < 1 \\ P_i + [2 - (D_i^{GA})^{-1}] & \text{for} \quad 1 \le D_i^{GA} < R_i \\ P_i + [R_i - (D_i^{GA})^{-1}] & \text{for} \quad D_i^{GA} \ge R_i \end{cases} \tag{8}
$$

where F_i^{GA} means the evaluation function with a given value of P_i in the fitness value.

It is important to make a genetic operator in order to transmit good genetic characteristics of parents to their offsprings. In this genotypic view, the 2-point crossover operator, which is usually used in evolutionary algorithms [20][22]. In evolutionary algorithms, a mutation operator acts on a single parent and produces an offspring by introducing small changes in order to ensure the diversity of potential solutions and to prevent a premature convergence to local optima [20][22]. In this genotypic view, however, the mutation is not used for the purpose of simplifying algorithm. The method of localized neighborhood interactions, which will be explained later, is used to promote diversity and search efficiency instead of the mutation operator.

Let $P_i^{GA}(t)$ be the parents of i user in the current generation of t. In the evolutionary process, maintaining diverse populations should be necessary for the long-term success of any evolutionary algorithm. A genetic algorithm (GA) with a diverse population can continue utilizing recombination in order to produce a new structure, and thus can avoid becoming trapped at local optima [20][22]. In order to promote diversity and search efficiency, in this genotypic view, we have modeled and designed the evolutionary system that is based on the localized neighborhood interactions within populations [23].

4   Computer Simulation Results

The DS-CDMA system with 19 base stations using omni-type antennas located in the centers of 19 hexagonal cells is used as a computer simulation system [15]. For a given time instance, a total of 190 mobile terminals are generated and the locations of which are uniformly distributed over the 19 hexagonal cells [15].

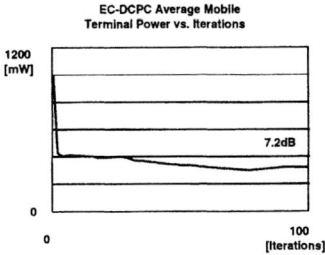

Fig. 1. Average mobile terminal power with mW unit at the EC-DCPC phenotypic algorithm in 100 genetic iterations.

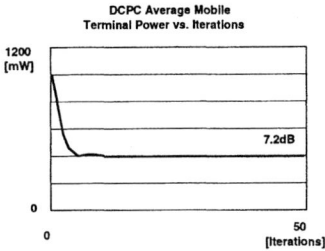

Fig. 2. Average mobile terminal power with mW unit at the DCPC reference algorithm in 50 iterations.

We consider the IS-95 and W-CDMA systems specification [17]-[19], where the spreading bandwidth is 1.2288MHz and the data transmission rate is 9.6Kbps including processing gain 21dB. The base station receiver noise is taken to be 10^{-12}. The relative maximum mobile terminal power is set to 1000mW.

4.1   EC-DCPC Phenotypic Algorithm Simulation

The target SINR with tolerance is set to 7.2dB for each mobile terminal. Employing the distributed constrained power control (DCPC) as a basic reference algorithm [6][9][12], we have implemented computational experiments on the DS-CDMA system. The simulation results indicate that the proposed EC-DCPC phenotypic algorithm significantly enhances the optimization and calculation speed of power control compared with the simple genetic algorithm (SGA) [20]. The computational results show that our proposed EC-DCPC phenotypic algorithm also has a high potential advantage for decreasing the mobile terminal power consumption and increasing the CDMA cellular radio network capacity as shown in Fig. 1 and 2 [23]. The average power of supported mobile terminals out of total mobile terminals is used as a performance measure. Fig. 1 shows the average mobile terminal power changes according to the genetic iteration using the proposed EC-DCPC phenotypic algorithm. Fig.2 shows the average mobile terminal power according to the iteration using the discrete DCPC basic reference algorithm.

As shown in Fig. 1, the average power consumption is about 350mW in 100 genetic iterations and those consumption power values should be less than about 400mW at

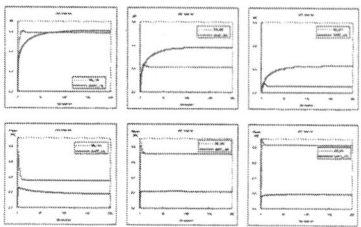

Fig. 3. Supportable rate at the upper graphs and power level with W unit at the lower graphs with the solid line using the GA-DCPC genotypic algorithm and the dashed line using the BB reference algorithm for the fixed target SINR at 8dB.

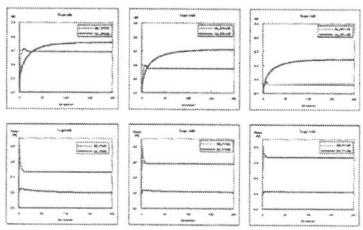

Fig. 4. Supportable rate at the upper graphs and power level with W unit at the lower graphs with the solid line using the GA-DCPC genotypic algorithm and the dashed line using the BB reference algorithm for the various target SINR at 9, 10, and 11dB.

the target SINR 7.2dB in 50 iterations as shown in Fig. 2. In addition, the average power consumption at the EC-DCPC should be more than about 200mW in 200 genetic iterations on the power control using the modified SGA [23]. However, simultaneously multiple mutation operations at the EC-DCPC can lead to more rapid optimization on power control linear systems of equations compared with optimization using a single mutation operation in the SGA [20][23].

Therefore, the average power consumption at the EC-DCPC is decreased by about 12.5% by comparison with the DCPC. Due to the different iteration numbers, the calculation time at the EC-DCPC in order to solve the power control linear systems of equations should be larger than that at the DCPC. However, the linear systems of equations should be solved in reasonable time. This result should be related to the EC-DCPC based on a stochastic search and the DCPC based on a deterministic search.

4.2   GA-DCPC Genotypic Algorithm Simulation

The two types of simulations are carried out. The first simulation is related to test the congestion performance in the DS-CDMA system as shown in Fig. 3. In order to evaluate this, each performance is measured as the number of mobile terminals (i.e., users) which are increased to 190, 380, and 570 with the target SINR fixed at 8dB. The second simulation is related to compare the performance by increasing the level of communications quality as shown in Fig. 4. Employing the bang-bang (BB) algorithm as a basic reference algorithm, each performance is measured as the target SINR is increased to 9dB, 10dB, and 11dB, when 190 mobiles exist in the DS-CDMA system. The other parameters are determined through preliminary experiments as shown in [23]

The supportable rate (M_s/M), the ratio of the number of supported mobile terminals (M_s) to that of total mobile terminals (M) at each genetic generation, is used as a performance measure. Each simulation has been repeated 100 times and then the average of those should be about 200mW as shown in Fig. 3 and 4, which show the results of the first simulation and the second simulation, respectively. As shown in Fig. 3 and 4, the upper graph represents the supportable rate and the lower graph represents the average power level over the generations. According to the results, the power levels of the GA-DCPC genotypic algorithm are smaller than those of the BB algorithm. The GA-DCPC genotypic algorithm outperforms the BB algorithm in terms of the supportable rate. From these simulations, it is concluded that the GA-DCPC genotypic algorithm shows the better performance than the BB algorithm, when the DS-CDMA system becomes congested and the requirement about the quality of service is increased.

5   Conclusions and Further Studies

This paper has proposed distributed power control (PC) algorithms that employ two evolutionary computation (EC) or genetic algorithm (GA) techniques in order to solve linear systems of equations for power update in CDMA cellular radio systems. The proposed algorithms are modeled on applying evolutionary computation algorithms with the phenotypic and genotypic views to the CDMA power control problem. Employing the distributed constrained power control (DCPC) and bang-bang (BB) algorithms as the basic reference algorithms, we have implemented computational experiments on the DS-CDMA system. The proposed EC-DCPC phenotypic algorithm is compared with the DCPC algorithm. The GA-DCPC genotypic algorithm is also compared with the BB algorithm used in the IS-95 and the W-CDMA systems.

From computer simulation results, it is concluded that the EC-DCPC phenotypic and GA-DCPC genotypic algorithms show the better performance compared with the DCPC and BB reference algorithms, respectively, when the DS-CDMA system becomes congested and the requirement about the quality of service should be increased. Furthermore, our proposed algorithms are fully distributed power control in that each mobile terminal can update its power without any communication with the other mobiles.

Acknowledgement. This work has been supported in part by the Korea Science and Engineering Foundation (KOSEF) on Ministry of Science and Technology (MOST) and the Korea IT Industry Promotion Agency (KIPA) on Ministry of Information and Communication (MIC) in Republic of Korea.

References

[1]   Z.Rosberg and J.Zander, "Toward a framework for power control in cellular systems," *ACM/Baltzer Wireless Networks Journal*, vol.4, pp.215–222, 1998.

[2]   N.Bambos, "Toward power-sensitive network architectures in wireless communications: Concepts, issues, and design aspects," *IEEE Personal Communications*, vol.5, pp.50–59, 1998.

[3]   J.Zander, "Performance of optimum transmitter power control in cellular radio systems," *IEEE Transactions on Vehicular Technology*, vol.41, pp.57–62, 1992.

[4]   J.Zander, "Distributed cochannel interference control in cellular radio systems," *IEEE Transactions on Vehicular Technology*, vol.41, pp.305–311, 1992.

[5]   S.A.Grandhi, R.Vijayan, D.J.Goodman, and J.Zander, "Centralized power control in cellular radio systems," *IEEE Transactions on Vehicular Technology*, vol.42, pp.466–468, 1993.

[6]   S.A.Grandhi, R.Vijayan, and D.J.Goodman, "Distributed power control in cellular radio systems," *IEEE Transactions on Communications*, vol.42, pp.226–228, 1994.

[7]   G.J.Foschini and Z.Miljanic, "A simple distributed autonomous power control algorithm and its convergence," *IEEE Transactions on Vehicular Technology*, vol.42, pp.641–646, 1993.

[8]   D.Mitra, "An asynchronous distributed algorithm for power control in cellular radio systems," *Proceedings of the 1993 WINLAB Workshop*, pp.249–259, 1993.

[9]   S.A.Grandhi, J.Zander, and R.Yates, "Constrained power control," *Wireless Personal Communications*, vol.1, pp.257–270, 1995.

[10] R.D.Yates and C.Y.Huang, "Integrated power control and base station assignment," *IEEE Transactions on Vehicular Technology*, vol.44, pp.638–644, 1995.

[11] S.V.Hanly, "An algorithm for combined cell-site selection and power control to maximize cellular spread spectrum capacity," *IEEE Journal on Selected Areas in Communications*, vol.13, pp.1332–1340, 1995.

[12] R.Yates, "A framework for uplink power control in cellular radio systems," *IEEE Journal on Selected Areas in Communications*, vol.13, pp.1341–1347, 1995.

[13] C.Y.Huang and R.D.Yates, "Rate of convergence for minimum power assignment in cellular radio systems," *ACM/Baltzer Wireless Networks Journal*, vol.1, pp.223–231, 1998.

[14] S.L.Kim and J.Zander, "Optimization approach to gradual removal in a cellular radio system with distributed power control," *IEEE Transactions on Vehicular Technology*, to be published.

[15] R.Jantti and S.L.Kim, "Second-order power control with asymptotically fast convergence," *IEEE Journal on Selected Areas in Communications*, vol.18, no.3, 2000.

[16] D.B.Fogel and R.W.Anderson, "Revisiting Bremermann's genetic algorithm: Simultaneous mutation of all parameters," *Proceedings of the 2000 Congress on Evolutionary Computation*, vol.2, 2000.

[17] *TIA/EIA Interim Standard-95: Mobile Station-Base Station Compatibility Standard for Dual-Mode Wideband Spread Spectrum Cellular System*, 1993.

[18] E.Dahlman, P.Beming, J.Knutsson, F.OvesjoOvesjo, M.Persson, and C.Roobol, "WCDMA – The radio interface for future mobile multimedia communications," *IEEE Transactions on Vehicular Technology*, vol.47, pp.1105–1118, 1998.

[19] A.J.Viterbi, *CDMA: Principles of Spread Spectrum Communication*, Addison-Wesley, 1995.

[20] D.E.Goldberg, *Genetic Algorithms in Search, Optimization, and Machine Learning*, Addison-Wesley, 1989.

[21] D.B.Fogel and J.W.Atmar, "Comparing genetic operators with Gaussian mutations in simulated evolutionary processes using linear systems," *Biological Cybernetics*, vol.63, pp.111–114, 1990.

[22] Z.Michalewicz, *Genetic Algorithms + Data Structures = Evolution Programs*, 2nd edition, Springer-Verlag, 1994.

[23] W.J.Song, S.J.Kim, B.H.Ahn, and M.K.Choi, "Phenotypic and Genotypic Evolutionary Computation Power Control Algorithms in CDMA Cellular Radio Networks," *Lecture Notes in Computer Science*, LNCS 2524, pp.470–481, 2003.

A Novel Multiobjective Evolutionary Algorithm Based on Min-Max Strategy*

Hai Lin Liu[1] and Yuping Wang[2]

[1] Department of Applied Mathematics, Guangdong University of Technology,
Guang Zhou, 510090, P. R. China
[2] Faculty of Science, Xidian University, Xi'an, Shaanxi 710071, P. R. China

Abstract. A new fitness function is proposed in the paper at first, in which the fitness of an individual is defined by the maximum value of the weighted normalized objectives. In order to get the required weights, the sphere coordinate transformation is used. The fitness constructed in this way can result in a group of uniform search directions in the objective space. By using these search directions, the evolutionary algorithm can explore the objective space uniformly, keep the diversity of the population and find uniformly distributed solutions on the Pareto frontier gradually. The numerical simulations indicate the proposed algorithm is efficient and has a better performance than the compared ones.

1 Introduction

Multi-objective optimization problem has wide applications in science, engineering, management, military and other fields. Evolutionary algorithm evolves a population of potential solutions and is hopeful to find multiple solutions in one run, thus it seems that it is especially suitable to multi-objective optimization problems. However, There are two important problems to need further research: How to design effective fitness functions and selection schemes such that they can guide the search effectively; How to find uniformly distributed solutions on the Pareto frontier.

In recent years, many efficient algorithms have been proposed for multi-objective programming problems (e.g., [1]~[5], [8], [9]), in which the algorithms using the weighted sum of objectives as the fitness function are the one of the simplest and the most easily usable ones ([1], [5]), but, this kind of algorithms usually can not find the solutions on the non convex parts of the Pareto frontier ([1], [2], [4], [6], [8], [9]). In order to overcome the drawbacks and keep the advantages, a new fitness function is proposed and it was defined by the maximum value of all the weighted normalized objectives, while the weights used are properly constructed by the sphere coordinate transformation and uniform design. As a result, a group of uniform search directions in the objective space can be

* This work was supported in part by the Natural Science Foundation of Shaanxi Province (No. 2001SL06), by the SRF for ROCS, SEM, and by the Doctoral Fund of Guangdong University of Technology.

generated. By using these search directions, the evolutionary algorithm can explore the objective space uniformly, keep the diversity of the population and find uniformly distributed solutions on the Pareto frontier gradually. The numerical simulations indicate that the proposed algorithm is efficient and has a better performance than the compared ones in [2], [4] and [5] no matter the Pareto frontier is convex, nonconvex or mixture of the convex and the nonconvex.

The paper is organized as follows. Section 1 gives a brief introduction. Section 2 describes transformed multi-objective programming problem and introduces the related results. A new kind of fitness functions is developed in Section 3, and a new evolutionary algorithm is proposed in Section 4. In Section 5 we do the simulations on the proposed algorithm and compare the results with other algorithms for three test functions. Section 6 gives the conclusions.

2   Transformed Multi-objective Programming Problem and Related Results

Consider the following multi-objective programming problem:

$$\min f(x) = (f_1(x), f_2(x), \cdots, f_m(x))$$
$$\text{s.t.} \quad x \in X \subseteq R^n, \tag{1}$$

where x is the decision variable and X is the hyper-rectangle in R^n.

Definition 1. *A vector* $a = (a_1, a_2, ..., a_m)$ *dominates a vector* $b = (b_1, b_2, ..., b_m)$ *if* $a_i \leq b_i$ *for any* i *and there is* j *such that* $a_j < b_j$. *A solution* $x^* \in X$ *is said to be Pareto optimal in* X *if and only if there is no* $x \in X$ *such that its image* $f(x)$ *dominates* $f(x^*)$. *The Pareto optimal set,* $E(f, X)$, *is thus the set of all* $x \in X$ *such that* $f(x)$ *is non-dominated in* $\{f(x) : x \in X\}$. *The Pareto frontier is the set* $\{f(x) : x \in E(f, X)\}$.

Definition 2. *For* $x^* \in X$, *if there exists no* $x \in X$ *such that* $f_i(x) < f_i(x^*)$ *for any* i, *then* x^* *is said to be weak Pareto optimal in* X. *The set of all weak Pareto optimal solutions is said to be the weak Pareto optimal solution set, denoted by* $E_w(f, X)$. *The set* $\{f(x) : x \in E_w(f, X)\}$ *is said to be the weak Pareto frontier.*

In order to get uniformly distributed solutions easily, we normalize all objective functions and transform problem (1) into the following problem:

$$\min g(x) = (g_1(x), g_2(x), \cdots, g_m(x))$$
$$\text{s.t.} \quad x \in X \subseteq R^n, \tag{2}$$

where

$$\begin{cases} g_i(x) = \dfrac{f_i(x) - f_i^*}{\max\limits_{x \in X}\{f_i(x) - f_i^*\}}, i = 1, 2, ..., m \\ g(x) = (g_1(x), g_2(x), ..., g_m(x)) \end{cases}$$

and $f_i^* = \min\limits_{x \in X} f_i(x)$ or f_i^* is a lower bound of $f_i(x)$ on X, $i = 1, \cdots, m$. Obviously, we have the following relation:

$$x \in E(f, X) \Leftrightarrow x \in E(g, X);$$

$$x \in E_w(f, X) \Leftrightarrow x \in E_w(g, X).$$

Thus the problem (1) is equivalent to problem (2).

Theorem 1. *If there exists $\bar{x} \in X$ and weights $w_i > 0$ $(i = 1, 2, ..., m)$ such that*

$$w_1 g_1(\bar{x}) = w_2 g_2(\bar{x}) = \cdots = w_m g_m(\bar{x}),$$

then

1) $\bar{x} \in E_w(g, X)$ if and only if

$$\min\limits_{x \in X} \max\limits_{1 \leq i \leq m} \{w_i g_i(x)\} = \max\limits_{1 \leq i \leq m} \{w_i g_i(\bar{x})\};$$

2) If $\bar{x} \in E(g, X)$, then

$$\min\limits_{x \in X} \max\limits_{1 \leq i \leq m} \{w_i g_i(x)\} = \max\limits_{1 \leq i \leq m} \{w_i g_i(\bar{x})\}.$$

when $\exists x^\star \in X$, $x^\star \neq \bar{x}$ satisfying

$$\min\limits_{x \in X} \max\limits_{1 \leq i \leq m} \{w_i y_i(x)\} = \max\limits_{1 \leq i \leq m} \{w_i y_i(x^\star)\},$$

then $q(\bar{x}) = g(x^\star)$.

3   The New Fitness Function

It can be seen from theorem 3 that if $\bar{x}$ is a Pareto optimal solution, then $\max\limits_{1 \leq i \leq m} \{w_i g_i(x)\}$ will attain the minimum at $\bar{x}$. Thus, if $\max\limits_{1 \leq i \leq m} \{w_i g_i(x)\}$ is used as the fitness function, it will guide the search to the Pareto optimal solution. Based on this, a new fitness function can be defined as follows:

$$F(x) = \max\limits_{1 \leq i \leq m} \{w_i g_i(x)\}, \tag{3}$$

where the weights $w_i > 0$ $(i = 1, ..., m)$ should satisfy the following conditions:

$$\begin{cases} w_1 w_2 \cdots w_m = 1, \\ w_1 g_1(x) = w_2 g_2(x) = \cdots = w_m g_m(x). \end{cases} \tag{4}$$

Using the sphere coordinate transformation to $g_1(x)$, $g_2(x), \cdots, g_m(x)$, we get

$$\begin{cases} g_1(x) = r\cos\theta_1, \\ g_2(x) = r\sin\theta_1\cos\theta_2, \\ \cdots \quad \cdots, \\ g_m(x) = r\sin\theta_1\sin\theta_2\cdots\sin\theta_{m-1}. \end{cases} \tag{5}$$

Then the weights can be determined by solving equations (4) and (5) and given by

$$\begin{cases} w_1 = \frac{1}{\cos\theta_1}\sqrt[m]{\prod_{i=1}^{m-1}\sin^{m-i}\theta_i\cos\theta_i} \\ w_2 = \frac{\cos\theta_1}{\sin\theta_1\cos\theta_2}w_1 \\ \cdots\ \cdots \\ w_m = \frac{\cos\theta_{m-1}}{\sin\theta_{m-1}}w_{m-1} \end{cases} \tag{6}$$

In objective space with objective function vector $g(x) = (g_1(x), ..., g_m(x))$ for problem (2), suppose that the intersection between the Pareto frontier and the line, on which the direction angles between axes and it are $(\theta_1, ..., \theta_{m-1}) = (\theta_{1j}, ..., \theta_{m-1,j})$ in the objective space, is $g(x_j)$. If $(\theta_{1j}, ..., \theta_{m-1,j})$ is put into formula (6) and the corresponding weights are denoted by $w_{1j}, w_{2j}, ..., w_{mj}$, and denote $F_j(x) = \max\limits_{1\le i\le m}\{w_{ij}g_i(x)\}$, then we have

$$F_j(x_j) = \min_{x\in X}F_j(x) = \max_{1\le i\le m}\{w_{ij}g_i(x_j)\}$$

by theorem 3. When we use uniform design ([7]) to choose M uniformly distributed direction angles of the weight vectors $(\theta_{1j}, ..., \theta_{m-1,j})$ for $j = 1, 2, ..., M$, we then can get a group of uniformly distributed Pareto optimal solutions on Pareto frontier.

Theorem 2. *For a given direction angle vector $(\theta_{1,0}, \theta_{2,0}, ..., \theta_{m-1,0})$, suppose that the corresponding weight vector obtained by (6) is $(w_{1,0}, ..., w_{m,0})$ and let us denote*

$$F_0(x) = \max_{1\le i\le m}\{w_{i,0}g_i(x)\},$$

then

1) *If the intersection of the Pareto frontier and the line, on which the direction angles between axes and it are $(\theta_{1,0}, ..., \theta_{m-1,0})$ in the objective space, is $g(x_0)$, where x_0 is the Pareto optimal solution for problem (2), then for any solution x_1 of $\min_{x\in X}F_0(x)$, we have $g(x_1) = g(x_0)$.*
2) *If the intersection of the weak Pareto frontier and the line, on which the direction angles between axes and it are $(\theta_{1,0}, ..., \theta_{m-1,0})$ in the objective space, is $g(x_0)$ and x_0 is the weak Pareto optimal solution for problem (2), then for any solution x_1 of $\min_{x\in X}F_0(x)$, we have $g(x_1) \le g(x_0)$.*

4   A Novel Multi-objective Evolutionary Algorithm

In the proposed algorithm, we adopt the crossover operator, mutation operator and selection operator in ([1]).

Step 1. (Initialization) Choose population size N and proper positive integer M. Generate initial population by uniform design ([1]). Given mutation probability p_m.

Step 2. (Crossover) Choose one best individual based on each fitness function, i.e., the one with the smallest fitness, then randomly choose another individual. Match these two individuals as a pair and use crossover operator to this pair to generate offspring.

Step 3. (Mutation) Execute mutation operator with the probability p_m.

Step 4. (Selection) Select the best $\lfloor \frac{N}{M} \rfloor$ individuals by each fitness function in current population and all offspring. Totally N individuals will be chosen by M fitness functions.

Step 5. (Termination) If termination conditions hold, then stop, and keep the best solution obtained as the global optimal solution of problem; otherwise, go to Step 2.

5   Simulation Results

Three test functions were chosen from ([6]). they are difficult for evolutionary algorithms ([6]). These function can be defined by the following form:

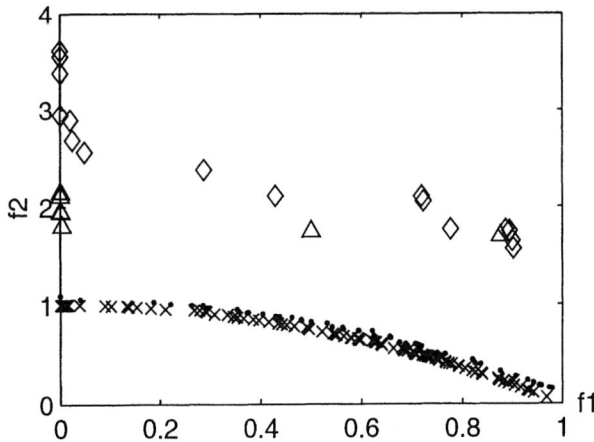

Fig. 1. Comparison among the algorithms in [2], [4], [5] and the proposed algorithm on function F_1.

$$\min F(x) = (f_1(x_1), f_2(x))$$
$$s.t. \ \ f_2(x) = g(x_2, ..., x_n) h(f_1(x_1), g(x_2, ..., x_n))$$
$$where \ \ x = (x_1, ..., x_n).$$

$F_1 : f_1(x_1) = x_1,$
$$g(x_2, ..., x_n) = 1 + 9 \sum_{i=2}^{n} x_i/(n-1),$$
$$h(f_1, g) = 1 - (f_1/g)^2, \ n = 30, \ x_i \in [0, 1].$$

$F_2 : f_1(x_1) = 1 - \exp(-4x_1) \sin^6(6\pi x_1),$
$$g(x_2, ..., x_n) = 1 + 9(\sum_{i=2}^{n} x_i/(n-1))^{0.25},$$
$$h(f_1, g) = 1 - (f_1/g)^2, \ n = 10, \ x_i \in [0, 1].$$

$F_3 : f_1(x_1) = x_1,$
$$g(x_2, ..., x_n) = 1 + 9 \sum_{i=2}^{n} x_i/(n-1),$$
$$h(f_1, g) = 1 - \sqrt{(f_1/g)}(f_1/g) \sin(10\pi f_1),$$
$$n = 30, \ x_i \in [0, 1].$$

These test functions were solved by some frequently cited algorithms. for example, by the algorithms ([2], [4] and [5]). We execute the proposed algorithm for

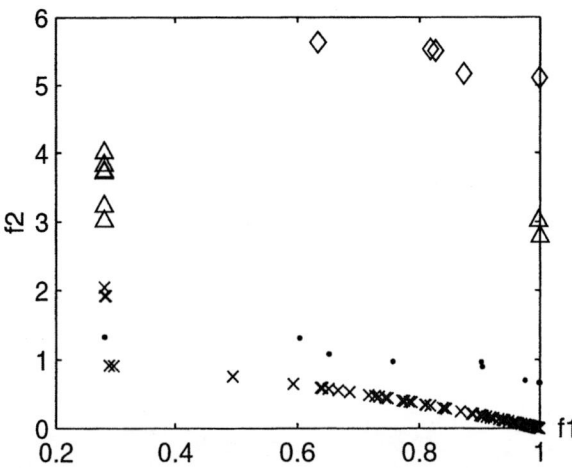

Fig. 2. Comparison among the algorithms in [2], [4], [5] and the proposed algorithm on function F_2.

these test functions and have a direct comparison with the algorithms in ([2], [4] and [5]) by using the existing results from web address:

$$http://www.tik.ee.ethz.ch/{\sim}zitzler/testdata.html.$$

Each function were run 30 times and the first 5 run's results were unified as one set of Pareto optimal solutions. The results are given by Figures 1, 2 and 3. In all the figures 1, 2 and 3, the Pareto optimal solutions found by algorithms in [2], [4], [5] and in this paper were represented by $\bullet$, $\triangle$, $\bigcirc$ and ∇, respectively. It can be seen from Figures 1, 2 and 3 that The Pareto solutions found by the proposed algorithm are better and more uniform along the Pareto frontier than those found by algorithms in [2], [4], [5].

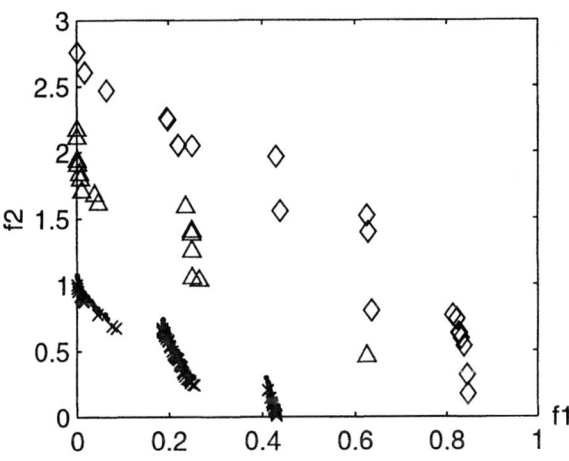

Fig. 3. Comparison among the algorithms in [2], [4], [5] and the proposed algorithm on function F_3.

6   Conclusions

A new evolutionary algorithm for multi-objective programming problem is proposed. It can explore the objective space uniformly, keep the diversity of the population and find uniformly distributed solutions on the Pareto frontier gradually. Simulations for 3 difficult test functions are also made, and the results obtained are compared with those reported in the related references. The comparison reveals that the proposed algorithm has better performance with accurate solutions scattering more uniformly along Pareto frontier.

References

1. Y.W. Leung, Y.P. Wang: Multiobjective programming using uniform design and genetic algorithm. IEEE Trans. on Syst., Man, Cybern. C. **30** (2000) 293–304.
2. E. Zitzler, L. Thiele: Multiobjective evolutionary algorithms: a comparative case study and the strength pareto approach. IEEE Trans. on Evolutionary Computation. **3** (1999) 257–271.
3. H. Ishibuchi, T. Murata: A multiobjective genetic local search algorithm and its application to flowshop scheduling. IEEE Trans. on Syst., Man, Cybern. C. **28** 1998 392–403.
4. C.M. Fonseca, P.J. Fleming: Multiobjective optimization and multiple constraints handling with evolutionary algorithms-Part 1: Unified formulation. IEEE Trans. on Syst., Man, Cybern. A. **28** (1998) 38–47.
5. P. Hajela, C.Y. Lin: Genetic search strategies in multicriterion optimal design. Structural Optimization. **4** (1992) 99–107.
6. K. Deb: Multiobjective genetic algorithms: Problem difficulties and construction of test functions Evolutionary Computation. **7** (1999) 205–230.
7. F.T.Fang, Y.Wang: Number-theoretic methods in statistics. Chapman & Hall, London, UK (1994)
8. E. Zitzler, K. Deb, and L. Thiele: Comparison of multiobjective evolutionary algorithms: Empirical results. Evolutionary Computation. **8** (2000) 173–195.
9. K. Deb, A. Pratap, S. Agarwal and T. Meyarivan: A fast and elitist multiobjective genetic algorithm: NSGA-II. In: M. Schoenauer, K. Deb, G. Rudolph, X. Yao, E. Lutton, J. J. Merelo and Hans-Paul Schwefel (eds.) Proceedings of the Parallel Problem Solving from Nature VI Conference. Springer-Verlag, Berlin Heidelberg New York (2000)

Dynamics of Gradient-Based Learning and Applications to Hyperparameter Estimation

Kwok Yee Michael Wong[1], Peixun Luo[1], and Fuli Li[2]

[1] Department of Physics, Hong Kong University of Science and Technology
Clear Water Bay, Hong Kong, China
{phkywong,physlpx}@ust.hk
[2] Department of Applied Physics, Xian Jiaotong University
Xian 710049, China
flli@xjtu.edu.cn

Abstract. We analyse the dynamics of gradient-based learning algorithms using the cavity method, considering the cases of batch learning with non-vanishing rates, and on-line learning. It has an an excellent agreement with simulations. Applications to efficient and precise estimation of hyperparameters are proposed.

1 Introduction

Many learning algorithms in information processing are based on parameter tuning or iteration directed by gradients of risk functions or likelihood functions. However, most theoretical analyses focused on their *steady state* behavior. The *dynamics* describing how the system approaches steady state in time was much less understood.

The two most common modes of learning are *batch* and *on-line* learning. In batch learning, gradient-directed iterations are made after the contributions of the individual components or examples have been summed up. In on-line learning, a gradient-directed iteration is made once the contribution due to an individual component or example has been computed. Significant theoretical progress has been made in the case of on-line perceptron learning of *infinite* training sets [1]. However, for the more realistic case of *recycled* examples, the analysis is complicated by the presence of temporal correlations of the weights in the learning history. In general, a theory with physical interpretations covering the dynamics of both batch and on-line learning is still lacking. More complicated cases such as multilayer perceptrons and natural gradient learning are not yet studied.

We present in this paper a general theory for the dynamics of learning algorithms. It is based on the *cavity method* [2,3], which was originally developed for magnetic systems and spin glasses. It has the advantages of a clear physical picture, and hence the potential to provide a unifying theory extendable to the more complicated cases mentioned above. We will also apply the cavity method to estimate the leave-one-out generalization error. This can be used to estimate hyperparameters without having to sweat through the tedious leave-one-out cross validation procedure.

J. Liu et al. (Eds.): IDEAL 2003, LNCS 2690, pp. 369–376, 2003.

2   Formulation

We consider a training set of p examples, each example $\mu = 1, \cdots, p$ consists of an N-dimensional input vector, which may be taken from the feature space in the case of SVM, or from the input space directly in the case of perceptrons. We assume that the inputs ξ_j^μ, $j = 1, \cdots, N$, are Gaussian variables with zero mean and unit variance.

In classification and regression applications, each example μ also consists of an output $\tilde{y}_\mu$. It is convenient to analyse the learning of examples generated by a teacher network with N weights B_j, $j = 1, \cdots, N$. For definiteness, we set $|\boldsymbol{B}| = 1$. The outputs $\tilde{y}_\mu$ are equal to $\mathrm{sgn}(y_\mu + \epsilon z_\mu)$ for classification, and $y_\mu + \epsilon z_\mu$ for regression. Here $y_\mu \equiv \boldsymbol{B} \cdot \boldsymbol{\xi}^\mu$ is the teacher activation, z_μ is a Gaussian variable with zero mean and unit variance, and ϵ is the noise amplitude.

The examples are learned by a student network with N weights J_j, $j = 1, \cdots, N$. In batch learning, the weights are modified according to

$$J_j(t + \Delta t) = J_j(t) + v\Delta t \left[\frac{1}{p} \sum_\mu F(x_\mu(t), \tilde{y}_\mu) \xi_j^\mu - \lambda J_j(t) \right], \qquad (1)$$

where the force $F(x_\mu, \tilde{y}_\mu)$ due to an example is generally a function of the student activation $x_\mu \equiv \boldsymbol{J} \cdot \boldsymbol{\xi}^\mu$ and the teacher activation y_μ, and is computed according to the gradient of the loss function due to the example. In particular, $F(x, \tilde{y}) = \tilde{y} - x$ for Adaline rule, and $F(x, \tilde{y}) = (\tilde{y} - x)\Theta(1 - x\tilde{y})$ for the Adatron, Θ being the step function. v is the learning rate and λ is the weight decay, often introduced to control the complexity of the student.

In on-line learning, one example in the training set is randomly drawn at each learning step. If the example drawn out at time t is $\sigma(t) = \mu$, then the weights and biases are modified according to

$$J_j(t + \Delta t) = J_j(t) + v\Delta t \left[F(x_\mu(t), \tilde{y}_\mu) \xi_j^\mu - \lambda J_j(t) \right]. \qquad (2)$$

3   Batch Learning

We have studied the dynamics of batch learning with vanishing learning rates [2]. Here we extend the study to large step batch learning, which was proposed as an alternative to speed up batch learning [4]. This can be done by increasing $v\Delta t$ in Eq. (1) to magnitudes of order 1. For convenience we choose $\Delta t = 1$, so that the time t takes integer values. Learning is expected to converge in a time scale of order 1. The number of updates of each example scales as order 1, a factor of order Δt less than that of batch learning with vanishing learning rates. Thus the computational load is comparable with that of on-line learning.

The cavity method uses a self-consistency argument to consider what happens when a new example, labeled by 0, is added to a training set. The central quantity in this method is the *cavity activation*, which is the activation of a new example for a perceptron trained without that example. Since the original network has no information about the new example, the cavity activation at time n, $h_0(n) \equiv \boldsymbol{J}(n) \cdot \boldsymbol{\xi}^0$, is a Gaussian variable for large N. Its covariance is given by the correlation function $C(n, m)$ of the weights at times n and m, i.e., $\langle h_0(n)h_0(m)\rangle = \boldsymbol{J}(n) \cdot \boldsymbol{J}(m) \equiv C(n, m)$, where ξ_j^0 and ξ_k^0 are assumed to be independent for $j \neq k$. Furthermore, it is specified by the teacher-student correlation $R(n)$, given by $\langle h_0(n)y_0\rangle = \boldsymbol{J}(n) \cdot \boldsymbol{B} \equiv R(n)$.

Now suppose the perceptron incorporates the new example at the batch-mode learning step at time m. Then the activation of this new example at a subsequent time $n > m$ will no longer be a random variable. Furthermore, the activations of the original p examples at time n will also be adjusted from $\{x_\mu(n)\}$ to $\{x_\mu^0(n)\}$ because of the newcomer, which will in turn affect the evolution of the activation of example 0, giving rise to the so-called Onsager reaction effects. This makes the dynamics complex, but fortunately for large $p \sim N$, we can assume that the adjustment from $x_\mu(n)$ to $x_\mu^0(n)$ is small, and linear response theory can be applied.

Suppose the weights of the original and new perceptron at time t are $\{J_j(n)\}$ and $\{J_j^0(n)\}$ respectively. The cavity method yields

$$J_j^0(n) - J_j(n) = \frac{v}{p} \sum_m G(n, m)F_0(m)\xi_j^0, \tag{3}$$

where $F_0(m) \equiv F(x_0(m), y_0)$ and $G(n, m)$ is the *Green's function*, which describes how the effects of a perturbation propagate from weight J_j at learning time m to a subsequent time n. In the present context, the perturbation comes from the gradient term of example 0, such that summing over the history gives the resultant change from $J_j(n)$ to $J_j^0(n)$. For large N the Green's function can be found by the diagrammatic approach [2].

Our key to the macroscopic description of the learning dynamics is to relate the activation of the examples to their cavity counterparts, which is known to be Gaussian. Multiplying both sides of (3) and summing over j, we have

$$x_0(n) - h_0(n) = \frac{v}{\alpha} \sum_m G(n, m)F_0(m), \tag{4}$$

where $\alpha \equiv p/N$. In turn, the covariance of the cavity activation distribution is provided by the so-called fluctuation response relations

$$R(n) = v \sum_{l \leq n} (1 - v\lambda)^{n-l} \langle F_\mu(l)y_\mu\rangle, \tag{5}$$

$$C(n, m) = v \sum_{l \leq n} (1 - v\lambda)^{n-l} \langle F_\mu(l)x_\mu(m)\rangle. \tag{6}$$

The above distributions and parameters are sufficient to describe the dynamics of learning. For Adaline learning, the Green's function is time translational invariant, i.e., $G(n, m) = G(n - m, 0)$. In this case, the dynamics can be solved by z-transform, and the Green's function consists of a spectrum of relaxation modes with rate x, i.e., $G(n) = \int dx\rho(x)(1 - x)^n$, where $\rho(x) \equiv \mathrm{Im}G(-x - i\epsilon)/\pi$ is the density of states. Hence for the dynamics to converge, the maximum relaxation rate $x_{\max}$ in the density of states must be less than 2. This condition yields a critical learning rate beyond which the magnitude of weights diverge asymptotically.

The training error $E_t(n)$ and the generalization error $E_g(n)$ can be computed from the values of $R(n)$ and $C(n,m)$. As shown in Fig. 1, they have an excellent agreement with simulations. When the learning rate v is close to v_c, the training and generalization errors oscillate.

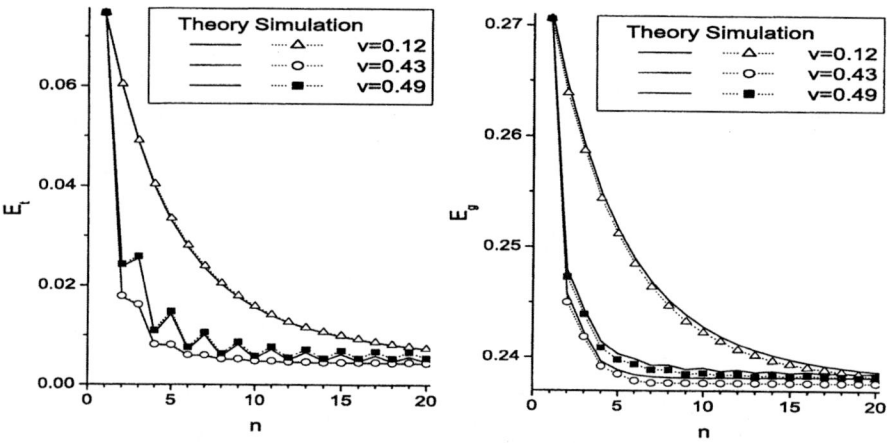

Fig. 1. The evolution of (a) training error E_t and (b) generalization error E_g for large step batch Adaline learning at $\alpha = 1.2$ and $\lambda = 0.42$, corresponding to $v_c = 0.49$. $N = 500$ for 500 samples in the simulation.

4   Online Learning

To adapt the cavity method from batch learning to on-line learning, there is a need to account for the following subtleties. (a) Averaging over the choice of sequencing the examples is now necessary. (b) The measurements of an example observed at an instant is now correlated with the instants when it was learned. This is due to the giant boost of that example at a learning step, which upsets the uniformity of the examples as in the case of batch learning.

Consider the evolution of the network $J_j^0(t)$ in which a new example 0 is added to the training set. For on-line learning, the new example appears as a Poisson event m times in time t with a mean t/α. Suppose this example appears in the new training sequence at $0 \leq t_m < \cdots < t_2 < t_1 \leq t$. Compared with the original network $J_j(t)$, the force due to the new example at these m instants now play the role of the stimulus. As a result, the student weight becomes

$$J_j^0(t) - J_j(t) = \frac{v}{N} \sum_{r=1}^{m} G(t, t_r) F(x_0(t_r), \tilde{y}_0) \xi_j^0. \qquad (7)$$

Multiplying both sides by ξ_{0j} and summing over j, we obtain the relation between the generic and cavity activations,

$$x_0(t) - h_0(t) = v \sum_{r=1}^{m} G(t, t_r) F(x_0(t_r), \tilde{y}_0). \tag{8}$$

The giant boosts received by an example are illustrated in Fig. 2(a). Up to $t = 3$, example 1 is drawn from the learning sequence $\sigma(t)$ 9 times, close to the Poisson average of $t/\alpha = 10$. The solid line describes the evolution of $x_1(t)$, which exhibits giant boosts at the 9 learning instants indicated by the vertical dashed lines. The dotted line describes the evolution of the cavity activation $h_1(t)$, which is obtained in a second network which uses the same learning sequence $\sigma(t)$, except that learning is paused when example 1 is drawn. Since example 1 and this network are uncorrelated, $h_1(t)$ evolves as a random walker with appropriate means and covariances. The filled circles indicate the values of the cavity activations predicted by Eq. (8), using the Greeen's functions derived in [2]. They show remarkable agreement with the simulated $h_1(t)$.

This introduces a subtlety in the derivation of the student-student correlation $C(t, s)$ via Eq. (6). There is now a correlation between the observation time s and the learning time t in the sequence average $\langle F_\mu(t) x_\mu(s) \rangle_\sigma |_{\sigma(t)=\mu}$. This *active average* is distinct from the *passive average* $\langle F_\mu(t) x_\mu(s) \rangle_\sigma$, where the example learned at time t is not necessarily μ. As illustrated in Fig. 2(a), the giant boosts of an example at its learning instants can give rise to a significant difference between these two kinds of averages. Indeed, we derived in [3] for Adaline learning that the active and passive correlations differ by a term generated by the force fluctuation $\langle F_\mu(t)^2 \rangle_\sigma$. Similarly, the force fluctuation creates an additional term in the passive correlation. Consequently, $C(t, s)$ consists of an additional component $\Delta C(t, s)$ due to the force fluctuation.

The generalization error can be computed using the parameters $R(t)$ and $C(t, t)$, analogous to the case of batch learning. However, there is no closed expression for the training error. Rather, we have to compute it by a Monte Carlo sampling procedure [3]. Figure 2(b) shows the generalization and training errors at the steady state. The theoretical predictions agree well with the simulation results. In contrast, in the mean-force approximation in [6], there is an increasing discrepancy when v becomes large.

An important result of this analysis is the existence of a critical learning rate v_c at which the fluctuations of the activations and weights diverge at the steady state. This predicted value of v_c agrees with the simulations, as shown in Fig. 2, and previous results [5], but is in contrast with the value predicted by the mean-force approximation in [6].

5   Hyperparameter Estimation

It is well known that correct choices of hyperparameters in classification and regression tasks can optimize the complexity of the data model, and hence achieve the best generalization. The common technique of hyperparameter estimation is

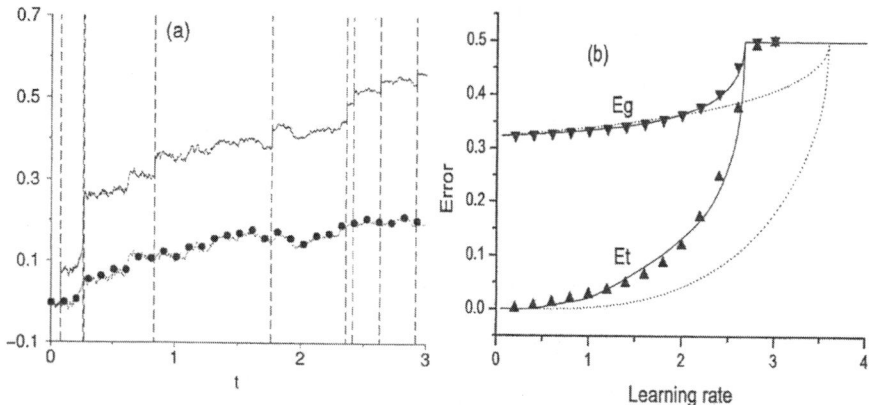

Fig. 2. (a) The evolution of the activations of example 1 in an Adatron. (b) The dependence of the steady-state generalization error E_g and training error E_t on the learning rate v for on-line Adaline learning at $\alpha = 0.5$, $\lambda=0.8$. Solid lines: the cavity method. Dotted lines: the mean-force approximation. Symbols: simulations averaged over 100 samples with $N = 1000$ and $t = 20$.

cross-validation or its variant, leave-one-out validation. While the leave-one-out procedure gives an almost unbiased estimate of the generalization error, it is nevertheless very tedious.

As an offshoot of the cavity approach to learning dynamics, we propose a new approach to hyperparameter estimation in large systems [8]. Here, we consider the optimal learning time in multilayer networks. As far as we are aware of, our method provides the only estimate of the hyperparameter beyond empirical stopping criteria and brute force cross-validation [7].

Early stopping addresses the problem of overtraining, when the generalization error decreases in the early stage of learning, reaches a minimum and then increases towards its asymptotic value [2]. Since the early stopping point sets in before the system reaches the steady state, most analyses based on the equilibrium state are not applicable.

In batch learning of two-layer perceptrons with n_h hidden nodes, the dynamical evolution of the estimated generalization error can be estimated from the cavity activations. At hidden node a of example 0, the cavity activation evolve according to an equation similar to Eq. (4),

$$x_{a0}(t) - h_{a0}(t) = \frac{v}{\alpha} \sum_b \int ds G_{ab}(t, s) F_{b0}(s), \qquad (9)$$

where $G_{ab}(t, s)$ is the time-dependent Green's function, which represents the response of a weight feeding hidden node a at time t due to a stimulus applied at the gradient with respect to a weight feeding node b at time s. To measure the Green's functions, we propose to monitor $n_h + 1$ learning processes, one being original and each of the other n_h processes having an initial homogeneous stimulus at the gradients with respect to one of the hidden nodes, i.e., for the learning process labeled by hidden node b, $\delta J_{aj}^{(b)}(t) = \eta\delta(t)\delta_{ab}$ for all a and j. Assuming normalized and independent inputs with $\langle\xi_j\rangle = 0$ and $\langle\xi_j\xi_k\rangle = \delta_{jk}$, the measurement $\langle J_{aj}^{(b)}(t) - J_{aj}(t)\rangle$ yields the quantity $\eta G_{ab}(t,0)$. Then the cavity activations are estimated in the approximation that the Green's functions are time-translational invariant.

An alternative way to measure the Green's function is to introduce constant homogeneous stimuli, i.e., $\delta J_{aj}^{(b)}(t) = \eta\delta_{ab}\Delta t$ for all a, j and t. Then assuming time-translational invariance, the time derivative of $\langle J_{aj}^{(b)}(t) - J_{aj}(t)\rangle$ yields the quantity $\eta G_{ab}(t,0)$.

Figure 3 shows the simulation results of 4 randomly generated samples. Three results are compared: the teacher's estimate, the cavity method with constant stimulus, and fivefold cross-validation. We see that the cavity method yields estimates of the early stopping time with comparable precision as fivefold cross-validation. Including the overhead of setting up the simulations, the overall CPU time of the cavity method is 11% less than that of fivefold cross-validation.

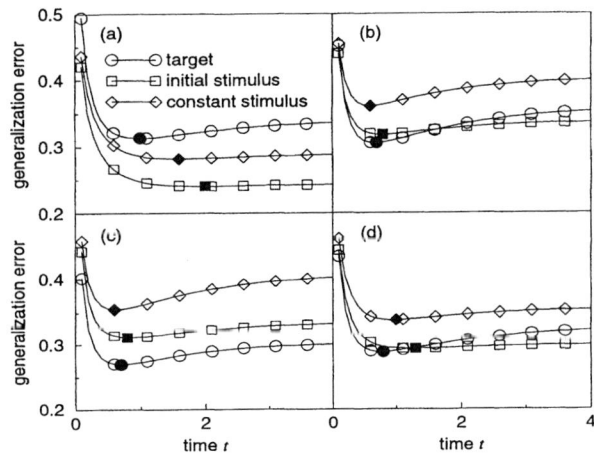

Fig. 3. (a-d) The evolution of the generalization error of the multilayer peceptron for $N = 200$, $n_h = 3$, $p = 500$ and $\sigma = 0.6$. The solid symbols locate the early stopping points estimated by the teacher (circle), the cavity method with constant stimulus (diamond), and fivefold cross-validation (triangle).

6   Conclusion

We have analysed the dynamics of learning with restricted sets of examples, studying the cases of batch learning with non-vanishing learning rates, and on-line learning. Using the cavity approach, we have derived equations for the macroscopic parameters describing the learning dynamics. They yield results which agree with simulations for Adaline learning.

Our work is a step forward from two recent treatments [5,6]. Compared with [5], we have made explicit the distribution of cavity activations, and that a functional relationship exists between the generic and cavity activations. As a result, our framework can be used to analyse the training error. Compared with [6], we have based our analysis on a more physical picture. For example, we have made explicit the difference between the active and passive averages unique to on-line learning. This enables us to analyse correctly the network behavior at large learning rates, when the mean-force approximation does not apply. The method has the potential to be extended to other paradigms of gradient-based iterative learning, such as BP or EM algorithms.

We have also proposed a method for the fast estimation of hyperparameters in large networks, based on the cavity method, combined with an empirical method of measuring the Green's function. The technique of hyperparameter estimation can be generalized to other learning systems, such as Gaussian processes and SVM.

This work is supported by the grant HKUST6157/99P and HKUST6153/01P from the Research Grant Council of Hong Kong.

References

1. D. Saad (ed.), *On-line learning in Neural Networks*, (Cambridge University Press, Cambridge MA, 1998).
2. K. Y. M. Wong, S. Li, and Y. W. Tong, Many-body approach to the dynamics of batch learning, *Phys. Rev. E* **62**, pp. 4036–4042 (2000).
3. P. Luo and K. Y. M. Wong, Dynamical and stationary properties of on-line learning from finite training sets, to appear in *Phys. Rev. E* **67**, 011906 (2003).
4. S. Bös and M. Opper, Dynamics of batch learning in a perceptron, J. Phys. A **31**, pp. 4835–4850 (1998).
5. D. Barber and P. Sollich, Online learning from finite training sets, in [1], pp. 279–302 (1998).
6. J. A. F. Heimel, and A. C. C. Coolen, Supervised learning with restricted training sets: a generating functional analysis, *J. Phys. A: Math. Gen.* **34**, pp. 9009–9026 (2001).
7. S. Amari, N. Murata, K.-R. Müller, M. Finke and H. H. Yang, Asymptotic statisitcal theory of overtraining and cross-validation, *IEEE Trans. on Neural Networks* **8**, pp. 985–996 (1997).
8. K. Y. M. Wong and F. Li, Fast parameter estimation using Green's functions, *Advances in Neural Information Processing Systems 14*, T. G. Dieterrich, S. Becker and Z. Ghahramani, eds., (MIT Press, Cambridge MA, 2002).

Nonlinear Multidimensional Data Projection and Visualisation

Hujun Yin

Dept. of Electrical Engineering and Electronics
University of Manchester Institute of Science and Technology
Manchester, M60 1QD, UK
h.yin@umist.ac.uk

Abstract. Multidimensional data projection and visualisation are becoming increasingly important and have found wide applications in many fields such as decision support, bioinformatics and web/document organisation. Various methods and algorithms have been proposed as either nonparametric or semiparametric approaches. This paper provides an overview of the subject and reviews some recent developments. Relationships among various key methods such as Sammon mapping, Neuroscale, principal curve/surface, SOM, GTM and ViSOM are analysed and their advantages and limitations are highlighted in the context of nonlinear principal component analysis and independent component analysis.

1 Introduction

Data projection and visualisation methods are becoming widely used tools in many fields such as decision support [8], financial analysis [1], information/knowledge management [11] and bioinformatics [51]. Searching for a suitable data mapping method has always been an integral objective of multivariate data analysis and pattern recognition. Projecting data on to its underlying subspace can detect its real structures, facilitate functional analysis, and help making a judgment. A great deal of research has been devoted to this subject and a number of methods have been proposed.

Classic projection methods include the linear principal component analysis (PCA) and the multidimensional scaling (MDS). The PCA projects the data onto its principal directions, which are represented by the orthogonal eigenvectors of the covariance matrix of the data. It is the optimal linear projection in the sense of minimum mean-square-error between the original data points and the projected ones on the principal subspace. But the PCA's linearity has limited its power for practical data, as it cannot capture nonlinear relationships defined by higher than second order statistics. If the input dimensionality is much higher than two, the projection onto a linear plane will provide limited visualisation power. An extension to nonlinear PCA, in principle, could tackle practical problems better. However there is no single and unique solution to nonlinear PCA [34]. Various methods have been proposed, for example the auto-associative networks [27], generalised PCA [20], kernel PCA [46], and the principal

J. Liu et al. (Eds.): IDEAL 2003, LNCS 2690, pp. 377–388, 2003.

curves and surfaces [14, 28]. Other mapping methods include the recently proposed local, geometric based grouping and averaging [49] and local linear embedding [43].

MDS tries to project data points onto a two-dimensional plane by preserving as close as possible the inter-point metrics [9, 42]. The mapping generally is nonlinear and can reveal the overall structure of the data. Sammon [45] mapping is a widely known example of MDS. However, like other MDS methods, the Sammon algorithm is a point-to-point mapping, which does not provide the explicit mapping function [45, 35].

Neural networks present another approach to nonlinear data analysis or projection. A feedforward neural network has been proposed to parametrise the Sammon mapping function and a back-propagation algorithm has been derived for training of the network and minimising the Sammon stress [35]. Neuroscale [33] is another realisation of the MDS using the radial basis function. The self-organising map (SOM) is an abstract mathematical model of the mapping between nerve sensory and cerebral cortex [24, 25]. The SOM has been widely used as a visualisation tool for dimensionality reduction (e.g. [52, 26]). The generative topographic mapping (GTM) [3] parametrises the SOM using mixture of Gaussians. The SOM's topology preserving property can be utilised to visualise the relative mutual relationships among the input. However, the SOM does not directly apply to scaling, which aims to reproduce proximity in (Euclidean) distance on a low visualisation space, as it has to rely on a colouring scheme to imprint the distances –that is very crude and often the distributions of the data points are distorted on the map. The recently proposed visualisation induced SOM (ViSOM) [54, 55] constrains the lateral contraction force between the neurons in the SOM and hence regularises the inter-neuron distances with respect to a scaleable parameter that defines and controls the resolution of the map. It preserves the data structure as well as the topology as faithfully as possible. The ViSOM provides a direct visualisation of both the structure and distribution of the data.

The remaining of the paper provides a review on various methods. The relationships among these methods are analysed and drawn. The advantages and drawbacks of these different approaches are also elucidated.

2 MDS and Sammon Mapping

Multidimensional scaling (MDS) is a traditional subject related to dimension reduction and data projection, which includes PCA as one of the projection methods. MDS tries to project data points onto a two-dimensional sheet or plot by preserving as close as possible the inter-point metrics [9, 42]. The projection is generally nonlinear and can reveal the overall structure of the data.

A general fitness function or so-called *stress* can be described as,

$$S = \frac{\sum_{i,j} [d_{ij} - D_{ij}]^2}{\sum_{i,j} D_{ij}^2} \tag{1}$$

where d_{ij} represents the proximity of points i and j in the original space, D_{ij} represents the distance (usually Euclidean) between mapped points i and j in the new space,.

There is no exact and unique procedure to find the projection. Instead, the MDS relies on an optimisation algorithm to search for a configuration that gives as low stress as possible. A gradient method is commonly used for this purpose. Inevitably, various computational problems such as local minima and divergence may occur to the optimisation process. The methods are also often computationally intensive. The final solution depends on the starting configuration and parameters used in the algorithm [5].

2.1 Sammon Mapping

Sammon mapping is a well-known example of MDS. The objective of Sammon mapping is to minimise the differences between inter-point distances in the original space and those in the projected plane. The Sammon mapping has been shown to be useful for data structure analysis (e.g. [45], [41]). However, like other MDS methods, the Sammon algorithm is a point-to-point mapping, which does not provide the explicit mapping function and cannot naturally accommodate new data points [45, 35]. It also requires to compute and store all the inter-point distances. This proves difficult or even impossible for many practical applications where data arrives sequentially, the quantity of data is large, and/or memory space for the data is limited.

In Sammon mapping intermediate normalisation (of original space) is used to preserve good local distributions and at the same time maintain a global structure. The transformation function is simply the Euclidean distance between points i and j in the original space. The Sammon stress is expressed as,

$$S_{Sammon} = \frac{1}{\sum_{i<j} d_{ij}} \sum_{i<j} \frac{[d_{ij} - D_{ij}]^2}{d_{ij}} \tag{2}$$

Sammon proposed a recursive learning algorithm using the Newton optimisation method for the optimal configuration [45]. It converges faster than the simple gradient method, but the computational complexity is even higher. It still has the local minima and inconsistency problems.

In addition to being computationally costly, especially for large data sets, and not adaptive, another major drawback of MDS methods including Sammon mapping is lack of an explicit projection function. Thus for any new input data, the mapping has to be recalculated based on all available data. Although some methods have been proposed to accommodate the new arrivals using triangulation [29, 5, 10], the methods are generally not adaptive.

2.2 Neural Approaches to MDS

Mao and Jain [35] have proposed to use a feedforward neural network, termed SAMANN, to parametrise the Sammon mapping function and a unsupervised training methods has been derived for training of the network. The derivation is similar to the back-propagation algorithm, by minimising the Sammon stress instead of the total errors between desired and actual output. The network takes a pair of input points at each time in the training. An evaluation has to be carried out, using all the data points, after a fixed number of iterations.

In the SAMANN, all the inter-point distances have to be normalised before being input to the network. This will result clamping of any new data points whose distances to previous data points are larger the initial normalising scale. The algorithm is a gradient descent method and relies on a good initialisation.

Neuroscale uses radial basis function (RBF) to generalise the MDS [33]. It minimises a simple unweighted stress function, i.e. Eq (1) without the denominator. A subjective element has also been incorporated into the objective function and produces a projection that takes into account of subjective perception of data attributes, if such a prior knowledge exists such as in grading systems.

3   Nonlinear Extensions of PCA and ICA

PCA is a classic linear data analysis method aiming at finding orthogonal principal directions from a set of data, along which the data exhibit the largest variances. By discarding the minor components, the PCA can effectively reduce data variables and display the dominant ones in a linear, low dimensional subspace. It is the optimal linear projection in the sense of the mean-square error between original points and projected ones, i.e.,

$$\min_{\mathbf{x}} \sum [\mathbf{x} - \sum_{j=1}^{m} (\mathbf{q}_j^T \mathbf{x}) \mathbf{q}_j]^2 \tag{3}$$

where $\mathbf{x}=[x_1, x_2, \ldots x_n]^T$ is the n-dimensional input vector, $\{\mathbf{q}_j, j=1,2, \ldots m, m{\leq}n\}$ are orthogonal vectors representing principal directions. They are the first m principal eigenvectors of the covariance matrix of the input. The second term in the above bracket is the reconstruction or projection of $\mathbf{x}$ on these eigenvectors. The term $\mathbf{q}_j^T \mathbf{x}$ represents the projection of $\mathbf{x}$ onto the j-th principal dimension. Traditional methods for solving eigenvector problem involve numerical methods. Though fairly efficient and robust, they are not usually adaptive and often require the presentation of the entire data set. Several Hebbian-based learning algorithms and neural networks have been proposed for performing PCA such as, the subspace network [37] and the generalised Hebbian algorithm [44]. The limitation of linear PCA is obvious, as it cannot capture nonlinear relationships defined by higher than the second order statistics. If the input dimension is much higher than two, the projection onto linear principal plane will provide limited visualisation power.

The extension to nonlinear PCA (NLPCA) is not unique, due to the lack of a unified mathematical structure and an efficient and reliable algorithm, in some cases due to excessive freedom in selection of representative basis functions [34, 20]. Principal curves and principal surfaces [14, 41] were primary nonlinear extension of PCA, but a valid algorithm is required for a good implementation. Several networks have been proposed for nonlinear PCA such as, the five-layer feedforward associative network [27] and the kernel PCA [46]. The first three layers of the associative network project the original data on to a curve or surface, providing an activation value for the bottleneck node. The last three layers define the curve and surface. The weights of the associative NLPCA network are determined by minimising the following objective function,

$$\min \sum_{\mathbf{x}} \| \mathbf{x} - \mathbf{f}\{s_f(\mathbf{x})\} \|^2 \qquad (4)$$

where $\mathbf{f}: R^1 \rightarrow R^n$ (or $R^2 \rightarrow R^n$), the function modelled by the last three layers, defines a curve (or a surface), $s_f: R^n \rightarrow R^1$ (or $R^n \rightarrow R^2$), the function modelled by the first three layers, defines the projection index.

The kernel-based PCA [46] uses nonlinear mapping and kernel functions to generalise PCA to NLPCA and has been used for character recognition. The nonlinear function $\Phi(\mathbf{x})$ maps data onto high-dimensional feature space, where the standard linear PCA can be performed via kernel functions: $k(\mathbf{x}, \mathbf{y})=(\Phi(\mathbf{x}) \cdot \Phi(\mathbf{y}))$. The projected covariance matrix is then

$$\overline{C} = \frac{1}{N} \sum_{i=1}^{N} \Phi(\mathbf{x}_i) \Phi(\mathbf{x}_i)^T \qquad (5)$$

The standard linear eigenvalue problem can now be written as $\lambda\mathbf{V}=\mathbf{K}\mathbf{V}$, where the columns of $\mathbf{V}$ are the eigenvectors and $\mathbf{K}$ is a NxN matrix with elements as kernels $K_{ij}:=k(\mathbf{x}_i, \mathbf{x}_j)=(\Phi(\mathbf{x}_i) \cdot \Phi(\mathbf{x}_j))$.

(Linear) ICA is another way to extend and generalise the PCA. With the assumption of linear mixtures, ICA can decompose and map data set into statistically independent components. It has been studied intensively recently. Many theories regarding various aspects of the linear ICA have been established and confirmed experimentally [30, 17, 12]. However, in general and for many practical problems, mixtures are more likely to be nonlinear or subject to some kind of nonlinear distortions due to sensory or environmental limitations. Extension of existing theories and methods to nonlinear ICA (NLICA) is not straightforward. There have been few initial attempts (e.g. [39]). ICA and NLICA can be approached through non-linear PCA (NLPCA), SOM, and mixture models, and some work has demonstrated tentative links [38, 15, 40, 53].

The generic NLICA problem can be formulated as $\mathbf{X}(t)=F[\mathbf{S}(t)]$, where $\mathbf{S}(t)$ are a set of unknown source signals and $\mathbf{X}(t)$ the observation or measurements, F is unknown and generally a nonlinear transformation. In real problems there is a noise process $\mathbf{V}(t)$ associated with either source or observed signals. This noise term can be additive and multiplicative, and with various distributions (either correlated or not with the source signals). The complexity of the noisy NLICA model suggests the use of a flexible method that may need to be tailored to the experimental context. Some research has addressed a compromise between standard linear and purely NLICA methods, such as the ICA mixture models [32] and the local linear ICA using k-means clustering [21]. The first tries to relax the independence assumption of the generic ICA model. While the second is closely related to the batch version of the SOM, but with standard k-means clustering used, because of the fairly small number of clusters involved.

Various neural networks have also been applied to the NLICA problem. The use of multilayer perceptrons (MLP) in biomedical applications has been studied [31], while earlier a two-layer perceptron was employed [6]. An RBF network [48] has been used to recover the unknown sources from their nonlinear mixtures in presence of cross-nonlinearities. This method appears robust against additive, uniformly distributed white noise, but a further noise suppression technique is necessary to denoise the separated source signals. SOMs have been used [15, 40] to extract independent components from nonlinearly mixed discrete or continuous sources. The network complexity increases with the number of neurons while the quantization error (interpolation error, in the continuous case) cannot be disregarded. A SOM-based NLICA method has been used to denoise multiplicative noise [13]. A post-nonlinear mixing has been proposed by [32] and [47]. In this case, the sources are assumed to be linearly mixed and then transformed by a nonlinear transfer channel. This parametric approach uses sigmoidal functions and MLP networks to approximate the inverse nonlinearity. However, the approach is limited to a certain class of nonlinear mixtures. A generalization to a rather larger class of functions has been given by [18] using the notion of conformal mapping into the complex domain. Generally existing NLICA methods can be classified into two categories. The first models the nonlinear mixing as a linear process followed by a nonlinear transfer channel. These methods are of limited flexibility as they are often parametrized. The second category employs parameter-free methods, which are more useful in representing more generic nonlinearities. A common neural technique in this second category is the SOM, which can be used to model and extract the underlying nonlinear data structures.

4 Principal Curves and Surfaces

The principal curves and principal surfaces (14, 28] are primary nonlinear extension of PCA, but a valid algorithm is required for a good implementation. The principal curve was first defined as a smooth and self-consistency curve, which does not intersect itself. Denote x as a random vector in R^n with density p and finite second moment. Let $f(\cdot)$ be a smooth unit-speed curve in R^n, parametrised by the arc length ρ (from one end of the curve) over $\Lambda \in R$, a closed interval.

For a data point x, its projection index on f is defined as

$$\rho_f(\mathbf{x}) = \sup_{\rho \in \Lambda}\{\rho : \|\mathbf{x} - f(\rho)\| = \inf_{\vartheta}\|\mathbf{x} - f(\vartheta)\|\} \tag{6}$$

The curve is called self-consistent or a principal curve of p if

$$f(\rho) = E[\mathbf{X} \mid \rho_f(\mathbf{X}) = \rho] \tag{7}$$

The principal component is a special case of the principal curves if the distribution is ellipsoidal. Although 1-D principal curves have been mainly studied, extension to higher dimension, e.g. principal surfaces is feasible in principle. However, in practice, a good implementation of principal curves/surfaces relies on an effective and efficient algorithm.

The principal curves/surfaces are more of a concept that invites practical implementations. The HS algorithm is a nonparametric method [14], which directly iterates the two steps of the above definition. It is similar to the LGB VQ algorithm, combined with some smoothing techniques.

HS algorithm:

Initialisation: Choose the first linear principal component as the initial curve, $f^{(0)}(\mathbf{x})$.

Projection: Project the data points onto the current curve and calculate the projections index, i.e. $\rho^{(t)}(\mathbf{x})=\rho_{f(t)}(\mathbf{x})$.

Expectation: For each index, take the mean of data points projected onto it as the new curve point, i.e., $f^{(t+1)}(\rho)=E[\mathbf{X}|\rho_{f(t)}(\mathbf{X})=\rho]$.

The projection and expectation steps are repeated until a convergence criterion is met, e.g. when the change of the curve between iterations is below a threshold.

For a finite data set, the density p is often unknown, the above expectation is replaced by a smoothing method such as the locally weighted running-line smoother or smoothing splines. For kernel regression, the smoother is,

$$f(\rho) = \frac{\sum_{i=1}^{N}\mathbf{x}_i\kappa(\rho,\rho_i)}{\sum_{i=1}^{N}\kappa(\rho,\rho_i)} \tag{8}$$

The arc length is simply computed from the line segments. There are no proofs of convergence of the algorithm, but no convergence problems have been reported, though the algorithm is biased in some cases [14]. Banfield and Raftery [2] have modified the HS algorithm by taking the expectation of the residual of the projections in order to reduce the bias. Kegl et al [23] have proposed an incremental, e.g. segment by segment, and arc length constrained method for practical construction of principal curves.

Tibshirani [50] has introduced a semi-parametric model for the principal curve. A mixture model was used to estimate the noise along the curve; and the expectation and maximisation (EM) method was employed to estimate the parameters. Other options for finding the nonlinear manifold include the GTM [3] and probabilistic principal surfaces (PPS) [7]. These methods model the data by a means of a latent space. They belong to the semi-parametrised mixture model, although types and orientations of the local distributions vary from method to method.

5 SOM, GTM, and ViSOM

The SOM is an unsupervised learning algorithm that uses a finite grid of neurons to frame the input space. As the map is often arranged in a low dimensional, e.g. 2-D, grid, it can be used for visualisation of potentially high dimensional data on a visible dimension. In the SOM, neighbourhood learning is adopted to form topological ordering among the neurons in the map. The mapping is generally nonlinear. The close data points are likely projected to nearby nodes. Thus the map can be used to show the relative relationships among the data points. However, the SOM does not directly show the inter-neuron distances on the map. For visualisation, the SOM requires assistance from a colouring scheme to imprint the inter-neuron distances and therefore the clusters and boundaries can be marked. The colour or grey tone of a node or a region between nodes is proportional to the mean or median of the distances between that node and its nearest neighbours. Such a colouring method has been used in many data visualisation applications, e.g. WEBSOM [16] and World Welfare Map [22]. The colouring methods indeed enhance the visualisation ability of the SOM. However, the cluster structures and distribution of the data shown on the map often are not apparent and appear in distorted and unnatural forms. Other techniques to mark the inter neuron distances include calculating the magnification factors or the Jacobians [4] and interpolation [57]. The SOM can serve as a visualisation map only in showing the relative closeness and relationships among data points and clusters. This is also the case for the GTM, which is a parametrised approach to the SOM [3]. It uses a set of RBFs to map a latent 2-D grid into the high dimensional data space,

$$Y(\mathbf{x}, \mathbf{W}) = \mathbf{W}\phi(x) \tag{9}$$

In the GTM, the data is modelled by a mixture of homoscedastic Gaussians. Then the EM algorithm is used to learn the parameters: the mapping $\mathbf{W}$ and the common variance σ of the Gaussians. The PPS [7] has adopted a general Gaussian mixture and oriented covariance noise model in the GTM and results in a better approximation to principla curves and surfaces. The recently proposed latent trait model (LTM) [19] generalises the GTM for both discrete and categorical data distributions. The SOM can also be directly parametrised using mixture of Gaussians such as the Bayesian SOM [58] for modelling the data density.

In many cases, however, a direct and faithful display of structure shapes and distributions of the data is highly desirable in visualisation applications. ViSOM has been proposed to directly preserve distances on the map [54, 55]. For the map to capture the data structure naturally and directly, the distance quantity must be preserved on the map, along with the topology. Ideally the nodes should be uniformly and smoothly placed in the nonlinear manifold of the data space. The map can be seen as a smooth and graded mesh embedded into the data space, onto which the data points are mapped and the inter-point distances are approximately preserved.

In the ViSOM, lateral contraction force is constrained in the learning rule,

$$\mathbf{w}_k(t+1) = \mathbf{w}_k(t) + \alpha(t)\eta(v,k,t)\{[\mathbf{x}(t) - \mathbf{w}_v(t)] + \beta[\mathbf{w}_v(t) - \mathbf{w}_k(t)]\} \tag{10}$$

where the simplest constraint can be $\beta := d_{vk}/(\Delta_{vk}\lambda) - 1$, with d_{vk} the distance in the input space, Δ_{vk} the distance on the map, and λ a resolution constant.

The ViSOM regularises the contraction force so that the distances between the nodes on the map are analogous to the distances of their weights in the data space. The aim is to adjust inter-neuron distances on the map in proportion to those in the data space, i.e. $\Delta_{vk} \propto d_{vk}$. When the data points are eventually projected on a trained map, the distance between point i and j on the map is proportional to that of the original space, subject to the quantisation error (the distance between a data point and its neural representive). This has a similar effect to Sammon mapping, which also aims at achieving this proportionality, $D_{ij} \propto d_{ij}$, though here D_{ij} represents the distance of two mapped data points. When the number of nodes increases, the quantisation errors reduces. The key feature of the ViSOM is that the distances between the neurons on the map (in a neighbourhood) reflect the corresponding distances in the data space. When the map is trained and data points mapped, the distances between mapped data points on the map will resemble approximately those in the original space (subject to the resolution of the map). This makes visualisation more direct, quantitatively measurable, and visually appealing. The size or covering range of the neighbourhood function can also be decreased from an initially large value to a final smaller one. The final neighbourhood, however, should not contain just the winner. The rigidity or curvature of the map is controlled by the ultimate size of the neighbourhood. The larger of this size the flatter the final map is in the data space.

The SOM has also been related to the discrete principal curve/surface algorithm [42, 36]. However the differences remain in both the projection and smoothing processes. In the SOM the data are projected onto the nodes rather than onto the curve. The principal curves perform the smoothing entirely in the data space –see Eq. (8). The smoothing process in the SOM and ViSOM, as a convergence criterion, is [56],

$$\mathbf{w}_k = \frac{\sum_{i=1}^{L} \mathbf{x}_i \eta(v,k,i)}{\sum_{i=1}^{L} \eta(v,k,i)} \tag{11}$$

The smoothing is governed by the indexes of the neurons in the map space. The kernel regression uses the arc length parameters $(\rho,\ \rho_i)$ or $\|\rho-\rho_i\|$ exactly, while the neighbourhood function uses the node indexes $(k,\ i)$ or $\|k-i\|$. Arc lengths reflect the curve distances between the data points. However, node indexes are integer numbers denoting the nodes or the positions on the map grid, not the positions in the input space. So $\|k-i\|$ does not resemble $\|\mathbf{w}_k-\mathbf{w}_i\|$ in the common SOM. In the ViSOM, however, as the inter-neuron distances on the map represent those in the data space (subject to the resolution of the map), the distances of nodes on the map are in proportion to the difference of their positions in the data space, i.e. $\|k-i\|\sim\|\mathbf{w}_k-\mathbf{w}_i\|$. The smoothing process in the ViSOM resembles that of the principal curves as shown below,

$$\mathbf{w}_k = \frac{\sum_{i=1}^{L} \mathbf{x}_i \eta(v,k,i)}{\sum_{i=1}^{L} \eta(v,k,i)} \approx \frac{\sum_{i=1}^{L} \mathbf{x}_i \eta(\mathbf{w}_v,\mathbf{w}_k,i)}{\sum_{i=1}^{L} \eta(\mathbf{w}_v,\mathbf{w}_k,i)} \tag{12}$$

The ViSOM is a better approximation to the principal curves/surfaces than the SOM is. The SOM and ViSOM are similar only when the data are uniformly distributed, or when the number of nodes becomes very large, in which case both the SOM and ViSOM will closely approximate the principal curves/surfaces.

6 Conclusions

Nonlinear projections of multidimensional data have been approached from various aspects such as MDS, nonlinear PCA, nonlinear ICA, and principal manifold such as principal curves and surfaces. Various realisation methods have been proposed and proved to be useful in various data modelling and visualisation applications. Among these methods, the SOM and ViSOM seem to be the most versatile and nonparametric methods not only in data visualisation, but also in capturing the nonlinear manifold of the data. The ViSOM is a natural algorithm for extracting discrete principal curves and surfaces.

References

1   Arciniegas, I., Daniel, B., Embrechts, M. J.: Exploring Financial Crises Data with self-organising maps. *Advances in Self-Organising Maps.* Allinson, N, Yin, H., Allinson, L. and Slack J. (Eds). (2001) 39–46

2   Banfield, J. D. and Raftery, A. E.: Ice floe identification in satellite images using mathematical morphology and clustering about principal curves. *Journal of the American Statistical Association*, 87 (1992) 7–16.

3   Bishop, C. M., Svensén, M., and Williams, C. K. I.: GTM: The generative topographic mapping. *Neural Computation*, 10 (1998) 215–235

4   Bishop, C. M., Svensén, M., and Williams, C. K. I.: Magnification factors for the SOM and GTM algorithms. *Proceedings of Workshop on Self-Organizing Maps (WSOM'97)*, 333–338.

5   Biswas, G., Jain, A. K., & Dubes, R. C.: Evaluation of project algorithms. *IEEE Trans. on Pattern Analysis and Machine Intelligence*, PAMI-3 (1981) 701–708

6   Burel, G.: Blind separation of sources: A nonlinear neural algorithm. *Neural Networks*, 5 (1992) 937–947.

7   Chang, K.-Y. and Ghosh, J.: A unified model for probabilistic principal surfaces, *IEEE Trans. on Pattern Analysis and Machine Intelligence*, PAMI-23 (2001) 22–41.

8   Condon, E., Golden, B, Lele, S., Raghavan, S, Wasil, E.: A visualization model based on adjacency data. *Decision Support systems*, 33 (2002) 349–362.

9   Cox, T. F., & Cox, M. A. A.: *Multidimensional Scaling*, Chapman & Hall (1994).

10   De Ridder, D. and Duin R.P.W.: Sammon mapping using neural networks: a comparison. *Pattern Recognition Letters* 18 (1997) 1307–1316

11   Freeman, R. and Yin, H.: Self-organising maps for hierarchical tree view document clustering using contextual information. *LNCS-2412*. Yin, et al (Eds). (2002) 123–128

12   Girolami, M.: *Self-Organising Neural Networks: Independent Component Analysis and Blind Source Separation.* Springer (1999).

13   Haritopoulos, M., Yin, H., and Allinson, N.M.: Image denoising using self-organising map –based nonlinear independent component analysis. *Neural Networks* 15 (2002) 1085–1098.

14   Hastie, T., & Stuetzle, W.: Principal curves. *Journal of the American Statistical Association*, 84 (1989) 502–516

15   Herrmann, M. and Yang, H. H.: Perspectives and limitations of self-organising maps in blind separation of source signals. *Proc. ICONIP'96* (1996) 1211–1216.

16   Honkela, T., Kaski, S., Lagus, K., and Kohonen, T.: WEBSOM-self-organizing maps of document collections. *Proceedings of Workshop on Self-Organizing Maps (WSOM'97)*, 310–315.

17   Hyvärinen, A, Karhunen, J. and Oja, E.: *Independent Component Analysis.* John Wiley & Sons, Inc. (2001).

18   Hyvärinen, A. and Pajunen, P.: Nonlinear independent component analysis: Existence and uniqueness results. *Neural Networks*, 12 (1999) 429–439.

19   Kaban, A. and Girolami, M.: A combined latent trait class and trait model for the analysis and visualisation of discrete data. *IEEE Trans. on Pattern Analysis and Machine Intelligence*, PAMI-23 (2001) 859–872.

20   Karhunen, J., and Joutsensalo, J.: Generalisation of principal component analysis, optimisation problems, and neural networks. *Neural Networks*, 8 (1995) 549–562.

21   Karhunen, J. and Malaroiu, S.: Local independent component analysis using clusternig. *Proc. 1st Int. Workshop on Independent Component Analysis and Signal Separation (ICA '99)* (1999) 43–48.

22   Kaski, S., and Kohonen, T.: Exploratory data analysis by the self-organizing map: Structures of welfare and poverty in the world. *Neural Networks in Financial Engineering*, Apostolos-Paul N. Refenes, Yaser Abu-Mostafa, John Moody, and Andreas Weigend (Eds.) World Scientific, (1996) 498–507.

23   Kegl, B., Krzyzak, A., Linder, T., and Zeger, K.: A polygonal line algorithm for constructing principal curves. *Neural Information Processing Systems (NIPS'98)*, 11 (1998) 501–507.

24   Kohonen, T.: Self-organised formation of topologically correct feature map. *Biological Cybernetics*, 43 (1982) 56–69.

25   Kohonen, T.: *Self-Organising Maps,* Springer: Berlin (Second edition). (1995).

26   Kraaijveld, M.A., Mao, J., and Jain, A.K.: A nonlinear projection method based on Kohonen's topology preserving maps. *IEEE Trans. Neural Networks*, 6 (1995) 548–559.

27   Kramer, M.A.: Nonlinear principal component analysis using autoassociative neural networks. *AICHE Journal*, 37 (1991) 233–243.

28   LeBlanc, M., and Tibshirani, R. J.: Adaptive principal surfaces. *J. Amer. Statist. Assoc.* 89 (1994) 53–64.

29   Lee, R.C.T., Slagle, J.R., and Blum, H.: A triangulation method for the sequential mapping of points from n-space to two-space. *IEEE Trans. on Computers*, 27 (1977) 288–292.

30   Lee, T.-W.: *Independent Component Analysis: Theory and Applications.* Kluwer Academic (1998).

31   Lee, T.-W., Koehler, B.-U. and Orglmeister, R.: Blind source separation of nonlinear mixing models. *Proc. IEEE Workshop on Neural Networks for Signal Processing (NNSP '97)* (1997) 406–415.

32   Lee, T.-W., Lewicki, M.-S. and Sejnowski, T.-J.: Unsupervised Classification with Non-Gaussian Mixture Models using ICA. *Advances in Neural Information Processing Systems*, 11 (1999) 508–514.

33   Lowe, D and Tipping, M.E.: Feed-forward neural networks and topographic mappings for exploratory data analysis. *Neural Computing and Applications.* 4 (1996) 83–95.

34   Malthouse, E. C.: Limitations of nonlinear PCA as performed with generic neural networks. *IEEE Trans. Neural Networks*, 9 (1998) 165–173.

35   Mao, J., and Jain, A. K.: Artificial Neural Networks for Feature Extraction and Multivariate Data Projection. *IEEE Trans. on Neural Networks*, 6 (1995). 296–317.

36   Mulier, F., and Cherkassky, V.: Self-organisation as an iterative kernel smoothing process. *Neural Computation*, 7 (1995) 1165–1177.

37   Oja, E.: Neural networks, principal components, and subspaces. *Int. Journal of Neural Systems*, 1 (1989), 61–68

38   Oja, E.: PCA, ICA, and nonlinear Hebbian learning. *Proc. Int. Conf. on Artificial Neural Networks (ICANN'95)* 89–94.

39   Pajunen, P. and Karhunen, J.: A maximum likelihood approach to nonlinear blind source separation. *Proc. Int. Conf. on Artificial Neural Networks (ICANN'97)* 541–546.

40   Pajunen, P., Hyvärinen, A. and Karhunen, J.: Nonlinear blind source separation by self-organising maps. *Proc. ICONIP'96,* 1207–1210.

41   Ripley, B. D.: *Pattern Recognition and Neural Networks,* Cambridge University Press: Cambridge, (1996).

42   Ritter, H., Martinetz, T., and Schulten, K.: *Neural Computation and Self-organising Maps: An Introduction.* Addison-Wesley Publishing Company (1992).

43   Roweis, S. T., and Saul, L. K.: Nonlinear dimensionality reduction by locally linear embedding. *Science,* 290 (2000) 2323–2326.

44   Sanger, T. D.: Optimal unsupervised learning in a single-layer linear feedforward network. *Neural Networks,* 2 (1991) 459–473.

45   Sammon, J. W.: A nonlinear mapping for data structure analysis. *IEEE Trans. on Computer,* 18 (1969) 401–409.

46   Schölkopf, B., Smola, A., & Müller, K. R.: Nonlinear component analysis as a kernel eigenvalue problem. *Neural Computation,* 10 (1998) 1299–1319.

47   Taleb, A. and Jutten, C.: Source separation in postnonlinear mixtures. *IEEE Trans. on Signal Processing,* 47 (1999) 2807–2820.

48   Tan, Y., Wang, J. and Zurada, J. M.: Nonlinear blind source separation using a radial basis function network. *IEEE Trans. on Neural Networks,* 12 (2001) 124–134.

49   Tenenbaum, J. B., de Silva, V., & Langford, J. C.: A global geometric framework for nonlinear dimensionality reduction. *Science,* 290 (2000) 2319–2323.

50   Tibshirani, R.: Principal curves revisited. *Statistics and Computation,* 2 (1992) 183–190.

51   Törönen, P., Kolehmainen, K., Wong, G., Castrén, E.: Analysis of gene expression data using self-organising maps. *FEBS Letters,* 451 (1999) 142–146.

52   Ultsch, A.: Self-organising neural networks for visualisation and classification. *Information and Classification,* O. Opitz, B. Lausen and R. Klar (Eds.) (1993) 864–867.

53   Xu, L, Cheung, C. C. and Amari, S.-I.: Learned parametric mixture based ICA algorithm. *Neurocomputing,* 22 (1998) pp. 69–80.

54   Yin, H.: Visualisation induced SOM (ViSOM). In: *Advances in Self-Organising Maps (Proc. WSOM'01),* N. Allinson, H. Yin, L. Allinson, & J. Slack (Eds.), Springer, 81–88.

55   Yin, H.: ViSOM-A novel method for multivariate data projection and structure visualisation. *IEEE Trans. on Neural Networks,* 13 (2002) 237–243.

56   Yin, H.: Data visualisation and manifold mapping using the ViSOM. *Neural Networks,* 15 (2002) 1005–1016.

57   Yin, H., and Allinson, N. M.: Interpolating self-organising map (iSOM). *Electronics Letters* 35 (1999) 1649–1650.

58   Yin, H., and Allinson, N. M.: Bayesian self-organising map for Gaussian mixtures. *IEE Proc. –Vis. Image Signal Processing,* 148 (2001) 234–240.

Comparative Study between Radial Basis Probabilistic Neural Networks and Radial Basis Function Neural Networks[1]

Wen-Bo Zhao[1,2], De-Shuang Huang[2], and Lin Guo[2]

[1] Department of Automation, University of Science and Technology of China
[2] Institute of Intelligent Machines, Chinese Academy of Sciences.
zwblp@163.com

Abstract. This paper exhaustively discusses and compares the performance differences between radial basis probabilistic neural networks (RBPNN) and radial basis function neural networks (RBFNN). It is proved that, the RBPNN is better than the RBFNN, in the following several aspects: the contribution of the hidden center vectors to the outputs of the neural networks, the training and testing speed, the pattern classification capability, and the noises toleration. Finally, two experimental results show that our theoretical analyses are completely correct.

1 Introduction

The radial basis function neural network (RBFNN) is a kind of widely used neural network model [1-3]. From the topology structure, as shown in Fig. 1, it can be seen that the RBFNN is a sort of feed-forward artificial neural network (FNN), which only includes a hidden layer. Generally, the synaptic weights (also called hidden centers vectors) between the input layer and the hidden layer do not require training but selecting from the training samples. For the pattern recognition problem the transfer function of the hidden layer of RBFNN is chosen as the kernel functions satisfying the probabilistic density estimate based on Parzen window function [4]. In essence the hidden layer is the key part of the RBFNN as accomplishing the nonlinear hyper-separation and function expansion. In addition, the outputs of the RBFNN are the linear combinations of the hidden layers output. Thus, the training of the synaptic weights between the hidden layer and the output layer is relatively simple [5,6]. And from the viewpoint of convergence, the RBFNN is faster than the other FNN's, especially the conventional multi-layer perception neural networks (MLPNN).

The radial basis probabilistic neural network (RBPNN) is a new neural network model proposed by Huang [7]. The topology structure of the RBPNN is shown in Fig. 2. It consists of four layers: the fist layer is an input layer, the second and the third layer are hidden layers, the forth layer is an output layer. Similar to the RBFNN, the two hidden layers are the key parts of the RBPNN. The essence of the first hidden layer is the same as the unique hidden layer of the RBFNN. The synaptic weights between the first hidden layer and the second hidden layer are the selective factors

---

[1] This work was supported by NSF of China and the Grant of "Hundred Talents Program" of Chinese Academy of Sciences of China

J. Liu et al. (Eds.): IDEAL 2003, LNCS 2690, pp. 389–396, 2003.
© Springer-Verlag Berlin Heidelberg 2003

doing the summations of the outputs of the first hidden layers, which do not need to be trained. The synaptic weights between the second hidden layer and the output layer are somewhat similar to the one of the RBFNN. Generally, the training speed for the RBPNN has also advantage over the other FNN's.

From the above analyses, it can be known that the RBFNN and the RBPNN are in structure similar to each other, the unique differences is that the RBPNN has more one hidden layer than the RBFNN. However, in performance, are there any differences between the two models? How to suitably apply them to solve more practical problems? These are the focus and the motivation of this paper.

2 Basic Differences between the RBPNN and the RBFNN

Assume that for the input vector x, the j-th output of the RBFNN, $y_j(x)$, can be expressed as:

$$y_j(x) = \sum_{i=1}^{M} w_{ji} z_i(x), \ j = 1, 2, \cdots, L \tag{1}$$

where w_{ji} is the synaptic weight between the i-th neuron of the hidden layer and the j-th neuron of the output layer; M, L respectively denotes the number of the hidden neurons and the number of the output neurons; $z_i(x)$ is the i-th output of the hidden layer of the RBFNN. As the hidden layer is composed of the hidden center vectors and the kernel functions, which are generally Gaussian kernel functions, $z_i(x)$ can be written as:

$$z_i(x) = K(\|x - c_i\|, \sigma_i) = \exp(-\frac{\|x - c_i\|_2^2}{\sigma_i}) \tag{2}$$

where c_i is the i-th hidden center vector; σ_i is the controlling parameter of the kernel function. The j-th output $y_j(x)$ of the RBFNN can be expressed as:

$$y_j(x) = \sum_{i=1}^{M} w_{ji} \exp\left(-\frac{\|x - c_i\|^2}{\sigma_i}\right) \tag{3}$$

For input vector x, the j-th output $y_j(x)$ of the RBPNN can be expressed as:

$$y_j(x) = \sum_{i=1}^{M} w_{ji} h_i(x) \tag{4}$$

where $h_i(x)$ is the i-th output of the second hidden layer of the RBPNN. According to the working principle of the RBPNN, $h_i(x)$ can be written as:

$$h_i(x) = \sum_{k=1}^{M_i} \exp(-\frac{\|x - c_{ik}\|_2^2}{\sigma_i}) \tag{5}$$

where c_{ik} and σ_i is respectively the k-th hidden center vector of the i-th pattern and the i-th controlling parameter.

So (4) can be written as:

$$y_j(x) = \sum_{i=1}^{M} h_i(x) w_{ji} = \sum_{i=1}^{M} w_{ji} \sum_{k=1}^{M_i} \exp(-\frac{\|x - c_{ik}\|_2^2}{\sigma_i}) \tag{6}$$

From (3) and (6), it can be seen that there exist some similarities and differences between the two kinds of neural network models.

From the topology structures and mathematical mappings of the two kinds of neural network models, it can be observed that there exist the common processing organizations, i.e., kernel processing units, for the two models. In [7], it had been proved that when the two neural network models were used to recognize the labeled pattern classification problems, the outputs of the neural networks could converge to the posterior probability estimation of the input samples after the networks converge to the given error accuracy. According to [7], for the labeled pattern classification problems, the kernel functions of the kernel units must satisfy the four following

conditions [4]: (1) $\sup_{-\infty < x < +\infty} |K(x)| < \infty$ (2) $\int_{-\infty}^{\infty} |K(x)| dx < \infty$ (3) $\int_{-\infty}^{+\infty} K(x) dx = 1$ (4) $\lim_{x \to \infty} |xK(x)| = 0$.

As for the selection of the kernel functions, the two neural network models have not almost differences, generally the Gaussian kernel functions are preferred. This kernel function has the advantages that, in the condition of different controlling parameters, the outputs have different recognition resolutions. Like the receptive field of optic nerves of human being, when the particular parts of objects need to be distinguished, the receptive field will turn small, otherwise, become large.

Although the two neural network models have the common properties above, there exist some differences in essence. The following discussions will be mainly focused on these key points.

2.1 The Differences between the Hidden Outputs of the Two Neural Network Models

As the above discussions, although the kernel functions of the two models choose the Parzen window functions for the labeled pattern classification problems, there exist differences between the two kernel unit layers. For the RBFNN, each neuron of output layers is determined by all the hidden center vectors. In other words, all the hidden centers of the RBFNN, take part in contributing to the output posteriori probability estimate of input samples. For the RBPNN, however, as the hidden centers with common characteristics are all concentrated on one pattern class in the structures, as a result, the pattern classification based on the hidden center vectors has almost been implemented. So when the RBPNN is used in the training and testing phases, it has the following characteristics. Firstly, the RBPNN classifies the input samples initially clustered by the hidden center vectors. If some input sample is close to the most hidden center members of some pattern class, the corresponding output value of the pattern class is obviously bigger than the ones of any other pattern classes numerically. This is the merit only with the RBPNN.

2.2 The Different Training Time and Converged Speed for the RBPNN and the RBFNN

Assumed that training set $\varnothing$ has L pattern classes, and the number of the hidden center vectors for each pattern class is respectively $N_1, N_2, \cdots, N_M$. For the RBFNN, the total number of the hidden center vectors is $N_H = N_1 + N_2 + \cdots + N_M$. When the RBFNN has L output neurons, the number of the synaptic weights from the hidden-to-output layer is $N_{RBFNN} = L \times (N_1 + N_2 + \cdots + N_M)$; For the RBPNN, the number of the synaptic weights between the second layer and output layer is $N_{RBPNN} = L \times M$. The

ratio is $\dfrac{N_{RBPNN}}{N_{RBFNN}} = \dfrac{N_1 + N_2 + \cdots + N_L}{M} \square\ 1$. From the viewpoint of computational complexity,

the RBPNN might be faster than the RBFNN in training and testing speed for the same pattern classification problems.

2.3 The Different Classification Ability for the RBPNN and the RBFNN

Assume that the input sample x_t is far away from all hidden center vectors of the RBFNN in distance, and its distances to the nearest hidden center vectors belonging to different classes are difficult to be distinguished in numeral, e.g., $z_j \approx z_k \square\ 1$ ($j \neq k$)(supposed that there are two classes among training samples set), although the synaptic weights between the two hidden units and output layers can be different from each other, their actual output can be very small, e.g., $y_j \approx y_k \rightarrow 0$ ($j \neq k$). So at this case the RBFNN can not correctly recognize the class property of the input sample.

For the RBPNN, as the selected hidden center vectors belong to different pattern classes, generally the corresponding hidden output results of the input training samples are obviously separate so that the fuzzy state can not appear. Even if in the especial condition, the two components of the output, $h(x) = [h_1(x), h_2(x), \cdots, h_M(x)]$, of the second hidden layer are very close and very small numerically, e.g., $h_j(x) \approx h_k(x) \square\ 1$ ($j \neq k$), because of normalized operator of the output neurons in this

hidden layer, e.g., $h'_j(x) = h_j(x) \Big/ \sum\limits_{t=1}^{M} h_s(x), h'_k(x) = h_k(x) \Big/ \sum\limits_{t=1}^{M} h_s(x)$, so the RBPNN

possesses also better classification ability.

2.4 Differences of Noises Toleration Performance of the RBPNN and the RBFNN

From the viewpoint of the structures of the RBPNN and the RBFNN, while only one hidden center vector for each pattern class is selected, the RBPNN turns into the RBFNN. So the RBFNN is a special case of the RBPNN.

As there exist more than one hidden center vector for each pattern class, it can assure that the RBPNN possesses better noise tolerance than the RBFNN. It is the hidden centers that provide the contribution to the noise tolerance or balance, which will be shown by the following experiments.

3 Experiments and Discussions

In order to validate the above analyses, two examples are conducted in this section. One is the telling-two-spirals-apart problem, the other is a time sequence predication problem.

3.1 Telling – Two-Spirals-Apart Problem

Telling-spirals-apart problem, proposed by Lang and Witbrock (1989) [8] is generally considered as a neural network testing benchmark, which is used to test the classification ability of some neural classifiers. In this paper, the RBPNN and the RBFNN are used to solve the problem so that their corresponding classification performance can be compared.

The raw data of two-spirals can be derived from [9], where the sizes (the length from the start point to the end one) of the two spirals were all set as 100 in this paper. From [9] it can also be known that (x^{2n}, y^{2n}) represents one point in one spiral, while (x^{2n-1}, y^{2n-1}) denotes a point in another spiral. Suppose that 100 sample points for each spiral are sampled, thus a total of 200 samples form the training samples set.

The RBFNN and the RBPNN were constructed as follows. They consisted of two input nodes, fitting the two dimensional input data, and two output nodes, representing the class of input samples in vector, that is, $[1, 0]^T$ expresses the input sample point that is part of the first spiral, otherwise, $[0, 1]^T$ indicates the input sample pertain to the second spiral.

Conveniently, the same optimizing method, recursive orthogonal least square algorithm (ROLSA) [10], was used to select the hidden center vectors of the two neural networks. And the error criterion of the RBPNN was same as the one of the RBFNN. Namely, after the actual output values of the training samples in the output layers of the two neural networks was rounded, the F-norms of the differences between the rounded actual outputs and desired signals must be zeros, e.g., $\left\| round(Y_A) - Y_S \right\|_F = 0$, where Y_A is the actual output matrix, Y_S is the desired signal matrix. So in the case of correct classification the actual difference between the two output nodes was made greater than 0.5, so that the optimized neural networks can be guaranteed to possess better classification performance.

By means of the ROLSA optimization, the least number of hidden centers of the RBFNN was 118, while the least of the RBPNN was 32. Furthermore, when all 200 training samples were input to two neural networks, the actual output values of the two neural networks (Supposed the operation of $round(\Box)$ be not utilized in the output layers of the two neural networks) were plotted in Figs. 3 and 4. So it can be deduced that the RBPNN is more optimal than the RBFNN, not only in the networks structure but also in classification ability.

In order to test the generalization capability of the RBFNN and the RBPNN, according to literature [9], a total of 1982 samples generated were mixed with the Gaussian white noises in the mean of zeros and the different variances to form the testing samples set. As stated above, the same error criterion was used during the testing process. The experimental results were shown in Table.1. From table, it can be seen that, in the way of generalization capability, the RBFNN constructed by 32 optimized hidden center vectors are significantly better than the RBFNN with 118 optimized hidden center vectors. So we can conclude that the classification capability of the RBPNN highly surpasses the one of the RBFNN.

3.2 The Time Sequence Prediction

In this subsection, the RBFNN and the RBPNN were applied to solve the predication of time sequence, Mackey-Glass. The training samples were generated from the following equation:

$$\frac{dx(t)}{dt} = -0.1x(t) + \frac{0.2x(t)}{1+x^{10}(t-\tau)} \tag{7}$$

where $\tau = -21$, when $0 \le t \le \tau$, $x(t-\tau) = 0.5$. By means of numerical integral method, there were 998 values of sequence x generated. Assume that the previous 8 sequence values were used to predict the next value. So the RBFNN and the RBPNN were built with the structures of 8 input nodes and 1 output node. So the 998 sequence values formed a 990 training samples set.

Here, the OLS [6] was used to select 15 key hidden center vectors of the RBFNN. According to the above statement, the RBPNN was designed as follows. There were 15 hidden nodes in the second hidden layer of the RBPNN. Based on the 15 selected hidden center vectors of the RBFNN, in a small neighborhood of each hidden center, another four samples from 990 training samples were also selected as the hidden center vectors of first hidden layer of the RBPNN, so that in the first hidden layer of the RBPNN, there exist totally 75 hidden center vectors. According to the working principle of the RBPNN, the outputs of every 5 hidden vectors of the first hidden layer can be summed to form the outputs of the second hidden layers.

The 990 training samples were employed to train the RBPNN and the RBFNN until they converged respectively to the fixed termination errors, e.g., $e\_rbp = 6.764 \times 10^{-4}$ and $e\_rbf = 5.167 \times 10^{-4}$.

In order to test the noise tolerance of the RBFNN and the RBPNN, the 990 training samples were mixed with the Gaussian white zero mean noises with different variances to generate the testing samples. The experimental results were shown in Fig. 5. From Fig.5, it can be found that although the converged error of the RBPNN was greater than the one of the RBFNN, the outputs of the RBPNN were closer to the real values than the RBFNN.

4 Conclusions

This paper mainly discussed the performance differences between the RBPNN's and the RBFNN's in theory and experiment. It can be concluded that the RBPNN's performance is obviously better than the RBFNN's in the following aspects:

(1)From the viewpoint of structure, the contributions of the hidden center vectors of the RBPNN's are more explicit than the ones of the RBFNN's.

(2)From the viewpoint of training time and convergent speed, the RBPNN's are mostly faster than the RBFNN's.

(3) For those complicated classification pattern problems, the RBPNN's possess stronger capability than the RBFNN's.

(4)From the viewpoint of noises toleration, the appropriately constructed RBPNN's are able to decrease the effect produced by input noise signals on the performance by comparing with the RBFNN's.

Future research works will include using the RBPNN's to solve more practical problems.

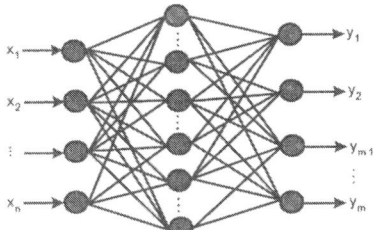

Fig. 1. The topology scheme of the RBFNN

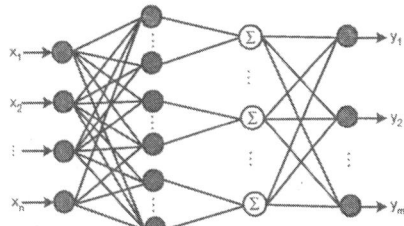

Fig. 2. The topology scheme of the RBPNN

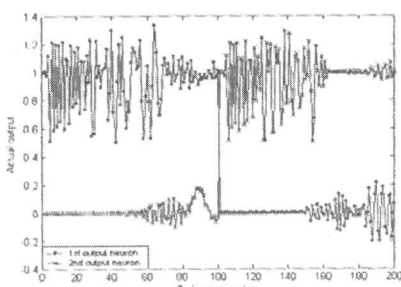

Fig. 3. The classification curves for telling-two-spirals-apart problem by the RBFNN (The crisscross signals represent the output of one neuron, the dot signals denote the other neuron output).

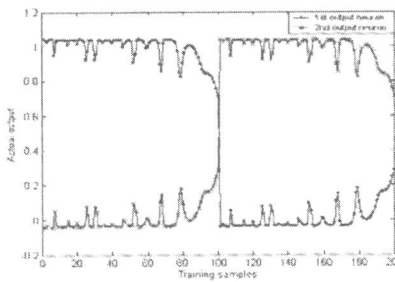

Fig. 4. The classification curves for telling-two-spirals-apart problem by the RBPNN (The crisscross signals represent the output of one neuron, the dot signals denote the other neuron output)

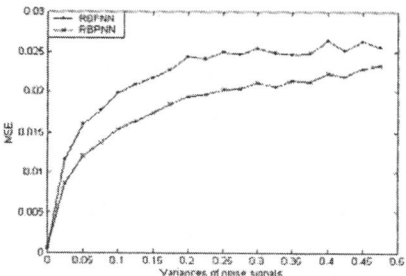

Fig. 5. The noise tolerance comparison between the RBPNN and the RBFNN for Mackey-Glass time sequence problem.

Table 1. The generalization capability comparison between the RBPNN and the RBFNN

Noise variances	class	RBFNN/RBPNN			Recognition rate (%)
		class1	class2	Rejection	RBFNN/RBPNN
$\sigma_1=0$	class1	978/991	0/0	13/0	98.69/100
	class2	0/0	971/991	20/0	97.98/100
$\sigma_1=0.01$	class1	767/980	171/6	52/5	77.4/98.89
	class2	104/11	728/985	159/0	73.46/99.39
$\sigma_2=0.1$	class1	322/510	309/451	380/30	32.49/51.46
	class2	292/477	320/534	379/0	32.29/53.88
$\sigma_3=0.2$	class1	252/435	264/450	475/106	25.43/43.90
	class2	237/483	206/474	548/34	20.79/47.83

References

1   Hush D. R., Horne B. G:, Progress in Supervised Neural Networks. IEEE Signal Processing Magazine (1993), 8–39..
2   Huang D. S.: Application of Generalized Radial Basis Function Networks to Recognition of Radar Targets. International Journal of Pattern Recognition and Artificial Intelligence (1999), 13(6), 945–962.
3   Huang D. S. , Bao Z., A Study of Recognition Technique of Radar Targets One-dimensional Images Based on Radial Basis Function Networks. Journal of Electronics (1995), 12(3), 200–210.
4   Parzen E.: On Estimation of A Probability Density Function Model. Ann. Math (1962), Stat. (33) 1065–1076.
5   Billings S. A., Zheng G. L.: Radial Basis Function Networks Configuration Using Genetic Algorithms. IEEE Trans. on Neural Networks (1995), vol. 8(6), 877–890.
6   Chen S., Cowan C. F. N., Grant P.M.: Orthogonal Least Squares Learning Algorithm for Radial Basis Function Networks. IEEE Trans. Neural Networks (1991), vol. 2, 302–309.
7   Huang D. S.: Radial Basis Probabilistic Neural Networks: Model and application. International Journal of Pattern Recognition and Artificial Intelligence (1999), 13(7), 1083–1101.
8   Lang K. J., Witbrock M. J. :Learning to Tell Ttwo Spirals Apart. In Proceedings of the 1988 connectionist models summer school. Morgan Kaufmann, San Mateo, CA, 52–59.
9   Zhao W. B., Huang D. S.: The Structure Optimization of Radial Basis Probabilistic Neural Networks Based on Genetic Algorithms. in WCCI2002 (IJCNN2002), Hilton Hawaiian Village Hotel, Honolulu, Hawaii, 1086–1091.
10 Zhao W. B., Huang D. S.: Application of Recursive Orthogonal Least Squares Algorithm to the Structure Optimization of Radial Basis Probabilistic Neural Networks.   *in Proceeding of ICSP2002* , Beijing, China, Aug. 26-30, 2002, . 1211–1214.

On Hadamard-Type Output Coding in Multiclass Learning

Aijun Zhang[1], Zhi-Li Wu[2], Chun-Hung Li[2], and Kai-Tai Fang[1]*

[1] Department of Mathematics,
[2] Department of Computer Science
Hong Kong Baptist University, Kowloon Tong, Hong Kong

Abstract. The error-correcting output coding (ECOC) method reduces the multiclass learning problem into a series of binary classifiers. In this paper, we consider the dense ECOC methods, combining an economical number of base learners. Under the criteria of row separation and column diversity, we suggest the use of Hadamard matrices to design output codes and show them better than other codes of the same size. Comparative experiments based on the support vector machines are made for some real datasets from the UCI machine learning repository.

Keywords. Multiclass learning, error-correcting output codes, Hadamard matrix, support vector machines.

1 Introduction

Many real-world classification problems require multiclass supervised learning. Most of machine learning algorithms, as developed for binary classification, could not be directly used for multiclass learning. Instead, the strategy of output coding is often considered, which reduces the multiclass problem to a series of binary problems, then makes the multiclass classification based on the binary outputs.

The simplest output code suggests to compare each class against all others, usually termed as one-per-call (OPC) output code. A more general type of output code (ECOC) with error-correcting properties is introduced by [6]. Both ECOC and OPC codes can be viewed as *dense* binary matrices and every binary classifier is obtained based on the full data. There are *sparse* output codes, e.g., the method of pairwise comparison [7]. A unifying framework of both dense and sparse codes is addressed in [1].

In this paper we restrict ourselves into the dense ECOC framework and consider a new type of output codes constructed from Hadamard matrices. In Section 2, a systematic study of ECOC methods is given, including Hamming decoding, goodness assessment and error analysis. In Section 3, we introduce Hadamard-type output codes and show them optimal in terms of row separation and column diversity. Finally, we show some experimental results for some public datasets from the UCI machine learning repository. The support vector machines are employed as our base learners, as they are widely believed to be stronger binary classifiers with good generalization performance.

---

* Corresponding author. `ktfang@math.hkbu.edu.hk`

J. Liu et al. (Eds.): IDEAL 2003, LNCS 2690, pp. 397–404, 2003.
© Springer-Verlag Berlin Heidelberg 2003

2   Error-Correcting Output Coding

2.1   ECOC and Hamming Decoding

Suppose $SS = \{(\mathbf{x}_i, y_i)\}_{i=1}^N$ is the set of N training examples, where each $\mathbf{x}_i \in \mathcal{X}$ contains the attributes and $y_i \in \mathcal{Y} = \{1, 2, \ldots, K\}$ is categorical. Denote an ECOC using L binary classifiers as $\mathbf{M} = (M_{kl})_{K \times L}$ with entries from $\{-1, 1\}$. Each class k in $\mathcal{Y}$ can be uniquely represented by a row M_{k*} of the ECOC matrix, which is also called as a codeword. For any two codewords $\mathbf{w}, \mathbf{u}$, their Hamming distance is defined by

$$d_H(\mathbf{w}, \mathbf{u}) = |\{j : w_j \neq u_j, 1 \leq j \leq L\}|. \tag{1}$$

The ECOC method consists of two stages: decomposition and reconstruction. In the first stage, the original training data (multiclass labeled) are partitioned into two superclasses according to each column M_{*l}: one superclass collects the examples with certain labels k's such that $M_{kl} = 1$, and the other superclass collects the rest examples. Running through all the columns, L sets of binary superclasses are obtained and therefore L binary classifiers $\hat{f}_1, \ldots, \hat{f}_L$ are trained.

At the stage of reconstruction, there are different schemes to recover the multiclass labels, typically Hamming decoding (i.e. majority vote) [6,9] and loss-based decoding [1]. The latter one is shown advantageous for margin-based classifiers, employing different loss functions of the margin. In this paper we mainly discuss how different output codes work with Hamming decoding, but the results are readily extended to loss-based decoding.

Given any observation $\mathbf{x}$, the vector of predictions $\hat{\mathbf{f}}(\mathbf{x}) = (\hat{f}_1(\mathbf{x}), \ldots, \hat{f}_L(\mathbf{x}))$ is called the target codeword. We predict $\mathbf{x}$ as from class k if $\hat{\mathbf{f}}$ and M_{k*} are closest in Hamming distance. Quite often there are more than one codewords in $\mathbf{M}$ attaining the smallest Hamming distance from $\hat{\mathbf{f}}$, so we need to define the following candidate set

$$\mathcal{C}(\mathbf{x}) = \left\{ k : d_H(\hat{\mathbf{f}}(x), M_{k*}) \text{ minimized} \right\}, \tag{2}$$

then assign $\mathbf{x}$ to every element of $\mathcal{C}(\mathbf{x})$ with probability $1/|\mathcal{C}(\mathbf{x})|$. This procedure is commonly referred to as Hamming decoding.

2.2   Goodness Assessment

Given an output code, two criteria of row separation and column diversity are commonly suggested [6] for the goodness assessment.

Row separation. Each codeword should be well-separated in Hamming distance from each of the other codewords;
Column diversity. Each column should be as uncorrelated with each of the other columns as possible.

There might be error bits in the target codeword, since not all binary classifiers can avoid making some wrong decisions. For Hamming decoding, small number of error bits may not result in a wrong multiclass decision if the target codeword keeps being closest to the true label. Therefore, a better row separation is expected in order to correct as many error bits as possible. In the coding theory [8], the minimum Hamming distance

$$d_{min} = \min_{1 \le i, k \le K} d_H(\mathbf{w}_i, \mathbf{w}_k) \qquad (3)$$

is a common measure of quality for error-correcting codes. The folloiwng lemma plays a key role in the framework of ECOC methods.

Lemma 1. *An ECOC matrix with minimum Hamming distance d_{min} can correct $\left[\frac{d_{min}-1}{2}\right]$ errors, where $[x]$ denotes the greatest integer not exceeding x.*

On the other hand, the criterion of column diversity is also essential for a good ECOC method. Otherwise, the training data partitioned according to identical (similar) would yield identical (similar) learned base classifiers, thus resulting in redundancy. We define

$$s_{max}(\mathbf{M}) = \max_{1 \le j, l \le L} |\mathrm{Corr}(M_{*j}, M_{*l})|, \qquad (4)$$

for monitoring the worst column diversity in ECOC, and use the minimax criterion $\min(s_{max})$ to search for the optimal ECOC with best column diversity.

Given the parameters K (cardinality of $\mathcal{Y}$) and L (number of binary classifiers), now we consider the optimality of the dense ECOC $\mathbf{M}_K(L)$. Denote as $\Omega(K, L)$ the set of $K \times L$ ECOC matrices with binary entries from $\{-1, 1\}$, i.e. $\Omega(K, L) = \{-1, 1\}^{K \times L}$. In terms of the criteria discussed above, we have the following definition of ECOC optimality.

Definition 1. *An ECOC $\mathbf{M}_K^*(L)$ is said to be optimal if*

$$\begin{cases} d_{min}(\mathbf{M}^*) \ge d_{min}(\mathbf{M}) \\ s_{max}(\mathbf{M}^*) \le s_{max}(\mathbf{M}) \end{cases} \quad \text{for all } \mathbf{M} \in \Omega(K, L). \qquad (5)$$

2.3 Error Analysis

For each learned binary classifier $\hat{f}_l(\mathbf{x})$, denote as ε_l, ρ_l the corresponding empirical and generalization losses, respectively. For the Hamming decoding, it is natural to define the empirical and generalization risks by

$$R_{emp}(\mathbf{M}, \hat{\mathbf{f}}) = \frac{1}{N} \sum_{i=1}^{N} \left(1 - \frac{\mathbf{1}_{y_i \in C(\mathbf{x}_i)}}{|C(\mathbf{x}_i)|}\right); R_{gen}(\mathbf{M}, \hat{\mathbf{f}}) = E\left(1 - \frac{\mathbf{1}_{y_i \in C(\mathbf{x}_i)}}{|C(\mathbf{x}_i)|}\right) \quad (6)$$

where the expectation in R_{gen} is taken with respect to the proper distribution of the unknown observation.

Basically, the error-correcting property in ECOC is supported by the pre-mentioned lemma [8]. More theoretically, since every codeword differs at least d_{min} positions from every other codeword, the Hamming balls of radius $\left[\frac{d_{min}-1}{2}\right]$ around each codeword are disjoint. Therefore, any target vector with at most $\left[\frac{d_{min}-1}{2}\right]$ error positions can be corrected. By these facts, we derive the following theorems concerning both empirical and generalization risks.

Theorem 1. *For the ECOC* $\mathbf{M}_K(L)$ *with minimum Hamming distance* d_{min}, *the empirical risk for the multiclass training is bounded above by*

$$R_{emp}(\mathbf{M}, \hat{\mathbf{f}}) \leq \min \left\{ 1, \frac{\sum_{j=1}^{L} \varepsilon_j}{\left[\frac{d_{min}-1}{2}\right] + 1} \right\}. \tag{7}$$

Proof. For $\hat{f}_j$, there are $N\varepsilon_j$ error bits male-classified among N empirical examples, so in total $N \sum_{j=1}^{L} \varepsilon_j$ error bits are distributed into the $N \times L$ virtual binary labels. Symbolically, we can think of these error bits are the nontrivial entries of a matrix $\mathbf{E}$ of size $N \times L$.

At the reconstruction stage, let us first consider an original training data $(\mathbf{x}_i, y_i)$. The ith row E_{i*} of matrix $\mathbf{E}$ corresponds to the error bits in the target codeword $\hat{\mathbf{f}}(\mathbf{x}_i)$. By Lemma 1, any increase in $R_{emp}(\mathbf{M}, \hat{\mathbf{f}})$ might be made only if the row has at least $\left[\frac{d_{min}-1}{2}\right] + 1$ error bits. Considering the worst-case of error distribution in $\mathbf{E}$ such that the number of problematic rows is maximized,

$$n_{max} = \left[\frac{N \sum_{j=1}^{L} \varepsilon_j}{\left[\frac{d_{min}-1}{2}\right] + 1} \right] \leq \frac{N \sum_{j=1}^{L} \varepsilon_j}{\left[\frac{d_{min}-1}{2}\right] + 1}.$$

Finally, by $R_{emp} \leq n_{max}/N$ and the fact $R_{emp} \leq 1$, we prove the claim. □

Theorem 2. *For the ECOC* $\mathbf{M}_K(L)$ *with minimum Hamming distance* d_{min}, *the generalization risk of multiclass reconstruction satisfies*

$$R_{gen}(\mathbf{M}, \hat{\mathbf{f}}) \leq 1 - \sum_{u} \prod_{r \in u} \rho_r \prod_{t \in u^c} (1 - \rho_t) \tag{8}$$

in which the subset $u \subset \{1, 2, \ldots, L\}$ *with its cardinality* $|u| \leq \left[\frac{d_{min}-1}{2}\right]$ *and* $u^c = \{1, 2, \ldots, L\} \setminus u$, *provided that the base learners associated with the column diverse ECOC are independent.*

Proof. We can justify this claim from the opposite direction. For a new observation $\mathbf{x}$, the jth element of its target codeword $\hat{\mathbf{f}}(\mathbf{x})$ has the probability ρ_j to be an error bit. Lemma 1 tells us that any subset u of error bits with the cardinality less than $\left[\frac{d_{min}-1}{2}\right]$ can be corrected, so the generalization accuracy should be at least $\sum_{u} \prod_{r \in u} \rho_r \prod_{t \in u^c} (1 - \rho_t)$ for all $|u| \leq \left[\frac{d_{min}-1}{2}\right]$, which leads to (8). □

For the generalization risk bound, it is straightforward to obtain the following corollary, which can be calculated easily and useful when the base learner behaves invariantly with respect to different decompositions. The corollary can be verified by combining the identical terms in (8).

Corollary 1. *Suppose all the base binary learners have the same generalization loss* $\rho_1 = \ldots = \rho_L = \rho$, *For the ECOC* $\mathbf{M}_K(L)$ *with* d_{min},

$$R_{gen}(\mathbf{M}, \hat{\mathbf{f}}) \leq 1 - B_\rho \left(L, \left[\frac{d_{min}-1}{2}\right] \right) \tag{9}$$

where $B_\rho(L, t)$ *denotes* $\sum_{j=0}^{t} \binom{L}{j} \rho^j (1 - \rho)^{L-j}$, *provided that the base learners are independent.*

3   Hadamard Output Codes

A square matrix $\mathbf{H}_n$ of order n and entries ± 1 is called a Hadamard matrix if $\mathbf{H}'_n \mathbf{H}_n = n\mathbf{I}_n$ where $\mathbf{I}_n$ is the nth order identity matrix. A Hadamard matrix $\mathbf{H}_n$ is often written in the normalized form with both the first row and column consisting of all $+1$'s. Some examples of Hadamard matrices are shown below. All Hadamard matrices $\mathbf{H}_K$ discussed in this paper can be downloaded from the web site of Sloane's collection [10].

$$
\mathbf{H}_2 = \begin{bmatrix} + & + \\ + & - \end{bmatrix}, \quad
\mathbf{H}_4 = \begin{bmatrix} + & + & + & + \\ + & - & + & - \\ + & + & - & - \\ + & - & - & + \end{bmatrix}, \quad
\mathbf{H}_8 = \begin{bmatrix} + & + & + & + & + & + & + & + \\ + & - & + & - & + & - & + & - \\ + & + & - & - & + & + & - & - \\ + & - & - & + & + & - & - & + \\ + & + & + & + & - & - & - & - \\ + & - & + & - & - & + & - & + \\ + & + & - & - & - & - & + & + \\ + & - & - & + & - & + & + & - \end{bmatrix}
$$

Deleting the first column from any normalized Hadamard matrix, we obtain a Hadamard output code. The important properties of a Hadamard output code $\mathbf{H}_K$ with $K \equiv 0(\mathrm{mod}\ 4)$ are two fold: a) every pair of codewords has the same Hamming distance of $d_{min} = \frac{K}{2}$, and b) every pair of columns are orthogonal, i.e., $H'_{*j} H_{*l} = \delta_{jl} K$ where $\delta_{jl} = 1$ for $j \neq l$ and 0 otherwise. Then we have

Theorem 3. *The Hadamard output codes $\mathbf{H}_K$ for $K = 4, 8, \ldots$ are optimal error-correcting output codes, within the pool of K-class output codes that combine $K - 1$ base learners.*

Proof. According to the Definition 1 of the optimal ECOC, we need to show the Hadamard designs satisfy the extreme conditions of both row separation and column diversity.

1. Maximum d_{min} in $\Omega(K, K - 1)$
   By the Plotkin's bound for any $\mathbf{M} \in \Omega(K, L)$ that is widely known in the coding theory (see page 41 of [8])

$$
K \leq 2 \left[\frac{d_{min}}{2d_{min} - L} \right],
$$

where $L = K - 1$ for $\Omega(K, K - 1)$, we have the following bounds

$$
d_{min} \leq \frac{L}{2} \frac{K}{K - 1} = \frac{K}{2}.
$$

Therefore, the minimum Hamming distance $d_{min} = \frac{K}{2}$ for $\mathbf{H}_K$ achieves the above upper bound. In another word, $d_{min}(\mathbf{H}_K) \geq d_{min}(\mathbf{M})$ for all $\mathbf{M} \in \Omega(K, K - 1)$.

2. Minimum s_{max} in $\Omega(K, K-1)$

Since every two columns are orthogonal in Hadamard output codes, we have

$$s_{max}(\mathbf{H}_K) = \max_{j \neq l} |\mathrm{Corr}(H_{*j}, H_{*l})| = \frac{1}{N} \max_{j \neq l} |H'_{*j} H_{*l}| = 0,$$

achieving the minimum value in the class of $\Omega(K, K-1)$. $\square$

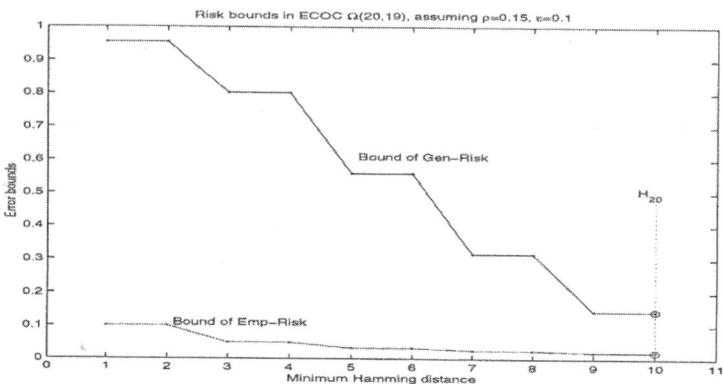

Fig. 1. Illustration of empirical and generalization bounds; the risk bounds for Hadamard output codes are circled on the right ends

The error bounds of multiclass reconstruction can be decreased by using the Hadamard output codes. Let ε denote the global average empirical losses for all the base learners, i.e. $\varepsilon = \sum_{j=1}^{L} \varepsilon_j / L$. Let ρ be defined in Corollary 1. Then we have the empirical and generalization risk bounds for Hadamard output codes

$$R_{emp}(\mathbf{H}_K, \hat{\mathbf{f}}) \leq \min\left\{1, \frac{4\varepsilon}{K}\right\}; \quad R_{gen}(\mathbf{H}_K, \hat{\mathbf{f}}) \leq 1 - B_\rho\left(K-1, \frac{K}{4}-1\right). \quad (10)$$

By Figure 1 that illustrates the risk bounds for both empirical and generalization bounds derived in Section 2.3, we see the Hadamard output codes can greatly decrease the risk bounds within the pool of $\Omega(K, K-1)$.

4   Experimental Results

The support vector machines (SVMs) are used as the base learners in our experiments for comparing different dense output codes, for the SVMs with flexible kernels are strong enough to classify various types of dichotomous data while keeping good generalization performance [5]. Plugged into the ECOC framework, the base SVM can be written as

$$f_j(\mathbf{x}) = \mathrm{sign}\left\{\sum_{i=1}^{N} M_{y_i j} \alpha_i^{(j)} \mathbb{K}_j(\mathbf{x}_i, \mathbf{x}) + b_j\right\} \quad (11)$$

where $\mathbb{K}_j(\mathbf{x}, \mathbf{w})$ is a selected kernel, b_j is the offset term and $\boldsymbol{\alpha}^{(j)} = (\alpha_1^{(j)}, \ldots, \alpha_N^{(j)})$ can be obtained by

$$\boldsymbol{\alpha}^{(j)} = \arg\max \left\{ L_j(\boldsymbol{\alpha}) = \sum_{i=1}^{N} \alpha_i - \frac{1}{2} \sum_{i=1}^{N} \sum_{r=1}^{N} \alpha_i \alpha_r M_{y_i j} M_{y_r j} \mathbb{K}_j(\mathbf{x}_i, \mathbf{x}_r) \right\}, \quad (12)$$

subject to the constraint of $0 \leq \alpha_i \leq C_j$. The constant C_j controls the trade-off between maximizing the margin and minimizing the training errors. In our experiments, we choose the Gaussian radian basis function (RBF) as the kernel $\mathbb{K}_j(\mathbf{x}, \mathbf{w}) = \exp\{-\gamma_j \|\mathbf{x} - \mathbf{w}\|^2\}$ with γ_j being used to further tune the RBF kernel. For each base SVM learner, we employed the LIBSVM software [4] for handling two tasks, a) using the default svm-train program in C language for solving the above optimization problem; b) using the grid program in Python language for tuning parameters (C_j, γ_j) in order to select SVM models by cross-validation (10-fold in our setups).

Table 1. Description of the datasets from the UCI repository

Datasets	#Classes	#Train Data	#Test Data	#Attributes
dermatology	6	366	-	34
glass	6	214	-	13
ecoli	8	366	-	8
vowel	11	528	-	10
yeast	10	1484	-	8
letter	26	16000	4000	16

Table 2. Experimental results using different output codes based on the support vector machines with Guassian RBF kernels

Datasets	Hadamard		One-per-class		Random	
	R_{emp}	R_{gen}	R_{emp}	R_{gen}	R_{emp}	R_{gen}
dermatology	0.0000	0.0121	0.0037	0.0633	0.0000	0.0170
glass	0.0498	0.1184	0.0265	0.1869	0.2329	0.2457
ecoli	0.0179	0.0159	0.0365	0.0450	0.0302	0.0387
vowel	0.0000	0.0013	0.0000	0.0121	0.0000	0.0028
yeast	0.0745	0.0685	0.2652	0.2873	0.1102	0.1203
letter	0.0000	0.0171	0.0089	0.1502	0.0000	0.0133

Our comparative experiments are carried on the real multiclass datasets from from the UCI Repository and a simple statistics is given in Table 1. We compare three types of dense output codes with economical number (around the number of classes) of decompositions: 1) Hadamard-type, pruning, if necessary, the last row(s) (up to 3) of Hadamard designs such that the number of rows in the output codes coincides with the cardinality of the polychotomy; 2) one-per-class, i.e., a square output code with diagonal entries of all +1's and off-diagonal entries of all -1's; and 3) random ECOC. The random error-correcting output codes are generated in the following way: generate 10,000 output codes in $\Omega(K, K)$ with entries uniformly at random from $\{-1, 1\}$, then choose the code with the largest d_{min} without identical columns. For demonstrating the different usages of output codes, both empirical and generalization risks for the multiclass reconstruction by Hamming decoding are evaluated for training and testing data, respectively. For the datasets without testing data offered, we use again the cross-validation as an estimate of R_{gen}. For the letter dataset, we choose only 2600 (100 per class) from the training data and 1300 (50 per class) from the testing data for the demonstration purpose. Results are given in Table 2, which shows that in general Hadamard-type output codes perform better than random error-correcting output codes, which in turn perform better than OPC codes. Then we may turn to ask: what happens to the traditional OPC methods? Our theories reveals that the OPC output codes have no error correcting properties because all their d_{min}'s slump to low 2 and $\left\lceil \frac{d_{min}-1}{2} \right\rceil = 0$!

References

[1] Allwein, E.L., Schapire, R.E. and Singer, Y.: Reducing multiclass to binary: a unifying approach for margin classifiers. *Journal of Machine Learning Research* **1** (2000) 113–141

[2] Blake, C.L. and Merz, C.J.: UCI Repository of machine learning databases. (1998) http://www.ics.uci.edu/~mlearn/MLRepository.html

[3] Box, G.E.P. and Hunter, W.G. and Hunter, J.S.: *Statistics for Experiments* (1978) Wiley, New York

[4] Chang, C.C. and Lin, C.J.: LIBSVM: a library for support vector machines. (2001) Software available at http://www.csie.ntu.edu.tw/~cjlin/libsvm

[5] Cristianini, N. and Shawe-Taylor, J.: *An Introduction to Support Vector Machines (and other kernel-based learning methods)*. (2000) Cambridge University Press

[6] Dietterich, T.G. and Bakiri, G.: Solving multiclass learning problems via error-correcting output codes. *Journal of Artificial Intelligence Research* **2** (1995) 263–286

[7] Hastie, T. and Tibshirani, R.: Classification by pariwise coupling. *The Annals of Statistics* **26**(2) (1998) 451–471

[8] MacWilliams, F.J. and Sloane, N.J.A.: *The Theory of Error-Correcting Codes* (1977) Elsevier Science Publishers

[9] Schapire, R.E.: The strength of weak learnability. *Machine Learning* **5** (1990) 197–227

[10] Sloane, N.J.A.: A Library of Hadamard Matrices (1999) AT&T http://www.research.att.com/~njas/hadamard/

An Adaptive Uniform Fractional Guard Channel Algorithm: A Learning Automata Approach

Hamid Beigy and Mohammad Reza Meybodi*

Soft Computing Laboratory
Computer Engineering Department
Amirkabir University of Technology
Tehran, Iran
{beigy, meybodi}@ce.aut.ac.ir

Abstract. In [1], a learning automata (LA) based call admission policy is given which accepts new calls as long as the pre-specified level of QoS is maintained. The simulation results show that this policy cannot maintain the upper bound on the level of QoS. In this paper, we propose a new LA based algorithm in which a LA is used to accept/reject new calls. This algorithm can be considered as an adaptive version of uniform fractional guard channel policy. In order to study the performance of the proposed call admission policy, computer simulations are conducted. The simulation results show that the level of QoS is satisfied by the proposed algorithm and the performance of given algorithm is very close to the performance of uniform fractional guard channel policy which needs to know all parameters of input traffic. Unlike the uniform fractional guard channel policy, the proposed policy is fully adaptive and doesn't require any information about the input traffics.

1 Introduction

Introduction of micro cellular networks leads to efficient use of channels but increases the expected rate of handovers per call. As a consequence, some network performance parameters such as *blocking probability of new calls* (B_n) and *dropping probability of handoff calls* (B_h) are affected. In order to maintain B_h and B_n at a reasonable level, *call admission algorithms* are used, which play a very important role in the cellular networks because directly control B_n and B_h. Since B_h is more important than B_n, call admission algorithms give the higher priority to handoff calls. This priority is implemented through allocation of more resources (channels) to handoff calls. A general call admission policy, called *fractional guard channel policy* (FG), accepts new calls with a probability that depends on the current channel occupancy and accepts handoff calls as long as channels are available [2]. Suppose that the given cell has C full duplex channels. The FG policy uses a vector $\Pi = \{\pi_0, \ldots, \pi_{C-1}\}$ to accept the new calls,

---

* This work is partially supported by Iranian Telecommunication Research Center (ITRC), Tehran, Iran.

J. Liu et al. (Eds.): IDEAL 2003, LNCS 2690, pp. 405–409, 2003.

where $0 \leq \pi_i \leq 1$, $0 \leq i < C$. The FG policy accepts new calls with probability of π_k when k ($0 \leq k < C$) channels are busy. There is no algorithm to find the optimal vector Π^*. A restricted version of FG is called *guard channel policy* (GC) [3]. The GC policy reserves a subset of channels, called *guard channels*, for handoff calls (say $C - T$ channels). Whenever the channel occupancy exceeds the certain threshold T, the GC policy rejects new calls until the channel occupancy goes below T. The GC policy accepts handoff calls as long as channels are available. It has been shown that there is an optimal threshold T^* in which B_n is minimized subject to the hard constraint on B_h [4]. An algorithm for finding such optimal threshold is given in [4]. In order to have more control on B_h and B_n, *limited fractional guard channel policy* (LFG) is introduced [2]. The LFG can be obtained from FG policy by setting $\pi_k = 1$, $0 \leq k < T$, $\pi_T = \pi$, and $\pi_k = 0$, $T < k < C$. It has been shown that there are an optimal threshold T^* and an optimal value of π^* for which B_n is minimized subject to the hard constraint on B_h [2]. The algorithm for finding such optimal parameters is given in [2]. In [5], a restricted version of FG policy, called *uniform fractional guard channel policy* (UFG), is introduced. The UFG policy accepts new calls with probability of π independent of channel occupancy. The UFG policy can be obtained from FG by setting $\pi_k = \pi$, $0 \leq k < C$. In order to find the optimal value of parameter π, a binary search algorithm is given [5].

All of mentioned call admission policies are static and assume that all parameters of traffic are known in advance. These policies are useful when input traffic is a stationary process with known parameters. Since the parameters of input traffic are unknown and possibly time varying, the adaptive version of these policies must be used. In order to have such adaptive polices, a learning automata based call admission policy is introduced [1]. This policy accepts new calls as long as the dropping probability of handoff calls is below of a pre-specified threshold. Simulation results show that, performance of this policy is very close to the performance of the UFG policy when the handoff traffic is low, but this policy cannot maintain the upper bound on the dropping probability of handoff calls.

In this paper, we propose an adaptive version of UFG policy which maintains the upper bound on the dropping probability of handoff calls. The proposed algorithm uses a learning automaton to accept/reject new calls and the pre-specified level of dropping probability of handoff calls is used to determine penalty/reward for selected action of automaton. The simulation results show that, the performance of the proposed algorithm is very close to the performance of the UFG policy which needs to know all traffic parameters in high handoff traffic conditions. It is shown that probability of accepting new calls converges to the optimal value found by the algorithm given in [5]. Since learning automaton is adaptive and doesn't require any information about its environment, the proposed algorithm is adaptive and doesn't need any information about input traffics.

The rest of this paper is organized as follows: Section 2 presents UFG policy and the adaptive UFG algorithm is given in section 3. The computer simulations is given in section 4 and section 5 concludes the paper.

2   Uniform Fractional Guard Channel Policy

UFG policy accepts handoff calls as long as channels are available and accepts new calls with probability π independent of channel occupancy. The description of UFG policy is given algorithmically in figure 1.

```
if (HANDOFF CALL) then
    if c(t) < C ) then
        accept call
    else
        reject call
    end if
end if
if (NEW CALL) then
    if (c(t) < C and rand (0,1) < π) then
        accept call
    else
        reject call
    end if
end if
```

Fig. 1. Unform fractional guard channel policy

The objective is to find a π^* that minimizes the blocking probability of new calls with the constraint that the dropping probability of handoff calls must be at most p_h. The value of p_h specifies the QoS of the network. It is too complex to obtain an exact solution for this problem. Hence, a search algorithm is given in [5] to determine the optimal value of π for given traffic and constraint p_h.

3   Adaptive UFG Algorithm

In this section, we introduce an adaptive version of UFG policy which uses a learning automaton. This algorithm is used to determine admission probability π when the parameters a and ρ (or equivalently λ_h, λ_n and μ) are unknown or probably time varying. The proposed algorithm adjusts parameter π as network operates. This algorithm gives the higher probability to handoff calls by allowing the handoff calls to be accepted with higher probability than new calls. This algorithm can be described as follows: The proposed algorithm uses one reward-penalty type learning automaton with two actions in each cell. The action set of this automaton corresponds to {ACCEPT,REJECT}. The automaton associated to each cell determines the probability of acceptance of new calls (π). Since initially the values of a and ρ are unknown, the probability of selecting these actions are set to 0.5. When a handoff call arrives, it is accepted as long as there is a free channel. If there is no free channel, the handoff call is dropped. When a new call arrives to a particular cell, the learning automaton associated to that cell chooses one of its actions. Let π be the probability of selecting action ACCEPT. Thus, the learning automaton accepts new calls with probability π as long as there is a free channel and rejects new call with probability $1 - \pi$. If action ACCEPT is selected by automaton and the cell has at least one free channel, the incoming call is accepted and action ACCEPT is rewarded. If there is no free channel to be allocated to the arrived new call, the call is blocked and action ACCEPT is penalized. When the automaton selects action REJECT, the incoming call is blocked and the base station estimates the dropping probability of handoff calls ($\hat{B}_h$). If the current estimate of dropping probability of handoff calls is less than the given threshold p_h, then action REJECT is penalized; otherwise action REJECT is rewarded. rewarded.

The main contribution of this paper is summarized in theorem 1, which is stated below and proved in [6].

Theorem 1. Adaptive UFG algorithm minimizes the blocking probability of new calls while the the dropping probability of handoff calls is smaller than p_h.

4   Simulation Results

In this section, we compare performance of the uniform fractional guard channel [5], the learning automata based call admission [1] policies and the proposed algorithm. The results of simulations are summarized in table 1. The simulation is based on the single cell of homogenous cellular network system. In such network, each cell has 8 full duplex channels ($C = 8$). In the simulations, new call arrival rate is fixed to 30 calls per minute ($\lambda_n = 30$), channel holding time is set to 6 seconds ($\mu^{-1} = 6$), and the handoff call traffic is varied between 2 calls per minute to 20 calls per minute. The results listed in table 1 are obtained by averaging 10 runs from $2,000,000$ seconds simulation of each algorithm. The objective is to minimize the blocking probability of new calls subject to the constraint that the dropping probability of handoff calls is less than 0.01. The optimal parameter of uniform fractional guard channel policy is obtained by algorithm given in [6].

By carefully inspecting the table 1, it is evident that for some range of input traffics, the performance of the proposed algorithm is close to the performance of the UFG policy and performs better than the algorithm given in [1]. Since in the low handoff traffic conditions, the UFG policy doesn't maintain the upper bound on the dropping probability of handoff calls, the blocking probability of new calls for the proposed algorithm is greater than the blocking probability of new calls for UFG. When the handoff traffic becomes high, the UFG policy maintains the upper bound on the dropping probability of handoff calls and the performance of UFG policy and the proposed algorithm is very close. In such situations, the probability of accepting new calls converges to the optimal value found by the algorithm given in [5].

Table 1. The simulation results

λ_h	UFG			LA Based Algorithm [1]			Proposed Algorithm		
	π^*	B_n	B_h	π^*	B_n	B_h	π^*	B_n	B_h
2	0.9759	0.0239	0.0246	0.9255	0.0881	0.0194	0.7609	0.2085	0.0100
4	0.9093	0.0898	0.0236	0.8960	0.1196	0.0216	0.7043	0.2609	0.0100
6	0.8424	0.1572	0.0222	0.6821	0.3152	0.0100	0.6366	0.3186	0.0100
8	0.7757	0.2238	0.0203	0.7352	0.2722	0.0165	0.6171	0.3652	0.0100
10	0.7091	0.2898	0.0192	0.6559	0.3579	0.0140	0.6712	0.3372	0.0155
12	0.6424	0.3568	0.0176	0.6268	0.3869	0.0155	0.5478	0.4698	0.0100
14	0.5758	0.4240	0.0163	0.5381	0.4764	0.0129	0.4808	0.5154	0.0102
16	0.5091	0.4899	0.0150	0.5263	0.4839	0.0158	0.4518	0.5505	0.0111
18	0.4425	0.5570	0.0139	0.5036	0.4994	0.0185	0.4128	0.5893	0.0120
20	0.3758	0.6237	0.0133	0.5029	0.5018	0.0234	0.3670	0.6238	0.0135

5   Conclusions

In this paper, we proposed a new learning automata based algorithm in which a learning automaton is used to accept/reject new calls. This algorithm can be considered as an adaptive version of uniform fractional guard channel policy. We studied the performance of the proposed call admission policy through computer simulations. Simulation results show that in high handoff traffic conditions for which the UFG policy maintains the level of QoS, performance of the proposed algorithm is very close to performance of the UFG policy. In such situations, the probability of accepting new calls converges to the optimal value. In low handoff traffic conditions, the proposed algorithm performs better than the UFG policy.

References

1. H. Beigy and M. R. Meybodi, *Call Admission Control in Cellular Mobile Networks: A Learning Automata Approach*, vol. 2510 of *Springer-Verlag Lecture Notes in Computer Science*, pp. 450–457. Springer-Verlag, Oct. 2002.
2. R. Ramjee, D. Towsley, and R. Nagarajan, "On Optimal Call Admission Control in Cellular Networks," *Wireless Networks*, vol. 3, pp. 29–41, 1997.
3. D. Hong and S. Rappaport, "Traffic Modelling and Performance Analysis for Cellular Mobile Radio Telephone Systems with Priotrized and Nonpriotorized Handoffs Procedure," *IEEE Transactions on Vehicular Technology*, vol. 35, pp. 77–92, Aug. 1986.
4. G. Haring, R. Marie, R. Puigjaner, and K. Trivedi, "Loss Formulas and Their Application to Optimization for Cellular Networks," *IEEE Transactions on Vehicular Technology*, vol. 50, pp. 664–673, May 2001.
5. H. Beigy and M. R. Meybodi, "Uniform Fractional Guard Channel," in *Proceedings of Sixth World Multiconference on Systemmics, Cybernetics and Informatics, Orlando, USA*, July 2002.
6. H. Beigy and M. R. Meybodi, "An Adaptive Uniform Fractional Guard Channel Algorithm: A Learning Automata Approach," Tech. Rep. TR-CE-2002-006, Computer Engineering Department, Amirkabir University of Technology, Tehran, Iran, 2002.

Empirical Comparison between Two Computational Strategies for Topological Self-Organization

Bonnie Kit Yee Chan, Wilson Wei Sheng Chu, and Lei Xu

Department of Computer Science and Engineering, Chinese University of Hong Kong,
Shatin, NT, Hong Kong, People's Republic of China,
{kychan2,wschu,lxu}@cse.cuhk.edu.hk

Abstract. The standard Self-Organizing Map (SOM) achieves self organization through incremental, stepwise update of its weight vectors. However, beginning with a randomly initialized map, the convergence speed of SOM is rather slow. It would be desirable to speed up the self-organization process. For this reason, a new strategy for topological self-organization (Xu, 2002) has been proposed to speed up the self-organization process. This paper empirically compares the two strategies. The new strategy is shown to speed up the self-organization significantly.

1 Introduction

Self-Organizing Map has been developed as a very powerful method for visualization and unsupervised classification. Being a computational mapping principle, SOM is able to approximate the original input space, by a much smaller set of prototypes only.

Although the resultant map is considered to be an excellent non-linear projection of the input space, the SOM algorithm is not perfect. Starting from an initial state of complete disorder, the convergence speed of SOM is rather slow. It would be desirable to speed up the self-organizing process. In the last decade, efforts have been made towards the speedup of SOM.

Recently, (Xu, 2002) has proposed a new topological self-organizing strategy. The new approach is based on the interchange of weight vectors, where a group of winners will cluster in one single step, instead of going through the process of updating its values in numerous iterations.

In some sense the two strategies are analogous to the way human live. In the conventional strategy, every neuron should adapt itself to his surrounding environment in order to get along with their neighbors; On the other hand, in the new strategy the neurons migrate and team up directly with the ones who possess similar characteristic. Therefore, they need not go through the process of adapting themselves slowly.

In this paper, the performace of the two strategies are compared empirically. This paper is organized as follows. In section 2, the algorithms of the new and the conventional strategies are presented. In section 3, empirical results comparing their self-organization speed are analyzed. Finally, we come to conclusion in section 4.

J. Liu et al. (Eds.): IDEAL 2003, LNCS 2690, pp. 410–414, 2003.

2   The Two Topological Self-Organization Strategies

2.1   The Conventional Strategy

The conventional topological self-organization algorithm (Kohonen, 2001), referred as "the conventional strategy" in this paper. It proceeds as follows:
    Step1: Define the $m_i(t)$ closest to $x(t)$:

$$c = \arg\min_i \{d(x(t), m_i(t))\} \tag{1}$$

where $x(t)$ is an n-dimensional input vector, $m_i(t)$ is a weight vector and $d(x(t), m_i(t))$ denotes the Euclidean distance measure between $x(t)$ and $m_i(t)$.
    Step 2: Correct the $m_c(t)$ and the $m_i(t)$ in the neighborhood of $m_c(t)$ on the grid towards $x(t)$:

$$m_j(t+1) = m_i(t) + h_{c,i}(t) * [x(t) - m_i(t)] \tag{2}$$

where $h_{c,i}(t)$ is the neighborhood function in Gaussian form, which also determines the learning rate of the map.
    From the equations above, it is observed the formation of SOM is based on three processes: competition, cooperation and adaptation (Haykin, 1999). With the three processes mentioned above, the map will eventually approximate the intrinsic features contained in the input patterns.

2.2   The New Strategy

The new topological self-organization strategy (Xu, 2002), referred as "the new strategy" in this paper, is a rapid correction process. It proceeds as follows:
    Step 1: Select the first $2^m + 1$ neurons which best match the input vector and let N_w be the set containing them.
    Step 2: Correct the neurons in the set N_w towards $x(t)$:

$$m_i(t+1) = m_i(t) + l_i(t) * [x(t) - m_i(t)] \tag{3}$$

where i is the index of these neurons, and $l_i(t)$ is the learning rate parameter.
    Step 3: Exchange the weight vectors of BMU's neighbors with the neurons in N_w, such that all the winning neurons will cluster together as neighbors with BMU at the centre.
    Comparing these two strategies, there is a trade-off between stability and speed. The new approach is faster but less stable than the conventional one. While eliminating the need of updating values incrementally does increase the speed, the original neighbors around the BMU are forced to leave and may therefore disrupt the harmony elsewhere in the map. For these reasons, (Xu, 2002) suggests the combination of these two approaches by using this approach in the early stage and the conventional strategy is used subsequently. Combination of the two yields the greatest benefit in terms of speed and performance.

3   Empirical Comparison between the New Strategy and the Conventional Strategy

In this section, we compare the new strategy and the conventional strategy using three different criteria: speed of self-organization, the topological quality of the map and the effect of dimensionality of input data on speed and topological quality. In order to investigate their relative performance given different input data, both normally distributed artificial data sets and real world data set(Johnson, 1995) are used.

3.1   Metric and Configurations

Measurement of Map Goodness. From (Kohonen, 2001), two evaluation criteria are used: resolution and topology preservation. To measure map resolution, quantization error is used as a metric. It is defined as the average distance between each data vector and its BMU. To measure topology preservation, topological error is used, which is defined as the proportion of all data vectors for which first and second BMUs are not adjacent units.

Time of Switch in the New Strategy. Switching is performed only after the rate of decrease of quantization error is below a "specified percentage" for 3 consecutive steps. From table 1, the time required will increase when the threshold is either too large or too small. Too large a threshold would switch the algorithm prematurely; conversely, time would be spent unnecessarily as the new approach makes little progress when the map has already been largely unfolded. Therefore, we conclude that 0.1% is the optimal choice for all experiments performed in this paper.

Table 1. Summary of the time required to converge given different threshold using 15-dimensional normal distributed data

Threshold	Time required to converge (seconds)
5	266.74
1	241.26
0.5	233.98
0.1	224.16
0.05	228.12
0.01	235.77

Miscellaneous. Firstly, the experiment is performed until the self-organization process finishes the ordering phase, where topological error decreases to almost zero. Secondly, all maps are randomly initialized before training starts. Thirdly, for the new strategy, m is set to 2 in these experiments.

3.2   Results and Analysis

Table 2 summerises the experimental data. Due to space limitation, we focus on the analysis of 2 sets of data in this paper, namely, 50-dimensional and real world data.

Table 2. Summary of the relative performance between the two strategies

Data Set	Conventional Strategy (seconds)	New Strategy (seconds)	Speed up (%)
5D	240.06	216.82	9.68
10D	253.13	224.5	11.31
15D	261.72	224.16	14.35
20D	279.98	231.1	17.46
25D	285.15	228.43	19.89
30D	303.54	234.55	22.73
35D	307.77	237.81	25.57
50D	319.43	222.54	30.3
Real world	638	556.91	12.7

Speed of Self-Organization. In all data sets, the new strategy gives a more desirable result. Moreover, from Fig.1 and Fig. 4, it is observed the shapes of two curves are rather similar. It comes at no surprise since except during the early stage, both strategies are in fact using the same algorithm. While the quantization error of both strategies decrease at the very beginning, the corresponding quantization error of the new strategy decreases much more sharply. After the rapid drop there is a period of relatively low speed of self-organization. It is where the switch occurs. It is the speed-up at its early stage which contributes to the overall acceleration of the self-organization speed in the ordering phase. Note that due to the more complex distribution of real world data set, more time is required to achieve convergence than that of the previous experiments. Nevertheless, the new strategy still excels.

Quality of Topological Preservation. From Fig.2 and Fig.5, it is observed that the topology is preserved. Although there are some vibrant fluctuations during the early stage when using the new strategy, it soon decreases at the rate similar to that of the conventional strategy. From these results, we can conclude that the speed-up is achieved without significant effect on its topological preservation property

Dimensionality. Interestingly, from the data collected above, it is observed the speed of self-organization tends to increase as the dimensionality of input data increases. Results in Table 2 illustrate this trend.

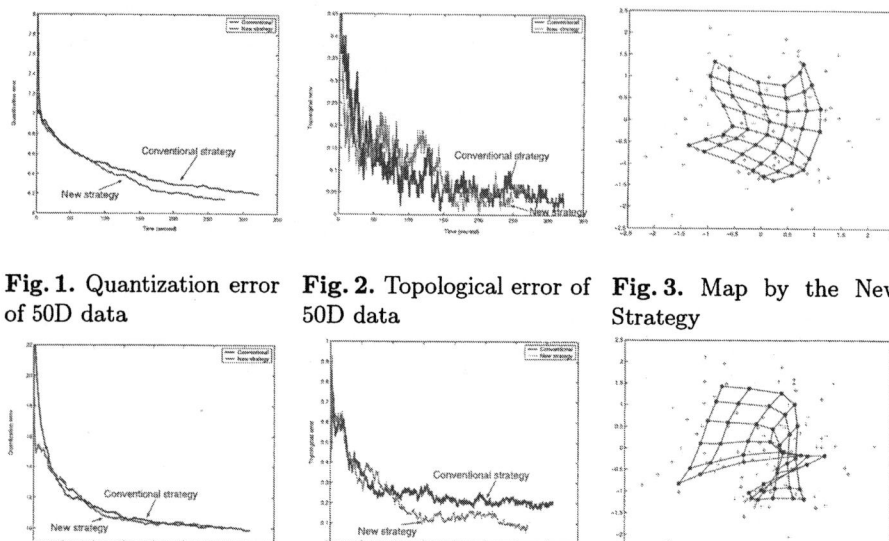

Fig. 1. Quantization error of 50D data

Fig. 2. Topological error of 50D data

Fig. 3. Map by the New Strategy

Fig. 4. Quantization error of real world data

Fig. 5. Topological error of real world data

Fig. 6. Map by the conventional strategy

The Resultant Maps from the Two Strategies. In order to provide a more intuitive comparison between the two strategies, the resultant maps of 2-dimensional normal distributed data are included as examples. It is observed that as map in Fig.3 is already unfolded, map in Fig.6 is still intermingled.

4   Conclusion

The performance of the two computational strategies for topological self organization has been analyzed in detail empirically. While the topological qualities of the resultant maps don't differ much, the new strategy does increase the pace of self-organization significantly. Moreover, the higher the input dimension, the better the performance of the new strategy.

References

1. Haykin, S.(1999). Neural networks: A comprehensive foundation, Prentice Hall, Second Edition, pp.443–483
2. Johnson, R.(1995). StatLib Datasets Archive, Carnegie Mellon University
3. Kohonen, T.(1990). The self-organizing map, Proceedings of the Institute of Electrical and Electronics Engineers
4. Kohonen, T.(2001). Self-organizing maps, Berlin: Springer-Verlag, Third Edition, pp.106–113
5. Xu, L.(2002). BYY harmony learning, structural RPCL, and topological self-organizing on mixture models, Neural Networks, 15, pp.1125–1151

A Novel Orthogonal Simulated Annealing Algorithm for Optimization of Electromagnetic Problems

Li-Sun Shu[1], Shinn-Jang Ho[2], and Shinn-Ying Ho[1]

[1] Department of Information Engineering, Feng Chia University,
Taichung, Taiwan 407, Republic of China
[2] Department of Automation Engineering, National Huwei Institute of Technology,
Huwei, Yunlin, Taiwan 632, Republic of China
[c] syho@fcu.edu.tw

Abstract. A novel orthogonal simulated annealing algorithm OSA for optimizations of electromagnetic problems is proposed in this paper. High performance of OSA mainly arises from an intelligent generation mechanism (IGM) based on orthogonal experimental design (OED). The OED-based IGM can efficiently generate a good candidate solution for next move by using a systematic reasoning method instead of the conventional method of random perturbation. It is shown empirically that OSA performs well in solving parametric optimization problems and in designing optimal electromagnetic devices, compared with some existing optimization methods using simulated annealing algorithms and genetic algorithms.

1 Introduction

Simulated annealing algorithm (SA) [1]-[7] and genetic algorithm (GA) [8]-[11] have been widely applied to the optimization of electromagnetic problems. Generally, simple SA always takes much computing time and is not acceptable for many engineering applications [2]. To improve the convergence of SA to some extent, many auxiliary techniques [3], [5]-[7] and combined strategy using GA [9] have been proposed to improve SAs. The convergence of SA is fairly slow [12]. Szu and Hartley proposed a fast SA (FSA) using Cauchy stochastic method [5]. Renyuan *et al.* [2] proposed an improved SA to avoid blindness in search.

GA has been shown to be efficient for exploring NP-hard or complex non-linear search spaces as an efficient optimizer relative to computer-intensive exhaustive search [11]. Chen *et al.* [8] proposed an improved GA (IGA) for global optimization of electromagnetic problems. It is shown empirically that the performance of IGA is better than the conventional SA, GA, and Tabu search [8].

In this paper, we propose a novel orthogonal simulated annealing algorithm OSA with an intelligent generation mechanism (IGM) based on orthogonal experimental design (OED). The OED-based IGM can efficiently generate a good candidate solution for next move by using a systematic reasoning method. It is shown empirically that OSA performs well in solving parametric optimization problems and in designing optimal electromagnetic devices, compared with FSA [5] and IGA [8], respectively.

J. Liu et al. (Eds.): IDEAL 2003, LNCS 2690, pp. 415–420, 2003.

2   Orthogonal Simmulated Annealing Algorithm OSA

OSA with IGM based on orthogonal experimental design (OED) can efficiently improve the exploring ability for an optimal solution. The orthogonal array (OA) and factor analysis (FA) of OED used in IGM are described in Section II.A. IGM and OSA are described in Sections II.B.

2.1   OA and FA Used in IGM

The three-level OA used in IGM is described as follows. Let there be N factors with three levels for each factor. All the optimization parameters are generally partitioned into N groups. One group is regarded as a factor. Generally, levels 1, 2 and 3 of a factor represent a group selected from three candidate solutions. Table 1 illustrates an example of OA $L_9(3^4)$. An algorithm of constructing OA can be found in [10]. After proper tabulation of experimental results, the summarized data are analyzed using FA to determine the relative effects of levels of various factors as follows. Let y_t denote an objective function value of the combination corresponding to the experiment t, where t = 1, ..., n. Define the main effect of factor j with level k as S_{jk} where j = 1, ..., N and k = 1, 2, 3: $S_{jk} = \sum_{t=1}^{n} y_t \cdot F_t$, where F_t = 1 if the level of factor j of experiment t is k; otherwise, F_t = 0. Considering the case that the objective function is to be minimized, the level k is the best when $S_{jk} = \min\{ S_{j1}, S_{j2}, S_{j3}\}$.

2.2   Intelligent Generation Mechanism IGM

Consider a parametric optimization problem of m parameters. According to a current solution $P_I=(S_1, ..., S_m)$ where S_i is a parameter value, IGM generates two temporary solutions $P_2=(S_1^1, ..., S_m^1)$ and $P_3=(S_1^2, ..., S_m^2)$ from perturbing P_I where S_i^1 and S_i^2 are $S_i^1 = S_i + \overline{S}_i$ and $S_i^2 = S_i - \overline{S}_i$, i=1, ..., m.   (1)

Each disturbing value $\overline{S}_i$ is generated by Cauchy-Lorentz probability distribution [5]. Using the same division scheme, partition all the m parameters into N non-overlapping groups. To efficiently use all columns of OA, N is generally specified as $N = (3^{\lfloor \log_3(2m+1) \rfloor} - 1)/2$ and the used OA is $L_{2N+1}(3^N)$ excluding the study of intractable interaction effects.

IGM aims at efficiently combining good groups of parameters from solutions P_1, P_2 and P_3 to generate a good candidate solution C_1 for next move. How to perform an IGM operation using P_1 with m parameters is described as follows:

Step 1: Generate two temporary solutions P_2 and P_3 using P_1.

Step 2: Adaptively divide each solution of P_1, P_2 and P_3 into N groups of parameters where each group is treated as a factor.

Step 3: Use the first N columns of an OA $L_n(3^{(n-1)/2})$, where $n = 3^{\lceil \log_3(2N+1) \rceil}$.

Step 4: Let levels 1, 2 and 3 of factor j represent the jth groups of P_1, P_2, P_3, respectively.

Step 5: Evaluate the objective function value y_t of the combination corresponding to the experiment t, where $t = 1, \ldots, n$.

Step 6: Compute the main effect S_{jk} where $j = 1, 2, \ldots, N$ and $k = 1, 2, 3$.

Step 7: Determine the best one of three levels of each factor based on the main effect.

Step 8: The solution C_1 is formed using the combination of the best groups from the derived corresponding solutions.

Step 9: Verify that C_1 is superior to the $n-1$ representative combinations of OA except P_1 according to the objective function value. If it is not true, select the best solution from these $n-1$ candidate solutions as the final solution C_1.

OSA employees a variable value of N_T, the number of trials per temperature. Without lose of generality, consider the case that the objective function f is to be minimized. The proposed novel OSA is described as follows:

Step 1: (Initialization) Randomly generate a starting point P_1. Initialize $T = T_0$, $N_T = N_0$, and cooling rate C. Let the number of trial be $I = 0$.

Step 2: (Generation) Perform an IGM operation to generate a candidate solution C_1.

Step 3: (Acceptance criterion) Accept C_1 to be the new P_1 with probability $P(C_1)$ which is given by

$$P(C_1) = \begin{cases} 1, & \text{if} \quad f(C_1) \le f(P_1) \\ \exp(\dfrac{-|f(P_1) - f(C_1)|}{T}), & \text{if} \quad f(C_1) > f(P_1) \end{cases} \qquad (2)$$

Step 4: (Iteration) Increase the value of I by one. If $I < \lceil N_T \rceil$, go to Step 2.

Step 5: (Reduction) Let the new values of T and N_T be $C \cdot T$ and $C \cdot N_t$. Reset I to zero.

Step 6: (Termination test) If a pre-specified stopping condition is satisfied, end the algorithm. Otherwise, go to Step 2.

3   Optimization Problems

All conducted experiments were run on a PC with CPU Celeron 1.2G under Windows 2000 using C language.

1) Case I: a parametric optimization problem

To directly compare with IGA [8], the benchmark function used in [8] is tested:

$$min \quad f(X) = k_1 \left\{ sin^2(k_2 \pi x_1) + \sum_{i=1}^{m-1} (x_i - k_3)^2 \left[1 + sin^2(k_4 \pi x_{i+1})\right] + (x_m - k_5)^2 \left[1 + sin^2(k_6 \pi x_m)\right] \right\} \quad (3),$$

where $m=5$, $k_1=0.1$, $k_2=3$, $k_3=1$, $k_4=3$, $k_5=1$, $k_6=1$, and $X=\{X \in R^5 | -5 \le x_i \le 5$, $i=1,2,\ldots,5\}$. There are about 15^5 local minima in the search space. The globally optimal solution is $X_{opt}=(1, 1, 1, 1, 1)$ and $f_{opt}= f(X_{opt})=0$. Let the control parameters of OSA be $C = 0.99$, $T_0 = 150$ and $N_0 = 4$. To compare with IGA, the stopping condition of OSA uses no more 15,390 function evaluations which are used by IGA. The average performances of 5 independent runs are shown in Table 2. All the reported data of Table 2 except those of OSA are gleaned from [10]. It reveals that OSA is superior to IGA in terms of the solution quality and robustness.

2) Case II: an electromagnetic problem

Fig. 1 shows a typical bar-plane electrode mode. One point charge and two semi-infinite line charges located in the z-axis are selected as turning parameters of the design problem.

Therefore, there are six parameters, the quantities (q_a, q_b, q_c) and z-directional coordinates (z_a, z_b, z_c) of the three charges. The effect of the grounded reference plane is considered using the image method [13]. The relevant parameters are given as follows: R, the radius of the end ring of the bar, is set to 1; G, the perpendicular distance between the end of the bar and the grounded plane, is set to 5; φ_*, the electric potential of the bar, is set to 1; and m is the number of randomly selected test points which are located on the surface of the bar. The locations of these test points are denoted as (r_i, z_i), $i=1, 2, ..., m$. Under these presumptions, the electrical potential at any testing point (r_i, z_i) produced by the equivalent charges can be determined by

$$\varphi(r_i, z_i) = \frac{1}{4\pi\varepsilon}\left[q_a\left(\frac{1}{\sqrt{r_i^2+(z_i-z_a)^2}} - \frac{1}{\sqrt{r_i^2+(z_i+z_a)^2}}\right) + q_b \ln\left(\frac{(z_b+z_i)+\sqrt{r_i^2+(z_b+z_i)^2}}{(z_b-z_i)+\sqrt{r_i^2+(z_b-z_i)^2}}\right) + q_c \ln\left(\frac{(z_c+z_i)+\sqrt{r_i^2+(z_c+z_i)^2}}{(z_c-z_i)+\sqrt{r_i^2+(z_c-z_i)^2}}\right)\right].$$

(4)

The objective function $f(X)$ is given as follows: $\min \quad f(X) = \sqrt{\sum_{i=1}^{m}\frac{1}{m}(\varphi_* - \varphi_i)^2}$ (5),

where $X=[q_a, q_b, q_c, z_a, z_b, z_c]^T$ denotes a solution, φ_i is the computed potential at the ith testing point, and $m = 100$. Let the control parameters of FSA and OSA be $C =0.99$, $T_0 =150$, $N_0=4$, and 10000 function evaluations. The experimental results of OSA using 20 independent runs are shown in Table 3. All the reported data of Table 3 except those of FSA and OSA are gleaned from [8]. It reveals that FSA and OSA are superior to IGA in terms of the solution quality in limited computation time. The comparison of convergence performance between FSA and OSA is shown in Fig. 2. It can show that OSA can efficiently design optimal bar-plane electrode models.

4   Conclusions

In this paper, we have proposed an orthogonal simulated annealing algorithm OSA with a novel intelligent generation mechanism (IGM) to solve electromagnetic optimization problems. High performance of OSA mainly arises OED-based IGM that can efficiently generate a good candidate solution for next move by using a systematic reasoning method instead of the random perturbation method. It has been shown empirically that OSA performs well. We believe that the proposed OSA can be widely used to solve various optimization problems of electromagnetic devices.

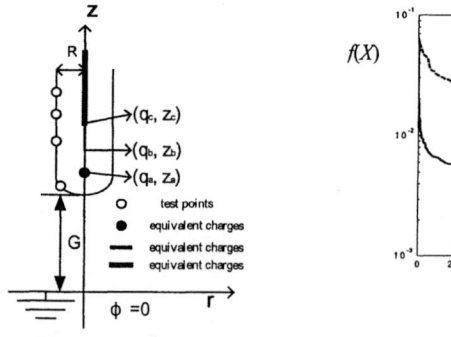

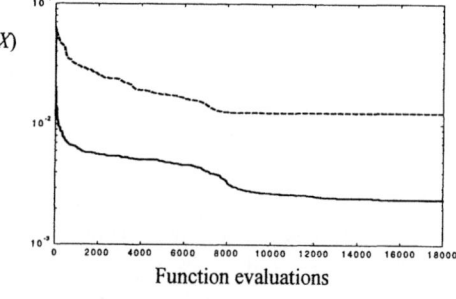

Fig. 1. Bar-plane electrode model   Fig. 2. The comparison of convergence

Table 1. Orthogonal array $L_9(3^4)$

Experiment no.	Factors				Observed Response
	1	2	3	4	
1	1	1	1	1	y_1
2	1	2	2	2	y_2
3	1	3	3	3	y_3
4	2	1	2	3	y_4
5	2	2	3	1	y_5
6	2	3	1	2	y_6
7	3	1	3	2	y_7
8	3	2	1	3	y_8
9	3	3	2	1	y_9

Table 2. Performance comparison among SGA, IGA, and OSA

Performance	SGA	IGA	OSA
X_{opt}	(0.999933, 0.979000, 1.016089, 0.994936, 1.000238)	(1.0000095, 1.000458, 0.999990, 0.998560, 1.000019)	(0.9999998, 0.9999997, 0.9999997, 0.9999998, 0.9999996)
f_{opt}	7.88×10^{-5}	6.13×10^{-7}	1.54×10^{-10}
$f_{avgerage}$	6.23×10^{-3}	8.97×10^{-7}	3.51×10^{-9}
$f_{standard\ deviation}$	6.69×10^{-3}	3.64×10^{-7}	3.26×10^{-9}
No. of function evaluations	381×90(=34290)	171×90(=15390)	15301

Table 3. Comparison of various algorithms for the Bar-Plane Electrode Model problem

	f_{opt}	$f_{avgerage}$	$f_{standard\ deviation}$	No. of evaluations
SGA	0.038915	0.056333	0.014887	221.6×90
IGA	0.022326	0.032890	0.009022	113.2×90
SA	0.22384	0.028500	0.005789	40916
Utabu	0.022072	0.022522	0.001418	11441
FSA	0.002203	0.012423	0.0064226	10000
OSA	0.001268	0.002699	0.000914	10000

References

[1] S. Yang, J.-M. Machado, G. Ni, S.-L. Ho and P. Zhou, "A self-learning simulated annealing algorithm for global optimizations of electromagnetic devices," *IEEE Trans. Magnetics*, vol. 36, pp. 1004–1008, 2000.

[2] T. Renyuan, S. Jianzhong and L. Yan, "Optimization of electromagnetic devices by using intelligent simulated annealing algorithm," IEEE Trans. Magnetics, vol. 34, no. 5, pp. 2992–2995, 1998.

[3] J. Simkin and C.-W. Trowbridge, "Optimization electromagnetic devices combining direct search methods with simulated annealing," *IEEE Trans. Magnetics*, vol. 28, no. 2, pp. 1545–1548, 1992.

[4] S. Kirkpatrick, C.-D. Gelatt and M.-P. Vecchi, "Optimization by simulated annealing," *Science*, vol. 220, pp. 671–680. 1983.

[5] H. Szu and R. Hartley, " Fast simulated annealing," *Physics Letters*, vol. 122, pp. 157–162, 1987.

[6] C. Tasllis and D. A. Stariolo, "Generalized simulated annealing," *Physica A,* vol. 233, pp. 395–406, 1996.

[7]   G. Gong, Y. Liu and M. Qian, "An adaptive simulated annealing algorithm," *Stochastic Processes and their Applications*, vol. 94, pp. 95–103, 2001.

[8]   X. Chen, J. Qia, G. Ni, S. Yang and M. Zhang, "An improved genetic algorithm for global optimization of electromagnetic problems," *IEEE Trans. Magnetics*, vol. 37, no. 5, pp. 3579–3583, 2001.

[9]   T. Renyuan, Y. Shiyou and L. Yan, "Combined strategy of improved simulated annealing and genetic algorithm for inverse problem," *IEEE Trans. Magnetics*, vol. 32, no. 3, pp. 1326–1329, 1996.

[10] Y. W. Leung and Y. Wang, "An orthogonal genetic algorithm with quantization for global numerical optimization," *IEEE Trans. Evol. Comput.*, vol. 5, no. 1, pp. 41–53, 2001.

[11] D. E. Goldberg, *Genetic Algorithms in Search, Optimization and Mechanism Learning*. Addison – Wesley Publishing Company, 1989.

[12] S. Geman and D. Geman, "Stochastic relaxation, gibbs distributions, and the bayesian restoration of images," *IEEE Trans. Pattern Analysis and Machines Intelligence*, vol. 6, pp. 721–741, 1984.

[13] S. Jianni, Numerical Analysis of Electromagnetic Field. Beijing: Academic, 1984.

Diversity Control to Improve Convergence Rate in Genetic Algorithms

Chaiwat Jassadapakorn and Prabhas Chongstitvatana

Department of Computer Engineering
Chulalongkorn University, Bangkok 10330, Thailand
chaiwat.ja@student.chula.ac.th, prabhas@chula.ac.th

Abstract. The diversity of the population affects the convergence rate in genetic algorithms. The determination of the proper diversity is still a trial and error process. The objective of this work is to study a method to find suitable population diversity automatically for a given problem. The proposed method is based on a modified restricted mating. A strategy to use diversity control is suggested using multiple subpopulations. Three well-known test problems, which have different requirement for diversity, are used to evaluate the proposed method.

1 Introduction

An important issue in applying genetic algorithms (GAs) to solve problems is a phenomenon called *premature convergence*. The most common cause of premature convergence is the lack of diversity coupled with ineffectiveness of the crossover operator to search for a new solution. The traditional GAs do not directly employ a method to maintain diversity during the evolutionary process. Without adequate diversity a few fitter individuals dominate the population in a short period of time. When the population diversity is lost, the evolutionary process cannot progress. It is because some necessary genetic materials, which may be the part of solution, are lost. To improve the performance of GAs, many works proposed enhanced strategies by embedding the diversity maintenance feature in different forms. The well known strategies are the sharing approach [1], the ranked space method [2], and the restricted mating [3,4,5].

All these works require the knowledge to setup parameters that effect the degree of population diversity in the evolutionary process such as the radius of neighborhood in sharing, conditions and threshold in restricted mating. Setting parameters incorrectly leads to unsuitable population diversity for the problem and causes poor performance.

The objective of this work is to study a method to find suitable population diversity automatically for a problem without using the knowledge of problem's structure. A modified restricted mating is used in conjunction with multiple subpopulations to control the diversity. The experiment is carried out on three test problems: one-max, multimodal function, and deceptive function to evaluate the proposed method.

J. Liu et al. (Eds.): IDEAL 2003, LNCS 2690, pp. 421–425, 2003.

2 Diversity Control

Two mechanisms are used to control diversity: a modified restricted mating and multiple subpopulations. In the modified restricted mating, each individual has a preference for its partner depends on "*preference type*" which is a parameter to control the degree of the difference of two individuals in the mating. By controlling the preference type, the diversity of the population can be influenced.

Given the first selected individual x_1 which is selected by a selection method (tournament selection in the experiment), the preference type is used to calculate the chance of another individual to be selected as its partner. Let d represents the difference between the first selected individual and a partner candidate, τ represents the preference type, and D represents a function of d and τ, called the "*difference function*". The candidate who has a higher D value has more chance to be selected as the second partner. The selection criterion depends on the difference function and the fitness value (Eq. 1).

$$x_2 = \underset{i \in s_t}{\mathrm{argmax}}[\, f(c_i) \cdot D(\tau, d_i)\,] \tag{1}$$

where x_2 represents the second selected partner, c_i is the ith candidate which are randomly selected from the population, f is the fitness function, and s_t is the tournament size. The linear difference function is used (Eq. 2).

$$D(\tau, d_i) = 0.5 + \frac{\tau}{\tau_{max}}\left(d_i - 0.5\right) \tag{2}$$

where τ_{max} is the maximum preference type, $0 \leq \tau \leq \tau_{max}$, and d_i is the difference between the first selected individual and the candidate c_i calculated from the equation:

$$d_i = \frac{h(c_i, x_1)}{l} \tag{3}$$

where h is the Hamming distance of two individuals, and l is the length of chromosome.

Please note that when τ is 0, the probability of selection does not depend on d, which is equivalent to a traditional selection method, the chance to be selected depends only on the fitness value. The higher value of τ gives more weight to the difference between individuals, which influences the population towards more diversity.

To determine the appropriate diversity value for a problem, multiple subpopulations are evolved using different diversity. They are in direct competition for the resource. Their effectiveness in solving the problem are evaluated. The subpopulation that performs well will be maintained. The subpopulation that is inferior will be eliminated. This scheme leads to the concentration of computational effort to the promising subpopulation.

3 Experiment and Discussion

The proposed method is evaluated using three test functions. They are well-known test problems in GAs: one-max problem, multimodal function (from [6]), and deceptive function (from [7]). These functions are range from easy, moderately difficult to very difficult and they require different degree of diversity in the population to solve them efficiently. The parameters used in the experiment are shown in Table 1.

Table 1. The parameters used in the experiment

Parameter	Value
Number of subpopulation	8 ($\tau = 0 - 7$)
Population size (for each subpopulation)	100
Copied individuals	10
Crossover individuals	90
Mutation rate	0.0333 per bit
Tournament size	3
Chromosome length	30 bits
Number of generation	200
Number of repeated run	500

The convergence rates of all problems are plotted to the generation 50, both the average fitness and the best individual fitness. The data is average from 500 runs. Only three lines of graph are shown: $\tau = 0$, $\tau = 3$ and $\tau = 7$, for maximum clarity of the presentation. The $\tau = 0$ is equivalent to a simple genetic algorithm. It is used as a reference method.

For one-max problem (Fig. 1), the best-performed subpopulation has the preference type $\tau = 0$ and the worst has $\tau = 7$. The best fitness plot is also agreed with the average fitness plot. For the multimodal function (Fig. 2) and the deceptive function (Fig. 3), the higher diversity yields better result. This can be seen in the best fitness plot where fitness of $\tau = 7$ is highest in both problems and $\tau = 0$ is lowest. However, the average fitness plots do not reflect this fact. The average fitness shows the better convergence for the lower diversity. These results show that the best fitness should be used to determine the proper diversity control.

How this observation can be used in improving the convergence rate of solving a problem? One strategy to perform diversity control is to use a number of subpopulations with different preference type to solve the problem and concentrate the computational effort to the promising subpopulation. All subpopulations are evolved and their effectiveness in solving the problem are evaluated. The subpopulation that performs well will be maintained. The subpopulation that is inferior will be eliminated.

The next question is how to determine when to evaluate the performance of subpopulation. Observing the best fitness plot of the deceptive function (Fig. 3), there is a certain period before the fitness value of each subpopulation tends to its final value. The line $\tau = 7$ surpasses $\tau = 0$ at the generation 22 and surpasses $\tau = 3$ at the 40th generation. This indicates that it is not a simple matter as using the best fitness at any time to evaluate the performance of a subpopulation. A certain amount of time must be allowed for a subpopulation to evolve before its performance can be compared properly with other subpopulations. For the experiments shown here, the generation 50th can be used as the judging point.

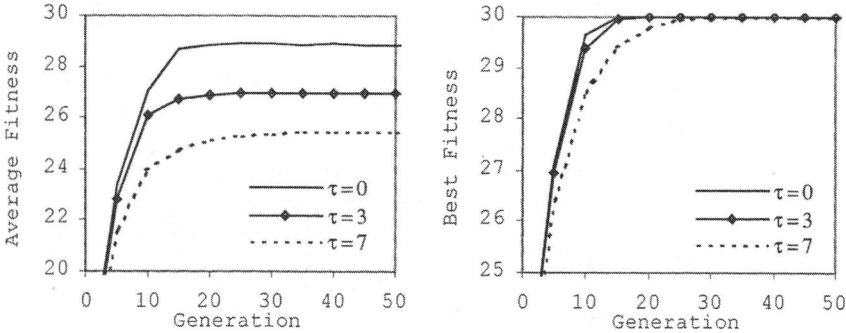

Fig. 1. The convergence of the one-max problem.

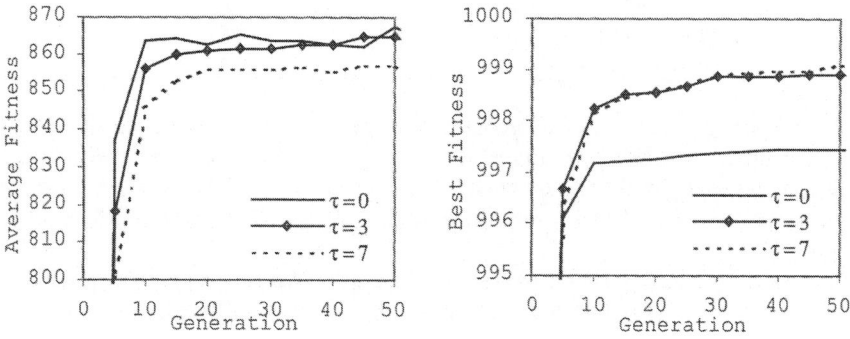

Fig. 2. The convergence of the multimodal function.

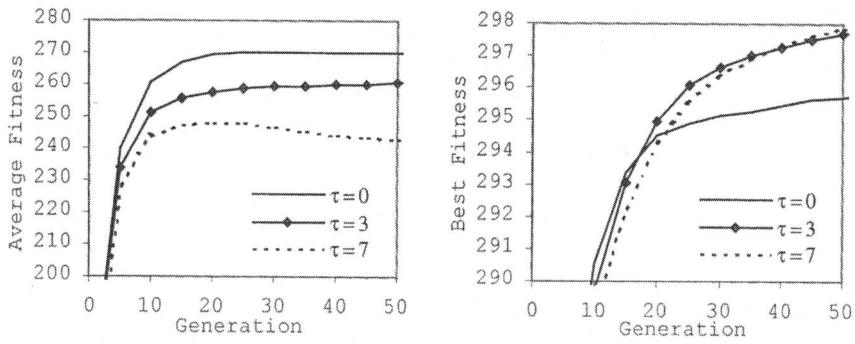

Fig. 3. The convergence of the deceptive function.

From Fig. 3, one can observe that the subpopulation with lower diversity is performing better early on and will compete with the subpopulation with higher diversity. However, eventually the higher diversity population will produce better results. Therefore, it is crucial to allow time for the higher diversity population to be developed before comparing its performance with the lower diversity population. This is more apparent for a more difficult problem such as the deceptive function.

4   Conclusion

The diversity control has been used to improve the convergence rate of Gas. A mechanism for diversity control has been proposed based on the modified restricted mating with linear difference function. The result is demonstrated through the experiment where multiple subpopulations with different diversity control are evolved. The strategy to concentrate the computational effort to the promising subpopulation is suggested. The subpopulation that performed well will be maintained and the under-performed subpopulation will be eliminated. The method to evaluate the performance of the subpopulation is proposed using the best fitness after a certain period of time to allow the subpopulation to progress. The actual method to determine this period is subjected to further study.

Acknowledgement. The first author would like to acknowledge the support of the Royal Golden Jubilee Ph.D. Graduates program by Thailand Research Fund organization.

References

1. Goldberg, D.E., Richardson, J.: Genetic Algorithms with Sharing for Multimodal Function Optimization. Proc. 2nd Int. Conf. Genetic Algorithms. (1987) 41–49
2. Winston, P.H.: Artificial Intelligence. 3rd edn. Addison-Wesley (1992)
3. Eshelman, L.J., Schaffer, J.D.: Preventing Premature Convergence in Genetic Algorithms by Preventing Incest. Proc. 4th Int. Conf. Genetic Algorithms. (1991) 115–122
4. Ronald, E.: When Selection Meets Seduction. Proc. 6th Int. Conf. Genetic Algorithms. (1995) 167–173
5. Matsui, K.: New Selection Method to Improve the Population Diversity in Genetic Algorithms. Proc. IEEE Int. Conf. Systems, Man, and Cybernetics. (1999) 625–630
6. Sareni, B., Krähenbühl, L.: Fitness Sharing and Niching Methods Revisited. IEEE Trans. Evolutionary Computation. 3 (1998) 97–105
7. Shimodaira, H.: DCGA: A Diversity Control Oriented Genetic Algorithm. Proc. 9th IEEE Int. Conf. Tools with Artificial Intelligence. (1997) 367–374

A Perception Evaluation Scheme for Steganography

Xiangwei Kong, Rufeng Chu, Xiaohui Ba, Ting Zhang, and Deli Yang

Dalian University of Technology, Dalian, 116023, China
kongxw@dlut.edu.cn; baxiaohui@yahoo.com.cn; rfchu@msn.com

Abstract. The aim of steganography is to conceal the very existence of hidden communication, so its demand on invisibility is serious. However there are not any corresponding perception evaluation methods. Most researchers still use Peak-Signal-to-Noise Rate (PSNR) for their perception evaluation, while ignoring the speciality of steganography. In this paper, we present an objective method of perception evaluation, which based on both characteristics of steganography and human visual systems (HVS). Extensive experimental results demonstrate that our method is superior to PSNR, which is consistent with HVS and can effectively evaluate the performance of steganographic algorithm.

1   Introduction

Steganography is the art of secret communication whose purpose is to hide the presence of communication [1]. It's important that the steganographic results don't contain any detectable artifacts due to message embedding.

There are many software that can be used to embed information within digital images. At present, there is still not a universal criterion for the performance evaluation of steganography. Most of researchers use the traditional image quality metrics such as PSNR, MSE, for their invisible evaluation. However these metrics are generally used in the fields of image compression and image communication, steganography is different with the fields described above, which demands the stego-image must not be suspected, namely, the demand of the quality of stego-image is more serious than that of watermarked image and compressed image. So we need a better image quality metrics. As for steganography, it is not necessary to resist any attacks, so there is a high correlation between the cover image and stego-image. Due to this property it will be more effective for the perception error measurement if we combine distortion with HVS model. Our method provides an evaluation criterion based on perception error for steganography, and we can find the drawbacks of steganographic software from our experimental results. We expect it can help to the development of more secure steganographic algorithm.

In the next section, we introduce the existing invisible evaluation criteria and overview the properties of human visual systems, then we give a detailed discussion on the speciality of steganography. In the section 3, a new evaluation is proposed to evaluate the perception of steganography. Experimental results and conclusion are given in Section 4 and 5 respectively.

J. Liu et al. (Eds.): IDEAL 2003, LNCS 2690, pp. 426–430, 2003.

2   Invisibly Evaluation Used for Information Hiding

There are two ways of measuring the perceptual quality, namely subjective quality assessment and objective quality assessment. We will discuss the latter in details.

2.1 Peak-Signal-to-Noise Rate

Global PSNR as well as mean square error (MSE) is the most widely used quality measure in the field of image and video coding and compression. One apparent argument used against PSNR is that it typically provides a single number for the entire image, and thus can't reflect spatial variations caused by message embedding. Fig.1 shows an extreme example, for a standard image, we add gauss noise evenly on one of the copy, while on another copy we concentrate the noise in the center. Here we can distinguish the difference easily, however, they have the same PSNR. Therefore, the PSNR is unsuitable for evaluating information hiding performance [2].

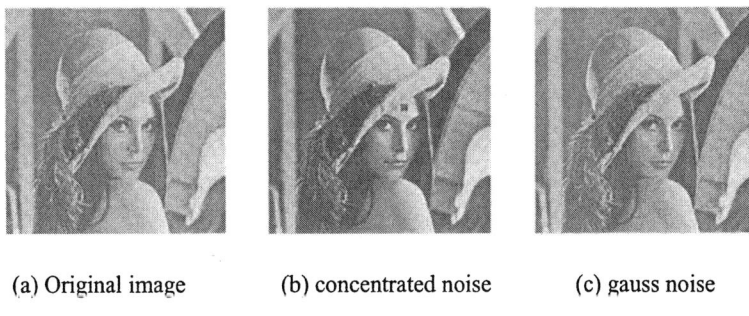

   (a) Original image   (b) concentrated noise   (c) gauss noise

Fig. 1. Contrast of Noisy Images (PSNR=37dB)

2.2 HVS Based Matrix

Over the past several decades, there have been many efforts to develop models or metrics for image quality that incorporate properties of the HVS. Most of the models incorporate frequency sensitivity, luminance sensitivity and contrast sensitivity of the HVS. These properties are summarized in the following.

Frequency sensitivity describes the human eye's sensitivity to sine wave gratings at various frequencies. Pereira and S.Voloshynovskiy[3] use noise visibility function (NVF) to compute Weighted PSNR (WPSNR) to evaluate visual quality of a watermarked image. The NVF characterizes the local texture of the image and varies between 0 and 1 where it takes 1 for flat areas and 0 for highly textured regions. The perceptual model applied here is based on the computation of a NVF that have local image properties.

Luminance sensitivity measures the effect of the detectability threshold of noise on a constant background. It typically involves a conversion to contrast, and is usually a nonlinear function of the local image characteristics. We denote relative contrast as C_R, we can get the following formula from [4]:

$$C_R = \frac{L_M - L}{L} = \frac{\Delta L}{L}$$

where L and L_M are denoted as the background luminance and image luminance respectively. We denote $C_{\min}$ as contrast sensitivity, which is the least relative contrast according to the perceptible difference of luminance.

2.3 Distortion Caused by Steganography

Steganography replaces redundant parts with embedded secret message to get an innocuous stego-object so that the existence of communication is concealed. Spatial domain method and transform domain method are two mainly used methods.

It is well known that different information hiding application has different property request. The aim of steganography is to conceal the very existence of hidden communication, so its demand on invisibility, undetectability and capacity are more serious than that of watermarking. But there is not a suitable evaluation criterion for invisibility. Because the difference calculated from origin image and stego-image can't precisely reflect human's perception's diversity caused by these two images□we must combine the distortion calculated from original image and stego-image with HVS models in order to precisely evaluate the image quality. This inspires us to put forward a new scheme of image quality metrics for steganography.

3   Evaluation Criterion

From above we can see that a good evaluation criterion should exploit the HVS properties to maximum extent so that the evaluation method will be the most exact to the steganographic system. Our method in this paper consists of the following six steps as shown in Fig.2.

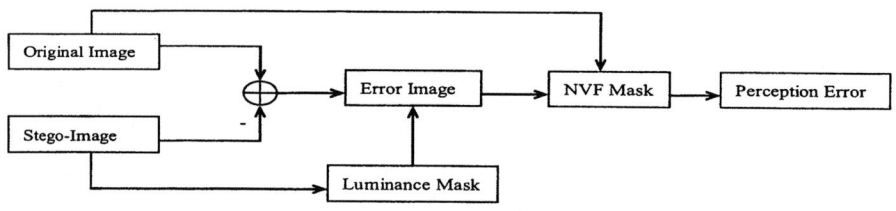

Fig. 2. The procedure of computing perceptual error

Step 1: We denote the cover image and stego-image as C and S respectively, whose size is $M \times N$, ΔX is denoted as the error matrix, which is be expressed as follows,

$$\Delta X = \left\{ \Delta x_{m,n} = \left| C_{m,n} - S_{m,n} \right| \, | \, 0 \le m < M; 0 \le n < N \right\},$$

then the error image ΔX is divided into $p \times p$ blocks,

$$MB = \{MB_{ij} = \frac{1}{p \times p} \sum_{m=0}^{p-1} \sum_{n=0}^{p-1} \Delta x_{i+m,j+n} \mid 0 \le i < \frac{M}{p}, 0 \le j < \frac{N}{p}\} \text{ denote as}$$

the mean of the block of ΔX.

Step 2: The stego-image S is divided into $p \times p$ blocks, then we compute the mean value of each block, let us denote those means of relative block as follows,

$$L = \{L_{ij} = \frac{1}{p \times p} \sum_{m=0}^{p-1} \sum_{n=0}^{p-1} C_{i+m,j+n} \mid 0 \le i < \frac{M}{p}, 0 \le j < \frac{N}{p}\}.$$

Then the luminance sensibility of each blocks is $C_{min}^{ij} = \frac{K}{\sqrt{L_{ij}}}$, K is a constant.

Step 3: MB_{ij} is processed by the luminance mask with the following rules, if

$\frac{MB_{ij}}{L_{ij}} < C_{min}^{ij}$, then $MB_{ij} = 0$, else keep MB_{ij} unchangeable.

Step 4: According to formula in [3], we can get NVF mask of the cover image. Then the NVF mask is divided into $p \times p$ blocks, $MBNVF$ is expressed as the mean of the NVF block, which describes the masking capability of the block.

$$MBNVF = \{MBNVF_{ij} = \frac{1}{p \times p} \sum_{m=0}^{p-1} \sum_{n=0}^{p-1} NVF_{i+m,j+n} \mid 0 \le i < \frac{M}{p}, 0 \le j < \frac{N}{p}\}$$

Step 5: We define the masking result as follows:

$$Mask = \{Mask_{ij} = MBNVF_{ij} \times MB_{ij} \mid 0 \le i < \frac{M}{p}, 0 \le j < \frac{N}{p}\}$$

Step 6: Compute stego-image quality evaluation ($SIQE$) as follows

$$SIQE = 10 \log \frac{\sum_{ij} Mask_{ij}^2}{\lfloor M/p \rfloor \times \lfloor N/p \rfloor}$$

It is obvious that the less the $SIQE$ is, the better the quality of the image is. If all the error can be masked, the $SIQE$ will be negative infinite (-Inf).

4 Experiment Results

In our experiments, K is 1, p is 8 and D is 80. In section 2, We describe two images that have same PSNR (Fig.1(b) and Fig.1(c)). Now we use our method to assess the two image, the $SIQE$ from Fig.1(c) is -1.0635, and the $SIQE$ from Fig.1(b) is 8.4078. This example shows that our method is better than PSNR.

We use several typical steganography software to hide different message into some standard image such as Lena, etc. Table1 summarizes our $SIQE$ results with some popular steganography software[5]. From the table 1, we can find that Hide in Picture, BPCS, are better than Jstegshell2.0. For BPCS, the size of embedded message is larger than the other methods. But with the increasement of the message size, the distortion also becomes serious. Through many experiments, we think that the $SIQE$ acceptable is less than 0.

Table 1. SIQE for different steganographic methods with varies embedding capacity

Software / Embedded Message	Hide in picture	JstegShell2.0	BPCS
2%	-Inf	5.3170	-Inf
5%	-Inf	5.5332	-Inf
10%	-Inf	5.6975	-Inf
20%	----	-------	-Inf
30%	---	-------	-8.7584
40%	---	-------	10.2677

5   Conclusion

For steganography, invisibility is the basic request, but there is not a corresponding perception error evaluation method. In this paper, we present an objective method for perception evaluation, which based on distortion and HVS. From the test results, we can see the method is effective for the perception evaluation of steganography.

References

[1] W. Bender, D. Gruhl, N. Morimoto, and A. Lu, "Techniques for data hiding," IBM Syst. J., vol. 35, 1996.
[2] Xingang You, Yunbiao Guo, Linna Zhou, PSNR is Unsuitable for evaluating information hiding performance. Information Hiding (Proceedings of CIHW2001), pp: 51–56, Xidian University Publish House, Xi'an, 2001
[3] S. Voloshynovskiy, A.Herrigel, N. Baumgaertner and T. Pun, "A stochastic approach to content adaptive digital image watermarking". In Lecture Notes in Computer Science: Third International Workshop on Information Hiding. Volume 1768 pages 211–236. 1999
[4] Chuanyao Tang. "Fundamentals of Image Electronics" published by Publishing House of Electronics Industry, Beijing, China in 1995.
[5] http://www.jjtc.com/Steganography/toolmatrix.htm

Clustering Individuals in Non-vector Data and Predicting: A Novel Model-Based Approach

Kedong Luo, Jianmin Wang, Deyi Li, and Jiaguang Sun

School of Software
Tsinghua University, Beijing, China
lkd99@mails.tsinghua.edu.cn

Abstract. In many applications, data is non-vector in nature. For example, one might have transaction data from a dialup access system, where each customer has an observed time-series of dialups which are different on start time and dialup duration from customer to customer. It's difficult to convert this type of data to a vector form, so that the existing algorithms oriented on vector data [5] are hard to cluster the customers with their dialup events. This paper presents an efficient model-based algorithm to cluster individuals whose data is non-vector in nature. Then we evaluate on a large data set of dialup transaction, in order to show that this algorithm is fast and scalable for clustering, and accurate for prediction. At the same time, we compare this algorithm with vector clustering algorithm by predicting accuracy, to show that the former is fitter for non-vector data than the latter.

1 Introduction

From the data mining perspective, clustering is a fine and common methodology in understanding and exploring large data sets. But existing algorithms are mostly oriented to vector measurements of fixed dimension.

But many applications have non-vector data, e.g. described in [2]. Some are easy to be converted to vector form, others are difficult for conversion which may lose too much information. For example, let's inspect into a tiny dice of dialup data—two customers' dialup events in one week—as Figure 1 shows.

In general, we use the term "individual" for a customer, a natural person, a mobile phone, and so on; and "event" for a customer's dialup, a personal basket, a phone call, and so on.

This type of dialup data is non-vector in nature, because it has not some significant characters by which many existing methods convert non-vector data to vector form. Firstly, it's difficult to assign events between individuals. Secondly, single individual's events are always sparse. Thirdly, it's not smooth for events of a customer changing over time. The last, fore-and-aft events aren't causal or correlative in the same customer.

We create a novel model fitted for dialup habit of a cluster of customers in order to cluster this type of non-vector data. Different from usual parametric model, our novel model can be estimated not only in parameters, but also in

J. Liu et al. (Eds.): IDEAL 2003, LNCS 2690, pp. 431–435, 2003.

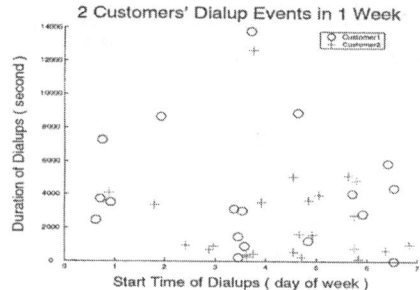

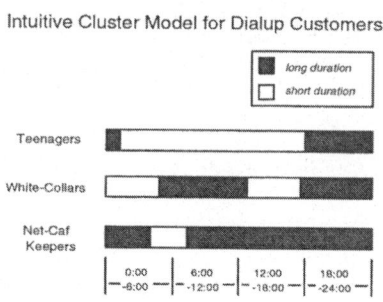

Fig. 1. Two customers' dialup events.

Fig. 2. Three clusters gained from common sense intuitively.

architecture, because agglomerations of dialup events are different from cluster to cluster.

Though novel model is fit for the non-vector data, we have to use a huge model. Fortunately, dialup data possesses a basic and important character—periodicity—that many types of time-series data also contain. So that, we can create a much smaller model adapted to dialup habit of a cluster of customers in a period of time.

As Figure 2 shows, we need a flexible model to cluster individuals in non-vector data. This model can be estimated both on architecture and parameters. The flexible model and estimating method are taken into account in Section 3. Given the novel model, we use a re-allocation algorithm to learn the architecture and parameters of cluster models.

Then, some experiments were done on dialup data to evaluate this method. We'll take prediction accuracy for new events as the measurement, since it's hard to view the clustering result under massive individuals.

The remainder of the paper is organized as follows. Section 2 gives a brief overview of the related work on non-vector clustering problem. Section 3 introduces our novel model and algorithm. Section 4 shows the experimental results. We conclude in Section 5.

2 Related Work

In past decade, many algorithms have given various solutions to cluster some certain types of non-vector data, as below.

One approach is mathematical transform approach. The pivot of this approach is how to draw out the features. Some significant papers adopted classical mathematical transforms. For example, [1] introduced Discrete Fourier Transform to gain the features of smooth sequence data.

Another approach introduces Markov model to hold the nature of a certain type of dynamic behaviors, in which fore-and-aft events are correlative. For instance, clustering web navigation patterns [2].

Since the domain of vector clustering is fully explored, some cases try to cluster non-vector data by forcing conversion from non-vector to vector form, even though the conversion will lose too much information.

The model-based clustering approach is also powerful for non-vector data, so long as you can define a rational and effective cluster model.

Consequently, this paper adopts model-based method to clustering individuals in non-vector dialup data. One reason is scalability. The other reason is that model-based methods can get a profile (model) for each cluster but distance-based methods can't.

3   Novel Model and Algorithm

Full-flexible architecture isn't practical. Thus we must trade off between flexibility and algorithm performance. So we adopts a agglomerative method to generate model, as Figure 3 shows. Firstly, we train the model in fine-granularity under owned events. Each cell estimates its parameter to fit for its owned events. After this step, many neighbors are similar and many cells have unknown parameters because they don't own events. Afterwards, we agglomerate similar neighbors and extend to unknown-parametric neighbors. Now we have effectively estimated a flexible model with its events.

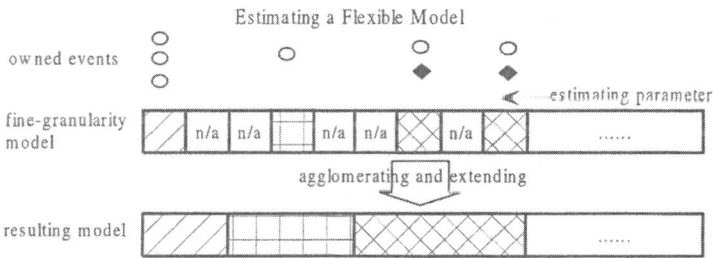

Fig. 3. Estimating model's architecture and parameters to suit for its owned events.

Given the novel model, we use a re-allocation algorithm to learn the architecture and parameters of cluster models. In general, this algorithm adopts the cycle between two steps: estimating architecture and parameters of cluster models, and allocating individuals to clusters; stop criterion is that cluster models are stable enough.

It's only left that how to compute match between an individual and a model. Assuming $m_{i,j}$ is the match between individual i and cluster model j, and $c_{i,j}$ is the total count that events of individual i match to model j, and C_i is the total event count of individual i. Whether an event matches to a cluster model depends on if the value of the event matches to the corresponding parameter of the model. Then $m_{i,j} = c_{i,j}/C_i$.

4   Experimental Results

Using the real non-vector data, we now evaluate the prediction accuracy, speed, and scalability of our clustering algorithm and compare with the vector method.

All these experiments were run on a 1.6GHz single processor Intel Pentium4 machine with 256M DRAM. The operation system was Windows 2000. The non-vector data in our experiments was China Telecom's nationwide dialup data. We arbitrarily defined fine-granularity an hour and model's period a week. So we start with the simplest case where events are categorized as *short* or *long* ones by a duration threshold.

The experiment depicts the algorithm performances, such as speed, scalability, and accuracy, and what the performances depend on, in Figure 4. In this experiment, we held the number of cluster models on 200. This non-vector algorithm is so fast to easily cluster tens of thousands of individuals within several minutes. Furthermore, the time complexity is linear in the number of individuals, while the predictions are still accurate enough.

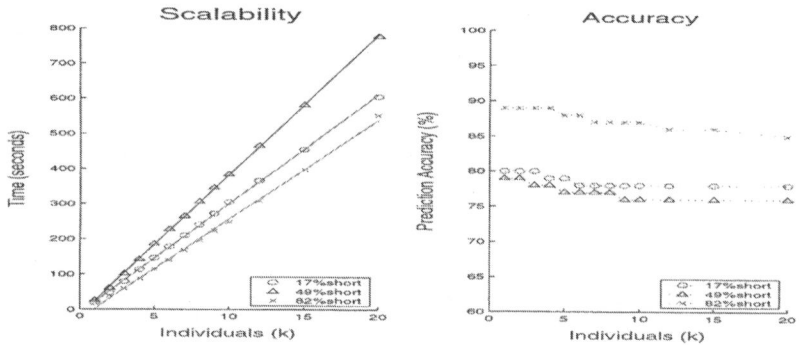

Fig. 4. The left depicts the speed and scalability of this algorithm. The right depicts the prediction accuracy in the same experiments.

Figure 5 is about the accuracy comparison to predict new dialup events using clustering result. The contrastive vector method is EM [3] clustering provided by WEKA [4]. The conversion from non-vector to vector is computing the average dialup durations group-by hours. There are 5000 customers and 226705 dialup events which would be divided to 100 clusters. This experiment makes sure that our clustering method is good at clustering and predicting in non-vector data. The vector method behaves badly, because the conversion from non-vector to vector has lost much information.

5   Conclusion

This paper presents a novel model-based algorithm for clustering individuals into groups with their non-vector events. The algorithm adopts a flexible cluster

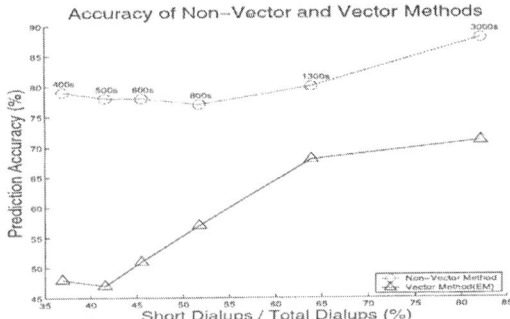

Fig. 5. The accuracy of non-vector clustering method to predict new dialup durations, in contrast to that of vector method.

model which is trained by a novel reallocation algorithm, in order to fit for the nature of non-vector data.

In contrast to vector clustering, this algorithm is fitter for non-vector data according to its better prediction accuracy for new events. Furthermore, it is fast, and its complexity is linear in the number of individuals. Using this method, we can rapidly process tens of thousands of individuals and millions of events. This algorithm can be broadly used on personalized non-vector data in many commercial or scientific applications.

Acknowledgments. This work is supported by the National High Technology Research and Development Program of China (863 Program) under Grant No.2002AA444120. The dialup data for this paper was provided by China Telecom. The EM clustering procedure for vector data is a part of WEKA [4].

References

1. R. Agrawal, C. Faloutsos, and A. Swami, "Efficient Similarity Search In Sequence Database", In *Proc. of 4th Int. Conf. of Foundations of Data Organization and Algorithms*, Chicago, IL, Oct. 1993
2. I. V. Cadez, D. Heckerman, C. Meek, P. Smyth, and S. White, "Visualization of Navigation Patterns on a Web Site Using Model-Based Clustering", in *Proc. of KDD 2000*, New York: ACM Press, pages 280–284.
3. A. Dempster, N. Laird, and D. Rubin, "Maximum Likelihood from Incomplete Data via the EM algorithm". *Journal of the Royal statistical Society*, Series B, 39(1): 1–38, 1977.
4. E. Frank, M. Hall, L. Trigg, R. Kirkby, G. Schmidberger, M. Ware, X. Xu, R. Bouckaert, Y. Wang, S. Inglis, I.H. Witten, et al, "Weka 3: Machine Learning Software in Java". *http://www.cs.waikato.ac.nz/ml/weka/*
5. J. Han and M. Kamber, *Data Mining: Concepts and Techniques*, Morgan Kaufmann, 2001.

A Fuzzy Multi-criteria Decision Model for Information System Security Investment

Vincent C.S. Lee

School of Business Systems, Monash University Clayton Campus,
PO Box 63B, Wellington Road, Victoria, Australia 3800
vincent.lee@infotech.monash.edu.au
Fax: (+ 61 3) 9905 5159, Tel: (+613) 9905 2360

Abstract. Decision on how much resources should be invested to curb information security threat at a specific risk level is contingent upon multiple criteria, some of which must be represented by linguistic variables. This paper aims to provide theoretical justifications for the various criteria and the need to use a fuzzy-logic based tool for their selection and classification.

1 Introduction

Hitherto, it remains extreme impracticable to establish a unified model for information security investment across all industries. Exploring the similarities of core business operations and strategic directions of firms in the same industry, it can be approximately generalised an information security investment model for an industry. Lee and Shao [1] proposed an information security investment model Y=F (X) that describes the relation between security investment Y and other independent variables or criteria, X ($x_1, x_2, x_3, \cdots x_n$), basing on the similarity of businesses in the same industry. This paper discusses the definition and research method used to identify variables Y and X.

2 The Proposed Fuzzy Multi-criteria Information Security Investment Model

Basing on the similarity of business operation, for firms in the same industry, we believe that it is possible to set up a generic model to meet mission critical business information security requirements. Using principal component analysis, the four key criteria: data importance (DI) level; information complexity (IC) and information intensity (II); and overall risk (OR) environment that jointly determine the information security threats. The driving dynamics behind these four key criteria are: i) The pur

J. Liu et al. (Eds.): IDEAL 2003, LNCS 2690, pp. 436–441, 2003.
© Springer-Verlag Berlin Heidelberg 2003

pose of a security system is to protect the business' viability both in short- and long-term; ii) These criteria are time dependent variables of which (OR) is the only exogenous variable, which is beyond a firm's control while the other three factors are endogenous; and iii) Other factors like technology, staff training and policy are short term in nature. Mathematically, Y%=F (II, IC, DI, OR)

3 Information Security Investment Ratio, Endogenous, and Exogenous Criteria

Information security investment (Y) is defined as the investment of protecting availability, integrity and confidentiality of the information asset in an organisation including technology, staff, education, policy and consulting etc.

The total information security investment, $Y = \sum (y_1 + y_2 \cdots y_n)$, in which each component cannot be analytically calculated but can be measured. It is easier to use a relative measure, investment ratio Y% defined as

$$Y\% = \frac{\sum_{i=1}^{n} y^i}{Total\ Asset} \quad (1) \quad or \quad Y\% = \frac{Y(1+b\%)^m}{TA(1+a\%)^n} \quad (2)$$

where b% and a% are the average investment increment speed, and n and m are number of years to start the investment ($n \geq m$). Data for all variables in (2) are normally partially disclosed in aggregated narrative form in annual firm report. The disaggregated data can however be obtained through confidential survey questionnaires or field studies. According to our experience, when Y% is reaching 16% to the total information security investment, we can say it is very high. Now, we will classify the Y% into 9 degrees: extremely high (A9), very high (A8), rather high (A7), high (A6), medium (A5), low (A4), rather low (A3), very low (A2), and extremely low (A1). For graphical representation, see the figure given as below.

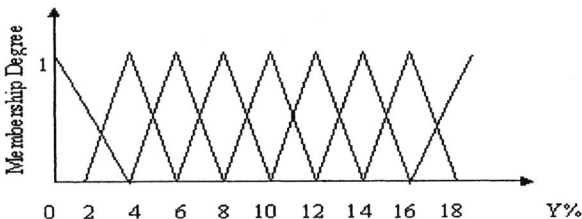

Therefore, we can write Y% into the following fuzzy equation.

$$\mu_{A1}(Y)=\begin{cases}\dfrac{4-Y}{4}, & Y<4 \\ 0, & Y\geq 4\end{cases} \qquad \mu_{A2}(Y)=\begin{cases}\dfrac{Y-2}{2}, & 2\leq Y\leq 4 \\ \dfrac{6-Y}{2}, & 4<Y<6 \\ 0, & otherwise\end{cases} \qquad (3)$$

Like wise, we can define the membership functions for $\mu_{A3}, \mu_{A4}, \mu_{A5}, \cdots \mu_{A9}$

3.1   Exogenous Criteria

The overall risk (OR) environment is exogenous to information risk investment, which is beyond the control by an individual organisation. By nature the overall risk environment is too complicated to measure exactly, we can therefore only devise a measurement instrument to give a general assessment of the overall risk (OR) as follows.

$$OR=\frac{\text{The combination of statistics data of CERT}}{\text{The total equipment or people in the specified zone can access the internet}} \qquad (4)$$

Note: CERT (computer emergency reaction team, based at USA). CERT's [2] statistics are available from year 1988-2002 including number of incidents, vulnerabilities, security alerts, security notes, mail message and hotline calls handled [3]. To classify the data from CERT, we propose to use the different weights assigned to different criteria used by experts' assessment. For example, we regard 1998's data as benchmark, and compare the rest of years' data to it.

Table 1. Basic and computed CERT Statistics

CERT data	Incidents Number	Vulnerability	Security Alerts	Mail handled	Environment OR index	Internet user (million)**
1998	3734	262	34	41871		77
1999	9859 (2.64)	417 (1.59)	22 (0.65)	34612 (0.83)	1.43 (0.826#)	133 (1.73)
2000	21756 (5.83)	1090 (4.16)	26 (0.76)	118907 (2.84)	3.40 (1.276#)	205 (2.66)
2001	52658(14.10)	2437 (9.30)	41 (1.21)	56365 (1.35)	6.49 (1.74#)	287 (3.73)

* Figures in brackets are the number of times of 1998's benchmark

** Data obtained Internet research report, Morgan Stanley [7,8]

\# Figures denote the number of times of OR index for Internet user compared with 1998's benchmark

Assuming equal weight is given for all years' data, the overall risk (OR) environments for years 1999 to 2001 are computed as given in 6th column of Table 1. With this method, one can get a time series of overall environment risk from 1998, which enables the model to have strong prediction ability.

3.2   Endogenous Criteria

There are three endogenous criteria to be determined. For one year time period, the change in exogenous risk can be regarded negligible. For the companies in the different industries, the method of their information flow and service, information intensity are different. Most of enterprise will adopt several kinds of data exchange methods and information service.

3.2.1 Information Complexity (IC)

Information complexity is the degree of information exchange and service. We propose four levels of IC: (i) Very simple (C1, Very basic information data exchange, such as E-mail service; (ii) Simple (C2, basic information exchange and service, e.g. large information exchange in the internal organization, providing homepage for custom, and establishing E-mail severs and FTP severs); (iii) Intermediate (C3, middle information service and exchange. Such as, E-commerce, VPN service, Transaction protection etc); and (iv) Complex (C4, complex information exchange and service, like digital signature, protecting customer privacy, very secure data transfer, hot backup, load balance etc).

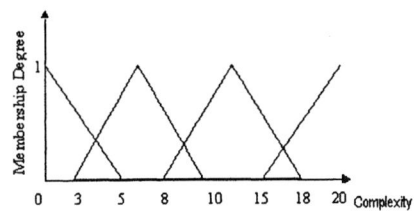

$$\mu_{C1}(c)=\begin{cases}\dfrac{5-c}{5},c\le 5\\[2mm]0,\qquad c>5\end{cases}$$

$$\mu_{C2}(c)=\begin{cases}\dfrac{c-3}{3.5},3\le c\le 6.5\\[2mm]\dfrac{10-c}{3.5},6.5<c\le 10\\[2mm]0\quad ,otherwise\end{cases}$$

$$\mu_{C3}(c)=\begin{cases}\dfrac{c-8}{5},8\le c\le 13\\[2mm]\dfrac{18-c}{5},13<c\le 18\\[2mm]0\quad ,otherwise\end{cases}$$

$$\mu_{C4}(c)=\begin{cases}\dfrac{c-15}{5},15\le c\le 20\\[2mm]1,\qquad c>20\end{cases}$$

3.2.2 Intensity of Information Flow (II)

The quantity of information flow is also varied in different enterprises. The information flow intensity can be calculated by the total quantity of information flow and total number of devices, which linked to the net [4, 5]. That is,

$$\text{Information intensity (II)} = \frac{\text{Total informtion flow (Mbyte)}}{\text{Total device number}} \tag{5}$$

We classify Information intensity into 5 categories: very large ($II5 \in [8.5, +\infty)$), large ($II4 \in [4,10]$), medium ($II3 \in [2,6]$), small ($II2 \in [1,3]$), very small ($II1 \in (0, 1.5]$).

3.2.3 Data Importance (DI)

Data importance implies different levels of the security. We will classify all kinds of data and give list by the property of business need. The importance of data could be expressed in two dimensions, (data use frequency, data loss due to insecurity). The frequency of use and severity can be written as follows.

Frequency of use {A, B, C, D, E, F, G}={1, 0.8, 0.6, 0.4, 0.2, 0.1, 0}
Severity, {I, II, III, IV, V}={1, 0.75, 0.5, 0.25, 0}. With those numerical situations, we get the following matrices.

Table 2. Frequency of use and severity of loss of information

	A	B	C	D	E	F	G
I	1	0.8	0.6	0.4	0.2	0.1	0
II	0.75	0.6	0.45	0.3	0.15	0.075	0
III	0.5	0.4	0.3	0.2	0.1	0.05	0
IV	0.25	0.2	0.15	0.1	0.05	0.025	0
V	0	0	0	0	0	0	0

Then we calculate and use $\dfrac{a_{ij}}{\sum\limits_{i,j=1}^{n,m} a_{ij}}$ for matrix normalisation and yielded Table 3.

Table 3. Frequency of use and loss information (in normalised data)

	A	B	C	D	E	F	G
I	0.129032	0.103226	0.077419	0.051613	0.025806	0.012903	0
II	0.096774	0.077419	0.058065	0.03871	0.019355	0.009677	0
III	0.064516	0.051613	0.03871	0.025806	0.012903	0.006452	0
IV	0.032258	0.025806	0.019355	0.012903	0.006452	0.003226	0
V	0	0	0	0	0	0	0

Table 4 assume same weights for each information type.

Table 4. Information weight matrix

Weight (if equal)	Information Type	Frequency	Severity if loss
1	Financial	C	II
1	Operational	B	III
1	...	...	...
1	Strategic	E	II

The data importance= $0.058065 \times 1 + 0.051613 \times 1 + ... + 0.019355 \times 1$

4   Conclusion

In this research, we demonstrated the process of identifying various exogenous and endogenous criteria in a generic information security investment model using fuzzy logic theory. With a clear definition of fuzzy membership function of those criteria, the relation can be disclosed with enough data collected.

References

[1.] Lee, V. C. S. and Shao, Linyi, (2003). "A Fuzzy Regression Inference design for optimal investment on enterprise information security", submitted to ISDA-03.
[2.] CERT/CC statistics (1988–2002) www.cert.org/stats/cert_stats.html.
[3.] Report of "Internet, Technology and Telecommunications", 2002 Internet research of Morgan Stanley August.
[4.] CIO magazine survey report (Sep 2002). Security Spending: how much is enough?
[5.] Briney, A. (Sept 2000). Report of Information Security Survey.

Blind Equalization Using RBF and HOS

Jung-Sik Lee[1], Jin-Hee Kim[1], Dong-Kun Jee[1], Jae-Jeong Hwang[1], and
Ju-Hong Lee[2]

[1] School of Electronic & Information Eng., Kunsan National University, Korea
{leejs,jhk0221,enigma64,hwang}@kunsan.ac.kr,
[2] School of Computer Science and Engineering, Inha University, Incheon, Korea
juhong@inha.ac.kr

Abstract. This paper discusses a blind equalization technique for FIR channel system, that might be minimum phase or not, in digital communication. The proposed techniques consist of two parts. One is to estimate the original channel coefficients based on fourth-order cumulants of the channel output, the other is to employ RBF neural network to model an inverse system for the original channel. Here, the estimated channel is used as a reference system to train the RBF neural network. The proposed RBF equalizer provides fast and easy learning, due to the structural efficiency and excellent recognition-capability of RBF neural network. Throughout the simulation studies, it was found that the proposed blind RBF equalizer performed favorably better than the blind MLP equalizer, while requiring the relatively smaller computation steps in training.

1 Introduction

For the last three decades, many of blind equalizers that do not use the known training sequence have been proposed in the literature beginning with Sato[1,2], because there are some practical situations when the conventional adaptive algorithms are not suitable for wireless communications during an outage

Most current blind equalization techniques use higher order statistics (HOS) of the received sequences, directly or indirectly, because they are efficient tools for identifying that may be the nonminimum phase[3,4]. The HOS based techniques have the capability to identify a nonminimum phase system simply from its output because of the property of polyspectra to preserve not only the magnitude but also the phase information of the signal.

This paper develops a new method to solve the problems of blind equalization, by combining the advantages of HOS and a RBF neural network[5,9]. The main purpose of the proposed blind RBF equalizer is to solve the obstacles of long time training and complexity that are often encountered in the blind MLP equalizers[6,7]. The proposed techniques firstly estimates the order and coefficients of the original channel based on the autocorrelation and the fourth-order cumulants of the received signals.

J. Liu et al. (Eds.): IDEAL 2003, LNCS 2690, pp. 442–446, 2003.

2 Blind RBF Equalizer

Assume that the received signal $\{y_k\}$ is generated by an FIR system described by

$$y_k = \sum_{i=0}^{p} h_i s_{k-i} + n_k = \hat{y}_k + n_k \tag{1}$$

where $\{h_i\}$, $0 \le i \le p$ is the impulse response of the channel and $\{s_k\}$ is i.i.d., non-Gaussian. Here, $\{s_k\}$ could be a two-level symmetric PAM sequence. The additive noise $\{n_k\}$ is zero mean, Gaussian, and statistically independent of $\{s_k\}$.

Firstly, the autocorrelation technique in [8] is used to estimate the channel order that is required to specify the number of centers in an RBF equalizer. Secondly, using the cumulants property[5], the following channel parameters are obtained

$$H = (C^H C)^{-1} C^H c \tag{2}$$

where C and c are the matrix and vector consisting of the estimated fourth-order cumulants, and H is the unknown coefficient vector. Fig. 1 shows the block diagram of the blind RBF equalizer system.

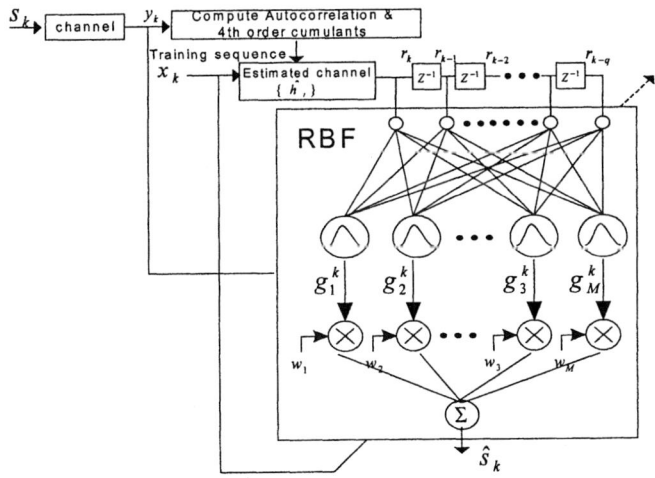

Fig. 1. The structure of blind RBF equalizer system

3 Simulation Results

For the computational convenience, it is assumed that the binary signals (+1 or -1) are generated at random with an additive white Gaussian noise. Firstly, the channel order is estimated with three different channel models. Autocorrelations of channel observations were computed and the results of them are illustrated in Fig.2. As shown in the Figures, channel orders were correctly revealed from their normalized sample autocorrelations. For the estimates of the channel coefficients, 5 different realizations with the training sequences equal to 512 are performed with SNR equal to 10 db. The mean value of the estimates is shown in the Table 1. Finally, the RBF equalizer is trained with the estimated channel model. Fig.3 shows the error rate comparison of linear equalizer and MLP and RBF neural network equalizers. As shown in the graph, the performance of the blind RBF equalizer is superior to that of the blind MLP equalizer and linear equalizer

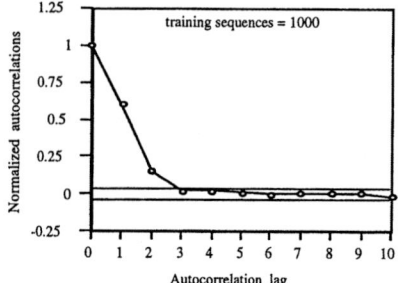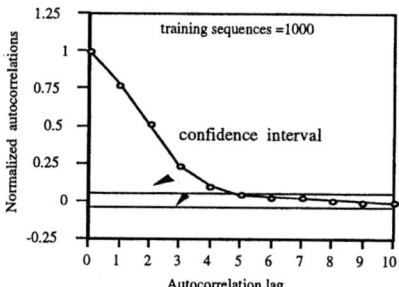

Fig. 2. Channel order estimation

4 Conclusion

In this paper, a blind equalization technique is discussed based on higher-order statistics and a RBF. The main procedures of the proposed blind equalizer consist of two parts. One is to estimate the order and coefficients of original channel using higher-order-cumulants; the estimated channel is used to generate the reference signal. The other part is to reconstruct the originally transmitted symbols (signals) after training the RBF neural network. The main purpose of the blind RBF equalize is to solve the obstacles of long time training and complexity that are often encountered in the MLP equalizers. The proposed RBF equalizer provides fast and easy learning, due to the structural efficiency and excellent recognition-capability of RBF neural network. Throughout the simulation studies, it was found that the proposed blind RBF equalizer performed favorably better than the blind MLP equalizer, while requiring the relatively smaller computation steps in training.

Acknowledgements. This Paper was partially supported by the Brain Korea 21 Project in Kunsan National University.

Table 1. Channel coefficient estimation

Original channel model	Estimated channel coefficient
$H(Z) = 0.5 + 1.0Z^{-1}$	$h_o = 0.50854$ $h_1 = 1.00076$
$H(z) = 0.348 + 0.87z^{-1} + 0.348z^{-2}$	$h_0 = 0.35706$ $h_1 = 0.87566$ $h_2 = 0.34682$

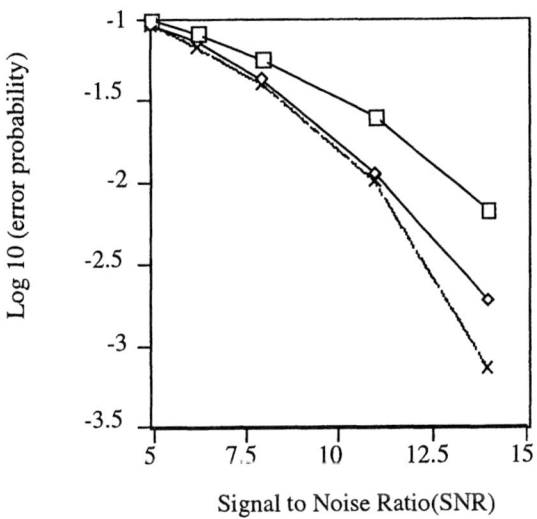

Fig. 3. Error rate comparison : $H(Z) = 0.5 + 1.0Z^{-1}$, □ : linear equalizer ◇ : MLP equalizer × : blind RBF equalizer

References

1. Y. Sato, "A Method of Self-Recovering Equalization for Multilevel Amplitude Modulation Systems," *IEEE Trans. Commun.,* vol. COM-23, pp.679–682, Jun. 1975.
2. A. Benveniste, Goursat, and G. Ruget, "Robust Identification of a Nonminimum Phase System: Blind Adjustment of a Linear Equalizer in Data Communications," *IEEE Trans. Automat. Contr.,* vol. AC-25, pp. 385–398, Jun. 1980.
3. J. M. Mendel, "Tutorial on Higher-Order Statistics (Spectra) in Signal Processing and System Theory: Theoretical Results and Some Applications," *Proceedings, IEEE,* 79, pp. 278–305, Mar. 1991.
4. F. B. Ueng and Y. T. Su, "Adaptive Blind Equalization Using Second and Higher Order Statistics," *IEEE J. Select. Areas Commun.,* vol. 13, pp. 132–140, Jan. 1995.

5. S. Mo and B. Shafai, "Blind Equalization Using Higher Order Cumulants and Neural Network," *IEEE Trans. Signal Processing*, vol. 42, pp. 3209–3217, Nov. 1994.
6. S. Chen, G. J. Gibson, and C. F. N. Cowan, and P. M. Grant, "Adaptive Equalization of Finite Non-Linear Channels Using Multilayer Perceptrons," *Signal Processing*, vol. 20, pp. 107–119, 1990
7. G. J. Gibson, S. Siu, and C. F. N. Cowan, "Application of Multilayer Perceptrons as Adaptive Channel Equalizers," *ICASSP*, Glasgow, Scotland, pp. 1183–1186, 1989
8. S. Chen, B. Mulgrew, and P. M. Grant, "A Clustering Technique for Digital Communications Channel Equalization Using Radial Basis Function Networks," *IEEE Trans. Neural Networks*, vol. 4, pp. 570–579, 1993.
9. J. Lee., C. Beach, and N. Tepedelenlioglu "A Practical Radial Basis Function Equalizer" *IEEE Trans. on Neural Networks*, pp. 450–455, Mar. 1999.

A Guided Monte Carlo Approach to Optimization Problems

C.I. Chou, R.S. Han, T.K. Lee, and S.P. Li

Institute of Physics, Academia Sinica, Taipei, Taiwan 115, R.O.C.

Abstract. We introduce a new Monte Carlo method by incorporating a guiding function to the conventional Monte Carlo method. In this way, the efficiency of Monte Carlo methods is drastically improved. We show how one can perform practical simulation by implementing this algorithm to search for the optimal path of the traveling salesman problem and demonstrate that its performance is comparable with more elaborate and heuristic methods. Application of this algorithm to other problems, specially the protein folding problem and protein structure prediction is also discussed.

Optimization problems arise in areas of science, engineering and other fields. Many of them are NP hard problems, in the sense that the number of computing steps required to solve the problem increases faster than any power of the size of the system. The traveling salesman problem (TSP)[1], the protein folding problem[2] and the Lennard-Jones microcluster problem[3] are some of the examples belonging to this class. Over the years, people have developed heuristic methods that can allow one to possibly obtain optimal solutions in some optimization problems, e.g. the TSP. However, these methods are usually specially designed for the problem that one is seeking to solve. We have recently developed a new algorithm by incorporating the Monte Carlo method with a guiding function. We have applied this to the TSP, the spin glass problem, X-ray crystallography problem and also the Lennard-Jones microcluster problem. All of them demonstrate the effectiveness of the present algorithm. We will briefly review our algorithm by implementing it in the TSP [4] in the following. We will then discuss how this algorithm can be applied to other problems, specially the protein folding problem.

The TSP is one of the oldest and most widely studied optimization problem. The task of the TSP is to find the shortest route through a given set of N cities. The conventional Monte Carlo rules [5] are that we accept a new solution over its old solution when the new solution is better fit than the old solution, i.e. when a new route has a shorter length over the old route. If a new solution is less fit than the old solution, we pick the new solution over the old solution with respect to a Boltzmann factor. The new substance in our algorithm is the addition of a guiding function to the conventional Monte Carlo method. This introduction of the guiding function is motivated from biology. Similar to the subject of evolutionary programming [6], this guiding function is based on the

J. Liu et al. (Eds.): IDEAL 2003, LNCS 2690, pp. 447–451, 2003.

cooperative effort of individuals. To begin with, we have a population of M randomly generated solutions. We let each of them evolve independently and according to the conventional Monte Carlo rules, i.e. we accept a new solution over its old solution when the new solution is better fit than the old solution. If a new solution is less fit than the old solution, we pick the new solution over the old solution with respect to a Boltzmann factor. At this point, it is equivalent to M individual runs of the Monte Carlo method. In each of the M individual runs, we keep record of its best fit solution while the individual solution is evolving.

After we perform a preset number of Monte Carlo steps, each of the M independent runs has its own best fit solution, or path. In each of these paths, we record the links between any two cities. There are a total of N links in each path and a total of MN links of the M best fit solutions. One has now a distribution function of the probability of appearance among all possible links that connects any two cities. This completes our first layer of Monte Carlo simulation. In our discussion, a layer of simulation always means a set of M individual Monte Carlo runs for a preset Monte Carlo steps plus the evaluation of the distribution function that we just mentioned. The distribution function that we obtain here will be used as a guiding function in the next layer of Monte Carlo simulation of M individual runs.

In the next layer of Monte Carlo simulation, a set of M individual Monte Carlo runs is again performed. An important point here is that we also start with M randomly generated solutions at the beginning of the simulation in this layer. There is however one more criterion here—that we pick the links which appear less frequent in the guided distribution function and try to change them into links with a higher probability of appearance. In practice, we pick one of the two cities that are connected with a less probable link and connect it to a city where this new link appears more often in the guided distribution function. The new solution will be compared with the old one to decide whether we keep or disgard it according to the conventional Monte Carlo method. The idea behind this is simple. The more (less) often that a certain link appears among the M best fit solutions, the more (less) likely that it would (not) appear in the optimal solution. One would then let a given solution evolve into solutions with links of high probability of appearance while avoiding links of low probability of appearance. The Monte Carlo method still allows enough fluctuation to search for optimal, or near-optimal solutions. After a preset number of Monte Carlo steps is performed, a new guiding function will again be obtained for the next layer simulation. In principle, the more Monte Carlo steps one performs in each layer, and the more layers of simulations one has, the better will be the result. For further detail, the reader is referred to [4]. Table 1 shows our result of some of the tested cases in TSP.

As can be seen in Table 1, the algorithm can locate the optimal paths in the two cases with fewest cities, i.e. d198 and lin318 while it can obtain near-optimal solutions for the other three cases within the number of Monte Carlo steps we preset. The above result will be improved if more Monte Carlo steps are used during the optimal search.

Table 1. Tests on 5 cases from TSPLIB. T is the temperature used for the Monte Carlo simulation, RQ([1]=% above the optimal solution) is the relative quality of the average length of the best paths obtained for the 100 trial runs with respect to the optimal solutions given in TSPLIB, *Best* is the shortest path length obtained in the 100 trial runs using the present algorithm and Op is the optimal solution given in TSPLIB.

Case	T	RQ	$Best$	Op
d198	10.0	0.0155%	15780	15780
lin318	37.5	0.30%	42029	42029
pcb442	27.5	0.67%	50798	50778
rat783	4.0	0.68%	8819	8806
fl1577	2.75	0.88%	22273	22249

To apply this method to other problems is straightforward. The important step is to construct the guiding function for subsequent layers of simulation. To construct such a guiding function, some knowledge about the solution we are looking for is always necessary. For example, we know that Lennard-Jones clusters will have most of its inner core atoms arranged with certain symmetry. The density of atoms is therefore a good parameter to use in our guiding function. In a similar fashion, one needs to identify the best parameters to use in the guiding function for the particular problem that one is studying. One of the most challenging and practical problems is the protein folding problem. We have recently implemented our algorithm in the protein folding problem [7] and the preliminary result is very encouraging. We will discuss it in the following briefly.

Protein folding [2] is one of the most outstanding problems in biology. Over the years, many simplified theoretical models [8] have been used to study this problem. Among them, lattice and off-lattice [9] protein models are the simplest models which have been playing important roles in the theoretical studies of protein folding. In these models, the protein chains are heteropolymers which live on two or three dimensional regular lattices. They are self-avoiding chains with attractive or repulsive interactions between neighboring unbonded monomers. In most simulations, people consider only two types of monomers—the hydrophobic (H) and polar (P) monomers. For more detailed discussion on these HP lattice and off-lattice models, the reader is referred to [8] and references therein.

As can be expected, there are many ways to construct a guiding function for these lattice and off-lattice protein models. For a real protein, we know that Ramachandran torsion angles are clearly good parameters to specify its orientation. Hence in the lattice and off-lattice models, we consider the angular distribution at each monomer or more appropriately the local substructures is used as our GF. In the lattice HP model, our method can obtain all the previous lowest energy states of the 2D lattice HP sequences [10,11] that we tested. We further found a new ground state and conformation in one of the lattice HP sequences that we tested [7]. In the off-lattice model, we have used an improved model which has the following form for the interaction

$$E = E_{HC} + E_{HB} + \epsilon E_{RR} \qquad (1)$$

where E_{HC} is the hard core term, E_{HB} is the backcone hydrogen-bond term and E_{RR} is the residue-residue interaction term. With this improved model and our GF, we can study in detail the formation of the substructures of the protein under study and compare with experiments. Figure 1 is the result of our simulated structure of protein (PDB ID: 1JLZ) and its structure in nature. One can see that the simulated structure captures the features of the alpha helix and the beta sheet of the real protein under study. Several other protein sequences from the PDB (Protein DataBank) is also studied and our algorithm can obtain the substructures in these sequences. Figure 2 is the Ramachandran plot (evolution of the guiding function) of the same protein sequence (PDB ID: 1JLZ), which demonstrates how our algorithm searches for the structure of the protein in subsequent layers (or generations).

In summary, we have presented a new approach to treat general OPs with continuous or discrete variables. We have demonstrated how one can use our algorithm by implementing it in the TSP. We have also used this algorithm in the study of protein folding and structure prediction. We are now in the process of developing more realistic protein models which should improve the predictive power of the present algorithm on protein structures. We believe our algorithm should be a powerful method to study the protein folding problem as well as protein structure predictions.

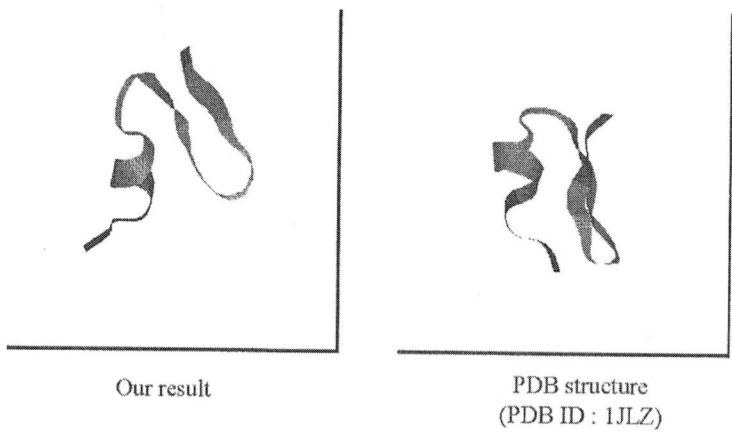

Our result   PDB structure
                                 (PDB ID : 1JLZ)

Fig. 1.

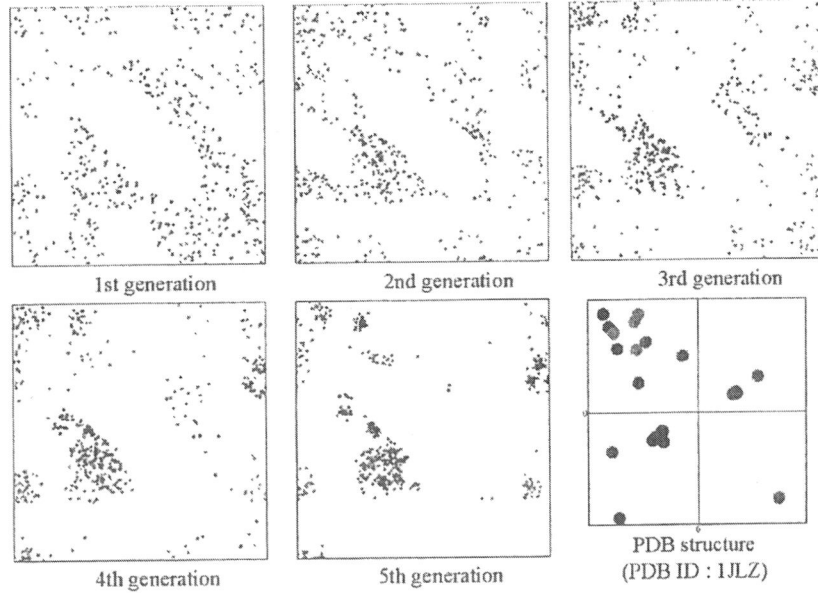

1st generation   2nd generation   3rd generation

4th generation   5th generation

PDB structure
(PDB ID : 1JLZ)

Fig. 2.

References

1. G. Reinelt, *The Traveling Salesman: Computational Solutions for the TSP Applications*, (Springer-Verlag, Berlin, 1994).
2. C. Levinthal, in *Mössbauer Spectroscopy in Biological Systems, Proceedings of a Meeting Held at Allerton House, Monticello, Illinois,* edited by J.T.P. DeBrunner and E. Munck (University of Illinois Press, Illinois, 1969), p.22.
3. D.J. Wales, J.P.K. Doye, A. Dullweber and F.Y. Naumkin, The Cambridge Cluster Database, URL http://brian.ch.cam.ac.uk/CCD.html.
4. S.P. Li (to be published in Int. J. Mod. Phys. C).
5. S. Kirkpatrick, C.D. Jr. Gelatt and M.P. Vecchi, Science **220**, 671 (1983); N. Metropolis, A. Rosenbluth, M. Rosenbluth, A. Teller and E. Teller, J. Chem. Phys. **21**, 1087 (1953).
6. See, e.g., Z. Michalewicz, *Genetic Algorithms + Data Structures = Evolution Programs* (Springer-Verlag, New York, New York, 1996).
7. C.I. Chou, R.S. Han, T.K. Lee and S.P. Li (in preparation).
8. See, e.g., H.S. Chan, H. Kaya and S. Shimizu in *Current Topics in Computational Biology*, (edited by T. Jiang et.al., MIT Press, 2002).
9. A. Irback, F. Sjunnesson and S. Wallin, Proc. Natl. Acad. Sci. USA, **97** 13614 (2000).
10. R. Unger and J. Moult, J. Mol. Biol. **231**, 75 (1993).
11. F. Liang and W. H. Wong, J. Chem. Phys., **115** 3374 (2001).

Editing and Training for ALVOT, an Evolutionary Approach

Jesús A. Carrasco-Ochoa and José Fco. Martínez-Trinidad

Computer Science Department
National Institute of Astrophysics, Optics and Electronics
Luis Enrique Erro No. 1 Sta María Tonanzintla, Puebla, CP: 72840, Mexico
{ariel,fmartine}@inaoep.mx

Abstract. In this paper, a new method, based on evolution strategies and genetic algorithms, for editing the sample data and training the supervised classification model ALVOT (voting algorithms), is proposed. Usually, this model is trained using Testor Theory, working with all available data. Nevertheless, in some problems, testors are not suitable because they can be too many to be useful. Additionally, in some situations, the classification stage must be done as fast as it is possible. ALVOT´s classification time is proportional to the number of support sets and the number of sample objects. The proposed method allows finding an object subset with associated features' weights, which maximizes ALVOT classification quality, and with a support sets system of limited size. Some tests of the new method are exposed. Classification quality of the results is compared against typical testors option.

1 Introduction

The edition process allows selecting some objects from the sample data, in order to be used to build a classifier. This process has as main objective to reduce the size of the sample used for training, and so, to speed both training and classification stages. Also, edition process tries to improve classifier accuracy. For ALVOT classification model, no method to sample edition has been developed. ALVOT [1, 2] is a supervised classification model developed in the framework of the logical combinatorial approach to pattern recognition [1]. This model is based on partial precedence. For ALVOT application it is necessary to define some parameters, including features' weights and the support sets system that indicates which parts of the objects are relevant to compare. There are several methods to estimate features' weights. In the framework of the logical combinatorial pattern recognition, these weights are calculated from the set of all typical testors. Usually the set of all typical testors is taken as the support sets system. The use of all typical testors as support sets system gives good results at the classification stage. However, there are two problems for using them, on the one hand, algorithms for calculating all typical testors have exponential complexity with regard to the number of features, so, for problems with many features applying them is very expensive. On the other hand, the number of typical testors has an exponential bound, for this cause, typical testors can be too many to be useful at the classification stage. Then, using them to calculate features'

J. Liu et al. (Eds.): IDEAL 2003, LNCS 2690, pp. 452–456, 2003.

weights becomes inadequate when they are too many, because of the number of typical testors is part of the denominator, in all expressions developed until now.

In this work, a new method based on genetic algorithms is proposed. This new method allows reducing the size of the sample data. Given a subset of objects, an evolution strategy is used to estimate values for features' weights. This strategy has as objective the classification quality maximization. To evaluate classification efficiency it is necessary to have a support sets system, but it will be incongruent to use the set of all typical testors. Therefore, a method based on genetic algorithms is used to estimate the support sets system for each step. The last process uses the selected objects as sample data, and as features' weights, the values that are being evaluated. Since the search strategy tries to maximize classification efficiency, the final values have high classification efficiency, many times better than the efficiency of using the set of all typical testors. Additionally, the size of the support sets system is bounded, on its cardinality, by the population size of the last genetic algorithm.

2   Typical Testors and Feature Weights Estimation

Into the framework of the Logical Combinatorial Pattern Recognition, feature selection is done using typical testors [1,3]. Testors and typical testor are defined as:

Definition 1. A subset of features T is a testor if and only if when all features are eliminated, except those from T, there is not any pair of equal subdescriptions in different classes.

Definition 2. A subset of features T is a typical testor if and only if T is a testor and there is not any other testor T' such that $T' \subset T$.

The approach based on Testor Theory was first proposed by Dimitriev et al. [4]. Let τ be the number of typical testors for a problem. Let $\tau(i)$ be the number of typical testors, which contain feature x_i. Feature's weight of x_i is given by (1).

$$P(x_i) = \frac{\tau(i)}{\tau} \text{ , where } i=1,...,n,\ x_i \in R. \tag{1}$$

3   Our Method

As we have explained, ALVOT requires an object sample, a support sets system and the features' weights. In this section, the new method based on evolution techniques, for estimating these parameters, is presented.

3.1   Genetic Algorithm to Compute a Support Sets System

The individuals handled by the genetic algorithm [5, 6] will be the support sets. These sets are represented as n-uples formed by the values 0 and 1 (genes), these values represent the absence or presence of a feature, and n represents the total number of features. The individuals are denoted as Ω_i $i=1,...,p$, where p is the number of individuals in the population. The *fitness function* used by the algorithm is (2):

$$\text{Fitness}(\Omega_i) = \frac{\text{Number of well classified objects}}{\text{Total number of classified objects}} \qquad (2)$$

This function evaluates how many objects were well classified by ALVOT regarding the total of classified objects. In this evaluation, the algorithm uses as support sets system $\{\Omega_i\}$; the features' weights W and the sample specified by E which are given as parameters. If an individual Ω_i (a support set) correctly classifies more objects, then it will be more capable. The crossover operator used in the algorithm is 1-point crossing. Also, the bit mutation is used

When the algorithm finishes, the efficiency of ALVOT is evaluated using: the computed support sets system (final population); the features' weights W, and the sample E. The algorithm returns this efficiency value because it will be used by the evolution strategy.

3.2   Evolution Strategy to Evaluate Feature's Weights

The individuals handled by the evolution strategy [7] will be the features' weights. These weights are represented as n-uples formed by values in $[0,1]$, these values represent the weight of each feature, and n is the number of features. We will denote the individuals as W_i $i=1,....,p$, where p is the number of individuals in the population.

The fitness function used by the strategy is the genetic algorithm above described, that is to say, $\text{Fitness}(W_i) = SSS\text{-}GA(W_i)$. In this case, the genetic algorithm ($SSS\text{-}GA$) computes a support set system $\{\Omega\}_i$ and jointly with W_i and E evaluates the classification efficiency of ALVOT, it will be used as fitness for W_i. If an individual W_i (using E and $\{\Omega\}_i$) correctly classifies more objects, then it will be more capable. The crossover operator used in the strategy is 1-point crossing. The bit mutation is used; this operator randomly takes an individual's gene and changes its value by a random number in the interval $[0,1]$.

When the strategy finishes, the efficiency of ALVOT is evaluated using the best individual W_i, their support set system $\{\Omega\}_i$ (returned by $SSS\text{-}GA$) and the sample E.

3.3   Genetic Algorithm for Editing a Sample

The individuals handled by this genetic algorithm are different selections of objects in a sample. These selections are represented as m-uples formed by values 0 and 1, these values represent the absence or presence of an object in the sample, and m represents the total number of objects. We will denote the individuals as E_i $i=1,...,p$, where p is the number of individuals in the population.

The fitness function used by the genetic algorithm is the evolution strategy above described, that is to say, $\text{Fitness}(E_i) = W\text{-}ES(E_i)$. In this case, the evolution strategy ($W\text{-}ES$) computes a set of features' weights W_i; their support sets system $\{\Omega\}_i$ and jointly with E_i evaluates the classification efficiency of ALVOT, which will be used as fitness for E_i. If with an individual E_i (using W_i, and their $\{\Omega\}_i$) ALVOT correctly classifies more objects, then it will be more capable. The crossover and mutation operators used by $W\text{-}ES$ are the same that those used by $SSS\text{-}GA$.

When the algorithm finishes, we select the best individual E_i and their correspondent W_i and $\{\Omega\}_i$ as solution.

4 Experimental Results

In this section, some experiments of sample edition with the described genetic approach are presented. A comparison of the classification efficiency using the parameters computed by our method against no edition options is made. No edition option tested were the estimation of the features' weights using the evolution strategy with the estimation of the support sets system using the genetic algorithm; and the typical testor option. The databases for experimentations were taken from [8].

The first experiment was carried out with the *zoo* database. This database contains 101 descriptions of animals grouped in 7 classes; each description is given in terms of 16 features. In this case, there are 33 typical testors. The efficiency of classification of ALVOT using these 33 testors as support sets system is of 1.0. The measure of efficiency was obtained classifying the training sample and taking the number of successes divided by the number of objects in the sample.

In the figure 1, the classification efficiency of ALVOT when E_f, the most capable individual in the last iteration of the genetic algorithm, W_f and $\{\Omega\}_f$ (the features' weights and the support set system associated to E_f) were used as parameters, is shown. In the figure 1a, it is seen that, for *zoo* database the efficiency cannot be improved, but with a population of only 3 support sets, the same efficiency can be achieved as with the 33 typical testors.

(a)   (b)

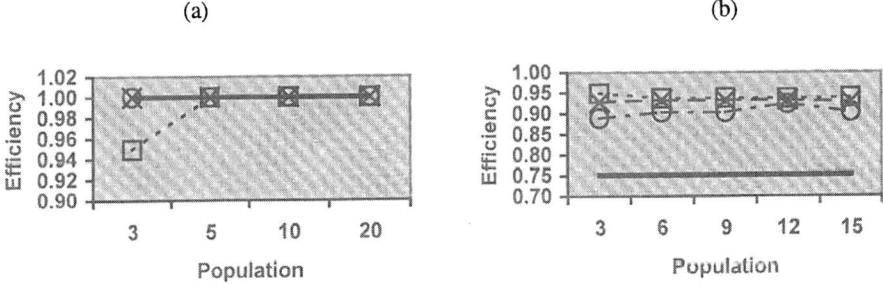

Fig. 1. Efficiency of ALVOT for a)*zoo* and b)*import85*, using the selected objects, features' weights and the support sets systems computed by our method. ⎯ no edition option using the typical testors and the features' weights computed on basis of them. □ no edition option with features' weights estimation using our method; × edition option discarding 10% of the objects; ○ edition option discarding 20% of the objects.

The second experiment was carried out with the *import85* database. This database has 205 car specifications and they are distributed in 7 classes, each specification is made using 25 features. The number of computed typical testors is 6. The classification efficiency of ALVOT using the 6 testors is 0.7512. In the figure 1b, the obtained results are shown.

5 Conclusions

Both, edition over all possible object subsets and training over all possible sets of features subsets are problems of combinatorial optimization. So, algorithms for exact solution search have a very high complexity, and then, alternative methods must be developed. In this paper, a new method, based on evolution strategies and genetic algorithms, for editing the sample and to estimate the features' weights and the support sets system for the model of supervised classification ALVOT, was presented.

From experimentation, we can conclude that a better classification efficiency than using typical testors, features' weights based on them, and all available objects, may be reached, and sometimes improved; but applying our method a training sample and a support sets system with lesser cardinality can be obtained.

Additionally, the problem of computing all the typical testors has exponential complexity and the proposed method can be proved that has polynomial complexity. Then for problems with many features may be impossible in the practice to calculate all typical testors, however the proposed method can be applied.

Another point to highlight is the fact that the number of typical testors is bounded exponentially, so that, in some cases they can be too many to be useful. Contrarily, in our method the size of the support sets system is one of the parameters, which allows fixing the size of the system according to the practical requirements.

The main application of our method is for big problems where using typical testors is not feasible. Since they cannot be computed or they turn out to be too many.

Acknowledgement. This work was financially supported by CONACyT (Mexico) through projects J38707-A and I38436-A.

References

1. Martínez-Trinidad J. F. and Guzmán-Arenas A. "The logical combinatorial approach to pattern recognition an overview through selected works", Pattern Recognition, Vol 34, No. 4, pp. 741–751, 2001.
2. Ruiz-Shulcloper J. and Lazo-Cortés M. "Mathematical Algorithms for the Supervised Classification Based on Fuzzy Partial Precedence", Mathematical and Computer Modelling, Vol. 29, No. 4, pp. 111–119, 1999.
3. Lazo-Cortes M., Ruiz-Shulcloper J. and Alba-Cabrera E. "An overview of the evolution of the concept of testor", Pattern Recognition, Vol. 34, No. 4, pp. 753–762, 2001.
4. Dmitriev A.N., Zhuravlev Y.I., Krendeliev F.P. "About mathematical principles of objects and phenomena classification", Diskretni Analiz Vol 7, pp. 3–15, 1966. (In Russian).
5. Mitchel M. An introduction to genetic algorithms. (MIT Press, 1996).
6. Goldberg D. Genetic algorithms in search, optimization and machine learning. (Addison Wesley, 1989).
7. Beyer H. G. Theory of Evolution Strategies. (Springer Verlag, 2001).
8. http://www-old.ics.uci.edu/pub/machine-learning-databases/

Consensus-Based Adaptive Interface Construction for Multiplatform Web Applications

Janusz Sobecki and Ngoc Thanh Nguyen

Department of Information Systems, Wroclaw University of Technology,
Wyb. St. Wyspianskiego 27, 50–370 Wroclaw, Poland
{sobecki,thanh}@pwr.wroc.pl

Abstract. In this paper a concept for multiplatform web application adaptive construction of user interfaces using consensus methods is presented. User interfaces are becoming the crucial element of every information system. It is obvious that because of the differences among users it is almost impossible to construct the single interface equally efficient interface for all them. Also differences in user platforms bring additional design problems. Adaptive interfaces could offer a possible solution in these circumstances. The adaptation is based on clique paradigm and the prediction is made by means of the consensus methods.

1 Introduction

The role of different web-based applications in the Information Society is ever increasing. Besides their technological effectiveness and availability, well-designed user interfaces are becoming essential for every successful information system [11]. There are however quite many reasons why this is very difficult to accomplish this requirement, i.e.: differences among the users of web-based systems [7], a great number of the available web-based systems and differences between system platforms that are used to access these systems. The differences among the users could have influence on their information needs and interaction habits [5]. It is believed that users that resemble each other in some sense have also resembling information systems requirements.

The Web technology is perceived by system developers as well as ordinary users as the most useful for information system implementation. In consequence it is used in all areas of human activities. Nowadays computer systems are all around us. The most popular are of course systems implemented on the PC platform, in form of a desktop or a notebook, but also other platforms such as information kiosks, workstations or even different types of mobile devices are also widely used. There are also other platforms such as different set-top boxes with TV sets as a display. All these platforms may have access to the Internet resources using different stationary or mobile technologies. These very differentiated system platforms could offer their users access to a great number of the web-based systems have many applications. The scope of these systems covers already almost all areas of people's interests.

J. Liu et al. (Eds.): IDEAL 2003, LNCS 2690, pp. 457–461, 2003.

The ever-increasing complexity of the web-based system user interfaces [10] and their users becoming naïve leads to the interface agent technologies application. Nowadays we can find quite many applications of the interface agents. For example, Letizia, an autonomous interface agent for Web browsing [4] and Apt Decision that learns user's real estates rental preferences to suggest him or her appropriate apartments [10]. Another type of interface agent is the collaborative filtering, also called recommended systems, which is built on the assumption that a proper way to find the relevant content for the particular user is to find other people that resemble somehow him or her, and then recommend titles that those similar people like [3].

In this paper we present the adaptive web-based user interface construction that is based on the consensus method used for appropriate prediction of the user classes' representations. In the consensus prediction also the interface usability measures that evaluate these interfaces is used for finding the optimal representation.

2 Interface Personalization and User Classification

Interface personalization is a common feature of many Internet portals, however many other information and entertainment services give users the opportunity to personalize them. The personalization enables users to set three basic elements of the system: the system information content, the way the information is presented to them and how the information is structured [3]. For example in the very popular Web portal - Lycos users are able to add and remove boxes with information (content), move them round the screen and change their sizes and colors (presentation) and making it the starting page (structure).

During the personalization process users are usually obliged to enter some demographic data about themselves, such as: name, address, occupation and interests. These types of data are called the user data and are used to model the user. Usually all types of data concerning users that are gathered by the system could be also called the user profile. The user profile could also contain the so-called usage data that may be observed directly from the users' interaction with Web-based systems, such as URL's of visited pages, links followed by the user and data entered by the user into the forms on the pages [2].

The user as well as usage data could serve as an input into the process of the user classification. The process of user classification results in grouping heterogeneous set of users $U=\{u_1,...,u_n\}$ into disjoint subsets of the set U by some measure of similarity or distance. Finding an appropriate measure, as well as a user representation, is key problems of users' classification. The process of classification could be computational difficult [1], so practically sub-optimal solutions are used. They usually are based on the selection of some initial partition, as for example, in the Dattola algorithm [8].

3 Determination of Interface Profiles' Consensus

The system personalization settings form the interface profile and the user data delivered by the users themselves as well as the usage data collected during the whole interaction process are used for the user classification. We must also remember that for each system platform different settings of the interface profile are appropriate, in consequence each system platform should be considered separately.

Having users classified and considerable set of the interface profiles collected, we can apply the clique idea [3] for adaptive interface construction. In the clique based filtering we can distinguish three phases: find similar neighbors, select comparison group of neighbors and finally compute prediction based on (weighted) representations of selected neighbors. In our adaptive interface construction method we propose not only to change the application (interface construction instead of a mail or retrieval results filtering) but we also propose to use the consensus methods for making the interface 'prediction' for each class of users. The consensus methods are known to give satisfactory results even if the number of elements that are basis for the prediction are not very large. Other known methods applied for solving similar problems, i.e. Bayes nets, do not have this useful property.

3.1 Definition of Conflict System for Interface Profiles

We assume that some real world is commonly considered by agents which are placed in sites of a distributed system. The subjects of agents' interest consist of events which occur (or have to occur) in the world. The task of these agents is based on determining the values of event attributes (an event is described by an elementary tuple of some type). The elements of the system defined below should describe this situation [6].

Definition 1. *By a conflict system in the web-based interactive systems we call the following quadruple: Conflict_Sys = (A, X, P, Z), where*

- A = {Agent, Class, A_1, A_2,..., A_n}: attribute Agent represents interface agents; Class represents classes of users; and A={A_1,A_2,...,A_n} is a set of attributes describing the interface profiles for user service.

- X – a finite set of conflict carriers, X ={$\Pi(V_a)$: $a \in A$}, where $\Pi(V_a)$ is an ordered subset with repetitions of values of attributes from the set A.

- P = {Profile$^+$, Profile$^-$}: Profile$^+$, Profile$^- \subseteq \Pi(V_{Agent}) \times \Pi(V_{Class}) \times \Pi(V_{A1}) \times \Pi(V_{A2}) \times....\times \Pi(V_{An})$.

- Z: Logical formulas representing conditions which have to be satisfied by the tuples belonging to the relations from P.

We interpret a tuple of relation *Profile$^+$*, for example, <*Agent*:a_1, *Class*:c_1, A_1:a_1, A_2:a_2,..., A_n:a_n> as follows: in opinion of agent a_1 the appropriate interface profile for serving users from class c_1 on the web-based information system should be the tuple <A_1:a_1, A_2:a_2,..., A_n:a_n>. A tuple <*Agent*:a_2, *Class*:c_1, A_1:a'_1, A_2:a'_2,..., A_n:a'_n> belonging to relation *Profile$^-$* means that according to agent a_2 on the information system for users from class c_1 the profile <A_1:a'_1, A_2:a'_2,..., A_n:a'_n> is inappropriate interface for their service.

The purpose of Definition 1 relies on representing two kinds of information: the first consists of information about conflicts in the distributed system, which requires solving, and the second includes the information needed for consensus determining. In the conflict system an event is described by an elementary tuple of type $B \subseteq A \backslash \{Agent\}$. The values of attributes represent the parameters of the event. For example the following tuple describes the event "*For the class c_1 the best interface should consist of the following parameters: the window size is 800x600, the sound volume – 0, the number of columns – 1 and the template - classical*".

3.2 Conflict Profiles

We define a conflict situation which contains information about a concrete conflict as follows:

Definition 2. *A conflict situation s is a pair* $<\{Profile^+, Profile^-\}, Class \rightarrow A>$.

According to the above definition a conflict situation consists of agents (conflict body) which appear in relations *Profile*$^+$ and *Profile*$^-$ (conflict content). These relations are the basis of consensus. Expression *Class* $\rightarrow$ *A* means that the agents are not agreed referring to combinations of values of attributes from the set *Class* with values of attributes from the set *A*.

For a given situation *s* we determine the set of these agents which take part in the conflict as follows: $Agent(s) = \{a \in V_{Agent}: (\exists r \in Profile^+)(r_{Agent}=\{a\}) \vee (\exists r \in Profile^-) (r_{Agent}=\{a\})\}$, and the set of *subject elements* (or *subjects* for short) as follows: $Subject(s) = \{e \in E\text{-}TYPE(Class):$

$$(e \neq \theta) \wedge [(\exists r \in Profile^+)(e \prec r_{Class}) \vee (\exists r \in Profile^-)(e \prec r_{Class})]\}.$$

Now for each subject $e \in Subject(s)$ let us determine sets with repetitions *Profile(e)*$^+$ and *Profile(e)*$^-$ which include the positive and negative knowledge of agents on subject *e*, as follows: $Profile(e)^+ = \{r_{A \cup \{Agent\}}: (r \in P^+) \wedge (e \prec r_{Class})\}$ and $Profile(e)^- = \{r_{A \cup \{Agent\}}: (r \in P^-) \wedge (e \prec r_{Class})\}$. These sets are called positive and negative profiles of given conflict subject *e*.

The set $\{Profile^+, Profile^-\}$ is then the basis of consensus, the attribute *Class* represents and the consensus subject, and set *A* describes the content of consensus. The interface quality evaluation is made by the usability measures. Usability, one of the basic notion of the domain HCI [5,7], according to the ISO norm 9241 could be measured as the extent to which the information system can be used by specific users to achieve specific goals with effectiveness, efficiency, and satisfaction in a specific context of use. Where the effectiveness expresses the accuracy and completeness with which users achieve specified goals, the efficiency considers the resources expended in relation to the accuracy and completeness with which users achieve goals and finally satisfaction reveals the users comfort and acceptability of use. In the adaptive user interface construction the usability must be measured automatically, but exact measures could be only given for the specified implementation.

3.3 Consensus Definition and Determination

Below we present the definition of consensus [6].

Definition 3. *Consensus on subject* $e \in Subject(s)$ *of situation* $s=<\{P^+, P^-\}, Class \rightarrow A>$ *is a pair of two tuples* $(C(s,e)^+, C(s,e)^-)$ *where* $C(s,e)^+, C(s,e)^- \in TYPE(\{Class\} \cup A)$ *and the following conditions are fulfilled:*

a) $C(s,e)^+{}_{Class} = C(s,e)^-{}_{Class} = e$; b) $C(s,e)^+{}_A \cap C(s,e)^-{}_A = \phi$; c) *Tuples* $C(s,e)^+$ *and* $C(s,e)^-$ *fulfill logic formulas from set* **Z**; d) *One or more of the postulates* **P1-P6**, *described in detail in* [6], *are satisfied.*

Let φ be a distance function between tuples from relations P^+ and P^-, the following theorem enables to determine a consensus satisfying all postulates **P1-P6**.

Theorem 1. *If there is defined a distance function* φ *between tuples of TYPE(B), then for given subject e of situation* $s=<\{P^+,P^-\}, \; Class{\rightarrow}A>$ *tuples* $C(s,e)^+$ *and* $C(s,e)^-$ *which satisfy conditions a)-c) of Definition 3 and minimize the expressions*

$$\sum_{r \in profile(e)^+} \varphi(r_A, C(s,e)^+_A) \quad and \quad \sum_{r \in profile(e)^-} \varphi(r_A, C(s,e)^-_A) \quad should \quad create \quad a \quad consensus$$

satisfying all of postulates **P1-P6**.

4 Conclusions

In this paper only the general methodology for constructing adaptive interfaces for the multi-platform web-based systems was presented. More precise procedures, however, could only be developed and applied for concrete applications. Nowadays, this methodology is used to design and implement several prototype web-based applications in the following fields: travel information service, car information system and web information service for our department.

References

1. Brown S.M., Santos E., Banks S.B., Oxley M.E.: Using Explicit Requirements and Metrics for Interface Agent User Model for Interface Agent User Model Correction. In: Proceedings of the 2nd international conference on Autonomous Agents, Minneapolis, Minnesota, USA (1998) 1–7.
2. Fleming M., Cohen R.: User Modeling in the Design of Interactive Interface Agents. UM99 User Modeling. In: Proc. of the 7th Int. Conference, Springer Vienna (1999) 67–76.
3. Kobsa A., Koenemann J., Pohl W.: Personalized Hypermedia Presentation Techniques for Improving Online Customer Relationships. The Knowledge Engineering Review **16**(2) (2001) 111–155.
4. Lieberman H.: Autonomous Interface Agents, Proc. CHI 97, ACM, (1997) 67–74.
5. Newman W., Lamming M.: Interactive System Design. Addison-Wesley, Harlow (1996).
6. Nguyen N.T.: Consensus System for Solving Conflicts in Distributed Systems. Information Sciences **147**(1-4) (2002) 91–122.
7. Nguyen N.T., Sobecki J.: Using Consensus Methods to Construct Adaptive Interfaces in Multimodal Web-based Systems. J. of Universal Access in the Inf Soc **2** (2003) 1–17.
8. Rijsbergen C v.: Information Retrieval. Butterworths, London, (1979) 2nd edition.
9. Schneiderman B., Maes P.: Debate: Direct Manipulation vs. Interface Agents. Interactions **4**(6) (1997) 42–61.
10. Shearin S., Lieberman H.: Intelligent Profiling by Example. In: Proc Intelligent User Interfaces New Orleans, LA USA, (2001) 9–12.
11. Sobecki J.: Interactive Multimedia Information Planning. In: Valiharju T. (ed.) Digital Media in Networks 1999, Perspectives to Digital World, Univ. of Tampere (1999) 38–44.

Portfolio Management for Pension Funds

Santiago Arbeleche, Michael A.H. Dempster, Elena A. Medova,
Giles W.P. Thompson, and Michael Villaverde

Centre for Financial Research, Judge Institute of Management, University of Cambridge,
Cambridge CB2 1AG
{sa269, mahd2, eam28, gwpt1, mv228}@cam.ac.uk
http://www-cfr.jims.cam.ac.uk/

Abstract. This paper introduces the use of dynamic stochastic optimisation for pension fund management. The design of such products involves econometric modelling, economic scenario generation, generic methods of solving optimization problems and modelling of required risk tolerances. In nearly all the historical backtests using data over roughly the past decade the system described (with transactions costs taken into account) outperformed the benchmark S&P500.

1 Introduction

Defined benefit pension plans and most state schemes are becoming inadequate to cover the gap between the contributions of people while working and their pensions once retired. A long-term minimum guarantee return plan with a variable time-horizon and with the possibility of making variable contributions during the lifetime of the product in addition to the initial contribution is a new investment instrument aimed at attracting investors who are worried about the volatility of financial markets. Although potentially highly profitable for the provider, the design of such instruments is not a trivial task, as it encompasses the need to do long-term forecasting for investment classes and handling a number of stochastic factors together with providing a guarantee. This paper shows that dynamic stochastic optimisation methodology is an ideal technique to solve these kinds of problems.

2 Critical Issues for Pension Fund Management

Asset liability management concerns optimal strategic planning for management of financial resources in stochastic environments, with market, economic and actuarial risks all playing an important role. Some of the most important issues a pension fund manager has to face in the determination of the optimal asset allocations over the time to product maturity include the stochastic nature of asset returns, long investment horizons (30 years), the risk of under-funding or the probability that the pension fund will not be able to meet its targets without resort to its parent guarantor and management constraints such as solvency and position limits.

J. Liu et al. (Eds.): IDEAL 2003, LNCS 2690, pp. 462–466, 2003.

3 Pension Fund Management through Stochastic Optimization

Most firms currently use *static* portfolio optimisation, such as the Markowitz mean-variance allocation [7], which is short-sighted and when rolled forward can lead to radical portfolio rebalancing unless constrained by the portfolio manager. By contrast, the dynamic stochastic programming models incorporated in the system described below automatically hedge current portfolio allocations against future uncertainties over a longer horizon, leading to more robust decisions and previews of possible future problems and benefits. It is this feature and its ability to incorporate different attitudes to risk that make dynamic stochastic optimisation the most natural framework for the effective solution of pension fund ALM problems.

3.1 Dynamic Stochastic Optimization Model

We focus here on strategic asset allocation which is concerned with allocation across broad asset classes such as equity and bonds of a given country. The canonical pension fund problem is that of maximizing utility subject to the constraints given a set of assets, a fixed planning horizon and a set of rebalance dates. Different pension plan instruments are given by alternative utility functions (fund risk tolerances) and the specification of risk management objectives through the constraints. A detailed specification of the model is given in [4].

Utility functions are used in our system to represent the general attitude to risk of the fund's participants over a specified fund horizon. We consider Exponential (CARA) and Downside-Quadratic utility functions. The basic constraints of the optimization model are those of the dynamic CALM model (*cf.* [2]). These include cash balance constraints, inventory balance constraints and wealth constraints. Besides these basic constraints, the fund may portfolio restrictions such as solvency constraints, cash borrowing/short selling limits, position limits and turnover or liquidity constraints.

For backtesting purposes we specify the following three types of constraint structures. T1 constraints have no position limits or turnover constraints, T2 constraints have position limits and no turnover constraints and T3 constraints contain both position limits and turnover constraints. Short selling and borrowing are not allowed in any of these constraint structures.

Another constraint the fund may face is a guaranteed return constraint. The return guarantee to an individual investor is absolute given the solvency of the guarantor. In the situation of a banking group such as the fund manager and its parent guarantor this necessitates strategies both to implement the absolute guarantee for individuals and to manage the investment strategy of the fund so as to ensure meeting the guarantee for all participants of the fund with a high probability. Mathematically, this latter goal can be met by imposing a *probabilistic* constraint of the *value at risk* type on the wealth process at specific trading dates, computing expected shortfall across scenarios which fail to meet the fund guarantee and adding the corresponding penalty terms to period objective functions. However, such scenario-based probabilistic constraints are extremely difficult to implement in that they convert the convex (deterministic equivalent) large scale optimisation problem to a *nonconvex* one. For practical purposes we have developed the *capital guaranteed products algorithm* implemented for a pension fund using parametric nested optimization techniques [4].

3.2 Asset Return Statistical Models

Our main *asset return model* used to generate scenarios for the ALM problem is called BMSIM. We *estimate* it econometrically (in the econometric estimation tradition initiated by Wilkie [9]) and *calibrate* the output of the simulation with history by various *ad hoc* or semi-formal methods of parameter adjustment. (See, for example, [3].)

The global structure of this model involves investments in the three major asset classes – cash, bonds and equities – in the four major currency areas – US, UK, EU and Japan (JP) – together with emerging markets (EM) equities and bonds. Each currency area is linked to the others *directly* via an exchange rate equation and *indirectly* through correlated innovations (disturbance or error terms). Detailed specifications of this model are given in [1] and [4]. Although linear in the parameters, this model is second order autoregressive and nonlinear in the state variables. Due to its linearity in the parameters this model may be estimated using the *seemingly unrelated regression* (SUR) technique, see e.g. [5, Chapter 11], recursively until a parsimonious estimate is obtained in which all non-zero parameters are statistically significant.

In light of Meese & Rogoff's [8] classical view on the inefficacy of macroeconomic explanations of exchange rates even at monthly frequency, after considerable single equation and subsystem analysis we have found that interest rate parity expressed as inter-area short and long rate differences – *together* with other local capital market variables – has significant explanatory power, while purchasing power parity expressed various ways has less (*cf.* [6]). Our main econometric finding is that the world's equity markets are linked simultaneously through shocks [1] and [4].

4 System Historical Backtests

A number of historical backtests have been run on variants of the global model, see [4] for complete details. The aims of these tests were several. First, we wished to evaluate how well the system would have performed had it been implemented in practice relative to a benchmark. Second, we wished to understand the impact of alternative utility functions on optimal portfolio decisions. Thirdly, we were interested in what effects imposing the practical diversification and liquidity (turnover) constraints would have on backtest returns. All portfolio rebalances are subject to a 1% value tax on transactions which of course does not apply to the benchmark index. Monthly data were available from July 1977 to August 2002.

Table 1 shows the results in terms of annualised returns of a typical backtest with a 2 year telescoping horizon and semi-annual rebalancing from February 1999 to February 2001. During this period the S&P500 returned 0 percent. With no position limits the model tends to pick the best asset(s) and so in this case a high annual historical return to the chosen low diversification portfolios is an indication of the predictive merits of the tuned econometric model used to generate the scenarios.

Table 1. Asset allocation backtests: Annualised returns from February 1999–2001.

Utility Function	Capital Markets		Capital Markets + Emerging Markets		Capital Markets + Emerging Markets + US Economic Model	
	No Limits	Limits	No Limits	Limits	No Limits	Limits
Linear	91%	9%	92%	10%	31%	11%
Downside-quadratic	54%	9%	70%	11%	29%	9%
Exponential	72%	9%	92%	10%	51%	11%

A summary of backtest results using the downside-quadratic utility function is given in Table 2.

Table 2. Summary of historical backtests[1].

Period	Asset Return Model	Horizon	Annualized Return %			S&P 500 Benchmark Annualised Return %
			T1	T2	T3	
1990-1995	3 areas (ex Japan)	telescoping	10.33	9.34	-	7.41
1996-2001	4 areas	telescoping	13.36	7.13	-	14.12
1999-2001	4 areas	telescoping	27.89	6.48	2.69	-2.3
1999-2001	above + Em. Mkts.	telescoping	16.98	5.72	3.38	-2.3
1999-2001	above + US econ.	telescoping	19.16	4.64	-0.38	-2.3
1996-2001	4 areas	telescoping	8.54	-	8.37	14.12

5 Conclusions

This paper has described the use of dynamic stochastic optimisation methodology for structured products for pension fund management. Practical solutions to the design of guaranteed return investment products for pension funds have been outlined. In nearly all the historical backtests using data over roughly the past decade the global asset allocation system outperformed the S&P500 when transactions costs are taken into account.

---

[1] "-" entries not calculated.

Acknowlegements. The authors would like to express their gratitude to the Pioneer Investments and its parent company UniCredito Italiano for their continuing support. The project could not have been undertaken without the creativity and contributions of our colleagues (past and present): S. Arbeleche, G. Cipriani, G. Consigli, M. Ferconi, J.E. Scott and G.W.P. Thompson, to whom we wish to record our heartfelt appreciation and thanks.

References

1. Arbeleche, S. & Dempster, M.A.H. (2003). Econometric modelling for global asset and liability management. Working Paper, Centre for Financial Research, University of Cambridge, in preparation.
2. Consigli, G. & Dempster, M. A. H. (1998). The CALM stochastic programming model for dynamic asset-liability management. In Ziemba & Mulvey (1998), *op. cit.,* 464–500.
3. Dempster, M. A. H. & Thorlacius, A. E. (1998). Stochastic simulation of international economic variables and asset returns: The Falcon Asset Model. *Proceedings of the 8th International AFIR Colloquium.* Institute of Actuaries, London, 29–45.
4. Dempster, M. A. H., Germano, M., Medova, E. A. & Villaverde, M. (2002). Global asset liability management. *British Actuarial Journal,* **9,** forthcoming (with discussion).
5. Hamilton, J. D. (1994). *Time series analysis.* Princeton University Press.
6. Hodrick, R. & Vassalou, M. (2002). Do we need multi-country models to explain exchange rate and interest rate and bond return dynamics. *Journal of Economic Dynamics and Control,* **26,** 1275–1299.
7. Markowitz, H. M. (1952). Portfolio selection. *Journal of Finance,* **7,** 77–91.
8. Meese, R. & Rogoff, K. (1983b). The out-of-sample failure of empirical exchange rate models. In *Exchange rates and international macroeconomics.* J. Frenkel, ed. University of Chicago Press.
9. Wilkie, A. D. (1986). A stochastic investment model for actuarial use. *Transactions of the Faculty of Actuaries,* **39,** 391–403.

Multiple Ant Colony Optimization for Load Balancing

Kwang Mong Sim[1] and Weng Hong Sun[2]

[1]Department of Information Engineering, The Chinese University of Hong Kong, Shatin, NT, Hong Kong. kmsim@ie.cuhk.edu.hk
[2]Business Information System, Faculty of Business Administration, University of Macau. Kevinsun@umac.mo

Abstract. This paper presents a *Multiple Ant Colony Optimization (MACO)* approach for load balancing in circuit-switched networks. Based on the problem-solving approach of ants in nature, Ant Colony Optimization (ACO) has been applied to solve problems in optimization, network routing and load balancing by modeling ants as a society of mobile agents. While traditional ACO approaches employed one ant colony for routing, MACO uses multiple ant colonies to search for alternatives to an optimal path. One of the impetuses of MACO is to optimize the performance of a congested network by routing calls via several alternatives paths to prevent possible congestion along an optimal path. Ideas of applying MACO for load-balancing in circuit-switched networks have been implemented in a testbed. Using fairness ratio as a performance measure, experimental results show that MACO is (1) effective in balancing the load, and (2) more effective than traditional ACO for load balancing.

1   Introduction

Inefficient bandwidth allocation and over-loading lower capacity nodes may lead to failure in establishing connections. Adopting the paradigm of *Ant Colony Optimization (ACO)* [1], this paper presents a *Multiple Ant Colony Optimization (MACO)* approach for load-balancing in circuit-switched networks [2]. Although by itself, an *ant* is a simple and unsophisticated creature, collectively a colony of ants can perform useful tasks such as building nests, and *foraging* (searching for food)[1]. Ants coordinate their problem solving activities by laying a chemical substance called *pheromone* [1] that can be sensed by other ants. In the interesting and emerging field of ACO, the problem-solving activities ant colonies are transformed into optimization/control techniques [1]. While traditional ACO approaches (such as [3]) employed one ant colony for routing, MACO uses multiple ant colonies to search for alternatives to an optimal path (section 2). The impetus of MACO is to optimize the performance of a congested network by routing calls over several alternative paths to prevent possible congestion along the optimal path p_o. If all calls are routed to p_o, degradation of network performance due to unregulated traffic along p_o may result. The idea of the MACO approach is to prevent every call from being 'selfishly' routed along p_o by search for alternatives to p_o. Ideas of MACO have been implemented in a testbed (section 3). Experiments conducted using the testbed demonstrated that MACO is an effective approach for load-balancing in circuit-switched networks (section 4).

J. Liu et al. (Eds.): IDEAL 2003, LNCS 2690, pp. 467–471, 2003.

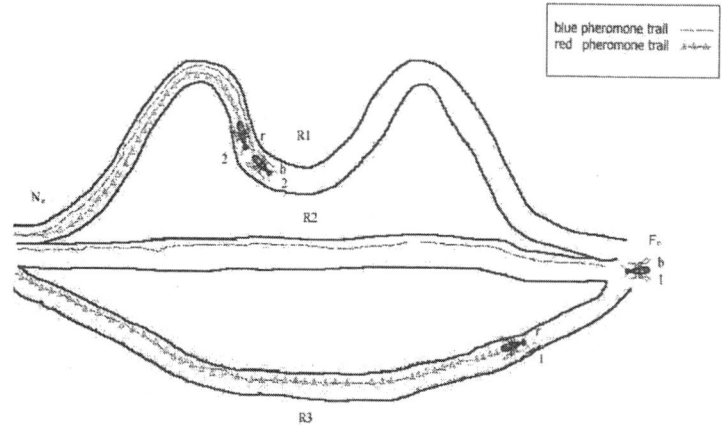

Fig. 1. *Multiple Ant Colonies*

2   Multiple Ant Colony Optimization (MACO)

In Multiple Ant Colony Optimization (MACO), more than one colony of ants are used to search for optimal paths, and each colony of ants deposits a different type of pheromone represented by a different color. An example is given as follows:

Suppose that there are 4 ants: A^r_1, A^r_2, A^b_1, and A^b_2; where A^r_1, and A^r_2 are red colony ants and A^b_1, and A^b_2 are blue colony ants. There are 3 routes R_1, R_2, and R_3 leading to a food source F_o, such that $R_1 > R_3 > R_2$. Initially, all ants are in the nest N_e, and they have to select from among $\{R_1, R_2, R_3\}$ to reach F_o.

1.   At N_e, A^r_1, A^r_2, A^b_1, and A^b_2 have no knowledge about the location of F_o. Hence, they randomly select from $\{R_1, R_2, R_3\}$. Suppose that A^b_1 and A^b_2 choose R_2 and R_1 respectively while A^r_1 and A^r_2 select R_3 and R_1 respectively. As they move along their chosen paths, they deposit a certain amount of pheromone. While A^b_1 and A^b_2 each deposits one unit of blue color pheromone τ_b along R_2 and R_1 respectively, A^r_1 and A^r_2 each deposits one unit of red color pheromone τ_r along R_3 and R_1 respectively (Fig. 1).

2.   Since $R_1 > R_3 > R_2$, A^b_1 reaches F_o before A^b_2, A^r_1, and A^r_2. To return from F_o to N_e, A^b_1 discovers that $\tau_b^{R2}=1$ and $\tau_b^{R1}=\tau_b^{R3}=0$ (there is one unit of blue pheromone along R_2, but there is no trace of blue pheromone along R_1 and R_3).

3.   Since $\tau_b^{R2} > \tau_b^{R1}$ and $\tau_b^{R2} > \tau_b^{R3}$, A^b_1 will choose R_2. As A^b_1 moves along R_2, τ_b^{R2} is increased to 2.

4.   Subsequently, since $R_1 > R_3$, A^r_1 reaches F_o before A^b_2 and A^r_2. To return from F_o to N_e, A^r_1 discovers that $\tau_r^{R3}=1$ and $\tau_r^{R1}=\tau_r^{R2}=0$ (it is reminded that A^r_1 cannot sense the blue pheromones, i.e., $\tau_b^{R1}=0$, $\tau_b^{R2}=2$ or $\tau_b^{R3}=0$). Since $\tau_r^{R3} > \tau_r^{R1}$ and $\tau_r^{R3} > \tau_r^{R2}$, A^r_1 selects R_3 again. As it moves along R_3, τ_r^{R3} is increased to 2.

5.   When A^b_2 and A^r_2 finally reach F_o and need to return to N_e, they select their return paths by sensing τ_b and τ_r respectively. Since A^b_2 discovers that $\tau_b^{R2} > \tau_b^{R1}$ and $\tau_b^{R2} >$

τ_b^{R3}, it will select R_2. In addition, A'_2 discovers that $\tau_r^{R3} > \tau_r^{R1}$ and $\tau_r^{R3} > \tau_r^{R2}$, it will select R_3.

6. When all 4 ants have returned to N_e, R_2 has the heaviest concentration of τ_b, while R_3 has the heaviest concentration of τ_r. Consequently, ants from the blue colony will prefer to select R_2 if they need to travel to F_o, while ants from the red colony will tend to select R_3.

3   MACO Testbed

While an optimal path p_o can be found by a single colony of *ants*, alternatives to p_o can be explored in parallel if multiple colonies of *ants* are used. Adopting the problem-solving paradigm of MACO, two sets of mobile agents (that act as routing packets) are used to established call connections in a circuit-switched network. The two groups of mobile agents correspond to two colonies of *ants* (e.g., the red colony and the blue colony), and each colony establishes its own routing preferences, deposits its own type of pheromone, and maintains and consults its own pheromone table. Although *ants* in a colony manipulate and respond to their own pheromone tables, interactions between pheromone types are also incorporated into the design of the MACO system to enable indirect exchange of information on network status between the colonies (details are given below). To formulate a MACO system for solving the load-balancing problem in circuit-switched networks, three kinds of ants: *allocator*, *deallocator*, and *destagnator* are implemented in each colony.

Allocator. An allocator A_k allocates bandwidth for a call request by acquiring the necessary bandwidths in all the intermediate links and nodes from the requesting station to the destination. At a node i, A_k selects the edge to move to next by consulting the pheromone table of its colony in i. Each entry in the pheromone table in i is defined by a probability function:

$$p_{ij}(t) = \frac{[\tau_{ij}(t)]}{\sum\limits_{k \in N_i} [\tau_{ik}(t)]}$$

where $\tau_{ij}(t)$ is the amount of pheromone in edge e_{ij} at time t, and N_i represents the set of neighbors of i. As A_k travels from a source s to a destination d, it deposits pheromone along every intermediate nodes between s and d. This is achieved by updating its corresponding pheromone tables in the intermediate nodes. Whenever A_k travels along a path R, it increases the pheromone concentration τ_R along R as follows: $\tau_R(t+1) \leftarrow \tau_R(t) + \Delta\tau$. This reinforces the preference of other allocators in the same colony for R. However, continuous reinforcement of pheromone may result in a very dramatic increase in pheromone concentration along R. This may lead to the problem of stagnation [4], in which many allocators travel along R, and ignore other paths, resulting in possible congestion of nodes and links along R. To resolve stagnation, a destagnation procedure is used. When A_k detects a congested node c (i.e., the load in c approaches its total capacity), it activates a destagnator.

Destagnator. A destagnator DS_k reduces the pheromone concentration in a path p leading to a congested node c. DS_k achieves pheromone reduction by depositing "anti-pheromone" τ_{ij}. Consequently, this reduces the probability that allocators in the same colony will travel to c via p. While the routing preference of allocators in the same colony can be influenced by stagnation, allocators from the other colony are insensitive to the pheromone reduction, since they are only influenced by their own pheromone type. To exchange the information that a node or a path is congested, a technique called pheromone redistribution is used. Pheromone redistribution facilitates inter-colony communication through the exchange of pheromones. Pheromone redistribution between 2 paths R_1 and R_2 is applied using the following pheromone transformation rule:

$$\alpha\, \tau_R(t) + \beta\, \tau_B(t) \rightarrow \tau_R(t+1) \text{ and } \beta\, \tau_R(t) + \alpha\, \tau_B(t) \rightarrow \tau_B(t+1) \quad \text{where } \alpha + \beta = 1$$

$\alpha + \beta = \gamma + \kappa$ ensures that no additional data traffic is directed to either R_1 or R_2 since the total pheromone concentration for both red and blue pheromones remains unchanged in both R_1 and R_2. Redistribution provides a form of indirect communications between the red and blue colonies. The pheromone exchange indirectly communicates information of network status (e.g., congestion or link failure) to the other colony. The reduction of a certain pheromone type (e.g., blue pheromone) using a destagnator, will only influence allocators in the same colony. To also discourage allocators from other colony (e.g., red colony) from not traveling along a congested path, pheromone redistribution should be applied in conjunction with destagnation.

Deallocator. When the duration of a call expires, a deallocator D_k is activated to release the reserved bandwidth. D_k travels from the call destination to the source. At every node it passes, it releases the bandwidth that was previously acquired for the call.

4   Experimental Results

A series of 30 experiments was carried out to demonstrate the effectiveness of applying MACO in load balancing in circuit-switched networks. In each experiment, a 30-node circuit-switched network with a different topology was used, and four sets of simulations were carried out to measure the performance of (1) a single ACO colony augmented with evaporation, (2) MACO augmented *with only* evaporation, (3) MACO augmented *with only* evaporation and destagnation, and (4) MACO augmented with evaporation, destagnation and pheromone redistribution. The four sets of simulations in each experiment (labeled as ACO1, ACO2, ACO3 and ACO4 respectively) were designed to compare: (1) the performance of MACO and single ACO colony (SACO), and (2) the effectiveness of using evaporation, destagnation and redistribution to refine the MACO approach. In the experiments, *fairness ratio* [5] is used as a performance measure for load-balancing. It is the ratio of a node's relative load over its relative capacity to the entire network. *Fairness* is based on the idea that, given a set of call requests, more bandwidths should be allocated to nodes with relatively higher capacities, to allow low-capacity nodes to handle smaller or lesser requests. To accommodate more connections, a load-balancing technique should generally allocate lesser bandwidth to nodes with lower available capacities when there are other nodes with higher available capacities. Fairness *fair(t)* represents the degree of evenness of bandwidths allocation in all the nodes taking into consideration their available capacities, with *fair(t)* = 1 being the optimal value. In each experiment, the absolute difference (|*fair*(*t*)-1|) between both the *measured* and the *ideal* global fairness ratio were recorded. On the average, ACO4 achieved |*fair*(*t*)-1| = 0.084, i.e. within only 8.4% of the ideal fairness. Both ACO2 and ACO3 achieved an average fairness ratio of within 10% of the ideal fairness compared to 12% achieved by ACO1. The results show that: (1) MACO generally achieved *better* fairness than SACO, (2) the performance of MACO can be enhanced by augmenting it with both destagnation and redistribution, and (3) MACO is generally effective for load-balancing.

5   Conclusion

The contributions of this research are listed as follows:
1. an approach based on Multiple Ant Colony Optimization (MACO) for load balancing was devised
2. ideas of MACO were implemented in a testbed with two colonies of ants each with three new types of ants were implemented
3. a series of experimentation was carried out using the MACO testbed

Experimental results demonstrated that MACO is an effective approach for load balancing in circuit-switched networks. The results also show that MACO generally achieved better fairness ratios than single ant colony optimization. In summary, the major advantage of MACO is that it achieves load balancing without significantly increasing the routing overhead.

References

[1] E. Bonabeau, M. Dorigo and G. Theraulaz, "Inspiration for optimization from social insect behavior", *Nature*, 406, Macmillan Publishers Ltd., July 6, 2000, p.39–42.
[2] K. M. Sim and W. H. Sun, "Multiple Ant-Colony Optimization for Network Routing", *in Proc. of the conference Cyberworld*, November, Tokyo, Japan, pp 277–281.
[3] R. Schoonderwoerd, O. Holland and J. Bruten, "Ant-like agents for load balancing in telecommunications networks", *in Proc. of Agents'97*, Marina del Rey, CA, ACM Press, p. 209–216.
[4] T. Stuzle and H. H. Hoos, "MAX-MIN Ant System", *Future Generation Computer Systems Journal*, 16(8):889–914, 2000.
[5] C. C. Han, K. G. Shin and S. K. Yun, "On Load Balancing in Multicomputer/Distributed Systems Equipped with Circuit or Cut-Through Switching Capability", *IEEE Transactions on Computers*, Vol. 49, No. 9, Sept 2000.

Exploring Memory Access Regularity in Pointer-Intensive Application Programs

Keqiang Wu, Resit Sendag, and David J. Lilja

Department of Electrical and Computer Engineering, University of Minnesota
200 Union Street S.E., Minneapolis, MN 55455, USA
{kqwu, rsgt, lilja}@ece.umn.edu

Abstract. Pointer-intensive and sparse numerical computations typically display irregular memory access behavior. This work presents a mathematical model, called the Self-tuning Adaptive Predictor (SAP), to characterize the behavior of load instructions in procedures with pointer-based data structures by using procedure call boundaries as the fundamental sampling frequency. This model incorporates information about the history of specific load instructions (temporal locality) and their neighboring loads (spatial locality) using a least-squares minimization approach. Simulation results on twelve of the most time-consuming procedures with pointer-based data structures from five of the SPEC2000 integer benchmark programs show that these pointer-based data structures demonstrate surprisingly regular memory access patterns. The prediction error at steady-state is within [-6%, +6%] on average.

1 Introduction

An important characteristic of Pointer-Based Data Structures (PDS) is that they are dynamically allocated and managed using a heap. Heap allocation allocates blocks of contiguous memory as requested by the program at run-time. Memory blocks are deallocated in any order either explicitly or via process termination. For example, elements in a linked data structure contain explicit fields that name all adjacent elements by address. This mode of connectivity allows the easy construction and manipulation of data structures of arbitrary shape, such as trees and graphs. Dynamic construction allows PDSs to grow arbitrarily large. However, this flexibility makes it challenging to characterize the memory access behavior of these structures. Their behavior has been traditionally classified as *irregular* or *arbitrary* [1-2].

The intuitive method for prediction is to track the memory allocation/deallocation behavior by analyzing the program execution path. The cache miss behavior for two specified data structures, a linked list and a binary tree, was analyzed by tracking the memory allocation/deallocation sequence in synthetic programs [3]. However, in large and real programs, interactions and branch patterns are difficult to predict. These factors add complexity in extending this previous analysis.

In this paper, we avoid the detailed analysis of program execution path and use a mathematical model to extract the path pattern based on the observed paths. The primary contributions of this paper are:

J. Liu et al. (Eds.): IDEAL 2003, LNCS 2690, pp. 472–476, 2003.

1. The regularity of memory access patterns for procedures with pointer-based data structures is observed when using procedure call boundaries as the sampling unit.
2. A mathematical model, the Self-tuning Adaptive Predictor (SAP), is proposed to correlate both temporal and spatial locality with the program counter (PC). This model optimizes predictions of future memory addresses referenced by the program using a least-squares minimization technique [4].

2   Model Formulation

Consider a general example of the procedure call sequence in Figure 1. The memory access behavior of *main( )* is complex as it jumps to different locations when different procedures are called. Its overall behavior depends on the behavior of all of the individual procedures. In the following analysis, a leaf procedure is a procedure that does not call other procedures. PC-correlated spatial locality occurs when the data address referenced by a load instruction at a PC (program counter) likely depends on memory addresses referenced by loads at nearby PCs. PC-correlated temporal locality occurs when the next memory address referenced by a load instruction at a certain PC is likely to depend on the previous memory addresses referenced by the same load instruction.

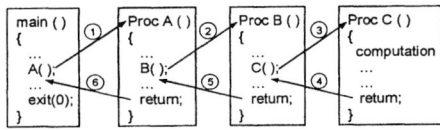

Fig. 1. Schematic of the calling procedure of a simple program.

This paper focuses on the memory access behavior produced by load instructions in leaf procedures using the procedure call as the fundamental sampling unit. The primary assumption is that, within some certain period, the behavior of memory accesses in a procedure depends on the history of both itself and nearby loads. This behavior can be represented as a linear system with constant but unknown parameters. At some point, the behavior changes which causes a consequent change in the specific parameter values. The goal of SAP is to detect such changes and automatically converge on the estimated parameter values as shown in Figure 2.

Consider the leaf procedure C in Figure 1. Suppose that there are r loads within procedure C with program counter (PC) values $p_1, p_2, ..., p_r$, respectively. Within the ith call of the procedure, the corresponding referenced addresses are denoted as $A_{i,1}$, $A_{i,2}, ..., A_{i,r}$. Within a certain range of consecutive calls, the behavior of memory accesses can be represented with the following equation, which takes both PC-correlated temporal and spatial localities into account:

$$A_{n,m} = \sum_{i=1}^{j} a_{i,m} A_{n-i,m} + \sum_{i=0}^{k_1} a_{i,1} A_{n-i,1} + ... + \sum_{i=0}^{k_l} a_{i,l} A_{n-i,l} \qquad (1)$$

where $1 \leq j \leq (n-1)$, $0 \leq k_i \leq (n-1)$ $(i=1,2,...,l)$, $0 \leq l \leq (m-1)$, and $1 \leq m \leq r$.

Without loss of generality, we consider the $l=1$ case in this paper. The prediction of a target load's address is based on the history of itself and one other nearby load. By letting $a_i=a_{i,m}$, $b_i=a_{i,l}$, $y(n)=A_{n,m}$, and $u(n)=A_{n,l}$, Equation (1) can be simplified to the following memory access function:

$$y(n) = a_1 y(n-1) + \ldots + a_j y(n-j) + b_0 u(n) + \ldots + b_k u(n-k) \qquad (2)$$

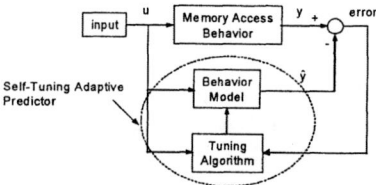

Fig. 2. Block diagram representation of the Self-tuning Adaptive Predictor (SAP).

3   Results and Discussion

The addresses actually accessed by load instructions are collected by modifying the SimpleScalar simulator [5]. We use the benchmark program *181.mcf* with the test input set for illustration. *181.mcf* exhibits the poorest data cache behavior among all benchmarks of the SPEC CINT2000 Benchmarks suite. Our simulation results show the total number of misses in the *bea_compute_red_cost* procedure constitutes 9.15% of the total misses in the program. The related code and data structures are schematically shown in Figure 3.

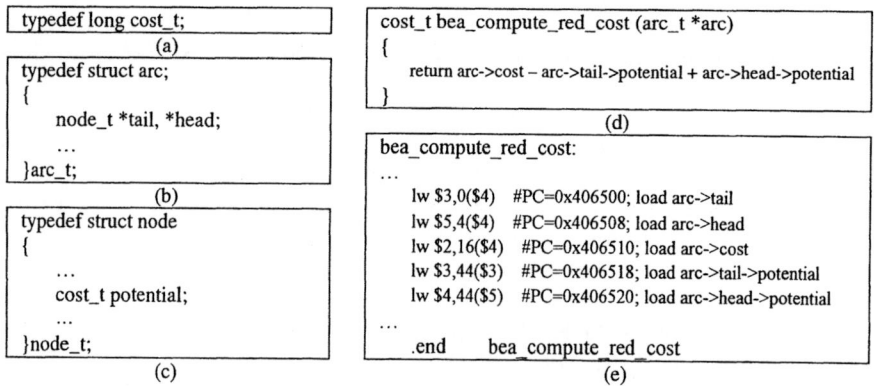

Fig. 3. Related C and assembly code of the procedure *bea_compute_red_cost* from 181.mcf.

The five PCs (p_i) shown in Figure 3(e) are defined as follows with the corresponding access addresses denoted as A_1, A_2, A_3, A_4, and A_5, respectively. Figures 3 (b), (c) and (e) show that the address relationship among *arc->cost*, *arc->tail*, and *arc->head* is determined at compile-time, but the correlation between *arc->tail->potential* and *arc->head->potential* are not known until *arc-> tail* and *arc->head* have been dereferenced at run-time. The memory addresses accessed by p_4

and p_5 depend on values stored in registers \$3 and \$5 respectively, and no correlation can be found from the source code. As prediction among A_1, A_2, and A_3 is trivial, our study focuses on A_2, A_4 and A_5. The prediction error is normalized based on the referenced address span of the same load instruction. Figures 4 and 5 show that these two loads display different access patterns at different call ranges. We have sampled several different call ranges and observed similar patterns.

p_1=0x406500; p_2=0x406508; p_3=0x406510; p_4=0x406518; p_5=0x406520.

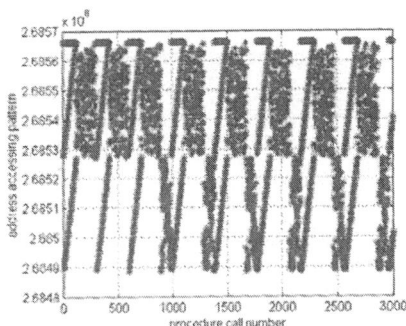   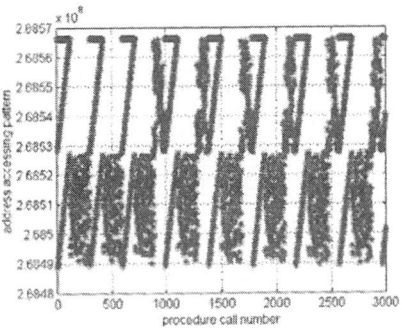

Fig. 4. Memory access pattern for p_4.   **Fig. 5.** Memory access pattern for p_5.

Empirical results [6] show that the regular memory access consists of different patterns at different call ranges and that different models can be effective during different phases of the memory access patterns. In this study, multiple versions of the SAP model run concurrently. Selection of a particular model with which to make a prediction is automated by observing the convergence rate of each component model.

Three models with different history depths of the target and reference loads are used as shown in Table 1. Figure 6 show that using A_2 as the reference, SAP provides good predictions in 55% of the total execution time for that procedure. Using A_4 as the reference, Figure 7 shows that the steady state error is within the ranges of [-5%, +5%]. We summarize the prediction performance in Table 2. The results show that using a reference load that has behavior similar to the target load is better for predicting the behavior of the target than naively selecting a reference load based on simple dependence relationships. The detailed discussion can be found in [6].

Table 1. History depths of the three models used in predicting A_5.

History Depth	Model 1	Model 2	Model 3
Target load	1	3	5
Reference load	2	4	6

4   Conclusions

This paper has proposed a Self-tuning Adaptive Predictor (SAP) model and examined the memory access patterns of leaf procedures with pointer-based data structures. By taking the procedure as the fundamental sampling unit, SAP incorporates temporal locality and spatial locality to dynamically adapt to the changing behavior of memory accesses. Our evaluations with a subset of the SPEC2000 integer benchmark programs showed that SAP is an accurate model for memory address prediction.

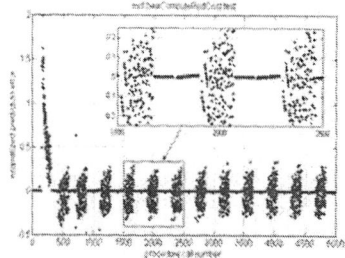

Fig. 6. Prediction of A_5 using A_2.

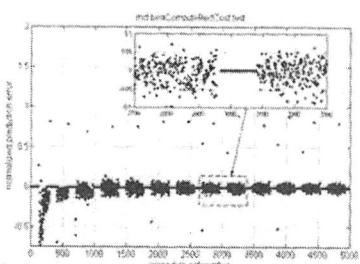

Fig. 7. Prediction of A_5 using A_4.

Table 2. Prediction performance of the procedures at steady state

Benchmark	Procedure	Error	Benchmark	Procedure	Error
164.gzip	pqdown_heap	[-3%, 3%]	175.vpr	alloc_linked_f_pointer	[-4%, 4%]
	gen_bitlen	[-11%, 11%]		net_cost	[-2%, 2%]
181.mcf	bea_compute_red_cost	[-5%, 5%]	255.vortex	chkgetchunk	[-8%, 8%]
	bea_is_dual_infeasible	[-4%, 4%]		memgetword	[-6%, 6%]
	compute_red_cost	[-6%, 6%]	256.bzip2	spec_getc	[-2%, 2%]
	sort_basket	[-14%, 14%]		spec_putc	[-2%, 2%]

Acknowledgments. This work was supported in part by National Science Foundation grants EIA-9971666 and CCR-9900605, the IBM Corporation, HP/Compaq's Alpha development group, and the Minnesota Supercomputing Institute

References

1. Chilimbi, T. M., Larus, J. R.: Using generational garbage collection to implement cache-conscious data placement. In Proceedings of the First International Symposium on Memory Management, volume 34(3) of ACM SIGPLAN Notices, October 1998.
2. Ding, C, Kennedy, K.: Improving cache performance in dynamic applications through data and computation reorganization at run time. In Proceedings of the SIGPLAN '99 Conference on Programming Language Design and Implementation, Atlanta, GA, May 1999.
3. Zhang, H., Martonosi, M.: A Mathematical Cache Miss Analysis for Pointer Data Structures. SIAM Conference on Parallel Processing for Scientific Computing, March 2001.
4. Draper, N. R., Smith, H.: Applied Regression Analysis. 2nd Ed.., John Wiley & Sons, 1981.
5. Burger, D. C., Austin, T. M., Bennett, S.: Evaluating future Microprocessors: The SimpleScalar Tool Set. Technical Report CS-TR-96-1308, University of Wisconsin-Madison, July 1996.
6. Wu, K., Sendag, R., Lilja, D. J.: Using a Self-tuning Adaptive Predictor to Characterize the Regularity of Memory Accesses in Pointer-Intensive Application Programs. University of Minnesota Technical Report: ARCTiC 03–04, April 2003.

Nonlinear Dimension Reduction via Local Tangent Space Alignment

Zhenyue Zhang[1]* and Hongyuan Zha[2]**

[1] Zhejiang University, Hangzhou 310027, P.R. China,
zyzhang@zju.edu.cn
[2] Penn State University, University Park, PA 16802, USA,
zha@cse.psu.edu

Abstract. In this paper we present a new algorithm for manifold learning and nonlinear dimension reduction. Based on a set of unorganized data points sampled with noise from the manifold, we represent the local geometry of the manifold using tangent spaces learned by fitting an affine subspace in a neighborhood of each data point. Those tangent spaces are aligned to give the internal global coordinates of the data points with respect to the underlying manifold by way of a partial eigendecomposition of the neighborhood connection matrix. We present a careful error analysis of our algorithm and show that the reconstruction errors are of second-order accuracy. Numerical experiments including 64-by-64 pixel face images are given to illustrate our algorithm.

1 Introduction

Many high-dimensional data in real-world applications can be modeled as data points lying close to a low-dimensional nonlinear manifold. Discovering the structure of the manifold from a set of data points sampled from the manifold possibly with noise represents a very challenging unsupervised learning problem [1,4,6, 8,9]. The discovered low-dimensional structures can be further used for classification, clustering, outlier detection and data visualization. The key observation is that the dimensions of the embedding spaces can be very high, the intrinsic dimensionality of the data points, however, are rather limited due to factors such as physical constraints and linguistic correlations.

Recently, there have been much renewed interests in developing efficient algorithms for constructing nonlinear low-dimensional manifolds from sample data points in high-dimensional spaces, emphasizing simple algorithmic implementation and avoiding optimization problems prone to local minima [6,9]. Two lines of research of manifold learning and nonlinear dimension reduction have emerged: one is exemplified by [1,9] where pairwise *geodesic* manifold distances are estimated, and then project the data points into a low-dimensional space that

* The work of this author was supported in part by the Special Funds for Major State Basic Research Projects (project G19990328) and NSF grants CCR-9901986.
** The work of this author was supported in part by NSF grants CCR-9901986.

best preserves the geodesic distances. Another line of research follows the long tradition starting with self-organizing maps[4], principal curves/surfaces[3], and topology-preserving networks [5]. The key idea is that the information about the global structure of a nonlinear manifold can be obtained from a careful analysis of the interactions of the *overlapping* local structures. In particular, the local linear embedding (LLE) method constructs a local geometric structure and seeks to project the data points into a low-dimensional space that best preserves those local geometries [6,7].

Our approach draws inspiration from and improves upon the work in [6,7]. In this paper, The basic idea of our approach is to use the tangent space in the neighborhood of a data point to represent the local geometry, and then align those local tangent spaces to construct the global coordinate system for the nonlinear manifold by minimizing the alignment error for the global coordinate learning. This minimization problem is equivalent to an eigenvalue problem that can be efficiently solved. We call the new algorithm *local tangent space alignment* (LTSA) algorithm.

2   The Local Tangent Space Alignment Algorithm

We assume that we are given a data set $X = [x_1, \ldots, x_N]$, $x_i \in \mathcal{R}^m$ sampled with noise from an underlying d-dimensional nonlinear manifold $\mathcal{F}$ embedded into a m-dimensional space with *unknown* generating function $f(\tau)$, $\tau \in R^d$, $d < m$,

$$x_i = f(\tau_i) + \epsilon, \quad i = 1, \ldots, N,$$

where $\tau_i \in \mathcal{R}^d$ are unknown. The objective for nonlinear dimension reduction is to reconstruct τ_i's from the data points x_i's without explicitly constructing f.

To this end, let us assume that the function f is smooth enough. Using first-order Taylor expansion at a fixed τ, we have

$$f(\bar{\tau}) = f(\tau) + J_f(\tau) \cdot (\bar{\tau} - \tau) + O(\|\bar{\tau} - \tau\|^2), \tag{1}$$

where $J_f(\tau) \in \mathcal{R}^{m \times d}$ is the Jacobi matrix of f at τ. Ignoring the second order term, the shifted coordinate $\bar{\tau} - \tau$ is a local coordinate of $f(\bar{\tau}) - f(\tau)$ with respect to the basis of the d column vectors of $J_f(\tau)$. Without knowing the function f, we can not explicitly compute the Jacobi matrix $J_f(\tau)$. However, if we know an orthonormal basis, say Q_τ in matrix form, of the tangent space $\mathcal{T}_\tau$ spanned by the columns of $J_f(\tau)$ and the coordinate θ_τ of $f(\bar{\tau}) - f(\tau)$ corresponding to Q_τ, we have

$$\bar{\tau} - \tau \approx L_\tau \theta_\tau$$

with (unknown) matrix $L_\tau = (Q_\tau^T J_f(\tau))^{-1}$ provided $J_f(\tau)$ is of full rank, i.e., $\mathcal{F}$ is *regular*. It is clear that the global coordinate τ can be extracted by minimizing

$$\int d\tau \int_{\Omega(\tau)} \|\bar{\tau} - \tau - L_\tau \theta_\tau\| d\bar{\tau}. \tag{2}$$

Here $\Omega(\tau)$ is a local neighborhood of τ and $\bar{\tau}$ can be taken as its mean.

The above approach can be applied to the data set X for approximately extracting the underline coordinates τ_i because the orthogonal basis Q_i of the tangent space with respect to τ_i and the local corresponding coordinate θ_i can be approximately determined by the neighborhood $x_{i_1}, \cdots, x_{i_k}$ of x_i. This can be done by finding the best d-dimensional affine subspace approximation for the data points $x_{i_1}, \cdots, x_{i_k}$

$$\min_{c_i, \theta_j^{(i)}, Q_i} \sum_{j=1}^{k} \left\| x_{i_j} - (c_i + Q_i \theta_j^{(i)}) \right\|_2^2.$$

The optimal solutions are given by $c_i = \bar{x}_i$, the mean of all the x_{i_j}'s, Q_i the d left singular vectors of $[x_{i_1} - \bar{x}_i, \cdots, x_{i_k} - \bar{x}_i]$ corresponding to its d largest singular values, and the orthogonal project $\theta_j^{(i)} = Q_i^T (x_{i_j} - \bar{x}_i)$.

To retrieval the global coordinates $\tau_i, i = 1, \ldots, N$, in the low-dimensional feature space based on the local coordinates $\theta_j^{(i)}$, the global coordinates should respect the local geometry determined by the $\theta_j^{(i)}$, $\tau_{i_j} = \bar{\tau}_i + L_i \theta_j^{(i)} + \epsilon_j^{(i)}$ with $\bar{\tau}_i$ the mean of $\tau_{i_j}, j = 1, \ldots, k$, corresponding to the neighborhood index set of x_i. In matrix form, $T_i = \frac{1}{k} T_i ee^T + L_i \Theta_i + E_i$ with $T_i = [\tau_{i_1}, \ldots, \tau_{i_k}]$, $\Theta_i = [\theta_1^{(i)}, \ldots, \theta_k^{(i)}]$, and $E_i = [\epsilon_1^{(i)}, \cdots, \epsilon_k^{(i)}]$ is the local reconstruction error matrix. To preserve as much of the *local* geometry in the low-dimensional feature space, we seek to find τ_i and the local affine transformations L_i to minimize the reconstruction errors $\epsilon_j^{(i)}$, i.e.,

$$\sum_i \|E_i\|^2 \equiv \sum_i \|T_i(I - \frac{1}{k} ee^T) - L_i \Theta_i\|^2 = \min. \tag{3}$$

This optimization problem is equivalent to an eigenvalue problem (4) if we impose an normalization constraint on τ_i's. Obviously, for a fixed T_i, the optimal alignment matrix L_i that minimizes the local reconstruction error $\|E_i\|_F$ is given by $L_i = T_i(I - \frac{1}{k} ee^T)\Theta_i^+ = T_i \Theta_i^+$ and therefore $E_i = T_i W_i$ with $W_i = (I - \frac{1}{k} ee^T)(I - \Theta_i^+ \Theta_i)$, where Θ_i^+ is the Moor-Penrose generalized inverse of Θ_i. Let $T = [\tau_1, \ldots, \tau_N]$ and S_i be the 0-1 selection matrix such that $TS_i = T_i$. Then $E_i = TS_i W_i$. To uniquely determine T, we impose the constraints $TT^T = I_d$. We then need to find T to minimize the overall reconstruction error,

$$\min \sum_i \|E_i\|_F^2 = \min_{TT^T = I_d} \text{trace}(TBT^T), \tag{4}$$

where

$$B = S_1 W_1 W_1^T S_1^T + \cdots + S_N W_N W_N^T S_N^T. \tag{5}$$

Note that the vector e of all ones is an eigenvector of B corresponding to a zero eigenvalue, therefore, the optimal T is given by the d eigenvectors of the matrix B, corresponding to the 2nd to $d+1$st smallest eigenvalues of B. Because of the sparse structure (5), it is not difficult to construct B.

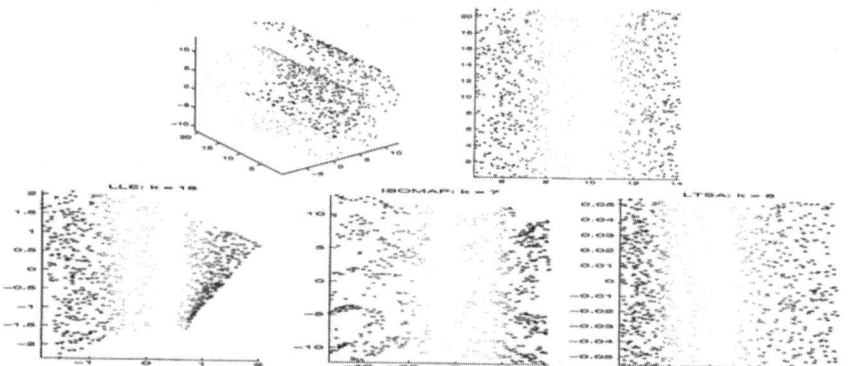

Fig. 1. Top line: Swiss roll data points and the coordinates. Bottom line: 2D coordinates computed by LLE (left, $k = 18$), ISOMAP (middle, $k = 7$), and LTSA (right, $k = 6$).

3   Experimental Results

We have applied our LTSA algorithm to many data sets. The test data sets include curves in 2D/3D Euclidean spaces and surfaces in 3D Euclidean spaces. To show that our algorithm can also handle data points in high-dimensional spaces, we also consider curves and surfaces in Euclidean spaces with dimension equal to 100 and an image data set with dimension 4096. Here we report two applications of the LTSA algorithm.

First we apply LTSA, LLE [6], and ISOMAP [9] to the swissroll data set constructed as $x_i = [t_i \cos(t_i),\ s_i,\ t_i \sin(t_i)]^T$ with t_i and s_i are randomly chosen in the interval $(3\pi/2,\ 3\pi)$ and $(0,\ 21)$, respectively. We set $n = 1000$. LTSA always produces coordinates T that has similar geometric structure as the generating coordinates. There are little geometric deformations in the coordinates generated by LTSA, see the bottom in Figure 1 for the swissroll data set. The surface has zero Gaussian curvature, and therefore it can be flattened without any geometric deformation, i.e., the surface is *isometric* to a 2D plane. In the left and middle in the bottom line of Figure 1, we also plot the results for LLE and ISOMAP, the deformations (stretching and compression) in the generated coordinates are quite prominent.

Now we look at the results of applying LTSA algorithm to the face image data set [9]. The data set consists of a sequence 698 64-by-64 pixel images of a face rendered under various pose and lighting conditions. Each image is converted to an $m = 4096$ dimensional image vector. We apply LTSA with $k = 12$ neighbors and $d = 2$. The constructed coordinates are plotted in the middle of Figure 2. We also extracted four paths along the boundaries of of the set of the 2D coordinates, and display the corresponding images along each path. It can be seen that the computed 2D coordinates do capture very well the pose and lighting variations in a continuous way.

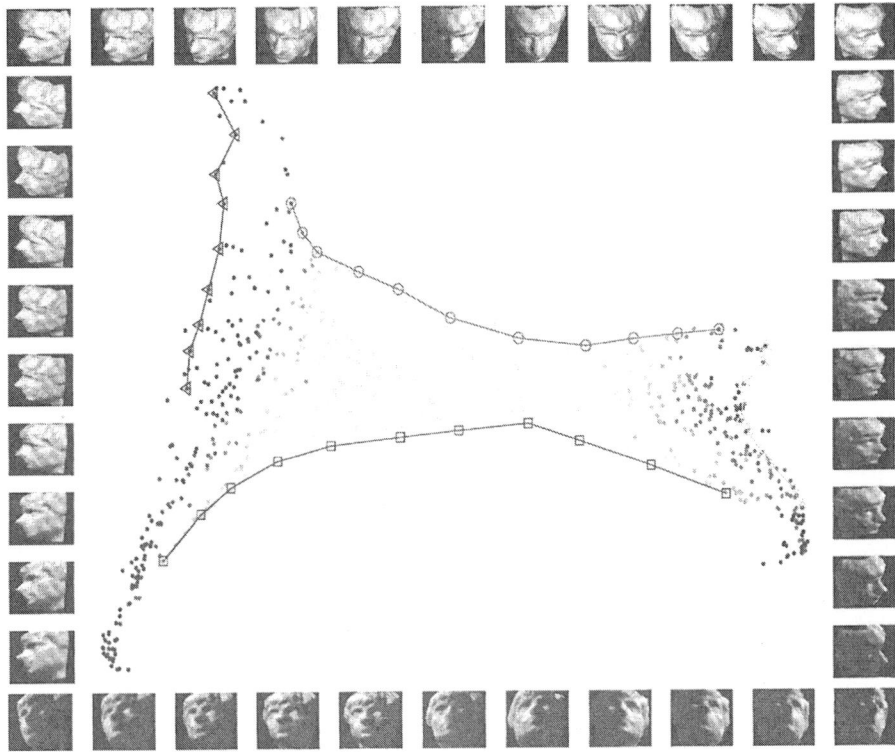

Fig. 2. Coordinates computed by Algorithm LTSA with $k = 12$ (middle) and images corresponding to the points on the bound lines (top, bottom, left, and right).

References

1. D. Donoho and C. Grimes. Local ISOMAP perfectly recovers the underlying parameterization for families of occluded/lacunary images. To appear in IEEE COMPUTER VISION & PATTERN RECOGNITION, 2003.
2. G. H. Golub and C. F. Van Loan. *Matrix Computations.* Johns Hopkins University Press, Baltimore, Maryland, 3nd edition, 1996.
3. T. Hastie and W. Stuetzle. Principal curves. *J. Am. Statistical Assoc.*, 84: 502–516, 1988.
4. T. Kohonen. *Self-organizing Maps.* Springer-Verlag, 3rd Edition, 2000.
5. T. Martinetz and K. Schulten. Topology representing networks. *Neural Networks,* 7: 507–523, 1994.
6. S. Roweis and L. Saul. Nonlinear dimension reduction by locally linear embedding. *Science,* 290: 2323–2326, 2000.
7. L. Saul and S. Roweis. Think globally, fit locally: unsupervised learning of nonlinear manifolds. Technical Reports, MS CIS-02-18, Univ. Pennsylvania, 2002.
8. Y. Teh and S. Roweis. Automatic Alignment of Hidden Representations. To appear in *Advances in Neural Information Processing Systems,* 15, MIT Press (2003).
9. J. Tenenbaum, V. De Silva and J. Langford. A global geometric framework for nonlinear dimension reduction. *Science,* 290:2319–2323, 2000.

System for Intelligent Processing and Recognition of Auditory Brainstem Response (ABR) Signals

Andrzej Izworski and Ryszard Tadeusiewicz

AGH University of Technology
Al. Mickiewicza 30, 30-059 Kraków, Poland
{izwa, rtad}@biocyb.ia.agh.edu.pl

Abstract. The registration of auditory brainstem response signals allows an objective analysis of processes taking place at particular levels of the neural part of the auditory system. The studies on hearing threshold using auditory brainstem response (ABR) comprise registration of a series of responses for stimuli of varying intensities and frequencies and then determination of the wave V detection threshold, which is directly correlated with the hearing threshold. The paper presents the currently realized system for analysis of ABR's registered during screening and diagnostic examinations. Presented are the methods of preliminary processing and analysis of ABR signals, the selected space of distinctive features describing these signals and the constructed techniques for classification and automated recognition of ABR signals. The system will allow collection and distribution of both raw and processed data for conducting the research work in the field of neuroacoustics and social medicine as well as the development and testing of electromedical equipment.

1 Introduction

Due to elaboration of extracranial registration techniques for ABR signals, which present a derivative of bioelectrical processes taking place at the brainstem and auditory cortex, it has become possible to construct objective diagnostic and research methods, which are able to provide a comprehensive assessment of functioning of the whole auditory system. That research is currently widely applied in clinical assessment of the hearing organs, and the progress in registration techniques and analysis of the ABR will probably lead to even wider dissemination of that technique, also in outpatients examinations. Unfortunately for that method the prospects for automation of the examination are not very promising. It is easy to elaborate an algorithm for automated acquisition and stimulation, it is however much more difficult to construct an algorithm for automated analysis of the results.

The examination of the hearing threshold using the ABR comprises registration of a sequence of responses for stimuli of varying intensities and frequencies and then the determination of the wave V detection threshold. The primary problem of the ABR threshold studies during analysis of the registered material is determination of the wave V threshold. The result of that determination is highly dependent on the experience of the person evaluating the examination results.

J. Liu et al. (Eds.): IDEAL 2003, LNCS 2690, pp. 482–489, 2003.
© Springer-Verlag Berlin Heidelberg 2003

Elaboration of a practical algorithm and detection procedure for wave V and its threshold is of great importance for persons with low/modest experience. Recently the number of early diagnostic centers, which implement the ABR method, has increased considerably. Further systematic growth of their number can be also expected, because of introduction of a massive program of auditory screening tests for newborn infants into clinical practice. Therefore construction of an automated method of wave V detection, which could be implemented into devices presently used by those centers, seems particularly useful.

The aim of the described project is the organization of a countrywide system for analysis of ABR signals registered during the screening tests and diagnostic examinations. Therefore the realization of the project required the following:

- Elaboration of methods for preliminary processing and analysis of ABR signals,
- Construction of the space of distinctive features, describing the signals,
- Elaboration of techniques for both classification and automated recognition of ABR signals,
- Elaboration of methods for collection and visualization of ABR data for the whole country

In the present paper the results for the first three items in the above "to-do" list has been described. At present the methods for ABR data storage and visualization are being prepared, which should enable the collection and distribution of both raw and processed data for the needs of scientific research in the fields of neuroacoustics and social medicine, development and testing of electromedical equipment, creation of standards and test sets, as well as training and improvement of the medical staff at all levels.

2 Preliminary Data Processing

Diagnosis of hearing impairment is primarily based on the analysis of the recording's morphology and the latency periods of particular waves. The second criterion seems to be much easier for formulation as a set of simple rules, allowing an instant determination whether a given recording can be classified as a regular one. At present it is assumed, that the latency periods of particular waves should be contained within the boundaries determined by examination of a great number of persons, exhibiting normal hearing abilities. However the determination of the limits and probability of error occurrence requires the examination of a great number of samples, and as a consequence brings on the need for automation of the ABR signal maxima determination process (Fig.1). Because of great individual variability, high level of low frequency noise and the occurrence of muscular artifacts, the task of latency period determination for a given wave becomes complicated, particularly for the low amplitudes of the stimulus signal (<50dB). For these cases it is very easy to take a noise peak or a random artifact for an actual wave occurrence. Up to now no characteristic features of the signal have been defined, which could allow a precise location of the particular wave's parameters. The registered potentials take the form of discrete   time recordings (see Fig.2). On the basis of the signals spectra analysis it has been found that the information is being carried in the 0-10kHz band.

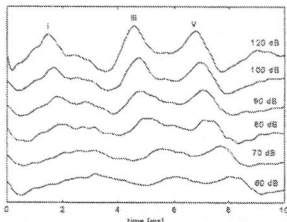

Fig. 1. Typical ABR signal recording obtained from a person with normal hearing abilities. On the right hand side the intensities of the stimulating signals have been denoted. With the decreasing intensity of the stimulus the amplitudes of particular waves decrease, while their latency periods increase.

In the preliminary stage the signal is filtered using a digital low-pass FIR-type filter, with the arbitrary cut-off frequency f_0=0.07Hz, what eliminates the high frequency noise. Then the average value and linear trend are eliminated from each sample. In order to eliminate the spurious local maxima, resulting from external disturbances or muscular artifacts the signal undergoes a further filtration. As a result the number of false maxima in the obtained signal is considerably reduced with respect to the original signal.

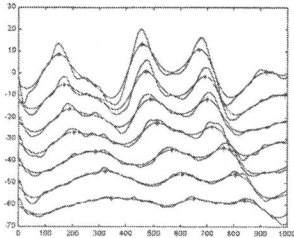

Fig. 2. The original and filtered signal recording

For determination of the latency periods for particular waves the oryginal algorithm has been used, allowing the detection of maxima in the ABR signal recording. The algorithm has been applied for 1144 samples, obtained from persons with normal hearing abilities, what allowed the determination of the latency period distributions for particular waves and their standard values, together with their respective standard deviations.

3   Signal Analysis Using SOM Networks

For purpose of the present study two sets of ABR signals have been constructed: the learning and test set, each consisting of 75 brainstem responses. The parameters of ABR recordings selected for the study were as follows: the triggering stimulus took the form of a cracking sound of intensity between 70 and 20dB, the signal size included 100 values.

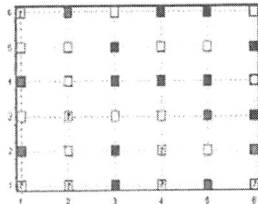

Fig. 3. Exemplary neural network after completion of the learning process. The non-active neurons are denoted as white, the neurons activated by signals containing wave V - black, the neurons activated by signals not containing the wave V - grey, and the neurons reacting to both types of signals are labelled by '?'.

As a result of the learning process the SOM neural network creates a mapping of the set of ABR signals onto a two-dimensional lattice of neurons, preserving the distance relations from the original space of the input signals. Such property of the SOM networks can be used for detection of clustering in the set of ABR signals.

Let's now consider for a particular example, what type of information about the set of ABR signals can be provided by the neural network. The results of learning for a network containing 36 neurons (6x6 neurons lattice) are presented in Fig. 3. It is easily noticed that 23 neurons have been activated in the learning process, and 6 of them recognised the signals not containing the wave V, 10 of them recognised the signals containing the wave V, and 7 reacted to signals belonging to both classes. After an additional calibration of the latter neurons finally 8 neurons recognised signals not containing wave V, and 15 neurons the signals in which wave V was visible. The obtained distribution of network's neurons (Fig.4) is very interesting.

The number of active neurons can be treated as the estimate number of groups in the set of ABR signals. This is obviously a possible approximation, however the number of obtained groups was in accordance with predictions estimating that the number of various groups of signals should not be less than:

*number of classes * number of stimulating intensities = 12*

The division into groups did not take place exactly according to the intensity of triggering stimulus, but anyway it has shown that the above considerations are correct, because in most cases the signals attributed to a given neuron were signals of identical values of the stimulus intensity or signals with neighbouring intensity values, e.g. for the neuron at (5,6) they were three signals of the stimulation intensity 60dB and three signals of 70dB.

The analysis of the way in which the set of signals is divided between particular neurons can also provide different information. There were 1 to 10 signals per one neuron, or average 3.3 signals per neuron. Only four neuron recognised single signals, and what's more in three cases they were signals not containing the wave V. For the latter signals there were 1.7 signals per neuron on the average.

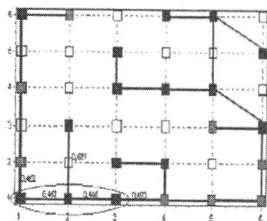

Fig. 4. The tree with the minimal span, connecting the active neurons of the network. An exemplary group of neurons has been denoted, which can be replaced by one neuron placed at (2,1). Selected distances between the neuron weights vectors, expressed in Euclidean metric, are also shown in the picture.

The above facts may lead to a conclusion that the class of signals not containing the wave V is more diversified than the class of signals containing it. Also that result is accordance with common sense conclusions, because to the class of signals with the wave V absent belong all the signals registered for low intensities of the triggering stimulus, the signals which are distorted as a result of defects of the brainstem auditory centres or the occurrence of various interfering signals during the measurements, e.g. muscular artefacts. After completion of the learning process and calibration of the network, it is possible to utilise the network for classification of ABR potentials. However the best recognition results obtained for the SOM network, i.e. 80.25% of correct answers for the test sets, are worse than the results obtained by multilayer networks learned by the error backpropagation method.

4 The Context Classification

In the task of automated recognition of the ABR potentials artificial neural networks have been applied, learned by the error backpropagation methods. The neurons exhibited a unipolar, sigmoidal activation function. The neural networks included one or two layers of hidden neurons.

Table 1. Results obtained for classification of signals 1000, 100 and 25 points in size

No.	Neural network architecture	No of epochs	RMS error	Accuracy of the classification [%]	
				Learning set	Test set
1	$1000 \times 12 \times 1$	260	0,63	100	83.12
2	$1000 \times 7 \times 2 \times 1$	325	3,70	92.11	85,71
3	$100 \times 8 \times 1$	479	0,09	100	85,71
4	$100 \times 7 \times 2 \times 1$	414	2,00	97.37	85,71
5	$25 \times 7 \times 1$	310	1,25	98.68	83,01
6	$25 \times 7 \times 1$	288	2,01	96.05	82,31

In table 1 selected results are shown of the automated classification of the ABR signals obtained in the previous research stages, oriented towards recognition of isolated signals by the artificial neural networks. The network's input have been fed with a signal describing the analysed ABR recording (it was a uniformly sampled set of momentary values of the signal of the normalised size of 100 points) and the network's output a single logical-type signal was expected, indicating the presence or absence of the wave V in the input signal. The studied network architectures exhibited the 100-n-1 structure (where n denotes the size of the optimised hidden layer) or alternatively 100-n-m-1 structure, for the cases when networks with two hidden layer were applied.

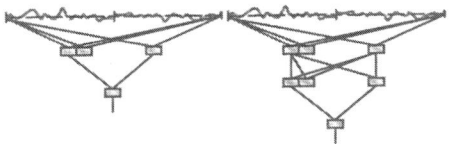

Fig. 5. The double and triple layer neural networks, in which the neurons are connected according to the "every with each other", doublets of signals are fed to the network's input

In order to take the context into account in the described study two signals have been fed at the same time to networks input: the presently analysed ABR signal and the previous, accompanying signal, obtained for the higher intensity of the acoustic stimulus. It could have been achieved using a simple multilayer neural network, but additionally attempts have been made to use in the recognition process neural networks of some more complicated architecture, modified according to the specific features of the considered task. Accordingly several various neural network structures have been proposed and studied. Their architectures will be presented and discussed below. The input vectors necessary for the context studies have been constructed in such a way, that to each of the ABR signals has been appended in the front part by the preceding signal, obtained in the same measuring sequence but for the higher amplitude of the acoustic stimulus. So the pairs of signals were created: 80 and 70dB, 70 and 60dB, etc. The length of such input vectors was of course 200 points.

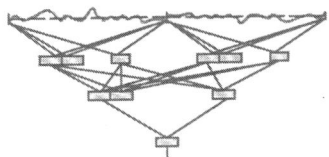

Fig. 6. Triple-layer network, the first hidden layer has been split, so that two consecutive ABR signals are fed separately to the network

The simplest architecture (Fig. 5), which provides the possibility of making use of the context during the recognition of signals of auditory response is a neural network to the input of which two signals are fed in sequence (i.e. vectors consisting of consecutive values of time samples of the considered signals, what leads the situation that the considered networks make use of the input vector being 200 points in size).

The network architecture described above have been later modified in such a way, that the first hidden layer has been split into two parts, and then two component signals of the input vector have been fed separately to each of the layers (Fig. 6). Due to such a procedure the split layers of the hidden layer preliminary process the signal to be recognised and its context signal, working independently.

In the course of the simulation the network's architecture has been optimised in order to provide the best results of the recognition. In table 1 several best results are shown (for comparison), obtained from the classification of single input signals. These results have already been published. The table 2 below shows the new results for the study of recognition of the ABR signals making use of the context signals.

Table 2. Selected best results of the classification for the networks presented in Fig.7 and 8

No	Neural network architecture	No of epochs	RMS Error	Accuracy of the classification [%]	
				Learning set	Test set
1	$200 \times 10 \times 1$	330	1.98	96.05	87,01
2	$200 \times 8 \times 1$	395	1.24	96,05	89,61
3	$200 \times 8 \times 1$	365	1.43	97,37	88,31
4	$200 \times 7 \times 2 \times 1$	1049	3.94	94,74	85,71
5	$(100+100) \times (4+4) \times 2 \times 1$	2080	3.87	94,74	87,01
6	$(100+100) \times (3+3) \times 2 \times 1$	1794	3.88	94,74	87,01
7	$(100+100) \times (3+3) \times 2 \times 1$	2250	3.87	94,74	88,31

After comparing the learning results, obtained during a few tens of simulation runs, quite a lot can be said about the influence of including the context and application of various network structures on the quality of ABR signals recognition results. From the completed research it follows that including the context has the strongest positive influence on the classification quality for the networks including one hidden layer, for which the improvement of the ABR recognition results was about 4-5%. The conclusion, which can be drawn, is that by the addition to the recognised signal only the information about the classification of the signal preceding the analysed signal leads to much worse effects than including the whole context signal.

5 Conclusions

The aim of the presented project was the creation of a unified technique for acquisition of ABR signals and elaboration of a method for their automated analysis. In further development the automation of ABR signals analysis was oriented towards the detection of wave V in the ABR signal, what is of key importance for the assessment of hearing abilities of the examined patients (mainly infants). The automated classification of ABR signals has been carried out by application of artificial neural networks of various architectures. Good results have been obtained only after application of neural networks with architectures allowing the application of context information. Deviation from the classical MLP type network resulted in much more satisfying solution of the considered task, then the solutions found without making use of the context information. It has been also found that increasing the network's complexity (by transition from triple layer to quadruple layer networks) does not lead to the expected improvement in the recognition quality, while considerably increasing the duration of the learning process. The neural network making use of the context data, which after the learning process were the best in classification of the ABR signals, have obtained the correct recognition in 92-94% cases. This result also shows that a search for methods of applications of neural networks with non-standard architecture may be rewarding, and once more it also proves the fact that it is possible to build a system based on neural networks, and capable of automated detection (with a satisfying reliability level) of the presence of wave V in the ABR signal.

Main efforts will be focused on the construction of visualization and distribution rules (in the countrywide scale) for the collected data together with their interpretation. The collected data will also allow the execution of several analyses assessing the health condition of the population subject to the screening tests. In the long run, due to the combination of that facility with the remote database access, it will be possible to create a decision support system, similar to an expert system, covering the area of whole Poland and providing the prospects for a considerable degree of unification and objectiveness of the ABR examinations.

This paper was supported by KBN/AGH grant 18.18.120.386

References

1. Izworski A., Tadeusiewicz R., Pasławski A.: The Utilization of Context Signals in the Analysis of ABR Potentials by Application of Neural Networks, Lecure Notes in Artificial Intelligence, No. 1810, Springer Verlag, 2000, pp.195–202
2. Izworski A. , R. Tadeusiewicz, A. Pasławski, Non-Standard Neural Network Architectures in the Analysis of Auditory Brainstem Response Potentials, First International Conference on: Advances in Medical Signal and Information Processing, Bristol, 2000, pp. 184–191
3. Izworski A., Tadeusiewicz R., Pasławski A.: Multidimensional Techniques of Nonlinear Processing of Auditory Brainstem Response, Proceedings of NSIP-01 2001 IEEE-EURASIP Workshop on Nonlinear Signal and Image Processing03.06.2001–06.06.2001, Baltimore, Maryland USA
4. Izworski A., Wochlik I., Bulka J., Paslawski A.: SOM Neural Networks in Detection of Characteristic Features of Brainstem Auditory Evoked Potentials (ABR), in: Advances in Systems theory, Mathematical Methods and Applications, Eds.: A. Zemliak, N.E. Mastorakis, WSEAS Press, ISBN 960-8052-61-0, 2002, pp. 158–162
5. Wochlik I., Bulka J., Tadeusiewicz R., Bania P., Izworski A.: Determination of Diagnostic Parameters in an Automated System for ABR Signal Analysis, Proceedings of the International Conference on Mathematics and Engineering Techniques in Medicine and Biological Sciences, METMBS'02, ISBN 1-892512-32-7, Vol. II, Las Vegas, Nevada, USA, June 24–27, 2002, pp.391–394

Protein Structure Modeling Using a Spatial Model for Structure Comparison

Sung-Hee Park[1], Keun Ho Ryu[1], and Hyeon S. Son[2]

[1] Database Laboratory, Chungbuk National University,
San 48 Kashin-dong, Hungduck-ku, Cheongju, 360-763, Korea
{shpark, khryu}@dblab.chugnbuk.ac.kr
[2] Center for Computational Biology & Bioinformatics,
Korea Institute of Science and Technology Information,
Eoeun-dong 52, Yuseong-gu, Daejeon city, 305-600, Korea.
hss@kisti.re.kr

Abstract. Features of newly emerging protein structure data are very large, extremely complex and multi dimensional. Furthermore, it is complicated to manage structural information with flat file for comparison and prediction of protein structure. Therefore, it is necessary to make a model of protein structures to store them into database and to represent spatial arrangements and topological relationships for providing analysis applications of protein structures with structural information.

This paper describes extracting structural features from flat file, making a model protein structures based on a network spatial model and querying relationships among protein structures using topological and geometric operators. Existing spatial DBMS can store and retrieve spatial features of protein structures with spatial index by protein structure modeling using spatial types.

1 Introduction

Newly emerging protein structure data are extremely complex, multidimensional, and incomplete. The volume and range of the data are ambiguous, and there are missing fields[6]. Therefore, there are some similarities as well as differences between protein structure data management and conventional data management.

There have been many studies on similarity and homology search[14] geared toward finding the methods to predict the 2D[9, 11]or 3D structure[7, 8, 10, 12] of protein from sequences and structures. However, these conventional researches ignored spatial characteristics, and did not treat high volume of protein structural data increased tremendously. Therefore, it is necessary to develop a data model and querying for protein structure data that can represent features and complexity of protein structure data such as spatial characteristics and relationships.

---

[1] This work was supported by Bioinformatics Center of Korea Institute of Science and Technology Information, University IT Research Center for Project, and KOSEF RRC (ChongJu Univ. ICRC) in Korea.

J. Liu et al. (Eds.): IDEAL 2003, LNCS 2690, pp. 490–497, 2003.
© Springer-Verlag Berlin Heidelberg 2003

In this paper, we propose a modeling of protein structures based on a network spatial model and describe queries for relationships among protein structures using topological and geometric operators. For the protein structure modeling, the protein 3D structures which have 3D coordinates of atoms, are considered spatial objects and represented with the spatial geometric type. A atom is presented with point, and a helix/sheet is a arc in the network spatial model. Therefore, the tertiary structure is the spatial network, which consists of nodes, arcs, points and lines, and has topological relationships.

2 Structural Feature Extraction from PDB Flat Files

This section describes a extraction of structural features used in prediction and comparison of protein structures from PDB flat files. It shows geometry and topology of protein structure in flat files for a extraction step. The feature extraction step is used to extract the identification, geometry and topology of protein structure from flat files. The identification information of protein structures is PDB identifier and molecule name and chain identifier.

The geometry of protein structures is different from that of structure levels. We consider relative positions of central atoms of a residue in a sequence, coordinates on atom, and SSEs (secondary structure element) which include the start and end position of SSE. Topology of protein structure presents element's order along the backbone and connectivity of residue(consecutive order of residue) in a sequence.

A sequences as primary structure is extracted from a SEQRES record in flat files. The SEQRES contains the amino acid or nucleic acid sequence in each chain of the macromolecule. In Helix record, chain Identifier, identifier of Helix, residue name and residue position (residue number) where helix starts and ends are extracted. Sheet identifier, strand identifier, residue name and residue position (residue number) where strand starts and ends, are also obtained from flat files. Structural information related to Turn and Loop is extracted as the same manner with Helix and Sheet. Chain identifier, residue number, atom number, and 3D coordinates of atoms are extracted as 3D structural information. Fields in flat file of mentioned geometry or topology of protein structure show in the Fig. 1.

3 Description of Protein Structures with Spatial Type

Arrangement of atoms in space have spatial topology and other spatial features. Therefore, This section describes the geometry and spatial topology of 3D structures in proteins with spatial geometry types.

The protein 3D molecule can be divided into one or more rigid substructures. Thus if we consider a molecule as a three dimensional graph, each atom is a node, each bond is an edge, and substructure is a block of the graph. This graph can be represented with the spatial network model which was first designed for representing the networks in graph-based application such as transportation services or utility management. In Fig. 2 tuples are denoted by [], lists by<>, and set by { }. Using this notation, protein structures can be summarized in Fig. 2.

In the primary structure of proteins, a sequence, can be defined as the polyline which is a finite set of line segments, such that end point of each segment is shared by exactly two segments when a residue corresponds to a point in spatial types. These polylines can not be considered spatial topologies between points and lists of points which are consist of extreme points of line segments. A point corresponds to a amino acid molecule in the backbone. Coordinates of point are coordinates of the C^α atom in a residue.

The elements of the secondary structure of proteins such as α-helix and β-sheet are represented with polylines which can have topologies and differ from polylines of the primary structure. In the spatial network model[2], polylines including an spatial topology denote arcs which start at a node and end at a node, and include a finite set of point. A node is a distinguished point that connects a list of arcs.

A start node corresponds to the C^α atom of a starting residue in a SSEs and an end node to the the C^α atom of a starting residue in a SSEs. If the secondary structures can be defined to polylines, the tertiary structure can be defined as a finite set of the elements of the secondary structure and there can be spatial topology relationships among them. Thus, the tertiary structure can denote a finite set of points, nodes, and arcs in the spatial network model.

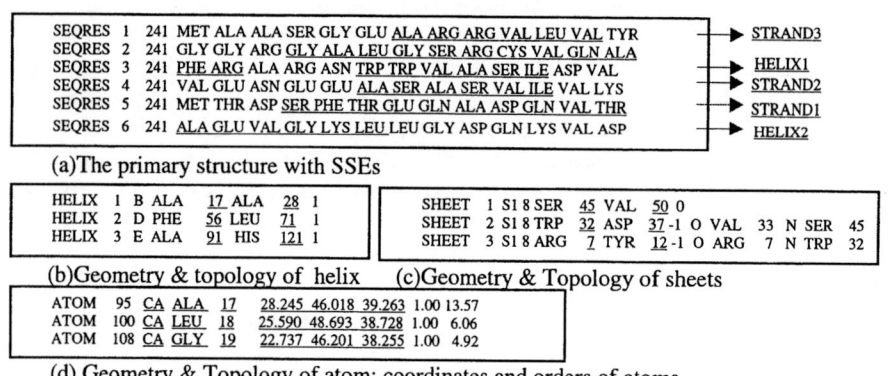

Fig. 1. Extracted structural features in PDB flat file

4 Protein Structure Modeling

It is time consuming step that features of structure are extracted from PDB flat file and parsed fields are inserted into specific tables or objects to be compatible with the designed schema. We divide modeling into two steps. The first step involves the modeling of extracting information of protein structures from flat files, and the second step is protein structure modeling represented by oracle spatial object types. Section 4.1 describes the first step of the modeling and representation of three dimensional structures using spatial types in ORACLE in order to implement the spatial geometry of protein which is referred to section 3. Section 4.2 describes queries using spatial operators to retrieve the structural information of proteins for the comparison of protein structures .

- primary structure of protein:
  < residue> = <polyline>
  <polyline> = <line-segment>
  <line-segment>=<start-point, end-point>
  <point> =[x:real, y:real, z:real]

- point: coordinates of C$^\alpha$ Atom in a residue

- secondary structure of protein:
  <α-Helixl β-Sheet> = <arc>
  <arc> =< [node-start, node-end, <point>] >

- node-start: C$^\alpha$ Atom of starting residue in an α-Helix

- node-end : C$^\alpha$ Atom of ending residue in an α-Helix

- point : C$^\alpha$ Atoms between starting residue and ending residue in an α-Helix

- tertiary structure of protein:
  <nodel arcl point >

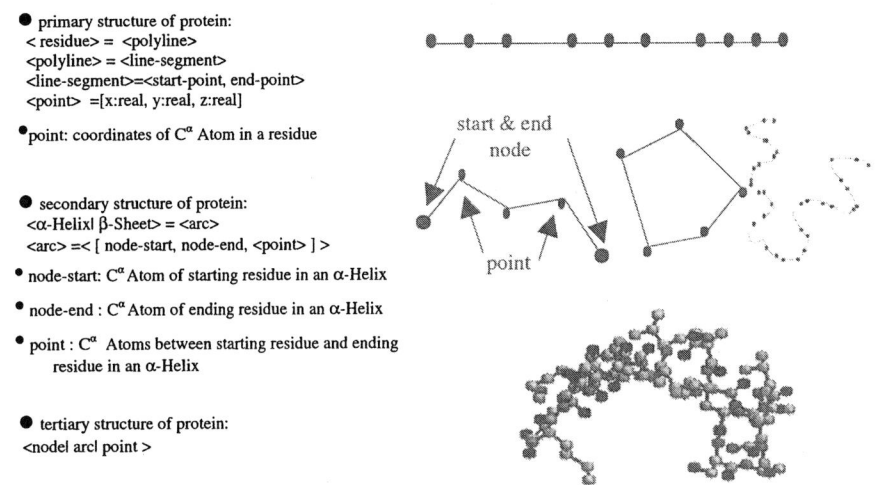

Fig. 2. Spatial geometries and topological relation of protein structures

4.1 Protein Structure Modeling with Oracle Spatial Type

Naïve protein structure modeling: Naïve modeling is a pre-processing step to store extracted fields of flat files into database a designed spatial schema. Format or type of a field in PDB flat files is often inconsistent, and value of filed is ambiguous. Therefore, this step is subtle, but also needs human interaction and inspection. This involves loading and extracting structural information into simple relations. The naïve schema for a database is referred to Park's paper[Park02]

A sequence is treated as the attribute of which the domain is a variable character. The length of variable character in ORACLE can be taken up to a maximum size of 4000 byte. The sequences that are longer than 4K are divided into two tuples. The strength of storing sequence data as a variable character is that the operator LIKE in SQL can be used.

Protein structure modeling based on oracle spatial type: The abstract definition is a mean to show intuitively the protein structures as geographic objects. Hence, a protein structure object consists of description of biological or chemical features and a spatial object part. The spatial objects do not correspond to any standard data type such as string or integer. They are represented by the topology and geometry with spatial data type. Arc, node, polygon, and region in spatial network model can be used and implemented with oracle spatial type.

Protein structure object ={description, spatial object of structural elements}
Spatial object of structural elements ={point, arc, node, polygon, region}
The Fig. 3 shows the spatial schema of protein structure modeling

---

• PM_COM_INFO(<u>PDB_IDcode,ChainID</u>,Classification, Title,)

•LHELIX(<u>PDB_IDcode, ChainID, HelixNum</u>,SerNum, initSeqNum, endSeqNum, **HARC**)

•LSTRAND(<u>PDB_IDcode, ChainID, StrandID</u>, SSNum, initSeqNum, EndSeqNum, **SARC**)

• PATOM(<u>PDB_IDcode, ChainID, SSENum, ANum</u>, AResidueNum, SSEType, **APoint**)

Fig. 3. Spatial schema for protein structure

The Table PM_COM_INFO as shown in Fig. 3, is the same table as PROTEIN in naïve modeling. LHELIX and LSTRAND contain attributes HARC and SARC that are spatial objects of a α-helix and β-sheet from tables HELIX and SHEET. HARC and SARC denote the geometric types of SDO_GEOMETRY in ORACLE8i Spatial, represented by geometric primitive type point and line string within SDO_GEOMTRY. The arc type can be represented with line string in ORACLE8i Spatial. PATOM contains a geometric representation of C^{alpha} atoms in each residue center as type POINT. Thus, table PATOM includes the spatial column APoint of object type POINT in ORALCE8i Spatial. The geometry of spatial object in ORACLE8i Spatial is stored as an object, in a single row, in a column of type SDO_GEOMETRY. The details of attribute in SDO_GEOMETRY are referred to ORACLE8i Spatial[3].

4.2 Querying Protein Structures Using Spatial Query

Query protein structure: Information related to protein structures can be obtained by querying spatial attributes that represent geometry of protein structures. The following queries demonstrate to find the coordinates of C^{alpha} atoms in Helix.
[Query 1] Query the coordinates of C^{alpha} atoms in Helix of protein.
SELECT PDB_IDCODE, APOINT.X, APOINT.Y, APOINT.Z
FROM PATOM
WHERE SSEType='HELIX'
In the above query, the coordinates C^{alpha} atom in an α-helix can be retrieved by querying the column of APOINT of spatial type POINT which has three columns, X, Y and Z. This query can lead to decrease join cost between table HELIX and table ATOM in naïve modeling due to a large number of tuples involved in ATOM.

Query structural relationships in proteins: The residue-residue(C^{alpha} atom-C^{alpha} atom) distance is a primitive operation at aligning steps for comparing rigid structures of proteins. Geometric operator such as SDO_DISTANCE and SDO_LENGTH can be calculated as an Euclidean distances between two spatial objects. To compare two protein structures, the superposition between two protein structures is examined[5]. The superposition of SSEs between proteins is evaluated by intersection of spatial geometry using topological operators of spatial objects represented the SSEs of protein. Topological operators[3] on spatial objects defined by Clementini can be used to find superposed SSEs, and

SDO.GEOM.RELATE operator provided by ORACLE 8i Spatial is used for executing 91M(Intersection Matrix)[13]. This operators are used for fast filtering many candidate protein objects at the comparison.

[Query 2] Find α-helices of protein, which superpose those of protein 1DHR.
SELECT H1.PDB_IDCODE, H1.SSENUM, H2.PDB_IDCODE, H2.SSENUM;
FROM LHELIX H1, LHELIX H2
WHERE SDO_RELATE(H1.HARC, H2.HARC, 'mask=ANYINTERACT
    querytype=JOIN')='TRUE'
AND H1.PDB_IDCODE!=H2.PDB_IDCODE
AND H1.HELIXNUM != H2.HELIXNUM AND H1.PDB_IDCODE='1DHR'
ORDER BY H1.PDB_IDCODE, H1.SSENUM, H2.PDB_IDCODE,
H2.SSENUM;

This query performs a spatial join operation between two common attributes in spatial relations, i.e., H1.HARC and H2.HARC. In addition, ANYINTERACT finds spatial objects that are not disjoint from H1.HARC to H2.HARC, and returns resulting objects sorted by the order of columns in ORDER BY clause. This query generates the candidate set for a refinement step of comparison with simple use of topological operators and without taking high cost.

5 Experiments and Results

In this section, we analyze the performance of proposed queries as mentioned in section 4.2. We have implemented the proposed spatial schema using java language on a Compaq ProliantML330e server, propagating structural information with spatial type from naïve database into ORACLE 8i DBMS.

5.1 Experiment 1

Query structural information in proteins: Our first experiment query is "To find the coordinates of C^{alpha} atoms in protein 1A1M of HIV like query1 in section 4.2. We evaluate execution time in two cases of the same size of protein structures: 1) query using spatial modeling, and 2) query with naïve modeling.

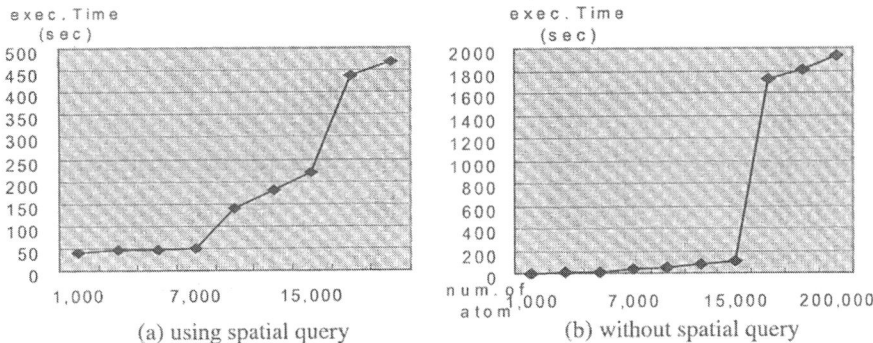

(a) using spatial query   (b) without spatial query

Fig. 4. Execution time for Retrieving the coordinates of atom

Fig. 4 (a) shows the execution time of retrieving the coordinates of atoms using spatial query after loading the protein structure information into spatial schema. When the number of atoms are over 50,000, the execution time was increased. However, as shown in Fig.4(b), the execution time of retrieving coordinates of atoms without a spatial query with naive schema was extremely high as compared to using spatial query as represented by Fig. 4(a). To compare the protein structures, retrieving coordinates of atoms included in secondary structure elements with naïve schema need the cost of joint operation between table atom and table helix. With spatial modeling, spatial index such as R tree and quad tree that facilitate the retrieving without joining, and performance of retrieving atom becomes efficient.

5.2 Experiment 2

Query topological relation of protein structures: Our second experiment query is "To find topological equivalent atom pairs in the α-Helix of the protein 1K6Y of HIV" using topological operator ANYINTERACT like Query2. This experiment restricts to N-terminal Zn binding domain of HIV integrase family which belongs to DNA/RNA-binding 3-helical bundle fold and all alpha class in the SCOP. We queried all the proteins within N-terminal Zn binding domain of HIV integrase family using ANYINTERACT operator. As a result the matched protein have the same as that of the SCOP except the 1K6Y PDB entry. In our result with Table1, 1K6Y PDB entry did not match with any protein in DNA/RNA-binding 3-helical bundle fold and 1K6Y matched with 1A00 PDB entry. The following table shows the same matched proteins between the SCOPE and our results.

Table 1. The result of query with a topological operator

Fold : DNA/RNA-binding 3-helical bundle			
Family: N-terminal Zn binding domain of HIV integrase Num. of atoms=136,352 Num of atom in helix=6,055 Num. of helix=1,625 Execution time=3.687 seconds			
SCOPE	This	SCOPE	This
1K6Y	**1A00**	1WJD	1WJD
1WJA	1WJA	1WJE	1WJE
1WJB	1WJB	1E0E	1E0E
1WJC	1WJC		

6   Conclusion

This paper described the protein structure modeling based on the network spatial model and showed queries for relationships among protein structures using spatial operators. For the protein structure modeling, the protein 3D structures were considered spatial objects and were represented with spatial geometric type. 3Dstructure represented spatial networks which consisted of nodes, arcs, points and lines and had topological relationships. Geometric and topological operators were treated as primitive functions for comparing protein structures. These operators can generate small candidate set to use at structural alignment steps, by filtering unrelated structures. To make a model for protein structures as spatial objects can facilitate comparison of protein structures with spatial index and operators. Thus, advanced conventional data management systems such as spatial databases can be applied to manage the newly emerging protein structure data.

The proposed modeling can be applied for classifications of 3D structures of proteins and structure prediction. In future work, spatial operations can be extended to classify the similar 3D structures of proteins.

References

1. Y. Han, S. H. Park, K. H. Ryu: Modeling of three Dimensional Structure in Protein based on Spatial Object Model. In Proc. of Korea Info. Sci. Soc., Vol.29 No.1 (2002) 73–75

2. P. Rigaus, M. School, A. Voisard: Spatial Databases with application to GIS. Academic Press, San Diego (2002) 29–61

3. Oracle Spatial User's Guide and Reference: Loading and Indexing Spatial Object Types. Release8.1.5, Oracle (2001)

4. H. M. Berman, J. Westbrook, Z. Feng, G. Gilliland, T. N. Bhat, H. Weissig, I. N. Shindyalov, P. E. Bourne: The Protein Data bank. J. Nucleic Acids Research., Vol. 28. Oxford University Press, New York (2000) 235–242

5. D. Higgins, W. Tailor: Bioinfomatics: Sequence, Structure, and databanks, 1st edn. Oxford University Press, New York (2000)

6. K. H. Ryu: Genome database & EST database. J. Scientific & Technological Knowledge Infrastructure, Vol.10. KORDIC (2000)48–61

7. L. Holm , C. Sander: Dali/FSSP classification of three-dimensional protein folds. Nucleic Acids Research., Vol. 25. Oxford University Press, New York (1997) 231–234

8. Levitt, M. : Competitive assessment of protein fold recognition and alignment accuracy. Int. J. Proteins Struct. Funct. Genet. 1 (1997) 92–104

9. Stultz, M., Nambudripad, R., Lathrop, H., White, V.: Predicting protein structure with probabilistic models. Int. J. Adv. Mol. Cell Biol. 22B (1997)447–506

10. Alexandrov, N., Nussinov, R., Zimmer, .M.: Fast Protein fold recognition via sequence to structure alignment and contact capacity protentials. In: Proc. of Pac. Symp on Biocomput. (1996) 53–72

11. Garnier, J., Gibrat, J.-F., Robson, B.: GOR method for predicting protein secondary structure from amino acid sequence. J. Method Enzymol. 266 (1996) 540–553

12. Johnson, M. S., May, A. C., Ridionov, M. A., Overington, J. P.: Discrimination of common protein folds: Application of protein structure to sequence/structure comparisons. J. Methods Emzymol. 266 (1996).575–598

13. E. Clementini, P. Felice, P. van Oostrom: A small set of formal topological relationships suitable for end-user interaction. In: Proc. of Spatial Databases Symp., Singapore (1993) 277–295

14. Altschul, S. F., Carrol, R. J., Lipman, D. J.: Basic local alignment search tool. J. Mol. Biol. 215 (1990) 403–410

DNA Algorithms for Rough Set Analysis

Alfons Schuster

School of Computing and Mathematics, Faculty of Informatics, University of Ulster
Shore Road, Newtownabbey, Co. Antrim BT37 0QB, Northern Ireland
a.schuster@ulster.ac.uk

Abstract. This paper presents work combining the fields of rough set analysis and DNA-computing. The paper includes brief introductions into the two areas and then presents some algorithms based on the DNA-computing paradigm that perform some basic rough set analysis.

1 Introduction

This paper investigates the application of DNA-computing to a data analysis technique that has gained increasing interest in the data analysis and machine learning community over the last years, namely rough set analysis. The strategy of the paper is to demonstrate potential solutions for simple problems, and to draw conclusions for more complex and also more realistic situations. We are aware of problems that can arise from an application of the proposed work in the real world such as large information tables with many records and attributes in rough set analysis, as well as engineering issues associated with DNA design. This paper is less concerned about these problems at the moment and advocates simplicity for the sake of ease of explanation. In this rather idealistic world it is possible, for example, to engineer genetic design processes and manipulations on DNA strands free of error. The remainder of the paper introduces major concepts from rough set theory and DNA-computing. The paper then presents a number of DNA algorithms performing rough set analysis tasks. The paper ends with a summary discussion. Finally, it is important to mention that to a large extent the paper adopts the terminology and uses examples that can be found in the work of Adleman, Lipton, Paun et al., and Pawlak et al. [1] [2] [3] [4].

2 Rough Set Analysis

Rough set analysis uses so-called *information tables* to represent decision-making scenarios. For example, records *r1*, *r2*, *r3*, *r4*, *r5*, and *r6* in Table 1 represent six individual decision-making scenarios. Table 1 could present a loan risk assessment analysis conducted by a bank, for instance. In this case a record might represent a client, attributes *A, B* and *C* could stay for *Age, Income*, and *Profession*, and *Out* for the final decision taken by the bank, e.g. loan granted *yes* or *no*. From now on Table 1 shall illustrate an imaginary scenario in which *Out*

J. Liu et al. (Eds.): IDEAL 2003, LNCS 2690, pp. 498–513, 2003.

Table 1. Information table

Record	A	B	C	Out
r1	1	1	1	2
r2	1	1	2	1
r3	1	1	3	1
r4	2	1	1	2
r5	2	2	2	2
r6	2	1	3	1

$= \{1, 2\}$, $A = \{1, 2\}$, $B = \{1, 2\}$, and $C = \{1, 2, 3\}$. Note that Table 1 is based on an example that can be found in [4].

Rough set analysis aims to extract information from such information tables. Its main motives are: (1) attribute reduction, (2) rule generation, and (3) prediction. To achieve these tasks rough set analysis uses the following constructs:

Indiscernibility and indiscernibility relations: Table 1 reveals that records r1, r2, and r3 can not be distinguished on the bases of attributes A and B only, because $A = 1$ and $B = 1$ for each of these records. They are indiscernible with respect to attributes A and B. The same accounts for records r4 and r6, because $A = 2$ and $B = 1$ for both of them. These observations describe an indiscernibility relation as a relation defining sets, where the elements of the sets are indiscernible from each other with respect to particular attribute values.

Elementary sets: Sets defined by an indiscernibility relation are called elementary sets. For example, the two attributes A and B in Table 1 define the elementary sets $\{r1, r2, r3\}$, $\{r4, r6\}$, and $\{r5\}$, with the latter being a singleton.

Definable sets: A definable set is a union of elementary sets. For example the set $\{r1, r2, r3, r5\}$ is definable, because its members can be identified by either $A = B = 1$, or, $A = B = 2$.

Redundant attributes: Imagine two indiscernibility relations on Table 1, the first on the bases of all three attributes (A, B, C), and the second using only the two attributes A and C. From Table 1 it can be extracted that both relations define the same elementary sets $\{r1\}$, $\{r2\}$, $\{r3\}$, $\{r4\}$, $\{r5\}$, and $\{r6\}$. This observation identifies attribute B as being redundant.

Minimal sets: A set of attributes containing no redundant attributes is called *minimal.*

Reducts: Let there be two sets $(M$, and $N)$ of attributes, where $M \neq N$. If the indiscernibility relations defined by both sets are identical, and set M is minimal, then M is called the reduct of N. In the example given before set $\{A, C\}$ is the reduct of set $\{A, B, C\}$. The identification of the redundant attribute (B) allows the reduction of Table 1 into Table 2.

It is important to realise that both information tables contain the same information. It is equally important to mention that so far the decision outcomes (*Out*) have been completely ignored. Rough set analysis achieves the inclusion of these outcomes by so-called *concepts.*

Table 2. Reduced information table

Record	A	C	Out
r1	1	1	2
r2	1	2	1
r3	1	3	1
r4	2	1	2
r5	2	2	2
r6	2	3	1

Concepts: The idea of an indiscernibility relation can be applied to decision outcomes as well. The elementary sets defined in this process are referred to as concepts. From Table 2 it is possible to extract the following concepts: $\{r1, r4, r5\}$ for $Out = 2$, and $\{r2, r3, r6\}$ for $Out = 1$. The elements of each set are indiscernible from each other with respect to the values of the attribute Out.

Is it possible now to draw any conclusions, or to extract any rules from Table 2 using the definitions given so far? In terms of rough set analysis this is possible, because all elementary sets defined by attributes A and C on Table 2 (which are $\{r1\}, \{r2\}, \{r3\}, \{r4\}, \{r5\}, \{r6\}$) are subsets of one of the two concepts ($\{r1, r4, r5\}$, and $\{r2, r3, r6\}$). For example, it is possible to extract the following rule, amongst other rules, from Table 2:

Rule: If $A = 1$ and $C = 1$ then $Out = 2$, because $\{r1\}$ is a subset of concept $\{r1, r4, r5\}$.

In order to explain further rough set constructs Table 2 is extended by two more records ($r7$ and $r8$) into Table 3.

Table 3. Extended (inconsistent) information table

Record	A	C	Out
r1	1	1	2
r2	1	2	1
r3	1	3	1
r4	2	1	2
r5	2	2	2
r6	2	3	1
r7	2	2	1
r8	2	3	2

Inconsistency: From Table 3 it can be extracted that the elementary sets defined by attribute A and C are $\{r1\}, \{r2\}, \{r3\}, \{r4\}, \{r5, r7\}$, and $\{r6, r8\}$. It is also possible to identify that the concepts in the table are $\{r1, r4, r5, r8\}$, and $\{r2, r3, r6, r7\}$. A look at these set reveals that neither elementary set $\{r5, r7\}$, nor elementary set $\{r6, r8\}$ is a subset of any of the two concepts. Table3 also illustrates that the outcome for record $r5$ and record $r7$ is contradicting ($Out(r5) = 2$, $Out(r7) = 1$), although both records are described by the same attribute values ($A = C = 2$). Record $r6$ and record $r8$ display a similar scenario. In the rough set analysis framework the consequences of these observations are that the concepts in Table 3 are not definable by attributes A and C. Table 3 is said to be inconsistent. Rough set analysis uses the constructs *lower approximation*, and *upper approximation* in order to deal with inconsistencies.

Lower approximation and upper approximation: Given a concept X, a lower approximation is defined by the smallest definable set in X. On the other hand, an upper approximation is defined by the greatest definable set in X. For instance, for the concept $\{r2, r3, r6, r7\}$ in Table 3 the lower approximation is given by $\{r2, r3\}$, and the upper approximation by $\{r2, r3, r5, r6, r7, r8\}$. For the second concept $\{r1, r4, r5, r8\}$, lower and upper approximation are $\{r1, r4\}$ and $\{r1, r4, r5, r6, r7, r8\}$, respectively. It is important to understand that both concepts define a **rough set**, that is, *a set that is undefinable by given attributes*.

Boundary region: A boundary region contains those elements from the upper approximation of a concept X that are not elements of the lower approximation of X. For example, the boundary region for the concept $\{r2, r3, r6, r7\}$ is given by $\{r5, r6, r7, r8\}$.

Certainty and possibility: Rules derived from the lower approximation of a concept are certainly valid. Rules derived from the upper approximation of a concept are possibly valid. For example, for the concept $\{r2, r3, r6, r7\}$ the following rules can be established:

Certain Rule: If $A = 1$ then $Out = 1$, because $\{r2\}$ and $\{r3\}$ are subsets of the concept.

Possible Rule: If $A = 2$ then $Out = 1$, because records $r5$ and $r8$ contradict to this rule.

3   Genetic Engineering

DNA is a rather important molecule in nature, because it facilitates two significant functions (a) the coding of proteins, and (b) it self-replicates so that an exact copy is passed on to offspring cells. From a chemical perspective DNA is a polymer chain of monomers called deoxyribonucleotides, or simply *nucleotides*. Nucleotides are chemical compounds including a chemical base, a sugar, and a phosphate group. According to their base four nucleotides are distinguished, *Adenine (A)*, *Guanine (G)*, *Cytosine (C)* and *Thymine (T)*. Nucleotides can combine or bond in two ways. The result is either: *single stranded* DNA, or *double stranded* DNA. Single stranded DNA is generated through the subsequent bonding of any of the four types of nucleotides and is often illustrated as a string of letters (e.g., AGCCAAGTT). Double stranded DNA is generated from a single stranded DNA strand and its complementary strand. This type of bonding also follows a rule, the so-called *Watson-Crick Complementary*. This rule says that base A only bonds with base T, base G only with base C, and vice versa. For example, for the single stranded DNA strand AGCCAAGTT mentioned before Watson-Crick Complementary produces the complementary strand TCGGTTCAA. The resulting double stranded DNA is often illustrated in one picture as two parallel strands. For example, it might be illustrated as: $\frac{AGCCAAGTT}{TCGGTTCAA}$ (with the fraction line symbolizing bonding).

Advances in genetic engineering allow the manipulation and design of single stranded DNA, as well as double stranded DNA. These manipulations are usually mediated by a specific class of enzymes, and include processes such as lengthening, shortening, cutting, linking, and multiplying of DNA, for example [3]. DNA-computing is based on the processing of these molecules. Its power and interest is largely based on two features: (1) DNA strands allow parallel computation, and (2) Watson-Crick Complementary, which was mentioned before. Major contributions in the field come from Adleman and Lipton [1] [2].

4   DNA-Computing and Rough Set Analysis

So far information was encoded numerically in information tables. The previous discussion allows the consideration of substituting this numerical encoding by genetically engineered DNA single strands. For example, it is possible to substitute attribute $A = \{1, 2\}$ by $A = \{\text{AAATCG, AAAGCT}\}$. Table 4 below illustrates a possible substitution for attributes $A = \{1, 2\}$, $B = \{1, 2\}$, $C = \{1, 2, 3\}$, and $Out = \{1, 2\}$ from Table 1 and Table 3.

Table 4. Substitution of input and output attributes by DNA single strands

Attribute	1	2	3
A	AAATCG	AAAGCT	-
B	TTTTCG	TTTGCT	-
C	CCCTCG	CCCGCT	CCCACT
Out	GGGTCG	GGGGCT	-

On the bases of Table 4 it is now possible to replace information Table 1 with Table 5 below. Note that the record numbers in Table 5 are also DNA encoded.

From Table 5 it is only a small step forward to imagine the design of a single DNA molecule that contains the entire information of a single row in Table 5. For example, for the first record in Table 5 this molecule is given by: GGGAAAAAATCGTTTTCGCCCTCGGGGGCT. In the same fashion it is possible to generate a molecule for each record in Table 5. From now on this paper uses the term *DNA record* for any such molecule. Further, although the

Table 5. Alternative representation of information table Table 1, using DNA single strands instead of numerical values

Record	A	B	C	Out
GGGAAA	AAATCG	TTTTCG	CCCTCG	GGGGCT
GGGAAG	AAATCG	TTTTCG	CCCGCT	GGGTCG
GGGAGA	AAATCG	TTTTCG	CCCACT	GGGTCG
GGGAGG	AAAGCT	TTTTCG	CCCTCG	GGGGCT
GGGGAA	AAAGCT	TTTGCT	CCCGCT	GGGGCT
GGGGAG	AAAGCT	TTTTCG	CCCACT	GGGTCG

amplification of a small amount of a specific fragment of DNA is a problem of genetic engineering, there exists a technique called *polymerase chain reaction* that solves this problem. Even if it begins with only one strand of a DNA molecule this technique can produce a million of copies of a desired DNA molecule within a short period of time. It it possible then to imagine some sort of container with a large number of copies of genetically engineered DNA records in it. From now on such a container is referred to as a *tube*. For example, imagine a tube that contains a large number of copies of DNA records generated from Table 5.

In order to come closer to the desired goal, that is DNA based rough set analysis, it is necessary to introduce a few more operations on DNA strands. Note that these definitions are adopted from [3].

- **amplify:** Given a tube N, produce two copies of it.
- **detect:** Given a tube N, return *true* if N contains at least one DNA strand, otherwise return *false*.
- **merge:** Given tubes N_1 and N_2, this operation forms the union $N_1 \cup N_2$ of the two tubes.
- **separate** or **extract:** Given a tube N and a DNA strand w composed of nucleotides $m \in \{A, T, C, G\}$, produce two tubes $+(N, w)$, and $-(N, w)$, where $+(N, w)$ consists of all strands in N which contain w as a consecutive substring and similarly, $-(N, w)$ consists of all strands in N which do not contain w as a consecutive substring.
- **length-separate:** Given a tube N and an integer n, produce the tube $(N, \leq n)$ consisting of all strands in N with length less then of equal to n.

4.1 DNA Algorithms for Rough Set Analysis

The definitions given before can be viewed as elements of a programming language. The following sections employ this language in order to perform some of the rough set operations introduced in Section 2 on Table 5. To avoid difficulties that may arise from a notation that uses lengthy DNA single strands, the forthcoming sections use set theory notation when referring to particular attributes and attribute values. For example, the attributes in Table 1/Table 5 are represented as: $A = \{a_i \mid i \in I\}$, where $I = \{1, 2\}$, $B = \{b_j \mid j \in J\}$, where

$J = \{1, 2\}$, $C = \{c_k \mid k \in K\}$, where $K = \{1, 2, 3\}$, $Out = O = \{o_l \mid l \in L\}$, where $L = \{1, 2\}$. $Record = R = \{r_m \mid m \in M\}$, where $M = \{1, 2, 3, 4, 5, 6\}$.

DNA: Indiscernibility and indiscernibility relation: Algorithm-1 below is used to model these rough set constructs.

(1) *input(N)*
(2) *amplify(N)* to produce N_1 and N_2
(3) $+(N_1, a_1) \rightarrow N_{a_1}$
(4) $+(N_2, a_2) \rightarrow N_{a_2}$
(5) **for** $m = 1$ **to** 6 **do begin**
(6) $+(N_{a_1}, r_m) \rightarrow N_{r_m}$
(7)   *detect*(N_{r_m})
(8) $+(N_{a_2}, r_m) \rightarrow N'_{r_m}$
(9)   *detect*(N'_{r_m})
(10) **end**

Fig. 1. Algorithm-1.

Algorithm-1 starts in line one with tube N, which is full of DNA records generated from Table 5. In line two tube N is amplified (copied). This amplification produces two new tubes, N_1 and N_2. Line three produces tube N_{a_1} from tube N_1, and line four produces tube N_{a_2} from tube N_2. Note that in tube N_{a_1} are only DNA records that include the string $a_1 = $ AAATCG as a consecutive substring, and similarly, tube N_{a_2} contains only DNA records that include the string $a_2 = $ AAAGCT as a consecutive substring (see Table 4 and Table 5).

Line five to line ten use the index variable m in a for-loop. Note that lines six and seven, as well as lines eight and nine in this loop always form a unit. The outcome in line six depends on the value of the index variable m. For example, $m = 1$ produces tube N_{r_1} from tube N_{a_1}. Note that tube N_{r_1} only contains DNA records that include the strings $a_1 = $ AAATCG **and** $r_1 = $ GGGAAA as consecutive substrings. Further, if tube N_{r_m} in line seven is not empty then *detect*(N_{r_m}) = *true*, otherwise *detect*(N_{r_m}) = *false*. Table 1, Table 4 and Table 5 illustrate that in line seven *detect*(N_{r_m}) = *true* for $m = 1, 2$, and 3, but *detect*(N_{r_m}) = *false* for $m = 4, 5$, and 6. Since r_1, r_2, and r_3 stand for records *r1, r2* and *r3*, and a_1 stands for attribute $A = 1 = $ AAATCG, it is possible to conclude that, looking at attribute A only, records *r1, r2* and *r3* are **indiscernible** from each other. Similar reasoning identifies that in line nine *detect*(N'_{r_m}) = *true* for $m = 4, 5$, and 6, and *false* otherwise. This observation however allows the conclusion that, looking at attribute A only again, records *r4, r5* and *r6* are also indiscernible from each other. Further, remember from Section 2 that records that are indiscernible from each other with respect to particular attributes and attribute values define elementary sets. So, Algorithm-1 establishes the two elementary sets $\{r1, r2, r3\}$, and $\{r4, r5, r6\}$.

Algorithm-1 can be extended to analyse more than only one attribute. for example, Algorithm-2 presents such an extension, and processes all three attributes A, B, and C.

(1) $input(N)$
(2) **for** $i = 1$ **to** 2 **do begin**
(3) $amplify(N)$ to produce a copy N'
(4) $+(N', a_i) \rightarrow N'_{a_i}$
(5) **for** $j = 1$ **to** 2 **do begin**
(6) $+(N'_{a_i}, b_j) \rightarrow N'_{a_i, b_j}$
(7) **for** $k = 1$ **to** 3 **do begin**
(8) $+(N'_{a_i, b_j}, c_k) \rightarrow N'_{a_i, b_j, c_k}$
(9) **for** $m = 1$ **to** 6 **do begin**
(10) $+(N'_{a_i, b_j, c_k}, r_m) \rightarrow N'_{r_m}$
(11) $detect(N'_{r_m})$
(12) **end**
(13) **end**
(14) **end**
(15) **end**

Fig. 2. Algorithm-2.

Similar to Algorithm-1, Algorithm-2 starts with tube N, which is full of Table 5 DNA records, but then depicts four for-loops. The four loops basically perform an exhaustive search on the three variables A, B, and C, and the records $r1$ to $r6$. The first loop initially generates a copy of tube N. The successive utilisation of the *separate* operator throughout the four loops finally generates tube N'_{r_m} in line ten. Line eleven detects whether tube N'_{r_m} is empty or not. Going through Algorithm-2 one can find that it produces the six elementary sets $\{r1\}$, $\{r2\}$, $\{r3\}$, $\{r4\}$, $\{r5\}$, and $\{r6\}$, the result expected from Section 2. Note that although Algorithm-2 immediately indicates one problem, namely that of increasing computational expense for increasingly larger information tables, it also demonstrates the potential of performing such a task in principle.

DNA: Elementary sets: It was already mentioned that the outcome of Algorithm-1 and Algorithm-2 can be interpreted as constituting elementary sets (see Section 2), and so this section does not need further commenting.

DNA: Definable sets: According to Section 2 a definable set is a union of elementary sets. Algorithm-2 described before established the six elementary sets $\{r1\}$, $\{r2\}$, $\{r3\}$, $\{r4\}$, $\{r5\}$, and $\{r6\}$. The set $\{r1, r2\}$ generated by the union of the two elementary sets $\{r1\}$, and $\{r2\}$ therefore depicts a definable set. The operator *merge* introduced earlier can be applied to facilitate such a union in the DNA environment. For instance, take the two elementary sets $\{r1\}$, and $\{r2\}$ again. Algorithm-2 identifies and detects these elementary sets in line ten and line eleven. In particular, for $\{r1\}$ line ten reads $+(N'_{a_{i=1}, b_{j=1}, c_{k=1}}, r_{m=1}) \rightarrow N'_{r_1}$, and line eleven as $detect(N'_{r_1}) = true$. On the other hand, for $\{r2\}$ line ten and eleven read as $+(N'_{a_{i=1},b_{j=1},c_{k=2}}, r_{m=2}) \rightarrow N'_{r_2}$, and $detect(N'_{r_2}) = true$. Given that tubes N'_{r_1} and N'_{r_2} are available it is possible to produce the tube $N''_{r_{1,2}}$ via the operation $merge(N'_{r_1}, N'_{r_2}) \rightarrow N''_{r_{1,2}}$. Tube $N''_{r_{1,2}}$ is **definable**, because for any DNA record in it yields,

either: $a_{i=1}$ = AAATCG, $b_{j=1}$ = TTTTCG, $c_{k=1}$ = CCCTCG, and $r_{m=1}$ = GGGAAA, which is equivalent to $A = 1$, $B = 1$, $C = 1$, and record $R = 1$,

or: $a_{i=1}$ = AAATCG, $b_{j=1}$ = TTTTCG, $c_{k=2}$ = CCCGCT, and $r_{m=2}$ = GGG-AAG, which is equivalent to $A = 1$, $B = 1$, $C = 2$, and record $R = 2$ (see Table 1, and Table 5).

To conclude, it is possible to use the DNA operation *merge* to produce a tube that contains a definable content, that is definable DNA records. This is similar to the definition for definable sets given in Section 2, which was based on the union of elementary sets.

DNA: Redundant attributes: An analysis of Table 1 in Section 2 identi-fied the redundant attribute B, because the two attributes A, and C did describe the same six elementary sets ($\{r1\}$, $\{r2\}$, $\{r3\}$, $\{r4\}$, $\{r5\}$, and $\{r6\}$) as the three attributes A, B, and C did.

One way of identifying redundant attributes in the DNA environment illus-trated by Table 5 is to produce a new set of DNA records. Encoded in these DNA records are elementary sets as well as the attributes defining them. The opera-tor *length* introduced in Section 4 can then be used to detect the shortest DNA record. The shortest DNA record contains the smallest number of attributes defining the elementary set. For example, imagine that there are DNA records available containing information about elementary sets and the attributes de-scribing them. In order to do so, it is necessary to introduce the following at-tribute encoding: A = AAAAAA, B = TTTTTT, and C = CCCCCC. This allows the design of the DNA records illustrated in Figure 3, for instance.

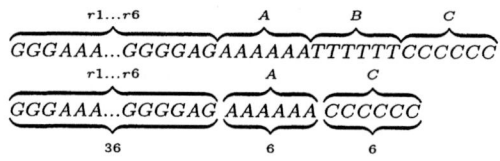

Fig. 3. DNA records representing elementary sets and their defining attributes.

Figure 3 illustrates that the encoding for the elementary sets $\{r1\}$ to $\{r6\}$ in each of the two DNA records is $6 * 6 = 36$ nucleotides long. Each of the three attributes A, B, or C adds another six nucleotides. Algorithm-3 takes advantage of this.

Algorithm-3 starts in line one with tube N, which contains a large number of copies of the DNA records illustrated in Figure 3. The for-loop uses the variable

(1) *input(N)*
(2) **for** $i = 1$ **to** 3 **do begin**
(3)   *length(N, $\leq 36 + 6*i$) $\rightarrow N_i$*
(4)   **if** *detect(N_i) = true* **then exit**
(5) **end**

Fig. 4. Algorithm-3.

i. Each iteration through the loop generates tube N_i in line three. The length of the DNA records in tube N_i depends on the value of the variable i in the *length* operation. For example, for $i = 1$ the length equals $36 + 6*1 = 42$ nucleotides, for $i = 2$ and $i = 3$ the strand lengths amount to 48 and 54 nucleotides, respectively. Line four exits the for-loop as soon as tube N_i is not empty, that is as soon as the operation *detect(N_i)* returns *true*. The DNA records illustrated in Figure 3 indicate that this is the case for $i = 2$. If Algorithm-3 runs through all iterations without the *detect* operation returning *true*, then there are no redundant attributes, otherwise there are redundant attributes.

DNA: Minimal sets: According to Section 2 a set of attributes containing no redundant attributes is called *minimal*. The outcome of Algorithm-3 is a tube containing DNA records with the possibly smallest number of attributes describing the elementary sets encoded in the DNA record. The set of attributes encoded in these DNA records therefore is *minimal*.

DNA: Reducts: Consider the two DNA records in Figure 3 and the definition for *reducts* given in Section 2 again. Both DNA records in Figure 3 describe the same elementary sets. They differ however in the number of attributes used to define these elementary sets. Further, Algorithm-3 established that the second DNA record in Figure 3 is *minimal*, and hence, is the *reduct* of the first DNA record in Figure 3.

DNA: Concepts: The concepts in Table 1 (Table 5) are elementary sets constructed on the bases of the single attribute *Out*. Since Algorithm-1 was used to establish elementary sets with respect to the single attribute A, an algorithm for the computation of the concepts in Table 5 can be derived from Algorithm-1 with only a few substitutions ($a_1 = o_1$, and $a_2 = o_2$). Algorithm-4 includes these substitutions, and, going through the algorithm, one can find that it produces the elementary sets $\{r1, r4, r5\}$, and $\{r2, r3, r6\}$ as expected from Section 2.

DNA: Inconsistency: The remaining rough set concepts are based on the reduced information Table 2 and the extended (inconsistent) information Table 3 in Section 2. Table 6 and Table 7 illustrate these two tables with the information DNA encoded.

Algorithm-5 is used to perform the task of identifying inconsistencies in Table 7. Algorithm-5 can be derived from Algorithm-2 with only a few modifications. The program code between line ten and line fifteen in Algorithm-5 actually indicates the significant modifications.

Similar to Algorithm-2, Algorithm-5 performs an exhaustive search through all attributes and records in Table 7. However, as soon as $detect(N'_{r_m}) = true$ in

(1) $input(N)$
(2) $amplify(N)$ to produce N_1 and N_2
(3) $+(N_1, o_1) \to N_{o_1}$
(4) $+(N_2, o_2) \to N_{o_2}$
(5) **for** $m = 1$ **to** 6 **do begin**
(6) $\quad +(N_{o_1}, r_m) \to N_{r_m}$
(7) $\quad detectN_{r_m}$
(8) $\quad +(N_{o_2}, r_m) \to N'_{r_m}$
(9) $\quad detectN'_{r_m}$
(10) **end**

Fig. 5. Algorithm-4.

Table 6. DNA representation of the reduced information Table 2

Record	A	C	Out
GGGAAA	AAATCG	CCCTCG	GGGGCT
GGGAAG	AAATCG	CCCGCT	GGGTCG
GGGAGA	AAATCG	CCCACT	GGGTCG
GGGAGG	AAAGCT	CCCTCG	GGGGCT
GGGGAA	AAAGCT	CCCGCT	GGGGCT
GGGGAG	AAAGCT	CCCACT	GGGTCG

line nine the program enters an if-then statement. Two new tubes are generated within this if-then statement, tube N'_{o_1}, and tube N'_{o_2}. If tube N'_{o_1} is not empty, then it contains only DNA records where the outcome $O = \text{GGGTCG} = 1$. Similarly, if tube N'_{o_2} is not empty, then it contains only DNA records where the outcome $O = \text{GGGGCT} = 2$. A situation where both tubes are not empty, that is in case $detect(N'_{o_1}) = detect(N'_{o_2}) = true$ indicates an **inconsistency**.

DNA: Upper approximation: Section 2 already identified the elementary sets and the concepts in Table 3. To repeat, the elementary sets defined by attribute A and C on Table 3 are $\{r1\}$, $\{r2\}$, $\{r3\}$, $\{r4\}$, $\{r5, r7\}$, and $\{r6, r8\}$, and the two concepts in the table are $\{r1, r4, r5, r8\}$, and $\{r2, r3, r6, r7\}$. By now, we assume that it is possible to establish the same results from Table 7 through the application of Algorithm-2, and Algorithm-4. Note that in order to achieve these results necessary modifications in the code of these algorithms are ignored at the moment. Further, imagine also the design of DNA records similar to those illustrated earlier in Figure 3. This time however the DNA records encode the elementary sets and the concepts mentioned before. Figure 7 illustrates these DNA records, and also uses a hyphen to distinguish individual DNA strands.

Figure 7 indicates that there are six DNA records describing elementary sets, and two DNA records for the concepts. Algorithm-6 is used to determine the upper approximation from these givens.

Table 7. DNA representation of the extended (inconsistent) information Table 3

Record	A	C	Out
GGGAAA	AAATCG	CCCTCG	GGGGCT
GGGAAG	AAATCG	CCCGCT	GGGTCG
GGGAGA	AAATCG	CCCACT	GGGTCG
GGGAGG	AAAGCT	CCCTCG	GGGGCT
GGGGAA	AAAGCT	CCCGCT	GGGGCT
GGGGAG	AAAGCT	CCCACT	GGGTCG
GGGGGA	AAAGCT	CCCGCT	GGGTCG
GGGGGG	AAAGCT	CCCACT	GGGGCT

Line one, two, and three provide Algorithm-6 with tubes N_e, N_c, and N. Tube N_e contains copies of **all** those DNA records that encode elementary sets in Figure 7. Tube N_c contains copies of **only one** of the concept DNA records in Figure 7, for example concept $\{r1, r4, r5, r8\}$. Tube N is **empty**. Algorithm-6 contains two for-loops, and each of the loops contains an if-then statement. Note that both for-loops go through the eight records in Table 7 and not through the six elementary sets in Figure 7.

Depending on the record in question, line five and six create tubes that are either empty or not empty. For example, for $i = 1$ tube N_{e,r_1} contains DNA records that include the coding for record $r1$, and hence also the coding for elementary set $\{r1\}$ as a consecutive substring. Tube N_{c,r_1} is not empty either and contains DNA records of the concept $\{r1, r4, r5, r8\}$, because the DNA strand for record $r1$ is contained as a substring in the DNA representation of this concept. On the other hand, for $i = 2$ tube N_{e,r_2} is not empty, but tube N_{c,r_2} is empty. This is because the DNA code for record $r2$ is a substring of the elementary set $\{r2\}$, but not a substring in the concept $\{r1, r4, r5, r8\}$.

The if-then statement in line seven uses the initially empty tube N. If tube N_{e,r_i} and tube N_{c,r_i} are not empty, then the content of tube N_{e,r_i} is merged with tube N, which generates tube N'. Line ten simply renames tube N' back to N.

What is the content of tube N after all iterations through the first for-loop? With the help of Table 7 and Figure 7 it is possible to extract that tube N contains the following elementary sets $\{\{r1\}, \{r4\}, \{r5, r7\}, \{r6, r8\}\}$, of course in the form of DNA records. The task of the second for-loop is relatively easy then. It goes through all records, if any of the records is in tube N, then tube N'_{r_i} is not empty, and the record belongs to the **upper approximation** $\{r1, r4, r5, r6, r7, r8\}$.

DNA: Lower approximation: According to Section 2 the lower approximation for a given concept X is defined by the smallest definable set in X. Section 2 determined that the lower approximations for the concepts $\{r1, r4, r5, r8\}$ and $\{r2, r3, r6, r7\}$ in Figure 7 are given by $\{r1, r4\}$, and $\{r2, r3\}$. Algorithm-7 aims to determine the lower approximation for the first concept $\{r1, r4, r5, r8\}$.

```
(1)  input(N)
(2)  for i = 1 to 2 do begin
(3)     amplify(N) to produce a copy N'
(4)     +(N', a_i) → N'_{a_i}
(5)     for k = 1 to 3 do begin
(6)        +(N'_{a_i}, c_k) → N'_{a_i,c_k}
(7)        for m = 1 to 8 do begin
(8)           +(N'_{a_i,c_k}, r_m) → N'_{r_m}
(9)           detect(N'_{r_m})
(10)          if detect(N'_{r_m}) = true then begin
(11)             +(N'_{r_m}, o_1) → N'_{o_1}
(12)             detect(N'_{o_1})
(13)             +(N'_{r_m}, o_2) → N'_{o_2}
(14)             detect(N'_{o_2})
(15)          end
(16)       end
(17)    end
(18) end
```

Fig. 6. Algorithm-5.

Algorithm-7 starts with tubes N_c, N_1, and N_2. Tube N_c contains copies of **only one** of the concept DNA records in Figure 7, for example concept {*r1, r4, r5, r8*}. Tube N_1 and tube N_2 are initially **empty**. Algorithm-7 contains three for-loops, and three if-then statements. Note that the first for-loop goes through the six elementary sets in Figure 7, whereas the second and the third loop run through the eight records in Table 7.

Line five introduces tube N_{e_i}, which contains copies of DNA records of **only one** of the six elementary sets in Figure 7. Line six enters the second for-loop. This loop uses the variable a, setting it to *true*. Line eight and line nine create new tubes on the bases of the DNA strand associated with record r_i.

elementary sets

{*r1*}	GGGAAA
{*r2*}	GGGAAG
{*r3*}	GGGAGA
{*r4*}	GGGAGG
{*r5, r7*}	GGGGAA-GGGGGA
{*r6, r8*}	GGGGAG-GGGGGG

concepts

{*r1, r4, r5, r8*}	GGGAAA-GGGAGG-GGGGAA-GGGGGG
{*r2, r3, r6, r7*}	GGGAAG-GGGAGA-GGGGAG-GGGGGA

Fig. 7. DNA records representing the elementary sets and the concepts extracted from Table 7.

(1) $input(N_e)$
(2) $input(N_c)$
(3) $input(N)$
(4) **for** $i = 1$ **to** 8 **do begin**
(5) $+(N_e, r_i) \rightarrow N_{e,r_i}$
(6) $+(N_c, r_i) \rightarrow N_{c,r_i}$
(7)   **if** $detect(N_{e,r_i}) = true$ **and**
(8) $detect(N_{c,r_i}) = true$ **then begin**
(9) $merge(N, N_{e,r_i}) \rightarrow N'$
(10) $N = N'$
(11)   **end**
(12) **end**
(13) **for** $j = 1$ **to** 8 **do begin**
(14) $+(N, r_i) \rightarrow N'_{r_i}$
(15)   **if** $detect(N'_{r_i}) = true$ **then begin**
(16)   {*record belongs to upper approximation*}
(17)   **end**
(18) **end**

Fig. 8. Algorithm-6.

Line ten to line sixteen contains an if-then statement. If any of the DNA records $r1$ to $r8$, is a substring of the current DNA encoded elementary set, but not an element of the DNA encoded concept, then the elementary set **is not** a subset of the concept. In this case the variable a is set to *false*, the for-loop is exited, and the next elementary set investigated. Note that the generated conclusion can be verified via the help of Figure 7 and Table 7.

On the other hand, if the variable a remains *true* throughout the second for-loop, then the elementary set **is** a subset of the concept, and the second if then statement in line eighteen comes into play. There are two processes in this statement. First, the initially empty tube N_1 is merged with tube N_{e_i} into tube N'_1, and second, tube N'_1 is renamed N_1.

What is the content of tube N_1 in the example, before Algorithm-7 enters the third for-loop in line twenty-five? With the help of Figure 7 and Table 7 again, it can be verified that the content are DNA records representing the two elementary sets $\{r1\}$ and $\{r4\}$.

The third for-loop finally identifies the records in tube N_1 via the detection of DNA strands, and establishes the final result, the **lower approximation** $\{r1,$ $r4\}$.

DNA: Boundary region: The boundary region contains those elements that are elements of the upper approximation, but not an element of the lower approximation. In the example the upper approximation is $\{r1, r4, r5, r6, r7, r8\}$ and the lower approximation $\{r1, r4\}$, which determines the boundary region $\{r5, r6, r7, r8\}$. The previous two sections demonstrated that it is possible to generate tubes for lower approximation and upper approximation. Algorithm-8 assumes the existence of such tubes.

(1) $input(N_c)$
(2) $input(N_1)$
(3) $input(N_2)$
(4) **for** $i = 1$ **to** 6 **do begin**
(5) $input(N_{e_i})$
(6)   **for** $j = 1$ **to** 8 **do begin**
(7) $a = true$
(8) $+(N_{e_i}, r_i) \rightarrow N_{e_i,r_i}$
(9) $+(N_c, r_i) \rightarrow N_{c,r_i}$
(10)   **if** $detect(N_{e_i,r_i}) = true$ **and**
(11) $detect(N_{c,r_i}) = false$ **then begin**
(12)   {*elementary set is not*
(13)   *a subset of the concept*}
(14) $a = false$
(15)   exit (second for-loop)
(16)   **end**
(17)   **end**
(18)   **if** $a = true$ **then begin**
(19)   {*elementary set is a*
(20)   *subset of the concept*}
(21) $merge(N_1, N_{e_i}) \rightarrow N_1'$
(22) $N_1 = N_1'$
(23)   **end**
(24) **end**
(25) **for** $i = 1$ **to** 8 **do begin**
(26) $+(N_1, r_i) \rightarrow N_2$
(27)   **if** $detect(N_2) = true$ **then begin**
(28)   {*record belongs to lower approximation*}
(29)   **end**
(30) **end**

Fig. 9. Algorithm-7.

Algorithm-8 starts with tubes N_u, and N_l. Tube N_u contains only copies of DNA records of the upper approximation, and tube N_l only copies of DNA records of the lower approximation. The for-loop runs through the eight records in Table 7. Tubes N_{u,r_i} and N_{l,r_i} are not empty in case tubes N_u, and N_l contain DNA strands of the form r_i. It can be extracted from the givens that if tube N_{u,r_i} is not empty, and tube N_{l,r_i} is empty, then the record encoded by r_i belongs to the **boundary region** {$r5, r6, r7, r8$}.

DNA: Certainty and possibility: A discussion about certainty and possibility would be similar to the discussion given in Section 2, and therefore is omitted here.

```
 (1) input(N_u)
 (2) input(N_l)
 (3) for i = 1 to 8 do begin
 (4)     +(N_u, r_i) → N_{u,r_i}
 (5)     +(N_l, r_i) → N_{l,r_i}
 (6)     if detect(N_{u,r_i}) = true and
 (7)        detect(N_{l,r_i}) = false then begin
 (8)        {record belongs to boundary region}
 (9)     end
(10) end
```

Fig. 10. Algorithm-8.

5   Discussion

The aim of the paper was to demonstrate that it is possible to perform operations that originate from rough set theory via DNA-computing algorithms. This aim was achieved and demonstrated on a simple information table. There are however a few problems and concerns, for example, engineering issues. The study was based on very idealistic assumptions. All genetic manipulations are expected to run error free. The encoding of DNA records was chosen more or less arbitrarily, and the problem of producing DNA strands for large information tables exists as well. There are also theoretical problems. For example, some of the algorithms perform an exhaustive search and so are computationally expensive. This is a known problem in rough set analysis too, but it may need further investigation. Also, the presented algorithms present ad hoc solutions, and it seems possible to solve one or the other problem more elegantly. For example, the program structure of some of the algorithms is not efficient, but can be improved by the use of recursive functions calls. Finally, and this may be a quite encouraging aspect, there is another potential source for improvement, namely DNA-computing and bio-technology themselves. Both sciences are relatively young, and so there may be developments in the future that provide new inside and approaches that may be useful for the problems investigated in this study.

References

1. Adleman L.M.: Molecular Computation of Solutions to Combinatorial Problems. Science **266** (November 1994) 1021–1024
2. Lipton J.L.: DNA Solution to Hard Computational Problems. Science **268** (April 1995) 542–545
3. Paun G., Rozenberg G., and Salomaa A.: DNA Computing – New Computing Paradigms. Springer-Verlag, Berlin Heidelberg New York (1998)
4. Pawlak Z., Grzymala-Busse J., Slowinski R., and Ziarco W.: Rough Sets. Communications of the ACM, Vol. 38 **11** (November 1995) 89–95
5. Watson J.D. and Crick F.H.C.: Molecular Structure of Nucleic Acids. Nature **171** (1953) 734–737

Input Selection and Rule Generation in Adaptive Neuro-fuzzy Inference System for Protein Structure Prediction

Yongxian Wang[1], Haiyan Chang[2], Zhenghua Wang[1], and Xiaomei Li[3]

[1] School of Computer, National University of Defense Technology
410073 Changsha, China
yongxian_wang@yahoo.com
[2] School of Life Science, Hunan Normal University
410081 Changsha, China
chang_haiyan@hotmail.com
[3] College of Command and Technology of Equipment
101416 Beijing, China
lxmcjh@sohu.com

Abstract. This work presents a method for input selection based on fuzzy clustering and for rule generation based on genetic algorithm (GA) in an adaptive neuro-fuzzy inference system (ANFIS) which is used for modeling protein secondary structure prediction. A two-phase process is employed in the model. In the first phase, the selection of number and position of the fuzzy sets of initial input variables can be determined by employing a fuzzy clustering algorithm; and in the second phase the more precise structural identification and optimal parameters of the rule-base of the ANFIS are achieved by an iterative GA updating algorithm. An experiment on three-state secondary structure prediction of protein is reported briefly and the performance of the proposed method is evaluated. The results indicate an improvement in design cycle and convergence to the optimal rule-base within a relatively short period of time, at the cost of little decrease in accuracy.

1 Introduction

In the literature, models for protein structure prediction are classified into two main categories [1]. The first class of methods, de novo or ab initio methods, predict the structure from sequence alone, without relying on similarity at the fold level between the target sequence and those of the known structures. The second class of protein structure prediction methods, including comparative modeling, artificial neural network (ANN), etc, rely on known structural information instead. In this class of method, many statistical models are developed in recent years. ANNs are applied for analysis of primary protein sequences and modeling structure prediction and classification [2,3,4]. The defect of this approach mainly lies in that the built model has no clear meaning which can be explained using domain related knowledge. Both the connection weights and the activation functions in ANNs can hardly expressed as the form of natural language which is easily understood by human.

J. Liu et al. (Eds.): IDEAL 2003, LNCS 2690, pp. 514–521, 2003.

Fuzzy set theory allows the use of linguistic concepts for representing quantitative values. Moreover, fuzzy systems can express the process of human reasoning by expressing relationships between concepts as rules. Several methods for the identification of fuzzy models have been reported in the literature ([5] among others). Adaptive neuro-fuzzy inference systems (ANFIS) is one of the most popular types of fuzzy neural networks, which combines the advantages of fuzzy system and neural network, in modeling non-linear control system [6]. However, ANFIS's inputs and rules must be preliminarily given by human experts before the learning process. For a real-world modeling problem, like protein structure prediction, it is common to have tens of potential inputs and more inference rules to the model under ANFIS construction. Without sufficient domain-related knowledge, it is hard to select inputs and to generate appropriate rules, except by using a trial-and-error method. To surmount these difficulties, the methods of selecting input variables and extracting fuzzy rules from original data have attracted many researchers to make efforts. [7] present a quick and straightforward way of input selection for ANFIS learning, and in [8], Sugeno and Yasukawa adopted a fuzzy clustering method, namely, fuzzy c-means, to identify the structure of a fuzzy model and extract the control rules by its input-output (I/O) data. In 1999, Fahn, Chin-Shyurng et al discussed a fuzzy rules generation method based on evolutionary algorithms (EA) and multilayer perceptions (MLP) [9].

In this paper, we propose a novel approach which has a two-phase processing, input selection phase and following fuzzy inference rule generation phase. A fuzzy clustering method is employed in the first phase to screen and choose appropriate indices in hundreds of physicochemical and biological properties of amino acids, and to select the inputs of the following generated rules. In the second phase, we use a method of optimization based on GAs, which result in a reasonable number of inference rules for training later.

This paper is organized with the following fashion. In the remainder of this section, we briefly introduce the concept of ANFIS and GA, while in Setc. 2 and Sect. 3 the method of input selection and rule generation in our model is described respectively. Application to the problems of protein secondary structure prediction and its experimental results are demonstrated in Sect. 4. Finally Sect. 5 gives concluding remarks.

1.1 ANFIS

The Sugeno neuro-fuzzy model was proposed in an effort to formalize a systematic approach to generating fuzzy rules from an input-output data set. A typical fuzzy rule in a Sugeno fuzzy model has the format

$$\text{If } x_1 \text{ is } A_1 \text{ and } x_2 \text{ is } A_2, \ldots, x_n \text{ is } A_n \text{ then } y = f(x_1, x_2, \ldots, x_n)$$

where x_is and y are input and output variables respectively, A_is are fuzzy sets in the antecedent, and f is a crisp function in the consequent.

To facilitate the learning of the model, Jang J.-S Roger proposed a five-layer network architecture to put the fuzzy interfence model into the framework of adaptive networks that can compute gradient vectors systematically. Fig. 1(a) illustrates graphically this reasoning mechanism, more details can be found in [7].

1.2   GAs

Genetic algorithms are search algorithms base on the mechanics of natural selection and natural genetics. Unlike many classical optimization techniques, genetic algorithms do not rely on computing local derivatives to guide the search process. GAs generally consist of three fundamental operators: reproduction, crossover and mutation. Given an optimization problem, GAs encode the parameters into finite bit strings, and then run iteratively using these three operators in a random way but based on the fitness function evolution to achieve the basic tasks. Readers may refer to [10] for more details about GAs.

GAs differ fundamentally from the conventional search techniques. For example, they (1) consider a population of points, not a single point, (2) use probabilistic rules to guide their search, no deterministic rules, (3) GAs include random elements, which help to avoid getting trapped in local minima, (4) Unlike many other optimization methods, GAs do not require derivative information and complete knowledge of the problem structure and parameters.

2   Input Selection

As mentioned earlier, a two-phase process is performed in modeling for protein structure prediction. As the first step, selecting the input variables of ANFIS is processed prior to generating fuzzy *if-then* rules. Because modeling such a problem involves tens of hundreds of potential inputs, and we need to have a way to quickly determine the priorities of these potential inputs and use them accordingly.

2.1   Feature Extraction and Training Data Selection

In the problem of protein secondary structure prediction, given a primary sequence of the target protein (i.e. the sequence of amino acid), we hope the final well-constructed model can assign a secondary structure type for each residue in the target sequence. In general, which secondary structure type should be assigned for a residue relies upon its position in the sequence, the types of neighbor residues and their physicochemical and biological properties.

The database AAindex (Amino Acid Index Database) is a collection of published indices of different physicochemical and biological properties of amino acids. Its AAindex1 section currently contains 494 indices [11]. A initial set containing 120 indices from AAindex database is carefully chosen by hand in our model, which covers the secondary structure propensities, the bias and hydrophobicity of every residue, and other physicochemical properties. A normal cluster analysis using the correlation coefficient as the distance between two indices results in a smaller set which only remains 32 indices. Those whose similarities are less than 0.85 are excluded such that only one representative index remains.

A followed normalization and fuzzification procedure is performed to make the range of each index lie in interval $[0, 1]$ and to make the modeling in a fuzzy style. We classify the domain of each normalized index into three fuzzy sets, denote "high", "midterm" and

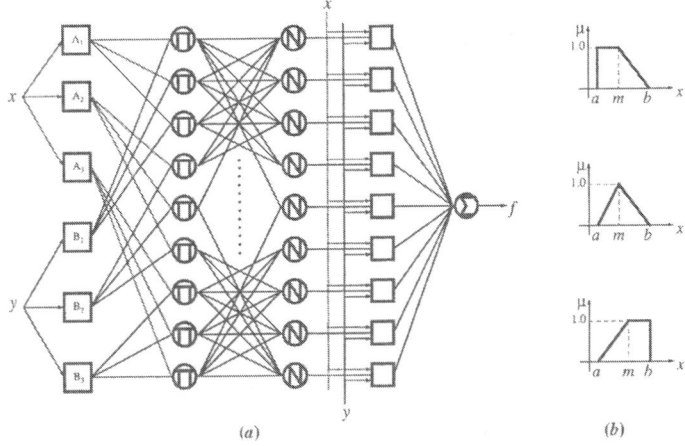

Fig. 1. ANFIS architecture and fuzzy sets. (a) ANFIS architecture of first-order Sugeno fuzzy model with 2-input, 1-output using grid partition of input space. (b) Membership functions of fuzzy sets used in our modeling protein secondary structure prediction, which describe "low", "medium" and "high", respectively.

"low" value, respectively. Three different membership functions are adopted illustrated as Fig. 1(b), each has three adjustable parameters to control its shape and range.

A high quality data set extracted from the Brookhaven Protein Data Bank (PDB) is used in our model [12]. We include entries which match the following:

– Those whose structure are determined by X-ray diffraction, since their high-quality in measure.
– Those program DSSP can produce an output which included in PDBFind database, since we want to use the PDBFind's assignment of protein secondary structure.
– The protein that physical chain has no break, in PDB, a minus sign ("-") indicates a break in the sequence of chain.
– Chains with a length of greater than 80 amino acids.

To avoid the disturbance of redundant information, a representative subset is selected from the extracted set of chains above, which contains entries included in PIR Non-Redundant Reference Protein Database (PIR-NREF) [13]. Furthermore, a smaller data subset consisting of 1000 distinct protein chains is picked out as train data and check data in our experiment described in Sect. 4.

2.2 Fuzzy Cluster Analysis of Inputs

The architecture of ANFIS used in our experiment takes as input a local N-mer (i.e. fixed-size window) of amino acids (the typical window width $N = 17$), centered around the residue for which the secondary structure is being predicted. This approach has been widely applied and proven to be quite successful in early work. However, we do not take directly the residues itself in the N-mer as the input variables, but as their certain attributes, thus more information is considered about the environment of the target residue. A problem in such a model is that the huge size of inputs will handicap the model construction and make the underlying model less concise and transparent.

For instance, if we use a 17-mer window, each residue has 32 attributes derived from selected indices mentioned earlier, then the total input of ANFIS will up to $17 \times 32 = 544$. Furthermore, if we employ an input-space grid partitioning and assign 3 fuzzy sets to each input in the following training phase, the number of candidate *if-then* rules will reach 3^{544} (an order of 10^{259}) ! It makes the training procedure painful, if not impossible.

A clustering strategy is used to overcome this problem. The candidate inputs are divided into groups and one or more representative members of each group may have the chance to entering the final input sets of our model under construction. Specifically, given a fixed number of groups, say, k, we use a fuzzy c-means clustering technique to fulfill this task. The method is as follow:

1. Chose the initial centers of k groups as their representative members. Firstly, we estimate the entropy of the joint distribution of each variable-pair (position in N-mer, attribute class) with respect to the appropriate type of secondary structure (for instance, α-helix, β-sheet, coil, etc) using a statistical method. Then we select k minimal values as the candidate centers of k groups.
2. Use standard fuzzy c-means clustering algorithm to divide the whole input-space into k subspace according to the initial centers chosen in the preceding step.
3. Depending on the complexity of modeling, one or more elements get the chance to enter the set of final inputs.

Virtually, if only one representative member is chosen from each group in step 3 described above, the better and more effective candidate member is the initial center of each group and as the result the fuzzy clustering in step 2 can be omitted.

3   Rule Generation

Generating fuzzy *if-then* inference rules based on GAs is the main task of second phase in modeling protein structure prediction. In [14] GAs are employed to optimize the fuzzy set and the shape and type of MFs, however, the conflict between the generated rules can occur during the iterative optimization procedure. Recently Yan Wu proposed a new similar method but the consequent of inference rule is restricted within a specific form. The method proposed here amends these drawbacks and optimize all the parameters and structures of the neuro-fuzzy system simultaneously. During the optimization the redundancy and conflict between temporarily generated rules can be cut off dynamically.

3.1   Encoding Method

Fig. 1(b) illustrates three types of MFs used in our model, each with three control parameters. The fuzzy *if-then* rule has the format described in Sect. 1.1 and the architecture of ANFIS has be shown in Fig. 1(a). The encoding of whole neuro-fuzzy system can be categorized two main parts, encoding fuzzy rules and encoding MFs of fuzzy sets.

For the convenience of the following process, we treat the 2-dimension input variable pair (position in N-mer, attribute class) of ANFIS as a flat one-dimension vector by rearranging it in a either row-first or column-first style. In the antecedent of each fuzzy rule, digit 1, 2 and 3 denote the fuzzy set "low", "medium" and "high", respectively, and a digit zero indicates the fuzzy set is non-existent. When consider the three class of secondary structure (i.e. α-helix, β-sheet and coil), they can be denoted by digit 1, 2 and 3, respectively. As an example, the rule " if x_1 is low and x_3 is high and x_4 is medium, then $y = p_0 + \sum_{i=1}^{4} p_i x_i$. " will encoding as digit string: "**1 0 3 2 1** p_0 p_1 p_2 p_3 p_4", where p_is are parameters in the consequent of rule encoding in a floating-point format.

Encoding the MFs of fuzzy sets concerns the centers of the MFs, the span of triangular MFs, the overlaps between two adjacent MFs, etc. All these parameters are encoded into decimal integer strings in the gene and each takes value in set $\{0, 1, 2, \ldots, 9, 10\}$.

3.2 Updating Rules

Let x be the variable to be concerned, $x \in [a, b]$, a dynamic interval. There are n fuzzy sets corresponding to variable x ranged on $[a, b]$. Initially the center of the i-th MF locates at

$$m_i = a + i * h \quad i = 1, 2, \ldots, n \qquad h = (b - a)/(n + 1).$$

During the iteration, the center of MF, the right-bottom corner of triangular MF, the factor of overlap of two adjective MFs and the left-bottom corner of triangular MF can be updated by (1)-(4), respectively:

$$m_i \leftarrow m_i + \omega * (c_j - 5), \tag{1}$$

$$b_i \leftarrow m_i + (m_{i+1} - m_i) \cdot (1 - c_j/10) + \Delta \tag{2}$$

$$\delta_{i,i+1} \leftarrow 0.3 + (1 - c_j/10) \cdot (0.8 - 0.3) \tag{3}$$

$$a_{i+1} \leftarrow b_i - (m_{i+1} - m_i) \cdot \delta_{i,i+1}/(1 - \delta_{i,i+1}) \tag{4}$$

where $i = 1, \ldots, n - 1$ and c_j denote the value of j-th gene in the chromosome, Δ and ω are some small adjustable variable ($\simeq 0.01$ in practice) as compensates for b_is and a_is respectively. The completeness of MFs in the system can be guaranteed [7].

Encoding of the whole neuro-fuzzy system can be expressed the concatenation of the two parts in a straight way. The common genetic operation can be applied in the GAs here. However, the crossover operation must be carefully processed to accord with the encoding characteristic here that every digit "bit" string must be limited in a fixed range predefined. To satisfy this requirement, given a pair of gene, a normalizing process takes precedence of the crossover operation to guarantee the gene value still in an appropriate range.

Moreover, the structure of neuro-fuzzy system can be optimized dynamically during the iteration. If the fitness increase very slowly in the optimization and updating the parameters takes little effect, then an additional fuzzy rule with random initial parameters will be added in the GAs.

We record the occurrence of activation for each rule in the learning and focus on zero-occurrence rules because they maybe have little use in the inference system and can be removed from rule set safely. However, those who have the same antecedent of rule but a different consequent should remain to improve the performance of the system.

4   Experiments and Results

The data set in our experiment is extracted as described in Sect. 2, the initial candidate inputs of ANFIS are organized into groups of 17-mer fragment of amino acid (a local window with width 17 residue). Each residue position is represented as 32 attributes which describe the physicochemical and biological properties of the corresponding amino acid. In the input selection phase, 50 inputs are chosen among 544 initial candidate inputs in the form of vector transformed from original two-dimension input matrix (row for position in 17-mer and column for index of residue). Even so there are still too many possible combinations in the set of rules if grid partitioning is employed in the input space. So in the following process, rule generation approach described in Sect.3 are applied. A cross-validation technique is employed in this process, wherein training data set include 900 entries derived from PDB as explained earlier and the remainder as the check data. We set the initial number of MFs for each input variable be 3 as shown in Fig. 1(b), and the number of rules be 100. After a time-consuming optimization iteration (500 epochs) as described in Sect. 3.2, the final model built contains 52 entries of inference rule. Defuzzification of the consequent of the resulting rule shows that nearly a half of the output is "α-helix" class.

Using such a model, a performance of MSE = 0.1028 for the train data and MSE = 0.0935 for the test data is obtained. The accuracy of the ensemble three-class prediction can up to 69.7%, more specifically, the accuracy of α-helix, β-sheet are 74.1% and 67.3%, and the performance is a little lower than that of model built earlier in our research group.

In another group of experiment we divided the problem into three sub-models, and each sub-model is used to predict only one class of protein secondary structure, that is, one for α-helix, another for β-sheet and the third for coil. The final result of prediction will be determined by outputs of three sub-model in a committee mechanism. However, the performance increases just a little more, 0.7% for α-helix and 1.3% for β-sheet.

5   Conclusions

This paper has described a method of structure identification and parameter optimization in an ANFIS. The main characteristics of the method is a two-phase processing technique, which includes the input selection phase based on fuzzy cluster and a rule generation approach based on GAs in the optimization of structure and parameters. An experiment on three-class secondary structure prediction of protein using this method is reported and the results indicate the method proposed has advantages of comprehensibility, high precision, good generalization and rapid convergence in rule generation. Compared with the traditional method of the same application, this method has a little decline of accuracy in prediction task. Future works include the use of a hybrid of gradient descent algorithms and the GAs for further optimization of parameters in consequent of *if-then* rules.

Acknowledgements. This work is supported partially by the National Natural Science Foundation of China (NSFC) under grant: 69933030.

References

1. Baker, D., Sali, A.: Protein structure prediction and structural genomics. Science **294** (2001) 93–96
2. Rost, B., Sander, C.: Improved prediction of protein secondary structure by use of sequence profiles and neural networks. Proceedings of the National Academy of Sciences of the USA **90** (1993) 7558–7562
3. Ding, C.H., Dubchak, I.: Multi-class protein fold recognition using support vector machines and neural networks. Bioinformatics **17** (2001) 349–358
4. Kaur, H., Raghava, G.: An evaluation of β-turn prediction methods. Bioinformatics **18** (2002) 1508–1514
5. Jang, J.S.R.: Neuro-fuzzy modeling for dynamic system identification. In: Fuzzy Systems Symposium, 1996. 'Soft Computing in Intelligent Systems and Information Processing'., Proceedings of the 1996 Asian. (1996) 320–325
6. Jang, J.S.R.: ANFIS: Adaptive-network-based fuzzy inference system. IEEE Transactions on Systems, Man and Cybernetics **23** (1993) 665–685
7. Jang, J.S.R., Sun, C.T., Mizutani, E.: Neuro-Fuzzy and Soft Computing: A Computational Approach to Learning and Machine Intelligence. Prentice Hall (1997)
8. Sugeno, M.; Yasukawa, T.: A fuzzy-logic-based approach to qualitative modeling. IEEE Transactions on Fuzzy Systems **1** (1993) 7–31
9. Fahn, C.S., Lan, K.T., Chern, Z.B.: Fuzzy rules generation using new evolutionary algorithms combined with multilayer perceptrons. IEEE Transactions on Industrial Electronics **46** (1999) 1103–1113
10. Michell, M.: An Introduction to Genetic Algorithms (Complex Adaptive Systems). MIT Press (1998)
11. Kawashima, S., Kanehisa, M.: AAindex: Amino acid index database. Nucleic Acids Research **28** (2000) 374
12. Berman, H., Westbrook, J., Feng, Z., Gilliland, G., Bhat, T., Weissig, H., Shindyalov, I., Bourne, P.: The protein data bank. Nucleic Acids Research **28** (2000) 235–242
13. Wu, C.H., Huang, H., Arminski, L., Castro-Alvear, J., Chen, Y., Hu, Z.Z., Ledley, R.S., Lewis, K.C., Mewes, H.W., Orcutt, B.C., Suzek, B.E., Tsugita, A., Vinayaka, C.R., Yeh, L.S.L., Zhang, J., Barker, W.C.: The protein information resource: an integrated public resource of functional annotation of proteins. Nucleic Acids Research **30** (2002) 35–37
14. Shi, Y., Eberhart, R., Chen, Y.: Implementation of evolutionary fuzzy systems. IEEE Transactions on Fuzzy Systems **7** (1999) 109–119

Quantification of Human Brain Metabolites from *In Vivo* ^{1}H NMR Magnitude Spectra Using Self-Organising Maps

Juhani Pulkkinen[1], Mika Lappalainen[2], Anna-Maija Häkkinen[3], Nina Lundbom[4], Risto A. Kauppinen[5], and Yrjö Hiltunen[6]

[1]Department of Biomedical NMR, A. I. Virtanen Institute, University of Kuopio, Finland
juhani.pulkkinen@uku.fi
http://www.uku.fi
[2] Pehr Brahe Software Laboratory, University of Oulu, Finland
mika.lappalainen@ratol.fi
http://www.pbol.org
[3]Department of Oncology, Helsinki University Hospital, Finland
Anna-Maija.Hakkinen@hus.fi
http://www.hus.fi
[4]Department of Radiology, Helsinki University Hospital, Finland,
Nina.Lundbom@hus.fi
http://www.hus.fi
[5]School of Biological Sciences, University of Manchester, England
Risto.Kauppinen@man.ac.uk
http://www.man.ac.uk
[6]Oulu Polytechnic, Raahe Institute of Computer Engineering and Business, P.O. Box 82,
FIN-92101 Raahe, Finland
yrjo.hiltunen@ratol.fi
http://www.oamk.fi/ratoli

Abstract. The self-organising map (SOM) analysis has been successfully applied in many fields of research and it is a potential tool also for analysis of magnetic resonance spectroscopy (MRS) data. In this paper we demonstrate that SOM-based analysis, can be applied for automated MRS data quantification. To this end, a set of experimental long echo time (TE=270 ms) *in vivo* ^{1}H MRS spectra were initially analysed by the lineshape fitting (LF) method to find out simulated spectra mathing to the experimental data. The results from simulated data sets show that clinically relevant metabolite quantification from human brain MRS can be obtained with the SOM analysis.

1 Introduction

A trend from single-volume ^{1}H MRS to multi-volume magnetic resonance spectroscopic imaging (^{1}H MRSI), producing several hundreds of spectra in each study, is underway. *In vivo* proton magnetic resonance spectroscopy (^{1}H MRS) [1] has proven unique potential as a non-invasive tool for both experimental and clinical neurochemistry [2-3]. For spectroscopic imaging manual spectral analysis is very time-consuming and therefore automated analysis without need for extensive spectroscopic expertise is expected to facilitate the use of spectroscopic data in clinical decision-making [4-11].

J. Liu et al. (Eds.): IDEAL 2003, LNCS 2690, pp. 522–529, 2003.
© Springer-Verlag Berlin Heidelberg 2003

Recent studies have shown that artificial neural network (ANN)-aided methods can provide efficient and highly automated alternative means for MRS data analysis [7-11]. In particular, clinical studies using standardised protocols are most likely to benefit from automated ANN analyses [12].

Training of ANNs can be accomplished either in a supervised or an unsupervised manner. A general problem related to the application of supervised ANN analysis in classification is that the classes need to be specified by the user *a priori*. A good understanding of the system is essential for this kind of approach and still some bias may be introduced via the pre-specified classes. The use of unsupervised ANN analysis would avoid bias and can thus provide a way of classification that is independent on *a priori* knowledge.

Here, we apply self-organizing maps (SOM) to the analysis of *in vivo* ^{1}H MR brain tumour spectra. In the study we have included some features of the supervised approach in the designed unsupervised method.

2 Methods

2.1 *In Vivo* ^{1}H NMR Spectroscopy

Our ^{1}H MRSI data set consisted of 191 spectroscopic images from 14 healthy controls and 71 glioma patients. ^{1}H MRSI measurements were performed in a 1.5 T MR scanner (Magnetom Vision, Siemens, Erlangen, Germany) using a standard circularly polarized head coil. For MRSI localization, 2D FLASH images in 3 orientations were acquired. A double spin echo sequence with 16 x 16 phase encoding steps was used with TR = 2600 ms and TE = 270 ms with 2 scans per phase encode with water suppression and a rectangular field of view of 160 mm^2. Volume pre-selection of 80/100x80/100x15 mm^3 with nominal voxel size 1.5 cm^3 was used including the tumour area. Spectral data were collected from one or two 15 mm thick slices covering the tumour volume as judged from the localizer MR images.

2.2 Data Processing and Lineshape Fitting Analysis of Experimental *In Vivo* Spectra

In order to remove the residual water signal from the experimental spectra, the Hankel Lanczos singular value decomposition [13] method was applied. Both real and imaginary parts were used for conversion of spectroscopic data into the magnitude mode. Fig. 1 shows some examples of experimental human brain proton spectra illustrating intensity variations in the spectral components.

The experimental magnitude spectra were analysed in the frequency domain by means of an automated analysis program (MRSTools Ltd, Kuopio, Finland) under a Matlab-software platform (Mathworks, Natick, MA, USA). The linewidths were constrained to be equal, because this approach has been shown to be more accurate especially for spectra with low signal-to-noise ratio [8].

2.3 Simulation of the Spectra

A total of 2500 long echo-time *in vivo* NMR magnitude spectra were simulated using Lorentzian lineshapes and varying frequencies, intensities, as well as half linewidths of three detectable metabolites, i.e. choline-containing compounds (Cho), creatine + phosphocreatine (Cr) and N-acetylaspartate (NAA). The complex spectrum can be written in the form of

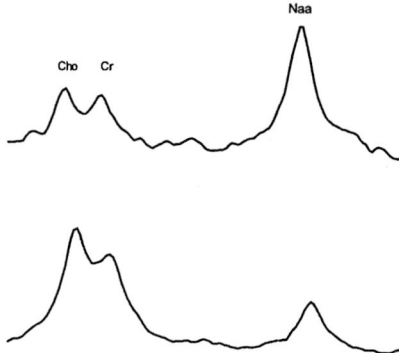

Fig. 1. Two *in vivo* ^{1}H MR spectra of human brain. (Cho) the choline-containing compounds, (Cr) creatine and phosphocreatine, and (NAA) N-acetyl aspartate.

$$F(v) = \text{Re}(v) + i \, \text{Im}(v) = |F(v)| \, e^{\, i\phi(v)}, \qquad (1)$$

where

$$|F(v)| = \left[\text{Re}^2(v) + \text{Im}^2(v) \right]^{1/2} \qquad (2)$$

and

$$\phi(v) = \tan^{-1}\left[\text{Im}(v) / \text{Re}(v) \right] \qquad (3)$$

$|F(v)|$ refers to the magnitude spectra and $\phi(v)$ to the phase angle. The following equations were used to calculate the real (Re) and imaginary part (Im) of the simulated spectra:

$$\text{Re}(v) = \sum_{i=1}^{3} ABS_i(v) = \sum_{i=1}^{3} \frac{a_i{}^2 I_i}{a_i{}^2 + 4(v - v_i)^2}, \qquad (4)$$

$$\text{Im}(v) = \sum_{i=1}^{3} DISP_i(v) = \sum_{i=1}^{3} \frac{2a_i I_i (v - v_i)}{a_i{}^2 + 4(v - v_i)^2}, \qquad (5)$$

in which a_i is the half linewidth, I_i the signal intensity, and v_i the resonance frequency. $ABS_i(v)$ stands for absorption and $DISP_i(v)$ for dispersion part of the Lorentzian i. To mimic the genuine *in vivo* spectra noise at a similar level as in experimental spectra was added. The half linewidths in each spectrum were the same for signals at the resonance frequencies of Cho, Cr, and NAA. Variations of parameters used in computations of simulated spectra are shown in Table 1. The simulated spectra agree with the experimental spectra except that the correct peak areas are known. Eq. (2) was used to form the magnitude spectra data sets for the SOM analysis.

Peak areas for the resonances, i.e. the actual outputs (A_i), were calculated using the equation as follows:

$$A_i = \frac{\pi}{2} a_i I_i \cdot \tag{6}$$

Table 1. Parameter variations of the data sets.

Data set	a^a	n^b	P_L	S/N_{Cho}	S/N_{Cr}	S/N_{NAA}
Experimental set	3.0-18.0	6623	± 1	0.0-34.4	0.0-26.8	0.2-40.6
Training set	3.1-14.4	1500	± 1	0.4-29.6	0.0-21.3	0.5-33.3
Test set	3.0-15.3	1000	± 1	0.6-25.6	0.3-18.3	0.5-29.1

[a] a is the half linewidth (in Hz).
[b] n is the number of spectra.
[c] P_L is the error estimate of frequency of the peaks (in Hz).
[d] S/N is the signal-to-noise ratio (intensity of signal/ standard deviation of noise).

2.4 SOM Analysis

SOM can be used to map n-dimensional input vectors to the neurons in a two-dimensional array, where the input vectors sharing common features end up on the same or neighbouring neurons [14]. This preserves the topological order of the original input data. The map reflects variations in the statistics of the data sets and to select good features to approximate the distribution of the data points. Each neuron is associated with an n-dimensional reference vector, which provides a link between the output and input spaces. The lattice type of array of neurons, i.e. the map, can be taken as rectangular, hexagonal, or even irregular. However, hexagonal organization is often suggested, as it best presents the connections between neighbouring neurons. The size of the map as defined by the number of neurons can be freely varied depending on the application; the more neurons the more details appear.

The SOM analysis includes an unsupervised learning process. First, random values for the initial reference vectors are sampled from an even distribution, where the limits are determined by the input data. During the learning, the input data vector is mapped onto a given neuron based on minimal n-dimensional distance between the input vector and the reference vectors of the neurons. The neighbours of the central activated neuron are also activated according to a network-topology-dependent neighbourhood function, a Gaussian function. The common procedure is to use an initially wide function, which is subsequently reduced in width during the learning to the level of individual neurons. Reference vectors of activated neurons will become updated after this procedure. This procedure features a local smoothing effect on the reference vectors of neighbouring neurons leading eventually to a global ordering [14].

The simulated human brain ^{1}H NMR spectral data set (n=2500) was divided into two subsets. The first subset (1500 spectra) was the training set, which was used for computing the reference vectors of the map. The other subset (1000 spectra) was the test set. 130 data points of each spectrum and 3 signal areas were used as an input for the SOM in training phase. The spectrum used in computations included chemical shift regions corresponding to Cho, Cr and NAA resonances. In the test phase signal areas were missing values, i.e. best matching neurons for the test sets were sought using only those 130 spectral points specified above. Predicted values for signal areas were obtained from the reference vectors of neurons.

The intensity of each frequency point in each spectrum was first divided by the maximum intensity of all spectra. Signal areas were scaled using variances of peak areas. Several SOMs were constructed for the analysis consisting of from 4 to 900 neurons in a hexagonal arrangement. A Gaussian function was used as a neighbourhood function and the learning rate was chosen to decrease linearly as a function of time. The maps were taught with 1000 epochs and the initial neighbourhood was at 3. The SOM Toolbox program (Version 2.0beta) was used in the training of the maps.

3 Results and Discussion

Experimental *in vivo* ^{1}H NMR magnitude spectra (n=6623) were analysed by the LF method so that the spectral qualities, as depicted by signal-to-noise ratio and linewidths, matched those in the simulated spectra. Simulated spectra (n=1000) of the test set were also quantified by the LF method yielding correlation coefficients with the actual output values of 0.986, 0.983, and 0.998 for Cho, Cr and NAA, respectively.

The SOM method was also investigated by training a self-organising map with 1500 simulated ^{1}H MR spectra and using the test spectra (n=1000) for validation of the maps. Fig. 2 shows the results for the test set using different numbers of neurons in the SOM analysis. These results illustrate that the SOM with 400 neurons gives results, which are almost identical to those obtained by a SOM with 900 neurons.

The SOM is a very robust algorithm as compared to many other neural network models [14], especially in the case of missing data of input vectors. Therefore we tested this feature leaving out different numbers of data points mimicking thus a missing value procedure. The results of these analyses are shown in Fig. 3.

The automated analysis methods should be able to deal with the low signal-to-noise ratio quite commonly associated with *in vivo* spectroscopic measurement. We investigated the effect of signal-to-noise ratio by varying the amplitude of noise, but keeping the signal areas constant in our data sets. The results are shown in Fig. 4 (a), where the correlation coefficients between the actual and SOM values are shown as a function of amplitude of noise. These data sets were also analysed using the LF method (Fig. 4 b).

For MRSI to become more widely used for clinical investigations, data processing methods need to become user-friendly. Automated methods are required that enable timely analysis of large numbers of spectra and that are robust to the low signal-to-noise. However, several automated spectral analysis methods have been proposed [4-11], it appears that the SOM-based method described here provides a new tool for spectral quantification. We have shown that this technique is robust in the presence of low signal-to-noise ratio. It should be noted, however, that the results in Fig. 4 strongly argue that the LF method is more difficult to use in the automated manner. Because our SOM method is also non-sensitive for the presence of missing values, it can be easily used for spectral analyses with different numbers of data points. Furthermore, SOM analysis does not require extensive knowledge of neural nets and it can be easily included in any kind of analysis software. An attractive property of SOM is also that it can be retrained, if new types of spectra are to be analysed.

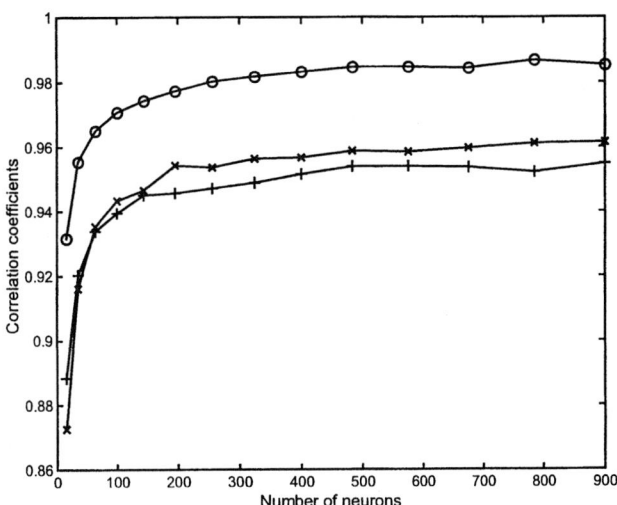

Fig. 2. The correlation coefficients between the actual and SOM method values for the human brain metabolites as a function of number of neurons. Symbols are as follows, Cho (x), Cr (+), NAA (o).

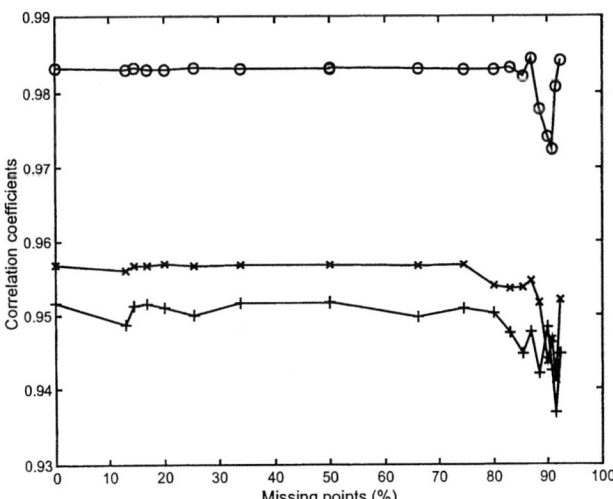

Fig. 3. The correlation coefficients between the actual and SOM method values for the human brain metabolites as a function of number of missing points. Symbols are as in Fig. 2.

4   Conclusion

The present results suggest that application of SOM can be extended to the automated quantification of human brain ^{1}H MR spectra. By doing so it is expected to play a significant role in biomedical MRS data analysis. It is feasible to construct a fully automated real-time quantifying analyser for long TE *in vivo* ^{1}H NMR spectra using this kind of method.

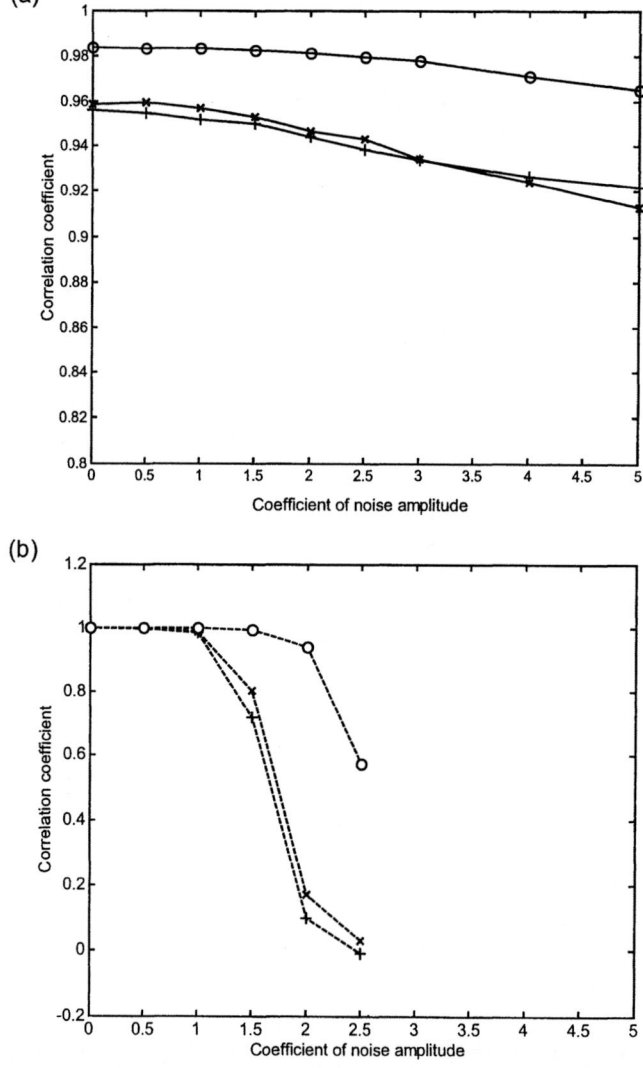

Fig. 4. The correlation coefficients between the actual and SOM (a) or LF (b) method values for the human brain metabolites as a function of noise. The symbols are as in Fig. 2.

Acknowledgments. This study was supported by the Academy of Finland, The Special Federal Grant no. TYH8224 of Helsinki University Central Hospital, the Magnus Ehrnrooth Foundation, the Alfred Kordelin Foundation.

References

1. Pfeuffer, J., Tkac, I., Provencher, S. W., Gruetter, R.: Toward an *in vivo* neurochemical profile: quantification of 18 metabolites in short-echo-time ^{1}H NMR spectra of the rat brain. J. Magn. Reson. **141** (1999) 104–120

2. Shulman, R.G., Rothman, D.L., Blamire, A.M.: NMR studies of human brain function. Trends Biochem. Sci. **19** (1994) 522–526

3. Hakumäki, J.M., Ala-Korpela, M., Kauppinen, R.A.: ^{1}H nuclear magnetic resonance spectroscopy: noninvasive neurochemistry for basic research and clinical applications. Curr. Top. Neurochem. **1** (1997) 59–85

4. Soher, B. J., Young, K., Govindaraju, V., Maudsley, A. A.: Automated spectral analysis. III. Application to in vivo proton MR spectroscopy and spectroscopic. Magn. Reson. Med. **40** (1998) 822–831

5. Zang, X., Heberlein, K., Sarkar, S., Hu, X.: A multiscale approach for analyzing in vivo spectroscopic imaging data. Magn. Reson. Med. **43** (2000) 331–334

6. Tate, A.R., Majos, C., Moreno, A., Howe, F.A., Griffiths, J.R., Arus, C.: Automated Classification of Short Echo Time in In Vivo ^{1}H Brain Tumor Spectra. Magn. Reson. Med. 49 (2003) 29–36

7. Usenius, J.-P., Tuohimetsä, S., Vainio, P., Ala-Korpela, M., Hiltunen, Y., and Kauppinen, R.: Automatic Classification of Human Brain Tumours by Neural Network Analysis Using In Vivo ^{1}H Magnetic Resonance Spectroscopic Metabolite Phenotypes. NeuroReport **7** (1996) 1597–1600

8. Kaartinen, J.; Hiltunen, Y.; Kovanen, P. T., Ala-Korpela, M: Classification of Human Blood Plasma Lipid Abnormalities by ^{1}H Magnetic Resonance Spectroscopy and Self-Organizing Maps. NMR Biomed. **11** (1998) 168–176

9. Kaartinen, J., Mierisova, S., Oja, J. M., Usenius, J.-P., Kauppinen, R. A., Hiltunen, Y.: Automated quantification of human brain metabolites by artificial neural network analysis from in vivo single-voxel ^{1}H NMR spectra. J. Magn. Reson. **134** (1998) 176–179

10. Hiltunen, Y., Kaartinen, J., Pulkkinen, J., Häkkinen, A.M., Lundbom, N., Kauppinen, R.: Quantification of Human Brain Metabolites from In vivo ^{1}H NMR Magnitude Spectra Using Automated Artificial Neural Network Analysis. J. Magn. Reson. **154** (2002) 1–5

11. Pulkkinen, J., Lappalainen, M., Häkkinen, A.-M., Lundbom, N., Kauppinen, R.A., Hiltunen, Y.: Automated Chemical Shift Correction of In Vivo ^{1}H NMR Spectra Using Self-Organizing Maps. Lecture Notes in Computer Science, Vol. 2412. Springer-Verlag, Berlin Heidelberg New York (2002) 423–428

12. Lisboa, P.J.G.: A review of evidence of health benefit from artificial neural networks in medical intervention. Neural Network **15** (2002) 11–39

13. Pijnappel, W.W.F., van den Boogaart, A., de Beer, R., van Ormondt, D.: SVD-based quantification of magnetic resonance signals. J. Magn. Reson. **97** (1992) 122–134

14. Kohonen, T.: *Self-organizing Maps*; Springer-Verlag, Berlin Heidelberg New York, (2001)

Probability Model Type Sufficiency

Leigh J. Fitzgibbon, Lloyd Allison, and Joshua W. Comley

School of Computer Science and Software Engineering
Monash University, Victoria 3800, Australia
{leighf,lloyd,joshc}@bruce.csse.monash.edu.au

Abstract. We investigate the role of sufficient statistics in generalized probabilistic data mining and machine learning software frameworks. Some issues involved in the specification of a statistical model type are discussed and we show that it is beneficial to explicitly include a sufficient statistic and functions for its manipulation in the model type's specification. Instances of such types can then be used by generalized learning algorithms while maintaining optimal learning time complexity. Examples are given for problems such as incremental learning and data partitioning problems (e.g. change-point problems, decision trees and mixture models).

1 Introduction

The formal specification of a statistical model type is an important ingredient of machine learning software frameworks [1]. In the interests of software reuse, robustness, and applicability the model type should encompass a general notion of a statistical model, and allow generalized machine learning algorithms to operate using any valid model type while still maintaining optimal time complexity. The model type should encourage and facilitate the decoupling of learning algorithms from the statistical models that they operate over, allowing the two to be plugged together as required depending on the problem and data involved. An intuitive example is that of a generalized decision tree algorithm that can operate with any valid model type in the leaves.

Sufficient statistics play an important role in reducing the time complexity of many machine learning algorithms. In this paper we investigate how the explicit inclusion of sufficient statistics in a model type allows machine learning algorithms to be generalized while maintaining optimal time complexity.

Code examples are given in the Haskell [4] programming language using a fixed width font. Footnotes are used to explain some of the semantics of the Haskell code.

J. Liu et al. (Eds.): IDEAL 2003, LNCS 2690, pp. 530–534, 2003.

2   A Basic Model Type

In this section we define the basic requirements for a model type that can be used for inference or learning. To perform probabilistic learning we need either the log-probability density/distribution function[1]:

```
lpr :: theta -> x -> Double
```

or the log-likelihood function[2]:

```
ll :: [x] -> theta -> Double
```

Since these can be derived from one another, having either the log-likelihood or log-probability function would allow one to do likelihood based inference. However, we are also interested in the time complexity of the basic model type and the implications this model type has on a system that is built around such a type. Note the difference in the order that the parameters are given in the two (curried) functions. The log-likelihood function requires the data-set as its first parameter, whereas the log-probability function requires the model parameters as the first parameter. This is because the log-likelihood function by definition is used for calculating *the log-likelihood of the parameters* whereas the probability function is used to calculate *the log-probability of the data*. These are conceptually two very different things. The log-likelihood function will be evaluated for different values of theta (e.g. numerical integration of parameters; simulation; optimisation - maximum likelihood, maximum posterior, minimum message length [7], minimum description length [6]), whereas we will generally evaluate the log-probability function for varied values of the data (e.g. numerical integration; optimisation - mode; moments; numerical entropy).

The log-likelihood function is used for inference, and if time complexity is of any importance then it needs to evaluate efficiently since it will be called frequently. Therefore the order of the parameters is important, the data must come first, for which a [minimal] sufficient statistic can be computed and stored, then the log-likelihood can be evaluated in optimal time for each call. It follows that a basic model type that explicitly includes sufficient statistics requires at least the following functions:

```
data ModelType x theta s = Model {
  lpr :: theta -> x -> Double,
  ss :: [x] -> s,
  ll :: s -> theta -> Double
}
```

---

[1] I.e. a function that given an element from the parameter space, and an element from the dataspace, returns the log-probability of the data element given the parameter.

[2] I.e. a function that given a vector of elements from the dataspace, and an element from the parameter space, returns the log-probability of the data elements given the parameter.

where ss is a function for computing the sufficient statistic for a given data-set.

There are many other operations that could be built into the model type. There are also important functions that are clearly distinct from model types yet are related. For example an estimator function with type:

```
type Estimator theta s = s -> theta
```

In the following sections we will show that having sufficient statistics as an explicit part of the model type allows for efficient implementations of a large class of popular algorithms.

3   Incremental Learning

Assume we initially observe some data x_1 and then estimate the model parameters according to some criterion (e.g. maximum likelihood). We might then observe more data, x_2, which is assumed to come from the same distribution. We then wish to revise our parameter estimate in light of the new data. We therefore wish to update the sufficient statistic to take into account the new data. The type of such a function would be:

```
type AddSs x s = s -> [x] -> s
```

Once the sufficient statistic has been update we can evaluate the likelihood function in best case time for the given sufficient statistic. If minimal sufficient statistics are used then these will typically be in the order of the dimension of the number of parameters being estimated.

More generally, we observe M data-sets incrementally $\{x_i : i = 1..M\}$ for which we make M estimates $\{\theta_i : i = 1..M\}$. Let the length of data-set x_i be denoted by N_i. We wish to estimate the parameters, θ_i, for each x_i using a known estimator function. Based on the data types defined so far we can describe the type of this incremental learning function (incLearn):

```
incLearn :: [[x]] -> (ModelType x theta s) ->
            (Estimator theta s) -> (AddSs x s) -> [theta]
```

which returns the vector of inferred parameters.

The incLearn function is able to perform incremental learning for any model type in optimal time[3].

4   Learning Models That Partition the Data

A large class of useful and popular inference algorithms partition the data-set into a pairwise disjoint set. Examples are change-point, decision tree, and mixture model algorithms. These algorithms can be efficiently implemented by storing a sufficient statistic for each subset and then updating the statistic as the subsets change (i.e. as data is added and removed). So as well as the AddSs function defined in the previous section, we also require a RemoveSs function:

---

[3] We ignore the function call overhead in the implementation language.

```
type RemoveSs x s = s -> [x] -> s
```

which allows for the removal of a set of data from a sufficient statistic.

Change-Point Algorithms. Change-point algorithms are quite common and can be found as the building blocks of more complex algorithms (e.g. decision trees). There are many algorithms for change-point problems that benefit from sufficient statistics. One example is the approximate binary search algorithm where the optimal location for a single change-point is found and then this is repeated recursively on each segment until some stopping criterion is reached. Another example is the dynamic programming algorithm (see e.g. [3]) which can identify the optimal change-point locations.

Using the types defined so far, a multiple change-point algorithm could be implemented that operates with arbitrary models in the segments. The algorithm could achieve optimal time complexity using the AddSs and RemoveSs functions.

Mixture Modelling. There is some research into versions of the EM algorithm that do not require all of the data to be visited. For these algorithms the use of sufficient statistics can improve the algorithm's time complexity. One example can be found in [5] where k-d trees and sufficient statistics are used to improve the time complexity of the algorithm for a specified class of distributions.

5   Revised Model Type

Given that incremental learning is a generic operation, and that data partitioning algorithms are extremely common one may consider including the update functions (addSs and removeSs) in the model type. There appears to be no downside to the inclusion of these functions in the model type especially since the data itself is a sufficient statistic and therefore a default implementation could simply manipulate the data. The Haskell code for the revised model type becomes:

```
data ModelType x theta s = Model {
  lpr :: theta -> x -> Double,
  ss :: [x] -> s,
  ll :: s -> theta -> Double,
  addSs :: s -> [x] -> s,
  removeSs :: s -> [x] -> s
}
```

For a large class of distributions (e.g. the Exponential Family [2]) the addSs and removeSs functions will be trivial, only involving addition and subtraction.

6 Parallelism

In probabilistic machine learning algorithms the likelihood function is the major (if not the only) link to the data. Through use of sufficient statistics we replace the high-dimensional data with a possibly low dimension sufficient statistic. If the algorithm is parallelised then the low dimensional sufficient statistic need only be transmitted between processors (instead of the data) thus reducing communication time as well as improving time complexity (over transmission and inference using the raw data). The revised model type defined in the previous section facilitates the use of sufficient statistics in generalized parallel algorithms.

7 Conclusion

We have investigated the explicit use of sufficient statistics in the definition of a statistical model type for machine learning software frameworks. A model type was defined and several examples explored in the functional language Haskell. The type explicitly includes a sufficient statistic which allows for the implementation of a class of generalized machine learning algorithms that have optimal time complexity.

References

1. L. Allison. Types and classes of machine learning and data mining. In M. Oudshoorn, editor, *Proceedings of the Twenty-Sixth Australasian Computer Science Conference*, volume 16, pages 207–215, February 2003.
2. J. M. Bernardo and A. F. M. Smith. *Bayesian Theory*. Wiley Series in Probability and Mathematical Statistics. John Wiley and Sons, Chichester, 1994.
3. L. J. Fitzgibbon, L. Allison, and D. L. Dowe. Minimum message length grouping of ordered data. In H. Arimura and S. Jain, editors, *Proceedings of the Eleventh International Conference on Algorithmic Learning Theory (ALT2000)*, volume 1968 of *Lecture Notes in Artificial Intelligence*, pages 56–70, Berlin, 2000. Springer-Verlag.
4. P. Hudak and J. H. Fasel. A gentle introduction to Haskell. *SIGPLAN Notices*, 27(5), May 1992.
5. A. Moore. Very fast EM-based mixture model clustering using multiresolution kd-trees. In *Advances in Neural Information Processing Systems (NIPS)*. MIT Press, December 1998.
6. J. J. Rissanen. Hypothesis selection and testing by the MDL principle. *Computer Journal*, 42(4):260–269, 1999.
7. C. S. Wallace and D. L. Dowe. Minimum message length and Kolmogorov complexity. *The Computer Journal, Special Issue - Kolmogorov Complexity*, 42(4):270–283, 1999.

Higher-Order Hidden Markov Models with Applications to DNA Sequences*

Wai Ki Ching, Eric S. Fung, and Michael K. Ng

Department of Mathematics, The University of Hong Kong
Pokfulam Road, Hong Kong
wkc,mng@maths.hku.hk

Abstract. Hidden Markov models (HMMs) have been applied to many real-world applications. Very often HMMs only deal with the first order transition probability distribution among the hidden states. In this paper we develop higher-order HMMs. We study the evaluation of the probability of a sequence of observations based on higher-order HMMs and determination of a best sequence of model states.

1 Introduction

Statistical methods of Markov source or hidden Markov modeling have become increasingly popular in the last forty years. Since the models are very rich in mathematical structure, they can form the theoretical basis for use in a wide range of applications [6]. Hidden Markov models (HMMs) provide a general structure for statistical analysis of a wide variety of DNA sequence analysis problems [5]. For instance, given a long piece of DNA sequence containing symbols A,C,G,T, how to find the CpG islands [2] in it or if there is any ? In a HMM, there is not a one-to-one correspondence between the states and the symbols. It is no longer possible to tell what state the model is in which the symbol is generated just by looking at the symbol. An HMM is usually characterized by the following elements [6]:

1. N, the number of states in the model. Although the states are hidden, for many practical applications there is often some physical significance to the states. For instance, the hidden states represent the CpG island and the non-CpG island in the DNA sequence. We denote the individual states as $\mathbf{S} = \{S_1, S_2, \cdots, S_N\}$, and the state at the length t as q_t.
2. M, the number of distinct observation symbols per state. The observation symbols correspond to the physical output of the system being modeled. For instance, A,C,G,T are the observation symbols in the DNA sequence. We denote the individual symbols as $\mathbf{V} = \{v_1, v_2, \cdots, v_M\}$.
3. The state transition probability distribution $A = \{a_{ij}\}$ where $a_{ij} = P[q_{t+1} = S_j | q_t = S_i]$, $1 \leq i, j \leq N$.

---

* supported in part by RGC Grant No. RGC Grant No. HKU 7126/02P, and HKU CRCG Grant Nos. 10203408, 10203501, 10203907, 10203919, 10204436.

J. Liu et al. (Eds.): IDEAL 2003, LNCS 2690, pp. 535–539, 2003.

4. The observation symbol probability distribution in state j, $B = \{b_j(k)\}$, where $b_j(k) = P[v_k \text{ at } t|q_t = S_j]$, $\quad 1 \leq j \leq N, 1 \leq k \leq M$.
5. The initial state distribution $\Pi = \{\pi_i\}$ where $\pi_i = P[q_1 = S_i]$, $\quad 1 \leq i \leq N$.

Given appropriate values of N, M, A, B and Π, the HMM can be used as a generator to give an observation sequence $O = O_1O_2 \cdots O_T$ where each observation O_t is one of the symbols from $\mathbf{V}$, and T is the number of observations in the sequence. For simplicity, we use the compact notation $\Lambda = (A, B, \Pi)$ to indicate the complete parameter set of the HMM.

According to the above specification, the first order transition probability distribution among the hidden states is used. However, in the DNA sequence analysis, higher-order Markov models are often used, see [3,7]. An mth order Markov process is a stochastic process where each event depends on the previous m events. Therefore, the above HMM specification is not sufficient to tackle modeling problems in DNA sequence analysis. The main aim of this paper is to develop higher-order HMMs. We will formulate higher-order HMMs. Based on the form of the higher-order HMM, we solve in this paper the following two classical problems for the HMM model to be useful in real-world applications.

- **Problem 1** Given the observation sequence $O = O_1O_2 \cdots O_T$ and a higher-order HMM, how to efficiently compute the probability of the observation sequence, given the higher-order HMM ?
- **Problem 2** Given the observation sequence $O = O_2O_2 \cdots O_T$ and a higher-order HMM, how to choose a corresponding state sequence $Q = q_1q_2 \cdots q_T$ which is optimal in certain sense ?

The rest of the paper is organized as follows. In Section 2, we formulate higher-order HMMs. We discuss how to solve the above two problems in higher-order HMMs and give practical techniques for solving these two problems. In Section 3, We test our higher-order HMMs for CpG islands in the DNA sequences. In particular, the model parameters based on the information of CpG island are used. Simulation results show the effectiveness of higher-order HMMs.

2   Higher-Order Hidden Markov Models

The main difference between the traditional HMM and a higher-order HMM is that in the hidden layer, the state transition probability is governed by the mth order higher-order Markov model $a_{i_{t-m+1}, \cdots, i_{t+1}} = P[q_{t+1} = S_{i_{t+1}} | q_t = S_{i_t}, \cdots, q_{t-m+1} = S_{i_{t-m+1}}]$. A higher-order HMM can be characterized by the elements in Section 1 except the above transition probabilities among hidden states and the initial hidden state distribution. We assume that the distribution Π of initial m states is given by $\pi_{i_1, i_2, \cdots, i_m} = P[q_1 = S_{i_1}, q_2 = S_{i_2}, \cdots, q_m = S_{i_m}]$. Next we present formal mathematical solution to the two problems for higher-order HMMs in Section 1.

For Problem 1, we calculate the probability of the observation sequence, $O = O_1O_2 \cdots O_T$, given the higher-order HMM, i.e., $P(O|\Lambda)$. The easiest way of doing this is through enumerating each possible state sequence of length T. However, this calculation is computationally infeasible even for small values of T and N. We apply the forward-backward procedure [1] to calculate this probability of the observation sequence.

We define the forward variable $\alpha_t(i_{t-m+1}, \ldots, i_t)$ as follows:

$$\alpha_t(i_{t-m+1}, \ldots, i_t)$$
$$= P[O_1 = v_1, \cdots, O_t = v_t, q_{t-m+1} = S_{i_{t-m+1}}, \cdots, q_t = S_{i_t} | \Lambda], \quad m \leq t \leq T$$

i.e., the conditional probability that the subsequence of the first t observations and the subsequence of last m hidden states ending at time t are equal to $v_1 \ldots v_t$ and $S_{i_{t-m+1}} \cdots S_{i_t}$ respectively, are given by the model parameters Λ. We see that if we can obtain the values of $\alpha_T(i_{T-m+1}, \cdots, i_T)$ for all $i_{T-m+1}, \cdots, i_T$, then $P[O|\Lambda]$ can be obtained by summing up all the values of $\alpha_T(i_{T-m+1}, \cdots, i_T)$. It is interesting to note that the values of $\alpha_T(i_{T-m+1}, \cdots, i_T)$ can be obtained by the following recursive equation and the details are given as follows:

- 1) Initialization: $\quad \alpha_m(i_1, i_2, \cdots, i_m) = \pi_{i_1, i_2, \cdots, i_m} \cdot \displaystyle\prod_{j=1}^{m} b_{i_j}(v_j)$.

- 2) Recursive Equation:

$$\alpha_{t+1}(i_{t-m+2}, i_{t-m+3}, \cdots, i_{t+1})$$
$$= \sum_{i_{t-m+1}=1}^{N} \alpha_t(i_{t-m+1}, \cdots, i_t) \cdot a_{i_{t-m+1}i_t, i_{t+1}} b_{i_{t+1}}(v_{t+1}).$$

- 3) Termination: $\quad P(O|\Lambda) = \displaystyle\sum_{i_{T-m+1}, \cdots, i_T = 1}^{N} \alpha_T(i_{T-m+1}, \cdots, i_T)$.

The initiation step calculates the forward probabilities as the joint probability of hidden states and initial observations. The induction step, which is the main part of the forward calculation. Finally, the last step gives the desired calculation of $P[O|\Lambda]$ as the sum of the terminal forward variables $\alpha_T(i_{T-m+1}, \cdots, i_T)$. This is the case since, by definition,

$$\alpha_t(i_{T-m+1}, \ldots, i_T)$$
$$= P[O_1, O_2, \cdots, O_T, q_{T-m+1} = S_{i_{T-m+1}}, \cdots, q_T = S_{i_T} | \Lambda]$$

and hence $P[O|\Lambda]$ is just the sum of the $\alpha_T(i_{T-m+1}, \cdots, i_T)$'s.

Problem 2 is the one in which we attempt to uncover the hidden part of the model, i.e., to find the "correct" state sequence. In practical situations, we use an optimality criteria to solve this problem as good as possible. The most widely used criterion is to find a single best state sequence, i.e., the maximize $P[Q|\Lambda, O]$. This is equivalent to maximizing $P[Q, O|\Lambda]$. We note that $P[Q|\Lambda, O] = \frac{P[Q, O|\Lambda]}{P[O|\Lambda]}$. Viterbi algorithm [8] is a formal technique for finding this single best state sequence $Q = \{q_1, q_2, \cdots, q_T\}$ for the given the observation sequence $O = \{O_1, O_2, \cdots, O_T\}$. We need to define the quantity:

$$\delta_t(i_{t-m+1}, \cdots, i_t)$$
$$= \max_{q_1, \cdots, q_{t-m}} P[q_1 = S_{i_1}, \cdots, q_t = S_{i_t}, O_1 = v_1, \cdots, O_t = v_t | \Lambda], \quad m \leq t \leq T$$

Here $\delta_t(i_{t-m+1}, \cdots, i_t)$ is the best score (highest probability) along a single best state sequence at time t, which accounts for the first t observations and ends in state S_{i_t}. By induction, we have

$$\delta_{t+1}(i_{t-m+2}, \cdots, i_{t+1})$$
$$= \max_{1 \leq q_{t-m+1} \leq N} \{\delta_t(i_{t-m+1}, \cdots, i_t) \cdot a_{i_{t-m+1}, \cdots, i_{t+1}}\} \cdot b_{i_{t+1}}(O_{t+1}) \qquad (1)$$

To actually retrieve the state sequence, we need to keep track of the argument which maximized (1) for each t and $i_{t-m+1}, \cdots, i_t$. We do this via the array $\beta_{t+1}(i_{t-m+2}, \cdots, i_{t+1})$. The complete procedure for finding the best state sequence can now be stated as follows:

- 1) Initialization: $\quad \delta_m(i_1, \cdots, i_m)\pi_{i_1, i_2, \cdots, i_m} \prod_{j=1}^{m} b_{i_j}(v_j), \quad 1 \leq i_1, i_2, \cdots, i_m \leq$
  N. Moreover, we set $\beta_m(i_1, \cdots, i_m) = 0$.
- 2) Recursion:

$$\delta_{t+1}(i_{t-m+2}, \cdots, i_{t+1})$$
$$= \max_{1 \leq q_{t-m+1} \leq N} \{\delta_t(i_{t-m+1}, \cdots, i_t) \cdot a_{i_{t-m+1}, \cdots, i_{t+1}}\} \cdot b_{i_{t+1}}(v_{t+1})$$

Moreover we have

$$\beta_{t+1}(i_{t-m+2}, \cdots, i_{t+1}) = \text{argmax}_{1 \leq q_{t-m+1} \leq N}\{\delta_t(i_{t-m+1}, \cdots, i_t) \cdot a_{i_{t-m+1}, \cdots, i_{t+1}}\},$$
$$m+1 \leq t \leq T \quad \text{and} \quad 1 \leq i_{t+1} \leq N.$$

- 3) Termination $\quad P^* = \max_{1 \leq q_{T-m+1}, \cdots, q_T \leq N}\{\delta_{q_{T-m+1}, \cdots, q_T}\}$

$$(q_{T-m+1}, \cdots, q_T^*) = \text{argmax}_{1 \leq q_{T-m+1}, \cdots, q_T \leq N}\{\delta_{q_{T-m+1}, \cdots, i_T}\}$$

3   DNA Applications

In this section, we test our higher-order HMMs for CpG islands in DNA sequences. We often focus on which part of the sequence belongs to CpG island and which part of the sequence belongs to non-CpG islands. As we can only observe the bases of the DNA sequence A,C,G,T, we cannot observe which part belongs to the CpG island, the classification of *CpG* island can be regarded as a hidden state. In the formulation, we have two hidden states ($N = 2$): $S_1 =$ CpG island and $S_2 =$ non-CpG island, and we have four observations symbols

Table 1. Comparisons among three HMMs.

	First-order	Second-order	reduced Second-order
$\log(P[O|\Lambda])$	-4.1254e03	-4.1237e03	-4.1249e03
$\log(P(Q|O,\Lambda))$	-1.32680e03	-0.5202e03	-1.0378e03

($M = 4$): $v_1 = A, v_2 = C, v_3 = G, v_4 = T$. In the evaluation, we have done 100 hidden and observation sequences to obtain the average values of the results (Table 1). Here the reduced second order model is proposed in [4].

In this paper, we have proposed higher-order HMMs. The hidden layer process is modeled by a higher-order Markov chain process. We have studied the evaluation of the probability of a sequence of observations based on higher-order HMMs and determination of a best sequence of model states. A major drawback of higher-order Markov model is that the number of model parameters increases exponentially with respect to the its order. Here we consider to use a model which involves less model parameters. Examples have shown that higher-order HMMs are quite effective. In this paper, we do not tackle the problem how to adjust the model parameters Π to maximize $P[O|\Lambda]$ or $P[Q|\Lambda, O]$. This part is an important issue in which we attempt to optimize the model parameters so as to best describe how a given observation sequence comes about. The observation sequence used to adjust the model parameters is called a training sequence since it is used to train the HMM. The training problem is the crucial one for most applications of HMMs. In the future, we plan to study how to create best models for real phenomena.

References

1. L. Baum and J. Egon, *An Inequality with Applications to Statistical Estimation for Probabilistic Functions of a Markov Process and to a Model for Ecology*, Bull. Amer. Meteorol. Soc. 73 (1967), pp. 360-363.
2. A. Bird, *CpG Islands as Gene Markers in the Vertebrate Nucleus*, Trends in Genetics, 3 (1987), pp. 342-347.
3. M. Borodovskii and D. Mcininch, *GeneMark*, Comp. Chem. 17, (1993), 123-133.
4. W. K. Ching, Eric S. Fung and Michael K. Ng, *Higher-order Markov Chain Models for Categorical Data Sequences*, submitted (2002).
5. R. Durbin, S. Eddy, A. Krogh and G. Mitchison, *Biological Sequence Analysis*, Cambridge University Press (1998).
6. L. Rabiner, *A Tutorial on Hidden Markov Models and Selected Applications in Speech Recognition*, Proceedings of the IEEE, 77 (1989) pp. 257–286.
7. S. Salzberg, A. Delcher, S. Kasif and O. White, *Microbial gene identification using interpolated Markov models*, Nuclei Acids Research, 26, (1998), 544-548.
8. A. Viterbi, *Error Bounds for Convolutional Codes and an Asymptotically Optimal Decoding Algorithm*, IEEE Trans. Information Theory 13 (1967), pp. 260–269.

Classification of the Risk Types of Human Papillomavirus by Decision Trees

Seong-Bae Park, Sohyun Hwang, and Byoung-Tak Zhang

School of Computer Science and Engineering
Seoul National University
Seoul 151-744, Korea
{sbpark,shhwang,btzhang}@bi.snu.ac.kr

Abstract. The high-risk type of Human Papillomavirus (HPV) is the main etiologic factor of cervical cancer, which is a leading cause of cancer deaths in women worldwide. Therefore, classifying the risk type of HPVs is very useful and necessary to the daignosis and remedy of cervical cancer. In this paper, we classify the risk type of 72 HPVs and predict the risk type of 4 HPVs of which type is unknown. As a machine learning method to classify them, we use decision trees. According to the experimental results, it shows about 81.14% of accuracy.

1 Introduction

Cervical cancer is a leading cause of cancer deaths in women worldwide. Since the main etiologic factor for cervical cancer is known as high-risk Human Papillomavirus (HPV) infection [5], it is now largely a preventable disease. There are more than 100 types of HPV that are specific for epithelial cells including skin, respiratory mucosa, and the genital tract. Genital tract HPV types are classified by their relative malignant potential into low-, and high-risk types [4]. The common, unifying oncogenic feature of the vast majority of cervical cancers is the presence of high-risk HPV. Therefore, the most important thing for diagnosis and therapy is discriminating whether patients have the high-risk HPVs and what HPV types are highly risky.

One way to discriminate the risk types of HPVs is using a text mining technique. Since a great number of research results on HPV have been already reported in biomedical journals [3], they can be used as a source of discriminating HPV risk types. Since there are a number of research results on HPV and cervical cancer, the textual data about them can be easily obtained. In this paper, we use the textual information describing the characteristics of various HPV types as document data, and decision trees as a learning algorithm to classify the their risk types. One advantage of this work is usefulness for designing the DNA-chip, diagnosing the presence of HPV in cervical cancer patients. Since there are about 100 HPV types, making the DNA chip needs to choose some dangerous ones related with cervical cancer among them. Therefore, this result classifying the risk of HPVs can be a big help to save time to understand information about HPV and cervical cancer from many papers and to choose the HPV types used for DNA chip.

J. Liu et al. (Eds.): IDEAL 2003, LNCS 2690, pp. 540–544, 2003.

<definition>
Human papillomavirus type 43 (HPV-43) E6 region.
</definition>
<source>
Human papillomavirus type 43 DNA recovered from a vulvar biopsy with hyperplasia.
</source>
<comment>
HPV-43 was classified by Lorincz et. al [435] as a "low-risk" virus. Prevalence studies indicate that HPV-44 and HPV-43 have been found in 4% of cervical intraepithelial neoplasms, but in none of the 56 cervical cancers tested. During an anlaysis of approximately 100 anogenital tissue samples, two new HPV types, HPV-43 and HPV-44, were identified. The complete genome of HPV-43 was recovered from a vulvar biopsy and cloned into bacteriophage lambda. The biopsy was taken from a woman living in the Detroit Michigan area. The DNA consisted of two fragments: a 6.3 kb BamHI fragment and a 2.9 kb HindIII fragment. The total quantity of unique DNA was 7.6 kb. Only the E6 region of the cloned sample has been sequenced, although all positions of the ORFs have been deduced and are consistent with the organization of DNA from HPV-6b. A possible feature of HPV types associated with malignant lesions is the potential to produce a different E6 protein by alternative splicing. This potential has been found in types HPV-16, HPV-18, and HPV-31. HPV-43 has both the potential E6 splice donor site at nt 233 and the potential splice acceptor at nt 413.
</comment>

Fig. 1. An example description of HPV43 from HPV sequence database.

2   Dataset

In this paper, we use *the HPV Sequence Database* in Los Alamos National Laboratory as a dataset. This papillomavirus database is an extension of the HPV compendiums published in 1994–1997 and provides the complete list of 'papillomavirus types and hosts' and the records for each unique papillomavirus type. An example of the data made from this database is given in Figure 1. This example is for HPV43 and consists of three parts: definition, source, and comment. The definition indicates the HPV type, the source explains where the information for this HPV is obtained, and the comment gives the explanation for this HPV. In the all experiments below, we used only comment. The comment for a HPV type can be considered as a document in text classification. Therefore, each HPV type is represented as a vector of which elements are $tf \cdot idf$ values. When we stemmed the documents using the Porter's algorithm and removed words from the stop-list, the size of vocabulary is just 1,434. Thus, each document is represented as a 1,434-dimensional vector.

To measure the performance of the results in the experiments below, we manually classified HPV risk types using the 1997 version of HPV compendium and the comment in the records above. The classifying procedure is as follows. First, we divided roughly HPV types by the groups in the compendium. Second,

Table 1. The manually classified risk types of HPVs.

Type	Risk	Type	Risk	Type	Risk	Type	Risk
HPV1	Low	HPV2	Low	HPV3	Low	HPV4	Low
HPV5	Low	HPV6	Low	HPV7	Low	HPV8	Low
HPV9	Low	HPV10	Low	HPV11	Low	HPV12	Low
HPV13	Low	HPV14	Low	HPV15	Low	HPV16	High
HPV17	Low	HPV18	High	HPV19	Low	HPV20	Low
HPV21	Low	HPV22	Low	HPV23	Low	HPV24	Low
HPV25	Low	HPV26	Don't Know	HPV27	Low	HPV28	Low
HPV29	Low	HPV30	Low	HPV31	High	HPV32	Low
HPV33	High	HPV34	Low	HPV35	High	HPV36	Low
HPV37	Low	HPV38	Low	HPV39	High	HPV40	Low
HPV41	Low	HPV42	Low	HPV43	Low	HPV44	Low
HPV45	High	HPV47	Low	HPV48	Low	HPV49	Low
HPV50	Low	HPV51	High	HPV52	High	HPV53	Low
HPV54	Don't Know	HPV55	Low	HPV56	High	HPV57	Don't Know
HPV58	High	HPV59	High	HPV60	Low	HPV61	High
HPV62	High	HPV63	Low	HPV64	Low	HPV65	Low
HPV66	High	HPV67	High	HPV68	High	HPV69	Low
HPV70	Don't Know	HPV72	High	HPV73	Low	HPV74	Low
HPV75	Low	HPV76	Low	HPV77	Low	HPV80	Low

Table 2. The performance of decision trees.

Trial	Accuracy (%)
1	86.7
2	86.7
3	66.7
4	73.3
5	92.3
Average	81.14 ± 10.68

if the group is skin-related or cutaneous, the members of the group are classified into low-risk type. Third, if the group is known to be cervical cancer-related HPV, the members of the group are classified into high-risk type. Lastly, we used the comment of HPV types to classify some types difficult to be classified. Table 1 shows the summarized classification of HPVs according to its risk. "Don't know"s in this table are the ones that can not be classified by above knowledge.

3   Experimental Results

Since we have only 76 HPV types and the explanation of each HPV is relatively short, *5-fold cross validation* is used to determine the performance of decision trees. That is, in each experiment, we used 58 examples as a training set, and the remaining 15 as a test set. As a learning algorithm of decision trees, Quinlan's C4.5 release 8 is used.

Table 2 shows the performance of decision trees. The average accuracy is 81.14±10.68%. Among the misclassified HPV types, 9 low-risk HPVs are classified as high-risk, and 5 high-risk HPVs are classified as low-risk. Four (HPV13, HPV14, HPV30, and HPV40) of 9 low-risk HPVs that are misclassied as high-risk have a potential to cause a laryngeal cancer, though they are not directly

Table 3. The misclassifed HPVs.

HPV Type	Real Type	Predicted Type	Characteristics
HPV2	Low	High	normal wart
HPV13	Low	High	oral infection, some progress to cancer
HPV14	Low	High	some progress to cancer
HPV18	High	Low	
HPV30	Low	High	laryngeal cancer
HPV40	Low	High	laryngeal cancer
HPV42	Low	High	genital wart
HPV43	Low	High	
HPV44	Low	High	
HPV53	Low	High	
HPV56	High	Low	
HPV59	High	Low	
HPV62	High	Low	mid-high-risk
HPV72	High	Low	mid-high-risk

Table 4. Risk type of the HPVs whose risk type is known as 'Don't Know'.

Trial	HPV26	HPV54	HPV57	HPV70	Accuracy (%)
1	Low	Low	Low	Low	75
2	Low	Low	High	Low	50
3	Low	Low	High	Low	50
4	Low	Low	Low	Low	75
5	High	Low	High	Low	25

related with cervical cancer. And, three (HPV59, HPV62, and HPV72) of 5 high-risk HPVs which are misclassified as low-risk are the ones which some clinical researchers classify them as mid-high-risk types. That is, they do not have many expression about cervical cancer, though we classify them as high-risk to make a problem simple. Therefore, if we exclude these 7 cases, the errors are only 5 low-risk HPVs (HPV2, HPV42, HPV43, HPV44, and HPV53) and 2 high-risk HPVs (HPV18 and HPV56). Table 3 summarizes these errors.

One point we should emphasize in classifying the risk-type of HPVs is that false negatives are far more important than false positives. That is, it is no problem to misclassify low-risk HPVs as high-risk, but it is fatal to misclassify high-risk HPVs as low-risk. In false negative case, dangerous HPVs are missed, and there is no further chance to detect cervical cancer by them. Because only 2 are false negatives in our experiments, the results are reliable.

Four HPVs in Table 1 are classified as "Don't Know" since their risk type is not certain. According to the other research results [1,2], their risk types are as follows.

Type	HPV26	HPV54	HPV57	HPV70
Risk	Low	Low	Low	High

When we classify their risk types by the decision trees, we obtain $55 \pm 20.92\%$ of accuracy. Table 4 summarizes this results. Especially, HPV70 is not correctly classified at all. This is because the comment for HPV70 does not describe its risk but explains that it is found at the cervix of patients and its sequence is analyzed.

4   Conclusions

In this paper, we classified the risk type of HPVs by decision trees. The accuracy is about 82%, which is a little bit higher than expected. But, if we are to use this result as not reference material but basic information before biomedical experiments, we need higher accuracy. In addition, it is no problem to classify low-risk HPVs as high-risk, but it is fatal to classify high-risk HPVs as low-risk. If we have about 20% of errors, we come to have too many misclassified high-risk HPVs. If the DNA-chips are designed only based on this result, some of them will cause misdiagnosis. Therefore, we suggest this result as reference material to design DNA-chips.

Because the virus is easy to mutate in order to survive within the host, most viruses have various types like HPVs and each type has different effect on serious diseases. Therefore, it is required to keep studying on classifying mutants of viruses like HPVs according to their relation with diseases. In case of HPV, it is an easy work because there are a number of research results and databases. But we need to study further how to classify the risk type of viruses when there is not such data available.

Acknowledgements. This research was supported by the Korean Ministry of Education under the BK21-IT Program, by BrainTech and NRL programs sponsored by the Korean Ministry of Science and Technology.

References

1. S. Chan, S. Chew, K. Egawa, E. Grussendorf-Conen, Y. Honda, A. Rubben, K. Tan and H. Bernard. Phylogenetic Analysis of the Human Papillomavirus Type 2 (HPV-2), HPV-27, and HPV-57 Group, Which is Associated with Common Warts. *Virology*, 239, pp. 296–302, 1997.
2. M. Favre, D. Kremsdorf, S. Jablonska, S. Obalek, G. Pehau-Arnaudet, O. Croissant, and G. Orth. Two New Human Papillomavirus Types (HPV54 and 55) Characterized from Genital Tumours Illustrate the Plurality of Genital HPVs. *International Journal of Cancer*, 45, pp. 40–46, 1990.
3. H. Furumoto and M. Irahara. Human Papilloma Virus (HPV) and Cervical Cancer. *The Jounral of Medical Investigation*, 49(3-4), pp. 124–133, 2002.
4. M. Janicek and H. Averette. Cervical Cancer: Prevention, Diagnosis, and Therapeutics. *Cancer Journal for Clinicians*, 51, pp. 92–114, 2001.
5. M. Schiffman, H. Bauer, R. Hoover, A. Glass, D. Cadell, B. Rush, D. Scott, M. Sherman, R. Kurman and S. Wacholder. Epidemiologic Evidence Showing That Human Papillomavirus Infection Causes Most Cervical Intraepithelial Neoplasis. *Jounral of the National Cancer Institute*, 85, pp. 958–964, 1993.

An Effective Rough Set-Based Method
for Text Classification

Yongguang Bao[1], Daisuke Asai[1], Xiaoyong Du[2], Kazutaka Yamada[1], and
Naohiro Ishii[1]

[1] Department of Intelligence and Computer Science, Nagoya Institute of Technology,
Nagoya, 466-8555, Japan
{baoyg, ishii}@egg.ics.nitech.ac.jp
[2] School of Information, Renmin University of China, 100872, Beijing, China
Duyong@mail.ruc.edu.cn

Abstract. A central problem in good text classification for IF/IR is the
high dimensionality of the data. To cope with this problem, we propose
a technique using Rough Sets theory to alleviate this situation. Given
corpora of documents and a training set of examples of classified documents, the technique locates a minimal set of co-ordinate keywords to
distinguish between classes of documents, reducing the dimensionality of
the keyword vectors. Besides, we generate several reduct bases for the
classification of new object, hoping that the combination of answers of
the multiple reduct bases result in better performance. To get the tidy
and effective rules, we use the value reduction as the final rules. This paper describes the proposed technique and provides experimental results.

1 Introduction

As the volume of information available on the Internet and corporative intranets
continues to increase, there is a growing need for tools finding, filtering, and managing these resources. The purpose of text classification is to classify text documents into classes automatically based on their contents, and therefore plays an
important role in many information management tasks. A number of statistical
text learning algorithms and machine learning techniques have been applied to
text classification.

However, a non-trivial obstacle in good text classification is the high dimensionality of the data. Rough Sets Theory introduced by Pawlak [3] is a non-
statistical methodology for data analysis. It can be used to alleviate this situation [5]. A. Chouchoulas and Q. Shen proposed a Rough Set Attribute Reduction
method (RSAR) to text classification that test E-mail messages. Given corpora
of documents and a set of examples of classified documents, the technique can
quickly locate a minimal set of co-ordinate keywords to classify new documents.
As a result, it dramatically reduces the dimensionality of the keyword space. The
resulting set of keywords of rule is typically small enough to be understood by a
human. This simplifies the creation of knowledge-based IF/IR systems, speeds
up their operation, and allows easy editing of the rule bases employed. But we

J. Liu et al. (Eds.): IDEAL 2003, LNCS 2690, pp. 545–552, 2003.

can see that with the increasing number of categories, its accuracy becomes to be an unacceptable level, from the experimental results of RSAR in [5]. A single reduct base which utilizes a single minimal set of decision rules to classify future examples may lead to mistake, because the minimal set of decision rules are more sensitive to noise and a small number of rules means that a few alternatives exit when classifying new objects. In order to enhance the classification accuracy, we generate several reduct bases instead of one reduct base for the classification of unseen objects, hoping that the combination of answers of multiple reduct bases result in better performance. Moreover, to get the tidy and effective rules, we develop the value reduction method as the final rules.

2   Information Systems and Rough Sets

2.1   Information Systems

An information system is composed of a 4-tuple as follow:

$$S =< U, Q, V, f >$$

Where U is the closed universe, a finite nonempty set of N objects $(x_1, x_2, ..., x_N)$, Q is a finite nonempty set of n features $\{q_1, q_2, ..., q_n\}, V = \bigcup_{q \in Q} V_q$, where V_q is a domain(value) of the feature q, $f : U \times Q \to V$ is the total decision function called the information such that $f(x, q) \in V_q$, for every $q \in Q$, $x \in U$.

Any subset P of Q determines a binary relation on U, which will be called an indiscernibility relation denoted by $INP(P)$, and defined as follows: $x I_B y$ if and only if $f(x, a) = f(y, a)$ for every $a \in P$. Obviously $INP(P)$ is an equivalence relation. The family of all equivalence classes of $INP(P)$ will be denoted by $U/INP(P)$ or simply U/P; an equivalence class of $INP(P)$ containing x will be denoted by $P(x)$ or $[x]_p$.

2.2   Reduct

Reduct is a fundamental concept of rough sets. A reduct is the essential part of an information system that can discern all objects discernible by the original information system.

Let $q \in Q$. A feature q is *dispensable* in S, if $IND(Q - q) = IND(Q)$; otherwise feature q is *indispensable* in S.

If q is an indispensable feature, deleting it from S will cause S to be inconsistent. Otherwise, q can be deleted from S.

The set $R \subseteq Q$ of feature will be called a *reduct* of Q, if $IND(R) = IND(Q)$ and all features of R are indispensable in S. We denoted it as $RED(Q)$ or $RED(S)$.

Feature reduct is the minimal subset of condition features Q with respect to decision features D, none of the features of any minimal subsets can be eliminated without affecting the essential information. These minimal subsets can discern decision classes with the same discriminating power as the entire condition features.

The set of all indispensable from the set Q is called $CORE$ of Q and denoted by $CORE(Q)$:

$$CORE(Q) = \cap RED(Q)$$

Similarly, we can reduce superfluous values of condition attributes from a attribute reduction to get a set of tidy and effective rules [3]. The process by which the maximum number of condition attribute values of a rule is removed without decreasing the classification accuracy of the rule is called as *Value Reduction*.

2.3 Discernibility Matrix

In this section we introduce a basic notions–a discernibility matrix that will help us understand several properties and to construct efficient algorithm to compute reducts.

By $M(S)$ we denote an $n \times n$ matrix (c_{ij}), called the *discernibility matrix* of S, such as

$$c_{ij} = \{q \in Q : f(x_i, q) \neq f(x_j, q)\} \text{for} \quad i,j = 1, 2, ..., n.$$

Since $M(S)$ is symmetric and $c_{ii} = \emptyset$ for $i = 1, 2, ..., n$, we represent $M(S)$ only by elements in the lower triangle of $M(S)$, i.e. the c_{ij} is with $1 \leq j < i \leq n$.

From the definition of the discernibility matrix $M(S)$ we have the following:

Proposition 1. $CORE(S) = \{q \in Q : c_{ij} = \{q\} \text{ for some } i,j\}$

Proposition 2. *Let* $\emptyset \neq B \in Q$. *The following conditions are equivalent:*
(1) For all i, j *such that* $c_{ij} \neq \emptyset$ *and* $1 \leq j < i \leq n$ *we have* $B \cap c_{ij} \neq \emptyset$
(2) $IND(B) = IND(Q)$ *i.e.* B *is superset of a reduct of* S.

3   The Proposed System

This paper proposes an effective method to text classification. The approach comprises three main stages, as shown in Fig. 1. The keyword acquisition stage reads corpora of documents, locates candidate keywords, estimates their importance, and builds an intermediate dataset of high dimensionality. The attribute reductions generation examines the dataset and removes redundancy, generates single or multiple feature reductions, leaves a dataset or rule base containing a drastically reduced number of pre conditions per rule. The value reductions generation computes the value of each rule in feature reducts, get the tidy and effective rules as the final rules

3.1   Keyword Acquisition

Text classification aims to classify text documents into categories or classes automatically based on their content. Perhaps, the most commonly used document representation is so called vector space model. In the vector space model, a

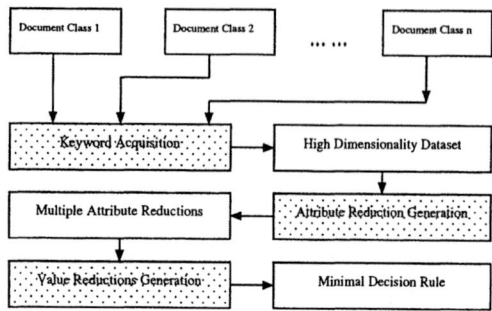

Fig. 1. Data flow through the system RSAR-MV

document is represented by vector of words. Usually, one has a collection of documents which is represented by a $M \times N$ word-by-document matrix A, where M is the number of words, and N the number of documents, each entry represents the occurrences of a word in a document, i.e.,

$$A = (\omega_{ik})$$

Where w_{ik} is the weight of word i in document k. Since every word does not normally appear in each document, the matrix is usually sparse and M can be very large. Hence, a major characteristic, or difficulty of text classification problem is the high dimensionality of the feature space.

The keyword acquisition subsystem uses a set of document as input. Firstly, words are isolated and prefiltered to avoid very short or long keywords, or keywords that are not words (e.g. long numbers or random sequences of characters). Every word or pair of consecutive words in the text is considered to be a candidate keyword. Then, the following weighting function is used for word indexing to generate a set of keywords for each document.

$$\omega_{ik} = \log(\frac{N}{N})f_i\omega_f$$

Where ω_{ik} is the weight of keyword i in document k; N is the total number of document and N_k is the number of documents containing keyword k; f_i is the frequency of the keyword i in document k; and ω_f denotes the current field's importance to the classification, which depends on the application and user preferences.

Finally, before the weighted keyword is added to the set of keywords, it passes through two filters: one is a low-pass filter removing words so uncommon that are definitely not good keywords; the other is a high-pass filter that removes far too common words such as auxiliary verbs, articles et cetera. This gives the added advantage of language-independence to the keyword acquisition algorithm: most similar methods rely on English thesauri and lists of common English words to perform the same function. Finally all weights are normalized before the keyword sets are output.

It must be emphasized that any keyword acquisition approach may be substituted for the one described above, as long as it outputs weighted keywords.

3.2   Generation of Feature Reductions

A reduct is a minimal subset of features, which has the same discernibility power as the entire condition feature. Finding all reducts of an information system is combinatorial NP-hard computational problem [4]. A reduct uses a minimum number of features and represents a minimal and complete rules set to classify new objects. To classify unseen objects, it is optimal to use the characteristics that different reducts use different features as much as possible and the union of these features in the reducts together include all indispensable features in the database and the number of reducts used for classification is minimum. Here, we proposed a greedy algorithm to compute a set of reducts which satisfy this optimal requirement. Our algorithm starts with the $CORE$ features, then through backtracking, multiple reducts are constructed using discernibility matrix. A reduct is computed by using forward stepwise selection and backward stepwise elimination based on the significance values of the features. The algorithm terminates when the features in the union of the reducts includes all the indispensable features in the database or the number of reducts is equal to the number determined by user. Since Rough Sets is suited to nominal datasets, we quantise the normalized weighted space into 11 values calculated by $floor(10\omega)$.

Let **COMP**(B, ADL) denotes the comparison procedure. The result of **COM P**(B, ADL) is 1 if for each element c_j of ADL has $B \cap c_j \neq \emptyset$ otherwise 0, m be the parameter of reducts number. The generation algorithm is shown in Fig. 2.

Step 1 Create the discernibility matrix $DM := [C_{ij}]$;

      $CORE = \cup\{c \in DM : card(c) = 1\}$; $i = 1$;

Step 2 **While** $(i \leq m)$ do begin

    $REDU = \emptyset$; $DL = DM - CORE$;

    $DL = DL - \cup REDU_i$;

    /* forward selection*/

    While $(DL \neq \emptyset)$ do begin

      Compute the frequency value for each feature $q \in Q - \cup REDU_i$;

      Select the feature q with maximum frequency value and add it to $REDU$;

      Delete elements dl of DL which $q \in dl$ from DL;

    End

    /* backward elimination*/

    $N = card(REDU - CORE)$;

    For $j = 0$ to $N - 1$ do begin

      Remove $a_j \in REDU - CORE$ from $REDU$;

      If **COMP**$(REDU, DM) = 0$ Then add a_j to $REDU$;

    End

    $REDU_i = REDU$; $i = i + 1$;

    End

Fig. 2. Algorithm: Generate Feature Reductions

3.3   Value Reductions Generation

For computing the value reducts, a method is suggested [6]. In there, we have to reduce superfluous values of condition attribute of every decision rule. To this end we have to compute core values of condition attributes and then compute value reducts in every decision rule, if necessary, remove duplicate rows. In the process of computing the value reducts we have to check the all subfamily of condition attribute. Unfortunately, the number of possible subsets is always very large when M is large because there are 2^{M-1} subsets for M condition attributes. In the following, we will propose an effective algorithm as shown in Fig. 3, based on the propositions of value reduction [6], to get the value reductions.

Step 1 $k = 1, n = card(C), L_1 = \emptyset, REDUCT = \emptyset, m = 0$;

Step 2 for all 1-elment subset c of C

    If $(card([x]C - c) = card([x]_{(C-c \cap D)}))$ then add c to L_1.

Step 3 For $(k = 2; k < n; k + +)$ do begin

    generate(L_{k-1}) /* generate candidates */

    for all $c \in C_k$ do

      if $(\exists$ a $(k - 1)$-subset s of c, s.t. $s \notin L_{k-1})$ then delete c from C_k,

    for all $c \in C_k$ do

      if $(card([x]_{C-c}) \neq card([x]_{(C-c) \cap D}))$ delete c from C_k ;

    for all $s \in L_{k-1}$ do if $(\exists$ a $t \in C_k$, s.t. $s \subset t)$ then delete s from L_{k-1};

    $L_k = C_k$;

    if $(card(L_k) < 2)$ break;

  end

Step 4 $\{C - s : s \in L_m, 1 \leq m \leq k\}$ are left part of the all value reductions.

Fig. 3. Algorithm: Compute Value Reduction

Where generate function take L_{k-1} as argument, join L_{k-1} p with L_{k-1} q as:

Insert into C_k **select** $p.item_1, p.item_2, \cdots, p.item_{k-1}, q.item_{k-1}$
from L_{k-1} p, L_{k-1} q
where $p.item_1 = q.item_1, \cdots, p.item_{k-2} = q.item_{k-2}, p.item_{k-1} < q.item_{k-1}$;

4   Experiments and Results

For evaluating the efficiency of our algorithm, we compared it with RSAR algorithm in [5] and the popular k-nearest neighbor algorithm in text classification. RSAR algorithm is a simple Rough Set-Based Approach, it just use one attribute reduction as rule to classify text. And for testing the efficiency of value reduction, we also compared multiple value reductions with multiple attribute reductions. The Reuters collection is used in our experiment, which is publicly available at http://www.research. att.com/ lewis/reuters21578.html. Five different corpora of the Reuters collection were used in our experiment. They are:

Cocoa: Training/test data number is 41/15.
Copper: Training/test data number is 31/17.
Cpi: Training/test data number is 45/26
Rubber: Training/test data number is 29/12.
Gnp: Training/test data number is 49/34.
In our experiment, we use 10 reducts, and for kNN, set parameter $k = 30$.

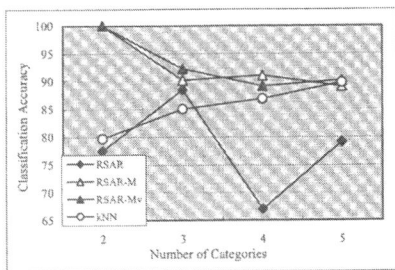

Fig. 4. Comparison of Classification Accuracy with RSAR and kNN

Fig.4. shows the experimental result. The "2-categories " shows the data includes cocoa and copper, the "3-categories" shows the data includes cocoa, copper and cpi, the "4-categories" shows the data includes cocoa, copper, cpi and gnp, the "5-categories" shows the data includes cocoa, copper, cpi, gnp and rubber. In the case of "5-categories", there are 4153 different words. After the preprocessing (remove tags, remove stopwords, perform word stemming), we get 2049 keywords. The RSAR curve means the result by algorithm RSAR. The RSAR-M curve means the result using 10 feature reducts. The RSAR-Mv curve means the result using value reduction based on 10 reducts. The kNN curve means the result using the basic k-nearest neighbor algorithm.

As can be see from Fig. 4., with the increasing the number of categories, the accuracy of RSAR becomes to be an unacceptable level. RSAR-M improves the performance of RSAR, and RSAR-Mv maintains the accuracy of RSAR-M. When compared with kNN, RASR-M/RSAR-Mv also achieves the higher accuracy.

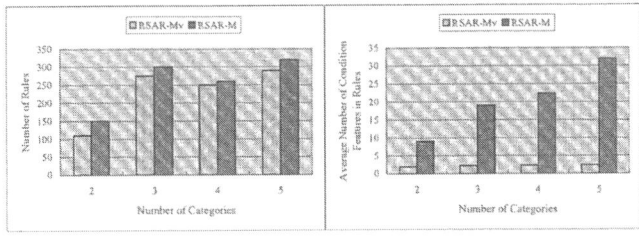

Fig. 5. Comparison of Number of Rules, Average Number of Condition Feature in Rule

Fig.5 shows the comparison of number of rules in RSAR-M with in RSAR-Mv and the comparison of average number of condition feature in rule. As it can be seen, using value reduction rule instead of simple attribute reduction rule can make an improvement in text classification. What may be concluded from the above figure is that RSAR-Mv decreases the number of rules and decrease size of rule more, but it can maintain the better performance of RSAR-M.

As it can be seen, using multiple reducts instead of single reduct can make a improvement in text classification, and using value reduction rule instead of attribute reduction rule can make a further improvement. What may be concluded from the above table and figures is that the proposed algorithm in this paper, is efficient and robust text classifier.

5 Conclusions

In this paper, an effective method for text classification has been presented based on Rough Set theory to classify new documents. Given corpora of documents and a set of examples of classified documents, the technique can quickly locate a minimal set of co-ordinate keywords to classify new documents. The resulting set of keywords of rule is typically small enough to be understood by a human. For the classification, we get high classification accuracy. The experimental results show that using several reduct bases instead of one reduct base make high improvement than RSAR algorithm, especially with the increasing the number of categories. And using value reduction rule instead of simple attribute reduction rule can make a further improvement. It also achieves the higher accuracy than the popular k-nearest neighbor algorithm in text classification.

References

1. T. Joachims, "Text Classification with Support Vector Machines: Learning with Many Relevant Features", ECML-98, 10th European Conference on Machine Learning, 1998, pp. 170–178.
2. Y. Yang, "An Evaluation of Statistical Approaches to Text Classification", Journal of Information Retrieval, 1, 1999, pp. 69–90.
3. Z. Pawlak, Rough Sets–Theoretical Aspects of Reasoning about Data, Kluwer Academic Publishers, Dordrecht. (1991)
4. A. Skowron & C. Rauszer, "The Discernibility Matrices and Functions in Information Systems", in R. Slowinski (ed.) Intelligent Decision Support – Handbook of Application and Advances of Rough Sets Theory, Kluwer Academic Publishers, Dordrecht, 1992, pp. 331–362.
5. A. Chouchoulas & Q. Shen, "A Rough Set-Based Approach to Text Classification", In 7th International Workshop, RSFDGrC'99, Yamaguchi, Japan, 1999, pp. 118–129.
6. N. Ishii & Y. Bao, "A Simple Method of Computing Value Reduction", Proceedings of CSITeA02, pp. 76–80, 2002,Brazil.

Abrupt Shot Change Detection Using Multiple Features and Classification Tree

Seung-Bum Hong, Won Nah, and Joong-Hwan Baek

School of Electronics, Telecommunication & Computer Engineering
Hankuk Aviation University, Koyang City , South Korea
{sbhong, nahwon, jhbaek}@mail.hangkong.ac.kr

Abstract. We propose an abrupt shot change detection method using multiple features and classification tree. Typical shot change detection algorithms have usually used single feature obtained between consecutive frames, and the shot change is determined with only one fixed threshold in whole video sequences. However, the contents of the video frames at shot changes such as intensity, color, shape, background, and texture change simultaneously. Thus multiple features have the advantage of single feature to detect shot changes. In this paper, we use five different features such as pixel difference, global and local histogram difference, and block-based difference. To classify the shot changes with multiple features, we use the binary classification tree method. According to the result of classification, we extract important features of the multiple features and obtain threshold value for feature at each node of the tree. We also perform the cross-validation analysis and drop-case method to confirm the reliability of the classification tree. An experimental result shows that our method has better performance than the existing single feature method for detecting abrupt shot changes.

Keywords: *Shot Change Detection, Multiple Features, Classification Tree*

1 Introduction

With an increase in the quantity of digital image and video data, shot change detection for effective information retrieval is applied to a video index, VOD, video edition, and video retrieval. A shot change means that a scene during a continuous camera operation changes to another scene. No change of contents can be detected inside a shot [1]-[3]. The shots may include a cut, where the shot change happens abruptly between two consecutive frames, or a fade, wipe, or dissolve, where the shot change is a gradual transition between several frames. In this paper we restrict ourselves to the study of the shot change detection only.

Many researchers have proposed the various methods for the shot change detection. There are methods mostly using the frame differences by the pixels or histogram differences, and the spatial-frequency domain by DCT coefficient or motion vector. The existing methods can perform well on the only special case because they use a single feature. So there is difficulty of applying the conventional methods to video sequences that include various cases [2], [4], [7].

J. Liu et al. (Eds.): IDEAL 2003, LNCS 2690, pp. 553–560, 2003.
© Springer-Verlag Berlin Heidelberg 2003

To overcome these problems of the existing shot change detection methods, [5], [6], and [7] suggested to detecting the enhanced shot change using the multiple features. But this approach is difficult to determine the relation among the features. Yusoff [5] et al suggested setting the threshold in term of the voting and behavior knowledge classification. Naphade [6] and Lee [7] et al clustered an abrupt shot change detection with the k-means algorithm that used the pixel and histogram difference. But their approach has some problems that the result of groups changes according to the initial central points.

In this paper, we focus on how to set the threshold value and classify the multiple features. We adopt the binary classification tree and multistage decision method to classify efficiently the multiple features. At the first stage of this classification method, the data is classified by selecting a feature variable that has the best performance of classification. At the next stage, the remaining data is classified again. This procedure is repeated until all of the terminal nodes are pure. The maximal tree is pruned back to obtain an optimal tree with given complexity. An optimal threshold value is determined at each stage. Cross-validation and drop-case methods are also used to confirm the reliability of the classification tree.

2   Related Works

Out of the conventional methods for shot-change detection, we select three methods: Firstly, we select the pixel-based method to detect the global luminance difference between consecutive frames. Secondly, we select the global and local histogram-based methods to detect the color and luminance difference. Finally, we select the block-based method to detect the motion of the camera and object. They are defined as below:

1. Pixel-based method [LPD]
Pixel difference [1]-[3] is a method that calculates the difference in corresponding pixel values between two consecutive frames. This method is easy to implement and acquires relatively good results. However, one problem with this method is false detection, as the pixel value difference becomes large when there exists fast object motion or fast camera movement.

2. Histogram-based method
The histogram-based method [1]-[4] is easy to implement and it has a low computational complexity. The advantage of this method is an insensitivity to object motion and camera movement. Also this method can fail to detect cuts when different shots have similar intensity distributions, or when there are sudden intensity changes within a shot.

We use 3 different histograms that are evaluated to generate relatively high performance. They are defined as below:

① Luminance Histogram Difference [IHD]
IHD is evaluated on luminance information with 256 bins for each frame histogram using the histogram difference.

② Local Luminance Histogram Difference [LHL]

LHL is evaluated on luminance information with 64 bins for each block histogram.

③ Hue Histogram Difference [HHD]

HHD is evaluated on hue information with 256 bins for each frame histogram.

3. Block-based method [LLR]

The block-based methods [1], [2], [4], [5] use local attributes to reduce the effect of noise and camera flashes. Here, each frame is partitioned into a set of r blocks. Rather than comparing a pair of frames, every block in the current frame is compared with the corresponding block in the previous frame. This method gives better performance than the pixel-based and histogram-based methods because the threshold value is decided at block level rather than at pixel level.

2.1 Analysis and Discussion

We evaluate and analyze the performance of each method, LPD, IHD, LHL, HHD, and LLR through an experiment. The data set used for the experiment consists of 37 cuts among total of 2716 frames. Note that this sequence is captured from VHS at a frame rate of 15 fps with 320x240 frame size and uncompressed in RGB format.

We use two indexes of *recall(re)* and *precision(pr)* to evaluate the performance of each method. We also define the evaluation index (*EI*) as follows.

$$EI = \frac{recall + precision}{2}$$

$$recall = \frac{S_C}{S_C + S_M}, \qquad precision = \frac{S_C}{S_C + S_F}$$

(1)

where, S_c is the number of correct detections, S_M is the number of missed detections, and S_F is the number of false detections. Note that closer to 1 is the *EI*, better performance is.

Table 1 shows the performance of each detection method. The respective threshold value is set for S_M and S_F to have minimum error ratio. From Table 1, we can see that LHL and LLR have best performance, but the other methods demonstrate poor performance. LPD shows poor performance when fast motion of camera and object exists in the sequence. IHD and HHD show poor performance in case of similar histogram at shot changes and reflection from light or noise, respectively. We investigate the cases of MD (missed detection) and FA (false alarm) from our experiment.

Fig. 1 shows examples of FA and correct detection. In the Fig. 1 (a), two cuts are detected at A^{th} and B^{th} frames, and one FA at C^{th} frame, which is caused by a noise of light. In Fig.1 (b), LPD detects the two cuts exactly with no FA. Fig. 2 illustrates the case of MD occurrence. Actual cuts occur at D^{th}, E^{th}, and F^{th} frames. All of the cuts are correctly detected when using LPD, HHD, and LHL methods, but D^{th} frame is missed when using IHD and LLR, which is due to the similar histogram.

Table 1. Comparison of the detection performance for each method

S_c	LPD		IHD		LHL		HHD		LLR	
	S_M	S_F	S_M	S_F	S_M	S_F	S_M	S_F	S_M	S_F
37	1	76	2	98	0	6	0	123	1	15
re/pr	0.97	0.33	0.95	0.27	1	0.86	0.95	0.23	0.97	0.74
EI	0.65		0.61		0.93		0.59		0.87	

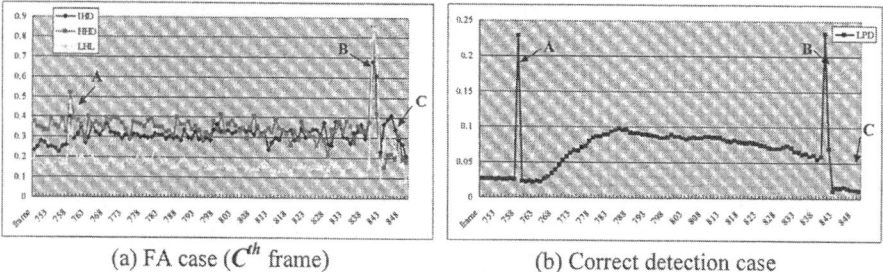

(a) FA case (C^{th} frame)   (b) Correct detection case

Fig. 1. Example of FA (Threshold values: IHD=0.391, LHL=0.332, HHD=0.423, and LPD= 0.166).

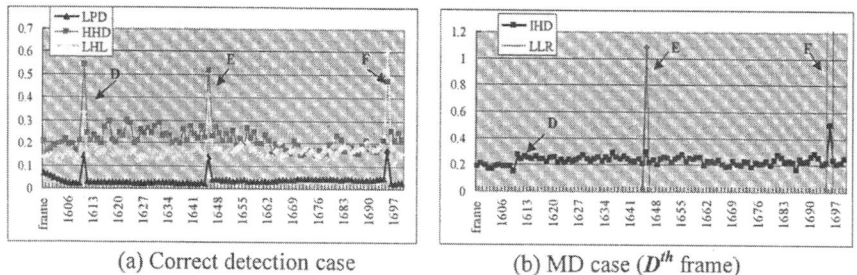

(a) Correct detection case   (b) MD case (D^{th} frame)

Fig. 2. Example of MD (Threshold values are same as in Fig. 2).

From two results so far explained, we note that combining several methods could eliminate FA and MD. The features can be classified by any classification methods. In this paper, binary classification tree method and multistage decision method are adopted. We can find an optimal threshold value and feature parameters during the classification. We present more details in section 3.

3   Binary Classification Method

The CART(Classification and Regression Tree) suggested by Breiman, et al [8],[9] is a tree-structured data mining technique that finds hidden relationships in data. This produces the binary classification tree in which each binary split of the data involves a splitting question of the form "Is $A \leq B$?" where A is one of the measurements, and B is a decision boundary. The root node of the tree contains all the training data; the various types are randomly mixed together in this node. The goal of the binary classification method is to successively subdivide the training set using binary splits in such a way that the data associated with the terminal nodes of the tree do not have a mix of various types; rather each node should be as 'pure' as possible. We used the Gini index of diversity to measure the impurity of a set of data. A simple rule is to assign the most popular class for each terminal node; this is called the plurality rule, and is what we used. When two different classes are tied for the most popular class in the node, we arbitrarily chose the lower numbered class as the class for that node.

To assess the reliability of predictive accuracy as applied to each of the data sets, we perform cross-validation analysis. This method proceeds by dividing the training sample into v roughly equal parts, each containing a similar distribution for the dependent variable. CART takes the first $v-1$ parts of the data, constructs the largest possible tree, and uses the remaining $1/v$ part of the data to obtain initial estimates of the error rate of selected sub-trees. The same process is then repeated (growing the largest possible tree) on another $(v-1)/v$ parts of the data while using a different $1/v$ part as the test sample. The process continues until each part of the data has been held in reserve one time as a test sample. The result of the v mini-test samples are then combined to form error rates for trees each possible size.

In order to predict for new test sample, we use the drop-case method. It uses the optimal classification tree grown by the training sample. Each observation is processed case-by-case, beginning at the root node. The splitting criteria are applied, and in response to each yes/no question the case moves down left or right until it reaches a terminal node. If the primary split criterion cannot be applied because the case is missing data, a surrogate split criterion is used. If no surrogates are available, the case moves down the tree with the priors-adjusted majority.

4 Experimental Results

The CART® software utilized for the analysis is Version 3.6.3(SP1) for Windows manufactured by Salford Systems, and runs on a personal computer with a 1.7GHz Pentium IV processor and 512MB of RAM.

To evaluate the appropriateness of constructed models, data is randomly divided into two different sets: a training set composed of 48 cuts and no gradual transition of 2167 frames captured from the movie "The Matrix" (1999), and a test set with 37 cuts of 2716 frames captured from a documentary. Note that these sequences are captured from VHS at a frame rate of 15 fps with 320x240 frame size and uncompressed in RGB format.

We compare the performance of each previous method with that of our method. We use five features of LPD, IHD, HHD, LHD and LLR. Resulting optimal tree is shown in Fig. 3. Each terminal node is indicated nsc(no shot change: white) or sc(shot change: gray) and the number of classes of a particular type in each node is indicated within the node. The optimal classification tree is grown by the three variables (LHL, LPD and HHD).

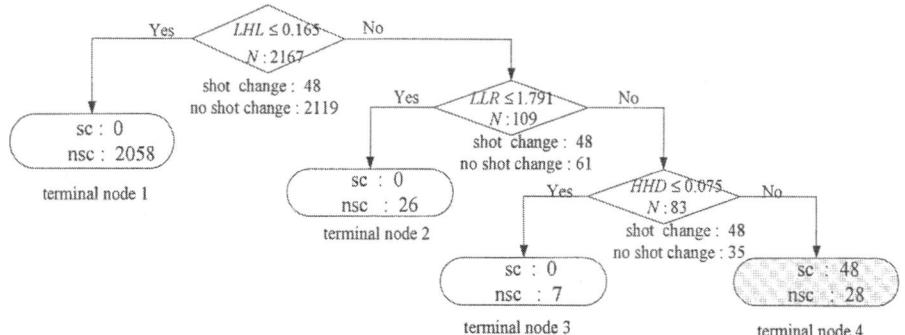

Fig. 3. The optimal classification tree trained with training sample. Where, *sc* denotes shot-change class and *nsc* is no shot-change detection.

Experimental result and cross-validation result are summarized in Table 2. For the training sample, *recall*, *precision*, and *EI* are 1.0, 0.63, and 0.815, respectively. So, we can say that the classifier shows high degree of success rate. Also, according to Table 2, the cross validation classification probabilities are 89.6% and 98.7% for *sc* class and *nsc* class, respectively. This means that we know how well any tree will perform on completely fresh data – even if we do not have an independent test sample. In this experiment, we set $v = 10$. We also use the drop-case method. We drop the samples of completely new video (documentary) down to the optimal tree built with the previous training sample. Classification results are given in Table 3.

Table 2. Experimental result and cross-validation

Actual Class	Actual Sample	Experimental Result		Cross Validation	
		sc	*nsc*	*sc*	*nsc*
sc	48	48	0	89.6%	10.4%
nsc	2119	28	2071	1.3%	98.7%
recall/precision		1.0	0.63		
EI		0.815			

Each observation is processed by the same criteria; that is, the splitting criteria used in the optimal classification tree of Fig. 3. Each threshold level for the LHL, LLR, and HHD among the multiple features is applied at each node of the optimal tree. In the Table 3-(a), the response statistics provide distributional information by terminal nodes. The response class means that each node assigned to what class. The probability indicates the occurrence rate about *sc* or *nsc*. *N* is the total number of the terminal node. And the correct means that the node has correctly 'pure' sample rate.

Table 3-(b) represents the predicted class such as the *sc* and *nsc* class using Table 3-(a). And the *correct* in Table 3-(b) indicates the accurately classified rates by the predicted class. Also, we compare the cross-validation performance in the Table 2 with drop-case *correct*. The cross validation classification probabilities are 89.6% and 98.7% for *sc* and *nsc* class, respectively. Thus, the classifier shows high degree of success rate while identifying the correct class type for new observations.

Next, we observe instances of FA and MD in our sample sequences. FA's occur due to sudden intensity change (flash), occlusion and fast motion of object. And MD's occur due to the similar histogram intensity distributions.

Table 3. Classification results of drop-case (documentary video samples)

(a) Response statistics

		Predicted class				Total
		Response	Prob.	N	Correct	
Terminal Node	1	*nsc*	0.859	2331	1.0	2331
	2	*nsc*	0.127	345	0.991	345
	3	-	-	-	-	-
	4	*sc*	0.015	41	0.829	41

(b) Case-by-case sample classification table

Actual Class	Predicted class		Actual Total
	sc	*nsc*	
sc	34	3	37
nsc	7	2672	2679
Predicted Total	41	2675	2716
Correct	0.919	0.997	
Total Correct	0.958		

5 Conclusions and Future Works

In this paper, we proposed an abrupt shot change detection method using supervised classification of the multiple features. First of all, we extracted 5 different features. To obtain the relationship among the multiple features, we used the binary classification tree and multistage decision method. Then we constructed an optimal tree using the features. According to the result of classification, we extracted the important features from the multiple features and obtained the decision-boundary for the feature at each node of the tree. Also, we performed cross-validation analysis and drop-case method to confirm the reliability of classification tree. An experimental result showed that the *EI* of our method performed 2% better than that of the conventional shot change detection methods. For future works, we will improve the performance of our method for the gradual transition such as fade, wipe, or dissolve.

Acknowledgements. This research was supported by IRC (Internet Information Retrieval Research Center) in Hankuk Aviation University. IRC is a Kyounggi-Province Regional Research Center designated by Korea Science and Engineering Foundation and Ministry of Science & Technology.

References

1. Idris, F., Panchanathan, S.: Review of Image and Video Indexing Techniques, Journal of Visual Communication and Image Presentation, Vol. 8, No. 2, (1997) 146–166
2. Gargi, U., Kasturi, S., Strayer, S. H.: Performance Characterization of Video-Shot-Change Detection Methods, IEEE Trans. on Circuit and Systems for Video Tech., Vol. 10, No 1, (2000) 1–13
3. Lupatini, G., Saraceno, C., Leonardi, R.: Scene break detection: a comparison, Proceedings of 8th International Workshop on Continuous-Media Databases and Application, (1998) 34–41
4. Yusoff, Y., Christmas, W., and Kitter, J.: A Study on Automatic Shot Change Detection, Proc. 3rd European Conference on Multimedia Applications, Services and Tech.(ECMAST), no. 1425 in LNCS, (1998) 177–189
5. Yusoff, Y., Kitter K., and Christmas, W.: Combining Multiple Experts for Classifying Shot Changes in Video Sequences, IEEE International Conference on Multimedia Computing and Systems, vol. 2, (1999) 700–704
6. Naphade, M. R., Mehrotra, R. , Ferman, A. M., Warnick, J. , Huang, T. S., and Tekalp, A. M., : A High-Performance Shot Boundary Detection Algorithm Using Multiple Cues, ICIP '98, vol 1, (1998) 4–7
7. Lee, H. C., Lee, C. W., Kim, S. D.: Abrupt Shot Change Detection Using an Unsupervised Clustering of Multiple Features, International Conference on Acoustics, Speech, and Signal Processing, Vol. 4, (2000) 2015–2018
8. Data Mining with Decision Trees: An Introduction to CART®, Salford Systems Training Manual
9. Dan, S., Phillip, C.,: CART® – Classification and Regression Tree, CA : Salford Systems, San Diego, (1997)

On a Lip Print Recognition by the Pattern Kernel with Multi-resolution Architecture

Jin Ok Kim[1], Kyong Seok Baik[2], and Chin Hyun Chung[2]

[1] School of Information and Communication Engineering, Sungkyunkwan University,
300, Chunchun-dong, Jangan-gu, Suwon, Kyunggi-do, 440-746, KOREA
jinny@ece.skku.ac.kr
[2] Department of Information and Control Engineering, Kwangwoon University,
447-1, Wolgye-dong, Nowon-gu, Seoul, 139-701, KOREA
chung@daisy.kwangwoon.ac.kr

Abstract. Biometric systems are forms of technology that use unique human physical characteristics to automatically identify a person. They have sensors to pick up some physical characteristics, convert them into digital patterns, and compare them with patterns stored for individual identification. However lip-print recognition has been less developed than recognition of other human physical attributes such as the fingerprint, voice patterns, retinal blood vessel patterns, or the face. The lip print recognition by a CCD camera has the merit of being linked with other recognition systems such as the retinal/iris eye and the face. A new method using multi-resolution architecture is proposed to recognize a lip print from the pattern kernels. A set of pattern kernels is a function of some local lip print masks. This function converts the information from a lip print into digital data. Recognition in the multi-resolution system is more reliable than recognition in the single-resolution system. The multi-resolution architecture allows us to reduce the false recognition rate from 15% to 4.7%. This paper shows that a lip print is sufficiently used by the measurements of biometric systems.

1 Introduction

Biometric systems are forms of technology that use unique human physical characteristics to automatically identify a person. They have sensors to pick up some physical characteristics, convert them into digital patterns, and compare them with patterns stored for his/her own identification. Non-sophisticated biometrics have existed for centuries. Parts of our bodies and aspects of our behavior have historically been used as important means of identification [1]. The study of finger images dates back to ancient China. A person is usually remembered and identified by his/her face or by the sound of his/her voice. His/her signature is one of the best-established methods of authentication in banking, for legal contracts and many other aspects of his/her life [2]. A system to analyze the unique pattern of the retinas was introduced in the mid 1980s. Biometric identification can eliminate such common problems as illicitly copied keys, lost or broken mechanical locks, and forged/stolen personal identification numbers which

J. Liu et al. (Eds.): IDEAL 2003, LNCS 2690, pp. 561–568, 2003.

can lead to automatic teller machine and checking fraud [3]. It can be used for identification purposes involving security access systems in information-services departments, government agencies, ATMs/banks, law enforcement, prisons, international border control, and military agencies [4] [5]. Biometric measurement systems typically include voice recognition/verification, fingerprint identification, palm prints, hand/wrist vein patterns, retinal/iris eye scans, hand geometry, keystroke dynamics or typing rhythms, and signature verification [6]. Each measurement has its own merits and faults. A lip print is included among measurements of biometric systems [7]. Each person's lip has a unique lip print and differs from others [8]. A new personal identification method is proposed by using lip print recognition with pattern kernels and multi-resolution architecture. Pattern kernels use some local masks in order to analyze a lip print by a pattern-recognition method based on computation of local autocorrelation coefficients [9]. The method has merits such as a small amount of data, and faster computation than template matching. The merit of lip print recognition by a CCD camera can be linked with other recognition systems such as the retinal/iris eye and the face, because those use the same sensors and are located in the human face.

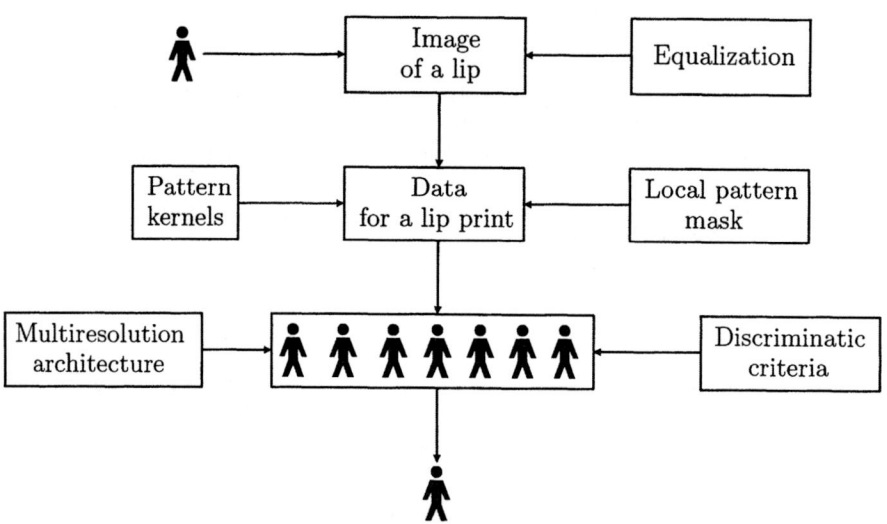

Fig. 1. Block diagram of a lip-print recognition system

Figure 1 illustrates a block diagram of a lip print recognition system with multi-resolution architecture. The image data from a lip print is considered a connective appearance with the directional local pattern [10] [11]. The local masks extract information from local patterns for a lip print, including the vertical, the horizontal, and the diagonal patterns. One of the advantages of the pattern kernels through the local masks is the small amount of data required to represent unique personal information for recognition. The discrimination criteria either recognizes a person from the classes of his/her input images or rejects him if the input image is mismatched [12] [13]. The multi-resolution architecture is proposed in order to reduce both the noise and false recognition rates.

2   Multi-resolution Architecture

The multi-resolution architecture is proposed to utilize the information vector at different image resolutions and to overcome the fault of the single-resolution system of a lip print recognition method. It is caused by the speciality of a lip print such as a chapped lip, and by an unexpected noise. A pre-process is used to reduce the noise by a histogram equalization. However, this method has limitations when removing the various noises from the image of the lip print. The multi-resolution system has more merits than the single-resolution, because of the robustness of the noise and the reliability of the system. The smoothing effect on averaging has proved to be more beneficial to the reduction of noise and the chapped lip.

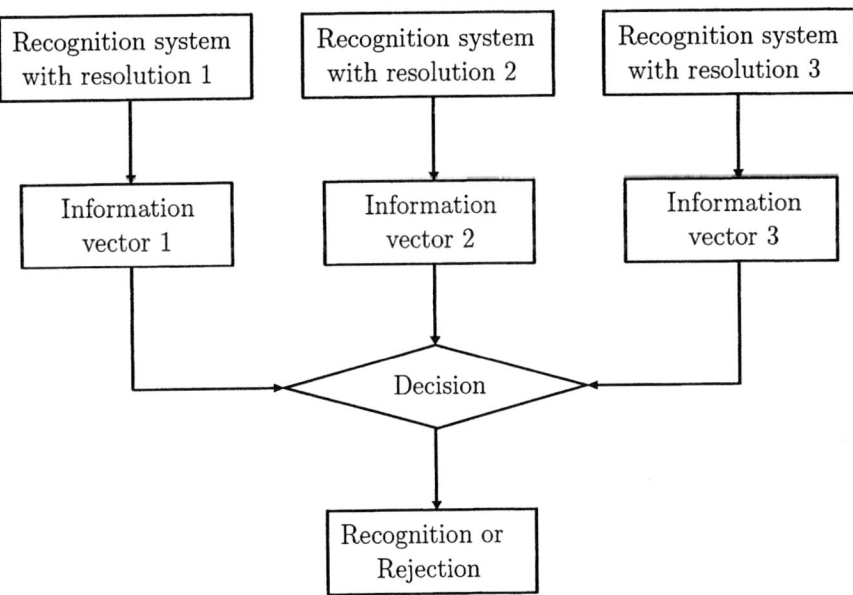

Fig. 2. Architecture of a multiresolution system

Figure 2 illustrates the architecture of the multi-resolution system. The recognition system corresponding to a resolution of the image produces a single information vector and discriminates its output. The last products of these modules are combined so as to decide the final result which indicates a recognition or a rejection. Recognition with a three- or two-resolution system is much more reliable than recognition with a single-resolution system.

The input image is composed of many pixels with the 8-bit-gray level. Its value ranges from 0 up to 255. In this paper, the image data maintains the 8-bit-gray level until all processes end, pre-processed with the histogram equalization for acquiring an enhanced image. The lip print holds some information in the small part inside the region.

If the input image is pre-processed with the threshold method, a part of the information on the lip print will vanish from the input image [14] [15] [16]. When the local pattern mask is compared with the pre-processed input image, it is not easy for the mask to find the same pattern of the input image because of its data with the 8-bit-gray level. This kind of difficulty can be resolved by using some statistical factors such as its mean and its standard deviation.

In Fig. 3, for example, mask 1 has 8 pixels marked in black and 8 pixels marked in white. The pixels marked in black are a part of the lip print. While mask 1 scans some regions of the image, its mean and its standard deviation can be computed. The computational results can be used for mask 1 to find out whether its region has the same pattern or not.

M_b, a mean of the pixel marked in black, is obtained by (1)

$$M_b = \frac{1}{8} \sum_{i=1}^{8} P_b. \tag{1}$$

where P_b is the pixel marked in black.

S_b, a standard deviation of the pixel marked in black, is obtained by (2)

$$S_b = \sqrt{\frac{1}{8} \sum_{i=1}^{8} (P_b - M_b)^2}. \tag{2}$$

M_w, a mean of the pixel marked in white, is obtained by (3)

$$M_w = \frac{1}{8} \sum_{i=0}^{8} P_w. \tag{3}$$

where P_w is the pixel marked in white.

S_w, a standard deviation of the pixel marked in white, is obtain by (4)

$$S_w = \sqrt{\frac{1}{8} \sum_{i=0}^{8} (P_w - M_w)^2}. \tag{4}$$

The statistical factors show a relationship of the pixels marked in black and white, and especially determine the output of the local pattern mask. It could be

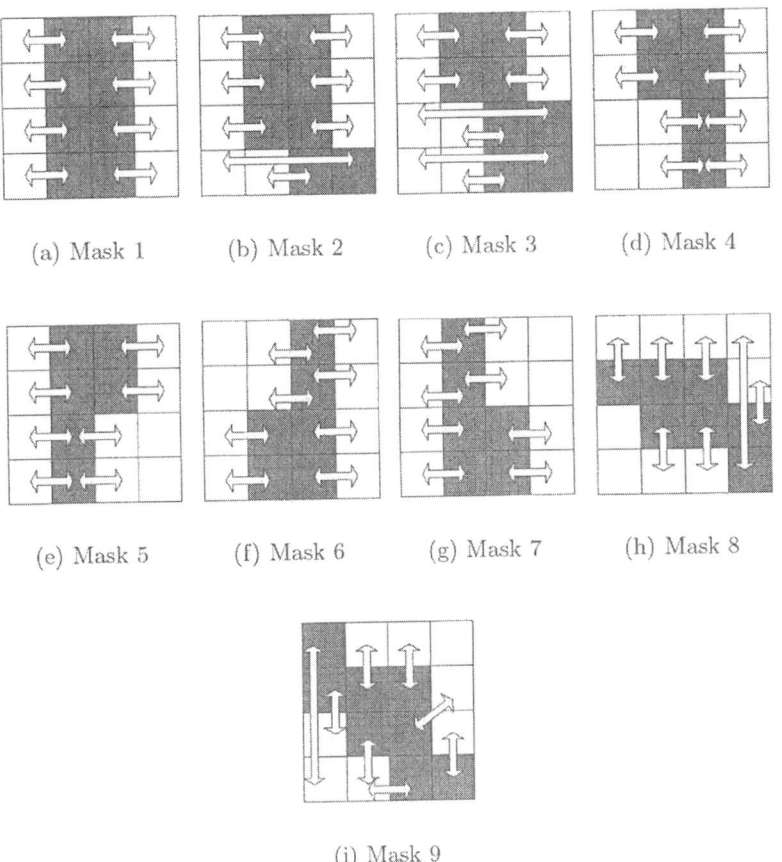

(a) Mask 1   (b) Mask 2   (c) Mask 3   (d) Mask 4

(e) Mask 5   (f) Mask 6   (g) Mask 7   (h) Mask 8

(i) Mask 9

Fig. 3. Example of the local pattern masks

true or false. If the output of any mask is true, the pattern kernel corresponding to a mask is computed in the region which includes a location of the detected mask. Since the number detected by the pattern kernel represents its frequency, it is converted into the vector data.

Some examples of a lip print are shown in Fig. 4, in which the pictures illustrate the various patterns of the lip print. Figure 4(a) shows the complex pattern of the lip print. The pattern of Fig. 4(a) consists of the horizontal direction pattern, the vertical direction pattern and the diagonal direction pattern. Fig. 4(d) shows the blurred pattern of the lip print. It is difficult to analyze the pattern of this lip print. However, if a combination of several pattern kernels is used, the characteristic features of its blurred pattern can be extracted. Each picture has the various shapes, frequencies and lengths of the lip print. These

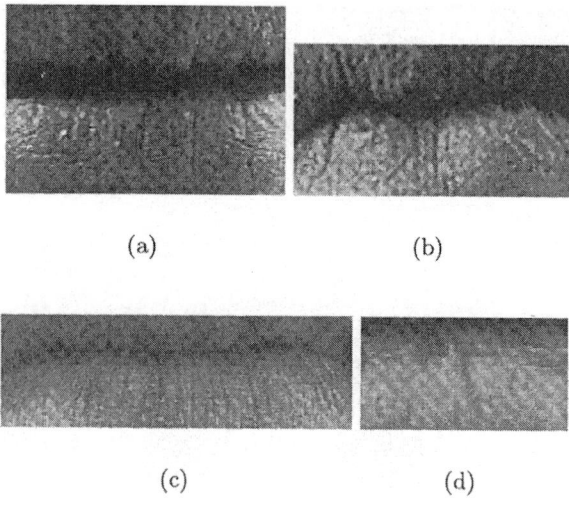

(a)   (b)

(c)   (d)

Fig. 4. Some samples of lip print patterns.

features should be analyzed and transformed to get the discriminative data by the pattern kernels.

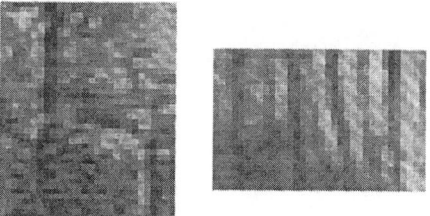

Fig. 5. Magnification of a lip print.

The magnifications of the vertical direction pattern and the WS(west-south) diagonal direction pattern are shown in Fig. 5, in which the pattern kernels inform us about the characteristics of the pattern. The vertical direction pattern inside the left image in Fig. 5 is detected by the pattern kernel 1 and the WS diagonal direction pattern is converted into digital data by the pattern kernel 3. For example, if a pattern in any location is matched with mask 1 or 4, the pattern kernel 1 will be computed to produce the information vector.

Table 1. Recognition rate (RR), false rejection rate (FRR) and false acceptance rate (FAR) of the recognition system

Resolution	RR	FRR	FAR
1	85.0%	11.3%	3.7 %
1, 2	90.6%	8.0%	1.4 %
1, 2, 3	95.3%	3.6%	1.1 %

3 Results and Conclusion

Figure 4(d) shows the blurred pattern of the lip print. It is difficult to analyze the pattern of this lip print. However, if a combination of several pattern kernels is used, the characteristic features of its blurred pattern can be extracted. Each picture has the various shapes, frequencies and lengths of the lip print. These features should be analyzed and transformed to get the discriminative data of the pattern kernels. Table 1 shows that the multi-resolution system with three modules achieves a recognition rate of 95.3%, but the single resolution system achieves a system error with a rate of 15%. Table 1 and Figure 6 show the multi-resolution architecture algorithm improves not only the recognition rate, the false recognition rate and the false acceptance rate but also the repeatabilty rate.

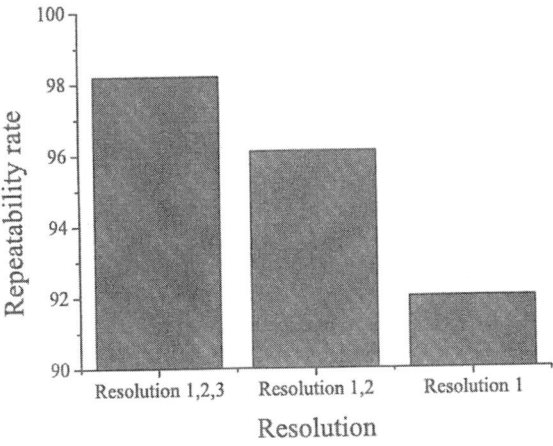

Fig. 6. Repeatability rate of the recognition system.

Its performance has been investigated for a lip print recognition based on the local pattern mask and the pattern kernels. The local pattern mask extracts information from the local pattern of a lip print. The pattern kernels detect information from the global pattern and convert a lip print into the digital data that can be discriminated by the criteria. The multi-resolution architecture allows us to reduce the false recognition rate from 15% to 4.7%. This paper shows that a lip print is sufficiently used by the measurements of biometric systems. The lip print recognition by a CCD camera has the merit of being linked with other recognition systems such as the retinal/iris eye and the face to make the system compensated. A system with plural attributes may have more reliability than a system with a singular one.

References

1. Wark, T., Sridharan, S., Chandran, V.: The use of speech and lip modalities for robust speaker verification under adverse conditions. In: IEEE MCS 1998, IEEE (1998)
2. Goudail, F., Lange, E., Iwamoto, T., Kyuma, K., Otsu, N.: Face recognition system using local autocorrelations and multiscale integration. IEEE Trans. Pattern Analysis and Machine Intelligence 18 (1996) 1024–1028
3. Lades, M., Vorbruggen, C., Buhmann, J., Lange, J., Wurtz, C.M.R.P., Konen, W.: Distortion invariant object recognition in the dynamic link architecture. IEEE Trans. Computers 42 (1993) 300–311
4. Brunelli, R., Poggio, T.: Face recognition: Features versus templates. IEEE Trans. Pattern Analysis and Machine Intelligence 15 (1993) 1042–1052
5. Lievin, M., Delmas, P., Coulon, P.Y., Luthon, F., Fristot, V.: Automatic lip tracking: Bayesian segmentation and active contours in a cooperative scheme. In: IEEE MCS 1998, IEEE (1998)
6. Oliver, N., Pentland, A.: Lafter: Lips and face real-time tracker. In: IEEE CVPR 1997, IEEE (1997)
7. Samal, A., Iyengar, P.A.: Automatic recognition and analysis of human faces and facial expressions: A survey. IEEE Trans. Pattern Recognition 25 (1992) 65–67
8. Valentin, D., Abdi, H., O'Toole, A.J., Cottrell, G.W.: Connectionist models of face processing: A survey. IEEE Trans. Pattern Recognition 27 (1994) 1209–1230
9. Pratt, W.K.: Digital Image Processing. 3 edn. John Wiley (2001)
10. Ashbourn, J.D.M.: Biometrics: Advanced Identify Verification: The Complete Guide. Springer Verlag, New York (2000)
11. Lucey, S., Sridharan, S., Chandran, V.: Initialized eigenlip estimator for fast lip tracking using linear regression. In: IEEE ICPR 2000, IEEE (2000)
12. Zhang, D.D.: Automated Biometrics: Technologies and Systems. Kluwer Academic Publishers, Boston, MA. (2000)
13. Jain, A., Bolle, R., Pankanti, S.: Biometrics: Personal Identification in Networked Society. Kluwer Academic Publishers, Boston, MA. (1999)
14. Abe, S.: Pattern Classification. Springer Verlag (2001)
15. Duda, R.O., Hart, P.E., Stork, D.G.: Pattern Classification. 2 edn. Wiley-Interscience (2000)
16. Javidi, B.: Image Recognition and Classification. Marcel Dekker (2002)

A XML-Based Data Communication Solution for Program Mining

Cunhao Fang, Yaoxue Zhang, Donglin Xia, and Kegang Xu

Department of Computer Science and Technology, Tsinghua University
Beijing 100084, P.R. China
fch@mails.tsinghua.edu.cn
http://inet-group.cs.tsinghua.edu.cn/

Abstract. This paper first discusses Program Mining, a new computing paradigm to achieve computing-on-demand in network environments. The basic
idea of Program Mining is making use of several task-specific software agents,
analyzing user's requests for computing, searching and retrieving candidates
from online component repositories, composing and reassembling them to form
programs to achieve computing on demand. XML is the standard format for
data exchange between applications on the Internet. In the implementation of
program mining, we have developed a XML messaging based dynamic agent
infrastructure, which applies XML to specify the messages among mobile
agents and define their tasks and access rights, to support multi-agent cooperation for program mining.

1 Introduction

For the past few years, the Internet is often regarded as a super information database,
where information related to a wide range of topics is disseminated and shared. To
help users find needed information on the Internet, many efforts have been made to
develop information on demand systems, such as news on demand, video on demand,
or other personalized or intelligent information retrieval systems. Some researchers
implement Data Mining techniques to discover knowledge from Web sites, we regard
it as knowledge on demand approach [1,4].

However, with the evolution of network technology, especially the prosperity of
Java, the Internet is emerging as a large-scale distributed computing platform, where
all kinds of Internet applications (web services) are deployed, providing various services for users. Traditionally, these applications often employ prepackaged monolith
systems containing any conceivable features, which are not easily extended and customized. Whereas in large scale distributed networks (e.g., the Internet), network
services and applications are diffused to a very large scope. This makes it necessary to
increase the customizability of services, so that different classes of users in heterogeneous networks can tailor the functionality and interface of a service according to their
specific needs [1]. An ideal solution to this problem is to implement applications as
component-based systems and deliver them at an on-demand manner, so that new

J. Liu et al. (Eds.): IDEAL 2003, LNCS 2690, pp. 569–575, 2003.

features can be added on demand at different granularities. Therefore, in Internet world, besides the need for personalized information, users have similar needs for computing. They need customized computing functionalities to process customized information. We regard it as the need for computing-on-demand at application level.

Based on these observations, we propose a new computing paradigm—Program Mining (PM) to deal with the increasing needs of computing-on-demand. The basic idea of PM is making use of several task-specific software agents, analyzing user's requests for computing, searching and retrieving candidates from online component repositories according to this request, composing and reassembling them to form programs that perform the expected computing. In this way, computing on demand can be provided for users, achieving great flexibility and customizability.

The rest of this paper organize as follows: In section 2, we present a more concrete concept of Program Mining; Based on this concept, we discusses and a multi-agent system framework for program mining. In section 3, we present the agent interaction mechanism for component retrieval with XML messaging. Finally, we summarize this paper by drawing a conclusion.

2   A Multi-agent System Framework for Program Mining

2.1   The Concept Diagram of Program Mining

In our proposal, software agents are utilized to discover programs among large amount of component resources. The users present what they want in terms of functionalities, which may be described in natural language and the concept of component is transparent to end users. The request is analyzed and the computing functionality is decomposed into smaller modules, possible components or component compositions that can realize these functional modules are identified. Then corresponding software agents are activated to search and retrieve potential component candidates, analyze and discover the dependencies among them, find out the possible component compositions that implement the needed computing logic. Just as Data Mining systems that discover implicit relations and patterns in a vast amount of data, Program Mining is to discover the dependencies and relationships among a great deal of software components, and compose executable programs using various task-oriented software agents. In the intermediary nodes of active networks, this mechanism can be used to dynamically discover programs that provide needed active services; in end systems, some network applications can also be composed on-the-fly using Program Mining. The concept of Program Mining is depicted in Fig.1.

2.2   The Multi Agent Architecture in Program Mining

In our scheme, many Program Mining tasks are carried out through cooperation and interaction between several software agents. According to the proposed system architecture, the agent deployment scenario on each host is depicted in Fig.2.

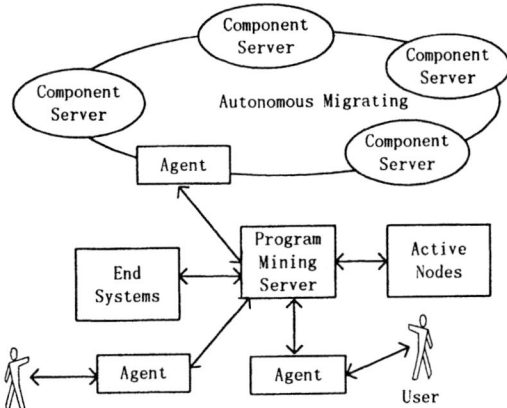

Fig. 1. Illustrates the basic concepts of Program Mining. We suppose that reusable software components have been organized in different component servers on the network. Software agents migrate autonomously among these servers to search and retrieve potential component candidates. On the Program Mining server, according to users' high-level requests, application level programs and network level computing logic can be discovered from the candidates. Particularly, in active nodes, active services are provided for the end users to perform customized computation, forming the programmable network API of active nodes. Software agents on the Program Mining server can carry out the composition of these services. In end systems, applications that utilize the underlying network services can also be composed using Program Mining mechanisms. Depending on the complexity of mining tasks, user intervention with agents might be needed when necessary.

On the directory server, a Directory Service Agent is set up to offer component directory service. On each component repository server, a Library Agent is configured to provide a standard interface for component access and meta-data registration. The library agents interact with the directory service agent to register and deregister components metadata when the repository server change the components supplied. The directory service agent can also poll the library agents to retrieve component information proactively. In this way, the metadata in the directory information base is kept up to date.

On the client side, a User Interface Agent is configured for the user to interact with the system. In our scheme, when a user or a client system need some programs or computing logics, the client-side entity can present its request through user interface agent. The interface agent accepts the request, making necessary pretreatments and forwarding it to a request analysis agent on the Program Mining server for further processing. On the client side, an Application Framework (AF) is also provided to host and activate the mined program.

On the Program Mining server, request analysis agent accepts user's request from the client side, searches the knowledge base to get the component composition scheme and the descriptions of component candidates. Based on this information, request analysis agent constructs component query terms and forwards them to one or more component retrieval agents. Component retrieval agent first interacts with directory service agent to get the exact descriptions and locations of component candidates matching the query terms. Then the agent migrates autonomously among corresponding component repository servers, communicate with the server locally to get the corresponding component candidates. At last, component retrieval agents return to the Program Mining server with retrieved components. A component composition agent receives these components and assembles them together in a Composition Environment (CE). The CE serves as a component container. It provides necessary services and adaptation mechanism for wiring components together to form the target program.

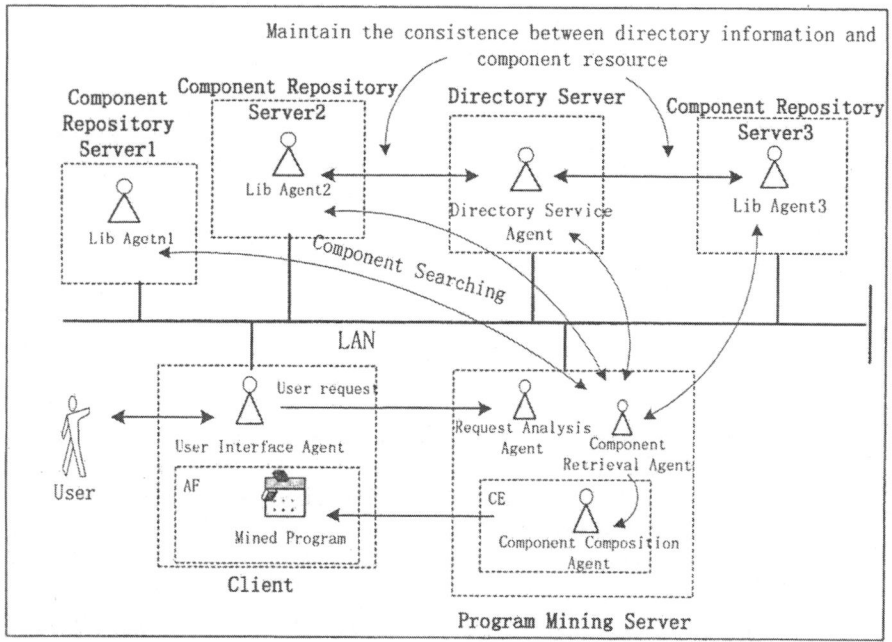

Fig. 2. Agent deployment scenario on each host in Program mining.

3   Agent Interactions for Component Retrieval with XML Messaging

Based on the component composition blueprint and function modules obtained in the previous stage of Program Mining, we can extract the description of corresponding components and construct query terms for component searching. The query terms are handed over to an agent responsible for component retrieval.

The query terms are handed over to an agent responsible for component retrieval. First, the agent accesses the component directory information base, gets the descriptions and locations of components that match the query terms. Then the agent migrates autonomously among corresponding component repository servers, communicate with the server locally to get the corresponding component candidates.

The component retrieval in the proposed multi-agent system is a two-step process. In the first step, the query terms are handed over to a Component Retrieval Agent (CRAgent) responsible for component retrieval. The CRAgent search for the component library advertisements ontology, which are stored in the Directory Service Agent (DSAgent), to discover the related component agents. The DSAgent, which is in fact a matchmaker, returns the component meta-knowledge descriptions. Such as names and addresses of the related component agents to the CRAgent. The CRAgent stores this knowledge as part of its coordination knowledge.

The component library advertisement ontology is used in the first step of component retrieval process. Using this ontology, users formulate a query to be sent to the DSAgent, to discover the Component Library Agent (LibAgent), which are wrapping the component libraries providing components in a specified domain and type. Then, the addresses of the related component agents are returned to the CRAgent by the DSAgent.

In the second step, the CRAgent, which is introduced in the first step, are queried LibAgent for the component meta-knowledge descriptions. These queries are formulated using the specified domain ontology's query interface. It maps the transferred ontology into its local knowledge base and creates the query interface related with that ontology. The query is formulated using this interface. The CRAgent migrates autonomously among corresponding component repository servers, communicate with the local LibAgent to get the corresponding component candidates. A number of component candidates are returned as the result of this query.

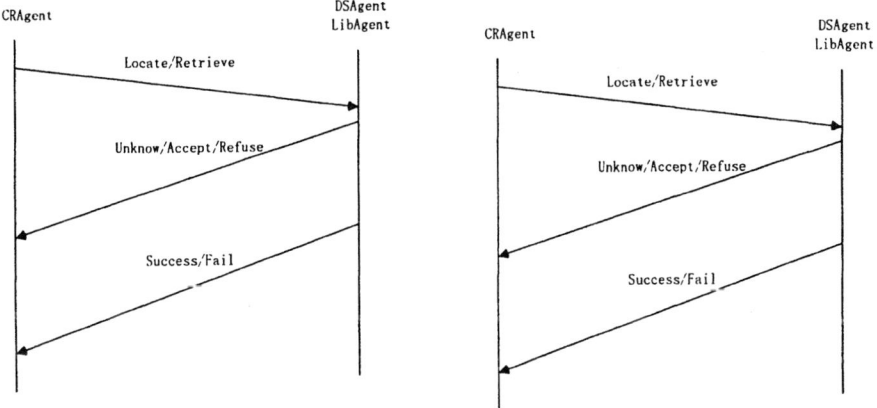

Fig. 3. Agent deployment scenario on each host.

3.1 Multi-agent Cooperation with XML Messaging

CRAgent, DSAgent and LibAgent cooperate by sending messages and using concepts from domain ontology. A standard message format with meaningful structure and semantics, and a mechanism for agents to exchange ontologies and message interpreters, are key issues. The message format should be accepted not only by the agent research community, but should be an industry standard that is likely to be adopted by information providers.

The extensive markup language, XML is a W3C standard that provides the universal format for structured documents and data on the Web, and is fast becoming the standard for data interchange on the Web. We chose XML, therefore, as the primary message format for dynamic agent communication. It has the following advantages:

Validation: By defining descriptor document DTD (Document Type Definition) [9], we can check whether a given XML-based Message is a valid agent communication message.

Translation: With appropriate XSL (eXtensible Stylesheet Language) [9] or CSS (Cascading Style Sheets) [9], the descriptor document can be transformed to other formats such as HTML, PDF, Microsoft Word, etc.

Uniformity: Using XML, agents from different models and frameworks can be interacted and integrated in the same way.

Therefore, XML is an ideal language for agent communication message descriptor presentation. The XML-based message format in agent cooperation is following:

Table 1. The message elements(tags) used in multi-agent cooperation.

Element name	Description
Message	root element
Type	message type
Sender	the sender agent of message
Receiver	the receiver agent of message
Protocol	agent communication protocol
Ontology	the specified domain ontology related with the message
Content	message content
Replywith	the ID of reply message(optional)
Language	coding language of message content

Example of a XML Message from CRAgent to LibAgent for a java-based, protocol implemetion Component in network ontology.

```
<?xml version="1.0">
<message>
 <type> request</type>
 <sender link=http://agent.tsinghua.edu.cn/~CRAgent>
  CRAgent
 </sender>
 <receiver link=http://bean.tsinghua.edu.cn/~LibAgent>
  DSagent
 </receiver>
 <ontology link=http://agent.tsinghua.edu.cn/~ontology>
     component </ontology>
 <content>
  <search>
   <application>network</application>
   <language>java</language>
   <function>protocol</function>
  </search>
 </content>
 <language link=http://agent.tsinghua.edu.cn/kif.html>
     ACML </language>
</message>
```

4 Conclusions

With the rapid development of computer networks and communication infrastructure, the Internet accessing technologies and devices are becoming more diverse. End users want to customize the functional feature sets of programs according to the network environment and resource constraints. Aiming at this problem, we propose a new computing paradigm— Program Mining to approach computing on demand in distributed environments.

We also discussed the basic concepts, a multi-agent system framework for Program mining general process in program mining. With the penetration of Internet into everyone's daily life, we believe that the change from information/knowledge-on-demand to computing-on-demand will be an important trend in the way people using Internet. More efforts should be made to achieve this goal. Program Mining is an initial attempt to approach it. Although the work in this paper represents only a beginning, we feel that Program Mining as a new computing paradigm offers a broad new field of research.

References

1. Alfonso Fuggetta, Gian Pietro Picco and Giovanni Vigna, "Understanding Code Mobility", IEEE Transactions on Software Engineering, Vol. 24, No. 5, May 1998.
2. D.Tennenhouse and D.Wetherall, "Towards an Active Network Architecture", Computer Communication Review, 26(2), April 1996.
3. L.A.Guedes, P.C. Oliveira, L.F. Faina and E.Cardozo, "An Agent-based Approach for Supporting Quality of Service in Distributed Multimedia Systems". Computer Communications 21 (1998) 1269–1278.
4. Minos N. Garofalakis, Rajeev Rastogi, S.Seshadri and Kyuseok Shim, "Data Mining and the Web: Past, Present and Future" WIDM99 Kansas City Mo USA.
5. RIG Uniform Data Model for Reuse Libraries (UDM), RPS-0002, Reuse Library Interoperability Group, January 1994.
6. Sanjiva Weerawarana and Matthew J. Duftler, "Bean Markup Language (Version 2.3) User's Guide", http://www.alphaWorks.ibm.com/formula/bml.
7. The Common Object Request Broker: Architecture and Specification, Version 3.0, CCM FTF Draft ptc/99-10-04, 29 October 1999.
8. Wienberg A, Matthes F and Boger M, "Modeling Dynamic Software Components in UML", UML'99, 1723: 204–219, 1999.
9. XMI http://www.software.ibm.com/ad/features/xmi.html.

Improving the Efficiency of Frequent Pattern Mining by Compact Data Structure Design

Raj P. Gopalan and Yudho Giri Sucahyo

Department of Computing, Curtin University of Technology
Kent St, Bentley
Western Australia 6102
{raj, sucahyoy}@computing.edu.au

Abstract. Mining frequent patterns has been a topic of active research because it is computationally the most expensive step in association rule discovery. In this paper, we discuss the use of compact data structure design for improving the efficiency of frequent pattern mining. It is based on our work in developing ·efficient algorithms that outperform the best available frequent pattern algorithms on a number of typical data sets. We discuss improvements to the data structure design that has resulted in faster frequent pattern discovery. The performance of our algorithms is studied by comparing their running times on typical test data sets against the fastest Apriori, Eclat, FP-Growth and OpportuneProject algorithms. We discuss the performance results as well as the strengths and limitations of our algorithms.

1 Introduction

Association rule mining aims to discover interesting relationships among sets of items in a transaction database [1]. The process of mining association rules consists of two main steps: 1) Finding the frequent item sets with a minimum support; 2) Using the frequent item sets to generate association rules that meet a confidence threshold. Step 1 is computationally expensive since the number of item sets grows exponentially with the number of items. A large number of increasingly efficient algorithms to mine frequent item sets have been developed over the years [5].

The frequent pattern mining algorithms use a variety of data structures. Most algorithms store the transaction database in memory using variations of array or tree structures. For example, FP-Growth represents the transactions in the FP-Tree, which is a prefix tree with links between nodes containing the same item [2]. H-Mine represents the transactions in H-struct, which consists of a set of arrays with links between each item and the next transaction that has the same item [3].

In this paper, we discuss the impact of improving the data structure design on the efficiency of frequent pattern mining. It is based on our work in developing fast algorithms that outperform the fastest available implementations of frequent pattern mining on some typical data sets at common support levels. We first designed a data structure named ITL that improved H-struct [3] for more efficient frequent pattern mining [6]. A prefix tree was then used for compressing transaction data before mapping to ITL [7]. The prefix tree was compacted further to improve the

J. Liu et al. (Eds.): IDEAL 2003, LNCS 2690, pp. 576–583, 2003.

compression and corresponding changes were made to the ITL structure. A basic algorithm was adapted to mine patterns using the different data structures. The algorithms we developed include three based on variants of ITL and one based on the compact tree structure. The performance of these algorithms was evaluated on typical test data sets. The ITL based algorithms were compared against the best available implementation of Apriori algorithm, OP [5], which is currently the fastest available pattern growth algorithm, and Eclat [4]. The tree based algorithm was compared against Apriori, Eclat and FP-Growth. The results of experiments show that our algorithms improve with changes to the data structure design and the fastest versions of our algorithm outperform other algorithms on typical data sets for most of the support levels we used. These results are discussed in more detail later in the paper.

The structure of the rest of this paper is as follows: In Section 2, we define the relevant terms. In Section 3, we discuss the data structures and their improvements. We describe the algorithms in Section 4, and present the performance study in Section 5. Section 6 contains conclusion and pointers for further work.

2 Definition of Terms

We give the basic terms needed for describing association rules using the formalism of [1]. Let $I=\{i_1,i_2,\ldots,i_n\}$ be a set of items, and D be a set of transactions, where a transaction T is a subset of I ($T \subseteq I$). Each transaction is identified by a *TID*. An association rule is an expression of the form $X \Rightarrow Y$, where $X \subset I$, $Y \subset I$ and $X \cap Y = \varnothing$. X and Y can consist of one or more items. X is the *body* of the rule and Y is the *head*. The proportion of transactions that contain both X and Y to those that contain X is the confidence of the rule. The proportion of all transitions that contain both X and Y is the support of the *support* of the item set $\{X, Y\}$. An item set is called a *frequent item set* if its *support $\geq$ support threshold* specified by the user, otherwise the item set is *not frequent*. An association with the *confidence $\geq$ confidence threshold* is considered as a valid association rule.

3 Design of Data Structures

In this section, we describe the initial design of our data structure and its subsequent modifications to improve the efficiency of our algorithm for frequent pattern mining. Our data representation is based on the following observations: 1) Item identifiers can be mapped to a range of integers; 2) Transaction identifiers can be ignored provided the items of each transaction are linked together.

The data structures are given in two parts. Section 3.1 describes the transaction tree based on the concept of prefix trees and the changes made to it. Section 3.2 deals with an array and link structure named ITL and its modifications. The initial version of our algorithm called ITL-Mine used only the basic ITL structure. It was subsequently modified to map transactions compressed using the transaction tree.

3.1 Transaction Tree Design and Its Modifications

Several transactions in a database may contain the same sets of items. Even if items of two transactions are originally different, early pruning of infrequent items could make their item sets identical. In addition, two transactions that do not contain an identical set of items may have a subset of the items in common. The transaction tree is designed to group such transactions.

Fig. 1a shows a full prefix tree for items 1-4. All siblings are lexicographically ordered from left to right. Each node represents a set consisting of the node element and all the elements on nodes in the path (prefix) from the root. It can be seen that the set of paths from the root to the different nodes of the tree represent all possible subsets of items that could be present in any transaction.

We further refined the transaction tree by reducing the number of nodes using a compression scheme. It is observed that a complete prefix tree has many identical subtrees in it. In Fig. 1a, we can see three identical subtrees *st1*, *st2*, and *st3*. Building a complete prefix tree will need a large amount of memory, and so we compressed the tree by storing information of identical subtrees together. We call this a compact transaction tree.

For example, we can compress the full prefix tree in Fig. 1a containing 16 nodes to the tree in Fig. 1b that has only 8 nodes, by storing some additional information at the nodes of the smaller tree. The number of paths from the root to various nodes corresponds to the transactions to be traversed during mining. So compressing the prefix tree in this way reduces the traversals of transactions thus improving the performance of the mining process.

Each node in the compressed tree has additional entries to keep the count of transactions represented by the node. For example, the entry (0,0) at the leaf node of the leftmost branch of the tree represents the item set 12345 that incidentally does not occur in the sample database. The first 0 in the entry indicates that the item set starts at level 0 in the tree with 1 as the first item. The second 0 indicates that no transaction in the database has this item set. Similarly, the entry (1,1) means there is one transaction with item set 2345 and (2,2) means there are two transactions with item set 345. In the implementation of the tree, the counts at each node are stored in an array so that the level for an entry is the array index that is not stored explicitly. The doted rectangles in Fig. 1b, that show the item sets corresponding to the nodes in the compressed tree are not part of the data structure.

3.2 Item-Trans Link (ITL) Data Structure

Our array based data structure called Item-Trans Link (ITL) has features of both vertical and horizontal data layouts (see Fig. 2). ITL consists of an item table (named ItemTable) and the transactions linked to it (TransLink) as described below.

1. ItemTable: It contains all individually frequent items (1-freq items). In Fig. 2, items with a minimum support of 2 in the sample database are represented. Each item is stored with its support count and a link to the first occurrence of that item in TransLink described below.

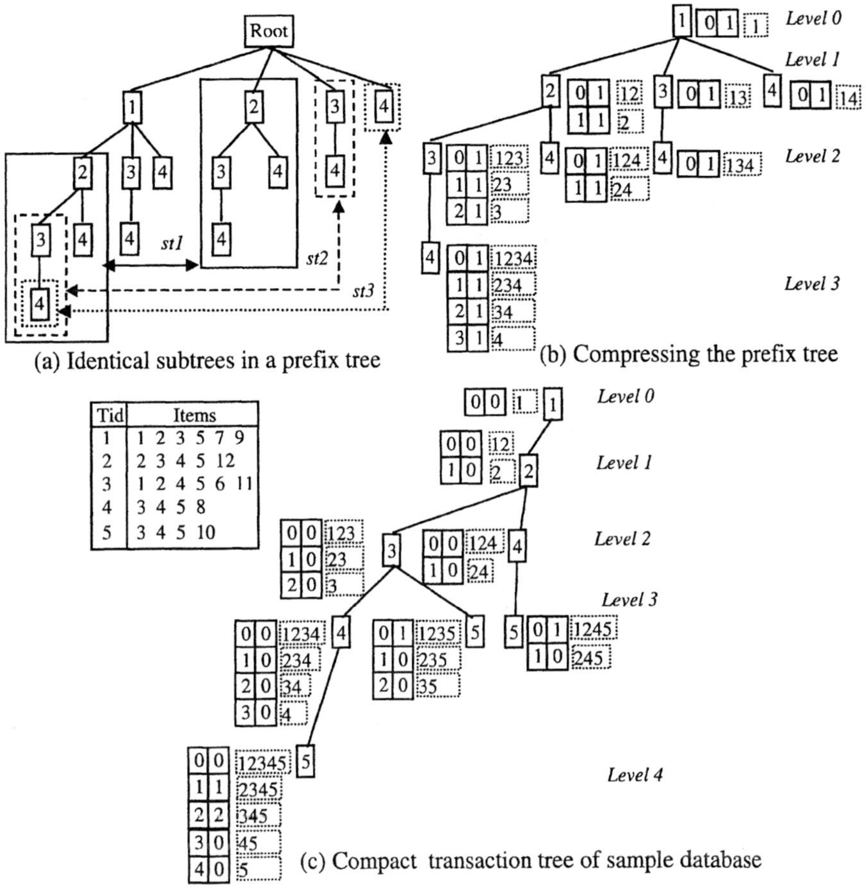

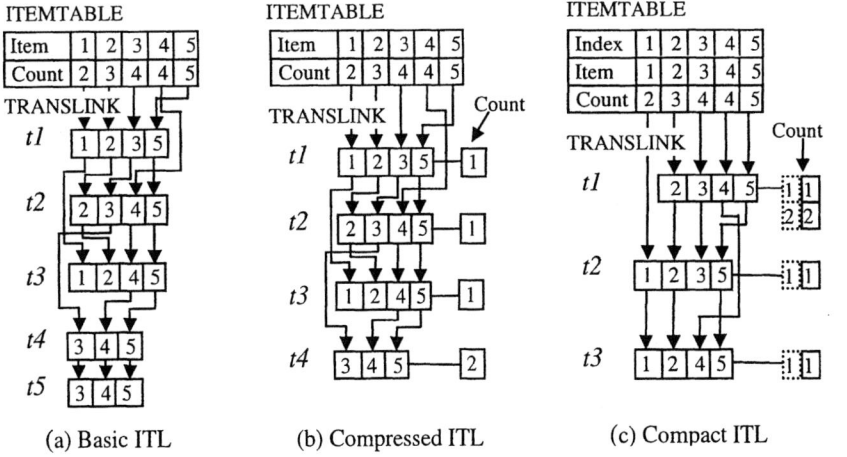

(a) Identical subtrees in a prefix tree

(b) Compressing the prefix tree

Tid	Items
1	1 2 3 5 7 9
2	2 3 4 5 12
3	1 2 4 5 6 11
4	3 4 5 8
5	3 4 5 10

(c) Compact transaction tree of sample database

Fig. 1. Prefix tree and compact transaction tree

(a) Basic ITL (b) Compressed ITL (c) Compact ITL

Fig. 2. The Item-TransLink (ITL) data structure and its modifications

2. TransLink: It represents each transaction of the database that contains the items of ItemTable. The items of a transaction are arranged in sorted order, and for each item, there is a link to its next occurrence in another transaction. For example, to get the occurrences of item 1, we can go to the cell of 1 in *t1* (see Fig. 2a), and then directly to the next occurrence of 1 in *t3* without traversing *t2*.

Fig. 2a shows the basic ITL for the sample database of Fig. 1c. It is constructed directly from the transaction database. Each transaction in the database is represented by a separate row. Fig. 2b shows the compressed ITL obtained by mapping the transaction tree of Fig. 1b. A count field is added to the basic ITL for mapping the transaction tree. Since each path in the transaction tree represents a group of transactions, each group is mapped as an entry in ITL with a count of transactions in the group.

For mapping the compact transaction tree, ITL is further modified to indicate the count of different subsets of items with each row. Fig. 2c shows the compact ITL mapped from the compact transaction tree of Fig. 1c. Additional information is attached to each row of TransLink, indicating the count of transactions that have different subsets of items. Each node in the tree that has a nonzero transaction count is mapped to a row in TransLink, with nonzero entries at the node attached to the row.

4   ITL-Mine, TreeITL-Mine, CT-ITL, and CT-Mine Algorithms

In this section, we briefly describe the algorithms based on the different data structures presented in Section 3. The ITL-Mine algorithm uses only the basic ITL data structure. TreeITL-Mine is a modification of ITL-Mine that uses the transaction tree and the corresponding compressed ITL. CT-ITL uses the compact transaction tree and the corresponding compact ITL. CT-Mine extracts frequent patterns directly from the compact transaction tree.

ITL-Mine. ITL-Mine uses the basic ITL data structure. There is a row in TransLink for every transaction that contains some 1-freq items. The steps of ITL-Mine are as follows:
1. Construct ItemTable and TransLink: The ItemTable and TransLink are constructed by a single scan of the transaction database. At the end of this step, the 1-freq items will be identified in the ItemTable from their support counts.
2. Prune: The infrequent items are pruned or deleted from the TransLink since they will not be useful in the next step, because of the anti-monotone property.
3. Mine Frequent Itemsets: All the frequent item sets of two or more items are mined by a recursive function following the pattern growth approach and using the tid-intersection method.

TreeITL-Mine. TreeITL-Mine uses the simple transaction tree to group transactions (see Fig. 1b). Each group of transactions is represented by a row in TransLink of compressed ITL that has a count field with each row. Number of entries in compressed ITL is usually less than the number of entries in basic ITL (see Fig. 2b). There are four steps in TreeITL-Mine as follows:

1. Identify the 1-freq items and initialize the ItemTable: The transaction database is scanned once to get the 1-freq items.
2. Construct the transaction tree: The transaction tree is constructed only from the occurrences of 1-freq items in the transaction database.
3. Construct ITL: The transaction tree is traversed to construct TransLink, which is attached to ItemTable.
4. Mine Frequent Itemsets: It is similar to Step 3 of ITL-Mine except for the use of tid-count-intersection for extracting longer patterns, instead of a simple tid-intersection.

TreeITL-Mine outperforms ITL-Mine on commonly used test data sets [7].

CT-ITL. CT-ITL algorithm is based on the compact transaction tree and compact ITL described in Section 3. There are four steps in CT-ITL as follows:
1. Identify the 1-freq items and initialise the ItemTable: The transaction database is scanned to identify all 1-freq items, which are recorded in ItemTable. All entries in the ItemTable are sorted in frequency ascending order and the items are mapped to new identifiers that are ascending sequence of integers. (The change of identifiers is not reflected in the example due to our choice of sample data.)
2. Construct the compressed transaction tree: Using the output of Step 1, only 1-freq items are read from the transaction database. They are mapped to the new item identifiers and the transactions inserted into the compact transaction tree.
3. Construct compact ITL: The compact transaction tree is traversed to construct the ItemTable and TransLink.
4. Mine Frequent Itemsets: It is similar to Step 4 of TreeITL-Mine.

A detailed description of CT-ITL is available in [8]. The performance of CT-ITL is better than other algorithms on dense data sets that contain relatively long patterns.

CT-Mine. There are three steps in the CT-Mine algorithm as follows:
1. Identify the 1-freq items and initialize the ItemTable: Same as Step 1 of CT-ITL.
2. Construct Compressed Transaction Tree: Same as Step 2 of CT-ITL.
3. Mining: All the frequent itemsets of two or more items will be mined in this step using a recursive function.

A detailed description of CT-Mine is given in [9].

5 Performance Study

We compare ITL-Mine, TreeITL-Mine, and CT-ITL with the fastest available implementation of Apriori algorithm representing the candidate generation-and-test approach, and OpportuneProject (OP), the fastest available program based on the pattern growth approach [5]. OP is an adaptive algorithm that can choose between an array or a tree to represent the transactions in the memory. Apriori 4.03 [10] uses a prefix tree for storing the transaction database while Apriori 4.01 is its earlier version without the prefix tree. Eclat is used in the evaluations because it uses tid-intersection similar to our algorithms. Since CT-Mine is a tree based algorithm, it is compared separately with Apriori, Eclat and FP-Growth which is the best known tree based algorithm.

All the programs are written in MS Visual C++ 6.0. All the tests were performed on an 866MHz Pentium III PC, 512 MB RAM, 30 GB HD running MS Windows 2000. In this paper, the runtime includes both CPU time and I/O time.

Several datasets were used to test the performance including Mushroom, Chess, Connect-4, Pumsb* and BMS-Web-View1. Due to space limitations, we show the results only on Connect-4 and Pumsb*. Connect-4 available from [11], is a dense dataset that produces many long patterns of frequent item sets for very high values of support. Pumsb*, downloaded from [12], contains census data from PUMS (Public Use Microdata Samples). It is less dense compared to Connect-4.

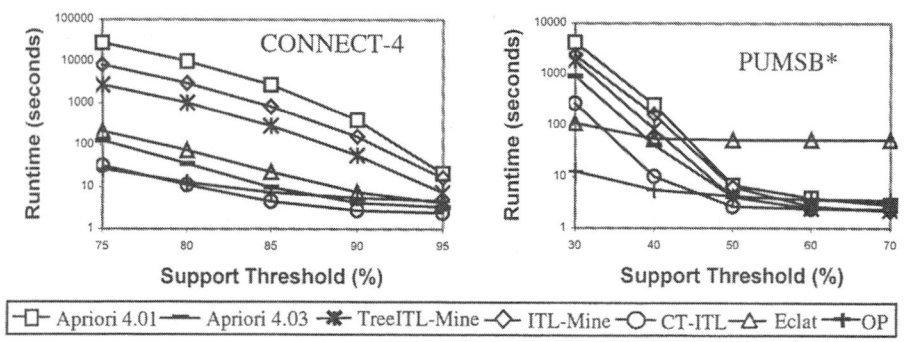

Fig. 3. Performance comparison of ITL algorithms with Apriori, Eclat and OP

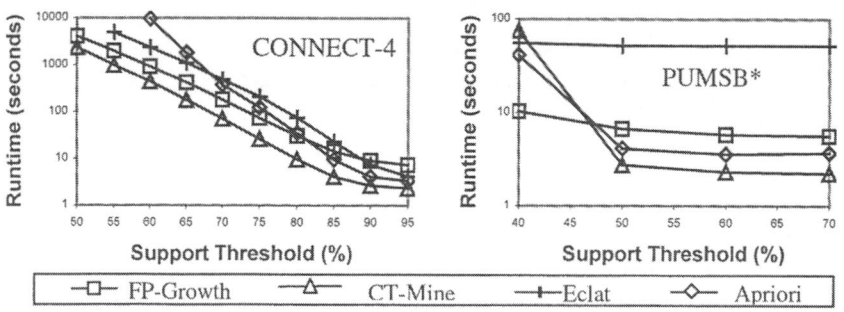

Fig. 4. Performance comparison of CT-Mine with Apriori, Eclat and FP-Growth

Run times of the algorithms on both datasets are shown in logarithmic scale along the y-axis in Fig. 3 and Fig. 4. CT-ITL outperforms OP and other algorithms at most support levels. On Connect-4, CT-ITL performs better than other algorithms because the number of TransLink entries is very low compared to the number of transactions in the original database. On Pumsb*, as with Connect-4, the reduction in number of TransLink entries by compressing transactions is very significant at support levels of 50-70 which helps CT-ITL perform better than other algorithms. Similarly, CT-Mine outperforms FP-Growth at most of the support levels because the compact transaction trees have less number of nodes than the corresponding FP-trees. However, at low support levels on relatively sparse data sets, the compression scheme of CT-Mine and CT-ITL does not provide the same degree of reduction in the cost of traversing the transactions. Therefore, algorithms like OP perform relatively better at lower support levels, especially on sparse data sets.

6 Conclusion

In this paper, we have discussed the influence of compact data structure design on the performance of frequent pattern mining. Starting with a basic prefix tree and an array based data structure called ITL, we presented a sequence of design changes and their impact on the performance of corresponding algorithms. Our algorithms were compared against Apriori, Eclat, OP and FP-Growth on various datasets and the results show that our fastest algorithms perform better than all others at several commonly used support levels.

To extend the CT-ITL and CT-Mine algorithms for very large databases, we plan to partition the tree to fit in available memory. This work is currently in progress. The relative performance of CT-ITL and CT-Mine on various practical data sets is also to be investigated. This work is part of a larger project for building a data mining query optimizer [8].

References

[1]   R. Agrawal, T. Imielinski, and A. Swami, "Mining Association Rules between Sets of Items in Large Databases", Proc. of ACM SIGMOD, Washington DC, 1993.

[2]   J. Han, J. Pei, and Y. Yin, "Mining Frequent Patterns without Candidate Generation", Proc. of ACM-SIGMOD, Dallas, TX, 2000.

[3]   J. Pei, J. Han, H. Lu, S. Nishio, S. Tang, and D. Yang, "H-Mine: Hyper-Structure Mining of Frequent Patterns in Large Databases", Proc. of IEEE ICDM, San Jose, California, 2001.

[4]   M. J. Zaki, "Scalable Algorithms for Association Mining", IEEE Transactions on Knowledge and Data Engineering, vol. 12, pp. 372-390, May/June 2000.

[5]   J. Liu, Y. Pan, K. Wang, and J. Han, "Mining Frequent Item Sets by Opportunistic Projection", Proc. of ACM SIGKDD, Edmonton, Alberta, Canada, 2002.

[6]   R. P. Gopalan and Y. G. Sucahyo, "ITL-Mine: Mining Frequent Itemsets More Efficiently", Proc. of 2002 Int. Conf. on Fuzzy Systems and Knowledge Discovery, Singapore, 2002.

[7]   R. P. Gopalan and Y. G. Sucahyo, "TreeITL-Mine: Mining Frequent Itemsets Using Pattern Growth, Tid Intersection and Prefix Tree", Proc. of 15th Australian Joint Conference on Artificial Intelligence, Canberra, Australia, 2002.

[8]   R. P. Gopalan, T. Nuruddin, and Y. G. Sucahyo, "Building a Data Mining Query Optimizer", Proc. of Australasian Data Mining Workshop, Canberra, Australia, 2002

[9]   R. P. Gopalan and Y. G. Sucahyo, "Fast Frequent Itemset Mining using Compressed Data Representation", Proc. of IASTED Int. Conf. on Databases and Applications, Innsbruck, Austria, 2003.

[10] http://fuzzy.cs.uni-magdeburg.de/~borgelt/.

[11] http://ww.ics.uci.edu/~mlearn/MLRepository.html.

[12] http://ugustus.csscr.washington.edu/census/.

Extraction of Dynamic User Behaviors from Web Logs

Younes Hafri[1], Bruno Bachimont[1], and Peter Stachev[3]

[1] Institut National de l'Audiovisuel, 4 avenue de l'Europe
94366 Bry-sur-Marne Cedex, France
{yhafri,bbachimont}@ina.fr
[2] Kettering University, USA
pstanchev@kettering.edu
3, Kettering University, Flint, MI 48504, USA

Abstract. Our paper proposes an approach which makes possible prediction of future states to be visited in k steps corresponding to k web pages hyper-linked, based on both content and traversed paths. To make this prediction possible, three concepts have been highlighted. The first one represents user exploration sessions by Markov models. The second one avoids the problem of Markov model high-dimensionality and sparsely by clustering web documents, based on their content, before applying Markov analysis. The third one extracts the most representative user behaviors (represented by Markov models) by considering a clustering method.

The original application of the approach concerns the exploitation of multimedia archives in the perspective of the Copyright Deposit that preserves French's WWW documents. The approach may be the exploitation tool for any web site.

1 Introduction

The future web sites, particularly web services, will amass detailed records of which uses their web documents and how people use them. However, this "new" future industry highlights the most ambitious effort yet to gather disparate bits of personal information into central databases containing electronic information on potentially every person who surfs the web bases. Profiling explorations are in the interest of the user, providing more customized and directed services through the web bases.

Profiling is a business concept from the marketing community, with the aim of building databases that contain the preferences, activities and characteristics of clients and customers. It has been for a long time a part of the commercial sector. It has developed significantly with the growth of e-commerce, the Internet and information retrieval. The goal of profiling web exploration is to have the most complete picture of the web users we can. Mining the web servers also achieves the used cookies, carries out profiling scenes off-line. The long-term objective is to create associations between potential commercial web sites and commercial

J. Liu et al. (Eds.): IDEAL 2003, LNCS 2690, pp. 584–595, 2003.

marketing companies. These sites make use of specific cookies to monitor client's explorations at the web site and record data that users may have provided to the exploration server. User likes, dislikes, browsing patterns and buying choices are stored as a profile in a database without user knowledge or consent.

The main technical contribution of the paper is the notion of probabilistic prediction, path analysis using Markov models, clustering Markov models and dealing with the high dimension matrix of Markov models in clustering algorithm. The paper provides a solution, which efficiently accomplishes such profiling. This solution should enhance the day-to-day web exploration in terms of information filtering and searching. More precisely, this paper proposes an approach that extracts automatically web user profiling based on user navigation paths. Web user profiling consists of the best representative behaviors, represented by Markov models. To achieve this objective, our approach is articulated around three notions: (1) Applying probabilistic exploration using Markov models. (2) Avoiding the problem of Markov model high-dimensionality and sparsity by clustering web documents, based on their content, before applying the Markov analysis. (3) Clustering Markov models, and extraction of their gravity centers. On the basis of these three notions, the approach makes possible the prediction of future states to be visited in k steps and navigation sessions monitoring, based on both content and traversed paths.

The paper contains the following sections. Section 2 situates our contribution among state of art approaches. Section 3 describes user-profiling based web exploration. Section 4 highlights the general framework of the system. Section 5 presented some implementation results. Finally, section 6 concludes the paper.

2   Related Works and Contribution

The problem of modeling and predicting user's accesses on web site has attracted a lot of research interest. It has been used to improve the web performance through various caching strategies such as [Agg 99], [Bad 98], [Fan 99], [Per 99] and prefetching [Fan 99], [Sch 99] [Pad 96]; adaptive web sites [Per 99], web log mining [Zai 98]; intelligent agents that detects user web topics [Chu 97]; extraction of the most interesting pages [Woo 96], [Sha 97]; recommend related pages improve search engines, personalize the browsing in a web site and continuous Markov models to influence caching priorities between primary, secondary and tertiary storages [Stu 98].

The analysis of sequential data is without doubts an interesting application area since many real processes show a dynamic behavior. Several examples can be reported, one for all is the analysis of DNA strings for classification of genes, protein family modeling, and sequence alignment.

In this paper, the problem of unsupervised classification of temporal data is tackled by using a technique based on Markov Models. MMs can be viewed as stochastic generalizations of finite-state automata, when both transitions between states and generation of output symbols are governed by probability distributions [Rab 89]. The basic theory of MMs was developed in the late 1960s, but only in the last decade it has been extensively applied in a large number of problems, as speech recognition [Rab 89], handwritten character recognition [Bro 96], DNA and protein modeling [Hug 96], gesture recognition [Eic 98], behavior analysis and synthesis [Jeb 00], and, more in general, to computer vision problems. Related to sequence clustering, MMs has not been extensively used, and a few papers are present in the literature. Early works were proposed in [Rab 89], [Lee 90], all related to speech recognition. The first interesting approach not directly linked to speech issues was presented by Smyth [Smy 97], in which clustering was faced by devising a distance measure between sequences using HMMs. Assuming each model structure known, the algorithm trains an HMM for each sequence so that the log-likelihood (LL) of each model, given each sequence, can be computed. This information is used to build a LL distance matrix to be used to cluster the sequences in K groups, using a hierarchical algorithm.

Subsequent work, by Li and Biswas [Bis 99], [Bis 00], address the clustering problem focusing on the model selection issue, i.e. the search of the HMM topology best representing data, and the clustering structure issue, i.e. finding the most likely number of clusters. In [Bis 99], the former issue is addressed using standard approach, like Bayesian Information Criterion [Sch 78], and extending to the continuous case the Bayesian Model Merging approach [Sto 93]. Regarding the latter issue, the sequence-to-HMM likelihood measure is used to enforce the within-group similarity criterion. The optimal number of clusters is then determined maximizing the Partition Mutual Information (PMI), which is a measure of the inter-cluster distances. In the second paper [Bis 00], the same problems are addressed in terms of Bayesian model selection, using the Bayesian Information Criterion (BIC) [Sch 78], and the Cheesman-Stutz (CS) approximation [Che 96]. Although not well justified, much heuristics is introduced to alleviate the computational burden, making the problem tractable, despite remaining of elevate complexity. Finally, a model-based clustering method is also proposed in [Law 00], where HMMs are used as cluster prototypes, and Rival Penalized Competitive Learning (RPCL), with state merging is then adopted to find the most likely HMMs modeling data. These approaches are interesting from the theoretical point of view, but they are not tested on real data. Moreover, some of them are very computationally expensive. Each visitor of a web site leaves a trace in a log file (see example bellow) of the pages that he or she visited. Analysis of these click patterns can provide the maintainer of the site with information on how to streamline the site or how to personalize it with respect to a particular visitor type. However, due to the massive amount of data that is generated on large and frequently visited web sites, clickstream analysis is hard to perform 'by hand'. Several attempts have been made to learn the click behaviour of a web surfer, most notably by probabilistic clustering of individuals with mixtures of Markov chains [Cad 00], [Smy 97], [Smy 99]. Here, the availability of a prior categorization of web pages was assumed; clickstreams are modelled by a transition matrix between page categories. However, manual categorization can be cumbersome for large web sites. Moreover, a crisp assignment of each page to one particular category may not always be feasible.

The core issue in prediction is the development of an effective algorithm that deduces the future user requests. The most successful approach towards this goal has been the exploitation of the user's access history to derive predictions. A thoroughly studied field in this area is Web prefetching. It shares all the characteristics that identify the Web prediction applications like the previously mentioned.

In general, there is two prefetching approaches. Either the client will inform the system about its future requirements or, in a more automated manner and transparently to the user, the system will make predictions based on the sequence of the client's past references. The first approach is characterized as informed and the latter as predictive.

3 User Profiling and Web Exploration

3.1 Web Features

We consider a robot named WPE (Web Profile Extractor) that extracts, invisibly, features from web user explorations. WPE is synchronized with the playing of scene that resulted from user browsing or queries.

To enable WPE to compile meaningful reports for its client web sites and advertisers and to better target advertising to user, WPE collects the following types of non-personally-identifiable feature about users who are served via WPE technology:

- User IP address. A unique number assigned to every computer on the Internet. Information, which WPE can infer from the IP address, includes the user's geographic location, company, and type and size of organization.
- User domain type (com, net or edu.).
- Standard feature included with every communication sent on the Internet. Information, which WPE can infer from this standard feature, includes user browser version and type (i.e., Netscape or Internet Explorer), operating system, browser language, service provider (i.e., Wanado, Club internet or AOL), local time, etc.
- Manner of using the scene or shot visit within a WPE client's site.
- Affiliated advertisers or web publishers may provide access with non-personally-identifiable demographic feature so that user may receive ads that more closely match his interests. This feature focuses on privacy protections as the access-collected non-personally-identifiable data. WPE believes that its use of the non-personally-identifiable data benefits the user because it eliminates needless repetition and enhances the functionality and effectiveness of the advertisements the users view which are delivered through the WPE technology.

3.2 Mathematical Modeling

Given the main problem "profiling of web exploration", the next step is the selection of an appropriate mathematical model. Numerous time-series prediction problems, such as in [Niz 00], supported successfully probabilistic models. In particular, Markov models and Hidden Markov Models have been enormously successful in sequence generation. In this paper, we present the utility of applying such techniques for prediction of web explorations.

A Markov model has many interesting properties. Any real world implementation may statistically estimate it easily. Since the Markov model is also generative, its implementation may derive automatically the exploration predictions. The Markov model can also be adapted on the fly with additional user exploration features . When used in conjunction with a web server, this later may use the model to predict the probability of seeing a scene in the future given a history of accessed scenes. The Markov state-transition matrix represents, basically, "user profile" of the web scene space. In addition, the generation of predicted sequences of states necessitates vector decomposition techniques. The figure 1 shows graph representing a simple Markov chain of five nodes and their corresponding transitions probabilities.

Markov model creations depend of an initial table of sessions in which each tuple corresponds to a user access.

```
INSERT INTO [Session] (id, idsceneInput)
SELECT[InitialTable].[SessionID],
      [InitialTable].[SessionFirstContent]
FROM OriginalTable
GROUP BY [InitialTable].[SessionID],
         [InitialTable].[SessionFirstContent]
ORDER BY [InitialTable].[SessionID];
```

3.3   Markov Models

A set of three elements defines a discrete Markov model: $< \alpha, \beta, \lambda >$

α corresponds to the state space. β is a matrix representing transition probabilities from one state to another. λ is the initial probability distribution of the states in a.

Each transition contains the identification of the session, the source scene, the target scene, and the dates of accesses. This is an example of transition table creation.

```
SELECT regroupe.Session_ID, regroupe.Content_ID AS idPageSource,
       regroupe.datenormale AS date_source,
       regroupe2.Content_ID AS idPageDest,
       regroupe2.datenormale AS date_dest INTO transitions
FROM [2] regroupe sessions from call4] AS regroupe,
     [2] regroupe sessions from call4] AS regroupe2
WHERE (((regroupe2.Session_ID)=regroupe!Session_ID)
       AND ((regroupe2.Request_Sequence)=regroupe!Request_Sequence+1));
```

The fundamental property of Markov model is the dependencies of the previous states. If the vector $\alpha(t)$ denotes the probability vector for all the states at time 't', then:

$$\alpha(t) = \alpha(t-1) \times \beta \tag{1}$$

If there are N states in the Markov model, then the matrix of transition probabilities β is of size N x N. Scene sequence modeling supports the Markov model.
In this formulation, a Markov state corresponds to a scene presentation, after a
query or a browsing. Many methods estimate the matrix β. Without loss of generality, the maximum likelihood principle is applied in this paper to estimate β
and λ. The estimation of each element of the matrix $\beta[v, v']$ respect the following
formula:

$$\beta[v, v'] = \phi(v, v')/\phi(v) \tag{2}$$

where $\phi(v, v')$ is the count of the number of times v' follows v in the training data.
We utilize the transition matrix to estimate short-term exploration predictions.
An element of the matrix state, say $\beta[v, v']$ can be interpreted as the probability
of transitioning from state v to v' in one step.

The Markovian assumption varies in different ways. In our problem of exploration prediction, we have the user's history available. Answering to which of
the previous explorations are *good predictors* for the next exploration creates the
probability distribution. Therefore, we propose variants of the Markov process to
accommodate weighting of more than one history state. So, each of the previous
explorations are used to predict the future explorations, combined in different
ways. It is worth noting that rather than compute β and higher powers of the
transition matrix, these may be directly estimated using the training data. In
practice, the state probability vector $\alpha(t)$ can be normalized and threshold in
order to select a list of *probable states* that the user will choose.

3.4 Predictive Analysis

The implementation of Markov models into a web server makes possible four
operations directly linked to predictive analysis. In the first one, the server supports Markov models in a predictive mode. Therefore, when the user sends an
exploration request to the web server, this later predicts the probabilities of the
next exploration requests of the user. This prediction depends of the history of
user requests. The server can also supports Markov models in an adaptive mode.
Therefore, it updates the transition matrix using the sequence of requests that
arrive at the web server.

In the second one, prediction relationship, aided by Markov models and
statistics of previous visits, suggests to the user a list of possible scenes, of
the same or different web bases, that would be of interest to him, and then the
user can go to next. The prediction probability influences the order of scenes. In
the current framework, the predicted relationship does not strictly have to be a
scene present in the current web base. This is because the predicted relationships
represent user traversal scenes that could include explicit user jumps between
disjointing web bases.

In the third one, there is generation of a sequence of states (scenes) using Markov models that predict the sequence of states to visit next. The result returned and displayed to the user consists of a sequence of states. The sequence of states starts at the current scene the user is browsing. We consider default cases, such as, if the sequence of states contains cyclic state, they are marked as "explored" or "unexplored". If multiple states have the same transition probability, a suitable technique chooses the next state. This technique considers the scene with the shortest duration. Finally, when the transition probabilities of all states from the current state are too weak, then the server suggests to the user, the go back to the first state.

In the fourth one, we refer to web bases that are often good starting points to find documents, and we refer to web bases that contain many useful documents on a particular topic. The notion of profiled information focuses on specific categories of users, web bases and scenes. The web server iteratively estimate the weights of profiled information based on Markovian transition matrix.

3.5   Path Analysis and Clustering

To reduce the dimensionality of the Markov transition matrix β, a clustering approach is used. It reduces considerably the number of states by clustering similar states into *similar groups*. The reduction obtained is about log N, where N is the number of scenes before clustering. The clustering algorithm is a variant of k-medoids, inspired of [19]. The particularity of the algorithm is the replacement of sampling by heuristics. Sampling consists of finding better clustering by changing one medoid. However, finding the best pair (medoid, item) to swap is very costly ($O(k(nk)2)$). That is why, heuristics have been introduced in [19] to improve the confidence of swap (medoid, data item). To speed up the choice of a pair (medoid, data item), the algorithm sets a maximum number of pairs to test (num_pairs), then choose randomly a pair and compare the dissimilarity. To find the k medoids, our algorithm begins with an arbitrary selection of k objects. Then in each step, a swap between a selected object O_i and a non-selected object O_h is made, as long as such a swap would result in an improvement of the quality of the clustering. In particular, to calculate the effect of such a swap between O_i and O_h , the algorithm computes the cost C_{jih} for all non-selected objects O_j. Combining all possible cases, the total cost of replacing O_i with O_h is given by: $T_{cih} = \sum C_{jih}$. The algorithm 1 is given bellow.

The algorithm go on choosing pairs until the number of pair chosen reach the maximum fixed. The medoids found are very dependant of the k first medoids selected. So the approach selects k others items and restarts num_tries times (num_tries is fixed by user). The best clustering is kept after the num_tries tries.

4   Approach Implementation

4.1   Data Set

The used data set is provided by KDDCup (www.ecn.purdue.edu/KDDCUP/) which is a yearly competition in data mining that started in 1997. It's objective is to provide data sets in order to test and compare technologies (prediction algorithms, clustering approaches, etc.) for e-commerce, considered as a "killer domain" for data mining because it contains all the ingredients necessary for successful data mining. The ingredients of our data set include many attributes (200 attributes), and many records (232000). Each record corresponds to a session.

More precisely, the data come from a concrete study carried out with truths users on a commercial site named www.gazelle.com (now on close state). The site sold data mining technologies. The data set describes Gazelle.com customer sessions that correspond to customer explorations.

4.2   Data Preparation

The provided data were generated by the requests of the users on the site and were recorded by the waiter web. We thus had a whole of tuples of which each one related to a request on the waiter. Each tuple was described by more than 200 attributes, as in the previous section, of which little was interesting for us.

Indeed, there was many information concerning the requests (execution time, chains of connection . . .), and also all the answers to a form of user information, that is to say in all more than 200 attributes. Thus, it was necessary to consider the attributes that are useful to create Markov model ingredients (states, transitions, probabilities), and to present them under a format useful for the treatments. For example, we deleted the attribute that calculates the number of entries in a web site, because it is not interesting, as we suppose that a web site has only one entry. Generally, all the users entered by the same page (main page).

The following database schema was used. It is composed of 19 attributes that are of interest for us to construct Markov models. So we reduced the number of attribute from 200 attributes to 19 attributes.

```
Number, Request Query String, Request Dates, Date_Time, Request
Sequence, Template Request, Visit Dates,Date_Time,Request Dates,First
Request Date_Time, Session Cookie ID,Session ID,Count,First Query
String,First Referrer, First Template, First ID,Content Level,Content
ID, Path
```

After selecting the suitable attribute, we create a table of sessions in the following way. The original data set is stored in a file "clicks.data" that contains large number of tuples. Each tuple contains a sequence of values of the attributes separated by commas. The file weigh is about 1.2 GB. Thus, it was impossible to load it in the central memory, and use it directly by the codes of our approach. That is why, we used relational database management system (Microsoft Access) to store the data set in a relational table. So the access to tuples is managed by the relational data base management system. We used such tool because it is easy to use, and it supports very powerful module of importation. The data set stored in the table concerns exclusively selected attributes. To identify the meaning of he values, we used the file "clicks.names" in which each line contains an attribute and its description.

The table contains some non-valid entries due to errors of importation (the corresponding tuples were unusable). We thus selected the good tuples and created another table under mySQL. So, from 232000 tuples that corresponds to discounted sessions, we obtained only 90785 sessions that are valid for Markov model modeling. That is due to the presence of null data in the file starting, and a significant number of sessions comprising only one request. We noticed that there is an average of 5 transitions by session, so an average of 5 pages from 90 pages by session.

4.3   Results

The tests were carried out on a PC Pentium III with 500 MHz and 256 MB of RAM on the Data set of sessions composed of 90785 sessions (individual Markov models). In our tests, we considered different number of classes, iterations and maximum number of neighbors to compute run time and clustering distortion. We will focus our results on run time and distortion obtained when varying the maximum number of neighbors. So we fixed the number of classes and iterations to respectively 4 and 5. For different numbers of classes and iteration, we obtain similar results.

We tested the approach is the data set composed of 90785 markov models, and we supposed that there are 4 typical user behaviors (number of classes equal to 4) and five iteration of the clustering algorithm (number of iteration equal to 5). Previous experiments [19] proved that the distortion is conversely proportional to the number of iterations. That is why we concentrate our experiments on Run time and distortion values on the basis of respectively numbers of classes (clusters) and iterations.

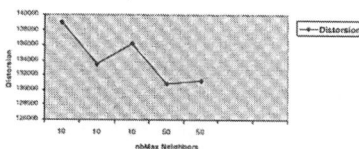

Fig. 1. Distortion conversely proportional to the number of the maximum neighbors

On the basis of the figure curve, we can highlight the following conclusions. The run time execution is proportional to the maximum number of neighbors. For 10 neighbors, we have 15 minutes run time. For 50 neighbors, we have 35 minutes of execution. We think that the run time will be very high when the number of iteration and classes are high. However the run time is less increasing than the maximum number of neighbors (figure ??). Another remark concerns the distortion (figure 1). The good quality of distortion is proportional to the maximum number of the neighbors. More generally, the results of tests showed some interesting points.

- The first point sub-lined the necessity to clean carefully the data set and to select the useful attribute before any application of the approach. In the data collections, we have a relation table with 200 attributes, and few of them are really useful to achieve our objective. We use only 19 attributes that specify the identification of the web pages, the identifier of the user session, the link relations between web pages and the time spent by the user in each web page.

- The second point sub-lined the necessity to create a new data set suitable for our approach. The original data set contain 230000 sessions, and only 90785 sessions are useful for our approach.

- The third point notes that the features of some attributes have been deleted, because they contain confidential information. So we don't know if they are useful or not in the quality of results as we don't know any thing about these attributes.

- The fourth point showed that the gravity centers of clusters are too small. The original sessions to be grouped are composed of 90 states that correspond to 90 pages visited or not by the user. However the gravity centers of clusters, obtained by our approach, are sessions composed of few pages, in several cases we obtain in our experiments gravity centers with less than 5 pages. We may explain this by the fact that the gravity center of a cluster represents the most typical session. And the most typical session is shared by the whole sessions in the cluster. And the shared point is necessary small when we consider a big number of sessions. The different tests showed that higher is the cardinality of the cluster, lesser is the volume of the gravity center. We think that this property is interesting to make accurate decision because the site administrator obtains simple and easy to interpret gravity centers, as they are composed of few states and transitions.

- The fifth point concerns the sparse property of the Markov models of sessions. The original Markov models are high dimensional and too sparse. Each session is represented by a high number of states (90 states) and transitions, however not all state are used. This is the result of the fact that the data set corresponds to a web site composed of many pages, and few number of these pages are used in a session. Our approach is addressed to such voluminous sites. The problem of the high dimension and sparse Markov model matrix is that it needs important resources: too large central memory, powerful processor and a clustering algorithm adapted to this high dimensionality. In our experiment, we considered 90 pages, however many commercial web sites consider hundred pages.

- The sixth point concerns how web site administrators may use the results of our experiments. That is good to obtain the most representative behaviors, but how the representative behaviors (gravity centers of behavior clusters) may be exploited in the real e-commerce environment.

5   Conclusion

The objective of this paper is to propose an approach that extracts automatically web user profiling based on user navigation paths. Web user profiling consists of the best representative behaviors, represented by Markov models. To achieve this objective, our approach is articulated around three notions: (1) Applying probabilistic exploration using Markov models. (2) Avoiding the problem of Markov model high-dimensionality and sparsity by clustering web documents, based on their content, before applying the Markov analysis. (3) Clustering Markov models, and extraction of their gravity centers. On the basis of these three notions, the approach makes possible the prediction of future states to be visited in k steps and navigation sessions monitoring, based on both content and traversed paths.

References

1. Rabiner, L.R.: A tutorial on Hidden Markov Models and Selected Applications in Speech Recognition. Proc. of IEEE 77(2) (1989) 257–286
2. Hu, J., Brown, M.K., Turin, W.: HMM based on-line handwriting recognition. IEEE Trans. Pattern Analysis and Machine Intelligence, 18(10) (1996) 1039–1045
3. Hughey, R., Krogh, A.: Hidden Markov Model for sequence analysis: extension and analysis of the basic method. Comp. Appl. in the Biosciences 12 (1996) 95–107
4. Eickeler, S., Kosmala, A., Rigoll, G.: Hidden Markov Model based online gesture recognition. Proc. Int. Conf. on Pattern Recognition (ICPR) (1998) 1755–1757
5. Jebara, T., Pentland, A.: Action Reaction Learning: Automatic Visual Analysis and Synthesis of interactive behavior. In 1st Intl. Conf. on Computer Vision Systems (ICVS'99) (1999)
6. Rabiner, L. R., Lee, C.H., Juang, B. H., Wilpon, J. G.: HMM Clustering for Connected Word Recognition. Proceedings of IEEE ICASSP (1989) 405–408
7. Lee, K. F.: Context-Dependent Phonetic Hidden Markov Models for Speaker Independent Continuous Speech Recognition. IEEE Transactions on Acoustics, Speech and Signal Processing 38(4) (1990) 599–609
8. Smyth, P.: Clustering sequences with HMM, in Advances in Neural Information Processing (M. Mozer, M. Jordan, and T. Petsche, eds.) MIT Press 9 (1997)
9. Smyth, P.: Clustering sequences with hidden markov models. In M.C. Mozer, M.I. Jordan, and T. Petsche, editors, Advances in NIPS 9, (1997)
10. Li, C., Biswas, G.: Clustering Sequence Data using Hidden Markov Model Representation, SPIE'99 Conference on Data Mining and Knowledge Discovery: Theory, Tools, and Technology, (1999) 14–21
11. Li, C., Biswas, G.: A Bayesian Approach to Temporal Data Clustering using Hidden Markov Models. Intl. Conference on Machine Learning (2000) 543–550
12. Schwarz, G.: Estimating the dimension of a model. The Annals of Statistics, 6(2) (1978) 461–464
13. Stolcke, A., Omohundro, S.: Hidden Markov Model Induction by Bayesian Model Merging. Hanson, S.J., Cowan, J.D., Giles, C.L. eds. Advances in Neural Information Processing Systems 5 (1993) 11–18
14. Cheeseman, P., Stutz, J.: Bayesian Classification (autoclass): Theory and Results. Advances in Knowledge discovery and data mining, (1996) 153–180

15. Law, M.H., Kwok, J.T.: Rival penalized competitive learning for model-based sequence Proceedings Intl Conf. on Pattern Recognition (ICPR) 2, (2000) 195–198
16. Cadez, I., Ganey, S. and Smyth, P.: A general probabilistic framework for clustering individuals. Technical report, Univ. Calif., Irvine, March (2000)
17. Smyth, P.: Probabilistic model-based clustering of multivariate and sequential data. In Proc. of 7th Int. Workshop AI and Statistics, (1999) 299–304
18. Ni, Z.: Normal orthant probabilities in the equicorrelated case. Jour. Math. Analysis and Applications, n° 246, (2000) 280–295
19. Ng, R.T. and Han, J.: CLARANS: A Method for Clustering Objects for Spatial Data Mining. TJDE 14(5), (2002) 1003–1016

SEMIR: Semantic Indexing and Retrieving Web Document Using Rhetorical Structure Theory

Kamel Haouam[1,2] and Farhi Marir[1]

[1] School of Informatics & Multimedia Technology, London Metropolitan University,
N7 8DB, U.K
f.marir@londonmet.ac.uk
[2] College of Computer and Information Sciences, King Saud University,
Riyadh, Saudi Arabia
haouam@ccis.ksu.edu.sa

Abstract. The amount of information available on the Internet is currently growing at an incredible rate. The lack of efficient indexing is, however, still a major barrier to effective information retrieval of documents from the web. This paper proposes the design of a technique for content-based indexing and retrieval of relevant documents from a large collection of documents such as the Internet. The technique aims at improving the quality of retrieval by capturing the semantics of these documents. It performs the conventional keyword-based indexing and introduces a thematic relationship between parts of text using a linguistics theory called Rhetorical Structure Theory (RST). The indexing and retrieval technique described in this paper is currently under development, and initial results obtained from a small number of documents has been found to be more satisfactory, compared to those obtained using keyword-based indexing and retrieval techniques we have been using.

1 Introduction and Previous Work

A lot of research has been expended on developing retrieval systems for use with the Web [1], [2], [3]. Albeit using all these indexing techniques, it has been reliably estimated that, on average, only 30% of the returned documents are relevant to the user's need, and that 70% of the returned documents in the collection are irrelevant [4]. These results are far from ideal considering that the user is still presented with thousands of documents pertaining to his keyword query. Existing indexing techniques, mainly used by search engines, are keyword based. In these techniques, each document is represented by a set of meaningful terms (also called descriptors, index terms or keywords) that are believed to represent its content. These keywords are assigned suitable weights depending on factors such as their expected frequency of occurrence in the needed documents [5][6][7]. The major drawback to keyword-based retrieval methods is that they only use a small amount of the information (i.e., keyword) associated with the needed documents as the basis for formulating the relevance criteria. As a consequence, irrelevant documents that contain the same keywords, but in a different

J. Liu et al. (Eds.): IDEAL 2003, LNCS 2690, pp. 596–604, 2003.

context, might be retrieved. Moreover, documents containing information relevant to these keywords might be missed. To achieve better performance, more semantic information about the documents needs to be captured. Some attempts at improving the traditional techniques using Natural Language Processing [8], logic [9] and document clustering [10] have yielded some improvements.

The aim of the work presented in this paper is to develop a method that uses a computational and linguistic technique called Rhetorical Structure Theory (RST) [11] to capture a more proper set of keywords, or index. The proposed technique will focus on capturing the content of the documents for accurate indexing and retrieval, resulting in an enhanced recall. This paper is composed of four sections. The first section is used for the introduction, and the second section details the RST technique, while the third section is devoted to explaining the proposed method. This will be followed by the conclusion and future work section.

2   Rhetorical Structure Theory (RST)

2.1   Background Information

Efficient document structuring goes back as far as Aristotle [13], who recognised that in coherent documents, parts of text can be related in a number of ways. A number of researchers have pursued this idea and developed theories

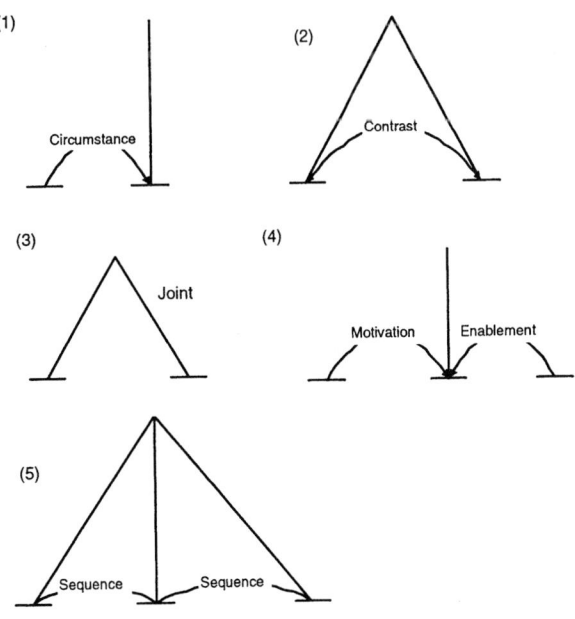

Fig. 1. RST five (5) schemas

to relate sentences. Amongst these theories, the theory developed by Mann & Thompson, called Rhetorical Structure Theory (RST) [11], which has a number of interesting characteristics. It postulates the existence of about twenty-five (25) relations, and is based on the view that these relations can be used in a top-down recursive manner to relate parts and subparts of text. RST determines relationships between sentences, and through these relationships the term semantics can be captured. In Table 1 some of the relationships used in RST are given. This top-down nature means that the documents can be decomposed into sub-units containing coherent subparts with their own rhetorical structure, and therefore opens up the possibility of extracting only relevant information from these documents. RST is a descriptive theory of a major importance in the organisation of natural text. It is a linguistically useful method for describing texts and characterising their structure. Using this theory two spans of text (virtually always adjacent, but exceptions can be found) are related such that one of them has a specific role relative to the other. A paradigm case is a claim followed by evidence supporting the claim. The claims span a *nucleus* and the evidence spans a *satellite* [14].

Rhetorical relations can be assembled into rhetorical structure trees (RS-trees), which may be organized into the five schemas shown in Fig. 1.

Table 1. Some RST common relationships between spans

Relation Name	Nucleus	Satellite
Contrast	One alternative	The other alternative
Elaboration	Basic information	Additional information
Background	Text whose understanding is being facilitated	Text for facilitating Understanding
Preparation	Text to be presented	Text which prepares the reader to expect and interpret the text to be presented

2.2   Rhetorical Relations

Rhetorical relations are often signaled by cue words and phrases [11], but emphasized that rhetorical relations can still be discerned even in the absence of such cues. Cue phrases are words and phrases, such as "first", "and", "now", that connects spans and adds structure to the discourse in text. They play an important role in signaling the basic structure of the text. Marcu [18] created a set of more than 450 cue phrases. Also Corston-Oliver [19] described a set of linguistic cues that can be identified in a text as evidence of discourse relations. Using only knowledge of cue phrases, an algorithm may be able to hypothesize the rhetorical relations. The relation Contrast can be hypothesized on the basis of the occurrence of the cue words "but", "however", etc. Table 2 presents a sample set of the cue phrases used in our system to identify rhetorical relations.

Table 2. Set of cues phrases

Contrast	Whereas, but, however
Elaboration	Also, sometimes, usually, for-example
Circumstance	After, before, while
Condition	If, unless, as long as
Sequence	Until, before, and, later, then

3   The SEMIR System

As mentioned earlier, the conventional indexing techniques lack in keyword semantics. We propose a technique that enhances the keyword-based retrieval techniques by capturing the relationships between units of text whenever keywords
appear in text. These relationships are established by using RST. RST has previously been used for text generation [12], but we are using it in our proposed
technique for text indexing. With the growing number of documents available to
users on the Web, and the advances in the Internet technology, more robust and
reliable document retrieval systems are needed. There is a growing need to understand the content of a document, compare it with the meanings of the query
and select it only if it is relevant. The proposed approach takes into account
the semantics, context and the structure of a document instead of considering
only keywords for the indexing. This approach indexes the content of a document in two phases. These are: keyword extraction and capturing the document
linguistic structure. The application of these phases is described in detail in the
next sections. We have borrowed three documents examples and these example
documents are used as running examples in this paper.

Document 1 [11] *"The next music day is scheduled for July 21 (Saturday),
noon midnight. I'll post more details later but this is a good time to reserve
the place on your calendar"*.

Document 2 [18] *"No matter how much one wants to stay a non-smoker, the
truth is that the pressure to smoke in junior high is greater than it will be
any other time of one's life. We know that 3,000 teens start smoking each
day, although it is a fact that 90% of them once thought that smoking was
something that they'd never do"*.

Document 3 *"After John went home, he smokes a cigarette"*.

3.1   Keyword Extraction

This technique is a basic keyword extraction technique, based on the term's
frequency of occurrence. It operates as follows:

- Eliminate common function words from the document texts by consulting a
  special dictionary, or a stop list, containing a list of high-frequency function
  words e.g. "and", "or", "but" etc.

- Stemming of the remaining words with the objective of removing affixes (i.e., prefixes and suffixes) and allowing the retrieval of documents containing syntactic variations of query terms (e.g., connect, connecting, connected, etc).
- Selection of index terms to determine which words will be used as indexing elements. In fact, noun words frequently carry more semantics than adjectives, adverbs, and verbs.
- Compute the term frequency (tf) for all the remaining terms T in each document D, specifying the number of occurrences of T in D.
- Choose a threshold frequency Th, and assign to each document D all terms T for which tf > Th.

Let's take the above example consisting of the three pieces of text. After performing the initial keyword extraction and the appropriate weight calculations, a table resembling the one in Table 3 would result. According to that table, document 2 and document 3 will be retrieved as an answer to a query with keyword "smoking" because the word "smoking " occurs four times in document 2 and one time in document 3. The problem is that there are a large number of documents, which are either relevant or irrelevant. In our case, we cannot decide if the subject of smoking is mentioned in document 3 or not. We also have the same problem of a query concerning the term "day" or the term "time". This is because single term indexing is not sufficient for representing a document's theme. Hence we need to capture the semantic relationship between parts of the text.

Table 3. Keyword Indexing Tables of the three Documents

Keyword	Doc	Freq	Weight
Calendar	1	1	0.47
Day	1	1	0.17
Detail	1	1	0.47
Good	1	1	0.47
July	1	1	0.47
Midnight	1	1	0.47
Music	1	1	0.47
Place	1	1	0.47
Post	1	1	0.47
Reserve	1	1	0.47
Saturday	1	1	0.47
Schedule	1	1	0.47
Time	1	1	0.17

Keyword	Doc	Freq	Weight
Day	2	1	0.17
Fact	2	1	0.47
Greater	2	1	0.47
High	2	1	0.47
Junior	2	1	0.47
Life	2	1	0.47
Matter	2	1	0.47
Pressure	2	1	0.47
Smoke	2	4	0.70
Start	2	1	0.47
Stay	2	1	0.47
Teen	2	1	0.47
Time	2	1	0.17
Truth	2	1	0.47

Keyword	Doc	Freq	Weight
Cigarette	3	1	0.47
Home	3	1	0.47
John	3	1	0.47
Smoke	3	1	0.17

Table 4. Scoring table

Relation name	Elaboration	Evidence	Justification	Concession	Restatement	Circumstance
Score	0.9	0.8	0.7	0.6	0	0

3.2 Capturing the Document Linguistic Structure

As a second step in this work, we suppose that the rhetorical relations are discerned only by the presence of the cue phrases. A computational discourse parser is used to achieve the analyses of large fragments of text. On the basis of the cue phrases, the principle of the parser consists in positing rhetorical relations between the identified clauses. These rhetorical relations are then used to assemble RST representations [16], [17]. Rhetorical Relations extracted from the text are expressed as a triplet: (relation name; span 1;span 2). The algorithm examines the text, sentence by sentence, and determines a set of potential discourse markers that occur in each sentence.

Document 1 [The next music day is scheduled for July 21 (Saturday), noon midnight. 1] [I'll post more details later 2] [but this is a good time to reserve the place on your calendar. 3]

$$rhet\_rel(concession; 2; 3); rhet\_rel(elaboration; 2; 1)$$
$$rhet\_rel(justification; 1; 2); rhet\_rel(justification; 1; 3)$$

Document 2 [No matter how much one wants to stay a non-smoker, 1] [the truth is that the pressure to smoke in junior high is greater than it will be any other time of one's life. 2] [We know that 3,000 teens start smoking each day, 3] [although it is a fact that 90% of them once thought that smoking was something that they'd never do. 4]

$$rhet\_rel(justification; 1; 2); rhet\_rel(justification; 4; 2)$$
$$rhet\_rel(evidence; 3; 2); rhet\_rel(concession; 3; 4)$$
$$rhet\_rel(restatement; 4; 1)$$

Document 3 [After John went home, 1] [he smokes a cigarette. 2]

$$rhet\_rel(circumstance; 1; 2)$$

3.3 RST in Document Indexing

Using conventional indexing techniques, documents are represented using keywords. Queries are also represented using keywords. For retrieval, a similarity computation is performed between the two sets of keywords and if they are sufficiently similar then the document is retrieved. These methods are term based, so documents that are not relevant but use a certain term are often retrieved. This is partly due to the lack of semantic relationships between different parts of texts. RST provides an analysis of any coherent, carefully written, text and such analysis provides a motivated account of why each element of the text has been included by the author. RST gives an account of textual coherence that is independent of the lexical and grammatical forms of the text. Therefore, it could be used for identifying relationships between the different units where certain keywords appear, stressing the importance of some and disregarding some. This could mean a major refinement to the number of documents retrieved resulting in an enhanced retrieval precision [15]. Intuitively, some relations are more compelling than others. To reflect this intuition, based on Mann and Thompson definitions, we assign numerical scores (with values ranging from 0 to 1) to each rhetorical relation.

3.4   Scoring Process

Based on the following definitions, we propose the scoring table shown in Table 4. The scores could be allowed to vary continuously between 0 and 1; the higher score assignments near 1 being used for the most important relation, whereas lower scores near 0 would characterize the less important relation. Using the RST analysis in Table 5, a preliminary selection excludes certain words for the reason that a circumstance or other relation with a low score occurs between the sentences where the word appears. It is clear that the last index table, Table 6, is more appropriate for the required retrieval. The query "smoking" is retrieved directly from document 2, which is more relevant for the user than document 3. Also the memory space required to store the last table is reduced.

Table 5. RST Indexing Tables of the three Documents

Keyword	Doc	RST_W
Calendar	1	0.6
Day	1	0.7
Detail	1	0.9
Good	1	0
July	1	0.7
Midnight	1	0
Music	1	0.7
Place	1	0.6
Post	1	0.9
Reserve	1	0.6
Saturday	1	0
Schedule	1	0
Time	1	0

Keyword	Doc	RST_W
Day	2	0
Fact	2	0
Greater	2	0
High	2	0
Junior	2	0
Life	2	0
Matter	2	0
Pressure	2	0
Smoke	2	0.7
Start	2	0.8
Stay	2	0.7
Teen	2	0.8
Time	2	0
Truth	2	0

Keyword	Doc	RST_W
Cigarette	3	0
Home	3	0
John	3	0
Smoke	3	0

Table 6. Final Indexing Table

Keyword	Doc	Freq
Detail	1	0.9
Post	1	0.9
Start	2	0.8
Teen	2	0.8
Day	1	0.7
July	1	0.7
Music	1	0.7
Smoke	2	0.7
Stay	2	0.7
Calendar	1	0.6
Place	1	0.6
Reserve	1	0.6

4   Conclusions

In this paper, we have presented a computational and linguistic technique for content-based indexing of documents from a large collection of text documents. We introduced an indexing method, based on a text description theory called rhetorical structure theory. RST was created in the late Eighties primarily for text generation. We here proposed to employ it for text indexing. Applying RST showed potential in improving the quality of current information retrieval systems. A system that indexes relations is able to yield higher precision than a system that utilizes keywords. The segmentation, the extraction of the rhetorical relations and the scoring could involve some pre-processing time during indexing. This time might be saved during the retrieval process. It is an undergoing project as it is at its conceptual level and so it has been conducted on a small number of documents. Future work includes the development of some experiments based on different document topics and sizes. A comparative study on bigger collections will follow. The study will compare the results of the proposed system to those of other retrieval systems including the ones used by search engines.

References

1. Pollitt, A. S, Information Storage and Retrieval Systems. Ellis Horwood Ltd., Chichester, The UK, 1989.
2. Salton Gerard, Automatic Text Processing, Addison-Wesley, USA, 1989.
3. Frants, Valery.I, Shapiro, Jacob and Voiskunskii, Vladimir G, Automated Information Retrieval: theory and Methods, Academic Press, California, 1997.
4. Sparck-Jones, Karen & Willet, Peter, Readings in Information Retrieval. Morgan Kauffman, California, USA, 1997.
5. Liu, G.Z. Semantic vector space model: implementation and evaluation. Journal of the American Society for Information Science, 48(5), 395–417, 1997.

6. Korfhage, R. Information Storage and Retrieval. John Wiley and Sons, London, 1997.
7. Losee, R.M. Comparing boolean and probabilistic information retrieval systems across queries and disciplines, Journal of the American Society for Information Science, 48(2), 143–156, 1997.
8. Smeaton, A.F. Progress in the application of natural language processing to information retrieval, The Computer Journal, 35, 268–278, 1992.
9. Lalmas, Mounia and Bruza, Peter, D. The use of logic in information retrieval modelling. The Knowledge Engineering Review, 13(3), 263–295, 1998.
10. Hagen, Eric, An Information Retrieval System for performing Hierarchical document Clustering, Thesis, Dartmouth college, 1997
11. Mann, W.C., & Thompson, S.A. Rhetorical Structure Theory: Towards a functional theory of text organization. Text , 8 (3). 243–28, 1988.
12. Rosener,D and Stede, M. Customizing RST for the Automatic Production of Technical Manuals. Lecture Notes in AI, 587, 199–214, 1992.
13. Aristotle. The Rhetoric, in W. Rhys Roberts (translator), The Rhetoric and Poetics of Aristotle, Random House, New York, 1954.
14. www.sil.org/linguistics/rst/index.htm
15. Vadera, Sand Meziane, F. From English to Formal Specifications. The Computer Journal, 37(9), 1994
16. Marcu, D. 1996 . Building up Rhetorical Structure Trees. In Proceedings of the Thirteenth National Conference on Artificial Intelligence, vol.2. 1069–1074, Portland, Oregon, August 1996
17. Marcu, D. 1997 a. The rhetorical parsing of natural language texts. In Proceedings of the 35th Annual Meeting of the Association for Computational Linguistics (ACL-97), 96–103.
18. Marcu, D. 2000 The theory and practice of discourse parsing and summarization. In Proceedings of the 35th Annual Meeting of the Association for Computational Linguistics (ACL-97), 96–103.
19. Simon H Corston-Oliver. 1998. ”Computing representations of the structure of written discourse”. In Technical report MSR-TR-98-15, Microsoft research, Microsoft corporation, One Microsoft way, Redmond, WA 98052. April 3, 1998

Generating Representative from Clusters of Association Rules on Numeric Attributes

Atsushi Hashizume[1], Bao Yongguang[1], Xiaoyong Du[2], and Naohiro Ishii[1]

[1] Department of Intelligence and Computer Science,
Nagoya Institute of Technology
Gokiso-cho, Showa-ku, Nagoya, 466-8555, Japan.
hashi@ics.nitech.ac.jp
[2] School of Information, Renmin Univercity of China
100872 Beijing, China.

Abstract. Association rule is useful to describe knowledge and information extracted from databases. However, a large number of association rules may be extracted. It is difficult for users to understand them. It is reasonable to sum up the rules into a smaller number of rules called representative rules. In this papar, we applied a clustering method to cluster association rules on numeric attribute and proposed an algorithm to generate representative rules from the clusters. We applied our approach to a real database, adult database. As the result, we obtained 124 rules divided into 3 clusters. We compared the rule generating method with another rule selecting method.

Keywords: Association rules, Representative rules, Rule clustering, Rule generation, Numeric attributes.

1   Introduction

Data mining has been recognized as an important area of database research to discover patterns of interest or knowledge from large databases. As a kind of important pattern of knowledge, association rule has been introduced. An association rule is an implication expression: $C_1 \Rightarrow C_2$, where C_1 and C_2 are two conditions. It means that when the condition C_1 is true, the condition C_2 is true with high possibility.

Assosiation rule is introduced in Agrawal et al.'s papers [AIS93,AS94]. They considered on bucket type data, like supermarket databeses where the set of items purchased by a single customer is recorded as a transaction. When we cover general databases like relational databases, we have to consider various types of data, especially continuous numeric data. We give you an example: $(age \in [40, 60]) \Rightarrow (own\_house = yes)$. In this case, we may find hundreds or thouthands of association rules corresponding to a specific attribute. Fig.1 shows all rules that we extracted from an adult database. The rule has the form "$fnlwgt \in [a, b] \Rightarrow (income < 50K)$", where $fnlwgt$ is a numeric attribute and $income$ is a decision attribute. The rules are ordered by the ranges in the left-hand side(LHS). It is difficult for users to understand all of them. To solve this

J. Liu et al. (Eds.): IDEAL 2003, LNCS 2690, pp. 605–613, 2003.

problem, optimized association rule is proposed by Fukuda et al.[FMMT96]. It extracts a single association rule from all candidates which maximaizes some index of the rules, for example, support. In many cases, however, it is just a common sense rule and has no value at all.

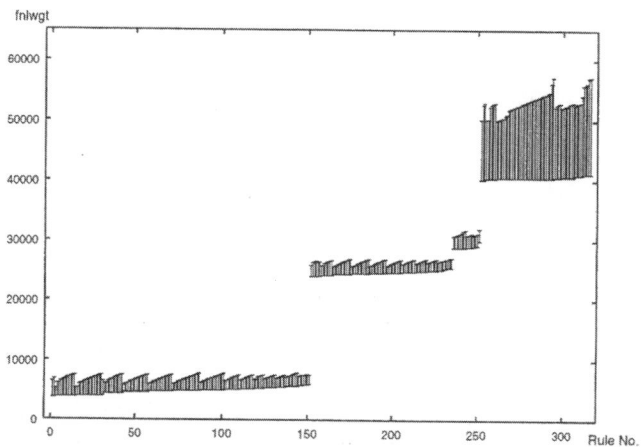

Fig. 1. Similar rules from an adult database

To overcome this shortcoming, it is reasonable to divide the process of descovering association rules into two steps: the first step is to find all candidates of which support and confidence are greater than the thresholds given by users; the second step is to generate some representative rules from all candidates. Although most of existing papers contributed to the first step, an incremental interesting has been paid on the second step [KMR+94,GB98,Kry98a,Kry98b]. Various measures for the value of association rules have been proposed.

Kiemettinen et al.[KMR+94] proposed a simple formalism of rule templates to describe the structure of interesting rules, like what attributes occur in the antecedent and what attribute is the consequent. Other authors choose to look for objective measures for rule selection. Gago et al.[GB98] defined a distance between two rules, and select n rules such that they are the most distinguished. Kryszkiewicz[Kry98a,Kry98b] defined a cover operator for association rule by bucket data, and found a least set of rules that covers all association rules by the cover operator. However, since downward closure property is not true for association rules on numeric attribute, the cover operation is not appropriate for rule selection. Xiaoyong Du et al.[DSI99] proposed the distance between rules, which is the objective measure for clustering association rules and selection representative rules.

Many association rules are extracted from databases. However, the rules are usually similar and we can devide them into some clusters. In addition, it is reasonable to define a representative rule for a set of similar rules.

In this paper, we focus on generation of association rules on numeric attributes. We assume that a set Ω of association rules have been extracted. We then generate a subset of Ω as representative rules of Ω. Our approach is first to cluster association rules according to the distance between rules, and then to generate a representative rule for each class. We propose the generation of representative rule using genetic algorithm.

This paper is organized as follows: In Section 2, we present basic terminology in the field of association rule and an overview of our work. Section 3 describes the definition of a distance between rules and the technique to get the clusters of rules. In Section 4, we propose how to generate the representative rule of clusters. In Section 5, we present some experimental results. Section 6 includes conclusions and our futhre works.

2 Preparation

2.1 Association Rule on Numerical Attributes

In this section we present basic terminologies for mining association rules on numeric attributes. Assume that there is a relation $D(A_1, A_2, \cdots, A_n, C)$, where A_i is an attribute name, and C is a decision attribute. For a tuple $t \in D$, $t.A_i$ denotes the value of A_i at t. An association rule is an expression of the form $C_1 \Rightarrow C_2$, where C_1 and C_2 are two expressions, called left-hand side(LHS) and right-hand side(RHS) of the rule, respectively. In this paper, we consider association rules on numeric attributes with the form:

$$R : (a_1 \leq A_1 \leq b_1) \wedge \cdots \wedge (a_n \leq A_n \leq b_n) \Rightarrow (C = yes)$$

where A_i is a numeric attribute and C is a boolean attribute. Without confusion, we usually denote a rule by an area P in the n dimension space. $t \in P$ means $(a_1 \leq t.A_1 \leq b_1) \wedge \cdots \wedge (a_n \leq t.A_n \leq b_n)$.

Two measures, *support* and *confidence*, are commonly used to rank association rules. The support of an association rule R, denoted by $supp(R)$, is defined by the following formula.

$$supp(R) = \frac{|\{t | t \in P \wedge t.C = yes\}|}{|D|}$$

It means how often the value of A occurs in the area P as a fraction of the total number of tuples. The confidence of an association rule R, denoted by $conf(R)$, is defined by the following formula.

$$conf(R) = \frac{|\{t | t \in P \wedge t.C = yes\}|}{|\{t | t \in P\}|}$$

It is the strength of the rule.

For a pair of *minsupp* and *minconf* specified by the user as the thresholds of support and confidence, respectively, an association rule is called "interesting" if both its support and confidence are over the minimal thresholds. Let Ω denote the set of all interesting association rules. That is $\Omega = \{R | supp(R) \geq minsupp \wedge conf(R) \geq minconf\}$.

2.2   Overview of Our Work

Our purpose is to extract a set of representative rules from Ω. Our approach consists of the following two steps:

1. Clustering. The set Ω of interesting association rules are clustered into some clusters by using the distance between rules and the diameter of clusters.
2. Generation. For each cluster, we generate one association rule as its representative rule. To generate representative rules we adopt genetic algorithm.

3   Clustering Association Rules

3.1   Definitions

In this section, we define distances between rules and clusters.

Definition 1. Let r_1 and r_2 be two rules. The distance between r_1 and r_2 is defined by

$$dist(r_1, r_2) = \sqrt{\sum_{i=1}^{n}((a_i^{(1)} - a_i^{(2)})^2 + (b_i^{(1)} - b_i^{(2)})^2)} \tag{1}$$

where $r_i = \{a_1^{(i)} \leq A_1 < b_1^{(i)}, \cdots, a_n^{(i)} \leq A_n < b_n^{(i)}\}$ for $i = 1, 2$.

In this definition, we view the left and right terminals of a range on a numeric attribute as two independent parameters. Thus a rule can be represented as a point in a $2n$ dimension space. The distance of two rules is defined as the distance of the two points in the space.

Definition 2. Let $C = \{r_1, \cdots, r_m\}$ be a set of rules, $r \in C$ be a rule. A (average) distance between r to C is defined by

$$dist(r, C) = \sum_{r_i \in C} dist(r, r_i)/m \tag{2}$$

Definition 3. Let C_1 and C_2 be two sets of rules. The (average) distance between C_1 and C_2 is defined by

$$dist(C_1, C_2) = \sum_{r_i \in C_1, r_j \in C_2} dist(r_i, r_j)/(|C_1| \cdot |C_2|) \tag{3}$$

where $|C_1|$ and $|C_2|$ are the numbers of rules in C_1 and C_2, respectively.

The diameter of a cluster is the average distance of all pairs of rules in the cluster.

Definition 4. Let C be a set of rules. A diameter of C is defined by

$$d(C) = \sum_{r_i, r_j \in C} dist(r_i, r_j)/(|C|(|C| - 1)) \tag{4}$$

Definition 5. Let $C = \{C_1, \cdots, C_k\}$, where $C_i \subseteq \Omega$. C is called a clustering of Ω if for a given threshold d_0, the followings are satisfied.

1. $C_i \cap C_j = \emptyset, (i \neq j)$
2. $d(C_i) \leq d_0$
3. $dist(C_i, C_j) \geq d_0, (i \neq j)$

3.2 Algorithm for Clustering Association Rules

In this section, we describe a heuristic approach to construct clusters. It is a hill-climbing method working on a matrix of which cells represent the distance between two rules. That is

$$D = (dist(r_i, r_j))_{n \times n} \tag{5}$$

We always select two clusters (or two rules) between which the distance is the minimal. Hence, this algorithm consists of a loop, each of which combines two rows/coloumns of the matrix of which cross point cell has the minimal value.

While combinig two clusters (or two rules), we have to recompute the distance between the combined cell and other rules. The following properties can be used for this incremental recomputing. They can be derived from the definitions of diameter and distance.

Property 1. Let $C_1 = \{r_1, \cdots, r_m\}$, $C_2 = \{s_1, \cdots, s_n\}$ be two sets of rules. Assume $d(C_1) = d_1$, $d(C_2) = d_2$, and $dist(C_1, C_2) = dist$. The diameter of $C_1 \cup C_2$ can be evaluated by the following formula.

$$\begin{aligned} d(C_1 \cup C_2) &= \frac{\sum_{r,s \in C_1 \cup C_2} dist(r, s)}{(m+n)(m+n-1)} \\ &= \frac{m(m-1)d_1 + n(n-1)d_2 + (2mn)dist}{(m+n)(m+n-1)} \end{aligned} \tag{6}$$

Property 2. Let $C_1 = \{r_1, \cdots, r_m\}$, $C_2 = \{s_1, \cdots, s_n\}$ be two clusters, C_3 be another cluster. Assume C_1 and C_2 are combined to a new cluster $C_1 \cup C_2$, then the distance between C_3 and $C_1 \cup C_2$ can be evaluated by the following formula.

$$\begin{aligned} dist(C_3, C_1 \cup C_2) &= \frac{\sum_{r \in C_3, s \in C_1 \cup C_2} dist(r, s)}{|C_3| \cdot |C_1 \cup C_2|} \\ &= \frac{md_1 + nd_2}{m+n} \end{aligned} \tag{7}$$

where $d_1 = dits(C_3, C_1)$, $d_2 = dist(C_3, C_2)$.

The algorithm consists of a loop of two steps. The first step is to select the minimal distance from the matrix D. If the value is less than threshold d_0 given by users, the corresponding clusters should be combined. The second step is to generate a new matrix which has smaller size. We sum up the algorithm in Fig.2.

4 Generating Representative Rules

Next phase of our approach is to generate a representative rule for each cluster. Since all rules in the same cluster are similar, it is reasonable to weave them into a single rule as a representative rule.

Xiaoyong Du[DSI99] prososed the method to select representative rules from clusters. However, if there is no rule which shows the feature of a cluster, the

(Input) a set of association rules: $\Omega = \{r_1, \cdots, r_n\}$
(Output) a set of clusters: $C = \{C_1, \cdots, C_m\}$
(Method)

1. let each rule r_i be a cluster C_i.
   for$(i = 1; i \leq n; i++)$
   $\quad C_i = \{r_i\}$
2. calculate distances between clusters.
   for$(i = 1; i \leq n; i++)$
   $\quad$**for**$(j = 1; j \leq n; j++)$
   $\quad\quad D(i,j) = dist(C_i, C_j)$
3. assume $D(s,t)$ is the minimal distance element of D.
   $D(s,t) = \min_{i \neq j}(D(i,j))$
4. **while** $(d \leq d_0)$ do {
   4-1. combine C_s and C_t, and let the new C_s be $C_s \cup C_t$
   $\quad C_s = C_s \cup C_t$
   4-2. delete C_t from C
   4-3. generate a new matrix D'.
   $$D' = \begin{cases} e_{s,s} = \frac{n_s(n_s-1)d_{s,s} + n_t(n_t-1)d_{t,t} + 2n_s n_t d_{s,t}}{(n_s+n_t)(n_s+n_t-1)} & \\ e_{s,j} = \frac{n_s d_{s,j} + n_t d_{t,j}}{n_s+n_t} & (j \neq s,t) \\ e_{i,j} = d_{i,j} & (i,j \neq s,t) \end{cases}$$

   $\quad$ where n_s and n_t are the size of the s-th and t-th clusters, respectively, and $d_{i,j}$ is the distance between C_i and C_j.
   4-4. find $D(s,t) = \min_{i \neq j}(D(i,j))$
   }
5. output C. Assume the final matrix is $D'_{m \times m}$.

Fig. 2. Algorithm for clustering

accuracy of the representative rule selected from the cluster is not high. To solve this problem ,we propose to generate a new rule as a representative rule.

We define a measure to evaluate the accuracy of a representative rule.

Definition 6. *Let* $C = \{r_1, \cdots, r_n\}$ *be a cluster of rules, and* R *be a rule. The coverage of* R *to* C *is defined by*

$$\alpha(R) = \frac{\sum_{r_i \in C} dist(R, r_i)}{|C|} \tag{8}$$

where $|C|$ *is the number of rules in the cluster* C.

The measure $\alpha(R)$ reflects the distance of the rule R to all rules in a cluster C. A rule R is called representative rule of C if $\alpha(R)$ is the minimal. Hence, our purpose is to find a rule of which $\alpha(R)$ is the minimal.

In this section, Genetic Algorithm(GA) is applied to find the representative rule. GA is the algorithm simulating the biological evolution, which searches the optimized solution by genes in the computer. The information is shown by the chromosome or the organism, which is called gene in the GA. The population of genes is shown in $G(t)$ at the generation t. The genetic operators on the $G(t)$, are the crossover operator, which makes a new gene by combining two old genes, and the mutation operator, which makes a new gene by changing the partial components in the old gene.

In the GA, the solution candidate of the gene, is represented with one-dimensional array of the components 0 or 1. The n-dimensional rule R is represented by using the numerical values a_i and b_j in the gene c as follows,

$$R : (a_1 \leq A_1 \leq b_1) \wedge \cdots \wedge (a_n \leq A_n \leq b_n) \Rightarrow (c = yes)$$

where a_i and b_j are represented by the binary numerals in the gene as follows,

$$c = (a_{1,1}, \cdots, a_{x,1}, b_{1,1}, \cdots, b_{x,1}, \cdots, a_{1,n}, \cdots, a_{x,n}, b_{1,n}, \cdots, b_{x,n})$$

and the parameter x of the suffix, is given under the condition of the solution accuracy.

```
generate initial population, G(0)
for(t = 1; t ≤ generation_max; t + +){
        evaluate G(t)
        select the elite gene randomly from G(t − 1) and add them to G(t)
        select another gene randomly from G(t − 1) and add them to G(t)
        apply crossover operation to G(t)
        apply mutation operation to G(t)
}
```

Fig. 3. Genetic algorithm for generating representative rule

5   Experiments

We apply our approach to analyse a set of association rules extracted from an adult database[Koh96]. The association rule has the form "$fnlgwt \in [a, b] \Rightarrow (income < 50K)$". The RHS of the rule can be view as a boolean attribute. The database contains 32560 tuples. When we set $minconf = 0.8$ and $minsupp = 0.02$, we obtained 128 association rules of which Ω consists, and represent them as points in a 2D space. We first applied the clustering algorithm to Ω and obtained 3 clusters(see Fig.4).

Next, we applied our rule generation algorithm to the clusters and three representative rules are generated form three clusters, respectively. We focus on Cluster 3 shown in Fig.5. Cluster 3 contains 91 association rules. To compare our rule generation algorithm with other rule selection algorithm. We show two

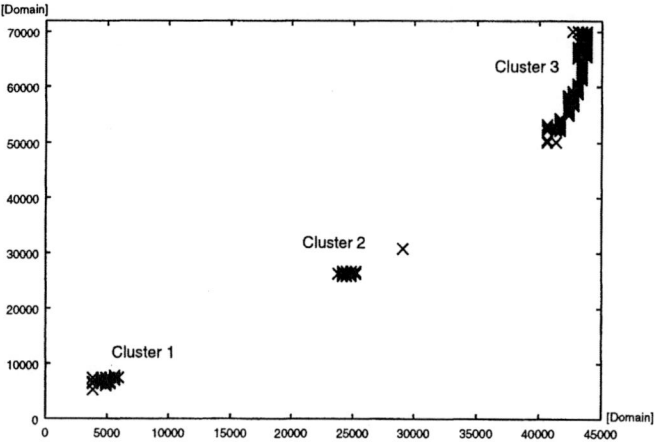

Fig. 4. Clustering of association rules

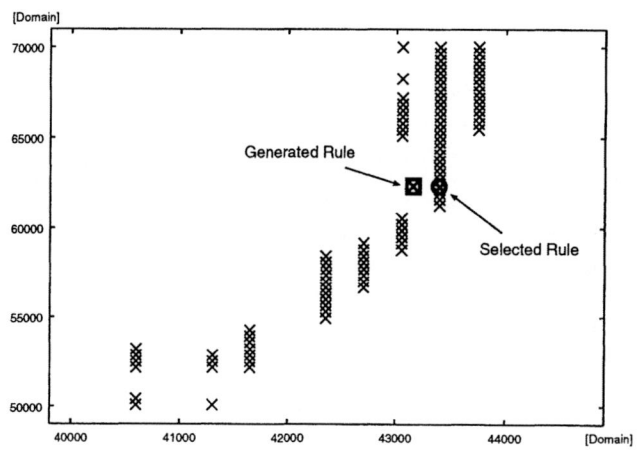

Fig. 5. Representative rule of Cluster 3

representative rules: one is generated by our algrithm and another one is selected by the selection algorithm of Xiaoyong Du[DSI99]. Since $\alpha(R)$ of the generated rule and the selected rule are 5417.7 and 5426.8, respectively. The rule generated by our algotithm is better than another one. The support and confidence of the generated representative rule are 0.021 and 0.80, respectively.

6   Summary and Conclusions

In this paper, we propose the generation of representative rules for clusters. A large number of association rules are usually extracted from database. These rules can be divided into some clusters. Since rules in the same cluster are similar, it is reasonable to generate a representative rule from each cluster. In the experiment, we showed that the generating rules is better method than selecting rules. This is because the selection doesn't work well, if there is no rule which shows the character of a cluster. The generating rules solved this problem.

References

[AIS93]   Rakesh Agrawal, Tomasz Imielinski, and Arun N. Swami. Mining associa-
             tion rules between sets of items in large databases. In Peter Buneman and
             Sushil Jajodia, editors, *Proceedings of the 1993 ACM SIGMOD Interna-
             tional Conference on Management of Data*, pages 207–216, Washington,
             D.C., 26–28 1993.

[AS94]   Rakesh Agrawal and Ramakrishnan Srikant. Fast algorithms for mining
             association rules. In Jorge B. Bocca, Matthias Jarke, and Carlo Zaniolo,
             editors, *Proc. 20th Int. Conf. Very Large Data Bases, VLDB*, pages 487–
             499. Morgan Kaufmann, 12–15 1994.

[DSI99]   Xiaoyong Du, Sachiko Suzuki, and Naohiro Ishii. A distance-based clus-
             tering and selection of association rules on numeric attributes. In *New
             Directions in Rough Sets, Data Mining, and Granular-Soft Computing
             (RSFDGrC'99)*, volume 1711 of *Lecture Notes in Artificial Intelligence*,
             pages 423–432, Yamaguchi, Japan, November 1999. Springer.

[FMMT96]   Takeshi Fukuda, Yasuhiko Morimoto, Shinichi Morishita, and Takeshi
             Tokuyama. Mining optimized association rules for numeric attributes. In
             *Proceedings of the 15th ACM SIGACT-SIGMOD-SIGART Symposium on
             Principles of Database Systems*, pages 182–191, Montreal, Canada, June
             1996. ACM Press.

[GB98]   P. Gago and C. Bento. A metric for selection of the most promising rules.
             In J.M. Zytkow and M. Quafaou, editors, *Principles of Data Mining and
             Knowledge Discovery(PKDD'98)*, volume 1510 of *Lecture Notes in Artifi-
             cial Intelligence*, pages 19–27, Nantes, France, September 1998. Springer.

[KMR⁺94]   Mika Klemettinen, Heikki Mannila, Pirjo Ronkainen, Hannu Toivonen,
             and A. Inkeri Verkamo. Finding interesting rules from large sets of dis-
             covered association rules. In Nabil R. Adam, Bharat K. Bhargava, and
             Yelena Yesha, editors, *Third International Conference on Information and
             Knowledge Management (CIKM'94)*, pages 401–407. ACM Press, 1994.

[Koh96]   Ron Kohavi. Scaling up the accuracy of Naive-Bayes classifiers: a decision-
             tree hybrid. In *Proceedings of the Second International Conference on
             Knowledge Discovery and Data Mining*, pages 202–207, 1996.

[Kry98a]   M. Kryszkiewicz. Representative association rules. In X. Wu, R.Kotagiri,
             and K.B. Korb, editors, *Research and Development in Knowledge Dis-
             covery and Data Mining(PAKDD'98)*, volume 1394 of *Lecture Notes in
             Artificial Intelligence*, pages 198–209, Melbourne, Australia, April 1998.
             Springer.

[Kry98b]   M. Kryszkiewicz. Representative association rules and mining condition
             maximum consequence association rules. In J.M. Zytkow and M.Quafafou,
             editors, *Principles of Data Mining and knowledge Discovery(PKDD'98)*,
             volume 1510 of *Lecture Notes in Artificial Intelligence*, Nantes, France,
             September 1998. Springer.

Grid-Based Indexing for Large Time Series Databases

Jiyuan An[1], Hanxiong Chen[1], Kazutaka Furuse[1], Nobuo Ohbo[1], and Eamonn Keogh[2]

[1] University of Tsukuba, Japan
{an,chx,furuse,ohbo}@dblab.is.tsukuba.ac.jp
[2] University of California - Riverside, USA
eamonn@cs.ucr.edu

Abstract. Similarity search in large time series databases is an interesting and challenging problem. Because of the high dimensional nature of the data, the difficulties associated with dimensionality curse arise. The most promising solution is to use dimensionality reduction, and construct a multi-dimensional index structure for the reduced data. In this work we introduce a new approach called grid-based Datawise Dimensionality Reduction(DDR) which attempts to preserve the characteristics of time series. We then apply quantization to construct an index structure. An experimental comparison with existing techniques demonstrate the utility of our approach.

1 Introduction

Similarity search in time series is useful in its own right as a tool for exploratory data analysis. The most promising similarity search techniques perform dimensionality reduction followed by the use of a SAM (Spatial Access Method) such as R-tree [7] and its many variants[4,8] in the transformed space. These techniques include Discrete Fourier Transform (DFT) [1], Piecewise Aggregate Approximation (PAA)[10] and Adaptive Piecewise Constant Approximation (APCA)[9]. They map each Fourier coefficient, aggregate segment and adaptive aggregate segment onto one dimension of an index tree. The efficiency of the above-mentioned indexes depends on the fidelity of the approximation in the reduced dimensionality space. The more accurate the approximation gets (i.e. the more coefficients retained), the higher the dimensionality of the transformed space becomes. Unfortunately, recent work by Chakrabarti[5], and others suggests that the R-tree and its variant multidimensional index structures have poor performance at dimensionality greater than 8 ~ 12. To overcome this difficulty, known as the *dimensionality curse*, a compressed indexing structure VA-file[12] has been proposed. Scanning a compressed index file generates a small set of candidates. The exact answer is obtained through refinement checking to this small candidate set, which needs fewer random accesses to data files. By taking into account that real datasets are always skewed, new versions of VA-file such as CVA-file[2], VDR-file [3] and C²VA[6] have been proposed. In these improvements, the techniques of dimensionality reduction and file compression are efficiently integrated.

J. Liu et al. (Eds.): IDEAL 2003, LNCS 2690, pp. 614–621, 2003.
© Springer-Verlag Berlin Heidelberg 2003

2   Approach

2.1   Notation and Terminology

We begin by summarizing the symbols and terms used in this paper. The data set of time series is $\mathcal{O}$, and an object $v \in \mathcal{O}$ is a time series which is represented by a sequence of values $v_1, v_2, \dots, v_n$. All objects in $\mathcal{O}$ have the same length n, which is also referred to as *dimensionality* in this paper. Each v_i of v is called a *data point*.

The main problem we are to address is to find k-NN of a query q from $\mathcal{O}$. This also implies that the length or dimensionality of q is also n.

3   Data Representation

In this section we discuss how to determine grids. First, the normalized values are quantized, then the lengths of segments are determined. To guarantee the admissibility when DDR is implemented as an index, upper and lower bounds are also considered.

3.1   The DDR Representation

We illustrate the representation of a given time series $(v_1, v_2, \dots, v_n)$ by using an example. For clarity of presentation, the explanation is separated to two steps.

As the example, suppose the time series is given as below.

$$(v_1, v_2, \dots, v_8) = (0.18, 0.24, 0.30, 0.62, 0.9, 0.45, 0.38, 0.32)$$

this series is approximated in the following way

1. **quantization:** The time series is quantized to 2^b intervals in the vertical axe, where b is the number of bits used for approximating v_i. In the example, if we assumed that $b = 3$, then by $\alpha_i = \lfloor v_i \times 2^b \rfloor$, the quantized time series of the example becomes

$$(\alpha_1, \alpha_2, \dots, \alpha_8) = ((001)_2, (001)_2, (010)_2, (100)_2, (111)_2, (011)_2, (011)_2, (010)_2)$$

2. **reduction:** If a value of a data point is close to that of its previous data point, then it is omitted. We use a tolerance parameter ϵ. Whether a data point is omitted or not is determined by Equation 1.

$$\alpha_{i+1} = \begin{cases} \text{omitted,} & -\epsilon \le v_{i+1} - \alpha_i' \times h \le h + \epsilon \\ \lfloor v_{i+1} \times 2^b \rfloor, & otherwise \end{cases} \tag{1}$$

$$(i = 1, 2, \dots, n)$$

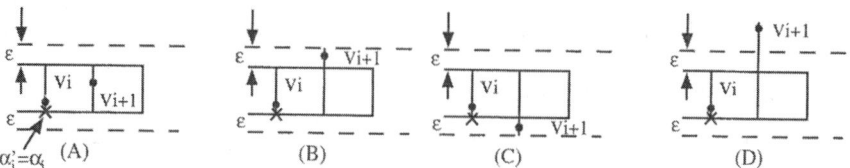

Fig. 1. Determination of Segments. (A) Since v_{i+1} has the same quantized value as v_i, it is omitted (grouped in the same segment as v_i). (B) Although quantized value of v_{i+1} is greater than v_i, it is also omitted because it is still in the error tolerance with respect to v_i. (C) This case is similar to case (B). (D) v_{i+1} is out of the error tolerance, and thus begins a new segment.

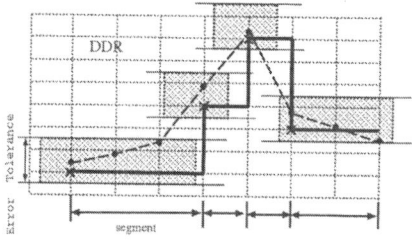

Fig. 2. Reduction of data points of v with DDR technique. The four gray rectangles represent the ranges of error tolerance.

In the equation, h is the height of grids $(= 1/2^b)$ and α_i' is the representative value of the segment in which data point v_i belongs. The representative value of each segments is the quantized value of the first data point in the segment.

Figure 1 shows four cases for determining segments of quantized time series. For the illustrative convenience, we assume that the previous quantized value α_i is not omitted.

To illustrate how to reduce the dimensions, the range of error tolerance is added as shown in Figure 2. The data points in a gray rectangle belong to a single segment, so their values are omitted except the first one. In this example, ϵ is set to $h/2 = 1/16$, and after the reduction, the time series becomes

$$(\alpha_1, \alpha_2, \ldots, \alpha_8) = ((010)_2, \times, \times, (100)_2, (111)_2, (011)_2, \times, \times),$$

where "$\times$" denotes the omission of the data points. By Equation 1, v_1 is out of range $[-\epsilon, \epsilon+h] = [-1/16, 3/16]$ (α_0 is initialized to 0), so α_1 must be stored. α_2 is omitted because $v_2 - \alpha_1 \times h = 0.24 - 0.125$ is in the range $[-1/16, 3/16]$. To determine whether v_3 can be omitted, α_1 is used because v_2 has been omitted. $v_3 - \alpha_1 \times h = 0.3 - 0.125 = 0.1775$ is also in the above range, thus α_3 is also omitted. Similarly, $v_4 - \alpha_1 \times h = 0.62 - 0.125$ exceeds the range so α_4 must be stored. The rest is calculated in the similar way.

There are two advantages of representing DDR based on the grid partition. First, data are stored in an index file effectively; second, unlike APCA technique, the omitted data point is easily determined.

Because the segments are variable-length, it is not known how many and which of the data points have been omitted. To record this information, an n-bit length bit pattern β is associated to the approximation of a time series data. If α_i is omitted, the corresponding bit β_i is set to 0. Otherwise it is set to 1. The structure of an entry representing one time series data is shown in Figure 3(A). In the case of the example above, the entry representing the series data is shown in Figure 3(B).

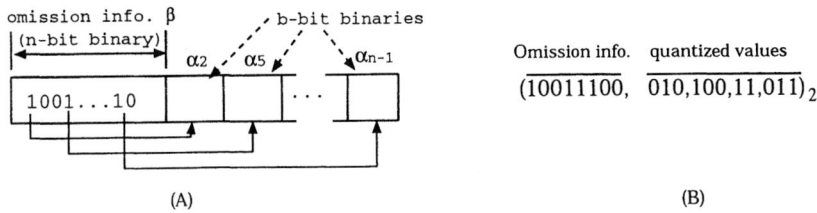

(A)   (B)

Fig. 3. Representation of one time series. n-bit binary denotes which data points in v is omitted or not. The following boxes indicate quantized value (α_i) of data points (v_i)

3.2 Distance Measures Defined for DDR

Consider a time series v, which we convert to DDR representation α, and a query time series q. Instead of computing the exact distance $D(q, v)$ between q and v, we want to estimate the bound between q and v to exclude as many irrelevant series as possible. In index files, since the quantized values of data points instead of exact values are stored, we have to define distance measures between q and α which approximates $D(q, v)$. The function has to avoid false dismissals, while maximizing the filtering effect. Functions $D_{LB}(q, v)$ and $D_{UB}(q, v)$ are defined so that they are lower and upper bounds of $D(q, v)$. These functions are used in the filtering phase for selecting candidates. $D_{LB}(q, v)$ is defined as:

$$D_{LB}(q, v) = \sqrt[p]{\sum_{i=1}^{n} (d_{LB}(q_i, v_i))^p} \tag{2}$$

where $d_{LB}(q_i, v_i)$ is the lower bound of two corresponding data points in q and v. Similarly, $D_{UB}(q, v)$ is defined as:

$$D_{UB}(q, v) = \sqrt[p]{\sum_{i=1}^{n} (d_{UB}(q_i, v_i))^p} \tag{3}$$

where $d_{UB}(q_i, v_i)$ is the upper bound value of two corresponding data points in q and v. To estimate the values of lower and upper bound, two cases are considered.

1. α_i **is stored.** The quantized value of v_i is available, because it is stored in an index file, As shown in Figure 4, $d_{LB}(q_i, v_i)$ and $d_{UB}(q_i, v_i)$ can be calculated by

$$d_{LB}(q_i, v_i) = \begin{cases} q_i - (\alpha_i + 1)h, & q_i > (\alpha_i + 1)h \\ 0, & \alpha_i h \le q_i \le (\alpha_i + 1)h \\ \alpha_i h - q_i, & q_i < \alpha_i h \end{cases} \qquad (4)$$

$$d_{UB}(q_i, v_i) = \begin{cases} q_i - \alpha_i h, & q_i > (\alpha_i + 1)h \\ max((\alpha_i + 1)h - q_i, q_i - \alpha_i h), & \alpha_i h \le q_i \le (\alpha_i + 1)h \\ (\alpha_i + 1)h - q_i, & q_i < \alpha_i h \end{cases} \qquad (5)$$

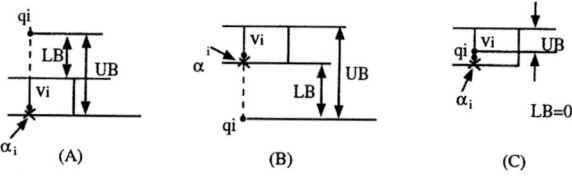

Fig. 4. Lower bound and upper bound. (A) q_i is larger than upper value of quantized value α_i of v_i. (B) q_i is smaller than lower value of quantized value α_i of v_i. (C) q_i has the same quantized value as α_i of v_i.

2. α_i **is omitted.** The value of v_i is estimated by α_i', the representative value of the segment to which v_i belongs. As mentioned above, representative value of a segment is the quantized value of the first data point in it. As shown in Figure 5, $d_{LB}(q_i, v_i)$ and $d_{UB}(q_i, v_i)$ are defined as

$$d_{LB}(q_i, v_i) = \begin{cases} q_i - (\alpha_i' + 1)h - \epsilon, & q_i > (\alpha_i' + 1)h + \epsilon \\ 0, & \alpha_i' h - \epsilon \le q_i \le (\alpha_i' + 1)h + \epsilon \\ \alpha_i' h - q_i - \epsilon, & q_i < \alpha_i' h - \epsilon \end{cases} \qquad (6)$$

$$d_{UB}(q_i, v_i) = \begin{cases} q_i - \alpha_{i-1} h + \epsilon, & q_i > (\alpha_i' + 1)h + \epsilon \\ max((\alpha_i' + 1)h + \epsilon - q_i, q_i + \epsilon - \alpha_i' h), & \alpha_i' h - \epsilon \le q_i \le (\alpha_i' + 1)h + \epsilon \\ (\alpha_i' + 1)h - q_i + \epsilon, & q_i < \alpha_i' h - \epsilon \end{cases}$$

$$(7)$$

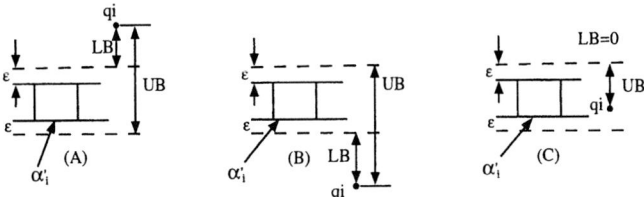

Fig. 5. Lower bound and upper bound. (A) q_i is larger than upper value of quantized value α_i' of v_i with addition of error tolerance ϵ. (B) q_i is smaller than lower value of quantized value α_i' of v_i with subtraction of error tolerance ϵ. (C) q_i has the same quantized value as α_i' of v_i in error tolerance.

4   Indexing DDR

In this section, we formally describe the algorithms using in the construction and search of DDR. DDR has a flat structure. It is a sequence whose entries correspond to the original series data one by one. Each entry contains a header of n-bit, indicating the presence or omission of quantized values by setting or unsetting the corresponding bit, respectively.

As CVA-file [2] technique, nearest neighbor queries are performed by scanning the quantized data file.

5   Experimental Evaluation

We performed all tests over a range of query lengths. In our experiments, 10-NN queries are used for queries of length 256, 512, 1024, respectively. The query sequences are extracted from the datasets randomly. L_2 is used as distance function. We use a page size of 8KB in all our experiments.

For testing whole matching, we converted subsequences by sliding a "window" of query length n along v. Though this causes storage redundancy, it simplifies the notation and algorithms. The dataset is a *"relatively clean and uncompli-cated"* electrocardiogram taken from the MIT Research Resource for Complex Physiologic Signals [11]. Totally, there are $100,000$ objects in the dataset. As mentioned earlier, data objects are normalized. That is, any data point has a real value between 0 and 1.

5.1   Experimental Result: Comparison on Number of Page Accesses

The comparisons with competing methods are illustrated here. Experiments are on a dataset of electrocardiogram. As the targets to compare, we implemented three indexing approaches other than our DDR-index. They are DFT-index, PAA-index, and linear scan. In DFT-index and PAA-index technique, we reduce dimensionality of the time series data using DFT and PAA as described in [10]. An index structure is built on the index dimensions for each technique. We adopt the SR-tree as the index structure. The k-NN search algorithm suggested by [2] is used. Two kinds of page accesses are considered: the one in accessing the index structure for getting the candidates of answer, and the one in accessing the full time series for refining the candidates.

Unlike other methods, our approach needs the refinement phase which makes random page accesses. The numbers in this phase for dimension $256, 512$ and 1024 are $49, 39$ and 16 respectively. To make the comparison fair, the total number of our page accesses is not simply the sum of the numbers in the two phases. Instead, we times the number of page accesses in the refinement phase by 10 before adding the number of filtering phase. Figure 6 illustrates the comparison for three kinds of queries lengths $1024, 512$ and 256. As can be seen from this figure, DDR retrieves much less pages than other methods. The difference is too wide so we have to plot in logarithm scale for comparing them in the same figure. Even taking the weight factor 10 into consideration, the small numbers ensure us that effects of the first phase are much more significant. The length b's of bit patterns quantizing coordinates are assighned to 6, 5 and 4 for original dimensionality 256, 512 and 1024, respectively.

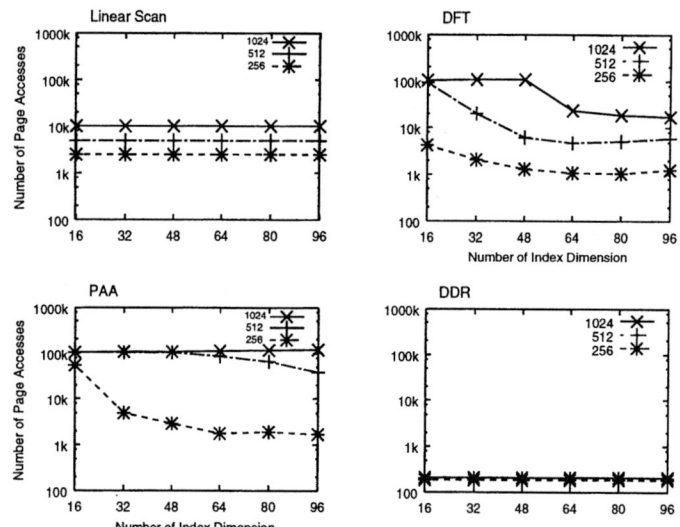

Fig. 6. Comparison on number of page accesses. Linear Scan and DDR are plotted in the same form as DFT and PAA for comparison. In fact, no dimensionality reduction happens in linear Scan, while the reduction in DDR is not fixed but depends on data.

6   Conclusions

In this paper we proposed an approach of dimensionality reduction for time series data. Combining with the technique of quantization, a grid-based indexing is designed and implemented. Experimental results are compared with some related works and confirm the efficiency of our method. As the future work, though the parameter b and tolerance ϵ are tuned to perform most effectively in the experiments, systematical determination is desirable. Furthermore, we plan to investigate formally properties and the cost model of the index structure. We are also planning to study statistical results on a wider range of data, because we believe it will enable us to predict the trends and improvement of the reduction. Affection of various definitions of distance functions other than L_p is also a potential avenue of further study.

References

1. R. Agrawal, C. Faloutsos, and A. N. Swami. Efficient similarity search in sequence databases. In *Proceedings of 4th conference on FODO*, pages 69–84, 1993.
2. J. An, H. Chen, K. Furuse, M. Ishikawa, and N. Ohbo. The convex polyhedra technique: An index strucrture for high-dimensional space. In *Proc. of the 13th Australasian Database Conference*, pages 33–40, 2002.
3. J. An, H. Chen, K. Furuse, M. Ishikawa, and N. Ohbo. A vector-wise dimensionality reduction for indexing high dimensional data. In *Proc. of Pan-Yellw-Sea International Workshop on Information Technologies for Network Era*, pages 135–142, 2002.
4. N. Beckmann, H. P. Kriegel, R. Schneider, and B. Seeger. The R*-tree:an efficient and robust access method for points and rectangles. In *Proceedings of the 1998 ACM SIGMOD International Conference on Management of Data*, pages 322–331, 1990.
5. K. Chakrabarti and S. Mehrotra. Locally dimensionality reduction: A new approach to indexing high dimensional spaces. In *Proceedings of 26th International Conference on Very Large Data Bases*, pages 151–162, 2000.
6. H. Chen, J. An, K. Furuse, and N. Ohbo. C^2VA:trim high dimensional indexes. In *Proc. WAIM2002*, pages 303–315, 2002.
7. A. Guttman. R-tree:a dynamic index structure for spatial searching. In *Proceedings of the 1984 ACM SIGMOD International Conference on Management of Data*, pages 47–57, 1984.
8. N. Katayama and S. Satoh. The sr-tree: An index structure for high-dimensional nearest neighbor queries. In *Proceedings of the 1997 ACM SIGMOD International Conference on Management of Data*, pages 369–380, 1997.
9. E. J. Keogh, K. Chakrabarti, S. Mehrotra, and M. J. Pazzani. Locally adaptive dimensionality reduction for indexing large time series databases. In *Proceedings of the 2001 ACM SIGMOD International Conference on Management of Data*, pages 151–162, 2001.
10. E. J. Keogh and M. J. Pazzani. A simple dimensionality reduction technique for fast similarity search in large time series databases. In *Proceedings of the Pacific-Asia Conference on Knowledage Discovery and Data Mining (PAKDD'00)*, pages 122–133, 2000.
11. G. Moody. Mit-bih database distribution [http://ecg.mit.edu/index.html]. In *Cambridge,MA.*, 2000.
12. R. Weber, H. J. Schek, and S. Blott. A quantitative analysis and performance study for similarity-search methods in high-dimensional spaces. In *Proceedings of 24th International Conference on Very Large Data Bases*, pages 194–205, 1998.

E.Coli Search: Self Replicating Agents for Web Based Information Retrieval

Derrick Takeshi Mirikitani and Ibrahim Kushchu

GSIM, International University of Japan
Yamato-machi, Minami Uonuma-gun
Niigata 949-7277 JAPAN
{dmirikit,ik}@iuj.ac.jp

Abstract. Although search engines are often used for information retrieval (IR) from the World Wide Web (WWW), current search engine technology seems obsolete. The quality of query results from today's search engines is unacceptable, creating a demand for new information search and retrieval techniques. The conventional IR methods often lack the flexibility to adapt to changes in the content of the WWW. This paper presents an overview of new developments in evolutionary and adaptive IR and proposes a system (E.Coli search) where an adaptive population of intelligent agents forage the web in search of relevant documents.

Keywords: Information Retrieval, evolutionary, adaptive agents, World Wide Web.

1 Introduction

The Internet (Web) is becoming an increasingly popular medium to disseminate information today. There is such an abundance of information available, yet how good is the information if it is inaccessible? The Web is massive, diverse, and dynamic and thus raises the issues of scalable and temporal complexity. The size of the Web is estimated at 8×10^8 documents and growing [14]. The continuous changing of documents makes the web extremely dynamic. Researchers [5] identified four common problems related to internet use; finding relevant information, creating new knowledge out of the information available on the web, personalization of the information, and learning about users and customers. By far, the largest problem Internet users commonly face when searching the Web for information is finding relevant information in a timely manner as the expansion of the Internet has outpaced the advances in information search and retrieval techniques.

The search engines of today use outdated search techniques developed in the previous fifty years including the probabilistic, vector space, and clustering models [11]. The static search paradigms of today cant keep up with the dynamic environment of the Web; if a page is moved it may take months before a search engine updates its database. The WWW has striking similarities with nature; it is in constant change, with documents continuously added, deleted, and moved. Furthermore, Bunde and Havlin [6] have found that the web obeys scaling laws characteristic of highly interactive self-organizing systems such as natural systems. Recently, a number of researchers

J. Liu et al. (Eds.): IDEAL 2003, LNCS 2690, pp. 622–629, 2003.
© Springer-Verlag Berlin Heidelberg 2003

[7,9,19,20,29] developed new adaptive search methodologies that aims to match this dynamic environment (see below for the review). They work on developing automated, intelligent, and adaptive methods that locate and retrieve information with respect to the users' individual preferences [9], and this paper proposes a new bacteriologically inspired model: E.Coli Search.

The E.Coli search paradigm is analogous to that of bacteria infecting a nutrient rich area (open wound etc.) The agents forage the web, and when a cluster of information-rich documents is found, the agents reproduce, infecting and infesting the cluster until most of the relevant documents (nurturance) are exploited (visited). When the majority of the relevant documents have been visited, the agents either find another information rich area or run out of energy and die. This paper proposes a new model called "E.Coli Search". Section 2 provides a brief overview of search engine mechanics. Section 3 introduces the E.Coli search engine. The experiments, results and discussions are presented in Section 4 and Section 5 concludes the paper by proposing directions for future work.

2   Search Engine Mechanics

Most search engines usually have a crawler. A crawler constantly searches the web, indexing between 3 – 10 million documents per day [3]. Some crawlers randomly search while others specifically look at previously indexed pages for new information. Typically, however, crawlers visit page addresses submitted by users. The crawler only takes part of a web page and copies it into a database. This means per user query, the search engine only analyzes part of each web page to determine page relevance. Search algorithms differ between engines. For instance, Excite web crawler parses as much as it can in 30 seconds, whereas Lycos takes the first 275 characters, and Infoseek takes the first 16kb for a reference [31]. Furthermore, each user query is compared against a static document representation in the search engines database. This explains why many links on search engines are out dated or irrelevant.

The efficiency of current search engines is based on indexing the web once, creating a snapshot of the web, and leveraging the cost of processing the index over a large number of queries. This model, which has led to the success of search engines, is also the cause of their limitations [19]. The index once, query many times, model is taken directly from earlier off-line information retrieval paradigms which assume the document collection is static. The web, on the other hand, is dynamic; with documents being constantly added deleted and changed. Crawlers work around the clock to update the index, revisiting every page. Regardless of the crawler's effort, the index can never be completely accurate. The large and increasing size of the web compounds this problem and prevents accurate responses to user queries. Users are often faced with low *precision* and *recall.* Users must spend significant time manually browsing for relevant documents.

3   E.Coli Search: Bacteriological Strategies for IR

The web can be thought of as a huge directed graph whose vertices are documents and whose edges are URL's that point from one document to another [2]. In [18], it is argued that in a distributed hypertext environment, the structure of link topology can assist autonomous agents in locating relevant documents. They go on to say that even in unstructured information spaces, documents about related topics tend to be clustered in information rich areas. It is found [2] that although the web is massive, the average distance between two pages is 19 links, further supporting argument [18] that topological clues from the structure of the web can assist search agents. Menczer and Blew [19] have shown that even random walking agents can effectively exploit web resources using link topology.

E.Coli search is a prototyped multi-agent information retrieval system for the World Wide Web. Each agent searches for documents relevant to the users query. Although, during the search there is no direct communication between agents, E.Coli search is able to simulate intelligent behavior both at the local level, by evaluating the relevance of the document with respect to the users query, and at the global level, through rapid reproduction leading to search agent infestation of information rich areas in the search space. In the E.Coli Search system, agents search through a collection of documents (document space) for specified words (keywords). The agents parse the HTML based web pages, extract "relevant" information, and use the vector space model to determine the page relevance. Based on static and predetermined thresholds, the agent can choose to return the page to the user, follow links on the page, or go back to the last page if the relevance is deemed low. Moving from page to page takes energy. If the page is irrelevant, the agent is punished with a subtraction of energy, thus, subsequent visits to irrelevant pages could mean death to the agent. On the other hand, if the page is relevant, the agent is rewarded with energy. Oh's [23] findings suggest keeping bandwidth usage to a minimum and thus in this experiment each agent only visits one page at a time. This work draws strong structural similarities to that of [8], [17] through [20]. Most work in this area assumes that related documents exist in clusters of information rich areas (link topology). We would like to extend our research to explore dynamics where clusters are not so well defined.

The extensive use of agents in E.Coli Search clearly lends it self to an object oriented design. The Java programming language was used for implementation as it is the latest object oriented language. All processing is carried out on the server. The user interface is an HTML page using a form to pass information and invoke a servlet. The servlet initializes the agents and the search is carried out. The results are written dynamically via servlet to the user.

Actual searching on the web is carried out at the local (Agent) level. Each agent is completely autonomous; there is no central control over the agents. Each agent makes its own decisions based on local conditions. A detailed explanation of the agent algorithm is given below:

Each agent is given the users query with stop words (a list of meaningless words with respect to the query) removed, and an initial supply of energy, steps (1,2). In step (4) Each agent parses its current document, stop words, formatting, and hyperlinks are removed. Next, in step (5), the agent analyzes the "meaningful" material of the document and compares it with the keyword query supplied by the user. Agents are rewarded with energy if the page is extremely relevant, and punished if the page is not relevant. Movement across the document space incurs energy, determined in step (8). In steps (10-17), if the page is extremely relevant, agents return the page, reproduce, and follow the chosen link to the next page. If the page is found to have moderate relevance, the agent will go to the next page. If the relevance is bad, the agent will go back. The process continues until the agent dies or visits a specified number of pages. The vector space class is used to determine the page relevance of each document. The vector space model is the defacto standard for information systems.

```
1.      HTML request to Servlet with key words
2.      initialize population, key word query and energy
3.      loop:
4.          parse page
5.          remove stop words
6.          determine page relevance
7.          choose a hyper link
8.          determine energy
9.          if (energy <0) die
10.         if(page is extremely relevant) {
11.             return page to user
12.             divide
13.             go to next page}
14.         if(page has ok relevance) {
15.             go to next page}
16.         if(page has little relevance) {
17.             go back to last page}
```

Each agent is given the users query with stop words (a list of meaningless words with respect to the query) removed, and an initial supply of energy, steps (1,2). In step (4) Each agent parses its current document, stop words, formatting, and hyperlinks are removed. Next, in step (5), the agent analyzes the "meaningful" material of the document and compares it with the keyword query supplied by the user. Agents are rewarded with energy if the page is extremely relevant, and punished if the page is not relevant. Movement across the document space incurs energy, determined in step (8). In steps (10-17), if the page is extremely relevant, agents return the page, reproduce, and follow the chosen link to the next page. If the page is found to have moderate relevance, the agent will go to the next page. If the relevance is bad, the agent will go back. The process continues until the agent dies or visits a specified number of pages. The vector space class is used to determine the page relevance of each document. The vector space model is the defacto standard for information systems.

4   Experiments and Results

Evaluation of a system such as E.Coli Search is complex. To evaluate its effectiveness in online and real-time information discovery, measurement of recall (the ratio of retrieved documents to the total amount of relevant documents) and precision (the ratio of the number of documents retrieved to the total number of documents) is nearly impossible when using the actual Web as the information space. We have tested E.coli search in a control environment acting as the web itself. The control environment used was a subset of the web consisting of linked HTML pages. The link structure of the test environment models a torus. This structure is similar to the automated game of life simulation by William Gosper [15].

Due to the large number of documents necessary to construct a suitable test environment, a program was written to generate the document space. The page generation program intentionally cerates information rich clusters with respect to a certain query. The information space contains a vocabulary of 5 words. Information clusters are formed for the keywords "risk management" and "horse". The other words (cat, fish) are distributed randomly. The document space was constructed such that per key word, there are as many randomly distributed documents as clustered documents. Out of many tests, we report two sets of 30 queries. In the first set we used 25 agents and in the second test we used 50 agents. The experiments aimed to test (1) the e-coli search can identify information rich clusters among web documents and (2) can adapt to changes in the position of the information rich clusters in the search space.

Testing with 25 agents: In the first test, an information rich cluster of 81 relevant documents with respect to the query "risk management" was placed in the information space. Also, 81 *randomly* placed documents relevant to the query "cat" was placed in the information space.

The first test was set to inoculate the information space with 25 agents. 30 queries each were submitted for "risk management" and "cat." The average precision rating for a search on a clustered query (risk management) was .78. On the other hand, the average precision rating for a search on a randomly distributed word was .16, a significant difference between the two. This shows that system is sensitive to information rich clusters. In other word E.Coli search was able to concentrate on the relevant documents more than documents scattered randomly.

To test the adaptive properties of the system, the information cluster was moved and second set of test was run. The results were almost exactly the same and the system was able to recognize the changes in the environment and respond to those changes.

Testing with 50 Agents: A second series of tests was run using a 50 agent initial population.

Surprisingly, there was no real increase in precision when querying for the information rich cluster.   As expected, there was an increase in precision for the randomly distributed documents. As done in the earlier test, the   information cluster was moved and documents were redistributed randomly. Again the system was able to recognize the changes in the document space.   The precision for both queries matched the previous test.

Table 1. Result Summary

Trial 1	Popsize 25		Popsize 50	
	query 1 risk m...	query 2 cat	query 1 risk m...	query 2 cat
mean	63.233	13.5	63.733	21.966
St.dev	1.006	6.986	0.449	6.195
precision	0.78	0.166	0.786	0.271
Trial 2				
mean	63.8	15.766	63.733	21.233
St.dev	1.095	6.29	0.639	6.344
precision	0.787	0.194	0.786	0.262

Table 1 summarizes what we have just described. The differences between the standard deviations show significant differences between queries for clustered documents and randomly distributed documents. The clustered documents had low standard deviations suggesting stable and predictable results whereas searches for non-clustered documents resulted in high standard deviations, suggesting varied results. These findings show that the system is able to exploit information rich structures efficiently on the web. Furthermore, these results support [19] argument for the value of link topology.

The document sample used for testing may be unrealistic; a vocabulary of 5 words. Nonetheless, this simplified experiment is useful in determining the effectiveness of the E.Coli Search in exploiting link topology. The results have shown agent convergence to information rich areas with high precision ratings.

5   Conclusions and Future Research Directions

This research was motivated by the belief that the rapid expansion of the web is outpacing current information retrieval technology, and that adaptive information retrieval paradigms should be used to match the dynamic nature of the web. This experiment has provided a simulation of dynamic, intelligent, and adaptive search of real web resources. The experiment has demonstrated the ability to exploit information rich link topology in an efficient manor. Evaluation of E.Coli Search provides encouraging support for further research in the area.

The experiment has focused on the behavior of agents in a carefully controlled environment. The findings of this experiment suggest that link topology can be exploited through a self replicating agent paradigm. Further testing is in order. First, more realistic pages in a larger information space must be used, and second, testing on the web must be carried out.

The collective behavior of the agents suggests a little systems intelligence, but at the local level, agents do not have the ability to learn. This is where artificial neural networks or genetic algorithms may fit in. Hyperlink estimation may make agent behavior more like that of a human, following links based on anticipation that a particular link will lead to a relevant document while disregarding those links that are thought to lead to irrelevant pages. The agent will try to learn from link based information during the search itself in an attempt to predict which link leads to the most relevant page [1].

Keyword vector mutation may also add significant intelligence for agents. A genetic algorithm or neural network may be useful in promoting learning of co-occurring words in documents that have a relationship to the search query. The system could then add these words to the query vector to enhance search.

We hope that through continuing work, we can support efforts in what is hopefully to become a new sub-field in computing science, Adaptive Information Retrieval. This paper is an attempt to establish a basis for a research in the area by providing a compilation of research resources including a literature review and a reproducible and expandable experiment. In the near future, we would like to include a learning mechanism in E.Coli search: adaptive information retrieval system for the Web based information retrieval.

References

1. Charu C Aggarwal, Fatima Al-Garawi, and Philip S Yu Intelligent Crawling on the World Wide Web with Arbitrary Predicates *WWW10* 2001 Hong Kong ACM 1-58113-348-0/01/005
2. Albert, Jeong, Barabasi, Diameter of the World Wide Web, In *Nature* Volume 401, 130, 1999
3. Michael W. Berry and Murry Browne Understanding Search Engines Mathematical Modeling and Text Retrieval *Society for Industrial and Applied Mathematics* Philadelphia 1999
4. Richard K. Blew Finding out About: a cognitive perspective on search engine technology *Cambridge University Press* 2000
5. H Blockeel and R Kosala. Web Mining Research: A Survey *SIGKDD Explorations. ACM SIGKDD,* 2000
6. A. Bunde and S. Havlin, Eds., Fractals in Science, *Springer*, Berlin, Heidelberg, New York, 1994
7. H. Chen, Y. Chung, M. Ramsey, and C. Yang. An intelligent personal spider (agent) for dynamic internet/intranet searching, 1998.
8. P. De Bra and Post Information retrieval in the world wide web: Making client-based searching feasible. In *1ˢᵗ International WWW Conference*, Geneva, 1994
9. Ibrahim Kuscu An Adaptive Approach to Organizational Knowledge Management *Knowledge and Information: Journal of the KMCI* Volume 01, number 2 2001
10. Kim Y. H., Kim S., Eom J. H., and Byoung-Tak Zhang. Scai experiments on trec-9. In *Proceedings of the Ninth Text REtrieval Conference (TREC-9)*, pages 392–399, 2000.
11. Sun Kim and Byoung-Tak Zhang. Evolutionary learning of web document structure for information retrieval. In *Proceedings of the 2001 Congress on Evolutionary Computation CEC2001*, pages 1253–1260, COEX, World Trade Center, 159 Samseong-dong, Gangnam-gu, Seoul, Korea, 27–30 May 2001. IEEE Press.
12. G. Pant and F. Menczer. Myspiders: Evolve your own intelligent web crawlers. *Autonomous Agents and Multi-Agent Systems*, 5(2):221–229, 2002.
13. Langton CG, Artificial Life: The Proceedings of an Interdisciplinary Workshop on the Synthesis and Simulation of Living Systems. Redwood City, Calif.: *Addison-Wesley* 1989.
14. Steve Lawrence and C. Lee Giles. Accessibility and Distribution of Information on the Web, *Nature* 400(6740): 107–109, July 8, 1999.
15. Steven Levy Artificial Life The Quest for a New Creation *Jonathan Cape* London 1992
16. Pattie Maes Agents that Reduce Work and Information Overload, Communications of the *ACM,* Vol. 37, No. 7, July 1994.
17. Flippo Menczer Complementing Search Engines with Online Web Mining Agents *Elsevier Science* 2002
18. Flippo Menczer and Richard K. Blew Adaptive Information Agents in Distributed Textual Environments *Agents'98: Proceedings of the Second International Conference on Autonomous Agents*, Minneapolis, MN 1998 ACM
19. Filippo Menczer and Richard K. Belew. Adaptive retrieval agents: Internalizing local context and scaling up to the web. *Machine Learning*, 39(2/3):203–242, 2000.
20. Filippo Menczer, Richard K. Belew, and Wolfram Willuhn. Artificial life applied to adaptive information agents. In *AAAI Spring Symposium on Information Gathering*, 1995.
21. Alexandros Moukas. Amalthaea: Information discovery and filtering using a multiagent evolving ecosystem. In *Proceedings of the Conference on Practical Applications of Agents and Multiagent Technology*, 1996.

22. Alexandros Moukas and Pattie Maes. Amalthaea: An evolving multi-agent information filtering and discovery system for the WWW. *Autonomous Agents and Multi-Agent Systems*, 1(1):59–88, 1998.

23. Jae C. Oh. Cooperating search agents explore more than defecting search agents in the internet information access. In *Proceedings of the 2001 Congress on Evolutionary Computation CEC2001*, pages 1261–1268, COEX, World Trade Center, 159 Samseong-dong, Gangnam-gu, Seoul, Korea, 27-30 May 2001. IEEE Press.

24. Luigi Pagliarini, Ariel Dolan, Filippo Menczer, and Henrik Hautop Lund. ALife meets web: Lessons learned. In *Virtual Worlds*, pages 156–167, 1998.

25. Praveen Pathak, Michael Gordon, and Weiguo Fan. Effective information retrieval using genetic algorithms based matching functions adaptation. In *HICSS*, 2000.

26. Francisco Pereira and Ernesto Costa. How learning improves the performance of evolutionary agents: a case study with an information retrieval system for a distributed environment.

27. Francisco B. Pereira and Ernesto Costa. How adaptive agents learn to deal with incomplete queries in distributed information environments. In *Proc. of the 2000 Congress on Evolutionary Computation*, pages 1329–1336, 2000. IEEE Press.

28. Reginald L. Walker. Assessment of the web using genetic programming. In Wolfgang Banzhaf, Jason Daida, Agoston E. Eiben, Max H. Garzon, Vasant Honavar, Mark Jakiela, and Robert E. Smith, editors, *Proceedings of the Genetic and Evolutionary Computation Conference*, volume 2, pages 1750–1755, Orlando, Florida, USA, 13-17 July 1999. Morgan Kaufmann.

29. Reginald L. Walker. Dynamic load balancing model: Preliminary assessment of a biological model for a pseudo-search engine. In *SPDP: IEEE Symposium on Parallel and Distributed Processing*. ACM Special Interest Group on Computer Architecture (SIGARCH), and IEEE Computer Society, 2000.

30. Reginald L. Walker. Parallel clustering system using the methodologies of evolutionary computations. In *Proceedings of the 2001 Congress on Evolutionary Computation CEC2001*, pages 831–938, COEX, World Trade Center, 159 Samseongdong, Gangnam-gu, Seoul, Korea, 27-30 May 2001. IEEE Press.

31. Reginald L. Walker. Search engine case study:searching the web using genetic programming. In *Parallel Computing*, volume 7. Elsevier, 2001.

An Efficient Mining Method for Incremental Updation in Large Databases*

Wan-Jui Lee and Shie-Jue Lee

Department of Electrical Engineering, National Sun Yat-Sen University, Kaohsiung 80424,
Taiwan
wrlee@water.ee.nsysu.edu.tw

Abstract. The database used in mining for knowledge discovery is dynamic in
nature. Data may be updated and new transactions may be added over time. As a
result, the knowledge discovered from such databases is also dynamic. Incremental
mining techniques have been developed to speed up the knowledge discovery
process by avoiding re-learning of rules from the old data. To maintain the large
itemsets against the incoming dataset, we adopt the idea of negative border to help
reduce the number of scans over the original database and discover new itemsets
in the updated database. A lot of effort in the re-computation of negative border
can be saved, and the minimal candidate set of large itemsets and negative border
in the updated database can be obtained efficiently. Simulation results have shown
that our method runs faster than other incremental mining techniques, especially
when the large itemsets in the updated database are significantly different from
those in the original database.

1   Introduction

Generally, mining of association rules was decomposed into two subproblems, discovering all large itemsets and generating the association rules from those large itemsets.
The second subproblem is straightforward once the large itemsets are known, and can
be done efficiently in a reasonable time. However, the first subproblem of discovering
all large itemsets is very tedious and computationally expensive for very large databases
and this is the case for many real life applications. Though, this high computational cost
may be acceptable when the database is static since the discovery is done off-line, and
several approaches to this problem have been presented in the literature. However, many
domains with streaming data, such as electronic commerce, web mining, stock analysis,
intrusion detection, fault monitoring, etc., impose time and memory constraints on the
mining process. In such domains, where the databases are updated continuously, running
the discovery program from scratch is infeasible, and having the user wait inordinately
long is unacceptable. Hence, there is a need for incremental mining techniques that can
effectively handle online updations of data. In [2], the concept of negative border, that
was introduced in [1], is used to compute the new set of large itemsets in the updated
database. The negative border consists of all itemsets that were candidates but did not

---

* Supported by the National Science Council under grants NSC-91-2213-E-110-024 and NSC-
91-2213-E-110-025.

J. Liu et al. (Eds.): IDEAL 2003, LNCS 2690, pp. 630–637, 2003.

have enough support while computing large itemsets in the original database. The availability of the negative border of the set of large itemsets and their counts in the original database can reduce the number of scans over the original database. If no itemset in negative border is promoted to the set of large itemsets in the updated database, there is no need to scan over the original database. However, if such an itemset exists, negative border will be repeatedly computed until there is no change in the negative border. However, recomputing negative border again and again deteriorates the performance of this method. Another method in [3] first counts the supports of itemsets in the set of large itemsets and negative border in the original database over the incremental database. If any itemset in the negative border is found to be large in the incremental database, then it computes all large itemsets of the incremental database and validates those against the original database by scanning it once. Its major advantage is that it does not scan the original database if there is no new itemset in the incremental database. However, we can only compute the negative border in the updated database until large itemsets are totally discovered. Therefore, to maintain the support counts of negative border, the second scan over the original database is necessary.

The methods described above do not have to scan over the original database if the incremental database is a good sample of the original database and no significant differences between the large itemsets of these databases. However, if there are new itemsets emerging, the computation of the negative border will become a problem. In applications like Point-of-Sales or databases containing patterns in seasonal nature, new large itemsets can be frequently discovered. To efficiently compute the negative border in different types of incremental databases, we propose a method to generate a candidate set of large itemsets and negative border in the updated database. Obviously, any large itemset in the updated database must at least be large in the original or incremental database. Therefore, using the information of large itemsets and negative border in the original database and the large itemsets in the incremental database, the search space of those candidate itemsets can be greatly reduced.

The rest of the paper is organized as follows. In Section 2, we describe our method in detail. Simulation results are presented in Section 3, and finally, a conclusion is given in Section 4.

2   Our Approach

Our method makes effective use of the information discovered during the earlier process of mining. Moreover, the knowledge of incremental database is also used by the algorithm to achieve better performance. The problem of incremental mining is to find the set L^{DB+db} of large itemsets in the updated database $DB + db$. L^{DB+db} may contain some new itemsets called emerged itemsets. Some itemsets from L^{DB}, called declined itemsets, may be absent in L^{DB+db}. Those itemsets which exist both in L^{DB+db} and L^{DB} are retained itemsets.

2.1   Description of Algorithm

In order to solve the update problem effectively, we maintain the large itemsets and the negative border along with their support counts in the database. That is, for every

$s \in L \bigcup NBD(L)$, we maintain $s.count$. Initially, we compute L^{db}. To compare with the incremental updation algorithm in [2], we use the Apriori method [4] to generate the large itemsets in db. Simultaneously, we count the support in db for all itemsets in $L^{DB} \bigcup NBD(L^{DB})$. If an itemset $s \in L^{DB}$ does not have minimum support in $DB \bigcup db$, then s is removed from L^{DB}. This can be easily checked since we know the support count for s in DB and db, respectively. The change in L^{DB} could potentially change $NBD(L^{DB})$ also. Therefore, we have to recompute the negative border using the negativeborder-gen function explained below.

---

function apriori-gen(L_k)
    $C_{k+1} = \emptyset$;
    for each $p \in L_k$ *do*
        for each $q \neq p \in L_k$ *do*
            if $(k-1)$ elements in p and q are equal *then*
                insert $p \cup q$ into C_{k+1};
    for each $c \in C_{k+1}$ *do*
        delete c from C_{k+1} if some k-subset of c is not in L_k;
end apriori-gen

---

function negativeborder-gen(L)
    Split L into $L_1, L_2,..., L_n$ where n is the size of the largest itemset in L;
    for all $k = 1, 2, ..., n$ *do*
        compute C_{k+1} using apriori-gen(L_k);
    $L \bigcup NBD(L) = \bigcup_{k=2,...,n+1} C_k \bigcup I_1$ where I_1 is the set of 1-itemsets;
end negativeborder-gen

On the other hand, there could be some new itemsets which become large in the updated database. Let s be an itemset which becomes a large itemset of the updated database. We know that s has to be in L^{db}. We also know that some subset of s must be moved from $NBD(L^{DB})$ to L^{DB+db}. If none of the itemsets in $NBD(L^{DB})$ gets minimum support, no new itemsets will be added to L^{DB+db}. If some itemsets in $NBD(L^{DB})$ get minimum support, they are moved to L^{DB+db} and the negative border is recomputed. If $L^{DB+db} \bigcup NBD(L^{DB+db}) \neq L^{DB+db} \bigcup NBD(L^{DB+db})$, we have to find the candidates of L^{DB+db} and $NBD(L^{DB+db})$, denoted as Can_L^{DB+db} and $Can\_NBD(L^{DB+db})$, respectively. Can_L^{DB+db} contains those itemsets in L^{db} but not in $L^{DB} \bigcup NBD(L^{DB})$. Then we use $Can\_L^{DB+db} \bigcup NBD(Can\_L^{DB+db} \bigcup L^{DB+db})$ to form $Can\_NBD(L^{DB+db})$. During the scan of the original database, all support counts of those candidate itemsets are computed. Finally, we can discover all itemsets in L^{DB+db}. Our algorithm is presented in a high-level description of program code as follows.

function Update-Large-Itemset(L^{DB},$NBD(L^{DB})$,db)

    Compute L^{db};

    for each itemset s$\in L^{DB} \bigcup NBD(L^{DB})$ *do*

      $t_{db}(s)$=number of transactions in *db* containing s;

    L^{DB+}=$\emptyset$;

    for each itemset $s \in L^{DB}$ *do*

      if $(t_{DB}(s)+t_{db}(s))\geq$minsup*$(|DB| + |db|)$ *then*

        L^{DB+}=$L^{DB+} \bigcup s$;

    for each itemset $s \in L^{db}$ *do*

      if $s \notin L^{DB}$ and $s \in NBD(L^{DB})$ and $(t_{DB}(s)+t_{db}(s))\geq minsup*(|DB| + |db|)$ *then*

        L^{DB+}=$L^{DB+} \bigcup s$;

    if $L^{DB+} = L^{DB}$ *then*

      $NBD(L^{DB+})$=$NBD(L^{DB})$;

    else

      $NBD(L^{DB+})$=negativeborder-gen(L^{DB+});

    if $L^{DB} \bigcup NBD(L^{DB}) \neq L^{DB+} \bigcup NBD(L^{DB+})$ *then*

      $Can\_L^{DB+db} = \emptyset$;

    for each itemset $s \in L^{db}$ *do*

      if $s \notin L^{DB}$ and $s \notin NBD(L^{DB})$ *then*

        Can_L^{DB+db}=$Can\_L^{DB+db} \bigcup s$;

    Max_L^{DB+db}=$Can\_L^{DB+db} \bigcup L^{DB+}$;

    $NBD(Max\_L^{DB+db})$=negativeborder-gen(Max_L^{DB+db});

    $Can\_NBD(L^{DB+db}) = Can\_L^{DB+db} \bigcup NBD(Max\_L^{DB+db})$;

    $L^{DB+db} = \{x \in Max\_L^{DB+db}|support(x) \geq minsup * (|DB| + |db|)\}$;

    //support(x) is the support count of x in $DB + db$

    $NBD(L^{DB+db})$=negativeborder-gen(L^{DB+db});

end Update-Large-Itemset

2.2 Validation of Candidate Generation

The prediction for the negative border candidates used earlier in our algorithm is based on the following property:

$$NBD(L^{DB+db}) \subseteq Can\_NBD(L^{DB+db}) \qquad (1)$$

where

$$Can\_NBD(L^{DB+db}) = Can\_L^{DB+db} \bigcup NBD(Can\_L^{DB+db} \bigcup L^{DB+}), \quad (2)$$

$$Can\_L^{DB+db} = \{s|s \in L^{db} \text{ and } s \notin (L^{DB} \bigcup NBD(L^{DB}))\} \qquad (3)$$

$$L^{DB+} = \{s|s \in (L^{DB} \bigcup NBD(L^{DB})) \text{ and } s \in L^{DB+db}\}. \qquad (4)$$

This property is derived below.

Note that

$$
\begin{aligned}
L^{DB+db} &= (L^{DB+} \bigcup L^{db+}) \\
&\subseteq (Can\_L^{DB+db} \bigcup L^{DB+}) = Max\_L^{DB+db}, \text{ where} \quad (5)
\end{aligned}
$$

$$
L^{db+} = \{s | s \in L^{db}, s \in L^{DB+db} \text{ and } s \notin (L^{DB} \bigcup NBD(L^{DB}))\}, \quad (6)
$$

$$
L^{db-} = \{s | s \in L^{db}, s \notin L^{DB+db} \text{ and } s \notin (L^{DB} \bigcup NBD(L^{DB}))\}, \quad (7)
$$

and

$$
Can\_L^{DB+db} = L^{db+} \bigcup L^{db-}. \quad (8)
$$

Also, we have

$$
L^{db-} \subseteq Can\_L^{DB+db}. \quad (9)
$$

To prove Eq.(1), we have to certify first that

$$
NBD(L^{DB+db}) \subseteq L^{db-} \bigcup NBD(Can\_L^{DB+db} \bigcup L^{DB+}). \quad (10)
$$

From Eq.(5), $\forall$ k-itemsets, we have

$$
L_k{}^{DB+db} \subseteq Max\_L_k{}^{DB+db}. \quad (11)
$$

Using the apriori-gen function, C_{k+1}^{DB+db} can be generated by L_k^{DB+db}, and hence the negative border of L_{k+1}^{DB+db} is derived with

$$
NBD(L_{k+1}^{DB+db}) = \text{apriori-gen}(L_k^{DB+db}) - L_{k+1}^{DB+db}. \quad (12)
$$

Also, the $(k + 1)$-itemsets of negative border candidates in Eq.(10) are determined by

$$
\begin{aligned}
&L_{K+1}^{db-} \bigcup NBD(Max\_L_{K+1}^{DB+db}) \\
&= L_{K+1}^{db-} \bigcup (\text{apriori-gen}(Max\_L_K^{DB+db}) - Max\_L_{K+1}^{DB+db}). \quad (13)
\end{aligned}
$$

By Eq.(5) and Eq.(8), we have

$$
\begin{aligned}
Max\_L^{DB+db} &= Can\_L^{DB+db} \bigcup L^{DB+} = (L^{db+} \bigcup L^{db-}) \bigcup (L^{DB+}) \\
&= L^{db-} \bigcup (L^{db+} \bigcup L^{DB+}) = L^{db-} \bigcup L^{DB+db}. \quad (14)
\end{aligned}
$$

From Eq.(14), Eq.(13) can further be rewritten as

$$
\text{apriori-gen}(Max\_L_K^{DB+db}) - L_K^{DB+db} + (L_K^{DB+db} \bigcap L_{K+1}^{db-}). \quad (15)
$$

By Eq.(11), it can be easily found that

$$
\text{apriori-gen}(L_k{}^{DB+db}) \subseteq \text{apriori-gen}(Max\_L_K^{DB+db}). \quad (16)
$$

Finally, from Eq.(12), Eq.(15), and Eq.(16), we conclude that $\forall$ k-itemsets,

$$NBD(L_{k+1}^{DB+db}) \subseteq L_{k+1}^{db-} \bigcup NBD(Can\_L_{k+1}^{DB+db} \bigcup L_{k+1}^{DB+}) \qquad (17)$$

from which Eq.(10) is derived. Finally, by Eq.(9) and Eq.(10), we can see that

$$NBD(L^{DB+db}) \subseteq Can\_L^{DB+db} \bigcup NBD(Can\_L^{DB+db} \bigcup L^{DB+})$$
$$= Can\_NBD(L^{DB+db}) \qquad (18)$$

and the property of Eq.(1) holds.

3   Experimental Results

We compare the performance of our approach with that of the incremental updation algorithm in [2] by running them with experiments on a PC with AMD Athlon XP CPU and 1.3G memory. In the experiments, we use synthetic data to form input databases to the algorithms. The database of size $|DB+db|$ is generated using the same technique as introduced in [4], and the first $|DB|$ transactions are used as DB and the next $|db|$ transactions as db. The $T10.I4.D100K.C25\%$ and $T10.I4.D100K.C10\%$ datasets are used in the experiments where T is the mean size of a transaction, I is the mean size of potential maximal large itemsets, D is the number of transactions in units of K, i.e., 1000, and C is the correlation between items in terms of percentage. In Figure 1, we compare the execution time of our incremental mining algorithm with respect to the incremental updation algorithm using 1% fractional size as the increment and running Apriori on the whole dataset. From Figure 1(a), our method shows better speedup than the incremental updation algorithm for low support thresholds. Note that the dataset $T10.I4.D100K.C25\%$ has strong correlations between items, and the incremental database is more possible a

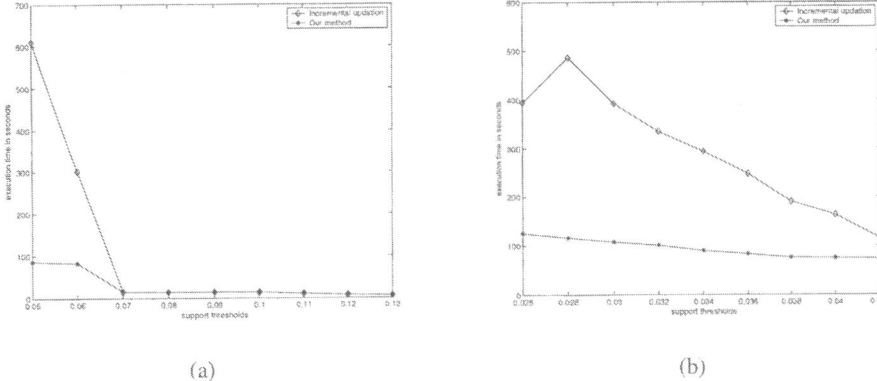

(a)   (b)

Fig. 1. Comparison of the two methods on execution time with different support thresholds for (a) dataset $T10.I4.D100K.C25\%$ and (b) dataset $T10.I4.D100K.C10\%$.

good sample of the original database. Therefore, at medium or high support thresholds, new large itemsets are rarely found and the scan of the original database is avoided. At low support thresholds, the probability of the negative border expansion is higher and as a result the performance of the incremental updation algorithm deteriorates. At medium or high support thresholds, like incremental updation, we do not have to scan over the original database since no negative border becomes large itemsets. Even if there is, we do not have to iteratively expand the negative border. In Figure 1(b), our method is much more efficient than the other two methods in all support thresholds. The dataset $T10.I4.D100K.C10\%$ has weak correlations between items, therefore there are many chances to discover new large itemsets in all support thresholds. In Figure 2, we show the speedup ratio SR of our method in comparison with the incremental updation algorithm for incremental sizes of 1%, 2%, 5% and 10%, respectively. The speedup ratio SR is calculated as follows:

$$SR = \frac{\text{time for the incremental updation algorithm} - \text{time for our method}}{\text{time for our method}}. \quad (19)$$

Figure 2(a) shows our speedup ratio for dataset $T10.I4.D100K.C25\%$. For smaller incremental sizes, our speedup is higher since a smaller incremental database will be less possible to be a good sample of the original and the negative border is more likely to expand. Figure 2(b) shows that, for dataset $T10.I4.D100K.C25\%$, our method runs much faster with all fractional sizes of incremental databases. Note that with our method, no iterations are needed for the expansion of negative border. However, iterations are needed for the incremental updation algorithm, as shown in Table 1.

In summary, our method performs better than the incremental updation algorithm for all types of incremental databases, especially in the case of smaller incremental sizes and thresholds.

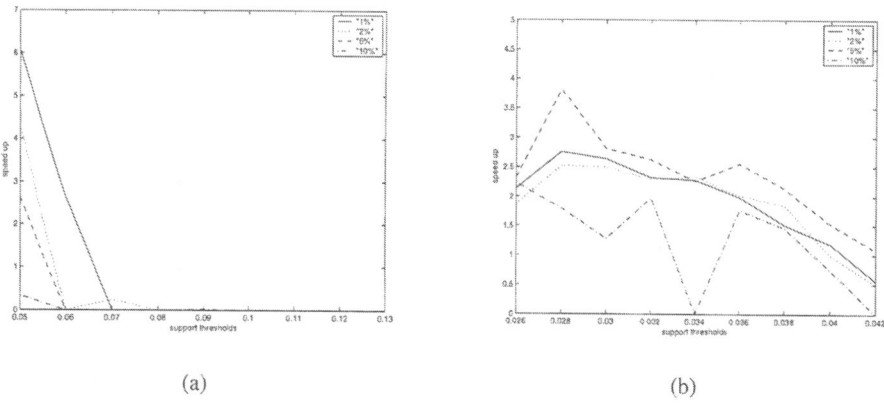

(a)   (b)

Fig. 2. The speedup ratio of our method in comparison with the incremental updation algorithm for incremental sizes of 1%, 2%, 5% and 10% with (a) dataset $T10.I4.D100K.C25\%$ and (b) dataset $T10.I4.D100K.C10\%$.

Table 1. Numbers of iterations for negative border expansion for the incremental updation algorithm with different incremental sizes and support thresholds on dataset $T10.I4.D100K.C10\%$.

incremental	support thresholds	2.6%	2.8%	3.0%	3.2%	3.4%	3.6%	3.8%	4.0%	4.2%
sizes of 1%	number of iterations	3	5	4	4	4	4	4	3	3
incremental	support thresholds	2.6%	2.8%	3.0%	3.2%	3.4%	3.6%	3.8%	4.0%	4.2%
sizes of 2%	number of iterations	3	5	4	4	4	4	4	3	3
incremental	support thresholds	2.6%	2.8%	3.0%	3.2%	3.4%	3.6%	3.8%	4.0%	4.2%
sizes of 5%	number of iterations	3	5	4	4	4	4	4	3	3
incremental	support thresholds	2.6%	2.8%	3.0%	3.2%	3.4%	3.6%	3.8%	4.0%	4.2%
sizes of 10%	number of iterations	4	3	2	2	0	2	2	2	1

4   Conclusion

We have proposed an incremental mining technique which can speed up the knowledge discovery process by avoiding re-learning of rules from the old data when the underlying database is dynamic. To maintain the large itemsets against the incoming dataset, we adopt the idea of negative border to help reduce the number of scans over the original database and discover new itemsets in the updated database. A lot of effort in the re-computation of negative border can be saved, and the minimal candidate set of large itemsets and negative border in the updated database can be obtained efficiently. Experimental results have shown that our method runs faster than other incremental mining techniques.

References

1. Hannu Toivonen, "Sampling large databases for association rules," In*Proceedings of the International Very Large Database Conference* , pp. 134–145, 1996.
2. Shiby Tomas, Sreenath Bodagala, Khaled Alsabti, and Sanjay Ranka, "An efficient algorithm for the incremental updation of association rules in large databases," In *Proceedings of the International Conference on Knowledge Discovery and Data Mining* , pp. 263–266, 1997.
3. N.L. Sarda and N.V. Srinivas, "An adaptive algorithm for incremental mining of association rules," In *Proceedings of DEXA Workshop* , pp. 240–245, 1998.
4. R. Agrawal and R. Srikant,"Fast algorithms for mining association rules," In *Proceedings of the International Very Large Database Conference* , pp. 487–499 , 1994.
5. N.F. Ayan, "Updating Large Itemsets With Early Pruning," M.Sc. Thesis, Bilkent University, 1999.
6. Margaret H. Dunham, "Data mining introductory and advanced topics," Pearson Education, New Jersey, 2003.

Selectivity Estimation for Optimizing Similarity Query in Multimedia Databases

Ju-Hong Lee[1], Seok-Ju Chun[2], and Sun Park[1]

[1] School of Computer Science and Engineering, Inha University
253, Yonghyun-dong, Nam-gu, Incheon, Korea
juhong@inha.ac.kr, sunpark@datamining.inha.ac.kr
[2] Department of Information and Communication Engineering
Korea Advanced Institute of Science and Technology, Taejon, Korea
chunsj@islab.kasit.ac.kr

Abstract. For multimedia databases, a fuzzy query consists of a logical combination of content based similarity queries on features such as the color and the texture which are represented in continuous dimensions. Since features are intrinsically multi-dimensional, the multi-dimensional selectivity estimation is required in order to optimize a fuzzy query. The histogram is popularly used for the selectivity estimation. But the histogram has the shortcoming. It is difficult to estimate the selectivity of a similarity query, since a typical similarity query has the shape of a hyper sphere and the ranges of features are continuous. In this paper, we propose a curve fitting method using DCT to estimate the selectivity of a similarity query with a spherical shape in multimedia databases. Experiments show the effectiveness of the proposed method.

1 Introduction

A query optimizer uses the selectivity estimation to choose an efficient execution plan among all possible plans by estimating the cost of each plan. The accuracy of selectivity estimation significantly affects the selection of an efficient plan.

Unlike queries of traditional databases, similarity queries are frequently used in multimedia databases [2,9,12]. Fagin [4,5] and Chaudhuri et al[3] studied the optimization of fuzzy queries for multimedia databases. Fuzzy queries are composed of several atomic conditions, for example (color = 'red') ∧ (shape='round'), where atomic conditions are combined with the logical AND or the logical OR. According to their studies, fuzzy queries can be performed using functions such as the graded search and the probe. First, some of the atomic conditions are processed using the search function to find the multimedia objects that satisfy the conditions. After that, the remaining atomic conditions are processed using the probe function in order to check whether each multimedia object satisfies the remaining conditions. The more complex the fuzzy queries is, the more explosively the number of execution plans of fuzzy queries increases. Therefore, the optimization strategy is required to select a good execution

J. Liu et al. (Eds.): IDEAL 2003, LNCS 2690, pp. 638–644, 2003.

plan. To do this, the selectivity estimation is essential for the search function of an atomic condition.

Let $distance_F(A,B)$ be a distance function between two features (A,B) in a feature vector space F. Then a similarity query is expressed as follow: Find a set of multimedia data X that satisfy $distance_F(Q,X) < d$ for a given multimedia data Q of a query. If the distance is given as the Euclidean distance in a feature vector space, the shape of a similarity query is a hyper sphere.

Until now, almost all estimation methods of the selectivity were focused on queries whose shapes are hyper rectangles. As a solution, Belussi et al [1] devised a method using the fractal dimension. They successfully estimate the average estimation of a query of any shape. However, when a data distribution is not uniform, selectivity is changed depending on location. Therefore we need to devise a new method that estimates the selectivity dependent on location and can be applied to a query of any shape, particularly, the hyper sphere.

In this paper, motivated from the above problems, we propose a novel approach for the multi-dimensional selectivity estimation of a similarity query in continuous dimensions of a multimedia feature space. Our previous paper [8] reported the results of our preliminary study on the multi-dimensional selectivity estimation. We, then, investigated an advanced method to support for the selectivity estimation of a similarity query of multimedia databases.

The contents and contributions are as follows: Compressed information from a large number of small-sized buckets is maintained using the discrete cosine transform (DCT). This enables low storage overheads and low error rates even in a high dimensionality. Small-sized buckets can achieve low error rates and low storage overheads can be achieved by compressing a large amount of bucket information.

Using the continuity property of DCT we can make a set of rectangles compactly contained in a hyper sphere in the feature space, then we can estimate the selectivity of a query by calculating and summing up all selectivities of the rectangles.

The paper is organized as follows: In Section 2, we define k-dimensional DCT and describe multi-dimensional selectivity estimation techniques. In Section 3, we propose the selectivity estimation method for the similarity queries frequently used in multimedia databases. In section 4, we devise the efficient greedy method to generate random points within a hyper sphere for estimating the common volume of a hyper rectangle and a hyper sphere. In section 5, we show experimental results. Finally, conclusions are made in Section 6.

2   Selectivity Estimation Using DCT

We define k-dimensional DCT [7,11] and the method using DCT to estimate the selectivity of a query whose shape is a hyper rectangle [8].

Let $[F]_k$ be $N_1 \times N_2 \times ... \times N_k$ k-dimensional data. Let $u(t)=(u_1,...,u_t) \subseteq (u_1,...,u_k)$ and $n(t)=(n_1,...,n_t) \subseteq (n_1,...,n_k)$ for $1 < t \le k$ and $u_i = 0,...,N_i-1, n_i = 0,...,N_i-1$ for $1 \le i \le k$. Let $[G]_k$ be DCT coefficients of $[F]_k$. We define $G(u(t))$, $F(u(t))$ as follows:

$$G(u(t)) = \sqrt{\frac{2}{N_t}} k_{u_t} \sum_{n_t=0}^{N_t-1} G(u(t-1)) \cos\left(\frac{(2n_t+1)u_t\pi}{2N_t}\right)$$

$$G(u(1)) = \sqrt{\frac{2}{N_1}} k_{u_1} \sum_{n_1=0}^{N_1-1} f(n_1,...,n_k) \cos\left(\frac{(2n_1+1)u_1\pi}{2N_1}\right)$$

$$F(n(t)) = \sqrt{\frac{2}{N_t}} \sum_{u_t=0}^{N_t-1} k_{n_t} F(n(t-1)) \cos\left(\frac{(2n_t+1)u_t\pi}{2N_t}\right)$$

$$F(u(1)) = \sqrt{\frac{2}{N_1}} \sum_{n_1=0}^{N_1-1} k_{n_1} g(u_1,...,u_k) \cos\left(\frac{(2n_1+1)u_1\pi}{2N_1}\right)$$

Then, k-dimensional DCT coefficients is given by $g(u_1,...,u_k) = G(u(k))$. And the inverse DCT transform is given by $f(u_1,...,u_k) = F(u(k))$.

Let q_k be a k-dimensional range query whose shape is a hyper rectangle. The range of the query q_k is $a_i \le x_i \le b_i$ for $1 \le i \le k$, which is represented as $(a_1\sim b_1,...,a_k\sim b_k)$. The x_i coordinate is devided into N_i partitions. Then the selectivity $S(q_k)$ is expressed as follows:

$$
\begin{aligned}
S(q_k) &= \int_{a_k}^{b_k}...\int_{a_2}^{b_2}\int_{a_1}^{b_1} f(x_1,x_2,...,x_k)dx_1 dx_2...dx_k \\
&\approx \sqrt{\frac{2}{N_1}}...\sqrt{\frac{2}{N_k}} \sum_{g(u_1,...,u_k)\in Z} k_{u_1}...k_{u_k} g(u_1,...,u_k) \int_{a_1}^{b_1}\cos(u_1\pi x_1)dx_1....\int_{a_k}^{b_k}\cos(u_k\pi x_k)dx_k
\end{aligned}
$$

where Z is the set of selected coefficients from zonal sampling [8].

3   Selectivity Estimation of Similarity Queries

In this section, we propose the selectivity estimation method for similarity queries whose shapes are hyper spheres.

The SR(Single Rectangle) method is the simplest. It makes only one hyper rectangle that has the same center and the same volume as those of a hyper sphere. We calculate the selectivity of the hyper rectangular query and regard it as the selectivity of the hyper spherical query.

The NOR (Non-overlapping Rectangles) method makes a set of hyper rectangles that are compactly contained in a hyper sphere and all hyper rectangles do not overlap with each other. We generate and store such hyper rectangles in advance. Let S be the hyper sphere of a query Q and let $R = \{ R_i | i=1,...,n \}$ be a set of hyper rectangles which are compactly contained in S. Let s_i be the selectivity of R_i, β_i =(the volume of the common region of R_i and S) / (the volume of R_i), and ρ = (the volume of S) / (the total volume of common regions of all R_is). Then the selectivity of a query Q is approximately $\rho \sum_{i=1}^{n} s_i \beta_i$.

The OR (Overlapping Rectangles) method allows an overlapping between rectangles but each overlapping region must be shared by only two rectangles. If we allow that an overlapping region is shared by more than two rectangles, we encounter the problems: There are too many shared regions, and it is too complex to calculate the total selectivity. Therefore, we do not allow it.

The following is an algorithm to make a set of hyper rectangles that are contained compactly in a hyper sphere:

Algorithm. Generating hyper rectangles

Generate a set N of many random points in a hyper sphere
$i \leftarrow 0$ // number of rectangles
while (cumulative $\alpha < \tau_\alpha$ or $i < \tau_n$)
    $i \leftarrow i+1$
    select $p,q \in N$ and make R_i using p,q such that $\beta_i > \tau_i$
    delete all points in R_i
    do   select $g \in N$ outside of R_i
                extend R_i to include g
    until ($\tau_i^L < \beta_i < \tau_i^H$
            and check if R_i to overlap with the previous rectangles $R_j, j < i$)
    delete all points in extended R_i
endwhile
End

It first generate a great many random points in a hyper sphere S whose radius is 1. Let N be the set of random points. It select two points p and q from N arbitrarily and make a hyper rectangle R_i whose end points are p, q. It calculate the ratio β_i of R_i. If the β_i is less than a given threshold value τ_i, it discard q and select another random point q and repeat to make another hyper rectangle. If the β_i is larger than τ_i, It discard all random points in R_i and try to extend R_i by selecting a random point g from N outside of R_i. It extend R_i so that R_i compactly contains g. It repeats until the ratio β_i is to be between the thresholds τ_i^L and τ_i^H. From the second rectangle, the same process is applied except one thing to consider. It must check whether a new rectangle overlaps with the rectangles made previously. In case of the NOR, a new one should not overlap with the other rectangles. In case of the OR, it can overlap with only one other rectangle. We define the ratio α_i = (the volume of the common region of R_i and S) / (the volume of S). And the cumulative α is the sum of α_i values of rectangles generated so far. We stop generating rectangles when the cumulative α reaches a given threshold τ_α or the number of rectangles is over a given number τ_n.

This process to make a set of rectangles is very time consuming. However it is not a problem since we can use the ready-made rectangles repeatedly for other hyper spheres after we make them just one time. It is necessary to translate and scale to adjust rectangles into an actual query, when we calculate the selectivity of a similarity query.

4   Generating Spherical Random Points

In this section, we devise an efficient greedy method to generate random points within a hyper sphere. The reason why this method is required is as follows: To estimate the selectivity of a query whose shape is a hyper sphere, we need to calculate the volume of common region between a hyper sphere and a hyper rectangle. When a query over-laps with the boundary of a feature space, we need to estimate the volume of the query that is in the feature space. It is very hard to do it analytically. As an alternative solu-tion, we use the Monte-Carlo method. It is used to estimate approximately and effi-ciently the volume of any object which has an arbitrary shape. The Monte-Carlo method generates random points distributed uniformly in total region and counts the number of points that are contained in an object region to estimate a ratio of the vol-ume of the object to the volume of total region. In addition, to make a set of hyper rectangles for using the NOR or the OR, we need to generate random points uniformly distributed in a hyper sphere. We have a simple method for these purposes: *Accept and Reject method.*

Accept and Reject method
    For each generated random point uniformly distributed in a hyper rectangle, test if it is contained in a hyper sphere. Accept it if true, otherwise, reject it.
    Procedure SphereRand(n, P, r)
    // n is the dimension, P is the center of the hyper sphere, and r is its radius.
    // $U(a,b)$: A function to generate a random number in the range $[a,b]$.
    do {   for i=1, n
                $X_i \leftarrow U(-1,1)$
    } while($\sum_{i=1}^{n} X_i^2 > 1$)
    scale and translate X to X' with the center P, the radius r.
    return $X' = (X_1', X_2', ..., X_n')$

The *Accept and Reject* method is efficient only at a low dimensionality. It is be-cause the higher the dimensionality is, the lower is the probability that a random point generated in a hyper rectangle is in a hyper sphere. Therefore we devised an efficient greedy method to directly generate random points that are distributed uniformly in a hyper sphere.

Greedy method
Let $X^{(n)} = (X_1, X_2, ... , X_n)$ be a random point in a hyper sphere whose center is $(0,0,...,0)$ and radius is 1, then it have to satisfy $\sum_{i=1}^{n} X_i^2 \leq 1$. Let $U(a,b)$ be a function to generate a random number uniformly distributed between two real numbers, a and b.
    For the d-dimensional random point $X^{(d)}$, we can generalize above results as fol-lows: For i=3,..,d, let $f_i(t) = a\left(1-t^2\right)^{(i-1)/2}$, where $a = 1 / \int_0^1 f_i(t)dt$. Then their cumula-

tive density functions are $F_i(t) = \int_0^t f_i(s)ds$. We use the numerical analysis technique to find the values of inverse functions. We generate random numbers as follows: $r_1 = U(0, \pi/2)$, $r_2 = \sqrt{U(0,1)}$, $X_d = F_d^{-1}(U(0,1))$, and $X_i = r_d r_{d-1} \cdots r_{i+1} F_i^{-1}(U(0,1))$ for $i = d-1, \dots, 3$. We get $X_1 = r_d r_{d-1} \cdots r_3 r_2 \cos(r_1)$, $X_2 = r_d r_{d-1} \cdots r_3 r_2 \sin(r_1)$, where $r_i = \sqrt{1 - X_i^2}$ for $i = d, \dots, 3$. We change the sign of each X_i with the probability 0.5 to make it be a random point in the hyper sphere.

5 Experiments

We used real bit map images as multimedia data. The number of images is about 60000. We extracted a feature for 4×4 RGB from each image. The dimensionality of the extracted feature is 4×4×3=48. We used the Karhunen Roeve Transform (KLT) to reduce the dimensionality of a feature[6], and made 3~7 dimensional features. We varied the number of DCT coefficients. We generated 30 queries and averaged their results. The query results are compared with the estimations using the method proposed in this paper. A percentage error is used for the accuracy of an estimation result:

As a query model for the probability distribution of queries [10, 1]: We used the biased model which assumes that queries are more highly distributed in high-density regions.

As we explained before, we used three methods, the SR, the NOR, the OR. Error rates of the SR method are affected by how large the common volume between a hyper rectangle and a hyper sphere is. The NOR method and the OR method make hyper rectangles that are compactly contained in a hyper sphere. Rectangles inevitably have regions that are outside of the hyper sphere.

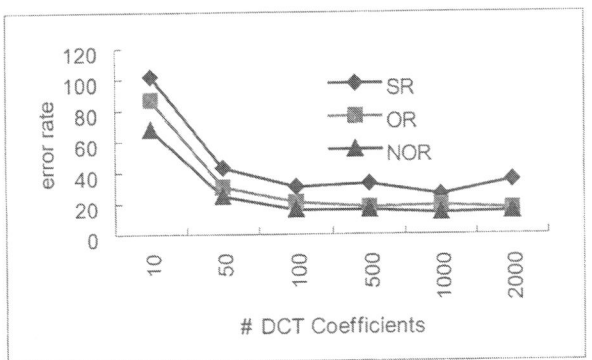

Fig. 1. 6-dimensional feature data

Figure 1 show the experimental results. From the results, the NOR is the best and the OR is the second and the SR shows the worst error rates.

6 Conclusions

In this paper, we proposed a novel approach for estimating the multi-dimensional selectivity of a similarity query in multimedia databases. We used the discrete cosine transform (DCT). It is continuous and integrable. Using these properties, we can easily and efficiently estimate the selectivity of a similarity query whose shape is a hyper sphere by constructing a set of hyper rectangles that are compactly contained in the hyper sphere. In addition, we devised an efficient greedy method to generate random points in a hyper sphere to estimate common volumes between hyper rectangles and hyper spheres. Experiments show that the proposed method produces error rates low enough to be used in real environments

Acknowledgement. This work was supported by INHA UNIVERSITY Research Grant. (INHA-22771-01)

References

1. Belussi, A., Faloutsos, C.: Estimating the Selectivity of Spatial Queries Using the 'Correlation' Fractal Dimension. *In the proceedings of the 21th International Conference on Very Large Databases*, Zurich (1995) 299–310.
2. Chang, W., Sheikholeslami, G., Zhang, A., Syeda-Mahmood, T.: Efficient Resource Selection in Distributed Visual Information Systems. *In the proceedings of the Fifth ACM International Multimedia Conference*, Seattle (1997) 203–213
3. Chaudhuri, S., Gravano, L.: Optimizing Queries over Multimedia Repositories. *In the proceedings of the 1996 ACM SIGMOD International Conference on Management of Data*, Montreal (1996) 91–102
4. Fagin, R.: Combining Fuzzy Information from Multiple Systems. *In the proceedings of the 5th ACM Symposium on Principles of Database Systems*, Montreal (1996) 216–226
5. Fagin, R.: Fuzzy Queries in Multimedia Database Systems. *In the proceedings of the 7th ACM Symposium on Principles of Database Systems*, Seattle (1998) 1–10
6. Flickner, M. (ed.): Query By Image and Video Content: The QBIC System. *IEEE Computer*, Vol. 28, No. 9 (1995) 23–32
7. Lim, J.S.: Two Dimensional Signal And Image Processing. *Prentice Hall* (1990)
8. Lee, J.H., Kim, D.H., Chung, C.W.: Multi-dimensional Selectivity Estimation Using Compressed Histogram Information. *In Proceedings of the 1999 ACM SIGMOD International Conference on Management of Data*, Philadelphia (1999) 205–214
9. Ortega, M., Chakrababarti, K., Porkaew, L., Mehrotra, S.: Supporting Ranked Boolean Similarity Queries in MARS. *IEEE Transactions on Knowledge and Data Engineering*, Vol.10, No.6 (1998) 905–925
10. Pagel, B., Six, H., Toben, H., Widmayer, P.: Towards an Analysis of Range Query Performance in Spatial Data Structures. *In the proceedings of the 2nd ACM Symposium on Principles of Database Systems*, Washington (1993) 214–221
11. Rao, K.R., Yip, P.: Discrete Cosine Transform Algorithms. Advantages, Applications. *Academic Press* (1990)
12. Sheikholeslami, G., Chang, W., Zhang, A.: Semantic Clustering and Querying Heterogeneous Features for Visual Data. *In the proceedings of the sixth ACM International Multimedia Conference*, Bristol (1998) 3–12

Related Factors of Document Classification Performance in a Highly Inflectional Language

Kyongho Min

School of Information Technology
Auckland University of Technology
Auckland, 1020 New Zealand
kyongho.min@aut.ac.nz

Abstract. This paper describes relationships between the document classification performance and its relevant factors for a highly inflectional language that forms monolithic compound noun terms. The factors are the number of class feature sets, the size of training or testing document, ratio of overlapping class features among 8 classes, and ratio of non-overlapping class feature sets. The system is composed of three phases: a Korean morphological analyser called HAM [11], an application of compound noun phrase analysis and extraction of terms whose syntactic categories are noun, name, verb, and adjective, and an effective document classification algorithm based on *preferred class score* heuristics. The best algorithm in this paper, W*eighted PCSICF* based on inverse class frequency, shows an inverse proportional relationship between its performance and the number of class feature sets and the number of ratio of non-overlapping class feature sets.

1 Introduction

Rapid increase of information on the world wide web causes the role of search engines to be more important. Two methods can improve the search engines: an effective indexing scheme for task document contents and an efficient ranking system of necessary information for users [12]. Both methods would be greatly improved by accurate document class information.

This paper discusses factors influencing the performance of an effective document classification system for Korean newspaper articles. The system called *PCS (Preferred Class Score)* is based on:

(a) HAM – Hangul (Korean) Analysis Module [11],
(b) a compound noun term analyser based on a longest substring algorithm [9] and an agenda-based chart parsing technique [6],
(c) extraction of document classification features based on syntactic categories such as entity terms (e.g. noun and names), verb, and adjective, and,
(d) a *preferred-class-scored* document classification algorithm without a training process but with two classification factors namely ICF (inverse class frequency) and IDF (inverse document frequency).

J. Liu et al. (Eds.): IDEAL 2003, LNCS 2690, pp. 645–652, 2003.

The term, *preferred class score,* means that each term used in classification process has its preferred score for a specific class on the basis of classification algorithms.

Many researchers have studied efficient text classification algorithms: vector space classification for a medical document filtering system with an IDF factor [16]; Okapi's *tf* score [1]; a neural network system with an ICF factor and χ-square (χ^2) algorithm [8]; a rule-based disjunctive production method based on term frequencies and boolean combinations of co-occurrence terms [2]; a context sensitive rule-based boolean method [5]; semantic classification based on conceptual models (e.g. Ling-soft's *Nptool* is applied by [3]) [4]; rule-based classification features based on important words, called field association words [7]; and comparisons of various classification algorithms [5], [10], [13], [18].

These previous researchers have studied the effects of the following factors of document classification: the number of features, the rareness of class documents, a term's frequency in a testing document, various learning algorithms to extract the best class feature sets, and different similarity measurement methods based on an ICF and IDF. For example, if the number of class features used in document classification increases, then the precision ratio of testing documents increases [13]. If the number of training documents increases, then the accuracy of document classification increases [10]. If the number of class features increase, then the recall ratio for testing documents increases [7]. In addition previous studies have shown that the performance of various classification methods has not been consistent because of different training techniques and testing environments employed [10], [13], [18].

This paper focuses on relationships between performance and classification factors such as the number of class features, the overlapping ratio among class features, and non-trained terms in the testing documents. The method of document classification based on preferred class score will be described in the next section. In section 3, experimental results of documents from an online Korean newspaper will be discussed and section 4 describes problems and possible further improvements of the current approach, and conclusions of this paper.

2   Method of Document Classification

This section describes a method of document classification that processes a document in three phases, namely morphological analysis based on the HAM (Hangul Analysis Module [11]) system, a term extraction method and analysis of compound noun terms, and document classification algorithms called *Preferred Class Score* (*PCS*). In this paper, the last phase will be discussed in detail (see [14] for the former two phases in detail).

2.1 Preferred Class Score Classification

Three basic classification algorithms were implemented. They were based on preferred class score with three weighted algorithms that use term frequency within the document [14]. They are a simple voting algorithm called a *PCSO&O* (Preferred Class Score based on One&Only), an algorithm based on inverse class frequency called *PCSICF* (PCS based on Inverse Class Frequency), and an algorithm based on inverse document frequency called *PCSIDF* (PCS based on Inverse Document Frequency). These algorithms consider each term's class score to decide which class is to be preferred rather than the probability of the term or the document's similarity measurement based on terms vectors.

PCSO&O (PCS One & Only) Algorithm

This algorithm classifies documents by a simple voting scheme. When the system applies the voting scheme to each term T_{ik} (i.e. term i extracted from testing document D_k), the frequency of term T_i in each class feature set C_j is retrieved to decide the class with a maximum frequency for term T_{ik}. If frequency $Cf(T_{ij})$ of term i in class j is highest among other class feature sets, then the preferred class score, $pcso\&o(T_{ik})(C_j)$, based on PCSO&O, 1 is allocated to class C_j and other classes have 0 of the preferred class score for term T_{ik}. After summation of each class's $pcso\&o(T_{ik})(C_j)$ over all terms in document D_k, the class with the maximum score of $pcso\&o(T_{ik})(C_j)$ is chosen for the document's class in formula 1.

$$PCSO\&O(D_k) = C_j, \text{ if } C_j \text{ maximises} \left\{ \sum_{i=1}^{m} pcso \& o(T_{ik})(C_j) \right\} \qquad (1)$$

The second algorithm (PCSO&OF in table 4) employs filtering heuristics based on the total frequency of a term, and uses the remaining 13.3% of terms as class features for document classification (see section 3.1). If a term's total frequency is less than 8 (i.e. total classes - 86.7% of total terms of the training data, see table 1), then the classification process discards the term from classification.

Algorithms based on Inverse Document or Class Frequency

These algorithms based on either Inverse Class Frequency (ICF) or Inverse Document Frequency (IDF) [8], [10], compute similarity of terms vector between a tested document and training data. In this paper the preferred class score method is employed to avoid complex computation of similarities of terms vectors between training data and testing data,. Two PCS algorithms, $PCSICF(D_k)$ and $Weighted\ PCSICF(D_k)$, are computed by formulae 2 and 3.

The class of a testing document is the class with maximum preferred class score (i.e. $pcsicf(T_{ik})(C_j)$) based on an ICF logarithm function. If the sum of the $pcsicf(T_{ik})(C_1)$ score of class C_1 is greater than the other class's $pcsicf(T_{ik})(C_{2...m})$ scores for the testing document, then the document's class is class C_1. For $PCSICF(D_k)$, N is the total number of classes (i.e. 8 in this paper).

$$PCSICF(D_k) = C_j, \text{ if } C_j \text{ maximise} \left[\sum_{i=1}^{m} Cf(T_{ij}) * \log(N / icf(T_i)) \right] \qquad (2)$$

$$Weighted\ PCSICF(D_k) = C_j, \text{ if } C_j \text{ maximise } \left\{ \sum_{i=1}^{m} Df(T_{ik}) * Cf(T_{ij}) * \log(N/icf(T_i)) \right\} \quad (3)$$

Weighted PCSICF algorithm (formula 3) weighs the positive local information so that more frequently occurring terms in each testing document are preferred for classification. For *PCSIDF* and *Weighted PCSIDF* algorithms, the logarithm function based on ICF (i.e. $\log(N/icf(T_i))$) in formulae 2 and 3 is changed to a logarithm function based on IDF (i.e. $\log(N/idf(T_i))$) where N is the total number of training documents – 720 in this paper).

3   Experimental Results

The system is implemented in Perl5.0 on a Linux platform. In this paper, the analysis of the experimental results focuses on the relationship between classification performance and the characteristics of testing and training documents. [14] showed the result of six various PCS algorithms and the simple voting classification algorithm performed well for the data, collected from an online Korean newspaper.

3.1 Analysis of Data and Class Feature Sets

From 8 topic classes from a major Korean daily newspaper in August 2002, 100 news articles for each topic were collected for training and testing the systems. The eight classes are domestic news (DSO), economy (DEC), world news (DIN), information and science (DIS), culture and life (DCL), political news (DPO), sports (DSP), and entertainment (DST).

Among 800 collected data, 720 data (90%) are used for training the system (i.e. data used for extracting the class feature sets) and the remaining data (80 articles, 10%) are used for testing the system. When extracting terms from training and testing documents, some words were not considered as either feature sets or terms for a document because of alphanumeric words (7.6% of training data) such as combination of Korean/English and numbers, and words combined with Korean and English.

Table 1. Number of Class Feature Sets

Class	DEC	DCL	DIN	DIS	DPO	DSO	DSP	DST	Total
Number	7284	3469	3962	4479	3729	1644	1223	1730	17470
%/total	41.7	19.9	22.7	25.6	21.3	23.8	20.9	29.4	-

From the 720 training data, 17470 class features were extracted and collected. Among total class feature sets, 51% of the terms occur once through the total training data and 13.3% occur more than 8 times in the training data. Table 1 shows the distribution of feature sets of each class obtained from the training data.

The class feature sets in each class overlaps one another. Table 2 shows the average overlapping number of class features and its ratio against the total class features. For example, the ratio (row '%/Total' in table 2) of overlapping features of DEC against the total number of feature sets (i.e. 17470) is 11% and the ratio (row '%/Class' in table 2) of overlapping features of DCL against total DCL class feature set (i.e. 3469 in table 1) is 42.5%.

Table 2. Average Overlapping Class Feature Sets

Class	DEC	DCL	DIN	DIS	DPO	DSO	DSP	DST	AVG
Overlaps	1917	1474	1607	1738	1577	1644	1223	1730	1614
%/Class	26.3	42.5	40.6	38.8	42.3	39.5	33.5	33.7	37.1
%/Total	11.0	8.4	9.2	10.0	9.0	9.4	7.0	9.9	9.2

The inverse class frequencies ($ICF(T_i)$) of all terms in the training sets are as follows: terms occurring in 1 class only are 10349 (59%), 2 classes 2892 (17%), 3 classes 1517 (9%), 4 classes 877 (5%), 5 classes 581 (3%), 6 classes 442 (3%), 7 classes 378 (2%), and 8 classes 434 (2%). Thus the algorithms based on the inverse class frequency do not use 2% of class features for classification.

Table 3. Non-training Terms from Testing Data (10 data per class)

Class	DEC	DCL	DIN	DIS	DPO	DSO	DSP	DST	Total
Total terms	2403	1412	2093	1825	2815	1548	1313	1261	14670
Unknown	427	66	136	203	150	88	104	85	1259
Ratio (%)	17.8	4.7	6.5	11.1	5.3	5.7	7.9	6.7	8.2

Table 3 shows the number of non-training terms found in the testing document. The class feature sets collected from a small number of training data resulted in about 8.2% of terms being unclassified. If these terms were classified as some class feature sets, then the classification performance would be different.

3.2 Result of Various Document Classification Algorithms

In terms of F-measurement (P*R/P+R, where P is a precision ratio and R is a recall ratio) of document classification with 80 sample documents (8 classes and each class has 10 sample documents), the best performance was obtained by *Weighted PCSICF* ([14] showed the precision and recall ratio of six algorithms). The simplest algorithm, PCSO&O, performs 2.6% worse than the best algorithm (Table 4).

To compare the performance of PCS document classification algorithm, the performance of each classification is sorted by ascending order and the sorted performance is compared with the factors such as *CFR/T* (each Class Features' Ratio against Total features), *CFOR/T* (each Class Features' Overlapping Ratio against Total features), *NOFR/C* (Non-Overlapping class Features' Ratio against each Class features), *NOFR/T* (Non-Overlapping class Features' Ratio against Total features), *DSR/T* (Testing Document's Size Ratio of each class against Total size of testing documents), *TDUTR/D* (Testing Document's Unknown Terms Ratio against total terms in testing

Documents), *TDSR/T* (Total Training Documents' Size Ratio of each class against the size of total Training documents).

Table 4. F-measurement of Recall/Precision Ratio

Algorithm	DCL	DEC	DIN	DIS	DPO	DSO	DSP	DST	Average
PCSO&O	25.0	37.5	31.2	31.2	39.1	30.4	50.0	21.4	33.2
PCS(ICF)	27.3	33.3	25.0	30.0	34.8	31.6	47.6	31.6	32.6
PCS(IDF)	26.1	37.5	28.6	29.4	38.5	30.4	47.6	30.0	33.5
Weighted PCS(ICF)	26.1	41.2	37.5	31.8	40.9	35.0	47.6	26.3	35.8
Weighted PCS(IDF)	25.0	37.5	33.3	33.3	40.0	34.8	47.6	22.2	34.2
PCSO&O F	25.0	35.3	26.7	31.2	39.1	29.6	47.4	15.8	31.3
Average	25.8	37.1	30.4	31.2	38.7	32.0	48.0	24.6	33.4

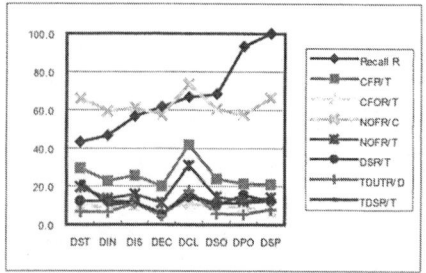

Fig. 1. Recall Ratios Relationships   **Fig. 2.** Precision Ratios Relationships

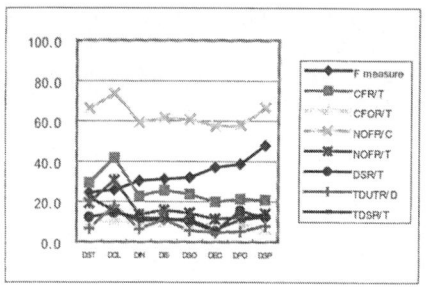
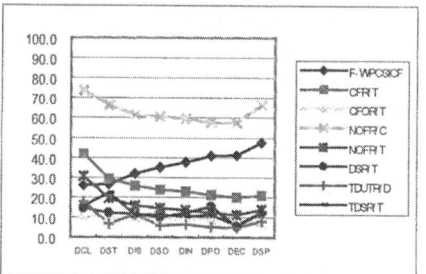

Fig. 3. F-measure Relationships   **Fig. 4.** F-measure WPCSICF Relationships

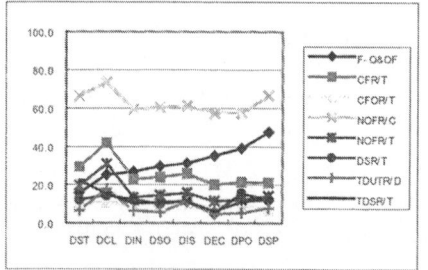
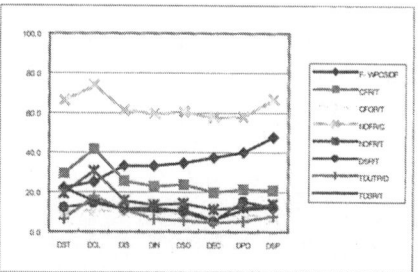

Fig. 5. F-measure PCSO&OF Relationships   **Fig. 6.** F-measure WPCSIDF Relationships

According to Figures from 1 to 6, the F-measurement of *Weighted PCSICF* is in inverse proportion to the number of class feature sets and the number of non overlapping class feature sets. The document size of training data and testing data and the ratio of non-trained terms from testing data do not show any consistent relationships to the sorted classification performance in this paper.

4   Further Improvement and Conclusions

In this paper, the simple classification algorithm PCSO&O shows good performance in comparison to the algorithms based on both *ICF* and *IDF* factors. However, the training data cannot cover 8.2% of terms in the testing document. If the system cannot provide class feature sets from training data enough to cover all terms in the documents classified, there would be unknown terms that do not belong to any class feature sets. In this case, a thesaurus or Korean Noun/VerbNet [15] would be one possible solution.

This paper focuses on the study of relationships between various classification performances (Recall Ratio, Precision Ratio, and F-measurement) and the number of class feature sets, the number of overlapping/non-overlapping class features, and the size of either training or testing documents. In the future, the employment of a shallow parsing system would help further accuracy of classification.

In conclusion, this paper describes a simple document classification algorithm without a complex learning and training processes, and related factors influencing document classification performances in a highly inflectional language. When extracting terms, the root forms of words of four categories (e.g. noun, verb, proper noun (i.e. name), and adjective) were extracted for class features and classification, after applying morphological/compound noun analysis to the document rather than the use of direct terms.

The performance of the best classification algorithm, *Weighted PCSICF*, is consistently in inverse proportion to the number of class feature sets and the number of non overlapping class feature sets. However, other five algorithms did not show any consistent relationships to influencing factors such as the number of class feature sets, the size of either training or testing document, the number of overlapping/non-overlapping class features in each class feature set.

Acknowledgement. I greatly appreciate the permission of Prof. Kang, S. from Kookmin University, to use the Linux version of his Korean Morphology Analysis, HAM. His application contributes to the implementation of document classification system in this paper.

References

1. Allan, J., Leuski, A., Swan, R., Byrd, D.: Evaluating combinations of ranked lists and visualizations of inter-document similarity. Information Processing and Management. 37 (2001) 435–458
2. Apte, C., Demerau, F., Weiss M.: Automated Learning of Decision Rules for Text Categorization. ACM Transactions on Information Systems. 12(3) (1994) 233–251
3. Arppe A.: Term Extraction from Unrestricted Text. http://www.lingsoft.fi/doc/nptool/ term- extraction. (1995)
4. Brasethvik, T., Gulla J.: Natural Language Analysis for Semantic Document Modeling. Data & Knowledge Engineering. 38 (2001) 45–62
5. Cohen, W., Singer, Y.: Context-Sensitive Learning Methods for Text Categorization, ACM Transactions on Information Systems, 7(2) (1999) 141–173
6. Earley, J.: An Efficient Context-Free Parsing Algorithm. CACM. 13(2) (1970) 94–102
7. Fuketa, M., Lee, S., Tsuji, T., Okada, M., Aoe, J.: A Document Classification Method by Using Field Association Words. Information Science. 126 (2000) 57–70
8. Han, K., Sun, B., Han, S., Rim, K.: A Study on Development of Automatic Categorization System for Internet Documents. The Transactions of The Korean Information Processing Society. 7(9) (2000) 2867–2875
9. Hirshberg, D.S.: Algorithms for the Longest Common Subsequence Problem. The Journal of ACM. 24(4) (1977) 664–675
10. Joachims, T.: A Probabilistic Analysis of the Rocchio Algorithm with TFIDF for Text Categorization. Proceedings of International Conference of Machine Learning (CIML97). (1997) 143–151
11. Kang, S.: Korean Morphological Analysis Program for Linux OS, http://nlp.kookmin.ac.kr. (2001)
12. Lewis, D., Jones, K.S.: Natural Language Processing for Information Retrieval. Communication of the ACM. 39(1) (1996) 92–101
13. Li, Y., Jain, A.: Classification of Text Documents. The Computer Journal. 41(8) (1998) 537–546
14. Min, K., Wilson, W.H., Moon, Y.: Preferred Document Classification for a Highly Inflectional/Derivational Language. In: McKay, B., Slaney, J. (eds.): AI2002: Advances in Artificial Intelligence. Lecture Notes in Artificial Intelligence, Vol. 2557. Springer-Verlag, Berlin Heidelberg (2002) 12–23
15. Moon, Y., Min, K.: Verifying Appropriateness of the Semantic Networks and Integration for the Selectional Restriction Relation. Proceedings of the 2000 MIS/OA International Conference. Seoul Korea (2000) 535–539
16. Mostafa, J., Lam, W.: Automatic classification using supervised learning in a medical document filtering application. Information Processing and Management. 36 (2000) 415–444
17. Salton, G., Singhal, A., Mitra, M., Buckley C.: Automatic Text Structuring and Summarization. Information Processing and Management. 33(2) (1997) 193–207
18. Yang, Y., Liu, X.: A Re-examination of Text Categorization Methods. Proceedings of ACM SIGIR Conference on Research and Development Retrieval. (1999) 42–49

Customer Loyalty on Recurring Loans

Vincent Ng and Ida Ng

Department of Computing, Hong Kong Polytechnic University
cstyng@comp.polyu.edu.hk

Abstract. Customer Loyalty has long been a pressing issue in today's competitive commercial arena. It is increasingly important as companies emphasize more on their customer relationship management. In this paper, we investigate the segmentation of bank customers in terms of their loyalty level; the sample dataset is the personal finance customers from a bank. Based on a loyalty definition, a model on the customer loyalty will be formulated. This loyalty function classifies customers into four levels. Statistical and neuro-fuzzy techniques will also be deployed to explore the relationships of customer demographics, loan approval information and transaction information towards customer loyalty.

Keywords: loyalty, neuro-fuzzy, regression analysis, customer relationship management

1 Introduction

In recent years, keen competition in the banking industry made the banks eager in their Customer Relationship Management (CRM). Large banks did a lot of empirical studies on their customers' profitability and default risk segmentation. From customer retention perspective, no one would argue that customer loyalty was the essential factor of doing business successfully. Customer Loyalty has long been a topic of interest. Its history extends back to Copeland's (1923) study of a phenomenon labeled "brand insistence". Among nearly 20 selected loyalty definitions, their ideas on customer loyalty are similar [4,7,10,11,12].

In a previous study, marketing scholar Gremler [6], found that, using a bank as the research sample, when fitting switching costs (independent variables) and service loyalty (dependent variable) into a regression model, the t-value of regression coefficient was 6.2, which was significantly greater than 2.0. The dependent variable is defined by a service loyalty definition. He suggested that switching costs and service loyalty had a significant correlation.

2 Loyalty Function

Loyalty function can be estimated on the basis of the loyalty indicators, pre-defined prior knowledge and loyalty definition. Our approach of customer loyalty is to define

J. Liu et al. (Eds.): IDEAL 2003, LNCS 2690, pp. 653–660, 2003.
© Springer-Verlag Berlin Heidelberg 2003

it as "repeated purchase, positive relationship with service provider, other purchases and less likely for the customer to defect". From a bank's perspective on customers with personal loans, the characteristics of a loyal customer can be reflected by the "current number of accounts" (CA), "total number of accounts"(TA), "total number of loan types"(TT), "refinance count" (RF), "early settlement count" (ES) and "charge off status" (CO). Hence, we have the following observations:

- The higher the CA, the greater the level of loyalty;
- The higher the RF, the greater the level of loyalty;
- The higher the net early settlement, ES-RF, the lower the level of loyalty;
- CO indicates the lowest loyalty level.
- The larger the number of previous account, TA-CA, the greater the level of loyalty.
- The larger the number of other purchases, TT-1, the greater the level of loyalty.
- The higher the percentage of net early settlement over total number of accounts, (ES-RF)/TA, the lower the level of loyalty.

Therefore, a loyalty function can be formulated like this:

$$LY = f(RF, CO, CA, TA, TT, ES) \tag{1}$$

In this research, customer loyalty will be categorized into 4 levels, i.e. 1, 2, 3 and 4; level 1 is the best while level 4 is the worst. The loyalty equation is:

$$LY = \ln(P_j/P4) = a_{0j} + \Sigma a_{ij}X_i, \text{ for } j = 1, 2 \text{ or } 3 \tag{2}$$

where X_i are loyalty indicated input variables

Based on the above prior knowledge of customer loyalty, our loyalty function would consist of 7 loyalty-indicated variables as follow:

$$LY_j = \ln(Pj/P4) = a_{0j} + a_{1j}(RF) + a_{2j}(CA) - a_{3j}(ES-RF) \tag{3}$$
$$+ a_{4j}(TA-CA) + a_{5j}(TT-1) - {}_{6j}[(ES-RF)/TA] - a_{7j}(CO)$$

For each combination of RF, CA, (ES-RF), (TA-CA), (TT-1), [(ES-RF)/TA], and CO, we can estimate the values of P1, P2, P3 and P4 based on the equations (3), (4) and (5). The highest Pj value of each combination will show its classification according to the design of multinomial logistic regression.

$$Pj = exp(ln(Pj/P4)) / 1 + \Sigma n \, exp(ln(Pn/P4)) \qquad for \, n = 1\text{-}3 \tag{4}$$

$$P4 = 1 - P1 - P2 - P3 \tag{5}$$

where Pj = probability to be classified as Class j

For each Pj, there are 8 unknown a_{ij}'s. Therefore, there are 4 equations and 28 unknown variables in this loyalty function. We then use at least 28 distinct combinations of loyalty indicators with well-classified loyalty level to estimate all the a_{ij}s and P_js. The classification of these 28 observations will be done manually based on the pre-defined prior knowledge of our research model.

After getting all the a_{ij}'s from these 28 observations, we can calculate and get the predicted LY classes or each customer based on the equation (3), (4) and (5). Before using the parameters, we need to ensure the LY classes are well predicted. If not, we have to modify the wrong classes and run the multinomial logistic regression again until we can the best a_{ij}'s to derive the LY classes.

The derived loyalty class of each customer will be utilized in step 2 as the input variable to study the relationships of customer personal data, financial data and transactional data and their loyalty levels. Firstly, a correlation analysis of the captioned data set and loyalty classes will be done. It aims for data filtering and selection. Both statistical and neuro-fuzzy data mining tools will be deployed to see the relationships between loyalty class and selected customer data.

3 Our Approach

A two-step model is proposed in our work. Firstly, we combine all the loyalty indicators to derive the loyalty classes. Next, we will use our customer data to estimate the loyalty classes. The derived loyalty class of each customer will be utilized in step 2 as the input variable to study the relationships of customer personal data, financial data and transactional data and their loyalty levels. Firstly, a correlation analysis of the captioned data set and loyalty classes will be done. It aims for data filtering and selection. Both statistical and neuro-fuzzy data mining tools will be deployed to see the relationships between loyalty class and selected customer data.

In our work, other than using statistical tools, neuro-fuzzy data mining technique will be also adopted for analysis. A new attempt on data mining project can bring in more fresh ideas on knowledge discovery in the banking industry. A two-step data-mining approach is adopted to segment personal finance customers in terms of loyalty level using both loyalty indicators and customer data. For different loyalty groups, we like to find out their customer characteristics to strengthen our knowledge on customer loyalty.

Only the personal finance customers were selected as our target sample. The data was extracted as a snapshot from the bank data warehouse as of 31st May 2001. The snapshot contained both past and existing customer information between 01st Jan 1999 and 31st May 2001. The whole dataset consists of 15654 rows and 42 columns and will be categorized into four types, including personal, financial, transactional and loyalty-indicated. From the whole data set, a 69.7% sample is randomly selected as development sample. Total sample size is 10917, i.e. 15654 x 69.7%. The entire 30.3% of the dataset is used as validation sample. Total sample size is 4737, i.e. 15654 – 10917.

4 Data Analysis

This study combines prior knowledge of the data with statistical and data mining techniques. We use SPSS to find out the loyalty function while NEFCLASS-J [2] is used to find patterns in the different classes of customers. In the training set, there are total 10917 observations. Out of these 10917 observations, there are 320 distinct combinations of loyalty indicators, i.e. RF, CA, ES-RF, TA-CA, TT-1, (ES-RF)/TA and CO. From these 320 combinations, 28 of them are selected for manual classification according to our model. For each loyalty class, 7 distinct combinations are classified.

Table 1. Rules for Expert Classification

Loyalty Class	CA	RF	ES-RF	TA-CA	TT-1	(ES-RF)/ TA	CO
Class 1	L	S to L	S	M to L	M to L	S	0
Class 2	M	M to L	M	S to M	S to M	M	0
Class 3	S	S to M	L	S to M	S to M	L	0
Class 4	--	--	--	--	--	--	1

L – Large; M – Medium; S – Small

With the expert classification of loyalty class, we can use the multinomial logistic regression to derive the parameter a_{ij}'s. Then we can get the Pj values by substituting the a_{ij}'s to the multinomial logistic regression formulas. With the calculated Pj values, all the training data has been classified in terms of loyalty classes. To validate the loyalty function, we apply the function on the testing data set, 4737 observations, to derive their loyalty classes.

After projecting the loyalty classes of each customer, we used multinomial logistic regression and neuro-fuzzy technique to examine the relationships of predicted loyalty level and customer data. Initially, we run the multinomial logistic regression on 14 input variables and loyalty class. We then calculated Pj values of each class for each observation.

The overall classification correctness is 79.6 %. As the classification correctness may not tell the whole story of the classification performance, we add a measurement to evaluate the classification accuracy. We divide the number of correct classification by the total number of predicted classification for its corresponding class. For example, 54.1% of Class 1 is the result of 33 divided by 61. The results show that the classification accuracy is better for Class 2 (82.2%) and Class 4 (90.5%) customers.

The multinomial logistic regression parameters have the following implications:
1.   Year of relation, total number of personal loans, 60-day and 90-day delinquency count, new loan in the past 6 months and settled loan in the past 6 months have greater effects on customer loyalty.
2.   The older the customer, the higher the loyalty level.
3.   The larger the debt-to-income ratio, the higher the loyalty level.
4.   The shorter the year of relation, the higher chance to be classified as Class 2.
5.   The larger the total number of personal loans, the lower the loyalty level.

6.   The larger the number of 14-day delinquent count, the higher the loyalty level.
7.   The larger the number of 21-day delinquent count, the higher the chance of being classified as Class 2 or Class 3.
8.   The larger the numbers of 60-day and 90-day delinquent count, the higher the chance of charge off.
9.   Customers without new loans in the past 6 months have lower loyalty.
10. Customers without settled loans in the past 6 months have higher chance to be classified as Class 2.
11. According to the source codes description table and parameter estimates, customer source from direct mailings and existing customers have higher loyalty. Customer source from advertisements of MTR, public vehicles, newspaper and magazine have lower loyalty. Pre-approved customers have higher chance to be classified as Class 3.
12. Customers approved by officers 2, 3, 9, 10, 14, 17, 18 and 19 have higher loyalty level. Customers approved by 1, 5, 8, 16, 20, 21, 23 and 24 tend to have lower loyalty level.

Table 2. Number of Fuzzy Sets for Selected Input Variables

Input Variable	Number of Fuzzy Sets	Remarks
Age	3	Eliminated during training
DI Ratio	6	
Source Code	--	Categorical Variable
Year of Relation	6	
Approval Officer	--	Categorical Variable
Total Number of PIL	4	
New Loan Flag	--	Categorical Variable
Settled Loan Flag	--	Categorical Variable
Total BLP	3	Eliminated during training
Delinquency 14-day	3	Eliminated during training
Delinquency 21-day	6	
Delinquency 30-day	6	
Delinquency 60-day	5	
Delinquency 90-day	5	

Nefclassj created a rule base containing 456 rules from the training data. There are 3187 misclassifications and the error is 6893.564713. We prune the classifier automatically and reduce the rule base to 242 rules. There are 3098 (28.38%) misclassifications and the error is 5085.415007. From the rule editor, we de-duplicate rules with similar meanings manually and then train the fuzzy sets to see the classification correctness. Finally, we further eliminate 21 rules and trim the rule base to 221 rules. The mis-classification drops to 3095 (28.35%) and the error is 5088.956098. Although the error is a little bit higher, the classification results are better for both training and testing data sets.

Table 3. High Frequency Rule Components for Loyalty Classes

Loyalty Class	Frequent Rule Components for Loyalty Classes
Class 1	• Source Code: fuzzy 5 • Settled Loan Flag: fuzzy 1 • Delinquency Count (21-90 days): Very Small or Extremely Small
Class 2	• Year of Relation: Small, Very Small • New Loan Flag: fuzzy 1 • Settled Loan Flag: fuzzy 1 • Delinquency Count (21-90 days): Very Small or Extremely Small
Class 3	• Year of Relation: Small or Very Small • Number of PIL: Small or Very Small • New Loan Flag: fuzzy 2 • Settled Loan Flag: fuzzy 1 • Delinquency Count (21-90 days): Very Small or Extremely Small
Class 4	• Number of PIL: Very Small • Year of Relation: Extremely Small • Delinquency Count (90 days): Small or Very Small

For the classification correctness, the best performance classes are Class 2 (79.9%) and Class 4 (81.6%). The overall correctness percentage is 71.65%. However, for the accuracy, the best performance classes are Class 3 (81.5%) and Class 4 (89.2). The overall accuracy is 76.6%. For the testing data set, the classification correctness and accuracy are more or less consistent with the results for training set. For classification correctness, the best performance classes are Class 2 (79.1%) and Class 4 (74.8%) while, for the accuracy, the best still are Class 3 (80.4%) and Class 4 (84.7%).

Results Implication
1. Age, total booked loan principle and 14-day delinquency count are eliminated during the classifier pruning process. They are not significant for loyalty classification.
2. From the membership function of source code, existing customer has higher probability in fuzzy set 5. That means existing customer, original source code 2, has higher probability to be classified as Class 1.
3. For settled loan in past 6 months, fuzzy set 1 means that there is no settled loan in the past 6 months. No settled loan in the past 6 months has higher probability to be classified as Class 1 to Class 3 customers.
4. Delinquency Count for 21-day to 90-day needs to be the smallest, either extremely small or very small, for Class 1 to Class 3 customers.
5. Customers with small or very small year of relation, ranged from 1 to 7 years, have higher probability to be classified as Class 2 and Class 3.
6. For new loan in the past 6 months, fuzzy set 1 means that there is new loan in the past 6 months. Customers with new loan in the past 6 months have higher probability to be classified as Class 2.
7. Fuzzy set 2 for new loan in the past 6 months means that there is no new loan in the past 6 months. Customers with no new loan in the past 6 months have higher probability to be classified as Class 3.
8. Customers with small or very small total number of personal loans, from 1 to 4, have higher chance to be classified as Class 3.

9. Customers with very small total number of personal loans, from 1 to 2, have higher chance to be classified as Class 4.
10. Customers with small 90-day delinquency count, either 1 or 2, have higher probability to be classified as Class 4.

Results Interpretability and Implication

1. Multinomial logistic regression uses 4 equations to derive the classification while neuro-fuzzy uses 221 rules and 14 fuzzy sets to derive the classification. If the rule base of neuro-fuzzy is large, it is hard for the user to grasp the relationships of input and output variables.
2. Multinomial logistic regression provides a series of numeric parameters. A user needs to have statistical background to interpret the parameters into human language. Neuro-fuzzy rules are in human language. A user can get the meaning directly. Below is the first rule from our neuro-fuzzy rule base.

> "if di_ratio is small and SOURCE is fuzzy1 and Yr_relation is very small and approve is fuzzy2 and nbr_pil is small and new_loan_6mth is fuzzy1 and settled_loan6 is fuzzy1 and delin_cycle3 is extremely small and delin_cycle4 is extremely small and delin_cycle5 is very small and delin_cycle6 is very small then LY2"

3. Both techniques exhibit that year of relation, total number of personal loans, 90-day delinquency count and settled loan flag in the past 6 months are the key factors to determine customer loyalty.
4. Multinomial logistic regression uses all the input variables and provides parameters for them; therefore, we can easily get an overall picture on the importance of each variable. Neuro-fuzzy technique interprets the knowledge in terms of rules and fuzzy sets. User has to study the rule base thoroughly to find out the importance of each variable.

Table 4. Comparisons of Classification Correctness and Accuracy between MLR and NF

Loyalty Class		MLR		NF		Strong/
		Train	Test	Train	Test	Stable
1	Correctness	18.1%	20.3%	21.4%	8.7%	MLR
	Accuracy	54.1%	46.7%	29.0%	12.0%	MLR
2	Correctness	76.6%	74.0%	**79.9%**	79.1%	NF
	Accuracy	82.2%	82.5%	72.6%	71.4%	MLR
3	Correctness	84.0%	85.0%	62.9%	61.4%	MLR
	Accuracy	76.1%	75.6%	**81.5%**	80.4%	NF
4	Correctness	85.5%	84.7%	81.6%	74.8%	MLR
	Accuracy	90.5%	87.3%	89.2%	84.7%	MLR

Multinomial logistic regression and neuro-fuzzy techniques are totally different types of techniques. In this work, the classification result of neuro-fuzzy technique is a little bit poor than that of multinomial logistic regression in terms of both correctness and accuracy. There may be a number of reasons. First of all, multinomial logistic regression are strong in uncover weak relationships between the input and output variables. As our problem domain, customer loyalty, does not have a strong relationship with input variables, it is much arduous for neuro-fuzzy technique to provide a good estimation. On the other hand, our customer loyalty measurement comes from several loyalty indicators, i.e. several variables are combined into one output variable. As the problem domain is so sophisticated, a medium level of classification correctness and accuracy is within our expectation.

5   Conclusion

We hope that, through this data-mining project, the bank can have more ideas on the customer loyalty so to design suitable loyalty or retention programs for its valuable customers. Although the overall classification accuracy of our work is around 75% to 80%, for individual class, like class 4, the classification accuracy achieves 90%. Therefore, we can say that this model is still useful to study the customers with less loyalty. For the model to have future improvement, we should add some input variables that are significant in classifying the highly loyal customers.

References

1.   Ulrike Nauck: Design and Implementation of a Neuro-Fuzzy Data Analysis Tool in Java. Technische Universitat Braunschweig, Institut fur Betriebssysteme and Rechnerverbund (1999).
2.   Ulrike Nauck: NEFCLASS-PC: Ein Neuro-Fuzzy Klassifikationstool unter MS-DOS. Studienarbeit, Technische Universitat Braunschweig, Institut fur Betriebssysteme and Rechnerverbund (1997).
3.   Charly Kleissner: Data Mining for the Enterprise. IEEE (1998).
4.   Anderson, Eugene W. and Mary W. Sullivan: The Antecedents and Consequences of Customer Satisfaction for Firms: Marketing Science, Vol. 12 (1993) Spring 125–143.
5.   Bitner, Mary: Evaluating Service Encounters: The Effects of Physical Surroundings and Employee Responses: Journal of Marketing, Vol. 54 (1990) October 95–106.
6.   Dwayne David Gremler: The Effect of Satisfaction, Switching Costs, And Interpersonal Bonds on Service Loyalty. Arizona State University (1995).
7.   Fornell, Clases: A National Customer Satisfaction Barometer: The Swedish Experience: Journal of Marketing, Vol. 56 (1992) January 6–21.
9.   Porter, Micheal E.: Competitive Strategy: Techniques for Analyzing Industries and Competitors. The Free Press, New York (1980).
10. Reichheld, Frederick F.: Loyalty-Based Management: Harvard Business Review, Vol. 71 (1993) March-April 64–73.
11. Reynold, Fred D., William R. Darden, and Warren S. Martin: Developing an Image of the Store-Loyal Customer: A Life-Style Analysis to Probe a Neglected Market: Journal of Retailing, Vol. 50 (1974-75) Winter 73–84.
12. Selnes, Fred: An Examination of the Effect of Product Performance on Brand Reputation, Satisfaction and Loyalty: European Journal of Marketing, Vol. 27 (1993) 9 19–35.
13. Biong, Harald: Satisfaction and Loyalty to Suppliers within the Grocery Trade: European Journal of Marketing, Vol. 27 (1993) 7 21–38.

Convolution Kernels for Outliers Detection in Relational Data

Mikhail Petrovskiy[1]

Computer Science Department of Lomonosov Moscow State University,
Building 2, MSU, Vorobjovy Gory, Moscow, 119899, Russia
michael@cs.msu.su

Abstract. There is a growing interest to kernel-based methods in Data Mining. The application of these methods for real-world data, stored in databases, leads to the problem of designing kernels for complex structured data. Since many Data Mining systems use relational databases, the important task is to design kernels for relational data. In this paper we show that for relational data the structure of single data instance in the input space can be described by nested relation schemes. For such data we propose the method for constructing kernels, which is based on convolution kernels framework developed by Haussler. For demonstration we construct the simple convolution Gaussian kernel and apply it, using k-nearest neighbor algorithm, for outliers detection problem in the sample relational database.

1   Introduction

The kernel-based methods for classification, regression, PCA and outliers detection have proved their effectiveness in many application domains [1]. There is a growing interest to these methods in Data Mining community. Hence, one of the serious issues obstructing applying kernel methods in Data Mining is that most kernels are designed for simple "flat" data, where each data instance is represented by fixed or varied length vector of attributes. But real-world problems, which are being solved using Data Mining tools, face the data of more complex structure.

Many application domains are best described by relational models, in which instances of multiple types are related to each other in the way defined by relation schema. Several authors proposed learning methods for relational data, using different techniques. For example, Koller et. al in [2] proposed a framework for probabilistic relational model, based on the "influence propagation" idea. Besides, several relational clustering algorithms have been suggested and applied in different application domains. Hence these techniques are reported to show good performance, our aim is the investigation of the problem how to apply particular kernel methods for relational

---

[1] Research is supported by RFBR grant # 03-01-00745

J. Liu et al. (Eds.): IDEAL 2003, LNCS 2690, pp. 661–668, 2003.

data. Kernel methods have several important advantages in comparison to other learning methods. Foremost, they allow deal with data instances geometrically, and thus apply geometrical algorithms, working in terms of distance metric and dot product. Secondly, the kernel function can be considered as a similarity measure. The freedom to choose it enables us to design a large variety of different similarity measures and analysis algorithms. Thirdly, using kernels allows us do not define the feature map explicitly, and thus do not store high dimensional feature vectors. It is very important in case of large datasets.

In this paper in Section 2 we briefly outline the main definitions and facts regarding kernels, feature spaces and Haussler's convolution kernels framework. In Section 3 the structure of the input space data instances for relational data is discussed and the convolution kernel for such data is proposed. Section 4 is devoted to the experiments with application convolution kernel to outliers detection in relational data.

2   Feature Space and Convolution Kernels

The basic idea of kernel methods is mapping data instances from the *input space X*, to the *feature space H*. The non-linear mapping is performed implicitly by means of *kernel function K*. Usually the feature space is a vector space of high or infinite dimension, or, generally speaking, it is a Hilbert space. The feature map φ is defined as:

$$\varphi : X \to H \tag{1}$$

This map associates with every x from the input space the image $\varphi(x)$ in the feature space. The kernel function corresponds to the dot product in the feature space:

$$K(x, y) = \langle \varphi(x), \varphi(y) \rangle \tag{2}$$

This definition of kernel function allows defining a distance metric as follows:

$$d(x, y) = \sqrt{K(x, x) - 2K(x, y) + K(y, y)} \tag{3}$$

The choice of kernel function is crucial in all kernel-based algorithms. Usually it is application specific and greatly depends on the ability of the feature space to capture the information relevant to the application domain. Though, the question of how to choose the best kernel even for particular data set has no good answer [1]. Another problem is designing kernels for discrete structured objects. Haussler in [4] investigated this problem and suggested the approach, which allows defining the kernel function for composite objects as a combination of kernels, defined on the "parts" of this object. The main idea of Haussler's method, called R-convolution kernels, is as follows. If $x \in X$ is a composite structure; $x_1, ..., x_D$ are "parts" of it, where $x_d \in X_d$ and K_d is a proper kernel function defined on $X_d \times X_d$, the R-convolution kernel K can be defined on $X \times X$ as

$$K(x, y) = \sum_{R} \prod_{1 \le d \le D} K_d(x_d, y_d) \qquad (4)$$

where the sum runs over all possible ways (allowed by R), in which we can decompose x into $x_1,...,x_D$ and y into $y_1,...,y_D$; that is, all $(x_1,...,x_D,y_1,...,y_D)$ such that $R(x_1,...,x_D,x)$ and $R(y_1,...,y_D,y)$. $R(x_1,...,x_D,x)$ is a relation, which stands for "$x_1,...,x_D$ constitute the composite object x". Haussler proved that if R is finite, the K, defined by formula (5), is a valid kernel.

3 The Input Space for Relational Data

Before defining the kernel function for relational data we have to identify the structure of data in the input space, i.e. what is the composite object x in our case. For relational data the object x is not a vector. We can consider the input space as a set of instances of different types and relations between them, where each instance represents the row from some relational table and relations between instances correspond to relations between tables. To apply kernel-based learning method we should choose what type of data instances we want to analyze. In other words, we should choose the case table and key attribute in this table. It allows us identify the data instances uniquely. That is, the input space in case of relational data consists of some structured objects, where each object x is a database record taken form specified case table, and a set of rows taken from other tables, related to the case table. Such structure can be represented by nested relation scheme, i.e. every instance in the input space can be represented as row from case table extended by nested table columns. Very similar approach is used in OLEDB for Data Mining specification [6] to describe data mining cases and data mining case set.

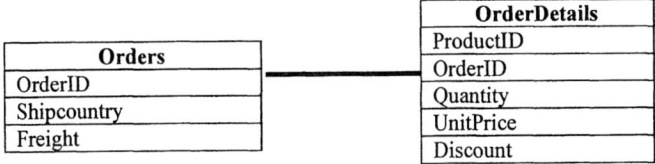

Orders						
OrderID	Shipcountry	Freight	OrderDetails			
			ProductID	Quantity	UnitPrice	Discount

Fig. 1. The example on this figure demonstrates the simple case, when two tables with single one-to-many relation exist.

To construct convolution kernel we should formally describe the structure of data instance in the input space. For that purpose we use the formal nested relational model, developed in [3] by Levene et. al. Below the main facts and definitions from [3] needed to construct our convolution kernel are listed.

Definition 1. Let $U = \{A_1,..., A_p\}$ be the universal set of attributes and let $W \subseteq U$. Then, a *schema tree*, T, defined over the set of attributes, W, is a rooted tree whose nodes are labeled by pairwise disjoint subsets of W. The following functions, which operate on schema tree, are defined.

Att(n) returns the set of atomic attributes associated with node n.

Root(T) returns the root node of T.

S(T) is the union of all *Att(n)* for all nodes in T.

Definition 2. The *nested relation schema*, represented by a schema tree, T, denoted by $R(T)$ is defined recursively as a set of attributes by:
1. If T is empty then $R(T)$ is empty.
2. If T contains the only node n and $V=Att(n)$ then $R(T)=V$.
3. If $V=Att(Root(T))$ and $T_1,...,T_s$ are the first-layer sub-trees of T then $R(T) = V \cup \{(R(T_1)^*),...,(R(T_s)^*)\}$.

Example. Let consider the relation schema, presented on Fig 1.
$U=W=\{$OrderID, ShipCountry, Freight, ProductID, Quantity, UnitPrice, Discount$\}$.
$R(T)=\{$OrderID, ShipCountry, Freight, ($\{$ProductID, Quantity, UnitPrice, Discount$\}$)*$\}$

Let $D = \{D_1,..., D_p\}$ be a set of domains, each consisting of atomic values. Domain $D_i = DOM(A_i)$ is associated with attribute A_i from the universe U. We consider the atomic attributes of two types – numerical, i.e. those for which the distance and the order are defined, and nominal (discrete), for which neither distance nor order are defined.

Definition 3. The domain for the nested relation schema $R(T)$, denoted by $DOM(R(T))$, is defined recursively:
1. If T is empty then $DOM(R(T))$ is empty.
2. If T contains the only node n and $V=Att(n)$ and $V = \{A_1,..., A_m\}$ then $DOM(R(T)) = DOM(V) = DOM(A_1) \times ... \times DOM(A_m)$.
3. If $V=Att(Root(T))$ and $T_1,..., T$ are the first-layer sub-trees of T then $DOM(T_1,..., T_s) = P(DOM(R(T_1))) \times ... \times P(DOM(R(T_s)))$, where $P(X)$ is finite powerset operator, and $DOM(R(T)) = DOM(V) \times DOM(T_1,..., T_s)$

4   Exponential Convolution Kernel for Relational Data

In this section we define the kernel for relational data using convolution kernels framework, developed by Haussler in [4]. Let x and y be the data instances from the input space, whose structure is described by nested relation scheme $R(T)$. The kernel function K is to be defined on $DOM(R(T)) \times DOM(R(T))$. We will define it recursively. We should consider two general cases, when $R(T)$ has nested relations, and when $R(T)$ has no nested relations.

Case I. *R(T)* has no nested relations.

In this case T contains the only node n. Let $V=Att(n)$ and $V = \{A_1,..., A \}$. Then $x, y \in DOM(V) = DOM(A_1) \times ... \times DOM(A_m)$ and we can define the kernel function using (4) as:

$$K_{DOM(V)}(x, y) = \prod_{1 \le j \le m} K_j(x_j, y_j) \tag{5}$$

where $x_j, y_j \in DOM(A_j)$. We consider two situations here, depending on type of attribute A_j, which is either nominal or numerical.

A_j is a numerical attribute

In this case we use the standard RBF kernel with the parameter q_j (kernel width) and normalized x_j and y_j:

$$K_j(x_j, y_j) = \exp\left(- q_j (x_j - y_j)^2 / \sigma_j^2\right) \tag{6}$$

A_j is a nominal attribute

Let A_j takes on m different values. We assume that the probability distribution is known or can be estimated. Let $p(x_j)$ be the probability that the value of the attribute A_j is equal to x_j. To handle nominal attributes we use standard approach. We consider the nominal attribute as a vector of m binary attributes, where the i-th component of vector is 1 iff the attribute value is equal to the i-th value from $DOM(A_j)$ and 0 otherwise. And now, as well as in the case with the numerical attribute, we use the standard exponential kernel function with the parameter q_j, and we get:

$$K_j(x_j, y_j) = \prod_{1 \le i \le m} \exp\left[- q_j (x_j^i - y_j^i)^2 / (\sigma_j^i)^2\right] \tag{7}$$

where σ_j^i is the variance of the i-th column. It is obvious that $K_j(x_j, y_j) = 1$ iff $x_j = y_j$. If $x_j \ne y_j$, let $x_j = i_x, y_j = i_y$ and we get:

$$K_j(x_j, y_j) = \exp\left[- q_j / (\sigma_j^{ix})^2\right] \exp\left[- q_j / (\sigma_j^{iy})^2\right] \tag{8}$$

Since $\sigma_j^{ix} = p(x_j)(1 - p(x_j))$, for $x_j \ne y_j$ we get:

$$K_j(x_j, y_j) = \exp\left[- q_j \left((p(x_j)(1 - p(x_j)))^{-2} + (p(y_j)(1 - p(y_j)))^{-2}\right)\right] \tag{9}$$

Thus, the final formula for calculating kernel for x and y in the case if $R(T)$ has no nested relations is:

$$K_{DOM(V)}(x, y) = \prod_{i \in Num} e^{-q_i \frac{(x_i - y_i)^2}{\sigma_i^2}} \prod_{j \in Discr \wedge x_j \ne y_j} e^{-q_j \left(\frac{1}{(p(x_j)(1-p(x_j)))^2} + \frac{1}{(p(y_j)(1-p(y_j)))^2}\right)} \tag{10}$$

where *Num* is the set of attribute indexes corresponding to numerical attributes, and *Discr* is the set of attribute indexes corresponding to discrete attributes.

Case II. R(T) has nested relations

Let $V=Att(Root(T))$ and $T_1,...,T_s$ are the first-layer sub-trees in T. In this case we should define the kernel function $K(x,y)$ for $x,y \in DOM(R(T))$, where $DOM(R(T)) = DOM(V) \times DOM(T_1,...,T_s)$. Using (4) we get:

$$K(x,y) = K_{DOM(V)}(x_V, y_V) \prod_{1 \le t \le s} K_t(x_t, y_t) \tag{11}$$

where $x_t, y_t \subseteq P(DOM(T_t))$ and s is a number of nested table attributes.

Let $Keys_t$ be the set of primary keys of the nested table attribute t corresponding to the sub-tree T_t; and the k-th tuple of x_t can be considered as $x_t(k) \in Dom(T_t)$, where $k \in Keys_t$. Thus, we can define $R^{-1}(x_t) = \{x_t(k) \mid k \in Keys_t\}$ and $R^{-1}(y_t) = \{y_t(k) \mid k \in Keys_t\}$. Therefore, using (4) and consider the additional condition that $K_t(x_t(k_x), y_t(k_y)) = 0$ if $k_y \ne k_x$, we get:

$$K_t(x_t, y_t) = \sum_{\vec{x} \in R^{-1}(x_t), \vec{y} \in R^{-1}(y_t)} K(\vec{x}, \vec{y}) = \sum_{k \in Keys(t)} K(x_t(k), y_t(k)) \tag{12}$$

The final recursive formulae for calculation the kernel function for x and y, whose structure is described by nested relation scheme $R(T)$ is:

$$K(x,y) = \prod_{i \in Num} e^{-q_i \frac{(x_i - y_i)^2}{\sigma_i^2}} \prod_{j \in Discr \wedge x_j \ne y_j} e^{-q_j \left(\frac{1}{(p(x_j)(1-p(x_j)))^2} + \frac{1}{(p(y_j)(1-p(y_j)))^2} \right)} \times$$

$$\times \prod_{t=1}^{s} \sum_{k \in Keys_t} K(x_t(k), y_t(k)) \tag{13}$$

where q_i is a width of the RBF kernel, which can be interpreted as a coefficient of importance of the i-th attribute. Since it controls how the deviation of the attribute affects the overall deviation of function K.

5   Experiments

For experiments we used the Northwind sample database [7], provided by Microsoft® Corporation with several its products, and freely distributed as a sample application. The Northwind database contains the sales data for a fictitious company called Northwind Traders, which imports and exports specialty foods from around the world. In the experiment we apply the kernel-based version of k-nearest neighbor outlier detection algorithm, which uses the distance metric (3) with kernel function (13). We added several artificial outliers to the dataset to test if the algorithm can discover them successfully.

5.1 Outlier Detection Algorithm Used in Experiments

The k-nearest neighbor algorithm is the state-of-the-art algorithm for mining distance-based outliers. In [5] the following definition of distance-based outliers is given: "An object o in a data set S is a *distance-based (DB) outlier* with parameters p and d, that is, $DB(p,d)$, if at least a fraction p of the objects in S lie at a distance greater than d from o". In other words, the outlier is the object having less than k "neighbors", where "neighbors" are defined depending on the distance from this given objects. To apply the *kNN* algorithm we need to define the distance metric. For that purposes the kernel-based distance (3) is used in our approach. We fix parameters k, d and q (the kernel widths for all attributes). After that the kernel matrix for all data instances from the dataset is calculated using (13) and then the pairwise distances are calculated using (3). After that *kNN* algorithm is applied to find outliers.

5.2 Experimental Setup and Results

From the Northwind database we took data related to detailed description of orders and the task was to find outliers among all orders. We used tables Orders, Order Details and Products. We performed attributes reduction [5] for these tables, left attributes ShipCountry and Freight for Orders, all attributes for Order Details, but ProductID attribute was generalized to product CategoryID. The structure is presented on the Fig 1. To test our algorithm we added several artificial outliers:

Outlier #1: all orders have from one to six items; the outlier #1 has ten items.

Outlier #2: the numeric attribute Freight has mean 78.2 and standard deviation 116. The outlier #2 has Freight attribute equal to 500.

Outlier #3: the outlier #3 has ShipCountry attribute which is not equal to any other among the dataset.

Outlier #4: the outlier #4 contains only one item with unique product, which is not included in any other order

Outlier #5: the outlier #5 contains item with Discount attribute equal to 0.3, when the average value of Discount attribute is 0.05 and standard deviation is 0.08.

In our experiment we set parameters $q=1$ for all numeric attributes and $q=0.01$ for ShipCountry. Generally, a good heuristic to set q for nominal is to set it in the order of $1/N^2$, where N is the size of the domain for this attribute. Total number of orders after inclusion artificial outliers is 835.

Table 1. The results of the experiments

Parameters	Total outliers (%)	Artificial Outliers discovered
d=3, k=1	22%	#1, #2, #3, #4, #5
d=3, k=5	31%	#1, #2, #3, #4, #5
d=4, k=1	6%	#1, #4
d=4, k=5	8%	#1, #4
d=5, k=1	1%	#4
d=5, k=5	2%	#1, #4

It is important to note that the capability of the algorithm to detect outliers of type #2, #3, #5 depends on the parameter q, i.e. the kernel width for corresponding attribute. So, the better performance may be achieved by tuning these parameters. On the other hand, the outliers of type #4 and #1 do not depend on any parameters, but the algorithm can discover them stably, that is promising result.

6 Conclusions and Future Work

This paper is devoted to the important problem of designing kernels for complex structured data, in particular, for relational data. The solution of this problem allows us apply the state-of-the-art kernel-based algorithms for real-world data, stored in relational databases. The structure of input space in case of relational data is discussed and the approach is suggested, which represents the structure of data instances in terms of nested relational model. For such model the method for constructing kernels, based on Haussler's convolution kernels framework, is developed. For demonstration purposes the simple Gaussian convolution kernel is constructed and applied, using k-nearest neighbor algorithm, for outlier detection problem. On sample data with artificially added outliers it has shown very promising results.

Future work involves designing more kernels, using suggested approach, and performing more experiments for outlier detection and other Data Mining tasks. It includes implementation and testing on real-world relational data other kernel-based algorithm and improving suggested kernels to support not only numeric and nominal, but ordered and other types of attributes.

References

1. Scholkopf, B., Smola, A., J.: Learning with kernels: Support Vector Machines, Regularization, Optimization and Beyond. The MIT Press Cambridge, Massachusetss (2000)
2. Friedman, N., Getoor, L., Koller, D. and Pfeffer, A..: Learning Probabilistic Relational Models, Proceedings of the 16th International Joint Conference on Artificial Intelligence (IJCAI), Stockholm, Sweden, pp. 1300–1307. (1999)
3. Levene, M., Loizou, G.: A Fully Precise Null Extended Nested Relational Algebra, Fundamenta Informaticae, Vol. 19, pp. 303–343, (1993)
4. Haussler, D.: Convolution kernels on discrete structures. Technical Report UCS-CRL-99-10, UC Santa Cruz, (1999)
5. Han, J., Kamber, M.: Data Mining : Concepts and Techniques. Morgan Kaufmann, ISBN 1-55860-489-8, (2000)
6. OLE DB for Data Mining Specification. Version 1.0. Microsoft Corporation, (2000). http://www.microsoft.com/data/oledb/dm.htm
7. Northwind Traders Sample Database. Microsoft Corporation, (2003) http://office.microsoft.com/downloads/9798/Nwind.aspx

Association Rule Mining Algorithms for Set-Valued Data

Christopher A. Shoemaker and Carolina Ruiz

Department of Computer Science. Worcester Polytechnic Institute
Worcester, MA 10609 USA
ruiz@cs.wpi.edu   http://www.cs.wpi.edu/~ruiz

Abstract. This paper presents an association rule mining system that is capable of handling set-valued attributes. Our previous research has exposed us to a variety of real-world biological datasets that contain attributes whose values are sets of elements, instead of just individual elements. However, very few data mining tools accept datasets that contain these *set-valued attributes*, and none of them allow the mining of association rules directly from this type of data. We introduce in this paper two algorithms for mining (classification) association rules directly from set-valued data and compare their performance. We have implemented a system based on one of these algorithms and have applied it to a number of biological datasets. We describe here our system and highlight its merits by means of comparing the results achieved with it and the failed attempts to mine association rules from those datasets using standard tools. Our system makes the creation of input files containing set-valued data much easier, and makes the mining of association rules directly from these data possible.

1 Introduction

Since the application of association rules to market basket analysis in [2], association rules have been the subject of active research in the data mining community, and the Apriori algorithm [1] has been the standard association rule mining algorithm. Apriori has been used to discover association rules from data in many different domains, but the tools that implement the Apriori algorithm always view the data in one of two forms: a list of transactions, where each transaction is a group of items, or a list of records, where each record has an individual elementary value for each attribute in the dataset. However, there are certain data types that do not easily fit into either of these two forms. Our research involves datasets from biological domains [13,14] that provide examples of these data types, because they contain set-valued attributes. *Set-valued attributes* are attributes whose values are sets of elements.

Sets are natural representations for the values of many important attributes in various datasets. One example of such a *set-valued attribute*, or simply, *set-attribute*, is the set of alleles present at a particular genomic location for each person in a database of people. Another example is the set of leading actors who starred in each movie of a movie database [8]. See Figure 1. We use here this toy dataset as a running example in order to provide simple illustrations of some of the concepts involved in mining association rules from set-valued data without the added complexity of the biology terminology. The value of a set-attribute is a set. We call this value a *set-value*. For example, the "Leading

J. Liu et al. (Eds.): IDEAL 2003, LNCS 2690, pp. 669–676, 2003.

Table 1. An example dataset with set-valued attributes

Movie Title	Leading Actors	Year
Rocky	{Sylvester Stallone}	1976
Lethal Weapon	{Mel Gibson, Danny Glover}	1987
Lethal Weapon 3	{Mel Gibson, Danny Glover}	1992
Lethal Weapon 4	{Mel Gibson, Danny Glover, Chris Rock}	1998

Actors" set-attribute for "Lethal Weapon" has set-value {Mel Gibson, Danny Glover}. A set-attribute can accompany other *normal* (non-set) attributes in a dataset, e.g. the year in which the movie was released.

Several other researchers have recognized both the prevalence of set-valued data in real-world applications and the lack of data mining algorithms and tools that accommodate set-valued data. [12] describes work on instance-based learning with set-valued attributes. [4] addresses rule induction from decision trees, where the attributes of the instances are set-valued. [7] covers induction of decision trees in numeric domains where attributes are set-values. To the best of our knowledge, none of the association rule mining tools directly support set-valued attributes.

In this paper we describe our data mining system, which is able to mine (classification) association rules directly from set-valued data. For this purpose, we introduce the *Set Based Apriori* (SBA) algorithm. In order to define a control environment for evaluating the performance of our SBA algorithm, we also describe techniques for transforming set-valued attributes into normal attributes that the Apriori algorithm can handle. We show how we have combined one of those transformations with Apriori to give Apriori access to set-valued data. We call this combination *Transformation Based Apriori* (TBA). We perform a complexity analysis of both TBA and SBA. This analysis motivates our system design decisions.

2   Background

The classical definition of association rules is as follows [2]: Let I be a set of items. Each *transaction*, T, is also a set of items, called an itemset, and $T \subset I$. The entire dataset, D, consists of uniquely identifiable transactions. An association rule is a rule of the form $A \Rightarrow B$ between the itemsets A and B, where $A \cap B = \emptyset$. Various metrics describe the utility of an association rule. The most common ones are the percent of all transactions containing $A \cup B$, called the *support*, and the percent of transactions containing B among transactions containing A, called the *confidence* of the rule. A *classification association rule* [9] is a rule whose consequent consists of a single value from a pre-specified collection of (target) values.

The *Apriori algorithm* [1] to mine association rules takes the dataset as input, along with minimum support and minimum confidence thresholds, and its final output is a list of all association rules whose confidence and support are above the minimum thresholds. As an intermediate step, it produces frequent itemsets. An itemset is *frequent* if its support is greater than or equal to the user-specified minimum support. An itemset of size k is called a k-itemset.

3   Our Algorithm: Set Based Apriori (SBA)

The basic idea of our algorithm is to separate the search for frequent combinations of set elements *within* the set-attributes from the search for frequent combinations of set-values *between* the set-attributes. The underlying assumption is that the dependencies within the set-attributes, i.e. the frequent set-values, are more interesting than some of the dependencies between elements from different set-attributes and dependencies between set-values and normal values. SBA first mines frequent sets within each set-attribute and then examines the dependencies between frequent set-values, normal values, and frequent set-values from other set-attributes. One result of this ordering is that the final rules contain literals that refer directly to set-values instead of only elements. An example of the type of rule mined by our algorithm is: Leading Actors = {Mel Gibson, Danny Glover} $\Rightarrow Year \geq 1980$. Our algorithm does not, however, limit the expressiveness of the rules.

SBA: Phase I. First, the SBA algorithm processes each set-attribute separately, producing set-values that will finally appear as literals in the association rules. This phase applies the Apriori principle. However, this phase differs from the Apriori algorithm by repeating the mining process for each set-attribute and by limiting the search to only the current set-attribute. Pseudocode for this phase is in Figure 1. While Apriori only counts an instance toward the support of an itemset if every item-value pair appears in the instance exactly as in the itemset, the SBA algorithm allows instances to contribute to the support of an itemset when every set-value in the itemset is exactly equal to *or a subset of* the corresponding set-value in the instance.

Input: D: all instances in a set-valued dataset; min_support: minimum support threshold
Output: F: a collection of all frequent set-values
Variables: C_k : set of candidate k-sets.
F_k : set of frequent k-sets. C_i : set of candidate itemsets in instance i.
i_A : set-value for set-attribute A in instance i. F_A : set of frequent set-values for attribute A.

```
for all set-attributes, A, in D {
        F₁ = {frequent elements of attribute A}
        for (k = 2; F_{k-1} ≠ ∅ ; k++){
            C_k = GenerateCandidates(F_{k-1})
            for all instances, i, i ∈ D {
                C_i = {c ∈ C_k|c ⊆ i_A}
                for all candidate itemsets, c, c ∈ C_i
                    c.count++ }
            F_k = {c ∈ C_k|c.count ≥ min_support} }
        F_A = ∪_k F_k }
return F = ∪_A F_A
```

Fig. 1. Phase I of the SBA algorithm

SBA: Phase II. When Phase I of SBA is complete, our algorithm uses the resulting frequent itemsets as input to a modified Apriori algorithm. The important aspect here is that the itemsets from the first phase become atomic items in the second phase. Itemsets in Phase II include or exclude entire itemsets from the first phase as indivisible items. The pseudocode for Phase II appears in Figure 2. Association rules are produced from the resulting frequent itemsets in the standard fashion described in [1].

Input: D: a dataset of instances
S: a collection of all the frequent set-values in D. min_support: minimum support threshold.
Output: F: a collection of all the frequent itemsets
Variables: C_k : collection of candidate k-itemsets
F_k : collection of frequent k-itemsets. C_i : collection of candidate itemsets in instance i.

```
for (k = 2; F_{k-1} ≠ ∅; k++) {
    C_k = GenerateCandidates(F_{k-1})
    for all instances, i, i ∈ D {
        C_i = Subset(C_k, i)
        for all candidate itemsets, c, c ∈ C_i
            c.count++ }
    F_k = {c ∈ C_k|c.count ≥ min_support}
    if (k = 2) then {
        j = 0
        for all frequent normal items, n ∈ F_1 {
            j + +
            B_n ={u ∈ S||u| = j}
            for all s ∈ B_n
                if (isFrequent(n ∪ s))
                    then F_2 = F_2 ∪ (n ∪ s)
                    else B_n ={B_n − t|s ⊆ t} } } }
return F = ∪_k F_k
```

Fig. 2. Phase II of the SBA algorithm

---

4   Transformation Based Apriori (TBA)

We need to establish a "control" environment in which we can compare our SBA algorithm to the Apriori algorithm on the same dataset. Since Apriori does not directly handle set-valued attributes, we need to use a consistent transformation of set-valued attributes into normal attributes. It is not trivial to decide which transformation to use.

The One-to-Many Transformation replaces a set-valued attribute with many normal attributes. k binary attributes replace a set-valued attribute whose element domain is of size k. Each binary attribute represents one element from the set-value's domain. The value for each of the normal attributes reflects whether the corresponding element is present in or absent from the original set-value. See Table 2.

We propose a combination of one-to-many transformation with Apriori to give Apriori access to datasets with set-values. We call it *Transformation Based Apriori* (TBA).

Table 2. The results of a one-to-many transformation

Movie Title	Stallone	Gibson	Glover	Rock	Year
Rocky	Yes	No	No	No	1976
Lethal Weapon	No	Yes	Yes	No	1987
Lethal Weapon 3	No	Yes	Yes	No	1992
Lethal Weapon 4	No	Yes	Yes	Yes	1998

Comparison of TBA vs. SBA. In order to compare SBA with TBA, we identify two alternative choices at the interface between Phase I and Phase II of SBA. The choice to be made is simply whether to pass all or just some of the frequent set-values from Phase I to Phase II. When Phase II of SBA uses all of the frequent set-values from Phase I, SBA examines the same combinations of set-values with normal values that transformational Apriori does. The order, however, is very different. When Phase II of SBA uses only some of the frequent set-values from Phase I, SBA might examine fewer combinations of set-values with normal values. The best strategy for selecting which frequent set-values to discard is generally domain specific. In order to maintain general applicability, we must allow a user to keep all of the frequent set-values. Since in this case SBA performs with the same computational complexity as TBA, we have chosen TBA as the basis for our rule mining system.

5   Implementation and Evaluation of Our Rule Mining System

We implemented our TBA system based on the excellent open-code provided with the WEKA [16] and the ARMiner [5] tools. We extended WEKA's attractive attribute-relation file format (ARFF) to include set-valued attributes. This extended format concisely and naturally represents set-valued data. We extended the ARMiner system to make it capable of mining classification rules and of mining rules from set-valued data.

5.1   The Spinal Muscular Atrophy (SMA) Dataset

Spinal muscular atrophy (SMA) is a genetic disease that affects cells in the spinal cord called anterior horn cells. It is estimated that 1 out of every 40 people carry the recessive gene for SMA. SMA is often fatal and death usually occurs in the very early childhood. There are different types of SMA, depending on the severity of the disease. Type I is the most severe. The SMA dataset for our experiments comes from [15] and gives the genotypic characteristics of 42 patients with SMA Types I, II, and III. The SMA dataset contains information about 9 types of SNP mutations and alleles for 2 microsatellite markers: C212 and Ag1-CA. C212 showed 15 different alleles and Ag1-CA showed 10 different alleles. The microsatellite marker for each person had between 2 and 4 allele values. The dataset also indicated with an underline which, if any, of the alleles came from the same parent as any observed mutation. For phenotypic characteristics, the dataset gives the SMA Type and the gender of the patient. See Table 3.

[6] mined classification rules, where the SMA Type (or severity) was the classification attribute. They transformed the original set-valued dataset into a normal one using what

Table 3. A reduced sample of the SMA dataset

ID	Sex	Mutation	C212	Ag1-CA	SMA Type
1	female	Y272C	31-<u>28 29</u>	102-<u>108 112</u>	I
2	male	Y272C	<u>28 29</u>-34	<u>108 112</u>-106	I
3	male	Y272C	27 29-<u>28 29</u>	114 116-<u>108 112</u>	II
4	male	Y272C	<u>28 29</u>-29 30	<u>108 112</u>-110	III
5	male	T274I	del-<u>25 29</u>	del-<u>108 114</u>	II
...	...	...	...	...	...

we call the one-to-many transformation. Their transformed dataset contains 71 binary attributes. They attempted to mine association rules using the original WEKA, but the tool could not complete the task due to the large number of frequent itemsets found in the transformed dataset, even when high values of minimal support were used. They then used CBA [3] to mine association rules from these data. Their results are difficult to interpret because since all of the alleles were absent more frequently than they were present, the rules which described allele absence "crowded out" rules that described allele presence. In constrast, the dataset represented in our extended ARFF contains just 6 attributes (2 of which are set-valued). We mined for classification rules with a support of at least 7% and a confidence of at least 50%. With these thresholds we discovered 120 rules, 56 of which had a confidence of 100%. A sample of the rules we discovered appear in Table 4. We found direct agreement with the literature stating that females were strongly association with the Type I SMA [11], and that alleles 28 and 29 for marker C212 and alleles 108 and 112 for marker Ag1-CA are related to SMA severity [15]. The allele 28 for marker C212 appears in 34 of the rules, while allele 29 occurs in 4 rules. For marker Ag1-CA, allele 108 is in 39 of the rules, and allele 112 is in 13 rules. Gender appeared in 52 of the 120 rules we mined.

Table 4. Sample classification rules obtained with our system for the SMA dataset.

Sample Rules	Supp %	Conf %
male & Mutation=none & Ag1-CA={108, 114} ⇒ SMA-III	14.3	100
C212={27, 28} ⇒ SMA-III	14.3	86
Ag1-CA={110} ⇒ SMA-III	14.3	75
female & C212={28u} & Ag1-CA={108u} ⇒ SMA-I	7.1	75

5.2   Gene Expression Data: The Promoters Dataset

We are interested in characterizing the expression patterns of genes based on their promoter regions. The promoter region of a gene controls both how and in which cells that gene is expressed. The collection of cells in which a gene is expressed is called the *expression pattern* of the gene. A gene is expressed when a protein binds to the gene sequence and copies it. The promoter region contains shorter subsequences called motifs to which gene regulatory proteins may bind. Therefore, the pattern of motifs in the promoter region is said to regulate the expression of the gene.

Phu [10] collected genetic information about the promoter regions of many of the genes of the nematode *C.Elegans*, a microscopic worm. From the gene sequences, Murphy et al. identified potential motif sequences. In this Promoters dataset, there is one instance for each gene sequence. The attributes of the dataset are only the name of the gene sequence, and two set-valued attributes: the expression pattern and the motif pattern. There were 78 gene sequences in the dataset. The expression pattern for each sequence was which of 7 different cell types the gene was expressed in; the motif pattern for each sequence was which of 368 motifs were contained, at least once, in the sequence. Figure 5 shows a small sample of the Promoters dataset.

Table 5. A sample of the Promoters dataset

Sequence	Expression Pattern	Motif Pattern
+c32e8.7	Pan-Neural	M10 M12 M14 M15 M18 . . .
+ceh-22	M-Cells	M1 M8 M10 M11 M17 M20 . . .
+che-3	OLL ASK ASE	M1 M2 M3 M4 M6 M10 . . .
+eat-4	OLL ASK	M1 M4 M6 M11 M20 M29 . . .

Murphy et al. tried to mine classification association rules using CBA. However, there was no straightforward way to represent the data for input to CBA. They ended up dividing the dataset into multiple datasets, one for each cell or cell type used for classification. They had to combine the results of multiple mining trials for the multiple datasets. They were also faced with the problem of what they called "irrelevant rules", that is rules that either referred to the absence of a motif or classified for the absence of expression in the cell type. For example, from the dataset for the OLL neural cell, CBA discovered 5596 classification rules, but they discarded 5518 of them as irrelevant.

In our experiments, we were able to exercise our system's ability to mine classification rules that classify for a set-valued attribute. We constrained our rules to have consequents that were subsets of the element domain of the expression pattern attribute. Some of the rules our system discovered from this dataset appear in Table 6. No "irrelevant" rules were mined.

Table 6. Classification rules that our system discovers for the promoters dataset

Sample Rules (set-valued classification)	Supp.	Conf.
{M1, M2, M10, M20, M29, M36} ⇒ {Pan-Neural}	10%	62%
{M1, M2, M20, M29} ⇒ {ASE}	10%	67%
{M1} ⇒ {OLL, ASK}	5%	6%
. . .	. . .	. . .

6   Conclusions

The main contributions of our work are: (1) We have developed a system that mines association rules directly from set-valued data. To the best of our knowledge, this is the first system with that property. (2) Our system is unique in its ability to mine *classification* rules from data with a set-valued classification attribute. (3) Our system discovers association and classification rules that are easier to read and to interpret than rules mined by standard systems over transformed data.

References

1. R. Agrawal and R. Srikant. Fast algorithms for mining association rules in large databases. In *Proc. 20th VLDB Conference*, pages 487–499, 1994.
2. Rakesh Agrawal, Tomasz Imielinski, and Arun Swami. Mining association rules between sets of items in large databases. *SIGMOD Records*, 22(2):207–216, June 1993.
3. Liu Bing, Wynne Hsu, Ma Yiming, Wong Ching Kian, Hu Minqing, Xia Yiyuan, and Liu Jing. Classification based on associations (CBA). http://www.comp.nus.edu.sg/~dm2/.
4. W. Cohen. Learning trees and rules with set-valued features. In *Proc. 13th AAAI Conf.*, 1996.
5. L. Cristofor and D. Cristofor. Association rules miner (ARMiner). http://www.cs.umb.edu/~laur/ARMiner/.
6. D. Doyle, J. Judecki, J. Lund, and B. Padovano. Genomic data mining. Undergraduate Graduation Project (MQP). Worcester Polytechnic Institute, April 2001.
7. D. Kalles and A. Papagelis. Induction of decision trees in numeric domains using set-valued attributes, 2000.
8. W. Lin, S.A. Alvarez, and C. Ruiz. Efficient adaptive–support association rule mining for recommender systems. *Data Mining and Knowledge Discovery*, 6(1):83–105, Jan. 2002.
9. Bing Liu, Wynne Hsu, and Yiming Ma. Integrating classification and association rule mining. In *Proc. 4th KDD Conf.*, pages 80–86, New York, August 1998.
10. B. Murphy, D. Phu, I. Pushee, and F. Tan. Motif- and expression-based classification of DNA. Undergraduate Graduation Project (MQP). Worcester Polytechnic Institute, April 2001.
11. G. Novelli, S. Semprini, F. Capon, and B. Dallapiccola. A possible role of naip gene deletions in sex-related spinal muscular atrophy phenotype variation. *Neurogenetics*, 1(1):29–30, 1997.
12. Terry R. Payne. Instance-based prototypical learning of set valued attributes, 1995. URL=citeseer.nj.nec.com/payne95instancebased.html.
13. C. Shoemaker, M. Pungliya, M. Sao Pedro, C. Ruiz, S.A. Alvarez, M. Ward, E. Ryder, and J. Krushkal. Computational methods for single point and multipoint analysis of genetic variants associated with a simulated complex disorder in a general population. *Genetic Epidemiology*, 21 (Suppl. 1):S738–S745, 2001.
14. C.A. Shoemaker, M.A. Sao Pedro, S.A. Alvarez, and C. Ruiz. Prediction vs. description: Two data mining approaches to the analysis of genetic data. In *Proc. 12th Genetic Analysis Workshop*, pages 449–453. Southwest Foundation for Biomedical Research, Oct. 2000.
15. B. Wirth, M. Herz, A. Wetter, S. Moskau, E. Hahnen, S. Rudnik-Schoeneborn, T. Wienker, and K. Zerres. Quantitative analysis of survival motor neuron copies: Identification of subtle smn1 mutations in patients with spinal muscular atrophy, genotype-phenotype correlation, and implications for genetic counseling. *American Jounal of Human Genetics*, 64:1340–1356, 1999.
16. Ian H. Witten and Eibe Frank. *Data Mining: Practical Machine Learning Tools and Techniques with Java Implementations*. Morgan Kaufmann Publishers, October 1999.

A Data Mining Based Intrusion Detection Model[*]

Jianhua Sun, Hai Jin, Hao Chen, Zongfen Han, and Deqing Zou

Internet and Cluster Computing Center
Huazhong University of Science and Technology, Wuhan, 430074, China
hjin@hust.edu.cn

Abstract. Intrusion Detection Systems (IDSs) have become a critical part of security systems. The goal of an intrusion detection system is to block intrusion effectively and accurately. However, the performance of IDS is not satisfying. In this paper, we study the issue of building a data mining based intrusion detection model to raise the detection performance. The key ideas are to use data mining techniques to discover consistent and useful patterns for intrusion and use the set of patterns to recognize intrusion. By applying statistics inference theory to this model, the patterns mined from a set of test data are effective to detect the attacks in the same category, and therefore can detect most novel attacks that are variants of known attacks.

1 Introduction

With the information increases explosively, many corporations and government entities build data warehouses to store the key information, and apply data mining techniques to make data-driven decisions. Once a warehouse is built, data mining techniques are frequently employed to identify trends in the warehouse that may not be readily apparent. In this paper we apply data mining techniques to security system and build a data mining based intrusion detection model.

Security of network systems is becoming increasingly important, and *Intrusion Detection System* (IDS) is a critical technology to help protect systems. There are two well-known kinds of intrusion detection systems: misuse intrusion detection system and anomaly intrusion detection system. Misuse intrusion detection system is efficient and accurate in detecting known intrusions, but cannot detect novel intrusions without unknown signature patterns [13]. Anomaly intrusion detection system can detect both novel and known attacks, but false alarm rate is high. Hence, misuse intrusion detection system and anomaly detection system are often used together to complement each other.

Many different approaches and techniques have been applied to anomaly intrusion detection. [8] presents risk-sensitive data mining techniques to detect intrusions and minimize the risks of false intrusion detection. [6] uses neural network to model normal data. Fuzzy theory is also applied to intrusion detection. [3] generates fuzzy association rules from new audit data to detect whether an intrusion occurs or not. In [2], the *fuzzy intrusion recognition engine* (FIRE) uses fuzzy logic to assess whether malicious activity is taking place on a network. Lee *et al.* apply data mining

---

[*] This research is supported by the Natural Science Foundation of Hubei Province under grant 2001ABA001.

J. Liu et al. (Eds.): IDEAL 2003, LNCS 2690, pp. 677–684, 2003.

techniques to audit to learn rules that accurately capture the behaviors of intrusions and normal activities [14][16]. Bridges *et al.* apply data mining techniques to the anomaly-based components [1].

After previous research on system calls sequences for intrusion detection [8], this paper focuses on analyzing and investigating the network behaviors of intrusion to achieve a higher detection performance. The rest of this paper is organized as follows. In section 2, we discuss the research background. Section 3 introduces a set of relevant statistics inference formulas, and builds a data mining based intrusion detection model. In section 4, we evaluate our intrusion detection model through experiments. Section 5 ends up with a conclusion.

2 Related Works

Most intrusions occur via network using the network protocols to attack their targets. For example, during a certain intrusion, a hacker follows fixed steps to achieve his intention, first sets up a connection between a source IP address to a target IP address, and sends data to attack the target. These kinds of connections are labeled attack connections and the rest connections are normal connection [11].

Generally, there are four categories of attacks [15]. They are:

- DOS (*denial-of-service*), for example, ping-of-death, syn flood, etc.
- PROBING, surveillance and probing, for example, port-scan, ping-sweep, etc.
- R2L, unauthorized access from a remote machine, for example, guessing password
- U2R, unauthorized access to local superuser privileges by a local unprivileged user, for example, various buffer overflow attacks.

DOS and PROBING attacks involve many connections to some hosts in a very short period of time. R2L and U2R attacks are embedded in the data portions of packets, and normally involve only a single connection. Attack connections and normal connections have their special feature values and flags in the connections head, and packets content can be used as signatures for normal determination and intrusion detection.

We can easily detect some intrusions through recording, analyzing, and charactering their connections. Intrusions belong to the same intrusion category have identical or similar attack principles and intrusion techniques. Therefore they have identical or similar attack connections and are significantly different from normal connections. Most novel attacks are variants of known attacks and the "signature" of known attacks can be sufficient to catch novel variants [11].

There are still two problems to resolve. One is how we get enough intrusions to represent most intrusion categories. The other is how we get suffice sample to character a kind of intrusion. Aim to these two problems, we use the data that was used by the 1999 KDD intrusion detection contest [11]. This database includes a wide variety of intrusions simulated in a military network environment. Being part of this database, test data file named corrected.gz contains a total of 38 training attack types. It consisted of approximately 300,000 data instances, each of which is a vector of extracted feature values from a connection record obtained from the raw network data gathered during the simulated intrusion and is labeled normal or a certain attack type.

3 A Data Mining Based Intrusion Detection Model

To evaluate the feature values of network attack behaviors, a set of relevant statistics inference formulas is introduced below. In statistical inference [5], parameter estimation involves the use of sample data in conjunction with some statistics to estimate the value of an unknown parameter. There are two ways of doing this: *point estimation* and *interval estimation*. In point estimation, one seeks an estimator that, based on the sample data, will give rise to a single-valued estimate of an unknown parameter value. In interval estimation, one determines an interval that is likely to contain the unknown parameter value. Such an interval is called a *confidence interval*. Let $L(\mathbf{X})$ and $U(\mathbf{X})$ be statistics that

$$P\{L(\mathbf{X}) \le \theta \le U(\mathbf{X})\} \ge 1 - \alpha. \tag{1}$$

Then the random interval $[L(\mathbf{X}), U(\mathbf{X})]$ is called a *confidence interval of level* $1 - \alpha$ for the parameter θ. For an interval estimator $[L(\mathbf{X}), U(\mathbf{X})]$ of a parameter θ, the coverage probability of $[L(\mathbf{X}), U(\mathbf{X})]$ is the probability that the random interval $[L(\mathbf{X}), U(\mathbf{X})]$ covers the true parameter, θ [9][10].

We next briefly calculate the attacks population expected value μ and population deviation σ^2 to represent the feature values of network attack behaviors.

3.1 Confidence Interval with Population Expected Value μ

Generally speaking, if the sample size is smaller than 30, it is called a small sample. Otherwise it is a large sample. Owning different probabilistic nature, small sample and large sample have different methods for interval estimation.

We first investigate the problem of finding a confidence interval for μ when a small sample coming from $N(\mu, \sigma)$, where μ and σ^2 are unknown, the random variable

$$T = \frac{\overline{X} - \mu}{S/\sqrt{n}} \tag{2}$$

has a Student t distribution with $n - 1$ degrees of freedom [5]. It is possible to determine the quantile value $t_{1 - \alpha/2, n - 1}$ of T for which

$$P(- t_{1-\alpha/2, n-1} < T < t_{1-\alpha/2, n-1}) = 1 - \alpha, \tag{3}$$

where the quantile value is such that $P(T < - t_{1 - \alpha/2, n - 1}) = \alpha/2$ and $P(T < t_{1 - \alpha/2, n - 1}) = 1 - \alpha/2$. Substituting T in (3), we have

$$P(\overline{X} - t_{1-\alpha/2, n-1} \frac{S}{\sqrt{n}} < \mu < \overline{X} + t_{1-\alpha/2, n-1} \frac{S}{\sqrt{n}}) = 1 - \alpha. \tag{4}$$

The interval $\overline{X} \pm t_{1-\alpha/2, n-1}(S/\sqrt{n})$ is a random interval, and the probability containing the true mean μ is $1 - \alpha$. Thus, given the data of a random sample of size n from which the estimates $\overline{x}$ and s^2 are computed, a $1 - \alpha$ confidence interval for μ is

$$\overline{x} \pm t_{1-\alpha/2,n-1} \frac{s}{\sqrt{n}} \tag{5}$$

Using similar derivations [4], for large sample a $1 - \alpha$ confidence interval for μ is

$$\overline{x} \pm z_{1-\alpha/2} \frac{s}{\sqrt{n}} \tag{6}$$

where Z is a random variable of $N(0, 1)$, and z is a observed value of Z.

3.2 Confidence Interval with Population Variance σ^2

We now consider a confidence interval for the population variance σ^2 when a small sample coming from $N(\mu, \sigma)$. The sampling distribution of $(n - 1)S^2/\sigma^2$ is chi-square with $n - 1$ degrees of freedom. It is possible to determine quantile values $\chi^2_{\alpha/2,n-1}$ $\chi^2_{1-\alpha/2,n-1}$ such that

$$P\left[\chi^2_{\alpha/2,n-1} < \frac{(n-1)S^2}{\sigma^2} < \chi^2_{1-\alpha/2,n-1}\right] = 1 - \alpha. \tag{7}$$

It follows that the interval

$$\left[\frac{(n-1)S^2}{\chi^2_{1-\alpha/2,n-1}}, \frac{(n-1)S^2}{\chi^2_{\alpha/2,n-1}}\right] \tag{8}$$

is a random interval that contains no unknown parameters and contains σ^2 with probability $1 - \alpha$ [5]. Based on the data of a random sample of size n, the estimate s^2 is computed and a $1 - \alpha$ confidence interval for σ^2 is

$$\left[\frac{(n-1)s^2}{\chi^2_{1-\alpha/2,n-1}}, \frac{(n-1)s^2}{\chi^2_{\alpha/2,n-1}}\right] \tag{9}$$

Using similar derivations [4], for large sample a $1 - \alpha$ confidence interval for σ is

$$s \pm z_{1-\alpha/2} \frac{s}{\sqrt{2n}} \tag{10}$$

where Z is a random variable of $N(0, 1)$, and z is a observed value of Z.

3.3 Data Mining Based Intrusion Detection Model

In order to mine patterns of network intrusion behaviors, we apply the above statistics inference formulas to KDD test data corrected.gz. Each data instance of test data has 42 fields, of which 35 fields are numeric valued features, and 7 fields are nominal valued features. Among the nominal valued features, fields such as attackname, protocol_type, service and flag are combined together to label one attack. We encode nominal attribute values as numeric integer values, and apply distance measures used in numeric clustering for computing proximity between object pairs [12].

Using the statistic and analyzing software SPSS, sample $\bar{x}$, s of 38 kinds of attacks are calculated. By applying these values to the statistics inference formulas in the above section, we get a confidence interval for population expected value μ and population variance σ^2 of the 38 kinds of attacks.

In order to illustrate conveniently, we number the 42 fields of each record in the corrected.gz file. Field 1 represents attackname, which means a certain attack name; and field 2 represents protocol_type, which means the protocol type.

Table 1. Values of Sample and Population Features for the Attack Guess_passwd

Field 5 - 42	$\bar{x}$	s	a confidence interval for μ	a confidence interval for σ
duration	4.06	.72	[4.04, 4.08]	[0.70, 0.74]
src_bytes	29.62	1.42	[29.57, 29.67]	[1.39, 1.45]
dst_bytes	94.25	12.40	[93.85, 94.65]	[12.12, 12.68]
logged_in	1.00	.00	[1.00, 1.00]	[0.00, 0.00]
count	1.02	.22	[1.01, 1.03]	[0.21, 0.23]
srv_count	1.00	.06	[1.00, 1.00]	[0.06, 0.06]
rerror_rate	.00	.02	[0.00, 0.00]	[0.02, 0.02]
same_srv_rate	.99	.06	[0.99, 0.99]	[0.06, 0.06]
diff_srv_rate	.01	.11	[0.01, 0.01]	[0.11, 0.11]
srv_diff_host_rate	.00	.05	[0.00, 0.00]	[0.05, 0.05]
dst_host_count	246.17	37.97	[244.94, 247.40]	[37.10, 38.84]
dst_host_srv_count	228.68	47.91	[227.12, 230.24]	[46.81, 49.01]
dst_host_same_srv_rate	.93	.13	[0.93, 0.93]	[0.13, 0.13]
dst_host_diff_srv_rate	.01	.01	[0.01, 0.01]	[0.01, 0.01]
Dst_host_same_src_port_r at	.00	.02	[0.00, 0.00]	[0.02, 0.02]
Dst_host_srv_diff_host_rat e	.00	.02	[0.00, 0.00]	[0.02, 0.02]
dst_host_rerror_rate	.02	.04	[0.02, 0.02]	[0.04, 0.04]
rest 21 fields	.00	.00	[0.00, 0.00]	[0.00, 0.00]

Table 1 lists the values for sample and population features for the attack guess_passwd (field 1), with tcp protocol (field 2), pop_3 (field 3) network service on the destination, SF (field 4) for the flag in network packets and number of records 3640 in file corrected.gz. The detail meanings of fields can be found at [11]. In table 1, the first column lists the rest 38 fields in a record. The second and third columns list the sample expected value and variance of each of the 38 fields. The last two columns list a confidence interval of level 0.95 for the population expected value μ and population variance σ of each of the 38 fields. In Section 4, we show how to use these values to produce patterns to detect intrusions.

4 Experiments and Performance Evaluation

We use the privileged process Sendmail in our experiment. This is because Sendmail is used widely and often becomes the target of hackers. Sendmail also provides various services that owns relatively more leaks and tends to be controlled easily. Because Sendmail is running on root privilege, and root processes have access to more parts of the system, therefore attackers aim at Sendmail to gain the root privilege.

In this experiment, we build a pattern database named NAP database containing *network attack patterns*, and then give an illustration of intrusion detection process and test the performance of our model.

4.1 NAP Database

Define $L(\mathbf{X}, \mu, i)$ the lower limit for the confidence interval for population expected value μ of the ith field; and define $U(\mathbf{X}, \mu, i)$ the upper limit for the confidence interval for population expected value μ of the ith field. In the same way, $L(\mathbf{X}, \sigma, i)$ is the lower limit for the confidence interval for population variance σ of the ith field; and $U(\mathbf{X}, \sigma, i)$ is the upper limit for the confidence interval for population variance σ of the ith field.

Records in the file corrected.gz were classified into the 38 kinds of attacks. For each of the 38 different kinds of attacks, we calculate a confidence interval of level 1 − α for the population expected value μ and population variance σ of each of the 42 fields. For each kind of attacks, we regard the intervals ($[L(\mathbf{X}, \mu, i)- L(\mathbf{X}, \sigma, i), U(\mathbf{X}, \mu, i)+ U(\mathbf{X}, \sigma, i)]$, $i = 1, 2, ..., 42$) as the patterns to describe this attack, and store the patterns in NAP database.

4.2 Detect Known and Novel Intrusions

In order to collect the same connection data as KDD database, Libpcap was used to collect network packets, and a program in C language was used to analyze network packets. We simulated several kinds attacks to the target while the program kept running.

To determine whether an intrusion occurred, we compare the test connections with the patterns in NAP database. For a test connection, if the number of fields values fell into the interval $[L(\mathbf{X}, \mu, i)- L(\mathbf{X}, \sigma, i), U(\mathbf{X}, \mu, i)+ U(\mathbf{X}, \sigma, i)]$ is larger than N_{match}, the connection is regarded as intrusion. N_{match} is a threshold value, above which a connection is regarded as intrusion. To detect intrusion effectively, we assign a large value to N_{match}.

In simulation experiment, we assign values to the parameters in formulas (5), (6), (9) and (10). The confidence coefficient $1 - \alpha$ value may change for different periods. For example, it may change with different levels of DEFCON which is borrowed from military, or if there is an increase in the number of hackers operating [7]. DEFCON stands for the whole military's defense readiness condition. DEFCON 5 means "normal readiness", DEFCON 1 means "maximum readiness", and DEFCON 3 means "an increase in force readiness above that required for normal readiness" [20].

Attacks simulated to a Sendmail service and an additional FTP service target include PROBING, DOS, U2R and R2L. Table 2 compares the detection rates for old intrusions and new intrusions. Here new intrusions refer to those who have little or no corresponding record in the training data, and attacks belonging to the same attack category have little or no corresponding record either, such as ftp_write has only one record in the training data. In table 2, percent refers to the rate of number of old intrusions or new intrusions to the whole number of attacks belonging to one category simulated in the test. It is very difficult to find a new intrusion for attacks belonging to DOS or PROBING. From Table 2, we can see that our model archives satisfying performance.

Table 2. Detection Rates for Different Intrusions

		DOS	PROBING	U2R	R2L
old intrusions	percent	100	100	87	72
	detection rate	92	84	82	90
new intrusions	percent	0	0	13	28
	detection rate	-	-	15	20

5 Conclusions

In this paper, we propose an intrusion detection model based on data mining to improve the accuracy of detection rate. To achieve the goal, NAP database is established. Through statistics inference formulas, the data in KDD database are transformed into attack patterns to describe intrusions. Empirical experiments show that our data mining based intrusion detection and deployment techniques are effective to detect the attacks in the same category, and therefore can detect most novel attacks that are variants of known attacks.

Intrusion detection model is a compositive model that needs various theories and techniques. One or two models can hardly offer satisfying results. We plan to apply other data mining theories and techniques in intrusion detection in our future work.

References

1. S. M. Bridges and R. B. Vaughn, "Fuzzy data mining and genetic algorithms applied to intrusion detection", *Proc. of the Twenty-third National Information Systems Security Conference*, Baltimore, MD, October 2000, pp.13–31.

2. J. E. Dickerson and J. A. Dickerson, "Fuzzy network profiling for intrusion detection", *Proc. of 19th International Conference of the North American, Fuzzy Information Processing Society*, 2000, pp.301–306.

3.   G. Florez, S. M. Bridges, and R. B. Vaughn, "An improved algorithm for fuzzy data mining for intrusion detection", *Proc. of NAFIPS Annual Meeting of the North American, Fuzzy Information Processing Society*, 2002, pp.457–462.

4.   F. Fu, J. Ni, H. Zhu, S. Wang, and Y. Huang, *Applied probability and statistical*, Renmin University of China Press, 1989, pp.254–275.

5.   G. C. Canavos, *Applied probability and statistical method*, Little, Brown, 1984, pp.417–420.

6.   A. Ghosh and A. Schwartzbard, "A study in using neural networks for anomaly and misuse detection", *Proc. of the Eighth USENIX Security Symposium*, 1999.

7.   J. E. Gaffney Jr. and J. W. Ulvila "Evaluation of intrusion detectors: a decision theory approach", *IEEE Symposium on Security and Privacy*, 2001, pp.50–61.

8.   H. Jin, J. Sun, H. Chen, and Z. Han, "A Risk-sensitive Intrusion Detection Model", *Information Security and Cryptology - Lecture Notes in Computer Sciences, Vol.2587*, Springer-Verlag, November 2002, pp.107–117

9.   J. R. Blum, *Probability and statistics*, Philadelphia: W. B. Saunders, 1972, pp.267–269.

10. G. Casella and R. Berger, *Statistical Inference*, Wadsworth & Brooks/Cole, Belmont, California, 1990, pp.260–270.

11. http://kdd.ics.uci.edu/databases/kddcup99/kddcup99.html

12. C. Li and G. Biswas, "Conceptual clustering with numeric-and-nominal mixed data – a new similarity based system", *IEEE Transactions on Knowledge and Data Engineering*, 1998.

13. N. Ye, X. Li, Q. Chen, S. M. Emran, and M. Xu, "Probabilistic techniques for intrusion detection based on computer audit data", *IEEE Trans. on Systems, Man, and Cybernetics - Part A: Systems and Humans*, Vol.31, No.4, July 2001, pp.266–274.

14. W. Lee and S. Stolfo, "Data Mining Approaches for Intrusion Detection", *Proc. of the Seventh USENIX Security Symposium (SECURITY '98)*, San Antonio, TX, January 1998.

15. W. Lee, S. Stolfo, and K. Mok, "A Data Mining Framework for Building Intrusion Detection Models", *Proc. of the 1999 IEEE Symposium on Security and Privacy*, Oakland, CA, May 1999.

16. W. Lee, S. Stolfo, and P. Chan, "Learning Patterns from Unix Process Execution Traces for Intrusion Detection", *Proc. of AAAI Workshop: AI Approaches to Fraud Detection and Risk Management*, July 1997.

17. W. Lee, S. Stolfo, P. Chan, E. Eskin, W. Fan, M. Miller, S. Hershkop, and J. Zhang, "http://www.cc.gatech.edu/~wenke/papers/dmids-discex01.psReal Time Data Mining-based Intrusion Detection", *Proc. of the 2001 DARPA Information Survivability Conference and Exposition (DISCEX II)*, Anaheim, June 2001, pp.85–100.

18. J. Marin, D. Ragsdale, and J. Surdu, "A hybrid approach to the profile creation and intrusion detection", *Proc. of DARPA Information Survivability Conference & Exposition II (DISCEX'01)*, Vol.1, 2001, pp.69–76.

19. L. Portnoy, E. Eskin, and S. J. Stolfo, "Intrusion detection with unlabeled data using clustering", *Proc. of ACM CSS Workshop on Data Mining Applied to Security (DMAS-2001)*, Philadelphia, PA, 2001.

20. http://www.ams.mod.uk/

Semantics Based Information Retrieval Using Conceptual Indexing of Documents

D. Manjula, Santhosh Kulandaiyan, Santosh Sudarshan, Ashok Francis, and
T.V. Geetha

manju@annauniv.edu, santhosh_cse@yahoo.com,
santosh_mvs@mailcity.com, ashoksmail@yahoo.com,
rctamil@annauniv.edu

Abstract. This paper proposes a technique for information retrieval using conceptual indexing of documents. A novel word sense disambiguation approach is applied to the set of input documents and the senses of the words are accurately determined using the senses present in the WordNet along with the contextual information present in the document. Once the senses are determined, the documents are indexed conceptually. The group of closely related synsets has been defined as a concept. The query is also conceptually disambiguated. Once the documents and the query are brought to the same format, retrieval of documents is performed and the results show improved effectiveness over other retrieval systems.

1 Introduction

In traditional IR systems, documents are indexed by words, and this leads to poor retrieval. This paper details a mechanism for efficient information retrieval using conceptual indexing. This is a coarse grained method of indexing as compared to the sense based indexing which works at a much fine grained level. The software aid used is WordNet, the lexical database for the English Language which captures all senses of a word and contains semantic information about the relation between words. The problem in WordNet is that it includes too much fine-grained sense distinctions and lack of domain information. The domain knowledge which is not available in WordNet can be taken from the gloss [1, 2]. This paper expands upon the work carried out by Julio Gonzalo et al [4] which deals with how to improve text retrieval by indexing with the WordNet synsets.

The rest of the paper is organized as follows. Section 2 deals with the background work that has been done in semantic indexing and information retrieval. Section 3 deals with the System Architecture. Sections 4 and 5 deal with WSD and conceptual indexing. Section 6 deals with the query disambiguation and sections 7 and 8 deal with the retrieval performance of the system and how it compares against other information retrieval methods. Section 9 concludes the work.

2 Related Works

Much work has been done in Information retrieval and Word Sense Disambiguation. With relevance to this paper, the work in document indexing can be classified into the following subsections.

J. Liu et al. (Eds.): IDEAL 2003, LNCS 2690, pp. 685–692, 2003.

2.1 Word Based Indexing

The documents are indexed based on the words alone and no semantic sense is imparted into the indexing process. Gonzalo et al [4] performed a number of experiments in word based indexing using the SMART system and the results they obtained showed that 48% of the correct documents were retrieved in first place.

2.2 Sense Based Indexing

In this method the documents are indexed based on the senses of the words as found in Wordnet. Much work was carried out by Mihalcea and Moldovan [3] in this direction. They observed a 16% increase in recall and 4% increase in precision while they used a combined word based and synset-based indexing, as opposed to basic word based indexing. Gonzalo [4] performed experiments with sense based indexing and synset based indexing and showed that the benefits obtained increased from a sense based approach to a synset based approach.

2.3 Conceptual Indexing

Gonzalo et al [4], performed experiments in conceptual indexing, where the concepts are represented by the synsets. Here, two words having equivalent word senses are represented with a unique identifier that denotes a synset number. This paper expands upon this idea of indexing by the synsets.

3   System Architecture

The figure shows the overall system architecture of the information retrieval system. The document repository is a collection of plain text documents that spans a variety of topics which include sports, place descriptions, career descriptions and historical events. The preprocessing phase does the initial preprocessing on the documents. This includes the stop word elimination, keyword identification and POS (Part of Speech) tagging. Once the key words are identified, the words are stemmed to their root forms. The important thing to be considered here is that the sentence information is also kept

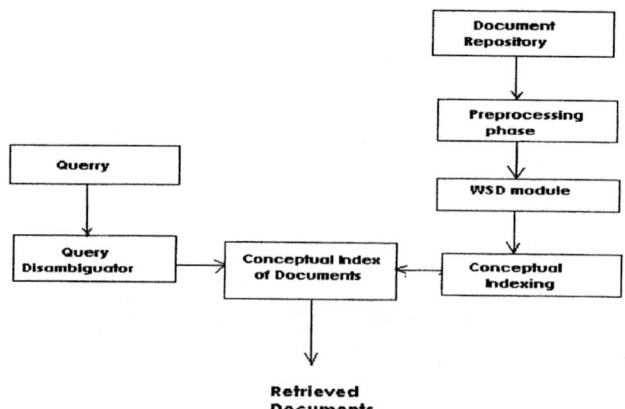

Fig. 1. The overall system architecture for the Information Retrieval system

track of in the keyword list. This information is used to identify the contextual information of the words that occur in a single sentence.

The WSD module disambiguates the words in the key word list using Wordnet. At the end of this phase, for every word in the keyword list, the following information is obtained:

Word | POS | offset | sense# | synset#

The 'Word' field denotes the actual word after it has been stemmed. The POS denotes the part of speech as already determined, the offset field denotes the offset in the document at which this word occurs. The sense# denotes the sense of the word that the WSD module has determined for the word and the synset# denotes the synset number that the sense comes under.

The Conceptual indexing module indexes the documents based upon the concepts that are obtained after WSD is completed on the set of keywords. The WSD and Conceptual Indexing are explained in subsequent sections.

Similarly the query is also disambiguated using the Wordnet senses along with the contextual information present in the query. Now the Query and the document have been converted from plain words to concepts. Using this conceptual information, retrieval is performed by matching the concept numbers.

4 Word Sense Disambiguation

This section explains the WSD module that is employed in the Information retrieval system. A word that appears in a document may have different senses depending upon the context and the following sub-sections explain how the senses of the words are determined using the contextual information present in the sentence.

4.1 Context Graphs

The context graphs are used to relate every possible sense of each key word in a sentence to every possible sense of every other key word in the same sentence. In this graph there are two kinds of nodes namely, outer nodes and inner nodes. The outer nodes represent the words that occur in a sentence while the inner nodes of a particular outer node represent the possible senses of the word that occurs in the outer node. Edges are possible only between the inner nodes of different outer nodes. The weight of an edge denotes the number of common words that occur in the definitions of the two senses which the edge connects. The definitions of the senses are taken from WordNet. The weight of an inner node is defined to be the sum of the weights of all the edges originating from that node. A *path* in a context graph is defined to be a set of adjacent edges originating from and terminating in inner nodes in such a manner that no two inner nodes in the path belong to the same outer node. A path is *closed* if the originating and ending inner nodes are one and the same. A path is said to be *complete* if the set of all outer nodes, whose inner nodes occur in the path, is the complete set of all the outer nodes of the graph. A path is said to be *complete closed* if it is both a closed and a complete path. The *weight* of a path is defined as the weight of all the edges in the path.

An Example: Consider a sentence which consists of 4 key-words W1, W2, W3 and W4. Let W1 have only 1 sense and the other three words have 2 senses each. Fig2 shows the context graph for the sentence.

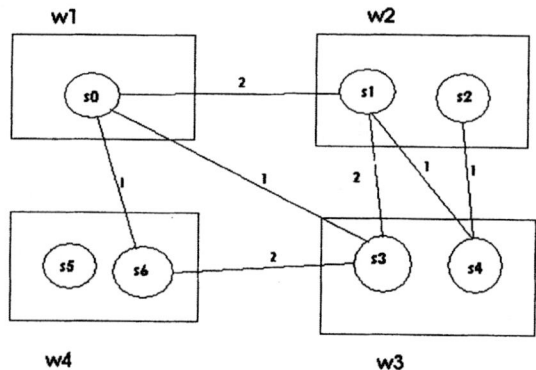

Fig. 2. Context graph for a sentence consisting of 4 words

Consider the edge labeled with a weight of 2 between the inner nodes s0 and s1. The number 2 denotes that there are 2 matching words between the meaning of the sense0 of word1 and the sense1 of word2.

4.2 Algorithm for WSD

Input: A set of words along with the sentence information. The words are stemmed to their root forms and POS tagged.

Output: A set of words that are semantically disambiguated using the contextual information present in the sentence. Each word will have the form: Word | POS | Offset | Synset# | Sense#

Algorithm:

1. For each sentence, the context graph is formed as explained in the previous section and the earliest possible step from 2 to 5 is carried out.
2. A complete closed path with maximum weight is determined and the corresponding senses are assigned to the words. The offset of the words and the synset number are also assigned.
3. A complete path with the maximum weight is determined and the corresponding senses along with the offset and synset number are assigned to the words.
4. A closed path with maximum weight that does not span all the outer nodes (words) is identified and the corresponding senses along with the offset and synset number are assigned to the words. For the remaining words the inner node that has the maximum weight associated with it is identified and that sense is applied to the word along with offset and synset numbers.
5. The path with the maximum weight is identified and the corresponding senses are assigned to the words along with offset and synset information. For all the remaining words, the sense of the word is taken to be the inner node with maximum weight.

For the hypothetical sentence of fig 2, the WSD algorithm identifies a complete cycle present in the graph between the inner nodes s0 s1 s3 s6 s0 and the weight of this cycle is 7. So the senses of the words are assigned as follows: W0 has sense s0, W1 has sense s1, W2 has sense s3 and W3 has sense s6.

5   Conceptual Indexing

A concept is a synset or a group of closely related synsets. The synsets present in the WordNet are manipulated and a concept list is created with each concept having a unique concept identifier. The synset number obtained after WSD is mapped to the appropriate concept number and the document is now represented as:

$$Concept\# \mid offset$$

Concepts in a document are given weights and this weight is determined by two factors namely,

1. *The spatial factor of the concept.* This factor denotes where exactly the concept occurs in the document. A concept is given more weightage if it occurs early in a document. This is due to our observation that the major ideas in a document are present in the initial part of the document.

2. *The frequency factor of the concept.* This denotes the frequency of occurrence of the concept in the document. A concept that occurs more often in a document should carry more weight than a concept that occurs less often.

Let S_i denote the spatial factor of the concept 'i' and let F_i denote the frequency factor of the concept 'i'. Then the following formula is used to calculate the weight of the concept (X_i).

$$X_i = S_i * F_i \tag{1}$$

The spatial factor is defined as

$$S_i = (\text{Total number of times the concept occurs in the document / average of the offsets at which the concept occurs}) \tag{2}$$

The Frequency factor is defined as

$$F_i = (\text{Number of times the concept occurs in the document / Total number of concepts in the document}) \tag{3}$$

Our experiments showed that this method of having weighted concepts led to a better representation of documents than what is obtained by sense based indexing or synset based indexing. From a set of words representation, the document has now been converted to a set of concepts, with a weight attached to each concept. The weights for each concept in the different documents are maintained as a conceptual index table.

6   Query Disambiguation

Initially the word sense disambiguation process for the query is the same as it is for the documents. The context graph for the query is constructed and the top few senses of the words as determined by the threshold value are chosen (since the query is considerably much shorter than the documents we choose a 'few' senses for the query instead of only the top sense).

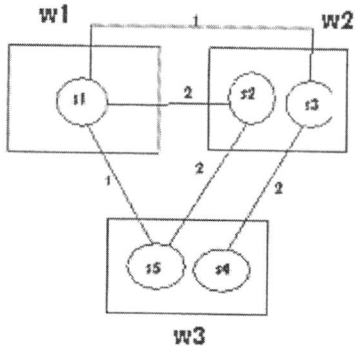

Fig. 3. Context graph for a query consisting of 3 words

Consider Fig3 which shows the context graph for a query consisting of 3 words w1, w2 and w3. The senses of the words and the related contextual information are shown as the inner nodes and the edges respectively. The threshold value for the number of different senses is taken to be 2. This means that 2 paths from the context graph can be chosen for assigning senses to the words in the query. A *disambiguated query set,* which is initially empty, is used to hold the different senses of the query that are chosen. For the above context graph, the paths {s1 – s2 – s5 – s1} and {s1 – s3 – s4} are chosen as the best possible paths. Weights of 5 and 3 are attached to the two paths respectively. The normalized weight of the first path is 5/8 and that of the second path is 3/8. From the senses just obtained using the modified word sense disambiguation algorithm, the concepts are identified as was done for the documents. For the example under consideration, there are two different concept sets corresponding to the 2 items in the disambiguated query set. The concept sets are denoted as CS1 and CS2. For our example CS1 contains the concepts {c121 and c767} with a weight of 5/8 and CS2 contains the concepts {c121 and c935} with a weight of 3/8. Thus, a conceptual representation of the query has been obtained, with a weight attached to each concept set of the query.

7   Retrieval of Documents

The documents are retrieved using the conceptually disambiguated query set created for the query and the conceptual index table created for the documents. During retrieval, the concepts that are present in a particular concept set of the query are matched against the concepts for a particular document in the conceptual index table. Two factors are taken into consideration during retrieval. One is that the sum of the weights in the conceptual index table should be as large as possible and the other is that the standard deviation for the weights should be as small as possible. This is primarily to give equal weights to all the concepts in the concept set of the query under consideration. If all concepts that are present in a concept set of a query cannot be matched against any document, then matching is performed for as many concepts as possible with the same consideration for the 2 factors as mentioned above. The weightage for the various concept sets of the query is used to output the results for the query. In the example for the query disambiguation of Fig3, the weights of the two concept sets are determined as 5/8 and 3/8. This means that for every 8 results that are displayed, 5 would carry the conceptual notion of the first concept set and 3 would carry the conceptual notion of the second concept set.

8   Results and Performance Evaluation

For our experiments the corpus consisted of documents relating to diverse fields like sports, career options, touring spots and historical events. 5 documents were taken in each of the sections mentioned above and each document consisted of approximately 1000 words. The average disambiguation rate obtained was very close to 90%.

The documents were evaluated against 3 general queries in the fields of the documents. For these 3 queries, the recall rate and the precision of the retrieved results were evaluated and are summarized in Table2. As Table2 shows, conceptual indexing of documents provides a better retrieval performance both in terms of recall rate and precision.

Table 1. Percentage of disambiguated words for the corpus which was considered. Disambiguation was carried out for 5 documents each from the set of articles which involved descriptions about sports, career options, touring palces and historical events. The average disambiguation rate was very close to 90%

	Sports Descriptions	Career Options	Touring Places	Historical Events
Doc1	94.12	88.45	91.35	90.33
Doc2	83.33	90.45	89.20	84.45
Doc3	92.18	92.18	87.66	92.34
Doc4	85.40	85.35	92.16	93.33
Doc5	90.24	84.24	84.33	88.65
Average	**89.05**	**88.13**	**88.94**	**89.82**

9   Conclusions and Future Work

Achieving perfect retrieval of documents by completely disambiguating all the words in a document is still an elusive goal. Our work is a step forward in realizing that goal, by indexing documents based on the concepts. The conceptual indexing method shows a high recall rate and precision as compared to the word based and sense based indexing for a similar set of documents.

Table 2. Recall rate and Precision for the three different queries. A comparision of conceptual indexing is made against the word based and sense based indexing

	Word Based Indexing		Sense Based Indexing		Conceptual Indexing	
	Re-call	Prec ision	Re-call	Prec ision	Re-call	Prec ision
Q1	80.33	55.46	85.45	60.66	85.45	63.23
Q2	76.54	53.34	83.33	62.33	86.66	65.33
Q3	82.34	57.75	86.92	61.13	87.12	64.50
Avg	**79.03**	**55.52**	**85.23**	**61.37**	**86.41**	**64.35**

The only drawback in the system is its inability to disambiguate words which don't have enough contextual information in the sentence. But as our observation shows, these words are few and far between in natural language text and the rest of the words are disambiguated with a high percentage of accuracy. However, disambiguation of such words with little or no contextual information can be performed by using a semantically tagged corpus such as Semcor. But that would mean an extra level of processing in the system, which is an overhead. Further work is needed in that direction.

References

1. P Malliga, D Manjula, T V Geetha : Semantic Based Text Mining, First International Conference on Global WordNet, Mysore (2002).
2. D Manjula, A Kannan, T V Geetha : Semantic Information Extraction and Querying from the World Wide Web, KBCS, Bombay (2002).
3. Rada Mihalcea, Dan Moldovan : Semantic indexing using WordNet senses, in Proceedings of ACL Workshop on IR & NLP, Hong Kong, October (2000).
4. Julio Gonzalo, Felisa Verdijo, Irina Chugur, Juan Cigarran : Indexing with Wordnet synsets can improve text retrieval, in Proceedings of the COLING/ACL Workshop on Usage of WordNet for NLP (1998).
5. Rada Mihalcea, Dan Moldovan : A Highly Accurate Bootstrapping Algorithm for Word Sense Disambiguation, in International Journal on Artificial Intelligence Tools, vol.10, no.1-2, (2001) pg. 5–21.
6. E.M Voorhes. Using WordNet for text retrieval. In WordNet, an electronic lexical database,. The MIT press. (1998). Pg. 285–303
7. E.M Voorhes. Natural Language Processing and information retrieval. In Information Extraction: towards scalable, adaptable systems. Lecture notes in artificial intelligence, #1714, (1999) .Pg32–48.
8. R Krovetz and W.B Croft. Lexical ambiguity and information retrieval. ACM transactions on information systems, 10(2): (1993) Pg.115–141.

Experiences of Using a Quantitative Approach for Mining Association Rules

Liang Dong and Christos Tjortjis

Department of Computation, UMIST, PO Box 88, Manchester, M60 1QD, UK
christos@co.umist.ac.uk

Abstract. In recent years interest has grown in "mining" large databases to extract novel and interesting information. *Knowledge Discovery in Databases* (KDD) has been recognised as an emerging research area. Association rules discovery is an important KDD technique for better data understanding. This paper proposes an enhancement with a memory efficient data structure of a quantitative approach to mine association rules from data. The best features of the three algorithms (the *Quantitative Approach, DHP,* and *Apriori*) were combined to constitute our proposed approach. The obtained results accurately reflected knowledge hidden in the datasets under examination. Scale-up experiments indicated that the proposed algorithm scales linearly as the size of the dataset increases.

1 Introduction

Progress in data acquisition and storage facilitated the explosive growth in the amount of data collected by businesses. The impetus to effectively harness the increased volumes of data now available has lead to the need for new data analysis techniques to build data characterisations and extract useful patterns and models. Consequently, the research field of KDD, also known as data mining, has arisen with *mining association rules* becoming one of the most prominent techniques within the context of extracting relationships among items hidden within datasets.

A promising algorithm for mining association rules in terms of accuracy and performance is the *Quantitative Approach* [9]. It generates the set of frequent itemsets by first partitioning the values of quantitative attributes and then using an interesting measure to prune any uninteresting candidate itemset.

In this paper, we present a combined approach which consists of various parts from existing algorithms, such as the *Quantitative Approach*, the hash-based technique from *DHP* (Direct Hashing and Pruning) algorithm [5], and the methodology for generating association rules from *Apriori* algorithm [2]. We present experimental results showing that the proposed approach precisely reflects the information hidden in the datasets. As the size of the dataset increases, the proposed approach scales-up linearly in terms processing time and memory usage. In section 2, some algorithms used within the framework of association rules are investigated. Encouraging results obtained by comparing the Quantitative Approach to other association rule algorithms are outlined in Section 3. The experimental results are analysed in Section 4. Conclusions and future work are discussed in Section 5.

J. Liu et al. (Eds.): IDEAL 2003, LNCS 2690, pp. 693–700, 2003.
© Springer-Verlag Berlin Heidelberg 2003

2 Related Work

This section aims at investigating six prominent algorithms for mining association rules: the *AIS* [1], *SETM* [2], *Apriori* [2], *AprioriTid* [2], *Quantitative Approach* [7], and *Boolean* Algorithm [10]. Advantages and disadvantages for each of them are discussed in terms of speed, accuracy, and suitability.

- Speed

Finding all frequent itemsets greatly affects the speed of algorithms, because it requires one or more database scans, which result in a time overhead for I/O connections to a database stored in a secondary storage device. Such overhead is much greater than that because of computation in the CPU [2].

In both *AIS* and *SETM* algorithms, candidate itemsets are generated "on-the-fly" during the first pass as data are being read. This results in unnecessarily generating and counting a lot of invalid candidate itemsets thus wasting a lot of time. In general, *Apriori*, *AprioriTid* and *Quantitative Approach* consider the itemsets found to be frequent in the previous pass, with no need to access the database again. Consequently, fewer candidate itemsets are generated. Taking the above statements into consideration, the *Apriori*, *AprioriTid*, and *Quantitative Approach* are superior to *AIS* and *SETM* for all problem sizes.

Although *Apriori* counts too many small sets in the second pass, this wastage decreases dramatically from the third pass onwards [2]. However, each iteration in *Apriori* requires a pass of scanning the database, incurring a severe performance penalty. The *Quantitative Approach* is similar to the *Apriori* algorithm, in this respect. In the *AprioriTid* algorithm a pass over the database is replaced by a pass over the set of candidate itemsets associated with *TIDs*[1] after the first pass. Hence, *AprioriTid* is more effective in later passes when the size of this encoding can become much smaller than that of the database. When the sets of this encoding fit in memory, *AprioriTid* is superior to *Apriori*; otherwise, *Apriori* beats *AprioriTid*.

The *Boolean* algorithm produces frequent itemsets without constructing candidate itemsets. In contrast, this construction of candidate itemsets is required by the "Apriori family" algorithms (for example, *AIS*, *SETM*, *Apriori*, *Quantitative Approach*, and *AprioriTid*). As a result, the *Boolean* algorithm should outperform the "Apriori family" algorithms for all problem sizes as reported on the literature [10]. However, when we applied this algorithm to mine quantitative association rules in a large dataset, it was found to be unsuitable for solving such problems (see Section 3).

- Accuracy

The *AIS*, *SETM*, *Apriori*, *AprioriTid*, and *Boolean* algorithms can only deal with Boolean Association Rules problems, while the *Quantitative Approach* can also deal with Quantitative problems. Since a transactional database often has richer attribute types like quantitative and categorical attributes, taking into account only Boolean attributes should result in a heavy loss of valuable information. Thus the *Quantitative Approach* is expected to be more accurate than the other algorithms discussed here.

- Suitability

Different algorithms suit different domains. The *AIS* and *SETM* are only effective in small databases [2]. As descendants of the *AIS* and *SETM*, the *Apriori* and *AprioriTid*

---

[1] It stands for Transaction Identifier, which is unique for each transaction in a dataset.

not only perform well in small databases, but also more efficiently in medium size databases [2]. The *Quantitative Approach* [7] is tailored to large databases.

Another important factor seldom mentioned in the literature is the memory usage, when different algorithms are applied to the same dataset [2, 7]. We investigate the scaling-up property of our approach on memory usage and discuss experimental results in Section 4.3.

3   Approach

We considered the following requirements to select a suitable algorithm.

- The algorithm should generate as many *interesting*[2] association rules as possible. All frequent itemsets must be identified based on the *minimum support threshold* specified by the end-users.
- The algorithm must have the ability to deal with quantitative and categorical values in addition to Boolean ones.
- The algorithm must perform well in medium or large databases.

Based on these requirements and the characteristics of the algorithms discussed in section 2, we decided to keep the advantage of *Quantitative Approach* in dealing with multiple data types and enhance this by using the *Boolean* algorithm to create the frequent itemsets.

However, a major shift on the initial selection and design of this approach arose. After investigation of the storage pattern involved in the *Boolean* algorithm, it was concluded that memory resources are wasted when the algorithm stores the quantitative and categorical values in the form of a truth table.

For example, suppose we have a table with three attributes that have a, b, and c possible values, respectively. As the *Boolean* algorithm stores the table content in the form of truth tables, $a \times b \times c$ truth tables are needed for all possible combinations of values for each attribute. This wastes memory resources especially as the datasets size grows. High performance achieved by the *Boolean* algorithm is offset by this deficiency. Consequently, the *Boolean* algorithm was abandoned in order to achieve better memory utilisation at the expense of processing speed.

Our final approach, therefore, can be decomposed into three parts (the first two parts are similar with the respective phase of the *Quantitative Approach*): a) Pre-processing the input dataset (such as the partition operation), b) creating frequent itemsets (the hash-based technique proposed by the *DHP* algorithm was introduced into this phase to reduce the number of the candidate k-itemsets examined), and c) generating association rules (this phase can be found in the *Apriori* algorithm). This approach was the most appropriate to satisfy all the requirements stated above. Nevertheless, the *Boolean* and *Quantitative Approaches* can be treated as a complementary alternative, in cases when the number of different attribute values is quite small.

---

[2] An association rule is *interesting* if it is unexpected and/or actionable [6].

3.1 Approach Decomposition

Let $I = \{i_1, i_2, \ldots, i_m\}$ be a set of attributes. Let P express the set of positive integers. Let I_v express the set $I \times P$. Let I_R express the set $\{<x,l,u> \in I \times P \times P \mid 1 \leq u,$ if x is quantitative; $l=u$, if x is categorical$\}$ [7].

As a result, a triple $<x,l,u> \in I_R$ represents an item which refers to either a quantitative attribute x with a value in the range $[l,u]$ or a categorical attribute x with a value l.

For any $X \subseteq I_R$, attributes (X) expresses the set $\{x|<x,l,u> \in X\}. \overset{\bullet}{X}$ is defined as a generalisation of X, if attributes (X)=attributes $(\overset{\bullet}{X})$ and $\forall x \in$ attributes(X)

$[<x,l,u> \in X \wedge <x,l',u'> \in \overset{\bullet}{X} \Rightarrow l' \leq l \leq u \leq u']$.

As mentioned above, this approach can be decomposed into three major phases: data pre-processing, creating frequent itemsets, and generating association rules.

3.1.1 Data Pre-processing

This can be divided into two tasks.

1)   Decide the number of partitions for each quantitative attribute.
     Assuming equi-depth partitioning [7], we get:

$$\text{Number of Intervals} = \frac{2 \times n}{\min \sup \times (K-1)} \qquad (1)$$

where K refers to partial completeness level which gives a handle on the amount of information lost by partitioning, *minsup* is the user supplied minimum support, and n means the number of quantitative attributes participating in the partition activity.

When K increases, there are fewer intervals (candidates for frequent itemsets) for the quantitative attributes. As a result, the number of frequent itemsets decreases. The number of rules based on those frequent itemsets decreases accordingly.

For categorical attributes, map the values to a set of consecutive integers. For quantitative attributes partitioned into intervals, the ranges are mapped to consecutive integers; otherwise the values of quantitative attributes are simply mapped to consecutive integers. In both cases, the order of ranges or values is preserved. The set of mapping rules, which are used throughout the rest of the algorithm, is then established.

2)   Calculate the support for each value or range of the attributes.
     In addition, adjacent values of quantitative attributes are combined as long as their support is less than the user-specified *maximum support*. All corresponding mapping rules are updated immediately to reflect the current state.

3.1.2 Creating Frequent Itemsets

This phase is similar to that of the *Apriori* algorithm except that the *interesting measure* is adopted at the end of the first database scan to prune all candidate 1-itemsets whose support is greater than $\frac{1}{R}$ in the partitioned quantitative attributes, where R refers to the interesting measure supplied by the user [7]. The frequent 1-itemsets are then identified as long as their support values are greater than, or equal to, the user-specified minimum support threshold and they pass through the examination of the interesting measure.

The subsequent *join-prune* procedure is composed of two steps: *Join* and *Subset Prune*. First, candidate itemsets are generated on the basis of the frequent itemsets found during the previous database scan. Let C_k represent the set of candidate k-itemsets and L_k the set of frequent k-itemsets. C_k is produced by joining any two different $L_{(k-1)}$ as long as their first lexicographically ordered (k-2) items are identical. Then, all candidate itemsets in C_k that have at least one (k-1)-subset not in L_{k-1} are removed. Next, a database scan calculates the support for each candidate itemset in C_k. Any candidate itemsets with support below the minimum support value are pruned, yielding the set of frequent itemsets L_k. Such set is stored into a *hash tree* in order to be used during the generation process of $C_{(k+1)}$. This procedure terminates when L_k becomes empty.

3.1.3 Generation of Association Rules

In this last phase, all strong association rules are created from frequent itemsets. The general idea can be expressed as follows:

First, generate all non-empty subsets for each frequent itemset l. Then, for every non-empty subset of l, the rule "$s \Rightarrow (l-s)$" holds if the ratio of

$$\frac{\sup port\_count(l)}{\sup port\_count(s)} \geq \frac{min\_conf}{K} \tag{2}$$

in which *min_conf* is the minimum confidence supplied by the user. The confidence for those rules can be easily obtained by accessing the hash tree established in earlier stages.

4 Experimental Results

To evaluate the effectiveness of our approach, we performed several experiments on a personal computer with CPU clock rate 800 MHz, 128MB of main memory, and running Microsoft Windows 2000. The performance of our approach was assessed in terms of parameter testing, scale-up testing, and memory usage testing. All the testing datasets used here were obtained from the UCI repository [9].

4.1 Parameter Testing

In order to assess the results of this approach in the case of some critical parameters varying, a public dataset, called *Abalone*, was used. It has eleven attributes: eight quantitative and three categorical. There are 5,000 records in this dataset with no missing values for any of the attributes.

Figure 1 shows the results obtained after performing twelve tests, in each of which the minimum support was set to 10%, maximum support to 20%, and minimum confidence to 30%. As expected in Section 3.1.1, the number of rules decreases as the partial completeness level increases.

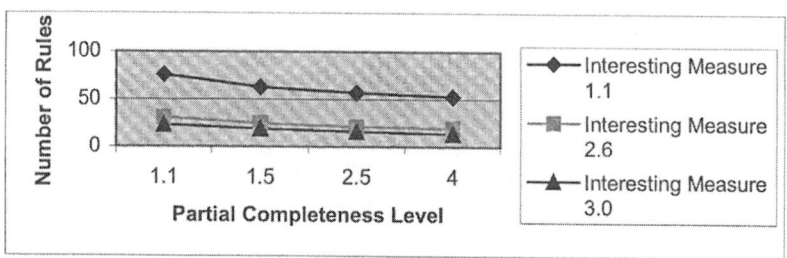

Fig. 1. Parameter Testing

4.2 Scale-up Testing

In order to evaluate the scale-up property of this approach, fifteen tests were performed using datasets with different sizes but the same structure as *Abalone* for comparison. In each of these tests, the partial completeness level was set to 1.1, interesting measure to 1.5, maximum support to 3%, and minimum confidence to 20%. Figure 2 shows the results obtained.

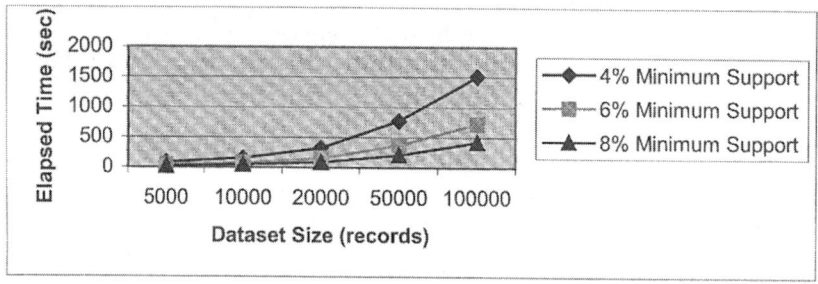

Fig. 2. Scale-up Testing

Increased minimum support prunes a number of frequent itemsets. Consequently, fewer rules are generated and the time spent on each phase decreases accordingly. Figure 2 confirms this by showing that the running time for this approach decreases as the minimum support increases. Figure 2 also shows that the whole processing time scales linearly as the size of the dataset increases from 5,000 records to 100,000 records by appending a number of different records to the same dataset.

4.3 Memory Usage Testing

Twelve tests used datasets with various sizes but the same structure as *Abalone*. That was achieved but reproducing randomly parts of this dataset. In each test, partial completeness was set to 1.1, maximum support to 8%, and interesting measure to 1.5. As shown in Table 1, similar results were achieved by varying the minimum support and confidence. Our approach uses memory when loading the dataset, saving the set of mapping rules, saving the frequent itemsets, and saving the association rules. As the dataset increases in size, the number of mapping rules, frequent itemsets, and association rules does not necessarily increase. When the size of the dataset becomes large enough, it will dominate the memory usage. Table 1 confirms this by showing that the total amount of memory usage does not double when the size of the dataset increases from 5.000 to 10.000 neither from 10.000 to 20.000 records.

Table 1. Memory Usage Testing (*Minsup* and *minconf* mean minimum support and confidence respectively)

Dataset Size	Total Memory Usage (MB)		
	Minsup=10% Minconf=10%	Minsup=10% Minconf=20%	Minsup=20% Minconf=20%
5.000	7.55	7.57	7.54
10.000	12.98	11.916	13.03
15.000	15.98	15.964	16.00
20.000	21.81	22.01	22.02

5 Conclusions and Further Work

We proposed an effective approach for mining association rules in large transactional databases. The main advantage of this approach over other prominent algorithms (such as *Apriori* and *AprioriTid*) is that it can deal with both Quantitative and Boolean Association Rule problems.

We also presented an alternative solution for the same problem: the enhancement of the Quantitative Approach using the part of the Boolean algorithm which creates frequent itemsets. This alternative was argued to be suitable for the cases when the number of potential different values for each attribute is small.

We conducted several experiments using datasets with different sizes. The results indicate that the performance of this approach can be regarded as satisfactory, as compared to the performance of the *Quantitative Approach*. We also concluded that the memory usage of this approach heavily depends on the size of the dataset.

A number of further improvements to the current approach are as follows:

- *Incorporation of alternative data structures*: The hash tree structure was chosen as part of our approach. However, it would be interesting to test other data structures used for mining association rules (for example, R^*-tree [3]).
- *Support for missing values*: We assumed that the input dataset has no missing values. However, this is not always the case in real life and missing values are also worth of investigation [8].

- *Improving the partitioning method*: the equi-depth partitioning method used performs well on evenly-distributed datasets. However, in the case of highly-skewed datasets, adjacent values whose behaviour would typically be similar might be split into different intervals. Consequently, for such cases we could use the *maximal appropriate abstraction* for partitioning numerical values into maximally extended intervals whose similarity is measured by the *interclass variance* between interval classes [4].
- *Incorporation of an incremental approach*: As our approach does not enable very large datasets to be loaded into the main memory as a whole, incorporation of incremental input could be beneficial.
- *Locating the breakpoint of the scale-up property*: Although the whole processing time of our approach scales linearly with the size of the dataset ranging between 5,000 and 100,000 records, it is worth finding the point when processing time starts to increase exponentially.

References

1.   Agrawal, R., Imielinski, T., and Swami, A., "Mining association rules between sets of items in large databases". *Proc. ACM SIGMOD Conf. on Management of Data*, 1993.
2.   Agrawal, R., and Srikant, R., "Fast Algorithm for Mining Association Rules in Large Databases", *Proc. Int'l Conf. on VLDB*, pp. 487–499, 1994.
3.   Beckmann, N., Kriegel, H.-P., Schneider, R., and Seeger, B., "The R*-tree: an efficient and robust access method for points and rectangles", *Proc. of ACM SIGMOD*, pp. 322–331, 1990.
4.   Narita M., Haraguchi M., and Okubo Y., "Data Abstractions for Numerical Attributes in Data Mining", *Proc. 3rd Int'l Conf. Intelligent Data Engineering Automated Learning*, 2002.
5.   Park, J. S., Chen, M. S., and Yu, P. S., "An Effective Hash Based Algorithm for Mining Association Rules", *Proc. of the ACM SIGMOD*, pp. 175–186, 1995.
6.   Silberschatz A. and Tuzhilin A., "On Subjective Measures of Interestingness in Knowledge Discovery", *Proc. Of the 1st Int'l Conf. on Knowledge Discovery and Data Mining*, 1995.
7.   Srikant, R., and Agrawal, R., "Mining Quantitative Association Rules in Large Relational Tables", *Proc. of the ACM SIGMOD Conf. on Management of Data*, 1996.
8.   Tjortjis C. and Keane J.A, "T3: an Improved Classification Algorithm for Data Mining", *Proc. 3rd Int'l Conf. Intelligent Data Engineering Automated Learning*, 2002
9.   UCI ML Repository, <http://www.ics.uci.edu/~mlearn/MLRepository.html>, last accessed: 15 September 2002.
10. Wur, S.Y., and Leu, Y., "An Effective Boolean Algorithm for Mining Association Rules in Large Databases", *Proc. 6th Int'l Conf. on Database Systems for Advanced Applications*, 1998.

Global B⁺ Tree Indexing in Parallel Database Systems

David Taniar [1] and J. Wenny Rahayu [2]

[1] Monash University, School of Business Systems, Vic 3800, Australia
David.Taniar@infotech.monash.edu.au
[2] La Trobe University, Department of Computer Science and Engineering, Australia
wenny@cs.latrobe.edu.au

Abstract. In this paper, we propose a global B⁺ indexing tree structure for parallel database systems, where the index tree is partitioned into multi processors with a possible overlap. We also present algorithms for maintenance of global B⁺ indexing trees (e.g. insertion and deletion of nodes), and describe operation algorithms (e.g. search and join) on tables that are indexed using global B⁺ indexing trees.

1   Introduction

Index is an important element in databases, and the existence of index is unavoidable. When an index has been built on a particular attribute, database operations (e.g. selection, join) on this attribute will become more efficient by utilizing the index. The aim of this paper is to study indexing schemes for parallel databases. In this paper, we propose a global B⁺ tree [1,2] for indexing in parallel database systems, called *Global Parallel Indexing (GPI)*.

2   Global Parallel Indexing (*GPI*) Schemes

Global Parallel Index (GPI) is where a complete index tree using B⁺ tree is maintained in parallel database systems. This means that each processor has a different part of the global index, and the overall structure of global index is still preserved. The ownership rule is that the processor owning a leaf node also owns all nodes from the root to that leaf. Consequently, the root node is replicated to all processors, and non-leaf nodes may be replicated to some processors. Additionally, if a leaf node has several keys belonging to different processors, this leaf node is also replicated to the processors owning the keys.

Global Parallel Indexing can be divided into three schemes: (*i*) a global index is built based on the same attribute as the table partitioning (we name it **GPI-1** for *Global Parallel Index* model 1), (*ii*) a global index is built on whatever records on each processing elements and assume that the table partitioning method is unknown (**GPI-2**), and (*iii*) a global index is built on a different attribute to the table partitioning (**GPI-3**).

2.1   GPI-1

As a running example, we use a table consisting of records of IDs and Names. The index is based on the ID attribute and is inserted based on the order of the records in the table. Assume the maximum number of node pointers from any non-leaf node is 4,

J. Liu et al. (Eds.): IDEAL 2003, LNCS 2690, pp. 701–708, 2003.

and the maximum number of data pointers from any leaf node is 3. An example of GPI-1 is shown in Figure 1. Assume the range partitioning rules used are that processor 1 holds IDs ranging from 1 to 30, processor 2 holds IDs ranging from 31 to 60, and the rest go to processor 3. Notice that the fifth leaf node (28, 33, 37) is replicated to processors 1 and 2 because key 28 belongs to processor 1, while keys 33 and 37 belong to processor 2. Also notice that some non-leaf nodes are replicated whereas others are not. It is also clear that the root node is fully replicated. The location of each leaf node is the same as where the actual record resides. For example, the left most leaf node (8,10,15) is located at processor 1 and so is the actual records of ID 8, 10, and 15.

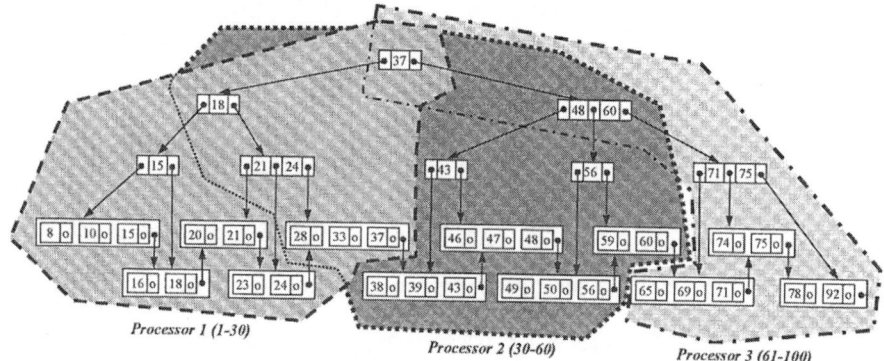

Fig. 1. Global Parallel Index model 1 (GPI-1)

2.2   GPI-2

In GPI-2 table partitioning can be unknown or not being used as an index partitioning attribute. For simplicity we assume the table is partitioned based on the Name attribute, which follows some partitioning function.

A global index based on GPI-2 is partitioned based on the location of the table fragment in each processor. For example, the first leaf node of (8, 10 and 15), key 8 is located at processor 1 (because employee Agnes is located in processor 1) whereas the other two keys are located at processor 2 (because employees Mary and Peter are located in processor 2). Consequently, this leaf node is replicated to both processors 1 and 2. As a result, more replication can be expected even at the leaf node level. Figure 2 gives an illustration of GPI-2. In this diagram, not all data pointers are shown in order to improve the readability of the diagram. We use numbers 1, 2 and 3 to correspond with the processor number.

2.3   GPI-3

GPI-3 is where the table is partitioned according to some rule on an attribute, which is different from the index partitioning attribute, or the partitioning rule for the table is not a range partitioning. Figure 3 shows an illustration of GPI-3. The global index tree for GPI-3 is the same as that for GPI-1, however the location of records may be different from location of index node. The node replication degree of GPI-3 may likely be less than in GPI-2.

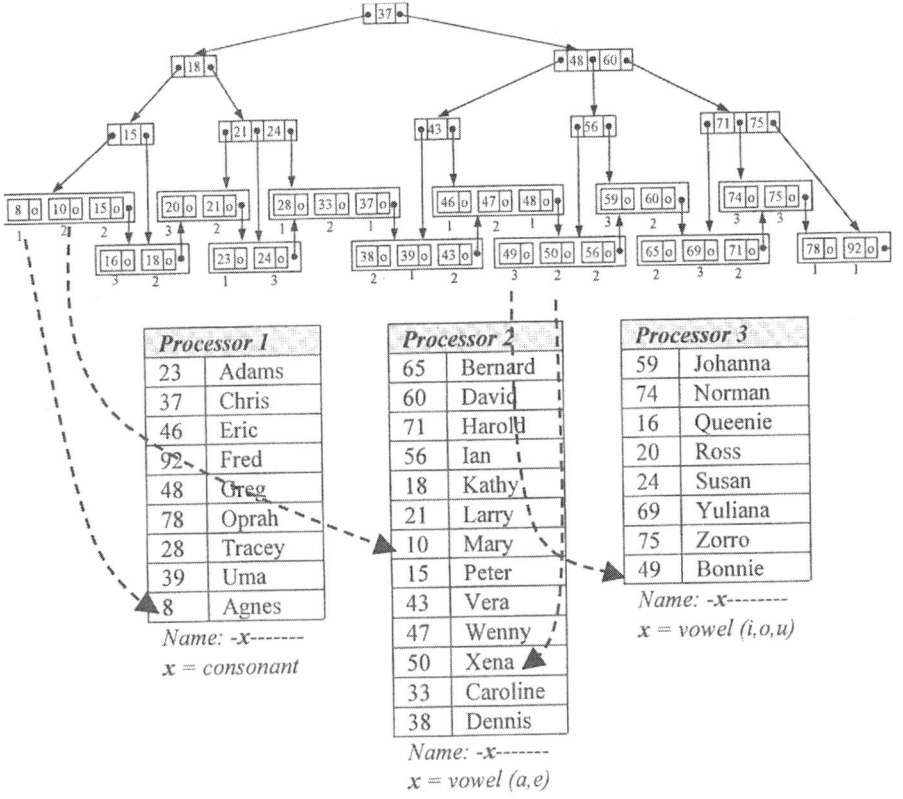

Fig. 2. Global Parallel Index model 2 (GPI-2)

3   Global Parallel Index Maintenance

Index maintenance includes insertion and deletion of nodes from the global parallel index tree. Insertion and deletion a key from an index tree are preceded by a searching the node where the desired key is located. Algorithm find_node illustrates a key searching on an index tree. The find_node basically starts from a root node and traces into the desired leaf node either at the local or neighbouring processor by recursively calling the find_node algorithm and passing a child tree to the same processor or following the trace to a different processor. Once the node is found an operation insert or delete can be performed.

After an operation is carried out to a designated leaf node, if the node is overflow (in the case of insertion) or underflow (in the case of deletion), a split or a merge operation must be done to the node. Splitting or merging nodes are performed in the same manner as splitting or merging nodes in single processor systems (i.e. single processor B⁺trees).

When splitting/merging non-leaf nodes, it is sometimes additional processors need to involve than initially used, since a node, especially non-leaf nodes may be replicated to several processors. For example, if we want to insert key 21 to a leaf-node, at first only processors 1 and 2 are involved. During the process, this new node is lifted up to non-leaf node, and subsequently processor 3 will need to involve. The problem is how processor 3 is notified to perform such operation whilst only processors 1 and 2 were involved in the beginning. This is solved by activating the find_node algorithm in each processor. Processor 1 will ultimately find the desired leaf node (18,23,37) in the local processor, and so will processor 2. Processor 3 however will pass the operation to processor 2 as the desired leaf node (18,23,37) located in processor 2 is referenced by the root node in processor 3. After the insertion operation (and the split operation) done to the leaf nodes (18,23,37) located at processors 1 and 2 is completed, the program control is passed back to the root node, due to the nature of a recursive algorithm. Since all processors were activated at start of the find node operation, each processor now can perform a split process (because of the overflow to the root node). Therefore, there is no special process whereby additional processor (in this case processor 3) needs to be invited or notified to involve in the splitting of the root node. Everything is a consequence of the recursive nature of the algorithm, which was initiated in each processor.

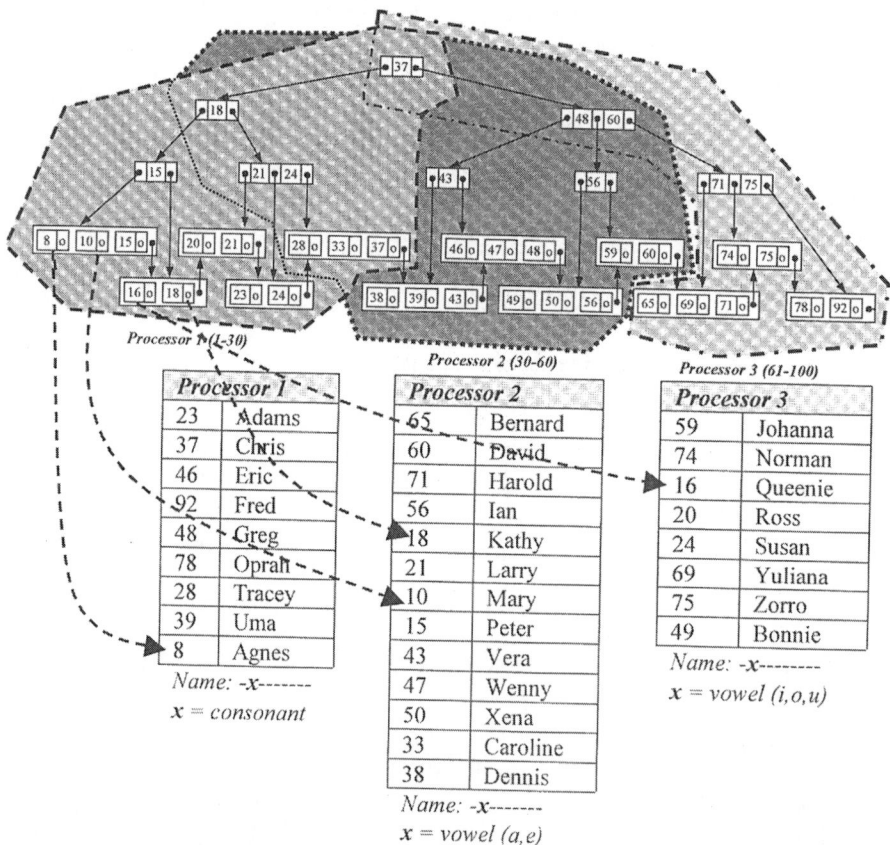

Fig. 3. Global Parallel Index model 3 (GPI-3)

```
Algorithm: Find a node initiated in each processor
1   find_node (tree, key, operation)
2       if (key is in the range of local node)
3           if (local node is leaf)
4               execute operation insert or delete on local node
5               if (node is overflow or underflow)
6                   perform split or merge on leaf
7           else
8               locate child tree
9               perform find_node (child, key, operation)
10              if (node is overflow or underflow)
11                  perform split or collapse on non-leaf
12      else
13          locate child tree in neighbour
14          perform find_node (neighbour, key, operation)
```

After the find_node algorithm (with an appropriate operation; insert or delete), it is sometimes necessary to restructure the index tree. The restructure algorithm is composed three algorithms. The main restructure algorithm calls the inorder algorithm where the traversal is done. The inorder traversal is a modified version of the traditional inorder traversal, because an index tree is not a binary tree.

For each visit to the node in the inorder algorithm, the proc_alloc algorithm is called, where the actual checking whether a right processor has been allocated to each node. The checking in the proc_alloc algorithm basically checks whether or not the current node should be located at the current processor. If not, the node is deleted (in case of a leaf node). If it is a non-leaf node, a careful checking must be done, because even when the range of (min,max) is not exactly within the range of current processor, it is not necessarily that the node should not be located in this processor, as its child nodes may have been correctly allocated to this processor. Only in the case where the current non-leaf node does not have child nodes, the non-leaf node should be deleted, otherwise a correct node pointer should be re-established.

```
Algorithm: Restructure in each local processor
1   restructure (tree)
2       perform inorder (tree)
```

```
Algorithm: Inorder traversal for non-binary trees (B+ trees)
1   inorder (tree)
2       if (local tree is not null)
3           for i=1 to number of node pointers
4               perform inorder (tree→node pointer i)
5               perform proc_alloc (node)
```

```
Algorithm: Processor allocation
1   proc_alloc (node)
2       if (node is leaf)
3           if ((min,max) is not within the range)
4               delete node
5       if (node is non-leaf)
6           if (all node pointers are either void or
7               point to non local nodes)
```

```
8               delete node
9          if (a node pointer is void)
10              re-establish node pointer to a neighbour
```

4   Query Operations Involving Global Parallel Index

4.1   Searching Operations

There are two searching types: (*i*) Exact Match Searching, and (*ii*) Range Searching. Range searching may exist in two forms: continuous or discrete range searching.

There are three important factors in *parallel exact match* search processing: processor involvement, index tree traversal, and record loading. If the indexing scheme of the indexed attribute is GPI-1 or GPI-3, we can direct the query into the specific processors. For GPI-2 scheme, since a global index is maintained, it becomes possible to traverse to any leaf node from basically anywhere. Therefore, only selected processors are used during the traversing of the index tree.

Searching is done through index tree traversal. The traversal starts from the root node and finishes either at a matched leaf node or no match is found. Depending on the indexing scheme used, there are two cases: traversal is isolated to local processor (GPI-1 or GPI-3), and traversal crosses from one processor to another (GPI-2).

Once a leaf node containing the desired data is found, the record pointed by the leaf node is loaded from disk. There are two cases: record loading is performed locally (GPI-1 or GPI-2) and record loading is performed remotely (GPI-3).

For *parallel continuous range* search, possibly more processors need to involve, as it needs to determine the lower and/or the upper bound of the range. For *parallel discrete range* search, each discrete value in the selection predicate is converted into multiple exact match predicates. Further processing follows the processing method for exact match search.

The algorithm for parallel index search processing is presented as follows.

```
Algorithm: Parallel-Search (Query Q and Index I)
Initialization - in the host processor:
1   Let Vexact be the search value in Qexact_match
2   Let Vlower and Vupper be the range lower and upper values
3   If Q is discrete range Then
4       Convert Qdiscrete into Qexact_match
5       Establish an array of Vexact []
Processor Allocation - in the host processor:
6   Let P be all available processors
7   Let PQ be processors to be used by query Q
8   Select PQ from P based on Q
Parallel Search - using processor PQ:
9   For each searched value V in query Q
10      Search value V in index tree I
11      If a match is found in index tree I Then
12          Put index entry into an array of index entry result
13          If Q is continuous range Then
14              Trace to the neighbouring leaf nodes
15              Put index entry into an array of entry result
```

```
Record Loading - using processor P_O:
16  For all entries in the array of index entry result
17      Trace the data pointer to the actual record r
18      If record r is located at a different processor Then
19          Load the pointed remote record r
20      Else
21          Load the pointed local record r
22      Put record r into query result
```

4.2 Join Operations

In join operations, one or both tables to be joined are indexed. If only one table is index (called *parallel one-index join*) and the other is not, the process can be done through a nested block index. If both tables are indexed based on the join attribute (called *parallel two-index join*), the process can be done by merging the two indexes.

Parallel One-Index Join processing, using a non-indexed table (say table *r*) and an indexed table (say table *s*), is a processing, whereby for each non-indexed record *r*, search for a matching index entry of table *s*. If a match is found, depending on the location of the record, record loading is performed. An algorithm for parallel one-index join processing is described as follows.

```
Algorithm: Parallel-One-Index-Join (table r and index s)
In each processor:
1   For each record r
2       Load record r and read join attribute value av
3       Search value av of record r in index tree of table s
4       If a match is found in index tree s Then
5           Trace the data pointer to the actual record s
6           If record s is located at a different processor Then
7               Load the pointed remote record s
8           Else
9               Load the pointed local record s
10          Concatenate records r and s into query results
```

Parallel Two-Index Join processing is where each processor performs an independent merging of the leaf nodes, and the final query result is the union of all temporary results gathered by each processor. Because there are three different models of GPI, it is possible that the two tables to be joined may have adopted different parallel indexing schemes, resulting in two different cases.

Case 1 is applicable to GPI-1 and GPI-3. We also assume that whichever parallel indexing scheme used, they must have adopted the same index partitioning function. Merging all leaf nodes in each processor can be performed by start scanning the left most leaf node and following the node pointer to the next leaf node on the right until all leaf nodes have been scanned. As merging involves leaf nodes only, non-leaf nodes contribute very little to the overall performance of the operation. An algorithm for parallel two-index join processing is presented as follows.

Algorithm: Parallel-Two-Index-Join Case 1 (indexes *r* and *s*)
In each processor:

```
1   Let starting and ending values of the range partitioning
    used are startval and endval
2   The starting node for comparison is the left most leaf node,
    and the ending node for comparison is the right most leaf
    node in each processor
3   Merge leaf nodes of indexes r and s from the respective
    starting leaf nodes
4   If matched Then
        Trace the data pointer to the base record.
        If the base record is located at a diff processor Then
            Load the pointed remote record
        Else
            Load the pointed local record
        Concatenate the two records into query results
5   Repeat steps 3-4 until one of the indexes' leaf nodes has
    run out, or contain an index entry ≥ endval
```

Case 2 is for GPI-2. If table *r* is indexed using GPI-2, and table *s* is indexed using GPI-1 or GPI-3, we ignore the index and assume table *r* is not indexed. Join processing then follows parallel one-index join processing. If table *r* and table *s* are both indexed using GPI-2, both indexes cannot be used, as described earlier. Hence, common parallel join processing without indexes (e.g. parallel hash join) is applied instead [6]. Therefore GPI-2 is useless to parallel two-index join query processing.

5   Conclusions

In this paper we have presented *Global Parallel Index* scheme (GPI), which is based on B+ tree structure designed especially for parallel database systems. We have described three models for GPI. We have described how maintenance can be done and some degree of complexity involved in splitting, merging, and index restructuring. We have described algorithms for parallel searching and parallel join on the indexed attribute.

References

1.   Bayer, R. and McCreight, E.M., "Organization and Maintenance of Large Ordered Indices", *Acta Informatica*, **1**(3):173–189, 1972.
2.   Comer, D., "The Ubiquitous B-Trees", *ACM Computing Surveys*, **11**(2):121–137, 1979.
3.   Rahayu, J.W. and Taniar, D., "Parallel Selection Query Processing Involving Index in Parallel Database Systems", *Proceedings of I-SPAN'02 Symposium*, IEEE CS, pp. 309–314, 2002.
4.   Taniar, D. and Rahayu, J.W., "A Taxonomy of Indexing Schemes for Parallel Database Systems", *Distributed and Parallel Databases*, **12**(1):73–106, 2002.
5.   Taniar, D. and Rahayu, J.W., "Parallel Join Query Algorithms Involving Index", *Parallel and Distributed Computing Applications and Technologies*, pp. 133–140, 2000.
6.   Wolf J. L., Dias D. M., and P. S. Yu, "A parallel sort-merge join algorithm for managing data skew", *IEEE Transactions On Parallel And Distributed Systems*, 4(1), 1993.

Efficient Execution of Parallel Aggregate Data Cube Queries in Data Warehouse Environments

Rebecca Boon-Noi Tan[1], David Taniar [2], and Guojun Lu[1]

[1] Gippsland School of Computing & IT, Monash University, Victoria 3842, Australia
{Rebecca.Tan, Guojun.Lu}@infotech.monash.edu.au
[2] School of Business Systems, Monash University, Victoria 3800, Australia
David.Taniar@infotech.monash.edu.au

Abstract. With the increasing emphasis on data warehouse systems, the efficiency of complex analytical queries in such systems has become an important issue. Such queries posed challenging performance problems that initiated the use of parallel database systems and parallel algorithms in data warehouse environments. Many of these have been proposed in recent years but a review of the literature to our knowledge has not revealed any literature describing parallel methods with detailed cost models for aggregate data cube queries in a data warehouse environment. This paper presents a detailed cost model based on parallel methods for aggregate data cube queries. The detailed cost model enables us to study the behaviour and evaluate the performance of the three methods and thus identify the efficient parallel methods for aggregate data cube queries.

1 Introduction

Data warehousing has gained prominence in today's dynamic business environment. Organisations recognise the value of corporate data as an important asset to achieve a competitive edge. With corporate data increasing exponentially, queries and analyses are becoming more complex. Hence there is a need to improve the query performance and to provide faster response times. There has been a great deal of interest in improving the query performance in the research community recently [1, 2, & 3]. However, the effective use of data warehouses should ensure acceptable response times for complex analytical queries. Such queries pose challenging performance problems that would require the use of parallel database system and also parallel algorithms [6].

Various parallel database systems as well as parallel algorithms for the improving the query performance and providing faster response times have been proposed in recent years [4, 5, & 6]. [4] proposed a parallel physical design for the data warehouse. [5] presented the design and implementation of a scalable parallel system for multidimensional analysis. In [6], the authors have proposed a dynamic query scheduling strategy that simultaneously considers both processors and disks in parallel data warehouses. However, to our knowledge, there is nothing to date in the literature describing parallel methods with detailed cost model for aggregate data cube queries in a data warehouse environment. This paper presents a detailed cost model

J. Liu et al. (Eds.): IDEAL 2003, LNCS 2690, pp. 709–716, 2003.

based on parallel methods for aggregate data cube queries. This model enables us to study the behaviour of the methods and identify the efficient parallel methods for aggregate data cube queries in a data warehouse environment.

2 Aggregate Data Cube Query: An Example

The following query to give a simple illustration of multi-join expansion aggregate data cube queries. The Query is to "retrieve product number by their city location where the sales amount is less than or equal to 10,000 and the count of the related cities less than or equal to 3". The Query will be used as a theme example throughout this paper.

QUERY:
    SELECT S.P#, S.U_City,
            (SELECT (COUNT (S.U_City) <= 3) FROM Sales S),
            (SELECT (SUM (S.amount) <= 10,000) FROM Sales S)
    FROM Sales S, Product P, Location L
    WHERE   P.P# = S.P#,
            L.L# = S.L#
    CUBE-BY S.P#, S.U_City

3 Algorithms and Cost Models for the Three Parallel Methods

The notations used by the cost models are presented in Table 1.

Table 1. Cost Notations

Symbol	Description	Symbol	Description
System and Data Parameters		*Time Unit Cost*	
N	Number of processors	IO	Effective time to read a page from disk
$Mips$	MIPS of the processor	t_r	Time to read a record
F	Fact Table size	t_w	Time to write a record
$|F|$	Number of records in table F	t_h	Time to compute hash value
D_1 & D_2	Dimensional Table size	t_a	Time to add a record to current aggregate value
$|D_1|$ & $|D_2|$	No. of records in table D_1 & D_2	t_d	Time to compute destination
P	Page size	t_j	Time to compare a record with a hash table entry
H	Maximum hash table entries		
Query Parameters		*Communication Cost*	
π_F, π_{D1} & π_{D2}	Projectivity ratio of the aggregation	m_p	Message protocol cost per page
σ_p	Selectivity ratio of local aggregate in a processor	m_l	Message latency for one page
σ_j	Join selectivity ratio		

3.1   Multi-join Partition Method with Cost Model

The Multi-join Partition method has two phases: the *distribution* phase and the *cube-by with multi-join* phase. Using the Query, the three tables to be joined are Sales, Product and Location based on attributes *P#* and *L#*, and the cube-by will be based on table Sales. For simplicity of notation, the table which forms the basis for cube-by is called the fact table F (e.g. table Sales), and the other tables are called D_1 and D_2 (e.g. tables Product and Location).

In the distribution phase, raw records from three tables are distributed based on the join/cube-by attributes according to two data partitioning functions. Once the distribution is completed, each processor will have records within specific group range identified by the cube-by/join attribute. Subsequently, the cube-by with multi-join phase calculates the aggregate values on each group via a sort or a hash function. After table F is grouped in each processor, it is joined with tables D_1 and D_2 in the same processor. After joining, each processor will have a local query result. The final query result is a union of all sub-results produced by each processor.

The cost components in the *distribution* phase consists of the sum of scan cost, select data cost, finding destination cost, and data transfer cost. There are presented as follows.

- *Scan cost* is the cost for loading data from local disk in each processor.

$$((F_i / P) \times IO) + ((D_{1i} / P) \times IO) + ((D_{2i} / P) \times IO). \tag{1}$$

- *Select cost* is the cost to retrieve the record from the data page.

$$(|Fi| \times (t_r + t_w)) + (|D_{1i}| \times (t_r + t_w)) + (|D_{2i}| \times (t_r + t_w)). \tag{2}$$

- *Determine destination* cost is the cost for calculating the destination of each record to be distributed from the processor in phase one to phase two.

$$(|F_i| \times t_d) + (|D_{1i}| \times t_d) + (|D_{2i}| \times t_d). \tag{3}$$

- *Data transfer cost* is the cost for sending records to other processors is given by the number of pages to be sent multiplied by the message unit cost.

$$((\pi_F \times F_i / P) \times (m_p + m_l)) + ((\pi_{D1} \times D_{1i} / P) \times (m_p + m_l)) + ((\pi_{D2} \times D_{2i} / P) \times \tag{4}$$
$$(m_p + m_l)).$$

- *Receiving records cost* from processors in the first phase is calculated by number of projected values of the three tables multiplied by the message unit cost.

$$((\pi_F \times F_i / P) \times m_p) + ((\pi_{D1} \times D_{1i} / P) \times m_p) + ((\pi_{D2} \times D_{2i} / P) \times m_p). \tag{5}$$

- *Aggregation and Multi-Join* costs involve reading, hashing, computing the cumulative value, and probing.

$$(|F_i| \times (t_r + t_h + t_a)) + (|D_{1i}| \times (t_r + t_h + t_j)) + (|D_{2i}| \times (t_r + t_h + t_j)). \tag{6}$$

- *Read/Write of overflow buckets* cost relates to the I/O costs associating with the limiting the main-memory to accommodate the entire hash table.

$$\left(1 - \min \left(\frac{H}{\sigma_F \times |F_i|}, 1 \right) \right) \times \left(\pi_F \times \frac{F_i}{P} \times 2 \times IO \right). \tag{7}$$

The overflow buckets associated with table D_1 are very similar. Assuming that the percentage of records overflown is the same as that of for table F, the overflow buckets for table D_1 becomes:

$$\left(1 - \min \left(\frac{H}{\sigma_F \times |F_i|}, 1 \right) \right) \times \left(\pi_{D1} \times \frac{D_{1i}}{P} \times 2 \times IO \right). \tag{8}$$

The term on left-hand side defines the percentage of overflow, while the term on right-hand side is the I/O cost associated with rewriting and reloading table D_1.

Assuming that the percentage of records overflown is the same as that of for tables F and D_1, the overflow buckets for table D_2 becomes:

$$\left(1 - \min \left(\frac{H}{\sigma_F \times |F_i|}, 1 \right) \right) \times \left(\pi_{D2} \times \frac{D_{2i}}{P} \times 2 \times IO \right). \tag{9}$$

- *Generate final result* cost is the number of selected records multiplied by the writing unit cost.

$$|F_i| \times \sigma_F \times |D_{1i}| \times \sigma_j \times |D_{2i}| \times \sigma_j \times t_w. \tag{10}$$

- *Storage cost* for storing final result is the number of pages to store the final aggregate values multiplied by the disk unit cost, which is:

$$(\pi_F \times F_i \times \sigma_F \times \pi_{D1} \times D_{1i} \times \sigma_j \times \pi_{D2} \times D_{2i} \times \sigma_j / P) \times IO. \tag{11}$$

3.2   Expansion Partition Method with Cost Model

The Expansion Partition Method consists of three phases: *local clustering* phase, *distribution* phase, and *final-amass* phase which performs the cube-by operation first before distribution.

In the local clustering phase, each processor performs its cube-by operation and calculates its local aggregate values on records in table F. In the distribution phase, the results of local aggregates from each processor, together with records of tables D_1 and D_2, are distributed to all processors according to the two partitioning function. The two partitioning function are based on the join/cube-by attributes, which in this case is attribute $P\#$ of the tables Product and Sales and also attribute $L\#$ of the tables Location and Sales. In the final-amass phase, two operations are carried out - final aggregate or grouping of F, and join with D_1 and D_2.

The cost components in the *local clustering* phase consist of scan cost, select data page cost, local aggregation cost, and generating local aggregation writing cost.

- *Scan cost* is associated with three tables F, D_1 and D_2, which is the same as that of the Multi-join partition method, and therefore **equation (1)** presented in the previous section can be used.

- *Select cost* is also associated with three tables F, D_1 and D_2, and it is identical to **equation (2)** in the Multi-join partition method.
- *Local aggregation* cost covers the reading, hashing, and accumulating aggregate values costs, which are as follows.

$$|F_i| \times (t_r + t_h + t_a). \tag{12}$$

- *Read/Write of overflow buckets* cost is similar to equation (7) in the Multi-join Partition method. The main difference is that the cube-by selectivity factor used here is now identified by σ_{F1} instead of σ_F.

$$\left(1 - \min\left(\frac{H}{\sigma_{F1} \times |F_i|}, 1\right)\right) \times \left(\pi_F \times \frac{F_i}{P} \times 2 \times IO\right). \tag{13}$$

- Generate results cost is:

$$|F_i| \times \sigma_{F1} \times t_w. \tag{14}$$

Cost components for the *distribution* phase are composed of finding destination costs, actual data transfer, and receiving costs.

- *Determine destination* cost is associated with three tables F, D_1 and D_2, since all the tables are distributed.

$$(|F_i| \times \sigma_{F1} \times t_d) + (|D_{1i}| \times t_d) + (|D_{2i}| \times t_d). \tag{15}$$

- *Data transfer cost* is the cost for sending local aggregate results and fragment of tables D_1 and D_2, from each processor.

$$((\pi_F \times F_i \times \sigma_{F1}/P) \times (m_p + m_l)) + ((\pi_{D1} \times D_{1i}/P) \times (m_p + m_l)) + ((\pi_{D2} \times D_{2i}/P) \times \quad (16) \\ (m_p + m_l)).$$

- *Receive records cost* is similar to the data transfer cost, but without the message latency overhead.

$$((\pi_F \times F_i \times \sigma_{F1}/P) \times m_p) + ((\pi_{D1} \times D_{1i}/P) \times m_p) + ((\pi_{D2} \times D_{2i}/P) \times m_p). \tag{17}$$

Cost components for the *final-amass* phase are as follows.

- *Aggregation and Multi-Join* costs involving reading, hashing, computing the cumulative value, and probing. The costs are as follows:

$$(|F_i| \times \sigma_{F1} \times (t_r + t_h + t_a)) + (|D_{1i}| \times (t_r + t_h + t_j)) + (|D_{2i}| \times (t_r + t_h + t_j)). \tag{18}$$

- *Read/Write of overflow buckets* cost is similar to equations (7), (8) and (9) described earlier.

$$\left(1 - \min\left(\frac{H}{\sigma_{F2} \times |F_i|}, 1\right)\right) \times \left(\pi_F \times \sigma_{F1} \times \frac{F_i}{P} \times 2 \times IO\right) + \left(1 - \min\left(\frac{H}{\sigma_{F2} \times |F_i|}, 1\right)\right) \times \left(\pi_{D1} \times \frac{D_{1i}}{P} \times 2 \times IO\right) \tag{19}$$

$$+ \left(1 - \min\left(\frac{H}{\sigma_{F2} \times |F_i|}, 1\right)\right) \times \left(\pi_{D2} \times \frac{D_{2i}}{P} \times 2 \times IO\right).$$

- *Generate final results* cost is the number of selected records multiplied by the writing unit cost, which is similar to **equation (10)**.
- *Storage cost* for storing the final result is the number of pages to store the final aggregate values multiplied by the disk unit cost, which is identical to **equation (11)**.

3.3   Early Expansion Partition with Replication Method with Cost Model

The Early Expansion Partition with Replication method is similar to the Expansion Partition method, as the cube-by processing has to be done before the distribution phase. However, the difference lies in the keyword "*Replication*" in this method as opposed to "*Partition*". The Early Expansion Partition with Replication Method, which also is comprised of three phases, works as follows.

The cost component of the second phase shows a major difference, since local aggregate results are now replicated. This cost component is purely associated with table F, as tables D_1 and D_2 are not at all moved from where they are stored.

- *Data transfer cost* is the cost for sending the local aggregate results of each processor to all processors.

$$((\pi_F \times F_i \times \sigma_{F1} \times (N\text{-}1) / P) \times (m_p + m_l)). \tag{20}$$

In the above equation, F_i is reduced by two factors, namely π_F and σ_{F1}. However, the replication cost is increased by the number of processors N-1.

- *Receive records cost* is as follows.

$$((\pi_F \times F_i \times \sigma_{F1} \times (N\text{-}1) / P) \times m_p). \tag{21}$$

The sum of the above two equations gives the total cost for phase two of the Early Expansion Partition with Replication method.

The third phase, the final-amass phase, is basically similar to that of the "Partition" method Cost components for the third phase (*final-amass* phase) are as follows.

- Aggregation and Multi-Join costs are as follows:

$$(|F| \times \sigma_{F1} \times (t_r + t_h + t_a)) + (|D_{1i}| \times (t_r + t_h + t_j)) + (|D_{2i}| \times (t_r + t_h + t_j)). \tag{22}$$

- *Read/Write of overflow buckets* cost is very similar to equation (19) except that F not F_i is used because of the replication.

$$\left(1-\min\left(\frac{H}{\sigma_{F2} \times |F|},1\right)\right) \times \left(\pi_F \times \sigma_{F1} \times \frac{F}{P} \times 2 \times IO\right) + \left(1-\min\left(\frac{H}{\sigma_{F2} \times |F|},1\right)\right) \times \left(\pi_{D1} \times \frac{D_{1i}}{P} \times 2 \times IO\right) \tag{23}$$

$$+ \left(1-\min\left(\frac{H}{\sigma_{F2} \times |F|},1\right)\right) \times \left(\pi_{D2} \times \frac{D_{2i}}{P} \times 2 \times IO\right).$$

The *generate final results* cost and *storage* cost are the same as those for the Expansion Partition method, which are also identical to those of the Multi-join Partition method. Hence, **equations (10)** and **(11)** can be used.

4   Performance Evaluation

Parameters. The system and data parameters consisted of 64 processors with 450 Mips each. The fact table F size (Sales) was 10GB with 1x10E8 records, the dimension table D_1 size (Product) was 30MB with 3x10E4 records, and the dimension table D_2 size (Location) is 2.5KB with 25 records. The page size was taken 4KB with a maximum hash table entry of 10,000 entries. Within the Query parameters, the projectivity ratio of the aggregation was 0.15; the join selectivity ratio was 2.5E-07.

Within the time costs parameters, the effective time to read a page from disk was 3.5 *ms*, while the time to read, write and add a record was 300/*Mips*, 100/*Mips*, and 300/*Mips* respectively. The time to compute a hash value or destination were 400/*Mips* and 10/*Mips* respectively while the time to compare a record with a hash table entry was 100/*Mips*. For the communication cost parameters, the message protocol cost per page was 100/*Mips* while the message latency for each page was 1.3 *ms*.

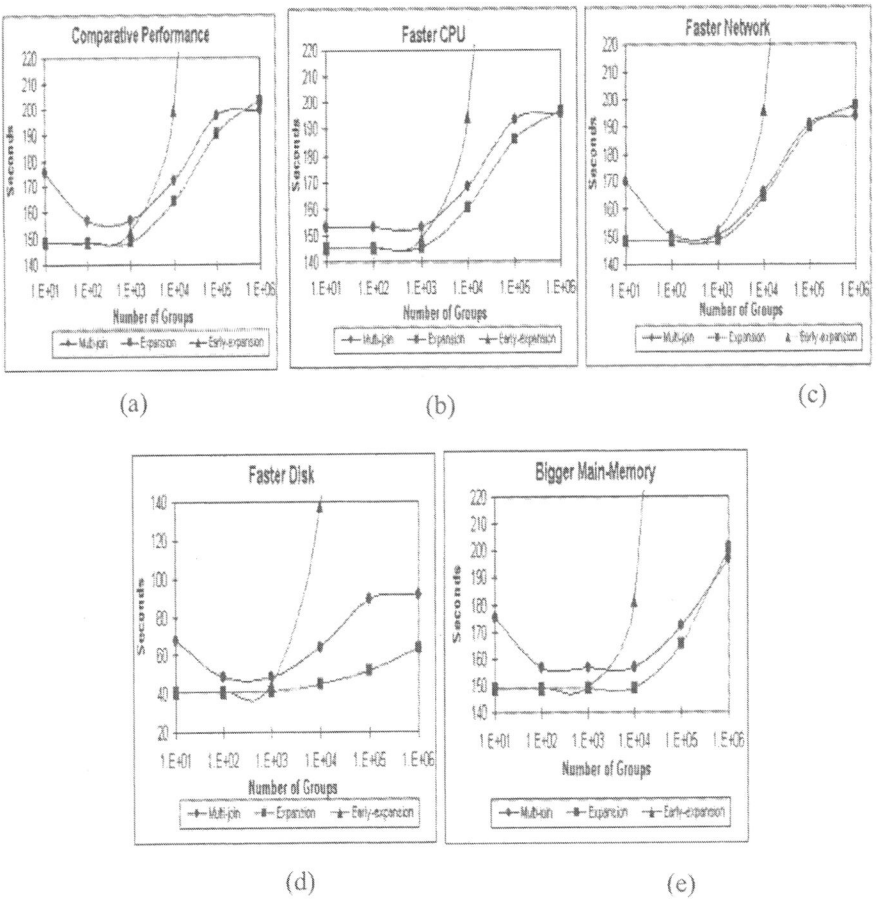

(a)   (b)   (c)

(d)   (e)

Fig. 1. Comparative Performance

Simulation result. The graphs in Figure 1 show the comparative performance between the three parallel methods by varied the Cube-By selectivity ratio.

Figures 1(a) to 1(e) were derived from the cost model of the sum of the Equations (1) to (23) (See Section 3). From the simulation result, we observed that the major portion of the data cost derived from the sum of the Equations 12, 13 and 14 of the Expansion Partition method did not have much impact on the overall performance when the number of groups is less than 1000 (see Figure 1). However the performance starts to decline when the number of groups increased beyond 1000. This conformed to the logic, that when number of groups produced increases, the data volume of data in second and third phases also increases.

As a variation was applied, for example the variation for a faster disk, the overall performance of all the methods improved significantly. This applied where the number of groups ranged from 0 to 1000. However, when the number of groups was greater than 1000, there was a significant decline of performance in the Early Expansion Partition with Replication method as compared to the other two methods. In general, the Expansion Partition method outperformed the others.

5 Concluding Remarks

In this paper, we have presented a detailed cost model based on the parallel methods for the aggregate data cube query. The detailed cost model enables us to study the behaviour of the methods and identify the efficient parallel methods for aggregate data cube queries in data warehouse environments. Based on the cost models, the performance evaluation results show that in most cases the Expansion Partition method offers better performance than the others. Our future work in this field will include implementation and testing of the methods.

References

1. Acharya S., Gibbons P.B., Poosala V. and Ramaswarmy S., "Join Synopses for Approximate Query Answering", *Proceedings of ACM SIGMOD International Conference on Management of Data*, pp.275–286, 1999.
2. Chan C.Y. and Ioannidis Y.E., "Hierarchical Cubes for Range_Sum Queries", *Proceedings of International Conference on VLDB*, Edinburgh, Scotland, pp. 675–686, September 1999
3. Chaudhuri S., Das G., Datar M., Motwani R. and Narasayya V., "Overcoming Limitations of Sampling for Aggregation Queries". *Proceedings of 17th International Conference on Data Engineering*, Heidelberg, Germany 2001
4. Datta A. and Moon B., "A case for parallelism in data warehousing and OLAP", *Proceedings of 9th International Workshop on Database Systems Applications*, 1998
5. Goil, S.; Choudhary A., "Design and implementation of a scalable parallel system for multidimensional analysis and OLAP", *13th International and 10th Symposium on Parallel and Distributed Processing, IPPS/SPDP Proceedings*, pp. 576–581, 1999
6. Martens H., Rahm E., and Stohr T, "Dynamic Query Scheduling in Parallel Data Warehouses", *Proceedings of 8th International conference on Euro-Par*, Paderborn, Germany, pp. 321–331, 2002.

An Optimal Approach to Mining Boolean Functions from Noisy Data

Murlikrishna Viswanathan[1] and Chris Wallace[2]

[1] Department of Computer Science and Software Engineering
University of Melbourne VIC 3010
murli@cs.mu.oz.au
[2] School of Computer Science and Software Engineering
Monash University VIC 3080
csw@csse.monash.edu.au

Abstract. Data Mining of binary sequences has been an area of profound research and is often used as a proof of concept in various aspects of computational learning theory. The inference task in this paper, a specialized version of the segmentation problem, is the estimation of a predefined Boolean function on the real interval $[0, 1]$ from a noisy random sample. The framework for this problem was introduced by Kearns et al. (1997) in an earlier empirical evaluation of model selection methods. This paper presents an optimal approach to mining for Boolean functions from noisy data samples based on the Minimum Message Length (MML) principle. The MML method is shown to be optimal in comparison to well-known model selection methods based on Guaranteed Risk Minimization, Minimum Description Length (MDL) Principle and Cross Validation after a thorough empirical evaluation with varying levels of noisy data.

1 Introduction

The segmentation problem occurs when there is a need to partition some data into distinct homogeneous regions. The specialized binary sequence problem framework considered in this paper was introduced by Kearns et al. [1]. An unknown Boolean function $f(x)$ is defined on the real interval $0 < x < 1$. The interval is partitioned into $(k + 1)$ sub-intervals by k "cut points" $\{c_j : j = 1..k\}$ which are uniformly and randomly distributed in $[0,1]$ and indexed so that $c_j < c_{j+1}$, $(j = 1..k - 1)$. The function $f(x)$ is defined to be 0 in even-numbered sub-intervals, and 1 in odd-numbered sub-intervals, the sub-intervals being numbered from 0 to k so that cut-point c_j separates sub-intervals $j - 1$ and j. Data is generated from this model at N sample points $\{x_i : i = 1..N\}$. The Boolean datum y_i generated at x_i differs from $f(x_i)$ with probability $p < (1/2)$. Thus the probability that $y_i = 1$ alternates between p and $(1 - p)$, depending on whether x_i lies in an even or odd sub-interval. The inference task is to infer an approximation to the function $f(x)$ from the data $\{x_i, y_i : i = 1..N\}$. That is, we wish to infer the number and position of the cutpoints (and, incidentally, the unknown "noise" rate, p).

J. Liu et al. (Eds.): IDEAL 2003, LNCS 2690, pp. 717–724, 2003.

The framework described above was originally employed by Kearns et al. [1] in their evaluation of different model selection methods. These selection methods included the two penalty-based methods, Vapnik's Guaranteed Risk Minimization (GRM) [5] and a version (KMDL) [1] of Rissanen's Minimum Description Length (MDL) Principle [4], and cross validation (hold out) [8]. Borrowing the framework from [1] this papers develops methods for model selection based on the Minimum Message Length (MML) principle. We improvize an approximation in KMDL, obtaining a slightly improved method which we term "CMDL", although it still employs a sub-optimal encoding scheme. Consistent with results from [1], we find both KMDL and CMDL to perform relatively poorly unless the sample is large (with CMDL slightly superior). Finally, we develop a more optimal method using the theoretical framework of the Minimum Message Length principle [2,3], with which we are more familiar. The sub-optimal behaviour of KMDL is again observed, but the MML method works well, and compares well with the cross-validation (CV) method which we implement in the same form as in [1].

2   Definitions

This section presents standard definitions for all the terms used in this paper.

1. S : training set, $\langle x_i, y_i \rangle$.
2. N : sample size.
3. p : true probability (noise rate).
4. $\hat{p}$: estimated probability.
5. k : number of cuts.
6. d : number of alternations of label in S ($d = k + 1$).
7. $f(x)$: true Boolean function from which S is generated.
8. $h(x)$: learning algorithm's estimate of $f(x)$ from S.
9. $H(x)$: binary entropy function given by $-(x \log x + (1 - x) \log(1 - x))$

We also define some standard error measures employed in the paper:

- $\epsilon(h)$ represents the generalization error of a hypothesis $h(x)$ with respect to the target function $f(x)$. $\epsilon(h) = KL(f(x) \parallel h(x))$, which is the Kullback-Leibler distance from $f(x)$ to $h(x)$.
- $\hat{\epsilon}(h)$ denotes the training error of h on sample S.
  $\hat{\epsilon}(h) = |\langle x_i, y_i \rangle \in S : h(x_i) \neq f(x_i)| / n$.

3   The Model Selection Problem

In order to test the various methods two main scenarios may be considered. The first scenario, tested in [1], is to chose a function $f(x)$ with 100 intervals each of length 0.01 (99 equally-spaced cutpoints). This function is the easiest to learn among all functions with 99 cuts. A randomly spaced set of cuts would increase the chance that some subintervals would contain few (or no) sample points, making them much harder to detect. In this study we consider the harder case and thus employ functions generating randomly-placed cuts. Note that none of the learning methods assume approximate or exact equality of subinterval lengths: they all assume the locations of the cuts to be random.

A single test problem is generated from $f(x)$ by fixing a sample size N and a noise probability, p. Then, N x-values are selected from the uniform distribution in $(0,1)$, and for each x_i, a Boolean datum y_i is generated as $f(x_i)$ XOR $ran(p)$, where $ran(p)$ is a random noise bit with probability p of being 1. Many replications of a problem with given N and p are generated by making different random selections of the sample points and noise bits. For a given sample S, one of the primary learning problems is the selection of a *model class*, where a class F_k is the set of all alternating functions with k cuts. That is, the essence is the estimation or selection of k. Within a class F_k, a simple dynamic programming algorithm suffices to find the model function $h'_k(x)$ with maximum likelihood, i.e. with minimum training error $\hat{\epsilon}(h'_k)$. Of course, the locations of the cutpoints of $h'_k(x)$ are determined only to within the interval between two adjacent sample points. In this work, we take the cutpoint of $h'_k(x)$ which lies between x_i and x_{i+1} to be midway between the sample points.

The learning task thus reduces to selecting a model from the set of model functions $\{h'_k(x); \ k = 1..k_{max}\}$, where k_{max} is the largest number of cuts resulting in any reduction in training error. This set of models is then given to the information-theoretic model selection methods (KMDL, CMDL and MML) for their preference. For the cross-validation method the sample S was divided randomly into a 90% fitting set and a 10% validation set. A set of maximum-likelihood models $\{h_k(x); \ k = 1..k^c_{max}\}$ was developed from the fitting sample, and the cross-validation method selected from that set the model with the lowest error on the validation sample. It is not claimed that this represents an optimal cross-validation, but it was chosen as a simple and representative application of the method. The generalization error for the model selected by each method was computed with respect to the problem target function $f(x)$.

4   The "KMDL" Method

We replicated the MDL encoding scheme employed by Kearns et al. in their paper. To distinguish from a modified method we consider later, we term it KMDL. Let h be a function with exactly k cut points. Description of $h(\cdot)$ first requires specification of its number k of cutpoints. The length of this description is neglected in KMDL. Given k, we can sufficiently describe $h(\cdot)$ by specifying the k sample points immediately before which $h(\cdot)$ changes value. Note that it makes sense for $h(\cdot)$ to have a cutpoint before the first sample point x_1, but not after the last, x_N. Thus, there are N places where $h(\cdot)$ may have cuts. Assuming, as in [1], that the cuts are equally likely to occur in any of these places, specifying their locations takes $\log_2 \binom{N}{k}$ bits. Given $h(\cdot)$, the training samples can simply be encoded by correcting the mistakes implied by $h(\cdot)$. Suppose $h(x)$ differs from $y(x)$ at m sample points, where $m = N \times \hat{\epsilon}(h)$. (KMDL neglects the cost of describing m.) Given m, the identity of the m sample points where y_i differs from $h(x_i)$ can be specified with $\log_2 \binom{N}{m}$ bits. Thus, KMDL arrives at a total description length of

$$\log_2 \left\{ \binom{N}{k} \times \binom{N}{m} \right\} \text{ bits}$$

In [1], expressions such as $\log_2 \binom{N}{m}$ are approximated by $N \times H(m/N)$ where $H()$ is the binary entropy function. Dividing by N leads to the KMDL choice of k:

$$k = argmin_k \{ H(k/N) + H(\hat{\epsilon}(h'_k)) \} \tag{1}$$

5   The "CMDL" Method

We attempt a modest improvement to the KMDL method, which we term CMDL. An important point that we note in developing our MDL approach is that as we are only considering the maximum-likelihood model in each class there cannot be any misses adjacent to a cutpoint. Therefore, we can safely assume that the number of cuts $k \leq N - 2m$. The encoding scheme includes the lengths needed for the description of k and m. The training error count m can certainly not exceed $N/2$, so the cost of encoding m is $N/2$ bits. The cost of specifying a cutpoint from $N - 2m$ potential cuts is $\log(N - 2m)$ bits. We also replace the binary entropy approximation in KMDL by the accurate log-combinations expression. Thus, CMDL selects

$$k = argmin_k \left\{ \log(N - 2m) + \log(N/2) + \log \binom{N - 2m}{k} + \log \binom{N}{m} \right\} \tag{2}$$

6   MML Based Model Selection

The Minimum Message Length (MML) [2,3,7] principle for inductive inference was pioneered by Wallace and Boulton in the 1960's. Founded on fundamental ideas from information theory, coding theory, and Bayesian learning, the MML principle suggests that the best theory or explanation (in some formal language) for a body of data is the one that best compresses a two-part encoding of the theory and data (assuming the theory is true) under an optimal encoding scheme. In essence, methods based on the MML principle seek to minimize a message length defined by the joint encoding of the model and data given the model. It will be more convenient now to measure lengths in nits rather than bits (1 nit $= \log_2 e$ bits) so now we switch to natural logs.

We start the message by stating the estimated k, with length $\log(N/2)$. (Henceforth, we use k and p to denote the estimated model quantities.) Next, the message states p, the estimated noise rate. This value determines that y-values agreeing with $h(x)$ will be encoded with length $-\log(1 - p)$ each, and those disagreeing, with length $-\log p$.

The MML principle [3,7] offers the following general expression for computing the MML message length for parameter vector $\boldsymbol{\theta}$ and data $\boldsymbol{x}$:

$$MessLen = -\log g(\boldsymbol{\theta}) - \log f(\boldsymbol{x}|\boldsymbol{\theta}) + 0.5 \log F(\boldsymbol{\theta}) - \frac{D}{2} \log 12 + \frac{D}{2} \qquad (3)$$

where $g(\boldsymbol{\theta})$ is the prior density on $\boldsymbol{\theta}$, $f(\boldsymbol{x}|\boldsymbol{\theta})$ is the likelihood of data $\boldsymbol{x}$ given $\boldsymbol{\theta}$, D is the number of parameters and $F(\boldsymbol{\theta})$ is the "Fisher Information". In this application of the MML principle, θ is the parameter p of a binomial sequence with n trials and m successes, so the relevant likelihood function is

$$f(m|p) = p^m (1-p)^{N-m} \qquad (4)$$

Since we assume $0 \le p \le 0.5$ but have no other prior information, we assume a uniform prior $g(p)$.

The Fisher Information $F(p)$ is easily shown [3] to be

$$F(p) = \frac{N}{p(1-p)} \qquad (5)$$

The value of p that minimizes the message length can be derived [3,2] by differentiating the expression for $MessLen$ to obtain,

$$p = (m + 0.5)/(N + 1.0) \qquad (6)$$

6.1   Encoding a Cut-Point

As the cut-points are real-valued, it would require an infinite number of bits to specify them precisely. Thus, we need to find an optimal precision for our parameter specification. Let δ be the precision (range) with which we want to specify our cut-point. We assume that the true cut-point lies within this range. We find the value of δ that yields the minimum message length to be (details have been left out due to lack of space),

$$\delta = \frac{4}{N(2p-1)\log \frac{p}{1-p}} \qquad (7)$$

The total cost of encoding all k cutpoints to precision δ is

$$\log(N - 2m) - k\log(\delta/N) - \log(k!)$$

since the order in which they are specified is immaterial and $k \le (N - 2m)$..

6.2   The Total Message

The length of the entire MML message can now be computed. The components are the statement of k, the statement of p to precision $\sqrt{12/F(p)}$ within the

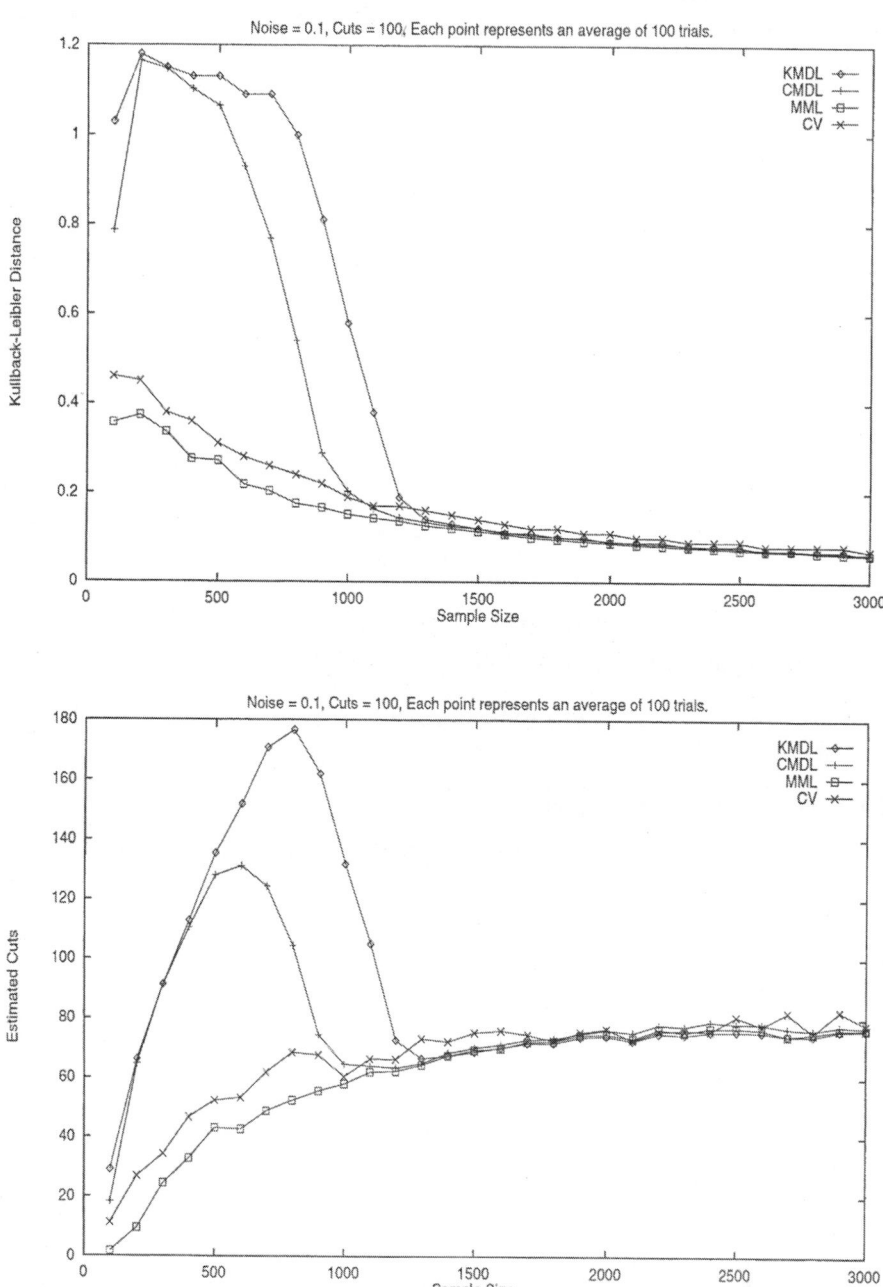

Fig. 1. Evaluation of Different Methods with Random Cutpoints

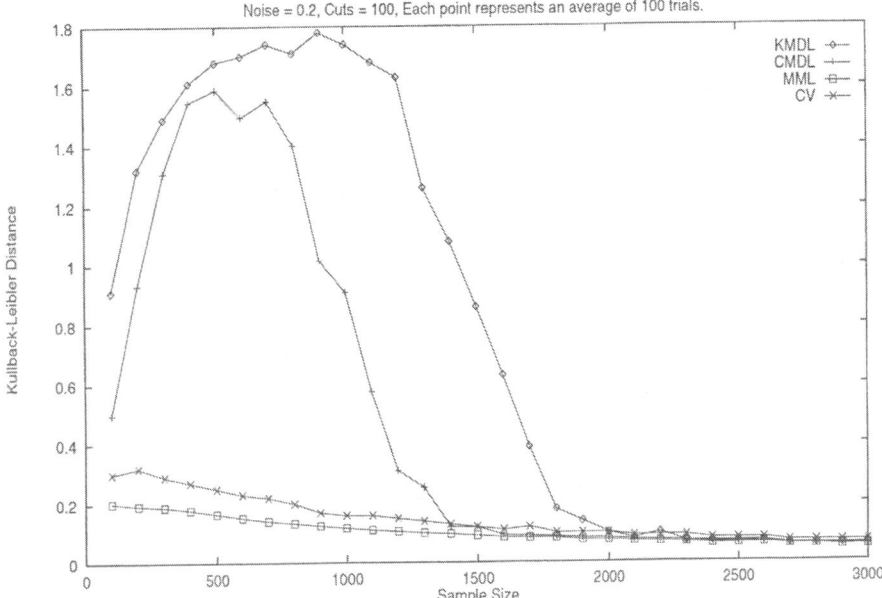

Fig. 2. Evaluation of Different Methods with Random Cutpoints

range $(0,1/2)$, the positions of the cutpoints to precision δ, and finally the expected *DataLoss* of one nit per cutpoint resulting from imprecise specification of cutpoints. Given m, the identity of the m sample points where y_i differs from $h(x_i)$ can be specified with code length $\log\binom{N}{m}$, which is included in the data part of our message.

In estimating the noise parameter p, the number of mistakes m made by the maximum-likelihood model $h'_k(x)$ is increased by the expected additional number of disagreements resulting from the imprecision of cutpoints. The resulting estimated error count is used in place of m in estimating p, which affects the choice of δ, and hence the estimated error count. A few iterations of these calculations converge quickly.

As a result, our estimate of the noise rate exceeds m/N. The effect seems to correct for the overfitting of the maximum-likelihood model which, in KMDL and CMDL, leads to an underestimate of p.

7   Results

All four methods — MML, KMDL, CMDL and CV — were compared on noise rates of 0, 0.1, 0.2, 0.3 and 0.4 with sample sizes ranging from 100 to 3000 in steps of 100. For each choice of p and N, 100 replications were performed. The true cutpoint model consisted of 100 either evenly-spaced or randomly generated cutpoints, but here, due to space restrictions, we only include results from evaluation of all our methods on random cutpoint models. All methods were compared on the basis of the number of estimated cuts and the Kullback-Leibler (KL) distance between the true and estimated model. Figures 1-2 include comparisons of the KL distance and the number of estimated cuts for noise rates of 0.1 and 0.2 respectively.

Each figure plots the generalization error as measured by the KL distance and the estimated number of cuts collated. All plots represent averages over 100 replications. With *no* noise (i.e., $p = 0$), all methods understandably performed well. But more important is how these methods perform given noise and random cut points. The robust performance of MML for small sample sizes in the presence of increasing noise values can be clearly observed from Figures 1-2. It is also important to observe that although MML tends to be conservative in estimating large numbers of cuts in comparison with CV, it does much better at minimizing the KL distance. Thus, in general, the MML approach performs significantly better than all the other methods evaluated when the models (cuts) are randomly distributed (as assumed in the problem framework). The results shown here demonstrate the generally improved performance of the MML-based method in the selection of the appropriate model class.

References

1. Kearns, M., Mansour, Y., Ng, A. Y., Ron, D., "An Experimental and Theoretical Comparison of Model Selection Methods", *Machine Learning*, 27, 7–50, 1997.
2. Wallace, C.S. and Boulton, D. M., "An information measure for classification", *Computer Journal*, 2:11, 195–209, 1968.
3. Wallace, C.S. and Freeman, P.R., "Estimation and Inference by Compact Coding", *Journal of the Royal Statistical Society*, B, 49: 240–252, 1987.
4. Rissanen, J., "Stochastic Complexity and Modeling", *Annals of Statistics*, 14, 1080–1100, 1986.
5. Vapnik, V., *Statistical Learning Theory*, Springer, New York, 1995.
6. Viswanathan, M. and Wallace, C. S., "A Note on the Comparison of Polynomial Selection Methods", in *Artificial Intelligence and Statistics 99*, Morgan Kaufmann, 169–177, 1999.
7. Wallace, C. S. and Dowe, D. L., "Minimum Message Length and Kolmogorov Complexity", to appear, Computer Journal.
8. Stone, M., "Cross-validatory Choice and Assessment of Statistical Predictions", *Journal of the Royal Statistical Society*, B, 36, 111–147, 1974.

Beyond Supervised Learning of Wrappers for Extracting Information from Unseen Web Sites*

Tak-Lam Wong, Wai Lam, and Wei Wang

Department of Systems Engineering and Engineering Management,
Ho Sin Hang Engineering Building,
The Chinese University of Hong Kong,
Shatin,
Hong Kong
{wongtl,wlam,wwang}@se.cuhk.edu.hk

Abstract. We investigate the problem of wrapper adaptation which aims at adapting a previously learned wrapper to an unseen target site. To achieve this goal, we make use of extraction rules previously discovered from a particular site to seek potential candidates of training examples for the target site. We pose the problem of training example identification for the target site as a hybrid text classification problem. The idea is to use a classification model to capture the characteristics of the attribute item of interests. Based on the automatically annotated training examples, a new wrapper for the unseen target Web site can then be discovered. We present encouraging experimental results on wrapper adaptation for some real-world Web sites.

Keywords: Text Mining, Web Intelligence, Information Extraction

1 Introduction

Maintenance of wrappers is a problem for existing wrapper learning techniques [3], [4]. The layout of Web pages changes from time to time. Wrapper constructed previously may become obsolete when the layout has changed. Lerman et al. [5] proposed an approach to solving the wrapper maintenance problem. When a wrapper is supposed to be invalid, it will identify probable target fragments from the Web page and re-learn a wrapper. However, the data to be extracted from the Web site is expected to be similar. Several systems have been proposed to address the preparation of training example problem. Muslea et al [7] proposed an active learning technique which can partially reduce the human effort in preparing training examples. Brin's DIPRE [1] tackled this problem

* The work described in this paper was substantially supported by a grant from the Research Grant Council of the Hong Kong Special Administrative Region, China (Project No: CUHK 4187/01E). This work was also partially supported by a grant from the Defense Advanced Research Projects Agency (DARPA), USA under TIDES programme (Grant No: N66001-00-1-8912), subcontract from City University of New York (Subcontract No: 47427-00-01A).

J. Liu et al. (Eds.): IDEAL 2003, LNCS 2690, pp. 725–733, 2003.

by continuously providing some concept pairs (e.g.: book title/author) to the system. Both systems can only partially solve the problem. For different Web sites, a separate effort is still required. ROADRUNNER [2] attempts to solve the problem by eliminating the need for training example preparation. The idea is based on the difference and the similarity of the text content of the Web pages. However, the semantic meaning and the relationship between the extracted data cannot be obtained by this method.

In order to tackle the above problems and reduce the effort users involved, we design a framework for wrapper induction and wrapper adaptation tasks. Our wrapper induction approach is based on our previous approach on hierarchical extraction rule learning algorithm [6]. By providing user annotated training examples, the system can learn the hierarchical record structure and extraction rules tailored to an information source automatically. It can handle both missing attribute items and multi-valued attribute items. The attribute items can also appear in different orders. Most of the existing wrapper induction techniques only consider the surrounding texts of the attribute item. Instead, our wrapper induction component also considers the content of the attribute item itself to enrich the expressiveness of the extraction rules.

Our wrapper adaptation approach aims at adapting a previously learned wrapper to an unseen target site. To achieve this goal, we make use of extraction rules previously discovered from a particular site to seek potential candidates of training examples for the target site. We pose the problem of training example identification for the target site as a hybrid text classification problem. The idea is to use a classification model to capture the characteristics of the attribute item of interests. Based on the automatically annotated training examples, a new wrapper for the unseen target Web site can then be discovered. We present encouraging experimental results on wrapper adaptation for some real-world Web sites.

2   Overview

Our framework is composed of two phases. The first phase is to induce a wrapper for a particular Web site from the provided training examples. The second phase is to adapt a learned wrapper to other unseen Web sites of the same domain. The adaptation technique is to make use of the knowledge discovered in the source Web site and learn a text classification model for discovering good training examples. These examples will then be used to induce a new tailor-made wrapper for the unseen target Web site.

Figure 1 shows an example of a Web page containing information about an electronic appliance catalog, particularly speakers products. The attribute items of interest are model number, descriptions, list_price, and our_price. The first product has a model number "LCONCEPT-6", description "6 1/2" 2-Way In-Wall Speakers", a list_price of "70.00" , and a our_price of "56.00" will also be extracted. Figure 2 depicts an excerpt of the HTML text document associated with the Web page shown in Figure 1. A user can simply provide examples of

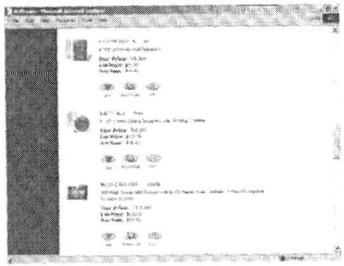

```
...
RCD-
CH1500</b></a>   <span
class="text">SHARP</span> </td></tr> <tr
valign=top><td> <p class="text">200 Watt
Tower Mini-System with 6-CD Player, Dual
Cassette, 3-Way Bi-Amplifier Speaker
System</p> </td></tr> <tr><td> <b
class=ourprice>Our Price:</b> <b
class=ouramount>216.00</b> <div
class=text><B>List Price:  </b>$270.00
<br><b>You Save:  
</b>$54.00</div> <table cellSpacing=0
cellPadding=0>
...
```

Fig. 1. An example of Web page about speaker products.

Fig. 2. An excerpt of the HTML texts for the Web shown in Figure 1

attribute items on the Web page via a graphical user interface. The system will induce a wrapper from the provided training examples and the HTML document. The learned wrapper is able to automatically extract precise information from different Web pages in the same site. Our previous work has presented the design of our wrapper induction method called HISER [6]. In this paper, we will focus on the wrapper adaptation approach in our framework.

2.1 Proposed Wrapper Adaptation

The goal of wrapper adaptation is to adapt a learned wrapper from one Web site (source site) to an unseen Web site (target site) of the same domain. This can reduce the human effort of providing training examples for unseen Web sites. This capability is also useful for wrapper maintenance when the layout of the Web site has been changed and the old wrapper can no longer be used correctly. Our adaptation approach first attempts to identify new training examples automatically for the the target site. After appropriate training examples are collected, a new wrapper for the target site can be learned.

To identify new training examples of the unseen target site, we pose this task as a hybrid text classification problem. One piece of information for this classification problem is to consider a set of Web documents generated from the same Web source, but containing different records of attribute items. Typically these Web documents are obtained by supplying different keywords or queries to the search engine provided by the same Web source. We call these kinds of generated Web documents *reference pages*. The text content of the reference pages provides very useful clues for seeking appropriate text fragments related to attribute item of interest. Generally the text content regarding the attribute items will not appear in different pages of the same Web site, while those text content regarding the format of the layout will probably be similar. This information gives a good indication in locating the attribute items of interest.

Other pieces of useful information for the hybrid text classification problem consist of the previously induced wrapper of the source site and the attribute item contents extracted from the source site. The induced wrapper of the source site embodies some knowledge about the pattern of an attribute item. Certain kind of knowledge may be useful for the target site to described the attribute items. The attribute item contents extracted from the source site can be viewed as a lexicon for the corresponding attribute item. This lexicon will be useful for identifying new training examples for the target site.

Our adaptation method has two major stages. The first stage is to seek the potential candidates of training examples from the target Web site. To achieve this task, we make use of extraction rules previously learned from the source site to locate potential candidate in the target site. The second stage is to classify the potential candidates using a hybrid text classification model. The hybrid text classification model consists of two components. The first component is the content classification model. This content classification model considers the reference page distance and the features related to the attribute items. The second component is the lexicon approximate matching. The content of previously extracted attribute items can be viewed as a lexicon. Lexicon approximate matching makes use of this lexicon to identify the "good" candidates. The overall degree of confidence of being "good" positive training examples for the target site can then be obtained by the combination of of the scores from content classification and lexicon approximate matching. After collecting the training examples, a new wrapper for the target site can be learned by HISER to extract records from the target site.

3   Seeking Potential Candidates

The basic idea of wrapper adaptation is to make use of the discovered knowledge in the source site to prepare training examples for the target sites. As mentioned before, the first stage of wrapper adaptation is to make use of extraction rules previously learned from a particular site to seek potential training example candidates for the target sites. Recall that a Web document can be regarded as a sequence of text tokens. A token can be a word, number, punctuation, date, HTML tag, specific ASCII character, or domain specific contents like such as manufacturer names. We define a *segment* to be a sequence of continuous tokens in a Web page not containing any HTML tags. For each attribute item of interest, our method will first try to locate potential candidates using the target component of the previously learned extraction rules. The initial candidate is the segment containing the pattern of the target component. Next, we try to produce a set of potential candidates by extending this segment forward and backward. A parameter T is used to control the seeking window size. The outline of the candidate identification algorithm is shown in Figure 3.

4   Hybrid Text Classification

A considerable number of candidates obtained by the above candidate seeking algorithm are actually noise. Hybrid text classification is employed to filter the candidates and only "good" candidates will be selected for subsequent processing. The hybrid text classification model consists of two major components. The

```
#  Function Candidate Identification
1  {Candidate} = {}
2  {Segment} = all segments in the Web page
3  Foreach s in {Segment}
4     {Pre-Candidate} = {After-Candidate} = {}
5     If t contains the pattern in the target component
6        seed = t
7        For i := 0 to T
8           {Pre-Candidate} = {Pre-Candidate} ∪ i-th token before seed
9           {After-Candidate} = {After-Candidate} ∪ i-th token after seed
10        {Candidate} = {Candidate} ∪ ({Pre-Candiate} × {After-Candidate})
```

Fig. 3. The outline of the candidate seeking algorithm.

first component is content classification. The second component is lexicon approximate matching.

4.1   Content Classification

We identify some features for characterizing the content of the attribute item. A text classification model can then be learned based on the training examples in the source site. Then the degree of confidence of a potential candidate being "good" training example can be predicted by the classification model.

We design two kinds of features. The first kind of features is related to reference pages. As mentioned in Section 2, reference page are a set of Web documents generated from the same Web source, but containing different records of attribute items. We define *main page*, M, as the original Web page where the records of interest are located. We then define *reference page*, $R(M)$, as a Web page under the same Web source as the main page M, but it contains different records from those in the main page. In fact, the candidates comes from the main page of the target site. The next step is to obtain a set of reference pages. A typical method to get the reference pages is supply different keywords or queries to the search engine provided by the Web site. From the reference pages, we can find a set of reference examples, by applying the candidate seeking algorithm discussed in Section 3 from the reference pages.

Suppose there are two examples $e_1 = t_{11}, \cdots, t_{1m}$ and $e_2 = t_{21}, \cdots, t_{2n}$, where t_{ij} is the j-th token in example i. We define the distance, $d(e_1, e_2)$, between the two examples e_1 and e_2 is as follows:

$$d(e_1, e_2) = \frac{k}{\max\{m, n\}}$$

where k is the number of tokens in e_1 matched with the tokens in e_2. For each example e, the reference page distance, ξ, is calculated by the following formula:

$$\xi = \max_r \{d(e_i, r)\}$$

where r is a reference examples obtained from the set of reference pages.

The second kind of features are related to the content of the attribute item. These features can be domain independent or domain dependent. We design the following features:

- F_1: the number of characters in the content
- F_2: the number of tokens in the content
- F_3: whether the content ends immediately before a punctuation
- F_4: whether the content starts immediately after a punctuation
- F_5: whether the content ends immediately before a HTML tag
- F_6: whether the content starts immediately after a HTML tag
- F_7: whether the content starts immediately after a certain semantic class
- F_8: whether the content starts with a capital letter
- F_9: whether the contents ends with a punctuation
- F_{10}: the proportion of uppercase characters in the content

The content classification model will return a score, f_1, which shows the degree of confidence being "good" training example for the target site of each candidate. f_1 will be normalized to between 0 and 1.

4.2   Training Data Construction

The content classification model is learned from a set of training samples composed of a set of positive and negative samples. The set of positive samples are those manually annotated obtained from the main page of the source site. We make use of the candidate seeking algorithm discussed in Section 3 to prepare the negative samples. Basically, we first apply the candidate seeking algorithm to the main page of the source site to get a set of samples. Those samples which are not in the positive samples are collected to from the set of negative samples. The next step is to obtain a set of reference pages under the same Web source. After the reference pages are obtained, the reference page distance, ξ, of each sample can be computed as discussed in Section 4.1. The values of the features $F_1, \cdots$, and F_{10} of each positive and negative sample can also be computed. As a result, a set of training data is prepared. To learn the content classification model, we employ Support Vector Machines [8] to learn the content classification model which demonstrates good performance for classification task.

4.3   Lexicon Approximate Matching

For each attribute item in the same domain, we maintain a lexicon by storing the items automatically collected from different sites. For example, there is a lexicon containing description entries for the description attribute in the electronic appliance domain. This previously discovered lexicon can help determine good training examples for an unseen site. Precisely, the content of a lexicon can be taken into consideration for classifying the potential candidates. Both of the lexicon and potential candidates need to be pre-processed in advance. First, stop words, such as *is, am, are, etc.*, are removed. Second, we emply stemming to reduce each word in different morphological forms to its word stem. After

Table 1.   Information sources for experiments (# is the total number of records.

	Web Site	URL	#
S1	4till9.com	www.4till9.com	210
S2	AAAprice.com	www.aaaprice.com	174
S3	AbtElectronics.com	www.abtelectronics.com	215
S4	American eSuperstore.com	www.americansuperstore.com	200
S5	BestBuyDigital.com	www.bestbuydigital.com	274
S6	CircuitCity.com	www.circuitcity.com	337
S7	Etronics.com	www.etronics.com	169
S8	Micro Warehouse Inc.	www2.warehouse.com	120
S9	Overstock.com	www.overstock.com	203
S10	Tek Gallery	www.tekgallery.com	200

that, the cosine similarity between the candidate and each of the entry in the lexicon will be computed and the lexicon approximate matching score, f_2, of the candidate will be the maximum value from all the similarity values.

In the hybrid text classification, the score from content classification and lexicon approximate matching will be computed. Then the final score $Score(C_i)$ of a potential candidate $C_i \in \{Candidate\}$ is given by:

$$Score(C_i) = wf_1 + (1 - w)f_2$$

where f_1 and f_2 are the score obtained in content classification and lexicon approximate matching respectively; w is a parameter controlling the weight of the content classification and lexicon approximate matching and $0 < w < 1$. After finding the scores of the candidates, the top N candidates will be selected as our training examples for the target site. User can optionally scrutinize discovered training examples to improve the quality of the training examples. In our experiment, we mainly perform deletion of some apparently invalid training examples. A new tailor-made wrapper to the target site can be learned by our wrapper induction approach HISER. The newly learned wrapper can then be applied to the remaining pages in the target site.

5   Experimental Results on Wrapper Adaptation

In order to demonstrate the capability of our wrapper adaptation approach, we have conducted experiments using the same Web site shown in Table 1.

We wish to evaluate the information extraction performance of a new information source when we adapt a previously learned wrapper to it. For each domain, we conducted two sets of experiments. The first set of experiment is to simply apply the hierarchical record structure and extraction rules learned from one particular source without adaptation to all other sources for information extraction. This experiment can be treated as a baseline for our wrapper adaptation approach. The second set of experiment is to adapt the hierarchical record structure and extraction rules learned from one particular source to other information sources by automatically annotating the training examples. Then each information source can learn their own hierarchical record structure and extraction rules for extraction. In all experiments, users are only required to provide a few training examples for one particular information source.

Table 2. Average extraction performance on *model number*, *price*, and *description* for the cases of without adaptation and with adaptation when training examples of one particular information source are provided. (Ave. R. and Ave. P. refer to average recall and average precision respectively.)

	model number				price				description			
	Without Adaptation		With Adaptation		Without Adaptation		With Adaptation		Without Adaptation		With Adaptation	
Source	Ave. R.	Ave. P.	Ave. R.	Ave. P.	Ave. R.	Ave. P.	Ave. R.	Ave. P.	Ave. R.	Ave. P.	Ave. R.	Ave. P.
S1	0.0	0.0	75.0	77.6	0.0	0.0	98.0	99.7	0.0	0.0	68.9	68.9
S2	33.2	33.3	55.5	55.5	33.3	33.3	98.0	99.6	32.8	32.7	86.4	88.3
S3	0.0	0.0	30.6	33.2	0.0	0.0	98.0	99.6	0.0	0.0	86.4	88.3
S4	33.3	33.3	66.7	66.4	33.3	33.3	98.0	99.6	32.8	32.4	86.4	88.2
S5	33.2	33.3	86.0	88.6	33.3	33.3	98.0	99.6	32.6	32.4	79.9	79.5
S6	0.0	0.0	22.2	22.2	0.0	0.0	92.1	92.0	0.0	0.0	87.5	87.2
S7	0.0	0.0	33.3	33.3	0.0	0.0	98.2	99.9	0.0	0.0	87.7	87.2
S8	0.0	0.0	19.5	22.1	0.0	0.0	98.0	99.6	0.0	0.0	0.0	0.0
S9	0.0	0.0	97.1	99.7	0.0	0.0	98.0	99.6	0.0	0.0	68.7	68.4
S10	33.2	33.3	63.9	66.4	33.3	33.3	98.0	99.6	32.5	32.2	64.3	66.0

Table 2 summarizes the average extraction performance on model number, price, and description respectively for the cases of without adaptation and with adaptation when training examples of one particular information source are provided. The first column shows the information sources where training examples are given. The columns labeled with "Without Adaptation" show the average recall and precision of an attribute item when the learned wrapper from the information source specified in column one are applied for extraction from all the remaining information sources. The columns labeled with "With Adaptation" show the average recall and precision of an attribute item when adapting the learned wrapper from the information source specified in column one to all the remaining information sources.

Except S2, S4, S5, and S10, the induced hierarchical record structure and extraction rules in a particular Web site cannot apply to others. Since S2, S4, S5 and S10 have very similar layout and formatting regularities, the extraction rules from any one of these Web sites can be applied to the others without adaptation. But in general, it is not true for most of the information sources. As we can see, in most of the cases of adapting a learned wrapper from a particular information source to the others. The extraction performance with adaptation is much better than that without adaptation.

References

1. S. Brin. Extracting patterns and relations from the World Wide Web. *Proceedings of SIGMOD Workshop on Databases and the Web*, pages 172–183, 1998.
2. V. Crescenzi, G. Mecca, and P. Merialdo. Roadrunner: Towards automatic data extraction from large web sites. *Proceedings of the 27th Very Large Databases Conference*, pages 109–118, 2001.
3. D. Freitag and A. McCallum. Information extraction with HMMs and shrinkage. *AAAI-99 Workshop on Machine Learning for Information Extraction*, July 1999.
4. N. Kushmerick. Wrapper induction: Efficiency and expressiveness. *Artificial Intelligence*, 118(1–2):15–68, April 2000.

5. K. Lerman and S. Minton. Learning the common structure of data. *Proceedings of the 17th National Conference on Artificial Intelligence*, pages 609–614, 2000.
6. W. Y. Lin and W. Lam. Learning to extract hierarchical information from semi-structured documents. *Proceedings of the Ninth International Conference on Information and Knowledge Management CIKM*, pages 250–257, November 2000.
7. Muslea, I., S. Minton, and C. A. Knoblock. Selective Sampling with Redundant Views. *Proceedings of the Seventeenth National Conference on Artificial Intelligence*, pages 621–626, 2000.
8. V. N. Vapnik. *The Nature of Statistical Learning Theory*. Springer, 1995.

Metasearch via Voting

Shanfeng Zhu[1], Qizhi Fang[2], Xiaotie Deng[1], and Weiming Zheng[3]

[1] Department of Computer Science, City University of Hong Kong,
Hong Kong, P. R. China
zhusf@cs.cityu.edu.hk
[2] Department of Mathematics, Ocean University of Qingdao,
Qingdao 266071, Shandong, P. R. China
[3] Department of Computer Science and Technology, Tsinghua University,
Beijing, P. R. China

Abstract. Metasearch engines are developed to overcome the shortcoming of single search engine and try to benefit from cooperative decision by combining the results of multiple independent search engines that make use of different models and configurations. In this work, we study the metasearch problem via voting that facilities multiple agents making cooperative decision. We can deem the source search engines as voters and all ranked documents as candidates, then metaseach problem is actually to find a voting algorithm to obtain group's preferences on these documents(candidates). In addition to two widely discussed classical voting rules: Borda and Condorcet, we study another two voting algorithms, Black and Kemeny. Since Kemeny ranking problem is NP-hard, a new heuristic algorithm has been proposed for metasearch. Some experiments have been carried out on TREC2001 data for evaluating these metasearch algorithms coming from voting.

1 Introduction

1.1 Background

Search engines are information retrieval systems that try to help users find documents satisfying their needs in the document collections (corpus). Early applications include bibliographical system in libraries and then online information service provided by database vendors DIALOG[1], LEXIS-NEXIS[2], and so forth. With the development of World Wide Web, Web search engines (e.g. Google)[3] become the most popular services on the Internet. Metasearch engines are developed to overcome the shortcoming of single search engine and try to benefit from cooperative decision by combining the results of multiple independent search engines, that make use of different models and configurations.

With respect to the overlap of collections in each source search engine, metasearch can be divided into three categories: data fusion, collection fusion

---

[1] http://www.dialog.com
[2] http://www.lexis-nexis.com
[3] http://www.google.com

J. Liu et al. (Eds.): IDEAL 2003, LNCS 2690, pp. 734–741, 2003.

and partial overlap fusion. Data fusion refers to the case that all source search engines operate on same collection, and collection fusion refers to the case that they operate on disjoint collections. In partial overlap fusion, there are arbitrary but not ignorable overlap among the collections, such as the case in the web search engines where each of them covers a different part of the web. In this work, we will concentrate on data fusion.

1.2   Related Work

Many studies have been carried out on desgining metasearch algorithms. Some of them [7,9,15] need fetch and analyze all documents for ranking, or establish protocols among source search engines on how to provide local statistical information for global computing. This type of algorithm consumes too much resources, and even worse, close collaborations sometimes are impossible due to the heterogeneities of source search engines. Another type of algorithms make use of relevant scores provided by each search engines to combine the search results, such as Min, Max and Average model [6], Logistic Regression model [14], Linear Combination Model[16]. In most cases, only the ranks of the documents in each search engine are available. Interleave method is a widely discussed algorithm in which the documents are selected from each source search engine's result in a round robin way[11,13]. In this work, we will focus on rank-based metasearch algorithm.

Metasearch problem can be modelled as a voting procedure in which we only need rank information. We can deem the source search engines as voters and all ranked documents as candidates, then meta-search problem is actually to select a voting procedure to make collective choices on these candidates. Voting procedures can be traced back to two centuries ago in Western Europe where elections for parliament and administrative were popular. Two famous voting algorithms, Borda rule [3] and Condorcet rule [4], are proposed to deal with sophisticated cases. In addition to these, other voting extensions, such as Black procedure [2], Kemeny [8], have been proposed and even widely employed in the elections of many countries.

Aslam and Montague [1,12] adopted Borda rule and Condorcet rule to build data fusion algorithm and carried out the experiments on the data in TREC3, TREC5 and TREC9. They found their algorithms usually outperform the best input system and are competitive with existing metasearch strategies. Dwork et. al. [5] studied Kemeny method [8] for metasearch on the Web, and found that the corresponding problem of computing optimal Kemeny ranking is NP-hard for given $k(k > 3)$ full (or partial) ranking $\tau_1, \cdots, \tau_k$ on N candidates. Spearman footrule distance is utilized to approximate the optimal Kemeny ranking.

This paper is organized as follows: In section 2, after we propose the voting model for metasearch, we introduce four typical voting algorithms: Borda, Condorcet, Black and Kemeny method. The algorithm issues of these methods are discussed in section 3. Since Kemeny ranking problem is NP-hard, a new heuristic algorithm has been proposed. In section 4, some experiments have been carried out on TREC2001 data for evaluating the effectiveness of these algorithms.

2   Voting Model for Metasearch

Here we give the formal model of voting for metasearch. Given a set of candidates (documents) $N = \{1, 2, \cdots, n\}$, a ranking τ with respect to N is a permutation of all elements of N which represents a voter's (search engine's) preference on these candidates(documents). For each $i \in N$, $\tau(i)$ denotes the position of the element i in τ, and for any two elements $i, j \in N$, $\tau(i) < \tau(j)$ implies that i is ranked higher than j by τ. Here we have a collection of k rankings $\tau_1, \tau_2, \cdots, \tau_k$ which are respectively provided by a set of voters (search engines) $V = \{1, 2, \cdots, k\}$. The voting (metasearch) algorithm is how to aggregate these k rankings into a "consensus" ranking π on these n candidates(documents). In this work, we will concentrate on four voting algorithms, Borda, Condorcet , Black and Kemeny.

- *Borda*

  It employs a point system to measure the difference among candidates. For each voter, the lowest candidate will be assigned a nonnegative integer score x. Then other candidates above will be scored with an interval of positive integer y, such as $x+y, x+2y, x+3y, \cdots, x+(n-1)y$. In a typical case, we give $x = 1, y = 1$. Then considering any two candidates $i, j \in N$ in aggregation ranking π , $\pi(i) < \pi(j)$ implies that $\sum_{l=1}^{k}(n+1-\tau_l(i)) > \sum_{l=1}^{k}(n+1-\tau_l(j))$

- *Condorcet*

  It considers relative majority between each pair of candidates, and proposed that the candidate defeating any other candidate in pairwise comparison should be elected as winner. That is to say, x is the winner of the election if for any other candidate $i \in N$, $|\{l \in V : \tau_l(x) < \tau_l(i)\}| > |\{l \in V : \tau_l(i) < \tau_l(x)\}|$. But Condorcet winner may not exist, since it may exist voting cycles (paradox) in the candidates. Montague, et. al. [12] extended it to a full ranking on candidates by partitioning them into different strongly connected components(SCC) which are actually different voting cycles. Therefore, the candidates in different SCC can be ranked according to Condorcet rule, and the candidates in the cycles will be ranked arbitrarily. Similar algorithms were discussed by Dwork et. al. [5].

- *Black*

  Black rule tries to incorporate both Borda and Condorcet in ranking the candidates. The winner of Black rule is Condorcet winner while existing, otherwise it will select Borda winner. Then for any two candidates $i, j \in N$ in aggregation ranking π by Black rule, $\pi(i) < \pi(j)$ implies that either they exist in same SCC(Voting Cycle) with i having a higher Borda score, or the SCC(Voting Cycle) for i have a higher grade than the one for j.

- *Kemeny*

  This algorithm is based on the concept of Kendall-τ distance between two rankings which counts the total number of pairs of candidates that are assigned to different relative orders in these two rankings. In other words, the Kendall-τ distance between two rankings τ_1, τ_2 is defined as

$$D(\tau_1, \tau_2) = |\{(i, j) : \tau_1(i) < \tau_1(j), \ and \ \tau_2(j) < \tau_2(i), \forall i, j \in N\}|$$

Kemeny ranking is an optimal ranking π with respect to the given k rankings $\tau_1, \tau_2, \cdots, \tau_k$ provided by the voters which minimizes the total Kendall-τ distance $D(\pi; \tau_1, \cdots, \tau_k) = \sum_{i=1}^{k} D(\pi, \tau_i)$

3   Algorithmic Issues

3.1   Borda

With the k rankings on n documents, we can first create n lists of k ranks given to each document respectively by k source search engines which takes time $O(nk)$. The computation of merged score for all documents takes time $O(n)$. Finally the documents can be ranked with respect to their merged scores by any sorting algorithm , such as QuickSort which takes time $O(n \log n)$. Then the total computation time will be $O(n \log n)$.

3.2   Condorcet

As Montague et. al. discussed in [12], they first establish a condercet graph by creating an edge from x to y for $\forall x, y \in N$, if $|\{l \in V : \tau_l(x) < \tau_l(y)\}| \geq |\{l \in V : \tau_l(y) < \tau_l(x)\}|$. This graph consists of many Strongly Connected Components(SCC) which identify different voting cycles. Then the ranking with respect to Condorcet rule is actually to find a Hamiltonian path in the graph. They propose an efficient algorithm without computing its SCC, but utilizing QuickSort algorithm by comparing the documents with Condorcet rule. The total computation takes $O(nk \log n)$. For detail algorithms, you can refer to [12].

3.3   Black

Black rule incorporates both Borda rule and Condorcet rule with breaking the Condorcet voting cycles by Borda rule. We need identify each Strongly Connected Component(SCC) in the Condorcet graph and assign a corresponding grade.

Step 1, a preprocessing step of establishing n lists of k ranks given to each document by k source search engines takes time $O(nk)$.

Step 2, as discussed in section 3.2, we can first construct a ranking according to Condorcet rule in time $O(nk \log n)$.

Step 3, for each candidate x, we assign a Condorcet grade by using **Algorithm 1** which takes time $O(kn^2)$.

Step 4, as discussed in section 3.1, we can construct a Borda merged score for each according to Borda rule in time $O(n)$.

Step 5, we sort the documents by Quicksort algorithm which consider both Condorcet grade and Borda score which takes $O(n \log n)$.

Therefore, the total computation time takes $O(kn^2)$.

Algorithm 1 Computing Condorcet grade for each candidate

Precondition: All candidates are ranked in Condorcet rule
and saved in $Doc[i], 1 \leq i \leq n$.

01: grade=n; $index = 1$;

02 Do

03:    Condorcet_Score[$index$]=grade;

04:    Flag=false;

05:    For $i = index + 1$ to n do

06:        Comparing Doc[index] with Doc[i] by Algorithm 1

07:        IF Doc[i] is better than Doc[index],

08:            Flag=true;

09:            break;

10:    IF (Flag)

11:        For $j = index + 1$ To $i - 1$ do

12:            Condorcet_Score[j]=grade;

13:        $index = i$;

14:    Else

15:        grade$--$;

16:        index++;

17: While $(index < n)$

3.4   Kemeny

Dwork et. al. [5] studied the complexity of finding a Kemeny optimal ranking and show that this is an NP-hard problem for even $k \geq 4$. They make use of optimal footrule distance aggregation to approximate the Kemeny problem which can be casted as a minumum cost bipartite matching problem. We propose a new heuristic algorithm Max-Diff(**Algorithm 2**), which are straightforward and easy for implementation.

For each candidate pair $(i, j)(i, j \in N)$, we define the preference value r_{ij} as the number of rankings which rank i higher than j, that is $r_{ij} = |\{\tau_l : \tau_l(i) < \tau_l(j), l \in V\}|$. Then the Optimal Kemeny ranking problem is to find a ranking π on N which maximize the total number of consistent candidate pairs $\Phi(\pi) = \sum_{i,j:\pi(i)<\pi(j)} r_{ij}$. For each candidate $i \in N$, let $P(i) = \sum_{j \in N} r_{ji}$, $Q(i) = \sum_{i \in N} r_{ij}$. Note that $P(i)$ and $Q(i)$ stand for the strength of voters putting candidate i in lowest position and the highest position, respectively. The main idea of Max-Diff (**Algorithm 2**) is,in every iteration, to arrange a candidate to the highest or lowest position, according to the largest difference of $P(i)$ and $Q(i)$.

The construction of matrix r_{ij} takes time $O(kn^2)$. With this matrix, the computation of P and Q takes time $O(n^2)$. At last, algorithm Max-Diff takes time $O(n^2)$. Thus, the total computation takes time $O(kn^2)$.

Algorithm 2 Max-Diff, a heuristic algorithm for Kemeny ranking problem

---

01: Let $S = N$, $u = 1$ and $v = n$.

02: Compute $\gamma = \max_{i \in S}\{|P(i) - Q(i)|\}$,

03: and denote i^* the candidate with the largest γ.

04: If $P(i^*) \leq Q(i^*)$,

05:　　$\pi(i^*) = u$,

06:　　$u \leftarrow u + 1$;

07: Else

08:　　$\pi(i^*) = v$,

09:　　$v \leftarrow v - 1$;

09: For each candidate $j \in S \setminus \{i^*\}$ do

10:　　$P(j) \leftarrow P(j) - r_{i^*j}$

11:　　$Q(j) \leftarrow Q(j) - r_{ji^*}$

12: $S \leftarrow S \setminus \{i^*\}$

13: If $v \geq u$,

14:　　go to Line 02;

15: Else

16:　　exit and output the ranking π.

---

4   Experiment

4.1   Experimental Setup

We compare the performance of these voting algorithms by using the retrieval system participating in Web track of Text REtrieval Conference 2001[17] as input. TREC [4] is an annually held conference since 1992, which provides testbed and benchmarks for retrieval systems on large document collections. Average precision is usually employed to evaluate the performance of the retrieval system. Since retrieval systems come from same company will decrease the performance of the Condorcet algorithm as reported in [12], we select top 10 independent retrieval systems in the web track of TREC2001 as input with respect to average precision. The id of the systems are fub01be2, JuruFull, ricMM, jscbtawt14, Lemur, ok10wt3, hum01tlx, msrcn1, tnout10t2 and iit01tfc.

In this work, we discuss four voting algorithms for metaseach: Borda, Condorcet, Black and Max-Diff. Since the ranking by Black algorithm also conforms to Condorcet rule, we only carried the experiments on three algorithms: Borda, Black and Max-Diff. There are total 9 runs in the experiment. In the first run, we select top 2 retrieval systems as input. Then we select top 3 retrieval systems as input. Finally, top 10 systems are chosen for metasearch. All 50 topics in TREC2001 web track are examined in the experiment. According to algorithms discussed in last section, we compute the top 1000 merged documents for each topic. Given these results, a program "trec_eval" provide by TREC will be executed to obtain performance information such as mean average precision for all 50 topics in the track.

---

[4] http://trec.nist.gov

4.2   Experimental Results

The experimental results are shown in the Fig. 1. First, it shows that these
three voting algorithms obtain benefits from cooperative decision that achieves
much high mean average precision than the best input retrieval system. Also
we notice that in this experiment three voting algorithms have small difference
in performance. We can find that Max-Diff is the most steadiest algorithm with
little deviation. In average, Borda is the best one in this experiment, than Black,
at last Max-Diff, but the difference is very small. In our experiment, we also
find that with the number of the input system increasing , the performance of
Metasearch systems adopting these three algorithms doesn't change much, which
is consistent with other researcher's result, such as Vogt[16], Montague[12].

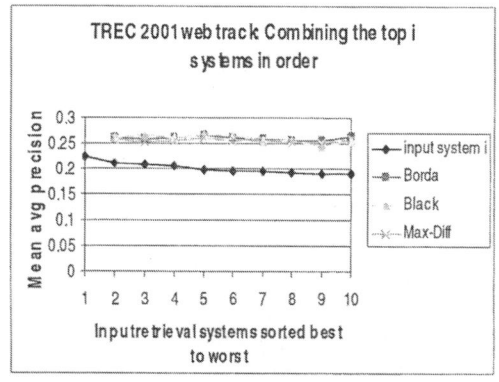

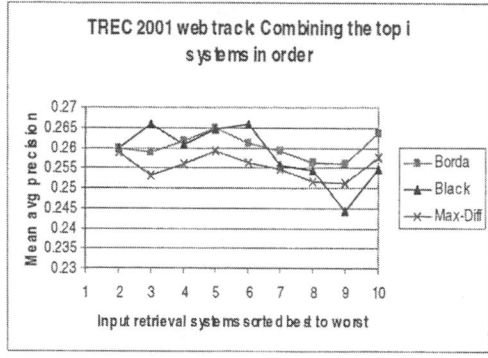

Fig. 1. Borda vs Black vs Max-Diff on TREC 2001 Web track data

5   Conclusion and Future Works

In this work, we study the metasearch problem via voting. In addition to two
widely discussed classical voting rules: Borda and Condorcet, we also study an-

other two voting algorithms, Black and Kemeny. Through the experiments on TREC2001 data, we find that these algorithms have small difference in performance, and Max-Diff, a new heuristic algorithm for Kemeny problem, behaves steadiest. Future works include exploring more voting algorithms for Metasearch.

Acknowledgement. This work is supported by a joint research grant (N_CityU 102/01) of Hong Kong RGC and NNSFC of China.

References

1. Javed A. Aslam , Mark H. Montague, Models for Metasearch, SIGIR 2001
2. Duncan Black, The Theory of Committees and Elections, Cambridge University Press ,1958
3. Borda, J. C., Mémoire sur les élections au scrutin, Memoires des l'Académie Royale des Sciences, 1781
4. Condorcet, M. de, Essai sur l'application de l'analyse à la Probabilité des Decisions Rendues à la pluralité des Voix. Paris, 1785
5. C. Dwork, R. Kumar, M. Naor and D. Sivakumar, Rank aggregation methods for the web, WWW10 (2001), 613–622.
6. Edward A. Fox and Joseph A. Shaw, Combination of multiple searches, The Second Text REtrieval Conference(TREC-2) U.S. Government Printing Office, Washington D.C. Editor D. K. Harman, pp243–249, March 1994
7. L. Gravano, C. Chang, H. Garcia-Molina, and A. Paepcke. STARTS: Stanford proposal for internet meta-searching, ACM SIGMOD, Tucson, May 1997, 207–218.
8. J. G. Kemeny, Mathematics without numbers, Daedalus 88, 1959, pp577–591.
9. S. Lawrence, and C . L. ,Giles : Inquirus, the NECI meta-search engine, WWW7 Conference, Brisbane, Australia, 95–105,1998.
10. Erik Warren Selberg. Towards Comprehensive Web Search. PhD thesis, University of Washington, 1999
11. Weiyi Meng, Clement T. Yu, King-Lup Liu, Building efficient and effective metasearch engines, ACM Computing Surveys,34(1) 2002,pp48–89
12. Mark Montague, Javed A. Aslam, Condorcet Fusion for Improved Retrieval, CIKM2002, Novemeber 4–9, 2002, McLean, Virginia, USA
13. B. Uygar Oztekin, George Karypis, Vipin Kumar, Expert Agreement and Content Based Reranking in a Meta Search Environment using Mearf. WWW2002, May 7–11, 2002, Honolulu, Hawaii, USA
14. Jacques Savoy, Anne Le Calvé and Dana Vrajitoru, Report on the TREC-5 experiment: Data fusion and collection fusion, The Fifth Text REtrieval Conference(TREC-5), Gaithersburg, MD, USA , U.S. Government Printing Office, Washington D.C. , EDITOR E. M. Voorhees and D. K. Harman", pp 489–502, 1997
15. E. Selberg and O. Etzioni , The MetaCrawler Architecture for resource aggregation on the web, IEEE Expert, Vol. 12(1), January-February 1997: 8–14.
16. Christopher C. Vogt and Garrison W. ottrell. Fusion via a linear combination of scores. Information Retrieval, 1(3):151–173, October 1999
17. E. Voorhees and D. Harman, Eds. (2002). Proceedings of the Tenth Text REtrieval Conference (TREC 2001). NIST Special Publication 500–250.

Peculiarity Oriented Mining in Multiple Human Brain Data

Ning Zhong[1], Akio Nakamaru[1], Muneaki Ohshima[1], Jing-Long Wu[2], and
Hiroaki Mizuhara[3]

[1] Dept. of Information Eng., Maebashi Institute of Technology, Japan
[2] Dept. of Intelligent Mechanical Systems, Kagawa University, Japan
[3] RIKEN Brain Science Institute, Japan

Abstract. In the paper, we investigate fMRI brain activations from the
view point of peculiarity oriented mining and propose a way of peculiarity
oriented mining for knowledge discovery in multiple human brain data.
The mining process is a multi-step one, in which various psychological experiments, physiological measurements, and data mining techniques are
cooperatively used to investigate human multi-perception mechanism.
We describe the initial results on transforming the multiple human brain
data obtained from visual and auditory psychological experiments by the
functional magnetic resonance imaging (fMRI) as well as using peculiarity oriented mining technique in such multi-data.

1   Introduction

In order to develop artificial systems which match human ability, it is necessary
to investigate human multi-perception mechanism systematically. It also is clear
that the future of cognitive science and neuroscience may be affected by the
ability to do large-scale mining of fMRI brain activations. The key issues are
how to design the psychological and physiological experiments for obtaining
various data from human multi-perception mechanism, as well as how to analyze
such data from multiple aspects for discovering new models of human multi-
perception.

Megalooikonomou et al. proposed an interesting method for mining associations between lesioned structures and concomitant neurological or neuropsycho-
logical deficits [6,7]. Their method can deal with the morphological variability
that exists between subjects and are scalable so that large longitudinal studies
can be performed. Tsukimoto et al. developed a novel method for mining classification rules by dividing brain images into meshes as condition attributes, and
treating functions as classes [8]. Thus, such rules like "if mesh A and mesh B
are active, then some function is positive" can be found. Their method consists
of two steps: (1) a nonparametric regression is applied on the training data and
(2) rules are extracted from the regression formula obtained by the regression
analysis.

We observe fMRI brain activations from the view point of *peculiarity oriented
mining* and propose a way of peculiarity oriented mining for knowledge discovery

J. Liu et al. (Eds.): IDEAL 2003, LNCS 2690, pp. 742–750, 2003.
© Springer-Verlag Berlin Heidelberg 2003

in multiple human brain data. The mining process is a multi-step one, in which various psychological experiments, physiological measurements and data mining techniques are cooperatively used to investigate human multi-perception mechanism. In particular, we describe the initial results on transforming the multiple human brain data obtained from visual and auditory psychological experiments by the functional magnetic resonance imaging (fMRI) as well as using peculiarity oriented mining technique in such multi-data.

The rest of the paper is organized as follows. Section 2 gives a global view of our methodology. Section 3 describes how to design fMRI visual and auditory calculation experiments. Section 4 introduces our peculiarity oriented mining approach. Then in Section 5, we discuss a result of mining in fMRI human brain data. Finally, Section 6 gives conclusions and further research directions.

2   Methodology

Figure 1 shows a global view of our methodology. First, we need to design the experiments for obtaining various raw data from human multi-perception mechanism. The experiments include psychometrics and physiometry. Then the data are transformed into the format in which data-mining techniques can be used efficiently, and stored in the databases, respectively. Such databases are called multiple data sources that can be used to discover new models of human multi-perception. Further, the discovered models can be tested and evaluated. Moreover, the process may repeat at different intervals when new/updated data come and/or the results are not good enough. We argue that the multi-phase process is an important methodology for knowledge discovery in the multi-media data obtained from the experiments with respect to human multi-perception mechanism. In the following, we focus on investigating how to obtain multiple data sources by fMRI visual and auditory calculation experiments and how to mine in such data sources.

3   Visual and Auditory Calculation Experiments

In the fMRI experiments, the mental arithmetic problems similar to the psychological experiments were used as auditory and visual stimuli, and we measured cortical areas of human calculate processing. The stimuli used in fMRI experiments are the mental arithmetic problems of addition as the "double figures plus double figures is equals triple figures" (for example, $56 + 75 = 131$). These stimuli are the most difficult task using in previous psychological experiments. The stimuli are presented to subjects according to the time chart as shown in Fig. 2. During first 30 sec., random figures are presented to subjects as auditory voice (Fig. 2a) or visual image (Fig. 2b). We define this presentation as "control" epoch. And after them, the mental arithmetic problems are presented during 30 sec. We define this presentation as "task" epoch. These task and control epochs are presented three times in one measurement. During the metal arithmetic problems are presented, the subjects are required to calculate the

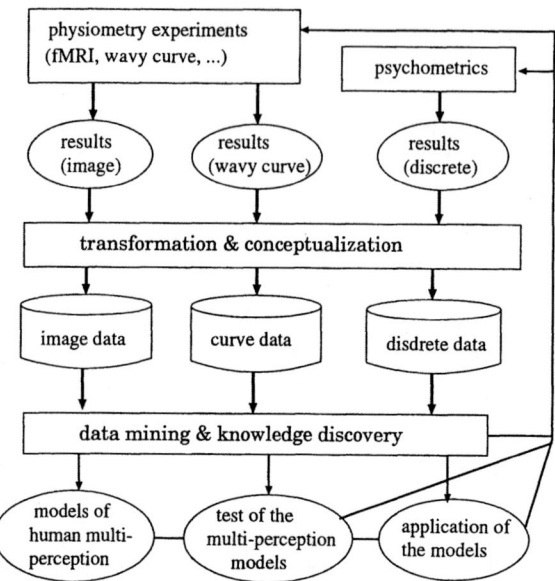

Fig. 1. A global view of our methodology to investigate human multi-perception

problems in his/her head without the response buttons. Conversely, during the random figures are presented, the subjects do not need to do any calculation.

Before the fMRI experiments, the rate of correct answers are measured by psychological experiments for all the subjects. In the fMRI experiments, the presenting speeds of the visual and auditory stimuli are decided to identify the rate of correct answer for each subject with using the results of the rate of correct answers measured by the psychological experiments. In the fMRI experiments, the presenting speed is used as the rate of correct answer both of the auditory and visual stimuli set at 85-90%. Numbers of stimuli presented and control epochs were decided by these presenting speed of the auditory and visual stimuli.

4   Peculiarity Oriented Mining

4.1   Peculiarity Rules

Peculiarity is a kind of interestingness. Peculiarity relationships/rules (with common sense) may be hidden in a relatively small number of data. Zhong et al. proposed *peculiarity rules* as a new class of association rules [12]. A *peculiarity rule* is discovered from *peculiar* data by searching the relevance among *peculiar* data. Roughly speaking, a data is *peculiar* if it represents a peculiar case described by a relatively small number of objects and is very different from other objects in a data set.

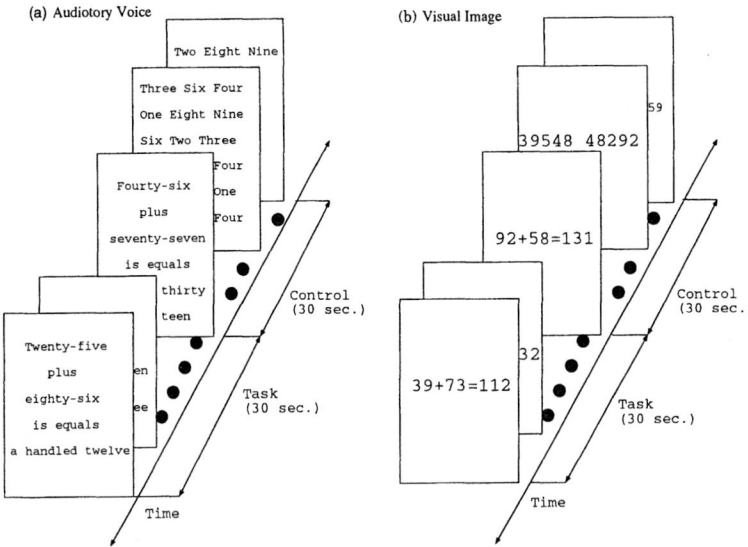

Fig. 2. Schematic illustration of stimuli in fMRI experiments. (a) Stimuli are presented to subjects as auditory voice. (b) Stimuli are presented to subjects as visual image.

We observe fMRI brain activations from the view point of peculiarity oriented mining. We argue that the *peculiarity rules* are a typical regularity hidden in a lot of scientific, statistical, and transaction databases. Sometimes, the general rules that represent the well-known fact with common sense cannot be found from numerous scientific, statistical or transaction data, or although they can be found, the rules may be uninteresting ones to the user since data are rarely specially collected/stored in a database for the purpose of mining knowledge in most organizations. Hence, the evaluation of interestingness (including surprisingness, unexpectedness, peculiarity, usefulness, novelty) should be done before and/or after knowledge discovery [3,5]. In particular, unexpected (common sense) relationships/rules may be hidden in a relatively small number of data. Thus, we may focus on some interesting data (peculiar data), and then we find more novel and interesting rules (peculiarity rules) from the data. For example, the following rules are the peculiarity ones that can be discovered from a relation called *Japan-Geography* (see Table 1) in a *Japan-Survey* database:

$rule_1$: *ArableLand(large)* & *Forest(large)* → *PopulationDensity(low)*.

$rule_2$: *ArableLand(small)* & *Forest(small)* → *PopulationDensity(high)*.

In order to discover the rules, we first need to search peculiar data in the relation *Japanese-Geography*. From Table 1, we can see that the values of the attributes *ArableLand* and *Forest* for Hokkaido (i.e. 1209 Kha and 5355 Kha) and for Tokyo and Osaka (i.e. 12 Kha, 18 Kha, and 80 Kha, 59 Kha) are very different from other values in the attributes. Hence, the values are regarded as peculiar data. Furthermore, $rule_1$ and $rule_2$ are generated by searching the relevance among peculiar data. Note that we use the qualitative representation for the quantitative values in the above rules. The transformation of quantitative to qualitative values can be done by using background knowledge on information granularity.

Table 1. Japan-Geography

Region	Area	Population	PopulationDensity	PeasantFamilyN	ArableLand	Forest	...
Hokkaido	82410.58	5656	**67.8**	93	**1209**	**5355**	...
Aomori	9605.45	1506	156.8	87	169	623	...
...	...	...	...	...	...	...	...
Tiba	5155.64	5673	1100.3	116	148	168	...
Tokyo	2183.42	11610	**5317.2**	21	**12**	**80**	...
...	...	...	...	...	...	...	...
Osaka	1886.49	8549	**4531.6**	39	**18**	**59**	...
...	...	...	...	...	...	...	...

4.2   Finding Peculiar Data

There are many ways of finding peculiar data. We here describe an attribute-oriented method.

Table 2 shows a relation with attributes A_1, A_2, ..., A_m. Let x_{ij} be the value of A_j of the i-th tuple, and n the number of tuples. The peculiarity of x_{ij} can be evaluated by the *Peculiarity Factor*, $PF(x_{ij})$,

$$PF(x_{ij}) = \sum_{k=1}^{n} N(x_{ij}, x_{kj})^{\alpha}, \tag{1}$$

where N denotes the conceptual distance, α is a parameter which can be adjusted by a user, and $\alpha = 0.5$ is used as default. Eq. (1) evaluates whether x_{ij} has a low frequency and is very different from other values x_{kj}.

Table 2. A sample table (relation)

A_1	A_2	...	A_j	...	A_m
x_{11}	x_{12}	...	x_{1j}	...	x_{1m}
x_{21}	x_{22}	...	x_{2j}	...	x_{2m}
⋮	⋮		⋮		⋮
x_{i1}	x_{i2}	...	x_{ij}	...	x_{im}
⋮	⋮		⋮		⋮
x_{n1}	x_{n2}	...	x_{nj}	...	x_{nm}

There are several advantages of the proposed method. One can handle both continuous and symbolic attributes based on a unified semantic interpretation.

Background knowledge represented by binary neighborhoods can be used to evaluate the peculiarity if such background knowledge is provided by a user. If X is a continuous attribute and no background knowledge is available, in Eq. (1) we use the distance,

$$N(x_{ij}, x_{kj}) = |x_{ij} - x_{kj}|. \tag{2}$$

If X is a symbolic attribute and the background knowledge for representing the conceptual distances between x_{ij} and x_{kj} is provided by a user, the peculiarity factor is calculated by the conceptual distances, $N(x_{ij}, x_{kj})$ [4,12]. The conceptual distances are assigned to 1 if no background knowledge is available.

There are two major methods for testing if peculiar data exist or not (it is called *selection of peculiar data*) after calculating peculiarity factors. The first is based on a threshold value:

$$threshold = mean\ of\ PF(x_{ij}) + \beta \times standard\ deviation\ of\ PF(x_{ij}), \tag{3}$$

where β can be adjusted by a user, and $\beta = 1$ is used as default. The threshold indicates that a data is a peculiar one if its PF value is much larger than the mean of the PF set. In other words, if $PF(x_{ij})$ is over the threshold value, x_{ij} is a peculiar data. By adjusting the parameter β, a user can define suitable threshold value. The other method for *selection of peculiar data* uses the chi-square test when the data size is sufficiently large [2].

Based on the preparation stated above, the process of finding peculiar data can be outlined as follows:

Step 1. Execute attribute oriented clustering for each attribute.
Step 2. For attributes 1 to m do
    Step 2.1. Calculate the peculiarity factor $PF(x_{ij})$ in Eq. (1) for all values of an attribute.
    Step 2.2. Calculate the threshold value in Eq. (3) based on the peculiarity factor obtained in *Step 2.1*.
    Step 2.3. Select the data that are over the threshold value as peculiar data.
    Step 2.4. If the current peculiarity level is enough, then goto *Step 3*.
    Step 2.5. Remove peculiar data from the attribute and thus, we get a new dataset. Then go back to *Step 2.1*.
Step 3. Change the granularity of peculiar data by using background knowledge on information granularity if the background knowledge is available.

Furthermore, the process can be done in a parallel-distributed mode for multiple attributes, relations and databases because this is an attribute-oriented finding method.

5 Application in fMRI Human Brain Data

5.1 Data Transformation

The existing multimedia data such as fMRI brain images and wavy curves might not be suitable for data mining. Therefore, a key issue is how to transform such image data into a unique representation format (i.e. table) so that the data can be stored in relational databases. For such transformation, we use software tools called MEDx (SPM) and Talairach daemon to interpret and conceptualize fMRI brain images, so that such images can be represented in a relational data model and stored in a relational database.

Brodmann assigned numbers to various brain regions by analyzing each area's cellular structure starting from the central sulcus (the boundary between the frontal and parietal lobes). Table 3 provides a general view of brain function that refers to the Brodmann map. In our experiments, the Brodmann map is used as prior knowledge to obtain the Brodmann area values from the Talairach daemon.

Table 3. Functional Areas of the Brain

Function	Brodmann Area
Vision	17, 18, 19, 20, 21, 37
Audition	41, 22, 42
Body Sensation	1, 2, 3, 5, 7
Sensation, tertiary	7, 22, 37, 39, 40
Motor	4, 6, 8, 44
Motor, tertiary	9, 10, 11, 45, 46, 47

5.2 Mining Process

The process of analyzing fMRI human brain data can be divided into the following steps.

Step 1. Analyze/transfer fMRI data by using the MEDx system.

Step 2. Obtain the Talairach daemon coordinate and active values from the MEDx data.

Step 3. Get Brodmann area values from the Talairach daemon.

Step 4. Create the visual and auditory calculation related databases, respectively, by using the Brodman area values. If there are multiple values in a Brodman area, use the sum of the values.

Step 5. Peculiarity-oriented mining in the visual and auditory calculation related databases, respectively.

Step 6. Compare/evaluate the results.

5.3 Results

Tables 4 and 5 shows a part of results of mining in *auditory* and *visual* calculation data, respectively, in which the data denoted in a bold type style are peculiar data (i.e., the activated values). By comparing results of mining in *auditory* and *visual* calculation data, we found an important feature of human information processing, that is, auditory information is usually transferred into visual information.

Table 4. A part of results of mining in *auditory* calculation data

Brodmann Area	ID of subjects								
	1	2	3	4	5	6	7	8	9
6	308.0	308.8	289.4	278.2	292.2	413.9	324.6	18.6	233.6
9	26.9	29.1	23.2	37.5	38.0	279.5	27.1	18.6	22.0
11	318.1	242.5	233.6	37.5	269.1	259.4	27.1	208.4	22.0
17	26.9	29.1	23.2	37.5	38.0	49.0	27.1	18.6	22.0
18	26.9	29.1	23.2	37.5	38.0	49.0	27.1	18.6	22.0
19	245.0	208.5	213.6	263.6	643.7	49.0	301.5	18.6	198.1
21	26.9	29.1	23.2	37.5	38.0	49.0	27.1	18.6	22.0
22	296.0	293.5	267.0	732.9	38.0	431.2	530.2	339.9	22.0
37	26.9	29.1	23.2	37.5	38.0	49.0	27.1	18.6	22.0
39	282.6	281.6	250.7	291.0	348.9	49.0	27.1	287.9	22.0
40	26.9	29.1	23.2	320.5	38.0	280.3	27.1	18.6	22.0
41	26.9	29.1	23.2	37.5	38.0	49.0	27.1	18.6	22.0
42	26.9	29.1	23.2	37.5	38.0	49.0	27.1	18.6	22.0
44	26.9	29.1	23.2	37.5	38.0	400.5	27.1	18.6	447.7
45	26.9	29.1	23.2	37.5	38.0	49.0	27.1	18.6	22.0
46	26.9	198.9	23.2	208.5	256.1	270.0	339.3	18.6	22.0
47	26.9	29.1	23.2	37.5	38.0	49.0	27.1	18.6	22.0

Table 5. A part of results of mining in *visual* calculation data

Brodmann Area	ID of subjects								
	1	2	3	4	5	6	7	8	9
6	312.3	222.5	279.5	123.4	64.1	301.6	503.9	29.8	45.9
9	205.4	263.4	17.1	61.6	64.1	285.6	52.1	29.8	279.0
11	319.5	241.8	17.1	301.2	64.1	51.5	52.1	29.8	45.9
17	248.0	287.5	17.1	61.6	581.7	51.5	52.1	29.8	45.9
18	602.2	50.6	274.7	692.4	692.1	591.1	600.7	464.1	584.5
19	595.2	305.7	17.1	279.0	64.1	561.5	335.0	381.3	464.4
21	77.6	50.6	17.1	61.6	64.1	51.5	288.9	188.7	45.9
22	77.6	50.6	17.1	264.2	64.1	227.2	52.1	224.3	45.9
37	77.6	372.6	200.3	61.6	64.1	51.5	52.1	29.8	347.7
39	77.6	50.6	17.1	307.5	363.6	229.9	52.1	29.8	45.9
40	77.6	195.9	187.2	301.0	240.8	51.5	52.1	206.4	45.9
41	77.6	50.6	17.1	61.6	64.1	51.5	52.1	29.8	45.9
42	77.6	50.6	17.1	61.6	64.1	51.5	52.1	29.8	45.9
43	77.6	50.6	17.1	61.6	64.1	51.5	52.1	29.8	45.9
44	245.5	50.6	17.1	61.6	64.1	51.5	52.1	29.8	45.9
45	77.6	50.6	17.1	61.6	64.1	51.5	52.1	29.8	45.9
46	77.6	50.6	17.1	221.4	240.1	200.7	419.1	29.8	45.9
47	77.6	199.9	17.1	61.6	231.5	51.5	52.1	29.8	244.4

6   Conclusions

We presented a new perspective of investigation on human multi-perception mechanism by using psychometrics and peculiarity oriented mining. We showed that multi-aspect analysis and mining in multiple data sources is an important way to investigate human multi-perception mechanism, systematically.

Since this project is very new, we just had a preliminary result in knowledge discovery from fMRI human brain data. Our future work includes peculiarity oriented mining in the visual and auditory calculation related databases without prior knowledge of Brodmann area, and comparing the results of using Brodmann area or not. We also will extend multiple information sources including brain wavy curves and other psychological experiments for multi-aspect analysis in various data mining approaches.

References

1. Agrawal R. et al. "Fast Discovery of Association Rules", *Advances in Knowledge Discovery and Data Mining*, AAAI Press (1996) 307–328.
2. Bhattacharyya, G.K. and Johnson, R.A. (1977) *Statistical Concepts and Methods*, John Wiley & Sons.
3. Freitas, A.A. "On Objective Measures of Rule Surprisingness" J. Zytkow and M. Quafafou (eds.) *Principles of Data Mining and Knowledge Discovery*, LNAI 1510, Springer (1998) 1–9.
4. Lin, T.Y., Zhong, N., Dong, J., and Ohsuga, S. "Frameworks for Mining Binary Relations in Data", L. Polkowski and A. Skowron (eds.) *Rough Sets and Current Trends in Computing*, LNAI 1424, Springer (1998) 387–393.
5. Liu, B., Hsu W., and Chen, S. "Using General Impressions to Analyze Discovered Classification Rules", *Proc. Third International Conference on Knowledge Discovery and Data Mining (KDD-97)*, AAAI Press (1997) 31–36.
6. Megalooikonomou, V., Davatzikos, C., and Herskovits, E.H. "Mining Lesion-Deficit Associations in a Brain Image Database", *Proc. Fifth International Conference on Knowledge Discovery and Data Mining (KDD-99)*, ACM Press (1999) 347–351.
7. Megalooikonomou, V., Ford, J., Shen, L., Makedon, F., and Saykin A. "Data Mining in Brain Imaging", *Statistical Methods in Medical Research*, 9 (2000) 359–394.
8. Tsukimoto, H. and Morita, C. "The Discovery of Rules from Brain Images", *Proc. First Inter. Conf. on Discovery Science*, LNAI 1532 (1998) 198–209.
9. Wu, J. and Zhong, N. "An Investigation on Human Multi-Perception Mechanism by Cooperatively Using Psychometrics and Data Mining Techniques", *Proc. 5th World Multi-Conference on Systemics, Cybernetics, and Informatics (SCI-01)*, Vol. X (2001) 285–290.
10. Yao, Y.Y. and Zhong, N. "Potential Applications of Granular Computing in Knowledge Discovery and Data Mining", *Proc. The 5th International Conference on Information Systems Analysis and Synthesis (IASA'99)*, edited in the invited session on Intelligent Data Mining and Knowledge Discovery (1999) 573–580.
11. Zadeh, L. A. "Toward a Theory of Fuzzy Information Granulation and Its Centrality in Human Reasoning and Fuzzy Logic", *Fuzzy Sets and Systems*, Elsevier, 90 (1997) 111–127.
12. Zhong, N., Yao, Y.Y., and Ohsuga, S. "Peculiarity Oriented Multi-Database Mining", J. Zytkow and Jan Rauch (eds.) *Principles of Data Mining and Knowledge Discovery*. LNAI 1704, Springer (1999) 136–146.

Automatic Classification and Clustering of Caenorhabditis Elegans Using a Computer Vision System

Seung-Bum Hong, Won Nah, and Joong-Hwan Baek

School of Electronics, Telecommunication & Computer Engineering
Hankuk Aviation University, Koyang City , South Korea
{sbhong, nahwon, jhbaek}@mail.hangkong.ac.kr

Abstract. In this paper, we introduce a computer vision system for automatic classification and clustering of C. elegans according to their behavioral phenotypes. We extract three kinds of features such as worm movement, body size, and body shape. A total of 117 features are extracted for each worm. Then the features are used to build an optimal classification tree using the CART(Classification and Regression Tree). We also try to find optimal clusters by using the gap statistic and hierarchical clustering method. For the experiment, we use 860 sample worms of 9 types (wild, goa-1, nic-1, egl-19, tph-1, unc-2, unc-29, unc-36, and unc-38). According to our experimental results, average success classification rate for wild, goa-1, nic-1, and egl-19 types is 92.3% while the rate for the other types is 70.3%. And the optimal number of clusters is 8 in our case.

Keywords: *Computer Vision, Classification, Clustering, C. elegans*

1 Introduction

Important application of quantitative image analysis to C. elegans neurobiology is to investigate molecular mechanisms of drug response. In [1], uncoordinated ('Unc') mutants are usually classified into a number of descriptive categories by a human observer. An experienced observer was able to subjectively distinguish worm types, but requirements for objective classification are now increasing. In the previous works [2],[3], classification was automated using the patterns from reliable egg-laying event timing data. In this paper, we introduce a computer vision system for automatic classification and clustering of C. elegans according to their behavioral phenotypes. The vision system consists of stereomicroscope, CCD camera, video recorder, video digitizer, stage controller, and tracking software. And we propose to use three kinds of features such as worm movement, body size, and body shape. Total of 117 features are extracted and used for constructing an optimal classification tree by using CART. In order to find an optimal number of clusters, we adopt gap statistic [4] and hierarchical clustering method [5].

J. Liu et al. (Eds.): IDEAL 2003, LNCS 2690, pp. 751–755, 2003.

2 Image Preprocessing and Feature Extraction

Binarization and preprocessing are the most important steps for the successful classification and analysis of C. elegans. First we perform binarization. Please refer to [6] for detailed information about the binarization. Then we use a 9×9 window for median filtering [7] to remove impulse noise in the binary worm image.

To remove the remaining noise, we propose a method that can distinguish between hole and noise. A hole is created when the worm loops or touches itself, while noise is located on the worm's body. Therefore, we can determine whether the region is a hole or noise by measuring the total thickness of the body enclosing the region. In order to measure the thickness, we define 16 vectors. We traverse and count the number of pixels ('0') from the centroid of a region in each vector direction until we reach the background ('1'). The total thickness is the sum of two opposite direction thicknesses. So, among the 8 total thicknesses, if the minimum is less than 25, the region is considered as noise, because we already know experimentally that the thickness of the worms used in this work is not larger than 25.

After detecting holes, we perform labeling [8] to remove the unwanted objects caused by worm's crawling tracks or eggs. Finally, we obtain the worm's skeleton by using the parallel thinning algorithm [7].

(a)   (b)   (c)   (d)

Fig. 1. (a) C. elegans gray image. (b) After binarization with median filtering. (c) Hole detection method using 16 vectors. (d) After hole detection and noise removal.

From the binary image and skeleton of a worm, we extract 3 kinds of features such as large-scale movement, body size, and body posture. Features for the large-scale movement are global moving distance and reversal frequencies during some intervals. Features related to body size are with and height of MER, worm's area, length, thickness, and fatness. Features related to body posture are the number of frames the worm is looped, amplitude of worm skeleton, angle change rate, and the number of frames with omega shape. Please refer to [6] for the detailed information about these features.

3 Classification Using CART and Clustering via Gap Statistic

The CART makes a binary classification tree using a learning sample. The root node of the tree contains all the training cases; the worm types are equally mixed together in this node. The goal of the CART is to successively subdivide the training set using binary splits in such a way that the data associated with the terminal nodes of the tree do not have a mix of worm types; rather, each node should be as pure as possible. In order to measure the impurity of a data set, the Gini index of diversity is applied. A simple rule is to assign the most popular class to each terminal node. To estimate the classification rate, the CART uses 10-fold cross-validation.

Estimation of the optimal number of clusters is one of major challenges in cluster analysis. In this paper, we adopt 'gap statistic' proposed by Hastie et al. [4]. We generate the reference features from a uniform distribution over a box aligned with the principal components of the data. For the computational implementation of the gap statistic, we take the following two steps: (1) Cluster the observed data, varying the total number of clusters from $k = 1, 2, \ldots K$, giving within dispersion measures $W_k, k = 1, 2, \ldots K$. (2) Generate B reference datasets, and cluster each one giving within dispersion measure W_{kb}^*, $b = 1, 2, \ldots B, k = 1, 2, \ldots K$. Compute the (estimated) gap statistic:

$$Gap(k) = (1/B)\sum_b \log(W_{kb}^*) - \log(W_k) \qquad (1)$$

Note that, in this paper, we adopt the hierarchical clustering method [5] for clustering the data.

4   Experimental Results

We use 9 different worm types (wild, goa-1, nic-1, unc-36, unc-38, egl-19, unc-2, unc-29, tph-1). Each worm type has 100 worms, except tph-1, which has 60 worms. So a total of 860 worms are used in this experiment. Primary features are extracted from each frame after preprocessing and skeletoning. Then, 117 features for a worm are computed from the primary features of 600 frames. Finally, the 860×117 variable set is fed into the CART for analysis and classification.

The CART creates a maximal tree and then prunes it back to obtain an optimal one. For our case, the optimal tree has 42 terminal nodes. To reduce the complexity of the tree, we set the complexity parameter to 0.007. The resulting classification tree has 13 terminal nodes. Table 1 shows the cross-validation classification probability table.

Table 1. Cross-validation classification probability table

Predicted / Actual	Wild	Goa-1	Nic-1	Unc-36	Unc-38	Egl-19	Unc-2	Unc-29	Tph-1
Wild	0.950	0.000	0.000	0.000	0.000	0.020	0.030	0.000	0.000
Goa-1	0.010	0.930	0.000	0.020	0.010	0.000	0.020	0.000	0.010
Nic-1	0.000	0.000	0.880	0.000	0.060	0.000	0.000	0.040	0.020
Unc-36	0.000	0.000	0.000	0.760	0.050	0.020	0.000	0.120	0.050
Unc-38	0.000	0.000	0.000	0.040	0.730	0.000	0.050	0.070	0.110
Egl-19	0.000	0.000	0.000	0.020	0.000	0.930	0.000	0.020	0.030
Unc-2	0.033	0.067	0.017	0.017	0.083	0.000	0.717	0.000	0.067
Unc-29	0.000	0.000	0.000	0.160	0.020	0.010	0.010	0.760	0.040
Tph-1	0.000	0.010	0.020	0.100	0.210	0.010	0.040	0.060	0.550

The success rates are listed along the shaded diagonal, while the off-diagonal entries represent the misclassification error rates. From this, we can see that wild, goa-1, nic-1 and egl-19 types have relatively high success classification rates (92.3%

on the average) comparing to the unc types (70.3% on the average). This is due to the fact that unc-36, unc-38, unc-2, unc-29, and tph-1 have similar behavioral characteristics.

In order to find the optimal number of clusters, first of all, we normalize each variable to $-1.0 \sim 1.0$, and then apply the hierarchical clustering method. For the gap statistic, 10 reference data sets are generated, and the number of the cluster centers k is varied from 1 to 10. Then the gap is computed by using Equation (1) for each k. Finally we select as the optimal number of clusters that value of k producing the largest gap: $\hat{k} = \arg\max_k Gap(k)$. Fig. 2 plots the gap verses the number of clusters. We can see that 8 is the optimal number of clusters.

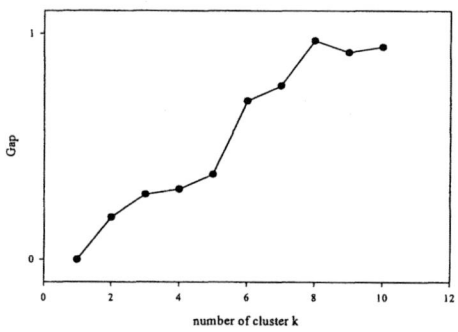

Fig. 2. Gap curve.

Table 2 shows the clustering results when the number of cluster is 8. We can see that unc-38 and unc-29 are aggregated.

Table 2. Clustering results when the number of clusters is 8

Cluster # / Worm type	1	2	3	4	5	6	7	8
1. Wild	82	18	0	0	0	0	0	0
2. Goa-1	1	21	76	2	0	0	0	0
3. Nic-1	0	0	0	0	98	1	1	0
4. Unc-36	0	1	0	80	0	11	8	0
5. Unc-38	0	1	0	9	1	11	78	0
6. Unc-29	0	9	0	12	0	39	40	0
7. Egl-19	0	1	0	3	0	11	1	84
8. Unc-2	0	0	0	27	1	58	13	1
9. Tph-1	0	56	0	0	2	0	2	0

5   Conclusions

In this paper, we introduced a computer vision system, which can measure C. elegans behavioral features quantitatively, and then classify them automatically. We extracted features related to worm's movement, body size, and body posture. A total of 117 features were computed from the primary features. Then the features were fed into the CART to create a classification tree. According to our experimental results, wild, goa-1, nic-1 and egl-19 types had relatively high success classification rates (92.3% on the average), but unc types and tph-1 had a low classification probability (70.3% on the average), which was due to the fact that unc types have very similar behaviors. We also found the optimal number of clusters using the gap statistic. First of all, we sought clusters from 860 worm samples by using the hierarchical clustering method. Then we computed the gap values varying the number of clusters from 1 to 10. From our experimental results, it was found that 8 clusters was optimal number of clusters in our case. For further works, more significant features for unc types and tph-1 are to be devised and extracted.

Acknowledgements. This research was supported by IRC (Internet Information Retrieval Research Center) in Hankuk Aviation University. IRC is a Kyounggi-Province Regional Research Center designated by Korea Science and Engineering Foundation and Ministry of Science & Technology.

Also, the authors are grateful to Prof. Pamela Cosman and Prof. William Schafer in University of California, San Diego, for their invaluable advice.

References

1. Hodkin, J.: Male phenotypes and mating efficiency in Caenorhabditis elegans. Genetics (1983) 43–64
2. Waggoner, L., et al.: Control of behavioral states by serotonin in Caenorhabditis elegans. Neuron (1998) 203–214
3. Zhou, G.T., Schafer, W.R., Schafer, R.W.: A three-state biological point process model and its parameter estimation. IEEE Trans On Signal Processing (1998) 2698–2707
4. Hastie, T., et al.: Estimating the number of clusters in a dataset via the Gap statistic. Tech. Report. Department of Statistics at Stanford University (2000)
5. Duda, R., Hart, P., Stork, D.: Pattern Classification. John Wiley & Sons, Inc., New York (2001)
6. Nah, W., Hong, S.B., Baek. J.H.: Feature Extraction for Classification of Caenorhabditis Elegans Behavioural Phenotypes. To be appeared in the proceedings of IEA/AIE-2003 (2003)
7. Gonzalez, R.C., Woods, R.E.: Digital Image Processing. Prentice Hall Inc., New Jersey (2002)
8. Jain, R., Kasturi, R., Schunck, B.G.: Machine Vision. McGraw-Hill Inc., New York (1995)

A Concept-Based Inter-lingua and Its Applications to Multilingual Text and Web Mining

Rowena Chau and Chung-Hsing Yeh

School of Business Systems,
Faculty of Information Technology,
Monash University, Clayton, Victoria 3800, Australia
{Rowena.Chau,ChungHsing.Yeh}@infotech.monash.edu.au

Abstract. In this paper, a novel concept-based approach for knowledge discovery from multilingual textual data is proposed and the potential applications of this approach in multilingual document mining and multilingual Web content mining are highlighted. The central idea is the generation of a concept-based inter-lingua encoding the multilingual concept-term relationship, using self-organizing map. Applying this concept-based inter-lingua as the multilingual linguistic knowledge base, conceptual content of arbitrary multilingual texts is then revealed using a novel multilingual conceptual indexing technique.

1   Introduction

Electronically accessible information is now available in an ever-increasing number of languages. With vast human knowledge being hidden beneath the largely untapped multilingual text, multilingual text mining methodology capable of discovering useful knowledge from multilingual textual data thus holds the key to open up the hidden treasure. Current text mining research is focused on processing monolingual text. The challenge of discovering knowledge from textual data which is significantly linguistically diverse has been well recognised [6]. In a multilingual environment, vocabulary mismatch among diverse languages implies that documents exhibiting similar concepts will not necessarily contain identical term patterns. Towards multilingual text mining, linguistic knowledge of concept-term relationships is essential in order to allow any knowledge relevant to the domain of a multilingual document collection to be exploited. To fulfil this requirement, we propose a novel concept-based approach using self-organising maps. The salient feature of this approach is its capability to automatically discover (a) the multilingual concept-term relationship with the construction of a concept-based inter-lingua and (b) the conceptual contents of multilingual texts using a novel multilingual conceptual indexing technique.

This paper is organised as follows. In Section 2, an overview of this approach is first presented. Details about the generation of the concept-based inter-lingua, and the multilingual conceptual indexing technique, are discussed in Sections 3 and 4. Section 5 and 6 discuss the application of this approach towards multilingual document mining and multilingual Web mining, followed by a conclusive remark in Section 7.

J. Liu et al. (Eds.): IDEAL 2003, LNCS 2690, pp. 756–760, 2003.

2 The Approach

The central idea of this approach to is: when a concept-based inter-lingua is represented by clusters of conceptually related multilingual terms, direct mapping of multilingual text within a common semantic space is facilitated. Hence, given a concept-
based indexing scheme, conceptual contents of multilingual texts can then be represented and revealed. This approach to multilingual text mining is realised using self-
organising map (SOM) [8]. First, multilingual linguistic knowledge in the form of
concept-term relationship is discovered with the generation of a concept-based inter-
lingua. To do so, a set of multilingual terms is first extracted from a parallel corpus.
By analysing co-occurrence statistics of these multilingual terms across the parallel
corpus, conceptual related multilingual terms are sorted into term clusters as they are
organised onto a self-organising map. Consequently, a concept-based inter-lingua is
formed. Second, to discover the conceptual content of arbitrary multilingual text, our
approach then proposes a language-independent concept-based text representation
scheme based on a novel multilingual conceptual indexing technique using the concept-based inter-lingua as the multilingual linguistic knowledge base. By representing
multilingual texts with the language-independent concepts in place of their original
language-specific index terms, conceptual content of all multilingual text can then be
universally represented and explicitly revealed.

3 Concept-Based Inter-lingua

Processing monolingual corpus for automatically constructing monolingual linguistic
knowledge bases, such as thesaurus, has been extensively studied [2][5]. For constructing multilingual linguistic knowledge base encoding lexical relationships among
multilingual terms, parallel corpora containing sets of documents and their translations in multiple languages is employed. Analysis of paired documents can be used to
infer the most likely translation of terms between languages in the corpus [1].

   Given a parallel corpus D consisting P pairs of parallel documents, meaningful
terms from every languages covered by the corpus are extracted. Each multilngual
term is then represented by a P-dimensional vector. Each feature value of the vector
corresponds to the occurrence of a term in the pth document in this term's own language version. When contextual contents of every multilingual term are well represented, they are used as the input into the self-organising map algorithm for constructing the concept-based inter-lingua.

   Let $\mathbf{x}_i \in R^N$ ($1 \leq i \leq M$) be the vector of the ith multilingual term, where N is
the number of documents in the parallel corpus for a single language (i.e. the total
number of documents in the parallel corpus divided by the number of languages supported by the corpus) and M is the total number of multilingual terms. The self-
organising map algorithm is applied to form a concept-based inter-lingua, using vectors of all multilingual terms as the training input. The map consists of a regular grid
of nodes. Each node is associated with an N-dimensional model vector. Let

$\mathbf{m}_j = \left[m_{jn} \middle| 1 \le n \le N \right] (1 \le j \le G)$ be the model vector of the jth node on the map.

The algorithm for forming the concept-based inter-lingua is given below.

Step 1. Select a training vector $\mathbf{x}_i$ at random.

Step 2. Find the winning node s with the vector $\mathbf{m}_s$ which is closest to $\mathbf{x}_i$ such that

$$\left\| \mathbf{x}_i - \mathbf{m}_s \right\| = \min_j \left\| \mathbf{x}_i - \mathbf{m}_j \right\| \tag{1}$$

Step 3. Update the weight of every node in the neighbourhood of node s by

$$\mathbf{m}_t^{new} = \mathbf{m}_t^{old} + \alpha(t)(\mathbf{x}_i - \mathbf{m}_t^{old}) \tag{2}$$

where $\alpha(t)$ is the gain term at time t ($0 \le \alpha(t) \le 1$) that decreases in time.

Step 4. Increase the time stamp t and repeat the training process until it converges.

After the training process is completed, each multilingual term is mapped to a grid node closest to it on the self-organising map and the conceptual similarities among multilingual terms are explicitly revealed by their locations and neighbourhood relationships on the map. A concept-based inter-lingua is thus formed.

4 Multilingual Conceptual Indexing

The objective of multilingual text mining is to reveal the conceptual content of arbitrary multilingual texts in accordance with the meanings they convey. This depends heavily on the support of an effective text representation scheme. To this end, a novel multilingual conceptual indexing technique is proposed. To achieve this, multilingual linguistic knowledge encoded in the concept-based inter-lingua is used. Within the concept-based inter-lingua, conceptually related multilingual terms have been organised into term clusters. These clusters, denoting concepts described universally in all languages, are thus used to index multilingual texts in place of these texts' original language-specific index terms. To carry out multilingual conceptual indexing, multilingual texts are indexed by mapping their original content, term by term, onto the concept-based inter-lingua whereby statistics of its 'hits' on each multilingual term cluster are recorded. This is done by counting the occurrence of each term on the concept-based inter-lingua at the node to which that term has been associated. As such, a concept-based index vector that explicitly expresses the conceptual context of a text regardless of its language can be obtained.

5 Application 1: Multilingual Document Mining

The objective of multilingual document mining is to reveals the conceptual content of a set of multilingual documents by organising them into document clusters. By using self-organising map, a multilingual document cluster map can be constructed to provide the conceptual overview of a multilingual document collection as a whole.

Let $\mathbf{y}_i \in R^G$ ($1 \le i \le H$) be the concept-based index vector of the ith multilingual document, where G is the number of nodes existing in the concept-based inter-lingua and H is the total number of documents in the multilingual document collection. In addition, let $\mathbf{m}_j = [m_{jn}|1 \le n \le G]$ ($1 \le j \le J$), be the G-dimensional model vector of the jth node on the map. The algorithm for forming the multilingual document cluster map is given below.

Step 1. Select a training multilingual document vector $\mathbf{y}_i$ at random.

Step 2. Find the winning node s with the vector $\mathbf{m}_s$ which is closest to document $\mathbf{y}_i$ such that

$$\|\mathbf{y}_i - \mathbf{m}_s\| = \min_j \|\mathbf{y}_i - \mathbf{m}_j\| \tag{3}$$

Step 3. After the winning node s is selected, update the weight of every node in the neighbourhood of node s by

$$\mathbf{m}_t^{new} = \mathbf{m}_t^{old} + \alpha(t)(\mathbf{y}_i - \mathbf{m}_t^{old}) \tag{4}$$

where $\alpha(t)$ is the gain term at time t ($0 \le \alpha(t) \le 1$) that decreases in time.

Step 4. Increase the time stamp t and repeat the training process until it converges.

The multilingual document cluster map is constructed to reflect the conceptual relationship among documents. Multilingual documents describing similar concepts will occur close to each other on the map. As such, when any arbitrary set of multilingual documents can be organised according to their conceptual contents on a multilingual document cluster map, global knowledge residing in all multilingual textual databases can be conveniently explored.

6 Application 2: Multilingual Web Content Mining

With the overwhelming amount of information in the multilingual WWW, not every piece of information is useful to a user. In the process of multilingual Web content mining, which aims exclusively at limited set(s) of useful multilingual Web documents, a user profile that models the user's information interest is required to filter out information that the user is not interested in.

Common approaches to user profiling build a representation of the user's information interest based on the distribution of terms found in some previously seen documents which the user has found to be useful [4]. However, such representation has difficulties in handling situations where a user is interested in more than one topic. In addition, in a multilingual environment, the vocabulary mismatch phenomenon across languages makes a language-specific term-based user profile insufficient for representing the user's information interest that spans multiple languages. To overcome these problems, we propose a concept-based representation for building user profiles.

To understand the user's information interests, the user's bookmark file from the browser is used as indicators of the user's preferences. Web documents pointed by the bookmarks are first retrieved. Applying the concept-based inter-lingua as the linguistic knowledge base, each Web document is then converted into a concept-based representation using the multilingual conceptual indexing technique. Given a multilingual Web page classifier, which is a multilingual document cluster map constructed to represent the conceptual document categories of a comprehensive training parallel corpus using the self-organising document clustering algorithm as described in Section 5, each concept-based index vector representing a bookmarked Web page is mapped onto it to find its winning node. After mapping all bookmarks' concept-based index vectors onto the multilingual document cluster map, the document categories relevant to the user's bookmark file are revealed. As such, these document categories can be interpreted as the user profile representing a user's information interest in multiple topics. By highlighting these document categories on the multilingual document cluster map, which is also used as a Web browsing interface, concept-based multilingual Web content mining is thus personalised.

7 Conclusion

We have presented a novel approach to multilingual text mining using self-organising maps. The approach is realised by two major developments, namely, the construction of a concept-based inter-lingua and the introduction of a multilingual conceptual indexing technique. Multilingual linguistic knowledge as encoded in the concept-based inter-lingua overcomes the vocabulary mismatch problem by enabling language-independent concept-based text representation using the multilingual conceptual indexing technique. By facilitating a unified text representation framework accommodating all languages, significant multilingual text mining tasks, including multilingual document mining and multilingual Web content mining can be realized.

References

1. Carbonell, J. G., Yang, Y., Frederking, R. E., Brown, R. D., Geng, Y. and Lee, D (1997) Translingual information retrieval: a comparative evaluation. In Pollack, M. E. (ed.) *IJCAI-97 Proceedings of the 15th International Joint Conference on Artificial Intelligence*, pp.708–714.
2. Jing, Y and Croft, W. B. (1994) *An Association Thesaurus for Information Retrieval*. Technical Report 94–17, Department of Computer Science, University of Massachusetts, Amherst.
3. Kohonen, T. (1995) *Self-Organising Maps*. Springer-Verlag, Berlin.
4. Lieberman, H., Van Dyke, N. W. and Vivacqua, A. S. (1999) Let's browse: A collaborative browsing agent. In *Proceedings of the 1999 International Conference on Intelligent User Interfaces, Collaborative Filtering and Collaborative Interfaces*, pp. 65–68.
5. Qiu, Y. (1995) *Automatic Query Expansion Based on a Similarity Thesaurus* .PhD thesis, Swiss Federal Institute of Technology.
6. Tan, A-H. (1999) Text Mining: The state of the art and the challenges. In *Proceedings of PAKDD'99 Workshop on Knowledge Discovery from Advanced Databases*, Beijing, April 1999, pp.65–70.

Flexible Decision Trees in a General Data-Mining Environment

Joshua W. Comley, Lloyd Allison, and Leigh J. Fitzgibbon

School of Computer Science and Software Engineering
Monash University, Clayton 3800, Australia
{joshc,lloyd,leighf}@bruce.csse.monash.edu.au

Abstract. We describe a new data-mining platform, CDMS, aimed at the streamlined development, comparison and application of machine learning tools. We discuss its type system, focussing on the treatment of statistical models as first-class values.
This allows rapid construction of composite models - complex models built from simpler ones - such as mixture models, Bayesian networks and decision trees. We illustrate this with a flexible decision tree tool for CDMS which rather than being limited to discrete target attributes, can model any kind of data using arbitrary probability distributions.

1 Introduction

This paper introduces the 'Core Data-Mining Software' (CDMS) system and a flexible decision tree inference program implemented as a CDMS 'plug-in'. CDMS is a general data-mining platform providing a tool-box of common operations such as data input and output, manipulation, and visualization. CDMS is being developed at Monash University, and although only in its early stages is already proving to be a useful environment for the streamlined implementation of a variety of machine learning and statistical analysis tools.

Many other machine learning and data-mining platforms exist (e.g. S-plus [7], R [5], and Weka [12]), but the unique handling and definition of statistical models by CDMS makes it a particularly interesting and powerful system. Section 2 describes CDMS and discusses its representation of values and data types. In section 3 we examine the characteristics of a CDMS model.

A statistical model is treated as a value by CDMS, meaning that it may be the subject or result of functions, or even a parameter for another model. By including models as parameters for other models, we can build powerful composite models. We illustrate this with a rather general decision tree 'plug-in', described in section 4, and give examples in section 5.

2 The Core Data Mining Software (CDMS) Platform

CDMS provides a framework in which to implement data-mining and machine learning tools, referred to in this paper as 'plug-ins'. It has a library of inbuilt

J. Liu et al. (Eds.): IDEAL 2003, LNCS 2690, pp. 761–767, 2003.

functions, models and other values which plug-ins can utilize and add to. CDMS is capable of performing input/output of data in various file formats, including standard delimited text files, Weka [12] '.arff' files, GenBank files and C5's [6] '.data' and '.names' files. It is implemented in Java and offers an intuitive graphical user interface. It is currently under development, but it is anticipated that a prototype will be available soon.

Data is represented in CDMS as values. CDMS defines various types of values using a class hierarchy. This includes simple types such as string, scalar - which has the sub-types of discrete and continuous - and 'Triv' (the null type of CDMS). In addition, the structured and vector types provide support for heterogeneous and homogeneous collections of values respectively. Functions are also treated as values in CDMS. They are characterized by a parameter type and result type. A function can be applied to any value which matches the parameter type, giving a new value which will match the result type. Because functions are values, one could build a vector of them, or even write a function which can be applied to a function, giving another function as a result.

3   CDMS Models

This section discusses another type of CDMS value - the model, which we define here to be a family of distributions (e.g. normal distributions). When predicting or generating data, or when obtaining a likelihood, the distribution to be used is determined by the parameters supplied to the model. For a discussion of closely related schemes for model types and operations, see [1], and [4].

Models are characterized by the kind of values they work with. This is broken down into the parameter space, data space, input space, and sufficient space.

The parameter space refers to the type of parameters the model requires. For example, a Gaussian model requires the mean and variance as parameters - which can be represented in CDMS using a structure of two continuous values.

The data space[1] is the type of data that is modelled - i.e.the data over which the model can give a probability density. This density is typically a function of the model's parameters, and often of some 'input' data as well.

The input space is the type of any 'input' or 'explanatory' data that the model requires (in addition to its parameters) to provide a probability of the observed target data. Examples include the explanatory attributes of a decision tree, or the 'independent' attributes in a polynomial regression.

The sufficient space refers to the type of data that can capture all the information needed by the model about a vector of input data, and a corresponding vector of output data. Such data are commonly referred to as a 'sufficient statistic'. For a more detailed discussion of sufficient statistics in relation to models, data types and efficient computations, see [4].

Any CDMS model should be able to perform the following operations: logprobability, prediction, generation, and 'get-sufficient'.

---

[1] referred to in this paper also as the 'target data' type, or 'output data' type

The 'log-probability' operation requires a model to compute the log-probability of some given output data, when also supplied with parameters and a vector of input data. Models are also required to perform this operation when given sufficient statistics in place of the vector of input and output data.

The prediction operation involves the model selecting the 'most likely' output vector, when presented with parameters and a corresponding input vector. Generation is similar to the prediction operation, but instead of returning the most likely output value, the model pseudo-randomly selects an output value by sampling from the predictive distribution.

When presented with a vector of input and output data, the 'get-sufficient' operation requires models to return the corresponding sufficient statistic.

4   Decision Trees

Decision trees model the correlation between the input and output attributes in order to predict likely output values for future 'test' data-sets where only the input values are known. Decision tree tools such as C5 [6], CART [3], and DTree [11] generally do this well, but are often only applicable to problems where the output attribute takes discrete values. Furthermore, rather than modelling the output attribute probabilistically some decision trees simply state the predicted value for each test case. Here we are concerned with a more general situation where the output attribute is not necessarily discrete, and where we wish to model it with a probability distribution.

The tree plugin has been designed to accept any CDMS model in the leaves, allowing us to use arbitrary distributions to fit the output data. A tree class is constructed from modular elements (described below) which are largely independent, making it easy to assemble decision tree classes to suit a range of data sets.

The **leaf model** of a decision tree class defines how the target attribute is to be modelled. Each leaf is likely to contain different parameters for this model, which are estimated using the tree's **leaf estimator function**, based on the training data pertaining to the leaf. Examples of simpler leaf models include Gaussian and multi-state distributions, but any CDMS model could be used. By choosing a leaf model with a (non-Triv) input space, e.g. a polynomial regression, interesting tree classes may be constructed, whose leaves model the target attribute as a function of one or more input attributes.

A tree class has a **branch method** for each attribute. This defines how the attribute will be tested at a branch node. Possible branch methods include 'hard' or 'soft' cut points for continuous attributes, 'pie-slice' cuts for cyclic attributes, or n-way branches for discrete n-valued attributes. The tree tool can accept any branch method so long as it can provide a fractional assignment over the branch's children when given the attribute to test.

The **cost function** is used by a search to cost each candidate tree. It is given a structure comprising the tree model, its parameters, and the data, and returns a penalty value which the **search function**[2] attempts to minimise.

It is interesting to note that the decision tree class, as well as using CDMS models in its leaves, can itself be seen as a CDMS model. The data space of the decision tree model is simply the target attribute, while the input space is a structured value of the explanatory attributes. The parameters of a decision tree model would include the topology of the tree, the input attribute to be tested at each branch node and any parameters pertaining to these tests, and the parameters for the model in each leaf. The search function, leaf estimator function, and tree costing function are not actually part of the decision tree model. Rather, they constitute an estimator function for it. Given the training data and this estimator function, one can obtain an estimate of the optimal parameters for the decision tree model.

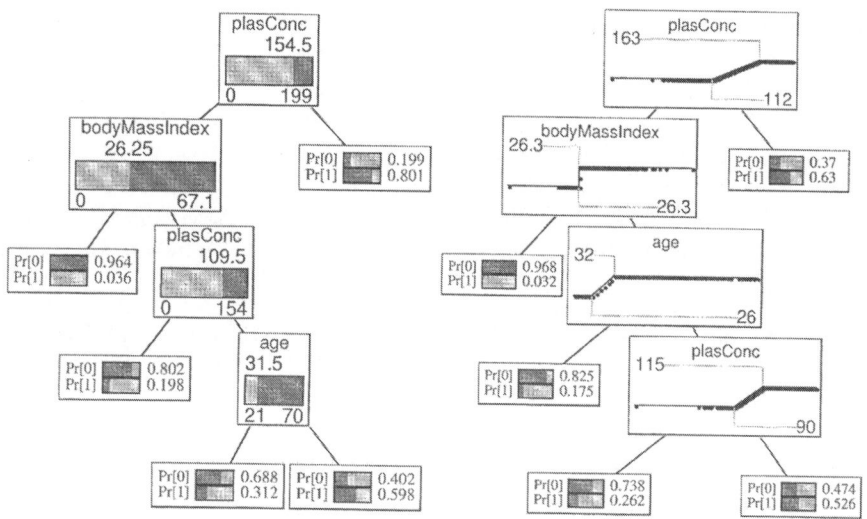

Fig. 1. Trees from two decision tree classes. The tree on the left uses 'hard' cut-points to test input attributes, while the tree on the right uses the 'soft' cuts.

5   Examples

This section briefly shows example trees from three CDMS decision tree classes. The first two trees were learnt from the "Pima Indians Diabetes Database", available from [2] and are depicted in figure 1. Both classes used a 2-state distribution as the leaf model, and a lookahead-0 search based on a Minimum Message

---

[2] Search functions provide a way to traverse the parameter space of a decision tree.

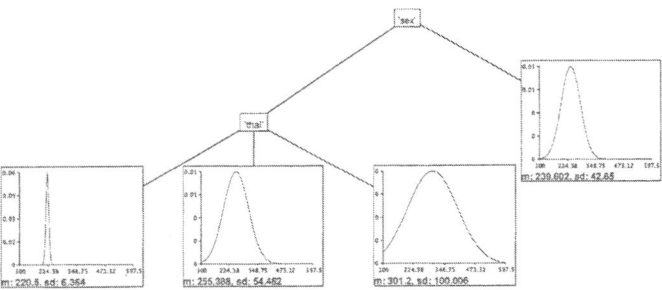

Fig. 2. This tree has been learnt from a cholesterol data set, obtained from the Weka website *http://www.cs.waikato.ac.nz/ml/weka/*. The data-set is a modified form of the Cleveland Heart Disease database collected by Dr Robert Detrano, available from [2].

Length (MML) [8,9,10] tree cost function, similar to that proposed in [11]. The difference is in the choice of branch methods. The tree on the left used the familiar 'hard' cut-point to test the continuous input attributes, while the tree on the right used 'soft' tests. The soft tests define a 'ramp' between two values a and b. Any item with a value less than a is assigned totally to the left-hand sub-tree, while any value greater than b is assigned totally to the right. Any value x between a and b is fractionally assigned to the right hand sub-tree with weight $(x - a)/(b - a)$.

Figure 2 illustrates a third class of decision tree. This tree uses discrete branch methods to test input attributes, and uses a Gaussian density function as the leaf model, supplying a probability density over the continuous target attribute.

6   Results

We now compare the performance of the two decision tree classes shown in figure 1 and that of C5 [6]. Five data sets were analysed - wine, iris, E-coli, pima, and glass - and are all available from [2]. Table 1 summarizes their characteristics. The data-sets chosen each had a categorical (discrete) target attribute, allowing easy comparison with C5 - which, unlike the tree classes presented here, is not able to model continuous data.

Table 1. A summary of the nature of the five data-sets.

Data-set	Target Attribute	Other Attributes
Wine	3-valued discrete	12 continuous attributes
Iris	3-valued discrete	4 continuous attributes
E-coli	8-valued discrete	7 continuous attributes
Pima	2-valued discrete	8 continuous attributes
Glass	7-valued discrete	9 continuous attributes

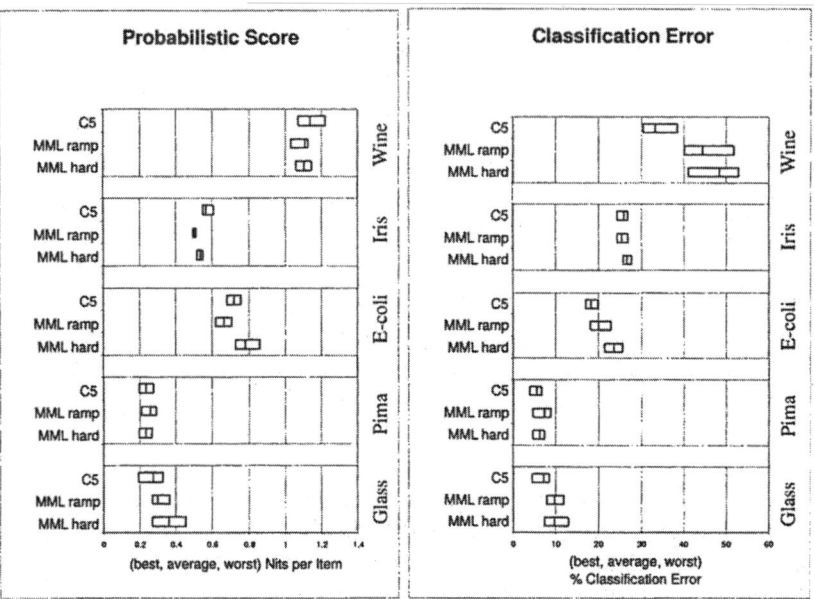

Fig. 3. A comparison of three decision tree methods. 'MML-ramp' refers to the tree class on the right in figure 1, using soft cut-points to test continuous input attributes. 'MML-hard' refers to the tree class on the left in figure 1, which like C5, uses hard cut-points to test continuous attributes.

We have assessed each method using both classification error and probabilistic score. Classification error simply measures the percentage of misclassified test cases (which only makes sense when dealing with discrete target attributes). Probabilistic score is a more general measure of performance, which penalises a method according to the negative logarithm of the probability the method assigns to the test data. This score rewards accurate estimates of probabilities, taking into account the certainty with which a prediction is made, rather than simply treating each prediction as 'right' or 'wrong'. Probabilistic score is thus more informative than classification error, and reflects our interest in *probabilistic* prediction. For many real-world instances, we would like to know not just the most likely outcome, but how likely this outcome is. For example, in a medical scenario, if we believed that a radical new treatment was 99% likely to succeed, the patient may feel differently than if the chance of success was believed to be only 51%.

For each data-set, we performed a 10-fold cross-validation experiment (with 90% training data, 10% testing data). The performance of each method was averaged over the 10 test-sets, resulting in a score, s. We then repeated this 10 times, recording for each method the best, worst, and average s. This is shown in figure 3.

Although C5 often yields superior classification error, we can see from the probabilistic score that it does not do so well at inferring accurate probabilities. An explanation for this is that it tends to estimate more extreme distributions, and may therefore make predictions with more certainty than is warranted. While assigning a near-zero probability to a test item does not impact greatly on classification error, it can have a disastrous effect on probabilistic score.

The results for the *iris*, *E − coli* and *wine* data-sets demonstrate the merits of a more general class of decision tree. In the probabilistic score especially, we can see that the 'soft ramp' branch tests significantly improve performance, providing a more accurate probabilistic model of the target attribute.

7   Conclusion

We have given an overview of a general data-mining platform that provides in-built support for statistical models in its type system. Using a decision tree 'plug-in' as an example, we have discussed how complex models can easily be constructed using simpler models as building blocks. This approach lets us quickly build a versatile library of machine learning tools that are tightly integrated with the system, rather than being stand-alone algorithms.

References

1. L. Allison. Types and classes of machine learning and data mining. In *Proceedings of the Twenty-Sixth Australasian Computer Science Conference (ACSC2003)*, pages 207–215, Adelaide, South Australia, 2003.
2. C. Blake and C. Merz. UCI repository of machine learning databases, 1998. http://www.ics.uci.edu/~mlearn/MLRepository.html.
3. L. Breiman, J. H. Friedman, R. A. Olshen, and C. J. Stone. *Classification and Regression Trees*. Statistics/Probability Series. Wadsworth Publishing Company, Belmont, California, U.S.A., 1984.
4. L. Fitzgibbon, L. Allison, and J. Comley. Probability model type sufficiency. In *Proc. 4th International Conference on Intelligent Data Engineering and Automated Learning*, 2003.
5. R. Ihaka and R. Gentleman. R: A language for data analysis and graphics. *Journal of Computational and Graphical Statistics*, 5(3):299–314, 1996.
6. J. R. Quinlan. C5.0. http://www.rulequest.com.
7. W. N. Venables and B. D. Ripley. *Modern Applied Statistics with S-PLUS*. Springer, 3 edition, 1999.
8. C. S. Wallace and D. M. Boulton. An information measure for classification. *Computer Journal*, 11:185–194, 1968.
9. C. S. Wallace and D. M. Boulton. An invariant Bayes method for point estimation. *Classification Society Bulletin*, 3(3):11–34, 1975.
10. C. S. Wallace and P. R. Freeman. Estimation and inference by compact coding. *J. Royal Statistical Society (Series B)*, 49:240–252, 1987.
11. C. S. Wallace and J. D. Patrick. Coding decision trees. *Machine Learning*, 11:7–22, 1993.
12. I. H. Witten and E. Frank. *Nuts and bolts: Machine learning algorithms in Java*. Morgan Kaufmann, 1999.

Developing a Directory of Search Engines for Meta-searching

Jacky K.H. Shiu, Stephen C.F. Chan, and Korris F.L. Chung

Department of Computing, The Hong Kong Polytechnic University
Hung Hom, Kowloon, Hong Kong.
{cskhshiu, csschan, cskchung}@comp.polyu.edu.hk

Abstract. Selecting the right search engine to use is critical to meta-searching. This paper discusses the development of a directory of search engines by linking search engines to appropriate topics in a hierarchy of search topics. A categorization algorithm based on probe queries is used to determine the relevancy of specific search engines to search topics. Output of the categorization algorithm is compared with human categorizations and results are promising.

1 Introduction

Search engines have become the most useful tools for the retrieval of Web documents on the Internet. However, even the largest search engines index only a fraction of the Internet [11]. As a result, meta-search engines such as MetaCrawler [16], Savvy-Search [6], Profusion [8, 15] and Dogpile [5] has been developed. While meta-searching increases the coverage, users find it difficult to find the target information in the large set of results returned. In this research, we developed an algorithm to build a hierarchical directory to help to select the appropriate search engine for specific queries in meta-searching.

One of the reasons that make it hard for general search engines to increase their coverage is that much of the documents available on the Internet are not "crawlable" to their software robots. Robots cannot index documents that are encapsulated by a search interface and generated dynamically by Web servers. In this research, we use the term *specialty search engines* [6] to represent such kind of searchable interfaces on the Web. Study shows that resources that are not indexed by general search engines are hundreds times greater than those indexed resources [2].

While general meta-search engines exploit general search engines, a number of meta-search engines have been developed for exploiting only specialty search engines. For instance, MetaXChem [12], LawBot [4], Ithaki [10] and Family Friendly Search [7]. Nevertheless, compare to the amount of all the covered resources on the Web, the resources discovered by each of the above meta-search engines are still limited. It is because each of them only exploits a small set of specialty search engines that are inside the same domain. Therefore, a meta-search engine that can exploit specialty search engines inside different domains is a possible solution.

J. Liu et al. (Eds.): IDEAL 2003, LNCS 2690, pp. 768–772, 2003.

In section 2 we present an algorithm that can automatically categorize specialty search engines into a hierarchical category tree. Section 3 discusses the validation of the categorization algorithm by comparison against manual categorization.

2   Search Engine Categorization

Instead of constructing a hierarchy from scratch, we utilize the largest and most comprehensive human-edited directory for the Web: the Open Directory [14]. In this paper, the sub-category "*Top / Computers / Software / Internet / Clients*" has been chosen for the implementation of the prototype.

2.1   Document Sampling

The sampling method we used here is based on *probe queries*, which has been used by many researchers in sampling text databases such as Callan et al. [3] and Hawking et al. [9]. The sample queries we used were generated using words from the selected Open Directory sub-category. To collect documents for a category *C*, a probe query *q* = {*name of C + name of parent of C*} will be formed and sent as search queries to the search engines. The documents listed in the search result will be downloaded as document samples.

2.2   Relevancy Calculation

The first step of our categorization algorithm calculates the relevancy of the documents (to a category) based on the *term-frequency* concept [1]. Let *q* be the probe query used, *S* be the search engine being categorized, and $D = \{d_1 \dots d_m\}$ be the set of documents returned by *S*. Then $tf_{i,q}$, the normalized term frequency of document d_i using *q* is determined by:

$$tf_{i,q} = \frac{freq_{i,q}}{\max freq_{l,q}} \tag{1}$$

where $freq_{i,q}$ is the raw frequency of *q* in d_i, and $\max(freq_{l,q})$ is the largest frequency of *q* found among all returned documents. Next, the corresponding ranking positions of the returned documents from the search engine are used as a factor for computing the relevance scores. Other researchers such as Mowshowitz & Kawaguchi [13] have also considered the ranking position when calculating the quality of search results. As a result, the value of *tf* will be amended by *w*, the ranking factor, as follows:

$$w_i = \frac{m - (\alpha \times o_i)}{m} \tag{2}$$

$$tf'_{i,q} = tf_{i,q} \times w_i \tag{3}$$

while m is the total number of documents in D, and o_i is the ranking position of d_i given by S. The value of w is used to weight the tf values and the importance of w is controlled by a constant α. For our experiments, we set $\alpha = 0.3$ which allows the rankings of the documents influence tf values by no more than 30%. After calculating the tf values for all the documents in D, the final term frequency value $tf_{s,q}$ for the search engine S using query q is determined by normalizing the values based on the largest tf value computed using q.

2.3   Relevancy Score

To improve the precision of the categorization process, we decided to exploit the hierarchy structure as extra information to compute the final relevancy score. Hence, the relevancy of search engine S to a category C should be affected by the relevancy of S to the child categories of C.

The first step of the algorithm will assign the relevancy scores for all the search engines in the *leaf node* categories equal to their tf values. For a search engine S inside a *leaf node* category LC, its relevancy score $R_{S,LC}$ will be equal to $tf_{S,LC}$.

Afterwards, the remaining search engines inside the *non-leaf node* categories will be processed. The relevancy score $R_{S,C}$ of the search engine S for the category C which has nc number of immediate child is given by:

$$R_{S,C} = tf_{s,c} + \sum_{i=1}^{nc} \beta \left(\frac{link_i}{L} \times R_{S,i} \right) \tag{4}$$

where $link_i$ is the number of links indexed in ODP for the child category i and L is the total number of links indexed for all the immediate child of C. β is a constant variable to control how the hierarchical information affect the final relevancy score.

2.4   Elimination of Irrelevant Search Engines

The final step of the categorization process is to eliminate search engines with low relevancy from the categories. For each category, there is a set of search engines that are ranked according to their relevancy scores. If there is any search engine has a score smaller than the standard deviation of relevancy scores of the category, it will be removed from the category.

After performing the procedures described above, the categorization process finished and a hierarchical directory of categories with associated search engines will be produced. Each category contains a number of sub-categories in a hierarchical structure. Each sub-category contains a number of relevant search engines. We believe that meta-search engines will benefit from such kind of search engine category in different ways.

3   Validation

The *Top / Computers / Software / Internet / Client* sub-category in the Open Directory was selected for implementation and validation of the proposed categorization algorithm. Within this category, there were 104 child categories. To reduce the size of the hierarchy, some child categories which we believed to be insignificant were manually excluded.

20 specialty search engines were selected for the implementation. Most of these search engines are computer-related. Using the categorization process as proposed, specialty search engines are categorized and ranked according to their relevancy scores.

Another set of rankings of those search engines are also obtained by human judgments, involving 20+ computer experts. The rankings produced by our proposed categorization algorithm were compared to the rankings produced manually. Results of the experiment indicate that the categorization algorithm ranks search engines stay close to human judgments.

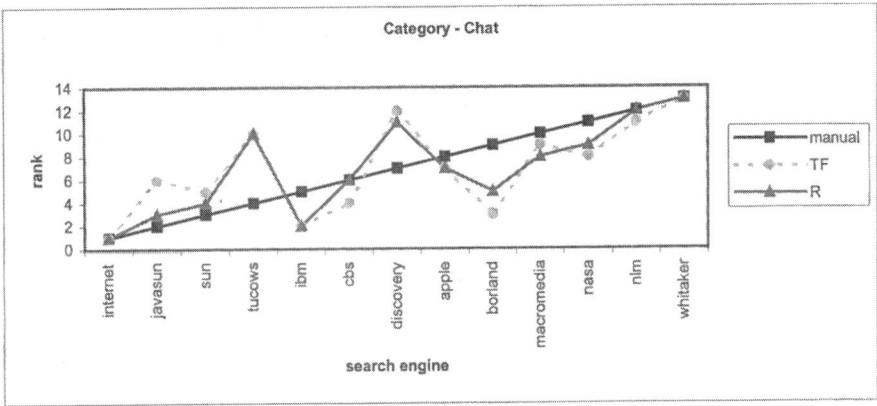

Fig. 1. Ranking produced by (1) human; (2) considering term frequency only; (3) the categorization based on relevancy score

Figure 1 shows the rankings assigned for one of the categories as an example to illustrate the performance of the proposed algorithm. Three groups of rankings for the category " *Top / Computers / Software / Internet / Clients / Chat* " are presented. The *"manual"* group is the rankings obtained from human judgments and it was used as the baseline; the *"TF"* group rank the search engines according to their term frequency values only and the *"R"* group rank the search engines according to their final relevancy scores.

As shown in the figure, both the *TF* and *R* groups rank search engines similar to those by human judgments. In particular, the rankings given by *R* are closer to the *manual* than those given by *TF*. This result demonstrates that when computing the relevancies of search engines, advanced performance can be obtained by including the hierarchical structure information.

4   Conclusion

An algorithm making use of probe queries has been developed to categorize specialty search engines. It has been used to create a hierarchical directory of search engines based on a branch of the Open Directory. Comparison with human categorization of the selected search engines has been encouraging. An experimental meta-search engine utilizing the hierarchical directory of search engines is being developed to further investigate the proposed methodology.

Acknowledgement. The research reported in this paper was partially supported by The Hong Kong Polytechnic University Research Grant G-W059.

References

1. Baeza-Yates, R. & Ribeiro-Neto, B. "Modern Information Retrieval". *ACM Press / Addison-Wesley Longman*, 1999.
2. Bergman, Michael K. "The Deep Web: Surfacing Hidden Value". *The Journal of Electronic Publishing*, Vol.7, Issue 1, 2001.
3. Callan, J., Connell, M. and Du, A. "Automatic Discovery of Language Models for Text Databases". *Proceedings of ACM-SIGMOD International Conference on Management of Data*, Philadelphia, Pennsylvania, USA, 1–3 June 1999, pp.479–490, 1999.
4. Debnath, S., Sen, S. and Blackstock, B. "LawBot: A Multiagent Assistant for Legal Research". *IEEE Internet Computing*, Vol.4, No.6, pp.32–37, 2000.
5. Dogpile, http://www.dogpile.com, 2003.
6. Dreilinger, D. and Howe, Adele E. "Experiences with Selecting Search Engines Using Metasearch". *ACM Transactions on Information Systems*, Vol.15, No.3, pp.195–222, 1997.
7. FamilyFriendlySearch, http://www.familyfriendlysearch.com, 2003.
8. Gauch, S., Wang, G. and Gomez, M. "Profusion: Intelligent fusion from multiple, distributed search engines". *Journal of Universal Computer Science*, Vol.2, No.9, pp.637–649, 1996.
9. Hawking, D. and Thistlewaite, P. "Methods for information server selection". *ACM Transactions on Information Systems*, Vol.17, No.1, pp.40–76, 1999.
10. Ithaki, http://www.ithaki.net, 2003.
11. Lawrence, S. and Giles, C. Lee. "Accessibility of information on the Web". *Nature*, Vol.400 pp.107–109, 1999.
12. MetaXchem, http://www.chemie.de/metaxchem, 2003.
13. Mowshowitz, A. and Kawaguchi, A. "Bias on the web". *Communications of the ACM*, Vol.45, No.9, 2002.
14. The Open Directory Project. *http://dmoz.org*, 2003.
15. Profusion, http://www.profusion.com, 2003.
16. Selberg, E. and Etzioni. O. "The MetaCrawler Architecture for Resource Aggregation on the Web". *IEEE Expert*, Vol.12, No.1, pp.8–14, 1997.

A Unified, Adjustable, and Extractable Biological Data Mining-Broker

Min-Huang Ho[1], Yue-Shan Chang[2], Ming-Chun Cheng[1],
Kuang-Lee Li[1], and Shyan-Ming Yuan[1]

[1]Department of Computer and Information Science, National Chiao-Tung University
1001 Ta Hsueh Road, Hsin-Chu, Taiwan 30050, R.O.C.
minhuang@ms4.hinet.net
[2]Department of Electronic Engineering, Minghsin University of Science & Technology
1 Hsin-Hsing Road, Hsin-Feng, Hsin-Chu, Taiwan 304, R.O.C.
ysc@must.edu.tw

Abstract. The document formats of biological data sources typically are more versatile and more complicated than the traditional data sources. It is hard to efficiently retrieve useful information from biological data sources by traditional information retrieval technologies. In this paper, we propose a unified, adjustable, and extractable Biological Data Mining-Broker mechanism. Based on XML methodology, the mechanism provides a federated forum model to overcome the heterogeneities of both form and meaning from those different diverse biological data sources. Furthermore, the mechanism also utilizes the feedback-based direct raw and meaningful extracted cache technique to improve the efficiency and accuracy of the system. The experimental results show that our proposed system has good performance, and it is a good choice for biological data mining process with multiple heterogeneous data sources, different mining applications, and knowledge analysts. It is highly useful for target discovery and bioinformatics research projects.

1 Introduction

The volume of biological data on the Internet is increasing in an extremely high pace nowadays. At the past decade we have seen an explosive growth in biological research. Also, there are many researches focused on biological data mining [1][2]. Meanwhile, there are lots of multiple heterogeneous data sources accessible for biological data mining processes. However, the format and structure of biological data mining queries and result sets are diverse among these different data sources. Furthermore, unlike the traditional keyword-based meta-search engine on the Internet, most of the structure of biological data mining query languages and processes are complex, and it is hard for concordant formulation by different knowledge analysts with different preference. Moreover, it is not easy to integrate the different biological data sources efficiently by the traditional mechanisms invented for keyword-based meta-search engines.

J. Liu et al. (Eds.): IDEAL 2003, LNCS 2690, pp. 773–777, 2003.

To overcome the problems mentioned above, in this paper, we propose an XML-based *federated model of Biological Data Mining-Broker mechanism*. The proposed mechanism supports coordination on the format of directory information, transparency of directory information, formulation of biological data mining language, planning of extraction format for mining applications and data sources, and knowledge acquisition among different knowledge analysts. Also, different mining applications and multiple heterogeneous biological data sources can perform the working of federated model underlying interactive discussion mechanism to enhance the meaningfulness and usefulness of information retrieval from Biological Data Mining-Broker. Finally, we utilize the de facto and well-known XML object model to archive *hard coding free* for designers of mining applications and data sources retrieval applications [4].

2   System Architecture

Based on our approach, the system architecture of BDMB is shown in Fig. 1.

As shown in Fig. 1, there are six basic components in the BDMB. They are BIO-Info. Interface (BIOII), Raw Data Cache (RDC), Directory & Extraction Cache (DEC), Federated Repository Center (FRC), Template Developer's Kits (TDK), and Mining Interface (MI). BIOII provides the interface for communicating with the integrated biological data sources. Through BIOII, the Biological Data Mining-Broker sends well-formed queries to each biological data source, and then receive perceivable result sets with meaningful extracted data from the same data source. The main purpose of RDC is to store the original raw data of each data source, and send

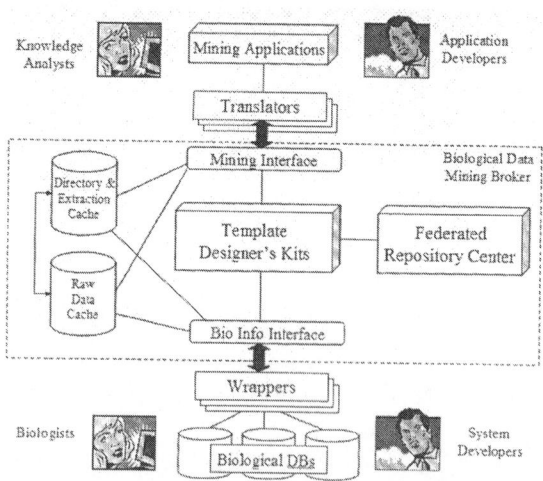

Fig. 1. The System Architecture of Biological Mining Broker

these data to mining application as they need. Utilize the rating condition in DEC, the mining application can access the meaningful raw data more efficient.

The DEC is composed of *Multi-source Directory (MD)* and *Extraction Cache Databases (ECD)*. While MD stores directory information about each data source, and ECD temporarily stores the extracted data into cache from each data source. Different to RDC, the DEC is more manageable and more meaningful, and it should have better rating condition and higher weight. It has also to be accessed by mining application earlier.

In FRC, *Federated Extraction Template (FET)* stores the definition of meaningful extracted data, *Federated Directory Template (FDT)* stores the definition of multi-source directory information, *Federated Query Template (FQT)* stores the definition of structured mining query, and *Federated Feedback Template (FFT)* stores the definition of pre-defined mining feedback form. In our system, it provides a set of toolkits called TDK to help the system developers developing his own mining applications. TDK includes *Extraction, Directory, Query, and Feedback template generators*. With the functionality of TDK, data sources and mining applications can share the templates in the federated model of Biological Data Mining-Broker, and it will help the developers to concord the format of documents used in wrapper and mining applications.

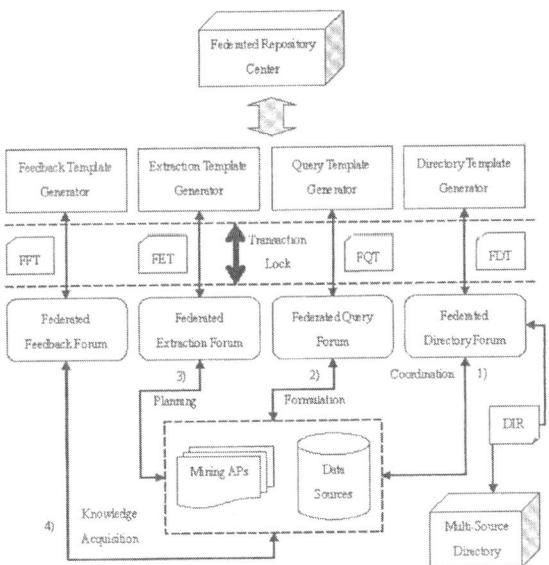

Fig. 2. Scenario of Federated Model

At the top of our BDMB architecture in Fig. 1, MI is the interface between BDMB and mining applications. BDMB can receive structured mining queries from mining applications, and send perceivable result sets with meaningful extracted data to mining applications through this interface.

This Federated Model of BDMB provides the support of coordination on the format of directory information, transparency of directory information, formulation of biological data mining language and planning of extraction format for mining applications and data sources, knowledge acquisition among different knowledge analysts. Fig. 2 shows the scenario of federated model. With this federated model, the Biological Data Mining-Broker establishes an interactive mechanism with discussion community for different mining applications, knowledge analysts and multiple heterogeneous data sources. The federated model provides flexibility, interactivity, transparency, maintenance and enhancement of meaningful and usefulness for directory information, BDMQL, extraction information and feedback information.

3   Experimental Results

These experiments perform numbers of different but related biological data mining querying toward Biological Data Mining-Broker with empty cache database initially and 3 data sources joined. The system simulates translators of mining applications and wrappers of data sources to process mining queries, extraction information and feedback forms. The public and demo data sources, *NCBI, DDBJ and EMBL*, used for experiments to sample test data from are denoted as DS_1, DS_2 and DS_3 respectively. For each data source, experiments randomly sample *1000 of biological data* from it. Each one of biological data costs about *700 KB to 800 KB* of disk space. Total biological test data sampled from three data sources are about *2.1 GB to 2.4 GB*. For more, there are three extraction cache databases for DS1, DS2 and DS3, cache size of each is 500 of extracted biological data.

Run	I_1	I_2	DS_1 I_2	DS_2 I_2	DS_3 I_2	I_4
R_1	{0.732s, 0}	{150.117s, 376}	{121.837s, 395}	{121.34s, 349}	{0.093s, 1120}
R_2	{1.11s, 450}	{121.657s, 381}	{112.303s, 383}	{122.207s, 367}	{0.083s, 830}
R_3	{1.189s, 785}	{121.38s, 327}	{114.423s, 352}	{120.946s, 332}	{0.09s, 1011}
R_4	{1.136s, 679}	{120.2s, 340}	{115.06s, 345}	{124.993s, 304}	{0.083s, 701}
R_5	{1.156s, 983}	{143.107s, 372}	{116.256s, 380}	{125.037s, 366}	{0.094s, 983}
R_6	{1.174s, 694}	{126.12s, 375}	{114.804s, 405}	{123.927s, 399}	{0.07s, 694}
R_7	{1.19s, 619}	{120.39s, 336}	{111.297s, 349}	{122.806s, 341}	{0.067s, 619}
R_8	{1.194s, 908}	{121.684s, 327}	{113.753s, 352}	{123.62s, 332}	{0.093s, 937}

Fig. 3. The Experimental Results

Fig. 3 shows the evaluation of simulation statistics for 10 rounds with 8 runs. The commentary descriptions of experiments with several test cases mentioned above are described as follows.

Each data source has its own RDBMS with indexing and cache mechanisms. The amount of biological data in each data source is 1000. On the other hand, the maximum amount of biological data in one extraction cache database of Biological Data Mining-Broker is 500. Thus the limitation of total amount of biological data in all extraction databases is 1500. The notation "{…, …}" in Fig. 3 means "*{execution time for a specific iteration of the run which starts from a simulated mining application sending a specific mining query and to it receiving related result sets, the amount of extracted or raw data result sets for a specific mining query}*." With the data shown in Fig. 3, obviously average time complexity of cache-based biological data mining querying is extremely lower than that of mining querying through data sources directly. This is because Biological Data Mining-Broker performs the working of cache-based biological data mining querying for extraction cache databases. Size of each extracted data is much smaller than size of each original raw biological data.

4   Conclusions

The goal of Biological Data Mining-Broker is not to replace human interpreters like knowledge analysts and functionalities of mining applications and data sources, but rather than to make biological data mining easier, faster and more efficient for domain experts through an integrated, flexible, transparent, interactive, federated, semantic and meaningful view supported by the unified, adjustable and extractable Biological Data Mining-Broker. As the experiments shows in Section 3, with the customized discussion mechanism, the Biological Data Mining-Broker makes biological data mining to meet the specific needs and considerations of varieties of individual and different mining applications and knowledge analysts.

References

1. Eckman, B. A., Kosky, A. S., Laroco, Jr., L. A.: Extending Traditional Query-Based Integration Approaches for Functional Characterization of Post-Genomic Data. bioinformatics, Vol. 17, No. 7. (2001) 587–601
2. The TAMBIS (Transparent Access to Multiple Biological Information Sources) System. http://bagel.cs.man.ac.uk/
3. Bertone, P., Gerstein, M.: Integrative Data Mining: The New Direction in Bioinformatics. IEEE Engineering in Medicine and Biology Magazine, Vol. 20, Issue: 4. (2001) 33–40
4. Reynaud, C., Sirot, J.-P., Vodislav, D.: Semantic Integration of XML Heterogeneous Data Sources Database Engineering & Applications. 2001 International Symposium. (2001) 199–208
5. Estivill-Castro, V.: Collaborative Knowledge Acquisition with a Genetic Algorithm: Tools with Artificial Intelligence. Proceedings of Ninth IEEE International Conference. (1997) 270–277

Nested State-Transition Graph Model of User Behaviors

Jia-Sheng Heh, Shein-Yun Cheng, and Nan-Chao Ma

Department of Information and Computer Engineering,
Chung Yuan Christian University
Chung Li, Taiwan, R.O.C.
{jsheh, cheng, erase}@mcsl.ice.cycu.edu.tw

Abstract. This paper proposes a systematic data mining approach to study users' Internet resource access actions for finding out behavior models as state-transition graphs. A series of Internet resource access actions are stored in a database of [user, resource-access-action, time] records. Such access actions are treated as basic behavior elements and form an action hierarchy which possesses different levels of radix codes. For every user, the data sequence is divided into a series of transactions and all the actions in a transaction constitute a special behavior pattern, called (inter-transaction) behavior. The behavior codes can be aggregated as behavior hierarchy also. Accordingly, each user can possess his/her own behavior model, formulated as a state-transition graph with behavior states and transition probability between behaviors. The overall mining process is computerized and validated by experiment. The example uses simulated sequential data to show how to combine AprioriAll algorithm and the proposed algorithm to construct a set of nested state-transition graphs.

1 Resource Access Actions

In the last decade of 20th century, the emergence of Internet and WWW makes all these data connected as a hyperlinked structure. Any form of learning material, no matter whether it is hypertext or hypermedia, is just one of Internet resources, which may encompass most general regions. General Internet resources can be formularized as a resource set with different kinds of Internet resources.

An atomic access action to access an Internet resource is called a *resource access action*. As mentioned in Agrawal and Srikant, these accessed resource actions will generally form a hierarchical taxonomy [1]. Without loss of generality, these access actions can be coded in a hierarchical way. Therefore, the coding of resource access actions λ's encircle two major parts: the access actions and their accessed resources.

2 User Behaviors

Formally, a real human or a computer-simulated agent, who is able to access the above Internet resources in $\Lambda 0$, is called a user or an individual, $\Psi_p \in \Psi$. Here, the user

J. Liu et al. (Eds.): IDEAL 2003, LNCS 2690, pp. 778–782, 2003.

set Ψ is a subset of user space $\Psi 0$, i.e. $\Psi \subseteq \Psi 0$. For example, $\Psi^A = \{ \Psi^A_1 = A$ (Arthur), $\Psi^A_2 = B$ (Buddy), $\Psi^A_3 = C$ (Clement), $\Psi^A_4 = D$ (Dian)$\}$.

An atomic access actions λ for user Ψ_p to access resource at time t is defined as a *behavior element* $\beta(p,\lambda,t) = [\Psi_p, \lambda, t]$, in which $t \in T=[t_0,t_f]$ is the time of access action, often dependent on the recording time of its resource server. Here, $T=[t_0,t_f]$ is the time interval within which resource access actions happen. For the example behavior $\beta(p,\lambda,t) = [$Buddy, FP1xx, $t_i]$ means the user B (Buddy) gets the text file 1xx at time t_i. The set of all possible actions λ for user Ψ_p to access resources resource at any time $t \in T \subseteq R^+ = [0,\infty)$ forms the overall discourse $\Psi 0 \times \Lambda 0 \times R^+$, which is the sample space of our database.

A series of behavior elements of a specific user $\Psi_p \in \Psi$ forms a *sequence of user behaviors* $\Theta(\Psi_p) = \{ \beta(p,\lambda,t) = [\Psi_p, \lambda, t]: \lambda \in \Lambda, t \in T \}$. For a simple behavior example can be $\Theta(\Psi_{A1}=$Arthur$) = \{$ [Arthur, WL101 = LOGIN, $t_1]$, [Arthur, BR001 = NEWS, $t_2]$, [Arthur, WL201 = VIDEO, $t_3]$, [Arthur, FP111 = HOMEWORK, $t_4] \}$, which describes the behavior of Arthur when reading news (001), listening a video lecture (201) and putting homework (111) on the given website. Such behavior sequence can be used to find the *user model* $\Xi(\Theta(\Psi_p) = \{[\Psi_p,\lambda,t]: \lambda \in \Lambda, t \in T \}$) in some formulation. Typical user models can be a *large sequence*, a *regular expression*, and so on. No matter which user model is selected, it is possibly applied to predict the fore-coming user behavior [1, 2, 7].

3 Assumptions and Preprocessing

For each kind of the above Internet resources on the resource server, a user can only access these resources when he/she invokes the corresponding client program on a so-called DTE (Data Terminal Equipment) [4]. As the access actions for a user to log on a DTE, three important factors -- access duration, transaction index, and action index - - can be defined under several suitable assumptions.

Assumptions for Analyzing Learning Behavior of Distance Education
The user Ψ_p uses (stays at) resource λ right from the time he/she gets (accesses) it until he/she fetches (accesses) the next resource λ', i.e. *access duration* $= t' - t$. When the access duration is less than or equal to a threshold, called *TransactionBoundary* [3]. Let the *transaction-indexed user behaviors* be $\Theta(\Psi_p, m) \equiv \{ \beta(p,m) = [n,\lambda,t]: \forall n(m(\Psi_p)), \lambda \in \Lambda, t \in T \}$, where the *action index* $n(\cdot)$ is defined as the sequence number for an action λ in its transaction $m(\cdot)$. As the time durations between transactions are large greater the time durations between actions in the same transaction, the action indices n's can be neglected. The transaction-indexed user behaviors satisfy Markov property, i.e. the mth behavior $\beta(p,m)$ of user is Ψ_p dependent only on the previous behavior, $\beta(p,m-1)$, but not on $\beta(p,m-2)$ [6].

With the previous assumptions, these three factors can be determined by the following algorithm.

Algorithm 1 (Algorithm for Determining Transaction Indices, Action Indices and Access Durations) Given a behavior elements in log database $DB = \{ \beta(p,\lambda,t):$ $\Psi_p \in \Psi, \lambda \in \Lambda, t \in T\}$ with all records of the same user are collected in the increasing order of time, to find the access durations $D(p,\lambda,m,n)$, transaction indices $m(\Psi_p)$ and action indices $n(m(\Psi_p))$.

1) $m(\Psi_p) = 1$ for each Ψ_p.
2) For two successive behavior elements $\beta(p,\lambda,t) = [\Psi_p, \lambda, t]$ and $\beta(p',\lambda',t') = [\Psi_{p'}, \lambda', t']$, carry out the following checks.
3) If $\Psi_{p'} = \Psi_p$ and $t' - t \leq TransactionBoundary$,
   then $D(p,\lambda,m,n) = t' - t$, $m(\Psi_p)' = m(\Psi_p)$ and $n(m(p))' = n(m(p)) + 1..$
4) If ($\Psi_{p'} = \Psi_p$ and $t' - t > TransactionBoundary$) or ($\Psi_{p'} \neq \Psi_p$),
   then $D(p,\lambda,m,n) = indeterminable$ and $m(\Psi_p) = m(\Psi_p) + 1..$

This algorithm can be used to transform the log database DB into a set of *transaction-indexed user behaviors* $\Theta(\Psi_p, m) \equiv \{ \beta(p,m) \}$. However, not all the behavior elements are qualified for later modeling. With selection criteria and assumption, the final set of transaction-indexed user behaviors can be determined. An example log database and its corresponding transaction-indexed user behaviors are listed to show the process of Algorithm 1 with *TransactionBoundary = 7200* (2 hours) and the filtering of selection criteria: *Twindow = [0,1500000]*, *DurationThreshold = 25*, *RAcenter = {WT,WM,BP,BR}* and *level=3*. Note that the resultant transaction-indexed user behaviors are: $\Theta(A) = '\beta(A,1) \rightarrow \beta(A,2)' = '\{WT\} \rightarrow \{WM\}'$, $\Theta(B) = '\beta(B,1)' = '\{WM,BP,BR\}'$, $\Theta(C) = '\beta(C,1) \rightarrow \beta(C,2)' = '\{WT\} \rightarrow \{BP\}'$, and $\Theta(D) = '\beta(D,1) \rightarrow \beta(D,2)' = '\{WM\} \rightarrow \{BP,BR\}'$.

4 Coding and Modeling for Learning Behaviors

To simplify the action expression, a radix representation for code hierarchy is proposed as $a(\lambda) = code(\lambda = [\lambda_1, ..., \lambda_l, ..., \lambda_L]) = \Sigma_{l=1...L} \lambda_l r^{L-l}$, where r is the *radix* and l is the *level* of each code. With this kind of coding, the scattering of behavior codes makes the behaviors with similar codes cluster together. By some elaborate design of the weights and radices, such coding can be extended to inter-transaction behaviors $\beta(p,m) = \{\lambda^n\}$. To aggregate the embedded access actions λ^n's, the radix coding $b(p,m)$ is accomplished by so-called *code summation strategy*: $b_{SUM}(p,m) = code(\beta(p,m)) = \Sigma_{l=1,L}(\Sigma_n \lambda_l^n) r^{L-l}$, or *code maximization strategy*: $b_{MAX}(p,m) = code(\beta(p,m)) = \Sigma_{l=1,L}(max_n\{\lambda_l^n\}) r^{L-l}$.

When the above radix coding is applied to the subsequence models of data sequencing, large sequences with 1 large itemset $\{\beta^i\}$ or 2 large itemsets $\{[\beta^{i1}, \beta^{i2}]\}$ of enough supports can be obtained in an easier way. Let $count(b^i_1=code(\beta^i)_1)$ and $count([b^{i2}_1=code(\beta^{i2})_1, b^{i2}_1=code(\beta^{i2})_1])$ be the *support count* of 1-element behaviors β^i and 2-element behavior sequence $[\beta^{i1}, \beta^{i2}]$ in user-behavior sequences, respectively. Under the Markovian of Assumption 4, *transition probability* $P(\beta^{i2}|\beta^{i1})$ for a user with the behavior β^{i1} to present the behavior β^{i2} in succession can be calculated from Bayesian rule: $P(\beta^{i2}|\beta^{i1}) = P([\beta^{i1}, \beta^{i2}]) / P(\beta^{i1}) = count(b^{i1}, b^{i2}) / count(b^{i1})$. For the previous example, we can have $P([\{WM2\} \mid \{WT1\}]) = P([\{WT1\}, \{WM2\}]) / P([\{WT1\}]) = (1/4)/(1/2) = 1/2$.

From the Bayesian viewpoint, $P([\beta^{i2} \mid \beta^{i1}])$ tell us how often the behavior β^{i2} will happen from the previous behavior β^{i1}. As the behaviors are defined as states in state-transition graph, this probability will describe such switching quantitatively. Therefore, the results of data sequences can be used to define the state-transition graphs of inter-transaction behaviors, as the following definition illustrated.

Definition 1 (State-transition Graphs of User Behaviors) For a user or a user cluster Ψ_p, $p=1,...,N_{user}$, *the state-transition graph of transaction-indexed user behaviors* is defined as STG(Θ,P), where $\Theta = \{ b(p,m), m=1,2,..., p=1,...,N_{user} \}$ is the set of intra-transaction behaviors and P $= [P([b^{i2} \mid b^{i1}]), b^{i1},b^{i2} \in \Theta]$ is the *transition probability matrix*.

The previous example with level-2 radix codes makes the behavior set be $\Theta^{2*} = \{\Theta^{21} = $ Wxxxx, $\Theta^{22} = $ Bxxxx$\}$ and their transition probability matrix be $P(\Theta^{2*}) == $

$$\begin{bmatrix} 1 & 2 \\ 0 & 0 \end{bmatrix} . / \begin{bmatrix} 4 & 4 \\ 3 & 3 \end{bmatrix} = \begin{bmatrix} 1/4 & 2/4 \\ 0 & 0 \end{bmatrix}$$

5 Experiment from Apriori Algorithm to State-Transition Graphs

In the experiment, the standard simulation method of sequential data is in the form of transition-indexed user behaviors. The hierarchical radix code of item taxonomy is [111, 112, 113, 121, 122, 131, 211, 212, 221, 222, 231, 232]. The simulation parameters are: the number of large itemsets $N_I = 25$, the number of large sequences $N_s = 50$, the number of customers $|D| = 10$, the size of an itemset is a Poisson distribution with mean $|I| = 1.25$, the size of a large sequence is a Poisson distribution with mean $|S| = 4$, the size of a transaction is a Poisson distribution with mean $|T| = 2.5$, the size of large sequence in a transaction is also a Poisson distribution with mean $|C| = 5$. For the simulated itemsets, the in-between correlation level is 0.25, each itemset is endowed a weight of exponential probability with mean 1, and an itemset in one transaction has corruption_level with normal distribution with mean 0.95 and variance 0.1.

In one simulation example, the resultant data sequence has 52 transactions for 10 customers. By the AprioriAll algorithm with minimal support 5, 36 maximal large sequences are found, such as $\{222, 231\} \rightarrow 231 \rightarrow 221$, $113 \rightarrow 231 \rightarrow 131$, $\{222, 231\}$ $\rightarrow \{222, 231\}$, $122 \rightarrow 131$ and $\{131, 211, 212\}$ [5]. The behaviors in these transactions can be coded in accumulated radix codes.

There are 19 behaviors with minimal supports greater than or equal to 5, collected in a behavior set Θ^{3*} (since the radix level is 3). Of course, the item taxonomy makes a behavior hierarchy through leveled radix codes. According to those k-element maximal large sequences across two transactions ($k\geq2$), the transition matrix Θ^{l*} ($l=3$) of 2-element behavior sequences $[\beta^{i1}_l, \beta^{i2}_l]$ with supports ≥ 5 can be obtained as Table 1 shown. It can be seen that the support counts of the transitions of all levels ($l=1,2,3$) are satisfies. Table 1 then successively shows some the corresponding transition probability matrices $P(\Theta^{l*})$, then the nested state-transition graphs can be established.

Table 1. Elements, counts and probabilities of nested state-transition graphs

β^{i1}_1	β^{i2}_1	count	$P(\Theta^{1*})$	β^{i1}_2	β^{i2}_2	count	$P(\Theta^{2*})$	β^{i1}_3	β^{i2}_3	count	$P(\Theta^{3*})$
1	1	16	0.1618	11	13	5	0.0725	113	131	5	0.0725
				12	13	5	0.0725	122	131	5	0.0725
				13	13	6	0.0870	131	131	6	0.0870
	2	44	0.1857	11	23	5	0.0323	113	231	5	0.0323
				12	22	5	0.1064	122	221	5	0.1351
				21	5	0.2000	131	211	5	0.2000	
				13	22	6	0.1277	131	221	6	0.1622
				13	23	23	0.1484	131	231	23	0.1484

6   Conclusion

For Internet users, this paper proposes an approach to transforming resource access actions to the behavior models of state-transition graphs. User accesses Internet resource through the action. Such access action forms behavior element with radix code. As the time differences are investigated, each data sequence can be divided into a series of (transaction-index, action-index) actions. For each transaction of a user, the inter-transaction behavior can be found with level code, thus his/her data sequence becomes a behavior sequence. As behavior sequences are aggregated as user-behavior codes, hence used in user clustering to find communities. For all users in a community, the transition probability matrices between behaviors are found and used in classifying the subgroups of user transition behaviors. Finally, the state-transition graph of is found. In section 5, the example shows how to find state-transition graphs in the successive steps of AprioriAll algorithm.

References

1. R. Srikant and R. Agrawal. Mining sequential patterns: Generalizations and performance improvements. *In Proc. EDBT conference* pages 3–17, Avignon, France, 1996.
2. M.J. Zaki. Efficient enumeration of frequent sequences. *In Proc. Of the ACM CIKM Conference*, pages 68–75, 1998.
3. A. K. H. Tung, H. Lu, J. Han, and L. Feng, Breaking the barrier of trans-actions: Mining inter-transaction association rules. *In Proc. KDD-99*, ACM, pages 297–301, 1999.
4. N. Halbwachs, Synchronous Programming of reactive systems (Kluwer 1993)
5. R. Agrawal and R. Srikant. Mining sequential patterns. *In Proc. of the IEEE International Coference on Data Engineering*, pages 3–14, 1995.
6. L. R. Rabiner and B. H. Juang. An introduction to hidden Markov models. *IEEE ASSP Magazine,* pages 4–17, 1986.
7. Heikki Mannila, Hannu Toivonen, and A. Inkeri Verkamo. Discovering frequent episodes in sequences. In *Proc. of the KDD conference*, pages 210–215, 1995

Design of Data-Mining Application Software Based on Object-Oriented Approach

Hon-Kwong Ho and Shiu Kit Tso

CIDAM, Department of Manufacturing Engineering and Engineering Management,
City University of Hong Kong
Hong Kong SAR, China
{mesktso}@cityu.edu.hk

Abstract. In connection with the need to extract useful knowledge from a large power-system database, an application software is developed for data mining. The design based on object-oriented approach is described which minimises wastage of development effort and facilitates modular expansion as the scope for solving data-mining problems evolves.

1   Introduction

Large databases exist in power systems which record periodically at short time intervals many analogue and discrete signals for monitoring, control or analysis purposes. The storage expands rapidly with time and with its expansion there is an increasing accumulation of valuable information and knowledge which will lie hidden in the hoard of data if not immediately used at or close to the time of acquisition.

Whenever there are system problems to be understood, or system features, behaviors or characteristics to be revealed, the databases may be consulted in terms of the systematic historical records available, provided that there is a ready means of extracting whatever is needed in a meaningful and systematic way.

This paper deals with a suitable object-oriented architecture proposed for implementing the mining of large industrial databases such as the databases in large power systems for information harvesting or knowledge extraction.

2   Object-Oriented Architecture for Data Mining

In the data-mining [1, 2] process, the problems to be analysed usually become clearer progressively and new ones keep unfolding themselves. As more information or knowledge is obtained, what appears even more important often become realised. The raw data to be used may also be different or rearranged as the investigation proceeds. It is hence highly advantageous to apply the object-oriented architecture for the data-mining implementation. The basic design and the codes are retained in the form of object modules with minimum waste or duplication of development effort. Expansion

J. Liu et al. (Eds.): IDEAL 2003, LNCS 2690, pp. 783–788, 2003.

is facilitated as the software system complexity grows. Because the Microsoft Windows operating system is employed in the present development, a framework for creating distinct classes and objects for the application is developed based on the Microsoft Foundation Classes (MFC) tool [3, 4]. The codes that manage the data for the mining application are separate from the user-interface display codes, as shown in Fig. 1. This document/view architecture is similar to the Smalltalk MVC (model = document) approach adopted by Xerox [3]. With a buffer between the document and the view entities, they become more independent in their operation, thereby simplifying their coordination and individual long-term maintenance.

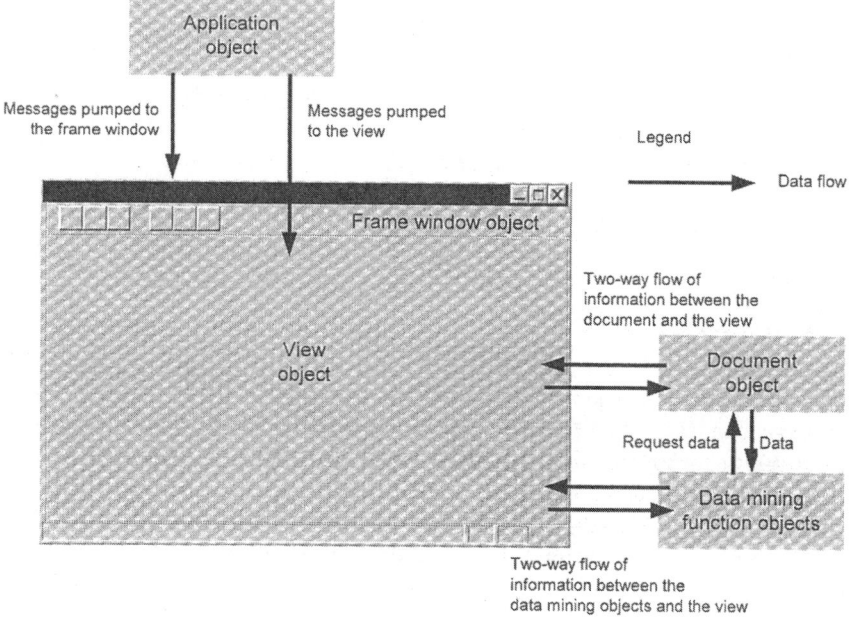

Fig. 1. Document/View Architecture

3   Data-Mining Function Objects

In the course of performing the data mining of the power system databases, the following objects or classes have been identified and created, among others:

- Cluster
- Correlation (two objects)
- Load Loss
- Deviation rate (dP/dV)
- Visualisation

The formation of the function objects is an evolving process associated with the need of the study.

With the Windows system, we create the CPwrSysApp object for this application. The MFC architecture provides four main types of components: documents, views, document/view frames, and document templates. These are created as the CPwrSys-App calls its own member function InitInstance( ) (Fig. 2, Fig. 3). The interaction between the view object (or document object) and the data-mining function objects is shown in Fig. 4 (or Fig. 5) in a star-like schema commonly used for relational database design. When the ShowWindow ( ) function is called, the application will be presented on the monitor screen.

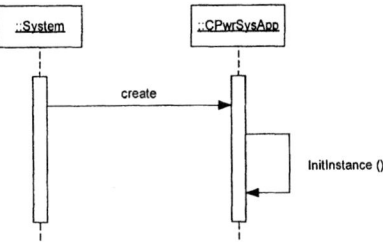

Fig. 2. Creation process

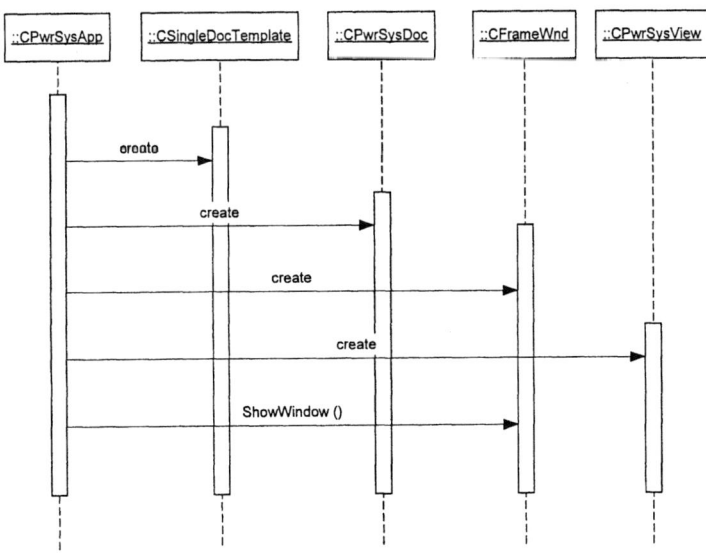

Fig. 3. Creation process (cont'd)

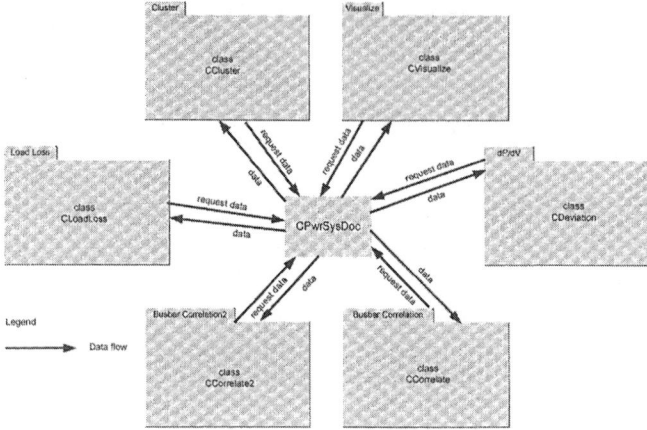

Fig. 4. Interaction between the document object and the data-mining function objects

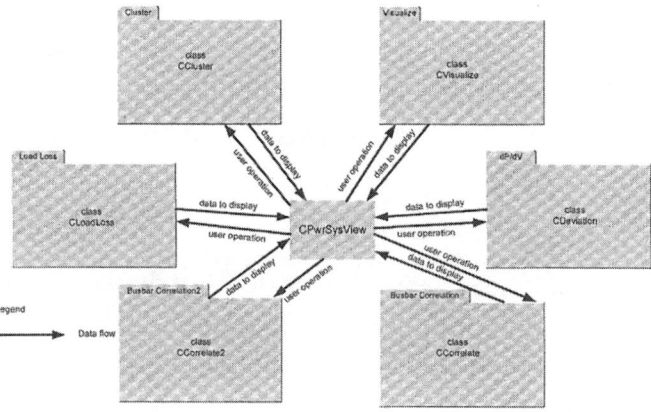

Fig. 5. Interaction between the view object and data-mining function objects

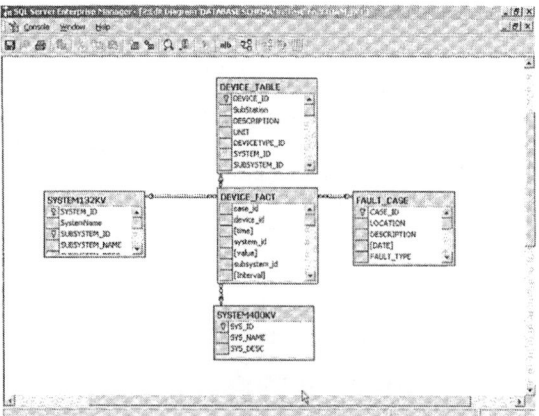

Fig. 6. Design of the data warehouse

4 Data Pre-processing for Data-Mining

Prior to formal data mining, the data will first be prepared for use. With the MS SQL Server [5, 6] used as the database backend, virtually any heterogeneous data sources may be extracted irrespective of its original format; transformed with suitable script language (in this vase VBScript [5]) irrespective of the number of source or destination fields associated with the data; then cleaned and validated using script language. The entire pre-processing stage can be carried out with the Data Transformation Services (DTS) tool [4] provided in the MS SQL Server. In this way the ASCII files in the power system database are converted and transferred to the data warehouse (Fig. 6).

A data warehouse contains one or more fact tables and dimension tables (used for analysing the fact tables). As mentioned above, the star schema design is used for convenience in this application. Fig. 6 shows that the DEVICE_FACT is the fact table at the center of the schema and is connected to the four dimension tables (DEVICE_TABLE, SYSTEM132KV, SYSTEM400KV and FAULT_CASE)

5 Conclusion

The approach described in this paper has been implemented in a power system database to extract knowledge associated with a number of chosen problems. The object-oriented architecture has proved extremely convenient for use with the Windows system. As the investigation proceeds, it is very easy to modify of add objects. Codes and designs can hence be reused or inherited from class to class. The DTS tool has played a useful role to convert the data into a consistent and validated form for populating the data warehouse, which can be reliably used again and again for the examination of various data-mining problems as identified in an evolving manner.

The proposed framework and organisation of the data-mining software, developed with relation to a specific power system database, can be extended with similar effectiveness to other types of applications where large volumes of time-series data are involved.

Acknowledgements. The work carried out in the City University of Hong Kong was supported by a Hong Kong CERG grant (9040490). The software was originally developed for special use with a power system database provided by Mr. C.M. Mak, CLP Power Ltd., in a joint project funded by the Innovation and Technology Commission, Hong Kong SAR and CLP Power Ltd. Appreciation is due to Mr. Mak and his collegues for their valuable contribution in this project.

References

1. J. Han, and M. Kamber, " Data Mining: Concepts and Techniques", Morgan Kaufmann Publishers, 2001.
2. David Hand, Heikki Mannila and Padhraic Smyth, *"Principles of Data Mining"*, MIT, USA 2001.
3. George Shepherd and Scot Wingo, "MFC Internals", Addison-Wesley, 1996.
4. Microsoft Corporation, "Microsoft SQL Server 7.0 Data Warehousing Training Kit", Microsoft Press, 2000.
5. Tony Bain. [et al.] "Professional SQL Server 2000 Data Warehousing with Analysis Services", Wrox, 2000.
6. Jeff Prosise, "Programming Windows with MFC", Microsoft Press, 1999.

Predicting Itemset Sales Profiles with Share Measures and Repeat-Buying Theory

Robert J. Hilderman

Department of Computer Science
University of Regina
Regina, Saskatchewan, Canada S4S 0A2
robert.hilderman@uregina.ca

Abstract. Given a random sample of sales transaction records (i.e., scanner panels) for a particular period (such as a week, month, quarter, etc.), we analyze the scanner panels to determine approximations for the *penetration* and *purchase frequency distribution* of frequently purchased items and itemsets. If the purchase frequency distribution for an item or itemset in the current period can be modeled by the *negative binomial distribution*, then the parameters of the model are used to predict sales profiles for the next period. We present representative experimental results based upon synthetic data.

1 Introduction

In this paper, we integrate the *share-confidence framework* for knowledge discovery from databases [1,5,6], which has been useful for detailed analysis of itemsets in market basket data [7], with *repeat-buying theory* [3,4], which has been useful for predicting the way in which consumers buy frequently purchased products/brands. The theory of repeat-buying is described in terms of individual alternative products/brands in a market basket. Here we investigate whether this individual product/brand model is also applicable to predicting consumer purchase behaviour involving frequent itemsets containing multiple products/brands. Generally, the methodology can be summarized as follows. Given a *random sample* of sales records for a particular period (i.e., week, month, quarter, etc.), we can determine the *parameters* for a repeat-buying model that describe the purchases made in the period. The parameters can then be plugged into the model to facilitate prediction of consumer purchase behaviour in the *next* period. Sales records are typically captured in *scanner panels* which record purchase histories on a per household basis [2]. By analyzing the scanner panels for individual consumers, the *penetration* (i.e., the observed proportion of households that buy the item or itemset in a given period) and *purchase frequency distributions* (i.e., the average number of times each household buys the item or itemset in a given period) can be determined. If the purchase frequency distribution can be modeled by the negative binomial distribution (NBD), then the parameters of the model are used to predict sales profiles for the next period.

J. Liu et al. (Eds.): IDEAL 2003, LNCS 2690, pp. 789–795, 2003.

2   Repeat-Buying Theory

Repeat-buying theory is a classical work in the application of the NBD to the analysis of market share and consumer choice behaviour. It describes a mathematical model based upon the NBD that can be used to analyze consumer choice behaviour. For example, Table 1 shows a purchase frequency distribution which can be fitted by the NBD, this being for an itemset obtained from synthetic scanner panels for a 2,000 household sample.

Table 1. Eight-week NBD purchase frequency distribution for a 2,000 household sample

No. of Purchases	No. of Households (Actual)	No. of Households (Predicted)
0	1,856	1,856
1	118	120
2	22	19
3	4	4
4	0	1
5+	0	0

The values for the predicted distribution in Table 1 are derived, as follows. Using an iterative formulation of the NBD, the probability, p_r, of observing r purchases is given by

$$p_r = \left(\frac{a}{1+a}\right)\left(1 - \frac{a-m}{ar}\right)p_{r-1},$$

where $a = m/k$ (parameters m and k must be estimated and are described in the next subsection) and p_0 is obtained from the observed distribution (p_0 is simply the number of non-buyers in the 2,000 household sample). In this case, $p_0 = 0.928$ (i.e., 1856/2000). Assuming the estimated values for $m = 0.087$ and $k = 0.251$, we have $a = m/k = 0.087/0.251 = 0.347$,

$$p_1 = \left(\frac{0.347}{1+0.347}\right)\left(1 - \frac{0.347-0.087}{(0.347)(1)}\right)0.928$$
$$= 0.060,$$

$$p_2 = \left(\frac{0.347}{1+0.347}\right)\left(1 - \frac{0.347-0.087}{(0.347)(2)}\right)0.060$$
$$= 0.0097,$$

etc. Thus, the number of households predicted to purchase the itemset one time is $(0.060)(2000) = 120$, two times is $(0.0097)(2000) = 19$, etc. The general method should now be clear.

We now describe a technique for estimating the parameters m (the average number of purchases per household) and k (the negative binomial exponent).

However, prior to deriving the parameter k, we must first calculate b (the observed proportion of households buying the itemset in the sample period), w (the observed average number of purchases per household that bought the itemset in the sample period), and p_0. These values can be easily calculated directly from the sample data. For example, the itemset in Table 1 was purchased 174 times by 144 of 2,000 sampled households in the eight-week period (the eight-week period, T, is known as the base period, so $T = 1$). So, $b = 144/2000 = 0.072$, $w = 174/144 = 1.208$, and $p_0 = 1 - b = 1 - 0.072 = 0.928$. The best estimate of m is simply the observed average number of purchases per household in the sample period. This value can be calculated as the product of b and w, so $m = bw = (0.072)(1.208) = 0.087$. Parameter k is estimated by solving the nonlinear equation $p_0 = (1 + (m/k))^{-k}$. This equation cannot be solved directly for k, but it can be estimated using an iterative approach, such as the bisection method. To determine an estimate for k, we substitute the observed values for p_0 and m into the equation for p_0 and rewrite it as

$$0 = \frac{1}{(1 + 0.087/k)^k} - 0.928$$

We then determine a value for k such that the right side of the above equation is approximately equal to zero within some specified tolerance ϵ. Choosing $\epsilon = 0.0001$, the bisection method generates $k = 0.251$.

3   Experimental Results

Real scanner panels were not used for this preliminary investigation into the application of repeat-buying theory to the analysis of itemsets. Instead, the synthetic data generator described in [7] was used to generate sample scanner panels which simulate customer purchase behaviour for 2,000 customers over a period of 32 weeks. Transactions were generated only for the 100 most frequently purchased items. A total of 108,825 transactions were generated containing 309,284 line items.

All 1- and 2-itemsets which could be modeled by the NBD were discovered for time periods of 1, 2, 4, 8, 16, and 32 weeks in length. The number of itemsets discovered is shown in Table 2. For each discovered itemset, a table was constructed showing the actual and predicted purchase frequency distributions (similar to Table 1). Table 1 actually corresponds to the purchase frequency distribution for the 2-itemset containing synthetic items 18 and 72.

The results that follow are based upon the purchase frequency distribution for the 2-itemset containing items 18 and 72 shown in Table 1. The values used for T, b, w, p_0, a, m, and k are those previously calculated in Section 2.

Number of Households Purchasing an Itemset. The proportion of households buying the itemset in the eight-week sample period (i.e., the penetration) is 0.072 (i.e., b). The predicted proportion of households buying in a period of

Table 2. Number of discovered itemsets that could be modeled by the NBD

Time Period (in weeks)	No. of 1-Itemsets	No. of 2-Itemsets
1	19	35
2	32	94
4	49	342
8	54	732
16	64	1411
32	66	2319

length T is given by $b_T = 1 - (1 + (Ta))^{-k}$, where T is the proportional to the base period. For example, the predicted penetration in a 16-week period (i.e., $T = 2$) is

$$b_2 = 1 - (1 + (2)(0.347))^{-0.251}$$
$$= 0.1238.$$

The predicted penetration is based upon the sample size of 2,000 households. If we assume there are 35,000 households in the trading area, then the predicted number of households purchasing the itemset in a 16-week period is $(0.1238)(35000)=4333$. The predicted penetration for periods ranging from eight to 32 weeks (i.e., $T = 1$ to $T = 4$) is shown in Table 3.

Table 3. Predicted number of households purchasing itemset $\{18,72\}$

Time Period (in weeks)	Penetration (%) (Actual)	Penetration (%) (Predicted)	No. of Households (Predicted)
8	7.20	7.197	2520
16	12.40	12.382	4333
32	21.30	19.613	6864

Number of Transactions Containing an Itemset. Households that buy an itemset more than once in the sample period are repeat-buyers, and the average purchase frequency is a measure of repeat-buying. The average purchase frequency per buyer in the eight-week sample period is 1.208 (i.e., w). The predicted average purchase frequency per buyer in a period of length T is given by $W_T = (Tm)/(1 - (1 + (Ta))^{-k})$, where T is proportional to the base period. For example, the predicted average purchase frequency in a 16-week period is

$$W_2 = (2)(0.087)/(1 - (1 + ((2)(0.347))^{-0.251})$$
$$= 1.405.$$

Since the predicted purchase frequency per buyer over a 16-week period is 1.405, and we know from the previous section that the predicted number of households purchasing the itemset is 4,333, then the predicted number of purchases of the itemset in a 16-week period is $(1.405)(4333)=6088$. The predicted number of

Table 4. Predicted number of purchases of itemset $\{18,72\}$

Time Period (in weeks)	Avg. Purchase Frequency (Actual)	Avg. Purchase Frequency (Predicted)	No. of Purchases (Predicted)
8	1.21	1.209	3047
16	1.34	1.405	6088
32	1.53	1.774	12177

purchases of the itemset for periods ranging from eight to 32 weeks is shown in Table 4.

Number of Light and Heavy Buyers. The predicted number of light and heavy buyers is a subjectively influenced measure, and is based upon the predicted proportion of households buying the itemset r times. From the sample data, we have $p_0 = 0.928$, and from the iterative method described in Section 2, we have $p_1 = 0.060$, $p_2 = 0.0097$, $p_3 = 0.0019$, and $p_4 = 0.0004$. If we consider a heavy buyer to be one that makes three or more purchases in the sample period, then $p_{3+} = 1 - (p_0 + p_1 + p_2) = 0.0023$. Similarly, if we consider a light buyer to be one that makes two or fewer purchases, then $p_{2-} = p_0 + p_1 + p_2 = 0.9977$. The proportions p_{3+} and p_{2-} are for all households in the sample and includes non-buyers. If we let p'_r represent the proportion of buyers who actually bought r times (i.e., the buyers), then $p'_r = bp_r$, $p'_{3+} = (0.072)(0.0023) = 0.0002$, and $p'_{2-} = (0.072)(0.9977) = 0.0718$. The predicted number of light and heavy buyers over the next eight-week period is shown in Table 5. The predicted proportion of sales to buyers who make r purchases in the next period is given by rp_r/m. For example, the predicted proportion of sales to buyers making two purchases in the next eight-week period is $(2)(0.0097)/0.087 = 0.223$.

Table 5. Predicted number of light and heavy buyers of itemset $\{18,72\}$

r	p_r	No. of Households (Predicted)	p'_r	No. of Buyers (Predicted)
0	0.928	32480	0.067	2345
1	0.060	2100	0.004	140
2	0.0097	340	0.0007	25
3	0.0019	67	0.0001	4
4+	0.0004	14	0.00003	1

Proportion of Households Who are Repeat-Buyers. While the average purchase frequency in the sample period is one measure of repeat-buying (see Number of Transactions Containing an Itemset), another form of repeat-buying is the incidence of households who buy in the sample period and again in the next period. The predicted proportion of households who buy in both periods is given by $b_R = 1 - 2(1+a)^{-k} + (1+2a)^{-k}$. For example, the predicted proportion of households who buy in the eight-week sample period and again in the next eight-week period is

$$b_R = 1 - 2(1 + 0.347)^{-0.251} + (1 + (2)(0.347))^{-0.251}$$
$$= 0.020.$$

While this cannot be verified directly from the sample data in Table 1, it is theoretically consistent with behaviour observed from thousands of products/brands [4].

Quantity Purchased by Repeat-Buyers. The predicted number of purchases made by repeat-buyers on a per households basis in the next period is given by $m_R = m(1 - (1 + a)^{-k-1})$. For example, the predicted number of purchases made by repeat-buyers on a per household basis in the next eight-week period is

$$m_R = (0.087)(1 - (1 + 0.347)^{-0.251-1})$$
$$= 0.027.$$

The predicted number of purchases that will be made by repeat-buyers in the next eight-week period is $(0.027)(35000) = 945$. If items 18 and 72 were each purchased 258 and 207 times in the itemset, respectively, then the average quantity of items 18 and 72 per buying household is $258/144 = 1.792$ and $207/144 = 1.438$, respectively. Thus, the predicted quantity of items 18 and 72 purchased by repeat-buyers in the next 8-week period is $(945)(1.792) = 1693.4$ or 1,693 and $(945)(1.438) = 1358.9$ or 1,359, respectively.

Quantity Purchased by New Buyers. The predicted average purchase frequency per new buyer (i.e., households who did not make a purchase in the previous period) on a per household basis in the next period is $m_N = m/(1+a)^{k+1}$. For example, the predicted average purchase frequency per new buyer on a per household basis in the next eight-week period is

$$m_N = 0.087/(1 + 0.347)^{0.251+1}$$
$$= 0.060.$$

The predicted number of purchases made by new buyers is $(0.060)(35000) = 2100$. The average quantities of items 18 and 72 purchased per buying household is 1.792 and 1.438, respectively. Thus, the predicted quantity of items 18 and 72 purchased by new buyers in the next 8-week period is $(2100)(1.792) = 3763.2$, or 3,763, and $(2100)(1.438) = 3019.8$, or 3,020, respectively.

References

1. C.L. Carter, H.J. Hamilton, and N. Cercone. Share-based measures for itemsets. In J. Komorowski and J. Zytkow, editors, *Proceedings of the First European Conference on the Principles of Data Mining and Knowledge Discovery (PKDD'97)*, pages 14–24, Trondheim, Norway, June 1997.

2. L.G. Cooper and M. Nakanishi. *Market-Share Analysis*. Kluwer Aacdemic Publishers, 1993.
3. A.S.C. Ehrenberg. The pattern of consumer purchases. *Applied Statistics*, 8:26–41, 1959.
4. A.S.C. Ehrenberg. *Repeat-Buying: Theory and Applications*. North Holland Publishing Company, 1972.
5. R.J. Hilderman, C.L. Carter, H.J. Hamilton, and N. Cercone. Mining association rules from market basket data using share measures and characterized itemsets. *International Journal on Artificial Intelligence Tools*, 7(2):189–220, June 1998.
6. R.J. Hilderman, C.L. Carter, H.J. Hamilton, and N. Cercone. Mining market basket data using share measures and characterized itemsets. In X. Wu, R. Kotagiri, and K. Korb, editors, *Proceedings of the Second Pacific-Asia Conference on Knowledge Discovery and Data Mining (PAKDD'98)*, pages 159–173, Melbourne, Australia, April 1998.
7. R. Srikant and R. Agrawal. Mining sequential patterns: generalization and performance improvements. In *Proceedings of the Fifth International Conference on Extending Database Technology (EDBT'96)*, Avignon, France, March 1996.

A Virtual Join Algorithm for Fast Association Rule Mining

Minho Kim, Gye Hyung Kim, and R.S. Ramakrishna

Department of Information and Communications, K-JIST
1 Oryong-dong, Buk-gu, Gwangju, 500-712, Republic of Korea
{mhkim, kgh4001, rsr}@kjist.ac.kr

Abstract. A new algorithm for improving ECLAT performance has been presented in this paper. The algorithm is based on the concept of a "virtual join". The virtual join algorithm avoids relatively expensive real joins, leading to enhanced performance. Experimental results demonstrate the effectiveness of the proposed algorithm.

1 Introduction

The first major algorithm for association rule mining, the Apriori [1] is based on the intuitive idea that all the subsets of a frequent itemset should be frequent.

However, Apriori and its variations are not known to be very efficient. In order to address the weaknesses of Apriori-based algorithms, some alternatives, such as ECLAT [4] or FP-growth [2], have been developed in recent times. ECLAT utilizes the inherent properties of equivalence classes (eqclass) in search spaces (lattices): FP-growth explores the FP-tree that compactly represents information needed to find all frequent itemsets in the original DB.

There have been some attempts to search only the frequent closed itemsets that represent all the frequent itemsets: for instance, CLOSET [3] and CHARM [5].

In this paper we propose a virtual join algorithm to improve ECLAT. ECLAT finds all frequent itemsets with only a single scan over a pre-calculated database (vertical tid-list database) by dividing the search space into independent eqclasses, each of which fits within the memory. With its simple intersection operations, it can also avoid excessive memory and computational costs incurred by Apriori-based algorithms due to the complex data structures that they employ.

The major computation in ECALT algorithm is the join operation. It involves the intersection of two sets of transaction ids (*tid-lists*) of two itemsets. The corresponding complexity is O(mn), where m and n are the lengths of the two tid-lists. This operation is required even if the newly generated itemset turns out to be infrequent and hence, need not be considered any longer.

The proposed virtual join algorithm can effectively avoid such unnecessary real joins through just a table lookup process. The experimental studies show that the virtual join algorithm discards about 55% of real joins, thereby considerably improving the performance of ECLAT.

J. Liu et al. (Eds.): IDEAL 2003, LNCS 2690, pp. 796–800, 2003.

2 Virtual Join Algorithms

The *Join* operation begins by combining two $(k–1)$-itemsets and ends with the determination of a frequent k-itemset. In the first step, a new candidate k-itemset is generated by combining two $(k-1)$-itemsets within an eqclass. Then, an intersection of tid-lists of the two $(k–1)$ itemsets is performed in order to find the tid-list of the candidate itemset. Finally, the support of the candidate itemset, that is, the size of the tid-list, is compared with the user specified minimum support, *min_sup*. If the support is greater than or equal to (less than) min_sup, the candidate itemset is frequent (infrequent).

Example: We assume we have eqclass $[A]$ = $\{AC, AD\}$ and tid-list(AC) = $\{1,2,3,4,5,6\}$, tid-list(AD) = $\{5,6,7,8,9\}$, and tid-list(CD) = $\{5,6\}$. Let min_sup be 3. In the first step of join of itemsets AC and AD, a new candidate itemset ACD is generated. Then, tid-list(ACD) is determined by combining tid-list(AC) and tid-list(AD). Thus, we have tid-list(ACD) = tid-list(AC) $\cap$ tid-list(AD) = $\{5,6\}$. Since sup(ACD) = |tid-list(ACD)| = 2 < min_sup = 3, the candidate itemset ACD is infrequent.

2.1 Observations

Several observations on the join operation are in order. First, the intersection operation is simple but relatively expensive, particularly when tid-lists are long. In order to reduce computationally expensive intersections, we can check the potential of a newly generated candidate itemset to be frequent. This approach is based on a well-known intuition that "*all the subsets of frequent itemset are frequent.*" That is, $\forall S \subset$ a frequent itemset, sup(S) $\geq$ min_sup. This means that if there exists even a single $S' \subset$ a candidate itemset with sup(S') < min_sup, then the candidate itemset cannot be frequent. Therefore, if we find any subset S' of the candidate itemset with sup(S') < min_sup before a real join, the candidate itemset is infrequent and thus, we can avoid the computationally expensive intersection. For instance, in the example above the support of CD, one of the subsets of the candidate itemset ACD, is less than min_sup. Thus, we can conclude that ACD is infrequent. Here, we need just one lookup into the support table, instead of computing the intersection.

This approach, however, has a drawback. As the size of a candidate itemset increases, the additional cost increases exponentially since the number of its subsets grows exponentially.

The costs are listed below.

1) the maintenance cost of all the support tables from 2-itemsets to $(k–1)$-itemsets;
2) the generation cost of all the subsets of the candidate itemset, and
3) the lookup cost for all the subsets.

There is another observation that can address this problem. In the example above, we do not need to check supports of all the subsets of the candidate itemset ACD in order to check the potentiality of ACD because we already know that AC and AD, which were used to generate ACD,were frequent. Thus, we only need to check the support of CD. The generalization of this observation is the following: Since the join of ECLAT is an equivalence class based operation, the generation of a new candidate itemset has the form $pX + pY = pXY$, where p is a prefix of length $(k–1)$. Since pX and pY are frequent, all the subsets of pX and pY are frequent and the newly generated size 2 subset of pXY is only XY. Also, we already have a lookup table of support of all 2-itemsets and it is always accessible. Therefore, we do not incur any extra cost for the virtual join algorithm except that of a single lookup of the table.

2.2 Virtual Join

Subsets of size 2 of a candidate itemset seem to be good candidates for checking whether the candidate itemset is frequent and in this case we need only a single lookup. This is the essence of the virtual join algorithm which is summarized below:

> (For the join of pX and pY, i.e., $pX + pY = pXY$)
>
> If support(XY) < min_sup,
>   goto the next join
> else (i.e., support(XY) ≥ min_sup),
>   do the real join

3 Experimental Results

This section presents a comparison of the performance of ECLAT with virtual join (ECLAT_VJ) with that of ECLAT without virtual join. All the experiments were performed on 733MHz Pentium III Computer with 256MB RAM, running LINUX. All the programs were written in C++.

Table 1. The average relative number of joins of ECLAT_VJ in terms of ECLAT

Experiment type	TxI4D400K	T20IyD400K	T10I4Dz	T10I4D400K (Sw)
Relative no. of joins	0.45	0.53	0.37	0.40

In the first experiment, the number of transactions contained in DB (database size) and the average number of items for a pattern itemset (pattern size) are fixed at 400K (D400K) and 4 (I4), respectively, and the average number of items in a transaction (transaction size) varies; that is, the transaction is Tx, where $x = \{10, 15, 20, 25, 30\}$. The user specified minimum support, min_sup, is 0.25%. This support is applied to all the experiments except those with varying min_sup. As summarized in table 1, the average relative number of real joins of ECLAT_VJ for this experiment (TxI4D400K) is just 45% of ECLAT. That is, the proposed virtual join algorithm discards 55% of real joins. And Fig. 1 (a) shows that the performance of ECLAT_VJ is always better than that of ECLAT and that the difference in runtime between ECLAT and ECLAT_VJ increases, as the average transaction size increases. These results are due to the fact that the complexity of a join operation is directly dependent on the transaction size. The results suggest that the runtime becomes shorter as the average transaction size increases.

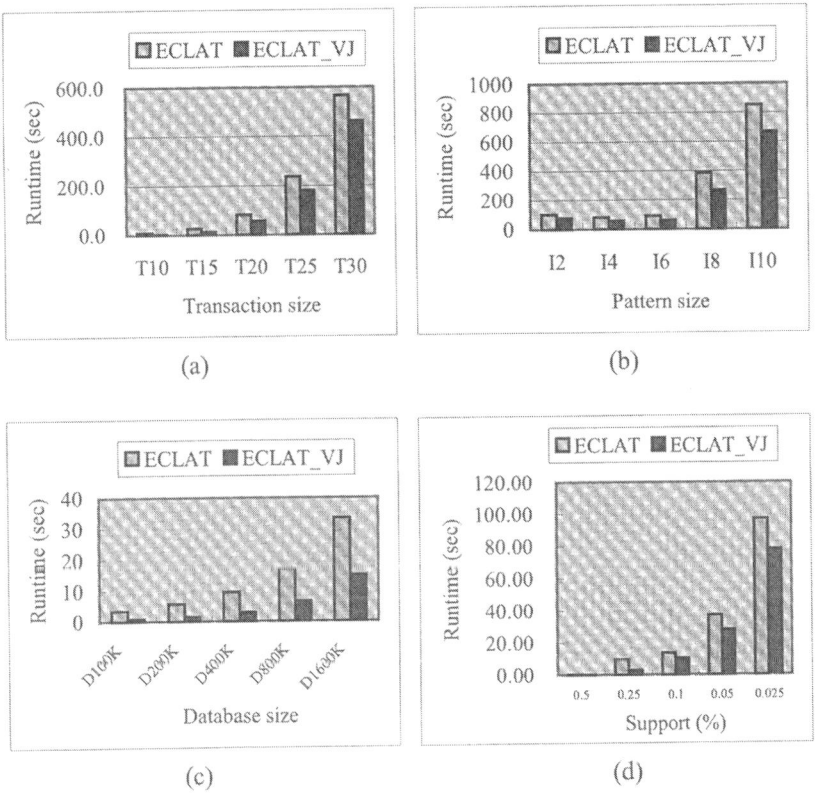

(a)

(b)

(c)

(d)

Fig. 1. Comparisons of runtime between ECLAT and ECLAT_VJ with varying transaction size (Tx), pattern size (Iy), database size (Dz), and user-specified minimum support (Sw).

In the second experiment, the transaction size and the database size are fixed at 20 (T20) and 400K (D400K), respectively. The pattern size Iy varies; in particular, $y = \{2, 4, 6, 8, 10\}$. Results in Fig. 1 (b) are similar to those of Fig. 1 (a). Since the pattern size varies up to 10, we selected 20 as the transaction size so as to easily accommodate the pattern in a transaction. As the pattern size increases, transactions in databases can contain longer patterns, which means more joins and iterations are required. Thus, the relative number of joins of ECLAT_VJ in table 1 increases. Also, the runtime in Fig. 1 (b) is longer than that in the first experiment.

In the third experiment, the transaction size and the pattern size are fixed at 10 (T10) and 4 (I4), respectively. The database size (Dz) varies over {100K, 200K, 400K, 800K, 1600K}. Since the min_sup is the percentage of support for an itemset fixed (0.25%) in a database, the real minimum support count of transactions for frequent itemsets increases as the database size increases. The virtual join approach shortens runtime more pronouncedly for larger databases. This means that the virtual join algorithm scales well with database size. The results are shown in Fig. 1 (c).

The final experiment pertains to scalability for user-specified minimum support, min_sup. The transaction size, the pattern size, and the database size are fixed at 10 (T10), 4 (I4), and 400K (D400K), respectively. The results in Fig. 1 (d) show that the virtual join algorithm also scales well with min_sup.

4   Conclusions

A virtual join algorithm for enhancing the performance of ECLAT was presented in this paper. The proposed algorithm avoids unnecessary joins.

The effectiveness of the algorithm increases with

(a)   increasing transaction size;
(b)   increasing pattern size and
(c)   increasing database size.

It is, therefore, felt that the virtual join algorithm for ECLAT would be very effective in association rule mining – especially frequent pattern mining – in the areas such as bioinformatics.

Acknowledgement. The authors wish to acknowledge Prof. Mohammed J. Zaki's help in this investigation. This work was supported by the Ministry of Education (MOE) through the Brain Korea 21 (BK21) project.

References

1. Agrawal, R., Srikant, R.: Fast Algorithms for Mining Association Rules. Proc. the 20th Int'l Conf. VLDB (1994) 487–499
2. Han, J., Pei, J., Yin, Y.: Mining Frequent Patterns without Candidate Generation. Proc. ACM SIGMOD Conf. on Management of Data (2000) 1–12
3. Pei, J., Han, J., and Mao, R.: CLOSET: An Efficient Algorithm for Mining Frequent Closed Itemsets. Proc. ACM SIGMOD Workshop on Data Mining and Knowl. Discovery. (2000) 21–32
4. Zaki, M.J., Parthasarathy, S., Ogihara, M., Li, W.: New Algorithms for Fast Discovery of Association Rules. Proc. the 3rd Int'l Conf. KDD (1997) 283–286
5. Zaki, M.J., Hsiao, C.-J.: CHARM: An Efficient Algorithm for Closed Itemset Mining. Tech. Rep. 99–10. (1999) Computer Science, RPI

Packet Filtering Using a Decision Tree Classifier

Chunyan Li, Wei Lin, and Yongtian Yang

College of computer science and technology, Harbin Engineering University,
Harbin, Hei Long Jiang, 150001, China
Li_cyan@hotmail.com

Abstract. Packet filtering is an important technology in firewalls and other relevant security devices. Traditional packet filtering just compares some fields of an input packet header with a given rlue-list in linear order and finds out the first matched rule, then follows the matched rule's policy to allow or block the packet. In this way, efficiency is low and rules in the rule-list are independent, so that information among them can not be used effectively. In this paper, a new idea using a decision tree classifier is proposed. It first builds a decision tree according to the rule-list and then searches the tree to find out the matched rule for an input packet. It can be illustrated that packet filtering using a decision tree classifier is more quickly and can study inductively from the rules, so it will make the packet filter firewall has some prediction ability.

1 Introduction

Packet filter firewall is the initial firewall model, although there are many new technologies come up, such as proxy, state inspection and others, packet filtering is also a necessary and basic technique for a firewall.

Every packet has a header and takes some information in the header fields. These information include source and destination IP addresses, transport layer ports, type of protocol and others. Packet filtering means that build a rule-list at first, these rules determine which packets are allowed to pass the firewall and which are blocked. Table 1 is part of a rule-list sample. When a packet is input, it will be examined whether its header information is matched with one of the rule in the list. If there is more than one rule matched with it, the highest priority rule will be taken. Then corresponding action will be executed. If there is no rule matched the packet then the default rule will be taken.

Table 1. Some rules in a rule-list

No.	Source IP	Destination IP	Source port	Destination port	Type of protocol	Action
R1	202.118.101.11	192.168.0.1	*	25 (SMTP)	6 (TCP)	A (allow)
R2	202.118.176.2	192.168.0.2	*	21 (FTP)	6 (TCP)	A (allow)
R3	*	192.168.0.3	*	80 (HTTP)	6 (TCP)	B (block)
R8	202.118.179.1	*	53	53	17 (UDP)	A (allow)

J. Liu et al. (Eds.): IDEAL 2003, LNCS 2690, pp. 801–805, 2003.

Traditional packet filtering is a linear search process. In linear search the rules are independent, which means that the former rules can not give any heuristic information to the latter. It is clear that the computing complexity is O(Nd) in worst condition, N denotes the amount of rules and d is the number of header fields used to check the packets[1]. When the rule-list becomes large, the searching speed will be very slow, so this linear search method just adapts to small rule-list firewalls.

2 Decision Tree Classifier

In fact, packet filtering can belong to classification problem. In this paper, we use decision trees as a classifier because it has simple structure and can easily be converted into IF-THEN rules, and it need not any other additional knowledge. So this method is efficient and suitable for real-time packet filtering with a large rule-list.

the ID3 [2]algorithm or other present algorithms[3,4] can not be used into packet filtering directly. Because the packet filtering has some special characters different from general classification problems, so we propose an improved algorithm for packet filtering classifier. The new packet filtering algorithm consists of two parts: building algorithm and searching algorithm.

2.1 Building Algorithm

The input is a rule list as a training set, the output is a decision tree.
1) For each non-categorical attributes A_i calculating information gain I_A;
2) Selecting the A_k with the maximal I_A as the dividing attribute and the root node;
3) According to the values of A_k, the rule list is divided into m sub-sets (m denotes the number of values of A_k). Then add m branches below the root labeled with v_i (i=1...m);
4) For each of the m sub-sets examine:
   if the rules in the sub-set are the same class
   or if the number of rules is small enough (e.g. less than 5)
   then end dividing , and each leaf refers to a two dimensions linear list in which stores the rest attributes and values of the sub-set rules.
   Else recursively execute this algorithm for each sub-set.
5) End.
   The information gain I_A is calculated by following formula:
   $I (U, V) = E (U) - E (U|V)$

   $$E(U) = -\sum_{i=1}^{c} p(Ui) \log p(Ui)$$

   $$E(U|V) = -\sum_{j=1}^{m} p(v_j) \sum_{i=1}^{c} p(Ui \mid v_j) \log p(Ui \mid v_j)$$

Here U_i (i=1...c) denotes classes, if there are only two kinds of class A and B, then c=2. And $p(.)$ denotes probability distribution of different part or different value. v_j(j=1...m) are distinct values of a non-attribute.

2.2 Searching Algorithm

The input is a decision tree and a coming in packet $p(v_1, v_2, \ldots v_k)$, the output is a matched rule. From the root begin:
1) Initializing a stack S called trace stack;
2) Initializing a matched rule set MRS;
3) If node N is not a leaf then
     For each branch of N
     If $V(N) = vi$ or $V(N) = *$ then
          Push corresponding child node into S;
4) If node N is a leaf then
     Lookup the linear list linked by N,
     If find out the matched rule then add it into MRS;
5) If S is not empty, then pull a node from S and goto 3);
6) If MRS is empty then the matched rule is default rule;
     Else find out the highest priority rule in MRS, which is the matched rule (the minimal No. is the highest priority.) Output it.
7) End.

3 Example of Packet Filtering Using the Decision Tree Classifier

In order to generalize the representation of the rule list, the rules are symbolized. For example, the first rule in table 1 <R1, 202.118.101.11, 192.168.0.1, *, 25, 6, A> can be symbolized as <1, SIP_1, DIP_1, *, $Dport_1$, T_1, A>. So a table like table 1 is converted into table 2 and Figure 1 shows a decision tree that is built by building algorithm according to the rules in table 2.

As inputs a packet $p(SIP_2, DIP_1, Sport_5, Dport_3, T_1)$, the searching processes is like the red dashed showing. Firstly the destination IP address is used to compare p with the branches. There are two branches satisfy the query DIP_1 and *. Going on lookup according to the searching algorithm, finally two leaves including four rules are got. When lookups the four rules, it can be determined that rule 3 is the matched rule. That is the same result to linear searching. As inputs $p(SIP_5, DIP_2, Sport_5, Dport_1, T_1)$, it just need to lookup four rules to get the result that p matches with the default rule. While it should lookup all rules in the list in linear searching algorithm.

Table 2. Symbolized rule list

No	Source IP	Dest IP	Source port	Dest port	Type of protocol	Action
1	SIP_1	DIP_1	*	$Dport_1$	T_1	A
2	SIP_2	DIP_2	*	$Dport_2$	T_1	A
3	*	DIP_1	*	$Dport_3$	T_1	B
4	SIP_3	DIP_3	*	$Dport_1$	T_1	A
5	SIP_4	DIP_4	*	$Dport_3$	T_1	B
6	*	DIP_3	*	$Dport_3$	T_1	A
7	SIP_1	DIP_5	*	$Dport_1$	T_1	A
8	SIP_5	*	$Sport_1$	$Dport_4$	T_2	A
9	*	*	$Sport_2$	$Dport_5$	T_3	A
10	*	*	$Sport_3$	$Dport_6$	T_3	A

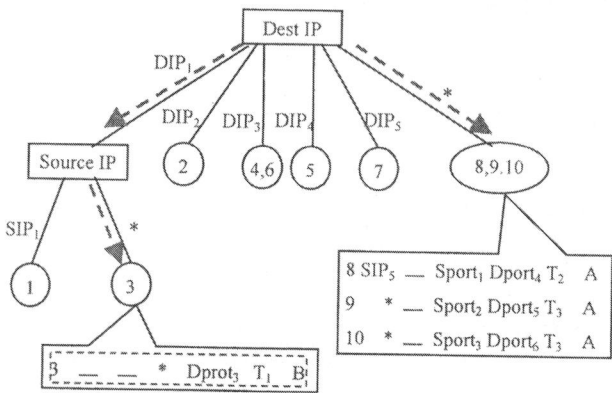

Fig. 1. A built decision tree and a packet searching process

4 Performance

The computing complexity of the building algorithm is similar to ID3 algorithm. That is a linear function of the product of the number of rules (N) and the number of attributes (d) and the number of nodes (V). Building a decision tree is finished in the preprocess time, so it has little effect on the efficiency of the real-time packet filtering.

The searching algorithm can be portioned into two parts. One is looking for the suitable leaves in a decision tree, and the other is lookup in the linear list that linked by these leaves. In fact, the former part is a traversal of a binary tree because there are no more than two branches matched the input packet each time. So the complexity of this part is less than the traversal complexity of a binary tree with the same levels, if there are L levels, it is $O(2^L)$. The latter part is a set of linear searching. Each searching complexity is $O(n(d-L))$, $n \leq N$ is the average of the rules in all satisfied leaves, and no more than 2^L leaves will be looked up.

So the total complexity of the two algorithms is no more than $O(2^L n(d-L))$.

5 Conclusion

Packet filtering using a decision tree classifier has less query complexity than the conventional linear searching in average and the worst conditions. And by making use of threshold to increase the depth of the decision tree, the number of rules in each leaf can be restricted to some scale. So that improves the searching speed.

In this paper, the exact match is still used in the packet filtering. But by using the decision tree classifier the packet filtering has some induction and prediction abilities, so a new packet filter firewall with some self-study abilities will be realized by it.

References

1. Robert L. Ziegler. Linux firewalls (2nd edition). New Riders Publishing, Indianapolis, USA, 2001
2. Quinlan J.R. Induction of decision trees. Machine Learning, 1986
3. Wang Xi-zhao, Hong Jia-rong. Learning algorithm of decision tree generation for interval-valued attributes. Chinese Journal of Software, vol.9, no.8: 638–640, 1998
4. Chen Enhong, Wang Qingyi and Cai Qingsheng. Test generation and discrimination of continuously-valued attributes in decision tree based learning. Chinese Computer Research and Development, vol.35, no.5: 403–407, 1998

An XML Query Mediator

Kyeung Soo Lee, Dong Ik Oh, Im Young Lee, and Yong Hae Kong

Division of Information Technology Engineering, Soonchunhyang University,
Asan-si, Choongnam, 336-745, Korea
{kslee, dohdoh, imylee, yhkong}@sch.ac.kr

Abstract. Proper query to XML documents is difficult because of different structures and properties. For effective query to XML documents, we developed an XML query mediator. Through conceptualizing information of a domain the query mediator expands XML queries suitable to various XML documents with the consideration of semantic association as well as structural dependency.

1 Introduction

Since XML documents may have different structures and properties for the same type information, accessing XML document is limited. Therefore, we propose a mediator that expands XML queries to effectively search from XML documents. We use domain information to expand a query into conceptual ones. The expanded queries can be comprehensively applied to various forms of XML documents. The query mediator is designed to have three components: query expansion by explicit conceptual inheritance, by implicit conceptual inheritance and by forced conceptual association. Finally, the expanded queries are tested by sample XML documents and they are more effective than raw queries in catching semantic information.

2 Domain Conceptualization

A domain can be described by concepts and attributes of concepts: [1],[2]. For example, a 'Music CD' domain has two parts. One part describes concept hierarchy where sub-concepts are inherited from a super-concept. Fig. 1 schematizes a hierarchical structure of concepts, where 'Object' is the super-concept of all other

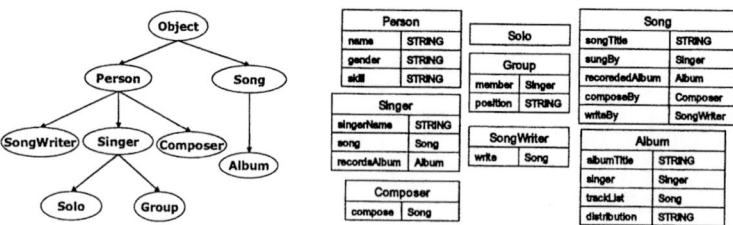

Fig. 1. Concept Hierarchy   **Fig. 2.** Attributes of Concepts

This research was supported by University IT Research Center Project

J. Liu et al. (Eds.): IDEAL 2003, LNCS 2690, pp. 806–810, 2003.

concepts. The other part describes attributes of concepts. Attributes of a concept are inherited to sub-concepts as well. In Fig. 2, concepts are semantically inter-related with these attributes: [3],[4].

3 XML Query Mediator

An XML Query Mediator consists of Inference Engine, Query Mediator and Query Engine. Inference Engine generates inferred rules and Query Mediator in turn expands queries using the rules inferred. For Query Engine, XQL(XML Query Language) engine is used. The mediator is depicted in Fig. 3 and the following steps of operations are conducted.

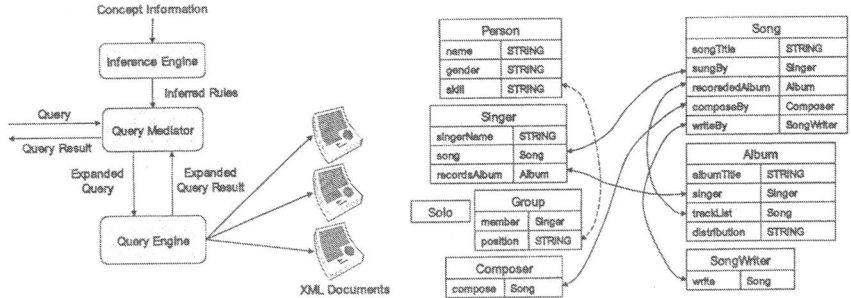

Fig. 3. XML Query Mediator   **Fig. 4.** Concepts Associations

Step1 Conceptualize a domain by a concept hierarchy and attributes
Step2 Inference Engine generates inherent rules by attribute analysis
Step3 Inference Engine generates forced rules by teaching association
Step4 Query Mediator expands a query based on the generated rules
Step5 Query Engine searches XML documents using the expanded queries

3.1 Query Expansion by Explicit Conceptual Inheritance

Structural variations of documents can be tolerated by considering explicit inheritances as follows.

Step1 Find a concept that corresponds to the element of query
Step2 Add the sub-concepts as elements to the query
Step3 Repeat Step1 and Step2 for all the sub-concepts recursively

Query '// Person[skill="song"]' for the concept of Fig.1 is expanded to '//(Person | Singer | SongWriter | Composer | Solo | Group)[skill="Song"]' which searches for all the occurrences of sub-concepts.

3.2 Query Expansion by Implicit Conceptual Inheritance

Implicit conceptual inheritance establishes associations among concepts, which is inherent semantic relations, as follows.

Step 1 Find a concept A whose attribute is another concept B
Step 2 If concept B has attribute of concept A, set an association between the two
Step 3 Repeat Step 1 – Step 2 until no more associations are made

In Fig. 2, an association can be established between the two concepts 'Singer' and 'Album' through implicit inheritance. This association generates an inference rule as shown below. That is, 'singer' of instance 'Song1' and 'recordedAlbum' of instance 'Pers1' is semantically identical.

FORALL Pers1, Song1
  Song1 : Album[singer ->> Pers1] <-> Pers1 : Singer[recordsAlbum ->> Song1]

All possible associations in Fig. 1 and Fig. 2 are depicted as solid lines in Fig. 4. With the following set of inferred rules corresponding to the solid lines of Fig. 4, query expansion can be done quickly without repeating the search process.

FORALL Pers1, Song1
  Song1 : Album[singer ->> Pers1] <-> Pers1 : Singer[recordsAlbum ->> Song1].
FORALL Pers1, Song1
  Song1 : Song[sungBy ->> Pers1] <-> Pers1 : Singer[song ->> Song1]
FORALL Pers1, Song1
  Song1 : Song[writeBy ->> Pers1] <-> Pers1 : SongWriter[write ->> Song1]
FORALL Pers1, Song1
  Song1 : Song[composeBy ->> Pers1] <->Pers1 : Composer[compose ->> Song1]
FORALL Song1, Song2
  Song2 : Album[trackList ->>Song1]<->Song1 : Song[recordedAlbum ->> Song2]

3.3 Query Expansion by Teaching Association

Forced associations are required when inherent associations are not enough to convey all the relations among concepts. Search for persons who play guitar in Fig. 4 is query '//Person[skill="Guitar"]'. However, the fact that 'position' attribute of concept 'Group' is 'Guitar' means that he has skill 'Guitar' too. Therefore, the teaching association is included by a dotted line in Fig. 4 and the following rule is generated.

FORALL Obj1, Obj2, data
  Obj1 : Person[skill ->> data] <-> Obj2 : Group[position ->> data]

3.4 Application Results

For the example XML document in Table 1, we tested the effectiveness of the query mediator. Query '//Singer[name="John Lennon"]' is structurally expanded to '//(Singer | Solo | Group)[name="John Lennon"]' by the mediator.

Table 1. Example of XML Document

<Song>	<position>Guitar</position>
<Person>	</Group>
<name>Tom Frazer</name>	<Album>
<skill>Guitar</skill>	<albumTitle>The Best Of
</Person>	</albumTitle>
<Singer>	<singer>Simon And Garfunkel
<name>Jessica</name>	</singer>
<song>Good Bye</song>	<songTitle>The Sound Of Silence
</Singer>	</songTitle>
<Singer>	</Album>
<name>Sting</name>	<sungBy>
<song>Shape Of My Heart</song>	<Singer>
</Singer>	<singerName>Simon And Garfunkel
<Group>	</singerName>
<singerName>Beatles</singerName>	<recordsAlbum>The Best Of
<name>Paul McCartney</name>	</recordsAlbum>
<name>Ringo Starr</name>	<song>Bridge Over Troubled Water
<name>John Lennon</name>	</song>
<name>George Harrison</name>	<song>Scarborough Fair</song>
</Group>	</Singer>
<Group>	</sungBy>
<singerName>Queen</singerName>	</Song>
<name>Brian May</name>	

For query '//Album[singer]', the mediator generates an additional query '//Singer[recordsAlbum]' by implicit conceptual inheritance. The query results are compared in Fig. 5.

Fig. 5. Results of Queries '//Album[singer]' and '//Singer[recordsAlbum]'

For query '//Person[skill="Guitar"]' that finds a person who can play guitar, the mediator first expands the query to structurally expanded one '//(Person | SongWriter | Composer | Singer | Solo | Group)[skill="Guitar"]'. Then, the expanded query successively expanded to '//Group[position="Guitar"]' by the teaching association as in Fig. 6.

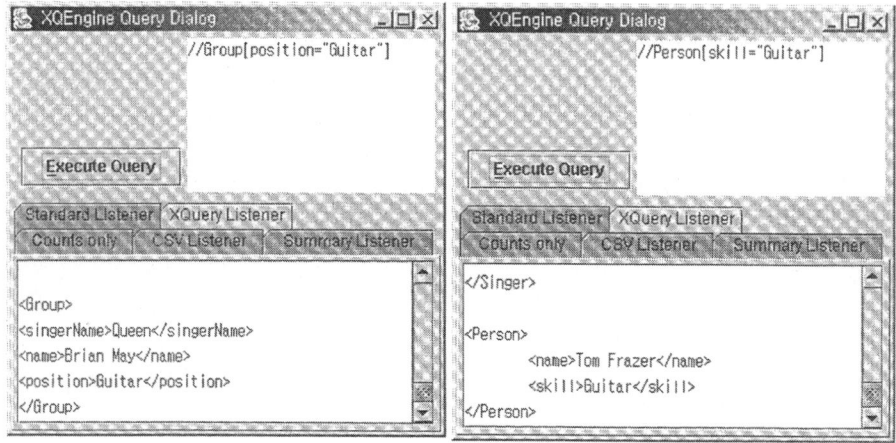

Fig. 6. Results of Queries '//Group[position="Guitar"]' and '//Person[skill="Guitar"]'

4 Conclusions

Properly interpreting XML documents is difficult because they have dissimilar properties and structures even though they represent identical objects. An XML query mediator is developed that expands XML queries comprehensively applicable to various forms of XML documents. For the system development, an application domain is conceptually modeled. Then, three modules are developed so as to expand a query by structuring and inherent/forced association. Once all the associations are built, then inferred rules are generated for quick references for prompt query expansion. Experiments using sample XML documents show the effectiveness of the mediator-generated queries by catching underlying information otherwise undetected.

References

1. Mena, E., Kashyap, V., Illarramendi, A., Sheth, A.: Domain Specific Ontologies for Semantic Information Brokering on the Global Information Infrastructure. Intl. Conf. on Formal Ontology in Information Systems, IOS Press (1998)
2. Gruber, T.R.: A Translation Approach to Portable Ontology Specifications. Knowledge Acquisition, Vol. 5. No. 2 (1993) 199–220
3. Kifer, M., Lausen, G., Wu, J.: Logical foundations of object-oriented and frame-based languages, Vol. 42. Journal of the ACM (1995) 741–843
4. Erdmann, M., Studer, R.: How to Structure and Access XML Document with Ontologies. Data & Knowledge Engineering, Vol. 36. No.3 (2001) 317–335

Potential Gains from Global Market Timing Involving Three or More Markets

Wei Li[1] and Kin Lam[2]

[1] Department of Business Studies, FBIS, Hong Kong Polytechnic University
Hung Hom, Kowloon, Hong Kong,
buwli@polyu.edu.hk
[2] Department of Finance and Decision Sciences, Hong Kong Baptist University,
Kowloon Tong, Kowloon, Hong Kong
lamkin@hkbu.edu.hk

Abstract. In this paper we evaluate the potential gains from international market timing. Empirical results show that the potential gain decreases as transaction cost increases and increases as the frequency of review schedule increases. However, the potential gain increases in a decreasing rate as the number of countries increases.

1 Introduction

Traditionally, market timing is an investment strategy which shifts funds between common stocks and cash equivalents within a domestic market with the objective of outperforming the market. Increasingly efficient communication technology and the dismantling of regulatory constraints have encouraged globalization in recent years. Nowadays, investors can more easily invest in international stock markets. Despite these develoments, there seems to be a lack on the studies on potential gains from "intermarket timing", in which the timing of the market is achieved by shifting common stock investments internationally from one stock market to another. The only available studies that involve more than one market are those of Kester (1991) and Wang and Tai (2000), which discussed the potential gains from shifting funds between two markets. In their researches, although there are two risky assets involved, e.g., two countries, there is no risk-free asset. Obviously, a successful globalized investment should involve a risk-free investment as well as allowing for investing in three or more markets. While the potential gain in expanding the investment from one country to two has been investigated, the potential of further globalization is not fully investigated. This paper intends to fill this gap by studying the potential gain from shifting between several markets.

This study deviates from the previous studies in the following two important aspects: (1) we do not limit the study to two assets only. (2) A truly perfect timing strategy under transaction costs will be considered.

J. Liu et al. (Eds.): IDEAL 2003, LNCS 2690, pp. 811–815, 2003.
© Springer-Verlag Berlin Heidelberg 2003

In this paper, we consider ten assets, nine equity markets and a risk-free asset, i.e., Australia (AU), Canada (CA), France (FR), Germany (GE), Hong Kong (HK), Italy (IT), Japan (JA), UK, USA markets and T-bills. In section 2, we argue that the traditional "perfect" timing strategy is not truly perfect. We will also show the growth optimal criteria as an international market timer's objective. Data and the empirical results are presented in Section 3. Section 4 gives the conclusion.

2 Truly Perfect Timing Strategy

In Sharpe (1975) and Jeffrey (1984)'s argument against timing the market, the perfect timing strategy has played a key role. To assess the potential reward of market timing, the strategy of solely investing in stocks or solely in cash equivalents is compared with a timing strategy with perfect predictive ability. The perfect timing strategy in the literature is commonly constructed as follows. Each year can be categorized as either a good or a bad year for stocks. In a good year, the excess return, i.e. the total return on stocks including dividends minus that on cash equivalents is positive. In a bad year the reverse holds. The perfect timing strategy when there is no transaction cost is one that holds stocks in a good year and holds cash equivalents in a bad year. In the presence of transaction costs, the overall transaction costs involved in the perfect timing strategy will be deducted from its return. The net return is then used as a benchmark based on which the likely gain from perfect timing is being calculated.

One main problem of the commonly accepted 'perfect' timing strategy is that the investment decision does not depend on transaction costs. It is obviously undesirable, since the same number of switches would be recommended even when transaction costs are high. Lam and Li (2001) pointed out that in the presence of transaction costs, the so-called 'perfect' timing strategy is actually less than perfect! However, they only solve for the case of shifting between two assets, a risky asset and a risk-free assets.

Using the optimal growth criterion, this paper will calculate the potential gain from the truly perfect timing strategy which can achieve the maximum long term growth for international market timing.

In this paper, we assume that decisions are made with full knowledge of future price movement. We also assume that investment decisions are to be made at discrete points in time ($t=0,1,2,...$), the time horizon is T, and there are m stock markets and one risk-free asset. At each time point t, the investor has to decide on the decision variable $\underline{d}_t = (d_t^1, d_t^2, ..., d_t^m)$, where d_t^i is the decision of investment in market i, $i=1,2, ..., m$. Note that the remaining proportion of $1 - \sum_{i=1}^{m} d_t^i$ is invested in the risk-free asset and denoted by d_t^0.

Similar to Li and Lam (2002), we use TR to denote the total return from investing in these m countries for the T periods, our objective is

$$\underset{d_t^i,t=1,...T,i=1,...m}{MAX} \quad TR = \sum_{t=1}^{T} r_t^0 (1 - \sum_{i=1}^{m} d_t^i) + \sum_{t=1}^{T}\sum_{i=1}^{m} r_t^i d_t^i - \sum_{t=1}^{T}\sum_{i=1}^{m} c_i |d_t^i - d_{t-1}^i|$$

$$s.t. \qquad \sum_{i=1}^{m} d_t^i \leq 1, t = 1,...,T$$

$$d_t^i \geq 0, t = 1,...T, i = 1,...m$$

$$d_0^i = 0, i = 1,...m$$

where r_t^i is the continuously compounded return of country i at time t, r_t^0 is the continuously compounded return of the cash equivalent at time t, d_t^i is the decision on market i at time t, c_i is the transaction costs for entering into and leaving market i.

3 Empirical Results

In this paper, we let the United States be the investors' home country. When investors invest in a foreign equity market, they are exposed to exchange rates risks. To monitor investors' performance, Morgan Stanley Capital International (MSCI) country indices are appropriate because the returns resulting from the indices are based on US currency.

In order to calculate the potential gains from international timing, we consider an investment horizon of 30 years from January 1970 to December 1999 and collect the monthly, quarterly, semiannual and yearly MSCI country index data. The corresponding US T-bills rates are also collected to reflect the return from a risk-free investment.

The one-way transaction cost may differ from one pair of countries to another. To simplify discussion, we assume a single transaction cost to apply to switching between all pairs of countries and let the transaction costs vary from 0.2% to 1.4%.

The first column in Table 3.1 gives the maximum annual return assuming that investors can have perfect timing between T-bills and the US equity market. For example, if the review schedule is yearly and the transaction cost is 1.4%, by perfectly timing, one can achieve a continuously compounded growth rate of 12.91%. It can be seen from Table 3.1 that as the review schedule becomes more frequent, i.e., from yearly to monthly, the potential gain of perfect market timing increases quite rapidly. Perfect timing can achieve a growth rate of 21.28% if a monthly review schedule is adopted.

We then adopt a sequential approach to include another country. The investors now have to time three assets: T-bills, the US, and one other country. We add the country offering maximum growth rates. The maximum growth rates so attained are reported in Table 3.1 in the second column. When a third country is added to the two

Table 3.1. Potential Gains and Investment Sequence

Frequency	cost	Number of countries								
		1	2	3	4	5	6	7	8	9
Monthly	0.002	0.2630 (US)	0.6384 (HK)	0.7906 (IT)	0.8838 (JA)	0.9450 (AU)	0.9903 (UK)	1.0259 (FR)	1.0369 (CA)	1.0621 (GE)
	0.004	0.2526 (US)	0.6195 (HK)	0.7665 (IT)	0.8567 (JA)	0.9155 (AU)	0.9589 (UK)	0.9928 (FR)	1.0033 (CA)	1.0277 (GE)
	0.006	0.2428 (US)	0.6020 (HK)	0.7432 (IT)	0.8310 (JA)	0.8876 (AU)	0.9293 (UK)	0.9614 (FR)	0.9710 (CA)	0.9947 (GE)
	0.008	0.2340 (US)	0.5858 (HK)	0.7211 (IT)	0.8059 (JA)	0.8607 (AU)	0.9006 (UK)	0.9311 (FR)	0.9407 (GE)	0.9634 (CA)
	0.010	0.2264 (US)	0.5712 (HK)	0.7011 (IT)	0.7820 (JA)	0.8348 (AU)	0.8728 (UK)	0.9023 (FR)	0.9113 (GE)	0.9334 (CA)
	0.012	0.2193 (US)	0.5575 (HK)	0.6828 (IT)	0.7591 (JA)	0.8096 (AU)	0.8458 (UK)	0.8741 (FR)	0.8826 (GE)	0.9038 (CA)
	0.014	0.2126 (US)	0.5452 (HK)	0.6663 (IT)	0.7379 (JA)	0.7854 (AU)	0.8209 (UK)	0.8477 (FR)	0.8558 (GE)	0.8759 (CA)
quarterly	0.002	0.1974 (US)	0.4532 (HK)	0.5404 (IT)	0.5948 (JA)	0.6244 (FR)	0.6437 (UK)	0.6583 (AU)	0.6680 (GE)	0.6738 (CA)
	0.004	0.1940 (US)	0.4468 (HK)	0.5317 (IT)	0.5844 (JA)	0.6128 (FR)	0.6320 (UK)	0.6465 (AU)	0.6560 (GE)	0.6617 (CA)
	0.006	0.1909 (US)	0.4408 (HK)	0.5235 (IT)	0.5743 (JA)	0.6012 (FR)	0.6204 (UK)	0.6347 (AU)	0.6441 (GE)	0.6496 (CA)
	0.008	0.1880 (US)	0.4350 (HK)	0.5156 (IT)	0.5643 (JA)	0.5897 (FR)	0.6090 (UK)	0.6230 (AU)	0.6323 (GE)	0.6377 (CA)
	0.010	0.1854 (US)	0.4297 (HK)	0.5082 (IT)	0.5549 (JA)	0.5789 (FR)	0.5981 (UK)	0.6118 (AU)	0.6208 (GE)	0.6260 (CA)
	0.012	0.1830 (US)	0.4247 (HK)	0.5010 (IT)	0.5456 (JA)	0.5682 (FR)	0.5873 (UK)	0.6007 (AU)	0.6096 (GE)	0.6145 (CA)
	0.014	0.1806 (US)	0.4196 (HK)	0.4941 (IT)	0.5367 (JA)	0.5585 (UK)	0.5789 (GE)	0.5909 (AU)	0.5987 (FR)	0.6033 (CA)
Semi-annually	0.002	0.1691 (US)	0.3501 (HK)	0.4103 (IT)	0.4342 (UK)	0.4483 (JA)	0.4592 (AU)	0.4680 (FR)	0.4765 (CA)	0.4823 (GE)
	0.004	0.1673 (US)	0.3473 (HK)	0.4068 (IT)	0.4294 (UK)	0.4432 (AU)	0.4539 (JA)	0.4625 (CA)	0.4707 (FR)	0.4761 (GE)
	0.006	0.1656 (US)	0.3446 (HK)	0.4034 (IT)	0.4248 (UK)	0.4384 (AU)	0.4488 (JA)	0.4573 (CA)	0.4650 (FR)	0.4700 (GE)
	0.008	0.1640 (US)	0.3420 (HK)	0.4000 (IT)	0.4203 (UK)	0.4337 (AU)	0.4436 (JA)	0.4522 (CA)	0.4594 (FR)	0.4640 (GE)
	0.010	0.1626 (US)	0.3394 (HK)	0.3966 (IT)	0.4163 (UK)	0.4294 (AU)	0.4388 (JA)	0.4474 (CA)	0.4540 (FR)	0.4581 (GE)
	0.012	0.1612 (US)	0.3368 (HK)	0.3932 (IT)	0.4125 (UK)	0.4253 (AU)	0.4342 (JA)	0.4427 (CA)	0.4486 (FR)	0.4524 (GE)
	0.014	0.1598 (US)	0.3342 (HK)	0.3898 (IT)	0.4087 (UK)	0.4213 (AU)	0.4297 (CA)	0.4381 (JA)	0.4435 (FR)	0.4469 (GE)
yearly	0.002	0.1351 (US)	0.2896 (HK)	0.3300 (IT)	0.3516 (JA)	0.3611 (UK)	0.3683 (FR)	0.3726 (AU)	0.3769 (GE)	0.3769 (CA)
	0.004	0.1341 (US)	0.2882 (HK)	0.3280 (IT)	0.3495 (JA)	0.3587 (UK)	0.3659 (FR)	0.3702 (AU)	0.3742 (GE)	0.3742 (CA)
	0.006	0.1331 (US)	0.2868 (HK)	0.3261 (IT)	0.3474 (JA)	0.3564 (UK)	0.3636 (FR)	0.3680 (AU)	0.3717 (GE)	0.3717 (CA)
	0.008	0.1321 (US)	0.2854 (HK)	0.3242 (IT)	0.3454 (JA)	0.3542 (UK)	0.3614 (FR)	0.3658 (AU)	0.3692 (GE)	0.3692 (CA)
	0.010	0.1311 (US)	0.2840 (HK)	0.3222 (IT)	0.3433 (JA)	0.3520 (UK)	0.3592 (FR)	0.3636 (AU)	0.3669 (GE)	0.3669 (CA)
	0.012	0.1301 (US)	0.2826 (HK)	0.3203 (IT)	0.3412 (JA)	0.3499 (UK)	0.3570 (FR)	0.3614 (AU)	0.3645 (GE)	0.3645 (CA)
	0.014	0.1291 (US)	0.2812 (HK)	0.3185 (IT)	0.3393 (JA)	0.3478 (UK)	0.3548 (FR)	0.3592 (AU)	0.3622 (GE)	0.3622 (CA)

countries that have been so identified, the maximum growth rates obtained are reported in the third column. We repeat the process and stop until we exhaust all countries. For the case of a yearly review schedule, when one can perfectly time all markets, one can obtain a maximum growth rate of 36.22%. Under a more frequent review schedule, the maximum growth rate can be boosted up to 87.59%.

Table 3.1 also reports the sequential order of countries that are being added. Take the yearly review schedule under a one-way transaction cost of 0.14% as an example. The first country to be added to the US equities and T-bills is the Hong Kong equity market. Then, investors should add Italy to US and Hong Kong and gain the most if they can time the three markets perfectly. The last country to be added in this sequential search of largest potential gain is Canada. It is interesting to note that the sequential ordering is very robust against levels of transaction costs and is relatively less robust against review frequencies.

As we can see from Tables 3.1, the potential gains increase as the number of counties increases. However, the rate of increase is slowing down and the marginal percentage increases beyond having more than 4 countries is rather small. Even though we can time all the markets perfectly, it does not pay too much by participating in all markets. In the case under study, participating in four markets is almost as good as participating in all nine markets. The results show that while it is very desirable to go international and participate in more than one market, it is sufficient to participate in three of four and to participate in more than four markets become not very meaningful.

4 Conclusion

In this paper we evaluate the potential gains from international market timing. Empirical results show that the potential gain decreases as transaction cost increases and increases as the frequency of review schedule increases. However, the potential gain increases in a decreasing rate. From our results, it does not pay very much by participating in five or more countries, even when investors can time all the markets perfectly.

References

1. Jeffrey, R. (1984), 'The Folly of Stock Market Timing', Harvard Business Review, (July/August), 689–706.
2. Kester, G.W. (1991), "Inter-market timing equity investments in the United States and Singapore", in Rhee, S.G. and Ghang, R. (Eds), Pacific-Basin Capital Markets Research, Vol. II, 297–308.
3. Lam, K. and Li, W. (2001), "Is the 'perfect' timing strategy truly perfect?", Conference Proceedings of the Eighth Annual Conference of Multinational Finance Society, June 23–27, 2001, Lake Garda, Verona, Italy.
4. Sharpe, W.F. (1975), 'Likely Gains from Market Timing', Financial Analysts Journal, 31, 2, 60–69.
5. Wong, K.A. and Tai, L.S. (2000), "Intermarket timing in equity investments: Hong Kong versus Singapore", Journal of Economic Studies, 27, 525–540.

Incremental Condition Evaluation for Active Temporal Rules

Kyong Do Moon[1], Jeong Seok Park[2], Ye Ho Shin[3], and Keun Ho Ryu[4]

[1]Galim Information Technology Co., Ltd.
58-17, Songpa-Dong, Songpa-Gu, Seoul, Korea
kdmoon@galimit.com

[2]Chongju National College of Science & Technology
24, Yongang, Jeungpyeong, Goesan, Chungbuk, Korea
jspark@cjnc.ac.kr

[3]School of Information & Telecommunication, Far East University
5 San, Wangjang, Gamgok, Emseong, Korea
snowman@kdu.ac.kr

[4]Database Laboratory, Chungbuk National University
48, Gaesin-dong, Cheongju, Chungbuk, Korea
khryu@dblab.chungbuk.ac.kr

Abstract. Active temporal database system extends temporal database to include active rule system. This system can be efficiently applied to high facility applications such as trend analysis forecasting the fault, financial system, flow control. However this system has to process multidimensional data space that has temporal data dimension, therefore those systems require a high rule processing cost. Improving the performance of rule system depends on the efficiency of condition evaluation methods. Above all, active temporal rule have to consider a temporal dimension of data, because the amount of temporal data will be increased depending on temporal region. Therefore in this paper, we not only consider the condition evaluation of active temporal rule for performance enhancing, but also propose the temporal incremental evaluating operation by difference. [1]

1 Introduction

Active temporal database system extends temporal database system[6] to include active rules system[4]. The framework of the active temporal database system can be efficiently applied to many different classes of high facility applications such as trend analysis, forecasting the fault, financial system, flow control. It is important to note that the integration of the both temporal database system and active database system have recently emerged to apply in a wide variety of applications. Thus, in this paper, we propose a new generic method of condition evaluation for the most processing cost to improve the performance of active temporal rules. That is, in order to improve the performance of active temporal rules, we suggest the operations of incremental

---

[1] This work was supported by Korea Research Foundation (KRF-2002-002-D00152).

J. Liu et al. (Eds.): IDEAL 2003, LNCS 2690, pp. 816–820, 2003.

condition evaluation such as selection, projection, insertion and deletion and join operation for extended temporal data dimension to use difference. Thus, these operations can be processed efficiently for the work on the active temporal database system.

The paper is organized as follows. Section 2 we mention some related work on the method of condition evaluation for active rules. Section 3 describes difference model for temporal databases. Section 4 defines the definition of difference and the state transition formula of database. Section 5 presents temporal incremental operation with difference. Section 6 contains our conclusion.

2   Related Work

In general, the focal point of improving the performance of active database system depends on the efficiency of condition for evaluation [1,4,6]. That is, the optional clause which describe the condition for the rules contain the join that require high processing cost because if the rule will be triggered once for each triggering statement, then it will be executed once, and the whole database is affected by the triggering event each time. The work [4] proposed the incremental condition for evaluation that is the sum of accumulated evaluation and evaluation for difference instead of evaluation for the whole database. There have been two major approaches to the method of incremental condition evaluation, one is based on the view materialization in the database, and the other is base on the artificial intelligence including the expert system [4]. The approach on this database uses the condition expression in order to obtain result for the accumulated evaluation and difference relation and to describe evaluation of updated current state. The work [2,3] defined the many of semantics for difference in the transaction.

The method of condition evaluation on the active rule does not concern about temporal data dimension in the temporal database. Thus, following the next section will examine condition evaluation for the active rule and describe the incremental condition evaluation for the temporal data in the temporal database.

3   Difference Model for Temporal Databases

Using the method of condition evaluation for active temporal rules, we have to understand temporal semantics for data. The graphical representation of circumstance which update the data in the temporal database are showed in figure 1, as follows. It is represented by three lines that are thick line, thin line, dotted line and depicts current tuple, transaction time is not terminated yet, and history tuple, transaction time is already terminated, and changed tuple from current tuple to history tuple. So, we can see the manipulation of database when inserting a new data, updating the old data and terminating the transaction time for logical deletion. Therefore, insert difference, delete difference and history difference are distinguished from among the difference in the temporal database.

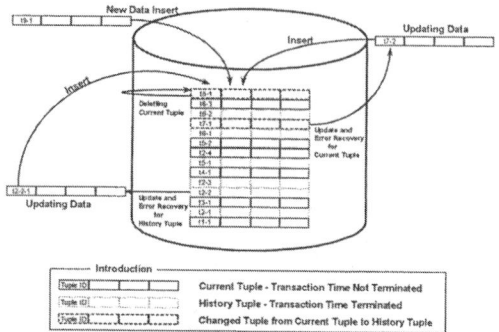

Fig. 1. Translation of data for temporal database

4   The Definition of Differential and State Transition Operation

Base on the difference model, described section 3, we represent the notation, as follows, in order to satisfy the preliminaries for the difference.

Definition 1   Difference and the notation of difference are as following :
- The notation and meaning of insert difference : $_t\Delta^+ = (a_1, a_2, ..., a_n \mid \{UC\} \times tv)$

    if $(a_1, ..., a_n)$ is newly inserted tuple and $\neg\exists t_b \{(\{UC\}, tv) \in t_b \wedge ((a_1, ..., a_n \mid t_b) \in r)\}$

    ※ The tuples represented thick line in figure 1.
- The notation and meaning of delete difference : $_t\Delta^- = \{(a_1, a_2, ..., a_n \mid (UC, c_v), ...)\}$

    if $(a_1, ..., a_n)$ is deleted tuple and $\exists t_b \{\{(UC, c_v), ...\} \in t_b \wedge ((a_1, ..., a_n \mid t_b) \in r)\}$

    ※ The tuples represented dotted line in figure 1.
- The notation and meaning of history difference :

    $_t\Delta^h = \{(a_1, ..., a_n \mid t_b - \{(<UC, c_v>, ...) \in t_b\})\}$

    if $\exists t_b \{\{(<UC, c_v>, ...) \in t_b\} \wedge \{(a_1, ..., a_n \mid t_b) \in r\}\}$ c_v is only random valid time particle in the relation.   ※ The tuples represented dotted thin in figure 1.

    Where the tv is the valid time particle to represent the valid time and tt is the transaction time particle to represent the transaction time through the data model. We define the set of the state for the database as follows.

Definition 2   The state transition operation that let $_tS$ be a state set of database, $_cS$ be a current state set of database and $_hS$ be a history state set of database. The $_tS$ is represented as $_tS = {_cS} \cup {_hS}$ and we can represent the state transition of database to use the definition 1 as follows

$$_tS_i = \{({_cS_{i-1}} - {_t\Delta_i^-}) \cup {_t\Delta_i^+}\} \cup \{{_hS_{i-1}} \cup {_t\Delta_i^h}\}$$

5   Temporal Incremental Operation with Difference

Now, in this section will extend the temporal database to include the incremental operation that base on the definition 1 and definition 2. This incremental operation incorporates temporal selection, temporal projection and temporal join operations.

Definition 3   Difference set with temporal meaning that the difference set for temporal meaning $_t\Delta$ is defined by the union of difference and definition 1 is represented as follows.

$$_t\Delta = {}_t\Delta^+ \cup {}_t\Delta^- \cup {}_t\Delta^h$$

Definition 4   Temporal difference operator $\oplus_t$ that the temporal difference operator $\oplus_t$ is defined by $_tS_i = {}_tS_{i-1} \oplus_t {}_t\Delta_i$ and the meaning is same as definition 2.

Base on the these definition, to represent the unit operation in the temporal database, let O and Q be a relation in the database, i be a start time points of index and $_t\Delta O$, $_t\Delta Q$ be a difference for the relation O and Q. Each of unit operations can define to use the temporal difference operator $\oplus_t$ as follows.

Proposition 1   The incremental temporal selection operation using temporal difference

$$\sigma_p(O_i) = \sigma_p(O_{i-1} \oplus_t {}_t\Delta O_i) = \sigma_p(O_{i-1}) \oplus_t \sigma_p({}_t\Delta O_i) \tag{1}$$

Proof 1   Proof of the incremental temporal select operation using the temporal difference operator

The formula $\sigma_p(O_{i-1} \oplus_t {}_t\Delta O_i)$ can be represented by difference operator $\oplus_t$ as follows.

$$\sigma_p[\{(_cO_{i-1} - {}_t\Delta O_i^-) \cup {}_t\Delta O_i^+\} \cup \{{}_hO_{i-1} \cup {}_t\Delta O_i^h\}] \tag{2}$$

Let us in above (1) expand using the distributive law for the operator $\cup$ and $-$. we have (formula 2) as follows.

$$\sigma_p(_cO_{i-1}) - \sigma_p({}_t\Delta O_i^-) \cup \sigma_p({}_t\Delta O_i^+) \cup \sigma_p({}_hO_{i-1}) \cup \sigma_p({}_t\Delta O_i^h) \tag{3}$$

On the other hand, a formula that is the right side of (1) $\sigma_p(O_{i-1}) \oplus_t \sigma_p({}_t\Delta O_i)$ is expanded by using the definition of temporal difference operator $\oplus_t$. Then we have :

$$[\sigma_p(_cO_{i-1}) - \sigma_p({}_t\Delta O_i^-) \cup \sigma_p({}_t\Delta O_i^+)] \cup [\sigma_p({}_hO_{i-1}) \cup \sigma_p({}_t\Delta O_i^h)] \tag{4}$$

If we rewrite the sub-parenthesis of (4), then it is equivalent to the (3). Thus, the (3) which is the result from treating the LHS of (1) and the (4) which is the result from treating the RHS of (1) are equals, so the proposition 1 that is the incremental temporal selection operation with using temporal difference is satisfied. The efficient method for incremental evaluation is presented and verified by as following.   □

Proposition 2   There are guarantee the performance that the method of incremental evaluation with using difference is more efficient method than the method without using difference.

Proof 2   There are two relations such as O and Q. Let $_\iota\Delta O$ be a difference for relation as O, $_\iota\Delta Q$ be a difference for relation as Q, n_c be a cardinality of current data for relation as O, n_h be a cardinality for history data, m_c be a cardinality of current data for relation as Q, m_h be a cardinality for history data., $\sigma\Delta n_c^+$, $\sigma\Delta n_c^-$, $\sigma\Delta m_c^+$, $\sigma\Delta m_c^-$ be a current version of cardinality and $\sigma\Delta n_h$, $\sigma\Delta m_h$ be a history version of cardinality. Then, The maximum cost for evaluation is as follows.

$$MaxCost(O_i \rhd \lhd_p Q_i) = (n_c + n_h) \times (m_c + m_h)$$
$$\leq \{ <\sigma n_{ci-1} \times \sigma m_{ci-1}> (+ <\sigma n_{ci-1} \times \sigma\Delta m_{ci}^-> + <\sigma\Delta n_{ci}^- \times \sigma m_{ci-1}> + <\sigma\Delta n_{ci}^- \times \sigma\Delta m_{ci}^->$$
$$+ <\sigma\Delta n_{ci}^h \times \sigma\Delta m_{ci}^h>) \mid (+ <\sigma n_{ci-1} \times \sigma\Delta m_{ci}^+> + <\sigma\Delta n_{ci}^+ \times \sigma m_{ci-1}> + <\sigma\Delta n_{ci}^+ \times \sigma\Delta m_{ci}^+>) \}$$

As we see above, the method of incremental evaluation with using difference is more efficient method than the method without using difference, and selection and projection operation can be compared by above the same comparison.   □

6   Conclusion

This paper considers the method of temporal incremental evaluation for the condition of active temporal rules that extends the method of incremental evaluation to include temporal dimension that affects the efficiency of rule system for the active temporal database system. This work applies to the method of incremental evaluation, suggests operation of temporal incremental evaluation extends the basic operations such as selection, projection and join to include temporal behavior and represents the algebraic formula. But it does not support the temporal and non-temporal aggregation function. So, further work is needed to extend for temporal and non-temporal aggregation function. In addition, base on the result from this paper, to develop the performing model and its implementation and evaluation for performance can be suggested feature research.

References

1.   U. Dayal, B. Blaustein, A. Buchmann, and S. Chakravarthy, The HiPAC project: Combining active database and timing constraints, ACM SIGMOD Record, Vol. 17, No. 1, March 1988.
2.   R.T. Snodgrass, Michael H. B hlen, Christian S. Jensen and Andreas Steiner, Transitioning Temporal Suport in TSQL2 to SQL3, A Time Center Technical Report, 1997.
3.   E. Hanson, Rule Condition Testing and action execution in Ariel, in Proceedings of the ACM SIGMOD International conference on Management of Data, 1992.
4.   Widom, S. Ceri, Introduction to Active Database System, Active Database Systems (Triggers and Rules), Morgan Kufman Publishin Inc., 1996.
5.   M Stonebraker and L. A. Rowe, THE DESIGN OF POSTGRES, ACM SIGMOD 86.
6.   R. T. Snodgrass and I. Ahn, Temporal Databases, IEEE Computer, September 1986.

Automatic Webpage Classification Enhanced by Unlabeled Data

Seong-Bae Park and Byoung-Tak Zhang

School of Computer Science and Engineering
Seoul National University
Seoul 151-744, Korea
sbpark@bi.snu.ac.kr

Abstract. This paper describes a novel method for webpage classification that uses unlabeled data. The proposed method is based on a sequential learning of the classifiers which are trained on a small number of labeled data and then augmented by a large number of unlabeled data. By taking advantage of unlabeled data, the effective number of labeled data needed is significantly reduced and the classification accuracy is increased. The use of unlabeled data is important because obtaining labeled data, especially in Web environment, is difficult and time-consuming. The experiments on two standard datasets show substantial improvements over the method which does not use unlabeled data.

1 Introduction

Due to the massive volume of online text documents available on the Web, it is important to classify or filter the documents. Especially, automatic webpage classification is of great importance to provide a Web portal service. For the most machine learning algorithms applied to this task, plenty of labeled webpages must be supplied [2]. However, it is very expensive and time-consuming to come by the labeled webpages because labeling must be done by human experts. On the other hand, the unlabeled webpages are ubiquitous and significantly easier to obtain than the labeled ones. Thus, in learning webpage classification, it is natural to utilize the unlabeled data in addition to the data labeled by the oracle.

This paper describes a novel method to classify webpages using both labeled and unlabeled data. We assume that the webpages are represented in the *bag-of-words*. In this scheme, the webpages are represented by the vectors in a space whose dimension equals the size of the *vocabulary*. For simplicity, we shall consider only binary classification problems. The label for a given document vector $\mathbf{x}$ is denoted by $y \in \{-1, +1\}$, where $+1$ represent that the document is relevant and -1 being irrelevant.

According to Cramér-Rao inequality, the mean squared error of unbiased estimator $T(\mathbf{x})$ of the parameter θ is bounded by the reciprocal of the Fisher information. That is, $\mathrm{var}(T) \geq \frac{1}{I(\theta)}$. Since the larger Fisher information produces the smaller variance and the expected error of the estimator is proportional to the variance [3], the larger Fisher information gets, the smaller the expected

J. Liu et al. (Eds.): IDEAL 2003, LNCS 2690, pp. 821–825, 2003.

Given unlabeled data set $U = \{\mathbf{x}_1, \ldots, \mathbf{x}_u\}$
and labeled data set $L = \{(\mathbf{x}_1, y_1), \ldots, (\mathbf{x}_l, y_l)\}$,

Train a classifier f_0 with $L_0 = L$.
Set $t = 0$ and $\tau_{-1} = 1$.
Do

1. **Calculate** $\tau_t = \tau_{t-1} \times \tau$, where τ is the probability given to the negative example in L_t with the highest probability.
2. **Sort** data in L_t according to $f_t(\mathbf{x} \in L_t)$.
3. **Sort** data in U_t according to $f_t(\mathbf{x} \in U_t)$.
4. **Delete** data in L_t and U_t such that $f_t(\mathbf{x}) > \tau_t$.
5. **Set** $s = |L_t|$.
6. **Set** U_{add} such that $U_{add} = \{(\mathbf{x}_1, y_1), \ldots, (\mathbf{x}_{l-s}, y_{l-s}) \mid \mathbf{x} \in U_t, y = f_t(\mathbf{x})\}$.
7. **Set** $L_{t+1} = L_t + U_{add}$.
8. **Train** f_{t+1} with L_{t+1}.
9. **Set** $t = t + 1$.

While ($|U_{add}| > 0$ and $\tau_t > 0.5$)
Output the final classifier: $f^*(\mathbf{x}) = \left(\prod_{i=1}^{k_{\mathbf{x}}-1} \tau_i \right) f_{k_{\mathbf{x}}}(\mathbf{x})$.

Fig. 1. The text classification algorithm using unlabeled data. $k_{\mathbf{x}}$ in the final classifier is an index to the best classifier of $\mathbf{x}$.

error of the estimator becomes. Shahshahani and Landgrebe [3] showed that the Fisher information using both labeled and unlabeled data, $I_{labeled+unlabeled}$, is $I_{labeled} + I_{unlabeled}$. Since the Fisher information and variance are reciprocal, using unlabeled data increases the accuracy of the estimator.

However, Zhang and Oles argued that $I_{unlabeled} = 0$ in the semi-parametric models [4]. They argued that active learning is helpful to maximize Fisher information of unlabeled data for the semi-parametric models, and proposed two principles to select informative unlabeled data points:

- Choose an unlabeled data of low confidence with the estimated parameter.
- Choose an unlabeled data that shall not be redundant with other choices.

2   Labeling Unlabeled Text by Sequential Learning

In order to measure the confidence of the unlabeled data, we adopt an idea from SEQUEL (SEQUEnce Learner) proposed by Asker and Maclin [1]. Assume that a classifier f_t produces a probability estimate. That is, $f_t(\mathbf{x})$ gives the probability that a document $\mathbf{x}$ is relevant. And, it has a threshold τ_t which is the probability given to the negative example with the highest probability. For a given data, if the output of the classifier is above the threshold, the classifier is considered *competent* to make a prediction. The confidence of a classifier is set by the number of positive examples such that $\mathbf{x} : f_t(\mathbf{x}) \geq \tau_t$, divided by the total number of examples above the threshold.

In SEQUEL, a set of classifiers for the ensemble is created by varying the set of features, since it considers only labeled data. In training SEQUEL, the first classifier labels some part of data as sure data. Such data have been given a probability of at least τ_t. To determine the next classifier in the sequence, all of the sure examples labeled by the first classifier are removed and the classifier with the highest confidence score for the remaining examples is chosen as the most confident classifier. This process is repeated until the best classifier's confidence score is less than a predetermined threshold.

Figure 1 shows a version of SEQUEL modified to utilize the unlabeled data. It takes two sets of examples as input. A set L is the one with labeled data and U is the one with unlabeled data, where $\mathbf{x}$ is a document and y in L represents the relevancy of $\mathbf{x}$. First of all, the first classifier f_0 is trained with L. After a classifier f_t is trained on labeled data, the threshold τ for the labeled data is calculated and the confidence of f_t is updated by $\tau_t = \tau_{t-1} \times \tau$. The data in both L_t and U_t are sorted according to their margin. The examples in L_t and U_t whose probability is larger than τ_t are removed from the sets, since they give no information in guiding the hyperplane. This coincides with the second principle. The remaining labeled data are augmented by some informative unlabeled data with the predicted labels, so that the number of labeled data for $(t+1)$th step is maintained to be that for tth step. With this new labeled data, a new classifier f_{t+1} is trained.

This process is repeated until the unlabeled examples are exhausted or τ_t gets lower than 0.5, the predefined threshold. For a given unknown document $\mathbf{x}$, the probability of $\mathbf{x}$ being produced by the best classifier, which is indexed by $k_{\mathbf{x}}$, is multiplied by the thresholds of all previous classifiers: $f^*(\mathbf{x}) = \left(\prod_{i=1}^{k_{\mathbf{x}}-1} \tau_i \right) f_{k_{\mathbf{x}}}(\mathbf{x})$.

3   Experiments

3.1   Data Sets

The first data set is the one used in "Using Unlabeled Data for Supervised Learning" workshop of NIPS 2000. This dataset has two kinds of webpage data for the competition of learning unlabeled data. The first problem (P2) is to distinguish the homepages of "http://www.micro soft.com" and those of "http://www.linux.org", and the second problem (P6) is to distinguish the homepages of "http://www.mit.edu" from those of "http:// www.uoguelph.ca". Table 1-(a) describes the NIPS 2000 workshop data set. Each document in the dataset is represented in $tf \cdot idf$.

The second data set for the experiments is a subset of "The 4 Universities Data Set" from "World Wide Knowledge Base Project" of CMU text learning group. It consists of 1,051 webpages collected from computer science departments of four universities: Cornell, University of Washington, University of Wisconsin, and University of Texas. The 1,051 pages are manually classified into *course* or *non-course* category. The categories are shown in Table 1-(b) with the number of webpages in each university. The baseline performance shows the accuracy achieved by answering non-course for all examples.

Table 1. The statistics for the dataset.

Data Set	P2	P6
# Labeled Data	500	50
# Unlabeled Data	5,481	3,952
# Test Data	1,000	100
# Terms	200	1000

(a) NIPS 2000 Dataset

Data Set	Course	Non-Course	Baseline
Cornell	40	203	83.5%
Texas	38	216	85.0%
Washington	74	220	71.1%
Wisconsin	78	220	73.8%
Total	230	821	78.1%

(b) WebKB Dataset

Table 2. The effect of removing the confident examples.

	Accuracy	Elapsed Time
Removing Confident Examples	99.5%	992 sec
Not Removing Confident Examples	99.4%	13,337 sec

3.2 Experimental Results

We use the multi-layer perceptron (MLP) as a classifier, since it can provide the framework of probabilistic learning model and shows reasonably high accuracy by itself. The proposed method is implemented on a PC with Pentium III 500MHz and 256MB RAM running Linux. Table 2 gives the advantage obtained by removing the confident examples. The accuracy of the final classifier on P2 of NIPS 2000 workshop data set is little changed though the informative examples are removed, whereas the training time is far reduced. In Web environment, since the input dimension is generally very large, it takes long time to train large number of training data. Thus, it is of great importance to reduce number of training data for practical use.

Table 3-(a) shows the experimental results on NIPS 2000 workshop data set. The result implies that the proposed method improves the classification accuracy for both problems in NIPS 2000 workshop data set by additionally using unlabeled data. The accuracy increase obtained by using unlabeled data is 0.7% for P2 and 15.0% for P6.

In the experiments on WebKB data set, the proposed method achieves the higher accuracy than using all labeled data, where the accuracy of the proposed method is measured when the accuracy is in its best for various ratios of the number labeled data (Table 3-(b)). The accuracy is increased by 0.8% for Cornell data set, 0.6% for Texas, 1.6% for Washington and 2.9% for Wisconsin, which is 1.5% improvement on the average. This also implies the better accuracy of 16.2% than the baseline on the average.

4   Conclusions

In this paper, we presented a novel method for classifying webpages that uses unlabeled data to supplement the limited number of labeled data. The proposed

Table 3. Accuracy of the proposed method.

Labeled Only		Labeled + Unlabeled	
P2	P6	P2	P6
98.8%	60.0%	99.5%	75.0%

(a) NIPS 2000 Dataset

Data Set	Labeled + Unlabeled	Only Labeled	Baseline
Cornell	**94.2%**	93.4%	83.5%
Texas	**97.1%**	96.5%	85.0%
Washington	**91.4%**	89.8%	71.1%
Wisconsin	**94.2%**	91.3%	73.8%
Average	**94.2%**	92.8%	78.1%

(b) WebKB Dataset

learning method first trains a classifier with a small training set of labeled data and the confidence of the classifier is determined. After that, a series of classifiers is constructed in sequence with unlabeled data. The labeled data and some informative unlabeled examples with their predicted labels are used to train the next classifier in the sequence, so that the method ovecomes the knowledge acquisition bottleneck.

We also showed empirically that unlabeled data enhace the learning method for webpage classification. The proposed method outperforms the method which does not use unlabeled data. The classification accuracy is improved by 7.9% for NIPS 2000 data set and up to 9.2% for WebKB data set.

Acknowledgements. This research was supported by the Korean Ministry of Education under the BK21-IT Program, by BrainTech programs sponsored by the Korean Ministry of Science and Technology.

References

1. L. Asker and R. Maclin. Ensembles as a Sequence of Classifiers. In *Proceedings of the Fifteenth International Joint Conference on Artificial Intelligence*, pp. 860–865, 1997.
2. M. Craven, D. DiPasquo, D. Freitag, A. McCallum, T. Mitchell and K. Nigam. Learning to Construct Knowledge Bases from the World Wide Web. In *Proceedings of the Fifteenth National Conference on Artifical Intelligence*, pp. 509–516, 1998.
3. B. Shahshahani and D. Landgrebe. The Effect of Unlabeled Samples in Reducing the Small Sample Size Problem and Mitigrating the Hughes Pheonomenon. *IEEE Transactions on Geoscience and Remote Sensing*, 32(5), pp. 1087–1095, 1994.
4. T. Zhang and F. Oles. A Probability Analysis on the Value of Unlabeled Data for Classification Problems. In *Proceedings of the Seventeenth International Conference on Machine Learning*, pp. 1191–1198, 2000.

Electricity Demand Forecasting Using Neural Networks

Sukhvinder Singh Panesar[1] and W. Wang[2]

[1]School of Informatics, University of Bradford (UK)
Energy Trading Information Systems, Npower Yorkshire Ltd (UK)

[2]School of Information Systems, University of East Anglia, UK

Abstract. This paper introduces a methodology to forecast electricity consumption. A Multi-Version System (MVS) methodology combines different data mining methods to compensate weaknesses of each individual method and to improve the overall performance of the system. The current benchmark forecasting system in use is a Regression system, which is in need of improvement after the structural as well as operational changes in the electricity supply markets. Experiments are Modelled on the Regression and the prototype Neural Network system. The results indicate that, in some cases, the Neural Network Model has performed better than the Regression System.

Keywords: Forecasting, Data Mining, Multi-Version System, Neural Networks, Decision Tree

1 Introduction

Accurate forecasting of electricity demand is essential for energy service providers to successfully participate in the deregulated retailed electricity markets. Forecasters need to know the sources of variation in their load requirements to evaluate cost and market risk. Energy service providers require the same information to plan long term power supplies, estimate end user service costs, price retail service, plan short term delivery schedules, assess market risk exposure, and ultimately determine the sources of imbalance charges due to forecast errors. Electricity forecasting can be very complex and difficult because it involves many uncertain factors. The forecasting accuracy depends on not only the performance of approaches applied but also the quality of the historical data used and the validity of the forecaster's basic assumptions, and the accuracy of the demand influencing factors. None of these are ever perfect.

2 The Data

- Data Collection

There are a number of effects that can be quantified as possible candidates used as inputs for neural net training and forecasting. Data is collected with special

J. Liu et al. (Eds.): IDEAL 2003, LNCS 2690, pp. 826–834, 2003.

monitoring equipment installed at each customer house or premises. This Equipment monitors the customer's electricity supply and records and logs measurements of Demand for each half-hour period during the day. There are also some other measurements, for example, the local temperature and time of sunset for the geographical region. Temperature and day length are considered to be very important factors in determining how half hourly average demand varies from day to day. The effect of temperature, day length and other factors on demand are calculated using regression analysis in the current forecasting system.

- Weather Effects

This includes temperature, wind velocity, cloud cover, rainfall and snowfall. It has been widely observed that, in most cases, there is a strong correlation between weather (especially temperature) and electricity demand. In most cases, as the temperature goes down, the demand for electricity goes up in the UK. Actual Temperature data was collected for the period 1 Jan 2000 – 1 Oct 2002. Data is for GSP Group Id _M (Leeds) and the Weather Station is Leeds. The data has been restricted to the Leeds because of the quantity of data.

- Calendar Effects

This includes hour of day, month of year, weekend and holiday effects. Most of the electricity load patterns shows a very consistent dependence on the calendar.

- Historical Demand Values

The consumption of electrical energy by homes and small businesses is usually measured in kilowatt-hours. Larger businesses and institutions sometimes use the megawatt-hour (MWh). The energy outputs of large power plants over long periods of time, or the energy consumption of states or nations, can be expressed in gigawatt hours (GWh). The kilowatt-hour (symbolised kWh) is a unit of energy equivalent to one kilowatt (1 kW) of power expended for one hour (1 h) of time. The kilowatt-hour is not a standard unit in any formal system, but it is commonly used in electrical applications. Future electricity demand can be obtained by using historical demand data and correlating it with all applicable and quantifiable inputs. Historical Data was collected for GSP Group Region _M (Leeds) for the period 1 Jul 2001 to 1 Jul 2002.

3   Forecasting Methodologies

3.1 Current Forecasting System

The current Forecasting system uses Linear Regression Method. Regression analysis is used to derive a linear relationship between the average demand per customer in the load research sample.
The system uses historical data of electricity demand as well as weather conditions to derive a set of regression coefficients for the function:

$Y(p,a,t,d) = B_1(p,a,t) + B_2(p,a,t)T(d) + B_3(p,a,t) \ s(d) + B_4(p,a,t)S(d)^2 + E(p,a,t)$,
where, $Y(p,a,t,d)$ is the sample average demand(KW) for Analysis *Class (a), Hour (t)*
calculated for the days included in analysis *class (a)* and *s(d)* the national average
Sunset value for day (d). The regression coefficients produced by the load research
sample are then used to calculate a number of specific profiles on a daily basis for
each region on each day, these are known as Profile Coefficients. Profile Coefficients
represent the proportion of annual consumption taken during a particular half hour in
a day. Profile Coefficients are then used to calculate demand. These have been
adjusted to reflect current climate conditions. Due to the non-linear nature of the
forecasting problem, it is not surprised to observe that this linear regression method
does not produce the required accuracy of forecast for most periods of a day because
the demand for electricity in these periods appears very non-linear. It is therefore
necessary to explore other methods that may do better, and neural network is one of
them.Neural Networks are capable of modelling nonlinear and non-parametric
problems because they have the ability to learn from data and to interpolate and
extrapolate along curves in the data without making any prior assumptions about the
relationship between dependent and independent variables.

3.2 Proposed Approaches

A key focus over the last two decades has been determining the conditions under
which various forecasting methods perform the best [Makridakis 1982]. In general no
single method dominated all other methods, but there seemed to be some clear
indication that simple methods performed the best [Makridakis 1982]. A Multiversion
System [Wang & Partridge 2000] is a system, which incorporates features of a
number of data mining techniques. Versions represent data mining models. All
versions are executed in parallel and the system output can be determined by a
decision strategy [Wang & Partridge 2000]. The properties of the versions must be
diverse to prevent problems occurring across the versions [Wang & Partridge 2000].
Electricity consumption is represented in continuous data ranges meaning we are
trying to predict a value or a range of values. It is envisaged that the versions for the
Multi-Version System are likely to encompass prediction tasks. Versions can be built
using any appropriate data mining approaches such as machine learning and statistics.
Machine Learning approach includes learning from examples, such as neural
networks and decision trees.

4 Forecasting System

4.1 Problem Mapping

Data for the Neural Network is sliced into periods. Each period represent a Network,
therefore in total the system creates 48 Neural Networks one for each half hour of the
day. The reason why the data in sliced into period dimensions is because the format of
the electricity load data is period based, therefore in order for the network to learn
historical data is would need to have inputs representing individual periods. The
Neural Network Model for the prediction of Half Hourly Demand for electricity

consists of 25 Inputs and one output. The input is historical data from previous data. The output is the demand for the next half hour. The diagram in <u>Figure 1</u> illustrates how the networks are generated. A Half Hour represents a Neural Network. Inputs are fed into the network a half hour at a time. The output for the network is saved to the database. For the purpose of this paper, a fully inter-connected neural network was created. This consisted of 25 Inputs, a hidden layer of 8 Neurons and an output layer of one neuron. The inputs were the half hour period of the day, calendar dates such as Special Days, Day, Week, Year enumeration's, the season and temperature. The network output would be a value between 0 and 1 (due to the use of the sigmoid function) and this would be multiplied by the average value of that half hour time period to give the forecast for the next half hour.

4.2 Forecasting System Design and Implementation

A demand forecasting system, named <u>Neural Network Forecasting System</u>, has been designed and implemented, which will be eventually used as one type of versions for building multiversion systems (Figure 1). The system can be used to forecast the load for periods that have actual data available.

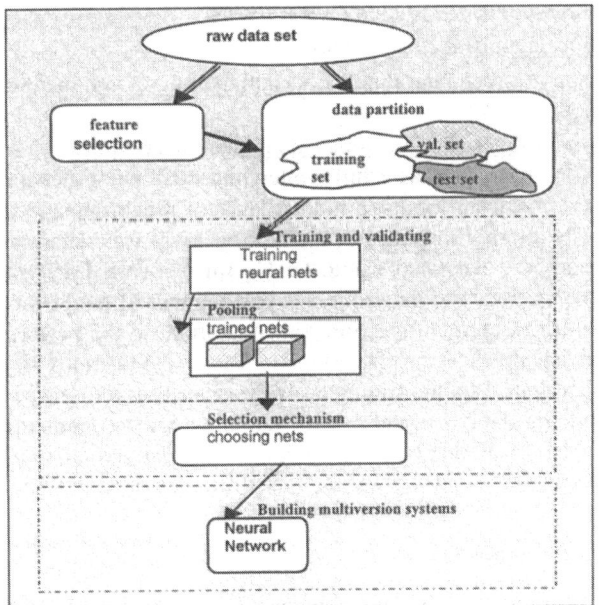

Fig. 1. Neural Network Model

Once the network has been trained then the user will able to forecast. Forecasting also is triggered from the main form. The main form has a button named Forecast. The date and period selection for the forecast are entered from this form. The user can select the period and date range to be forecasted. The method used to forecast is year on year mapping _time of day model_, $Y_0 * N$, where Y_0 is the Year on Year mapping value and N is the Network output. Using the output for the network for each input and hidden layer the actual value year on year ago is multiplied to give the forecast value.

5 Experimentals and Discussions

To test the forecasting system four types of experiments have been designed and conducted. As a result, four different types of populations of neural networks were trained using the developed Neural Network Forecasting System software and each ANN model was assigned to forecast the half-hourly demand. Firstly the data were randomly divided into 3 data sets: training, testing and production. The training and testing sets were used for the actual training of the model. The training set is what the model trains on, the testing set is what the model periodically tests itself on, to see if it is correctly learning from the data. The third set is the production set. This set is used as a final indication of how well the model will perform on data that it has never seen before.

A population of neural networks were developed for each of following experiments.

- Effect of the number of hidden nodes in Hidden Layer Nodes
- Effect of the number of hidden layers.
- Performance against Actual Values
- Comparison between neural networks and the Regression method.

Experiment 1 – Number Hidden Nodes in Hidden Layer Nodes
The design of the network was a fully -interconnected neural network. This consisted of an input layer with 25 inputs, a hidden layer of 8 neurons and an output layer of one neuron. The number of nodes in the hidden layers was determined by a series of experiments and was designed using the Neural Network Forecasting System. The aim of the experiments is to determine the best number of nodes for the network. The numbers of nodes in hidden layers are very important to the performance of a neural network [Xiri Zhand & Kurt Thearling].   Table 1 illustrates the experiments on different hidden units. 10000 training cycles was used for all networks. Data used was 12 Months training data, 6 months cross validation and 6 months test data. Training data was from the 1 Jul 2001 to 1 Jul 2002, cross validation data was for the 1 Jan 2002 to the 1 Jun 2002 and the test data used was for the 1 Jul 2002 to 31 Jul 2002. The test data was for a period where actual demand values could be attained. The inputs for the experiments were the half-hour period of the day, the day of the week, the season, average daily temperature. The network output would be a value between 0 and 1 (due to the use of the sigmoid function) and this would be multiplied by the average value of that half hourly time period.

Table 1. Neural Network Hidden Unit Experiment

Inputs	Hidden Layers	Training Error	Test Error
20	7:5	0.6339	0.6714
20	10:10	0.6202	0.6609
20	20:20	0.5997	0.6468
20	30:30	0.6129	0.6486

From the results of the experiments 2 hidden layers of 20 units each produced the best prediction, with a mean square error of 0.5997. On the whole there were only small differences between the different experiments.

Experiment 2 – Number of Hidden Layers

The second experiment conducted on the <u>Neural Network Forecasting System</u> was to determine the number of hidden layers. The previous work on neural network design suggests increasing the number of hidden layers tends to slow neural network performance [Xiri Zhand & Kurt Thearling]. Specifying too many hidden nodes can result in poor models, which tend to memorise the training set rather than learn relationships [Xiri Zhand & Kurt Thearling]. First we compare networks of different hidden layers on the identical training test sets,

Table 2. Neural Network Topology Experiments

Topology	Training Error	Test Error
10:10:1	0.6846	0.7319
10:7:5:1	0.6453	0.6915
10:6:5:4:1	0.6486	0.6943

For this problem increasing the number of hidden layers to three did not improve the accuracy of forecasting but slowed down the training significantly.

Experiment 3 – Neural Network performance against Actual Values

The choice of dates and inputs for this experiment was purely arbitrary based on past experiences and industry knowledge. The first neural network test-bed used the following parameters.

Table 3. Neural Network Dates

Dates	Value
Forecast Period	(17-05-2002) - (15-06-2002)
Training Period	(01-01-2002) - (16-05-2002)
Profile Curve	(17-05-2001) - (15-06-2001)

A profile load curve was generated between 17/5/2001 – 15/6/2001, which gives a load curve for May and June 1997. This curve gives the shape for demand year ago. The training period was selected as 01/01/2002 – 16/05/2002. On running these parameters the network simulated a forecast for May and June 2002, once completed, the output of the network was compared to the actual for May and June 2002, using the year on years model. The ANN model performed well on the production data set. It had a r^2 (Pearson product moment correlation coefficient) value of 0.895. It also was able to predict within 10% on average of the actual electricity demand in all cases within the production set, and 89% of the time it was within 5% of the actual electricity demand. Initial results over-forecasted in periods 12 - 15. Reasons could be with noisy or anomalies in the data. Certain periods required more training cycles than others. Reasons could be data, network topology or Parameters or the network could have over trained in certain half-hours

Experiment 4 – Neural Network performance against Regression Methods

The final experiment conducted was to compare the Neural Forecast with the Current Regression forecasting system. There are huge differences in the way Regression and Neural Network techniques forecast. Standard Linear Regression depends on several assumptions, one of which is that the relations ship between independent and dependent variables is always Linear. The dates used for the experiment are shown in the Table 4.

Table 4. Experiment 4 Run Dates

Dates	Value
Forecast Period	(17-05-2002) - (15-06-2002)
Training Period	(01-01-2002) - (16-05-2002)
Profile Curve	(17-05-2001) - (15-06-2001)

The best forecasting result achieved from the 2 systems is given in the Table 5, for the period 1 Sept 2002 – 31 Sept 2002.

Table 5. Forecast Comparison Results

Forecast Method	Forecast MAPE
Neural Network	6.45%
Regression	4.12%

The results from the Regression system were better than Neural Network based on the sample data used. It does not necessarily mean that the Neural Network model is worse than the regression model. When the relationship between various factors is not clear or too complex to use the Neural Network model is a good choice. However if dependencies between factors are relatively obvious then Linear Regression may be a better choice. Complexities in relationships between inputs can mean that forecast are better for certain time periods than others. Each half-hour has it's own complexity. For example switching between tariffs can cause sudden fluctuations in demand increasing the complexity in demand for the period. It is possible that there are certain periods in the day when the neural network is having difficulty understanding patterns possibly due to random observations.

Generally the Regression and Neural Forecast seem to follow a similar trend. There are differences during certain days with the Neural

Forecast consistently *over forecasted* on about 50% of the days in the sample. Certain random factors during the day could cause the forecast to under or over forecast. For example Figure 2 illustrates the forecast for periods 16 – 19 (8:00 – 9:30), the peak hours in the morning.

The results suggest that the Neural Forecast is under forecasting over these periods. It seems that the Neural Forecast is also under forecasting considerably during the periods 30 –36.

In contrast the forecast for period 38-44 represents a different shape. The Neural forecast appears to be a lot closer to the regression and actual values.The results from this experiment suggest that random effects during certain periods during the day could have a significant effect on Neural Forecasting. Because these effects are random the neural network finds it difficult to learn the patterns. Certain half hour during the day seem to forecast better than a neural network model. The results indicate that the neural network model performs better during the daytime periods where there are greater random effects, in contrast Linear Regression performed better during night time hours where weather and other factors are more constant.

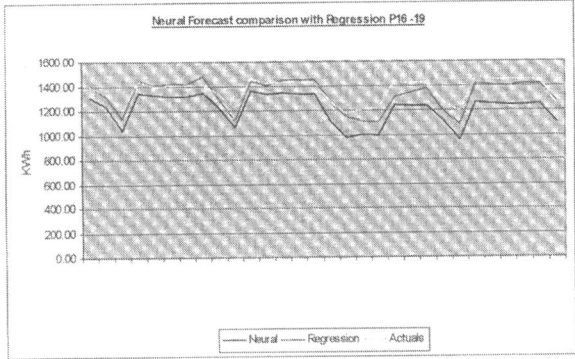

Fig. 2. Periods 16-18 Compared

6 Conclusions

The methodology under development represents enhancements to the traditional load forecasting approaches. Eventually, different forecasting methods will be coupled in a single system for predicting peak loads. While 24hr forecasts are in the focus of the present work the approach is easily extended to longer forecast periods. Further work is required. First, to experiment further, using different network topology, design and parameters. Second, to test the electricity demand models on-line at NPower Yorkshire Ltd, to see how well they can perform with real-time data and thirdly to introduce new methods into the Multi-Version System prototype.

Acknowledgements. The authors would like to thank Rod Fisher from Npower for providing the necessary data for this paper.

References

1. Amstrong, J (1970): Exploratory Analysis of Marketing Data : Trees vs. Regression Journal of Marketing Research (1970), 487-492
2. Bishop, C. M. (1995): Neural networks for pattern recognition. Oxford Press.1995
3. Bigus, J (1996): Data Mining with Neural Networks McGraw-Hill Publishers. 1996

4. Kamber, H, Data Mining, Concepts and Techniques Morgan Kaufmann Publishers. 2000
5. Quinlan, J. R. (1986): Induction of decision trees. Machine learning, vol.1, pp81-106.
6. Linoff, B: Data Mining Techniques (1997) Wiley Computer Publishing
7. Makridakis, S, A (1982): The M2 competition: A real time judgementally based Forecasting competition. Journal of Forecasting, 9, 5–22
8. Morgan, M (1995) : Forecasting Electricity demand using non-linear mixture of experts Universite Paries, Research Centre SAMOS
9. Remus, W (1998): Neural Networks for Time Series Forecasting, Principles of Forecasting May 1998
10. Wang, W. & Partridge, D. (2000):Multiversion systems of neural networks and decisions tree. Proceedings of the IASTED International Conference on Neural Networks Pittsburgh, USA.
11. Williams, M (1998):The use of Profiles in the Electricity Market Electricity Pool

An Extended Multivariate Data Visualization Approach for Interactive Feature Extraction from Manufacturing Data

S. Rezvani[1], G. Prasad[1], J. Muir[2], and K. McCraken[2]

[1] Intelligent Systems Engineering Laboratory, School of Computing and Intelligent Systems, University of Ulster, Londonderry BT48 7JL, N. Ireland, UK.
s.rezvani@ulst.ac.uk
[2] Perfecseal Ltd., Springtown Industrial Area, Londonderry, N. Ireland, UK

Abstract. Awareness about interconnectivities and interactions among parameters is vital for the identification of the optimal manufacturing routes and economic factors within a manufacturing system. Within this context, multidimensional data projection methods, Principal Component Mapping (PCM) and Sammon's Mapping, have been scrutinized for visualizing multivariate interaction patterns. As a new approach, these techniques were employed in such a way that interactive multi-layer maps could be created. Each layer within the generated map matches to a specific attribute and characteristic of the dataset. Individual layers within the map can be interactively selected and superimposed to show multiple and partial interactions.

1 Introduction

The main objective of the project is to build a generic system, which helps to identify the interrelationship between performance factors in relation to constituents and manufacturing processes. This approach allows improving product formulations (PF), process routes and economic factors. The initial system included a relational database along with a Case Based Reasoning application for an efficient product recommendation. This however is insufficient for analyzing multivariate interactions among parameters in a detailed way. Furthermore such a system does not take into account the variability associated with the statistical distribution of values for each parameter.

As an extended approach to multivariate data projection, we developed an Interactive Visual Feature Extraction System (IVFES) based on Principal Component Mapping (PCM) and Sammon's Mapping (SM). These methods in connection with the original dataset are utilized to generate interactively selectable layers, which characterize specific features of the projected clusters. Each cluster represents a particular PF. Apart from the visualization of shapes and distributions of clusters within the multi-dimensional dataset, the new system facilitates the analyses of interactions between parameters through interactive activations and superimpositions of layers. It also provides the tool to select desirable PFs and to examine the consistency of product quality.

J. Liu et al. (Eds.): IDEAL 2003, LNCS 2690, pp. 835–839, 2003.

2   IVFES Based on Principal Component Mapping

To reduce a high dimensional and complex dataset to a simpler and less complex data image, which reflects most of the coherent information about PFs in the database, we utilized Principal Component Analysis (PCA) as a multidimensional data projection method [1] for obtaining the linear combinations of the original variables [2], [3], [4]. The basic idea of IVFES based on PCM is to generate an interactive graph of the scaled Principal Component (PC) scores π_{ik} (equation 1) obtained from those PFs in the database, which belong to the same category.

$$\pi_{ik} = s_{m,m+1} \sum_{i=1}^{n} (a_{ik}\theta_{ik})' z_n \tag{1}$$

Here, a'_{ik} is the eigenvector corresponding to k^{th} eigenvalue (λ_i) and the ith variable, z_n is the normalized variables, θ_{ik} is the scaling factor for the eigenvector and $s_{m,m+1}$ is an index proportional to PC similarity between clusters m and $m+1$.

The optimal graph ideally should show each PF as a separate entity and minimize cluster overlapping. The overlapping indicates an inexplicable sub-dimensional data space. To overcome this problem in connection with low overlapping clusters, we introduced the Principal Component Zooming (PCZ), obtaining PC scores from ambiguous areas and $s_{m,m+1}$ index, which discriminates similar formulations. In the case of high cluster overlapping, however, non-linear projection or Vector Quantization algorithms are preferred [5]. The PCA, in general term, is suboptimal for non-gaussian. Compared to non-linear projection methods however, the linear PC scores can be obtained easily, fast and reliably. The fact that PCA should be performed on datasets with a Gaussian distribution [6], however, applies for inferential analyses and is less relevant for descriptive tasks [4].

IVFES based on PCM can be divided into 3 groups, namely constituents specific map C showing the proportion of raw materials used in formulations, process specific map P and response specific map R. Furthermore, each PF is delineated within a specific cluster. To discover the interconnectivity between C, P and R, we superimpose R and C. R put on top of P shows graphically the interaction between process attributes and the performance. In accordance with the empirical and theoretical knowledge about the area of specification, each parameter k can be categorized into membership values "M" showing different parameter intensities. The locations of these intensities c_n can be highlighted with selected colors and shades (see equation 2).

$$\{c_1,....,c_n\} \hat{=} \{c \mid c \in \pi_{ik} \wedge m_{low} \leq X(:,k) \leq m_{high} \wedge m \subseteq M\} \tag{2}$$

In contrast to ordinary PC plots, IVFES based on PCM suggests that those isolated PFs, which do not show any intersection with any other PFs, can be reliably represented by 2 or 3 PC levels. If there is any intersection between membership areas of a single variable that section should be analyzed in depth by applying PCZ. The main advantage of IVFES based on PCM is the interactive selection of layers of different colors and shades, which display product features within PF clusters. The intersection of layers corresponding to membership areas of different variables $(V_1 \cap V_2)$ in proportion to the occupied area $(V_1 \cup V_2)$ is a measure for the interaction between the represented variables. In the same manner, ideal PFs – intersection of layers $(V_i \cap V_n)$ with desirable attributes - can be selected for further examination. The lack of space precludes presentation of detailed figures. These, however, are similar to the plots shown in the next section.

3   IVFES Based on Sammon's Mapping

Sammon's Mapping (SM) [7] is a nonlinear data projection method, which emulates the internal structure of an n-dimensional dataset onto a non-linear subspace of n-k dimensions $(0<k<n)$ and preserves internal-pattern distances within the projection [8]. SM algorithm is used to minimize the cost function E through a function approximation with Artificial Neural Network (ANN) (see equation 3).

$$E = \frac{1}{\sum\limits_{i=1}^{n-1}\sum\limits_{j=i+1}^{n} d_{ij}} \sum_{i=1}^{n-1} \sum_{i=j+1}^{n} \frac{(d_{ij} - \partial_{ij})^2}{d_{ij}} \tag{3}$$

where, d_{ij}: Euclidean distance between input vectors, ∂_{ij}: projected distance in the output space

SM is still one of the best projection techniques [9], [10]. The data projection is neat and shows minimal overlapping areas with regard to different PFs. SM however involves a high computational load. Compared to Curvilinear Component Analysis (CCA), PCA and Self-Organizing Maps (SOM) [11], SM presupposes a stricter sample and parameter reduction prior to any analysis. An initialization of Sammon's algorithm with PC-scores, eigenvectors or SOMs [12] can improve the computational efficiency. Mao and Jain have suggested a two-layer perceptron feed-forward Neural Network (SAMANN) based on back propagation and gradient descent learning rules, which is initialized with PC-scores [13]. Lerner et al. [14], [15], however, imply that the efficiency of the SM can be improved by employing eigenvectors of the sample covariance instead of PC-scores. A further disadvantage of the basic SM is the fact that the addition of new observations presupposes a repetition of the entire mapping procedure. To overcome this problem, SAMANN, Triangulation Algorithm and standard feed- forward ANN have been suggested in the literature [16]. To improve interpretability, predictability and the filtering of outliers, a fuzzy logic approach to SM non-linear projection can be employed [17]. As a new approach, Dzemyda [12] applied a correlation matrix to visualize the interlocation of parameters with the help of SOM initialized SM. The interpretation of parameter clusters within this approach seems to be casual and should be done with care. Within our case study, the application of feature layers using IVFES reflected the true nature of the data and added meaning in term of performance, raw material and process attributes to each cluster.

IVFES based on SM resulted in the best projection of PF in comparison with PCA, SOM and CCA. Here, we applied a projection using ANN with 100 iterations and with an iteration step size of 0.2. Each product can be distinguishably displayed on a two-dimensional map taking a specific location. The mapping process however involved a very high computational load, forcing us to cut the amount of observations to 700 and the amount of parameters to 31. Figure 1 shows an example for PF maps in connection with polymeric adhesive coated substrates. Figure 2 is a case for response specific map, representing areas of different permeability. Examples for raw material and process specific maps are given in figures three and four. These maps as a multivariate projection of original dataset can be interactively selected and superimposed to generate areas of desirable PFs and to represent interactions between variables. To improve the computational load, we have initialized SM with PC-scores accounting for 85% variability. Here, we could double the number of observations.

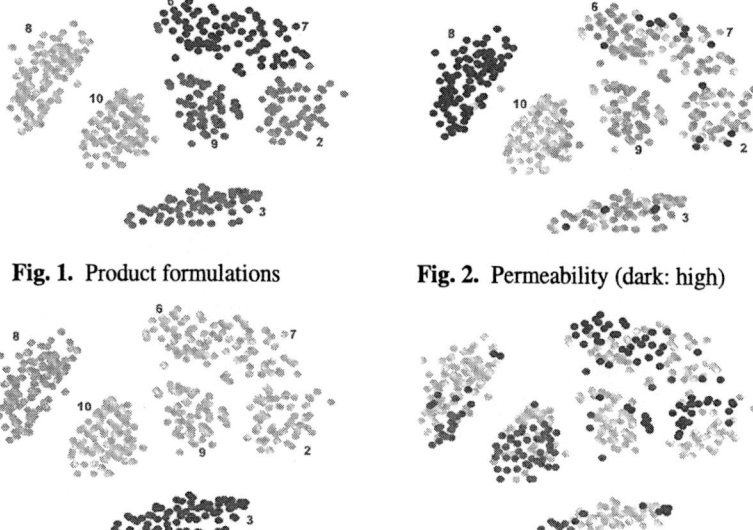

Fig. 1. Product formulations   **Fig. 2.** Permeability (dark: high)

Fig. 3. Water content (dark: high)   **Fig. 4.** Substrate tension (dark: high)

4   Conclusion

In comparison to conventional data processing methods and multivariate data visualisation techniques, the proposed approach provides a realistic and simplified picture of the data, describing the variation of all the PFs, their tendencies toward special attributes and the similarity of observations or attributes. Within the scope of this research work, the locations of favourable performances, associated with particular process parameter and raw material proportions were determined. The interaction between variables were visualised by interactive selections and superimpositions of colours and shades. The intersections of desirable attributes within the plot indicated cases with the best overall characteristics. To generate projected layers, IVFES based on SM delivered the best picture of the multidimensional dataset. However, computationally it was the slowest and most intensive process. PCM involved the lowest computational load although the generated layers are less sharp than the nonlinear methods. A non-linearity, however, could be emulated through PCZ, which allowed generating a clearer picture of those areas with high ambiguity.

References

1. Ralston, P., DePuy, G., Graham, J.H., Computer-based Monitoring and Fault Diagnosis: Chemical Process Case Study, ISA Transactions, Vol. 40 (2001) 85–98,
2. Jackson, J.E., A User Guide to Principal Components, John Wiley & Sons Inc (1991)
3. Aggarwal, C.C., On the Effects of Dimensionality Reduction on High Dimensional Similarity Search, IBM T.J. Watson Research Centre, Yorktown Heights NY 10598
4. Bai, Z., Demmel J., et al., Templates for the solution of algebraic Eigenvalue Problems: a practical guide, Siam (2000)
5. Vesanto, J., SOM-Based Data Visualization Methods, Intell. Data Anal., Vol. 3(2) (1999)
6. Jolliffe, I.T., Principal Component Analysis, Springer Verlag (1986) 41–46
7. Sammon, JW, A non-linear mapping for data structure analysis. IEEE Transactions on Computers; Vol. 18 (1969) 401–409
8. Rider D.D., Duin, R. P., Pattern Recognition Letters, Vol. 18 (1997) 1307–1316
9. Biswas, G., Jain, A.K., Dubes, R.C., Evaluation of Projection algorithms, IEEE Trans. Pattern Anal. Mach. Intell., Vol. 3(6) (1981) 701–708
10. Bezedek, J.C., Pal, N.R., An index of topological preservation for feature extraction, Pattern Recognition, Vol. 28 (1995) 381–391
11. Kohonen, T, Self-Organizing Maps, Second Edition, Springer Verlag (1997)
12. Dzemyda, G., Visualisation of a set of parameters characterized by their correlation matrix, Computational Statistics & Data Analysis (Elsevier), Vol. 36 (2001) 15–30
13. Mao, J., Jain, AK., Artificial Neural Networks for feature extraction and multivariate data projection, IEEE Transactions on Neural Networks, Vol. 6 (1995) 296–317
14. Lerner, B., et al., Pattern Analysis & Applications (Springer) Vol. 3 (2000) 61–68
15. Lerner, B., et al., On Pattern Classification with Sammon's Nonlinear Mapping – An Experiemental Study, Pattern Recognition (Pergamon), Vol. 31, No. 4 (1998) 371–381
16. Lee, R.C.T., J. R. Slagle et al., A triangulation method for sequential mapping of points from n-space to two-space, IEEE Transactions on Computers, Vol. 27 (1977), 288–299
17. Pal, N.R., et al., Fuzzy Logic Approaches to Structure Preserving Dimensionality Reduction, IEEE Transactions on Fuzzy Systems, Vol. 10, No. 3 (June 2002)

Determining the Semantic Orientation of Web-Based Corpora

Arno Scharl[1], Irene Pollach[2], and Christian Bauer[3]

[1] University of Western Australia, Graduate School of Management & Information
Management and Marketing Department; 35 Stirling Highway, Crawley, WA 6009, Australia
arno.scharl@uwa.edu.au

[2] University of Economics and Business Administration,
Department of English Business Communication; Augasse 9, A-1090 Vienna, Austria
irene.pollach@wu-wien.ac.at

[3] University of Notre Dame Australia, School of Information Technology;
19 Mouat St, Fremantle, WA 6959, Australia
bauer@webLyzard.com

Abstract. The Web media monitoring methodology underlying this paper provides linguistic descriptives by automatically mirroring, processing and comparing large samples of Web-based corpora. Since May 1999, the database of the *webLyzard* project has continually been extended and now comprises more than 3,700 sites, which are being monitored in monthly intervals. The wealth of information contained in these sites is converted into aggregated representations through structural and textual analysis. Based on word frequencies and distance measures, perceptual maps and the semantic orientation of Web-based corpora towards particular concepts are computed.

1 Introduction

In previous research the foundations have been laid for gathering and analyzing structure and content of large samples of Web-based information systems [1-3]. Due to their flexible nature, the methods underlying this paper cover a wide range of problem formulations, independent of the investigated system's level of technical sophistication. Only a few operations need to be adapted to specific situational parameters; e.g., word stemming, which requires a language-specific list of lemmas (groups of related word forms that are all derived from one common stem word).

When investigating large collections of empirical data, the term *'mining'* has become increasingly popular in recent years. Text and data mining are part of the more general field of information mining, reflecting the wide variety of forms information may take [4]. The demarcation between exploratory data analysis and the more application-oriented concept of data mining is difficult to discern. Activities such as association, classification, clustering, estimation, optimization, segmentation, sequencing, prediction, or visualization, which today come under the umbrella term data mining, have been used for many years [5, 6]. Exploratory data analysis and data mining share much of their methodology and are both concerned with the inductive discovery and visualization of patterns and non-obvious relationships between data elements that might be useful in a particular context [7, 8]. With special regard to the World Wide

J. Liu et al. (Eds.): IDEAL 2003, LNCS 2690, pp. 840–849, 2003.
© Springer-Verlag Berlin Heidelberg 2003

Web, mining tasks often extend traditional media and marketing research [9]. They can be classified into three categories [4]: *Web content mining,* which analyzes a site's textual and/or audiovisual content, *Web structure mining,* which performs an analysis of the hypertext and its navigational mechanisms, and *Web usage mining,* which focuses on behavioral data such as hits, visits, or individual clickstreams from server log-files or client state cookies. Some authors treat Web structures as part of Web content and only distinguish two aspects: content and usage [10, 11]. Excluding previously investigated aspects of usage and structure [2, 12], this paper concentrates on online media monitoring and the textual analysis of Web-based corpora.

2 Methodology

The highly dynamic nature of the World Wide Web requires rapid collection of data, limiting manual approaches to consider little beyond the introductory homepage [13]. The more specific the measure, the greater the need to revise manual methods prior to each evaluation cycle. Thus a high level of detail is inconsistent with the objectives of longitudinal studies and necessitates automated alternatives to acquire empirical data. Automated data gathering is also an essential prerequisite for obtaining samples of appropriate size. The volume and constantly changing character of Web-based information systems entails ongoing analysis. Between May 1999 and December 2002, the overall sample size of the *webLyzard* project (http://www.webLyzard.com) has continually been increased to more than 3,700 Web sites that are now being monitored on a monthly basis. Scalability, speed, consistency, rigorous structure, and abundance of data are assured if the processes of gathering and extracting information are automated by means of software tools. The existing prototype captures and measures the characteristics of Web-based information systems, determines their specific importance, and stores them in a relational database.

Sample specification and *sample maintenance* are vital to the success of Web evaluation projects. The analyst needs to upload new sites, update third party rankings, and regularly check the validity of primary and secondary (redirected) addresses. In the *data gathering* phase, Web sites are mirrored in regular intervals while respecting the wishes of site owners with regards to limits where robots may search as stipulated in the *robots.txt* file [14]. The algorithm, which ignores graphical data and multimedia files, follows a site's hierarchical structure until a limit of either 10 megabytes for site analysis or 50 megabytes for media monitoring is reached. Only textual information is considered, which includes both visible (raw text including headings, menus, or link descriptions) and invisible text (embedded markup tags, scripting elements, and so forth). These limitations help to compare systems of heterogeneous size, and to manage available local storage space. Specialized information found in hierarchical levels below that limit does not belong to the primary user interface and thus can be disregarded for most analytical objectives. In the *data extraction* phase, actionable knowledge is derived from processing the mirrored data. The computation of ratios, means and variances reduces data redundancy and provides aggregated parameters that are easier to interpret. Statistical and other analytical methods can then be applied on the preprocessed output. Automated coding removes subjective interpretations and many of the questionable aspects of manual coding from the analytical process. It renders the problems of time-consuming and expensive coder training or intra- and intercoder reliability obsolete, as the process does not involve human coders who could disagree on particular attribute values. Automated approaches also tend to increase a project's overall reliability, understood as the degree to which three basic criteria are met [15, 130ff., 16]: *Stability* (process and its results are invariant or unchanging over time), *reproducibility* (process can be recreated under varying circumstances), and *accuracy* (process functionally conforms to a known standard and yields what it is designed to yield). The very nature of the object to be analyzed – i.e., Web-based information systems that are publicly available – does not require interviewing members of the organization or privileged access to the computing or communication resources of third parties beyond those available to regular Web users. While the integration of external data sources and a comprehensive structural investigation of Web-based information systems is an important component of automated Web-assessment as shown in Fig. 1, the following sections emphasize textual Web analysis: representing electronic documents, generating frequency-ordered word lists, lemmatization (word stemming), automated language identification, and the computation of a site metric that denotes the semantic orientation of a site towards particular concepts.

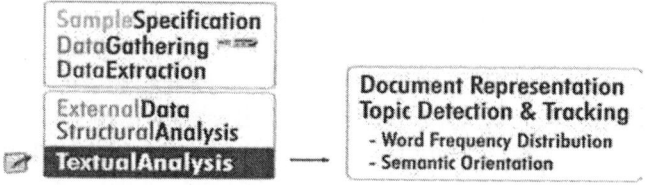

Fig. 1. Automated analysis of Web-based corpora

3 Representation of Electronic Content

From a theoretical perspective, there are many different approaches to analyzing electronic content. Most approaches have grown out of the meeting of a variety of disciplines including corpus linguistics, discourse analysis, statistics, computer science, Web engineering, and socio-economic survey analysis [17]. While the study of traditional media has moved beyond the point where further descriptions of content are needed, the situation differs when investigating electronic sources: "We have no real idea what Web content consists of, and it is arguably important ... to obtain that knowledge before we chase after the content trying to superimpose theories upon it" [18]. Textual Web data contains valuable information about industry trends and competitive strategies. By concentrating on the structure and technical implementation of Web-based information systems, equally important opportunities to grasp contextual meaning are often neglected. To overcome this shortcoming, the media monitoring architecture introduced in this section aims at discovering and visualizing regularities in textual Web data. It applies and extends a set of methods that originate from the fields of corpus linguistics and textual statistics [19, 20].

Context and Coding Units

The textual aspect of the analysis requires the conversion of a stream of characters (= the original text) into a stream of coding units (= words). Coding units represent the smallest segments to be analyzed. The context unit is the body of material surrounding the coding unit [21-25]. There is a broad range of potential *context units*, comprising both spoken and written language [19]. Biber et al. present a methodological overview of corpus-based studies, which are characterized by large context units, and a comparison to other linguistic approaches [20]. The empirical, corpus-based set of methods presented in this paper analyzes natural texts occurring in an organization's hierarchical structure of published documents. In contrast to process-oriented investigations (e.g., discourse analysis), which focus on conversational units like utterances or speaking turns [21], coding units for content-oriented approaches are usually identified on the basis of their graphical form. These textual pieces of information are often referred to as strings or tokens and belong to one of the following categories [26, 27]: Syntagms (sequences of words – paragraphs, sentences, repeated segments), lexemes (single words or lemmas), or graphemes (sequences of consecutive characters in a document – prefixes, suffixes, infixes; the term *n-gram* is used for partial sequences of *n* characters). *Tokens* represent the number of all running words encountered when processing the text file. Each word is counted as a string of valid letters with a separator at each end. *Types* are distinct words identified when first processing the text; they represent the system's complete vocabulary (a Web site containing one million running words might comprise less than 50,000 distinct occurrences).

Document Conversion

The first requirement for quantitative textual analysis is converting the text to be analyzed into an adequate, machine-readable representation. In comparison to the time-consuming process of scanning printed material, this seems to be straightforward in the case of Web-based information systems. Nevertheless, a number of transformations are needed prior to any statistical analysis. First, the hypertext documents are converted into plain text. In a second step, the derived textual chain is segmented into minimal units, removing coding ambiguities such as punctuation marks, the case of letters, hyphens, or points occurring within abbreviations. A sequence of non-delimiters whose bounds at both ends are delimiters is referred to as an occurrence. To obtain an automatic segmentation of a text into occurrences of graphical forms, a subset of characters is specified as delimiting characters. Most regular texts contain paralinguistic items such as word delimiters (blanks), sequence delimiters (weak punctuation marks), and sentence separators (strong punctuation marks). All other characters contained in the text are then considered to be non-delimiting characters. Two or more identical series of non-delimiters constitute two or more occurrences of the same word [17]. Frequently, numeric coding is employed to identify words in a more memory-efficient way. The third step, identification, groups identical units together by counting the number of their occurrences – i.e., a word list is created. Such an exhaustive index regularly uses decreasing frequency of occurrence as the primary sorting criterion and lexicographic order as secondary criterion.

Language Identification

Automatic treatment of textual content often necessitates a preliminary identification of the language(s) used. The algorithm should be able to classify both multilingual sites – i.e., localized versions of the same content – and multilingual content within one particular document [28]. For this classification problem, several techniques have been proposed with those based on trigrams and common short words being the most popular. The trigram technique calculates the frequency of sequences of three letters within a document and compares them with typical distributions for particular languages. Similarly, common short words such as determiners, conjunctions or prepositions are good clues for guessing a language. As the results of both methods are nearly identical for textual segments comprising more than ten words [29], we use the computationally less intensive technique based on short words.

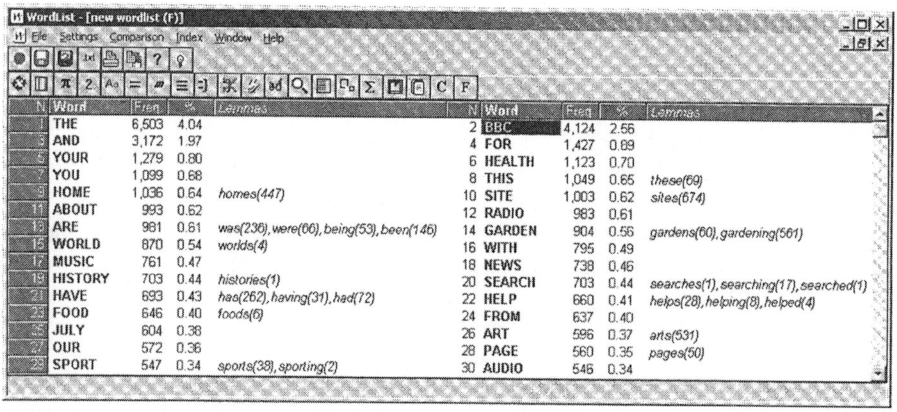

N	Word	Freq	%	Lemmas	N	Word	Freq	%	Lemmas
1	THE	6,503	4.04		2	BBC	4,124	2.56	
3	AND	3,172	1.97		4	FOR	1,427	0.89	
5	YOUR	1,279	0.80		6	HEALTH	1,123	0.70	
7	YOU	1,099	0.68		8	THIS	1,049	0.65	*these(69)*
9	HOME	1,036	0.64	*homes(447)*	10	SITE	1,003	0.62	*sites(674)*
11	ABOUT	993	0.62		12	RADIO	983	0.61	
13	ARE	981	0.61	*was(236),were(66),being(53),been(146)*	14	GARDEN	904	0.56	*gardens(60),gardening(561)*
15	WORLD	870	0.54	*worlds(4)*	16	WITH	795	0.49	
17	MUSIC	761	0.47		18	NEWS	738	0.46	
19	HISTORY	703	0.44	*histories(1)*	20	SEARCH	703	0.44	*searches(1),searching(17),searched(1)*
21	HAVE	693	0.43	*has(262),having(31),had(72)*	22	HELP	660	0.41	*helps(28),helping(8),helped(4)*
23	FOOD	646	0.40	*foods(6)*	24	FROM	637	0.40	
25	JULY	604	0.38		26	ART	596	0.37	*arts(531)*
27	OUR	572	0.36		28	PAGE	560	0.35	*pages(50)*
29	SPORT	547	0.34	*sports(38),sporting(2)*	30	AUDIO	546	0.34	

Fig. 2. Lemmatized word list of BBC News (07/2001)

Lemmatization (Word Stemming)

Plurals, gerund forms, and past tense suffixes are syntactical variations that complicate the interpretation of word lists. This problem can be partially solved by lemmatizing the text, which puts verb forms into the infinitive, nouns into the singular, and removes elisions. For compiling the example of *BBC News* shown in **Fig. 2**, a lemma list containing 40,569 tokens in 14,762 lemma groups was used [30]. The word frequency and the rank order of the list have changed considerably. More sophisticated approaches for eliminating ambiguities concerning the syntactic function or semantic nature of tokens require grammatical analysis of the sentence structures. While being indispensable for socio-linguistic or morpho-syntactic studies, the computational overheads introduced by such methods render them less useful for general Web assessment. Lemmatization reduces the number of tokens as compared to the initial text. While the vocabulary of a text consists of the entire set of distinct occurrences, its size (or length) depends on the total number of occurrences. Both lemmatizing texts and applying a frequency threshold for words considerably reduce the size of the vocabulary by grouping words of similar meaning together and discarding occurrences that only appear once (hapaxes) or rarely used expressions. The patterns obtained are more significant and the accuracy of statistical tests increases [17].

4 Topic Detection and Tracking

In the context of online media monitoring, topic detection refers to the identification of semantic clusters in continuous streams of raw text that correspond to new or previously unidentified events [4]. The dynamic characteristics of such agglomerations can be illustrated using temporal histograms, concordances, or perceptual maps based on correspondence analysis.

Cross-Sectional Comparison

Comparing the acquired data across sectors helps determine opinion leaders regarding various technologies, uncover subtle trends in the coverage of particular events and topics, and derive recommendations on how to improve Web-based information systems. On the basis of cumulated term frequencies as of June 2001, **Fig. 3** contrasts the coverage of various energy sources within four sub-samples: the Fortune Global 500 (n=492), an international media sample (n=15), a set of major solar power companies (n=22), and a sample comprising environmental non-profit organizations (n=30). The energy categories represent cumulative frequency data (AE = Alternative Energy). Percentages for the *solar* category, for example, integrate the number of occurrences of the terms *solar, photovoltaic*, and *photovoltaics*.

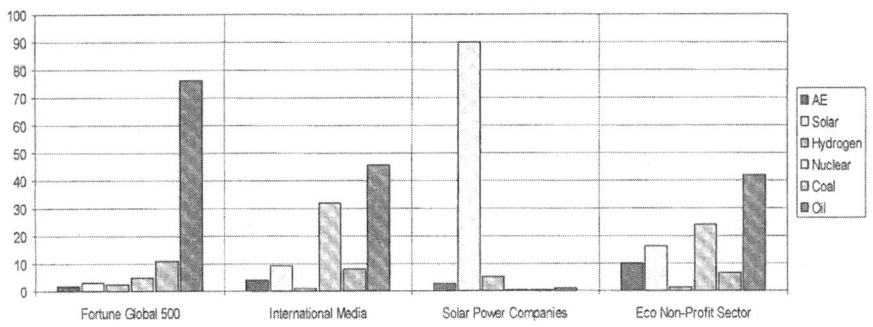

Fig. 3. Relative coverage of traditional vs. alternative energy sources by sector

Semantic Orientation

Unfortunately, statistics based on term frequencies are limited since they do not consider the usage context of a particular term. Both the environmental non-profit sector and the Fortune Global 500 companies, for example, show an extensive coverage of fossil fuels in Fig. 3. Although intuitively the non-profit sites have a more negative orientation towards fossil fuels, this assumption can neither be supported nor rejected by the available evidence.

Thus a logical next step is to automatically determine not only the term frequency, but also the semantic orientation of a site towards specific concepts. Fig. 4 documents this process for the term 'gasoline' as identified on the CNN Web site (September 2002). This particular example has been chosen since the low number of occurrences (2) makes it easier to demonstrate the underlying concept. A positive semantic orientation implies desirability and can be inferred from semantic association. The semantic orientation is computed from the strength of a term's association with a set of positive words, minus the strength of its association with a set of negative words. As the full raw text is available, the semantic association can be measured by means of distances to the positive and negative words within a sentence (as compared to representing documents as word lists or vector space models, which often restricts these techniques to measuring co-occurrences within a document).

In a first step, only those documents of a site that contain text of the language under consideration are selected and broken into individual sentences. Subsequently, each sentence with at least one occurrence of the target term is processed. Within each sentence, a distance measure (DIST) is computed from the relative positions (POS) of the target term and the evaluative words. Based on this distance and the orientation of the evaluative word (SVALUE=+/-1), the semantic orientation (SO) is approximated and added to the overall site metric (SO_TOTAL).

---

site: **CNN**
language_id: **ENGLISH**
country_id: **U.S.**
region_id: **NORTH AMERICA**
industry_id: **News | Media | Content (50MB)**

SENTENCE: Some agencies will not rent to people over 70 or under 25, and **gasoline** is **expensive** abroad.

POS: **14**; WORD: **expensive**; SVALUE: **-1**; POS: **16**; DIST: **2**; SO: **-0.25**

SENTENCE: Three **distinct** historic trains, including a steam engine and vintage **gasoline** motorcars, journey along forty miles of track through Northern California country and the towering redwoods.

POS: **11**; WORD: **distinct**; SVALUE: **1**; POS: **2**; DIST: **9**; SO: **0.056**

TERM: **gasoline**; FREQ: **2**; SO_TOTAL: **-0.194**

Fig. 4. Semantic orientation of CNN ('gasoline', 09/2002)

The list of evaluative words (positive and negative) used for the computation was adapted from the tagged dictionary compiled for the *General Inquirer*, a computer-assisted tool for content analysis developed at *Harvard University's Department of Psychology*. The *General Inquirer* dictionary contains a total of 182 tag categories, including for example "Positive", "Negative", "Negate", "Power", "Affiliation" or "Hostility" [31, 32]. An inherent problem in computer-assisted content analysis is that high-frequency words tend to carry different meanings in different contexts and may thus belong to several tag categories, possibly even with conflicting tags. Typically, high-frequency words have a positive/negative meaning only in some contexts, but may have a neutral or even opposite meaning in other contexts (Stone et al. 1966). Examples include *mean* (*to denote* [neutral] vs. *evil* [negative]), *good* (*product* [neutral] vs. *fine* [positive]), or cheap (*inferior* [negative] vs. *low-priced* [positive]). The underlying approach to semantic orientation circumvents the problem of multiple entries, as it focuses only on the mutually exclusive attributes *positive* and *negative*. The list compiled draws on the *General Inquirer* categories "Positive", "Negative" and "Negate". The entries in the latter two categories were combined to represent one category, as they largely overlap. Originally, these three categories contained (1,915), (2,291) and (217) entries, respectively. A number of words had to be eliminated, as they showed varying degrees of certainty regarding their positive or negative orientation or were found in both categories. Therefore, the list was adjusted to reflect only those terms whose semantic orientation shows a probability of at least 99%. The resultant list contains 1,474 positive and 1,952 negative words.

The scatterplot of Fig. 5 visualizes frequency versus semantic orientation for the term *'gasoline'*, as measured from an international media sample in September 2002. It is interesting to note that publications of scientific character frequently use particular terms, but tend to employ a neutral language. Both commercially oriented magazines such as *Fortune* or *Business Week* and sites with an environmental focus such as *Environmental News Service* or *Earth Times* have a more biased approach.

5 Conclusion and Outlook

With the media monitoring methodology described in this paper, thousands of Web-based information systems can be processed without human intervention. The mirroring of the general sample will continue in monthly intervals, while for particular sites a higher frequency might be required – i.e., weekly or daily intervals, depending on the dynamic characteristics of the observed media. Such repeated evaluations support the tracking of dynamic trends within certain sectors. Preliminary results based on an international media sample (n=180) have been presented. We will extend and leverage the existing architecture to derive theoretical knowledge and advance existing theories about the nature and dynamics of Web content in general and of specific focus areas in particular. Similar to traditional media research, further research will focus on building theories concerning organizational influences on the production, their connections to the final content, and on inter-relationships between content and target audience. Both snapshot and longitudinal studies regarding electronic content on the macro-level (comparative analyses within industries and specific groups of media) and the micro-level (trends in the coverage of certain topics, benchmarking organizational efforts to implement and maintain Web-based information systems, etc.) will facilitate and complement this theory building process.

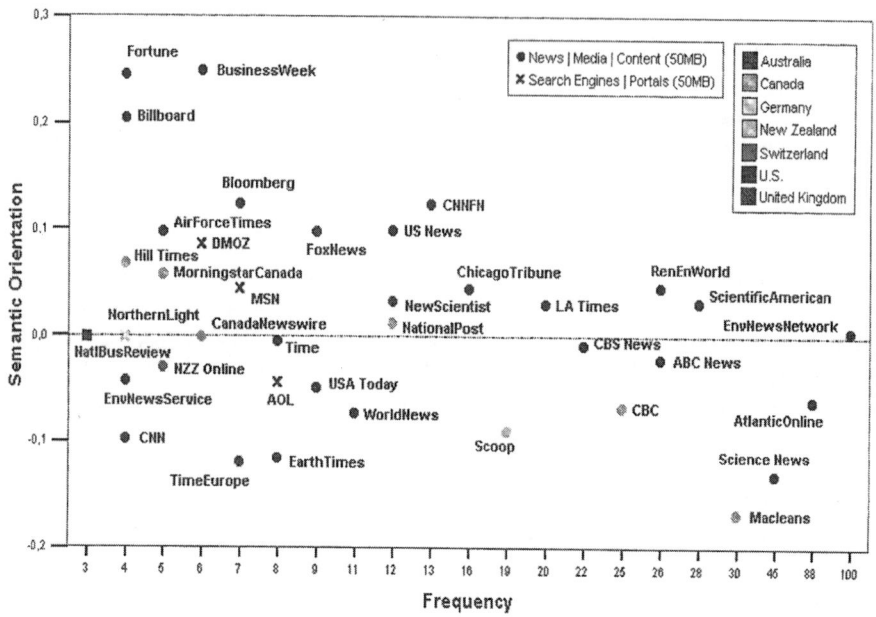

Fig. 5. Frequency vs. semantic orientation ('gasoline': media sample, 09/2002)

References

1. Bauer, C., Scharl, A.: Quantitative Evaluation of Web Site Content and Structure. Internet Research: Networking Applications and Policy 10 (2000) 31–43
2. Scharl, A.: Evolutionary Web Development. Springer, London (2000)
3. Scharl, A., Bauer, C.: Explorative Analysis and Evaluation of Commercial Web Information Systems. In: Proc. 20th International Conference on Information Systems (1999) 534–539
4. Chang, G., Healey, M. J., McHugh, J. A. M., Wang, J. T. L.: Mining the World Wide Web – An Information Search Approach. Kluwer Academic Publishers, Norwell (2001)
5. Mena, J.: Data Mining Your Website. Digital Press, Boston (1999)
6. Turban, E., Aronson, J. E.: Decision Support Systems and Intelligent Systems. 5th edn. Prentice-Hall, Upper Saddle River (1998)
7. Pyle, D.: Data Preparation for Data Mining. Morgan Kaufmann, San Francisco (1999)
8. Kleinberg, J., Papadimitriou, C., Raghavan, P.: A Microeconomic View of Data Mining. Data Mining and Knowledge Discovery 2 (1998) 311–324
9. Murphy, J., Hofacker, C. F., Bennett, M.: Website-generated Market-research Data: Tracing the Tracks Left Behind by Visitors. Cornell Hotel and Restaurant Administration Quarterly 42 (2001) 82–91
10. Mobasher, B., Dai, H., Nakagawa, M., Luo, T.: Discovery and Evaluation of Aggregate Usage Profiles for Web Personalization. Data Mining and Knowledge Discovery 6 (2002) 61–82
11. Han, J., Kamber, M.: Data Mining: Concepts and Techniques. Morgan Kaufmann, San Francisco (2001)

12. Bauer, C., Scharl, A.: Acquisition and Symbolic Visualization of Aggregated Customer Information for Analyzing Web Information Systems. In: Proc. 32nd Hawaii International Conference on System Sciences (1999)
13. McMillan, S. J.: The Microscope and the Moving Target: The Challenge of Applying Content Analysis to the World Wide Web. Journalism and Mass Communication Quarterly 77 (2000) 80–98
14. Koster, M. Evaluation of the Standard for Robots Exclusion [Online]. Available: http://www.robotstxt.org/wc/eval.html
15. Krippendorf, K.: Content Analysis: An Introduction to Its Methodology. Sage, Beverly Hills (1980)
16. Potter, J. W., Levine-Donnerstein, D.: Rethinking Validity and Reliability in Content Analysis. Journal of Applied Communication Research 27 (1999) 258–284
17. Lebart, L., Salem, A., Berry, L.: Exploring Textual Data. Kluwer Academic Publishers, Dordrecht (1998)
18. Potter, R. F.: Measuring the "Bells & Whistles" of a New Medium: Using Content Analysis to Describe Structural Features of Cyberspace. In: Proc. 49th Annual Conference of the International Communication Association (1999)
19. McEnery, T., Wilson, A.: Corpus Linguistics. Edinburgh University Press, Edinburgh (1996)
20. Biber, D., Conrad, S., Reppen, R.: Corpus Linguistics - Investigating Language Structure and Use. Cambridge University Press, Cambridge (1998)
21. Tesch, R.: Qualitative Research: Analysis Types and Software Tools. Falmer Press, New York (1990)
22. Terveen, L. G., Hill, W. C., Amento, B.: Constructing, Organizing, and Visualizing Collections of Topically Related Web Resources. ACM Transactions on Computer-Human Interaction 6 (1999) 67–94
23. Baeza-Yates, R., Ribeiro-Neto, B.: Modern Information Retrieval. ACM Press Books, Harlow (1999)
24. Titscher, S., Wodak, R., Meyer, M., Vetter, E.: Methoden der Textanalyse: Leitfaden und Überblick. Westdeutscher Verlag, Opladen (1998)
25. McMillan, S. J.: The Microscope and the Moving Target: The Challenge of Applying a Stable Research Technique to a Dynamic Communication Environment. In: Proc. 49th Annual Conference of the International Communication Association (1999)
26. Aarseth, E. J.: Nonlinearity and Literary Theory. In: G. P. Landow, (ed.) Hyper/Text/Theory. Johns Hopkins University Press (1994) 51–86
27. Pearce, C., Miller, E.: The TELLTALE Dynamic Hypertext Environment: Approaches to Scalability. In: C. Nicholas and J. Mayfield, (eds.): Intelligent Hypertext: Advanced Techniques for the World Wide Web. Springer (1997) 109–130
28. Hull, D. A., Grefenstette, G.: Querying Across Languages: A Dictionary-based Approach to Multilingual Information Retrieval. In: Proc. 19th Annual International ACM SIGIR Conference on Research and Development in Information Retrieval (1996) 49–57
29. Grefenstette, G.: Comparing Two Language Identification Schemes. In: Proc. 3rd International Conference on Statistical Analysis of Textual Data (1995) 263–268
30. Someya, Y. (1999) e_lemma.txt [Online]. Available: http://www.lexically.net/downloads/e_lemma.zip
31. Stone, P. J., Dunphy, D. C., Smith, M. S., Ogilvie, D. M.: The General Inquirer: A Computer Approach to Content Analysis. MIT Press, Cambridge (1966)
32. Stone, P. J. The General Inquirer [Online]. Available: http://www.wjh.harvard.edu/~inquirer/

Dynamic Subspace Clustering for Very Large High-Dimensional Databases

P. Deepa Shenoy[1], K.G. Srinivasa[1], M.P. Mithun[1],
K.R. Venugopal[1], and L.M. Patnaik[2]

[1] University Visvesvaraya College of Engineering, Bangalore-560001.
shenoypd@yahoo.com, kgs.cse@msrit.edu, vkrajuk@vsnl.com
http://www.venugopalkr.com
[2] Microprocessor Application Laboratory, Indian Institute of Science ,
Bangalore-560012, India.
{lalit@micro.iisc.ernet.in}

Abstract. Emerging high-dimensional data mining applications needs
to find interesting clusters embeded in arbitrarily aligned subspaces of
lower dimensionality. It is difficult to cluster high-dimensional data objects, when they are sparse and skewed. Updations are quite common in
dynamic databases and they are usually processed in batch mode. In very
large dynamic databases, it is necessary to perform incremental cluster
analysis only to the updations. We present a incremental clustering algorithm for subspace clustering in very high dimensions, which handles
both insertion and deletions of datapoints to the backend databases.

1 Introduction

Clustering is a useful technique for the discovery of data distribution and patterns in the underlying database. A cluster is a collection of data objects that
are similar to one another within the same cluster and are dissimilar to the
objects in the other clusters. A cluster of data objects can be treated as one
group. Applications like data warehousing, market research, customer segmentation and web search involve the collection of data from multiple sources, which
are frequently updated. All cluster patterns derived from the above applications
have to be changed as the updation to backend database occurs. Since backend
databases are very large in size, it is highly desirable to perform the changes to
the previous patterns incrementally.

In high dimensional spaces all the dimensions may not be relevant to a given
cluster. Further, a single set of subspaces may not be enough for discovering all
the clusters because different set of points may cluster better for different subsets of dimensions [2]. In the algorithm used in [1] *arbitrarily ORiented projected
CLUSter generation*, the best projection for each cluster is determined by retain-
ing the greatest amount of similarity among the points in the detected cluster.
This algorithm is used as the base for our Dynamic Clustering algorithm.

The base algorithm [1] generates clusters in a lower dimensional projected
subspace for data of high dimensionality. It is assumed that the number of output

J. Liu et al. (Eds.): IDEAL 2003, LNCS 2690, pp. 850–854, 2003.

clusters k and the dimensionality l of the subspace in which each cluster exists are the user defined input parameters to the algorithm. The output of the algorithm is the set $C := \{C_1, \ldots, C_k, \Psi\}$ of the data points such that the points form the clusters $\{C_1, \ldots, C_k\}$ each of the cluster of dimensionality l and the set of outliers Ψ (outliers are the points that do not belong to any cluster). Let $\varepsilon_i := \{\varepsilon_i{}^1, \varepsilon_i{}^2, \ldots, \varepsilon_i{}^l\}$ denote the set of $l \leq d$ orthogonal vectors defining the subspace associated with cluster C_i. The vectors for the outlier set Ψ are empty. Let N be the total number of data points, d the dimensionality of the input data, k_0 the initial number of clusters, $C_i := \{x_1, x_2, \ldots, x_t\}$ be the set of points in the cluster i.

The paper is organized into the following sections. Section 2 presents the algorithm DPCA, section 3 shows the performance analysis and results of the algorithm. Finally section 5 presents the conclusions.

2   Dynamic Projected Clustering Algorithm(DPCA)

Consider a large backend database D of high dimensionality d consisting of a finite set of records $\{R_1, R_2, \ldots, R_m\}$. Each record is represented as a set of numeric values. Let δ^+ be the set of incremental records added to D and δ^- be the set of records deleted from D.

Let Ψ: set of outlier points, Υ: set of non-classified points i.e., the points that do not belong to any of the existing clusters, ξ_i: $E\ (C_i, \varepsilon_i)\ /\ E(U, \varepsilon_i)$ i.e., the ratio of projected energy of the cluster C_i to that of the universal set of points U in the subspace ε_i, and τ: the value of ξ_i for which the cluster C_i is *wellformed*. The objective is to generate new cluster patterns $D + \delta^+$ or D - δ^- without considering D. The datapoints can either be inserted into or deleted from the database, that can affect the cluster patterns in the following way.

Insertions:
a) *Absorption*: For any $p \in \delta^+$, $C_i = C_i \bigcup p$, $(1 \leq i \leq k$).
b) *Creation*: New cluster C_{k+1} gets added to the set of existing clusters C.
c) *Outliers*: For $p \in \delta^+$ and $p \notin C_i$ $(1 \leq i \leq k)$, p becomes an outlier.

Deletions:
a) *Reduction*: For any $p \in \delta^-$, $C_i = C_i$ - p and $\xi_i \leq \tau$ $(1 \leq i \leq k$).
b) *Removal*: For any $p \in \delta^-$, $C_i = C_i$ - p and $\xi_i > \tau$ $(1 \leq i \leq k$).
c) *Split*: A particular cluster C_i may split into γ clusters, $\gamma \geq 2$.
d) *Outliers*: Undeleted points of a cluster C_i become outliers when $\xi_i > \tau$.
The base algorithm is initially executed on the backend database. The clusters formed have the *cluster sparsity coefficient* less than one. To determine whether a particular cluster C_i is *wellformed*, ξ_i the ratio of the projected energy of the cluster C_i in the subspace ε_i to that of the projected energy of the universal set of points U in the same subspace is determined. If $\xi_i > \tau$, it indicates that the average spread of the points in the subspace is almost same as that of the universal set of points of the database and the cluster thus formed is sparse [7]. Therefore it is meaningless to consider C_i as a cluster. Further if $\xi_i \leq \tau$, the cluster C_i is dense and said to be *wellformed*.

Algorithm *IncrementData* (δ^+)
$\quad\quad \Upsilon = \delta^+ \bigcup \Psi;$
$\quad\quad$ **while** (*true*) **do**
$\quad\quad\quad\quad$ **for** each Point $p \in \Upsilon$, **do** //classify p as merged or non-merged point
$\quad\quad\quad\quad\quad\quad$ *Classify* $(p, \Upsilon);$
$\quad\quad\quad\quad$ $O = CalculateCentroid(\Upsilon);$ //nearest centroid to O
$\quad\quad\quad\quad$ $\nu = CalculateInterCentroidDistance(O);$
$\quad\quad\quad\quad$ **for** each point $p \in \Upsilon$, **do**
$\quad\quad\quad\quad$ **if** (*distance* $(p, O) \le \nu$) //point p gets absorbed into cluster C_{k+1}
$\quad\quad\quad\quad\quad\quad$ *AddPoint* $(p, C_{k+1});$
$\quad\quad\quad\quad\quad\quad$ $\Upsilon = \Upsilon - \{p\};$
$\quad\quad\quad\quad$ **endif**
$\quad\quad\quad\quad$ $\xi_{k+1} = E\ (C_{k+1}, \varepsilon_i)\ /\ E\ (U, \varepsilon_i);$
$\quad\quad\quad\quad$ **if** $(\xi_{k+1} \le \tau)$ //new cluster is formed
$\quad\quad\quad\quad\quad\quad$ $k = k + 1;$
$\quad\quad\quad\quad$ **else**
$\quad\quad\quad\quad\quad\quad$ $\Psi = \Upsilon;$ //neglect C_{k+1} , end of iteration$\}$
$\quad\quad\quad\quad\quad\quad$ **return;**
$\quad\quad\quad\quad$ **endif;**
$\quad\quad\quad\quad$ **for** $i = 1$ to k **do**
$\quad\quad\quad\quad\quad\quad$ Recompute the eigenvectors and eigenvalues for C_i ;
$\quad\quad\quad\quad\quad\quad$ Recompute centroid for C_i ;
$\quad\quad$ **End Algorithm** *IncrementData*

Lemma: For all $p \in \delta^+$, p may join the existing cluster C_i iff $dist_i\ (p) \le$ $\min\{dist_i\ (\overline{X}_j\ ),\ 1 \le j \le k$ and j $\ne i$ $\}$ where $\overline{X}_j$ is the centroid of cluster C_j.
Proof: Assume $p \in C_i$. If $dist_i\ (p) > \min\{dist_i\ (\overline{X}_j\ ),\ 1 \le j \le k$ and j $\ne i$ $\}$ where $\overline{X}_j$ is the centroid of cluster C_j, p becomes an outlier. Therefore p cannot join any of the existing clusters. Hence the contradiction.
IncrementData(): The increments are assumed to be in batch mode. The input set of points δ^+ are classified into merged and non-merged points. Merged points get absorbed into the existing clusters when their distance from the centroid of the parent cluster is less than or equal to the shortest intercentroid distance between the parent and the remaining clusters [*Lemma*]. The remaining points may form a new cluster or become outliers. The datapoint nearest to the arithmetic mean of the non-merged points will form a potential seed for the new cluster. The nearest centroid (these centroids correspond to the centroids of the existing clusters) to this potential seed is calculated(ν). The distance between the non-merged points and the seed is calculated(g). If $g < \nu$, the points get added to the cluster. The remaining points become outliers, but they are not discarded because they may form new clusters in future updations.

$\quad\quad$ The dimensions of the newly formed cluster C_{k+1} are reduced to check whether it is wellformed or not. Next ξ_{k+1} the ratio of the projected energy of the cluster C_{k+1} in the subspace ε_{k+1} to the projected energy of the universal set U of points in the same subspace is calculated. If $\xi_{k+1} \le \tau$, cluster C_{k+1} is added to the set of existing clusters. The centroids and the eigenvectors corresponding to the least spread subspaces are recomputed for all the clusters. This iteration is repeated for the remaining set of outliers. If $\xi_{k+1} > \tau$ the cluster C_{k+1} is discarded and the iteration stops. The points of C_{k+1} are added to the outlier set.

The deletion of points can be treated as an indirect insertion into the database. For each set δ^- deleted from the database, ξ_i the ratio of energies of the clusters with the universal set of points is determined. The clusters with $\xi_i > \tau$ are discarded. The points of the discarded clusters are added to the outlier set Ψ and these set of points are given as input for reinsertion. This step is required mainly to handle the *split situation*(cluster may split into two or more clusters).

3   Performance Analysis

The algorithm DPCA was implemented using C++ and tested on an Intel PIII 900MHz machine with 128MB memory. The data was stored on a 20GB hard-disk. We determined the performance of DPCA with respect to the accuracy of clustering with variable number of updations, the running time requirements for insertions and the speedup factor of our algorithm over the base algorithm. The algorithm was tested using synthetic data.

Table 1. Confusion Matrix: ORCLUS

OC IC	A	B	C	D	E	F	G
1	0	0	0	17453	0	0	0
2	0	0	0	0	0	16447	0
3	0	0	0	0	0	0	15414
4	0	0	0	0	17487	0	0
5	0	0	0	0	0	0	0
6	14263	0	0	0	0	0	0
7	0	0	0	0	0	0	0

Table 2. Confusion Matrix: Insertion

OC IC	A	B	C	D	E	F	G
1	0	0	0	16768	0	0	0
2	0	0	0	0	0	15682	0
3	0	0	0	0	0	0	14600
4	0	0	0	0	16638	0	0
5	0	0	0	0	0	0	0
6	13557	0	0	0	0	0	0
7	0	982	0	0	0	0	0

The algorithm was tested for variable number of updations and the corresponding *Confusion matrices* were obtained. The *Confusion Matrix* indicates the mapping of input clusters to the output clusters. The rows(A, B, ...) and columns(1, 2, ...) correspond to the output clusters(OC) and input clusters(IC) respectively. *Quality of clustering* of a particular input cluster is defined as the number of points that are present in the non-dominant columns of a particular input cluster in the confusion matrix. The algorithm was executed for 0.1 million backend database. The *Confusion matrices* are shown for the base algorithm (Table 1) and for an insertion of 5000 points(Table 2). The dominance of a particular column in each row indicates that the particular cluster is wellformed.

The execution time of DPCA versus number of increments for different sizes of backend databases is depicted in Fig. 1. The running time of DPCA shows that the algorithm scales linearly with increase in number of insertions into the database. The performance of DPCA versus the base algorithm is evaluated and *speedup factors* are derived for typical parameter values. Let $f_{ins} :=$ the total cost for running the base algorithm for both backend database(D) and the increments(δ^+), $f_{base} :=$ Cost of running the base algorithm only for the backend database(D), $f_{DPCA} :=$ Cost of running DPCA only for the increments(δ^+) . Therefore,

$$Speedup\ factor = (\ f_{ins}\ -\ f_{base}\ )\ /\ f_{DPCA}\ .$$

The speedup factor indicates the degree of improvement of DPCA over the base algorithm with respect to the running time for a specified size of increments. Fig. 2 shows that the speedup factor increases with an increase in the size of increments (δ^+). Also the speedup factor decreases with the increase in the size of backend database(D).

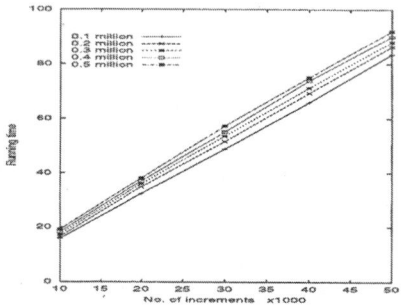
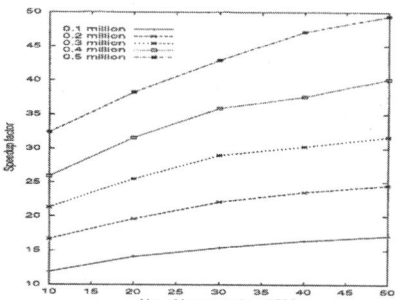

Fig. 1. Execution time vs Increments   **Fig. 2.** Speed up factor vs Increments

4   Conclusions

In this paper, we have proposed an Dynamic Subspace Clustering Algorithm (DPCA) for dynamic updations. DPCA addresses sparse and skewed databases of high dimensionality. The results of DPCA show that the algorithm is stable for dynamic updations with respect to the quality of clusters formed and is also scalable to large databases. Significant speedup factors are achieved over the base algorithm for variable number of increments.

References

1. Charu C. Aggarwal, and Philip S. Yu, "Redefining Clustering For High Dimensional Applications," *IEEE Transactions on Knwoledge and Data Engineering*, Vol 14, No. 2, pp. 210–224, 2002.
2. Anil K. Jain, Richard C. Dubes, "Algorithms for Clustering Data ," *Prentice Hall, Englewood Cliffs, New Jersey*, 1998.
3. P. Deepa Shenoy, Srinivasa K. G, Venugopal K. R, L. M Patnaik, "An Evolutionary Approach for Association Rule Mining on Dynamic Databases," *Proc. Int. Conf. on PAKDD, LNCS, Springer Verlag, 2003.*
4. Jiawei Han, Micheline Kamber,"Data Mining : Concepts and Techniques ," *Academic Press*, 2001.

Spatial Information in Histograms for Shape Representation

Atul Sajjanhar

School of Information Technology
Deakin University
221 Burwood Highway
Burwood, VIC 3125
Australia
atuls@deakin.edu.au
http://www.deakin.edu.au/~atuls

Abstract. Histograms have been used for Shape Representation and Retrieval. In this paper, the traditional technique has been modified to capture additional information. We compare the performance of the proposed method with the traditional method by performing experiments on a database of shapes. The results show that the proposed enhancement to the histogram based method improves the effectiveness significantly.

1 Introduction

Retrieval of images based on the shape of objects in images is an important part of Content based image retrieval (CBIR). Recently, a contour based method for shape representation and retrieval was used by Fan [1]. We propose to modify this method so that more information is contained in the indices for shapes. We show that the proposed method has better effectiveness.

In Section 2, we describe the traditional histogram method. In Section 3, we describe the proposed method. The Experimental Setup and Results are presented in Section 4. We provide the conclusion in Section 5.

2 Histogram Method

Fan [9] has proposed a method of using distance histograms for shape representation and retrieval. In this method, points are sampled along the shape boundary and their distances are computed from the centroid. The centroidal distances obtained are discretised into buckets. The resulting histograms are used for shape representation and retrieval. A histogram is represented as below.

$$D : (d_0, d_1 \ldots d_{N-1}) \tag{1}$$

J. Liu et al. (Eds.): IDEAL 2003, LNCS 2690, pp. 855–859, 2003.

Where N is the number of buckets in the histograms and d_i is the number of centroidal distances, which were discretised into bucket i.

The distance between two shapes is measured as the Euclidean distance below.

$$Dist(D_1, D_2) = \sqrt{\sum_{i=0}^{N-1}(d_{1i} - d_{2i})^2} \tag{2}$$

Each shape has N buckets, from 0 to N-1, d_{1i} is the count in bucket i for histogram D_1 and d_{2i} is the count in bucket i for histogram D_2.

3 Proposed Method

There is no spatial information about the centroidal distances in the method described in Section 2. Hence, two shapes, which are entirely different, may have the same distance histograms.

We propose to incorporate spatial information when discretising the centroidal distances into a histogram. We draw an analogy from Color Coherence Vectors (CCV) proposed by Pass and Zabih [2]. CCV is used for image retrieval based on colour. Pass et al [2] defined colour coherence of pixels as the degree to which pixels of that colour are members of a large similarly coloured region. Pixels are classified as coherent or incoherent. Coherent pixels are part of a sizable contiguous region of similar colour while incoherent pixels are not.

In the case of shape representation, we define "shape coherence" of pixels on the shape boundary. If the centroidal distance of a sample point on the shape boundary is part of a segment in which all the sample points have the same discretised centroidal distance then it is coherent. On the other hand, if the discretised centroidal distance of a sample point is different from the discretised centroidal distances of it's immediate neighbours then it is incoherent. The number of consecutive sample points, which should belong to the same bucket for the comprising sample points to be coherent is given by a variable τ. Hence, if τ consecutive sample points have centroidal distances belonging to the same bucket then these pixels will be coherent.

In the method described in Section 2, each bucket in the histogram has one count. This count represents the number of pixels, which had their centroidal distances, discretised into that bucket. In the proposed method, we classify the pixels in each bucket into coherent and incoherent. Hence, there will be two counts for each bucket (refer Eqn 5). One count will represent the coherent pixels and the other will represent the incoherent pixels.

During the indexing process, N equi-spaced points are sampled along the shape boundary. The distance between a sample point $s_i(x_i, y_i)$ and the centroid $c(x_c, y_c)$ is computed as below.

$$d(s_i, c) = \sqrt{(x_c - x_i)^2 + (y_c - y_i)^2} \tag{3}$$

The distances thus obtained are invariant to rotation and translation. However, the distance needs to be normalised for scale. To normalise the distance for scale, we scale them from 0 to 100. Thus, the minimum distance will be 0 and the maximum will be 100. The normalisation is done as shown in Eqn 4 below.

$$norm\_dist = \left[\frac{dist - dist_{min}}{dist_{max} - dist_{min}} \right] \times 100 \tag{4}$$

Where $norm\_dist$ is the normalised centroidal distance for $dist$. $dist_{max}$ is the maximum centroidal distance and $dist_{min}$ is the minimum centroidal distance.

The normalised centroidal distances of the pixels are discretised into buckets. The pixels in each bucket are divided into coherent and incoherent. For instance, bucket "i" will have α_i coherent pixels and β_i incoherent pixels. The total number of pixels in the bucket is $(\alpha_i + \beta_i)$. A histogram for a shape is represented as follows.

$$D : [(\alpha_0, \beta_0), (\alpha_1, \beta_1) \ldots (\alpha_{N-1}, \beta_{N-1})] \tag{5}$$

Where N is the number of buckets in the histogram. The distance between the two shapes represented by histograms D_1, D_2 is computed as below.

$$Dist(D_1, D_2) = \sum_{i=0}^{N-1} \left(|\alpha_{1i} - \alpha_{2i}| + |\beta_{1i} - \beta_{2i}| \right) \tag{6}$$

4   Experimental Setup and Results

The SQUID database [3] is used to perform experiments and test the proposed method. This database consists of 1100 fish shapes and has been extensively used by researchers for testing. Indexing and Retrieval experiments are performed on the database for the traditional method and the proposed method. We use 150 sample points along the shape boundary. Distances are computed for the sample points from the centroid. The distances are then scaled for each shape such that all distances are in the range 0 to 100. 10 buckets are created. τ is defined to be 3 pixels.

Queries are performed using the traditional method and the proposed method. The shapes in the database, which are perceptually similar to the query shapes are noted. We obtain the rank of the relevant shapes for each query, using both methods. The change in the rank of the relevant shapes retrieved is used to compare the effectiveness of the proposed method with the traditional method. We make six queries for both the methods. The six query shapes are #736, #675, #1090, #1072, #264, #706. The results obtained for the six queries are shown in figures 1 to 6.

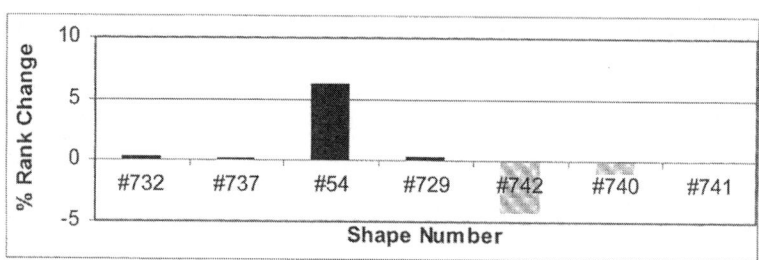

Fig. 1. Result for Query Shape #736

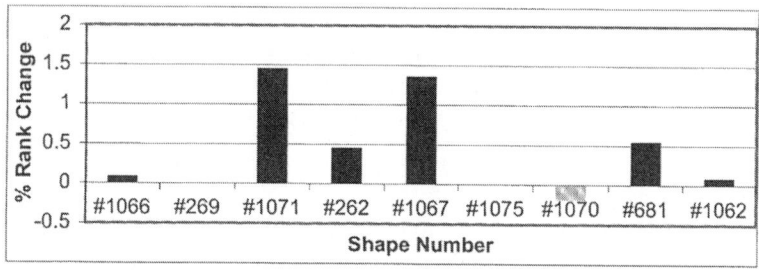

Fig. 2. Result for Query Shape #675

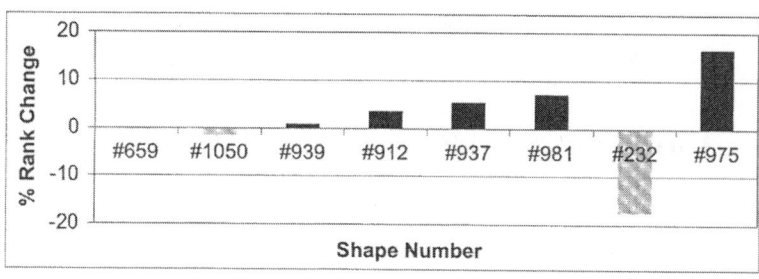

Fig. 3. Result for Query Shape #1090

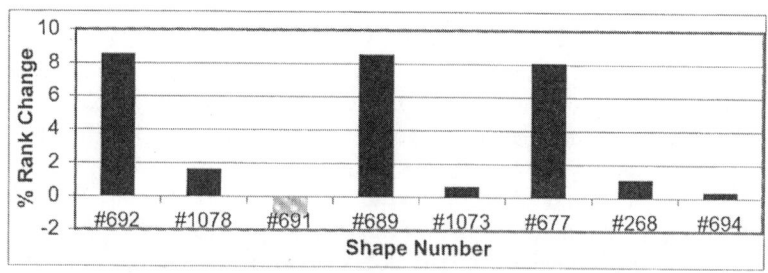

Fig. 4. Result for Query Shape #1072

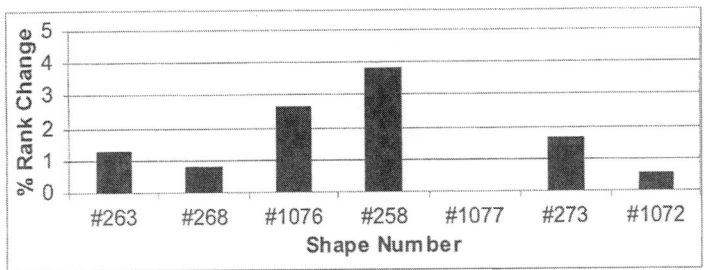

Fig. 5. Result for Query Shape #264

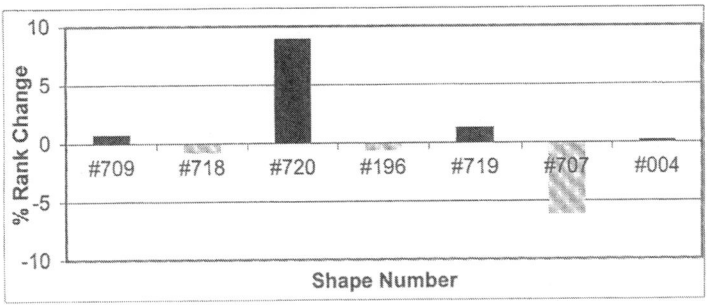

Fig. 6. Result for Query Shape #706

5 Conclusion

From the experimental results we see that the proposed method is effective. In most cases, there is significant improvement in the ranking of the relevant shapes retrieved when using the proposed method.

References

1. Fan, S.: Shape Representation and Retrieval using Distance Histograms, Technical Report – University of Alberta (2001)
2. Pass, G., Zabih, R.: Histogram refinement for content-based image retrieval, IEEE Workshop on Applications of Computer Vision (1996) 96–102
3. SQUID: http://www.ee.surrey.ac.uk/Research/VSSP/imagedb

From Competing Associations to Justifiable Conclusions[*]

Choh Man Teng

Institute for Human and Machine Cognition
University of West Florida
40 South Alcaniz Street, Pensacola FL 32501, USA
cmteng@ai.uwf.edu

Abstract. The standard formulation of association rules is suitable for describing patterns found in a given data set. These rules may each be adequately supported by the evidence, yet provide conflicting recommendations regarding an unseen instance when considered together. We proposed an alternative formulation called *interval association rules*, and developed a set of principles to adjudicate between conflicting rules.

1 Association Rules

One of the active research areas in data mining and knowledge discovery deals with the construction and management of association rules. We will call the formulation typified in [Agrawal *et al. 1993*] the *standard* formulation. A *standard association rule* is a rule of the form

$$X \Rightarrow Y,$$

which says that if X is true of an instance in a database Δ, so is Y true of the same instance, with a certain level of significance as measured by two indicators, *support* and *coverage*:

[**support**] proportion of XY's in Δ;
[**coverage**] proportion of Y's among X's in Δ.

(Note that "*coverage*" is typically called "*confidence*" in the standard association rule literature. However, we will be using "confidence" to denote the level of certainty associated with an interval derived from a statistical procedure. To avoid confusion, we will refer to the above measure of rule accuracy as the *coverage* of the rule, and restrict the use of the word "confidence" to terms such as "the confidence interval" as are traditionally used in statistics.)

In [Teng and Hewett, 2002,Teng, 2003] we advanced the interval association rule framework as an approach to deriving associations that is grounded in the theory of statistical inference. Instead of standard point based measures, association coverage is given in terms of an interval, encompassing a range of values

---

[*] This work was supported by NASA NCC2-1239 and ONR N00014-03-1-0516.

J. Liu et al. (Eds.): IDEAL 2003, LNCS 2690, pp. 860–864, 2003.

in which we can claim the true rule coverage in the parent population falls with a certain level of confidence. An *interval association rule* is a rule of the form

$$X \Rightarrow Y \quad [l, u] : 1 - \alpha,$$

where $[l, u]$ denotes a range of coverage values, and $1 - \alpha$ denotes a level of confidence. The size and range of the interval associated with a rule are derived from, in addition to the level of confidence required, both the rule coverage obtained from the data set as well as the absolute size of the relevant portion of the data. The larger the sample, the narrower the width of the interval.

What sets our approach apart is that instead of using statistical measures as a descriptive summary of the characteristics in the sample data set, or as a way to select a subset of more relevant rules from the exhaustive set of standard association rules, or as a handle to deal with numeric data, we relate explicitly the rule coverage in the given sample data to the rule coverage in the population.

Further details of the interval association rule framework can be found in [Teng and Hewett, 2002,Teng, 2003].

2   Choosing among Competing Rules

One of the acute problems with association rules is that there can be any number of rules generated at any time, more than can ever be reasonably inspected by either human or even machine. Various methods have been devised to pick out the more interesting and relevant rules from the huge pool of acceptable rules. Alternative measures to determine the fitness of a rule include, for instance, correlation, gain, Gini, Laplace, χ^2, lift, and conviction. These metrics provide grounds to pre- or post-prune the standard association rules in order to arrive at a smaller set of rules. [Klemettinen *et al.*, 1994,Silberschatz and Tuzhilin, 1996, Fukuda *et al.*, 1996,Brin *et al.*, 1997,Ng *et al.*, 1998,Bayardo and Agrawal, 1999, Liu *et al.*, 1999,Zaki, 2000, for example].

The *real* problem however, at least from the point of view of performing inferences, is not so much that there are too many rules, but that little has been said about how we should interpret or *make use of* them. The rules may each be adequately supported by the evidence, yet provide conflicting recommendations regarding an unseen instance when considered together. Let us look at a few scenarios illustrating the complications involved.

Suppose our knowledge discovery system provided us with, among others, the following standard association rules. (For simplicity, we omit the support measure here.)

$$\text{coke} \Rightarrow \text{potato chips:} \quad 0.75 \text{ coverage;} \qquad (^*1)$$
$$\text{coke and nachos} \Rightarrow \text{potato chips:} \quad 0.60 \text{ coverage;} \qquad (^*2)$$
$$\text{coke and dip} \Rightarrow \text{potato chips:} \quad 0.70 \text{ coverage.} \qquad (^*3)$$

Given that we know Sam is buying both coke and nachos, what probability would we attribute to his also buying potato chips?

We will take these relative frequencies or coverage values as generic probabilities. Rules (*1) and (*2) both apply to Sam. However, the two rules each asserts a different value for the probability that Sam is also buying potato chips. At first glance, a simple rule of thumb would be to go with the most *specific* rule, in this case, rule (*2). By the same token, Susan, who buys both coke and dip, would have rule (*3) applied to her. We thus conclude that there is a 60% chance that Sam buys chips and a 70% chance that Susan does the same.

However, standard association rules, using only point probability estimates, do not tell enough of the story. We need to know how substantiated the rules are before we can make a rational decision. Suppose the interval association rules corresponding to rules (*1)–(*3) with 95% confidence are as follows. (We will omit the confidence parameter in the rules.)

$$\text{coke} \Rightarrow \text{potato chips:} \quad [0.72, 0.78]; \quad (*4)$$
$$\text{coke and nachos} \Rightarrow \text{potato chips:} \quad [0.55, 0.65]; \quad (*5)$$
$$\text{coke and dip} \Rightarrow \text{potato chips:} \quad [0.45, 0.95]. \quad (*6)$$

Now reconsider the two cases, Sam and Susan. For Sam, we may still prefer the more *specific* rule (*5) to the general rule (*4). The intervals associated with the two rules *conflict*, and we would adhere to the recommendation provided by the more specific rule.

For Susan, however, we note that rule (*6), although concerning a class of people that is more specific than that of rule (*4), is also *vaguer*. The interval associated with rule (*6) is not in conflict with the interval associated with rule (*4). The former interval is merely wider and includes the latter interval, perhaps because there are relatively few occurrences of coke-dip purchases in our data set. This observation should cast reasonable doubt on the utility of rule (*6). The additional information, the purchase of dip, is irrelevant to the relationship between coke and potato chips. We would be well-advised to instead prefer the more general rule (*4) in such a situation.

In the interval rule framework, different choices are made according to the different relationships between the applicable rules and their intervals. For Sam, we prefer rule (*5) for the additional information contained in this more specific rule. For Susan, on the other hand, we prefer the general rule (*4) to the vaguer rule (*6), whose specificity is misleading. Standard point-based association rules are not equipped with the information required to make such distinctions.

3   Principles for Resolving Conflicts

We developed a set of principles to adjudicate between conflicting reference classes in an evidential probability setting [Kyburg and Teng, 2001]. These principles take into account such information as the taxonomy of the reference classes, the width and set inclusion relationship between the intervals, and the conditioning on prior distributions. Analogous principles can be developed to resolve conflicts between competing interval association rules.

We will outline below the principles for tackling specificity and vagueness based on interval association rules. Two interval rules are said to *compete* if their consequents are identical, for example,

$$X_1 \Rightarrow Y : [p_1, q_1]; \tag{*7}$$
$$X_2 \Rightarrow Y : [p_2, q_2]. \tag{*8}$$

Even though the two rules sanction the same consequent Y, they differ in the *strength* of the inference, as indicated by their supporting intervals. We need to select the rules whose strengths are the most justifiable from among competing rules with respect to a particular situation.

Given two intervals $[p_1, q_1]$ and $[p_2, q_2]$, $[p_1, q_1]$ is *nested* in $[p_2, q_2]$ iff $p_2 \leq p_1 \leq q_1 \leq q_2$. The two intervals *conflict* iff neither is nested in the other. The *cover* of two intervals $[p_1, q_1]$ and $[p_2, q_2]$ is the interval $[\min(p_1, p_2), \max(q_1, q_2)]$. We consider three cases in adjudicating between the competing rules (*7) and (*8).

1. X_1 is a specialization of X_2, i.e., all X_1's are X_2's.
   There are three subcases according to the relationship between p_1, p_2, q_1, and q_2.
   a) Conflict: $(p_1 \leq p_2$ and $q_1 \leq q_2)$ or $(p_2 \leq p_1$ and $q_2 \leq q_1)$.
      Rule (*7) is preferred when X_1 is known. Rule (*8) applies when we only know the more general X_2.
   b) Vague information about the more specific class X_1: $p_1 \leq p_2 \leq q_2 \leq q_1$.
      Only rule (*8) is sanctioned, and it applies to all X_2's regardless of the truth value of X_1.
   c) Specific information about the more specific class X_1: $p_2 \leq p_1 \leq q_1 \leq q_2$.
      Again rule (*7) is preferred for X_1's, and the more general rule (*8) applies only when the more specific rule for X_1 cannot be applied.
2. X_2 is a specialization of X_1, i.e., all X_2's are X_1's.
   This is symmetrical to Case (1).
3. Neither X_1 nor X_2 is a specialization of the other.
   Again there are three subcases.
   a) Conflict: $(p_1 \leq p_2$ and $q_1 \leq q_2)$ or $(p_2 \leq p_1$ and $q_2 \leq q_1)$.
      Rules (*7) and (*8) apply respectively to cases where the object in question is known to satisfy X_1 or X_2 but not both. When both X_1 and X_2 are satisfied, we take the supporting interval to be the cover of the conflicting intervals $[p_1, q_1]$ and $[p_2, q_2]$ of the competing rules (*7) and (*8).
   b) Nested intervals: $p_1 \leq p_2$ and $q_2 \leq q_1$.
      Rule (*8), the rule supported by the tighter interval, is preferred whenever X_2 is known. Rule (*7) applies when only X_1 is known.
   c) Nested intervals: $p_2 \leq p_1$ and $q_1 \leq q_2$.
      This is symmetrical to Case (3b).

Based on the relationship between the rules and the characteristics of the particular situation we need to make inferences about, we can pick out the preferred rules according to the above guidelines. We remove from the set of competing rules the less specific and vaguer rules. Of the remaining we take the cover of their associated intervals. This approach provides normative guidance to the application of interval association rules. The preferred rules are systematically selected based on the underlying statistics.

Our approach extends the capability of association rule mining beyond data description. Interval association rules are statistically grounded, and the principles described here provide us with a constructive mechanism to make justifiable conclusions from conflicting yet each individually well supported associations.

References

[Agrawal *et al.* *1993*] R. Agrawal, T. Imielinski, and A. Swami. Mining association rules between sets of items in large databases. In *Proceedings of the ACM SIGMOD Conference on the Management of Data*, pages 207–216, 1993.

[Bayardo and Agrawal, 1999] R. Bayardo and R. Agrawal. Mining the most interesting rules. In *Proceedings of the ACM SIGKDD Conference on Knowledge Discovery and Data Mining*, pages 145–154, 1999.

[Brin *et al.*, 1997] S. Brin, R. Motwani, and C. Silverstein. Beyond market baskets: Generalizing association rules to correlations. In *Proceedings of the ACM SIGMOD Conference on the Management of Data*, pages 265–276, 1997.

[Fukuda *et al.*, 1996] Takeshi Fukuda, Yasuhiko Morimoto, Shinichi Morishita, and Takeshi Tokuyama. Data mining using two-dimensional optimized association rules: Scheme, algorithms, and visualization. In *Proceedings of the ACM SIGMOD Conference on the Management of Data*, pages 13–23, 1996.

[Klemettinen *et al.*, 1994] M. Klemettinen, H. Mannila, P. Ronkainen, H. Toivonen, and A. I. Verkamo. Finding interesting rules from large sets of discovered association rules. In *Proceedings of the Third International Conference on Information and Knowledge Management*, pages 401–407, 1994.

[Kyburg and Teng, 2001] Henry E. Kyburg, Jr. and Choh Man Teng. *Uncertain Inference*. Cambridge University Press, 2001.

[Liu *et al.*, 1999] B. Liu, W. Hsu, and Y. Ma. Pruning and summarizing the discovered associations. In *Proceedings of the ACM SIGKDD Conference on Knowledge Discovery and Data Mining*, pages 125–134, 1999.

[Ng *et al.*, 1998] Raymond T. Ng, Laks V. S. Lakshmanan, Jiawei Han, and Alex Pang. Exploratory mining and pruning optimizations of constrained association rules. In *Proceedings of the ACM SIGMOD International Conference on Management of Data*, pages 13–24, 1998.

[Silberschatz and Tuzhilin, 1996] A. Silberschatz and A. Tuzhilin. What makes patterns interesting in knowledge discovery systems. *IEEE Transactions on Knowledge and Data Engineering*, 8(6):970–974, 1996.

[Teng and Hewett, 2002] Choh Man Teng and Rattikorn Hewett. Associations, statistics, and rules of inference. In *Proceedings of the International Conference on Artificial Intelligence and Soft Computing*, pages 102–107, 2002.

[Teng, 2003] Choh Man Teng. A comparison of standard and interval association rules. In *Proceedings of the Sixteenth International Florida Artificial Intelligence Research Society Conference*, 2003. To appear.

[Zaki, 2000] Mohammed Javeed Zaki. Generating non-redundant association rules. In *Proceedings of the Sixth ACM SIGKDD Conference on Knowledge Discovery and Data Mining*, pages 34–43, 2000.

Line Chart Recognition and Data Extraction Technique

Md. Khademul Islam Molla[1], Kamrul Hasan Talukder[2], and
Md. Altab Hossain[1]

[1] Department of Computer Science and Technology, University of Rajshahi, Rajshahi 6205,
Bangladesh
{khadem_ru, altab75}@yahoo.com
[2] Computer Science and Engineering Discipline, Khulna University, Khulna 9208, Bangladesh
kamrul9375@yahoo.com

Abstract. This paper presents a system for recognizing line chart and extraction of data from the chart. This system includes three parts: preprocessing of the chart image, detection of line chart area bounded by the coordinate axes and the extraction of data from the detected chart area. The axes are detected using the projection method taking over the chart image. Then all the texts are filtered by connected component analysis. The data are extracted from the chart using sequential scanning process through the region of the line chart and calculating the relative distance of the data points from the both axes.

1 Introduction

Chart is a powerful representation of data relationship between variables. It is very easy to understand the affinity among the entities come out from any experiment by observing the chart rather than the entire data table used to generate the chart. Charts are usually used to represent the result and information of scientific and business experiments in many books, research papers, newspapers etc. [1]. Though textual information is still the major source of data, there has been an increasing trend of introducing graphs, pictures and figures into the information pool [2].

In document image processing, form or table recognition has been a topic of intensive research in the last decade. But charts have not yet drawn much attention. Most of the work in the graphics recognition of document images has been reported in circuit diagrams, geographic maps, engineering drawings [3]. The major reason for the difficulty of chart recognition is the variety of chart styles. Among different types of charts, line chart is widely used for graphical representation of text data. Our work focuses on the recognition and data extraction from a single-line chart image.

In this paper a simple model is presented for the general single-line chart. Matching the model with the input chart recognizes the data area of the line chart. Then the data is extracted by sequential scanning through the recognized data area and finally it is represented as a tabular form after some post processing.

2 Preprocessing and Chart Area Recognition

The document image containing the line chart is scanned and saved as 8 bit gray level image to make the input image file. The gray levels of the image are scaled and

J. Liu et al. (Eds.): IDEAL 2003, LNCS 2690, pp. 865–870, 2003.

translated into the binary range 0 to 1 for better processing efficiency [4]. Any line chart does not contain only the graph line. It is also composed of chart tittle, axes tittles, labels of the axes values, scaling lines, comments of the graph properties etc. as shown in Fig 1(a).

For any given line chart we search for the above components regions. By data area or chart area we mean the region containing the graph line of the chart. The coordinate axes and the origin are detected to find the data area of the chart using the projection method. The projection is very much like to the histogram of an image in which each line indicates the number of foreground pixels along that line in image. The horizontal and vertical projection along with chart is shown in Fig 1(b).

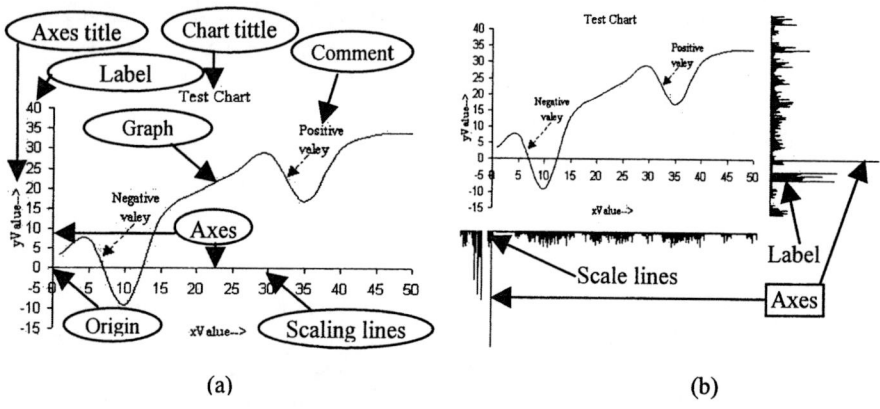

(a)   (b)

Fig. 1. (a) Simple model of line chart. (b) Line chart and its horizontal and vertical projections

Usually the axes are the largest continuous lines in a line chart and produce the largest peak in the projections. From the projection data the position of the axes are easily determined. The starting and ending points of every long line (longer than a specified threshold length related to the dimension of the graph image) are also settled. To detect the long lines we have also considered any small breaking of lines due to noise in the input image. Now we are discussing some different situations that may be occurred in the line graph image.

(a) When the axes are appeared as a rectangle as shown in Fig 2(a), then two long lines are produced in each projection. The lower one in the horizontal projection is selected as the x-axis and the left one is the y-axis in the vertical projection.

(b) When the whole chart is bounded by a rectangle as shown in Fig 2(b), then there exist two extra lines in both vertical and horizontal projections. These lines do not have the scale lines (projection) adjacent to the projection of the long lines. Then the search is preceded for the next long line, which has the scale lines adjacent to its projection. These lines are selected as the axes lines by same procedure as described above.

The vertical projection is scanned from left to right and from bottom to top for the horizontal one. The final model of sequence to detect the axes is: long line or not→some text elements→scale lines→long line connected with the scale lines. The last long line is the axis line and it is located in the first half of the chart projection. The starting and ending points of the axes are already determined during the computation of the projection.

Also the scale line area is marked to be used in the data extraction process. Solving the straight-line equations of the axes, the origin is settled down. The chart area or data area is the rectangular area bounded by the axes lines determined here as shown in Fig 2(b). In the chart area there exists many other text and graphics elements along with the graph line. The next section describes the process to filter out the components rather than the graph line from the chart area.

3 Graph Line Detection

The graph line is extracted by filtering out the other components using connected component

labeling and separation. Connected components labeling scans an image and groups its pixels into components based on pixel connectivity [5]. Once all groups have been determined, each group of pixels is labeled with a distinct number or level to identify each connected component. Extracting and labeling of various disjoint and connected components in an image is central to many automated image analysis applications [6]. The labeling operator scans the image until it comes to a point p of value 1 where p denotes the pixel to be labeled in the binary image. We have used 8-connectivity for foreground and 4-connectivity for background pixels.

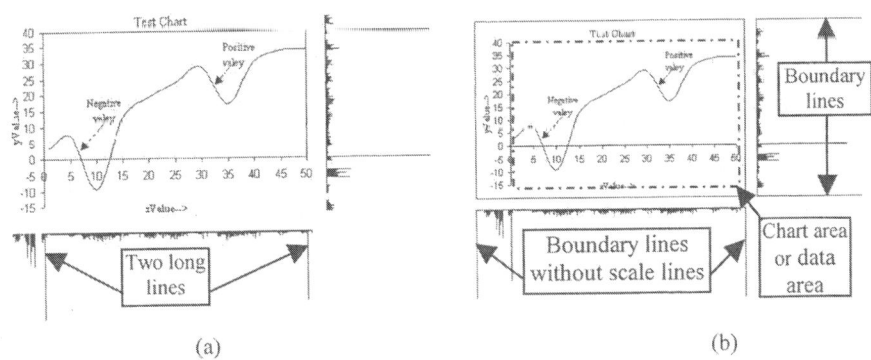

Fig. 2. (a) Line chart and its projection with rectangular type axes. (b) The graph bounded by the rectangle and its projections

To formulate the adjacency criterion for connectivity, we first introduce the notation of neighborhood. For a pixel p with the coordinates (x, y) the set of pixels given by $N_4(p) = \{(x+1, y), (x-1, y), (x, y+1), (x, y-1)\}$, is called its 4-neighbors. Its 8-neighbors are defined as $N_8(p) = N_4(p) \cup \{(x+1, y+1), (x+1, y-1), (x-1, y+1), (x-1, y-1)\}$. Two pixels p and q, both having values from a set V are 4-connected if q is from the set $N_4(p)$ and 8-connected if q is from $N_8(p)$. An example of a binary image with two connected components which are based on 4-connectivity is shown in Fig 3(a). If the connectivity were based on 8-connectivity, the two connected components would merge into one. The connected component labeling algorithm uses the well-known recursive procedure to assign an individual label to each component [7].

During the labeling process the mass (total number of on pixels) and the dimension (width and height) of all the components are determined. The small graphics components (small arrow, lines etc.) are filtered out by mass filtering. Dimensions and mass are collectively used for text-graphics separation by choosing some thresholds. Fig 3(b) shows the chart after filtering out all the components from the data area except the graph line.

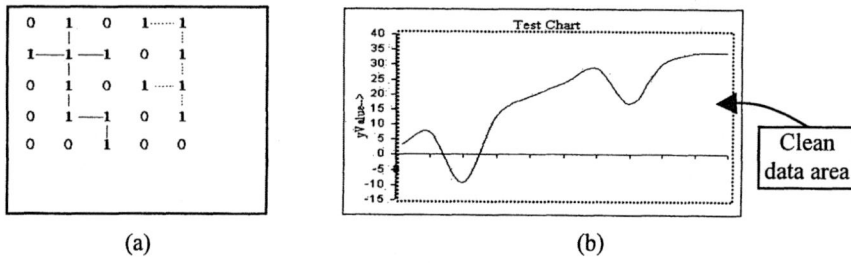

(a)   (b)

Fig. 3. (a) Two connected components based on 4-connectivity. (b) Chart image after filtering out the additional components (*clean data area*)

4 Data Extraction

We have already detected the position of the axes lines as well as the area containing the scale lines adjacent to it. The data extraction is performed easily by sequential scanning from the upper left corner to lower right corner of the clean data area. When the pointer encounters axis line or the scale line region, it just skips the region. If it meets any foreground pixel on the graph line, the distances of that pixel from both the axes are calculated. The distance from the y and x axis represent the x and y coordinates respectively of the pixel located point. The scanning process scans the graph line for every pixel along the x-axis whereas it tabulates the values with a significant deviation of the y axis values. Sometimes it appears the different values of y coordinate for the same value of the x coordinate as shown in Fig 4.

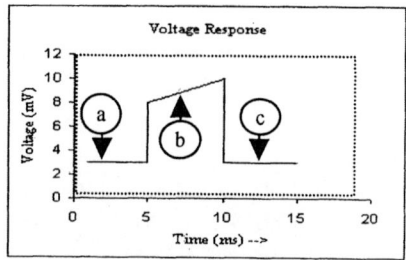

Fig. 4. Line chart with sharp line along both the axes

In the data area of Fig 4 does not contain any axis since whole the graph line contained in the positive portion of the both axes. For the regions 'a' and 'c' of the graph, there is no deviation of the y value. Avoiding the redundant values, only the starting and ending points of theses regions are tabulated as the extracted data. For the part 'b', considering the threshold value of the y deviation more than two values are tabulated. For the sharp lines along y axis, no deviation is encountered in the x values. Theses regions are tabulated by inserting two end points of the each line for the same value of x coordinate. The extracted data from the line chart of Fig 4 is tabulated in Table 1. The tabulated x and y values represent the pixel distances for the y and x axis respectively.

Table 1. Data extracted from the Chart of Figure 4

x	10	51	51	59	69	79	92	103	103	154
y	30	30	80	83	87	91	96	100	30	30

We have tested this system using different types of line charts from various books and journal papers. The efficiency of the recognition is with a reasonable scale. This system can be easily used for practical data extraction from line chart if the data is converted to the real scale data.

5 Conclusions

This system is very useful for the data extraction from any two variables line chart. If any OCR is used to detect and recognize the text which we have filtered out the relative data can
easily be converted to the real data table from which the chart is drawn. One limitation of this system is that it is unable to detect the axes as well as the chart area if the chart is slanted by a greater amount of degree. In future work, we are expecting to overcome this limitation by using line detection algorithm instead of projection method as well as to recognize legend based multi line chart.

References

1. Md. Khademul Islam Molla, Ramesh Chandra Debnath and M. Ganjer Ali: Data Extraction from Graph-Image and Formation of Equation. International Conference on Computer and Information Technology (ICCIT), pp 11–15, Shahjalal University, Sylhet, Bangladesh (1999)
2. Y. Zhou, Chew Lim Tan: Learning-Based Scientific Chart Recognition. Graphics Recognition Workshop (GREC), pp. 482–492, Kingston, Ontario, Canada (2001)
3. Y. Zhou, Chew Lim Tan: Hough Technique for Bar Charts Detection and Recognition in Document Images. ICIP 2000 International Conference on Image Processing, Vol. II, pp. 605–608, Vancouver, Canada (2000)

4. Kamrul Hasan Talukder, Md. Khademul Islam Molla: Performance Analysis of Back-Propagation Learning Algorithm for Handwritten Digit Classification. INMIC2002 International Multi Topic Conference (IEEE—KIIT) Karachi, Pakistan (2002)
5. Md. Khademul Islam Molla, Kamrul Hasan Talukder: Bangla Number Extraction and Recognition from Document Image. International Conference on Computer and Information Technology (ICCIT), East West University, Dhaka, Bangladesh (2002)
6. Dacheng Wang, Sargur N. Shihari: Analysis of Form Images. Department of Computer Science, State University of New York at Buffalo, Buffalo, NY 14228-2567, USA.
7. R. Mukundan: Binary Vision Algorithms in Java. Faculty of Information Technology, Multimedia University, 75450 Melaka, Malaysia.

List Representation Applied to Sparse Datacubes for Data Warehousing and Data Mining

Frank Wang[1], Frahi Marir[1], John Gordon[2], and Na Helian[1]

[1]Department of Computing
London Metropolitan University
166-220 Holloway Road
London N7 8DB, United Kingdom
f.wang@londonmet.ac.uk

[2]e-Science Centre
CCLRC Rutherford Appleton Laboratory
Didcot
Oxfordshire OX11 0QX, United Kingdom
j.c.gordon@rl.ac.uk

Abstract. Typically 80% of the data in the logical OLAP datacube, the core engine of data warehouses, are zero. When it comes to sparse, the performance quickly degrades due to the heavy I/O overheads in sorting and merging intermediate results. In this work, we first introduce a list representation in main memory for storing and computing datasets. The sparse transaction dataset is compressed as the empty cells are removed Accordingly we propose a new algorithm for association rule mining on the platform of list representation, which just needs to scan the transaction database once to generate all the possible rules. In contrast, the well-known apriori algorithm requires repeated scans of the databases, thereby resulting in heavy I/O accesses particularly when considering large candidate datasets. In our opinion, this new algorithm using list representation economizes storage space and accesses.

1   Introduction

With huge amounts of data collected in various kinds of applications, data warehouse is becoming a mainstream information repository for decision support and data analysis mainly because a data warehouse facilitates on-line analytical processing (OLAP). The core engine of data warehouses is the datacube. This model views data in the form of a data cube. A data cube allows data to be modeled and viewed in multiple dimensions. It is defined by dimensions and facts. In general terms, dimensions are the perspectives or entities with respect to which an organization wants to keep records. The fact table contains the names of the facts, or measures, as well as keys to each of the related dimension table.

Typically 80% of the data in the logical OLAP cube are zero[1]. When it comes to sparse data cubes, the performance quickly degrades due to the heavy I/O overheads in sorting and merging intermediate results. So a simple way is to compress the sparse array such that the empty cells are removed. In this work, we introduce an efficient method of list representation for storing and computing datasets to support OLAP and data mining.

J. Liu et al. (Eds.): IDEAL 2003, LNCS 2690, pp. 871–875, 2003.

2   List Representations

There are several list implementations. The linked list consists of a series of nodes, which are not necessarily adjacent in memory. Each node contains the element and a link to a node containing its successor[2]. We might need to examine every node of the list when searching a linked list. To execute find(x), we merely start at the first node in the list and then sequentially traverse the list by following the next links. The operation is clearly linear-time. To avoid such a proportional increase in search time, skip-lists[3] have been introduced. In a linked list every other node has an additional link to the node two ahead of it in the list. Because of this, at most [N/2]+1 nodes are examined in the worst case. We can extend this idea. Here, every fourth node has a link to the node four ahead. Only [N/4]+2 nodes are examined. In general, every 2ith node has a link to the node 2i ahead of it. The total number of links has only doubled, but now at most [logN] nodes are examined during a search. It is not hard to see that the total time spent for search is O[logN], because the search consists of either advancing to a new node or dropping to a lower link in the same node. Each of these steps consumes at most O[logN] total time during a search. Notice that the search in this data structure is essentially a binary search. Roughly half the nodes are level 1 nodes, roughly a quarter are level 2, and, in general, approximately ½ nodes are level i. To perform a find, we start at the highest link at the header. We traverse along this level until we find that next node is larger than the one we are looking for (or NULL). When this occurs, we go to the next lower level and continue the strategy. When progress is stopped at level 1, either we are in front of the node we are looking for, or it is not in the list.

3   A New Algorithm for Association Rule Mining

Association rule mining is a powerful method for so-called shopping basket analysis, which aims at finding regularities in the shopping behaviour of customers of supermarkets, mail-order companies, on-line shops and the like. With the association rules one tries to find sets of products that are frequently bought together, so that from the presence of certain products in a shopping cart one can infer (with a high probability) that certain other products are present. Such information, expressed in the form of association rules, can often be used to increase the number of items sold, for instance, by appropriately arranging the products in the shelves of a supermarket (they may, for example, be placed adjacent to each other in order to invite even more customers to buy them together)[4]. Among the best known algorithms is the apriori algorithm[5]. This algorithm works in two steps: In a first step the frequent itemsets are determined. These are sets of items that have at least the given minimum support (i.e., occur at least in a given percentage of all transactions). In the second step association rules are generated from the frequent itemsets found in the first step. Usually the first step is the more important, because it accounts for the greater part of the processing time. In order to make it efficient, the apriori algorithm exploits the simple observation that no superset of an infrequent itemset (i.e., an itemset not having minimum support) can be frequent (can have enough support). It is generally acknowledged that the apriori technique works well in terms of reducing the candidate set. However, there are some criticisms[6] where there are many patterns, long patterns or low support thresholds: 1. Many candidate items sets must still be generated; 2. Requires repeated scans of the databases thereby resulting in heavy I/O accesses particularly when considering large candidate sets.

In this paper we proposed a new association rule mining algorithm on the platform of list representation, which just needs to scan the transaction database once to generate all the possible rules. In order to find the frequent itemsets, we have to count the transactions. The simplest way of processing the transactions is to handle them individually and to apply to each of them the recursive counting procedure described in apriori algorithm[5]. However, the recursion is a very expensive procedure involving frequent I/O operations and degrading the system performance. On the other hand, it does not suit the naturally linear data structure of the list representation, which is introduced to make the data mining more space efficient. In a linked list, we might need to examine every node of the list when searching for a desired node. The time to perform such a search (a sequential node-by-node procedure) is proportional to the number of nodes that have to be examined, which is at most N (the length of the list). Therefore it is worth considering how it can be improved.

Our algorithm is a purely sequential (rather than recursive) count procedure which is well compatible with the list representation. To count a certain transaction (represented by a list), we merely start at the first node (item) in the list and then sequentially traverse the list by following the next links. In computing the counters for 1-itemset a, b, c, d, e, we will have scanned each of the 5 items in the transaction. "Is there a way to avoid having to rescan all these items for the computation of other counters, such as ab, abc, abcd and abcde?" The answer is. When the any item (if exists) is scanned, its contribution will be comprehensively taken into account. For example, when the first item (a) in the transaction is being scanned (say, for the computation of the counter for the 1-itemset a), all of other $k(k>1)$-itemsets ab, ac, abc, abcd and abcde, relating to a (inversely, a is subset of these k-itemsets), can be simultaneously computed. That is, each counter of the four 2-itemsets, ab, ac, ad and ae, each counter of the six 3-itemsets, abc, abd, abe, acd, ace and ade, each counter of the four 4-itemsets, abcd, abce, abde and acde, the counter of the 5-itemset, abcde, should be incremented then as well. In other words, such a multiway computation aggregates to each of the relating $k(k>1)$-itemsets while a 1-itemset is being examined. In computation, the counter for the 1-itemset a is incremented by 1. Note that the counter for the 2-itemset ab should be incremented by 0.5 only as a=1 just contributes 1/2 to the 2-itemset ab, and so on. Similarly the counter for the 3-itemset abc is incremented by 0.334 (0.334 rather than 0.333 is used to compensate the machine representation error of the decimal number) as a=1 contributes 1/3 to abc. For 4-itemset 1/4 is incremented; for 5-itemset 1/5 is incremented, and so on. After the first item a is examined, the second item b of the transaction, currently being scaned, is examined in a similar way. When b=1, ab=ab+0.5 is carried out, which makes the final count number in the counter ab is 1, fairly reflecting the contribution from its two subsets a and b. After the current transaction is completely inspected, a post-processing is needed. A function floor(x), which finds the largest integer not greater than x, is carried out to rounds down each counter. The insufficient contributions (less than 1) will be removed, which implies the corresponding itemset is not supported by the current transaction.

After the whole database is scanned, the counters for the all possible itemsets, organised in a full itemset tree, is obtained. This is a full itemset tree for the five items a, b, c, d and e. It is not hard to see that this tree is equivalent to the provided transaction database in terms of finding the frequent itemsets. Organising the counters in a full itemset tree not only allows us to store them efficiently (using little memory), but also supports generating the rules. Each canonical attribute sequence S denotes a counter for an itemset S. The circled itemsets (infrequent itemsets) will be pruned since they do not have minimum support.

4   Experiment Results

The performance of a data mining system is determined by two criteria: processing time and memory utilization. The association rule mining algorithm using list representation is designed to economize storage space and accesses, and we must show that this overriding concern for speed is compatible with a reasonable utilization of available space. Our experiment with association rule mining algorithm using list representation is based on a simulation program coded in Borland C++ 5.02. For ease of displaying results graphically, the two-dimensional case and the three-dimensional case are considered. Because what we use are a group of one-dimensional arrays, the performance would not be worse in higher dimensional grid space in principle. The program runs on an Intel Pentium III machine under the Windows XP operating system. The CPU frequency is 1.2 GHz. The physical memory size is 512 MB and virtual memory size is 1GB.

Table 1. Experiment results on Windows XP machine. While disk-block accesses are involved, the average retrieval time increase dramatically.

No. of transactions	Items/ transaction	Sparse ratio (non-zero/total)	Memory Storage	Transaction Preparation(ms)	Rule Mining (ms) [5 itemset max]	Memory Used(MB)	Disk Access?
100000	1000	10%	Array	2804	3014	382	No
100000	1000	20%	Array	3034	3084	382	No
100000	1000	25%	Array	3145	3054	382	No
100000	1000	30%	Array	3265	3074	382	No
100000	1000	60%	Array	3915	3105	382	No
100000	1000	10%	List	2193	2273	147	No
100000	1000	20%	List	4527	4857	294	No
100000	1000	25%	List	5608	5798	367	No
100000	1000	30%	List	6730	7060	440	Yes
100000	1000	60%	List	40989	158468	990	Yes

Since the association rule mining algorithm using list representation is designed to handle large volume of data, real-time visualization of memory usage by far the most important point. For this purpose, the Performance Monitor in the system tools was used. The sample spaces used in the experiments are as follows: item values of each transaction are determined by a small program generating the database repeatedly.

Table 1 summarizes the experiment results on Windows XP machine. The simulation confirms that the mining time against a list is proportional to its sparse ratio whereas the mining time against an array is independent of its sparse ratio. The simulation also confirms that the memory space against a list is proportional to its sparse ratio whereas the memory space against an array is independent of its sparse ratio. The mining time increases dramatically when the sparse ratio exceeds 30%. This is because 512MB (physical memory size) is an important threshold for main memory databsets. While the data mining application space (commit memory) plus operating system space (kernel memory) is below this threshold, all the operations are internal without accessing the external storage devices. It takes limited amount time. When the threshold is overtaken, virtual memory technique would be activated and frequent disk-block accesses would be involved. It takes a relatively long time to fulfill an operation. Normally we just count the number of disk accesses into access time.

5   Conclusions

The new association rule mining algorithm, specially designed on the platform of list representation, just needs to scan the transaction database once to generate all the possible rules. To count a certain transaction (represented by a list), we merely start at the first node (item) in the list and then sequentially traverse the list by following the next links. The contribution from each node (item) will be comprehensively taken into account. However, it is not without drawback with this new algorithm. In the first step of finding frequent itemsets, we even count those itemset which are not frequent although they will be pruned eventually. Based on the observation that if any given set of attributes S is not adequately supported, any superset of S will also not be adequately supported and consequently any effort to calculate the support for such supersets is wasted. However, considering the advantage of space saving brought by the introduction of list representation and another advantage of performance improving brought by avoiding heavy I/O operations as the transaction database is just scanned once, this new algorithm using list representation presents us with a broad range of trade-offs based on speed requirement and storage requirement.

References

[1]   G.Colliat, OLAP, relational and multidimensional database system, SIGMOD Record, 25:64–69, 1996

[2]   Clifford A. Shaffer, Data Structures and Algorithm Analysis, Prentice Hall, 2001

[3]   William Pugh, Skip Lists: A Probabilistic Alternative to Balanced Trees, Communications of the ACM, 33(6):668–676, June 1990

[4]   Christian Borgelt and Rudolf Kruse, Induction of Association Rules: Apriori Implementation, Accepted to the 14th Conference on Computational Statistics (Compstat 2002, Berlin, Germany)

[5]   Agrawal, R., Imielienski, T., and Swami, A., Mining Association Rules between Sets of Items in Large Databases. In: Proc. Conf. on Management of Data, 207–216. New York: ACM Press, 1993

[6]   Han, J., Pei, J., and Yin, Y., Mining Frequent Patterns without Candidate Generation. In: Proc. Conf. on the Management of Data (SIGMOD'00, Dallas, TX). New York: ACM Press,

A Fast Algorithm for Incremental Principal Component Analysis[*]

Juyang Weng, Yilu Zhang, and Wey-Shiuan Hwang

Department of Computer Science and Engineering
Michigan State University
East Lansing, MI 48824, USA

Abstract. We introduce a fast incremental principal component analysis (IPCA) algorithm, called candid covariance-free IPCA (CCIPCA), to compute the principal components of a sequence of samples incrementally without estimating the covariance matrix (thus covariance-free). This new method is for real-time applications where no iterations are allowed and high-dimensional inputs are involved, such as appearance-based image analysis. CCIPCA is motivated by the concept of statistical efficiency (the estimate has the smallest variance given the observed data). The convergence rate of CCIPCA is very high compared with other IPCA algorithms on high-dimensional data, although the highest possible efficiency is not guaranteed because of the unknown sample distribution.

1 Introduction

A well-known computational approach to principal component analysis (PCA) involves solving an eigensystem problem, i.e., computing the eigenvectors and eigenvalues of the sample covariance matrix, using a numerical method such as the power method and the QR method [1]. This approach requires that all the training images are available before the principal components can be estimated. This is called a batch method. This type of methods no longer satisfy an upcoming new trend of computer vision research [2], in which all visual filters are incrementally derived from very long online real-time video stream, motivated by the development of animal vision systems. Further, when the dimension of the image is high, both the computation and storage complexity grow dramatically. For example, in the eigenface method, a moderate grey image of 64 rows and 88 columns results in a d-dimensional vector with $d = 5632$. The symmetric covariance matrix requires $d(d + 1)/2$ elements, which amounts to 15,862,528 entries! A clever saving method can be used when the number of images is smaller than the number of pixels in the image [3]. However, an online developing system must derive principal components from an open number of images and adapt to the possible non-stationary (changing) characteristic of the data. Thus,

---

[*] The work is supported in part by National Science Foundation under grant No. IIS 9815191, DARPA ETO under contract No. DAAN02-98-C-4025, and DARPA ITO under grant No. DABT63-99-1-0014. The authors would like to thank Shaoyun Chen for his codes to do batch PCA.

J. Liu et al. (Eds.): IDEAL 2003, LNCS 2690, pp. 876–881, 2003.

an incremental method is required to compute the principal components for observations arriving sequentially, where the estimate of principal components are updated by each arriving observation vector.

2   The Algorithm

Suppose that sample vectors are acquired sequentially, $u(1), u(2), \ldots$, possibly infinite. Each $u(n)$, $n = 1, 2, \ldots$, is a d-dimensional vector. Without loss of generality, we can assume that $u(n)$ has a zero mean (the mean may be incrementally estimated and subtracted out). The proposed candid covariance-free incremental PCA (CCIPCA) algorithm is shown in Fig. 1.

For $n = 1, 2, \ldots$, do,
  1. $u_1(n) = u(n)$.
  2. For $i = 1, 2, \ldots, k$, do,
    2.1. If $i < n$,

$$v_i(n) = \frac{n-1-l}{n} v_i(n-1) + \frac{1+l}{n} u_i(n) u_i^T(n) \frac{v_i(n-1)}{||v_i(n-1)||}, \tag{1}$$

$$u_{i+1}(n) = u_i(n) - u_i^T(n) \frac{v_i(n)}{||v_i(n)||} \frac{v_i(n)}{||v_i(n)||}. \tag{2}$$

    2.2. If $i = n$, initialize the ith eigenvector, $v_i(n) = u_i(n)$.
    2.3. If $i > n$, initialize the ith eigenvector, $v_i(n) = 0$.

Fig. 1. The CCIPCA algorithm to compute the first k dominant eigenvectors, $v_1(n), v_2(n), \ldots, v_k(n)$, directly from $u(n)$, where $n = 1, 2, \ldots$. l, an amnesic parameter, gives more weight on new data so that old data will gradually fade out.

The derivation of CCIPCA is motivated by statistical efficiency. An unbiased estimate $\hat{Q}$ of the parameter Q is said to be the *efficient estimate for the class D of distribution functions* if for every distribution density function $f(u, Q)$ of D the variance $D^2(\hat{Q})$ (squared error) has reached the minimal value given by

$$D^2(\hat{Q}) = E[(\hat{Q} - Q)^2] \geq \frac{1}{n \int_{-\infty}^{+\infty} \left[\frac{\partial \log f(u,Q)}{\partial Q} \right]^2 f(u, Q) du}. \tag{3}$$

The right side of inequality (3) is called Cramér-Rao bound. It says that the efficient estimate is one that has the least variance from the real parameter, and its variance is bounded below by the Cramér-Rao bound. For example, the sample mean, $\bar{w} = \frac{1}{n} \sum_{i=1}^{n} w(i)$, is the efficient estimate of the mean of a Gaussian distribution with a known standard deviation σ [4].

If we define $w_i(n) = u_i(n) u_i^T(n) \frac{v_i(n-1)}{||v_i(n-1)||}$ and ignore the amnesic parameter, $v_i(n)$ can be viewed as the mean of "samples" $w_i(n)$. That is exactly why our method is motivated by the statistical efficiency in using averaging. In other words, statistically, the method tends to converge most quickly or the estimate has the smallest error variance given the currently observed samples. Of course, $w_i(n)$ is not necessarily drawn from a Gaussian distribution independently and thus the estimate using the sample mean in the algorithm is not strictly efficient. However, the estimate $v_i(n)$ still has a high statistical efficiency and has a fairly low error variance as we will show experimentally.

IPCA algorithms have been studied by several researchers [5] [6] [7] [8]. An early work with a rigorous proof for convergence was given by Oja & Karhunen [7] [8], where they introduced their stochastic gradient ascent (SGA) algorithm. SGA computes,

$$\tilde{v}_i(n) = v_i(n-1) + \gamma_i(n)u(n)u^T(n)v_i(n-1) \tag{4}$$

$$v_i(n) = \text{orthonormalize } \tilde{v}_i(n) \text{ w.r.t. } v_j(n), j = 1, 2, \dots, i-1 \tag{5}$$

where, $v_i(n)$ is the estimate of the i-th dominant eigenvectors of the sample covariance matrix $A = E\{u(n)u^T(n)\}$, and $\tilde{v}_i(n)$ is the new estimate. In practice, the orthonormalization in Eq.(5) can be done by a standard *Gram-Schmidt Orthonomalization* (GSO) procedure. The parameter $\gamma_i(n)$ is a stochastic approximation gain.

SGA is essentially a gradient method, associated with which is the problem of choosing $\gamma_i(n)$, the learning rate. Simply speaking, the learning rate should be appropriate so that the second term (the correction term) on the right side of Eq. (4) is comparable to the first term, neither too large nor too small. Contrasted with SGA, the first term on the right side of Eq. (1) is not normalized. In effect, $v_i(n)$ in Eq. (1) converges to $\lambda_i e_i$ instead of e_i as it does in Eq. (4), where λ_i is the i-th dominant eigenvalue and e_i is the corresponding eigenvector. The statistical efficiency is realized by keeping the scale of the estimate at the same order of the new observations (the first and second terms properly weighted on the right side of Eq. (1) to get sample mean), which allows fully use of every observation in terms of statistical efficiency. Note that the coefficient $(n-1)/n$ in Eq. (1) is as important as the "learning rate" $1/n$ in the second term to realize sample mean. Thus, one does not need to worry about the nature of the observations. This is also the reason that we used "candid" in naming the new algorithm. It is true that the series of parameters, $\gamma_i(n)$, $i = 1, 2, ..., k$, in SGA can be manually tuned in an off-line application so that it takes into account the magnitude of $u(n)$. But an online algorithm must automatically compute data-sensitive parameters.

In SGA, the higher order eigenvectors are computed by a GSO procedure, which is time-consuming. Further, breaking-then-recovering orthogonality slows down the convergence compared with keeping orthogonality all along. We know eigenvectors are orthogonal to each other. So, it helps to generate "observations" only in a complementary space for the computation of the higher order eigenvectors. For example, to compute the second order eigenvector, we first subtract from the data its projection on the estimated first order eigenvector $v_1(n)$, $u_2(n) = u_1(n) - u_1^T(n)\frac{v_1(n)}{||v_1(n)||}\frac{v_1(n)}{||v_1(n)||}$, where $u_1(n) = u(n)$. The obtained residual, $u_2(n)$, which is in the complementary space of $v_1(n)$, serves as the input data to the iteration step. In this way, the orthogonality is always enforced when the convergence is reached, although not exactly so at early stages. A similar idea has been used by some other researchers [9] [10]. However, in both cases, the statistical efficiency was not considered.

3   Empirical Results on Convergence

We conducted several experiments to study the statistical efficiency of the new algorithm as well as the existing IPCA algorithms, especially for high dimensional data such as images. Because of space limit, presented here are only the results on the FERET face data set [11]. This data set has frontal views of 457 subjects. Most of the subjects have two views while 34 of them have four views and two of them have one view, which results in a data set of 982 images. The size of each image is 88-by-64 pixels, or 5632 dimensions.

We computed the eigenvectors using a batch PCA with QR method [12] and used them as our ground truth. Since the real mean of the image data is unknown, we incrementally estimated the sample mean $\hat{m}(n)$ by $\hat{m}(n) = \frac{n-1}{n}\hat{m}(n-1) + \frac{1}{n}x(n)$, where $x(n)$ is the nth sample image. The data entering the IPCA algorithms are the scatter vectors, $u(n) = x(n) - \hat{m}(n), n = 1, 2, \ldots$.

To record intermediate results, we divided the entire data set into 20 subsets. When the data went through the IPCA algorithms, the estimates of the eigenvectors were saved after each subset was passed. In SGA, we used the learning rate suggested in [7, page 54]. Since only the first five γ_i were suggested, we extrapolated them to give $\gamma_6(n) = 46/n$, $\gamma_7(n) = 62/n$, $\gamma_8(n) = 80/n$, $\gamma_9(n) = 100/n$, and, $\gamma_{10}(n) = 130/n$. In GHA, we set $\gamma(n)$ as $1/n$.

The correlation between the estimated unit eigenvector v and the one computed by the batch method v', also normalized, is represented by their inner product $v \cdot v'$. Thus, the larger the correlation, the better. Since $\|v - v'\| = 2(1 - v \cdot v')$, $v = v'$ iff $v \cdot v' = 1$. As we can see from Fig. 2, SGA does not seem to converge after fed all images. GHA shows a trend to converge but the estimates are still far from the correct ones. In contrast, the proposed CCIPCA converges fast. Although the higher order eigenvectors converges slower than earlier ones, the 10th one still reaches about 70%.

To examine the convergence of eigenvalues, we use the ratio, $\frac{\|v_i\|}{\lambda_i}$, the length of the estimated eigenvector divided by the estimate computed by the C Recipe batch method. The results for eigenvalues show a similar pattern as in Fig. 2. For conciseness, we only shown the eigenvalue result of the proposed CCIPCA in Fig. 3. The ratio between the summation of the first 10 eigenvalues and the variance of the data is 58.82%, which means that about 60% of the data variance falls into the subspace spanned by the first 10 eigenvectors.

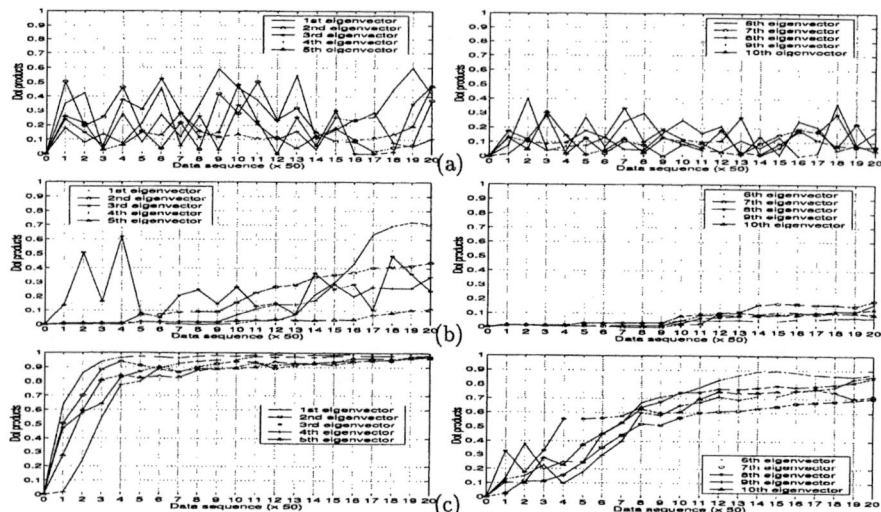

Fig. 2. The correctness, or the correlation, represented by dot products, of the first 10 eigenvectors computed by (a) SGA (b) GHA (c) the proposed CCIPCA with the amnesic parameter $l = 2$.

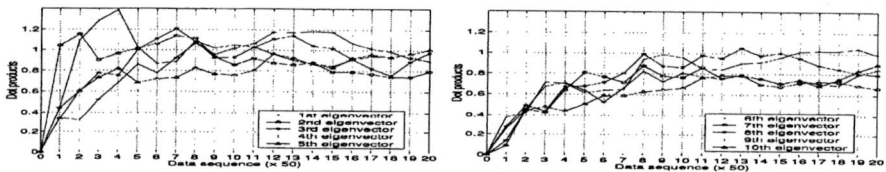

Fig. 3. The correctness of the eigenvalue, $\frac{\|v_i\|}{\lambda_i}$ by CCIPCA.

4   Conclusions

This short paper concentrates on a challenging issue of computing dominating eigenvectors and eigenvalues from incrementally arriving high dimensional data stream without computing the corresponding covariance matrix and without knowing data in advance. The proposed CCIPCA algorithm is fast in convergence rate and low in the computational complexity. Our results showed that whether the concept of the efficient estimate is used or not plays a dominating role in convergence speed for high dimensional data.

References

1. G. H. Golub and C. F. van Loan, *Matrix Computations*, The Johns Hopkins University Press, Baltimore, MD, 1989.
2. J. Weng and I. Stockman (eds), *Proceedings of NSF/DARPA Workshop on Development and Learning*, East Lansing, Michigan, April 5–7, 2000.

3. I. Sirovich and M. Kirby, "Low-dimensional procedure for the caracterization of human faces," *Journal of Optical Society of America A*, vol. 4, no. 3, pp. 519–524, March 1987.

4. M. Fisz, *Probability theory and mathematical statistics*, John Wiley & Sons, Inc., New York, third edition, 1963.

5. N.L. Owsley, "Adaptive data orthogonalization," in *Proc. IEEE Int'l Conf. Acoust., Speech and Signal Processing*, Tulsa, Oklahoma, April 10–12 1978, pp. 109–112.

6. P.A. Thompson, "An adaptive spectral analysis technique for unbiased frequency estimation in the presence of white noise," in *Proc. 13th Asilomar Conf. on Circuits, System and Computers*, Pacific Grove, CA, 1979, pp. 529–533.

7. E. Oja, *Subspace Methods of Pattern Recognition*, Research Studies Press, Letchworth, UK, 1983.

8. E. Oja and J. Karhunen, "On stochastic approximation of the eigenvectors and eigenvalues of the expectation of a random matrix," *Journal of Mathematical Analysis and Application*, vol. 106, pp. 69–84, 1985.

9. E. Kreyszig, *Advanced engineering mathematics*, Wiley, New York, 1988.

10. T.D. Sanger, "Optimal unsupervised learning in a single-layer linear feedforward neural network," *IEEE Trans. Neural Networks*, vol. 2, pp. 459–473, 1989.

11. P. J. Phillips, H. Moon, P. Rauss, and S. A. Rizvi, "The FERET evaluation methodology for face-recognition algorithms," in *Proc. IEEE Conf. Computer Vision and Pattern Recognition*, Puerto Rico, June 1997, pp. 137–143.

12. W.H. Press, B.P. Flannery, S.A. Teukolsky, and W.T. Vetterling, *Numerical Recips in C*, University Press, New York, 2nd edition, 1986

A Database-Independent Approach of Mining Association Rules with Genetic Algorithm

Xiaowei Yan, Chengqi Zhang, and Shichao Zhang

Faculty of Information Technology
University of Technology, Sydney
PO Box 123, Broadway, Sydney NSW 2007, Australia
{xyan, chengqi, zhangsc}@it.uts.edu.au

Abstract. *Apriori*-like algorithms for association rules mining rely upon the minimum support and the minimum confidence. Users often feel hard to give these thresholds. On the other hand, genetic algorithm is effective for global searching, especially when the searching space is so large that it is hardly possible to use deterministic searching method. We try to apply genetic algorithm to the association rules mining and propose an evolutionary method. Computations are conducted, showing that our *ARMGA* model can be used for the automation of the association rule mining systems, and the ideas given in this paper are effective.

1 Introduction

Association rule mining has been investigated by many researchers and practitioners for many years [1,?,?,?,2]. One widely-used approach is the support-confidence framework [1], where an association rule is an implication between two sets of items, and the interestingness of a rule is measured by two factors, its support and confidence. A rule is excavated out if and only if both of its confidence and support are greater than the minimum confidence and the minimum support, respectively. Therefore, users need to appropriately specify these two thresholds before they start their mining job. There are also other interestingness measures for association patterns. Although these measures are effective on mining interesting association rules, it is difficult for users to apply them if the users know little about the database to be mined. These models are consequently called to be database-dependent.

On the other hand, genetic algorithm is an efficient tool to do global searching work, especially when the searching space is too large to use deterministic searching method. This paper proposes an approach to mine the acceptable association rules by using a genetic algorithm. In the following sections, we begin with some reviews of applications of genetic algorithms on the field of data mining in Section 2. Then the details of our model are described in Section 3, followed by computational results in Section 4. Finally, we'll conclude our work in Section 5.

J. Liu et al. (Eds.): IDEAL 2003, LNCS 2690, pp. 882–886, 2003.

2   Some Related Work

There have been many applications of genetic algorithms in the field of data mining and knowledge discovery. Most of them are addressed to the problem of classification.

Usually, genetic algorithms for rules mining are partitioned into two categories according to their encoding of rules in the population of chromosomes [3]. One encoding method is called Michigan approach, where each rule is encoded into an individual. Another is referred to as Pittsburgh approach, with which a set of rules are encoded into a chromosome. For example, Fidelis et al gave a Michigan type of genetic algorithm to discover comprehensible classification rules, having an interesting chromosome encoding and introducing a specific mutation operator [4]. Pei et al, on the other hand, used the Pittsburgh approach for discovery of classes and feature patterns [5]. Other applications can be demonstrated by *SIAO1*, which finds the first-order-logic classification rules by generalizing a seed example [6]. A recent work which is also worthy to mention is the *dAR*, designed by W. Au and K. Chan for mining association rules or more exactly for discovering changing patterns in historical data [7].

Although it is known that genetic algorithm is good at searching for undetermined solution, it is still rare to see that genetic algorithm is used to mine association rules.

3   Algorithm

3.1   Modelling

Let $I = \{i_1, i_2, ..., i_n\}$ be a set of literals. i_k is called an item, where $k = 1, ...n$. An itemset is a set of items. The length of an itemset is the number of the items in the itemset. Itemset of length k is denoted as k-itemset. Then a transaction can be viewed as an itemset with variable length, and a database D can be defined as a set of transactions over I. The support of an itemset X, written as $supp(X)$, is the proportion of transactions in D, that contain X. An association rule is an implication, $X \rightarrow Y$, where $X, Y \subset I$, and $X \cap Y = \emptyset$. X is its antecedent and Y the consequent. Rule $X \rightarrow Y$ is a k-rule if $X \cup Y$ is a k-itemset. The support of the rule is defined as $supp(X \cup Y)$, and the confidence as $supp(X \cup Y)/supp(X)$.

The traditional task of mining association rules is how to find all rules $X \rightarrow Y$, such that the supports and confidences of the rules are larger than, or equal to, a minimum support, *minsupp*, and a minimum confidence, *minconf*, respectively.

In our model, called *ARMGA*, we require that the confidence $conf(X \rightarrow Y)$ should be larger than, or equal to, $supp(Y)$, because we only deal with positive association rules of the form $X \rightarrow Y$. Hence, we define the positive confidence of the rule as

$$pconf(X \rightarrow Y) = \frac{supp(X \cup Y) - supp(X)supp(Y)}{supp(X)(1 - supp(Y))}.$$

We now re-state the above mining task as follows. Given a rule length k, we search for some high-quality association k-rules, with their $pconfs$ acceptably maximized, by using a genetic algorithm.

3.2   Encoding

First we number and quote all items in $I = i_1, i_2, ..., i_n$ by their indexes. In other words, we can assume that the universal itemset $I = 1, 2, ..., n$. Given an association k-rule $X \rightarrow Y$, where $X, Y \subset I$, and $X \cap Y = \emptyset$, we encode it to an individual as

$$ j \quad A_1 \quad ... \quad A_j \quad A_{j+1} \quad ... \quad A_k $$

where j is an indicator that separates the antecedent from the consequent of the rule. That is, $X = A_1, ..., A_j$ and $Y = A_{j+1}, ..., A_k, 0 < j < k$. Therefore, a k-rule $X \rightarrow Y$ is represented by $k+1$ positive integers.

3.3   Operators

Operator $select(c, ps)$ acts as a filter of chromosome with considerations of their fitness and probability ps. It returns **TRUE** if chromosome c is successfully selected with probability ps, and otherwise **FALSE** if failed.

Operator $crossover(pop, pc)$ uses two-point strategy to reproduce offspring chromosomes at a probability of pc from population pop, and returns a new population. These two crossover points are randomly generated, such that any segment of chromosome may be chosen.

Operator $mutate(c, pm)$ occasionally changes genes of chromosome c at a probability of pm, besides considering the fitness of c as an additional weight.

3.4   Fitness Function and Initialization

We define the fitness function as

$$ fitness(c) = \frac{supp(A_1 ... A_k) - supp(A_1 ... A_j)supp(A_{j+1} ... A_k)}{supp(A_1 ... A_j)(1 - supp(A_{j+1} ... A_k))} $$

for a given chromosome c.

Given a seed chromosome s, we use the $mutate(s, pm)$ function to produce an initial population $pop[0]$, where we have $pm = 1$.

3.5   *ARMGA* Algorithm

Suppose that the current population is pop[i]. We first apply the $select$ operator to $pop[i]$, and produce a new population $pop[i+1]$. Then any pair of chromosomes in $pop[i + 1]$ are crossed over at a probability of pc to reproduce two offspring. Each new chromosome mutates at a probability of pm. *ARMGA* generates a population at last, with high-quality chromosomes.

population $ARMGA(s, ps, pc, pm)$
begin
    $i \leftarrow 0;$
    $pop[i] \leftarrow initialize(s);$
    while not $terminate(pop[i])$ **do**
    begin
        $pop[i + 1] \leftarrow \emptyset;$
        $pop\_temp \leftarrow \emptyset;$
        for $\forall c \in pop[i]$ **do**
            if $select(c, ps)$ **then**
                $pop[i + 1] \leftarrow pop[i + 1] \cup c;$
        $pop\_temp \leftarrow crossover(pop[i + 1], pc);$
        for $\forall c \in pop\_temp$ **do**
            $pop[i + 1] \leftarrow (pop[i + 1] - c) \cup mutate(c, pm);$
        $i \leftarrow i + 1;$
    end
    return $pop[i];$
end

$ARMGA$ stops, that is, the $terminate()$ function returns a non-zero value, if and only if one of the following cases occurs:

1) The difference between the best and the worst chromosome is less than a given value, α, which is small enough.
2) The number of iterations, i, is larger than a given maximum number $maxloop$.

4   Computation

We use the Mushroom database from **UCI** at $http://www.ics.uci.edu/\tilde{}mlearn$ to show the effectiveness of algorithm $ARMGA$. The dataset contains 8124 records and 23 attributes. We choose $ps = 0.95, pc = 0.85, pm = 0.01, k = 3, n = 118, s = (1, 34, 86, 85)$, etc.

    We run the program when $maxloop$ is given from 10 to 100 stepped with 10, from 100 to 1000 stepped with 100, and from 1000 to 9000 stepped with 1000, respectively. For example, some results when $maxloop$ is 10 are listed as follows.

$$34 \; 85 \; < - \; 86 \; (90\%)$$
$$34 \; < - \; 98 \; 86 \; (100\%)$$
$$34 \; < - \; 78 \; 86 \; (100\%)$$
$$\cdots \cdots \cdots$$

Results under other $maxloop$ values are similar. We also run a traditional $Apriori$-like algorithm when rule length is fixed to 3, the minimum support is set to 0%, and the minimum positive confidence is specified as 90%. The number of returned rules is 445978. Of course, the chromosomes, returned by $ARMGA$ with their positive confidence equal to or larger than 90%, are all among those mentioned above by the *Apriori*-like algorithm. Consequently, we can see that *ARMGA* is able to find some desired association rules with acceptable quality.

Moreover, we find that much different populations can be obtained each time we run *ARMGA*, even when the generation number grows up to 9000. The reason might be that there are too many rules with high quality according to the fitness function we defined in Section 3.4. Therefore we need to define a more strict fitness function. One of possible approaches is to additionally consider the minimum support threshold. In fact, the support measure is statistically significant, and requisite in the light of traditional association rules mining area. When the minimum support increases to 60%, the *Apriori*-like algorithm generates only 8 rules.

5   Summary

Existing approaches of association rules mining are usually database-dependent. It is difficult for users or even experts to appropriately specify the minimum support and minimum confidence as thresholds. In this paper, we investigate the possibility of applying genetic algorithm to association rules mining and propose the *ARMGA* algorithm. Computation results show that our *ARMGA* model is effective and promising, and there are many problems with *ARMGA* we need to study further. We need to do more computation at various databases and different parameters selections. We need to improve the fitness function.

References

1. Agrawal, R., Imielinski, T., Swami, A.: Mining association rules between sets of items in large databases. Proceedings of the 1993 ACM SIGMOD International Conference on Management of Data, Washington, DC, May 1993, 207–216
2. Wu, X., Zhang, C., Zhang, S.: Mining both positive and negative association rules. Proceedings of 19th International Conference on Machine Learning, Sydney, Australia, July 2002, 658–665
3. Freitas, A.: A survey of evolutionary algorithms for data mining and knowledge discovery. Advances in Evolutionary Computation, Springer-Verlag, Berlin, (2002)
4. Fidelis, M., Lopes, H., Freitas, A.: Discovering comprehensible classification rules with a genetic algorithm. Proc. of the 2000 Congress on Evolutionary Computation, La Jolla, CA, USA, July 2000, 805–810
5. Pei, M., Goodman, E., Punch, W.: Pattern discovery from data using genetic algorithm. Proc. 1st Pacific- Asia Conf. Knowledge Discovery and Data Mining, Feb. 1997
6. Augier, S., Venturini, G., Kodratoff, Y.: Learning first order logic rules with a genetic algorithm. Proc. 1st Int. Conf. Knowledge Discovery and Data Mining, Montreal, Canada, (1995) 21–26
7. Au W., Chan, C.: An evolutionary approach for discovering changing patterns in historical data. Proc. of 2002 SPIE **4730** (2002) 398–409

Discovering Process Models from Execution History by Graph Matching

Kevin C.W. Chen and David Y.Y. Yun

Laboratory of Intelligent and Parallel Systems
College of Engineering, University of Hawaii
H492, 2540 Dole Street, Honolulu, HI 96822
dyun@spectra.eng.hawaii.edu[1]

Abstract. Process engineering and workflow analysis both aim to enhance business operations, product manufacturing and software development by applying proven process models to solve individual problem cases. However, most applications assume that a process model already exists and is available. In many situations, though, the more important and interesting problem to solve is that of discovering or recovering the model by reverse engineering given an abundance of execution logs or history. In this paper, a new algorithmic solution is presented for process model discovery, which is treated as a special case of the Maximal Overlap Sets problem in graph matching. The paradigm of planning and scheduling by resource management is used to tackle the combinatorial complexity and to achieve efficiency and practicality in real world applications. The effectiveness of the algorithm, for this generally NP (nondeterministic polynomial) problem, is demonstrated with a broad set of experimental results.

1 Introduction

There has always been ample interest in Process Engineering as a vehicle to improve production optimization, software development and business operation. Process defines a description and ordering of small activities across time and space to yield specific results. Observations confirm that up to 90% of the elapsed time in some business processes is actually wait and transfer time [H&C94]. Therefore, the quality and accuracy of a business process significantly affects the performance of an enterprise. Most of the current process research assumes the existence of a formal model of a process. However, constructing a desired process model is time-consuming, expensive, and in most cases requires the assistance from experts. A fast-prototyping program that can generate an approximate model from a given past history of execution logs would be a major driving force for process automation. Solving this model discovery/recovery problem is, unfortunately, difficult, costly, and error prone, whether performed by human experts or by computer processing. A few studies attempt to break this barrier by enabling model discovery/recovery from a given set of past executions with dependency constraints in execution logs, under a simplifying assumption that no duplicate activities are allowed.

J. Liu et al. (Eds.): IDEAL 2003, LNCS 2690, pp. 887–892, 2003.

Agrawal et al. [AGL98] proposed to compute the process model by data mining and achieve optimal solutions that minimize the edge number in the derived process model for cases where no duplicate activities are allowed. Cyclic graph is proposed to avoid combinatorial matching among execution logs for a more general case with duplicate activities. In order to remove limitations introduced by cyclic graph representation, this paper proposes a graph matching based solution that discovers directed acyclic graph for process model with duplicated activities. The Maximal Overlap Sets (MOS) algorithm is used to resolve the combinatorial matching among the execution logs. The paper is organized as follows. The Process Model Discovery from Execution (ProMODE) problem and the MOS problem are defined in Section 2. Then a new MOS algorithm is introduced in Section 3 and applied for process model discovery in Section 4. An assessment of the effectiveness for process model discovery is shown in Section 5, followed by some conclusions.

2 Problem Definition and Analysis

Activities-based ***process*** (as in [AGL98]) can be represented as a directed acyclic graph (DAG) $G_p=(V_p, E_p)$, with modifications made to accommodate repetitive activities, where the labeled vertex set $V_p = V_1, ...,V_n$ denotes the activities, and the directed edges $E_{ij}(V_i, V_j)$ denote the dependency.   Finite times of multiple appearances of the same activities are allowed and represented with distinct vertices of the same label. The discovery of the process model is carried out by examining a set of execution logs that can either be the past execution history of the process. An ***execution log*** is a list of records that keeps track of a single execution of the activities of a process. A process model graph **G** is ***conformal*** for the given execution log **L** if all of the following conditions hold:

- *Dependency completeness*: For each dependency in **L**, there exists a path in **G**
- *Independence separation*: There is no path in **G** between any independent activities
- *Execution completeness*: **G** is consistent with every execution in logs

Clearly, the conformal graph for a given log **L** is not unique. In particular, for a single execution log, two extreme cases of conformal graphs (CFG) exist (Figure 1).

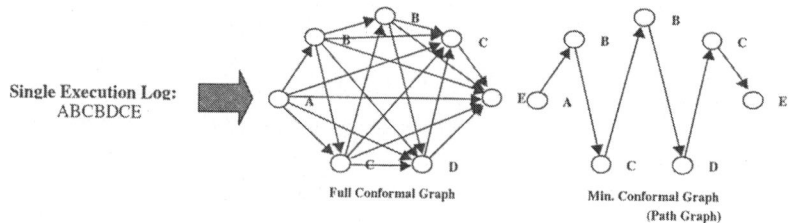

Single Execution Log:
ABCBDCE

Full Conformal Graph

Min. Conformal Graph
(Path Graph)

Fig. 1. Example of Conformal Graphs

The ***minimal conformal graph*** (or ***path graph***) in Figure 1 contains the most compact dependency information given by the execution log, e.g. *AB* and *BC* implies *AC* , which is not shown.   One thing to note is that, when more than one execution is presented, certain dependencies among activities in one execution may contradict with what shown in the others, i.e., they are independent.   Such dependencies then need to be removed. With the use of conformal graph, the problem of ***Process Model Discovery from Execution History*** can be defined as: Given a sufficiently informative set of execution logs, *Process Model Discovery from Execution (ProMODE)* generates a conformal DAG with minimal number of edges that reflects dependencies implied in the logs, or each log can be derived from the DAG.

Agrawal et al. [AGL98] proposed to use cyclic representation, where all duplicate activities are to be merged together, to avoid the matching problem. However, acyclic representation has several advantages over the cyclic representation.

For example, when an explicit execution path (Figure 2a) is represented using cyclic representation (Figure 2b), several spurious execution sequences such as ($A{\rightarrow}D$, $A{\rightarrow}B{\rightarrow}C{\rightarrow}A{\rightarrow}B{\rightarrow}C{\rightarrow}A{\rightarrow}D$, ...) can be inferred.   Moreover, once an acyclic representation is generated, the corresponding cyclic representation can be easily derived in polynomial time. On the other hand, deriving a

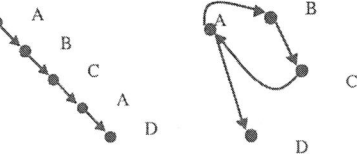

Fig. 2. **(a)** Acyclic vs. **(b)** Cyclic Representations

minimal acyclic model from cyclic representation is expected to be NP-complete, and there is no known algorithm for this problem. Therefore, when a process model is expected to have finite times of multiple appearances of same activities, we feel that acyclic graph is a better representation.

One appropriate concept directly applicable to model discovery/recovery is the problem of Maximal Overlap Sets (MOS), which is defined as that of finding an isomorphic *edge-induced* sub-graph of two labeled graphs that has the maximal number of edges. An example of MOS is shown in Figure 3, where the MOS of graphs G_1, and G_2 consists of the solid edges. Conformal graphs can be regarded as labeled graphs with activities as node labels, and with direction as edge labels. By maximizing the overlap (or intersection) between graphs, the resultant union conformal graph will be minimized.

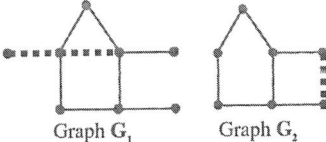

Graph G_1 Graph G_2

Fig. 3. Example of MOS

3   Maximal Overlap Sets Algorithm

Maximal Overlap Sets (MOS) problem itself is an NP-hard problem. The only MOS algorithm appeared in literature is the one by McGregor [McGr82]. In his work, a branch-and-bound search algorithm was proposed to find the matched edges and nodes. The algorithm is known to be applicable only to small graphs. Barrow et al. [B&B76] proposed a transform to convert the dual problem of MOS, the maximal common subgraph (MCS) problem, into the Maximum Clique (MC) problem by constructing the '*correspondence graph*' from the two to-be-matched graphs. The solution of MOS then corresponds to the largest clique (full connected subgraph) in the correspondence graph. Recently, Kann [Kann92] showed in his dissertation work that MOS can also be transformed into the MC.   This theoretical result is less practical since it generates a large correspondence graph. Independent from his work, the authors [C&Y98, Chen99] devised a similar transform from MOS to MC by a two-stage reduction process that results in smaller correspondence graphs in practical cases (details omitted here).

Once the correspondence graph of the two given graphs is derived, we can then apply a MC algorithm, called CRP-MC, to discover the MOS. We found that graph minimum coloring provides a perfect dual problem that allows iterative convergence towards finding both MC and Min-Coloring (also MC) solutions. By utilizing the duality concept, we developed a dual-MC algorithm called **CRP-MC** that couples two sub-algorithms, **COLORING** and **CLIQUE-FINDING** [Yun00, C&Y98]. The two algorithms are executed alternatingly in an iterative loop controlled by a tested, efficient resource management technique, *Constraint Resource Planning* (CRP) [Yun02, K&Y89]. In general, the iterative process of **CRP-MC** terminates when (1) the clique size equals the number of colors used, since no larger clique can be possible (Lemma 2), or (2) no node can get a smaller color degree, since no more improvement is possible from this iterative refinement process. Once the process terminates, the maximal overlap sets of the two graphs can be transformed back from the maximum clique in the correspondence graph.

4 Process Model Discovery from Execution Logs

Transitive reduction removes all the redundant dependencies that can be implied by the other non-redundant ones. In this work, we use an efficient transitive reduction algorithm with complexity of $O(VE)$ (V is the number of activities in the execution, and E is the number of dependency edges) that is discussed in [AGL98]. Compare to the $O(VE)$ complexity of the transitive reduction, the major bottleneck in the previous method apparently is the complexity for computing the pairwise MOS. The size of the correspondence graph for each MOS sub-problem in this case could be as large as E^2, while the complexity of the MOS algorithm is at least the square of the problem size (the actual complexity is not determinable because of its iterative nature). Therefore, reducing the input graph sizes for the MOS problem appears to be very critical for this solution to be practical. Instead of working on the full conformal graphs and performing reduction on those graphs is proposed in previous section, we propose to use the path graphs in a constructive fashion. The follow algorithm finds the minimal conformal model graph: The correctness and convergence proof is omitted for space considerations.

Algorithm ProMODE2s

<u>Input</u>: a set of execution logs $\{L_i\}$ of a process, where the process contains V
  activities, and each activity appears once and only once in each log

<u>Output</u>: a DAG process model with minimal number of edges

1. Start with an empty graph **G(V,E)** with **V** nodes and edge $\mathbf{E} = \varnothing$.
2. For each execution log $\mathbf{L_i}$,
  generate the path graph $\mathbf{P_L}$
  For each edge (u,v) in $\mathbf{P_i}$, add (u,v) to **E**

3. For all strongly connected component in **G**, remove all edges in such component
4. For each path graph P_{L_i}, let Gi be the induced graph of G, and Ei = Pi - Gi
    For each edge $E_{ij}(u,v)$ in E_i (where the edge starts from u and ends at v)
    Trace along the path in P_i until the source node, if there is no edge connecting v with any node along the path in **G**, add a directed edge in **G** between the closest node to v and v itself so that the edge was not removed in Step 3.
    Do the same for u.
5. The resultant DAG is the desired process model.

To generalize the idea to the case where same activities may appear more than once in a single execution, the proposed MOS algorithm is introduced to resolve the maximal matching problem. With the help of MOS algorithm, the largest intersection between path graphs can be found, consequently reduce the size of the union graph. Most importantly, because we use the path graph instead of full graph, the size of the correspondence graph for each MOS sub-problem is significantly reduced from E^2 to V^2, which is the minimum size achievable when MOS solution is desired. The modified algorithm is ProMODE2 (omitted here).

5 Empirical Results

Due to the abundance of software program flow charts in the academic environment, in contrast to the lack of ample workflow execution logs in the production or business

Execution Logs:

LOG1: ABCF   LOG5: ADCEF

LOG2: ACDF   LOG6: AEBCDF

LOG3: ADEF   LOG7: ACF

LOG4. AECF   LOG8: AEBCF

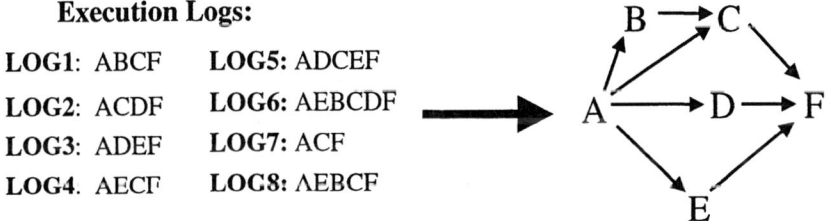

environment, our experiments focused on verifying the software reverse engineering process. An example of software (subroutine) execution log history and the discovered flow dependency graph are shown below. Such software reverse engineering process has been found to be specifically valuable for verifying the program design/organization and flow correctness of student projects. The execution times for these problems show a near linear behavior to the number of edges (relations) in the graph representation. This efficiency significantly enhances the confidence for the computational model discovery tool and opens the door for testing the approaches in the manufacturing and business arena.

Solving Maximal Overlap Set (MOS) problems have been of great interest to many fields due to the capability of extracting the largest common substructure, the ease to match the problems, and the flexibility to incorporate constraints. However, the lack of efficient algorithms for solving these difficult problems has limited the uses to small problems, both in space and in time complexity. The algorithm, MOS, presented here solves MOS problems in the maximum clique (MC) domain using CRP-MC and CRP-GC (Graph Coloring) as complementary solvers. Although the problem is NP-hard, it's shown to reach near linear speed for a wide spectrum of benchmark cases.   Moreover, a generic pre-processing and dynamic-accessing technique is developed to further circumvent the space/time overhead. The result is shown to be a new and effective data-mining tool for discovering/recovering process models. The ProMODE algorithm presented here is shown to successfully bring the graph-based approach to solve important real-world problems and is expected have more applications in assisting the discovery of new knowledge in related areas.

References

[AGL98] Rakesh Agrawal, Dimitrios Gunopulos, Frank Leymann, "Mining Process Models from Workflow Logs", *Proc. of the 6th Int'l Conf. on Extending Database Technology (EDBT)*, Valencia, Spain, 1998.

[B&B76] H. G. Barrow and R. M. Burstall, "Subgraph Isomorphism, Matching Relational Structures and Maximal Cliques," *Information Processing Ltrs*, vol.4, no.4, pp.83–4, 1976.

[Chen99] C. W Chen, "Algorithms for Maximal Common Subgraph Problem Using Resource Planning", Ph.D. dissertation, University of Hawaii, Aug. 1999

[C&Y98] Chao-wen Chen and David Yun, "Unifying Graph-Matching Problems with a Practical Solution," *International Conference on Systems, Signals, Control, Computers*, Durban, South Africa, Sept. 1998.

[H&C94] M. Hammer, and J. Champy, Business Reengineering – Die Radikalkur fur das Unternehmen. – Campus Franfurt/M, 3. Auflage, 1994.

[Kann92] V. Kann, "On the Approximability of NP-complete Optimization Problems," PhD. Thesis, Department of Numerical Analysis and Computing Science, Royal Institute of Technology, Stockholm, 1992.

[K&Y89] Keng, N. P. and D. Y. Y. Yun, "A Planning/Scheduling Methodology for the Constrained Resource Problem," *Proceedings of the Eleventh International Joint Conference on Artificial Intelligence*, (1989), 20–25.

[Yun00] D. Y. Y. Yun, "Solving a Family of Graph Matching Problems using the Constrained Resource Planning Paradigm", Ft. Laud., FL: *Congressus Numerantium*, pp.142–7, 2000.

[Yun02] D. Y. Y. Yun, Achieving Computational Intelligence by Resource Optimization, (Invited Paper) *Proc. 2002 World Congress on Computational Intelligence, International Joint Conference on Neural Networks*, May 2002.

Constructing UML Galaxy Diagram
for Conceptual Data Integration in Web Mining

Zhe Zhang [1], Xiaoyuan Huang[1], and Liang Zhang[2]

[1] Faculty of Business Administration, Northeastern University, Shenyang, China
zhangz27@hotmail.com
[2] Department of Information Systems, City University of Hong Kong, Kowloon, Hong Kong,
SAR
iszhang@is.cityu.edu.hk

Abstract. In Web mining conceptual data integration rather than physical integration is necessary in many situations. XML is becoming the new standard for data representation and exchange on the World Wide Web quickly. The rapid emergence of XML data on the web, e.g., business-to-business (B2B) e-commerce, is making it necessary for OLAM Web mining and other data analysis to handle XML data. In this paper a multidimensional model, the UML galaxy diagram describing the multidimensional structure of the conceptual integrating data at the conceptual level, is proposed.

Keywords: UML galaxy diagram, conceptual data integration, XML, Web mining, e-commerce

1   Introduction

In data cube, data mining is operated in multiple dimensions and layers to mine knowledge flexibly and support decision. Online analytical mining (OLAM) is built on the multidimensional data model [1][2]. OLAM Web mining is one of the important application fields and research topics. In processing of Web mining data integration at the conceptual level is becoming increasingly important as more business-related data such as e-commerce appear on the web.

Web mining must have semi-structured data model and semi-structured data model extraction technology as the prerequisite. The newest WWW technology based on XML is directly related to Web data. It is not only compatible with the former Web applications, but also facilitates the realization of information sharing and exchange in the Web more smoothly. Extensible Markup Language (XML) can be regarded as a kind of semi-structured data model that can relate document descriptions of XML and attributes of relational database easily to conduct accurate enquiry and model extraction. Thus, the problems of integration and enquiry of heterogeneous data in the Web could be solved [3]. The XML 1.0 Recommendation is used in this paper [4].

Integrating web-based data at the conceptual level is more suitable for use by system designers and end users. The most widespread conceptual model is the Unified Modeling Language (UML) which is used in this paper [5][6]. The research findings

J. Liu et al. (Eds.): IDEAL 2003, LNCS 2690, pp. 893–897, 2003.

of Jensen et al. provide indications for future research directions [7] [8]. Data integration conceptual design can be implemented with the aid of UML tool [9].

The basic idea for conceptually integrating XML data and relational data into UML galaxy diagram is described below. At first, UML diagrams are used to describe XML data sources and relational data sources. As for XML data sources, DTDs (Document Type Definition) for describing XML documents structure should be taken into account. It is assumed that the logical structure of an XML document is described by a DTD and the XML document is validated by a DTD. The DTDs should be transformed into UML diagrams. The approach of converting DTDs to UML diagrams has already been realized [7]. As for the relational data sources, some design tools can aid the process of transforming relational schemas into UML diagrams. In this paper it is assumed that UML diagrams can describe the relational data. Then conceptual integration is conducted on the base of data representation of UML diagrams with the result of the multidimensional data concept model for OLAM Web mining— the UML galaxy diagram.

The remainder of the paper is organized as follows. Section 2, on the conceptual level, defines UML galaxy diagram capturing the multidimensional structure of data cube of Web-based MDDB (Multidimensional Databases) schema on XML and relational data sources. Simulation analysis and results are stated in section 3. Finally, in section 4 conclusions and future research suggestions are given.

2   Constructing UML Galaxy Diagram

This section describes a UML galaxy diagram and defines a set of rules defining how to construct a UML galaxy diagram consisting of data elements from XML and relational data sources. The UML galaxy diagram is composed entirely of UML classes and constitutes the schema of web_based data cube for OLAM Web mining. Moreover, the UML model is a high_level semantic data model with a graphical notation, making it convenient to illustrate relationships between data elements. When constructing the UML galaxy diagram, some design patterns related with some structural properties of XML can aid the model design process [10].

2.1   Definition of UML Galaxy Diagram

A UML galaxy diagram is an n_roots graph consisting of UML classes. Each root graph is a UML snowflake diagram [8]. Each root graph has a root_class and many subgraphs. The root_class is termed a *fact_class*. Each fact_class is a subject_oriented class that is commonly designated by designer based on a subject. Each subgraph is termed a *dimension* and each path $class_1$, $class_2$, ... , $class_n$ from root to leaf in a subgraph is termed a *concept hierarchy*. $Class_i$ in the path define a *concept hierarchy level* for the dimension.

In UML galaxy diagram, there are two common types of concept hierarchy. They are schema hierarchy and set_grouping hierarchy that describe total order and partial order (lattice) of hierarchy level for the dimension. The UML galaxy diagram allows dimension to be shared between fact_classes. The nesting structures of XML documents are modeled as aggregations. Moreover, the constraint on the UML galaxy diagram is to ensure data generalization.

2.2   UML Galaxy Diagram Sets

The sets used to describe a UML galaxy diagram are defined as follows. As a galaxy diagram is n_roots graph consisting of UML classes satisfying definition 2.1 conditions, galaxy diagram class should be defined. In UML galaxy diagram there are two types of galaxy diagram classes: fact classes and concept hierarchy level classes.

$GalaxyDiagram = \{(GalaxyDiagram\ class_1), (GalaxyDiagram\ class_2), ...,$
$\qquad\qquad (GalaxyDiagram\ class_i), ... , (GalaxyDiagram\ class_n)\}$

$GalaxyDiagram\ class = \{(class\_Name, class\_AttList, class\_Link)\}$
  Class_Name: a distinct name identifying the class;
  class_AttList: a set of attributes associated with a specific class;
  class_Link: a set of links between classes.

$class\_AttList = \{(AttName, AttType, MissingValues, AttLocation, CalcAtt,$
$\qquad\qquad LinkPath, AttClassification, AggFunction) \}$
  AttName: a distinct name identifying the attribute;
  AttType: the data type of the attribute;
  MissingValues: whether or not null values are allowed for the attribute,

$$MissingValves \in \{NULL, NonNULL\};$$

  AttLocation: the location of the attribute (the URI of the data source);
  CalcAtt: a formula used for calculating the attribute *AttName*;
      NULL indicating the *AttName* need not any calculations to get;
  LinkPath: a list of *AttLocations*, attribute names or *Relationships* when adding
      attributes to a class; NULL indicating that the attribute is native within
      the class;
  $Relationship=\{(UMLclassName, RelationshipType, RelationshipRole)\}$
  Relationship: a set describing relationship between two classes in a UML diagram;
    UMLclassName: the name identifying the class for which a link exist;
    RelationshipType: association or aggregation;
    RelationshipRole: an association type link;
  AttClassification: measure or descriptive attribute;
  AggFunction: for measure attribute, it is the default aggregation function;
        for descriptive attribute, it is NULL;

$$AggFunction \in \{SUM, COUNT, MIN, MAX, AVG, NULL\}.$$

$class\_Link = \{(LinkClassName, LinkType, SourceCardinality, TargetCardinality)\}$
  LinkClassName: the name identifying the class for which a link exist;
  LinkType: association or aggregation;

$SourceCardinality \in \{0..*, 1..*\};$

$TargetCardinality = 1.$

2.3 Constructing UML Galaxy Diagram

The designer constructs the UML galaxy diagram by choosing elements from various data sources describing the domain of the model. Each data source is described by a

UML diagram (as assumed in section 1) and the designer creates classes in the UML galaxy diagram by choosing one or more UML classes from UML diagrams. The UML galaxy diagram is n_roots graph. Each root (fact class) in the UML galaxy diagram is constructed by choosing one class in a UML diagram as the foundation. This class is extended by adding attributes from other UML classes, either from the same diagram or from UML classes originating from other data sources.

When constructing classes in the UML galaxy diagram, sometimes it is necessary to add additional attributes to the UML galaxy diagram class. If a UML class R is extended with additional attributes from another UML class C_n, There exists a path of UML classes C_1, C_2, ..., C_n ($n \geq 1$). The following OQL expression describes how to redefine class R to R', which includes the attributes from class R and a_1, a_2, ..., a_p from a UML class C_n.

SELECT $A \in R, C_{m+1}.C_{m+2}. \cdots .C_n.a_1, \cdots, C_{m+1}.C_{m+2}. \cdots .C_n.a_p$

FROM $R, C_1, C_2, \cdots, C_n$

WHERE $R.att_R = C_1.att_{C_1}$ AND $C_1.C_2. \cdots .C_i.att_{C_i} = C_{i+1}.att_{C_{i+1}}$

AND $C_{i+1}.C_{i+2}. \cdots .C_j.att_{C_j} = C_{j+1}.att_{C_{j+1}}$ AND ... AND

$C_k.C_{k+1}. \cdots .C_m.att_{C_m} = C_{m+1}.att_{C_{m+1}}$

3   Simulation Analysis

The example of 2_roots UML galaxy diagram is provided as follows. The example concerns retailers and suppliers of PC products. The retailer sells PCs to end users and buys PCs from a number of different suppliers. Meantime the retailer provides service corresponding to sale PC products. Sale data and service data provided by retailer and PC products data provided by suppliers are stored as XML documents. The retailer stores information about customers in a relational database. Based on the above data, the goal is to construct a 2_roots UML galaxy diagram in order to enable analysis of sales and customers for the retailer.

The UML galaxy diagram is constructed from two different XML documents and one relational data source. One subject is the sale profit of various types of PCs, and another subject is the service benefit corresponding to sale PC products. The DTDs describing the structures of sale document, service document, code_mapping document and product document and the schema of the customer table and the contents of XML documents and relational table are omitted. The galaxy diagram is shown in Figure 1. The UML galaxy diagram set is omitted.

4   Conclusion

The research constructing UML galaxy diagram for conceptual data integration in Web mining is a theoretical exploration and the system design and realization of it have wide research fields. Furthermore, since DTD exists limitations in aspects of validation function and flexibility, it would be researched to consider using XML schema instead of DTD describing XML data and redesign generating UML class from XML data algorithm.

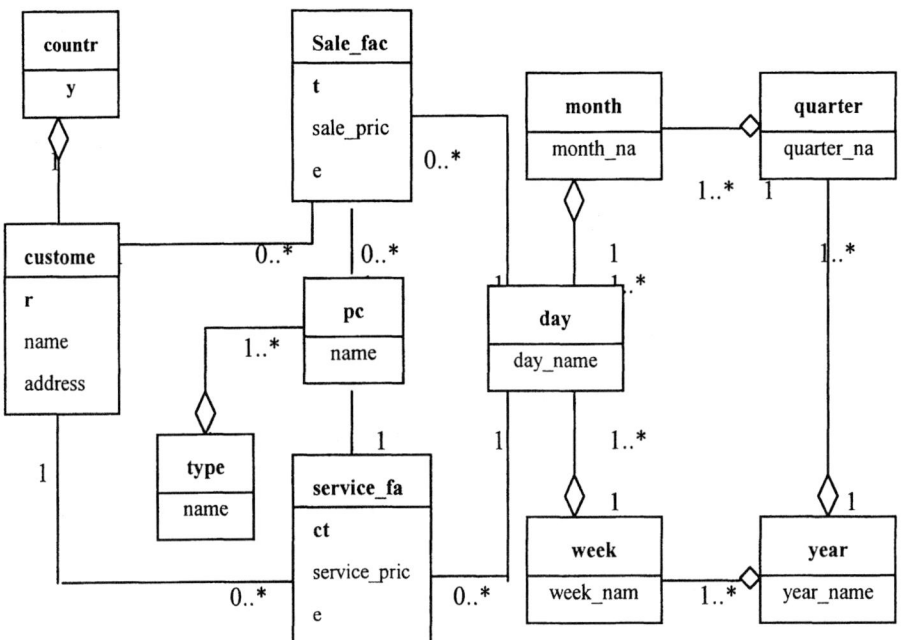

Fig. 1. UML galaxy diagram

References

1. Han, J.W.: Towards On-Line Analysis Mining in Large Databases. ACM SIGMOD Record, Vol.27. (1998) 97–107
2. Shi, L., Shi, Y.: The Research and Development of a Unified Framework for OLAP and Data Mining. Computer Science, Vol.27. (2000) 45–49
3. Yao, Q.D., Chen, N.L.: A XML-Based Data Storage Solution. Computer Science, Vol.27. (2000) 49–52
4. World Wide Web Consortium (W3C): Extensible Markup Language (XML)1.0. 2nd edn. W3C Recommendation,
   http://www.w3.org/TR/2000/REC-xml-20001006 (2001)
5. Object Management Group: OMG Unified Modeling Language Specification 1.3
   http://www.rational.com/uml/resources/ documentation/index.jsp (2001)
6. Fowler, M., Scott, K.: UML Distilled: A Brief Guide to the Standard Object Modeling Language. 2nd edn. Addison-Wesley, MA (2000).
7. Jensen, M.R., MØller, T.H., Pedersen, T.B.: Converting XML data to UML diagrams for conceptual data Integration. Proceedings of the First International Workshop on Data Integration Over The Web, (2001a) 17–31
8. Jensen, M.R., MØller, T.H., Pedersen, T.B.: Specifying OLAP Cubes on XML Data. Journal of Intelligent Information Systems, Vol.17. (2001b) 255–280
9. Boggs, W., Boggs, M.: Mastering UML with Rational Rose 2002. Sybex, CA(2002)
10. Gamma, E., Helm, R., Johnson, R., Vlissides, J.: Design Patterns: Elements of Reusable Object-Oriented Software. Addison Wesley, MA(1994)

MLPCA Based Logistical Regression Analysis for Pattern Clustering in Manufacturing Processes

Feng Zhang and Daniel Apley

Department of Industrial Engineering
Texas A&M University
College Station, Texas 77843-3131, USA
zhangfeng@neo.tamu.edu

Abstract. This article proposes a method of improving pattern clustering accuracy combined with a logistical regression model for manufacturing processes with binary inspection outputs. A latent variable model was incorporated into the classical logistical regression model, involving the use of Maximum Likelihood Principal Component Analysis (MLPCA) to identify the underlying variation sources governing the behaviors of the high dimensional measurable variables. The highly correlated continuous measurable predictors are projected onto a lower dimensional latent space, followed by a more precise pattern clustering algorithm to the inspected manufacturing products for in-line process monitoring. The example of the visual inspects from semiconductor manufacturing processes is shown that this new pattern clustering algorithm could help identify the root causes of the variations.

1 Introduction

Visual defect metrology is an in-line process monitoring technique used to assess process capability in semiconductor manufacturing [2]. The inspections are performed by automated inspection equipment given statistical sampling methods, and the results are used for low yield analyses. Often, pattern recognition systems are able to identify systematic and correlated visual defects on individual wafers and across multiple lots.

In semiconductor manufacturing processes, several hundred IC's are fabricated simultaneously on a printed circuit board (PCB), and each chip on every wafer would have tens or even hundreds of solder joints which are declared to be either good or defective. The goal of this article is to develop methods for routinely monitoring these binary visual inspection data to detect the presence of significant spatially clustered defects. This paper describes a latent variable model based method and uses binary test data at the PCB level to estimate the size and location of clusters of defective solder joints, without assuming any particular distribution for the size, shape and location of clusters.

J. Liu et al. (Eds.): IDEAL 2003, LNCS 2690, pp. 898–902, 2003.

2   Logistic Regression

Logistic regression is a workhorse of statistics and is closely related to methods used in Machine Learning [3], the objective of which is to find the maximum-likelihood coefficients estimate.

$$p\{y = \pm 1 \mid x, \beta\} = \sigma(y\beta^{T}x) = \frac{1}{1 + \exp(-y\beta^{T}x)}. \tag{1}$$

It can be used for binary classification or for predicting the certainty of a binary outcome. Given a data set $(x, y) = [(x_1, y_1), \ldots, (x_n, y_n)]$, one efficient method to estimate the coefficients vector β is the Newton method,

$$\beta_{new} = \beta_{old} + (\mathbf{X}\mathbf{A}\mathbf{X}^{T})^{-1} \sum_{i=1}^{n} (1 - \sigma(y_i\beta^{T}x_i))y_i x_i \tag{2}$$

where $a_{ii} = \sigma(\beta^{T}x_i)(1 - \sigma(\beta^{T}x_i))$.

This efficient implementation is also called Iteratively Reweighted Least Squares (IRLS), which takes $O(nd^2)$ time per iteration where d is the dimensional size of β.

Logistic regression models are used mostly as a data analysis and inference tool, where the goal is to understand the role of the input variables in predicting or explaining the binary response data. Typically many of these input measurements are correlated due to some underlying physical phenomena, which encourage us to identify such latent variables as parsimonious inputs to determine the effects on the outcomes. That is, these input variables themselves can also been explained by the underlying variables with the latent linear model introduced in the next section.

3   Latent Variable Model and MLPCA

Linear principal component analysis (PCA) is a widely used statistical data analysis tool for identifying relationships and patterns in multivariate data sets. In most manufacturing processes, there exist strong correlations between many of these observation variables x, which indicate the presence of some underlying root causes which explain such interrelated manners among x. The purpose of a latent variable model is to relate a d dimensional observed data vector x to an underlying p - dimensional random vector v, labeled as latent variables by a linear model [1]

$$x = Cv + w, \tag{3}$$

where $C = [c_1, c_2, \ldots, c_p]$ is an $n \times p$ constant and $v = [v_1, v_2, \ldots, v_p]^{T}$ is a $p \times 1$ zero-mean random vector with independent components, each scaled without loss of generality to have unit variance. In general, $p < d$ such that the dependencies among the observation data x could be explained by a smaller number of latent variables v, and w is the x-independent process noise, representing the aggregated effects of measurement noise and any inherent variation not attributed to the sources. The vectors v and w, and thus x, are assumed to be zero-mean. The model parameters may be determined by some maximum-likelihood estimating methods.

Here, we assumed the latent variables to be Gaussian distributed with unit variance, i.e., $v \sim \mathcal{N}(0, I)$, and the noise is also Gaussian with isotropic covariance, $w \sim \mathcal{N}(0, \sigma_w^2 I)$. Given these model assumptions, it has been shown that the columns of the maximum-likelihood estimator C_{ML} would span the principal subspaces of the observation data x.

The log-likelihood of sample data under the above model is

$$L = \sum\nolimits_{n=1}^{N} \log(p(x_n)) = -\frac{N}{2}\left\{d\log(2\pi) + \ln|\Sigma| + \mathrm{tr}\{\Sigma^{-1}S\}\right\}.$$

Here $\Sigma = \sigma_w^2 I + CC^T$ and S is the sample covariance matrix for observation data. It was shown [4] that the maximum likelihood estimates of C and σ_w^2 can be calculated by the EM (Expectation-Maximization) iterative algorithm, that is,

$$\tilde{C} = SC(\sigma_w^2 I + M^{-1} + C^T SC)^{-1}, \tag{4}$$

$$\tilde{\sigma}^2 = \frac{1}{d}\mathrm{tr}(S - SCM^{-1}C^T), \tag{5}$$

where $M = (\sigma_w^2 I + C^T C)$.

One thing to point out here is how to determine the effective dimensional size p accurately and efficiently. The probabilistic PCA model itself does not provide a mechanism for determining the dimensionality p. The cross-validation to compare all possible values of p offers a possible approach, however it would be time-consuming and complex when d increases. We suggest using the following rule to determine the value of p and then substitute this p into the above EM iterative procedures.

$$\hat{p} = \inf_{j}\left\{ \frac{\dfrac{1}{j+1}\sum_{k=1}^{j+1}\lambda_k - \dfrac{1}{j}\sum_{k=1}^{j}\lambda_k}{\dfrac{1}{j}\sum_{k=1}^{j}\lambda_k - \dfrac{1}{j-1}\sum_{k=1}^{j-1}\lambda_k} \gg 1 \right\}.$$

4 MLPCA Logistic Regression Clustering Algorithm and Application

One fundamental objective considered in large multivariate data analysis is to identify as precisely as possible the nature of each distinct variation pattern and explain the root causes of variation patterns with the above linear variation model. Combining the classical logistic regression method and linear latent variable model, we would like to obtain or calculate the effects onto the process measurement or characteristic from the underlying latent variation sources, which is based entirely on the data sample with no a priori knowledge of the patterns. Proper identification of the patterns can provide much insight into the interdependencies and correlations between the different observable variables and, ultimately, the phenomena that cause the patterns.

With the same assumption as above, let $x = [x_1, x_2 \ldots x_d]'$ be a $d \times 1$ random vector that represents the measured variables in a part or product. Let x_k be a sample of N observations of x. The interpretation is that there are p independent variation sources $\{v_j : j = 1, 2 \ldots p\}$ that affect the measurement vector x, which further explain the binary inspection data y. The effect of the jth source is represented by the variation pattern vector c_j. Since v_j is scaled to have unit variance, c_j also indicates the magnitude or severity of the jth source. Then $\beta_v = \mathbf{C}^T \beta$ refers to the latent variable v, which then are partitioned into some spatial clusters such that the inspected parts in visual detection stage are more closely related to a specific vriation source v_i.

Now, given the calculated logistic regression coefficients β_v, we are going to apply the clustering analysis approach to determine the spatial subgroups for all of the n inspected measurable points in a part or product. For example, when $p = 2$, it can be seen that the coefficients $[\beta_{v1} \ \beta_{v2}]^T$ around $[0 \ 1]^T$ indicating that the corresponding measurable points are mainly affected by the latent variable or variation source v_2 only. Also, the larger v_2 is, the more probable that these points are to be labeled as "fail" by the visual defect inspection due to the logit model

Thus, the proposed MLPCA logistic regression method can be used to obtain accurate estimates for the logistic regression coefficient for the underlying variation sources v without much prior knowledge about the latent variables.

In semiconductor manufacturing processes, electronic components can be placed on the board only after the solder pastes are applied to the pads. And the amount of paste to the pad is crucial to the quality of the electrical connection. In the screen printing process, solder pastes are deposited on the board automatically by some printing machines, then registered with the screen and printed, where some uncontrolled factors or environmental noise would play roles on the production of solder balls in the paste, and hence lead to some failures of the final components. The typical solder joints profiles include solder thickness or volume, shape of heel fillet, shape of toe or center fillet, alignment between pad and lead, etc. For simplicity, here we choose 10 variables as the intermediate measurable variables x, that is, $d = 10$.

The above spatial clustering approach facilitate identify the relationship between solder joints location coordinates of defects and the spatial patterns, when the defects of solder joints on a PCB are not completely spatially random. Through such spatial clustering analysis, the information about defect generating mechanisms could be gained to improve the solder joints production quality.

The presented spatial clustering algorithm is illustrated for a region of PCB consisting of more than 3, 000 solder joint. And the final results are easy to interpret in an intuitive graphical way. We could estimate the logistic regression coefficients $\beta_v = \mathbf{C}_{\text{ML}}^T \beta$ corresponding to the variation sources or causes v based on the collected data, and aggregate the solder joints coordinate data into 2 different clusters, shown in the Fig. 1.

It can be seen that there are 2 underlying variation sources which govern the variation pattern among the solder joints, denoted by '+' and '×' respectively. We may conclude that the variation source v is the screen printing direction which is taken into account for the clusters in Fig. 1 classified based on the solder pastes' horizontal and vertical coordination.

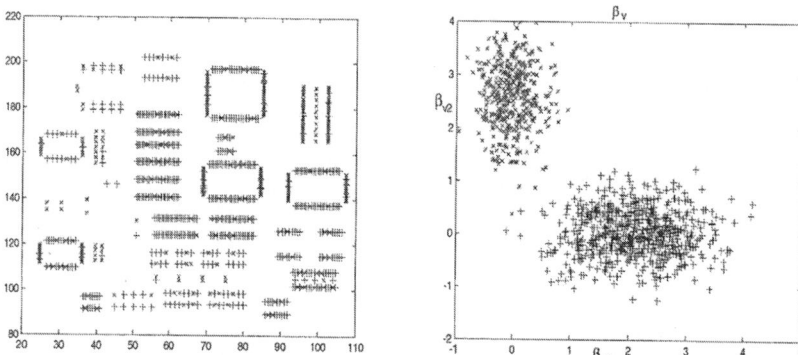

Fig. 1. Layout of the clustered point coordinates (*Left*) and corresponding logistic regression coefficients scatter plot (*Right*)

5 Conclusion

The improved statistical clustering method presented here provide a more thorough understanding of defect mechanisms than traditional defect count and defect density statistics. Learning the causes of defects and their effects on yield lie on the maximum likelihood PCA estimation and logistic regression model, which provide a proper understanding of the underlying process variation patterns. This spatial clustering algorithm is easily applied in current process control systems with affordable computational effort. Also, there are some benefits from calculating the probability of transition from normal production quality to defect for each solder joint influenced by some specific assignable cause.

References

1. Bartholomew, D. J. and Knott, M., Latent Variable Models and Factor Analysis. Oxford University Press Inc., New York (1999).
2. Cunningham, S.P. and MacKinnon, S., Statistical Methods for Visual Defect Metrology, IEEE Transactions on Semiconductor Manufacturing. 11(1998) 48–53.
3. Minka, T. P., Algorithms for maximum-likelihood logistic regression. CMU Statistics Tech Report 758 (2001).
4. Tipping, M. E. and Bishop, C. M., Mixtures of Probabilistic Principal Component Analyzers. Neural Computation. 11(1999) 443–482.

Graph-Based Data Clustering: Criteria and a Customizable Approach

Yu Qian[1], Kang Zhang[1], and Jiannong Cao[2]

[1]Department of Computer Science
The University of Texas at Dallas
Richardson, TX 75083-0688, USA
{yxq012100, kzhang}@utdallas.edu

[2]Department of Computing
The Hong Kong Polytechnic University
Hung Hom, Kowloon, Hong Kong
csjcao@comp.polyu.edu.hk

Abstract. A graph model is often used to represent complex relational information in data clustering. Although there have been several kinds of graph structures, many graph-based clustering methods use a sparse graph model. The structure and weight information of a sparse graph decide the clustering result. This paper introduces a set of parameters to describe the structure and weight properties of a sparse graph. A set of measurement criteria of clustering results is presented based on the parameters. The criteria can be extended to represent the user's requirements. Based on the criteria the paper proposes a customizable algorithm that can produce clustering results according to users' inputs. The preliminary experiments on the customizability show encouraging results.

1 Introduction

The purpose of data clustering is to find smaller and more homogeneous groups from a huge heterogeneous collection of data [2]. A variety of techniques have evolved to discover the relational information among the given data. Such techniques often adopt graph models. The vertices of a graph model represent the points of the data and the edges represent the relations among the data points. In the simplest case, the graph is complete: all vertices are connected to each other; the main information lies within the edge weights. As pointed out by Harel and Koren [4], many clustering methods prefer to model the data using sparse graphs[1], which contain only a small subset of the edges of the complete graph, mostly those corresponding to higher similarity values. The limitation on the number of the edges has two advantages [4]: first, it reduces the time and space complexity. Second, the structure of a sparse graph reflects spatial proximity and expresses the arrangement of the data. The information implied by a sparse graph can be divided into two categories: structural information, i.e., the

---

[1]   A rough definition of sparse graphs is that the number of the edges in a sparse graph is much less than the square of the number of the vertices in it [3], i.e., $|E|<<|V|^2$, for a graph $G(V, E)$, where $|V|$ is the number of vertices, $|E|$ is the number of edges.

J. Liu et al. (Eds.): IDEAL 2003, LNCS 2690, pp. 903–908, 2003.

connectivity of the vertices such as the degree of a vertex; and weight information, i.e., quantitative relation such as the distance between two vertices. All clustering algorithms based on sparse graphs must take both kinds of information as the criteria for judging the boundary of a cluster. Unlike the explicit edge weight information, the graph structure is implicit and elusive. This has increased the difficulty but also flexibility of clustering. This paper will examine sparse graph based data clustering from a user-centric perspective, aiming at maximizing the flexibility to produce satisfactory clustering results.

There have been many clustering methods in the literature. Few of them, however, perform in-depth analysis on the role of the user in the process of clustering. As observed by Jain *et al.* [5], there is a dilemma on the clustering algorithm: on the one hand, the more information the user has about the data at hand, the more likely the user would be able to succeed in assessing its true structure. On the other hand, minimizing the number of input parameters would simplify the clustering algorithm [7]. This dilemma leads to two different paradigms on clustering criteria: user-centric and data-centric. The former paradigm uses a user specified set of clustering criteria while the latter adopts some application-independent criteria such as high cohesiveness, low coupling, less noises, and etc., which are independent from the domain knowledge and practical situation.

Compared with the aforementioned clustering measurements, our criteria have two major features: first, the cluster analysis is graph-based. By modeling data with a graph, this paper proposes a set of graph-based clustering criteria, which can control and measure the clustering process. As a result, the derived clusters can meet users' requirements and be easily visualized. Second, our approach is customizable. In our approach we consider the user's requirement as the basis of our clustering criteria.

The rest of this paper is organized as follows. Section 2 proposes a set of criteria for clustering measurement and a corresponding clustering algorithm. Section 3 reports the experimental results. Section 4 concludes the paper.

2   Clustering Criteria

The criteria proposed in this paper are extended from our previous criteria for unweighted graphs [6]. The extended criteria introduced here can be applied to both weighted and unweighted graphs.

2.1   Graph Model and Measurements

Given a graph $G = (V, E)$, $|V| = n$, is the number of vertices, $|E| = m$, is the number of edges. A *clustering* of G partitions the vertices of G into k disjoint sets $C_1, C_2, C_3,...,$ C_k. Each set C_i $(1 \leq i \leq k)$ is called a *cluster*. $|C_i|$ is the number of vertices of cluster C_i. A *clustered graph* is a graph with a recursive clustering, or partitioning, of the vertex set of G. A *clique* (or a complete graph) is a simple graph in which there exists one edge between every pair of vertices.

Given $u, v \in V$, $(u, v) \in E$, we say that edge (u, v) is *inside* C_i iff both u and v are in C_i. The number of edges inside cluster C_i is denoted as E_i. The maximal possible number of edges inside C_i is denoted as M_i, $M_i = |C_i|(|C_i|-1)/2$, when C_i is a clique. For weighted graphs a weight function $w: E \rightarrow R$ is used to represent the relation between a graph edge and its corresponding weight.

1. **Cohesiveness** is the minimum value of ratio of E_i to M_i, for the ith cluster C_i, denoted as a real number α, $0<\alpha\leq 1$. For weighted graphs, *cohesiveness* is the minimum product of the ratio of E_i to M_i and the sum of the weights of all the edges inside a cluster C_i, denoted by a real number α_w. α measures whether every cluster is a cohesive group. The goal is to maximize the value of α for the clustering result. For unweighted graphs, the cluster is a clique when $\alpha=1$.

2. **Coupling Bound** is the biggest number of inter-cluster edges, represented by an integer U_{inter}. For weighted graphs, *coupling bound* is the maximal sum of the weights of inter-cluster edges, denoted by an integer U_{inter_w}. U_{inter} represents the clustering quality between every pair of clusters. A lower U_{inter} helps maintaining the natural clustering.

3. **Coupling Ratio** is the ratio of the total number of inter-cluster edges to the total number of edges in G, denoted as a real number β, $0<\beta<1$ For weighted graphs, *coupling ratio* is the ratio of the total weight of inter-cluster edges to the total weight of all edges in G, denoted as β_w. β is used to measure an overall cohesiveness for a graph. A smaller β means less inter-cluster edges/weight and more intra-cluster edges/weight.

4. **Granularity** is defined as the number of clusters, denoted by an integer k. *Granularity* indirectly measures the flexibility and the adaptability of the clustering result. Different applications may require different *granularities*.

The concept of **Clustering Measurement (CM)** is defined as a 4-tuple (α, U_{inter}, β, k), where α, U_{inter}, β, k are defined as above. The definition of **Clustering Requirement (CR)** is extended from **CM**. A **Clustering Requirement (CR)** is a 5-tuple (α', U_{inter}', β', K_{min}, K_{max}). α' represents the requirement on *cohesiveness*; U_{inter}' represents the requirement on *coupling bound*; β' describes the requirement on *coupling ratio* while K_{max} and K_{min} are a pair of integers measuring the upper bound and the lower bound of the number of clusters respectively.

2.2 A Customizable Approach to Clustering

We have implemented a corresponding algorithm according to our criteria. Due to the space limit we only provide a simple explanation here. The algorithm is composed of 4 steps. Step 1 of our algorithm uses the k-core approach [1]: the big graph is partitioned into cores. Step 2 creates the corresponding matrix for every produced core. Step 3 combines the resulting small matrices into a big matrix. Step 4 accepts the user's specifications and requirements as a goal to decide the final clusters in the matrix.

3   Preliminary Experimental Results

3.1 Customizability Tests

The purpose of customizability tests is to evaluate the ability of our algorithm to produce corresponding results for different user inputs. According to the *CM* defined in Section 2, the quality of a clustering can be judged from the following aspects:

1.   Intra-cluster quality, i.e., high cohesiveness,
2.   Inter-cluster quality, i.e., less coupling, and
3.   Appropriate granularity.

Therefore the user's requirements can be classified according to their emphases on the 3 aspects of the quality. To simplify the tests, for each aspect of the quality, the user has two choices: emphasize and not. Without losing generality, two choices on three aspects produce $2^3 = 8$ combinations of requirements. As a result, every user requirement can be classified to one of the 8 combinations. Table 1 compares the 8 clustering results and the 8 sets of different requirements for the same graph.

Among the 8 sets of requirements, the ones in rows 5,6,7,8 require the produced clusters to be cohesive vertex groups, which mean a high α (α=0.5). The ones in rows 3,4,7,8 say they need low coupling between the clusters, implying a low β (β=0.1) and a low U_{inter} (U_{inter}=20). The ones in rows 2,4,6,8 imply a strict limit on the number of clusters, indicating that K_{min} and K_{max} are close. For those in rows 1,2,3,4,5, and 6, our algorithm produced satisfactory result. For the ones in rows 7 and 8, our algorithm could not find any result meeting the coupling bound requirement ($U_{inter}{\leq}20$). In fact, such kind of result does not exist in the given graph.

Table 1. The clustering outcomes with 8 different user requirements.

	Clustering Requirements					Clustering Measurements				Satisfy?
	α	U_{inter}	β	K_{min}	K_{max}	k	β	α	U_{inter}	
1	0.15	30	0.2	2	25	18	5.3e-2	0.154	16	Yes
2	0.15	30	0.2	20	23	20	6.7e-2	0.217	18	Yes
3	0.15	20	0.1	2	25	20	6.7e-2	0.217	18	Yes
4	0.15	20	0.1	20	23	20	6.7e-2	0.217	18	Yes
5	0.5	30	0.2	2	25	23	9.0e-2	0.509	21	Yes
6	0.5	30	0.2	20	23	23	9.0e-2	0.509	21	Yes
7	0.5	20	0.1	2	25	N/A	N/A	N/A	N/A	No
8	0.5	20	0.1	20	23	N/A	N/A	N/A	N/A	No

3.2   Parameter Priority Tests

For priority tests, we use the same input graph with different parameter priorities to see how different the clustering results are. The purpose is to show that the *cohesiveness, coupling*, and the *granularity* are 3 orthogonal measurements. In other words, the best *cohesiveness* does not mean the best *coupling*, larger *granularity* does not mean a better or worse *cohesiveness* or *coupling*, and vice versa. So the way to evaluate the relation of the parameters is to see if the clustering results are different when applying different priorities. We assign extreme values to each parameter to simply verify this.

Table 2 reveals that different priorities have generated different clustering results. The smallest granularity (K_{min}=1) produces a bad cohesiveness (α=0.057) while the biggest granularity (K_{max}=300) produces the worst coupling ratio (β=1). The best cohesiveness (α=1) leads to the highest coupling bound (U_{inter}=22); the best coupling (β=0) causes a bad cohesiveness (α=0.057). We also notice that in Table 2 the clustering results of the last two rows are the same. This test therefore has verified empirically that granularity, cohesiveness, and coupling are orthogonal while coupling ratio and coupling bound are related. This is consistent with what these parameters are intended for.

Table 2. The clustering outcomes with different priorities.

Priority	Clustering Measurements			
	k	α	β	U_{inter}
Granularity K_{min}	1	5.7e-2	0	0
Granularity K_{max}	300	1	1	1
Cohesiveness α	24	1	9.9e-2	22
Coupling ratio β	2	5.7e-2	0	0
Coupling bound U_{inter}	2	5.7e-2	0	0

3.3   Comparison Tests

For comparison tests, we apply k-core algorithm and our hybrid algorithm to the same input graph. This can be regarded as a comparison between data-centric and user-centric paradigms. The input graph is an ideal one for the k-core approach that contains 23 cliques and an isolated vertex. So we can easily find if our approach fails to find any natural cluster produced by the k-core approach. Further, we use a normal requirement (0.5, 30, 0.2, 2, 25) to see if our result is better than that of k-core. In terms of *CM*, our result is (0.509, 21, 0.090, 23) while the result of the k-core approach is (1, 22, 0.099, 24). Fig. 1 illustrates the cohesiveness values of all the clusters produced by the two algorithms. Fig. 1 indicates that only one cluster produced by our approach is worse on *cohesiveness* than that by the k-core approach. Most of the clusters produced by the k-core approach have been maintained. With the same input

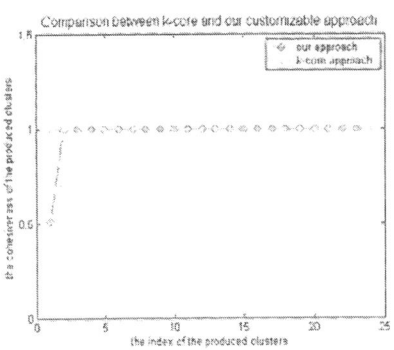

Fig. 1. Comparison with k-core approach.

graph, our hybrid algorithm can produce a more desirable value on *coupling ratio* and *coupling bound* (0.090<0.099, 21<22). Since our algorithm takes user's inputs, it is more suitable for practical applications. The tests show two positive results: (1) our customizable partitioning approach may be used to handle the output from any data-centric approach to produce user-desired results, (2) combining the k-core approach and our partitioning approach is effective.

4   Conclusion

This paper attempts to provide such a set of criteria and a corresponding solution for the general clustering algorithms. The proposed criteria have four features: first, it can represent the user's requirements. Second, it can measure the quality of a clustering result. Third, it combines the application-independent criteria and the user's specific needs. Last, it provides a guideline for more customizable clustering algorithms. Our experiments have shown encouraging results. Future work includes the visualization of clusters and automatic requirements processing.

References

1. V. Batagelj, A. Mrvar, and M. Zaversnik, Partitioning Approaches to Clustering in Graphs, *Proc. GD'1999*, LNCS, pp. 90–97(2000).
2. M. J. A. Berry and G. Linoff, *Data Mining Techniques – for Marketing, Sales, and Customer Support*, John Wiley & Sons, NY, USA (1997).
3. T. H. Cormen, C. E. Leiserson, and R. L. Rivest, *Introduction to Algorithms*, The MIT Press (1989).
4. D. Harel and Y. Koren, Clustering Spatial Data Using Random Walks, *Proc. 7th Int'l Conf. Knowledge Discovery and Data Mining (KDD-2001)*, ACM Press, New York, pp. 281–286 (2001).
5. A. K. Jain, M. N. Murty, and P. J. Flynn, Data Clustering: A Review, *ACM Computing Surveys*, Vol. 31, No. 3, pp. 264–323 (1999).
6. Y. Qian and K. Zhang, A Customizable Hybrid Approach to Data Clustering, *Proc. of 18th ACM Symposium on Applied Computing (SAC03)*, ACM Press (2003).
7. O. R. Zaiane, A. Foss, C. Lee, and W. Wang, On Data Clustering Analysis: Scalability, Constraints and Validation, *Proc. of the Sixth Pacific-Asia Conference on Knowledge Discovery and Data Mining (PAKDD'02)*, Springer-Verlag, pp. 28–39 (2002).

Study of United Mileage Agent in E-commerce[1]

Jang-Mi Baek and In-Sik Hong

Division of Information Technology Engineering Soonchunhyang Univ. 646,
Eupnae-ri, Shinchang-myun, Asan-si, Choongchungnam-do, 336-745, KOREA
bjm1453@empal.com, ishong@sch.ac.kr

Abstract. E-commerce is becoming more popular on the Internet, smart cards
have been used for safe transfers and transactions. Especially, business models
using smart cards are actively being developed and the expense transaction
method using smart card is becoming diverse since these various business
models such as payment agent. So, in this paper, we propose the efficient
mileage agent on the Internet, using smart card. This agent offers security for
data and the simplicity of application development. Also, It is an independent
program saved on Java Card and can calculate and save mileage, although the
characteristic of the mileage is different from others through the calculating
process of the Card.

1 Introduction

As E-commerce is becoming more popular on the Internet, personal authentic
information and the data related to transactions are more important than before in
security. As a result of this, smart cards are being used for safe transfers and
transactions on E-commerce, popularly. Especially, business models using smart
cards are actively being developed. Payment agent is basic model in smart card. So,
we propose the efficient united mileage agent on E-commerce using Java Card. Java
Card considered as COS for the next generation, must take advantage of the good
points of Java Language by using this language and making programs asked for, by
various demands. Also, the Java Card is a better follow-up to USIM(Universal
Subscriber Identity Module) in IMT-2000 terminal. The suggested mileage agent is a
personal independent program. Using the calculating process of Java Card, users
themselves can calculate and save unified mileage that has different characteristics for
other Internet cyber malls. Also the agent is aimed to encourage the efficient use of
the agent after comparing and contrasting it with other existing agents and the newly
designed one, in simulation. The simulative environment is incarnated in J Builder
made by Java Language and based on the specification of ISO 7816. Gemxpress 211
assisting the COS of the Java Card and manufactured by Gemplus is used for
simulation as a basic card and a terminal[1][2][3].

---

[1] This research was supported by University IT Research Center Project.

J. Liu et al. (Eds.): IDEAL 2003, LNCS 2690, pp. 909–913, 2003.

2 Java Card Technology

Java Card technology offers a way to overcome obstacles hindering smart card acceptance. Java Card applets are written on top of the Java Card platform and thus are smart card hardware independent. A Java Card can host multiple applets, such as an electronic purse and loyalty from different service providers. Java Card is based on the standard ISO 7816, so it can easily support smart card system and applications that are generally compatible with ISO 7816[4][5][7][10].

3 United Mileage Management Agent

Accordingly, as the expansions of commercial activities develop on Electronic commerce, the services for users have been offered vigorously. Users especially receive good quality service by getting mileage from a cyber mall when they purchase goods. Most cyber malls give mileage to purchasers but they can only spend the mileage at the participating branches and consequently the users need places where they can spend their mileage anytime. For an example of mileage services in Korea, there are OKcashbag and easycash, considered as popular cases of mileage services. Although the two companies have carried out management service of mileage, they have failed to give users satisfaction because of the inconvenient management by a server. Compared with many established agents, the newly designed agent is intended for better planning of mileage accumulation.

3.1 Protocol of Mileage Management Agent

Figure 1 is Protocol of united mileage agent. A user can access a cyber mall through smart card and a terminal. To confirm personal authentication, the user should send his/her certificate to the cyber mall. After finishing the confirmation of the authentication, the user can save mileage on the website and send the mileage saved, through the mileage management program on his/her card. Every mileage saved at a cyber mall should have both the balance of mileage and the total mileage that the user has earned and spent, because the user's qualification for earning mileage is different from other users, according to the mileage policy. A cyber mall should receive authentication from the CA, so the security of mileage is guaranteed by the organization. CA's main role is to authenticate mileage factors from a cyber mall and to manage the authenticated data of cyber malls through a directory server.

Figure 2 is mileage accumulation stage. Java Card has each shop's each mileage and integration mileage. Authentication of transaction needs for Non-Repudiation.

Figure 3 is mileage consumption stage. Accumulated mileage can be used like cash. User can pay integrate mileage and cash at the time. When the store receives the information of mileage from user, store requests illegality of mileage to CA. CA confirms illegality of mileage. If mileage is illegal, user can't use mileage. Then, user's Java Card run reversing process that delete illegal mileage from mileage list in

Java Card. If illegal mileage notified from mileage CA store sends illegal mileage message.

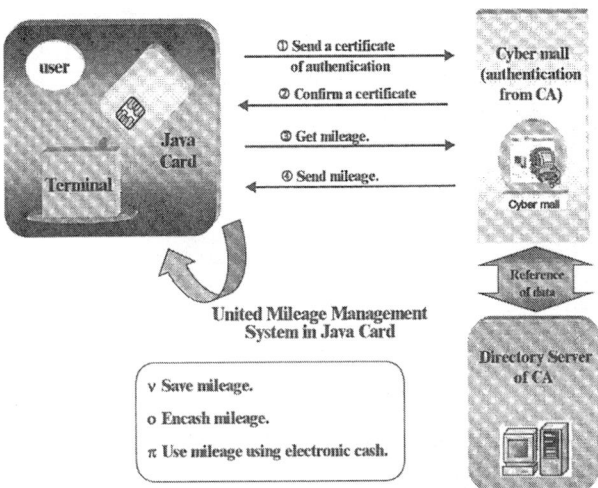

Fig. 1. Protocol of United Mileage Agent

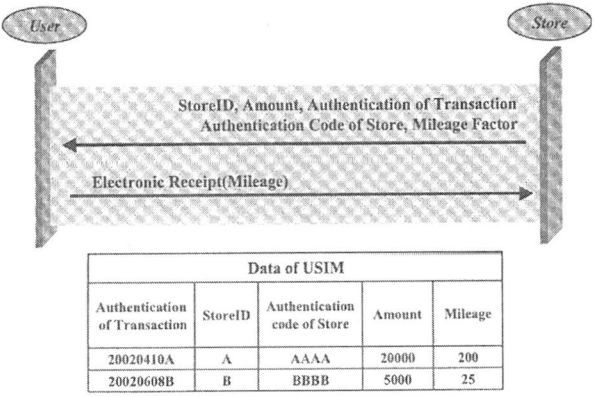

Fig. 2. Mileage Accumulation Stage

4   Simulation

The simulation is to demonstrate the efficiency of the agent. As Java Language on J Builder programs, the simulation, APDU is used for communication between a card and a terminal. Cards and application use orders such as command and response to communicate. Applet has its own AID, Application Identifier. The process of authentication is required when cards and terminals are connected. A cyber mall is not only realized by applet, but is also able to communicate with the mileage management agent by using communicating protocols such as TCP/IP. All mileage factors from cyber malls are saved in the memory of the card. With the balance of mileage in the memory, mileage of each cyber mall can be converted into money. The balance of mileage should be visible to a user to confirm his/her balance and it should be possible for the user to spend his/her mileage as cash promptly, after being connected with electronic currency such as Wallet[6][8][9].

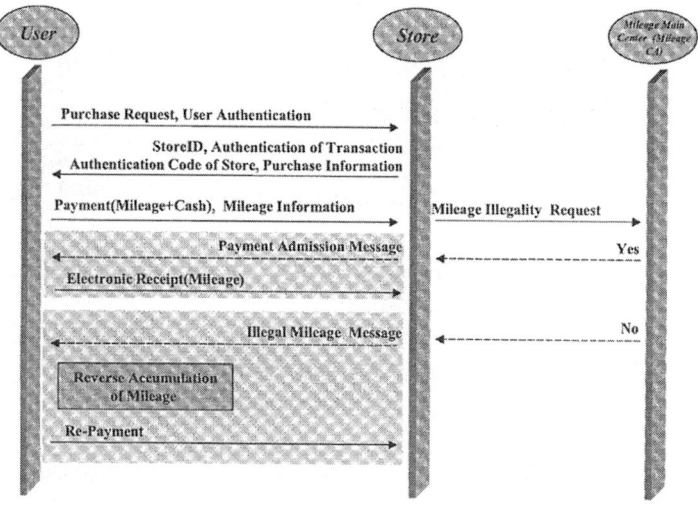

Fig. 3. Mileage Consumption Stage

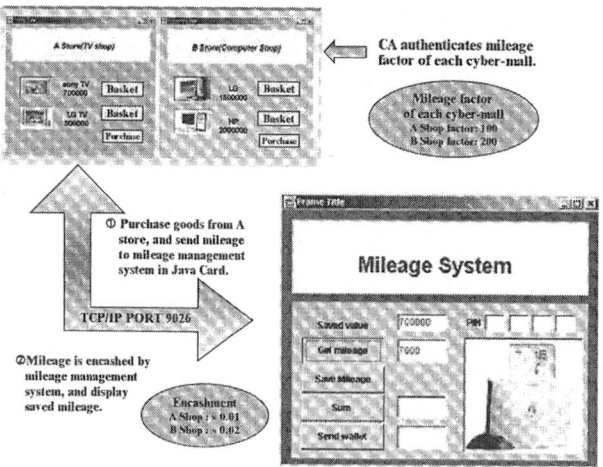

Fig. 4. Simulation of Saving Mileage Stage

Figure 4 is simulation of saving mileage stage. Mileage factors from a cyber mall are saved in the memory of Java Card. The transferred balance of the mileage should be recorded and calculated exactly because each mall provides its members with different qualification. That means that the user can earn larger or smaller mileage than other users according to the condition of the mileage policy.

Figure 5 is simulation for sum and using mileage. Saved mileage can be transferred and spent in other application such as Wallet.

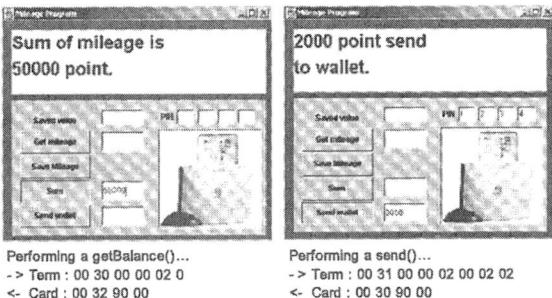

Performing a getBalance()...
-> Term : 00 30 00 00 02 0
<- Card : 00 32 90 00

Performing a send()...
-> Term : 00 31 00 00 02 00 02 02
<- Card : 00 30 90 00

Fig. 5. Simulation for Sum and Using Mileage

5 Conclusion

In this paper, suggests a new agent of mileage management, which works more efficiently and perfectly on the Java Card. This project suggests a new efficient agent after comparing and analyzing the differences between the existing agents and a newly designed one. The agent is a personal independent program saved on the Java Card that has personal authentic information and mileage factors of cyber malls. Additionally the agent realizes that mileage can be saved and converted into money by using the calculating process of the CPU. Through simulation, we showed how effectively this application could use available space of Java Card. It seems that the marketing of smart cards is in its infancy.

References

[1] Zhiqun Chen, "Java Card Technology for Smart Cards", Addison-Wesley, 2000
[2] Wolfgang Effing, Wolfgang Rankl, "Smart Card Handbook", John Wiley & Sons, 2000
[3] Mike Hendry, "Smart Card Security and Application", Artech House Publishers, 1997
[4] P. Biget, P. George, and J. Vandewalle, "How Smart-Cards Can Take Benefits From Object-Oriented Techonogies", In Hartel et al, pp. 175–194, 1999
[5] Frank Seliger and Martin Scott Nicklus, "Smart Card Application Development Using Java", Springer Verlag, 1999
[6] Ivor Horton, "Beginning Java2", WROX, 2000
[7] Eric Vetillard, "Java™ Card 2.1 general presentation", Gemplus Developer Conference, 1999
[8] Hawlitzek, Florian, "Java 2", Addison-Wesley, 2001
[9] Third Generation Partnership Project, http://www.3gpp.org/
[10] Gemplus, http://www.gemplus.com/

Verifying the Payment Authorization in SET Protocol

Qingfeng Chen, Chengqi Zhang, and Shichao Zhang

Faculty of Information Technology
University of Technology, Sydney
P.O. Box 123, Broadway, NSW 2007, Australia
{qchen, chengqi, zhangsc}@it.uts.edu.au

Abstract. The Secure Electronic Transaction (SET) protocol is a protocol designed to conduct safe business over Internet. We present formal verification of the Payment Authorization in SET by using ENDL (extension of non-monotonic logic) [1]. The analysis uncovers some subtle defects that may incur malicious attacks. To overcome these vulnerabilities, some feasible countermeasures are proposed accordingly.

1 Introduction

In the past decade, Electronic commerce has been changing the way in which consumers, merchants, and business interact and transact. According to International Data Corp (IDC), worldwide e-commerce reached more than $ 600 billion in 2001 and expects to pass the $ 1 trillion mark in 2002.

However, E-commerce also causes enormous challenges to the safety of online shopping. In the past few years, those companies studied with web-based sales have been the victims of information losses, theft of data or trade secrets. Regarding these security issues, a variety of security protocols have been developed. In spite of that, some protocols have been found to have security flaws years after they were published [2]. Thus it is imperative to design method for the validation of security protocols.

Formal verification of security protocols has received much attention in recent years. Below is a summary to the works based on the survey of Gritzalis [3].

Existing approaches to validating security protocols consist of two categories. The *Attack-construction approach* is the construction of probable attack sets based on the algebraic properties of a protocol algorithm, involving the work of Dolev-Yao model and the NRL Analyzer. The *Inference-construction approach* utilizes modal logics similar to those that have been developed for the analysis of the evolution of knowledge and belief in distributed systems. This includes the BAN logic and the GNY logic. The BAN logic is simple and has been successfully applied to discover flaws in a variety of authentication protocols. The GNY logic is a rather complicated approach, which increases the scope of BAN logic.

However, there are two limitations in existing methods. (a) The attack-construction approach has low-efficiency in detecting attacks for its huge state

J. Liu et al. (Eds.): IDEAL 2003, LNCS 2690, pp. 914–918, 2003.
© Springer-Verlag Berlin Heidelberg 2003

space. (b) The inference-construction approach is still too complicated to be used.

In addition, there have been attempts to model more realistic protocols. Bella, Massacci etc.[4] have verified the Cardholder Registration in SET. However, the methods for verification of e-commerce protocols are not quite as mature as those used for authentication protocols. The new type of threats, such as payment card transaction, will be a significant challenge to the analysis of e-commerce protocols. To our knowledge, existing tools cannot cover these problems in many cases. This paper gives a formal analysis of the Payment Authorization in SET.

The rest of this paper is organized as follows. In Section 2, we presents the terms and notations. Section 3 gives the verification to the Payment Authorization. Finally, Section 4 concludes this paper.

2   Basic Terms and Notations

Uppercase X, Y, and CA (Certificate Authorities) range over particular principals; m_1, m_2, ... , and m_n denote specific messages; T denotes a specific timestamp; $CertS()$ denotes the signature certificate; $CertK()$ denotes the key-exchange certificate; k denotes the encryption, or decryption, keys; $Generate$ and $Send$ denote specific actions.

Function word:

$e(m, k)$: This represents the operation that message m is encrypted by the symmetric (communication) key k.

$E(m, k)$: This represents the operation that message m is encrypted by the public key k, namely $Kpb(X)$ and $Spb(X)$ listed below.

$S(m, k)$: This represents the operation that message m is encrypted by the private key k, namely $Kpv(X)$ and $Spv(X)$ listed below.

$H(m)$: This represents the message digest of message m encoded by the one-way hashing algorithm $H(x)$.

$Kpb(X)$: This represents the public key-exchange key of X.

$Kpv(X)$: This represents the private key-exchange key of X.

$Spb(X)$: This represents the public signature key of X.

$Spv(X)$: This represents the private signature key of X.

$m_1, ... , m_n$: This represents the combination of messages m_1, ... , and m_n.

Action is applied to describe the communication process in which a principal is the executant of action and tries to execute some appointed tasks.

$Generate(X, m)$: Applied to represent that X generates the message m.

$Send(X, Y, m)$: Applied to represent that X sends the message m to Y after X has successfully generated the message m.

Predicate is applied to express the knowledge state and belief relation of principals. There are four kinds of predicate listed below:

$Know(X, m)$: This represents that X knows message m.

$Auth(X, Y, m)$: This represents that X authenticates message m sent by Y. If X can authenticate m is valid, then the return value is true; otherwise the return value is false.

3   The Verification of Payment Authorization

3.1   Authorization Request

In order to authorize a transaction, the merchant generates an Authorization Request *AuthReq*. The *AuthReq* contains the payment instructions *PI*, which are then combined with the transaction identifiers *TransIDs* and the hash of the order information *OI*. The merchant digitally signs *AuthReq* and encrypts it with a randomly generated symmetric key. Then this key is encrypted with the *Kpb(P)*. Let *AuthReq* = *<TransIDs, PI, HOD, HOIData>*

α_1 = *Generate(M, k_2)* ∘ *Generate(M, AuthReq)* ∘ *Send(M, P, E(k_2, Kpb(P)))* ∘
     Send(M, P, <CertS(C), CertS(M), CertK(M)>) ∘
     Send(M, P, e(<AuthReq, S(H(AuthReq), Spv(M))>, k_2)) ∘
     Send(M, P, e(S(<PI, H(OI), H(<H(OI), H(PI)>)>, Spv(C)), k_1)) ∘
     Send(M, P, E(<k_1, PAN>, Kpb(P)))

Finally, the merchant transmits the authorization request to *P*.

3.2   Processing of Authorization Request

The gateway decrypts the symmetric key k_2, then decrypts authorization request using k_2. He uses the *Spb(M)* to verify the merchant digital signature. The gateway also need to verify the certificates.

Next the gateway decrypts k_1 and cardholder account information with gateway private key-exchange key, and then decrypts the *PI* using k_1.

The gateway verifies the dual signature using the supplied hash of payment instruction. The gateway can validate the Cardholder's account number using the Cardholder's certificate. The gateway also verifies that the transaction identifier received from the merchant matches the one in the cardholder payment request.

The *OI* and *PI* are protected from the malicious attacks due to the application of dual signature. The dual signature on *PI* is stored during the purchase request. It ensures the message really comes from the merchant and has not been altered. However, we are concerned with the replay attack on *AuthReq*.

(1)$M \rightarrow Z(P)$: *E(k_2, Kpb(P))*
(2)$M \rightarrow Z(P)$: *e(<AuthReq, S(H(AuthReq), Spv(M))>, k_2)*
(1')$Z(M) \rightarrow P$: *E(k_2', Kpb(P))*
(2')$Z(M) \rightarrow P$: *e(<AuthReq', S(H(AuthReq'), Spv(M))>, k_2')*

Actually, the intruder *Z* can intercept the encrypted *AuthReq* and replace it with an old authorization request, which was intercepted from the previous transaction. Finally, *Z* impersonates *M* to send an outdated message (1') and (2').

The authorization request is digitally signed by merchant. SET does not provide the mechanisms to ensure the freshness of the authorization request. To prevent the replay attack, it is necessary to attach a timestamp *T* to the authorization request [5]. By this way, we can protect the authorization request against the replay attacks by checking the timestamp.

3.3   Authorization Response

If the cardholder's financial institution agrees on the authorization request the gateway generates authorization response message *AuthRes* and digitally signs it. Actually, the authorization response message includes *AuthCode*, *AuthAmt*, *XID*, and *LID_M*.

Gateway encrypts the *AuthRes* with k_3, which is then encrypted with *Kpb(M)*. The gateway creates capture token and digitally signs it with *Spv(P)*, then encrypts it with k_4. This key and the cardholder account information are then encrypted with *Kpb(P)*. Finally, the gateway transmits encrypted authorization response to merchant.

$\alpha_2=$ *Generate(P, AuthRes)* ∘ *Generate(P, k_3)* ∘ *Generate(P, k_4)* ∘
   Generate(P, CapToken) ∘ *Send(P, M, E(<k_4, PANToken>, Kpb(P)))* ∘
   Send(P, M, E(k_3, Kpb(M))) ∘ *Send(P, M, CertS(P))* ∘
   Send(P, M, e(<AuthRes, S(H(AuthRes), Spv(P))>, k_3)) ∘
   Send(P, M, e(<CapToken, S(H(CapToken), Spv(P))>, k_4))

Business Description of SET explicitly includes the *CapToken* in the authorization response. However, its Programmer's Guide states that the *CapToken* is optional and just generated by the *P* if the merchant does not request an immediate capture of the funds upon authorization. Thus, a message indicating the merchant's decision should be presented.

When the merchant receives the authorization response message, it decrypts k_3, and then decrypts the *AuthRes* with k_3. Then merchant verifies the digital signature with the *Spb(P)* and stores encrypted capture token for later capture processing.

However, the intruder can repeat the similar attacks happened in authorization request. Next we present the verification of *AuthRes*.

(1) *Send(P, M, E(k_3, Kpb(M)))*   [action]
(2) *Send(P, M, e(<AuthRes, S(H(AuthRes), Spv(P))>, k_3))*   [action]
(3)   *Know(M, E(k_3, Kpb(M)))*   (1)
(4)   *Know(M, e(<AuthRes, S(H(AuthRes), Spv(P))>, k_3))*   (2)
(5)   *Know(M, k_3)*   (3)
(6)   *Know(M, <AuthRes, S(H(AuthRes), Spv(P))>)*   (4)(5)
(7) $\rightharpoondown$ *Auth(M, P, AuthRes)*   (6)

The verification fails for the lack of timestamp *T*. On the other hand, the gateway may alter k_3 or the authorization response as *P* wonders they have been masqueraded or the network is blocked. Under this circumstance, whether the principals have the memory function to message or not is critical. We cannot give the whole analysis in this paper, and therefore just list three cases below:

(1) *P* alters *AuthRes* , but does not modify k_3;
(2) *P* alters k_3, but does not change *AuthRes*;
(3) *P* alters k_3 and *AuthRes*.

In case (1), the gateway creates a new *AuthRes*. If P does not let M know what have been changed or notices M the modification but the contents is not identical to the original one, M will fail to authenticate the *AuthRes*; in case (2), P generates a new key k_3. If P does not let M know the alteration about k_3, M will fail to authenticate *AuthRes*; in case (3), P alters the two messages. If P does not let M know the modification or lets M know the changes but the content is not identical to the original one, M will fail to authenticate *AuthRes*. At that time, the merchant should stop the processing of *AuthRes*. In the end, the participants have to risk the unending dispute with each other.

4   Conclusions

E-commerce has played an important role in global economic growth today. Meanwhile, it has resulted in the increase of both the vulnerability of e-commerce system to security violations and the damages that such violation may cause. Some secure transaction protocols have been found to be subject to attacks. Thus a variety of formal methods have been developed to verify them.

The traditional formal approaches cannot qualify for the analysis of secure transaction protocols because it involves some new processes, such as payment card transaction. In this paper, we present how to verify the payment authorization in SET using ENDL. Some potential flaws are detected during the verification. It is mainly because the specifications of SET do not provide the detailed description and sometimes are misleading. Thus, it is inevitable that some potential flaws can be utilized by the intruder. In addition, some practicable solutions are proposed to the protocol designer accordingly.

References

1. Chen Q.F, Zhang C.Q, Zhang S.C., A Logical Framework ENDL for Verifying Secure Transaction Protocols. *Journal of Knowledge and Information Systems*, Springer, accepted, forthcoming.
2. Needham R. and Schroeder M., Using Excryption for Authentication in Large Networks of Computers. *Comm. of the ACM*, 21(12), pages 993–999, Dec 1978.
3. Gritizalis S., Security Protocols over Open networks and distributed systems: Formal methods for their Analysis, Design, and Verification, *Computer Communications*, 22(8), pages 695–707, May 1999.
4. Bella G., Massacci F., Paulson C., Tramontano P., Formal Verification of Cardholder Registration in SET. 6th *European Symposium on Research in Computer Security*, LNCS 1895, pages 159–174, Springer, 2000.
5. Denning D., Sacco G., Timestamp in Key Distribution Protocols,Communications of ACM, 24(8), 533–536, August 1981.

Heuristic Methods for Portfolio Selection at the Mexican Stock Exchange

Cesar A. Coutino-Gomez, Jose Torres-Jimenez, and Brenda Ma. Villarreal-Antelo

Tec de Monterrey, Campus Ciudad de Mexico, Departamento de Computacion,
Calle del Puente 222, Col. Ejidos de Huipulco,
Tlalpan, D.F., Mexico, 14380
{ccoutino, jtj, brenda.villarreal}@itesm.mx

Abstract. Portfolio selection represents a challenge where investors look for the best firms of the market to be selected. This research presents a real world application at the Mexican Stock Exchange (La Bolsa) using a set of heuristic algorithms for portfolio selection. The heuristic algorithms (random, genetic, greedy, hill-climbing and simulated annealing) were implemented based on the Markowitz Model where the investor can select the size of the portfolio as well as the expected return.

1 Introduction

Portfolio selection is the activity involved in selecting a portfolio of stocks that meets or exceeds an investor's stated objectives [1]. This process is fundamentally based on two variables, expected return and risk. Markowitz established that investors would optimally hold a mean variance efficient portfolio [2]. This is a portfolio with the highest expected return for a given level of variance. Markowitz assumed that investors are risk averse, this means accepting higher risk only if they get higher expected return. Therefore, investors will prefer a portfolio that offers at least the same expected return than a single stock but with an overall lower risk. This is named diversification. Unsystematic risk is generated by the performance of the companies or industries; therefore, a good selection of the companies is important for the performance of the portfolio.

One of the most important tasks in portfolio selection is the selection of the firms that will be part of the portfolio. This research presents a set of heuristic algorithms to obtain the assets (firms) that will be part of the portfolio with the minimum risk at a certain level of expected return. In other words, portfolio selection is presented as an optimization problem trying to minimize the risk subject to the size of the portfolio and expected return established by the investor.

This article is organized as follows: Section 2 establishes the problem as well as the mathematical formulation. Section 3 presents the set of heuristic algorithms used in this research. Section 4 shows the experiment using real data from the Mexican Stock Exchange. Section 5 discusses our findings and conclusions.

J. Liu et al. (Eds.): IDEAL 2003, LNCS 2690, pp. 919–923, 2003.
© Springer-Verlag Berlin Heidelberg 2003

2 Mathematical Formulation

In this section, it is presented the mathematics of mean-variance efficient sets, which will be needed to find portfolios at the efficient frontier. The complete solution can be consulted at Campbell 1997 [2].

3 The Heuristic Algorithms

3.1 The Genetic Algorithm

The portfolios are constructed using a vector of integers where each stock is represented by an integer number from 0 to n where n represents the size of the market. The size of the vector is determined by the preferences of the investor. The initial population of the algorithm is generated at random, and for this implementation 300 portfolios are used as the population of the algorithm.

The fitness function for this algorithm is the risk calculated from the variance and covariance matrix. See Equation (2).

Two basic genetic operators are used for this implementation, crossover and mutation. The mutation operator alters one stock within the portfolio based on the probability of mutation. On the other hand, the crossover operator needs to work with modified portfolios to prevent duplicated stocks. An extra algorithm was developed to move from real portfolios realm to modified portfolios realm and vice versa to be successful while applying the crossover operator.

On the other hand, the selection method is tournament selection. The tournaments take place between three portfolios, the winner is copied to the next generation.

Finally, the parameters of this implementation are shown in Table 1.

Table 1. The genetic algorithm parameters

Parameter	Value
Population size	300
Generations	200
Probability of mutation	0.75
Probability of crossover	0.01

3.2 The Random Algorithm

The random algorithm is implemented by generating random portfolios within a loop and keeping the best portfolio.

In this implementation MAX=60,000 which is taken from population times generation from the genetic algorithm.

3.3 The Hill-Climbing Algorithm

The hill-climbing solution is an approach that looks for a local optimum. For this implementation MAX=60,000 to have the same opportunities.

3.4 The Greedy Algorithm

Greedy algorithms attack a problem by constructing the complete solution in a series of steps [3]. This algorithm is very simple to implement and very fast to run, but assumes that taking optimum decision at each step is the best solution overall.

3.5 The Simulated Annealing Algorithm

The simulated annealing algorithm can be seen as an extended hill-climbing algorithm where it can escape from local optima. This algorithm takes an additional parameter named temperature that changes the probability of moving from one point of the search space to another [3][4]. This approach allows exploring new areas of the function being evaluated.

4 The Experiment at the Mexican Stock Exchange

The Mexican Stock Exchange (MSE) has about 180 firms. The main purpose of the MSE is to provide the infrastructure and services to handle the processes of issuing, offering, and trading securities and instruments listed in the National Registry of Securities and Intermediaries

Companies that need funds for expansion can turn to the securities market in search of money by issuing securities (stocks) which are offered to the public. These stocks are traded (bought and sold) on the MSE, under a free market environment which offers equal opportunities for all participants.

For this research we worked with a pool of 80 stocks and the data was from March 1, 2001 to May 16, 2002. This represents 300 days of operation. The sample was restricted due to the size of the market, where some of the firms does not have enough days of trading.

The following assumptions were taken:
- Investors are risk averse.
- Closing price is taken for each day.
- Short selling is allowed
- Dividends are not included

Thirty nine portfolios were calculated for each algorithm:
- Genetic algorithm.
- Hill-climbing.
- Random.

– Greedy.
– Simulated Annealing.

Each portfolio was repeated 20 times (except by the greedy) and the result of the portfolio with the minimum risk was reported. The search space for each portfolio is between 2.168E+25 and 7.157E+118.

Figure 1 and Table 3 show the comparison of the heuristic algorithms evaluated. The performance of the algorithms based on the risk obtained by each portfolio size. The random and hillclimbing algorithm are the worst, then the genetic and simulated annealing found good portfolios after they have 15 stocks. Finally, the greedy algorithm found the best portfolios.

Table 2. The search space

Portfolio size	Greedy	Random	Hill-climbing	Sim. Annealing	Genetic
5	0.003935	0.004385	0.004265	0.004193	0.004193
10	0.003202	0.003640	0.003584	0.003269	0.003309
15	0.002943	0.003401	0.003398	0.002988	0.002982
20	0.002816	0.003142	0.003207	0.002836	0.002848
30	0.002664	0.002942	0.002928	0.002685	0.002688
35	0.002615	0.002829	0.002800	0.002627	0.002630
40	0.002583	0.002747	0.002760	0.002596	0.002597

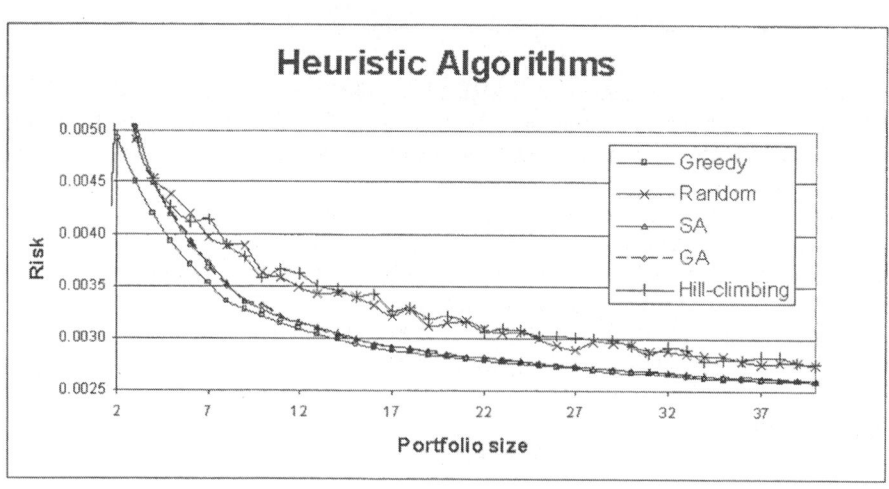

Fig. 1. Comparison of the heuristic algorithms: *portfolio size* versus minimum *risk* performance

5 Conclusions

The random algorithm did perform as expected; the only way to reduce the risk by using this approach was by increasing the size of the portfolio, even though sometimes did not improve. The first unexpected result was the behavior of the hill-climbing algorithm which found the portfolios quite similar to the random approach. This performance can be explained due to the fact that we considered only one neighbor to compete with the current portfolio. It is feasible to increase de overall performance by increasing the number of neighbors.

The genetic algorithm as well as the simulated algorithm did a very similar performance. They found superior solutions even though the genetic was slowest algorithm. On the other hand, the simulated annealing did require a heating process in order to find good portfolios.

The greedy algorithm did find the best portfolios with the minimum CPU time for each portfolio size. However, the drawback of this approach is to find the portfolio seed which is needed to begin the search.

The findings of this research are undoubtedly very surprising. The greedy algorithm which is very simple was able to find the portfolios with lowest risks. In addition, this algorithm offers the fastest result compare to the rest of algorithms. However, the key factor for the greedy algorithm to succeed is to identify the first couple of stocks of the portfolio.

Finally, this approach can be very valuable for people with little knowledge of the stock market to select firms based on historical data, as well as and additional tool for people currently in the stock market to have a second source of information for the decision making process.

References

1. Ghasemzadeh, F., Archer, N.P.: Project Portfolio Selection through Decision Support. Decision Support Systems. Elsevier (2000) 73–88
2. Campbell, J., et al: The Econometrics of Financial Markets. Princeton University Press, Princeton, New Jersey (1997)
3. Michalewicz, Z., Fogel, D.B.: How to Solve It: Modern Heuristics. Springer-Verlag, Berlin Heidelberg New York (1996)
4. Michalewicz, Z.: Genetic Algorithms + Data Structures = Evolution Programs. 3rd edn.

The Knowledge-Base of a B2B E-commerce Multi-agent System

Nelly Kasim, Chunyan Miao, and Angela Goh

School of Computer Engineering, Nanyang Technological University
Nanyang Avenue, Singapore 639798
{G938819, ascymiao, asesgoh}@ntu.edu.sg

Abstract. Businesses must be able to customise their services in order to compete in the global economy. An intelligent Multi-Agent has been implemented to perform dynamic scheduling and data gathering, data analysis and recommendation. We present an application involving an Airline Ticketing System which allows customisation of an Agent Inference Model. Data analysis is performed through a decision-making process by representing factors in a knowledge-base derived from the agent model. The paper focuses on the capture, representation and interpretation of the knowledge-base.

1 Introduction

Arising from economic globalisation, Business-to-Business (B2B) e-Commerce, which includes dynamic supply chain management, business technology and virtual organizations, has grown considerably in the past few years. In order to stay competitive and to tap potential markets, it is necessary to enable consumers to customise their ever-changing demands. While most of the literature about software agents describes the use of agents to assist end users in Business-to-Consumer B2C e-Commerce, we propose autonomous agents that can provide personalised information, undertake automated negotiations, and perform planning and scheduling functions [5] to support B2B e-Commerce.

The term 'intelligent agent' can be defined as an entity that is able to act rationally [8]. It has abilities to monitor the environment, to perform inference (reasoning), and to act rationally. Agents that work together in a community form as a multi-agent system(MAS) [7]. Within a MAS, agents collaborate to achieve a common goal.

The foundation of our proposal is the Agent Inference Model, AIM, [4] which captures knowledge as a collection of factors and impacts between the factors. It infers and makes decisions by manipulating factors and the impacts via a connected graph with one node representing a decision. Thus, AIM is a directed graph, which consists of two basic types of objects: *factor,* denoted by nodes, and *impact,* denoted by directed, signed and weighted arcs. *Factor* represents all the factors that the intelligent agent has to take into account when modeling a real world problem. There are two

J. Liu et al. (Eds.): IDEAL 2003, LNCS 2690, pp. 924–928, 2003.

types of factors: *cause factor* and *effect factor*. The direction of the impact edge shows which factor "causes" or "has impact on" the other.

In AIM, the factors and impacts are application dependent. Each factor has its own state value set, defined as a discrete value set or a fuzzy set. The membership functions of a value set are discrete value functions that can play the role of mapping each point onto a discrete set in real interval [0,1]. The mapping is based on fuzzification. The fuzzy state value sets that represent factors enable AIM to have the ability to characterize various kinds of fuzzy concepts used by human beings. In addition, AIM also supports the temporal concept, which allows the factors to have a time dimension (t). Thus, in AIM, each factor has an input/output function to interact with the environment; a fuzzification (mapping) function to map a real causal activation value to its state value and a decision function to determine the state value.

The paper aims to describe the implementation of a multi-agent system with a specific focus on its knowledge-base. The goal is to perform purchase recommendation. This is achieved by specifying a graph which represents the knowledge-base of the agent system. Section 2 describes the B2B application used to illustrate the system. Section 3 gives a brief overview of the multi-agent system, with its ability to perform data gathering. Section 4 describes the details of the knowledge-base. This is followed by a brief conclusion.

2   Case Study Scenario

Our scenario is based on transactions between the suppliers and the customer-end businesses. The latter are the buyers, acting as the 'customer' in B2B context. Although in a complete business model, the customer-end businesses are considered as the middlemen (the distributors), they are referred throughout this paper as the 'Customer'.

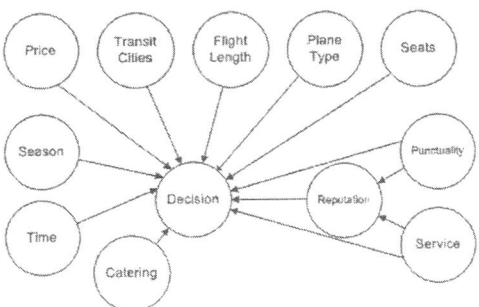

Fig. 1. The Knowledge-base of the Customer Agent in the Airline Ticketing System

To illustrate a typical distribution model, the following scenario is presented. The customers are travel agencies who wish to block-book tickets for tour groups. The system, which will be referred to as *Airline Ticketing System*, assists the customers to process a multitude of flight information, schedules, and offerings from airlines around the world in order to make a recommendation that will suit the customers' needs and preferences. The system uses the knowledge graph to depict the factors involved in the decision making process as shown in Figure 1. Data gathering is performed by the system through queries to various suppliers. The queries include the origin and destination of the flight, number of seats requested, and the date and time preferable for the flight. A scheduling mechanism is incorporated in the system to initiate automatic data gathering cycles to acquire fresh sets of data at regular intervals. This data analysis process simulates a decision-making process that users normally carry out when presented with flight information. Through the data analysis process, each set of data is assigned a recommendation value. Based on these recommendation values, undesirable data (data with low recommendation value) are filtered, and the final set of more-desirable data is presented to the user.

3 Architecture

We have assumed that all the businesses involved in the B2B e-Commerce transaction have agreed upon and will adhere to a certain communication protocol including

- The sequence of actions involved in communication (communication etiquette).
- The content and the format of the messages used in communication (the *vocabulary* and the *grammar*). In an agent system, the vocabulary corresponds to an ontology, and the grammar corresponds to the specific standard of communication protocol used.

In this scenario, there are two independent agent systems, namely, the customer and the supplier. These agents serve as the building blocks of the multi-agent system. At first glance, the system architecture may resemble a traditional client-server architecture. In reality, the architecture is not in the form of N-tier system as there is an equal standing between agents. Communication between agents lies solely on message passing. There is strictly no invoke-and-run type of operation. The supplier agents have the right not to respond to the customer agents' requests. From the customer viewpoint, its agents communicate with the supplier systems to achieve its goals. Queries are sent to the supplier systems to gather information regarding flight schedules and so on.

The agents involved in the customer agent architecture include:

- Information Gathering Agent (IGA) and its sub-agents (SIGAs) - The agent and its sub-agents will perform data gathering from various supplier's agents.
- Analyser Agent - Performs data analysis and recommendation on data gathered by IGA. This represents the agent that implements the knowledge-base.
- Scheduler Agent - Performs schedule management and scheduling.
- Master Agent - Performs tasks such as status check and synchronization.

In order to promote interoperability with other agent systems, our system adheres to the FIPA Specification on the Agent Management Reference Model and ACL Message specification [1]. JADE API [3]was used to implement the Agent Management Reference Model as it provides a platform that is FIPA compliant.

4   Creating the Knowledge Base

Before any analysis is performed, the user must specify the knowledge graph that represents the purchase decision. The graph is created in the *graph creation phase*, where the factors that influence the purchase decision are added to the graph. There are different types of factors, each with its own characteristics and properties. For example, the *Airline Ticketing System* graph involves 12 factors, including the 'decision' factor. However, there may exist connections between two nodes. For example, a higher reputation of the airlines may imply a higher price. Thus, a connection may exist between the Price node and the Reputation node.

After the graph creation phase, the user specifies the way these factors influence the decisions. This phase is known as the *graph parameters specification phase*. In this phase, the importance of every factor in the graph is defined. The 'importance' value determines the extent to which the factor affects the decision. For example, if the user considers Price to be more important than Reputation in the purchase decision, the connection between Price and Decision nodes has a higher weight value than the connection between Reputation and Decision nodes.

Factors have been categorised and treated in a manner appropriate to its meaning. **Range factors** are factors where the user specifies a range of values as the preferred value, for example, preferred price to be between $0 to $2,000. If the data returns a value that falls within the range, the factor is assigned to the maximum value. Everything that falls outside the range will have a factor value that decreases gradually as its value moves further away from the range, until the factor value is zero.

Number factors have expected values defined as an integer. This category is further divided into sub-categories: Exact factor; Minimum factor; Maximum factor. Taking the Minimum Factor as an example, if 'Seats' is defined as 8, the user expects to have at least 8 available seats. Values with 8 or above will be assigned the maximum factor value while results below 8 will be mapped to decreasing factor values.

An example of **mapping factors whose value can be defined in numbers** is Reputation. The reputation quality of the airlines can be quantified and normalized to a scale ranging from minimum to maximum values. In our tests, the reputation values of twelve admired airline companies in the Airlines industry were taken from the website of Fortune [2]. The values of the other factors such as Catering, Service, Punctuality were taken from Skytrax, the World Airline Site [6].

An example of **mapping factors whose values are defined as a series of concepts** is Season. As the factor value could refer to specific months or periods within a year, it requires intermediate processing before the information can be translated into factor value. The system provides various simple-to-use input maps similar to the one shown in Figure 2(a). In the Graph Specification phase, the user specifies the importance of each factor to the purchasing decision using values such as *'Not Important'*, *'Important'*, *'Very Important'* and so on. These importance values are specified through a slide-bar similar to those in Figure 2(b). The values must be defuzzified to determine the corresponding weight of the arc connecting the factor node to the decision node. When the user sets the factor to *'Not Important'*, the factor has no effect on decision and the connection weight is set to zero. A GUI, shown in Figure 2(b), was developed to provide a convenient means through which the user can customize his/her preferences without having to delve into lower-level details.

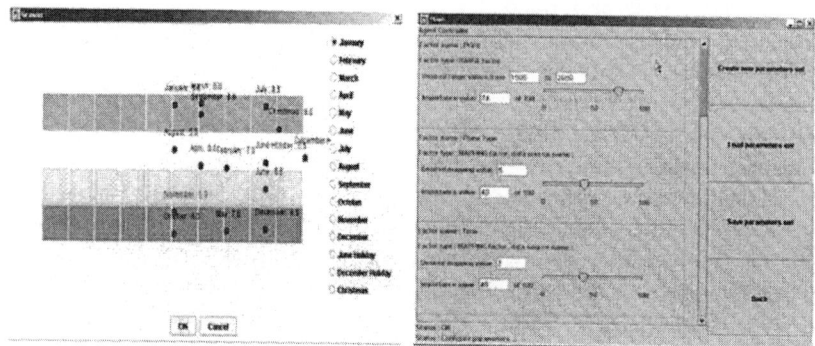

Fig. 2. (a) Graphical method of specifying requirements **(b)** Graph Parameter Specification

Testing was carried out using data collected from various airline websites and the other sites in [2, 6]. Variation of the factors and their importance was made to test out the effects on the final recommendation. The recommendation values corresponded with expected results.

5 Conclusion

An intelligent multi-agent system has been successfully developed. With the use of knowledge which is based on AIM (Agent Inference Model), the decision making process is simulated through the factors and the relationships between factors. Through the assistance and customisation provided by the agent system, the decision-making process can be more efficient as consumers are relieved of the tedium of information gathering and analysis.

References

1. FIPA (Foundation for Intelligent Physical Agent). http://www.fipa.org.
2. Fortune Website. http://www.fortune.com/lists/globaladmired/indsnap_3.html.
3. JADE Specification for Interoperable Multi-Agent System. http://jade.cselt.it/
4. Miao, C.Y., Goh, A., Miao, Y. and Yang, Z.H., Agent that Models, Reasons and Makes Decisions, Knowledge-Based Systems, Vol. 15, No.3. Elsevier Science, 2002
5. Schafer, J. B., Konstan, J. A. and Riedl, J., E-commerce recommendation applications, Data Mining and Knowledge Discovery, Vol.5, pp115–152, 2001.
6. Skytrax, the World Airline Site. http://www.airlinequality.com, 2002.
7. Stone, P. and Veloso, M., Multi-agent Systems: A Survey from a Machine Learning Perspective, Autonomous Robotics, Vol. 8, No. 3, pp. 345–383, 2000.
8. Wooldridge, M., Reasoning about Rational Agents, The MIT Press, July 2000.

Trading Futures with the Largest Equity Drawdown Method

Paul Lajbcygier and Eugene Lim

School of Business Systems, Monash University, Clayton, Victoria, 3168, Australia,
Paul.Lajbcygier@infotech.monash.edu.au

Abstract. The focus of this work is on money management: that is, given a trading system, how much should be risked per trade? Whilst many studies study trading systems and their ability to generate profits, few consider the equally important question of money management. In this work a method of money management is considered which depends on the largest expected draw- down (LEED). The properties of the LEED method are studied using a well- known technical trading rule applied to Canadian dollar futures.

1 Introduction

In the trading of commodities or derivative instruments, a trader needs to make two critical decisions: the direction to trade (i.e. whether to buy or sell); and, secondly, the amount to wager. The amount a trader wages determines the extent to which he is exposed to movements in prices. If the trade is profitable, a trader would want to place as large a stake as possible to capitalize on the upside gain, however if the trade is a loosing one, large stakes would mean large losses. The fact that traders will not know with certainty the outcome of each trade implies that decisions on exposure should be made judiciously — in such a way that draw downs (i.e. peak-to-valley losses) are minimized if the trade turns sour. This level of exposure should also be sufficiently large such that it allows the trader to reap profits in the event of a win. Techniques used to determine an optimal level of exposure are referred to as Money Management (MM) techniques.

In the past, money management decisions were not made with the same care as trading decisions and were often characterized by loose collections of rules of thumb. Recently however, practitioners and academics have proposed numerous techniques that aim to provide discipline to this decision. A technique, developed by William Gallacher [1] and for the purposes of this work, referred to as LEED (Largest Expected Equity Draw-down), is a statistically based method that estimates a trader's largest tolerable potential drawdown using statistical re-sampling.

It is the purpose of this paper to introduce and measure the performance of the LEED technique.

J. Liu et al. (Eds.): IDEAL 2003, LNCS 2690, pp. 929–933, 2003.

2 Money Management and Futures Trading

The decision of how many contracts to trade for a given trading account balance is a dilemma that faces traders and is the problem that money management addresses. It is possible to put boundaries on this decision. For example, given a starting account of $100,000 and a margin requirement of $2000 per contract, traders may decide to be highly leveraged (HL) in their trading approach and trade at minimum margin requirements by taking on 50 contracts ($100,000/ $2000). In this situation, the account could be subject to over trading because the trader is assuming a very high level of risk. HL is risky as it will provide the greatest return in the event of a winning trade, but will suffer the greatest loss if it is a loosing one. When the account is marked to market the loss will force the trader to obtain new funds so that minimum margins can be maintained[1]. At the other extreme, the trader can trade thinly or under leveraged (UL) and take on only one contract. UL is the safest bet but will not increase account growth by much because winnings are only compounded by a factor of 1.

More realistically, what determines the money risked per futures contract depends on a number of factors. The minimum monetary requirement consists of the initial margin, in this case $2,000. Add to that, $3,000 which is an estimate of the largest single drawdown that the contract will face over the trading horizon. Thus, when the account suffers a drawdown of $3,000, the margin requirement is still met and trading can continue (provided another drawdown does not follow). Further to these two amounts, another buffer should be added as a guard against estimation error. Estimation error is that uncertainty associated with the point estimate of the maximum drawdown. For example, the $5,000 (i.e. $2,000 + $3,000 discussed above) may be multiplied by a factor of three to provide a buffer. Using this method, a trader would require $15,000 in order to safely trade a single futures contract. This is the trader's reasonably expected financing requirement per contract.

Finally, given this financing requirement, the trader has to convert these requirements into actual number of contracts to trade. In this case, the trader should take on only 8 contracts ($100,000 / $15,000) in order to have a position that is neither too risky nor under leveraged. The aim of money management techniques, such as LEED, are to provide a more accurate estimate of the number of contracts to trade.

2.1 Largest Expected Equity Drawdown Method

There are four steps required to use LEED (the reader is referred to Ch.8 of [1]):

Step 1: Determine the contract's price volatility and designate it as R.
R is the average daily trading range.

---

[1] Many text-books are available that introduce futures trading concepts such as margins (e.g. [2])

Step 2: Obtain a distribution of wins and losses for sampling.
Once R has been estimated, a trader will have to review his trading strategy and ascertain the distribution of profits and losses that it generates(Figure 2). These would form the distribution range from which re-sampling is done.

Step 3: Obtain numerous trade series through re-sampling plotting each LEED observed in a probability distribution.
[2] states that it is possible to objectively estimate, at a given level of probability, the worst equity drop a trader can ever expect to encounter. Having determined the distribution of profits and losses, new trading series are generated through a bootstrap process (re-sample with replacement). For each bootstrapped series of profits and losses, a LEED must be calculated (
Fig. 2).

Step 4: Determine financing requirement through by identifying comfortable risk boundaries.
One aspect of this technique is that it requires an arbitrary risk tolerance level to be set. Given the probability distribution for LEEDs (Figure 1), and applying a traders risk preference will result in a worst case drawdown (represented in multiples of R) that the trader must prepare for, over a given horizon (e.g. In Figure 1 there is a 25% chance (or less) of a 50% drawdown over 5 years, if there is 2*12R dollars of capital).

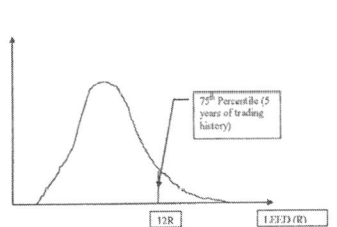

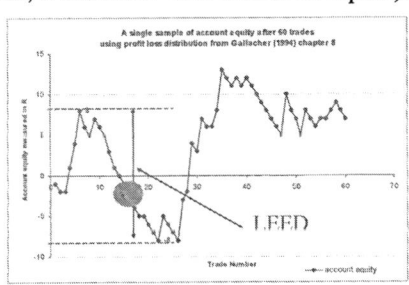

Fig. 1. This shows the distribution of LEEDs bootstrapped from trading P&L.

Fig. 2. This figure shows the LEED for a trading rule.

3 Empirical Results

In this section, the LEED technique is applied in practice. To do this, LEED is applied to a technical trading rule that has been shown to be profitable (see [2]) on Canadian dollar futures. Furthermore, to show the utility of LEED, it is compared with a naive money management approach using the same trading rule and data.

3.1 Replicating the Levich and Thomson Trading Rule

[2] has shown that it is possible to generate statistically and economically significant profits using simple technical trading rules traded on various global futures markets. As a starting point, we replicate these results and apply the same successful moving average cross-over rule (MACR[2]) (with the same parameter configuration) on the same data set (Canadian Dollar) as [2].

The reason we do this is because it makes no sense, whatsoever, to apply money management techniques to rules that are not expected to be profitable.

The MACR trading rule is applied to Canadian dollar futures. The data series spans from January 1, 1976 through to December 31, 1990, which covers 3800 daily observations. This 15-year data set is split into three sub periods. LEED is calculated on each sub period. PERIOD 1 is from the 1st Jan 1976 to the 31 Dec 1980; PERIOD 2 is from the 1st Jan 1981 to the 31 Dec 1986; and, PERIOD 3 is from the 1 Jan 1986 to the 31 Dec 1990.

3.2 Trade Simulation Results Using LEED

The risk parameters used by traders in this work are consistent with risk such that the trader would only trade so long as there is only a 25% chance (or less) of experiencing a drawdown of more 50% of capital over a trading horizon of 5 years.

For the sake of comparison, this research also implements both extreme financing situations (discussed earlier) using null model 1 "under leveraged" (UL), which trades using only 1 contract (regardless of the capital under management); and, null model 2, "highly leveraged" (HL), which will be the maximum number of contracts allowed by the exchange, given the account's starting balance. The trading results from these null models are compared to results obtained when accounts trade a fixed number of contracts derived through the application of money management techniques.

---

[2] The technical trading rule we focus on in this study is the most profitable in [2]'s study of technical trading rules. The moving average cross over rule (MACR) is a type of trading breakout technique that encompasses a support and resistance level. A support level is a price level a commodity has difficulty falling below while a resistance level is a price level that a financial instrument has difficulty rising above. The basic idea is that a "breach" of either of these levels signals that the market is trending and 1rading such breakouts involves buying and selling in the direction of a trend. As trends are temporary, it is important for traders to monitor price levels to trade with the trend and avoid losses. In using the moving average cross over rule, several parameters need to be considered. For the purposes of this research, the 5 day / 20 day parameters are used as they are of medium length and should be sufficient to filter out sudden price movements in the system. Furthermore, these parameters generated more significant returns than the others did in [2].

To facilitate the illustration of results the following indicators are used to represent various MM values. LEED P1 represents the LEED value derived from the period 1 sample and used in periods 2 and 3. LEED P2 represents the LEED value derived from the period 2 sample and used in period 3. LEED P3 represents the LEED value derived from the period 3 which cannot be tested out-of-sample. Margin refers to those accounts traded at (minimum) margin requirements (i.e. HL).

Figure 3 shows actual trading performance with varying money management techniques. The ending equity for the margin account (i.e. HL) is only $2406, for the one contract account (i.e. UL) it is $115,000 whilst for the each LEED account (only Pl is shown, Table 1 has the entire results) it is substantially more — admirably demonstrating the utility of the LEED approach.

Table 1. MACR trading characteristics using different LEEDs in period 3.

	LEED P1	LEED P2	LEED P3
Ending equity	$ 501,070	$ 244,170	$ 252,290
Mean returns	0.031	0.017	0.018
Standard Deviation	0.150	0.072	0.078
Coefficient of Variation	0.207	0.237	0.227
Sharpe Ratio	4.829	4.216	4.406

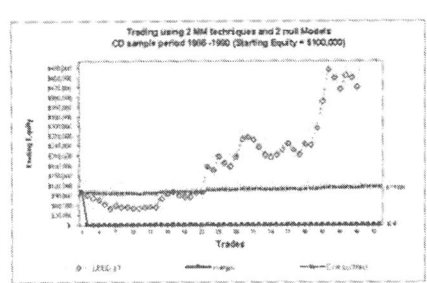

Fig. 3. Comparison of ending equity for both money management techniques using a $100,000 on CD futures.

4 Conclusion

We have seen in this work how money management, although often neglected, is very important for the purposes of trading. In particular, we considered the LEED method of money management, have discussed its application and shown it to be superior to two naive methods of money management. Further work will consist of extending this technique to other currencies and trading rules and comparing competing methods of money management such as optimal f.

References

1. Gallacher W R (1994) Winner Take All. Sydney: McGraw-Hill.
2. Levich R M and Thomas (III) L R (1993) The significance of technical trading-rule profits in the foreign exchange market: a bootstrap approach, Journal of International Money and Finance, October, pp.451–74.

Intraday Analysis of Portfolios on the ASX Using ICA

Kevin Lo and Richard Coggins

Computer Engineering Laboratory,
Electrical and Information Engineering, University of Sydney, Australia
richardc@ee.usyd.edu.au,
http://www.sedal.usyd.edu.au/~richardc

Abstract. In this paper we address the problem of forecasting non-gaussian portfolio returns over multiple time scales. We apply a relatively new technique for estimating portfolio returns by considering higher order mutual information. This technique is based on two methodologies: Independent Component Analysis and Gaussian mixtures. We apply this model to intraday data from the ASX. Our findings illustrate that this model is particularly useful in estimating portfolio returns over a short time scale when the distribution is highly non-Gaussian.

1 Introduction

The standard covariance framework for modeling the distribution of portfolio returns over an investment period assumes the distribution of returns is Gaussian, however it completely disregards the effects of higher order correlation among stocks. Therefore, it may not be appropriate when the returns distribution becomes non-Gaussian, particularly over the short time scales of intra-day data. This suggests the need for a more sophisticated approach to approximating non-Gaussian return distributions. One model suggested by Chin, Weigend and Zimmermann [1] is to combine two data modelling techniques - *ICA* and *Mixtures of Gaussians* to take into account the non-gaussianity of the distributions. We denote this technique *ICA-MOG modelling*.

The organization of this paper is as follows. In section 2, we discuss the procedure for using the model. Section 3 describes the context of our experiment when we apply the ICA-MOG model to intra-day data on the Australian Stock Exchange (ASX). The gaussianity of portfolios over different time scales is discusssed in section 4. We then analyse the performance of the model on the intra-day data over multiple time scales, and detail the in-sample and out-of-sample results in section 5 and section 6 respectively. We conclude our discussions in section 7.

2 Description of the ICA-MOG Model

This model makes use of the property that ICA can take into account higher order signal correlations, and a mixture of Gaussian functions to approximate non-Gaussian distributions. The model is constructed in the following steps:

J. Liu et al. (Eds.): IDEAL 2003, LNCS 2690, pp. 934–938, 2003.

1. *Independent Component Analysis* - ICA linearly transforms the asset returns into a set of statistically independent components (ICs). Each IC is non-normal and is mutually independent from the others.
2. *Mixtures of Gaussians* - To capture the non-gaussianity of each independent component, each IC is modelled with a mixture of Gaussians.
3. *Convolution* - Calculating the weighted sum of individual Gaussian distributions corresponds to evaluating the convolution of all ICs. This is used to obtain the return distribution of any desired portfolio.

ICA, also known as Blind Source Separation, corresponds to representing the asset return time series $r(t)$ as a linear transformation of statistically Independent Components (or sources) $s(t)$ as shown in equation 1. One popular ICA algorithm is the FastICA algorithm [2], its advantage lies in its computational efficiency and stability.

$$r_i = \sum_j a_{ij} s_j(t) \tag{1}$$

The financial portfolio returns are now represented by a set of independent components, with each component being non-Gaussian distributed. The mixture of Gaussian densities was shown to approximate non-Gaussian density distributions effectively by Kon [3]. Each of the independent components can be represented by a mixture of Gaussians as shown in equation 2. The parameters: mean μ_k, variance σ_k^2, and γ_k of the underlying Gaussians can be estimated by the Expectation Maximisation (EM) Algorithm.

$$s_j \sim \sum_{k=1}^{K} \gamma_k N(\mu_k, \sigma_k) \tag{2}$$

The final step is convolution of the component densities to recover the portfolio return distribution. This step relies on the statistical independence of the independent component. The portfolio return distribution is now made up of a mixture of Gaussians, and because of the statistical independence of independent components, calculating the weighted sum of individual Gaussian distributions corresponds to evaluating the convolution of all the components (Refer to Chin, Weigend and Zimmermann(1999) equations 18 to 29 for convolution formulae).

3   The Experiment and Data

Data Preprocessing - The main aim of our experiment is to apply the ICA-MOG model to portfolio returns over different time scales. The time scales we study are 1, 2, 4, 8, 16, 32 and 64 weeks. The data selected are intra-day data of the top 50 stocks on the ASX from October 1999 to May 2002. The time interval is 15 minutes, which gives 24 intervals per trading day. The opening prices are omitted since they do not represent the actual trading prices and incorporate overnight volatility which would benefit from separate modelling. From the price series, a continuous compounded log returns series is calcuated.

The experiments - For each of the time scales, 5 different portfolios are constructed based on the non-gaussianity of the stocks. The 50 stocks are ranked in order of increasing kurtosis, with Set 1 containing the 5 least non-gaussian stocks and Set 5 containing the 5 most non-gaussian stocks. For each portfolio set, the portfolio weight of each stock is calculated based on the market capitalisation of each stock. We have also found that there is no obvious relationship between the market capitalisation of the stocks and its non-gaussanity, as the largest stocks do not contribute to the most non-gaussian or the least non-gaussian portfolio (see results in [4]). For computational simplicity in our experiment, the number of Gaussians is chosen such that the in-sample mixture VaR error (see below for a definition) is somewhat smaller than the case of a single Gaussian model. This will not ensure the number of Gaussians chosen is the optimal number, but will ensure the ICA-MOG model performance can be better than the single Gaussian case.

Post-experiment Analysis - We compare the performance of the ICA-MOG model and the single Gaussian model numerically by using a popular risk measure called Value at Risk (VaR) [1]. VaR measures the worst expected returns over a specific time interval at a given confidence level or a given probablity. For the case of a Gaussian mixture, VaR can be expressed mathematically as:

$$p^{VaR} = 1 - C^{VaR} = \int_{-\infty}^{r^{VaR}} \sum_{k=1}^{K} \gamma_k N(r, \mu_k, \sigma_k) dr \qquad (3)$$

r^{VaR} represents the worst case return up to a specified confidence level C^{VaR}. The VaR from the mixture model and single model are computed at some specific confidence levels, and then compared to the empirically observed VaR. Empirical VaR is calculated by ranking the empirical log return series from highest to lowest. For example, empirical VaR at 95% corresponds to the worst 5% return over the duration.

4   Portfolio Gaussianity over Different Time Scales

An interesting finding from the distribution of the ASX intra-day data is that there is a trend of increasing kurtosis (as a measure of non-gaussanity) as the time period increases in all ASX top 50 stocks (see results in [4]). This suggests that the ICA-MOG model should be suitable over trading windows of 4 weeks or more as the distribution is highly non-Gaussian. However, when the time period becomes very short, (i.e. over a period of 1 to 2 weeks), the distribution of intraday returns could be better described as a discrete probability mass function with a high probability for zero returns. This is illustrated in Figure 1.

5   In-Sample Results

The in-sample results indicate the performance of ICA-MOG model in evaluating historical portfolio returns. Figure 2 (a) shows that the error made by the ICA-MOG model is much smaller than single model at 95% confidence level. Results

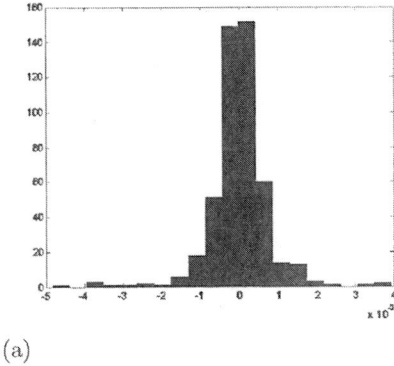
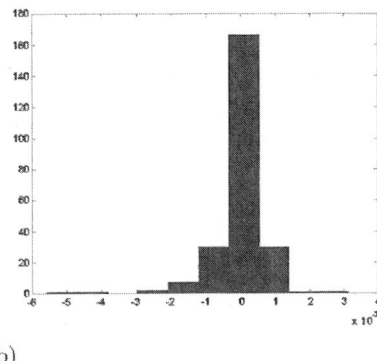

(a)   (b)

Fig. 1. (a) Histogram of portfolio distribution over 4 weeks (intraday data). (b) Histogram of portfolio distribution over 1 week (intraday data) Figure (a) is non-Gaussian distributed. Figure (b) can be described as a discrete mass function.

from other confidence levels also suggest the same findings. There is also an indication that the stronger the non-Gaussian behaviour of the portfolio returns, the better the fit of the mixture model over the single model.

In summary, both the mixture and the single model are appropriate in modelling portfolio returns that are Gaussian, however if the distribution is more non-Gaussian, the mixture of Gaussian model is the superior model. The reason being the mixture model takes into account asymmetric risk and fat tails in the distribution, while the single Gaussian model ignores asymmetry and assumes portfolio risk is symmetrical.

6 Out-of-Sample Results

The out-of-sample results shows the ICA-MOG model used for forecasting future returns and verifies that we are not overfitting the return distributions. To test the models we take the risk measure estimates from the in-sample set, and evaluate the performance with respect to the empirical measures of the next out-of-sample set (we chose a out-of-sample size equal to the in-sample length). In doing this we also investigate over what trading horizon the mixture of gaussian model should be used in forecasting future portfolio returns.

The results at 95% confidence level of figure 2 (b) shows that the mixture model is best in forecasting over a trading window of around 8 to 32 weeks, the reason being the mixture of gaussian model is able to capture the non-gaussianity in the testing set. However, over an even shorter time scale of 1-2 weeks, the return time series become more discrete, so the continuous assumption of the mixture model breaks down. On a much longer time scale, the mixture model still outperforms the single Gaussian approach perhaps due to increased in kurtosis. Results from other confidence levels also suggest the same findings.

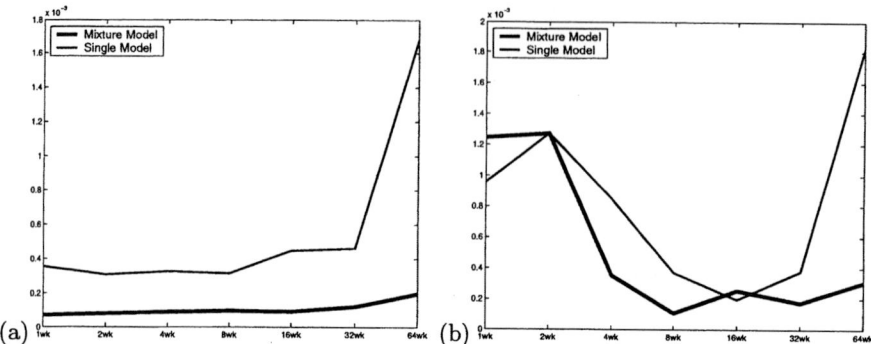

Fig. 2. (a) In-sample: Deviation of calcuated VaR from empirical VaR at 95% confidence (Average across the 5 portfolios) (b)Out-of-sample: Deviation of calculated VaR from empirical VaR at 95% confidence. The forecasting error is smaller around 8 to 30 weeks which suggests the model is best in forecasting over a trading window over these periods of time. (Average across the 5 portfolios)

7   Conclusion

Our results show that the ICA-MOG model is a superior technique in both evaluating intraday in-sample returns and forecasting out-of-sample returns. The ICA-MOG model has shown to be particularly useful in forecasting over a trading window of 8 to 32 weeks. Future work could be done on including some measures of transaction costs in the model and to develop a mutlinomial model for very short time scales of 1 to 2 weeks.

Acknowledgments. We acknowledge the provision of the intra-day price data and the software for preprocessing provided through the Australian Capital Markets Co-operative Research Centre (CMCRC) and its industry partners. We would like to thank Mr. Adam Blazejewski for his assistance in preprocessing the data.

References

1. E. Chin, A. Weigend and H. Zimmermann: *Computing portfolio risk using Gaussian mixtures and Independent Component Analysis*, Proceedings of the 1999 IEEE/IAFE/INFORMS, CIFEr'99, New York, March 1999, pp. 74–117.
2. A. Hyvarinen, J. Karhunen and E. Oja, *Independent Component Analysis*, John Wiley & Sons, 2001.
3. S. Kon: *Models of Stock Returns – A Comparison*, Journal of Finance Volume 39, pp.147–165
4. K. Lo, R. Coggins, *Intraday Analysis of Portfolios on the ASX using ICA*, Technical Report, CEL, School of Electrical and Information Engineering, University of Sydney, March 2003

Case-Based Reasoning: An Intelligent Approach Applied for Financial Crises Warning

Ying Wei[1] and Feng Li[2]

[1] Department of Systems Engineering and Engineering Management,
Chinese University of Hong Kong,Hong Kong
ywei@se.cuhk.edu.hk
[2] Institute of System Science and Engineering,
Huazhong University of Science and Technology, China
FengLee_Jeff@hotmail.com

Abstract. This paper presents case-based reasoning approach for financial crises warning. Unlike problem solving processes of the traditional rule-based reasoning approach, in which users directly obtain the problem's solution by rule series, CBR is a methodology providing adaptive solu-tions by systematic comparison between current situation and the simi-lar cases stored in the case library. Three critical techniques of CBR are studied intensively in this paper, namely: knowledge representation, re-trieval of similar cases and case learning. At the end of the paper, an implementation of the Case-based Financial Crises Warning Prototype System (CFCWPS) is described in summary.

1 Introduction

In the past decades, financial crises, such as the Southeast Asia financial crises, had taken great damages to the regional and even to the global financial market, counteracting the countries' economic development greatly. So it becomes an urgency of taking the precaution of financial crises and establishing the monitor mechanisms to keep crises away.

Currently there are four representative methods for financial crises predicting as followed, namely: "Signals Approach" by Graciela Kaminsky[1],[2],[3]; "a probit-based alternative model" by Frankel and Rose[2]; "STV approach" by Sachs, Tornell and Velasco[2]; and at last, "Subject Probability" by Liu Zunyi[2]. Although their research have devoted much to the field of crises forecasting research, few of them worked in the East Asia currency crises in 1997.

In the research of the financial crises warning, two kinds of considerations should be taken into account. The first one is the limits of general features of macroeconomics, which refers to the half-structured description of problems, difficulties of transferring experiences to rules and describing nonlinear character of features. The second one is the unique limits of crisis events, particularly including the fluctuation periods of crisis events and the influences of outbreaks. However, the recent research of financial crises predicting, majoring in linear

J. Liu et al. (Eds.): IDEAL 2003, LNCS 2690, pp. 939–943, 2003.

economic predicting model and rule-based expert system, cannot solve the presented contradiction before.

An intelligent machine learning method, Case-based Reasoning (CBR) method, is introduced to the financial crises warning in this paper. CBR is a reasoning method solving analogous problems and similar questions, first introduced by Schank (1982). Unlike problems solving processes of the traditional rule-based reasoning approach, in which users directly obtain the problem's solution by rule series, CBR is a methodology providing adaptive solutions by systematic comparison between current situation and the similar cases stored in the case library.

Applying CBR method to financial crises warning can overcome the difficulties mentioned above. Firstly, CBR can solve half-structured and non-structured problems, which avoids incomplete information caused by normal structured description. Secondly, presumed by the irrelevance of different attributes, CBR avoids considering the linear relationship only. At last, regarding the influences of outbreaks as solution adjusting, CBR calculates the unique limits of crisis events.

The research in this paper is an attempt to develop an alternative feasible method to financial crises warning problems. The remainder of the paper is organized as follows. First, we introduce the reasoning process of CBR briefly in Section 2. Then three critical techniques of CBR application are discussed intensively in Section 3. Section 4 describes the implementation of the Case-based Financial Crises Warning Prototype System (CFCWPS). Finally, section 5 gives the results and conclusion of this paper.

2   Reasoning Process of CBR in Financial Crises Warning

Similar to the process of human knowledge recognizing, the working flow of CBR is a process of drawing adaptive solution using the experiences and knowledge. The reasoning process of CBR in financial crises warning can be described as followed:

- Firstly, inputting financial problems to be predicted;
- Secondly, matching the problem cases and the old financial cases in case library, obtaining similarities;
- Thirdly, comparing the similarities and retrieving the matching cases;
- Fourthly, revising the solutions of matching cases according to the influence of outbreak and the character of input problems;
- Fifthly, outputting the solutions as the results of predicting.

3   Applying CBR for Financial Crises Warning

Three critical techniques are considered as the crucial part in CFCWPS (Case-based Financial Crises Warning Prototype System): knowledge representation, retrieval of similar cases and case learning. They will be discussed in detail in the following parts.

3.1 Knowledge Representation

In order to describe a country's financial status in any given time, including all the information needed, an effective way of case representation is required, which can not only describe the structural attributes, but also present the nonstructural attributes at the same time. A frame-based financial knowledge representation approach is presented in the paper. Serving as a data structure of storing information and knowledge of a given object or conception entity, frame-based representation is able to satisfy the basic hierarchy structured requirements for describing financial cases. Table1 shows a brief description.

Table 1. Frame-based financial event representation

Financial Event
Slot1: Country Information
Facet1:Country Name
Facet2: Year
$\cdots$
Slot2: Financial Status Information
Facet1: Basic Economic Indicators
Value: GDP growth, Inflation,$\cdots$
$\cdots$
Slot3: Case Related Knowledge
Facet1:Crises Origin
Facet2:Crises Process
$\cdots$

3.2 Case Retrieval

Case retrieval is the core of CBR reasoning process. The ability of retrieving an adaptive solution is often regarded as the criteria of evaluating a Case-based system's efficiency. A good retrieving strategy can accelerate speed of system retrieving, reduce computer resource expenditure and gain the maximized utility. Choosing case retrieving strategy is based on the foundation of case match algorithm. This paper selects Nearest Neighbor Algorithm (NN), which is the most widely used for its simple computing process and easy understanding, and has been used in many CBR applications. The formula below shows the rules of NN computing:

$$Sim_i = \sum_{i=1}^{n} \omega_j \cdot Sim_{ij} \quad (i = 1, \ldots, n; \; j = 1, \ldots, m) \tag{1}$$

The NN computing process in case-based financial crises warning can be described as follows:

- Inputting the new case and data preprocessing
- Acquiring weights of each indicator
- Computing similarities of indicators separately
- Aggregating similarities of the old cases and Ranking by similarities
- Retrieving matching cases by ranking
- Outputting the matching cases' solutions

3.3   Case Learning

Case learning is the process of obtaining new cases and diminishing old cases in the case library.

Two thresholds, reasoning threshold and restoring threshold are introduced in the case learning process. Reasoning threshold is used for judging whether the result case matches the input case. At the time when the similarity is greater or equal to the threshold, the result case is considered matched successfully; otherwise, failed. Restoring threshold determines whether the input case should be added to the case library. If similarity is under the threshold, input cases are added; otherwise, abandoned. These two thresholds value from 0 to 1, which should be set before each reasoning process.

When the similarity is smaller than the reasoning threshold and the input case cannot get a matching case in the library, it is considered unsuccessful reasoning, the case learning is then achieved by the domain expert giving the solutions and added to the case library.

4   Implementation of CFCWPS Based on CBR Method

Fig. 1 shows the system structure of CFCWPS based on the CBR method, including two function modules: Knowledge mining and Financial cases reasoning subsystem.

Knowledge mining module completes the preprocessing of data and analysis of knowledge, transfers the original data to applicable knowledge and sets up the case library as the knowledge foundation of subsequent reasoning.

Financial cases reasoning module implements the process of case reasoning, including input cases representation, case retrieval, revising solutions of matching cases and case learning process. The warning signal is sent out by adaptive solutions of existed crises.

5   Results and Conclusions

Using the financial data of East Asia countries and Latin American in the 90's, a forecasting test on Thailand's 1997 financial warning was taken and the results showed the possibility of crises in Thailand, 1997, was above 70 percent, much higher than the KLS method mentioned before.

The results imply that CBR method is applicable for financial crises warning. With the development of Artificial Intelligence (AI) technique applied to macroeconomic forecasting, more and more AI methods will show their advantages in this field. Combining CBR method with other AI approach, e.g., Artificial Neural Network (ANN) and genetic algorithm (GA), will probably optimize the retrieving and matching process of CBR and get some improved results. That will be a promoting exploring to macroeconomic forecasting and business intelligence.

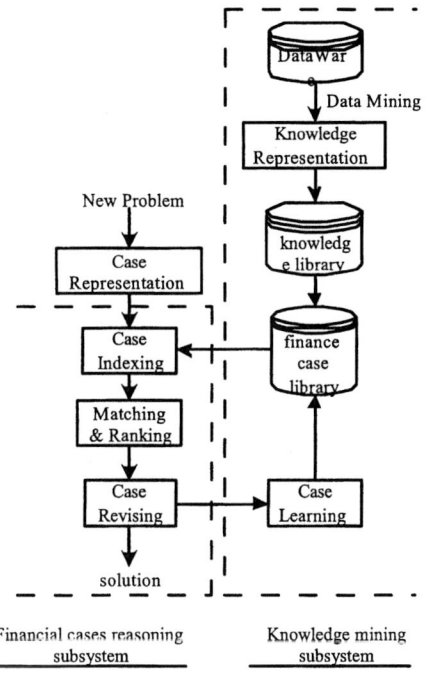

Fig. 1. Layer modeling for the proposed system

References

1. Andrew Berg,Catherine Pattillo:Predicting currency crises: The indicators approach and an alternative. Journal of International Money and Finance. Vol. 18.(1999) 561–586.
2. Liu Zhiqiang:Evaluation to the methods of forecasting currency crises.World Economy. Vol. 7,(2000) 16–21.
3. Graciela L. Kaminsky, Saul Lizondo, Carmen M. Reinhart:Leading Indicators of Currency Crises. IMF WorkPaper 97/79
4. David W. Aha:The omnipresence of case-based reasoning in science and application. Knowledge-based systems. Vol. 11,(1998) 261–278
5. Irma Becerra-Fernandez, David W. Aha:Case-Based Problem Solving for Knowledge Management System. Proceedings of the 12th Annual International FLAIRS, NCARAI Technical Report AIC-99-005
6. Watson,I.:Case-based reasoning is a methodology not a technology. Knowledge-Based Systems Vol. 12,(1999) 303–308

Pattern Recognition in Classification of Intelligent Composites during Smart Manufacturing[*]

Nasser Esmaili[1] and Afshad Talaie[2]

[1]Artificial Intelligence Department, University of New South Wales, Sydney, NSW,
Australia   nasser@cse.unsw.edu.ai
[2]Department of Intelligent Materials Engineering, Osaka City University, Osaka, Japan
iriaus@hotmail.com

Abstract. The development of an on line computer based classification system for the real time classification of different composites is addressed in this study. Different parameters were collected simultaneously when embedded sensors (dielectric, optical fibre, and piezoelectric sensors) were used within two different composite matrices during the curing process. The measurements were used by an algorithm-based software as a logged data file, resulting in to induction of a decision tree. Later, a systematic software is designed based on the rules derived from this decision tree, to recognise the type of composites used in the experiment together with recognition of their physical and mechanical characteristics. This is a new approach to data acquisition in intelligent materials produced by smart manufacturing system.

Keywords. Computer modelling, process controls, smart composites, smart manufacturing.

1 Introduction

During the manufacturing of the thermoset composite materials, the curing process is always given special attention since it is crucial to the quality of structural component of the thermoset composites. Beyond any doubt on line/real time techniques are required for *in situ* monitoring of the curing process to study the kinetics and characteristics of the process from both chemical and physical/mechanical properties points of views. Curing is a chemical reaction in nature to form a cross-linked molecular structure that increases the molecular weight together with viscosity and modulus. If within a manufacturing process one can control the viscosity and modulus together with the changes in strain of the composite under process such that an intelligent material can be produced with desired mechanical/physical properties, then such a system can be denoted as "smart manufacturing system". This could be

---

[*] The authors would like to thank NEDO (New Energy and Industrial Technology Development Organisation, Japan) and RIMCOF (R & D Institute of Metals and Composites for Future Industries) for supporting the project. Also, we are thankful to Tatsuro Kosaka[2] , Nobuo Oshima[2] , Katsuhiko Osaka[2] , Youichi Asano[2] and Takehito Fukuda[2] for providing the chemical data for this study.

J. Liu et al. (Eds.): IDEAL 2003, LNCS 2690, pp. 944–958, 2003.
© Springer-Verlag Berlin Heidelberg 2003

only possible via the use of smart sensors/actuators within an on-line adoptive control of the manufacturing process (intelligent manufacturing) [1-3].

Smart composites have been widely used in advanced engineering products such as airplanes, space structures and military ships. The moulding process of thermosetting resins includes the curing process, in which liquid monomeric resin becomes a rigid solid by chemical cross-linking under proper conditions. Since the curing process of the thermosetting polymers governs mechanical properties and integrity of the final products, it is very important to determine optimum conditions in the moulding process. These conditions have been obtained mainly by trial and error and thereby it makes the curing process inefficient. The inefficiency increases the manufacturing cost of polymeric composites. Therefore, the efficient (short time) and optimally controlled cure processing techniques of polymers and composites need to be introduced. The cure monitoring is performed to monitor chemical or/and mechanical properties in the curing process of thermosetting resin. Consequently a variety of sensors have been developed over the past decade for on line/real time measurements to name few piezoelectric, dielectric and optical fibre sensors [4]. Besides these sensors integration of a computerised system within the curing system is required for controlling the mechanical properties of the composites during the process. The integrated system needs to be supported by an algorithm by which pattern recognition process and online modelling is possible.

Due to the instability of the sensor response, quantification can often only be accomplished by use of either calibration curves or standard addition approach. While these approaches may yield useful quantitative data, they do not fully utilise the capability of the sensors. More significantly, the adoption of these quantitative approaches defeat some of the purposes of modern sensing technology in terms of speed, repeatability, reusability and ease of use. These problems require the adoption of novel strategy for the fabrication of sensors with artificial intelligence that will enable the identification, characterisation and classification of the response pattern. Such pattern recognition approach, if feasible, will enable reliable determination of the mechanical and physical properties of the composites during the curing process and reduce the emphasis or concern on the variation of sensor response with repeated use.

The principles of "artificial intelligence" methods based on statistical pattern recognition are similar to those used in human decision making. This usually involves collection of information for a known set of cases during the experiments. However, instead of adopting a subjective approach in synthesising, the information is replaced by equations derived from the data and used to classify cases into groups. Hence, unlike human decision making, a pattern recognition approach is objective and reproducible. The development of appropriate artificial intelligence methods that can use comprehensive information from the sensor response rather than just the signal magnitude will therefore provide a considerable progress towards realisation of the optimum performance of these new devices. These sensors (piezoelectric, optical fibre and dielectric sensors) have been recently integrated to monitor impedance, strain and viscosity profiles of the reinforced plastics during the curing process by using a new SISI [4] method and DOP [4] sensing element. However, no information on integration of a computer-aided system to control any deviation from the desired properties for composites has been reported. Deviations from the optimum cure conditions can lead to laminates with undesirable levels of built-in stresses due to differences in fibre and matrix expansion coefficients as the composite is cooled after curing. Such information would be of considerable value to the manufacturers of composite who need an *in situ* signal that can be fundamentally correlated to the processing parameters in order to guide the process along a desired path. The SISI system with its DOP sensing element enables us to control any deviation from the desired process during the curing process if it is supported by a machine learning program which is the thrust of this paper.

2 Experimental

To study the characteristics of the piezoelectric element the mixture of melts, epoxy resin and a cure agent were transferred in to a thin rectangular tank where the piezoelectric ceramics was also located. The experiment was carried out at 40°C in a thermostatic oven. An LCR meter was used to measure the impedance of the piezoelectric ceramics, supplying the alternating voltage and to measure the electronic data (impedance, and phase angle) as outputs. For the measurement of the internal strains, FTI-Buss500 strain measurement system was used [4]. The GFRP laminate used for the internal strain measurement is a unidirectional laminate consisting of 20 plies of SCOTCHPLY™.

The C4.5 program [5], used for model production in these experiments, was executed under a SUN operating system. The program works based on an algorithm, generating an initial decision tree from a set of training cases. The C4.5 rule generator program using this decision tree produces rules for the modelling of the desired system. We have used different settings and various combinations of recorded data for the model generation, and the results will be discussed further.

Several experiments have been performed, during which two composites have been tested and five attributes for each composite have also been measured. These attributes are temperature, strain, permittivity, loss factor, ion viscosity (in Log form), impedance and phase-angle, which are referred to as *Temp*, *Strn*, *Perm*, *Loss*, *LogI*, *Imp*, and *Phase* respectively hereafter. We will call the composites *Composite1* and *Composite2*. These composites have different commercial names and chemical structures [4]. During the experiments, the measurements for each composite have been logged in to an individual data file, which are later pre-processed before being applied to the C4.5 program. The program has been executed on an IBM-compatible machine under SUN-Sparc operating system. C4.5 can generate decision tree and rule set based on the collected data. The decision tree and/or the rules generated for the experiments are used generally for modelling purposes.

3 Results and Discussions

The files containing measurements for Temp, Strn, Perm, Loss and LogI were logged separately in each experiment for each composite. In addition to the mentioned attributes, the time of the measurement readings were also logged along. However, the time recordings have not been used for modelling. In figures 1 to 4, a set of graphs for the attributes on the basis of the time (hour) has been presented. As can be seen from the figures 1 and 2, the Temp, LogI and the Strn changes for both are very similar. However, the Perm and Loss data are very different for each composite. So, it is very natural to see the lesser effect for those two in the modelling criteria.

The files later were copied in to one file and pre-processed in order to have all the attributes along with the name of composite on one line for each measurement, which from now on will be called one training case. The pre-processing also involves the change of format to be recognised by the C4.5 programs. A sample of this file is shown below. In case there are any missing values for a particular reading, they are replaced with '?', so that the program knows the values are not to be used for the modelling decisions in those particular training cases. Every line contains Temp, Perm, Loss, LogI, Strn, Imp values, Phase values and the name of the composite. The last field is called a *'class'* while the other ones are known as *'attributes'*.

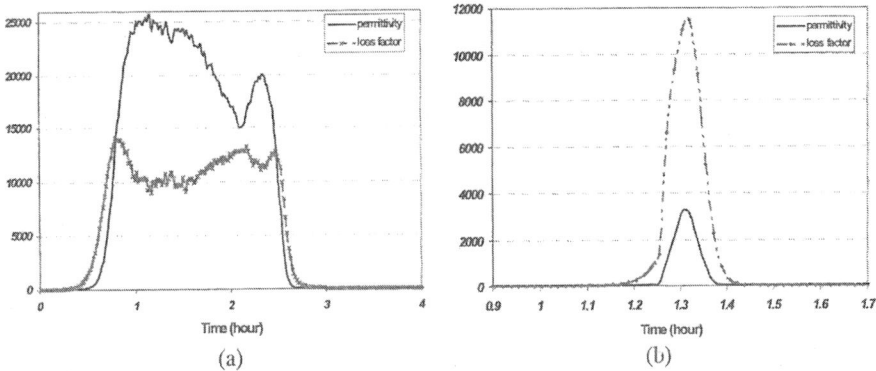

(a)   (b)

Fig. 1. Permittivity and Loss Factor profiles vs. Time during the curing process of composites (a) Comp_A   (b) Comp_B

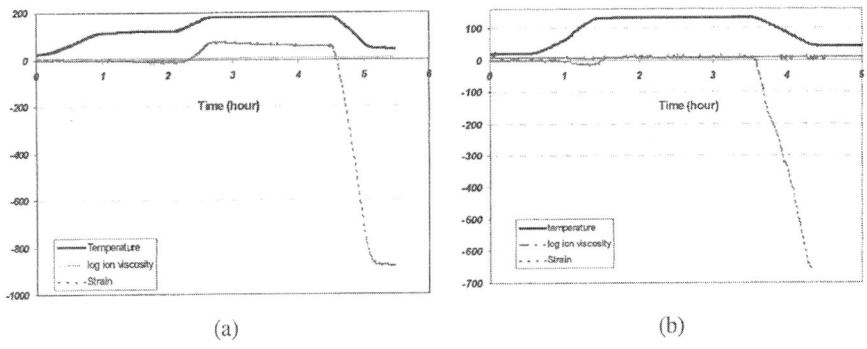

(a)   (b)

Fig. 2. Temperature, Log-Ion-Viscosity and Strain profiles vs. Time during the curing process of composites   (a) Comp_A   (b) Comp_B

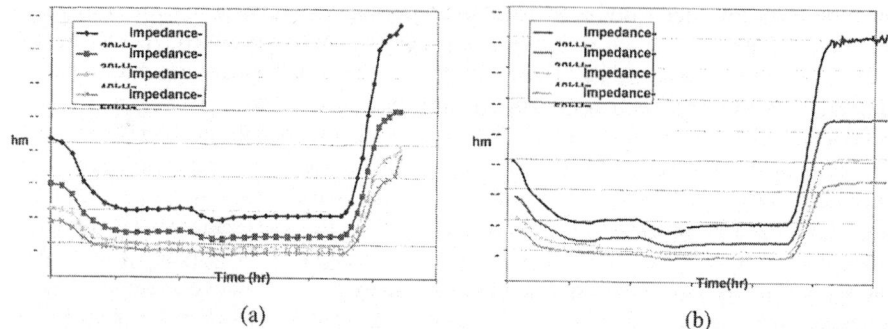

Fig. 3. Impedance profiles vs. Time during the curing process of composites   (a) Composite1
(b) Composite2

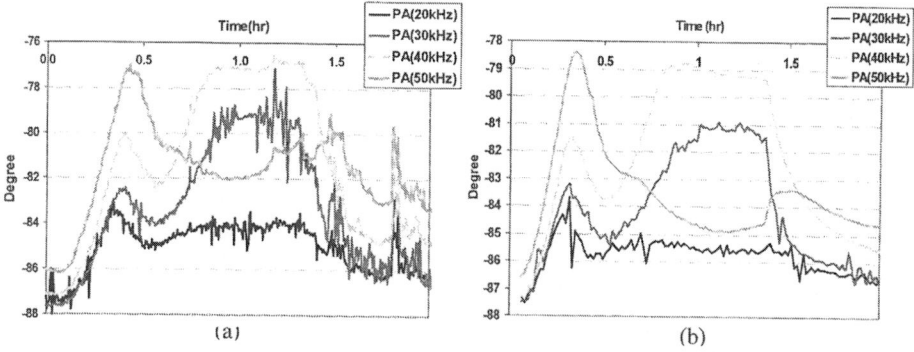

Fig. 4. Phase-angle profiles vs. Time during the curing process of composites AO represents
the Phase-Angle   (a) Composite1 (b) Composite2

Table 1. A sample of training/test cases logged during the curing process

		...			
41.87	16.932	0.382	8.672	...	Composite2
41.848	17.616	0.388	8.665	...	Composite2
41.774	17.179	0.852	8.324	...	Composite2
41.725	17.568	0.904	8.298	...	Composite2
101.95	21099.8	16414.7	4.039	...	Composite1
103.11	22510.5	15912.7	4.053	...	Composite1
103.339	18855.1	13615.7	4.121	...	Composite1
104.17	23840.4	14910.1	4.081	...	Composite1
104.64	21.135	0.935	8.284	...	Composite1
		...			

In addition to the data file containing training cases, C4.5 program also needs a name
file, which provides the name and specification of each attribute and the classes in the
data file. The name file for this experiment is shown below:

```
Composite1,
Temp: continuous.
Perm: continuous.
Loss: continuous.
LogI: continuous.
Strn: continuous.
Imp-20K: continuous.
Imp-30K: continuous.
Imp-40K: continuous.
Imp-50K: continuous.
Phase-20K: continuous.
Phase-30K: continuous.
Phase-40K: continuous.
Phase-50K: continuous.
```

The classes are declared on the first line of the file as Composite1 and Composite2. The rest of the lines present the name and the type of the attributes. All the attributes in the provided data file are considered continuos values (natural numbers) which mean numeric values. C4.5 program summarises the training cases provided by the data file in to a decision tree and later to a set of rules by means of the name of the attributes provided in the name file. The data file can either be used as a whole or can be divided into two separate files, training cases and unseen (or test) cases. In the first option, the summarised decision tree is finalised by simplifying it, while in the second option the decision tree is summarised based on the training cases and then tested against the unseen cases which will result in a smaller decision tree.

Two different modelling procedures have been performed. In first model, only Temp, Strn, Perm, Loss and LogI have been used, while the second model benefits from the Imp and Phase values for different frequencies. Appendices A to C are related to the first model, while Appendix D is from the second modelling. For each modelling level, two sets of operations was executed, only training cases and training cases plus the unseen/test cases. However as shown at the end of Appendix A and B, the rate of error (both present and estimated) for the decision tree with test cases is less than the one for training cases only. The total number of cases [*each training/test case is a combination of recorded attributes which are located on the same line, as shown in Table 1*] logged for the first model during the experiments are 958, out of which 862 is kept in the data file (training cases) and 96 cases have been used in the test file (unseen cases).

As can be seen from both appendices A and B, the size of the decision tree for training and test cases is less than training cases only, 33 branches against 45 (classification table, located at the bottom of appendices A and B). Furthermore, the classification table at the end of Appendix B clearly shows that 65 cases have been classified as Composite1 and 31 as Composite2, which is very successful and there is no error. However, the overall estimated error against unseen cases remains 2.8% according to the original decision tree, which is worked out only based on the 862 training cases. This point has to be added here that the test cases have been randomly selected from the original training cases. The selection process has been achieved by using a UNIX program from every 10 lines. By observing the final decision tree from the training and test cases, it was noted that the tree did not show any dependency on the Loss and LogI attributes. In order to test this theory, the modelling was repeated on the following situations, no Loss data, no LogI data and finally without either data present in the training cases. Table 2, in previous page, shows the corresponding estimated error for each case.

Table 2. Comparison table on the summaries of the decision trees, deduced during the modelling process

Before Pruning		After Pruning			
Size	Errors	Size	Errors		
45	3 (0.3%)	37	6 (0.6%)	(3.3%) <<	← Training cases only (958 cases) – all attributes
33	1 (0.1%)	33	1 (0.1%)	(2.8%) <<	← Training and test cases (862 train.) – all attributes
33	0 (0.0%)	33	0 (0.0%)	(2.8%) <<	← Training and test cases (96 test) – all attributes
43	3 (0.3%)	43	3 (0.3%)	(3.1%) <<	← Training cases only (958 cases) – No Loss
35	4 (0.5%)	31	4 (0.5%)	(3.1%) <<	← Training and test cases (862 train.) – No Loss
35	1 (0.1%)	31	1 (0.1%)	(3.1%) <<	← Training and test cases (96 test) – No Loss
35	20 (2.1%)	31	20 (2.1%)	(4.5%) <<	← Training cases only (958 cases) – No LogI
25	17 (2.0%)	19	17 (2.0%)	(3.8%) <<	← Training and test cases (862 train.) – No LogI
25	4 (4.2%)	19	4 (4.2%)	(3.8%) <<	← Training and test cases (96 test) – No LogI
39	1 (0.1%)	39	1 (0.1%)	(2.9%) <<	← Training cases only (958 cases) – No Loss & LogI
31	2 (0.2%)	31	2 (0.2%)	(2.8%) <<	← Training and test cases (862 train.) – No Loss & LogI
31	1 (1.0%)	31	1 (1.0%)	(2.8%) <<	← Training and test cases (96 test) – No Loss & LogI

The first and third columns show the size of the decision trees before and after pruning, while the second and forth provide the information on the errors produced by the un-matching cases against the produced decision tree. In x $(y\%)$ under Errors columns, x represents the number of un-matching cases and y shows the error rate caused by the un-matching cases. The first raw of each block is the outcome for training cases only used, while the second and third are for the training and test cases used. Furthermore, the algorithm used in the program can provide an estimate of error caused by future unseen cases. As a result and based on the probability theorems, the estimate error is more than the calculated errors on presented training and test cases. Referring to the Appendices A to C, the reader can clearly see a number at the end of each leaf of the decision trees. The numbers are enclosed in brackets. Either (N) or (N/E), in which, N represents the number of training cases covered by the leaf and E specifies the predicted errors if N set of unseen cases were classified by the decision tree. Table 3 shows the confusion matrix for the training and test cases for all four generated models. For more information on the error estimates, the reader should refer to [5].

Table 2 clearly shows that the first and last models show the very similar performances. While the all attributes model has an estimated error rate of 3.3%, the overall estimated error of the no-Loss&LogI model is 2.9%. However, the confusion matrix in Table 3 suggests that based on the produced model, the no-Loss&LogI model classifies one of the Comp-B cases as Comp-A. But, overall the two models perform very closely. So far, in order to establish the reliability of the classification model, we divided the logged data into training and test sets, built the model using only the training set, and examined its performance against the unseen cases (test set). This method is quite satisfactory when we have a vast amount of data logged during experiments. However, it is likely to have some difficulties in the more common circumstances when we have lesser data. If we choose to use the majority of the collected data as test cases to get a very accurate fix on estimated error rate, then the training set will be so small that can produce such inaccurate classification model. In addition, when the number of logged cases is limited, different separations of data into training and test cases can produce large difference in the estimated error rates on the unseen cases. So, in order to accomplish a better accuracy on the test cases, we can use cross-validation procedure.

Table 3. Confusion matrices resulted from the four previously described modelling processes

All attributes		No Loss		No LogI		No Loss&LogI		← classified as
(a)	(b)	(a)	(b)	(a)	(b)	(a)	(b)	
65		65		65		65		(a): class Composite1
	31	1	30	4	27	1	30	(b): class Composite2

Table 4. Outcome for Cross-Validation on entire of data

Siz	Errors	Siz	Errors	Estimate	
33	1(0.1%)	33	1(0.1%)	(2.8%)	<<
33	0(0.0%)	33	0(0.0%)	(2.8%)	<<
35	3(0.3%)	31	3(0.3%)	(2.9%)	<<
35	0(0.0%)	31	0(0.0%)	(2.9%)	<<
35	4(0.5%)	35	4(0.5%)	(3.3%)	<<
35	2(2.1%)	35	2(2.1%)	(3.3%)	<<
35	1(0.1%)	35	1(0.1%)	(2.9%)	<<
35	1(1.0%)	35	1(1.0%)	(2.9%)	<<
33	4(0.5%)	33	4(0.5%)	(3.2%)	<<
33	5(5.2%)	33	5(5.2%)	(3.2%)	<<
27	1(0.1%)	27	1(0.1%)	(2.4%)	<<
27	1(1.0%)	27	1(1.0%)	(2.4%)	<<
27	2(0.2%)	27	2(0.2%)	(2.5%)	<<
27	1(1.0%)	27	1(1.0%)	(2.5%)	<<
37	0(0.0%)	37	0(0.0%)	(2.9%)	<<
37	3(3.1%)	37	3(3.1%)	(2.9%)	<<
33	1(0.1%)	33	1(0.1%)	(2.7%)	<<
33	1(1.1%)	33	1(1.1%)	(2.7%)	<<
41	1(0.1%)	41	1(0.1%)	(3.2%)	<<
41	2(2.1%)	41	2(2.1%)	(3.2%)	<<
Train: 33.6	1.8(0.2%)	33.2	1.8(0.2%)	(2.9%)	<<
Test 33.6	1.6(1.7%)	33.2	1.6(1.7%)	(2.9%)	<<

In cross-validation procedure, we have tried to break the data into 10 blocks of cases with as much possible unified cases and class distribution. Then 10 different classification models were made, as explained before, in which one block of data is used as test set. This will make sure that each test case only appears in exactly one test set. In this case, we believe that the average error rate on unseen cases can be a good factor for the error rate of the model built from all data.

However, this factor can give a rather overestimate of the error rate, since each model is made from a subset of the whole data. The result of the cross-validation process is a number of different decision trees (in this case 10). The deduced trees are based on the provided training cases, and since those are different sets in each time the tree is produced the tree will be different. As a result, the size and error rate for each tree will be different, too. However, the average for each item can be obtained. Able 4 represents the outcome of the 10-way cross-validation procedure on the whole of data, showing that the average size of the decision tree before and after pruning are 33.6 and 33.2, respectively.The average error rate on training cases is 1.8 (0.2%) while the same for the test cases has been 1.6 (1.7%). This in turn will cause the system to estimate an error rate of 2.9% for the unseen cases. For comparison purposes, the 10-way cross-validation was also performed for the no-Loss&LogI data.

Table 5. Outcome for Cross-Validation on the no-Loss&LogI data

	Size	Errors	Size	Errors	Estimate	
	37	1(0.1%)	37	1(0.1%)	(3.1%)	<<
	37	0(0.0%)	37	0(0.0%)	(3.1%)	<<
	39	2(0.2%)	39	1(0.1%)	(3.2%)	<<
	39	1(1.0%)	39	1(1.0%)	(3.2%)	<<
	33	1(0.1%)	33	1(0.1%)	(2.8%)	<<
	33	2(2.1%)	33	2(2.1%)	(2.8%)	<<
	37	1(0.1%)	37	1(0.1%)	(3.1%)	<<
	37	0(0.0%)	37	0(0.0%)	(3.1%)	<<
	37	2(0.2%)	37	2(0.2%)	(3.2%)	<<
	37	3(3.1%)	37	3(3.1%)	(3.2%)	<<
	37	1(0.1%)	37	1(0.1%)	(3.1%)	<<
	37	1(1.0%)	37	1(1.0%)	(3.1%)	<<
	33	1(0.1%)	33	1(0.1%)	(2.7%)	<<
	33	1(1.0%)	33	1(1.0%)	(2.7%)	<<
	37	2(0.2%)	37	2(0.2%)	(3.2%)	<<
	37	2(2.1%)	37	2(2.1%)	(3.2%)	<<
	31	1(0.1%)	31	1(0.1%)	(2.6%)	<<
	31	1(1.1%)	31	1(1.1%)	(2.6%)	<<
	27	1(0.1%)	27	1(0.1%)	(2.4%)	<<
	27	3(3.2%)	27	3(3.2%)	(2.4%)	<<
Train	34.8	1.3(0.1%)	34.6	1.2(0.1%)	(2.9%)	<<
Test	34.8	1.4(1.5%)	34.6	1.4(1.5%)	(2.9%)	<<

As previously explained, the whole data is used without the loss factor and log-ion-viscosity related readings. The whole set of data has 958 training cases and while excluding the two attributes does not change the number of cases, hence the overall procedure is the same as the previous case. Table 5 is the outcome of this cross-validation procedure. As can be seen from the average results in both tables, the model constructed based on the data without the Loss and LogI related measurements is more reliable. The average estimated error rate is 2.9% for both models, while the number decision tree's branches as well as the errors on unseen cases and training cases are lower for the second model. This proves that these two attributes have a little effect on the classification model.

And, this is very clear from the above graphs (Figure 5), which show the LogI related measured data for Composite1 (on the left) and Composite2 (on the right). Figure 5 illustrates the loss factor profiles for both composites. it is clear from the graphs that the loss factor values for the composites are completely different. Consequently the best model is the one constructed based on the whole data without the Loss and LogI attributes. So, the final data files used to construct the desired classification model, will only include *Temp, Strn, Perm* and the *class*. A complete copy of the decision tree concluded for this classification model is presented in Appendix C.

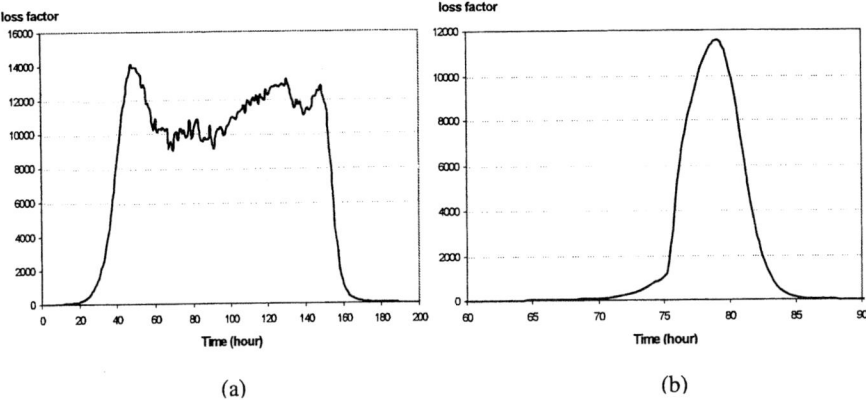

Fig. 5. Loss Factor profile vs. Time   (a) Comp_A   (b) Comp_B

In order to examine the possibility of any internal correlation between the impedance and phase-angle values, once more the data files were split and two new models were created. Table 6 summarises the deduced models. The top part is for the whole of data, the middle part model only has phase-angle values, while the last part is related to the impedance data only.

Table 7 represents the confusion matrix for the three models. It clearly shows that the all-attributes and impedance-only models have very similar performances. While the first model has an estimated error rate of 2.5%, the overall estimate error of the second model is 5.5%. All together, the above confusion matrix suggests that the all-attributes model has a better classification for Composite2. This is also confirmed by the total estimated error for the first model from table 6.

Once again, to confirm this theory, a 10-way cross validation on the whole of data for frequency related attributes was performed. As a result, the average size of the decision trees before and after pruning are 27.6 branches. The average error rate on training cases is 5.9 (6.0%), while the same for the test cases has been 1.8 (1.5%). This in turn will make an error estimate rate of 2.3% for the unseen cases. For comparison purposes, the 10-way cross validation test for impedance only data provided 32.4 branches for decision tree, 50.6 (4.7%) error rate for training and 7.6 (6.4%) error rate for test cases. The estimated error rate for this model was 6.9%, which is much more than the first one. This fact confirms the previous finding that all the frequency related attributes are necessary for a reliable model of the system.

Finally, based on the above discussion, it is possible to make a system to automatically monitor the temperature, strain and permittivity using sensors, and maintain the correct levels using attached actuators to the test platform. Using this system, it will be possible to produce composite to match a desired model with desired properties.

4 Conclusion

Based on the above discussion it can be concluded that an integrated computerised/sensing/control system is necessary to produce smart materials with desired properties for advanced technologies. In this system an online/real time sensing technique is combined with a powerful computer system to enable us on line pattern recognition and therefore control of mechanical properties of the products.

Table 6. Comparison table on the summaries of the decision trees, deduced during the modelling process

Before Pruning		After Pruning			
Size	Errors	Size	Errors	Estimate	
3	3 (0.3%)	33	3 (0.3%)	(2.1%) <<	← Training cases only (1193 cases) :: all attributes
2	9 (0.8%)	23	9 (0.8%)	(2.5%) <<	← Training and test cases (1073 train.) :: all attributes
2	2 (1.7%)	23	2 (1.7%)	(2.5%) <<	← Training and test cases (120 test) :: all attributes
5	33 (2.8%)	43	36 (3.0%)	(5.8%) <<	← Training cases only (958 cases) :: Phase-Angle
6	17 (1.6%)	63	17 (1.6%)	(5.5%) <<	← Training and test cases (862 train.) :: Phase-Angle
6	5 (4.2%)	63	5 (4.2%)	(5.5%) <<	← Training and test cases (96 test) :: Phase-Angle
2	60 (5.0%)	25	60 (5.0%)	(6.9%) <<	← Training cases only (958 cases) :: Impedance
3	55 (5.1%)	25	56 (5.2%)	(7.2%) <<	← Training and test cases (862 train.) :: Impedance
3	5 (4.2%)	25	5 (4.2%)	(7.2%) <<	← Training and test cases (96 test) :: Impedance

Table 7. Confusion matrices resulted for three modelling processes

All attributes		Phase-angle Only		Impedance Only		
(a)	(b)	(a)	(b)	(a)	(b)	← classified as
84		83	1	84		(a): class Composite1
2	34	4	32	5	31	(b): class Composite2

References

[1] N. Esmaili, A. Talaie, and F. Talaie: "Real Time Computer Based Communication with Conducting Polymers: An Artificial Intelligence Approach", *Analytical Proceedings Including Analytical Communications*, (1995) Vol. 32, 405–414.

[2] N. Esmaili, A. Talaie, J.A. Romagnoli, and T. Taguchi: "Towards Real Time Ion Classification Using a Machine Learning Algorithm (C4.5): A case Study of a conducting Polymer Ion Detector", *Iranian Polymer Journal*, (1997) Vol. 6 (3-17), 185–194.

[3] A. Talaie, T. Kosaka, N. Oshima, K. Osaka, Y. Asano and T. Fukuda: "Report on simultaneous ion viscosity, strain, and impedance measurement technique using a novel integrated DOP sensing element for on line characterisation of smart structures", *Smart Material Structure*, to be published.

[4] A. Talaie, T. Kosaka, N. Oshima, K. Osaka, Y. Asano and T. Fukuda: "Towards dual in situ sensing using an integrated piezoelectric wafer and optical fibre sensor: a new approach towards an online/real time smart manufacturing for production of intelligent structures for aerospace applications", *ICCE 7*, Denver, USA, (2000) 627–630.

[5] J.R Quinlan, *C4.5: Programs for Machine Learning.*, Morgan Kaufmann (1993).

Appendix A: (Decision tree for training cases only)

Read 958 cases (5 attributes) from data_notest.data

Decision tree

```
Loss <= 4.544 :
|  Strn <= -23 :
|  |  Strn <= -673 :
|  |  |  Temp <= 43.602 : Composite2 (7.0)
|  |  |  Temp > 43.602 : Composite1 (61.6/0.6)
|  |  Strn > -673 :
|  |  |  Temp <= 76.706 : Composite2 (27.6)
|  |  |  Temp > 76.706 :
|  |  |  |  Temp > 129.33 : Composite1 (18.0)
|  |  |  |  Temp <= 129.33 :
|  |  |  |  |  Strn > -297 : Composite2 (20.0)
|  |  |  |  |  Strn <= -297 :
|  |  |  |  |  |  Perm > 22.74 : Composite2 (4.0)
|  |  |  |  |  |  Perm <= 22.74 :
|  |  |  |  |  |  |  Temp > 83.621 : Composite1 (20.0)
|  |  |  |  |  |  |  Temp <= 83.621 :
|  |  |  |  |  |  |  |  Strn <= -508 : Composite1 (4.0)
|  |  |  |  |  |  |  |  Strn > -508 : Composite2 (3.0)
|  Strn > -23 :
|  |  Logl > 7.672 : Composite2 (197.2)
|  |  Logl <= 7.672 :
|  |  |  Perm <= 26.815 : Composite2 (8.7)
|  |  |  Perm > 26.815 : Composite1 (2.0)
Loss > 4.544 :
|  Perm <= 25.879 :
|  |  Temp <= 146.65 : Composite2 (13.0/1.0)
|  |  Temp > 146.65 : Composite1 (13.0)
|  Perm > 25.879 :
|  |  Strn <= -11 :
|  |  |  Strn <= -14 : Composite2 (13.0)
|  |  |  Strn > -14 : Composite1 (16.0)
|  |  Strn > -11 :
|  |  |  Logl <= 7.362 :
|  |  |  |  Strn > -10 : Composite1 (466.0/1.0)
|  |  |  |  Strn <= -10 :
|  |  |  |  |  Tomp <- 125.37 : Compooito1 (36.0)
|  |  |  |  |  Temp > 125.37 : Composite2 (3.0)
|  |  |  Logl > 7.362 :
|  |  |  |  Strn > 25 : Composite1 (12.0)
|  |  |  |  Strn <= 25 :
|  |  |  |  |  Strn > 1 : Composite2 (2.0)
|  |  |  |  |  Strn <= 1 :
|  |  |  |  |  |  Temp <= 79.39 : Composite1 (8.0)
|  |  |  |  |  |  Temp > 79.39 : Composite2 (3.0/1.0)
```

Simplified Decision tree

```
Loss <= 4.544 :
|  Strn <= -23 :
|  |  Strn <= -673 :
|  |  |  Temp <= 43.602 : Composite2 (7.0/1.3)
|  |  |  Temp > 43.602 : Composite1 (61.6/2.0)
|  |  Strn > -673 :
|  |  |  Temp <= 76.706 : Composite2 (27.6/1.4)
|  |  |  Temp > 76.706 :
|  |  |  |  Temp > 129.33 : Composite1 (18.0/1.3)
|  |  |  |  Temp <= 129.33 :
|  |  |  |  |  Strn > -297 : Composite2 (20.0/1.3)
|  |  |  |  |  Strn <= -297 :
|  |  |  |  |  |  Perm > 22.74 : Composite2 (4.0/1.2)
|  |  |  |  |  |  Perm <= 22.74 :
|  |  |  |  |  |  |  Temp > 83.621 : Composite1 (20.0/1.3)
|  |  |  |  |  |  |  Temp <= 83.621 :
|  |  |  |  |  |  |  |  Strn <= -508 : Composite1 (4.0/1.2)
|  |  |  |  |  |  |  |  Strn > -508 : Composite2 (3.0/1.1)
|  Strn > -23 :
|  |  Logl > 7.672 : Composite2 (197.2/1.4)
|  |  Logl <= 7.672 :
|  |  |  Perm <= 26.815 : Composite2 (8.7/1.3)
|  |  |  Perm > 26.815 : Composite1 (2.0/1.0)
Loss > 4.544 :
|  Perm <= 25.879 :
|  |  Temp <= 146.65 : Composite2 (13.0/2.5)
|  |  Temp > 146.65 : Composite1 (13.0/1.3)
|  Perm > 25.879 :
|  |  Strn <= -11 :
|  |  |  Strn <= -14 : Composite2 (13.0/1.3)
|  |  |  Strn > -14 : Composite1 (16.0/1.3)
|  |  Strn > -11 :
|  |  |  Strn > -10 : Composite1 (491.0/7.4)
|  |  |  Strn <= -10 :
|  |  |  |  Temp <= 125.37 : Composite1 (36.0/1.4)
|  |  |  |  Temp > 125.37 : Composite2 (3.0/1.1)
```

Evaluation on training data (958 items)

Before Pruning		After Pruning		
Size	Errors	Size	Errors	Estimate
45	3 (0.3%)	37	6 (0.6%)	**(3.3%) <<**

Appendix B: (Decision tree for training and test cases)

Read 862 cases (5 attributes) from data_test.data
Decision tree

```
Loss <= 3.824 :
|   Strn > -69 : Composite2 (187.3)
|   Strn <= -69 :
|   |   Temp <= 43.602 : Composite2 (15.4)
|   |   Temp > 43.602 :
|   |   |   Strn <= -673 : Composite1 (55.6/0.6)
|   |   |   Strn > -673 :
|   |   |   |   Temp <= 76.706 : Composite2 (16.7)
|   |   |   |   Temp > 76.706 :
|   |   |   |   |   Strn <= -410 : Composite1 (15.0)
|   |   |   |   |   Strn > -410 :
|   |   |   |   |   |   Temp > 124.29 : Composite1 (14.0)
|   |   |   |   |   |   Temp <= 124.29 :
|   |   |   |   |   |   |   Strn > -324 : Composite2 (14.0)
|   |   |   |   |   |   |   Strn <= -324 :
|   |   |   |   |   |   |   |   Temp <= 100.097 : Composite2 (4.0)
|   |   |   |   |   |   |   |   Temp > 100.097 : Composite1 (5.0)
Loss > 3.824 :
|   Perm <= 25.812 :
|   |   Temp <= 143.85 : Composite2 (14.0/1.0)
|   |   Temp > 143.85 : Composite1 (14.0)
|   Perm > 25.812 :
|   |   Strn <= -10 :
|   |   |   Perm <= 7628.3 : Composite2 (14.0)
|   |   |   Perm > 7628.3 : Composite1 (48.0)
|   |   Strn > -10 :
|   |   |   Perm > 27.323 : Composite1 (397.0)
|   |   |   Perm <= 27.323 :
|   |   |   |   Temp > 150.78 : Composite1 (37.0)
|   |   |   |   Temp <= 150.78 :
|   |   |   |   |   Temp <= 79.28 : Composite1 (6.0)
|   |   |   |   |   Temp > 79.28 : Composite2 (5.0)
```

Evaluation on training data (862 items)					Evaluation on test data (96 items)				
Before Pruning		After Pruning			Before Pruning		After Pruning		
Size	Errors	Size	Errors	**Estimate**	Size	Errors	Size	Errors	**Estimate**
33	1 (0.1%)	33	1 (0.1%)	**(2.8%) <<**	33	0 (0.0%)	33	0 (0.0%)	**(2.8%) <<**

(a)	(b)	←classified as
65		(a): class Composite1
	31	(b): class Composite2

<u>Appendix C:</u> (Decision tree for training and test cases – no-Loss&LogI)

Read 862 cases (3 attributes) from no_LossLogI_test.data

<u>Decision tree</u>

```
Perm <= 25.879 :
|  Strn <= -23 :
|  |  Strn <= -673 :
|  |  |  Temp <= 43.602 : Composite2 (6.3)
|  |  |  Temp > 43.602 : Composite1 (55.5/0.5)
|  |  Strn > -673 :
|  |  |  Temp <= 76.706 : Composite2 (25.4)
|  |  |  Temp > 76.706 :
|  |  |  |  Temp > 129.57 : Composite1 (17.0)
|  |  |  |  Temp <= 129.57 :
|  |  |  |  |  Strn <= -358 : Composite1 (20.0/1.0)
|  |  |  |  |  Strn > -358 :
|  |  |  |  |  |  Temp <= 121.8 : Composite2 (16.0)
|  |  |  |  |  |  Temp > 121.8 :
|  |  |  |  |  |  |  Strn <= -194 : Composite1 (3.0)
|  |  |  |  |  |  |  Strn > -194 : Composite2 (4.0)
|  Strn > -23 :
|  |  Temp <= 150.78 : Composite2 (194.7/1.0)
|  |  Temp > 150.78 : Composite1 (11.0)
Perm > 25.879 :
|  Strn <= -10 :
|  |  Perm <= 7628.3 : Composite2 (14.0)
|  |  Perm > 7628.3 : Composite1 (48.0)
|  Strn > -10 :
|  |  Perm > 27.323 : Composite1 (397.0)
|  |  Perm <= 27.323 :
|  |  |  Temp > 150.78 : Composite1 (35.0)
|  |  |  Temp <= 150.78 :
|  |  |  |  Temp <= 79.28 : Composite1 (6.0)
|  |  |  |  Temp > 79.28 : Composite2 (9.0)
```

Evaluation on training data (862 items)					Evaluation on test data (96 items)				
Before Pruning		After Pruning			Before Pruning		After Pruning		
Size	Errors	Size	Errors	Estimate	Size	Errors	Size	Errors	Estimate
31	2 (0.2%)	31	2 (0.2%)	(2.8%) <<	31	1 (1.0%)	31	1 (1.0%)	(2.8%) <<

(a)	(b)	←classified as
65		(a): class Composite1
1	30	(b): class Composite2

Appendix D: (Decision tree for training and test cases)

Read 1073 cases (8 attributes) from Poly_test.data

Decision tree

```
Imp-30kHz <= 62.9 : Composite2 (144.0/1.0)
Imp-30kHz > 62.9 :
|  Imp-30k > 265 : Composite1 (374.0)
|  Imp-30k <= 265 :
|  |  Phase -40k <= -87.2 : Composite2 (75.0)
|  |  Phase -40k > -87.2 :
|  |  |  Phase-50k <= -83.4 :
|  |  |  |  Imp-20k <= 192 : Composite2 (75.0/1.0)
|  |  |  |  Imp-20k > 192 :
|  |  |  |  |  Imp-30k > 196 : Composite2 (4.0)
|  |  |  |  |  Imp-30k <= 196 :
|  |  |  |  |  |  Imp-30k > 132 : Composite1 (32.0)
|  |  |  |  |  |  Imp-30k <= 132 :
|  |  |  |  |  |  |  Phase20K <= -86.9 : Composite2 (2.0)
|  |  |  |  |  |  |  Phase20K > -86.9 : Composite1 (10.0)
|  |  |  Phase50k > -83.4 :
|  |  |  |  Imp-20k <= 112 : Composite1 (222.0)
|  |  |  |  Imp-20k > 112 :
|  |  |  |  |  Phase20K > -85.2 : Composite1 (105.0/7.0)
|  |  |  |  |  Phase20K <= -85.2 :
|  |  |  |  |  |  Imp-30k <= 123 : Composite2 (24.0)
|  |  |  |  |  |  Imp-30k > 123 : Composite1 (6.0)
```

Evaluation on training data (1173 items)					Evaluation on test data (120 items)				
Before Pruning		After Pruning			Before Pruning		After Pruning		
Size	Errors	Size	Errors	Estimate	Size	Errors	Size	Errors	Estimate
23	9 (0.8%)	23	9 (0.8%)	(2.5%) <<	23	2 (1.7%)	23	2 (1.7%)	(2.5%) <<

(a)	(b)	←classified as
84		(a): class Composite1
2	34	(b): class Composite2

Fuzzy Logic Aided Gesture Recognition

Tapio Frantti and Sanna Kallio

Technical Research Center of Finland,
Kaitoväylä 1, PL 1100,
FIN-90571,Oulu, Finland.
{tapio.frantti, sanna.kallio}@vtt.fi
http://www.vtt.fi

Abstract. This paper describes a fuzzy logic based gesture recognition procedure for a user interface of a mobile terminal. In the presented solution, a terminal includes three acceleration sensors positioned like *xyz* co-ordinate system in order to get three-dimensional acceleration vector, $\overline{xyz}$ (gesture). The acceleration vector is used as an input to a reasoning unit for classification. The method is compared to the *fuzzy c-means* and to the *hidden Markov model* methods. The advantages of the developed fuzzy method, which classified successfully the test sets, are computational effectiveness, lower data sample rate requirement, simple implementation and reliability. Therefore, the gesture recognition can be applied to the terminals to replace traditional keyboard functions. The computational effectiveness and low sample rate requirement also increases the operational time of device. The easy implementation and reliability are important factors for the success of the new technology's spreading on the mass market of terminals.

1 Introduction

Target of the gesture recognition as a part of user interface research is to replace keyboard functions with gestures. Replacement of keyboard functions with controlled movements is especially important in very small and simple devices without keyboard and screen. Furthermore, it is very useful in 'normal' size devices with keyboard and screen, like mobile phones, as an optional choice for the traditional user interface. For example, the incoming calls can be initiated via lifting the phone to the ear and hang up via transferring it back to the pocket without pressing any keys or giving voice commands. However, the gesture recognition has several problems like unreliability of recognised gestures, quite heavy computational load and high data sample rate requirement. The gesture recognition is usually performed via *hidden Markov model (HMM)* method. Even if this method is quite a reliable at the high data sample rate (data sample rate frequency around 80 Hz), it is computationally heavy and slow. Hence, it is not optimal for the real time systems with very limited resources.

In this application gestures are composed of time series data of acceleration sensors. Sensors are positioned on 90° angle with each other in order to get 3-dimensional voltage signal, *i.e.*, acceleration vector $\overline{xyz}$. For the *fuzzy rule*

J. Liu et al. (Eds.): IDEAL 2003, LNCS 2690, pp. 959–966, 2003.

classification method the vector is autocorrelated and Fourier transformed to get Doppler spectrum. Fractions $\frac{Dopplerspectrum_{max}}{Dopplerspread}$ are then used as input values to a *reasoning* module. For the comparative *HMM* method, the $\overline{xyz}$ vector is filtered, normalised and quantised before HMM -modelling. For the *fuzzy c-means*, different features are extracted from the vector and used as an input for FCM -algorithm. Different data preprocessing methods for different classification methods were selected according to the best results achieved for the method. In figure 1 has presented a simplified architecture of the research.

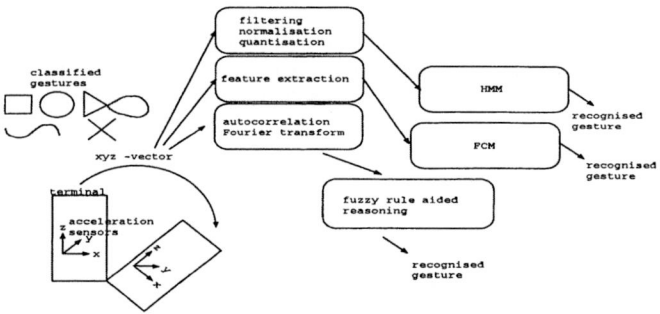

Fig. 1. Simplified architecture of the research arrangement.

The organisation of the rest of paper is: section 2 briefly summarizes the basic principles of the fuzzy set theory and fuzzy logic as well as fuzzy methods and techniques used in this application. Section 3 describes shortly HMM method as a part of gesture recognition. Section 4 presents the acceleration vectors and the Doppler spectrums of the example gesture and describes implementation environment of the model. Results and discussions of the selected approaches are presented in section 5 and conclusions are drawn in section 6.

2   Fuzzy Set Theory and Fuzzy Logic

Fuzzy set theory was originally presented by L. Zadeh in his seminal paper "Fuzzy Sets" [1]. The name *fuzzy sets* are used to distinguish them from the *crisp sets* of the conventional set theory. The characteristic function of a crisp set C, $\mu_C(u)$, assigns a discrete value (usually either 0 or 1) to each element u in the universal set U. The characteristic function can be generalized so that the values assigned to the elements u of the universal set U fall within a prespesified range (usually to the unit interval [0, 1]) indicating the degree of membership of these elements in the set. The generalized function is called *membership function* and the set defined with the aid of it is a *fuzzy set*, respectively.

In this paper the elements u of the universal set U in the *fuzzy rule aided classification* of gesture recognition research are fractions $\frac{Dopplerspectrum_{max}}{Dopplerspread}$. In other words, the fractions are used as input values to a fuzzy reasoning module. Fuzzy membership functions are approximated using quadrangle shape functions. Hence, the input variable is:

$$I_i = \frac{max_{f_i} X(f_i)}{\langle X(f_i) \rangle} \tag{1}$$

where $X(f_i)$ is the Doppler spectrum and the $\langle X(f_i) \rangle$ denotes the width of it (Doppler spread). Doppler spectrum for each component of acceleration vector can be defined as

$$X(f_i) = \frac{1}{2\pi} \int_0^{2\pi} x(t_i)^2 \times e^{j\omega t_i} dt \tag{2}$$

where $x(t_i)$ is the time series of x, y or z component and $X(f_i)$ is Fourier transformed autocorrelation function, respectively.

2.1   Inference of the Grade of Membership

In the systems, where the knowledge can be expressed in a linguistic form, a language-oriented approach is possible for a model generation. The idea of fuzzy modelling is to use of expert's knowledge for a rule base creation which is usually presented with linguistic conditional statements, i.e., if-then rules. However, in this paper we present rule base in a matrix form and we use linguistic equations (see more details from the [2] and [3]) in order to make calculations faster.

Reasoning can be done either using composition based or individual based inference. In the former all rules are combined into an explicit relation and then fired with fuzzy input whereas in the latter each rules are individually fired with crisp input and then combined into one overall fuzzy set. Here we used individual based inference with Mamdani's implication [4]. Main reason for the choice was its easier implementation (the results are equivalent for the both methods when Mamdani's implication is used). In the individual based inference the grade of membership of each fired rule can be formed by taking the T-norm value from the grades of membership of the inputs for each fired rule. Its definition is based on the intersection operation and the relation R_c (c for conjunction defined by the T-norm)

$$\mu_{R_c}(x, y) = T^*(\mu_A(x), \mu_B(y)), \tag{3}$$

where x and y denotes input variables whereas A and B are meanings of the x and y, respectively [4]. The meaning of the whole set of rules is given by taking the S-norm value of grade(s) of membership from the rules with the same output value to form output set with only linguistically different values.

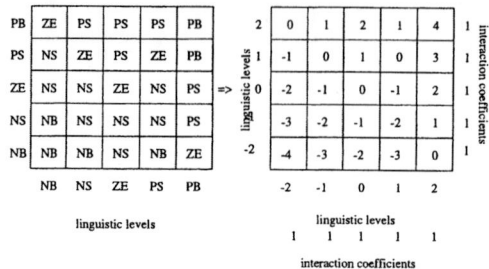

Fig. 2. The mapping of linguistic relations to linguistic equations.

2.2 Linguistic Equations

In the framework of linguistic equations a linguistic model of a system can be described by groups of linguistic relations. The linguistic relations form a rule base of the system that can be converted into matrix equations. Suppose, as an example, that X_j, $j = 1,..., m$ (m is uneven number), is a linguistic level (*e.g.,negative big (NB), negative small (NS), zero (ZE), positive small (PS), and positive big (PB)*) for a variable. The linguistic levels are replaced by integers $\frac{-(j-1)}{2},...,-2,-1,0,1,2,...,\frac{(j-1)}{2}$ (see Figure 2 and more details in [3]). The direction of the interaction between fuzzy sets is presented by coefficients A_i $\{-1,0,1\}$, $i = 1,..., m$. This means that the directions of the changes in the output variable decrease or increase depending on the directions of the changes in the input variables [5]. Thus a compact equation is:

$$\sum_{i,j=1}^{m} A_{ij}X_j = 0. \tag{4}$$

2.3 Fuzzy C-Means Algorithm

The *fuzzy c-means* clustering algorithm can be performed by starting from some initial partitioning and improving that using so called *variance criterion*, which measures the dissimilarity between the points in a cluster and its center point by *Euclidean distance*. *Variance criterion* minimize the squared *Euclidean distances* and for fuzzy *c-partitions* it can be stated as follows:

$$min\, z(\widetilde{U},v) = \sum_{i=1}^{c}\sum_{k=1}^{n}(\mu_{ik})^m\|x_k - v_i\|_G^2 \tag{5}$$

such that

$$v_i = \frac{1}{\sum\limits_{k=1}^{n}(\mu_{ik})}\sum_{k=1}^{n}(\mu_{ik}^m x_k),\; m \geq 1, \tag{6}$$

where z = variance criterion (measures the dissimilarity between the points in a cluster and its center by the Euclidean distance), $\tilde{U}$ = c -partitioning matrix, ($\tilde{U} = [\mu_{ik}] \in V_{cn}$, V_{cn} is the set of all real cxn matrices), v = vector of all cluster center points, c = partitioning number, n = number of elements in data set, μ_{ik} = degree of membership of classified object x_k in a fuzzy subset S_i (i=1,...,c), m = weight value (≥ 1) and v_i = mean of the x_k m -weighted by degrees of membership (clusters centers) [6]. Subindex G informs the chosen norm.

Systems described by equations above cannot be solved analytically. However, there exist iterative *fuzzy c -means algorithm* for that (see detailed explanations from [6] and [7]), which define the clusters center points, as mentioned above. The lacks of method are that number of clusters should be known in advance, which, however, was not the problem on the described application and undefined processing time due to iterative nature of algorithm.

3 Gesture Recognition with HMM

Hidden Markov Model (HMM) is based on the Markov chain theory. In the Markov chain theory each state generates an observation and the goal of the *HMM* is to infer the hidden state sequence. *HMM* can be formally expressed as

$$\lambda = (A, B, \pi), \tag{7}$$

where A represents the state transition probability matrix, B denotes the observation symbol probability matrix and π is the initial state probability vector. The specification of the *HMM* involves choosing the number of states, number of discrete symbols, and definition of three probability densities with matrix A, B, and π [8].

HMM has been widely used in speech and handwritten character recognition as well as in gesture recognition on video-based and glove-based systems [9]. We used a simple left-to-right discrete *HMM* with 5 states to model test set gestures. Therefore, system uses 5 different HMMs for 5 different gestures. The recognition result is the *HMM* with the highest probability for the given observation sequence. Parameters of each *HMM* are estimated by using the Baum-Welch algorithm whereas the Viterbi algorithm is used to evaluate the trained *HMM*.

Collected acceleration data is first lowpass filtered and normalized thereafter. Vector quantization is needed to map the filtered and normalized 3-dimensional gesture sequence onto one dimensional sequence of discrete symbols by using a codebook. The codebook was built using *k-means* clustering algorithm and the size of a codebook used here was 16 and 32 (see Table 1). Block diagram of the *HMM* system is presented in Figure 3.

4 System Model

A simplified architecture of research arrangement has been described in Figure 1. Three acceleration sensors were embedded into a mobile terminal according

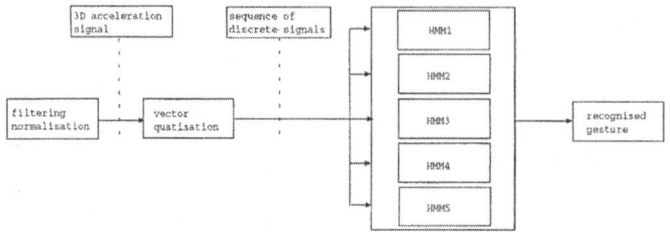

Fig. 3. Block diagram of a hand gesture HMM recognizer.

to the direction of co-ordinate axes (x, y, z). The acceleration data was sampled from each sensors at the frequency of 20 Hz. The Doppler spectrum and Doppler spread of data vector $\overline{xyz}$ were defined and the relation of these was used as an input value to the developed fuzzy reasoning module, as also shown in the Figure 1. The fuzzy reasoning module classifies preprocessed $\overline{xyz}$ vectors and gives recognised gesture as an output.

Acceleration components of *circle* gesture and Fourier transforms from the autocorrelation functions of the x, y and z components of *circle* movement are presented as an illustration in Figure 4. The ranges of linguistic variables for the x, y and z -components of *circle* movement are $[55, 284]$, $[20, 261]$ and $[55, 237]$, respectively.

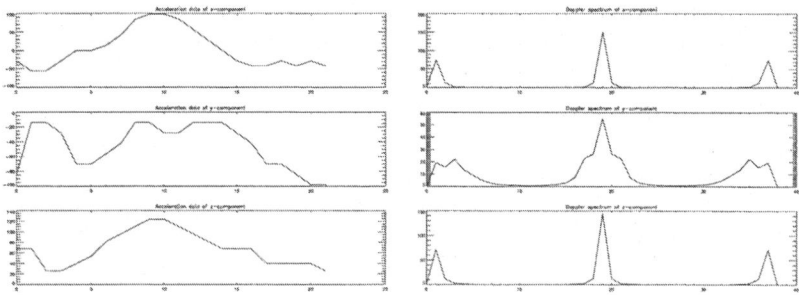

Fig. 4. Acceleration components of the *circle* and Doppler spectrums of the z, y and z components of the *circle*.

As an example, suppose that user performs *circle* movement (Figure 4) in order to open terminals' menu. The reasoning module must now classify the gesture to find out the desired action ('open the menu') and signal it to the user interface control unit. The fuzzy reasoning module includes/requires only one rule for each gesture. For the *circle* movement the required rule is: **IF** linguistic label x **IS** 0 **AND** linguistic label y IS -1 **AND** linguistic label z IS 0 **THEN** gesture **IS** circle. Therefore, the rule base is very compact. Due to that and linguistic equations the computation time is very short, which is necessary for the real-time terminals with limited resources.

5 Results

The main motivation of this research was to find out reliable and computationally light method to replace computationally heavy *hidden Markov modelling (HMM)* in gesture recognition. Therefore, we compared our method against existing *fuzzy c-means FCM* algorithm and the *HMM*. Results of the recognition can be seen in Table 1.

Table 1. Recognition results (%) of HMM, FCM and fuzzy rule aided classification method.

gesture	HMM-codebook 32/16	FCM-1	FCM-2	Fuzzy method
circle	73.3/96.6 %	72.0 %	98.0 %	100.0 %
square	93.3/90.0 %	60.0 %	100.0 %	100.0 %
bend	90.0/100.0 %	100.0 %	100.0 %	100.0 %
fish	80.0/90.0 %	98.0 %	100.0 %	100.0 %
x	100.0/100.0%	96.0 %	100.0 %	100.0 %

In the *FCM -method*, parameters for gestures were extracted in two different ways. Firstly, the Doppler spectrums and spreads were defined to get a 3-dimensional feature vector. Secondly, for each of the acceleration components were calculated minimum, mean, standard deviation, absolute mean of differentials and maximum values to get a 15-dimensional feature vector. Results of these are also presented in Table 1. The developed *fuzzy classification procedure* with the fractions $\frac{Dopplerspectrum_{max}}{Dopplerspread}$ as an input recognises different gestures with 100 % accuracy (Table 1).

The importance of results are especially emphasized for the user interface research of terminals with very limited resources. The developed method with very compact rule base and linguistic equations is computationally light, fast and survives with low data sample rate. Moreover, it is very reliable which make the applicability and acceptance of it in the commercial mobile terminal markets more probable.

6 Conclusions

The developed *fuzzy gesture recognition procedure* for the intelligent user interface of a mobile terminal increases significantly reliability of gesture recognition.

Moreover, fuzzy method is computationally effective and simple to implementat. The computational effectiveness increases the operational time of device as well as does the low data sample rate requirement. Therefore, the method can be applied to the real time systems.

In the presented solution, a mobile terminal includes acceleration sensors positioned like xyz -straight angle co-ordinate system. Fractions $\frac{Dopplerspectrum_{max}}{Dopplerspread}$ are used as an input vector to a fuzzy reasoning unit. The reasoning unit classifies different gestures according to theirs properties. The output of it is signaled to the user interface control unit in order to get proper functioning of user equipment.

Acknowledgments. Technical Research Centre of Finland is acknowledged for the finance of research.

References

1. L. Zadeh, "Fuzzy sets," *Information and Control*, vol. Vol. 8, No. 4, pp. 338–353, 1965.
2. E.K. Juuso, "Linguistic equations framework for adaptive expert systems," in *Modelling and Simulation 1992, Proceedings of the 1992 European Simulation Multiconference*, J. Stephenson, Ed., 1992, pp. 99–103.
3. T. Frantti and P. Mähönen, "Fuzzy logic based forecasting model," *Engineering Applications of Artificial Intelligence*, vol. 14(2), pp. 189–201, 2001.
4. D. Driankov, H. Hellendoorn, and M. Reinfark, *An Introduction to Fuzzy Control*, Springer-Verlag, New York, 2nd edition edition, 1996.
5. E.K. Juuso, "Linguistic simulation in production control," in *UKSS'93 Conference of the United Kingdom Simulation Society*, R. Pooley and R. Zobel, Eds., Keswick, UK, 1993, pp. 34–38.
6. H. J. Zimmerman, *Fuzzy Set Theory and Its Applications*, Kluwer Academic Publishers, Massachusetts, USA, 5th edition, 1992.
7. P. Mähönen and T. Frantti, "Fuzzy classifier for star-galaxy separation," *Astrophysical Journal*, vol. 541, pp. 201–203, 2000.
8. I.-C. Kim and S.-I. Chien, "Analysis of 3d hand trajectory gestures using stroke-based composite hidden markov models," *Applied Intelligence*, vol. Vol. 15, No. 2, pp. 131–143, 2001.
9. F. Hoffman, P. Heyer, and G. Hommel, "Velocity profile based recognituon of dynamic gestures with discrete hidden markov models," in *Proceedings of Gesture Workshop '97*, 1997.

On the Choices of the Parameters in General Constrained Learning Algorithms[1]

De-Shuang Huang[1,2] and Horace H.S. Ip[2]

[1] Institute of Intelligent Machines, Chinese Academy of Sciences,
P.O.Box 1130, Hefei, Anhui 230031, China
huangdeshuang@yahoo.com
[2] AIMtech Centre, Department of Computer Science, City University of Hong Kong,
83 Tat Chee Avenue, Kowloon Tong, Hong Kong,
cship@cityu.edu.hk

Abstract. This paper addresses the constrained learning algorithm (CLA) proposed by Perantonis et al, which is an efficient and fast back propagation (BP) algorithm formed by imposing the constraint condition, referred to as the *a priori* information, implicit in the issues into the conventional BP algorithm. It is found, through analyzing the CLA, that the choice of the values of the three learning parameters $\{\delta P, \theta_p, \eta\}$ in the algorithm is critical to successful application of the technique. Otherwise, the algorithm will not be able to converge within a limited time, or even diverge. This paper will discuss how to choose the three learning parameters based on an exhaustive understanding on the CLA. Finally, several computer simulation results show that our analyses and conclusions are completely correct.

1 Introduction

It is well known that the backpropagation (BP) learning algorithm is a popular method in the training multiple layer perceptron networks (MLPN)[1]. However, in essence, BP algorithm (BPA) is a gradient descent algorithm. Therefore, fundamentally, it suffers from the potential problem of being trapped in the local minima on the error surface [2,3]. It could also not overcome the difficulty of lengthy training time. These unfavorable factors largely limit the further applications of FNN's. Therefore, some effective and efficient training algorithms must be sought. Although these algorithms are of more superior performances to the conventional BPA, they are always very slow for problems that lack the *a priori* information. As a result, it is very difficult for those issues that need to be processed in real time to converge to the exact solutions within a limited time. In other words, to reach reasonable values with very high accuracy, a large amount of time will have to be taken.

---

[1] This work was supported by NSF of China and the Grant of "Hundred Talents Program" of Chinese Academy of Sciences of China.

J. Liu et al. (Eds.): IDEAL 2003, LNCS 2690, pp. 967–974, 2003.
© Springer-Verlag Berlin Heidelberg 2003

It is easily thought that the most important reason for the slow training is that the corresponding *a priori* information implicit in given problems had not been sufficiently extracted and incorporated into the BPA. In 1995, Perantonis *et al* proposed using constrained learning BP techniques, simply referred to as constrained learning algorithm (CLA), to train FNN's [4], and applied this algorithm to performing factorization of 2-D polynomials [5]. Moreover, we have successfully applied this algorithm to finding the roots of polynomials [6,7]. It can be found, however, through our work on applying CLA to finding the roots of polynomials, that if the three learning parameters $\{\delta P, \theta_p, \eta\}$ in the CLA are not appropriately chosen, then the algorithm will converge very slow, even oscillate or diverge.

In this paper we first generalize the real CLA to the complex domain so that the algorithm can be more generally applicable to practical problems. Further, this paper focuses particularly on how to choose the three learning parameters in the CLA. By carefully and exhaustively analyzing the theoretical foundation of CLA, we can deduce that the training speed of CLA will gradually reduce as the three parameters increase. Moreover, through experiments we showed that the experimental results are completely consistent with our theoretical results.

2 Complex Constrained Learning Algorithm

2.1 Constrained Learning Algorithm

For an outer-supervised learning FNN shown in Fig.1, considering a general version of complex variables, assume that an error cost function is defined at the output of the FNN:

$$E(w) = \frac{1}{2P} \sum_{p=1}^{P} \left| e_p(w) \right|^2 = \frac{1}{2P} \sum_{p=1}^{P} \left| o_p - y_p \right|^2 \tag{1}$$

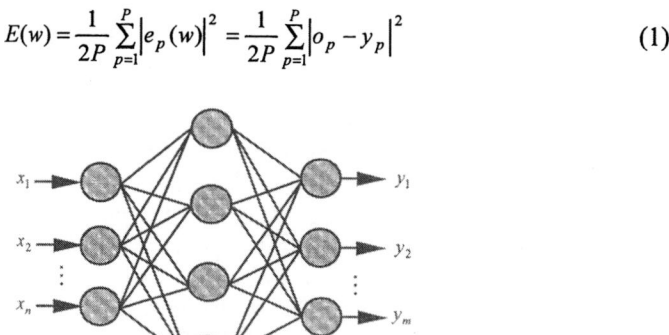

Fig. 1. The structure of feedforward neural network

where w is the set of all weights in the   network; o_p denotes the target (outer-supervised) signal; y_p denotes the actual output of the network; $p = 1,2,\cdots,P$ (P is the total number of training samples) is an index labeling the training patterns and $|\cdot|$ is the Euclidean norm (2-norm).

To introduce the CLA, here assume that the additional information (also called as the *a priori* information) available implicit in the issues can be expressed as the following constraint relations $\Phi = 0$, where $\Phi = [\Phi_1, \Phi_2, \cdots, \Phi_m]^T$ (T denotes the transpose of a vector or matrix) is a vector composed of the constraint conditions from the issues at hand. In addition, another constraint is assumed as $\sum_{i=1}^{n} |dw_i|^2 = (\delta P)^2$, where dw_i denotes the change of weight w_i, δP is a constant.

Before proceeding to the CLA, assume $d\Phi$ to be equal to a predetermined vector quantity δQ, designed to bring Φ closer to its target (zero). In addition, we introduce a vector $V = [v_1, v_2, \cdots, v_m]^T$ of Lagrange multipliers for the constraints in $\Phi = 0$ and another Lagrange multiplier μ for $\sum_{i=1}^{n} |dw_i|^2 = (\delta P)^2$. To ensure the maximum possible change in $|dE(w)|$ at each epoch, we introduce a function ε. Consequently, $d\varepsilon$ is defined as follows $d\varepsilon = dE(w) + (\delta Q^H - d\Phi^H)V + \mu \left[(\delta P)^2 - \sum_{i=1}^{n} |dw_i|^2 \right]$, where the superscript H denotes the conjugate transpose of a vector or matrix.

Let $w = [w_1, w_2, \cdots, w_n]^T$, by expanding the terms on the right hand side of $d\varepsilon$, we easily obtain:

$$d\varepsilon = \sum_{i=1}^{n} J_i dw_i + (\delta Q^H - \sum_{i=1}^{n} dw_i F_i^H)V + \mu \left[(\delta P)^2 - \sum_{i=1}^{n} |dw_i|^2 \right] \qquad (2)$$

where $J_i = \dfrac{\partial E(w)}{\partial w_i}$, $F_i = [F_i^{(1)}, F_i^{(2)}, \cdots, F_i^{(m)}]^T$, $F_i^{(j)} = \dfrac{\partial \Phi_j}{\partial w_i}$ ($i = 1,2,\cdots,n, j = 1,2,\cdots,m$).

Similar to the derivation of [5], we can derive the following relation:

$$dw_i = \frac{J_i}{2\mu} - \frac{F_i^H V}{2\mu} \qquad (3)$$

Eqn.(3) forms the new weight update rule called as complex CLA instead of the conventional BPA. Furthermore, the values of Lagrange multipliers μ and V in

eqn.(3) can be readily evaluated $\mu = -\dfrac{1}{2} \left[\dfrac{I_{JJ} - I_{JF}^H I_{FF}^{-1} I_{JF}}{(\delta P)^2 - \delta Q^H I_{FF}^{-1} \delta Q} \right]^{1/2}$ and

$V = -2\mu I_{FF}^{-1} \delta Q + I_{FF}^{-1} I_{JF}$, where $I_{JJ} = \sum_{i=1}^{n} |J_i|^2$ is a scalar, I_{JF} is a vector whose

components are defined by $I_{JF}^{(j)} = \sum_{i=1}^{n} J_i F_i^{(j)}$,($j = 1,2,\cdots,m$). Specifically, I_{FF} is a

matrix, whose elements are defined by $I_{FF}^{jk} = \sum_{i=1}^{n} F_i^{(j)} F_i^{(k)*}$ ($j,k = 1,2,\cdots,m$), where *

denotes the complex conjugate.

2.2 The Choices of Three Learning Parameters in Constrained Learning Algorithm

Generally, the parameter δP is often selected as a fixed value. However, the vector parameters $\delta Q_j (j = 1,2,\cdots,m)$ are often selected as proportional to Φ_j, i.e., $\delta Q_j = -k\Phi_j$ ($j = 1,2,\cdots,m$, $k > 0$), which ensures that the constraints Φ move towards zero at an exponential rate as the training progresses.

From μ, we note that k should satisfy $k \le \delta P (\Phi^H I_{FF}^{-1} \Phi)^{-1/2}$. In fact, the simplest choice for k is $k = \eta \delta P / \sqrt{\Phi^H I_{FF}^{-1} \Phi}$, where $0 < \eta < 1$ is another free parameter of the algorithm apart from δP. In fact, according to the above discussion, we can propose an adaptive parameter adjustment scheme for the parameters δP as [8] $\delta P(t) = \delta P_0 (1 - e^{\frac{\theta_p}{t}})$, where δP_0 is the initial value for δP, which is usually chosen as a larger value; t is the time index for training, θ_p is the scale coefficient of time t, which is usually set as $\theta_p > 1$.

Therefore, when one uses this complex CLA, there are the three learning parameters $\{\delta P, \theta_p, \eta\}$ that will have to be carefully chosen. Now the problem is how to choose these three parameters.

First, we can easily prove that $\xi = I_{JJ} - I_{JF}^H I_{FF}^{-1} I_{JF} \ge 0$, thus, we have the following:

$$\mu = -\frac{1}{2\delta P(t)} \cdot \frac{\xi}{\sqrt{1-\eta^2}} \qquad (4)$$

Approximately, it can be derived that when $\mu \to 0$, the original V becomes $V \approx I_{FF}^{-1} I_{JF}$, then eqn.(3) can be rewritten as

$$dw_i \approx \frac{J_i - F_i^H I_{FF}^{-1} I_{JF}}{2\mu} \qquad (5)$$

which is similar to the gradient descent formula of the BPA apart from the second term $-F_i^H I_{FF}^{-1} I_{JF} / 2\mu$ related to the *a priori* information of the problem itself. When $\mu \to \infty$, the original V becomes $V \approx -2\mu I_{FF}^{-1} \delta Q$, then eqn.(3) can be rewritten as

$$dw_i \approx F_i^H I_{FF}^{-1} \delta Q \qquad (6)$$

which is more dependent on the *a priori* information from the problem. From the above theoretical analyses, we can discuss three cases as follows:

Case I. The Effects of δP_0 on the performance of the CLA. When δP_0 dynamically increases, μ moves towards zero so that the iteration for the connection weights switches to the gradient descent searching phase. Owing to $\delta P(t)$ being adaptively chosen, it will take longer training time for the bigger δP_0 before the iteration for the connection weights switches to the *a priori* information searching phase.

Consequently, the convergent speed will certainly become slower for the bigger δP_0. From eqn.(4), we can further deduce that

$$\overline{\mu} = \left|\frac{\mu}{\xi}\right| = \frac{1}{2\delta P(t)\sqrt{1-\eta^2}} \qquad (7)$$

Fig.2 (a) shows five sets of logarithmic learning parameter (δP_0) curves for different times $t = 5.0, 15.0, 25.0, 35.0, 45.0$. From this figure the same conclusions respect to our theoretic analyses can be observed, i.e., $\overline{\mu}$ rises or drops down with t or δP_0 goes up.

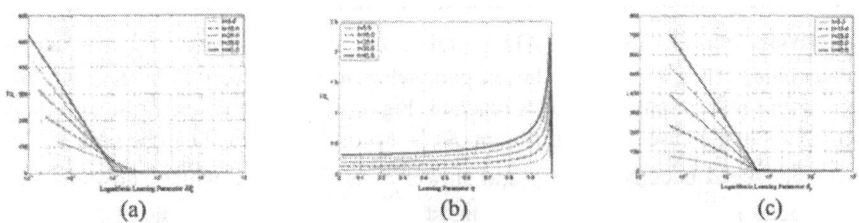

(a)   (b)   (c)

Fig. 2. The logarithmic learning parameter curves for different times. (a) δP_0, (b) η, (c) θ_p

Case II. The Effects of η on the performance of the CLA. Since $\delta P(t)$ is adaptively chosen, the learning process is always to start from $\mu \to 0$ (the gradient descent based phase) to $\mu \to \infty$ (the *a priori* information searching based phase) If $\eta (0 < \eta < 1)$ is chosen as a bigger value, from eqn.(4) $|\mu|$ also becomes bigger. As a result, the role of η is dominant in the gradient descent based phase so that the bigger η will result in a slower searching on the error surface. On the other hands, when the learning processing switches to the *a priori* information searching based phase, the role of $\delta P(t)$ becomes dominant. Obviously, during this phase, the distinct η will not effect on the convergent speed. Therefore, from the analyses above, it can be deduced that the convergent speed will drop with the parameter η goes up.

Fig.2 (b) shows five sets of logarithmic learning parameter (η) curves for different times $t = 5.0, 15.0, 25.0, 35.0, 45.0$. From this figure the same conclusions with our theoretic analyses are also observed, i.e., $\overline{\mu}$ rises with t and δP_0 goes up.

Case III. The Effects of θ_p on the performance of the CLA. Since δ t is the functional of θ_p and a bigger θ_p corresponds to a bigger δ t , therefore, similar to Case I, the convergent speed will certainly become slower for the bigger θ_p. Fig.2(c) shows five sets of logarithmic learning parameter (θ_p) curves for different times $t = 5.0, 15.0, 25.0, 35.0, 45.0$. From this figure it can be seen that the conclusions similar to Fig.2 are observed.

3 Experimental Results and Discussions

To verify the efficiency and effectiveness of our approach, we take an arbitrary 6-order test polynomial with unknown roots $f_3(x) = x^6 + 2.3ix^5 + (0.3 - 1.6i)x^2 + 1.7 - 2.9$ as an example to investigate the effects of the parameters on the complex CLA. In the following experiments, we always suppose that (1) The termination error is fixed at $e_r = 1 \times 10^{-7}$ for all cases, and (2) Three sets of different values for each parameter of $\{\delta P_0, \theta_p, \eta\}$ in the CLA are in turn chosen while keeping other two parameters unchanged.

Case I. The parameters $\theta_p = 3.0$ **and** $\eta = 0.3$ **are kept unchanged while** δP_0 **is respectively chosen as** $5.0, 10.0, 15.0$ **and** 20.0 . For this case, we design the corresponding CLA with these chosen parameters to respectively train the FNN root finder until the termination error is reached. Fig.3 (a) shows the logarithmic learning error curves in the case of four different δP_0's. From this figure, it can be seen that the convergent speed becomes slower and slower as δP_0 increases, which shows that our experimental results are completely consistent with theoretic analysis. Table 1 lists the estimated roots and the iterating number. From Table 1, it can be seen that the iterating number becomes bigger and bigger as the parameter δP_0 increases.

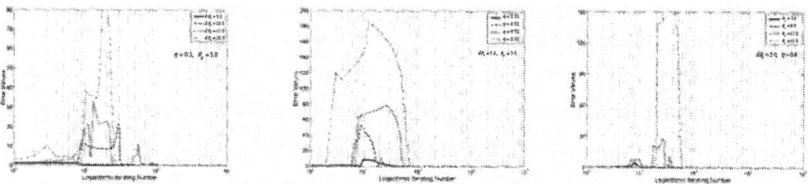

Fig. 3. The logarithmic learning error curves in the case of four different parameters. (a) δP_0, (b) η , (c) θ_p .

Case II. The parameters $\delta P_0 = 5.0$ **and** $\theta_p = 3.0$ **are kept unchanged while** η **is respectively chosen as** $0.32, 0.52, 0.72$ **and** 0.92 . Likewise, we design the corresponding CLA with these chosen parameters to train the FNN root finder until the termination error is reached. Fig.3 (b) shows the logarithmic learning error curves in the case of four different η's. From this figure, it can be seen that the convergent speed becomes slower and slower as the parameter η increases, which are completely consistent with the theoretic analyses. Table 2 shows the estimated roots, the iterating numbers. From Table 2, it can be observed that the iterating number becomes bigger and bigger as the parameter η increases.

Case III. The parameters $\delta P_0 = 5.0$ **and** $\eta = 0.4$ **are kept unchanged while** θ_p **is respectively chosen as** $3.0, 8.0, 13.0$ **and** 16.0 . Likewise, after the FNN root finder converges to the given termination error. Fig.3 (c) illustrates also the logarithmic learning error curves in the case of four different θ_p's. From this figure, it can be seen that the convergent speed drops with θ_p increases, which also shows that our experimental results are completely consistent with the theoretic analyses. Table 3 shows the estimated roots, the iterating numbers. From Table 3, it can be also observed that the iterating number increases as the parameter θ_p increases.

Table 1. The estimated roots and the iterating numbers in the case of four different δP_0's

Indices	$\delta P_0 = 5.0$ ($\theta_p = 3.0, \eta = 0.3$)	$\delta P_0 = 10.0$ ($\theta_p = 3.0, \eta = 0.3$)	$\delta P_0 = 15.0$ ($\theta_p = 3.0, \eta = 0.3$)	$\delta P_0 = 20.0$ ($\theta_p = 3.0, \eta = 0.3$)
Estimated Roots	(0.8436, -0.5457)	(0.8436, -0.5457)	(0.8436, -0.5457)	(0.8436, -0.5456)
	(-0.9225, 0.2034)	(-0.9225, 0.2036)	(-0.9224, 0.2036)	(-0.9225, 0.2034)
	(-0.7320, -1.1353)	(-0.7321, -1.1353)	(-0.7320, -1.1353)	(-0.7319, -1.1353)
	(0.9378, 0.5036)	(0.9378, 0.5036)	(0.9377, 0.5036)	(0.9377, 0.5036)
	(0.1573, -2.3383)	(0.1573, -2.3383)	(0.1573, -2.3383)	(0.1573, -2.3383)
	(-0.2841, 1.0120)	(-0.2841, 1.0120)	(-0.2841, 1.0120)	(-0.2842, 1.0120)
Iterating Number	1004	9686	10754	17405

Table 2. The estimated roots and the iterating numbers in the case of four different η's

Indices	$\eta = 0.32$ ($\delta P_0 = 5.0, \theta_p = 3.0$)	$\eta = 0.5$ ($\delta P_0 = 5.0, \theta_p = 3.0$)	$\eta = 0.7$ ($\delta P_0 = 5.0, \theta_p = 3.0$)	$\eta = 0.9$ ($\delta P_0 = 5.0, \theta_p = 3.0$)
Estimated Roots	(0.8435, -0.5456)	(0.8436, -0.5456)	(0.8436, -0.5456)	(0.8435, -0.5456)
	(-0.9224, 0.2035)	(-0.9226, 0.2034)	(-0.9225, 0.2035)	(-0.9224, 0.2034)
	(-0.7320, -1.1352)	(-0.7320, -1.1353)	(-0.7320, -1.1353)	(-0.7320, -1.1352)
	(0.9378, 0.5036)	(0.9377, 0.5036)	(0.9377, 0.5036)	(0.9377, 0.5036)
	(0.1573, -2.3383)	(0.1573, -2.3383)	(0.1573, -2.3382)	(0.1573, -2.3383)
	(-0.2841, 1.0120)	(-0.2841, 1.0121)	(-0.28410, 1.0120)	(-0.2841, 1.0120)
Iterating Number	797	3069	10709	25906

4   Conclusions

This paper revisited the constrained learning algorithm (CLA), which was constructed by imposing the *a priori* information, from the issues, into the output error cost function of the FNN, and extended the CLA to a more general complex version. Specifically, we study the choice method of the three parameters $\{\delta P_0, \theta_p, \eta\}$ in the CLA's, and discuss their effects on the CLA's. The experimental results, by applying this CLA's with varying the learning parameters to solve the complex roots of arbitrary polynomials, show that the training speeds will be sped up with these three parameters increase while the estimated accuracies have not been significantly effected.

Table 3. The estimated roots and the iterating numbers in the case of four different θ_p 's

Indices	$\theta_p = 3.0$ ($\delta P_0 = 5.0, \eta = 0.4$)	$\theta_p = 8.0$ ($\delta P_0 = 5.0, \eta = 0.4$)	$\theta_p = 13.0$ ($\delta P_0 = 5.0, \eta = 0.4$)	$\theta_p = 16.0$ ($\delta P_0 = 5.0, \eta = 0.4$)
Estimated Roots	(0.8436, -0.5456)	(0.8437, -0.5456)	(0.8436, -0.5457)	(0.8436, -0.5457)
	(-0.9225, 0.2035)	(-0.9226, 0.2035)	(-0.9225, 0.2035)	(-0.9225, 0.2035)
	(-0.7320, -1.1353)	(-0.7321, -1.1353)	(-0.7320, -1.1352)	(-0.7320, -1.1353)
	(0.9377, 0.5036)	(0.9378, 0.5037)	(0.9378, 0.5036)	(0.9377, 0.5036)
	(0.1573, -2.3383)	(0.1572, -2.3382)	(0.1572, -2.3383)	(0.1573, -2.3382)
	(-0.2841, 1.0120)	(-0.2840, 1.0120)	(-0.2841, 1.0121)	(-0.2841, 1.0121)
Iterating Number	525	8069	29875	118445

References

1. D.E. Rumelhart, G.E. Hinton, and R.J. Williams: Learning Representations by Backpropagating Errors. Nature, Vol.323 (1986) 533–536
2. D.R.Hush and B.G.Horne: Progress in Supervised Neural Networks. IEEE Signal Processing Magazine (1993) 8–39
3. D.S.Huang: Systematic Theory of Neural Network for Pattern Recognition. Publishing House of Electronic Industry, Beijing, China (1996)
4. D.A.Karras and S.J. Perantonis: An Efficient Constrained Training Algorithm for Feedforward Networks. IEEE Trans. Neural Networks, Vol.6 (1995) 1420–1434
5. S.J. Perantonis, N. Ampazis, S.J. Varoufakis and G. Antoniou: Factorization of 2-D Polynomials Using Neural Networks and Constrained Learning Techniques. Proceedings of the IEEE Int. Sympos. on Industrial Electronics, ISIE'97 (1997) 1276–1280
6. D.S. Huang: Application of Neural Networks to Finding Real Roots of Polynomials in One Element. ICONIP-2000 Proceedings, Taejon, Korea, Nov.14-17, Vol.II (2000) 1108–1113
7. D.S.Huang: A Neural Network Based Factorization Model for Polynomials in Several Elements. 2000 5th Int. Conf on Signal Processing Proceedings (WCC2000-ICSP2000), Aug.21-25, Beijing, China (2000) 1617–1622
8. D.S.Huang: Revisit to Constrained Learning Algorithm. The 8th Int. Conf. on Neural Information Processing (ICONIP), Shanghai, China, Vol. I, Nov. 14-18 (2001) 459–464

Strict Monotone of an Edge Intensity Profile and a New Edge Detection Algorithm

Eun Mi Kim[1] and Cherl Soo Pahk[2]

[1] Dept. of Computer Science, Howon Univ., Korea
ekim@mail.howon.ac.kr
[2] Dept. of Visual Optics and Optometry, Daebul Univ., Korea
pcs@mail.daebul.ac.kr

Abstract. As a characteristic behavior of edge signal intensity, the strictly monotonic variation of intensity across an edge is employed to propose a new criterion for identifying edges beyond scaling. Instead of the usual local operator such as the gradient, we extend the directional derivative to define a nonlocal operator, in terms of which we can describe a new edge detection algorithm adaptive to the variation of edge width.

1 Introduction

Because of the low frequency mode effect and its non-uniformity, the edges in the real image may have widely varying ramp width or acuity. Thus, in order to detect edge features precisely in real images, various advanced algorithms for the optimal edge detector has been developed. A significant early contributions to this subject was made by Marr and Hildreth[1], and further developed by Canny[2] employing different scales in the inspection of intensity changes. Some additional operational refinements of their strategy have been accomplished by using the matched filter for detecting edges[3][4][5][6].

In the Gaussian model of edge template, the profile of edge signal intensity is described by the integral of a Gaussian added to a fixed background, where we assume the *strictly monotonic* intensity profile of edge and two parameters for the edge detector. The one is the amplitude of Gaussian representing the contrast between the regions bounded by the edge, and the other is the variance of Gaussian indicating the signal slope i. e. the edge acuity. Therefore in order to handle the varying edge width, we may employ the Gaussian variance as a scale parameter of the edge detector adjusting the filter length in practice[3][4][5][6][7].

In this paper, we modify the directional derivative extensively to introduce an extended (nonlocal) directional derivative of gray level as the signal attribute characterizing an edge, which is to be referred to as *adaptive directional derivative of gray level*. In terms of this attribute, we can detect an edge by verifying the presence of a region with strictly monotonic change of intensity

J. Liu et al. (Eds.): IDEAL 2003, LNCS 2690, pp. 975–982, 2003.

without bothering to adjust the edge width parameter such as the Gaussian variance. In order to locate a single edge pixel, we find the *local center of directional derivative of gray level* within the edge width. We note that the proposed scheme of edge detection can provide a truthful detection of edges even without taking bothersome steps such as the hysteresis thresholding or scale space combination since it responds to all scales.

2   Directional Derivative and Some Detectors for Objects

The edge pixels correspond to the boundary points located between some regions representing objects or background in the image. Therefore, the neighborhood of an edge point always includes some points belonging to each of the different regions. On the contrary, an interior pixel of a region in the 2-dimensional image should have all of its 8 neighboring pixels similar in the intensity of image. Hence the pixel is an edge point only if it has at least one neighboring pixel whose intensity is different from the others in the neighborhood (or the pixel itself, equivalently) more than the threshold value T allowed by a certain similarity criterion. For the sake of the simplicity in discussion. we assume that the image is gray-scaled. With respect to the set of nonnegative integers Z_+, let (i, j) be the spatial rectangular coordinates of a digitized image in pixel units with $i, j \in Z_+$. Then, the image function is defined as a mapping f from $(i, j) \in Z_+ \times Z_+$ to $f(i, j) \in G$, which is the grayscale intensity of a pixel at (i, j) quantized into l levels of $G = \{0, 1, \cdots, l - 1\}$.

We introduce the pixel position vector $\boldsymbol{p} = (i, j)$ and eight direction vectors

$$\boldsymbol{u}_{\pm x} \equiv \pm(1, 0), \qquad \boldsymbol{u}_{\pm y} \equiv \pm(0, 1),$$

$$\boldsymbol{u}_{\pm +} \equiv \pm(1, 1), \qquad \boldsymbol{u}_{\pm -} \equiv \pm(1, -1), \tag{1}$$

to define the directional derivative of gray level(DDGL) from the image function f at $\boldsymbol{p}$ in the pixel space as

$$v_\theta \equiv f(\boldsymbol{p} + \boldsymbol{u}_\theta) - f(p) = -v_{-\theta}(\boldsymbol{p} + \boldsymbol{u}_\theta) \tag{2}$$

where θ parametrizes the eight directions to the neighboring pixels of $\boldsymbol{p}$ with $\boldsymbol{u}_{\pm\theta} = \pm\boldsymbol{u}_\theta$ in the above definition (1). This quantity can be used to identify the boundary features of the image. Since the gray level difference between the edge pixel and at least one of its neighboring pixels is larger than a certain threshold value T, *we can identify the pixel $\boldsymbol{p}$ as an edge pixel only if the criterion $|v_\theta(\boldsymbol{p})| \geq T$ with respect to the absolute value of a DDGL for one of θ directions at $\boldsymbol{p}$ is satisfied.* The edge pixels detected by this criterion is gathered and linked to construct an edge or the other boundary features such as points and lines. Therefore, it can be easily seen that we can detect all of these features by using this criterion alone without employing any other special masks for each of them. For example, the usual point detection mask[8][9] is applied to the pixel p producing the response $R_P = -\sum\limits_{\theta} v_\theta(p)$

and $R_{L,y} = - \sum\limits_{(k=0,u_{\pm y})} (v_x(p+k) + v_{-x}(p+k))$ is the response of the usual line detection mask in the y direction[8][9]. With respect to the typical point and line, $v_\theta(p)$ and $v_{\theta'}(p+u_{\theta''})$ in the above reponses have similar values with the same signs due to the geometrical characteristics of the objects. Therefore, a certain relevant threshold values for the absolute values of the above mask responses results in the equivalents to our simple criterion by $v_\theta(p)$. In order to detect discontinuities in general, we can use the gradient of the image f. Using the Sobel mask[8][9], the x component of the gradient is represented as

$$G_x(p) = 2(v_x(p+u_{-x}) + v_x(p)) \\ + v_+(p+u_{-+}) + v_+(p) + v_-(p+u_{--}) + v_-(p). \tag{3}$$

With respect to the typical sharp edge normal to x direction for example, the y component of the gradient $G_y(p) \simeq 0$, and the DDGL's $v_\theta(p)$ and $v_{\theta'}(p+u_{\theta''})$ in $G_x(p)$ of (3) have the values of the same sign or near zero. Therefore the result from the usual detection criterion by the magnitude of the gradient $\sqrt{G_x^2 + G_y^2}$ is equivalent to our simple criterion by $v_\theta(p)$.

3   New Criterion for Ramp Edge Detection

The criterion by the DDGL with a simple threshold may not detect a ramp edge with gradually changing gray level. In order to detect ramp edges in general, we modify the DDGL to define the adaptive directional derivative of gray level (ADDGL)

$$\triangle_\theta(p) \equiv [1 - \delta_{s_\theta(p),s_\theta(p-u_\theta)}] \sum_{k=0}^{\infty} \delta_{k+1,N_\theta(p,k)} v_\theta(p+ku_\theta), \tag{4}$$

where

$$N_\theta(p,k) \equiv \sum_{n=0}^{k} |s_\theta(p+nu_\theta)| \delta_{s_\theta(p),s_\theta(p+nu_\theta)} \tag{5}$$

$$s_\theta(p) \equiv \begin{cases} v_\theta(p)/|v_\theta(p)| & \text{at } v_\theta(p) \neq 0 \\ 0 & \text{at } v_\theta(p) = 0 \end{cases} \tag{6}$$

and $\delta_{(\cdot,\cdot)}$ is the Kronecker delta. According to this definition, $\triangle_\theta(p)$ has a non-vanishing value only when p is the starting pixel of a strictly monotonic interval of the profile of f in the θ direction. If f starts to increase or decrease strictly at p and ends at $p+wu_\theta$ from $f(p)$ to $f(p+wu_\theta)$ along the θ direction then

$$\triangle_\theta(p) = \sum_{n=0}^{w-1} v_\theta(p+nu_\theta)$$

$$= f(\boldsymbol{p} + w\boldsymbol{u}_\theta) - f(\boldsymbol{p}). \tag{7}$$

Since the ADDGL is defined nonlocally over some consecutive pixels in general, the normalization irregularity of $\boldsymbol{u}_\theta$ is not significant. We note that $\boldsymbol{p}$ and w in (7) change by scaling the image but the value of $\triangle_\theta(\boldsymbol{p})$ is left invariant. That is, the ADDGL is independent of scaling. Applying the property $v_\theta(\boldsymbol{p}) = -v_{-\theta}(\boldsymbol{p}+\boldsymbol{u}_\theta)$, of (2) to the equation (7), we can easily show that $\triangle_\theta(\boldsymbol{p}) = -\triangle_{-\theta}(\boldsymbol{p} + w\boldsymbol{u}_\theta)$. According to the definition, $\triangle_{\pm\theta}(\boldsymbol{p} + h\boldsymbol{u}_\theta) = 0$ for $0 < h < w$. Hence we can notice that the ADDGL $\triangle_\theta(\boldsymbol{p})$ specifies the strictly monotonic change of intensity and the corresponding interval $[\boldsymbol{p}, \boldsymbol{p}+w\boldsymbol{u}_\theta]$ along the fixed θ direction.

In the Gaussian model of a ramp edge, the edge signal is described by the integral of a Gaussian added to a fixed background. For the directional derivative in the direction normal to an edge, this implies a functional form of template

$$\partial_n f \equiv v_n(q_n) = \frac{A}{\sqrt{2\pi}\sigma} \exp\left(-\frac{q_n^2}{2\sigma^2}\right) \tag{8}$$

in terms of the length parameter q_n along the edge normal direction. Here, the amplitude A indicates the sign and magnitude of the transition in the image intensity across the edge and the standard deviation σ describes the slope of edge signal or edge width. We also note that the absolute value $|v_n(q_n)|$ is equal to the magnitude of gradient $\sqrt{G_x^2 + G_y^2}$. Then, the directional derivative of the direction with angle ϕ from the edge normal direction(ϕ-direction) has the template function

$$\partial_\phi f \equiv v_\phi(q_\phi) = (\cos\phi)\partial_n f$$
$$\equiv \frac{A}{\sqrt{2\pi}\sigma_\phi} \exp\left(-\frac{q_\phi^2}{2\sigma_\phi^2}\right) \tag{9}$$

where $\sigma_\phi \equiv \sigma/\cos\phi$ and $q_\phi \equiv q_n/\cos\phi$. Since $|v_\phi(q_\phi)| = |\cos\phi \cdot v_n(q_n)| \le |v_n(q_n)|$ and $v_\phi(q_\phi)$ is equivalent to $v_\theta(\boldsymbol{p})$ for some ϕ, the previous criterion $|v_\theta(\boldsymbol{p})| \ge T$ reduces to the usual one employing the magnitude of gradient

$$|v_n(q_n)| = \sqrt{G_x^2 + G_y^2} \ge T, \tag{10}$$

With respect to an ramp edge described by the template function (9), the condition (10) is rewritten as

$$|v_\theta(0)| = \frac{|A|}{\sqrt{2\pi}\sigma} \ge T(\sigma), \tag{11}$$

where we note that the threshold value T should be parametrized according to the edge width or the length scale of edge detection filter described by σ in such a way as $T(\sigma) = T_0/(\sqrt{2\pi}\sigma)$ in order to detect the edge signals with varying widths. That is, the significant change of image intensity by $|A| \ge T_0$ across the ramp edge can be detected as an edge by adjusting the edge detector parameter $T(\sigma)$ in terms of the edge width parameter σ. In the actual application, the criterion (11) can cause multiple identification of edge pixels at a single crossing of the ramp edge and demand an extra thinning to locate an exact edge pixel p with $q_n = 0$.

We can employ our ADDGL as the signal attribute characterizing an edge. With respect to the ramp edge satisfying the equation (9), for example, the ADDGL in the θ direction is estimated as

$$\triangle_\phi(\boldsymbol{p}) = \begin{cases} A & \text{at } \phi \neq \pi/2 \\ 0 & \text{at } \phi = \pi/2 \end{cases} \tag{12}$$

if the θ direction corresponds to the ϕ-direction at the starting pixel p of the strictly monotonic change of gray level in the ramp edge profile, which is independent of σ. Therefore, we can find that $\triangle_\theta(\boldsymbol{p})$ can detect the ramp edges which are strictly monotonic in gray level along the θ direction except the edge parallel to the θ direction, which can be detected by another $\triangle_{\theta'}(\boldsymbol{p})$ with a different direction θ', regardless of the edge width. In order to identify ramp edges, we thus implement a new criterion by $\triangle_\theta$:

(CRE) *The absolute value of an adaptive directional derivative of gray level at p is larger than T, i.e.* $| \triangle_\theta(\boldsymbol{p})| \geq T$ *for one of θ directions.*

Employing this criterion, the local maximal length interval $[\boldsymbol{p}, \boldsymbol{p}+w\boldsymbol{u}_\theta]$ of strictly monotonic gray level along the $\pm\theta$ directions satisfying $|f(\boldsymbol{p}+w\boldsymbol{u}_\theta) - f(\boldsymbol{p})| \geq T$ is identified to belong to the width of a ramp edge, and one of $w+1$ pixels in the interval is determined as the edge pixel. Since the ADDGL $\triangle_{\theta_1}(\boldsymbol{p})$ or $\triangle_{\theta_2}(\boldsymbol{p})$ of two non-parallel directions θ_1 and θ_2 can detect the edges of all directions, we can use the two fixed directions $\theta_1 - x$ and $\theta_2 = y$ in practice. Hence we can describe our edge detection strategy as the following procedure:

P1 We scan the image along the x direction to find the strictly monotonic intervals such as $[\boldsymbol{p}, \boldsymbol{p}+w_x\boldsymbol{u}_x]$ over which $|\triangle_x(\boldsymbol{p})|$ i.e. the variation of intensity $|f(\boldsymbol{p} + w_x\boldsymbol{u}_x) - f(\boldsymbol{p})|$ satisfies the criterion (CRE).
P2 Locate an edge pixel within the interval $[\boldsymbol{p}, \boldsymbol{p} + w_x\boldsymbol{u}_x]$.
P3 Repeat the procedures with respect to the y direction to find the strictly monotonic interval such as $[\boldsymbol{q}, \boldsymbol{q}+w_y\boldsymbol{u}_y]$ and locate an edge pixel in between.

Here, we note that this procedure can detect an edge regardless of spatial blurring or scaling which are concerned with the edge width parameter σ, and extract the exact edge only if a relevant method of locating edge pixels within the strictly monotonic intensity variation of ramp edges is provided.

4   Location of Edge Pixels and Edge Detection Algorithm

In order to complete the edge detection algorithm, we have to be provided with a way how to locate an edge pixel exactly as stated in the above procedure. In the scan of image along the θ direction, the range of location of exact edge is restricted to the strictly monotonic interval $[\boldsymbol{p}, \boldsymbol{p}+w\boldsymbol{u}_\theta]$ of ramp edge intensity. In order to locate an edge pixel within that interval, we define the local center of DDGL(LCDG) as

$$\boldsymbol{p}+k_c\boldsymbol{u}_\theta \equiv \frac{\displaystyle\sum_{k=0}^{w-1}[\boldsymbol{p}+k\boldsymbol{u}_\theta]v_\theta(\boldsymbol{p}+k\boldsymbol{u}_\theta)}{\displaystyle\sum_{k=0}^{w-1}v_\theta(\boldsymbol{p}+k\boldsymbol{u}_\theta)}$$

$$= \boldsymbol{p}+\frac{\displaystyle\sum_{k=0}^{w-1}kv_\theta(\boldsymbol{p}+k\boldsymbol{u}_\theta)}{\triangle_\theta(\boldsymbol{p})}\boldsymbol{u}_\theta. \tag{13}$$

In the pixel space, k_C should be rounded off to obtain the integer value

$$(k_C) \equiv \text{round}\left[\sum_{k=0}^{w-1}kv_\theta(\boldsymbol{P}+k\boldsymbol{u}_\theta)/\triangle_\theta(\boldsymbol{p})\right] \tag{14}$$

and the edge pixel is determined as $\boldsymbol{p}+(k_C)\boldsymbol{u}_\theta = \boldsymbol{p}+k_C\boldsymbol{u}_\theta - [k_C - (k_C)]\boldsymbol{u}_\theta$. We can expect that this pixel determined by the LCDG can locate the edge of single pixel width out of the ramp edge without employing an extra thinning mechanism.

With respect to strictly increasing intervals, we apply the strictly increasing edge detection (SIED) procedure to detect and locate an edge pixel, which is suspended at the end pixel $\boldsymbol{p}_F$ of the line and specified in the following pseudo code:

Procedure SIED

1. While $v_\theta(\boldsymbol{p}) > 0$ and $\boldsymbol{p} \neq \boldsymbol{p}_F$ with respect to the value $v_\theta(\boldsymbol{p})$ of DDGL from successive scan pixel by pixel along the θ direction, do
   a) Put $\varSigma kv = 0$ and $\varSigma kv = 0$ initially.
   b) Calculate $\varDelta = \sum_{\mathbf{p}} v_\theta(\boldsymbol{p})$.
   c) Count the scanned pixels to get the value of k.
   d) Add $v_\theta(\boldsymbol{p})\boldsymbol{p}$ and $kv_\theta(\boldsymbol{p})$ to $\varSigma vp$ and $\varSigma kv$ respectively to obtain their new values.
2. When $v_\theta(\boldsymbol{p}) \leq 0$ for $\boldsymbol{p} = \boldsymbol{p}_F$ (i. e. at the end of the strictly increasing interval), if $\varDelta \geq T$,
   a) Calculate $(k_C) \equiv \text{round}\,[\varSigma kv/\varDelta]$
   b) Write $\dfrac{\varSigma vp}{\varDelta} - \left[\dfrac{\varSigma kv}{\varDelta} - (k_C)\right]\boldsymbol{u}_\theta$ as an edge pixel.

With respect to strictly decreasing intervals, we apply the strictly decreasing edge detection (SDED) procedure, which is obtained simply by replacing $-v_\theta(\boldsymbol{p})$ in the SIED procedure. In order to construct the algorithm for detecting edge pixels from scanning the whole of a single line in the θ direction, we combine the SIED and SDED procedures as the sub-procedures for the pixels with $v_\theta(\boldsymbol{p}) > 0$

and $v_\theta(\boldsymbol{p}) < 0$ respectively, together with the bypassing procedure for the pixels with $v_\theta(p) = 0$. We then obtain the edge pixels identified with the LCDG from the SIED or SDED procedures as the output of this algorithm for edge detection from single line scan (EDSLS). Then, the complete edge detection algorithm of an image is constructed by the integration of the EDSLS algorithm over all the lines of x and y directions.

We illustrate the application of our algorithm to a 2-D image and the effects of noise reduction techniques such as median filtering or Gaussian smoothing in Fig. 1. In the result Fig.1(b) we have the edges of original image detected with $T = 30$ without preprocessing, The result Fig. 1(c) represents the pertinent detection of edges for principal objects with single pixel (noise) objects eliminated by the median filtering with filter size of 3 pixels using $T = 30$ again. In the result Fig. 1(d) from Gaussian smoothing with the filter size of 7 pixels, we can find that some elaborate edges of Fig. 1(c) disappear even with $T = 15$

Fig. 1. Application of the algorithm and the results from noise reduction techniques.

5   Conclusions

Simply by applying the proposed algorithm, we can extract exact edge pixels regardless of the acuity of edge. Although it employes the nonlocal operator ADDGL, the calculational expense is not so great since the procedure is carried out by single one-way scan of image in each of x and y directions. The preprocessing such as median filtering should be carried out to eliminate the fatal speckle noise or isolated pixel noise, which can be detected simultaneously together with the principal objects regardless of the size by this algorithm. Although the use of Gaussian smoothing can partly improve the connectivity in edge linkage, it may suppress some edges and should be used restrictively in applying our edge detection algorithm.

In using the ADDGL as the characteristic attribute of edge signal, the gradual change of intensity over large area of a single surface, which can be caused by the nonuniformity in scene illumination, may be recognized as a false edge. In order to prevent this false positive effect in particular, we need the unsharp masking or flat-fielding procedure before applying the edge detector[7][8].

Acknowledgments. This work was supported by a grant from the Howon University.

References

1. D. Marr and E. Hildreth, "Theory of edge detection," Proc. R. Soc. London B207, 187–217 (1980).
2. J. Canny, "A computational approach to edge detection," IEEE Trans. Pattern Anal. Mach. Intell. PAMI-8, 679–698 (1986).
3. R. A. Boie, I. Cox and P. Rehak, "On optimum edge recognition using matched filters," in Proceedings of the IEEE Conference on Computer Vision and Pattern Recognition (IEEE, New York, 1986), pp. 100–108.
4. R. A. Boie and I. Cox, "Two dimensional optimum edge recognition using matched and Wiener filters for machine vision," in Proceedings of the IEEE First International Conference on Computer Vision (IEEE, New York, 1987), pp. 450–456.
5. R. J. Qian and T. S. Huang, "Optimal Edge Detection in Two-Dimensional Images." IEEE Trans. Image Processing, vol. 5, no. 7, pp. 1215–1220 (1996).
6. Z. Wang, K. R. Rao and J. Ben-Arie, "Optimal Ramp Edge Detection Using Expansion Matching." IEEE Trans. Pattern Anal. Machine Intell., vol. 18, no. 11. pp. 1586–1592 (1996).
7. M. Seul, L. O'Gorman and M. J. Sammon, "Practical Algorithms for Image Analysis." Cambridge U. Press, Cambridge (2000) and references therein.
8. R. C. Gonzalez and R. E. Woods, "Digital Image Processing," 2nd ed. Prentice Hall, Upper Saddle River, N. J. (2000) and references therein.
9. J. R. Parker, "Algorithms for Image Processing and Computer Vision." Wiley (1997) and references therein.

Model-Based Pose Estimation of Human Motion Using Orthogonal Simulated Annealing

Kual-Zheng Lee, Ting-Wei Liu, and Shinn-Ying Ho

Department of Information Engineering, Feng Chia University
100 Wenhwa Rd., Taichung, Taiwan 407
syho@fcu.edu.tw

Abstract. Model-based pose estimation of human motion in video is one of important tasks in computer vision. This paper proposes a novel approach using an orthogonal simulated annealing to effectively solve the pose estimation problem. The investigated problem is formulated as a parameter optimization problem and an objective function based on silhouette features is used. The high performance of orthogonal simulated annealing is compared with those of the genetic algorithm and simulated annealing. Effectiveness of the proposed approach is demonstrated by applying it to fitting the human model to monocular images with real-world test data.

1   Introduction

Model-based pose estimation of human motion in video is one of important tasks in computer vision, having a wide range of applications in virtual reality, surveillance systems, and motion analysis [1-4]. A human model is composed of a set of rigid components connected at joints that allow some degrees of freedom. Generally, there are two approaches for representation the geometric structure of human body: the stick- and surface-based models [1]. The purpose of pose estimation is to establish the coherent relations between given sensory data and model features [5].

Existing methods dealing with pose estimation can be categorized into the following three methods: divide-and-conquer method [6,7], parametric method [8-11], and constraint fusion method [5]. In parametric method, the constraints of neighboring components are expressed implicitly by free parameters that the number of free parameters equals the degree of freedom of the model. The pose estimation problem can be simultaneously solved by solving the parameter optimization problem which consists of both model and viewpoint parameters [8-11]. A drawback of this method is the difficulty in finding the correct free parameters increasing with the number of constraints and with the number of parts participating in each constraint [5]. It is pointed out that there are a number of directions in which the parametric method would be further improved [9]. One is in dealing with models that have a very large number of variable parameters.

In this paper, a novel approach using an orthogonal simulated annealing (OSA) is proposed to effectively solve the pose estimation problem. The investigated problem is formulated as a parameter optimization problem which is equivalent to finding an optimal solution in high-dimensional space where each point represents a vector of

J. Liu et al. (Eds.): IDEAL 2003, LNCS 2690, pp. 983–991, 2003.

model and viewpoint parameters. A surface-based objective function is defined using the silhouette features [10,11] obtained from a background subtraction method. OSA with an efficient generation mechanism (EGM) can generate a set of candidate solutions using a number of perturbation operations and then systematically reasons a good solution for each iteration based on orthogonal experimental design [12,13]. The high performance of OSA is compared with those of the genetic algorithm (GA) [10,11] and simulated annealing (SA) [14]. Effectiveness of the proposed OSA-based approach is demonstrated by applying it to fitting the surface-based human model to monocular images with real-world test data.

2   Parameter Solving as an Optimization Problem

2.1   3D Human Modeling

In this paper, a 3D surface-based human model having 45 model parameters is used, which can directly fit the features of real-world human motions. The model is supported by the software package Life Forms^{TM} of Credo Interactive Inc., as shown in Fig. 1, which consists of 7146 polygons and eighteen revolute joints Z_i, i=1, ..., 18. The representation of the entire model uses a camera-center coordinate system (CCS) where point Q is the center of CCS. According to the definition of Life Forms^{TM}, the DOF=1 for joints Z_i, i=7, 11, 14, 17, DOF=2 for joint Z_4, and DOF=3 for joints Z_i, i=1, 2, 3, 5, 6, 8, 9, 10, 12, 13, 15, 16, 18. All the joints are defined using rotation parameters where each rotation parameter $\theta \in [\theta_{min}, \theta_{max}]$. The feasible ranges of these parameters are derived from Life Forms^{TM}. The parameters θ_{kx}, θ_{ky}, and θ_{kz} are the angles of rotation at Z_k about the X, Y, and Z axes, respectively. Therefore, the parameterized human body model has totally 51 parameters consisting of 45 model parameters and 6 viewpoint parameters (R_x, R_y, R_z for orientation and T_x, T_y, T_z for localization). The simplified feasible ranges of parameters used in these experiments are defined as follows: R_x, R_y, $R_z \in [-90°, 90°]$; T_x, $T_y \in [-90, 90]$; and $T_z \in [850, 1150]$. Generally, the viewpoint parameters can be estimated using heuristic approaches. For example, the localization parameters (T_x, T_y) can be estimated by the center of moving object and T_z can be determined using the size of silhouettes. The orientation parameters (R_x, R_z) can be estimated by checking the included angle between the main axis of silhouette and image plane. The value of R_y can be also estimated by the moving direction of human.

2.2   Objective Function

A variety of features can be used to establish correspondence between model and image remains. In this paper, silhouette features are obtained using an adaptive background subtraction [15]. The basic idea of background subtraction is to maintain a running statistical average of the intensity at each pixel and construct a static background. When the value of a pixel in a frame image differs significantly from average, the pixel is flagged as potentially containing a moving object (foreground).

There are various candidates for the similarity measurement between the extracted silhouette and the human model [1]. In this study, a similarity function proposed by Ohya and Kishino [10] is used as the objective function. Let H_m be the projected binary image of the human model corresponding to the parameter solution S and H_d be the image of the extracted silhouette. The similarity between two binary images H_m and H_d is calculated as follows [10]:

$$F(S) = \frac{\Omega(H_m \cap H_d)}{\Omega(H_m \cup H_d)} \ ,$$

(1)

where Ω denotes the operator counting non-zero elements of its argument set. The similarity F to be maximized takes values in the range $[0,1]$.

2.3 Parameter Encoding Scheme

In the investigated problem, strong interaction effects exist among parameters representing one joint or neighboring joints because these parameters simultaneously determine the appearance of the corresponding rigid component. Therefore, these parameters should not be separated and evaluated individually. For the used human model, there are 13 joints having DOF=3. There exists strong interaction among the three model parameters θ_{kx}, θ_{ky}, and θ_{kz} representing one joint Z_k. In our system, some parameters with strong interaction are put together as a group, such as orientation parameters (R_x, R_y, R_z), localization parameters (T_x, T_y, T_z), cervical vertebra (Z_3, Z_4), and clavicle shoulder, (Z_5, Z_6) and (Z_9, Z_{10}). The other parameters representing one joint are treated as a single group. The domain knowledge about reducing the interaction effects is incorporated in the parameter encoding, as shown in Fig. 2.

3   Orthogonal Simulated Annealing

The proposed OSA integrates the advantages of simulated annealing and EGM. In this section, the concepts of OED, EGM, and OSA will be presented.

3.1 Concepts of OED

An efficient way to study the effect of several factors simultaneously is to use OED with both orthogonal array (OA) and factor analysis [12,13]. OA is a factorial matrix, which assures a balanced comparison of levels of any factor or interaction of factors. It is a matrix of numbers arranged in rows and columns where each row represents the levels of factors in each experiment, and each column represents a specific factor that can be changed from each experiment. The array is called orthogonal because all columns can be evaluated independently of one another, and the main effect of one factor does not affect the estimation of the main effect of another factor [12].

Factor analysis using the OA's tabulation of experimental results can allow the main effects to be rapidly estimated, without the fear of distortion of results by the effects of other factors. Factor analysis can evaluate the effects of individual factors on the evaluation function, rank the most effective factors, and determine the best level for each factor such that the evaluation function is optimized.

3.2   OA and Factor Analysis for EGM

The two-level OA used in EGM is described below. Let there be γ factors with two levels for each factor. The total number of experiments is 2^{γ} for the popular "one-factor-at-a-time" study. To establish an OA of γ factors with two levels, we obtain an integer $\omega = 2^{\lceil \log_2 (\gamma+1) \rceil}$, build an orthogonal array $L_{\omega}(2^{\omega-1})$ with ω rows and $\omega-1$ columns, use the first γ columns, and ignore the other $\omega-\gamma-1$ columns. Table 1 illustrates an example of OA $L_8(2^7)$. The algorithm of constructing OAs can be found in [13]. The number of OA experiments required to analyze all individual factors is only ω where $\gamma+1 \leq \omega \leq 2\gamma$.

After proper tabulation of experimental results, the summarized data are analyzed using factor analysis to determine the relative effects of levels of various factors. Let y_t denote an objective value of the combination corresponding to the experiment t, where $t = 1, \ldots, \omega$. Define the main effect of factor j with level k as S_{jk} where $j = 1, \ldots, \gamma$ and $k = 1, 2$:

$$S_{jk} = \sum_{t=1}^{\omega} y_t \times f_t, \qquad (2)$$

where $f_t=1$ if the level of factor j of experiment t is k; otherwise, $f_t=0$. Considering the case that the objective function is to be maximized, the level 1 of factor j makes a better contribution to the objective function than level 2 of factor j does when $S_{j1} > S_{j2}$. If $S_{j1} < S_{j2}$, level 2 is better. If $S_{j1} = S_{j2}$, levels 1 and 2 have the same contribution. After the better one of two levels of each factor is determined, an intelligent combination consisting of all factors with the better level can be easily derived. OED is effective for development design of efficient search for the intelligent combination of factor levels.

3.3   Efficient Generation Mechanism

The conventional simulated annealing conducts a random perturbation operation on a current solution to generate a new solution for each iteration. The proposed OSA uses EGM to generate a set of candidate solutions using a number of perturbation operations and then systematically reasons a good solution for each iteration based on OED. EGM considers γ perturbation operations on a current solution S simultaneously. Based on OED, EGM can determine the effective ones of γ operations and reason a good candidate solution Q by performing these selected operations for the next move using ω objective function evaluations. How to perform an EGM operation is described as follows:

Step1: Randomly select one parameter in each group from the current solution S. Then randomly select γ values as perturbation candidates to these parameters. One perturbation operation is treated as a factor.

Step 2: Use the first γ columns of an OA $L_{\omega}(2^{\omega-1})$. Let level 1 (level 2) of a factor represent that the corresponding perturbation is disabled (enabled).

Step 3: Evaluate the objective function value y_t of the combinations corresponding to the experiment t, where $t=1, \ldots, \omega$.

Step 4: Compute the main effect S_{jk} where $j=1, \ldots, \gamma$ and $k=1, 2$.

Step 5: Determine the better one of two levels of each factor based on the main effect.

Step 6: The reasoned combination R consists of all factors with the better levels.

Step 7: The candidate solution Q is selected from the best one of the combinations corresponding to the experiments 2 to ω, and R if $R \neq S$. The combination of experiment 1 corresponds to the solution S.

3.4   Orthogonal Simulated Annealing

A single iteration of OSA consists of three phases: perturbation, evaluation, and decision. The proposed OSA for pose estimation is described as follows:

Step 1: Randomly generate a set of model parameters as the initial solution S. Initialize the temperature T, the number of trials per temperature N_T, cooling rate C, inner counter $I_c=0$.

Step 2: (Perturbation) Perturbed the current solution S to yield another candidate solution Q using EGM.

Step 3: (Evaluation) Evaluate the objective value for the candidate solution Q.

Step 4: (Decision) Accept Q to be the new S with probability min. $\{1, \exp(-|F(S)-F(Q)|/T)\}$.

Step 5: Increase the value of I_c by one. If $I_c<\lceil N_T \rceil$, go to Step 2.

Step 6: Let the new values of T and N_T be $C{\times}T$ and $C{\times}N_T$. Reset I_c to zero.

Step 7: If a pre-specified stopping condition is satisfied, stop the algorithm. Otherwise, go to Step 2.

Sine the human poses in neighboring frames of a video sequence are similar, the differences of extracted silhouettes in neighboring frames would be also small. In order to effectively obtain accurate estimation results of the following frames, OSA with an inheritance mechanism is proposed for two continuous frames in a video based on the accurate estimation of the first frame. The basic idea of inheritable OSA is to solve the pose estimation problem using two stages for the first and following frames. The procedure of inheritable OSA is described as follows:

Stage 1: Apply OSA to solve the pose estimation problems of the first frame to obtain an accurate solution S_{best} consisting of values of model and viewpoint parameters.

Stage 2: Reapply OSA using the initial solution inherited from S_{best} to solve the pose estimation problem for the second frame.

4   Experimental Results

In this section, two experiments are conducted to demonstrate the high performance of the OSA-based approach, including comparisons with those of GA [10,11] and SA [14]. An image sequences are obtained using a stationary camera with 320×240 pixel resolution and 15 frames/sec. Some frames are shown in Fig. 3.

4.1 Comparison of Pose Estimation

In this experiment, the model parameters are involved in the parameter solving problem. The number of factors of OSA is 15. The parameters of GA with elitist strategy are as follows: population size N_{pop}=100, selection rate P_s=0.1, crossover rate P_c=0.6, and mutation rate P_m=0.01. For OSA and SA, the starting temperature is T=0.0001, cooling rate is C=0.99, the number of trials per temperature is N_T=200. Note that the number of evaluations (EVLs) per iteration of SA, OSA, and GA are 1, 16, and 160, respectively. Therefore, for comparison, the numbers of iterations of SA, OSA, and GA are set to 16000, 1000, and 100, respectively.

In order to compare the performances of SA, GA, and OSA, an initial solution corresponding to a standing pose that all values of model parameters are zero is used. The objective values of SA, GA, and OSA are 0.554, 0.581, and 0.606, respectively. The estimated results and convergences are reported in Fig. 4(a). Note that the obtained objective values are not close to 1.0 because the artificial model is not specially designed for the walking human and some shadow effects occur during human motion. Experimental results show that the performance of OSA with a highest value is superior to those of SA and GA.

4.2 Performance of Inheritable OSA

In this experiment, the performance of the proposed inheritable OSA is tested for estimating the human pose in continuous frames. The human pose in the first frame is estimated by OSA, as shown in Section 4.1. The initial solution of the following frames is inherited from its front frame. The convergences of the inheritable OSA corresponding to the image sequences are shown in Fig. 4(b). The initial and obtained objective values of first frame are 0.376 and 0.606, respectively. The obtained results of first frame are inherited to the second frame, which has objective value of $F(S)$=0.514. It can be found that the computation cost of the second frame is significantly reduced because it has better initial parameters. Note that the objective value between frames 5 and 10 are not high due to the effects of shadow are large. The estimated results are shown in Fig. 5, where the superimposition denotes the fitting result of the OSA-based method. It reveals that the proposed inheritable OSA can effectively solve the pose estimation problem in continuous frames.

5 Conclusions

This paper proposes a novel approach using an orthogonal simulated annealing to effectively solve the pose estimation problem. The investigated problem is formulated as a parameter optimization problem and an objective function based on silhouette features is used. The proposed approach with OSA performs better than genetic algorithm and simulated annealing based approaches. Experimental results show the effectiveness of the proposed approach in real-world images.

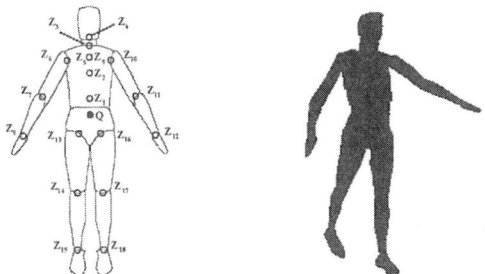

Fig. 1. The used surface-based human model and an example of the projected model with a set of known model and viewpoint parameters.

Factor no.	1	2	3	4	5	6	7	8	9	10	11	12	13	14	15	16	17
Parameters	T_x T_y T_z	R_x R_y R_z	θ_{1x} θ_{1y} θ_{1z}	θ_{2x} θ_{2y} θ_{2z}	θ_{3x} θ_{3y} θ_{3z} θ_{4x} θ_{4y}	θ_{5x} θ_{5y} θ_{5z} θ_{6x} θ_{6y} θ_{6z}	θ_{7x}	θ_{8x} θ_{8y} θ_{8z}	θ_{9x} θ_{9y} θ_{9z} θ_{10x} θ_{10y} θ_{10z}	θ_{11x}	θ_{12x} θ_{12y} θ_{12z}	θ_{13x} θ_{13y} θ_{13z}	θ_{14x}	θ_{15x} θ_{15y} θ_{15z}	θ_{16x} θ_{16y} θ_{16z}	θ_{17x}	θ_{18x} θ_{18y} θ_{18z}

Fig. 2. Representation of the chromosome for the human model. For example, the parameters θ_{1x}, θ_{1y}, and θ_{1z} are encoded together as a group and correspond to the third factor.

Table 1. Orthogonal array $L_8(2^7)$.

Experiment Number	Factor							Objective Value
	1	2	3	4	5	6	7	
1	1	1	1	1	1	1	1	y_1
2	1	1	1	2	2	2	2	y_2
3	1	2	2	1	1	2	2	y_3
4	1	2	2	2	2	1	1	y_4
5	2	1	2	1	2	1	2	y_5
6	2	1	2	2	1	2	1	y_6
7	2	2	1	1	2	2	1	y_7
8	2	2	1	2	1	1	2	y_8

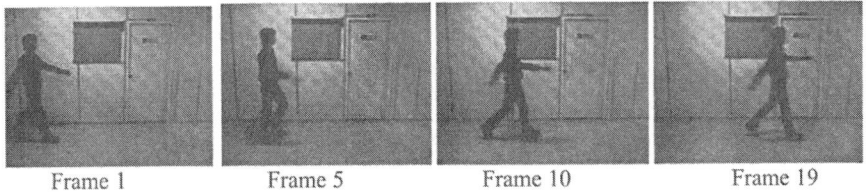

Frame 1   Frame 5   Frame 10   Frame 19

Fig. 3. Some frames of the test image sequences.

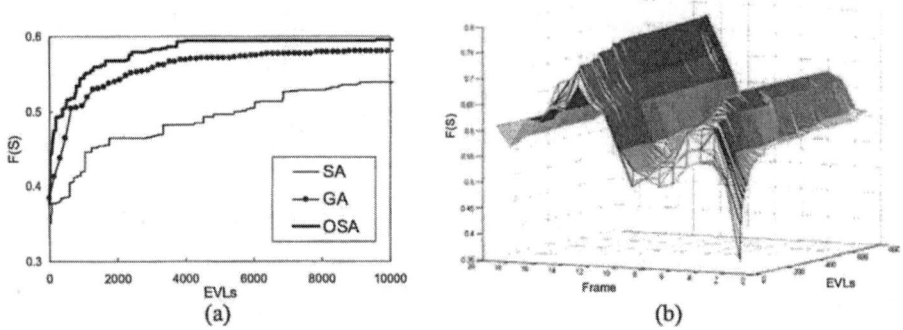

(a)   (b)

Fig. 4. Convergences of SA, GA, OSA, and inheritable OSA. (a) Estimation results of the first frame using SA, GA, and OSA. (b) Estimation results of the image sequences using the proposed inheritable OSA.

Fig. 5. Estimation results of frames 1 to 10 using the proposed inheritable OSA.

References

[1] D. M. Gavrila, "The visual analysis of human movement: a survey," *Computer Vision and Image Understanding*, vol. 73, no. 1, pp. 82–98, Jan. 1999.
[2] J. K. Aggarwal and Q. Cai, "Human motion analysis: a review," *Computer Vision and Image Understanding*, vol. 73, pp. 428–440, 1999.
[3] T. Moeslund and E. Granum, "A survey of computer vision based human motion capture," *Computer Vision and Image Understanding*, vol. 81, pp. 231–268, 2001.
[4] L. Wang, W. Hu, and T. Tan, "Recent developments in human motion analysis," *Pattern Recognition*, vol. 36, pp. 585–601, 2003.
[5] Y. Hel-Or and M. Werman, "Constraint fusion for recognition and localization of articulated objects," *International Journal of Computer Vision*, vol. 19, pp. 5–28, 1996.
[6] W. E. L. Grimson, "On the recognition of parameterized 2-D objects," *International Journal of Computer Vision*, vol. 2, pp. 353–372, 1989.
[7] T. Shakunaga, "Pose estimation of jointed structures," in *Proc. Conference on Computer Vision and Pattern Recognition*, pp. 566–572, 1991.
[8] R. A. Brooks, "Model-based 3-D interpretation of 2-D images," *IEEE Trans. Pattern Analysis and Machine Intelligence*, vol. 5, pp. 140–150, 1983.

[9] D. G. Lowe, "Fitting parameterized three-dimensional models to images," *IEEE Trans. Pattern Analysis and Machine Intelligence*, vol. 13, pp. 441–450, 1991.

[10] J. Ohya and F. Kishino, "Human posture estimation from multiple images using genetic algorithm," in *Proc. International Conference on Pattern Recognition*, pp. 750–753, 1994.

[11] C. Hu, Q. Yu, Y. Li, and S. Ma, "Extraction of parametric human model for posture recognition using genetic algorithm," in *Proc. Fourth International Conference on Automatic Face and Gesture Recognition*, pp. 518–523, 2000.

[12] S. H. Park, *Robust Design and Analysis for Quality Engineering*. Chapman & Hall, 1996.

[13] Y. W. Leung and Y. Wang, "An orthogonal genetic algorithm with quantization for global numerical optimization," *IEEE Trans. Evolutionary Computation*, vol. 5, pp. 41–53, 2001.

[14] P. J. M. Laarhoven and E. H. L. Aarts, *Simulated Annealing: Theory and Applications*. MA: Kluwer Academic Publishers, 1987.

[15] I. Haritaoglu, D. Harwood, and L. S. Davis, "W4: real-time surveillance of people and their activities," *IEEE Trans. Pattern Analysis and Machine Intelligence*, vol. 22, pp. 809–830, 2000.

PCA Fuzzy Mixture Model for Speaker Identification

Younjeong Lee[1], Joohun Lee[2], and Ki Yong Lee[1]

[1]School of Electronic Engineering, Soongsil University, Dongjak-ku, Seoul, 156-743, Korea
yjlee@ctsp.ssu.ac.kr, kylee@ssu.ac.kr
[2]Dept. of Internet Broadcasting, Dong-Ah Broadcasting College, Anseong, 456-880, Korea
[2]vincelee64@hanmail.net

Abstract. In this paper, we proposed the principal component analysis (PCA) fuzzy mixture model for speaker identification. A PCA fuzzy mixture model is derived from the combination of the PCA and the fuzzy version of mixture model with diagonal covariance matrices. In this method, the feature vectors are first transformed by each speaker's PCA transformation matrix to reduce the correlation among the elements. Then, the fuzzy mixture model for speaker is obtained from these transformed feature vectors with reduced dimensions. The orthogonal Gaussian Mixture Model (GMM) can be derived as a special case of PCA fuzzy mixture model. In our experiments, with having the number of mixtures equal, the proposed method requires less training time and less storage as well as shows better speaker identification rate compared to the conventional GMM. Also, the proposed one shows equal or better identification performance than the orthogonal GMM does.

1 Introduction

Both the GMM [1,2] and the fuzzy GMM (FGMM) modified from a fuzzy c-means (FCM) [3,4] are increasingly used for both speaker identification and verification. These models generally assume diagonal covariance matrices. And higher dimensional feature vectors are used to enhance the performance of the speaker recognizer. However, the elements of feature vectors extracted from a given speech signal are much correlated. So a large number of mixtures have to be used in order to model this correlation. The increase in the numbers of the mixture and the dimension of feature vector requires more parameters to characterize the classifier and more storage. Furthermore, larger amount of data is needed for training of such a recognizer.

The PCA is one of the feature extraction methods to reduce the dimension of feature vectors and the correlation among feature vectors [5]. The orthogonal GMM using PCA shows better performance than the conventional GMM in speaker identification [6,7].

This paper proposes a PCA fuzzy mixture model for speaker identification. The proposed method is defined from the combination of the PCA and the fuzzy version of mixture model with diagonal covariance matrices. The fuzzy mixture model is different from the FGMM obtained from modification of FCM [3,4]. In the proposed

J. Liu et al. (Eds.): IDEAL 2003, LNCS 2690, pp. 992–999, 2003.

method, the feature vectors are first transformed by PCA so that the correlation among the elements can be reduced. The speaker's fuzzy mixture model is obtained from these transformed feature vectors. The effectiveness of the proposed method is shown through comparative experiment results among the proposed method, the conventional GMM and the orthogonal GMM.

2 PCA Fuzzy Mixture Model

To reduce the correlation and the dimensionality of the feature space of speaker's data set, we individually take the PCA for each speaker. Namely, the output feature set of a system is linearly transformed to the input feature set.

Assume x_t is an n-dimensional feature vector and $X = \{x_1, \cdots, x_T\}$ is the feature vector set of speaker data. That is, in PCA, a set of the observed X is reduced to a set of L-dimensional feature vector y_t by a transformation matrix Φ_s of s-th speaker as

$$y_t = \Phi_s^T(x_t - E[x]) \tag{1}$$

where $L \leq n$, $E[x]$ is mean as

$$E[x] = \frac{1}{T}\sum_{t=1}^{T} x_t.$$

$\Phi_s = (\phi_1, \cdots, \phi_L)$ and the vector ϕ_k is the eigenvector corresponding to the k-th largest eigenvalue of the sample covariance matrix

$$\Sigma = \frac{1}{T}\sum_{t=1}^{T}(x_t - E[x])(x_t - E[x])^T$$

such that $\Sigma\phi_k = \lambda_k\phi_k$. The L principal axes Φ_s are those orthonormal axes onto which the retained variance under projection is maximal. In (1), the transformation matrix Φ_s of each speaker is unique.

For speaker identification, we consider a PCA fuzzy mixture model which is derived from the combination of the PCA transformed data $Y = \{y_1, \cdots, y_T\}$ and the fuzzy version of mixture model, which is performed onto the PCA transformed space as

$$b(y_t|\Theta_s) = \left[\sum_{i=1}^{M}(w_i p_i(y_t))^\alpha\right]^{1/\alpha} \tag{2}$$

where $p_i(y_t)$ is a Gaussian component parameterized by a mean vector, μ_i, and covariance matrix, Σ_i^y, and w_i is a linear combination coefficient of the i-th component, and α is called the degree of fuzziness, $\alpha > 0$. $p_i(y_t)$ can be modeled by a Gaussian function as

$$p_i(y_t) = \frac{1}{(2\pi)^{L/2}|\Sigma_i^y|^{1/2}} \exp\left\{-\frac{1}{2}(y_t - \mu_i)^T \Sigma_i^{y^{-1}}(y_t - \mu_i)\right\}.$$

(3)

The weights satisfy the constraint that $\sum_{i=1}^{M} w_i = 1$.

In general, the form of Σ_i^y is not truly diagonal. Since the PCA feature vector y_t is decorrelated due to the orthogonality of the transform matrix Φ_s, however, Σ_i^y is a more diagonal dominated than the covariance matrix Σ_i^x of X. Then, the PCA fuzzy mixture model for speaker model are parameterized by the mean vectors, covariance matrices and mixture weights as

$$\Theta_s = \{\theta_i\}, \quad i = 1, \cdots, M,$$

(4)

where $\theta_i = \{w_i, \mu_i, \Sigma_i^y\}$.

3 Training Method of Speaker Model with pca Fuzzy Mixture Model

The fuzzy objective is to find the speaker model which has the maximum of the PCA fuzzy objective function for a given transformation feature can be represented as

$$J(Y) = \sum_{t=1}^{T} \log\{b(y_t \mid \Theta_s)\}$$

$$= \sum_{t=1}^{T} \log\left\{\sum_{i=1}^{M}[w_i p_i(y_t)]^\alpha\right\}^{1/\alpha}$$

(5)

The basic idea in the proposed method is to maximize J over the parameters θ_i. The maximization of J is obtained by setting the derivative of J with respect to the parameter θ_i, $i = 1, \cdots, M$, as

$$\frac{\partial J}{\partial \theta_i} = \frac{1}{\alpha}\sum_{t=1}^{T}\left(\left.(w_i p_i(y_t))^\alpha \middle/ \sum_{m=1}^{M}(w_m p_m(y_t))^\alpha\right)\right)\frac{\partial}{\partial \theta_i}\log(w_i p_i(y_t)) = 0$$

Therefore, the following formulas are obtained:

- Mixture Weight:

$$w_i = \frac{1}{T}\sum_{t=1}^{T} f_{t,i}$$

(6.a)

- Means:

$$\mu_i = \frac{\sum_{t=1}^{T} f_{t,i} y_t}{\sum_{t=1}^{T} f_{t,i}} \tag{6.b}$$

- Variances:

$$\Sigma_i^y = \frac{\sum_{t=1}^{T} f_{t,i} (y_t - \mu_i)(y_t - \mu_i)^T}{\sum_{t=1}^{T} f_{t,i}} \tag{6.c}$$

In (6), the fuzzy membership function for i-th component is given by

$$f_{t,i} = \frac{(w_i p_i(y_t))^\alpha}{\sum_{m=1}^{M} (w_m p_m(y_t))^\alpha} \tag{7}$$

When $\alpha = 1$ and $L=n$, PCA fuzzy mixture model becomes to the orthogonal GMM [6] which can be considered as a special case of our model. When α approaches infinity, $f_{t,i}$ becomes a hard membership, and the method becomes the traditional K-means clustering method.

4 Speaker Identification

As a typical model-based approach, the PCA fuzzy mixture model has been used to represent speaker's characteristic in the form of probabilistic model [1]. For speaker identification, a group of S speakers $S= \{1,2,\cdots,S\}$ is represented by $\Theta_1, \Theta_2,...,\Theta_S$ of PCA fuzzy mixture model.

To evaluate the performance, a sequence of feature vectors is divided into overlapping segments of N feature vectors for the identification [1,8]. The first two segments from a sequence would be

Segment l

$$\overbrace{y_l, y_{l+1}, \cdots, y_{l+N-1}, y_{l+N}}, \cdots$$

Segment $l+1$

$$y_l, \overbrace{y_{l+1}, \cdots, y_{l+N-1}, y_{l+N}, y_{l+N+1}}, \cdots$$

For a segmental test sequence $Y^{(l)} = \{y_l, y_{l+1}, \cdots, y_{l+N-1}\}$, the log-likelihood function of a PCA fuzzy mixture model is as following:

$$L(Y^{(l)}, \Theta_s) = \sum_{t=l}^{l+N-1} \log b(y_t | \Theta_s)$$

$$= \sum_{t=l}^{l+N-1} \log \left\{ \sum_{m=1}^{M} [w_m p_m(y_t)]^\alpha \right\}^{\frac{1}{\alpha}} \quad s = 1, \cdots, S \tag{8}$$

Thus, $Y^{(l)}$ is assigned to a label of identified speakers, s^*, on the basis of the maximum likelihood principle; that is

$$s^* = \arg\max_{1 \leq s \leq S} L(Y^{(l)}, \Theta_s). \tag{9}$$

The identified speaker of each segment was compared to the actual speaker for the test utterance the number of segments that were correctly identified was tabulated. The final performance evaluation was then calculated as the percent of correctly identified N-length segments over all test utterances.

$$\text{Identification rate [\%]} = \frac{\text{\# correctly identified segments}}{\text{total \# of segments}} \times 100. \tag{10}$$

Each speaker had approximately equal amounts of testing speech so the performance evaluation was not biased to any particular speaker.

5 Experimental Results

We did speaker identification experiments to show the effectiveness of the proposed method. In the experiment, the speech database consists of Korean words uttered by 100 speakers (50 male, 50 female) at three time sessions over four months. Each of these speakers uttered 5 times same password per session. The speech data was sampled at 11 kHz and was parameterized using 12 LPC cepstrum and 13 delta cepstrum. The analysis window size was 20ms with 10ms overlap. 50 sentences uttered at the first time session were used for training. Each 250 password uttered at the second and the third time sessions were used for evaluation. The proposed method needs extra $L \times n$ storage for the transform matrix.

Table 1 shows the relationship between the speaker identification rate and the values of α in the conventional GMM and the proposed method. From the table, the speaker identification rate changes with the value of α.

At $\alpha = 1.0$, the speaker identification rate for the proposed method without PCA is same as conventional GMM. And at $\alpha = 1.1$, the speaker identification rate has the best performance by the proposed method.

The number of parameters required in the proposed method and the conventional GMM is presented in Table 2. Even the proposed method needs $M_p(1+2L)+L \times n$ storage and the conventional GMM needs $M_c(1+2n)$ storage for speaker model, respectively, but the former needs less parameter than the latter. For example, on the same performance level, as $M_p = 16$, $M_c = 32$, $L = 15$, $n = 25$, the proposed method and the conventional method have the parameters of 871 and 1632, respectively.

Although the proposed method needs the extra steps to obtain the transform matrix, the computational costs of all these steps are negligible. In the test phase, our method needs a transformation cost a transformation for all test vectors. However, this small calculation overhead has no noticeable influence on the response speed.

Table 1. The relationship between the speaker identification rate and the value of α ($M=32$, $L=25$)

| α | Speaker identification rate [%]   for | |
	The proposed method without PCA	The proposed method with PCA
0.7	91.88	93.13
0.8	91.50	92.50
0.9	92.13	92.88
1.0	92.38	92.90
1.1	92.50	93.25
1.2	92.75	93.21

Table 2. The required numbers of parameters for the proposed method and the conventional GMM

Proposed Method	Conventional GMM
$M_p(1 + 2L) + L \times n$	$M_c(1 + 2n)$

M_p : The number of mixtures in the proposed method

M_c : The number of mixtures in the conventional GMM

Figure 1 shows the relationship between the speaker identification rate and the numbers of mixture. From the figure we see that, when the same number of mixtures is used, the proposed method always gives higher identification rate than the conventional GMM and the orthogonal GMM do. On the same performance level, the conventional GMM needs about two times larger the number of mixtures used by the proposed method.

Figure 2 shows the speaker identification rate to the dimension of transformed feature vector. From the figure the PCA methods with $11 \le L \le 25$ are better than the conventional GMM with $n=25$. And the proposed method has the same or better identification rate compared to the orthogonal GMM.

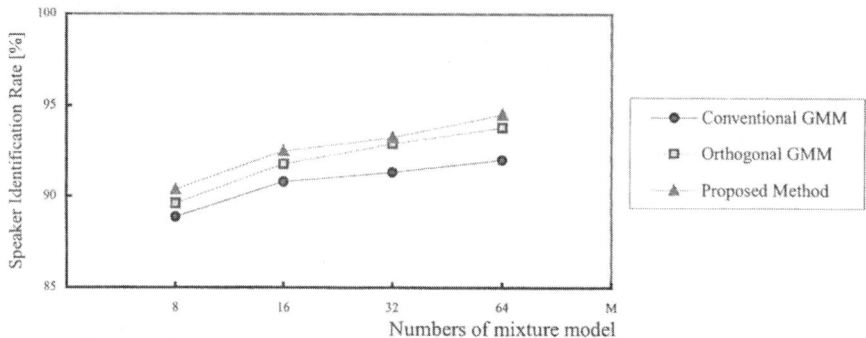

Fig. 1. The relationship between the speaker identification rate and the numbers of mixture ($\alpha = 1.1$, $L=25$)

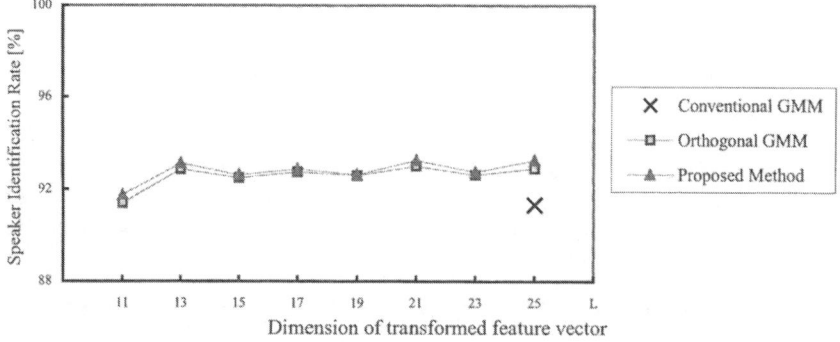

Fig. 2. The relationship between the speaker identification rate and the dimension of transformed feature vector ($\alpha = 1.1$, $M=32$)

6   Conclusions

The PCA fuzzy mixture model is proposed for speaker identification. To reduce the dimensions, the transformation matrix for speaker is individually taken. A PCA fuzzy mixture model is defined from the combination of the PCA and the fuzzy version of mixture model with diagonal covariance matrices. With $\alpha = 1$, the proposed method becomes the orthogonal GMM that can be considered as a special case of our method.

From the experimental results, with the number of mixtures being same, the proposed method needs less training time and less storage as well as shows better speaker identification rate compared to the conventional GMM. Also, the proposed one shows equal or better identification performance than the orthogonal GMM does.

Acknowledgment. This research was supported in part by University IT Research Center Project.

This research was supported in part by Biometrics Engineering Research Center, (KOSEF).

References

1. D.A.Reynolds and R.C. Rose, "Robust text-independent speaker identification using Gaussian mixture speaker models," *IEEE Tr. SAP.*, 3, 1, (1995) 72–82.
2. D.A. Reynolds, "Speaker identification and verification using Gaussian mixture speaker models", *Speech Comm.,* vol.17, (1995) 91–108.
3. D.Tran, T.V.Le, and M.Wagner, "Fuzzy Gaussian mixture models for speaker recognition," *Proc. ICSLP*, vol.3, (1998) 759–762.
4. D.Tran and M.Wagner, "A robust clustering approach to fuzzy Gaussian mixture models for speaker identification, " *Proc. KES'99* , Adelaide, Australia, (1999) 337–340.
5. I.T.Jolliffe, "Principal component analysis," *Springer-Verlag* (1986)
6. L.Liu and J.He, "On the use of orthogonal GMM in speaker recognition," *Proc. ICASSP*, (1999) 845–849.
7. C. Seo, K.Y.Lee and J.Lee, "GMM based on local PCA for speaker identification," *IEEE Electronic Letters*, vol.37, no.24, (2001)1486–1488.
8. L.Wang, K.Chen and H.S.Chi, "Capture interspeaker information with a neural network for speaker identification", *IEEE Tr. Neural Network*, vol.13, no. 2, Mar. (2002)

GMM Based on Local Fuzzy PCA for Speaker Identification

JongJoo Lee[1], JaeYeol Rheem[2], and Ki Yong Lee[1]

[1]School of Electronic Engineering, Soongsil Univ., Korea
jjlee@ctsp.ssu.ac.kr, kylee@ssu.ac.kr
[2]School of Information Technology, Korea University of Technology and Education, Korea
rheem@kut.ac.kr

Abstract. To reduce the high dimensionality required for training of feature vectors in speaker identification, we propose an efficient GMM based on local PCA with Fuzzy clustering. The proposed method firstly partitions the data space into several disjoint clusters by fuzzy clustering, and then performs PCA using the fuzzy covariance matrix in each cluster. Finally, the GMM for speaker is obtained from the transformed feature vectors with reduced dimension in each cluster. Compared to the conventional GMM with diagonal covariance matrix, the proposed method needs less storage and shows faster result, under the same performance.

1 Introduction

The Gaussian mixture model (GMM) with diagonal covariance matrix is increasingly being used for both speaker identification and verification [1]. Since the elements of feature vectors extracted from a speech signal are correlated, larger number of mixtures is necessary in order to provide a good approximation. Also, a higher dimension of the feature set is preferable to enhance the performance of the speaker recognition system [2]. However, the increase of the numbers of feature vectors and mixtures has caused several problems. First, the recognizer with higher dimension of feature set and a larger number of mixtures set requires more parameters to characterize the classifier, so needs more storage. The increases of the complexity and the cost make its real-time implementation difficult, as well as, require a larger amount of speech data for training.

To reduce the dimension of feature vector, the speaker recognition method based on principal component analysis (PCA) has been proposed by [3,4]. PCA is one of feature extraction methods, which reduces the dimension of feature vector and the correlation among the feature vectors by projecting the original feature space into a smaller subspace through a transformation.

In this paper, for speaker identification, we propose an efficient GMM based on local PCA with fuzzy clustering to get the efficiently reduced dimension of feature vectors. First, the proposed method partitions the feature space into several disjoint clus-

J. Liu et al. (Eds.): IDEAL 2003, LNCS 2690, pp. 1000–1007, 2003.
© Springer-Verlag Berlin Heidelberg 2003

ters by Fuzzy clustering [5,6,7]. Second, the new feature vector with reduced dimension is obtained by PCA applied to each cluster [4]. The PCA transforms the original p-dimensional feature vector into the L-dimensional linear subspace that is spanned by the leading eigenvectors of the covariance matrix of feature vector in each cluster ($L<p$). Finally, the GMM with diagonal covariance matrix is obtained from these transformed feature vectors.

The effectiveness of the proposed method is shown through the results of the comparative experiments between the proposed method and the conventional GMM

2 Fuzzy PCA Based on Fuzzy Clustering

Let $X = \{x_1, \cdots x_T\}$ be a set of feature vectors in the p-dimensional space, and $U = [u_{jt}]$ be a matrix whose elements are memberships of x_t in the j-th cluster R^j. *Fuzzy K-partition* space for X is the set of matrices U such that

$$0 \le u_{jt} \le 1, \qquad j = 1, 2, \cdots, K, \quad t = 1, 2, \cdots, T$$

$$\sum_{j=1}^{K} u_{jt} = 1, \forall t, \qquad 0 < \sum_{t=1}^{T} u_{jt} < T, \forall j \tag{1}$$

where $0 \le u_{jt} \le 1, \forall j, t$ means it is possible for each x_t to have an arbitrary distribution of membership among the K fuzzy clusters [8].

The most well known objective function for fuzzy clustering in X is the *least-squares* function - the infinite family of fuzzy K-means functions generalized from the function J_1

$$J_m(U, C; X) = \sum_{t=1}^{T} \sum_{j=1}^{K} (u_{jt})^m d^2(x_t, c_j) \qquad K \le T \tag{2}$$

where $U = [u_{jt}]$ is a fuzzy K-partition of X, m (>1) is a weighting exponent on each fuzzy membership u_{jt} and is called the degree of fuzziness. The c_j is the centroid of the j-th cluster R^j. In (2), $d^2(x_t, c_j)$ is the distance between x_t and c_j and is defined as:

$$d^2(x_t, c_j) = \| x_t - c_j \|_F^2$$
$$= (x_t - c_j)^T F_j^{-1}(x_t - c_j) \tag{3}$$

where F_j is the fuzzy covariance matrix of the j-th luster.

The fuzzy K-means algorithm is based on minimization of $J_m(U, C; X)$ over U and C on the assumption that matrix U as a part of optimal pairs for $J_m(U, C; X)$ identifies good partitions of the data X. Minimizing the fuzzy objective function $J_m(U,C;X)$ in (2) gives:

$$u_{jt} = \frac{\left[\dfrac{1}{d^2(x_t,c_j)} \right]^{1/(m-1)}}{\displaystyle\sum_{i=1}^{K} \left[\dfrac{1}{d^2(x_t,c_i)} \right]^{1/(m-1)}} \tag{4}$$

$$c_j = \frac{\displaystyle\sum_{t=1}^{T}(u_{jt})^m x_t}{\displaystyle\sum_{t=1}^{T}(u_{jt})^m} \tag{5}$$

$$F_j = \frac{\displaystyle\sum_{t=1}^{T} u_{jt}(x_t - c_j)(x_t - c_j)^T}{\displaystyle\sum_{t=1}^{T} u_{jt}} \tag{6}$$

Then, the fuzzy PCA can be obtained by computing the eigenvalues and the eigenvectors of fuzzy covariance matrix. Since the importance of any transformed coordinate is measured by the magnitude of its eigenvalue, only L principal eigenvectors which are associated with the largest eigenvalues, are taken. They are used to transform the feature vector into the optimal one.

During training and testing, each input feature vector for GMM is transformed as

$$y_{t_j} = \Phi_j x_t, \qquad \text{if } x_t \in R^j \tag{7}$$

where $\Phi_j = (\phi_1 \phi_2 \cdots \phi_L)_j$ is $L \times p$ weight matrix whose rows are the L principal eigenvectors of the j-th cluster R^j and the vector ϕ_i is the eigenvector corresponding to the i-th largest eigenvalue of the F_j. The covariance matrix of (7) has a diagonal form.

3 GMM Based on Local Fuzzy PCA

For a sequence of T_j training vectors $Y_j = \{y_{t_j=1}, \cdots, y_{t_j=T_j}\}$ in j-th cluster R^j, the Gaussian mixture density is defined by a weighted sum of M_j component densities as

$$p(y_{t_j}|\lambda) = \sum_{i=1}^{M_j} p_{j,i} b_i(y_{t_j}) \tag{8}$$

where $b_i(y_{t_j}) = \dfrac{1}{(2\pi)^{\frac{L}{2}}|\Sigma_{j,i}|^{\frac{1}{2}}} \exp\left\{-\dfrac{1}{2}(y_{t_j} - \mu_{j,i})^T \Sigma_{j,i}^{-1}(y_{t_j} - \mu_{j,i})\right\}$ with mean $\mu_{j,i}$ and variance

matrix $\Sigma_{j,i}$. The mixture weights satisfy the constraint that $\displaystyle\sum_{j=1}^{K}\sum_{i=1}^{M_j} p_{j,i} = 1$.

Given $Y = \{Y_1, \cdots, Y_K\}$, the complete GMM for speaker model is parameterized by the mean vectors, covariance matrices and mixture weights from all component densities. The notation collectively represents these parameters

$$\lambda = \{p_{j,i}, \mu_{j,i}, \Sigma_{j,i}\} \quad i = 1,2,\cdots,M_j \quad \text{and} \quad j = 1,2,\cdots,K \tag{9}$$

Then, the GMM likelihood can be written as

$$p(Y|\lambda) = \prod_{t_1=1}^{T_1} p(y_{t_1}|\lambda) \cdots \prod_{t_K=1}^{T_K} p(y_{t_K}|\lambda) \tag{10}$$

Parameter estimates can be obtained iteratively using EM algorithm [1]. On each EM iteration, the following reestimation formulas are used which guarantee a monotonic increase in the model's likelihood value:

- Mixture Weights:

$$p_{j,i} = \frac{1}{T}\sum_{t_j=1}^{T_j} p(j,i|y_{t_j},\lambda) \tag{11.a}$$

- Means:

$$\mu_{j,i} = \frac{\displaystyle\sum_{t_j=1}^{T_j} p(j,i|y_{t_j},\lambda) y_{t_j}}{\displaystyle\sum_{t_j=1}^{T_j} p(j,i|y_{t_j},\lambda)} \tag{11.b}$$

- Variance:

$$\Sigma_{j,i} = \frac{\displaystyle\sum_{t_j=1}^{T_j} p(j,i|y_{t_j},\lambda)(y_{t_j} - \mu_{j,i})(y_{t_j} - \mu_{j,i})^T}{\displaystyle\sum_{t_j=1}^{T_j} p(j,i|y_{t_j},\lambda)} \tag{11.c}$$

The *a posteriori probability* for acoustic class i in j-th cluster is given by

$$p(j,i|y_t,\lambda) = \frac{p_{j,i}b_i(y_{t_j})}{\sum\limits_{i=1}^{M_j} p_{j,i}b_i(y_{t_j})} \tag{12}$$

When $L = p$ and $K = 1$, the proposed method is equal to the method of [2]. The method proposed by [2] is considered as a special case of the proposed method.

4 Speaker Identification

For speaker identification, each of S speakers is represented by GMMs $\lambda_1,\cdots,\lambda_S$, respectively. The objective of speaker identification is to find the speaker model which has the maximum *a posteriori probability* for a given feature sequence as

$$\hat{s} = \max_{1 \le l \le S} \sum_{t=1}^{T} \log p(y_t|\lambda_l)$$
$$= \max_{1 \le l \le S} \sum_{j=1}^{K} \sum_{t_j=1}^{T_j} \log\left(\sum_{i=1}^{M_j} p_{j,i}b_i(y_{t_j})\right) \tag{13}$$

5 Experimental Result

We did speaker identification experiments to show the effectiveness of the proposed method. The speech data used in this experiment were gathered from three sessions over four months. The 100 speakers (50 males, 50 females) uttered their own sentence five times at each session. The speech data were sampled at 11kHz and were parameterized by using 12 LPC cepstrum and 13 delta cepstrum coefficients (p=25). The analysis window size was 20ms with 10ms overlap. The utterances from the first session were used for training and the others were used for testing.

The number of parameters required in the proposed and the conventional GMM is presented in Table 1. Even the proposed method needs extra $K \times L \times p$ storage for the transform matrix and $K \times p$ storage for fuzzy clustering, but it needs less parameter than the conventional GMM does. For example, as $M_p = 16$, $M_c = 64$, $K = 2$, $L = 17$, and $p = 25$, the proposed method needs 1460 parameters, however, the conventional method needs 3264 parameters.

Table 2 shows speaker identification performance for the numbers of mixtures and clusters. The total number of mixtures of the fuzzy PCA GMM with M mixtures and K clusters is similar to that of the conventional GMM with $M \times K$ mixtures, but the performance of the fuzzy PCA GMM with M mixtures and K clusters is better than the latter.

Figure 1 shows the relationship for the speaker identification performance and the number of mixtures when speaker model is trained. In here, $L=17$ in the Original PCA [2] and $L=17$, $K=2$ in the proposed method. From figure 1, we can observe that speaker identification performance of the proposed method is better than the other methods. Moreover, the conventional GMM method shows lower speaker identification performance than either the conventional PCA methods [2] or the proposed method does.

Figure 2 shows the speaker identification performance for the dimension L of transformed feature vector. From the figure the proposed method with reduced dimension $(11 \leq L \leq 25)$ has the same or better performance compared to the conventional GMM with $p=25$.

Table 1. The required numbers of parameters for the proposed and the conventional GMM Font sizes of headings.

Proposed GMM	Conventional GMM
$M_p(2L+1)+Kp(L+1)$	$M_c(2p+1)$

Table 2. The speaker identification performance for the numbers of mixtures and clusters with $L = p$.

M \ K	1	2	3	4
4	91.74	93.72	94.05	94.62
8	91.81	95.73	95.29	95.37
12	93.65	95.85	95.88	95.99
16	93.72	96.36	96.01	96.76
32	95.07	96.53		
64	95.98			

6 Conclusion

In this paper, we propose an efficient GMM based on local PCA with fuzzy clustering to get the efficiently reduced dimension of feature vectors for speaker identification.

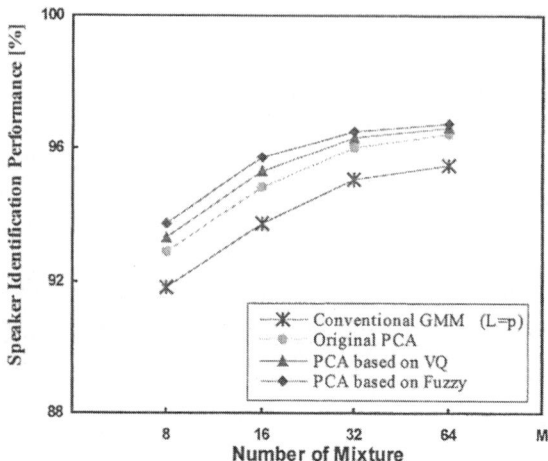

Fig. 1. The relationship between speaker identification performance and the number of mixtures (*L*=17, *K*=2)

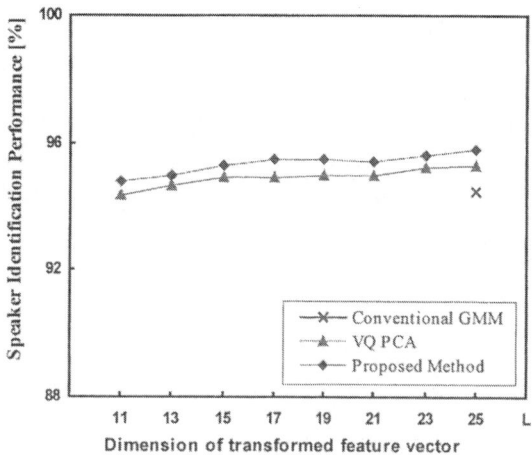

Fig. 2. The relationship between the speaker identification performance and the dimension of transformed feature vector (*M*=16, *K*=2)

The proposed method partitions the data space into several disjoint clusters by fuzzy clustering, and then performs PCA using the fuzzy covariance matrix in each cluster. Finally, the GMM for speaker is obtained from the transformed feature vectors with reduced dimension in each cluster. Compared to the conventional GMM with diagonal covariance matrix, the proposed method needs less storage and shows faster result, under the same performance.

The results of the comparative experiments between the proposed method and the conventional ones shows the proposed method is effective.

Acknowledgement. This research was supported in part by University IT Research Center Project. This research was supported in part by Biometrics Engineering Research Center, (KOSEF)

References

1. D. Reynolds and R. Rose : Robust text-independent speaker identification using Gaussian mixture speaker models. IEEE Transactions on Speech and Audio Processing, vol. 3, no. 1, pp. 72–82. 1995.
2. L. Liu and J. He, : On the use of orthogonal GMM in speaker recognition. International Conference on Acoustics, Speech, and Signal Processing, pp. 845–849, 1999.
3. Y. Ariki, S. Tagashira and M. Nishijima : Speaker recognition and speaker normalization by projection to speaker subspace. International Conference on Acoustics, Speech, and Signal Processing 96, pp. 319–322., 1996.
4. C. W. Seo, K. Y. Lee and J. Lee: GMM based on Local PCA for Speaker Identification. Electronics Letters 37, 24, pp. 1486–1488., 2001.
5. E. E. Gustafson and W. C. Kessel: Fuzzy clustering with a fuzzy covariance matrix. Proc. IEEE CCD, An diego, CA, pp. 761–766, 1979.
6. I. Gath and A. B. Geva : Unsupervised optimal fuzzy clustering. IEEE Trans. on Patt. Anal. & Mac. Intel., vol.11, no. 7, pp.773–781, 1981.
7. D. Tran and M. Wagner : Fuzzy Entropy Clustering,.Proceedings of the FUZZ-IEEE'2000 Conference, vol. 1, pp. 152 157, May, 2000.
8. J. C. Bezdek : Pattern Recognition with Fuzzy Objective Function Algorithms. Plenum Press, New York and London, 1981.

Fast Pattern Selection Algorithm for Support Vector Classifiers: Time Complexity Analysis

Hyunjung Shin and Sungzoon Cho

Department of Industrial Engineering, Seoul National University,
San 56-1, Shillim-Dong, Kwanak-Gu, 151-742, Seoul, Korea
{hjshin72, zoon}@snu.ac.kr

Abstract. Training SVM requires large memory and long cpu time when the pattern set is large. To alleviate the computational burden in SVM training, we propose a fast preprocessing algorithm which selects only the patterns near the decision boundary. The time complexity of the proposed algorithm is much smaller than that of the naive M^2 algorithm

1 Introduction

In SVM QP formulation, the dimension of kernel matrix $(M \times M)$ is equal to the number of training patterns (M). A standard QP solver has time complexity of order $O(M^3)$ and a decomposition method has (*the number of iterations*)$\cdot$ $O(Mq + q^3)$ where q is the size of the working set. Of course, "the number of iterations" is supposed to increase as M increases [3,4].

One way to circumvent this computational burden is to select only the training patterns, in advance, that are more likely to be support vectors. In a classification problem, the support vectors are distributed near the decision boundary. Therefore, selecting those patterns (potential support vectors) prior to SVM training is quite desirable. Recently, we proposed to select the patterns near the decision boundary based on the neighborhood properties [5]. The first property dictates that a pattern located near the decision boundary tends to have more heterogeneous neighbors. The second property dictates that a pattern on the correct side of the decision boundary tends to belong to the same class as its neighbors. Two measures utilizing these properties reduced the number of patterns significantly, thus reduced the training time. However, a naive algorithm evaluating kNNs for all patterns took $O(M^2)$, so the pattern selection process itself was time consuming.

In this paper, we propose a fast algorithm. Here, we just compute the kNNs of the patterns near the decision boundary, not all training patterns. The idea comes from another neighborhood property that the neighbors of the pattern located near the decision boundary tend to be located near the decision boundary as well. The time complexity of the fast algorithm is approximately $O(bM)$, where b is the number of patterns in the "overlap" region around decision boundary. In most practical problems, $b \ll M$ holds.

J. Liu et al. (Eds.): IDEAL 2003, LNCS 2690, pp. 1008–1015, 2003.

This paper is structured as follows. In section 2, we propose the fast algorithm which selects the patterns near the decision boundary. In section 3, we provide the time complexity analysis of the algorithm. In section 4, we present the empirical results confirming the time complexity of our algorithm. In the last section, we conclude the paper with the discussion of the limitations.

2   Fast Algorithm Based on Neighborhood Properties

The first neighborhood property is that a pattern located near the decision boundary tends to have heterogeneous neighbors. Thus, the degree of pattern x's proximity to the decision boundary can be estimated by "**Neighbors_Entropy(x)**", which is defined as the entropy of pattern x's k-nearest neighbors' class labels (see Fig. 1). A pattern with a positive Neighbors_Entropy(x) value is assumed to be located near the decision boundary. *The second neighborhood property* is that a pattern on the correct side of the decision boundary tends to belong to the same class as its neighbors. If a pattern's own label is very different from those of its neighbors, it is likely to be incorrectly labeled. The measure "**Neighbors_Match(x)**" is defined as the ratio of x's neighbors whose label matches that of x. Only those pattern xs are selected that satisfy Neighbors_Match(x) $\geq \beta \cdot \frac{1}{J}$ (J is the number of classes and $0 < \beta \leq 1$) among the patterns with positive Neighbors_Entropy(x) values.

LabelProbability(x) {

    /* For x, calculate the label probabilities of kNN(x) over J classes, $\{C_1, C_2, \ldots, C_J\}$, where kNN(x) is defined as the set of k nearest neighbors of x.*/

    $k_j = |\{x' \in C_j | x' \in k\text{NN}(x)\}|, \quad j = 1, \ldots, J.$

    return $\left(P_j = \frac{k_j}{k}, \forall j \right).$

}

Neighbors_Entropy(x) {

    /* Calculate the neighbors-entropy of x with its nearest neighbors' labels. In all calculations, $0 \, log_J \frac{1}{0}$ is defined to be 0. */

    Do **LabelProbability(x)**.

    return $\left(\sum_{j=1}^{J} P_j \cdot log_J \frac{1}{P_j} \right).$

}

Neighbors_Match(x) {

    /* Calculate the neighbors-match of x. j^* is defined as the label of x itself.*/

    $j^* = \arg_{j}\{C_j \mid x \in C_j, j = 1, \ldots, J\}.$

    Do **LabelProbability(x)**.

    return (P_{j^*}).

}

Fig. 1. Neighbors_Entropy and Neighbors_Match functions

A naive algorithm was presented in [5] where the kNNs of all patterns were evaluated. This algorithm is easy to implement and also runs in a reasonable amount of time as long as the size of training set, M, is relatively small. However, when the size of training set is large, the computational cost increases in proportion to the size. Let us assume that the distance between any two points in d-dimensional space can be computed in $O(d)$. Then finding the nearest neighbors for "each pattern" takes sum of distance computation time DT, $O\left(d(M-1)\right)$, and search time ST, $O\left(k(M-1)\right)$. The total time complexity of the naive algorithm for all patterns, therefore, is $O\left(M \cdot (DT+ST)\right)$. Roughly speaking, it is $O(M^2)$ if we suppose $d \ll M$ and $k \ll M$. There is a considerable amount of literature on efficient nearest neighbor searching algorithms for large data sets of a high dimension. Most approaches focus on reducing DT or ST. See [1,2,6].

Our approach, on the other hand, focuses on reducing the first M of $O(M \cdot M)$. The idea comes from yet *another neighborhood property* that the neighbors of a pattern located near the decision boundary tend to be located near the decision boundary as well. Given a set of randomly selected patterns, we examine the patterns near the decision boundary and their neighbors only. This successive "neighbors" only evaluation of the "current" pattern set is repeated until all the patterns near the decision boundary are chosen and evaluated. A pattern is "expanded" or a pattern's neighbors are evaluated when its Neighbors_Entropy is positive. This "selective kNN expanding" procedure is shown in Fig. 2 using notations displayed in Table 1.

Table 1. Notation

Symbol	Meaning
$\mathbf{D}$	the original training set whose cardinality is M
$\mathbf{D}_\mathbf{e}^i$	the evaluation set at i-th step
$\mathbf{D}_\mathbf{o}^i$	a subset of $\mathbf{D}_\mathbf{e}^i$, the set of patterns to be "expanded" from $\mathbf{D}_\mathbf{e}^i$ each element of which will compute its k nearest neighbors to constitute the next evaluation set, $\mathbf{D}_\mathbf{e}^{i+1}$
$\mathbf{D}_\mathbf{x}^i$	a subset of $\mathbf{D}_\mathbf{e}^i$, the set of patterns "not to be expanded" from $\mathbf{D}_\mathbf{e}^i$, or $\mathbf{D}_\mathbf{x}^i = \mathbf{D}_\mathbf{e}^i - \mathbf{D}_\mathbf{o}^i$
$\mathbf{D}_\mathbf{s}^i$	the set of "selected" patterns from $\mathbf{D}_\mathbf{o}^i$ at i-th step
$\mathbf{S}_\mathbf{o}^i$	the accumulated set of expanded patterns, $\bigcup_{j=0}^{i-1} \mathbf{D}_\mathbf{o}^j$
$\mathbf{S}_\mathbf{x}^i$	the accumulated set of non-expanded patterns, $\bigcup_{j=0}^{i-1} \mathbf{D}_\mathbf{x}^j$
$\mathbf{SS}^i$	the accumulated set of selected patterns, $\bigcup_{j=0}^{i-1} \mathbf{D}_\mathbf{s}^j$ the last of which $\mathbf{SS}^N$ is the reduced training pattern set
$k\mathbf{NN}(\boldsymbol{x})$	the set of k nearest neighbors of $\boldsymbol{x}$
$\mathbf{B}$	the set of patterns located in the "overlapped" region characterized by $Neighbors\_Entropy\,(\boldsymbol{x}) > 0$
$\mathbf{B}^+$	the set of k nearest neighbors of patterns belonging to $\mathbf{B}$

Selective-kNN-Expanding() {

[0] Initialize $\mathbf{D}_e^0$ with randomly chosen patterns from $\mathbf{D}$.
Constants k and J are given. Initialize i and various sets as follows:
$i \leftarrow 0$, $\mathbf{S}_o^0 \leftarrow \emptyset$, $\mathbf{S}_x^0 \leftarrow \emptyset$, $\mathbf{SS}^0 \leftarrow \emptyset$.

while $\mathbf{D}_e^i \neq \emptyset$ do

[1] Choose x satisfying [Expanding Criteria].
$\mathbf{D}_o^i \leftarrow \{x \mid Neighbors\_Entropy(x) > 0,\ x \in \mathbf{D}_e^i\}$.
$\mathbf{D}_x^i \leftarrow \mathbf{D}_e^i - \mathbf{D}_o^i$.

[2] Select x satisfying [Selecting Criteria].
$\mathbf{D}_s^i \leftarrow \{x \mid Neighbors\_Match(x) \geq \beta/J,\ x \in \mathbf{D}_o^i\}$.

[3] Update the pattern sets: the expanded, the non-expanded, and the selected.
$\mathbf{S}_o^{i+1} \leftarrow \mathbf{S}_o^i \cup \mathbf{D}_o^i$, $\mathbf{S}_x^{i+1} \leftarrow \mathbf{S}_x^i \cup \mathbf{D}_x^i$, $\mathbf{SS}^{i+1} \leftarrow \mathbf{SS}^i \cup \mathbf{D}_s^i$.

[4] Compute the next evaluation set $\mathbf{D}_e^{i+1}$.
$\mathbf{D}_e^{i+1} \leftarrow \bigcup_{x \in \mathbf{D}_o^i} k\mathrm{NN}(x) - (\mathbf{S}_o^{i+1} \cup \mathbf{S}_x^{i+1})$.

[5] $i \leftarrow i + 1$.
end
return $\mathbf{SS}^i$}

Fig. 2. Selective kNN Expanding algorithm

3 The Time Complexity Analysis of the Fast Algorithm

Now, we show that the fast algorithm terminates within a finite number of steps and its time complexity is significantly smaller than that of the naive algorithm.

Lemma 1. *Different evaluation sets are disjoint:*
$$\mathbf{D}_e^i \cap \mathbf{D}_e^j = \emptyset,\ \forall\, i \neq j. \tag{1}$$

Proof. Consider step [4] of the algorithm shown in Fig.2,

$$\mathbf{D}_e^i = \left(\bigcup_{x \in \mathbf{D}_o^{i-1}} k\mathrm{NN}(x) \right) - (\mathbf{S}_o^i \cup \mathbf{S}_x^i). \tag{2}$$

Since $\mathbf{S}_o^i$ and $\mathbf{S}_x^i$ are defined as $\left(\bigcup_{j=0}^{i-1} \mathbf{D}_o^j \right)$ and $\left(\bigcup_{j=0}^{i-1} \mathbf{D}_x^j \right)$ respectively,

$$\mathbf{S}_o^i \cup \mathbf{S}_x^i = \bigcup_{j=0}^{i-1} \left(\mathbf{D}_o^i \cup \mathbf{D}_x^i \right) = \left(\bigcup_{j=0}^{i-1} \mathbf{D}_e^j \right). \tag{3}$$

By replacing $(\mathbf{S}_o^i \cup \mathbf{S}_x^i)$ in Eq.(2) with Eq.(3), we get

$$\mathbf{D}_e^i = \left(\bigcup_{x \in \mathbf{D}_o^{i-1}} k\mathrm{NN}(x) \right) - \left(\bigcup_{j=0}^{i-1} \mathbf{D}_e^j \right). \tag{4}$$

Eq.(4) clearly shows that $\mathbf{D}_e^i$ does not share patterns with any of its earlier sets.∎

Lemma 2. *The union of all $\mathbf{D}_e^i$'s is equivalent to the set of kNN's of the union of all $\mathbf{D}_o^i$'s.*

$$\left(\bigcup_{i=1}^{n}\mathbf{D}_e^i\right) = \left(\bigcup_{x\in\mathbf{D}_o^0\cup\mathbf{D}_o^1\cup\cdots\cup\mathbf{D}_o^{n-1}} kNN(x)\right). \tag{5}$$

Proof. From Eq.(4) in Lemma 1, we get

$$\bigcup_{i=1}^{n}\mathbf{D}_e^i = \bigcup_{i=1}^{n}\left(\bigcup_{x\in\mathbf{D}_o^{i-1}} kNN(x)\right) - \bigcup_{i=1}^{n}\left(\bigcup_{j=0}^{i-1}\mathbf{D}_e^j\right). \tag{6}$$

Since in general

$$\left(\bigcup_{x\in\mathbf{A}_1} kNN(x)\right)\bigcup\left(\bigcup_{x\in\mathbf{A}_2} kNN(x)\right) = \left(\bigcup_{x\in\mathbf{A}_1\cup\mathbf{A}_2} kNN(x)\right) \tag{7}$$

holds, we get

$$\left(\bigcup_{i=1}^{n}\mathbf{D}_e^i\right) = \left(\bigcup_{x\in\mathbf{D}_o^0\cup\mathbf{D}_o^1\cup\cdots\cup\mathbf{D}_o^{n-1}} kNN(x)\right) - \left(\bigcup_{i=0}^{n-1}\mathbf{D}_e^i\right). \tag{8}$$

If we union $\left(\bigcup_{i=0}^{n-1}\mathbf{D}_e^i\right)$ to both sides of Eq.(8), then

$$\left(\bigcup_{i=0}^{n}\mathbf{D}_e^i\right) = \left(\bigcup_{x\in\mathbf{D}_o^0\cup\mathbf{D}_o^1\cup\cdots\cup\mathbf{D}_o^{n-1}} kNN(x)\right)\bigcup\left(\bigcup_{i=0}^{n-1}\mathbf{D}_e^i\right) \tag{9}$$

results. Since $\mathbf{D}_e^i \subseteq \bigcup_{x\in\mathbf{D}_o^{i-1}} kNN(x)$, $i = 1,\ldots,n$, $\left(\bigcup_{i=1}^{n-1}\mathbf{D}_e^i\right)$, the last $n-1$ components of the second factor of the right hand side may vanish. Then, we finally have

$$\left(\bigcup_{i=1}^{n}\mathbf{D}_e^i\right)\bigcup\mathbf{D}_e^0 = \left(\bigcup_{x\in\mathbf{D}_o^0\cup\mathbf{D}_o^1\cup\cdots\cup\mathbf{D}_o^{n-1}} kNN(x)\right)\bigcup\mathbf{D}_e^0. \tag{10}$$

If we consider only the relationship after the first iteration, then $\mathbf{D}_e^0$ from both sides of Eq.(10) is not to be included. Now, the lemma is proved.   ∎

Lemma 3. *Every expanded set $\mathbf{D}_o^i$ is a subset of $\mathbf{B}$, the set of patterns in the overlapped region.*

$$\mathbf{D}_o^i \subseteq \mathbf{B}, \forall i \tag{11}$$

Proof. Recall that in the proposed algorithm, $\mathbf{D}_o^i$ is defined as

$$\mathbf{D}_o^i = \{x \mid Neighbors\_Entropy(x) > 0, x \in \mathbf{D}_e^i\}. \tag{12}$$

Compare it with the definition of $\mathbf{B}$

$$\mathbf{B} = \{x \mid Neighbors\_Entropy(x) > 0, x \in \mathbf{D}\}. \tag{13}$$

Since $\mathbf{D}_e^i$'s are subsets of $\mathbf{D}$, $\mathbf{D}_o^i$'s are subsets of $\mathbf{B}$.   ∎

Lemma 4. *Different expanded sets $\mathbf{D}_o^i$'s are disjoint.*

$$\mathbf{D}_o^i \cap \mathbf{D}_o^j = \emptyset, \ \forall i \neq j \tag{14}$$

Proof. Every expanded set is a subset of the evaluation set by definition (see step[1] in the algorithm)

$$\mathbf{D}_o^i \subseteq \mathbf{D}_e^i, \ \forall i. \tag{15}$$

By Lemma 1, $\mathbf{D}_e^i$'s are disjoint from others for all i's. Therefore, their respective subsets are disjoint, too. ∎

Theorem 1. *(Termination of the Algorithm) If the while loop of the proposed algorithm exits after N iterations, then N is finite.*

Proof. We show that $N < \infty$. Inside the while-loop of the algorithm(Fig.2), condition $\mathbf{D}_e^{i+1} \neq \emptyset$ holds. Therefore, $\mathbf{D}_o^i \neq \emptyset$, $i = 0, \ldots, N-1$. That means $n(\mathbf{D}_o^i) \geq 1$, $i = 0, \ldots, N-1$. Since $\mathbf{S}_o^i$ is defined as $\bigcup_{j=0}^{i-1} \mathbf{D}_o^j$, and $\mathbf{D}_o^j$'s are disjoint (Lemma 4), we get

$$n(\mathbf{S}_o^i) = \sum_{j=0}^{i-1} n(\mathbf{D}_o^j). \tag{16}$$

Since $n(\mathbf{D}_o^i) \geq 1$, $i = 0, \ldots, N-1$, $n(\mathbf{S}_o^i)$ is monotonically increasing. In the meantime, the union of all the $\mathbf{D}_o^i$'s generated in the while loop is bounded by $\mathbf{B}$ (Lemma 3). So, we obtain

$$\bigcup_{j=0}^{N-1} \mathbf{D}_o^j \subseteq \mathbf{B}. \tag{17}$$

Now, Lemma 4 leads us to

$$\sum_{j=0}^{N-1} n(\mathbf{D}_o^j) \leq n(\mathbf{B}). \tag{18}$$

Combination of Eq.(16) and Eq.(18) results in

$$n(\mathbf{S}_o^N) \leq n(\mathbf{B}). \tag{19}$$

Since $n(\mathbf{B}) \ll M$ and finite, $n(\mathbf{S}_o^N)$ is finite. Thus, N is finite. ∎

Theorem 2. *(The Number of Pattern Evaluation) The number of patterns whose kNNs are evaluated is $(r \cdot n(\mathbf{B}^C) + n(\mathbf{B}^+))$, where $\mathbf{B}^C$ is the complement set of $\mathbf{B}$ or $\mathbf{D} - \mathbf{B}$, and r is the proportion of initial random sampling, $(0 < r < 1)$.*

Proof. The number of patterns whose kNNs are evaluated is denoted as $\sum_{i=0}^{N} n(\mathbf{D}_e^i)$. Let us first consider cases from $i = 1$ to N. We have

$$\sum_{i=1}^{N} n(\mathbf{D_e^i}) = n\left(\bigcup_{i=1}^{N} \mathbf{D_e^i}\right) \qquad \text{by Lemma 1}$$

$$= n\left(\bigcup_{x \in \mathbf{D_o^0} \cup \mathbf{D_o^1} \cup \cdots \cup \mathbf{D_o^{N-1}}} kNN(x)\right) \qquad \text{by Lemma 2}$$

$$\leq n\left(\bigcup_{x \in \mathbf{B}} kNN(x)\right) \qquad \text{by Lemma 3}$$

$$= n(\mathbf{B^+}). \tag{20}$$

Let us include the case of $i = 0$.

$$\sum_{i=0}^{N} n(\mathbf{D_e^i}) \leq n(\mathbf{D_e^0}) + n(\mathbf{B^+}), \tag{21}$$

where $n(\mathbf{D_e^0})$ is approximately $r \cdot n(\mathbf{D})$ because $\mathbf{D_e^0}$ is randomly chosen from $\mathbf{D}$. In the meantime, some patterns of $\mathbf{D_e^0}$ are already counted in $n(\mathbf{B^+})$. The number of those pattern amounts to $n(\mathbf{D_o^0})$ since $\mathbf{D_o^0} = \{x \mid Neighbors\_Entropy(x) > 0, \ x \in \mathbf{D_e^0}\}$ and $\mathbf{D_o^0} \subseteq \mathbf{B} \subseteq \mathbf{B^+}$. To get a tighter bound, therefore, we calculate $n(\mathbf{D_e^0} - \mathbf{D_o^0})$ ($\leq n(\mathbf{D_e^0})$)

$$n(\mathbf{D_e^0} - \mathbf{D_o^0}) = n(\mathbf{D_e^0}) - n(\mathbf{D_o^0})$$

$$\approx n(\mathbf{D_e^0}) - n(\mathbf{D_e^0}) \cdot \frac{n(\mathbf{B})}{n(\mathbf{D})}$$

$$= r \cdot n(\mathbf{D}) - r \cdot n(\mathbf{D}) \cdot \frac{n(\mathbf{B})}{n(\mathbf{D})}$$

$$= r \cdot n(\mathbf{B^C}), \tag{22}$$

where $\mathbf{D_o^0} \subseteq \mathbf{D_e^0}$ and $n(\mathbf{D_e^0} - \mathbf{D_o^0})$ denotes the number of the patterns which do not belong to $\mathbf{B}$. Thus, we get the following bound by Eq.(20) and Eq.(22):

$$\sum_{i=0}^{N} n(\mathbf{D_e^i}) \leq r \cdot n(\mathbf{B^C}) + n(\mathbf{B^+}). \qquad \blacksquare$$

The time complexity of the fast algorithm is $(r \cdot b^C + b^+) \cdot M$ where $b^C = n(\mathbf{B^C})$ and $b^+ = n(\mathbf{B^+})$. Practically, b^C is almost as large as M, i.e., $b^C \approx M$. But the initial sampling ratio r is usually quite small, i.e., $r \ll 1$. Thus the first term $r \cdot b^C M$ may be assumed to be insignificant. In most real world problems, b^+ is just slightly larger than b, thus the second term $b^+ M$ can be approximated to bM. In short, $(r \cdot b^c + b^+)M$ can be simplified as bM, which of course is much smaller than M^2 since $b \ll M$.

4   Experimental Results

The fast algorithm runs in bM, roughly speaking. We now show whether the complexity stands in the practical situations through experiments. A total of M patterns, half of M from each class, were randomly generated from a pair of two-dimensional uniform distributions:

$$C_j = \left\{ \boldsymbol{x} \mid U\left(\left[\frac{-1}{(\frac{-1+(-1)^{j+1}}{2} + \frac{(-1)^j b}{2M})} \right] < \boldsymbol{x} < \left[\frac{1}{(\frac{1+(-1)^{j+1}}{2} + \frac{(-1)^j b}{2M})} \right] \right) \right\}, \ j = 1, 2.$$

We set b to every decile of M, i.e. $b = 0, 0.1M, 0.2M, \cdots, 0.9M, M$. Fig. 3 shows the actual computation time for various values of b when (a) M=1,000 and (b) M=10,000, respectively. Compare with the Naive algorithm's computation time that is constant regardless of b. They clearly show that computation time is exactly proportional to b.

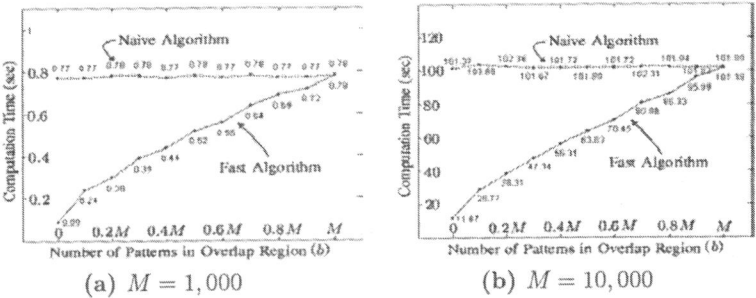

(a) $M = 1,000$ (b) $M = 10,000$

Fig. 3. Actual computation time for various values of b

5   Conclusion

We proposed a fast pattern selection algorithm which takes $O(bM)$ time. Currently, however, there are two limitations. First, the proposed algorithm was developed under the assumption that the classes are overlapped. Therefore, if one class is remote and clearly separable from the other, an empty set will be returned as a selected pattern set. Second, the number of neighbors, k, was empirically set to 4 in the experiment. A more scientific method is currently under investigation.

References

1. Arya, S., Mount, D.M., Netanyahu, N.S. and Silverman, R., (1998). An Optimal Algorithm for Approximate Nearest Neighbor Searching in Fixed Dimensions, *Jornal of the ACM*, vol. 45, no. 6, pp. 891–923.
2. Grother, P.J.,Candela, G.T. and Blue, J.L, (1997). Fast Implementations of Nearest Neighbor Classifiers, *Pattern Recognition*, vol. 30, no. 3, pp. 459–465.
3. Hearst, M.A., Scholkopf, B., Dumais, S., Osuna, E., and Platt, J., (1998). Trends and Controversies - Support Vector Machines, *IEEE Intelligent Systems*, vol. 13, pp. 18–28.
4. Platt, J.C. (1999). Fast Training of Support Vector Machines Using Sequential Minimal Optimization, *Advances in Kernel Methods: Support Vector Machines*, MIT press, Cambridge, MA, pp. 185–208.
5. Shin, H.J. and Cho, S., (2002). Pattern Selection For Support Vector Classifiers, *Proc. of the 3rd International Conference on Intelligent Data Engineering and Automated Learning (IDEAL)*, Manchester, UK, pp. 469–474.
6. Short, R., and Fukunaga, (1981). The Optimal Distance Measure for Nearest Neighbor Classification, *IEEE Transactions on Information and Theory*, vol. IT–27, no. 5, pp. 622–627.

Novelty Detection Approach for Keystroke Dynamics Identity Verification

Enzhe Yu and Sungzoon Cho

Department of Industrial Engineering, Seoul National University,
San 56-1, Shillim Dong, Kwanak-Gu, Seoul 151-744 Korea
{enzhe | zoon}@snu.ac.kr

Abstract. Password is the most widely used identity verification method in computer security domain. However, due to its simplicity, it is vulnerable to imposter attacks. Keystroke dynamics adds a shield to password. Discriminating imposters from owners is a novelty detection problem. Recent research reported good performance of Auto-Associative Multilayer Perceptron(AaMLP). However, the 2-layer AaMLP cannot identify nonlinear boundaries, which can result in serious problems in computer security. In this paper, we applied 4-layer AaMLP as well as SVM as novelty detector to keystroke dynamics identity verification, and found that they can significantly improve the performance.

1 Introduction

Password is the most widely used identity verification method in computer security domain. However, due to its simplicity, it is vulnerable to imposter attacks. Keystroke dynamics adds a shield to password. Keystroke dynamics is a biometric-based approach that utilizes the manner and rhythm in which each individual types passwords to create a biometric template. It measures the keystroke rhythm of a user in order to develop a template that identifies the authorized user. When a user types a word, for instance a password, the keystroke dynamics can be characterized by a "timing vector", consisting of the durations of keystrokes and the time intervals between them. The owner's timing vectors are collected and used to build a model that discriminates between the owner and imposters. This idea steps originally from the observations that a user's keystroke pattern is highly repeatable and distinct from others'. The only disadvantage has been a relatively low rate of accuracy.

All biometrics-based approaches have two types of error, the false acceptance rate (FAR) and the false rejection rate (FRR). FAR denotes the rate that an imposter is allowed access, and FRR denotes the rate that the legitimate user is denied access. Because one type of error can be reduced at the expense of the other, an appropriate tradeoff point is usually used as a threshold based on the relative cost of the errors.

In 1980, Gaines et al. [2] first proposed the approach using keystroke dynamics for user authentication. Experiments with a population of 7 candidates were conducted. Later on, Leggett et al.[6] conducted similar experiments by applying a long string of 537 characters, and reported a result of 5.0% FAR and 5.5% FRR. Recently, through the use of neural networks, a comparable performance of 12% to 21% was achieved using short strings such as real-life names [2]. Obaidat et al. reported a 0% error rate

J. Liu et al. (Eds.): IDEAL 2003, LNCS 2690, pp. 1016–1023, 2003.

in user verification using 7-character-long login name [7]. However, both the imposter's typing patterns and the owner's patterns were used training, and the training data set was much larger (6300 owners and 112 negatives). Also, the training and test patterns were not chronologically separated. In [1], a novelty detection model was built by training owner's patterns only, and was used to detect imposters using some sort of a similarity measure, and a 1.0% FRR and 0%FAR was reported. Furthermore, some products have been marketed, such as Net Nanny's BioPassword (http://www.biopassword.com).

In this paper, we propose: (1) A 4-layer autoassociative multilayer perceptron (AaMLP) to improve the performance of the novelty detector, and (2) Application of support vector machine (SVM) novelty detector to keystroke dynamics identity verification. Timing vectors from an owner were collected and used to build a neural network model that outperformed a generally applied single layer neural network model, i.e. 2-layer AaMLP. Model performances are compared between the two approaches. This paper is structured as follows. In session 2, descriptions on the neural network based novelty detector, the descriptions of the limitations of 2-layer AaMLP and the proposed 4-layer AaMLP are presented. The following session is about the SVM for novelty detection. After the explanation of the data, experimental results and performance comparison between neural network and SVM novelty detector are shown in session 4. A summary and acknowledge conclude this paper.

2   Autoassociative Multilayer Perceptron Novelty Detector

In an AaMLP, the input vectors are also used as targets during training, and the network is forced to encode the input vector in the hidden layer and then decode it back in the output layer. This model can be used for identity verification as follows. The owner's patterns are use to train the network to become an autoassociator by employing a timing vector as both an input and output. The AaMLP is trained to learn to encode certain properties only present in the owner's timing vectors at the hidden layer. When a previously 'unseen' timing vector for the owner arrives, the network will output a vector that is reasonably close to the input. When an imposter's pattern arrives, the network will output a vector that is far from the input. Then, it is possible to distinguish a pattern as either genuine or forged. This can be measured by the closeness of the vectors to the owner's pattern, that is, a timing vector X is classified as the owner's if and only if,

$$\|X\text{-}M(X)\| < \varepsilon, \tag{1}$$

where $M(X)$ and ε denote the MLP's output for X and a threshold.

In [3], Hwang and Cho studied the properties of AaMLP that are essential for a novelty detector: (1) Uncountably infinite input vectors exist for which AaMLP produces the same output vector; (2) The "output-constrained hyperplane" exists on which all the output vectors are projected. As long as AaMLP uses a bounded activation function such as a step function, the output-constrained hyperplane is bounded; (3) Minimizing the error function leads the hyperplane to be located in the vicinity of the training pattern, etc.

A 2-layer MLP is, however, computationally limited since all the output vectors are projected onto a hyperplane. In a situation like Figure 1, where the distribution of the training patterns (shaded area) is concave or nonlinear, the misclassification rate will increase greatly. The output constraining hyperplane is denoted by O. All the patterns located inside the surrounding ellipse are classified as "normal." Thus, these patterns from the areas denoted as A, B, and C are incorrectly classified. In a security problem like computer access or electronic commerce, such false acceptance of imposters, i.e. A, B and C, is very dangerous and must be avoided. In order to overcome such shortcomings of 2-layer AaMLP, a 4-layer AaMLP model, which is capable of nonlinear reconstruction, is proposed.

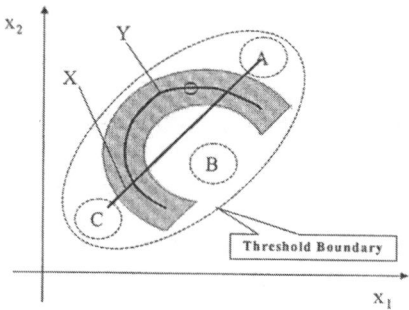

Fig. 1. Misclassification Resulted from a Concave Distribution Patterns

In a 2-layer AaMLP, although a sigmoid activation function is used in the hidden layer, but it only plays the role of bounding the output value, and the model cannot reflect the nonlinearity of the input patterns. The serious problem shown in Figure 1 is due to the incapability of 2-layer AaMLP's nonlinear pattern mapping. However, if the network can map the input patterns onto the curve Y, rather than the line X, then such misclassification problem is solved. A 4-layer AaMLP, is supposed to model the nonlinear input patterns, therefore improve the novelty detection capability of the network. The structure of a 4-layer AaMLP is shown in Figure 2.

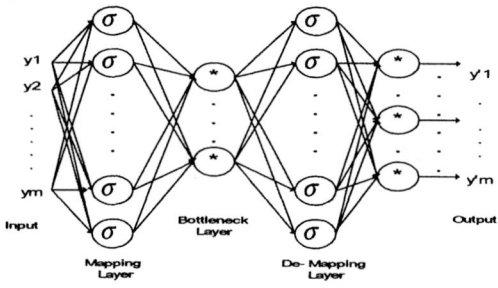

Fig. 2. The Structure of 4-layer AaMLP

In the *mapping* and *de-mapping* process, a sigmoid activation functions are used, and linear activation functions are applied to other layers. Specially, the output b_i of the unit i in the bottleneck layer, and the output y_i' of unit i in the output layer are computed as follows:

$$b_k = \sum_j w_{kj} f_\sigma (\sum y_i w_i) \qquad (1)$$

$$y_l' = \sum_j w_{lj} f_\sigma (\sum w_{ji} b_i)\tag{2}$$

where $f_\sigma(x) = \dfrac{1}{1+e^{-x}}$, and w_{kj} is the connection strength from unit j to unit k.

The bottleneck layer is the one that has the least number of nodes. Through learning, a "redundancy compression and non-redundancy differentiation" effect appears. Ikbal et al. [4] studied the characteristics of AaMLP, and argued that as network size increases, the nonlinearity level of the subspace and hypersurface increases accordingly.

In the past researches, 4-layer AaMLP is mainly applied for the purpose of dimension reduction [5]. The compressed dimensions are from the bottleneck layer, which is extracted by way of nonlinear PCA (NLPCA). Some researches have reported the limitations of 4-layer AaMLP in dimension reduction. One of the limitations is that the 4-layer AaMLP shows strong capability in interpolation, but is weak in extrapolation. However, given enough *normal* patterns, a 4-layer AaMLP is supposed to give excellent novelty detection performance. Accordingly, the limitation raised from dimension compression will play an important role in novelty detection.

3 Support Vector Machine for Novelty Detection

SVM is commonly used to solve two- or multi- class classification. While for the keystroke dynamics identity verification problem, only the user's normal data is available. Therefore, a model has to be built for user only, and it is used to detected imposters' intrusion. Recently, Schölkopf et al. [8, 9] extended support vector machine methodology to "one-class" classification, i.e. novelty detection problem. Our approach is based on their one-class classification algorithm.

The essential of Schölkopf et al.[8, 9, 10] is to map the data into the feature space corresponding to the kernel, and to separate them from the origin with maximum margin. The algorithm returns a decision function f that takes the value +1 in a "small" region capturing most of normal data, and -1 elsewhere. For a new point x, the value $f(x)$ is determined by evaluating which side of the hyperplane it falls on, in feature space.

Let $X_1, X_2, ..., X_l \in X$, where $l \in N$ is the number of normal data, X denotes one class and is a compact subset of R^N. Let Φ be a feature map $X \rightarrow F$, which transforms the training data to a dot product space F such that the dot product in the image of Φ can be computed by evaluating some simple kernel ,

$$k(x, y) = ((\Phi(x) \cdot \Phi(x)),\tag{1}$$

such as the Gaussian kernel $k(x, y) = e^{-\|x-y\|^2/s}$.

To separate the normal data set from the origin, one needs to solve the following quadratic programming problem,

$$\min_{w \in F, \xi \in R^l, \rho \in R} \frac{1}{2}\| w \|^2 + \frac{1}{\upsilon l}\sum_i \xi_i - \rho\tag{2}$$

subject to $(w \cdot \Phi(x_i)) \geq \rho - \xi_i, \ \xi_i \geq 0.$ (3)

Since nonzero slack variables ξ_i are penalized in the objective function, we can expect that if w and ρ solve this problem, then the decision function

$$f(x) = \text{sgn}((w \cdot \Phi(x)) - \rho)$$ (4)

will be positive for most examples x_i contained in the training set, while the SV type regularization term $\|w\|$ will still be small. The trade-off between these two goals is controlled by $v \in (0, 1)$.

If v approaches 0, the upper boundaries on the Lagrange multipliers tend to infinity, the problem then resembles the corresponding hard margin algorithm; If v approaches 1, then the constrains only allow one solution, that where all α_i are at the upper bound $1/(vl)$. In this case, for kernels with integral 1, the decision function corresponds to a Parzen windows estimator with threshold.

4 Experiment Results

Experiments were carried out to compare the novelty detection capability of 2-layer AaMLP, 4-layer AaMLP and SVM. Also, a comparison regarding learning time was made between the two different approaches, i.e. neural network vs. SVM.

4.1 The Data

The data was captured by a program in X window environment on a Sun Sparc-Station, in which the keystroke duration times and interval times is measured. The keystroke duration and interval times are captured at the accuracy of milliseconds (ms). A timing vector consists of keystroke duration times and interval times. A password with n-character long, length of the timing vector would be $(2n+1)$, where the *Enter* key is also included. For instance, a password *abcd*, which is 4-character long (n=4), together with the *Enter* key, results in a timing vector of 9 dimensions. An example of a timing vector is [30, 60, 70, 135, 60, -35, 75, 40, 55]. When the next key is stroked before the previous key is released, the keystroke interval time is represented as negative (<0).

The data for both the owners and the imposters were collected. The owners' data was collected from 21 participants with different passwords, whose length ranges from 6 to 10. Each participant was asked to type his password 150 to 400 times, and the last 75 timing vectors were collected for testing, whereas the remaining ones were used as training patterns. As for the novelty data, 15 imposters were asked to type each of the given 21 passwords 5 times without any practice, resulting in 75 impostor timing vectors for each password. We call those imposters as *"imposters without practice."*

Furthermore, these imposters were given passwords beforehand, and were asked to practice typing these passwords. After that, 21 sets of timing vectors from practiced imposters were collected, each of which consists of 75 timing vectors as was mentioned above. These are called 'imposter with practice.'

A novelty detection model is built under the assumption that the owner's typing follows a consistent pattern. However, the training data is not as clean as expected due to owner's inconsistency. If any of its elements was deviated to upper or lower 10%, however, the vector was classified as an outlier and discarded. Depending on the owner's consistency, a discard rate of 20%~50% was applied.

4.2 Experiment Results

Two models were built for every owner, i.e. 2-layer AaMLP and 4-layer AaMLP. All the networks, i.e. 2-layer and 4-layey, were trained with *Resilient backpropagation* algorithm, with a learning rate of 0.1, a momentum term of 0.25.

For the 2-layer networks with the structure of $N - h - N$, the number of hidden nodes ranged from 6 to 8 according to the performance of the network over different patterns. A 4-layer AaMLP has the structure of $N - l - h - l -N$, where N is the input dimension, l is the mapping or de-mapping layer, and h is the bottleneck. Depending on the input pattern, number of the nodes in l ranged from 12 to 25, and that in h ranged from 6 to 10. As we can see from *Table 1*, some owners only have a small number of useful patterns after data cleaning, say less than 100. In such a case, a *10-fold cross-validation* method was applied. Performances of the models were measured by FRR, when FAR is reduced to zero.

Shown in *Table 1* are the error rate comparisons for 2-layer AaMLP and 4-layer AaMLP, in terms of FRR when FAR was reduced to *zero* .

For the *unpracticed imposters,* 4-layer AaMLP showed 18 perfect authentications out of 21 owners. The worst performance was with the error rate of 2.67%. The average error rate was 0.25%. However, 2-layer AaMLP only achieved 6 perfect authentications. The worst performance was 4.00%, and the average error rate was 1.71%. In this situation, i.e. owner *vs* unpracticed imposters, though 4-layer AaMLP performed better in general, no significant difference was shown between the two models. In the situation of *owners vs practiced imposters,* 4-layer AaMLP showed its advantages over 2-layer AaMLP. 4-layer AaMLP showed an average performance of FRR=1.21, with the worst error rate of 4.00%, average error rate of 1.21% and 9 perfect authentications. While 2-layer AaMLP reported worse: the maximum error rate of 17.33%, average error rate of 5.71%.

Performance of SVM novelty detector was also evaluated and compared with neural network model, regarding both accuracy and learning time. Experiments with linear, sigmoid, polynomial and radial basis kernels were all carried out. Among them, models with radial basis kernel showed robustness and best performance, and only the results of these models are shown here. By comparison, the performance of SVM is comparable with that of improved neural network model, i.e. 4-layer AaMLP.

Furthermore, SVM is less computationally intensive than neural networks, and accordingly needs much less time for learning. On average, SVM only needs less than 0.1 *second* to construct a model, whereas 2-layer AaMLP and 4-layer AaMLP need 17 *seconds* and 124 *seconds*, respectively.

Table 1. Performance Comparison for the Respective Models

Owner ID	Dim- ension	Num. of Training Patterns	FRR* (FAR=0) imposter without practice			FRR* (FAR=0) imposter with practice		
			2L AaMLP	4L AaMLP	SVM	2L AaMLP	4L AaMLP	SVM
Atom	15	178	4.00	1.33	1.16	10.67	2.67	2.37
Bubugi	17	312	1.33	0.00	0.00	4.00	2.67	2.53
Celavie	17	330	0.00	0.00	0.00	1.33	4.00	3.64
Crapas	19	165	0.00	0.00	0.00	2.67	0.00	0.93
Dry	19	328	0.00	0.00	0.93	1.33	1.33	0.83
Flower	13	202	2.67	1.33	1.16	2.67	1.33	0.00
Gmother	17	101	2.67	0.00	0.00	4.00	1.33	0.87
Gusegi	15	231	2.67	0.00	0.00	9.33	1.33	0.33
Jmin	17	95	2.67	0.00	0.00	5.33	0.00	0.00
June	17	144	0.00	0.00	0.00	2.67	0.00	0.00
Jywoo	15	297	1.33	0.00	0.94	1.33	1.33	0.93
Megadet	17	329	4.00	2.67	0.74	14.6	1.33	0.52
Oscar	17	365	0.00	0.00	0.00	0.00	0.00	0.00
Perfect	17	86	2.67	0.00	0.26	4.00	0.00	1.16
Shlee	17	309	1.33	0.00	0.00	2.67	0.00	0.00
Sjlee	13	205	0.00	0.00	0.00	6.67	0.00	0.00
Woo	13	143	1.33	0.00	0.00	4.00	0.00	0.00
Wooks	17	81	4.00	0.00	0.26	17.33	0.00	0.33
Yanwen	17	108	2.67	0.00	0.00	9.33	2.67	0.00
Ysoya	17	260	1.33	0.00	0.00	10.67	1.33	1.92
Zeronine	21	135	1.33	0.00	0.53	5.33	2.67	0.74
Average			1.714	0.254	0.299	5.711	1.142	0.814
Minimum			0.00	0.00	0.00	0.00	0.00	0.00
Maximum			4.00	2.67	1.16	17.33	4.00	3.64

* FRR = False Rejection Rate, FAR = False Acceptance Rate, measured by *percentage* (%).

5   Conclusion

In this article, we applied SVM novelty detector to keystroke dynamics identity verification, and proposed a nonlinear novelty detector, i.e. 4-layer AaMLP to improve the performance of user authentication using keystroke dynamics. The performance of the proposed 4-layer AaMLP was compared with SVM and the commonly used 2-layer AaMLP, which is a linear model. Also, computational effectiveness was compared between SVM and neural network model.

Experiments were carried out in two situations, i.e. (a) owner *vs.* unpracticed imposters, and (b) owner *vs.* practiced imposters. The 4-layer AaMLP beat 2-layer AaMLP in both situations. SVM and 4-layer AaMLP showed similar novelty detection performance. However, the computational effectiveness of SVM is much higher than that of neural network model: a SVM model only needs less than 0.1 second for training, whereas neural network model usually needs more than 100 seconds to achieve similar accuracy.

Further investigation is necessary regarding the following issues: First, the quality of the owner's patterns must be satisfied. More participants are preferred for experiments. Also, standard keystroke dynamics data like UCI data is called for. Second, in order to reduce the complexity of the model, a feature extraction or dimension reduction method shall be applied. Irrelevant or redundant features do not help for generalization of the discovered models, feature extraction particularly shows this importance in some practical problems, where there is limited number of data. Third, model selection process needs to be automated. Since a different password requires a different set of model parameters, an automated optimization method, i.e. genetic algorithm, for the selection of SVM setting or neural network structure is also a requirement.

Acknowledgement. This research was supported by Brain Science and Engineering Research Program sponsored by Korean Ministry of Science and Technology, and (in part) by KOSEF through Statistical Research Center for Complex Systems at Seoul National University.

References

[1] S. Cho, C. Han, D. Han, and H. Kim, Web-based keystroke dynamics identity verification using neural network, *Journal of organizational computing and electronic commerce 10(4)*, 295–307, 2000.

[2] R. Gaines, W. Lisowski, S. Press, and N. Shapiro. Authentication by keystroke timing: some preliminary results. Rand Report R-256-NSF. Rand Corporation, 1980.

[3] B. Hwang and S. Cho, "Characteristic of Autoassociative MLP as a Novelty Detector," *International Joint Conference on Neural Networks*, Washington DC USA, July, 1999.

[4] M. Ikbal, H. Misra, and B. Yegnanarayana, Analysis of sutoassociative mapping neural networks, Proceedings of International Joint Conference on Neural Networks, #854, 1999.

[5] M. Kramer, Nonlinear principal component analysis using autoassociative neural networks, *AIChE Journal, Vol. 37, No. 2*, Feb. 1991.

[6] J. Leggett, G. Williams, M. Usnick, and M. Longnecker, Dynamic identity verification via keystroke characteristics, *International Journal of Man-Machine Studies, vol. 35*, pp. 859–870, 1991.

[7] M. Obaidat and S. Sadoun, Verification of computer users using keystroke dynamics, *IEEE Transactions on Systems, Man and Cybernetics, Part B:P Cybernetics, vol. 27*, no. 2, pp. 261–269, 1997.

[8] B. Schölkopf, J. Platt, J. Shawe-Taylor, A.J. Smola, and R.C. Williamson. Estimating the Support of a High-Dimensional Distribution, Technical Report MSR-TR-99-87. Microsoft Research, Redmond, WA, 1999.

[9] B. Schölkopf, R. C. Williamson, A.J. Smola, J. Shawe-Taylor and J.C. Platt: Support vector method for novelty detection. Advances in Neural Information Processing Systems 12, 582–588. (Eds.) S.A. Solla, T.K. Leen and K.-R. Müller, MIT Press, 2000.

[10] L. M. Manevitz, Malik Yousef, One-Class SVMs for Document Classification, Journal of Machine Learning Research 2 (2001) 139–154.

An Image Retrieval Method Based on Collaborative Filtering

Xiangdong Zhou, Qi Zhang, Liang Zhang, Li Liu, and Baile Shi

Department of Computing and Information Technology
Fudan University
Shanghai, China, 200433
000382@fudan.edu.cn

Abstract. Relevance feedback plays an important role in image retrieval. As a short-term learning strategy, it learns from the user's relevance evaluation on the current retrieval's output result to improve the retrieval performance. Nowadays using long-term learning strategy to improve image retrieval attracts more and more attention. In this paper, we present a composite image retrieval approach using both of them to improve image retrieval. Our approach is based on on-line analysis of feedback sequence log, the archive of the user's feedback evaluation data sequence created in the past. For long-term learning, Collaborative Filtering is adopted to predict the semantic correlations between images. During CF process, we make use of Edit Distance to evaluate the similarity between the feedback sequence records. Experiments over 11,000 images demonstrate that our method achieves significant improvement in retrieval effectiveness compared with conventional method.

1 Introduction

With a great amount of images produced, stored and spread, content-based image retrieval(CBIR) has become one of the most significant research areas in the last decades. Owing to its automaticity, CBIR enjoys obvious superiority. However, CBIR has not been widely used in practice as the result of the complexity of an image's internal semantic information, i.e. the disparity between the user's semantic understanding of an image and its visual features extracted by the system.

To address the above problem, a short-term learning strategy, user's Relevance Feedback (RF) has been borrowed from textual Information Retrieval (IR), which is an interactive and iterative process for adjusting query parameters to improve the retrieval's performance based on user's relevance evaluation on the output results.

The early methods were primarily based on heuristic ideas [8]. Ishikawa et al [4] used optimization method to estimate the query parameters. Rui et al [9] took into consideration the multi-level image model and formulated a unified relevance feedback framework. Some machine learning methods have also been employed in image retrieval.

Recently, using long-term learning strategy to exploit historical feedback information to improve retrieval performance is attracting growing attention [6,1,

J. Liu et al. (Eds.): IDEAL 2003, LNCS 2690, pp. 1024–1031, 2003.

12]. Unlike the known works, this paper proposes an retrieval approach based on the on-line analysis of feedback sequence log using collaborative filtering. In our approach, feedback sequence (composed of feedback samples' numbers) concerning each retrieval session is recorded into log file during relevance feedback process. Upon retrieval, the edit distance between current retrieval's feedback sequence and the prefixes of the log records are calculated to measure their similarities. The most frequent images in the top k similar feedback records have higher semantic correlation with current retrieval. Integrated with the method based on generalized Euclidean distance, the performance of image retrieval can be improved apparently. A prototype is implemented to test and demonstrate the performance of our method. Experiments on a database with 11,000 images demonstrate that our method achieves significant improvement in retrieval performance compared with the traditional methods.

The rest of the paper is organized as follows. Section 2 provides introduction of background and related works. Section 3 introduces the definition of the sequence pattern of RF log as well as our log analyzing method. In Section 4, we describe the new retrieval approach. Experimental results are presented and analyzed in Section 5. Section 6 concludes the paper.

2   Background and Related Works

Generally, there are two kinds of strategies for relevance feedback: query point movement and re-weighting. Query point movement can be described by Rocchio's equation. The idea of Rocchio's method is to move the query point toward the positive points leading to a better result and far away from the negative ones. Rui's layered method [8] is a way to update the weights.

Optimization method was adopted to estimate the "optimal" weight matrices[4]. It was proved that the weight matrix is an optimal full matrix only when the number of the feedback samples is no less than that of the feature dimensions. However, under most practical circumstances, the dimension of the feature vector is usually far more than the positive samples users can provide. To solve this problem, we use the semantic correlation obtained from log analysis to facilitate the expansion of the positive sample set so that feedback efficiency and retrieval precision can be greatly improved.

In Viper [6], the relevance factor in similarity metric was altered according to the log analysis. The basic idea of parameter modification is quite similar to that of Rocchio's. Yang et al[12] present a system using a peer index which is built from the user's feedback. The tf/idf method is used for long-term learning to acquire the semantic correlation between images.He et al. [3] set up a latent semantic sub-space by exploiting the user relevance feedback records. With the extracted latent semantic feature from the feedback data, on-line training is performed using a learned classifier.

In consideration of the personality issue of image system, Kohrs and Merialdo [5] presented an adaptive web image browsing system based on recommendation approach. The evaluation data given by the user in the past is analyzed by collaborative filtering, then the web pages are adjusted according to the user's preference.

3   Semantic Correlation Prediction with RF Sequence Logs Analysis

3.1   Collaborative Filtering Model

Collaborative filtering (CF), named by D. Goldberg [2] in a mail filtering system, is a method for predicting the preference or characteristics of unknown user (object) by using the information about the user group (related object group) already known. It is based on the following common-sense hypothesis: if different people share views on some objects, it is likely that they also share views on other objects. According to the above idea, we make use of collaborative filtering to perform a prediction of semantic correlation between images in the database and the current retrieval as follows:

In image retrieval, user feedback (only positive samples are considered here) regarding certain retrieval tends to be an iterative process with several feedback iterations. When the retrieval session is finished, the system gets a series of image numbers (relevant images), which can be regarded as an evaluation record (referred to as feedback record). After many retrieval sessions, feedback records will form a feedback information database. Such a database stores the particulars of each retrieval and represents users' evaluation, i.e. classification, of images as well. Let I be the image set in an image database with $|I| = n$. Let matrix $R_{m \times n}$ represent the feedback database with rows as feedbacks and columns as images, whose element r_{ij} stands for the relevance evaluation made in retrieval i on image j. Therefore, a single row of R represents user's relevance evaluations on images during certain retrieval, i.e. its particulars. Let d_i be the set of images evaluated by the user in retrieval i. Thus $\bar{r}_i = \frac{1}{|d_i|} \sum_{j \in I} r_{ij}$ is the average evaluation of images in retrieval i. Assuming a to be the feedback vector of current retrieval, the expectation value of relevance evaluation of image j concerning the current retrieval can be described by the following equation [10,5]

$$P_{a,j} = \bar{r}_a + \lambda \sum_{i=1}^{m} w(a, i)(r_{ij} - \bar{r}_i), \tag{1}$$

where m is the number of feedback records in relevance feedback database, the weight $w(a, i)$ represents the similarity degree between a and other feedback records and λ is the normalization factor. It can be seen from eq.(1) that $w(a, i)$ determines the relevance degree between an image and the current retrieval step, so the similarity measure of feedback records in feedback database is very important.

3.2   User Relevance Feedback Sequence Pattern

Generally, log file records users' operation sequences[6]. Thus, we can use these logged feedback operation sequences to describe the corresponding retrieval (represented as a series of numbers of feedback samples). We have the following definition:

Definition 1 (User feedback sequence pattern) Let $U, |U| = m$ denote the retrieval set, $I, |I| = n$ denote the item set of the database. Suppose the query is $a, a \in U$,and the query a contains l feedback iterations. For the ith iterantion $i \in 1, \ldots, l$, the positive sample set of a_i is denoted with $d_{ai}, |d_{ai}| = k, d_{ai} \subseteq I$, and the similarity metric function is $E : d_{ai} \to R^+$. Let p_i be a permutation on d_{ai} such that $E(p_i(c_1)) \geq E(p_i(c_2)) \geq \ldots E(p_i(c_k)), c_j \in d_{ai}, j = 1, \ldots, k$. Then the RF pattern for query a's ith feedback iteration can be defined by a k-tuple:

$w(a_i) =< p_i(c_1), p_i(c_2), \ldots, p_i(c_k) >$.

The feedback sequence pattern of retrieval a can be defined by a l-tuple:

$w(a) =< w(a_1), w(a_2), \ldots, w(a_l) >$.

For convenience, we use the sequence of RF samples' number as the RF pattern, and use w_i to represent the ith retrieval's sequence pattern accordingly.

3.3   Similarity Metric for Sequence Pattern Based on Edit Distance

Taking the form of a sequence pattern, RF record can be properly measured using the Edit Distance metric, which is originally employed in similarity matching between character strings. The following are some basic concepts about edit distance:

For any character strings A, B, the distance between A and B is defined as the minimum cost of the transformation from A to B through some character insertions, deletions and replacements necessary to make two strings equal.

Let γ be the cost function about edit operation $a \to b$. Then for an operation sequence S, $\gamma(S) = \sum_{i=1}^{m} \gamma(s_i)$.

We define the edit distance between string A and B,denoted by $\delta(A, B)$, as the minimum cost of the operation sequence transforming A to B, namely:

$$\delta(A, B) = min\gamma(S) \tag{2}$$

The classical dynamic programming algorithm for Edit Distance was improved by Ukknoen [11] to a complexity of $O(s \times n)$, where s is the edit distance. In this paper, searching for similar sequence patterns is managed by computing the edit distance between the sequences' prefixes. The related concepts are defined below:

Definition 2 The k-prefix of sequence w_i is the sub-sequence of w_i composed of the first k elements, which is represented as $[w_i]^k$.

We use the prefixes of the pattern records instead of the whole ones when matching with the current RF sequence.

Definition 3 Similarity between current RF pattern c and pattern w_i in log file is defined as:

$$sim(c, w_i) = 1 - \frac{\delta(c, [w_i]^{|c|})}{|c|} \tag{3}$$

where $|c|$ is the length of c, $[w_i]^{|c|}$ stands for the $|c|$-prefix of sequence w_i.

Suppose that the top k similar records to the current retrieval constitute the candidate record set U; and let P denote the candidate image set, which is composed of all the images included in the records of U. Let $d(r)$ denote the images set identified by record r, and another set $U_p = \{r \in U | p \in d(r), p \in P\}$, refers to those RF records in U containing $p \in P$. Thus according to equ. 3, we have:

Definition 4 The semantic correlation between image p in P and the current RF pattern c is defined as:

$$cor_p = \sum_{i=1, w_i \in U_p}^{|U_p|} \frac{sim(c, w_i)}{|w_i \setminus c|} \tag{4}$$

where $|w_i \setminus c|$ stands for the number of new images brought by w_i.

It is noticeable that c tends to be a short sequence in the first several rounds of feedback. Hence some longer sequence with the same prefix as c will win high correlation, namely many images brought by these longer sequences will also have very high correlation. So it is likely that these sequences will prematurely dominate the whole retrieval session. To avoid such a problem, $|w_i \setminus c|$ is added into the equation as a denominator to penalize long sequences.

3.4   Generation Semantic-Correlated Image Set

Suppose the images of database is denoted as $I = \{I_1, I_2, \ldots, I_n\}$, and the RF log is composed of m pieces of RF sequences. Let $d(r_i)$ represent the image set determined by sequence $r_i, i = 1, \ldots, m$, and c represent the RF sequence of the current retrieval. Then, the most similar k records with c in R make up the neighbor set $NB, r_{i_j} \in NB$, where $j = 1, \ldots, k$. Let $w(c, r_{i_j})$ represent the relevance degree between c and r_{i_j}. Let I' denote the set of images which appear in NB, i.e. $I' = \bigcup_{j=1,\ldots,k} d(r_{i_j})$, Then for each $p \in I'$, we can calculate the semantic correlation $cor(p, c)$ between p and c according to Equ. 4.

4   Cooperative Retrieval Framework

Rui [9] have presented a universal relevance feedback framework. let q represent the query sample, q_i represent the vector of feature i ,$\{x_1, \ldots, x_N\}$ represent the image set gained from user feedback, where x_{ni} is the vector of feature i of feedback image n . Let $\pi = \{\pi_1, \ldots, \pi_N\}$ represent the correlation of feedback samples, then the optimal retrieval vector of feature i is:

$$q_i^{T'} = \frac{\pi^T X_i}{\sum_{n=1}^{N} \pi_n} \tag{5}$$

In the above formula, X_i is an $N \times K_i$ feedback sample matrix corresponding to feature i, where K_i is the dimension of feature i. The optimal weight matrix is

$$W_i^* = (det(C_i))^{\frac{1}{K_i}} C_i^{-1} \tag{6}$$

where C_i is the covariance matrix of X_i.

According to section 3.4, we can get two output sets for correlation images, the set of image number and the set of correlation degree. Suppose we denote them as p_i and $correlation(p_i)$ respectively. Then the expanded RF sample set is $x = d_c \cup p_i$, the corresponding correlation degree is $\pi = \pi \cup correlation(p_i)$, where d_c is the sample set provided by the users, and π_c is its corresponding correlation degree set. By using the computed x and π into Equ.5 and Equ.6, we can obtain the new query and weight, therefore with these new parameters inputted into the Rui's method, we finally get the retrieval result. It is noticeable that when there is no RF records available, which is just the case for the initial condition of the system, our method is reduced to one of the previously described low-level feedback approaches as a special case. But with more and more RF record accumulated, the retrieval performance can be rapidly improved.

5 Experiment and Analysis

5.1 Experiment

Our experimental system is based on the visual features of color and texture, being represented by color histogram and standard deviations of each sub-band's wavelet coefficients. As to color feature, the following transformed color space is used: $u = \frac{R}{R+G+B}, v = \frac{G}{R+G+B}$. Both u and v are divided into 16 bins respectively, and thus a 32-dimension vector is formed. Meanwhile, each image is decomposed into three wavelet levels, thus having 10 sub-bands. For each sub-band, the standard deviation of the wavelet coefficients is extracted, therefore the 10 standard deviations form a 10-dimension vector. The feedback model proposed by [9] is adopted to refine both the query and the weights. Based on the above, the retrieval method addressed in this paper is realized.

Our image testing set consists of 11,000 various images[1]. It is classified into several subjects, each of which embodies 100 images. In our experiment, we choose 6 classes as the testing subjects, which are: birds, ocean fish, castles, planes, horse racing, and trains. For the purpose of comparison, the method previously cited [9] has been also implemented, which is referred to as the default method in the following part. And for our testing use, we pre-logged 700 feedback records about 10 different subjects(including the above 6 subjects) into the feedback database.

In the research on CBIR, the commonly adopted metrics for performance evaluation are Recall and Precision. Given that each subject contains 100 relevant images, only the top 100 output images are counted for relevant ones serving as both recall and precision. Since they are numerically equal in this experiment, we refer to both as accuracy(or precision).

5.2 Result and Analysis

Improvement of Performance. First, we observe the retrieval performance of our system. Experiments were conducted on both our method and the con-

---

[1] Thanks for Dr. James WANG providing images test set
http://jzw.standford.edu/IMAGE/download/corel1m.60k.tar

ventional one. For all the subjects, 10 random queries were performed, each with 5 or 6 feedback iterations. The comparison of retrieval performance is shown in Fig.1. Obviously, our method achieves a better retrieval accuracy.

Accuracy Improvement According to Number of RF Rounds. The improvement of accuracy is defined as[1]

$$prc_{gain} = (\frac{prc(CF)}{prc(default)} - 1) \times 100 \tag{7}$$

where prc_{gain} represents the times of improvement, $prc(CF)$ represents the accuracy of our method, and $prc(default)$ represents the accuracy of the conventional method. The statistical result is shown in Fig.2. We can see that our method gains most of its improvement at round 3. Actually, such a feature of our system properly fits the users' feedback habit in that users are often reluctant to provide feedback samples for more than 3 rounds.

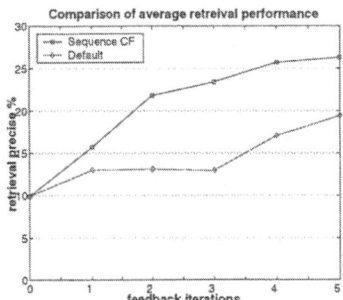

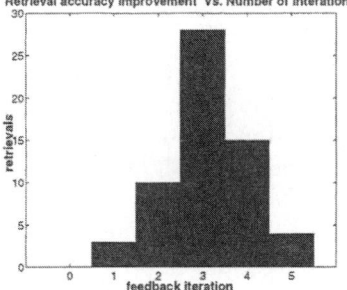

Fig. 1. Comparison of the average retrieval performance. After the second RF iteration, the accuracy of our method has surpassed the final accuracy of the default method at the 5th iterations

Fig. 2. The histogram of the feedback iteration with the maximum accuracy improvement compared with default method. In most cases,our method gets the most accuracy improvement around the 3rd iteration

6   Conclusions

Relevance feedback plays an important role in content-based similarity query. In this paper, we proposed a method to predict the semantic correlation between query sample and database images based on analysis of RF patterns using collaborative filtering. Experimental results show that our method achieves significant improvement in retrieval performance compared with conventional methods.

Acknowledgments. This work was supported by the National Natural Science Foundation of P.R.China under grant no.69933919.

References

1. I.Bartolini, P.Ciaccia and F.Waas: FeedbackBypass:A New Approach to Interactive Similarity Query Processing. In: Proceedings of 27th VLDB, September 2001, Roma, Italy. Morgan Kaufmann 2001 pp.201–210.
2. D.Goldberg,D.Nichols,B. Oki, and D.Terry: Using collaborative filtering to weave an information tapestry. Communications of the ACM, 35(12)61–70,1992
3. X.He,O.King,W.-Y.Ma, M.Li and H.-J.Zhang "Learning and Inferring a Semantic Space from User's relevance feedback for image retrieval", In Proc. of the 10th ACM Int'l Conf. Multimedia Conference, France. ACM Press, 2002
4. Y.Ishikawa, R.Subramanya and C.Faloustos: MinderReader:Query database through multimple examples. In: Proc. Of VLDB 1998,pp.218–227
5. A.kohrs and B.Merialdo: Improving Collaborative Filtering with Multimedia Indexing Techniques to create User-Adapting Web Sites. In: Proc. of the 7th ACM Conf. on Multimedia. ACM press, 1999
6. H.Muller,W.Muller and D.Squire: Learning Feature Weights from User Behavior in Content-Based Image Retrieval. In: Proc. of the Int'l Workshop on Multimedia Data Mining, USA.August 2000
7. J.Rocchio: Relevance feedback in information retrieval. The SMART retrieval system- experiments in automatic Document Processing, p313–323, 1971
8. Y.Rui,T.S.Huang and S.Mehrotra: Content-based Image Retrieval with Relevance Feedback in MARS. In: Proc. of IEEE Int'l Conf. on Image Processing , 1997. pp.II815–818,
9. Y.Rui and T.S.Huang: A Novel Relevance Feedback Technique in Image Retrieval. In: Proc. of the 7th ACM Conf. on Multimedia. ACM press, 1999. pp. 67–70,.
10. B.Sarwar, G.Karypis, J.Konstan and J.Riedl: Analysis of Recommendation Algorithms for E-commerce. In: Proc. of the 2nd ACM Conf on Electronic Commerce, USA. ACM Press, 2000. pp. 158–167.
11. E.Ukkonen: Algorithms for approximate string matching. Information and Control 64, pp.100–118,1985.
12. J.Yang, Q.Li and Y.Zhuang: Image Retrieval and Relevance Feedback using Peer Index. In: Proc. of IEEE Int'l Conf. Multimedia and Expo, Lausanne, Switzerland, Aug,2002.

Learning Neural Network Ensemble for Practical Text Classification

Sung-Bae Cho and Jee-Haeng Lee

Dept. of Computer Science, Yonsei University,
134 Shinchon-dong, Sudaemoon-ku, Seoul 120-749, Korea
sbcho@cs.yonsei.ac.kr, easygo@candy.yonsei.ac.kr

Abstract. Automated text classification has been considered as an important method to manage and process a huge amount of documents in digital forms that are widespread and continuously increasing. Recently, text classification has been applied by machine learning technologies such as k-nearest neighbor, decision tree, support vector machine, and neural networks. However, most of the investigations in text classification are studied not on real data but on well-organized text corpus, and do not show their usefulness. This paper suggests and analyzes text classification method for a real application, FAQ text classification task, by combining multiple classifiers. We propose two methods of combining multiple neural networks that improve performance by maximum combining and neural network combining. Experimental results show the usefulness of proposed methods for real application domain.

1 Introduction

Text classification (TC) has been investigated as a field of information storage and retrieval since early 1960's. Until the late 1980's, the most effective approach to the problem seemed to be that of manually building automatic classifiers by means of knowledge engineering techniques. Since the early 1990's, due to an increased interest and to the availability of more powerful hardware, TC has become a major field of investigation in the information systems discipline [1, 2, 3].

Recently, the machine learning technologies to automated TC has emerged and superseded the knowledge engineering approach. The advantage of machine learning approach lies in accuracy comparable to human performance [1]. k-nearest neighbor (kNN), decision tree (DT), support vector machine (SVM), and neural networks (NN) are effective machine learning technologies used actively in automated TC tasks [3].

TC has been applied in real applications: topic spotting systems of news articles and customer email routing system [1, 4] are some of the examples. However, most of TC investigations are studied not on real data but on well-organized text corpus. Real-world document sets have much noise, extreme imbalance of the number of documents between categories, and many documents that do not satisfy orthographical rules.

We attempt to achieve automated classification system of FAQ texts using multiple neural networks (MNN). In many pattern recognition problems, MNN approaches perform better than a single neural network [5, 6]. Especially, MNN

J. Liu et al. (Eds.): IDEAL 2003, LNCS 2690, pp. 1032–1036, 2003.
© Springer-Verlag Berlin Heidelberg 2003

approach is more favorable for the learning of noisy and imbalanced data sets [6]. In this paper, we divide TC problem to subtasks per category and combine them effectively. We combine the results with choice of maximum and combination by neural networks.

2 Neural Network Ensemble

2.1 Neural Network Classifier

The proposed text classification method is to model each category using a single NN and combine the results of all NNs. Figure 1 shows the text classification system.

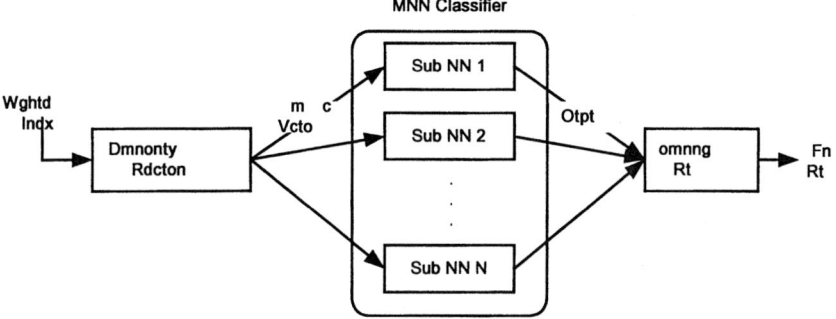

Fig. 1. Multiple neural network classifier

Key component of this method lies in task decomposition [5, 6]. Simple subtasks decomposed from a complex task can be learned effectively. First of all, the number of categories is problematic to solve the problem by a single NN. If the number of categories is too large like in this paper, the MNN approach that we propose can be one of powerful approaches because this does not deteriorate the performance due to the number of categories.

In addition, the hanmail.net FAQ texts are imbalanced per category. Learning the imbalanced data set by a single NN can lead difficulty of learning: learning cost and accuracy [6]. MNN approach does not have such problems and we can construct NNs according to the complexity of each subtask.

Finally, the features of each category can be selected through dimensionality reduction. It is possible to select features of each category separately. Optimized features by dimensionality reduction can lead to the improvement of performance because small and effective features are better for learning and it can eliminate noise terms [4]. Therefore, we can obtain overall improvement of learning capability and efficiency by this approach.

2.2 Learning

Neural network ensemble should be learned toward not only optimizing subtask by sub NN but also obtaining overall classification performance. This learning criterion can be derived by maximum mutual information (MMI) [7]. MMI of category c is simply defined as follows.

$$I_c = log\,P(D_c\,|\,\lambda_c\,) - log \sum_{x=1}^{N} P(D_c\,|\,\lambda_x\,) \qquad (1)$$

where D_c is document set in category c, N is the number of categories, λ_c is the model of category c. MMI criterion in which the average mutual information I_c between the document set D_c and the complete set of models $\lambda = \{\lambda_1, ..., \lambda_N\}$ is maximized.

By summing over all training data, one would hope to obtain the most separate set of models. Thus a possible implementation would be as follows.

$$I = \sum_{c=1}^{N} \left\{ log\,P(D_c\,|\,\lambda_c\,) - log \sum_{x=1}^{N} P(D_c\,|\,\lambda_x\,) \right\} \qquad (2)$$

To maximize mutual information I, we maximize the positive term and minimize the negative term. Consequently, overall learning of MNN should be achieved by maximizing the probability of documents for its category's sub NN and minimizing the probability of documents for other NNs.

To satisfy this learning condition we divide the document set to D_c which is in the category c and D_c' which is not when training sub NN λ_c. If a document is in D_c, sub NN λ_c propagates output 1 and otherwise, λ_c propagates output 0. Consequently, each sub NN solves a two-class problem.

3   Experimental Results

To evaluate the performance of the classifiers, we collect hanmail.net FAQ texts for a month. Among 2204 documents, we use 1718 documents as train data and 463 documents as test data. There exist categories that should be forwarded to the administrator. We regard the categories, which do not need any response and rarely encounter, as a reject category. We construct sub NN per each category including a reject category. We decide the number of hidden nodes by trial and errors.

3.1   Performance of Classifiers

We compare the classification performance in hanmail.net FAQ texts. We experiment on kNN, DT, SVM, SOM and MNN including single NN. We use the method of choosing the maximum of MNNs for objective comparison with other classifiers. Table 1 shows the results.

We compare the classifiers by the measures used in information retrieval area: precision, recall and F-measure. F-measure is defined as follows.

$$F_\beta = \frac{(\beta^2 + 1)\cdot Pr\cdot Re}{\beta^2 \cdot Pr + Re} \qquad (3)$$

where Pr is precision, Re is recall and β is the parameter that controls the importance of precision and recall. We use F_1 and $F_{0.3}$ to evaluate the classifiers. $F_{0.3}$ means that we regard precision as more important than precision. This property of $F_{0.3}$ satisfies with our overall classification purpose. MNN, NN and kNN produce promising results with more than 0.9 precision score.

Table 1. Performance of classifiers by measure of IR (F_1: Maximize F_1-measure, $F_{0.3}$: Maximize $F_{0.3}$-measure)

Classifiers		F_1	$F_{0.3}$	Precision	Recall
MNN	F_1	0.739	0.775	0.783	0.669
	$F_{0.3}$	0.614	0.837	0.903	0.465
KNN	F_1	0.692	0.744	0.755	0.639
	$F_{0.3}$	0.500	0.835	0.962	0.331
DT		0.690	0.697	0.699	0.682
SVM	F_1	0.500	0.714	0.780	0.368
	$F_{0.3}$	0.437	0.753	0.878	0.288
SOM	F_1	0.428	0.674	0.761	0.298
	$F_{0.3}$	0.425	0.691	0.786	0.294
NN	F_1	0.783	0.761	0.766	0.712
	$F_{0.3}$	0.614	0.837	0.903	0.464

3.2 Performance of Neural Network Ensemble

Table 2 shows the experimental results of combining MNN. We can achieve the improvement of NN combining methods. 0.849 is the best $F_{0.3}$ score over all classifiers in this paper.

Table 2. Results of combining MNN

Methods	F_1	$F_{0.3}$	Precision	Recall
Maximum	0.614	0.837	0.903	0.465
NN combining	0.649	0.849	0.904	0.507

4   Concluding Remarks

In this paper, we have proposed a text classification system with combining methods to solve the practical problem. The hanmail.net FAQ text set has much noise and extreme imbalance of the number of documents between categories, and many documents do not keep orthographical rules. To classify this practical data set, we propose neural network ensemble with combining methods. With reject strategy, we can obtain better results than any other classifiers.

We evaluate the method intensively from a practical point of view. We analyze the confidence of classification by several measures such as recognition rate, reliability, precision, recall, F_1, $F_{0.3}$ and so on. We can conclude that our classification method can be applied to practical application domains.

Acknowledgements. This work was supported by Biometrics Engineering Research Center and Brain Science and Engineering Research Program sponsored by Korean Ministry of Science and Technology.

References

1.   F. Sebastiani, "Machine Learning in Automated Text Categorisation," *Techical Report. IEI-B4-31-1999*, Istituto di Elaborazione dell'Informazione, Consiglio Nazionale delle Ricerche, Pisa, IT, 1999.
2.   G. Salton, *Automatic Text Processing: The Transformation, Analysis, and Retrieval of Information by Computer*, Addison-Wesley, 1988.
3.   Y. Yang and X. Liu, "A Re-examination of Text Categorization Methods," *Proc. of the 22h Annual Int. ACM SIGIR Conf. on Research and Development in Information Retrieval (SIGIR 99)*, pp. 42–49, 1999.
4.   S. M. Weiss, et al., "Maximizing Text-Mining Performance," *IEEE Intelligent System*, pp. 63–69, July/August 1999.
5.   A. J. C. Sharkey, "Multi-Net Systems," In A. J. C. Sharkey (Ed.), *Combining Artificial Neural Nets: Ensemble and Modular Multi-Net Systems*, Springer-Verlag, pp. 1–30, 1999.
6.   R. Anand, et.al., "Efficient Classification for Multiclass Problems Using Modular Neural Networks," *IEEE Trans. on Neural Networks*, vol. 6, no. 1, pp. 117–124, 1995.
7.   Y. Ephraim and L. R. Rabiner, "On the Relations between Modeling Approaches for Speech Recognition," *IEEE Trans. on Information Theory*, vol. 36, no. 2, pp.372–380, March 1990.

Filtering of Text Blocks in Web Images

Seongah Chin

#147-2, anyang-8 Dong, Manan-Gu, Anyang-City, Kyunggi-Do, Korea
Division of Multimedia, Sungkyul University
solideo@sungkyul.edu

Abstract. In this paper extracting text blocks in various Web images is presented here. The basic idea in our approach is to use knowledge of various characteristics of fonts, such as bitmap fonts and scalable fonts. Regardless of the font system there exists a somewhat fixed width of stroke to height ratio, independent of the characters. The algorithms associated with the technique work without prior knowledge of the text orientation, size or font. For verification of the proposed method, we have conducted a number of experiments.

1 Introduction

As broadband network tends to extend among internet users, various contents of the Web are constantly growing. In addition, very large amount of images on the Web are increasingly provided, conveying quite meaningful textual contents. Unfortunately, most existing search engines merely detect plan text information without seeking into Web images. Web images carry vast amounts of information and many images contain embedded or overlaid text. Therefore the task of text image segmentation is one of the primary stages of most document processing [1],[2],[3],[5], [6].

The complexity of character segmentation stems from the wide variety of fonts, the varying size of fonts, the poor quality of binary images and multiple character sets such as different languages, and special symbols. Recent text segmentation schemes from Web images are very few since interest on this topic has been driven lately [7]. The basic idea in our approach is to use knowledge of various characteristics of fonts, such as bitmap fonts and scalable fonts, also referred to as object oriented fonts or vector fonts. Regardless of the font system there exists a somewhat fixed width of stroke to height ratio, independent of the character including special symbols and different languages. Since the distance of a combination of curves or lines determines the segment width, we strive to compute segment widths and their number of appearance in order to identify font density function. Each font system has its own font density function, which makes it possible to identify fonts by the fact that mainly occupied segment widths of each font are accompanied with high probability in the density function. We note text can be aligned any orientation with skew angles. Shape moments based skew estimation and corrections are developed in order to detect the main skew. The aim of this research is to propose general schemes, which make it possible to obtain textual information in Web images.

J. Liu et al. (Eds.): IDEAL 2003, LNCS 2690, pp. 1037–1041, 2003.

2 Text Block Detection

The text block detection algorithm begins with operating on $f(x, y)$, an input image Text areas in an image consist of narrow scans that contain sequences of several segments of equal width. Segments in this context are image strips of uniform gray level and a scan is linear progression through the image along some orientation. The ratio of the height, of an aggregation of segments of equal width, to the width itself is an important feature for text segmentation. The first step is to create a derivative image so that image regions that have significant changes in gray intensity are highlighted. We expected the boundary of text characters to be identified with this operation. The next step is to detect a skew (i.e is not horizontally aligned) enabling the directional edge image is rotated so that the text is aligned correctly $(e'_{\theta,\pi}(x', y'))$. These images discriminate increasing intensity edges from decreasing intensity edges rising and falling edges respectively. Upon the selection of an orientation angle θ as shown in Figure 1, we will apply affine transformations, i.e. a translation along the X axis and a rotation counter clockwise by the angle $(\pi/2-\theta)$. Now the edge matrix will be mapped into another matrix coordinate system, which is defined with respect to the text orientation angle θ. We explore the method, which adjusts for a skew text image using transformations. Detection of text orientation is obtained by calculation of shape moments as shown in (1).

$$\theta = \frac{1}{2}(tan^{-1}\frac{2\mu_{11}}{\mu_{20}-\mu_{02}})$$

(1)

$$\mu_{pq} = \int_{-\infty}^{\infty}\int_{-\infty}^{\infty}(x-x_c)^p(y-y_c)^q e_\theta, \tau_e(x,y)dxdy$$

Since we have to transform all points in the edge matrix, we can proceed in two steps. At first, we calculate the combined transformation matrix, $T_{(Mcos\theta, 0)}R_{(\pi/2-\theta)}$ then we use this combined matrix on each point. This combined matrix saves calculation time by using a single matrix multiplication at each point. We rotate the image matrix by $(\pi/2-\theta)$ radians counter clockwise and translate $Mcos\theta$ units in the X direction. Now, we realize that new transformed image matrix size has been changed from N to $Nsin\theta+Mcos\theta$ and from M to $Msin\theta+Ncos\theta$ respectively as shown in Figure 1. The equation (1) explains the procedure performs transformation based on homogeneous coordinate system and calculation of new image size. First of all, we rotate with angle $(\pi/2-\theta)$ and translate to X axis with $Mcos\theta$. But we use the combined matrix for reduce calculation time. We denote new N and M as $N'= Nsin\theta + Mcos\theta$ and $M'=Msin\theta + Ncos\theta$. At this point, we change some notations as N to N', M to M', x to x', y to y', $e_{\theta,\pi}(x,y)$ to $e'_{\theta,\pi}(x', y')$. By examining the edge matrix, $e_{\theta,\pi}(x, y)$ we introduce two new edge index matrices, which store the column locations of individual edges.

$$\begin{bmatrix} x' \\ y' \\ 1 \end{bmatrix} = \begin{bmatrix} x \sin \theta - y \cos \theta + M \cos \theta \\ x \cos \theta + y \sin \theta \\ 1 \end{bmatrix} \qquad (2)$$

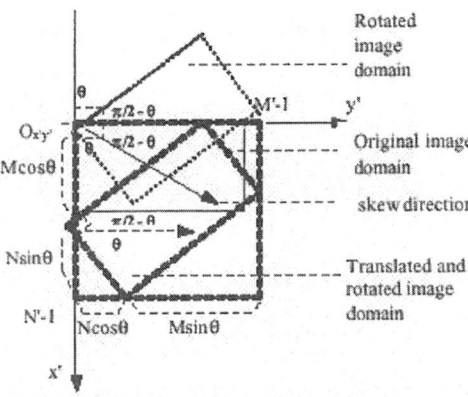

Fig. 1. Relationship of the translated and rotated image to the original image and skew angle θ

Edge index matrices, $K_s(x, c)$ and $K_e(x, c)$ hold the column indices of certain non zero elements of the matrix.

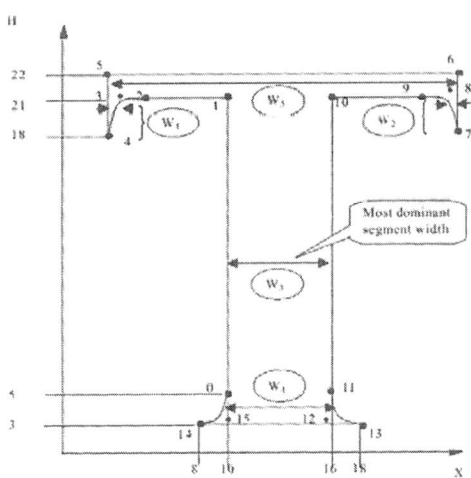

Fig. 2. Various types of segment width and dominant segment width W_3

In order to specify these matrices we need to define valid and invalid segments. Valid segments are scan line segment in the image that either starts with a +1 element in the edge matrix and ends with a −1 element or starts with a −1 element in the edge matrix and ends with a +1 element. Invalid segment starts and ends with +1 and +1 or −1 and −1 respectively. Now, $K_s(x, c)$ stores the image column index of the start of the cth valid segment in the Xth scan line. Similarly, $K_e(x, c)$ starts the image column index of the end of the cth valid segment.

Fig. 3. Experimental Results (a) – (f) Input Web Images and Text Extracted

Now, we define $S(x, c)$ as the cth valid segment width in x^{th} horizontal scan. Generally, segment width is the distance between the column locations of edges of which transition occurs either −1 to 1 or 1 to −1. $S(x, c) = K_e(x, c) - K_s(x, c)$. When the segment matrix contains many segment widths with the same or similar value then there exists a possibility that these segments are textual segments based on the proposed principle. In Figure 2 we have seen various types do segment width of letter 'T' with dominant segment width W_3. We will construct histograms of the scan lines and select as candidate typeface widths the modes of these histograms. The region $\Re$ in the height/width space represents valid text.

3. Experimental Results

Experiments as shown in Figure 3.have been conducted on a number of Web image files in order to evaluate correctness of the proposed schemes under Pentium4 Compaq Desktop workstation operated by Window 2000 professional environments. Web images goes into the algorithm without capturing stage. In our experiments we found that 10 to 12 point size of text mostly used in documents should be captured with a minimum of 300dpi (dot per inch) resolution since lower resolution cause significant data loss especially with small type fonts. Text in all other types of images is good enough to be extracted with 96dpi resolution. We solved skew angle estimations for images that contain text that is not aligned horizontally using shape moments. In addition we have evaluated the algorithm properly works with noise added images.

4 Conclusions

We have proposed a method for filtering of text blocks in Web images working without prior knowledge of the text orientation, size or font. We endeavor to calculate segment widths and their number of appearance in order to identify font density function. This algorithm can also work for with skew images by performing the can lead to image database retrievable system by automatically reading of text in Web images.

References

1. Amamoto, N., Torigoe, S., Hirogaki, Yoshitaka, "Block Segmentation and Text Area Extraction of Vertically/Horizontally Written Document", *IEEE Proceedings,* pp. 739–742, July 1993
2. Antonacopoulos, Apostolos, "Page Segmentation Using the Description of the Background" *Computer Vision and Image Understanding,* Vol. 70. No. 3, pp.350–369, June 1998
3. Chen, Francine R. and Bloomberg , Dan S., "Summarization of Imaged Documents without OCR" *Computer Vision and Image Understanding,* Vol. 70. No. 3, pp. 307–320, June 1998
4. Doermann, David, "Indexing and Retrieval of Document Images": *A Survey Computer Vision and Image Understanding,* Vol. 70. No. 3, pp. 287–298, June 1998
5. Etemad, K., Doermann, David and Chellappa , Rama "Multiscale Segmentation of unstructured Document Pages Using Soft Decision Integration", *IEEE Transaction on Pattern Analysis and Machine Intelligence,* Vol. 19, No 1, pp. 92–96, Jan. 1997
6. 13. O'Gorman, Lawrence and Kasturi, Rangachar, "Document Image Analysis", *IEEE Computer Society Press,*1995
7. Okun, O. and Pietikainen, Matti., "Text Localization in WWW images", *Proc. of the 5ᵗʰ Multiconference on Systemics, Cybernetics and Informatics,* Vol XIV, July, pp301–306 2001
8. Jain, Anil K., Yu , Bin, "Document representation and its Application to Page Decomposition" *IEEE Transaction on Pattern Analysis and Machine Intelligence,*Vol. 20 No.3, pp. 294–308, March 1998
9. Lu, Zhaoyang, "Detection of Text Regions from Digital Engineering Drawing", *IEEE Transactions on Pattern Analysis and Machine Intelligence,* Vol. 20, No. 4, pp. 431–439, April 1998
10. Kise, K. Sato, Akinori, and Iwata, Motoi "Segmentation of Page Images Using the Area Voronoi Diagram" *Computer Vision and Image Understanding,* Vol. 70. No. 3, pp. 370–382, June 1998

Towards a Terabyte Digital Library System

Hao Ding[1], Yun Lin[1], and Bin Liu[2]

[1]Department of Computer and Information Science,
Norwegian University of Science and Technology, 7491, Trondheim, NORWAY
{haowing,yunl}@idi.ntnu.no

[2] Digital Media Research Center, Chinese Academy of Sciences, Beijing 100080, P.R.China
bliu@ict.ac.cn

Abstract. In China-US Million Book Digital Library, output of the digitalization process is more than one terabyte of text in OEB and PDF format. To access these data quickly and accurately, we are developing a distributed terabyte text retrieval system. To solve the interoperability and extensibility among different information resources, we introduced our solutions of three kinds of metadata schemes. Furthermore, because of the complexity in Chinese language, we made an approach in word segment methods to increase the efficiency and response time of the DL system. In the testbed, we put an extra layer in the cache server and designed a new algorithm based on VSM. With the query cache, system can search less data while maintaining acceptable retrieval accuracy.

1 Introduction

As the sharp growth of the content in the Internet and especially, in the digital library system, the traditional full text search engines cannot cope with the increasing data scale. In the architecture perspective, therefore, many research and IR system come out, Hawking[1] used multiprocessor systems to response a single query less than a second on 100GB collection. Zhihong Lu[2] used simulation to experiment with a terabyte of text data, giving some promising performance of partial replication distributed IR system. TREC (Text Retrieval Conference) also provides the VLC2 (Very Large Collections version 2) that contains about 100GB text data for study.

In China-US Million Book Digital Library, output of the digitalization process is more than one terabyte. To provide information and knowledge service to any people at any time in any place, it is important to access any text data in the library quickly and accurately within a terabyte text retrieval system.

The structure of this paper is organized as follows. Section 2 briefly describes the system framework and the query cache mechanism. Section 3 shows our approach in the metadata set. Section 4 gives one of our approaches in retrieving documents. Section 5 comes with the conclusions and our future work.

J. Liu et al. (Eds.): IDEAL 2003, LNCS 2690, pp. 1042–1046, 2003.
© Springer-Verlag Berlin Heidelberg 2003

2 Architecture

In the system, we have collected millions of books in OEB format [3] which is based on XML. These XML formatted files are stored in the source library. Fig.1 shows the framework of the distributed text retrieval system.

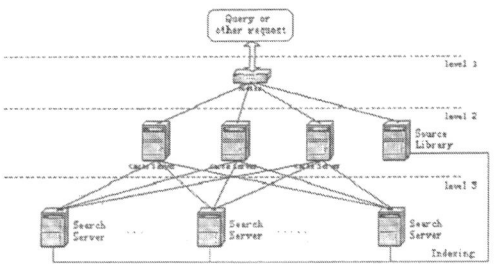

Fig. 1. Framework of the distributed text retrieval system

Although we use Gigabit Ethernet to transmit data, it cannot keep up with increasing users and expanding book collections. Based on recent research results [4,5], we put the indexes of different books on different search servers. Each search server can deal with about tenths of gigabyte text data with a full-text search engine. Fig 1 is the framework. To search less data, we built a query cache, which contains query logic as well as a subset of the documents or their summaries. We adopt cascading caches pattern because hit rates can be increased and resource consumption can be reduced by this infrastructure [7]. If a cache at a certain layer cannot satisfy a request, it forwards the request to its upstream cache and so forth. The cache infrastructure cuts down on the required network bandwidth and the I/O load caused by queries but does not attack the bandwidth requirements between different servers.

3 Approach on Metadata

Excellent metadata scheme should be interoperable and extensible. That is the core of the digital library technological scheme. In our digital library project, there are numerous resources which have different characteristics. There are ordinary books, publications, rare books, photos, audio and video materials. Among them, some have intact CNMARC written down already, some adopt peculiar metadata to describe, such as the Rare Books (RB) which is designed by ourselves, and yet some have not ready-made metadata. To those books which have CNMARC indices, CNMARC can offer very good content and forms to describe the digital objects. But to those resources which need re-process and re-organization, such as Chinese folk photo library and music libraries, it is not appropriate to import MARC again. This is not merely because there are not existing MARC to describe those records, but also because it is not wise to carry out MARC labeling again on such a large number of resources. Furthermore, MARC [10] itself pays much attention to the characteristic of the style, so it is not suitable to be used to describe the content the resources. In this case, Dublin Core then will have its strengths [6]. So, In the de facto digital library system, we adopt Dublin Core as the core metadata set, and also support other two metadata sets - CNMARC and RB. We use the former one to describe Chinese almanacs. Fig 2 gives the schema of the metadata sets in our DL system.

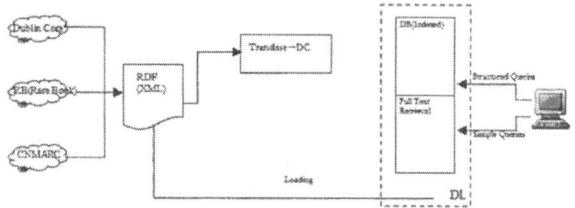

Fig. 2. Metadata Sets Scheme

In Fig 2, we have shown three kinds of metadata which are used to describe different information resources. As to rare books, we use the specific RB metadata scheme. To the folk photo dictionaries and national periodicals, we use Dublin Core. And to those digital resources (such as almanacs) which have been digitalized in the early period, we resort to the CNMARC to describe them. One of the critical point in the figure is using RDF [8] to wrap up the metadata. It is can not only help us enable the encoding, exchange and reuse of the metadata sets , but also make much use of the original resources (most of them are CNMARC wrapped records). In the framework of RDF, we can choose different metadata scheme according to the different demands of the resources. These metadata sets can also be seamlessly integrated, and we can give more detailed description on the contents of the resources. Here is an example as follows:

```
<?xml version="1.0" ?>
<rdf:RDF
    xmlns:rdf="http://www.w3.org/1999/02/22-rdf-syntax-ns#"
    xmlns:dc="http://purl.org/metadata/dublin_core#"
    xmlns:rb="http://159.226.42.116/metadata/rarebook_cn#"
    xmlns:sdl="http://159.226.42.116/metadata/Million_DL#">
<rdf:Description ID="4628-A-1">
<dc:Title>Thoughts on the countryside</dc:Title>
<dc:Subject >Countryside, Guang Dong</dc:Subject>
<dc:Subject Scheme="CNMARC">F323.4</dc:Subject>
<dc:Creator>Zhou Sen</dc:Creator>
<dc:Source>Southern China(1998)(4)(p2-5)</dc:Source>
<sdl:collection>National Magzine</sdl:collection>
<sdl:content>
<rdf:Seq>
<rdf:li resource="bk-image/4628/1998/F0040001.tif"/>
</rdf:Seq>
</sdl:content>
</rdf:Description>
</rdf:RDF>
```

Fig. 3. RDF description on the contents of the resources

4   Retrieval Documents

In the full text retrieval system of full text, the choice of indexing item is a basic one, also a very important problem. The first thing which has to be done is to segment, and then making out the relevant degree. In European Languages, full text retrieval system, segmenting documents or queries into items will take less work because there are separators (such as the blank) between the words. But in so called CJK (Chinese-Japanese-Korean) ideographs, it is much more complicated to do the segmentation [9]. Which kind of segment unit should we use? Most of the researchers think that we should have *word* as the segment unit at current research step because it is in accordance with the way that people think. Furthermore, using *word* as index item can reuse the existing theory and methods in the English full text retrieval system.

However, in Chinese platform, the retrieval results always can not meet people's needs. The most important factor is that there are no separators in Chinese. That is why the Chinese people also use *stroke ordering* and *Pinyin* (But not all Chinese people know Pinyin). So, in the segmenting phrase, we have to resort to the dictionary. But on the other hand, Chinese is very flexible, the number of the Chinese *symbol* is countless and it is nearly impossible to build a well structured dictionary.

In China-US Million Book Digital Library System, we use a subset. We add an extra layer which using the Chinese *symbol* as the segment unit to help digging out the coarse result set. According the encoding standard GB2312, there are totally 6763 Chinese *symbols*. Those *symbols* are frequently used in the daily life. And, comparably, the indexing set will not be that large. This method will greatly speed up the searching efficiency but on the other hand, it is almost manifest that we can not achieve high precisions. In order to obtain a high precision with a lower time cost, we used the K-NN retrieval method. And in order to decrease computational complexity, we have modified the VSM algorithm slightly. Following is the key points in the Chinese symbol based segmenting method we used in the system.

Firstly, we make an index according to the file name in the repository. The index method is based on the *Uniform Chinese Books Category Method*. The style is just as follows.

```
fileA        fileB        fileC      ....
S512.305     S512.306     S512.307   ....
```

Then, setting up the multi-indexing structure, the data structure is as follows:

```
filename indexing:
fileA   a1 f1,a2 f2, ... a20 f20   ?freqsA2
fileB   b1 f1,b2 f2, ... b20 f20   ?freqsB2
....

Word indexing:
word1   file.a1,file.a2,....
word2   file.b1,file.b2,....
....
```

In the filename indexing, for each file in the collection, we pick out top 20 frequent symbols, such as a1, a2, etc. and the corresponding frequences, such as f1, f2, etc. And then, we calculate the sum of the square of those frequences. Inversely, for each symbol, we select the top 20 files in which such symbol appears at least once.

We can make a rough calculation on the size of the indexing files. The size of the filename indexing file: $10^6 \times (4 + (2+2) \times 20 + 4) \approx 88M$; The size of the word indexing file is: $10^6 \times 20 \times 4 \approx 80M$. (Note: assuming the gross number of the books is 10^6). It is quite affordable for the cache server to put the indexed files into the cache. When calculating the Similarity, we extend the classical Vector Space Model (VSM).

$$\cos\theta = Sim(X_i, X_n) = \frac{<X_i \cdot X_n>}{|X_i| \cdot |X_n|} \xrightarrow{ext.} \frac{x_{i1} \cdot x_{n1} + x_{i2} \cdot x_{n2} + ... + x_{i,20} \cdot x_{n,20}}{x^2_{n1} + ... + x^2_{n20}} \qquad (1)$$

In (1), $|X_i|$ is constant variable, $|Xn|$ has been calculated. So, we can only multiply the weights of the words which appear. Furthermore, it is not necessary for us to calculate the $|X_i|$ once more, and extract the value of $<X_i \cdot X_n>$ because the value of $|X_i|$ is the same in each calculation and we only need the value of $<X_i \cdot X_n>$ for comparing the values. It will be time consuming to calculate them.

We have collected stochastically *10000* files from the repository as the test set. And the response time is satisfactory. Result can be reached at

5 Conclusion and Future Work

A terabyte text retrieval system in China-US Million Book Digital Library should meet both functions and performance needs. This article presents the challenges we have met in our work, such as the distributed large-scale system architecture, the metadata and retrieval method. Our future works are to explore some new retrieval models and text clustering approaches in the Digital Library.

References

1. Peter Bailey, David Hawking, A Parallel Architecture for Query Processing Over A Terabyte of Text. Australian National University, Technical Report, 1996
2. Zhihong Lu, Scalable Distributed Architectures for Information Retrieval. University of Massachusetts at Amherst, Ph.D. dissertation, 1999
3. Open eBook Publication Structure Specification 1.0.1. http://openebook.org/oebps/
4. Evangelos P. Markatos, On Caching Search Engine Query Results. Computer Communications, 24(2), Jan 2001, pp137–143
5. Yinglian Xie, David O'Hallaron, Locality in Search Engine Queries and Its Implications for Caching. Carnegie Mellon University, Technical Report, 2001
6. The Dublin Core Home Page: http://purl.oclc.org/dc/documents/rec-dces-19990702.htm
7. Thomas Gschwind, Manfred Hauswirth, A Cache Architecture for Modernizing the Usenet Infrastructure, Proceedings of the 32nd Hawai'i International Conference On System Sciences, January 5–8, 1999, Maui, Hawaii.
8. W3C Resource Description Framework (RDF) Schema Speci_cation. http://www.w3.org/TR/PR-rdf-schema/
9. Zhu Dexi, Lecture of Chinese Syntax, Commercial Press, 1982
10. Zhuang Leibo, Ji Lu'en, The difference between Dublin Core and USMARC, Journal of the Theory and Research, 2001–7–13, http://www.libnet.sh.cn/magzine/00-10/p17.htm

A Neural System Prototype for Data Processing Using Modified Conjugate Directional Filtering (MCDF)

Wanwu Guo and Anthony Watson

School of Computer and Information Science, Edith Cowan University
2 Bradford Street, Mount Lawley, Western Australia 6050, Australia
{w.guo, a.watson }@ecu.edu.au

Abstract. Modified conjugate directional filtering (MCDF) is a method proposed by us recently for digital data and image processing. By using MCDF, directional-filtered results in conjugate directions can be not only merged into one image that shows the maximum linear features in the two conjugate directions, but also further manipulated by a number of predefined generic MCDF operations for different purposes. In this paper, we report the progressive result of our MCDF study, which shows that a neural system can be used to implement the MCDF operations. We provide the trial work on applying this MCDF neural system to the processing of a digital terrain model (DTM) in central Australia. The trial work shows that the MCDF provides the power of integrating information in different forms, and thus presents more information in a single image than the conventional methods do.

1 Introduction

Guo and Watson recently reported the trial work using a method called the modified conjugate directional filtering (MCDF) [1][2][3]. By using MCDF, directional-filtered results in conjugate directions can be not only merged into one image that shows the maximum linear features in the two conjugate directions, but also further manipulated by a number of predefined generic MCDF operations for different purposes.

Although several generic MCDF operations were also defined to carry out this method, however, there was no consideration in how to implement this method given in our previous paper [1]. Our further study shows that neural networks can be used to implement the MCDF method. When the directional-filtered data are made available by a separate program, a MCDF interface based on a neural network design can be used to carry out and coordinate all the MCDF operations. In this paper, we first present the general structure of the neural system that is used to carry out the MCDF operations. To verify its usefulness and applicability to digital signal and image processing, we apply this neural system to the processing of a digital terrain model in central Australia, incorporating the use of some commonly used conventional processing methods. This enables a comparison on the advantages and disadvantages in using the MCDF and traditional operations to be made.

J. Liu et al. (Eds.): IDEAL 2003, LNCS 2690, pp. 1047–1051, 2003.
© Springer-Verlag Berlin Heidelberg 2003

2 Design of the MCDF Neural System

Assuming f_0 to be the original data file, f_1 and f_2 to be the directional-filtered data files in the two conjugate directions, the general operation of the MCDF can be expressed as [1]

$$MCDF = W_0{}^*f_0 + F_2[W_1{}^*F_1(f_1), W_2{}^*F_1(f_2)]; \qquad (1)$$

where W_0, W_1 and W_2 are selective constants; F_0, F_1 and F_2 are pre-defined generic functions.

We first assume that directional filtering has been applied to an original file (f_0) in two conjugate directions and the resultant files are f_1 and f_2. Consequently, the structure of a MCDF neural system is illustrated in Figure 1a. This system consists of five parts: initial transfer F_1, logical operator L, initial neuron N_1, final transfer F_2, and final neuron N_2.

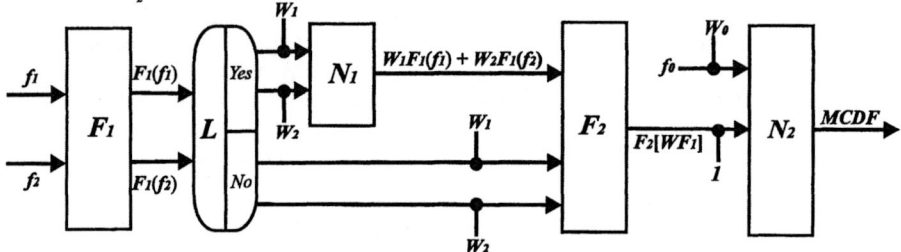

Fig. 1. Schematic diagram of the MCDF neural system

When the two data files of directional filtering in conjugate directions are firstly input into the system, they are manipulated by the same transfer function F_1. The pair of outputs, $F_1(f_1)$ and $F_1(f_2)$, is then used as the input to the logical operator L that determines whether the first neural operation is needed before the final transfer function is called. This is because some MCDF methods may require only one neural operation in the end of the process. If a *No* decision is made, the pair is directly sent to the final transfer unit F_2 for processing. If a *Yes* decision is made, the pair is directed to the initial neural unit for neural processing. During this process, a zero bias and two selective weights are merged with $F_1(f_1)$ and $F_1(f_2)$, respectively. The output $N_1 = F_1(f_1) + F_1(f_2)$ from the neuron N_1 is then sent to the final transfer unit F_2. Data into the final transfer unit F_2 are further manipulated there, and the output is $F_2[W \bullet F_1]$, which is then input into the final neuron with a constant weight 1.0, along with the weighted input of original data f_0. The output, $W_0{}^*f_0 + F_2[W \bullet F_1]$ from the neuron N_2, is as same as formula (1), i.e., the result of MCDF operations.

3 Digital Terrain Model (DTM) Processing

Figure 2a is the greyscale image of the original DTM in central Australia. The dark grades indicate the lowlands whereas the light grades indicate the highlands in this region. Figure 2b is the greyscale 3D relief image of the same model. The illumination is applied vertically so that no shading effect bias to any directions is made. This image indeed gives a strong impression on the topographic relief of the region that cannot be seen in the original DTM image. However, we should notice it is hardly to estimate the real scale of the terrain relief on this image, just as we cannot estimate how high a tall building is if we are looking down right over it in the air.

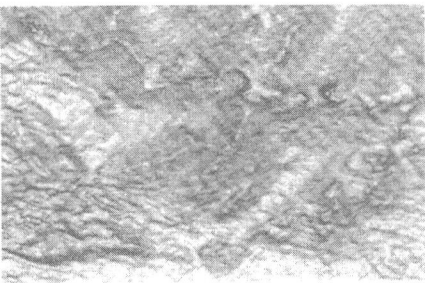

Fig. 2. Original DTM image (a, left) and the 3D image illuminated vertically (b, right)

More interesting observations come from the changes in illuminating orientations. Figure 3a shows a 3D shaded-relief image of the same model as being illuminated from northeast at an angle of 45°, whereas Figure 3b is the result as being illuminated from northwest at an angle of 45°. For the same model, being illuminated from different directions, it is expected that different images should be produced. However, what is unexpected is that the difference between these two images is so significant that one could easily regard them as showing two different regions. When comparing these two images with Figure 2b, one would question which 3D image should be regarded as the 'true' presentation of the DTM.

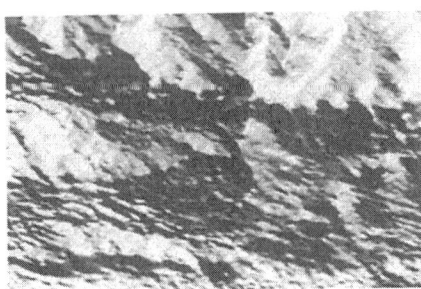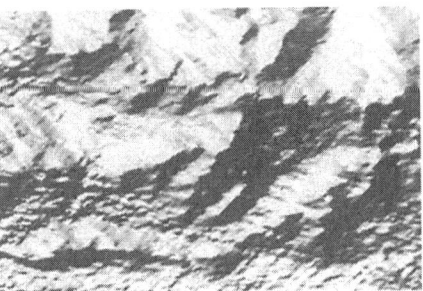

Fig. 3. Shaded-relief DTM images illuminated from NE (a, left) and NW (b, right)

Figure 4 shows the image after applying a conventional edge detection operation on the same terrain model [4][5]. It looks like a real topographical map with contours indicating the terrain relief. This image gives us some indication on the real scale of the terrain relief in this region by counting the number of the contours. However, the gray patterns as direct indication of terrain relief shown in the original image are lost. Furthermore, the impressive 3D shaded-relief features cannot be retained even to a little extent. This implies that by using any single conventional operation we may have an enhanced image that shows either quantitative information as contours, or qualitative information as gray patterns or 3D shades on terrain relief, but cannot contain both even to a little extent.

Fig. 4. Edge detected DTM image of the original terrain model

The MCDF processing is based on the system designed in Figure 1. Although several MCDF operations are defined [1], we only use MCDF(add1) and MCDF(add3) to process the DTM data in this paper. The MCDF(add1) operation can produce an image with 3D effect to some extent, which is especially useful in presentation of terrain relief. The MCDF(add3) operation is able to outline the gradient changes that indicate the topographic variation in DTM.

Firstly, directional filtering is applied in both the NE and NW directions to the original DTM data. The output (f_{NE} and f_{NW}) is then put into the neural system illustrated in Figure 1 for MCDF processing. Figure 5a shows the image processed using MCDF(add3). The system parameters for this operation are: $W_0 = 1$, $W_1 = W_2 = 3$, $F_1 =$ abs, $F_2 = 1$, and $L =$ yes. Essentially, the MCDF(add3) image is equivalent to a combination of the original DTM image (Fig. 2a) and the edge-detected DTM image in a ratio of 1:3. As a result, both gray patterns and contours are contained in this image. As we mentioned before, any single traditional operation is not capable of producing such an image. Since the directional filtering is applied in the conjugated NE and NW directions, linear features in these two directions are especially enhanced. However, this image does not show any 3D effect.

Figure 5b shows the image processed using MCDF(add1). The system parameters for this operation are: $W_0 = 1$, $W_1 = W_2 = 3$, $F_1 = F_2 = 1$, and $L =$ yes. In addition to the enhanced features shown in the MCDF(add3) image (Fig. 5), the MCDF(add1) image shows 3D effect to some extent, although its impression is far less than any 3D shaded-relief image presented before in this paper. However, we should notice that the MCDF operations indeed indicate the capability in integrating information in different patterns and formats into a single image, of which any single traditional operation is not capable.

Fig. 5. MCDF(add3) image (a, left) and MCDF(add1) image (b, right)

4 Discussions and Conclusion

Both conventional and MCDF operations have been used to process a DTM image. The 3D shaded-relief method produces visually impressive images, but the presentation difference caused by applying illumination from different directions on the same model could be so great that those images could be easily regarded as representing different models (Figs. 2b & 3).

Edge detection operation produces a relatively quantitative presentation of terrain relief by means of contours. However, no gray patterns and 3D effect can be retained on such an edge-detected image (Fig. 4). Furthermore, any single conventional operation is hardly able to produce an image that contains both qualitative and quantitative forms of information.

Application of the MCDF neural system to the DTM image demonstrates that by selecting appropriate system parameters, MCDF operations are able to partly combine both qualitative and quantitative forms of information into a single image. The MCDF(add3) image contains both contours and gray patterns (Fig. 5a), whereas the MCDF(add1) image shows terrain relief information in forms of contours, colours, and 3D effect (Fig. 5b). This system is also scalable in absorbing any new generic operations, and potentially it offers support for parallel processing.

References

1. Guo, W., Watson, A.: Modification of Conjugate Directional Filtering: from CDF to MCDF. Proceedings of IASTED Conference on Signal Processing, Pattern Recognition, and Applications. Crete, Greece (2002) 331–334.
2. Guo, W., Watson, A.: Conjugated Linear Feature Enhancement by Conjugate Directional Filtering. Proceedings of IASTED Conference on Visualization, Imaging and Image Processing. Marbella, Spain (2001) 583–586.
3. Watson. A., Guo, W.: Application of Modified Conjugated Directional Filtering in Image Processing. Proceedings of IASTED Conference on Signal Processing, Pattern Recognition, and Applications. Crete, Greece (2002) 335–338.
4. Jahne, B.: Digital Image Processing: Concepts, Algorithms and Scientific Applications. Springer-Verlag, Berlin Heidelberg (1997).
5. Proakis, J.G., Manolakis, D.G.: Digital Signal Processing: Principles, Algorithms and Applications. Prentice-Hall, Upper Saddle River New York (1996).

Prediction Error Context-Based Lossless Compression of Medical Images

Jae-Jeong Hwang, Sang-Gyu Cho, Chi-Gyu Hwang, and Jung-Sik Lee

School of Electronic and Information Eng., Kunsan National University,
68 Miryong-dong, Kunsan, 573-701, Korea
{hwang, hcgdino, leejs}@kunsan.ac.kr

Abstract. This paper presents a new context formation and lossless compression of medical images in which has huge number of pixels and 2-byte pixel depth. We analyze various prediction techniques and compare their performance. The initial prediction is used for the context to update and correct the prediction error. The results show that diagonal edge detection-based prediction does not perform well in medical images and the proposed scheme outperforms JPEG-LS and DMED in terms of compression ratio up to 2.2%.

1 Introduction

Compression of medical images to reduce their storage and transmission bandwidth requirements is of great interest in the implementation of systems such as PACS(Picture Archival and Communication System) and DR(Digital Radiography). To guarantee correct medical examination and treatment by a doctor, images obtained by an image detector must be coded in a lossless or near-lossless way.

Several methods are available for the lossless compression of images. A method that is currently popular in DICOM(Digital Imaging and Communications in Medicine) is the JPEG(Joint Photographic Exterts Group) standard based on discrete cosine transform resulting in lossy compression rather than lossless. Well-known DPCM(Differential Pulse Code Modulation) can be used for lossless compression with limited compression ratio.

JPEG has been evolved to JPEG-2000 that the wavelet transform adopted [1]. JPEG-2000 enables one lots of functions but does not perform well in the lossless compression of images, since the transform-based methods yield high performance with lossy quantization. In 1995, new technique was proposed named CALIC(Context-based Adaptive Lossless Image Codec) [2]. It is a rather elaborated coding scheme compared with others like JPEG, but the complexity is so high for real application. LOCO-I(Low Complexity lossless compression for Images) is the algorithm at the core of the ISO/IEC standard, JPEG-LS which was motivated from CALIC and reduced the complexity [3]. The schemes use the initial prediction to be updated and corrected by context modeling. The most important points are how to design the initial fixed predictor and how to design contexts for each pixel from surrounding pixels.

J. Liu et al. (Eds.): IDEAL 2003, LNCS 2690, pp. 1052–1055, 2003.

2 Prediction Schemes in Data Domain

2.1 Median Edge-Based Prediction

The JPEG-LS used the median edge detection (MED) predictor, which is adapted in the presence of local edges. MED detects horizontal and vertical edges by examining the North (R_b), West (R_a) and North-West (R_c) neighbors of the current pixel $I(x, y)$.

$$P_{x,y} = \begin{cases} \min(R_b, R_a) & \text{if } R_c \geq \max(R_b, R_a) \\ \max(R_b, R_a) & \text{if } R_c \leq \min(R_b, R_a) \\ R_b + R_a - R_c & \text{otherwise} \end{cases} \tag{1}$$

The MED predictor has also been called MAP(median adaptive predictor) and selects the median of a set of three predictions in order to predict the current pixel. It always chooses either the best or the second-best predictor among the three candidate predictors. In an extensive evaluation, the MED predictor was observed to give superior performance over most linear predictors[4]. However problems still remains for the diagonal edges that the MED could not respond enough and replace them with a planar prediction, average operation, since it's performance will be the best in the flat area rather than the diagonal edge areas.

2.2 The GAP Prediction

The CALIC proposal [2] included a gradient-adjusted predictor (GAP) which adapts the prediction according to local gradients and hence gives a more robust performance compared to the linear predictors. GAP weights the neighboring pixels of $I(x, y)$ according to the estimated gradients in the neighborhood : West(W), West-west(WW), North(N), North-west(NW), North-east(NE), North-north(NN), and North-north-east(NNE).

$$d_h = |W - WW| + |N - NW| + |N - NE|$$
$$d_v = |W - NW| + |N - NN| + |NE - NNE| \tag{2}$$

2.3 Diagonal Edge Detection and Prediction

Edirisinghe et al proposed diagonal edge based prediction in [5]. First, in the presence of a diagonal edge the two gradients ($R_b - R_d$) and ($R_a - P_{x,y}$) are equalized as :

$$(R_b - R_d) = (R_a - P_{x,y}) \rightarrow P_{x,y} = R_a + R_d - R_b \tag{4}$$

where the diagonal direction of 45 degree can be detected by this operation, while that in the conventional MED detects only 135 degree edges.

3   Prediction Error Context Coding

Contexts in JPEG-LS are formed by first computing the differences of neighboring four pixels : $D_1 = R_d - R_b$, $D_2 = R_b - R_c$, and $D_3 = R_c - R_a$. The three differences are then quantized into nine regions (labeled –4 to +4) symmetric about the origin consisting of only the difference 0 (region 0). Between the two adjacent regions threshold values are defined, i.e., three thresholds are used, T_1, T_2, and T_3 that can be changed by the user. Given nine possible values for each component of the context vector, this results in $9 \times 9 \times 9 = 729$ possible contexts. In order simplify the process, the number of contexts is reduced by replacing any context vector $\mathbf{Q} = [D_1, D_2, D_3]$ whose the first nonzero element is negative by $-\mathbf{Q}$. Whenever this happens, a variable $SIGN$ is also set to -1. Otherwise it is set to $+1$. This reduces the number of contexts to 365.

After initial prediction $P_{x,y}$ is computed, it is corrected according to the correction value which is a function of quantized difference values, depending on $SIGN$. The correction value is derived from the bias that the prediction value and the conditional expectation obtained from the past pixels might have some discrepancy. An error feedback mechanism cancels prediction biases in different contexts.

The MED predictor refers only three pixels, left, above, and left-above and the contexts include right-above pixel as well. Thus, the context obtained from this pixel does not match to the prediction values. We assume two constraints. First, the context formation and the prediction mechanism have to be closely related, since the correction of prediction by the context is performed by the conditional probability of the context. Other thing is the quantized value of the context has to be smaller to reduce the quantization error.

To meet these constraints we propose the prediction error context formation from the prediction value $P_{x,y}$ as following equations:

$$D_1 = R_d - P_{x,y}$$
$$D_2 = R_c - P_{x,y} \qquad (1)$$
$$D_3 = (R_b + R_a) - 2P_{x,y}$$

The first difference of R_d and $P_{x,y}$ represents that the prediction obtained by the left and above pixels and the right-above (45 degree diagonal component) form a context. Thus, more number of pixels in surrounding area are participated in the correction process and the quantized context can be smaller to meet the second constraint. Due to the similar reason, the second difference value can be justified. The third difference only belongs to the area where the MED use to get the context, i.e., the two mechanisms are already closely related.

4   Simulation Results

We choose 10 typical images obtained by digital radiography with more than 8 bits per pixel quantization and more than 1760 in horizontal and vertical resolution. In comparison with the proposed PEC scheme, Table 1 lists the lossless bit rates of CALIC, JPEG-LS, and DMED, the proposed PEC algorithm in terms of compression ratio. The PEC is superior to JPEG-LS and DMED and slightly inferior to CALIC.

Table 1. Simulation results of the four lossless compression schemes : CALIC, JPEG-LS, DMED, and PEC

Image	CALIC	JPEG-LS	DMED	PEC
Chest1	3.46	3.38	3.39	3.41
Chest2	5.95	5.83	5.84	5.86
Femur1	5.30	5.12	4.96	5.12
Femur2	5.19	5.00	4.89	5.00
L-spine1	4.30	4.18	4.20	4.21
L-spine2	3.71	3.62	3.64	3.64
Mammo1	16.43	15.94	15.85	16.03
Mammo2	16.98	16.42	16.30	16.50
Mammo3	6.21	6.03	6.01	6.07
Mammo4	5.84	5.63	5.61	5.69
Average	7.337	7.115	7.069	7.153

5 Conclusions

In this paper, we described the context-based lossless image compression techniques. Most of them use the initial fixed predictor, e.g., MED, DMED, structural predictor. After the prediction, it is corrected by context model derived by using the conditional probability. We analyze the conventional schemes and proposed a prediction error context-based lossless image compression scheme. It shows higher performance than JPEG-LS and DMED system and comparable to CALIC system.

References

[1] ISO/IEC JTC1/SC29/WG1, N2412, The JPEG-2000 still image compression standard, Sept. (2001)
[2] Wu, X., Memon, N., Sayood, K.: A context-based, adaptive, lossless /nearly-lossless coding scheme for continuous-tone images (CALIC). (1995)
[3] ISO/IEC JTC1/SC29/WG1, FCD 14495, lossless and near-lossless coding of continuous tone still images (JPEG-LS). (1997)
[4] Memon, N., Wu, X.: Recent developments in context-based predictive techniques forlossless image compression. The Computer Journal, vol. 40, no. 2/3, (1997) 127–135
[5] Edirisinghe, E.A., Bedi, S., Grecos, C.: Improvements to JPEG-LS via diagonal edge based prediction. SPIE Visual Commun. and Image Proc., vol. 4671, (2002) 604–613

Improving Feature Extraction Performance of Greedy Network-Growing Algorithm

Ryotaro Kamimura[1] and Osamu Uchida[2]

[1] Information Science Laboratory
and Future Science and Technology Joint Research Center, Tokai University,
1117 Kitakaname Hiratsuka Kanagawa 259-1292, Japan
ryo@cc.u-tokai.ac.jp
[2] Department of Human and Information Science,
School of Information Technology and Electronics, Tokai University,
1117 Kitakaname Hiratsuka Kanagawa 259-1292, Japan
o-uchida@tokai.ac.jp

Abstract. In this paper, we propose a new network-growing method to extract explicit features in complex input patterns. In [1], we have so far proposed a new type of network-growing algorithm called *greedy network-growing algorithm* and used the sigmoidal activation function for competitive unit outputs. However, the method with the sigmoidal activation function is introduced to be not so sensitive to input patterns. Thus, we have observed that in some cases final representations obtained by the method do not necessarily describe faithfully input patterns. To remedy this shortcoming, we employ the inverse of distance between input patterns and connection weights for competitive unit outputs. As the distance is smaller, competitive units are more strongly activated. Thus, winning units tend to represent input patterns more faithfully than the previous method with the sigmoidal activation function.

1 Introduction

In this paper, we propose a new computational method for the greedy network-growing algorithm. The method is called "greedy network-growing algorithm," because a network with this algorithm grows while absorbing as much information as possible from outside[1]. Contrary to conventional network-growing methods, we use an information theoretic method to grow networks, and thus, our method is considerably different from conventional methods.

Information theoretic approaches have been introduced in various ways into neural computing, for example, a principle of maximum information preservation (e.g. [2]), a principle of minimum redundancy [3] and spatially coherent feature detection (e.g. [4]). In conventional information theoretic methods, maximum possible information is determined before learning. It is impossible to increase information beyond a predetermined point, and thus, information theoretic methods have not been used in network growing. However, when we see self-organization processes in living systems, information capacity should be increased. We can intuitively see that, as living systems develop, their complexity

J. Liu et al. (Eds.): IDEAL 2003, LNCS 2690, pp. 1056–1061, 2003.

becomes larger; that is, their information capacity is larger. In our network-growing method, the number of competitive units can be increased in learning, and accordingly, the maximum possible information is increased in learning. Because we define information directly for the competitive units, information can be increased, as the number of competitive units is larger. This permits networks to adopt them flexibly to new input patterns.

In the previous model[1], we used the sigmoidal activation function to obtain competitive unit outputs. The sigmoidal activation function is a very powerful tool to realize competitive processes. Because multiple negative connections are generated in a course of information maximization. These negative connections can be used to turn off the majority of competitive units except a few number of winning units. However, one problem is that the sigmoidal function is introduced to be not so sensitive to input patterns, and thus, final competitive units in some cases do not represent input patterns faithfully. To remedy this shortcoming, we use the inverse of the distance between input patterns and connection weights. As the distance between input patterns and connection weights is smaller, competitive units are more strongly activated. Thus, winning units represents input patterns more faithfully.

2   Growing Network and Information Maximization

In the greedy network-growing algorithm, we suppose that a network attempts to absorb as much information as possible from the outer environment, because in the outer environment, there are many destructive forces against artificial systems. To absorb information on the outer environment, the systems gradually increase their complexity until no more complexity is needed. When no more additional information can be obtained, the network recruits another unit, and then it again tries to absorb information maximally. Figure 1 shows an actual process of growing by the greedy network-growing algorithm.

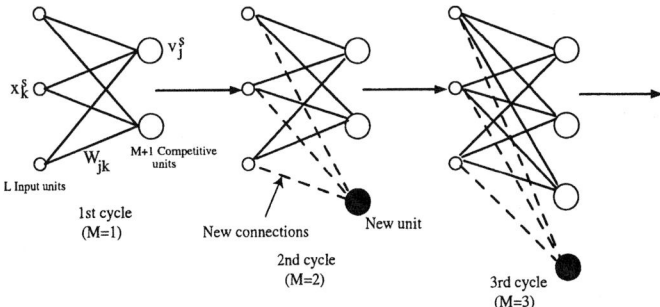

Fig. 1.   A process of network growing by the greedy network-growing algorithm.

Now, we can compute information content in a neural system. We consider information content stored in competitive unit activation patterns. For this purpose, let us define information to be stored in a neural system. Information stored in the system is represented by decrease in uncertainty [5]. Uncertainty decrease, that is, information $I(t)$ at the tth epoch, is defined by

$$I(t) = -\sum_{\forall j} p(j;t) \log p(j;t) + \sum_{\forall s}\sum_{\forall j} p(s)p(j \mid s;t) \log p(j \mid s;t), \qquad (1)$$

where $p(j;t)$, $p(s)$ and $p(j|s;t)$ denote the probability of the jth unit in a system at the tth learning cycle, the probability of the sth input pattern and the conditional probability of the jth unit, given the sth input pattern at the tth epoch, respectively.

Let us present update rules to maximize information content in every stage of learning. For simplicity, we consider the Mth growing cycle, and t denotes the cumulative learning epochs throughout the growing cycles. As shown in Figure 1, a network at the tth epoch is composed of input units x_k^s and competitive units $v_j^s(t)$. The output from the jth competitive unit can be computed by

$$v_j^s(t) = \frac{1}{\sum_{k=1}^{L}(x_k^s - w_{jk}(t))^2}, \qquad (2)$$

where L is the number of input units, and w_{jk} denote connections from the kth input unit to the jth competitive unit. The output is increased as connection weights are closer to input patterns. The conditional probability $p(j \mid s;t)$ at the tth epoch is computed by

$$p(j \mid s;t) = \frac{v_j^s(t)}{\sum_{m=1}^{M+1} v_m^s(t)}, \qquad (3)$$

where M denotes the Mth growing cycle. Since input patterns are supposed to be given uniformly to networks, the probability of the jth competitive unit is computed by

$$p(j;t) = \frac{1}{S}\sum_{s=1}^{S} p(j \mid s;t). \qquad (4)$$

Information $I(t)$ is computed by

$$I(t) = -\sum_{j=1}^{M+1} p(j;t) \log p(j;t) + \frac{1}{S}\sum_{s=1}^{S}\sum_{j=1}^{M+1} p(j \mid s;t) \log p(j \mid s;t). \qquad (5)$$

As information becomes larger, specific pairs of input patterns and competitive units become strongly correlated. Differentiating information with respect to input-competitive connections $w_{jk}(t)$, we have

$$\Delta w_{jk}(t) = -\beta \sum_{s=1}^{S} \left(\log p(j;t) - \sum_{m=1}^{M+1} p(m \mid s;t) \log p(m;t) \right) Q_{jk}^s(t)$$

$$+\beta \sum_{s=1}^{S} \left(\log p(j \mid s;t) - \sum_{m=1}^{M+1} p(m \mid s;t) \log p(m \mid s;t) \right) Q_{jk}^s(t) \quad (6)$$

where β is the learning parameter and

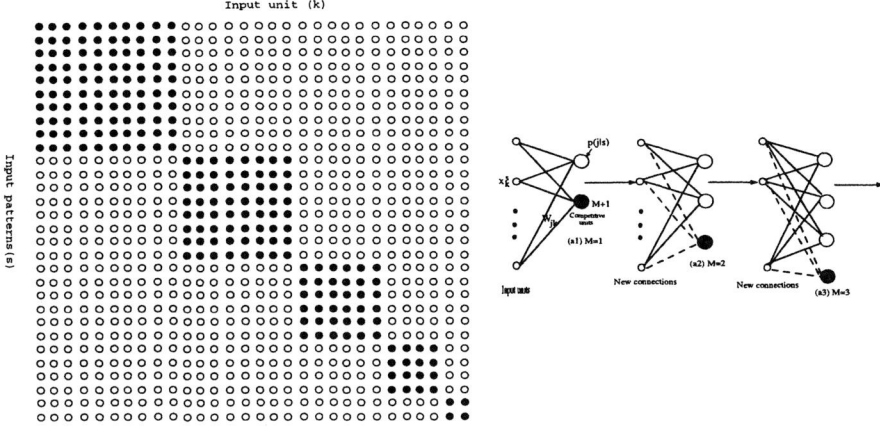

Fig. 2.   Artificial data for the experiment.

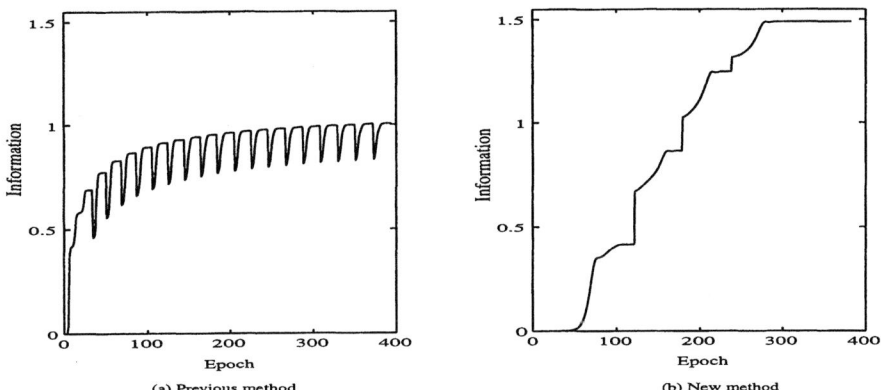

(a) Previous method

(b) New method

Fig. 3.   Information by the previous greedy algorithm (a) and the novel algorithm (b).

$$Q_{jk}^s(t) = \frac{2(x_k^s - w_{jk}(t))}{S \sum_{m=1}^{M+1} v_m^s(t) \left(\sum_{k=1}^{L}(x_k^s - w_{jk}(t))^2\right)^2}. \tag{7}$$

Finally, we should state how to add a new competitive unit, that is, the network shifts to the next cycle. Relative increase in information $R(t)$ is computed by

$$R(t) = \frac{|I(t) - I(t-1)|}{I(t-1)}, \tag{8}$$

where $t = 2, 3, \dots$. If $R(t)$ is less than a certain point ϵ for three consecutive epochs, the network recruits a new competitive unit.

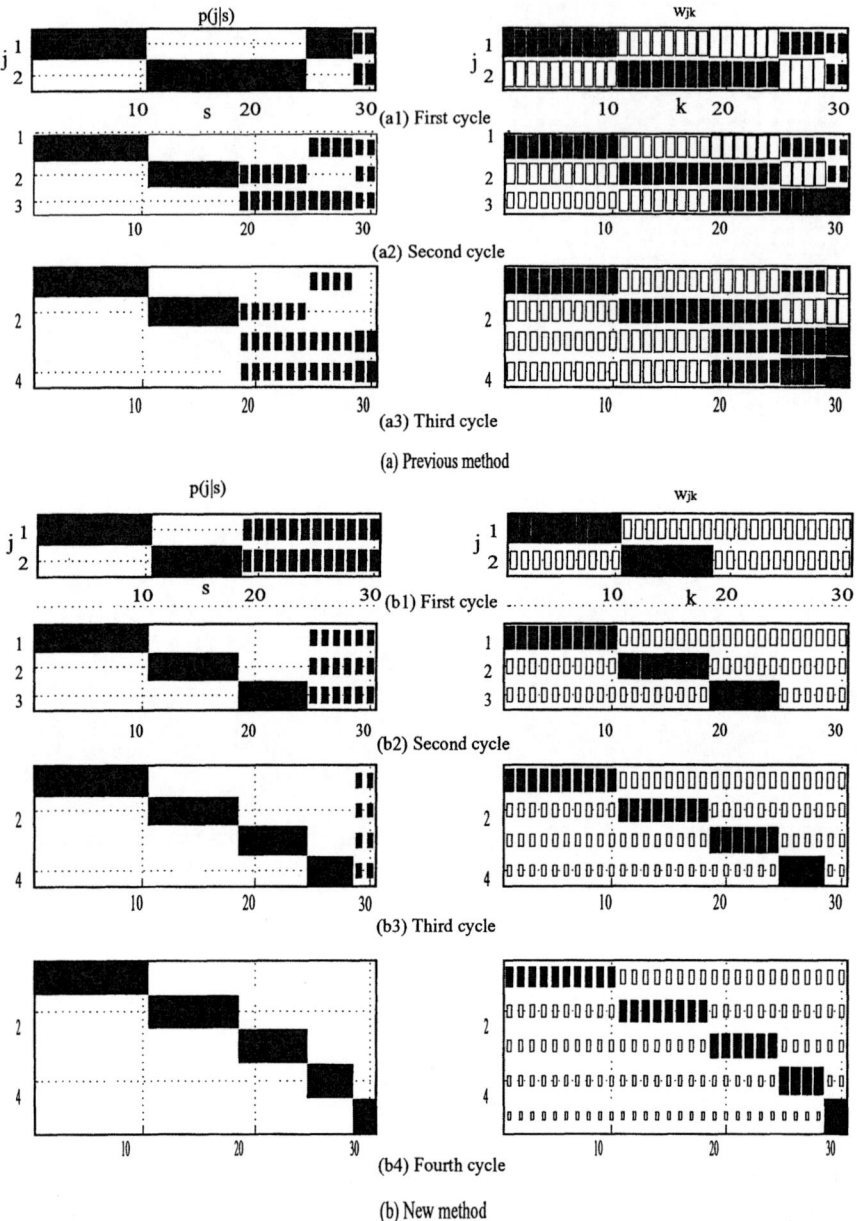

Fig. 4. Competitive unit activation patterns $p(j|s)$ and connection weights w_{jk} by (a) the conventional and (b) the novel method. Black squares represent normalized competitive unit activations (probabilities) $p(j \mid s)$, and their size denotes the activation level. In connection weights, black and white squares show the strength of positive and negative connections.

3   Experimantal Results

In this experiment, we attempt to show that a problem cannot be solved by the conventional greedy network-growing algorithm. In the problem, we have the 30 input patterns shown in Figure 2. The number of competitive units is increased gradually up to 20 with 19 growing cycles. The number of input units is 30. The learning parameter β is 1 for the previous and the new method. To make difference between two methods clearer, input patterns were adjusted to have zero mean and unity standard deviation[1].

Figure 3(a) shows information as a function of the number of epochs by the previous greedy network growing method. Information is rapidly increased in the first growing cycle, and then increase in information in the later growing cycles is significantly decreased. This means that it becomes difficult to extract features by the previous method. On the other hand, Figure 3(b) shows information as a function of the number of epochs by the new method. As shown in the figure, information is significantly increased during different learning cycles and reaches its stable point in about 300 epochs. We can see that information is significantly larger than that achieved by the previous model.

Figure 4(a) show competitive unit activations $p(j|s)$ and connection weights w_{jk} from the first to the third growing cycle by the previous method. In the first and the second growing cycle, features are gradually extracted. However, from the third growing cycle, no additional features can be observed in competitive unit activations as well as connection weights. Figure 4(b) shows competitive unit activations and connection weights from the first to the fourth growing cycles by the new method. As can be seen in the figure, distinct features are gradually extracted. Especially, when we see connection weights, five features are clearly separated.

References

1. R. Kamimura, T. Kamimura, and H. Takeuchi, "Greedy information acquisition algorithm: A new information theoretic approach to dynamic information acquisition in neural networks," *Connection Science*, vol. 13, pp. 323–347,2002.
2. R. Linsker, "Self-organization in a perceptual network," *Computer*, vol. 21, pp. 105–117, 1988.
3. J. J. Atick and A. N. Redlich, "Toward a theory of early visual processing," *Neural Computation*, vol. 2, pp. 308–320, 1990.
4. S. Becker, "Mutual information maximization: models of cortical self-organization," *Network: Computation in Neural Systems*, vol. 7, pp. 7–31, 1996.
5. L. L. Gatlin, *Information Theory and Living Systems*. Columbia University Press, 1972.

---

[1] Without normalization, the new method as well as the conventional method can extract features correctly. We normalized the data for demonstrating clearly the good performance of the new method.

Online Signature Verification Based on Dynamic Feature Segmentation and 3-Step Matching

Heeyong Kwon[1], Eunyong Ha[1], and Heeyeung Hwang[2]

[1] Dept. of Computer Science, Anyang University, Anyang-Shi, 430-714 KOREA
{hykwon, eyha}@aycc.anyang.ac.kr
[2] Dept. of Electronic Engineering, Hoseo University, 337-850 KOREA

Abstract. We propose a new on-line signature verification system based on dynamic feature segmentation and 3 step matching. Conventional segmentation methods are based on the shape of an input signature and it can be forged easily. Since our segmentation method is based on dynamic features such as speed and pressure of a pen, it makes a signature difficult to forge. Then the segments are associated with those of model signatures using augmented dynamic programming (DP) which exploits static features as a restriction condition in order to increase the reliability of matching between two segments. Also whole matching procedure is composed of three steps to minimize two types of errors, Type I and Type II. Our method is very useful to discern a forgery from input signatures. Experiments show the comparing results among on-line signature features, the basis of weights decision for each feature, and the validity of segmentation based on dynamic feature points.

1   Introduction

Signature verification is a part of biometrics widely studied as security systems and becomes more important to authorize on-line transactions and authenticate human identity. With its availability, on-line signature is an effective and practical personal identification method. There are lots of approaches to implement it: Fourier transform, Parametric and Non-parametric approaches, Structural analysis, Tree matching, GA, Neural Network, Fuzzy theory, and DP. They are, except for global feature approaches such as Fourier transform and Parametric ones, implemented by seeking the distance between each pair of corresponding segments after segmenting input signatures. It is well known that segmentation before matching two signatures is very useful for the precise operation because even two on-line signatures generated by a person are different in spatial and time domain [1,2,3]. DP algorithm has been used widely for this purpose. It, however, tends to find the best alignment between two signals [4] and does not reflect the structural information of the signal. Therefore, it has difficulty in discerning a forgery from input signatures.

J. Liu et al. (Eds.): IDEAL 2003, LNCS 2690, pp. 1062–1065, 2003.

In this paper, we propose a new segmentation method based on dynamic features and show why it is better than conventional one. Also we propose a three step matching system that minimizes trade-off between Type I and Type II errors. The remaining sections are organized as follows: Section 2 introduces the proposed system structure. The result of feature analysis and the new segmentation examples are presented in section 3. Finally, the conclusion is described.

2   Online Signature Verification

2.1   Preprocessing

Input signals of an on-line signature are inadequate for verification because of instrumental and user's factors. In the preprocessing step, it is necessary to remove the unstable factors in an input signal and make the successive process efficient. Preprocessing for on-line signature is composed of smoothing, concatenation, slant and size normalization.

2.2   Segmentation

There are two approaches for matching two signatures; one is based on global features and the other on local features. 'Matching after segmentation' as a unified method that exploits pros of both is known as an effective way. Conventional segmentation methods are mainly based on shapes of input signature such as acute angle points. A signature, however, might be forged easily because the segmentation position can be conjectured. Also the segmentation can be incorrect by misalignment between two signatures when the signatures have complicated forms.

To solve these problems, we propose a new segmentation method. First, it extracts points that the speed of input is over the sum of the average and the variance of them.

$$V(p_i) > Vm + Vd \qquad (1)$$

In here, $V(p_i)$ is the speed of i-th point, Vm the average speed of a signature and Vd the variance of a signature. After extracting such points from reference signatures and input signature, matching pairs are selected using DP algorithm. The static features are used for complementing the drawbacks of dynamic features like speed.

$$d(i, j) = \begin{cases} |a_i - b_i|, & \text{if ang }(a_i, b_i) < 135 \\ P, & \text{if ang }(a_i, b_i) > 135 \,. \end{cases} \qquad (2)$$

In this equation, a_i and b_i are lists of points of reference and input signatures respectively, $d(i, j)$ is the speed difference between point i and j, ang(a_i, b_i) is the direction difference, and P is a penalty for undesirable matching.

2.3   Feature Extraction

Features and its extraction methods for on-line signature verification have been studied widely. There are 75 extractable features in an on-line signature [5]. Most studies base on the subset of them as input features. In this paper, we calculate averages and variances of them, and compute the ratio between the two for each feature respectively (Fig. 1). Then we assign high weights to small ratio features.

2.4   Three Step Matching

Matching is the procedure that measures similarity between two signatures and decides whether they are from the same person or not. The higher criterion it has, the more secure it is, but the more difficult to pass, even the owner is. They are known as Type I and II errors. They are trade-off relation and not reduced simultaneously. We divide the whole procedure into three steps. In the first and the second steps, we reduce Type II error. In the last step, we reduce Type I error.

   In the first step, the spent time and the number of the strokes for two signatures are compared. In the second step, static features of each segment are compared with corresponding one, too (Eq. 3) .

$$S = \sum_i \sum_j \sum_k (|M_{ijk} - I_{ijk}|) \tag{3}$$
$$If(S < S_{th}) \text{ then PASS else REJECT,}$$

where S is a similarity (distance) between two static features, S_{th} is a threshold of each feature comparing, i is a stroke number, j is a segment number, k is a static feature number, M is a reference signature and I is a input signature.

In the last step, dynamic features are compared in the same way with the second step.

3   Experiments

Two experiments show the effectiveness of the proposed method. First, to compare and analyze 75 features of signatures, we gather 10 one-stroke signatures of two persons each. We divide each signature into three segments, and calculate the average, the variance and its ratio (Fig. 1). In the figure, the values are limited under 300 (over for minus). Next, to show the effectiveness of the proposed segmentation method, we present the segmentation results of the two persons' signatures (Fig. 2).

4   Conclusion

Conventional on-line signature verification methods that compare similarity between corresponding segments after segmentation, are based on the static features and might be forged easily. Proposed method uses dynamic features for segmentation. It is, therefore, difficult to make a forgery and the same person's signatures are segmented consistently as in Fig. 2. Experimental results show the effectiveness of the system. Also we present the feature selection criterion for the segment matching through the analysis of 75 features. It is used for deciding the weights of each feature. The most difficult thing in signature verification is that most users are not familiar with an electric pen. We are currently modifying the system as an adaptive one.

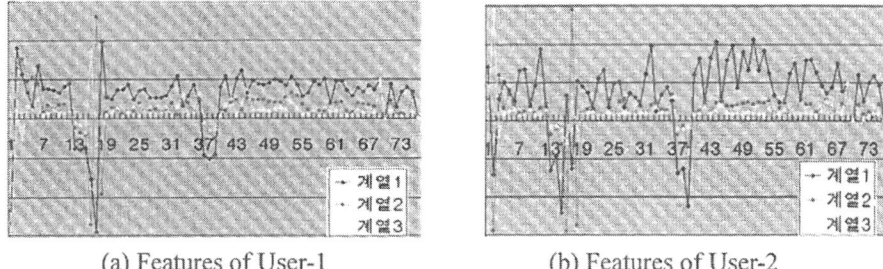

(a) Features of User-1   (b) Features of User-2

Fig. 1. 75 features of 3 segments of 2 users.

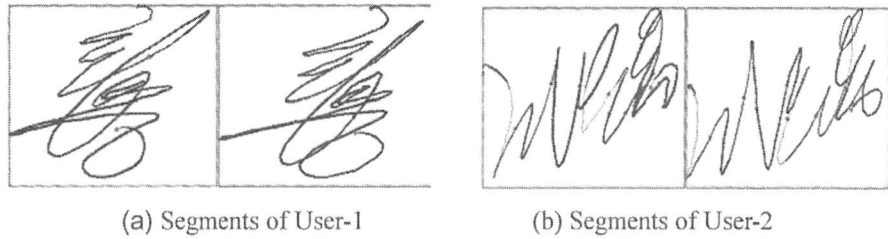

(a) Segments of User-1   (b) Segments of User-2

Fig. 2. Comparison of segmentation results of 2 users.

References

1. Rhee, T., Cho, S., and Kim, J.: 'On-Line Signature Verification Using Model-Guided Segmentation and Discriminative Feature Selection for Skilled Forgeries', Sixth International Conf. on Document Analysis and Recognition (2001) 645–649

2. Lee, W., Mohankrishnan, N., and Paulik, M.: 'Improved Segmentation through Dynamic Time Warping for Signature Verification using a Neural Network Classifier', ICIP98, Vol.2 (1998) 929–933

3. Yue, K., and Wijesoma, W.: 'Improved Segmentation and Segment Association for On-line Signature Verification', International Conf. on Systems, Man, and Cybernetics, Vol.4 (2000) 2752–2756

4. Parizeau, M., and Plamondon, R.: 'A Comparative Analysis of Regional Correlation, Dynamic Time Warping, and Skeletal Tree Matching for Signature Verification', IEEE Trans. on PAMI, Vol. 12, No. 7, Jul. (1990) 710–717

5. Hewitt D. Crane and John S. Ostrem: 'Automatic Signature Verification Using a Three-Axis Force-Sensitive Pen', IEEE Trans. on SMC, Vol. 13, No. 3, May. (1983) 329–337

Investigation of ART2-Based Audio-to-Visual Conversion for Multimedia Applications

Jin-Jang Lin, Chi-Wen Hsieh, and Tai-Lang Jong

Dept. of Electrical Engineering, National Tsing Hua University, Hsinchu, Taiwan, ROC
tljong@ee.nthu.edu.tw

Abstract. Audio-to-visual synchronization is important for multimedia applications involving talking human, either natural or synthetic. Close correlation exists between the acoustic speech signal and visible lip movement that can be exploited in developing real-time audio-to-visual conversions. In this article, we apply ART2 and a multi-audio-frame technique to derive lip movement sequence from its corresponding audio speech stream. The training process of ART2 is fast and it is capable of learning new things without necessarily forgetting things learned in the past. In the case of multi-user adaptation, we proposed a system which uses one user's ART2 model as the reference model together with audio adapting and visual learning mechanism for new user adaptation. The audio adaptation maps new user's audio features into reference model audio features, and the visual learning makes the reference ART2 model learn the new speech characteristics of the new user. Experimental results had shown that the proposed ART2-based method is both fast and effective for single user and multiuser.

1 Introduction

Research on creating friendly human interfaces between a human and a computer, or between human in distant locations flourished lately, partly because of the advances in computer, multimedia and internet technologies. One such style involves using an avatar, others might use a synthetic animated human face to provide an effective and efficient "face-to-face" multimodal communication channel in the distributed collaboration environments. Most of them adopt a real-time speech-driven face animation technique to avoid the need of directly transmitting the much larger-sized video data in order to meet the real time interpersonal communication requirement. The audio-to-visual conversion plays an important role in such real-time speech-driven face animation systems. In this article, we focus on the study of deriving the lip movement of a human user from its corresponding speech signal used in a speech-driven facial expression animation system. Many methods have been reported in the past for solving this problem. Generally, they maybe categorized into three approaches: (1) Classification-based approach, e.g., VQ, LVQ [1][2], and neural networks [1][2]. This approach treats the audio-visual conversion as a classification

J. Liu et al. (Eds.): IDEAL 2003, LNCS 2690, pp. 1066–1070, 2003.

problem. (2) Regression-based approach. The second approach treats the problem as a nonlinear regression one and tries to build the functional mapping between the audio input and visual output. The multi-layer perceptron [2], the Gaussian mixture model [3][4][5], and the time delay neural network [6] belong to this category. The MLP and TDNN used back-propagation algorithm to find the audio-visual mapping by minimizing the mean square-error. The GMM tries to build the joint Gaussian probability distribution function of the audio and visual features by utilizing the expectation-maximization algorithm to find the maximal likelihood estimate of the mixture model parameter.   (3) Speech recognition-based approach. The third approach first uses speech recognition techniques to process audio input signal. Then a mapping is used to find the visual output from the recognized speech. The Hidden Markov Model [7][8] is frequently used in this approach. Generally, this approach requires a lot of computations.

ART [9][10] is a kind of classification-base conversion, operating like human's memory. ART network has a good ability not only to memorize past knowledge but also to learn new object. In the real-time interpersonal multimedia communication, the transmitting efficiency is dominant in internet, however to accomplish constructing an enough database for modeling is a complicated challenge practically. Fortunately, ART algorithm can reduce the computational complexity of training that incremental learning is possible. The classification capability of ART2 can nicely segment the audio-visual training data into many small independent groups, thus decreases the complexity of the training for the audio-to-visual conversion system. Consequently, to combine all training patterns and new model retraining can be ignored when new training patterns are input. The complexity of training phase and the transmitting efficiency will be decreased and increased, alternatively.

2 Adaptive Resonance Theory 2

The architecture of ART2 contains two major subsystems: the attention subsystem and orienting subsystem. The attention subsystem includes F1 layer and F2 layer. The buffer 'r' belongs to the orienting subsystem. Patterns of activity that develop over the units in the two layers of the attention subsystem are called short time memory (STM) traces because they exist only in association with a single application of an input vector. The weights associated with bottom-up and top-down connections between F1 and F2 layers are called long time memory (LTM) traces because they encode information that remains a part of the network for an extended period. The main processes of ART2 consist of four steps as summarized below:

Preprocess. Normalize and encode the input pattern. This process works in the F1.

Choice. Find in LTM, and choose the best match data trained in the past. This work proceeds between LTM and F2 layer.

Match. Decide the best match data is similar enough to input pattern. This process acts in buffer 'r' block.

Adaptation. If the best match data and input pattern matches, adapt the LTM. If input data mismatch for any data in the past, add the input data into LTM.

3 Audio-Visual Conversion in Single-User Case

The ART2 model is used to build the mapping of lip movement sequence from its corresponding audio speech features for a single user. To illustrate the effectiveness of the proposed method, an English speech collection downloaded from CMU at http://amp.ece.cmu.edu/_download/Intel/feature_data.html was used as our database There are ten subjects (seven males and three females) in this collection, and each subject speaks seventy-eight isolated vocabularies for ten times. The speech format is 16 bit 44.1k Hz PCM. The corresponding positions of the lips are given as six lip parameters describing the left and right corner coordinates of the mouth and heights of the upper and lower the lips in a rate of 30 frames per second. We use first eight pronunciations of each vocabulary for each subject as the training data, and last two times as the testing data. The audio speech waveforms are first resampled from 44.1kHz stereo to 8kHz mono to reduce data size. The size is further reduced as the extracting the speech features. The line spectral pair of the speech signal was used as audio features in our experiments. 12 orders of LSP were calculated for each 240 samples audio frame. The ART2 was then used to classify the audio features. After the completion of ART2 training, the audio features were segmented into several separated classes. Each output neuron of the F2 layer represents a class of the audio signals. The width and height of the corresponding lips movement for each class of audio signals are then built from the training data.

In simulation, we try to compare the effect of single audio frame vs. multi audio frames. It is known that coarticulation plays an important role in establishing the audio-visual mapping model. To show this effect, the audio signals to ART2 are extended from a single basic frame to three frames, and five frames to grasp the temporal variations. The results indicate that with the increase of the audio frame number, the error ratio in estimating the corresponding lips height and width will decrease for all users because the effect of coarticulation.

In the second case, the training data set is partitioned into two equal parts and the first part is submitted for training alone. After converged, the second part is submitted as new data to ART2 for training. In the third case, the training data is partitioned into 4 equal parts and submitted to ART2 for training one by one after the previous part has reached convergence. The last case treats the training data as 8 separate equal parts and similar training procedure repeats for each part. If ART2 should forget the already-learned patterns while learning new ones, the final audio-visual conversion will suffer an obvious degradation in error ratio, which did not occur in our experiment. The error ratios for all four cases are roughly the same, which supports the fact that ART2 do have the incremental learning capability.

Finally, for comparison purpose, we compare the results of ART2 with those of a commonly used Gaussian Mixture Model (GMM) method. The GMM is based on the expectation-maximization (EM) algorithm and is widely used in speech recognition and audio-visual conversion [3]. The EM algorithm can find the likelihood estimate of GMM parameter. The process of GMM is listed in [3]. The comparison is made based on different views (i.e., time for training, time for testing, error ratio, size of model parameters) as listed below. In the simulations, the GMM uses six mixture models and its training epoch is 500. For ART2, the number of classes is less then 1500.

(1). Time for training. Since the GMM can only find local optimal solution, one has to guess the initial GMM parameters as many times as possible to find a better solution, which is not necessary for ART2. Therefore, in the learning phase, ART2 is faster than GMM.

(2). Time for testing.   When the size of testing pattern is 30 and the dimension of pattern is 12, the testing time is as follows (executed on an AMD Althelon 700 PC) ART2 (1500 class) : 0.0333 sec, and GMM (6 mixture models) : 0.0402 sec

(3). Error ratio. Fig. 4 plots the error ratio of ART2 and GMM. The ART2 and GMM almost have the same error ratio for all users.

(4). Size of model parameters. ART2: 12*1500+1500+1500=21000 byte, and GMM: 14*6+6*14*14+6=1266 byte

4 Multi-user Adaption

It is known that the audio and visual features are person dependent. A simple way to accommodate multi-users in the audio-driven face animation system is to include an audio-visual mapping model for each user. In simulation, we discuss the effects of different training steps to this system. The reference ART2 model was built using Database1 (Anne), and the new user is Chris (Database 3). The first eight pronunciations of each word of Database 3 is used as the training data for audio adapting and building the output mapping table, the remaining ones are used as testing data. Each audio feature consists of 5 frames with 12 orders LSP coefficients per frame. The first experiment uses no adaptation. In the second experiment, we adapt the audio feature only without visual learning. In the third experiment, we adapt both audio and visual features. The result is much better than that with only audio adaptation. Moreover, once the reference ART2 model has been built, a new user would require only 3024 bytes for establishing its audio and visual adaptation parameters, a drastic reduction from 21000 bytes per user if we build a separate ART2 model for each new user, as shown below. Therefore, the proposed scheme is suitable for multi-user applications.

   Single user: 12*1500+1500+1500 = 21000 byte
   Multi-users: 12+12+1500+1500 = 3024 byte

   The second simulation, the effect of choosing different user as reference model will be discussed. The average testing error is between 5.5 % and 6% for choosing different user as reference model. The small difference in average error again justifies the validity of the audio-adapting and visual-learning idea.

5 Conclusion

In this article, we have presented methods using the ART2 for exploiting audio-visual correlation to derive lip movement from its corresponding audio speech signal. Temporal effect of audio signal is considered by using multi-audio-frames in the mapping process. The advantages of ART2 are its fast training process and capable of learning new things without necessarily forgetting things learned in the past. The size of output mapping table might be its disadvantage. In the case of multi-user adaptation, we proposed a system which uses one user's ART2 model as the reference model together with audio-adapting and visual-learning mechanism for new user adaptation. The audio-adaptation maps new user's audio features into reference model audio features, and the visual-learning makes the reference ART2 model learn the new speech-lip movement characteristics of the new user. Experimental results had shown that the proposed ART2-based method is both fast and effective in performing audio-to-visual conversions for single user and multi-user situations.

Acknowledgement. This work is supported in part by the National Science Council of Taiwan under Grants NSC 91-2219-E-007-021.

References

1. D. G. Stork, G. Wolff, and E. Levine, "Neural network lipreading system for improved speech recognition," in *Proc. Int. Joint Conf. Neural Networks,* pp. 285–295, 1992.
2. Simon Haykin, "Neural Networks," Prentice Hall, pp. 156-255, pp. 466–473, 1999.
3. Ram R. Rao, Tsuhan Chen, "Audio-to-Visual Conversion for Multimedia Communication," *IEEE Transactions on Industrial Electronics*, Vol. 45, No.1, pp. 15–22, Feb. 1998.
4. Ram R. Rao, Tsuhan Chen, "Audio-to-Visual Integration in Multimedia Communication," *Proceedings of the IEEE*, Vol. 86, No.5, pp. 837–852, May 1998.
5. Yao-Jen Chang, Chih-Chung Chen, Jen-Chung Chou, and Yung-Chang Chen, "Virtual Talk: A Model-Based Virtual Phone Using a Layered Audio-Visual Integration," *IEEE Multimedia and Expo, 2000. ICME 2000. 2000 IEEE International Conference on Multimedia and Expo ,* Volume: 1 , vol.1, pp. 415–418, 2000.
6. Fabio Lavagetto, "Time-Delay Neural Networks for Estimating Lip Movements From Speech Analysis: A Useful Tool in Audio-Video Synchronization," *IEEE Transactions on Circuits and systems for Video Technology*, Vol. 7, No.5, pp. 786–800, 1997.
7. R. Rao, R. Mersereau, Tsuhan Chen, "Using HMM's in Audio-to Visual Conversion," *IEEE 1997 First Workshop on Multimedia Signal Processing*, pp. 19–24, 1997.
8. KyoungHo Choi, Jeng-Neng Hwang, "Baum-Welch Hidden Markov Model Inversion for Reliable Audio-to-Visual Conversion", *IEEE 3rd Workshop on Multimedia Signal Processing (MMSP99)*, pp. 175 –180, Copenhagen, Denmark, pp. 13–15, Sep.1999
9. G. A. Carpenter, S. Grossberg, "Art2:Self-organization of stable category recognition codes for analog input patterns" *Applied Optics*, 26(23): 4919–4930, 1997.
10. G. A. Carpenter, S. Grossberg, "The art of adaptive pattern recognition by self-organizing neural network," *IEEE computer*, 21(3):77–88, March 1988.

Spatiotemporal Restoration of Regions Occluded by Text in Video Sequences

Chang Woo Lee[1], Hyun Kang[1], Kyung Mi Lee[1], Keechul Jung[2], and
Hang Joon Kim[1]

[1]Dept. of Computer Engineering, Kyungpook National University,
Daegu, 702-701, Korea
{cwlee, hkang, kmlee, kimhj}@ailab.knu.ac.kr
[2]School of Media, College of Information Science, Soongsil University,
Seoul, 156-743, Korea
kcjung@ssu.ac.kr

Abstract. Occasionally, there is a case in which text inserted manually in a video sequence for convenience of viewers is unnecessary for reuse of that video. For reusability, we propose an approach for automatic detection and removal of caption text using an SVM and spatiotemporal restoration in video sequences. After detecting text using an SVM, we restore the regions occluded by the text using a spatiotemporal restoration scheme. The proposed approach includes many applications such as translation of captions and replacement of indirect advertisements in videos.

1 Introduction

These days, indirect advertisements are prevalent and easily found in TV programs and movie scenes. Recently, several approaches to the automatic detection and removal of objects of interest have been proposed [1-5]. Objects of interest in these fields include blotches, scratches, flaws, noises, or text characters in images or videos.

Detection and removal of blotches and line scratches in an image sequence is closely related to text detection [6, 8, 9] and removal in video sequences [1]. Bertalmio et al. presented a method that used a partial differential equation to the inpainting problem, and applied it to remove pre-specified regions and artificially inserted text in images [2]. Chan and Shen [3] proposed a similar approach based on curvature driven diffusions. As the application part of the flaw removal in photographs, films, and images, Wei and Levoy [4] used tree-structured vector quantization for texture synthesis. These approaches may hardly produce good results in cases in which the surrounding areas of the region to be restored are poorly textured. Irani and Peleg [5] used image motion information extracted from an image sequence for image enhancement and reconstruction of occlusion.

In this paper, we describe an approach for spatiotemporal restoration of the occluded regions by text in which text detection and removal techniques are incorporated in video sequences. We need two techniques for this purpose; one for detecting text regions in an image, and the other for removing the text regions and simultaneously

J. Liu et al. (Eds.): IDEAL 2003, LNCS 2690, pp. 1071–1075, 2003.
© Springer-Verlag Berlin Heidelberg 2003

restoring the background occluded by the text in the video sequence. For detecting the text in an image we use an SVM-based text detection method. For restoring the background regions, we perform temporal restoration between consecutive frames and then spatial restoration in the rest. We call it *spatiotemporal restoration*. Fig. 1 shows how to perform the automatic text detection and removal using the combined technique which the input is a video sequence including text and the output is the text removed video sequence.

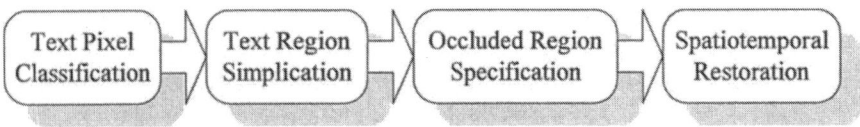

Fig. 1. Flow of the combined technique for spatiotemporal restoration.

2   Text Detection

We classify the pixels in an image into text pixels and non-text pixels using the SVM in which the textural properties of its local neighborhood are trained. The reader may refer to [6, 7] for more details.

As in previous works [7, 8], we also simplify the output of the SVM. First, we produce the potential text regions using four-connected component analysis. The boundaries of each potential text region are adjusted using the histogram distribution of the text pixels included in each bounding box. For example, in the left boundary, the new boundary is set to the left-most position when the vertical projection value of text pixels exceeds 1/10 of the width of that bounding box. The same strategies are applied in each left, right, top, and bottom boundaries of all the bounding boxes. Then, among the potential text regions, non-text regions that hardly include text are removed using several heuristics as follows:

(1) In a text region, the number of pixels classified as a text pixel should be larger than 1/3 of the area of the bounding box.

(2) The height of a text region should be larger than 1/30 of the height of the image.

(3) The width of a text region should exceed half of the height of the text region.

Regions violating these three rules are not text regions anymore. The results of the bounding box filtering step are rectangular bounding boxes representing text regions.

The target region of the spatiotemporal restoration is not the whole of a detected text region, but only the text pixels in the region not including the background. In order to extract only text pixels from a text region we use a simple thresholding scheme on the assumption that the text color in a text region is brighter than that of the background. Usually, the artificially inserted text has black boundary pixels to emphasize itself and distinguish itself from the similarly colored background. Therefore, to include the highlighting pixels and remove small holes, we expand the extracted text pixels by using a morphological operation (dilation). We call these expanded text regions the occluded regions.

3   Text Removal Using Spatiotemporal Restoration

We perform occluded region restoration using a combined method of temporal restoration in consecutive frames and spatial restoration in the residual regions. The spatiotemporal restoration is completed as a weighted sum of the spatial restoration and temporal restoration as following Eq. (1).

$$\hat{I}(i,j,t) = \alpha \hat{I}_T(i,j,t) + (1-\alpha)\hat{I}_S(i,j,t), \tag{1}$$

where α is a weighting coefficient, $\hat{I}_T(i,j,t)$ and $\hat{I}_S(i,j,t)$ are the results of temporal restoration and spatial restoration at time t for a pixel value in position (i, j) respectively.

To restore the occluded regions in a video sequence, we use both spatial and temporal information associated with the text regions. For the temporal restoration, we use the text motions estimated in the sequence classification, and the background motions selectively estimated using a BMA. The temporal restoration at time t using motion estimation results is performed as following Eq. (2).

$$\hat{I}_T(i,j,t) = I(i+d_1^b, j+d_2^b, t-1), \tag{2}$$

where $(i+d_1^b, j+d_2^b) \notin TextArea(i,j,t-1)$. $TextArea$ stands for the occluded regions in each frame and $TextArea(i,j,t-1) = TextArea(i+d_1^t, j+d_2^t, t)$. $I(i,j,t-1)$ is the pixel value of the position (i, j) at time t-1. d^t and d^b are the text motion vector and the background motion vector of the block including (i,j), respectively.

For estimating motion vectors we assume the background and the text regions have only simple linear motion so we can use a simple translational model, minimum absolute difference (MAD). In the background motion estimation step, even though a block includes only one text pixel, we do not estimate the background motion of the block. Instead, the motions of the occluded regions are approximated to the average of 8-neighboring background motions in which the text blocks are excluded. After forward mapping from the previous frame to the current frame using estimated motion vectors, the text pixels in the occluded regions in a current frame are restored temporally by copying the corresponding background pixels in the previous frame. If the pixels to be copied in a previous frame are the text pixels, we do not copy them.

To remove the occluded pixels remaining after the temporal restoration, we use the 'image inpainting' algorithm as the spatial restoration algorithm. The image inpainting algorithm devised by Bertalmio et al. [2] is a method for restoring damaged parts of an image and automatically filling in selected regions with surrounding information. Since the topology of text regions is hardly known in advance and the surrounding texture is degraded in the video sequences dealt with in the proposed method, we use the inpainting algorithm that is insensitive to the surrounding texture and the topology of the region to be filled-in.

4 Experimental Results

We have tested the proposed method using video clips collected from movies and animations. The sizes of the video frames used during the experiments ranged from 352×240 to 720×400. In this investigation, we tested the proposed method using four types of video sequences: stationary text on stationary background, stationary text on dynamically varying background, moving text on stationary background and moving text on dynamically varying background. We estimated text motion using a region-based model and the background motions using a block-based model. In spatiotemporal restoration, if a pixel at (i, j) is temporally restored, α in Eq. (1) is set to 1, otherwise 0. During the spatial restoration, anisotropic diffusion was interleaved with one per tenth inpainting loop to ensure noise insensitivity and preserve the sharpness of edges [2, 10].

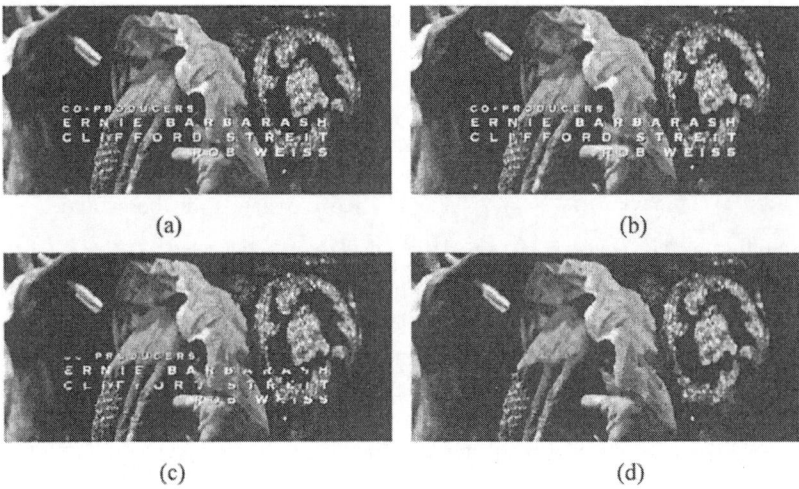

(a)   (b)

(c)   (d)

Fig. 2. Results of the spatiotemporal restoration; (a) current frame, (b) previous frame, (c) result of temporal restoration, and (d) final result of spatiotemporal restoration.

In the case of a video sequence in which the text is stationary on a dynamically varying background as shown in Fig. 2, we can restore only the uncovered regions caused by the background movement. Fig. 2 (a) and (b) are a current frame and a previous frame sized 640×304, (c) shows the temporal restoration result. Fig. 2 (d) shows the result of the spatiotemporal restoration. If we directly restore the occluded region without performing temporal restoration, the computational complexity in the spatial restoration is high. Due to the temporal information, the results of the restoration become more reliable and information in the previous frame can be utilized.

5 Conclusion

In this paper, we proposed an approach for spatiotemporal restoration of the regions occluded by text in a video sequence in which the text detection and removal techniques are incorporated. Experimental results suggest potential uses of the automatic text detection and removal in digital videos. The proposed method can be adapted to text removal in still images and stationary/moving text on the stationary/dynamically varying background as well. If it is needed to erase text, captions, or brand marks in video frames, the proposed method makes the whole process automatic.

Acknowledgement. This work was supported by the Soongsil University Research Fund.

References

1. Kokaram A. C. , Morris R. D., Fitzgerald W. J., and Rayner P. J. W., 1995. Interpolation of Missing Data in Image Sequences. IEEE Transaction on Image Processing, 4 (11), 1509–1519.
2. Bertalmio M., Sapiro G., Vicent Caselles and Coloma Ballester, 2000. Image Inpainting. Siggraph 2000 Conference Proceedings, 417–424.
3. Chan T. and Shen J., "Inpainting, zooming, and edge coding, 2001. Special Session on Inverse Problems and Image Analysis at the AMS Annual Conference, January.
4. Wei L. Y. and Levoy M., 2000. Fast Texture Systhesis using Tree-structured Vector Quantization. Siggraph 2000 Conference Proceedings, 479–488.
5. Irani M., Peleg S., 1993. Motion Analysis for Image Enhancement: Resolution, Occlusion, and Transparency. Journal on Visual Communications and Image Representation, 4 (4) 324-335.
6. Kim K. I., Jung K., Park S. H., and Kim H. J., 2001. Support Vector Machine-based Text Detection in Digital Video. Pattern Recognition, 34 (2), 527–529.
7. Kim K. I., Jung K., Park S. H., Kim H. J., 2002. Support Vector Machines for Texture Classification. IEEE Transactions on Pattern Analysis and Machine Intelligence, 24 (11), 1542–1550.
8. Jeong, K. Y., Jung, K., Kim, E. Y., and Kim, H. J., 1999. Neural Network-based Text Location for News Video Indexing. Proceedings of International Conference of Image Processing.
9. K. Jung, 2001. Neural network-based Text Location in Color Images, Pattern Recognition Letters, Vol. 22, No. 14, pp 1503–1515.
10. Perona P. and Malik J., 1990. Scale-space and edge detection using anisotropic diffusion. IEEE Trans. on Pattern Analysis and Machine Intelligence, 12 (7), 629–639.

A Non-parametric Image Segmentation Algorithm Using an Orthogonal Experimental Design Based Hill-Climbing

Kual-Zheng Lee, Wei-Che Chuang, and Shinn-Ying Ho

Department of Information Engineering, Feng Chia University
100 Wenhwa Rd., Taichung, Taiwan 407
syho@fcu.edu.tw

Abstract. Image segmentation is an important process in image processing. Clustering-based image segmentation algorithms have a number of advantages such as continuous contour and non-threshold. However, most of the clustering-based image segmentation algorithms may occur an oversegmentation problem or need numerous control parameters depending on image. In this paper, a non-parametric clustering-based image segmentation algorithm using an orthogonal experimental design based hill-climbing is proposed. For solving the oversegmentation problem, a general-purpose evaluation function is used in the algorithm. Experimental results of natural images demonstrate the effectiveness of the proposed algorithm.

1 Introduction

Image segmentation is one of the most important tasks in image processing, having a wide range of applications in pattern recognition, motion analysis, and image coding [1,2]. A large amount of segmentation algorithms with different segmentation criteria have been developed [3], which be categorized into four classes: edge-based [4], region-based [5,6], clustering-based [7,8], and split/merge approaches [9,10]. In this paper, a non-parametric image segmentation algorithm OEDIS using an orthogonal experimental design (OED) based hill-climbing is proposed, which belongs to clustering-based approaches. OEDIS can generate a set of candidate solutions using a number of perturbation operations and then systematically reasons a good solution for each iteration based on OED [11,12]. The high performance of OEDIS is compared with those of the K-means [7], FCM [8], GA, and SA.

2 Evaluation of Segmentation Quality

The incorporated criteria of image segmentation are: 1) the regions must be uniform and homogeneous; 2) the region's interiors must be simple, without too many small holes; and 3) adjacent regions must present significantly different values for uniform characteristics. Borsotti *et al.* proposed a general-purpose evaluation function [13] for evaluating the segmentation quality of color images, which is defined as:

J. Liu et al. (Eds.): IDEAL 2003, LNCS 2690, pp. 1076–1081, 2003.
© Springer-Verlag Berlin Heidelberg 2003

$$\min F(S) = \frac{1}{10000(W \times H)} \sqrt{R} \times \sum_{i=1}^{R} \left[\frac{e_i^2}{1 + \log A_i} + \left(\frac{R(A_i)}{A_i} \right)^2 \right], \tag{1}$$

where the symbols are defined as follows: 1) S, the solution of the segmented image; 2) $W \times H$, the image size; 3) R, the number of regions of the segmented image; 4) e_i, the average color error of the i-th region; 5) A_i, the area of the i-th region; and 6) $R(A_i)$, the number of regions having exactly area A_i. In this paper, Eq.(1) is used as the objective function of OEDIS.

3   Orthogonal Experimental Design Based Hill-Climbing

3.1   Orthogonal Array and Factor Analysis

The proposed orthogonal experimental design based hill-climbing can generate a set of candidate solutions based on OED. An efficient way to study the effect of several factors simultaneously is to use OED with both orthogonal array (OA) and factor analysis [11,12]. In this section, the concepts of OA and factor analysis will be presented. The two-level OA used in the OED based hill-climbing is described below. Let there be γ factors with two levels for each factor. The total number of experiments is 2^γ for the popular "one-factor-at-a-time" study. To establish an OA of γ factors with two levels, we obtain an integer $\omega = 2^{\lceil \log_2(\gamma+1) \rceil}$, build an orthogonal array $L_\omega(2^{\omega-1})$ with ω rows and $\omega-1$ columns, use the first γ columns, and ignore the other $\omega-\gamma-1$ columns. The algorithm of constructing OAs can be found in [12].

After proper tabulation of experimental results, the summarized data are analyzed using factor analysis to determine the relative effects of levels of various factors. Let y_t denote an objective value of the combination corresponding to the experiment t, where $t = 1, \ldots, \omega$. Define the main effect of factor j with level k as S_{jk} where $j = 1, \ldots, \gamma$ and $k = 1, 2$:

$$S_{jk} = \sum_{t=1}^{\omega} y_t \times f_t, \tag{2}$$

where $f_t = 1$ if the level of factor j of experiment t is k; otherwise, $f_t = 0$. Considering the case that the objective function is to be minimized, the level 1 of factor j makes a better contribution to the objective function than level 2 of factor j does when $S_{j1} < S_{j2}$. If $S_{j1} > S_{j2}$, level 2 is better. If $S_{j1} = S_{j2}$, levels 1 and 2 have the same contribution. After the better one of two levels of each factor is determined, an intelligent combination consisting of all factors with the better level can be easily derived. OED is effective for development design of efficient search for the intelligent combination of factor levels.

3.2   OED Based Hill-Climbing

The proposed OED based hill-climbing is described as follows:

Step 1: Randomly select γ perturbation candidates from a current solution S. One perturbation operation is treated as a factor.

Step 2: Use the first γ columns of an OA $L_\omega(2^{\omega-1})$. Let level 1 (level 2) of a factor represent that the corresponding perturbation is disabled (enabled).

Step 3: Evaluate the objective function value y_t of the combinations corresponding to the experiment t, where $t=1,\ldots,\omega$.

Step 4: Compute the main effect S_{jk} where $j=1,\ldots,\gamma$ and $k=1, 2$.

Step 5: Determine the better one of two levels of each factor based on the main effect.

Step 6: The reasoned combination R consists of all factors with the better levels.

Step 7: The candidate solution Q is selected from the best one of the combinations corresponding to the experiments 2 to ω, and R if $R \neq S$. The combination of experiment 1 corresponds to the solution S.

3.3   Proposed OEDIS

For 8-bits gray-scale images, a solution is a bit string consisting 255 elements whose values are g_i, $i \in \{0, 1\}$. The number of 1's element in a solution is fixed to γ. If $g_i=1$ then the gray value i is a parting between two clusters. The search space of this encoding method is $C(255, \gamma)$. In this paper, a simple swap scheme is applied as perturbation operations, which is performed by randomly select γ (0, 1) pairs in a solution S and swap it. The proposed OEDIS is described as follows:

Step 1: Input a test image and transfer it into gray-scale type.

Step 2: Characterized the image into a histogram with gray value and pixels of similar gray values.

Step 3: Randomly generate γ 1's elements and $(255-\gamma)$ 0's elements as an initial solution S.

Step 4: Perform the OED based hill-climbing on S to generate a solution Q.

Step 5: Accept Q to be the new S if $F(Q) > F(S)$.

Step 6: If a pre-specified stopping condition is satisfied, stop the algorithm. Otherwise, go to Step 3.

Step 7: Output the segmentation results.

4   Experimental Results

In this study, the performance of OEDIS is demonstrated by comparing with K-means, FCM, GA, and SA. These algorithms are coded using Borland C++ Builder language on an AMD K7-800 computer. Ten test images of RGB color type demoted as IMG-1 to 10 are selected from the USC-SIPI image database (e.g., http://sipi.usc. edu) and the Berkeley segmentation dataset (e.g., http://www.cs.berkeley.edu/~dmartin/

segbench/), as shown in Fig. 1. All the images are resized to 512×512 pixels. For K-means, the stopping criterion uses ε=0.01. For FCM, the maximum number of iterations is 100. For GA, the generations, population size, selection rate, crossover rate, and mutation rate are 20, 10, 0.2, 0.6, and 0.01, respectively. For SA, the starting temperature is 100, cooling rate is 0.9, the number of trials per temperature is 2, and the termination criterion is 120 iterations. For OEDIS, the maximum number of iterations is 30. The number of objective function evaluations is denoted as EVLs.

In order to compare the performance of these algorithms, a fixed cluster number K=4 is used [7]. The best, average, worst, and variance values of objective function F using ten independent runs are shown in Table 1. The dark mark denotes the best average value of objective function among these algorithms. It reveals that the objective values of K-means and FCM are not high in most images due to oversegmentation problems. On the other hand, GA and SA can obtain better results but larger variances than K-means and FCM due to random search and parameter settings. Although variance of OEDIS is larger than GA and SA in most case, it can obtain best results without setting parameters. The segmentation results of OEDIS are shown in Fig. 2. Experimental results of natural images demonstrate the effectiveness of the proposed algorithm.

5   Conclusions

Image segmentation is an important process in image processing. In this paper, a non-parametric image segmentation algorithm OEDIS using an OED based hill-climbing and a general-purpose evaluation function is proposed. OEDIS can generate a set of candidate solutions using a number of perturbation operations and then systematically reasons a good solution for each iteration based on orthogonal experimental design. Experimental results of natural images demonstrate the effectiveness of the proposed OEDIS comparing with K-means, FCM, GA, and SA.

Fig. 1. Test images (Top: IMG-1 to IMG-5, bottom: IMG-6 to IMG-10).

Fig. 2. Experimental results of OEDIS corresponding to Fig. 1.

Table 1. Comparisons of K-means, FCM, GA, SA, and OEDIS.

		IMG-1	IMG-2	IMG-3	IMG-4	IMG-5	IMG-6	IMG-7	IMG-8	IMG-9	IMG-10
K-means	A	283.05	52.52	323.67	119.08	279.82	300.23	158.69	178.49	544.61	163.12
	B	275.26	51.99	316.95	119.08	279.70	297.27	100.02	84.03	525.13	158.13
	W	288.24	53.45	340.32	119.08	279.90	312.08	213.19	454.58	553.04	173.19
	V	44.92	0.47	37.19	0.00	0.01	38.99	2568.76	22401.52	180.75	25.06
FCM	A	285.69	53.49	326.76	113.73	279.70	307.93	147.31	98.07	561.40	343.30
	B	285.69	53.49	326.76	113.73	279.70	307.93	100.02	84.03	561.40	315.27
	W	285.69	53.49	326.76	113.73	279.70	307.93	194.60	99.63	561.40	371.33
	V	0.00	0.00	0.00	0.00	0.00	0.00	2484.83	24.34	0.00	872.97
GA	A	233.99	40.14	204.09	111.60	310.33	303.43	107.55	104.04	425.73	173.98
	B	231.67	39.31	200.34	109.88	298.57	298.30	106.62	100.36	406.09	168.57
	W	254.88	40.97	219.11	114.21	338.22	309.77	109.82	109.25	456.52	185.35
	V	53.88	0.72	62.66	1.45	224.29	15.18	1.45	10.55	474.49	45.77
SA	A	244.86	39.68	186.77	95.29	255.69	304.91	82.11	76.69	309.49	147.73
	B	230.78	38.16	176.06	89.84	222.86	298.03	77.55	70.41	241.35	138.34
	W	262.52	41.61	212.10	100.98	297.59	316.53	85.68	85.58	342.13	157.52
	V	111.83	1.43	104.47	15.05	416.01	29.14	5.32	23.65	727.17	40.48
OEDIS	A	237.97	38.47	186.21	95.01	252.42	300.04	83.44	76.66	308.31	146.63
	B	223.03	37.54	174.56	92.74	231.59	290.94	77.18	69.80	241.26	130.44
	W	258.68	40.13	199.65	97.78	290.03	306.10	89.57	82.40	334.31	155.94
	V	193.75	0.71	62.24	2.58	313.65	21.19	9.83	19.13	662.82	46.57

Note: (A)verage, (B)est, (W)orst, (V)ariance.

References

[1] R. C. Gonzalez and R. E. Woods, *Digital Image Processing* (2nd Ed.). Prentice Hall, 2001.

[2] L. Wang, W. Hu, and T. Tan, "Recent developments in human motion analysis," *Pattern Recognition*, vol. 36, pp. 585–601, 2003.

[3] R. Pal and S. K. Pal, "A review on image segmentation techniques," *Pattern Recognition*, vol. 26, pp. 1277–1294, 1993.

[4] J. F. Canny, "A computational approach to edge detection," *IEEE Trans. Pattern Analysis and Machine Intelligence*, vol. 8, pp. 679–698, 1986.

[5] S. A. Hojjatoleslami and J. Kittler, "Region growing: a new approach," *IEEE Trans. Image Processing*, vol. 7, pp. 1079–1084, 1998.

[6] K. Haris *et al.*, "Hybrid image segmentation using watersheds and fast region merging," *IEEE Trans. Image Processing*, vol. 7, pp. 1684–1699, 1998.

[7]   T. N. Pappas, "An adaptive clustering algorithm for image segmentation," *IEEE Trans. Signal Processing*, vol. 40, pp. 901–914, 1992.

[8]   Y. A. Tolias and S. M. Panas, "Image segmentation by a fuzzy clustering algorithm using adaptive spatially constrained membership functions," *IEEE Trans. Systems, Man and Cybernetics*, vol. 28, pp. 359–369, 1998.

[9]   D. N. Chun and H. S. Yang, "Robust image segmentation using genetic algorithm with a fuzzy measure," *Pattern Recognition*, vol. 29, pp. 1195–1211, 1996.

[10] S.-Y. Ho and K.-Z. Lee, "Design and analysis of an efficient evolutionary image segmentation algorithm," *Journal of VLSI Signal Processing*, vol. 35, pp. 29–42, 2003.

[11] S. H. Park, *Robust Design and Analysis for Quality Engineering*. Chapman & Hall, 1996.

[12] Y. W. Leung and Y. Wang, "An orthogonal genetic algorithm with quantization for global numerical optimization," *IEEE Trans. Evolutionary Computation*, vol. 5, pp. 41–53, 2001.

[13] M. Borsotti, P. Campadelli, and R. Schettini, "Quantitative evaluation of color image segmentation results," *Pattern Recognition Letters*, vol. 19, pp. 741–747, 1998.

A Qualitative Discriminative Cohort Speakers Method to Reduce Learning Data for MLP-Based Speaker Verification Systems

Tae-Seung Lee, Sung-Won Choi, Won-Hyuck Choi, Hyeong-Taek Park,
Sang-Seok Lim, and Byong-Won Hwang

Hankuk Aviation University, School of Electronics, Telecommunication and Computer
Engineering, Seoul, Korea
thestaff@hitel.net, {swchoi, whchoi, htpark, sslim,
bwhwang}@mail.hangkong.ac.kr

Abstract. Although multilayer perceptrons (MLPs) present several advantages against other pattern recognition methods, MLP-based speaker verification systems suffer from slow enrollment speed caused by many background speakers to achieve a low verification error. To solve this problem, the quantitative discriminative cohort speakers (QnDCS) method, by introducing the cohort speakers method into the systems, reduced the number of background speakers required to enroll speakers. Although the QnDCS achieved the goal to some extent, the improvement rate for the enrolling speed was still unsatisfactory. To improve the enrolling speed in this paper, the qualitative DCS (QlDCS) has been proposed by introducing a qualitative criterion to select less background speakers. An experiment for both methods is conducted to use the speaker verification system based on MLPs and continuants, and speech database. The results of the experiment show that the proposed QlDCS method enrolls speakers in shorter time than the QnDCS does.

1 Introduction

Speaker verification systems require real-time speaker enrollment as well as real-time verification to provide satisfactory performance. To use speaker verification system to be used in daily life, it is necessary to consider a very fast verification since the system must be used frequently. In addition to it, the user convenience criterion for speaker verification system requests fast enrollments of speakers. Most users want to use verification services just after enrolling themselves for the system. If they have to wait for a long time for the first usage, they may quit their enrolling process.

Unlike parametric-based speaker verification systems, the systems based on multilayer perceptrons (MLPs) more quickly conduct the computation needed to verify identities but slowly to enroll speakers [1], [2]. The structure of MLPs inspires a fast verification process even with low-computational capability. On the other hand, it is difficult to settle the optimal values of the internally weighted connections to

J. Liu et al. (Eds.): IDEAL 2003, LNCS 2690, pp. 1082–1086, 2003.

achieve best behaviors of MLPs. And the number of background speakers required for an MLP to learn an enrolling speaker slow down the enrolling speed further.

To remedy the large learning data problem of MLPs, Lee et al. proposed the discriminative cohort speakers (DCS) method [3]. The DCS method adopted the cohort speakers concept into MLP-based speaker verification systems and attempted to reduce the number of background speakers required to enroll a speaker for the system. While the method achieved the goal to reduce the number of background speakers without losing any advantages of MLPs mentioned above, the improvement rate in speed was only about 30% and was not fully satisfactory.

This paper proposes an improved version of the DCS. The DCS presets the number of background speakers to be selected for comparatively learning an enrolling speaker. This makes the DCS inefficient because the density of background speaker population is not uniform and the number of background speakers facing an enrolling speaker varies with enrolling speakers. Such selection criterion of the previous DCS might be considered quantitative. On the contrary, newly proposed method selects background speakers in qualitative manner. This method selects background speakers on the basis of similarity. Thus many background speakers are selected when an enrolling speaker is located in a dense background speaker population and a few speakers are selected otherwise. Such a qualitative criterion reduces background speakers further and enables speakers to enroll in shorter time for MLP-based speaker verification systems.

The paper is organized as follows. In section 2, the quantitative DCS is briefly presented and the new qualitative DCS method is proposed. For illustration of the proposed method, an experiment was carried out and the results are analyzed in section 3. Finally, section 4 concludes the paper.

2 The Qualitative DCS

In the previous DCS, called the quantitative DCS (QnDCS) in this paper, the process of selecting the background speakers similar to an enrolling speaker is as follows:

$$S_{Cohort} = Sel_{1,N,I}(Sort_{Dec}(M_{MLP}(S_{BG} \mid \mathbf{X}))), \quad S_{BG} = \{S_i \mid 1 \le i \le I\}. \quad (1)$$

where, $\mathbf{X}$ is the speech of enrolling speaker, S_{BG} the set of background speakers S_i of which population is I and $Sort_{Dec}$ the function which sorts given values set in descending manner. $Sel_{1,N,I}$ denotes the function which selects the first N elements from background speakers set, S_{Cohort} the set of selected background speakers, namely, cohort and M_{MLP} the MLP function that evaluates likelihoods for each background speaker to given $\mathbf{X}$. The MLPs to calculate M_{MLP} are called MLP-I and the MLPs to learn an enrolling speaker using the background speakers selected by MLP-I MLP-II.

Generally, the distribution of the speaker population is not uniform, though it might vary as to the number and selection criterion of background speakers. When a speaker with ordinary voice is enrolled for verification system, there would be abundant background speakers facing the enrolling speaker. In contradiction to it, when a speaker with unusual voice is enrolled, only a few background speakers would have similarity to the enrolling speaker. Therefore, fixing the number of background speakers to be selected like the QnDCS might be inefficient for not accommodating such variety of background speaker population, even though the minimum number of background speakers is selected for minimum verification error. The reason is that too many for unusual speakers though a proper number of background speakers are selected for ordinary ones.

This paper proposes an improved learning method in which MLP-II utilizes the information of M_{MLP}. In this method, the M_{MLP} evaluates the likelihoods of all background speaker in Eqn. 1 and the background speakers presenting likelihoods beyond certain level can be selected. The preset likelihood level should be so high that the background speakers enclose the current enrolling speaker. This level is determined for experimental speech database. The higher the level is, the more background speakers are selected. Hence, the maximum likelihood must be selected to obtain the minimum verification error. Employing this concept, we can rewrite Eqn. 1 as:

$$S_{Cohort} = Sel_{M_{MLP} \geq \theta, I}(Sort_{Dec}(M_{MLP}(S_{BG} \mid \mathbf{X}))), \quad S_{BG} = \{S_i \mid 1 \leq i \leq I\}. \quad (2)$$

where, $Sel_{M_{MLP} \geq \theta, I}$ is the function to select the background speakers of the maximum number of background speakers I whose M_{MLP} s exceed the preset threshold θ. In this paper, the method is called the qualitative DCS (QlDCS). If the preset θ is appropriate, the QlDCS can reduce effectively the number of background speakers useless for MLPs to learn the current enrolling speaker.

3 Experiment

This paper uses an MLP-based speaker verification system and a speech database described in [3], and experiments on them with the same experiment condition to [3] in order to prove the effect of the QlDCS proposed in the previous section. In the experiment, the QlDCS is compared with the QnDCS and online mode error backpropagation (EBP) algorithm [2]. Also, enrolling time improvements by the QlDCS are measured.

The experiment is conducted for two cases: one is to compare the QnDCS with the online mode EBP algorithm and the other to compare the QlDCS with the QnDCS. The first experiment measures the improvement rate of the QnDCS and the second experiment the rate of the QlDCS to the QnDCS.

In the first experiment, measurements are recorded as the number of background speakers in cohort for the QnDCS is decreased by every 3 speakers. The experimental results are presented in Fig. 1. In the figure, it is clear that the learning speed improves near-linearly as the number of cohort speakers decreases. However, the improvement is meaningful above 20 background speakers in cohort because the error rate increases as the cohort speakers decrease less than 20. The maximum improvement rate of enrolling speed is recorded as 27.1%.

In the second experiment, measurements are recorded for various likelihood thresholds when the QlDCS is used. Fig. 2 displays the errors and learning times for the QlDCS and the QnDCS with respect to the number of speakers in cohort. In this figure, it is noted that although the transitions for the learning time are nearly the same for both the QnDCS and QlDCS, the QlDCS achieves the similar error rate for less speakers. As a result, the numbers of speakers in cohort for the QnDCS and QlDCS, at the same error rate of the online EBP, are 19 and 14.3, respectively. Similarly, the learning times for them are 1.18 and 0.93sec, respectively.

Fig. 3 shows the comparative results of the online EBP, QnDCS and QlDCS. It is clearly observed that the improvement rate of the QlDCS to the online EBP is two times higher than that of the QnDCS. This demonstrates that the method can effectively improve slow enrolling speed of the QnDCS method under variable distribution of background speakers.

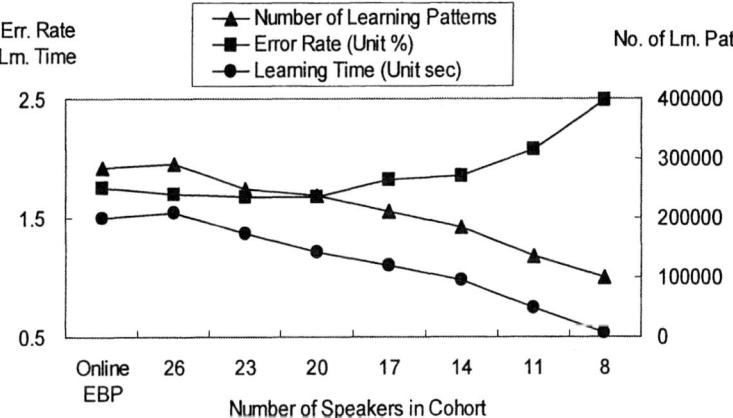

Fig. 1. Comparing result of the QnDCS to the online EBP in the first experiment

4 Conclusions

So far studies have been devoted to enhance the speaker enrollment speed of MLP-based speaker verification systems. In spite of several advantages of MLPs against other pattern recognition methods, MLP-based speaker verification systems suffer from slow enrollment speed due to large background speaker population to acquire a good verification rate. To cope with this problem, the QnDCS introduced the cohort speakers method and was able to reduce the number of background speakers required to enroll speakers. Although the QnDCS achieved the goal to some extent, the improvement for the enrolling speed was unsatisfactory. To improve the enrolling speed further in this paper, the qualitative criterion of the QlDCS has been proposed. To evaluate the QlDCS, the experiment was conducted to use the speaker verification system based on MLPs and continuants, and speech database. It is clearly observed from the results that the QlDCS achieves faster enrolling speed than the QnDCS does.

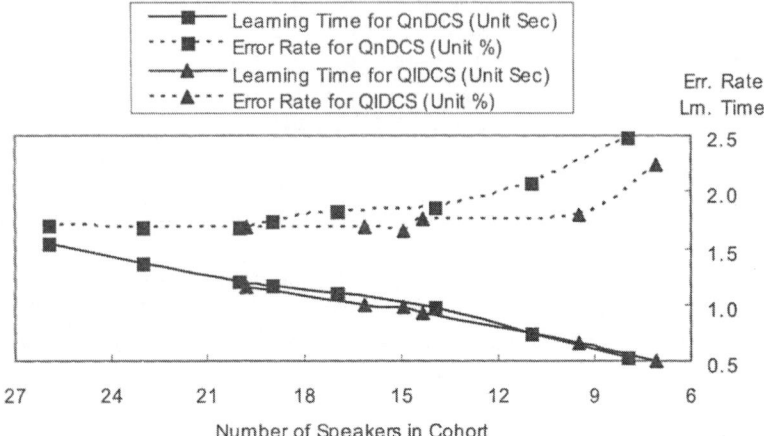

Fig. 2. Comparison of the QlDCS with the QnDCS for the second experiment

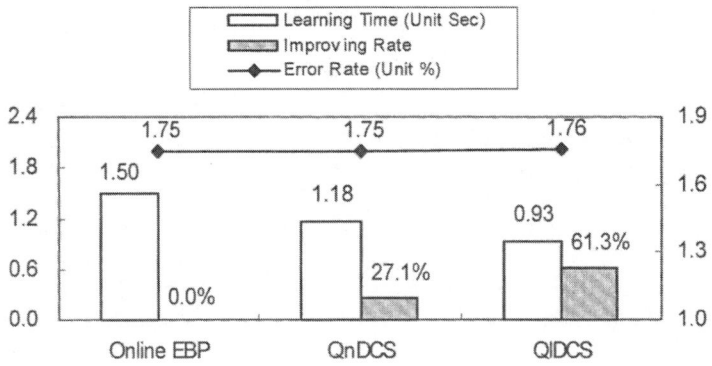

Fig. 3. Learning times and improving rates of the QnDCS and QlDCS against the online EBP

References

1. Rosenberg, A. E., Parthasarathy, S.: Speaker Background Models for Connected Digit Password Speaker Verification. IEEE International Conference on Acoustics, Speech, and Signal Processing. **1** (1996) 81–84
2. Bengio, Y.: Neural Networks for Speech and Sequence Recognition. International Thomson Computer Press, London (1995)
3. Lee, T. S. et al.: Faster Speaker Enrollment for Speaker Verification Systems Based on MLPs by Using Discriminative Cohort Speakers Method. To be published on Lecture Notes in Artificial Intelligence, Springer-Verlag, Berlin Heidelberg New York (2003)

Inheritance Transformation of XML Schemas to Object – Relational Databases

Nathalia Devina Widjaya[1], David Taniar[1], and J. Wenny Rahayu[2]

[1] Monash University, School of Business Systems, Vic 3800, Australia
{Nathalia.Widjaya, David.Taniar}@infotech.monash.edu.au
[2] La Trobe University, Department of Computer Science and Engineering,
wenny@cs.latrobe.edu.au

Abstract. XML (eXtensible Markup Language) is fast emerging as the dominant standard for describing data and interchanging data between various systems and databases on the Internet. Nevertheless, to enable efficient business application development in large-scale e-Commerce environments, XML needs to have databases to keep all the data. Hence, it will inevitable be necessary to use methods to describe the XML schema in the Object Relational Database (ORDB) formats. The paper discusses the modelling of XML and why we need the transformation. Then, a number of transformation steps from the XML schema to the ORDB, with the emphasis on the transformations of inheritance relationships are presented. Two perspectives regarding this conceptual relationship (single and multiple inheritance) and their transformations are mainly discussed.

1   Introduction

The eXtensible Markup Language (XML) is increasingly finding acceptance as a standard for storing and exchanging structured and semi-structured information [4]. XML has emerged and is gradually accepted as the standard for describing data and interchanging data between various systems and databases on the Internet [5].

The remainder of the paper is organised as follows. Section 2 discusses about the overview over OO concepts and OO in XML schemas. Then, we review some closely related work. Section 3 presents several generic-transforming rules from XML schema to ORDB with the emphasis on the transformation of inheritance relationship. We discuss the transformation steps and give example for each of them. Section 4 concludes the paper and further work that can be done.

2   Background and Related Work

In XML Schemas, there are static aspects from object-oriented conceptual model that we can find. The inheritance relationship is one of OOCM features that we will discuss in this paper.

The *inheritance* relationship (refer to Figure 1) represents "inherited" relationship, indicating that an object or a relation inherits the attribute (and methods) of another object [9]. This kind of relationship exists commonly in XML documents. XML assumes that data is hierarchically structured. One element may contain sub-elements,

J. Liu et al. (Eds.): IDEAL 2003, LNCS 2690, pp. 1087–1091, 2003.

which may sequentially contain other elements. ORDB in Oracle 9*i* also has a feature that can support inheritance relationship. Therefore, we can easily map inheritance relationship in XML Schema onto ORDB in Oracle 9*i*.

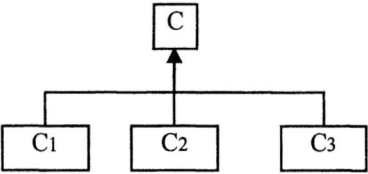

Fig. 1. A one-levelled Inheritance relationship rooted at C

In this paper, we discuss two types of inheritances such as *single inheritance and multiple inheritance*. Single inheritance means the sub class only has one superclass. Multiple inheritance means the sub class has multiple superclass.

Most existing work has focused on a methodology that has been designed to map a relational database to an XML database for database interoperability. There are many works that explain about the mapping from relational databases to XML. Some of them still use DTD [1, 3] and some of them use XML schema [1].

The way to model XML and to transform the OO conceptual models into XML Schema have been discussed in [4]. The writers choose the OO conceptual model because of its expressive power for developing a combined data model. They come out with several generic-transforming rules from the OO conceptual model to XML schema, with the emphasis on the transformations of generalization and Inheritance relationships. The XML Schema code that is presented below, in this paper, is adopted from the existing work that is done previously. In addition, our paper is done to improve what has been done in [4].

The work reported in this paper is distinguishes from this work in the following aspects. First, we focus the transformation from XML schema to ORDB. Second, our transformation target using OO features in Oracle 9*i* not just the general OO features. The similarity is we take inheritance relationships into consideration (single and multiple inheritance).

3   Inheritance Transformation from XML Schema to ORDB: The Proposed Methodology

3.1 Single Inheritance Relationship Transformation

In this example, we will use the mutual exclusion single inheritance implementation. This type of inheritance declares that a group of sub-classes in an inheritance relationship are pairwise disjointed. Account class is the superclass and it has 2 sub classes which are saving account and current account. The steps below explain how to transform the generalization relationship from XML Schema to ORDB:

i.   For the superclass C in the generalization relationship, create it as an object based
     on a complextype name C in XML schema. Then create its attributes based on the
     element name in XML Schema after `<xsd:sequence>`. Add another attribute
     called C_type and write `Not Null` beside it.

ii. In the XML Schema there is an extension base `<xsd:extension
     base=Ctype>` to show the element name, that is mentioned before it, is
     inheritance with Ctype. Create a table for superclass C and create its attributes for
     it (such as C_id and assign it as a Not Null). For every element that is inheritence
     with the superclass and null, we need to check it whether it has C_type in it. Then
     create a primary key for that table (such as C_id).

iii. Next, using 'under' to show the inheritance relationship for its subclass and the
     superclass in the Oracle. Declared its attributes type based on the element name
     under the sub class section in the XML schema.

Below is the full example of single inheritance relationship mapping.

XML Schema for single inheritance relationship	*ORDB for single inheritance relationship*
| ```xml
<xsd:complexType name="AccountType"/>
   <xsd:Sequence>
   <xsd:element name = "AccountNo" type
= "xsd:integer"/>
   <xsd:element name = "Name" type =
"xsd:string"/>
   <xsd:element name = "Balance" type =
"xsd:decimal"/>
   </xsd:sequence>
</xsd:complexType>

<xsd:element name = "Saving Account" type =
"SavingAccountType"/>
   <xsd:complexType name =
"SavingAccountType"/>
   <xsd:complexContent>
         <xsd:Extension base =
"AccountType">
            <xsd:element name =
"InterestRate"
            type = "xsd:decimal"/>
         </xsd:extension>
   </xsd:complexcontent>
   </xsd:complextType>
<xsd:element name = "CurrentAccount" type =
"CurrentAccountType"/>
   <xsd:complexTypename=
"CurrentAccountType"/>
   <xsd:complexContent>
      <xsd:extension base = "AccountType">
<xsd:element name = "OverDraftLimite" type =
"xsd:decimal"/>
   </xsd:extension>
   </xsd:complexContent>
   </xsd:complexType>
``` | ```
Create Or Replace Type Account_T As Object
   (AccountNo          varchar2 (10),
   Name    varchar2 (20),
   Balance          number,
   Account_Type     varchar2    (10)) Not
Final
Create Table Account of Account_T
   (AccountNo       varchar2 (10)
   Account_Type
CHECK            (account_type         In
('Saving_Account', 'Current_Account',
Null)),
   Primary key (id));
Create  or  Replace  Type  Saving_account
Under Account_T
   (Interest_rate     number)
Create  or  Replace  Type  Current_account
Under Account_T
   (OverDraftLimite  number)
``` |

3.2 Multiple Inheritances

The example that we use for this transformation is Administration class.
Administration is the superclass and it has 2 sub classes which are project assistant
and coordinator. ISI People class can be said to be inheriting from overlapping
classes, because basically a ISI People can be a Project Assistant who is also a

coordinator member. There are 3 steps to transform the XML Schema into ORDB in Oracle 9*i*.

i.   For the superclass C in the generalization relationship, create it as an table based on a complextype name C in XML schema. Then create its attributes based on the element name in XML Schema after `<xsd:sequence>`. The id for each table needs to be created as a Not Null. In the create table for the superclass, create a primary key and put id as its primary key.

ii. In the XML Schema there is an extension base `<xsd:extension base=Ctype>` to show the element name, that is mentioned before it, is inheritance with Ctype. Create a table for subclass C1 and create its attributes for it (such as C_id and assign it as a Not Null). Then, create 2 keys, one is primary key and the other one is foreign key that refer to the superclass id.

iii. Lastly, create the table for the subclass that has multiple parents. This table also has 2 keys, primary key and foreign key that refer to the superclass C id.

Below is the full example of multiple inheritance relationship mapping

**XML Schema for single inheritance relationship**	_**ORDB for single inheritance relationship**_
```<xsd:complexType name="AccountType"/> <xsd:Sequence> <xsd:element name = "AccountNo" type = "xsd:integer"/> <xsd:element name = "Name" type = "xsd:string"/> <xsd:element name = "Balance" type ="xsd:decimal"/> </xsd:sequence></xsd:complexType> <xsd:element name = "Saving Account" type = "SavingAccountType"/> <xsd:complexType name = "SavingAccountType/> <xsd:complexContent> <xsd:Extension base = "AccountType"> <xsd:element name = "InterestRate" type = "xsd:decimal"/> </xsd:extension> </xsd:complexcontent> </xsd:complexType> <xsd:element name = "CurrentAccount" type = "CurrentAccountType"/> <xsd:complexTypename= "CurrentAccountType"/> <xsd:complexContent> <xsd:extension base = "AccountType"> <xsd:element name = "OverDraftLimite" type = "xsd:decimal"/> </xsd:extension> </xsd:complexContent> </xsd:complexType>```	```Create Or Replace Type Account_T As Object (AccountNo varchar2 (10), Name varchar2 (20), Balance number, Account_Type varchar2 (10)) Not Final Create Table Account of Account_T (AccountNo varchar2 (10) Account_Type CHECK (account_type In ('Saving_Account','Current_Account', Null)), Primary key (id)); Create or Replace Type Saving_account Under Account_T (Interest_rate number) Create or Replace Type Current_account Under Account_T (OverDraftLimite number)```

4   Conclusion and Future Work

In this paper, we have investigated the transformation from XML schema to the ORDB by using Oracle 9*i*. We emphasis the transformation of *Inheritance* *relationship* to help people easily understand the basic object conceptual mapping that we proposed. This transformation is important because people always eliminate the object-oriented conceptual features when they transform XML schema to the database.

Our future work is being planned to investigate more transformation from XML schema to ORDB for other XML Schema features that has not been discussed in this paper. In addition, further research should be done to create a query from XML schema to get the data from the Oracle 9*i* databases.

References

1. Dillon T and Tan PL, *"Object Oriented Conceptual Models"*. Prentice Hall, 1993
2. Fong J., Pang F., and Bloor, C., "Converting Relational Database into XML Document". *Proceedings. 12th International Workshop on Database and Expert Systems Applications*, 2001, pp. 61–65, 2001
3. Klettke M. and Meyer H., " XML and Object Relational Database System". *Lecture Notes in Computer Science*, vol 1997, Springer-Verlag Berlin Heidelberg, pp.151–170, 2001
4. Mani M., Lee D. and Muntz R., " Semantic Data Modelling Using XML Schemas". *Lecture Notes in Computer Science*, vol 2224, Springer-Verlag Berlin Heidelberg, pp.149–163, 2001
5. Stonebraker, M., and Moore, D., *"Object-relational DBMSs:the next great wave"*. Mogran Kaufmann Publishers. San Francisco, 1996
6. Xiao R., Dillon T., Chang E., and Feng L., " Modelling and Transformation of Object-Oriented Conceptual Models into XML Schema". *Lecture Notes in Computer Science*, vol 2113, Springer-Verlag Berlin Heidelberg, pp.795–804, 2001

Wavelet-Based Feature Extraction from Character Images

Jong-Hyun Park and Il-Seok Oh

Department of Computer Science, Chonbuk National University, S. Korea
{jhpark, isoh}@dahong.chonbuk.ac.kr

Abstract. A wavelet-based feature extraction algorithm is proposed for
character images. The contours of character contain most of information
that discriminates the different classes of characters. The proposed algorithm is primarily based on the notion that the wavelet transformation
decomposes a 2-dimenional image into three high-frequency sub-bands
representing the vertical, horizontal, and diagonal edges. Several schemes
of partitioning the sub-bands into blocks are presented that are mesh-
like or slice-like. The moments are extracted from each of the blocks
and they are taken as the features. The low-frequency sub-band is also
used to compute the moments. Experiments performed with two character recognition problems showed promising results and the comparison
with other features revealed a superior recognition rate of the proposed
algorithm.

1 Introduction

The feature extraction is one of the most important tasks in pattern recognition, computer vision, and multimedia retrieval. Lots of techniques have been
developed and an excellent survey can be found in [1]. Tang et al. proposed ring-
projection scheme that transforms 2-dimensional image signal into 1-dimensional
signal [2]. Zhang et al. proposed a recognition method for similar objects that
transforms the 2-D image into shape matrix obtain the rotation and scaling invariance [3]. Chen and Bui represented the image in the polar-coordinate and
performed 1-dimensional FFT with respect to the angle [4].

In this paper, we propose a wavelet-based feature extraction algorithm for character images. The input character images are first size-normalized and then
wavelet-transformed. The Haar and Daubechies's kernels are applied and their
effectiveness on discrimination power is evaluated through the empirical studies. Our algorithm partitions each sub-band using one of mesh-like and slice-like
schemes. In the mesh-like partition, a sub-band is divided both in vertical and
horizontal directions into a set of the same-sized blocks. The slice-like partition
scheme divides a sub-band vertically or horizontally depending on the sub-band's
edge direction into a set of the same-sized slices. In each of the blocks or slices,
the moments of wavelet coefficients are computed and they are taken as features.
The proposed algorithm was tested using handwritten numeral recognition and
printed Hangul(Korean language) character recognition problems. The algorithm

J. Liu et al. (Eds.): IDEAL 2003, LNCS 2690, pp. 1092–1096, 2003.

was compared with other wavelet-based algorithm and edge direction-based algorithm. We used the modular MLP classifier for recognition experiments. The results illustrated that our algorithm is superior to the conventional algorithms.

2   Wavelet Decomposition of Character Images

For the convenience of wavelet transformation, the $L \times M$ image is first size-normalized into $N \times N$ one where N is 2^k. In our implementation, N was 64. An input pattern P is size-normalized by superimposing a 64×64 grid mesh R onto the $L \times M$ mesh. Several grids in P may overlap with a grid in R at different overlapping ratios. The value of a grid in R is computed using all the overlapped grids in P. The value is computed by summing the weighted values of the overlapping pixels of P where the weights are the overlapping ratios. After the values of all the grids in R have been computed, they are normalized into a value between 0.0 and 1.0. By considering all the overlapped pixels according to the amount of their overlap, information loss could be minimized during the size normalization process.

The wavelet transformation is applied to the size-normalized images. Two different kernels are used, Haar and Daubechies. The transform is performed recursively. At each level, 4 quadrants are available and the top left one is recursively decomposed while other three quadrants are not decomposed. The three quadrants contain the edge information; the top right, bottom left, and bottom right ones have the vertical, horizontal, and diagonal edge information, respectively. The magnitude of coefficient value represents the edge strength. The sign represents the edge direction at that position. For example, the pixel with positive (negative) coefficient in the top right quadrant (i.e. vertical edge quadrant) has the edge pointing to the left (right) direction.

3   Feature Extraction

3.1   Partitioning Schemes and Feature Descriptor

A quadrant is partitioned into several blocks in various ways as described below. Fig. 1 explains various schemes. (1) Mesh partitioning: In this scheme, a quadrant is divided into a non-overlapping $m \times m$ mesh, and as a result m^2 blocks are produced. (2) Overlapping mesh partitioning: This scheme divides a quadrant as in Fig. 1(b) where the blocks are allowed to overlap. The blocks are the same as the scheme (1). They are called the basic blocks. In addition to the basic blocks, there are $(m - 1)^2$ extra blocks that are located at the center of four adjacent basic blocks. So it produces $m^2 + (m - 1)^2$ blocks. (3) Slice partitioning: A quadrant is sliced vertically or horizontally. A quadrant with vertical edge information (i.e. top right quadrant) is horizontally sliced. The one with horizontal edges is vertically sliced. The scheme is adopted so that the features can tolerate the translational variations of character strokes.

A block produced by the partitioning schemes contains several pixels. The pixels have the wavelet coefficients that represent the edge information. In the

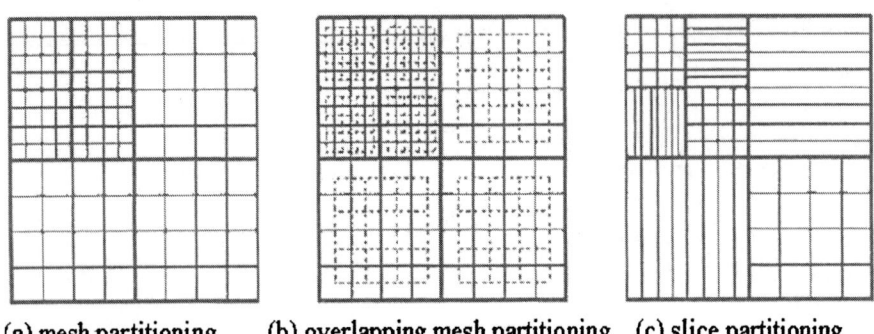

(a) mesh partitioning   (b) overlapping mesh partitioning   (c) slice partitioning

Fig. 1. Partitioning schemes

block, moments are computed and they are taken as the features. The first and second moments defined below are used where $b(x, y)$ represents a block sub-image.

$$\mu = \frac{1}{n^2} \sum_{i=0}^{n-1} \sum_{j=0}^{n-1} b(x, y), \sigma = \sqrt{\frac{1}{n^2} \sum_{i=0}^{n-1} \sum_{j=0}^{n-1} [\mu - b(x, y)]^2} \tag{1}$$

The pixels in a block are one of two types depending on their signs. Two kinds of moments are extracted. The first one ignores the sign and computes the moments from the absolutes pixel values. The features are denoted by *unsigned*. The other one divides the plus pixels and minus pixels and computes the moments from each of them. They are denoted by *signed*.

3.2   Algorithm

Here we will describe a complete procedure. In Section 4, experimental performance will be presented for each of the options. In the step 5, both the moments extracted from the high-frequency quadrants and low-frequency quadrant are taken as the features. Notice that the low-frequency quadrant has an averaged version of the original image and it also contains effective information for discriminating the characters.

Algorithm : wavelet-feature-extraction
Input : arbitrary-sized character image with binary or grayscale tone.
Output : wavelet features.
Procedure :
1. Size-normalize the input image into 64 × 64 image.
2. Perform wavelet transformation using **Haar or Daubechies** kernels by 2-levels.
3. Partition the quadrants using one of **mesh, overlapping mesh, or slice schemes**.
4. Compute the moments from the blocks by *unsigned* or *signed* schemes.
5. Take the moments as the features.

Table 1. Recognition for the numerals (by modular MLP without rejection)

		Haar		Daubechies	
		Train set	Test set	Train set	Test set
Nonoverlapping mesh	unsigned	95.45	93.50	99.20	95.56
	signed	97.90	92.05	99.03	94.20
Overlapping mesh	unsigned	95.03	94.02	99.28	95.30
	signed	97.00	94.50	99.25	96.00
Slice	unsigned	95.03	92.00	97.30	93.05
	signed	96.00	90.60	98.00	92.65

Table 2. Recognition rates for the Hangual characters (by k-NN without rejection)

		Haar	Daubechies
Nonoverlapping mesh	unsigned	84.68	90.15
	signed	85.50	89.55
Overlapping mesh	unsigned	84.38	94.10
	signed	86.28	93.50
Slice	unsigned	82.63	83.00
	signed	83.25	84.00

Table 3. Comparisons with other features

	Numeral		Printed Hangul
	Train set	Test set	
Mesh	98.13	93.25	80.12
Simple wavelet	97.50	92.97	84.03
Gradient	99.33	95.30	87.05
Our method	99.25	96.00	94.10

4   Experiments

Our experiment used two character recognition problems, handwritten numeral recognition and printed Hangul character recognition. For the numeral recognition, the CENPARMI database was used. For the Hangul recognition, database that was constructed in our laboratory was used. It has 2350 model characters collected from a Korean word processor and 4115 test samples collected from the actual document images. The modular MLP classifier in [7] was used for the handwritten numeral recognition. For the Hangul recognition, 1-NN classifier was used. Three conventional features described below were chosen for the comparison purpose. The gradient feature was chosen since they also used the edge information and is conceptually similar to our algorithm.

(1) Mesh features: For the mesh features, the character image was size-normalized to be 16×16. So the feature vector has 256 dimensions.

(2) Simple wavelet features in [5]: The Haar wavelet was used as a basis function. All the wavelet coefficients in the wavelet-transformed image were taken as the features. They are called as the simple wavelet features.

(3) Gradient features in [6]: The gradient feature is computed by suing the gradient magnitude map and gradient direction map.

Tables 1 and 2 illustrate the recognition rates for the handwritten numerals and printed Hangul characters, respectively. Several options were tested. The Daubechies kernel outperformed Haar kernel by 2~4%. For the numerals, the overlapping mesh scheme and signed moments scheme gave the best performance, 96.00%. For the Hangul characters, the overlapping mesh and unsigned moments schemes produced the best result, 94.10%. The overlapping mesh gave the best performance among three partitioning schemes while the slicing scheme was the worst. Table 3 compares four different features. For numerals, the proposed algorithm outperformed the gradient features by 0.7%. For the Hangul characters, our algorithm is much better than the gradient. The gap was 7.05%.

5 Conclusions

A wavelet-based feature extraction method for the character images was proposed and evaluated. The method was based on the notion that the wavelet transform contains different quadrants representing the edge information in vertical, horizontal, and diagonal directions. Some sub-band partitioning schemes was proposed. Finally the moments were extracted as the features. Experiments performed with the actual character databases revealed promising results.

References

1. O.D. Trier, A.K. Jain, and T. Taxt, "Feature extraction methods for character recognition-A survey," Pattern Recognition, Vol. 29, No.4, pp. 641–662, 1996.
2. Yuan Y. Tang, Bing F. Li, Hong Ma, and Jiming Liu, "Ring-projection-wavelet-fractal signatures: A novel approach to feature extraction," IEEE Transactions on Circuits and Systems, Vol. 45, No. 8, pp. 1130–1134, 1998.
3. P. Zhang, T.D. Bui, and C.Y. Suen, "Recognition of similar objects using 2-D wavelet-fractal feature extraction," International Conference on Pattern Recognition, Vol. 2, pp. 316–319, 2002.
4. Guangyi Chen and Tien D. Bui, "Invariant fourier-wavelet descriptor for pattern recognition," Pattern Recognition, Vol. 32, No. 7, pp. 1083–1088, 1999.
5. S.W. Lee, C.H. Kim, H. Ma, and Y.Y. Tang, "Multiresolution recognition of unconstrained handwritten numerals with wavelet transform and multilayer cluster neural network," Pattern Recognition, Vol. 29, No. 2, pp. 1953–1961, 1996.
6. G. Srikantan, S.W. Lam, and S.N. Srihari, "Gradient-based contour encoding for character recognition," Pattern Recognition, Vol. 29, No. 7, pp. 1147–1160, 1996.
7. Il-Seok Oh and Ching Y. Suen, "Distance features for neural network-based recognition of handwritten characters," International Journal on Document Analysis and Recognition, Vol. 1, No. 2, pp. 73–88, 1998.

Illumination Invariant Shot Boundary Detection

Laiyun Qing[1,2], Weiqiang Wang[2], and Wen Gao[1,2]

[1]Graduate School of Chinese Academy of Sciences, Beijing, China, 100039
[2]Institute of Computing Technology, Chinese Academy of Sciences, Beijing, China, 100080
{lyqing, wqwang, wgao}@ict.ac.cn

Abstract. Illumination variation poses a serious problem in video shot detection. It causes false cuts in many shot detection algorithms. A new illumination invariant measure metric is proposed in this paper. The metric is based on the assumption: the outputs of derivative filters to log-illumination are sparse. Thus the outputs of derivative filters to log-image are mainly caused by the scene itself. If the total output is larger than a threshold, it can be declared as a scene change or a shot boundary. Although this metric can detect gradual transitions as well as cuts, it is applied as a post-process procedure for a cut candidate because an illumination change is usually declared as a false cut.

1 Introduction

Shot detection is a crucial step in many content-based video browse and retrieval applications. The shot boundaries mark the transition from one sequence of consecutive images to another. According to the duration of the shot boundary, there are two types: cuts and gradual transitions.

Shot boundaries can be detected by employing a metric to measure the difference between two consecutive frames. This is based on the fact that the content remains nearly the same in an identical shot. If the difference is larger than a certain threshold, it is most likely that the two frames belong to different shots. Therefore an appropriate measure metric is the key of a shot detection algorithm.

For a good metric, it is almost the same inside a shot while the difference of two frames in different shots is large. Many efforts have been devoted to shot boundary detection and many measure metrics have been proposed. A comparison can be found in [1] and a survey, especially for gradual transitions can be found in [2]. The most popular measure metrics include pixel or block based temporal difference, difference of color histogram, edge and motion. Because histograms are easy to compute and robust to object motion, many researchers have declared that it could achieve a good tradeoff between accuracy and speed.

All the above measure metrics use pixel color directly except edge. They are sensitive to incident illumination variation. Even a simple light change will result in abrupt changes in the above metrics. The shot detection algorithms based on the above metrics will declare a false shot boundary when illumination changes in a shot.

This paper proposes an illumination invariant measure metric for detecting scene change. Although this metric can detect gradual transitions as well as cuts, it is

J. Liu et al. (Eds.): IDEAL 2003, LNCS 2690, pp. 1097–1101, 2003.

applied as a post-process procedure for cut candidates here because an illumination change is usually declared as a false cut.

The rest of this paper is organized as follows: Some related work about illumination in shot detection is overviewed in section 2. In section 3, the details of the proposed algorithm are presented. Experimental results are given in section 4. At last, the paper concludes with a summary.

2 Related Work

Edge metric uses the color difference between two pixels and is insensitive to illumination variation to a certain extent. Some algorithms [3][4]are based on edge metric. Zabih's feature-based algorithm [3] detects the appearance of intensity edges that are far from edges in the previous frame. This is based on the assumption that: during a cut or a dissolve, new intensity edges appear far from the locations of old edges and old edges disappear far from the location of new edges. The algorithm runs slow however. Li's algorithm [4] uses ABEM (area of boundary in edge map) as a measure for content difference between frames. ABEM is the area of non-edge pixels. The computation of ABEM is simple and fast. But it does not explore the intrinsic nature of the relations between image, illumination and scene.

Temporal property is adopted in [4] and [5] to detect flashlight. The algorithms are based on the fact that a flashlight usually occurs during several consecutive frames and vanishes quickly. Yeo [5] declared that there were two largest differences between frames corresponding to flashlight occurring and vanishing, and the two differences are much larger than the average difference (in 2m+1 sliding window). Zhang etc. [6] used a cut model and a flash model to distinguish the histogram difference resulted by cut and flash. These methods are effective for flash detection but they cannot handle more general illumination variation.

More general illumination variation might be handled by preprocessing with a color constancy algorithm. Font and Finlayson[7] studied the use of CRH (color ratio histogram) for indexing image database and it was adopted in shot detection. CRH is based on local light constancy, that is, when a pixel is lightened, the pixels around that one are also lightened, but the ratio changes little. Finlayson and Xu[8] proposed a non-iterative efficient comprehensive normalization approach to remove the effects of lighting geometry and light color. Its core idea is that the multiplication dependencies due to lighting geometry and light color turn into addition after applying the log operation. Then the log image is projected to subspace that is orthogonal complement of the space spanned by lighting geometry change and light color change. Color constancy algorithms can handle some kinds of illumination variations but their computing costs are very high.

3 The Proposed Metric

We use $I(x,y)$ to denote an input image. The image can be represented by the multiplication of its reflectance image $R(x,y)$ and the illumination image $L(x,y)$, like:

$$I(x,y) = L(x,y)R(x,y). \tag{1}$$

$R(x,y)$ contains the information of the scene. If $R(x,y)$ has little change, we declare that the scene is the same even if $I(x,y)$ changes much. In a video stream, if two consecutive frames change much while the two scene images $R_i(x,y)$ and $R_{i+1}(x,y)$ change little, we declare that the two frames are in the same shot.

If we take log on both sides of the equation (1), and let i(x,y)=log(I(x,y)), r(x,y)=log(R(x,y)), l(x,y)=log(L(x,y)), we get

$$i(x,y) = l(x,y) + r(x,y). \tag{2}$$

Assume that we have derivative filters in horizontal and vertical directions: $f_h=(0,1,-1)$ and $f_v=(0,1,-1)^T$. We denote the filter outputs by $o_n=f_n*i(x,y)$, $l_n=f_n*l(x,y)$ and $r_n=f_n*r(x,y)$. Therefore

$$o_n(x,y) = l_n(x,y) + r_n(x,y). \tag{3}$$

The idea in this paper is motivated by recent work on the statistics of natural illumination [9] and computer vision [10]. We use the same prior assumption that: when derivative filters are applied to natural illumination images, the filter outputs tend to be sparse. Figure 1 illustrates such a fact: different images have histograms that are peaked at zero and fall off much faster than a Gaussian. These prototypical histograms can be well fit by a Laplacian distribution. An interpretation of this assumption is that in a scene, light difference between neighbor pixels is little. In the extreme case, the light of every pixel is same, that is, the scene is lighted by constant illumination. It has also been proved that in a Lambertian scene, only the low frequent illumination (9D) contributes to imaging [11].

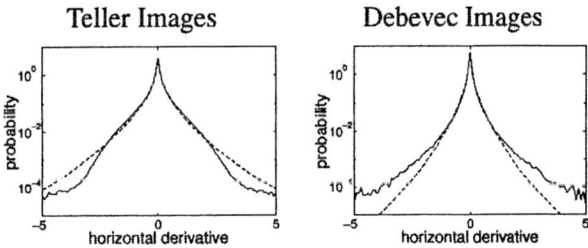

Fig. 1. Statistics of natural illumination: Solid lines indicate distribution of horizontal derivatives for log luminance illumination maps. Dashed lines are generalized Laplacian fits (From [9])

We can see that the difference of image pixels $o_n(x,y)$ is the sum of that of $l_n(x,y)$ and $r_n(x,y)$. As the difference of $l_n(x,y)$ is very little, it can be concluded that the difference of $o_n(x,y)$ is mainly caused by $r_n(x,y)$. That is, a large difference of $o_n(x,y)$ indicates that the scene changes. In a video clip, it can be declared as a shot boundary.

In fact $o_n(x,y)$ contains the edge information of the scene. Then a metric similar to ABEM in [4] can be used in our method, but edges are derived by subtraction of $i(x,y)$ instead of that of $I(x,y)$. Positive and negative values $o_n(x,y)$ indicate the direction of edges; therefore we compute the positive edge number and the negative edge respectively. The feature vector of a frame f_i is represented by V_i: $<pAbem_h, nAbem_h, pAbem_v, nAbem_v>$, where $pAbem_n=\#(o_n>T)$, $nAbem_n=\#(o_n<-T)$. T is a threshold and #

is a sum operator for the number of pixels. Denoting the size of the frame by N, the difference of two consecutive frames can be defined as:

$$diff(f_t, f_{t+1}) = |V_{t+1} - V_t| / N. \tag{4}$$

For instance, the feature vectors for the images of the same scene under different illuminations in Figure 2 are <6483, 6800, 10895, 108267> and <6905, 7080, 11402, 11479> respectively when $T=0.5$. The difference of the two frames is 0.55%. Although the second image is obviously brighter than the first one, the difference is very small using the metric, which indicates they belong to the same scene.

Fig. 2. An example of illumination varying

To evaluate the proposed metric, we take a statistical analysis on the different cases as shown in Table 1. We can see that the average difference is very little if two frames belong to an identical shot, even with illumination change. The statistics also show the average difference on shot boundaries is very large. Thus the metric is effective in distinguishing scene changes.

Table 1. Comparison of the average difference under various cases

Cases	Average pAbemn difference (Image size: 704*480)
The identical shot without illumination change	525
The identical shot with illumination change	798
Shot boundary	2458

As the gray values of the pixels in an image/frame are in the range of [0, 255], the log operation can be computed for each integer in the range [0,255] and store them as a look-up table. Therefore the computation cost doesn't increase much for the total video stream.

4   Experimental Results

We use three video clips as the experimental data, which include many flashlights. Two come from two days' CCTV News and the last from the "Harry Potter". The experimental results are tabulated in Table 2. The fifth column list the false cuts due to illumination changes, and the last column counts the number of such false cuts which have been corrected. In the experiment we found the proposed metric does not discard any true cuts. The proposed metric can filter 2/3 false cuts successfully without discarding any true cuts. For the other false cut declarations, our further analysis show that the energy of the flashlights in them is so high that the pixels are over saturated and the equation $I(x,y) = L(x,y)R(x,y)$ is not satisfied. In the case, we can use the metric in a sliding window similar to the flash model in [6].

Table 2. Experimental results of shot boundary detection

Video clips	Frames	True cuts	Detected cuts	False cuts	Detected false cuts
Clip1	10284	40	58	19	12
Clip2	5492	20	22	2	2
Clip3	951	7	25	18	13

5 Summary

In this paper, an illumination invariant metric is proposed to measure scene changes. Illumination variation in a video stream often results in false cuts. For cut candidates generated by many histogram-based shot detection algorithms, the metric can be exploited to refine the results further as a post process. It has been proven by the experiments that this metric is effective in distinguish the same scene under various illumination and different scenes.

References

1. Boresczky J. S. and Rowe L. A.: A comparison of video shot boundary detection techniques. In Proceedings to Storage & Retrieval for Image and Video Databases IV, SPIE 2664, pages 170–179 (1996)
2. Lienhart R.: Reliable transition detection in videos: a survey and practitioner's guide. International Journal of Image and Graphics, 1(3):469–486 (2001)
3. Zabih R., Miller J. and Mai K.. A feature-based algorithm for detecting and classifying production effects. ACM Journal of Multimedia Systems, 7(2):119–128 (1999)
4. Li D. L., and Lu H. Q.: An illumination invariant measure in detecting scene breaks. Journal of Software, 12(8):1120–1128 (2001)
5. Yeo B. L. Liu B.: Rapid scene analysis on compressed video. IEEE Transactions on circuits and systems form video technology, 5(6):533–544 (1995).
6. Zhang D., Qi W. and Zhang H. J.: A new shot boundary detection algorithm. Proceedings of the second Pacific Conference on Multimedia, pages 63–70, Beijing (2001).
7. Funt B. V., Finlayson G. D.: Color constant color indexing. IEEE Transactions on PAMI, 17(5):522–529, (1995)
8. Finlayson G., Xu R.: Non-iterative comprehensive normalization. Proceedings of The First European Conference on Color in Graphics, Imaging and Vision, Poitiers, France (2002)
9. Dror R. O.:, Leung T. K., Adelson E. H., and Willsky A. S.: Statistics of real-world illumination. Proceeding of CVPR2001, Kauai, Hawaii (2001)
10. Weiss Y.: Deriving intrinsic images from image sequences. Proceedings of ICCV2001, Vancouver, Canada (2001)
11. Basri R., and Jacobs D.: Lambertian reflectance and linear subspaces. In Proceedings to ICCV2001, Vancouver, Canada (2001)

Modified Chamfer Matching Algorithm

Abdul Ghafoor[1], Rao Naveed Iqbal[2], and Shoab A Khan[2]

[1]Department of Electrical Engineering, College of Electrical and Mechanical Engineering,
National University of Sciences and Technology,
Rawalpindi, Pakistan
a_ghafoor30@yahoo.com
[2]Department of Computer Engineering, College of Electrical and Mechanical Engineering,
National University of Sciences and Technology,
Rawalpindi, Pakistan
{rao_naveed,kshoab}@yahoo.com

Abstract. Image matching is an important task. There are many available methods for occluded image matching. In this paper we propose new simple image-matching algorithm, modified chamfer matching algorithm (MCMA). Distance transform and conventional chamfer matching algorithm are explained. Examples to demonstrate the algorithm and necessary results are also included. Proposed MCMA is robust, and to an extent rotation, scale and rotation invariant method.

1 Introduction

Matching between objects remains a central problem in the pattern recognition, image analysis, robotics and computer vision. Based on the level of image feature extraction, the matching methods developed in the past can be divided into three classes: algorithms that use image pixel values directly; algorithms that uses low level features; and algorithms that uses high level features.

The methods making use of image pixel value directly are sensitive to changes between images, e.g., a slight change in illumination may make matching between, otherwise, equal scenes impossible. The same structures in images from different sensors can not be identified. High level matching methods are very insensitive to these disturbances. But it is difficult to extract high level features.

Chamfer matching [1] is a technique for finding the best fit of edge points from two different images, by minimizing a generalized distance between them. The original idea has several good properties but also had false matching. Measure of correspondence between patterns to be matched has been improved to have fewer false matches [2]. As the matching problem is computation intensive, [3]-[4] to speed up the computation considerably. Image matching using Hausdorff distance [5] and its variants [6]-[7]. Hausdorff matching is the only robust method of the known literature for occluded images to an extent. Other available matching schemes are chamfer matching [1]- [4] and wavelet decomposition method [8].

MCMA is low level feature based method, in which edge points or low level feature points are extracted from digital images (using any suitable edge extraction

J. Liu et al. (Eds.): IDEAL 2003, LNCS 2690, pp. 1102–1106, 2003.
© Springer-Verlag Berlin Heidelberg 2003

scheme), converted to binary images, which are distance transformed, and then distance transform is used for matching. The distance transform of template is superimposed on the distance transform of the model and values are subtracted pixel wise and matching is found by minimizing the rms average.

This paper is organized in 5 sections. Section-2 describes the basic concept regarding distance transform and chamfer matching. Proposed MCMA is explained in Section-3, simulation results in section-4 and finally conclusion in section-5.

2   Basic Concepts

Two binary images based on feature and non-feature points, are to be matched. The feature can be any well defined object visible in both images. The two images are not treated symmetrically [4], [5]. One is called predistance (distance transformed) and other is called prepolygon with arbitrary assignation in most of the cases. The predistance (distance transform) image is formed by assigning each non-edge pixel a value that is a measure of to the nearest edge pixel.

2.1   Distance Transform

The process of converting a binary image to an approximate distance image is called distance transformation (DT). The true Euclidian distance is resource demanding (memory) to compute, therefore an approximation is used. For the matching algorithm, it is important that DT is a reasonably good approximation of the Euclidean distance. Chamfer distances are the distances between horizontal/vertical neighbors and two local distances in a 3x3 neighborhood.

In the binary edge image each edge pixel is first set to zero and each non edge pixel is set to infinity. If the DT is computed by parallel propagation of local distances then at each iteration each pixel obtains a new value using the expression in equation (1)

$$v^k_{i,j} = \text{minimum}(v^{k-1}_{i-1,j-1} + 4, v^{k-1}_{i-1,j} + 3, v^{k-1}_{i-1,j+1} + 4, v^{k-1}_{i,j-1} + 3, v^{k-1}_{i,j}, v^{k-1}_{i,j-1} + 3, v^{k-1}_{i+1,j-1} + 4, v^{k-1}_{i+1,j} + 3, v^{k-1}_{i+1,j+1} + 4)$$ (1)

where $v^k_{i,j}$ is the value of the pixel in position (i,j) at iteration k. The iteration continues until no value changes and is proportional to the longest distance in image.

To speed up the distance computation process, sequential DT algorithm [4] is used where two passes are made: "forward" left to right; "backward" right to left.

2.2   Prepolygon

In the prepolygon image, the edge pixels are extracted and converted to a list of coordinate pairs, each pair being the row and column numbers of an edge pixel. From this list the edge points that are actually used are later chosen according to some criterion, which is application dependent.

2.3   Matching Measures

The polygon is superimposed on the distance image. An average of the pixel values that the polygon hits is the measure of correspondence between the edges, called the edge distance. A perfect fit between the two edges will result in edge distance zero, as each polygon point will then hit an edge pixel. The actual matching consists of minimizing the edge distance. There are many variants of matching measure averages, e.g. arithmetic, root mean square and median.

$$\text{Arithmetic average distance} = (v_1 + v_2 + \ldots + v_N)/N \tag{2}$$

$$\text{Root mean square average distance} = \{(v_1^2 + v_2^2 + \ldots + v_N^2)/N\}^{1/2}/3 \tag{3}$$

where N is total number of points in polygon and $v_1, v_2, \ldots, v_N$ are pixel values of corresponding coordinate pairs.

Each position of the polygon corresponds to an edge distance. The position with minimum edge distance is matching position. The translation and rotational parameters defines the polygon matching position.

3   MCMA

Like conventional chamfer matching, MCMA is low level feature based method. Unlike conventional chamfer matching, where model image is translated to distance transform, and template image which is polygon is superimposed onto the model and matching is found as per matching measure, we propose MCMA, in which edge points or low level feature points are extracted from digital images (using any suitable edge extraction scheme), converted to binary images, which are distance transformed, and then distance transform is used for matching. The distance transform of template is superimposed on the distance transform of the model and values are subtracted pixel wise and matching is found as per the metric.

3.1   Algorithm

Consider a reference image A of size MxN and a template image B of size OxP with elements $a_{m,n}$ and $b_{o,p}$ respectively.   Assume A≥B; m=1,2,...,M; n=1,2,...,N; o=1,2,...,O; p=1,2,...,P; range1>range2. We can define C, such that C=oϵ O, pϵP [$c_{o,p}$] for all o and p.
for q=0: m-o
    for r=0: n-p
            C= oϵ O, pϵP[[$a_{o+q,p+r}$]-B]
            Measure=rms average [oϵ O, pϵP [$c_{o,p}$]]
    end
end

3.2   Matching Measure

The DT of template is subtracted from DT of reference and using matching measure, object is matched. Algorithm also provides confidence level, which is useful parameter in certain applications relating to image matching.

By computing the RMS average (3) of all the numbers and finding the minimum value localizes the template on reference. If minimum RMS value is zero at a specific translation we have perfect match with 100% confidence level. A non zero rms average will give us less than 100% confidence level according to rms average value.

4   Experimental Results

In this section we present the experimental results for evaluating the efficiency of the proposed modified chamfer matching algorithm. All experiments are implemented on a personal computer with Pentium IV, 1.7GHz processor. The images (reference/template) were applied soble operator for edge detection. After finding the DT image, templates were matched to the reference as per the matching measures. Results were simulated in Matlab 6.1.

Fig.1. is a 415X321, 8 bit gray level reference image. Fig.2. is a 223x196, 8 bit gray level template image. Template is rotated and perturbed with noise. These edge images are then converted to 3-4 DT images, applied as input to MCMA, and translation parameters are found as per matching measure. It took about 124 seconds for producing the match including about 68 seconds DT computation time. Fig.3. shows that template is matched to reference. Only translational parameter is used for matching. A rotated image was also perfectly matched with 92.3% confidence level.

5   Conclusions

In this paper we proposed a modification in existing chamfer matching algorithm, MCMA. We discussed conventional chamfer matching algorithm and MCMA. Experimental results show MCMA is robust, to an extent rotation and scale invariant.

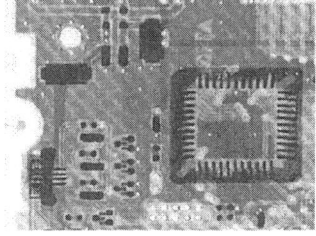

Fig. 1. 415X321, 8 bit gray level reference image

Fig. 2. 223x196, 8 bit gray level template image

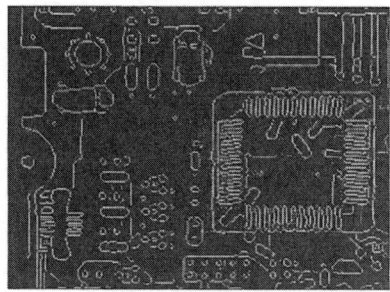

Fig. 3. Match

References

1 H.G. Barrow, J.M. Tanenbaum, R.C. Botles and H. C. Wolf, "Parametric correspondence and chamfer matching: Two new techniques for image matching," In *Proceedings of 5th International Joint Conference on Artificial Intelligence*, Cambridge, MA, pp. 659–653,1977.
2 G. Borgefores, "An improved version of the chamfer matching algorithm," *in 7th Int. Conf, Pattern Recognition* , Montreal, P.Q.,Canada, pp. 1175–1177, 1984.
3 A. Rosenfeld, "Multi resolution image representation", in *Digital Image Analysis*, S. Levialdi, Ed., London: Pitman, pp. 18–28, 1984.
4 Gunnila Borgefores, "Hierarchical chamfer matching: A parametric edge matching algorithm", *IEEE transaction on Pattern Analysis and Machine Intelligence*. Vol. 10, no. 6, pp. 849–856, 1988.
5 Daniel P. Huttenlocher, Gregory A. Klanderman, and William J. Ruklidge, "Comparing images using the Hausdorff distance", *IEEE Trans. Patt. Anal. Machine Intell.*, vol 15, no 9, pp 850–863,1993.
6 D.P. Huttenlocher, K. Kedem, M. Sharir, "The upper envelope of Voronoi surfaces and its applications, *Discrete Comput. Geom. 9*, pp 267–291, 1993.
7 L.Paul Chew, Kalara Kedem, "Getting around a lower bound for the minimum Hausdorff distance", *Computational Geometry 10*, pp197–202, 1998.
8 D. M. Tsai ,C. H. Chiang, "Rotation invariant pattern matching using wavelet decomposition", *Pattern Recognition Letters 23*, pp 191–201, 2002.

Design and Implementation of Alert Analyzer
with Data Mining Engine

Myung Jin Lee[1], Moon Sun Shin[1], Ho Sung Moon[1], Keun Ho Ryu[1], and Ki Young Kim[2]

[1]Department of Computer Science, Chungbuk National University,
48, Gaesin-dong, Cheongju, Chungbuk, Korea
{mjlee, msshin, hsmoon, khryu}@dblab.chungbuk.ac.kr

[2]Network Security Department,
Electronics and Telecommunications Research Institute, Korea
kykim@etri.re.kr

Abstract. This paper describes an alert analyzer based on data mining techniques. The security policy server has to analyze and manage the alert messages received from policy enforcement system in Policy-Based Network Management framework. We develop an alert analyzer that supports security policy server for the available alert analysis. Also we design and implement mining system to help the alert analyzer for the security policy management. The alert analyzer with data mining engine is a useful system to manage the fault users or hosts. *

1 Introduction

As network-based computer systems play increasingly vital roles these days, they have become the targets of intrusions. There are many penetration points for intrusions to take place in network system. Because of large traffic volume, IDS often needs to be extended and be updated frequently and timely. Currently building effective IDS is an enormous knowledge engineering task. Some of the recent researches have started to apply data mining techniques to the IDSs. Because of the sheer volume of audit data, efficient and intelligent data analysis tools are required to discover the behavior of system activities. Data mining generally refers to the process of extracting useful information from large stores of data. The aim of our research is to develop mining system for the analysis of alert data.

This paper describes the idea of applying data mining techniques to analyze alert data. So we propose an alert analyzer with data mining engine. We first outline related work. Section 2 presents the framework for policy-based network security management and alert correlation analysis of IDSs. In section 3 we mention the basic idea of our work. Section 4 and 5 describes the implementation of the alert analyzer with data mining system and the experimental results. In the last section, we will summarize our works.

---

* This work was supported by University IT Research Center Project, KOSEF RRC Project(Cheongju Univ. ICRC) and ETRI in Korea

J. Liu et al. (Eds.): IDEAL 2003, LNCS 2690, pp. 1107–1112, 2003.
© Springer-Verlag Berlin Heidelberg 2003

2 Related Works

Policy-Based Network Security Management

Policy-based network management is a network management based on policy. Policy is defined as an aggregation of policy rules. Each policy rule consists of a set of conditions and a corresponding set of actions. So, we can use policy for modification of system behavior.

Architecture of the policy-based network management for network security has hierarchical structure, and there are at least two levels. One is the management layer that includes security policy server system, and the other is enforcement layer that executes intrusion detection to perceive and prepare the hacking traffic between the connection points.

Alert Correlation

In the response to the attacks and potential attacks against networks, administrators are increasingly deploying IDSs. IDSs products have become widely available in recent years. But the intrusion detection techniques are still far from being perfect. These systems should monitor hosts, networks and critical files, and must deal with a potentially large number of alerts. They should report all alerts to the security policy server or operator. So the security policy server has to manage the reporting alerts in order to build the new security policy rule. But current intrusion detection systems do not make it easy for operators to logically group the related alerts. To solve these critical problems, the intrusion detection community is actively developing standards for the content of the alert messages and some researches is on going about the alert correlation. In [9] they introduced probabilistic approach for the coupled sensors to reduce the false alarm. An aggregation and correlation algorithm is presented in [8] for acquiring the alerts and relating them. The algorithm could explain more condensed view of the security issues raised by the intrusion detection systems. Whereas actual alerts can be mixed with false alerts and also the amount of alerts will also become unmanageable. As a result, it is difficult for the human users or intrusion response systems to understand the intrusions behind the alerts and take the appropriate actions. In [10] they propose the intrusion alert correlator based on the prerequisites of intrusions.

In this paper, we propose an alert analyzer with mining engine. We design and implement the alert analyzer module that is a part of the policy-based network security management framework. Also we implement mining system that analyzes alert data efficiently and supports high-level analyzer for the security policy server.

3   Basic Idea of Applying Data Mining to Analyze Alert

The recent rapid development in data mining has made available a wide variety of algorithms, drawn from the fields of statistics, pattern recognition, machine learning and databases. Some algorithms are particularly useful for mining audit data. In the other cases of alert data, these algorithms are also useful. Follows are the several data mining areas that support IDS;

- Association rules: determines relationships between fields in the database records.
- Frequent episodes: models sequential patterns. These algorithms can discover what time-based sequence of audit events and frequent episodes.
- Clustering: gathers similar patterns to the same group. These algorithms can measure similarity of sequence.
- Classification: maps data item into one of several predefined categories. An ideal application in intrusion detection will be to gather sufficient "normal" and "abnormal" audit data for a user or a program.

Especially, clustering is a useful technique that identifies interesting distribution or mining groups of underlying data.

Table 1 presents an example of alert correlation after mining task. Here we can find out the correlations among alert data inter-records or intra-records. These rules have some confidence information. For example, the first rule means that there is a close correlation between "attack id" 102 and "destination port" 21. That also implies the strong relation between attributes "attack id" and "destination port". Therefore we are able to extract the relationships between attributes using association rules. We can also find sequential pattern of events as results. In the example, we might guess the fact that attack 5009 brings about attack 5002.

Table 1. Example of Alert Correlation

Alert Correlation Rule	Meaning
102<=>21 (supp:49, conf:100%,)	Attribute 102(Atid) correlated with attribute 21(dsc_port)
5009:210.155.167.10:21:tcp=> 5002:210.155.167. 10.21 :tcp (fre:10, conf:100%, time:10sec)	If 5009(Ftp Buffer Ovrflow) occur, then 5002(Anonymous FTP) occur together.

So, in this paper, we design and implement the alert data mining system that consists of three components. The association rule miner performs link analysis of alert data and the frequent episodes miner can discover time based sequence of alert events. The cluster miner can measure similarity of alert sequence.

4 Alert Analyzer with Mining Engine

Implementation of Alert Analyzer

The alert data mining system was implemented on the base of windows XP as operating system and Oracle 8i as database. And it was implemented by Java language. The security policy server system uses relational DBMS for storing alert data that were sent by security policy enforcement system. The PEP detects intrusions and sends information about intrusions to the security policy server system. These data were stored in databases by Alert Manager, and analyzed by Alert Analyzer and Black List Watcher. The High-Level Analyzer, Alert Manager and Blacklist Watcher systematically co-work together using the alert data in database. We design the schema of alert data to be stored in table 2.

Table 2. Schema of Alert Data

Attribute name									
ALID	SID	ATID	ATTYPE	DDATE	SADDR	DADDR	SPORT	DPORT	PROTO

It is an important faculty of the security policy server that analyzes the alert data from security policy enforcement system and responses against those. For supporting these analysis and detecting various intrusions, we need the modules that analyze the correlation of alert data. Correlation analysis of alert data extracts the relationships among alert data, and covers analysis of behavior as well as similarity. Behavior analysis analyzes the correlation behavior[1, 2, 3]. Details are as follows: repetitive analysis, similarity analysis, potentiality analysis and behavior analysis.

Alert Data Mining System

In order to support the security policy server we propose an alert data mining system that consists of three modules such as association rule miner, frequent episode miner and clustering miner. Association rule miner can find the correlation among attributes in record, although frequent episode miner searches event patterns in records. In addition, clustering miner discovers similar attack patterns by grouping alert data with the similarity among alert data. We improved the basic mining algorithms to create candidate item sets that included only interesting attributes.

We expanded Apriori algorithm without grouping items by T_id because of the characteristics of the alert data. So rules can be generated only with attributes of interest. The process of the expanded algorithm is composed of three steps. The process of the association rule miner has three steps.: Finding all frequent item sets composed of interesting attributes, generating strong association rules from the frequent item sets and generating final rules.

An episode is defined by a sequence of specific events that occurs frequently. Using episodes, an infiltration detection system can detect frequently repeated patterns, and apply them to the rule or use them as guidelines for service refusal attacks. Frequent episode mining is carried out through the following 3 steps.:

1) Generating candidate episodes: The tuples composed of attributes of interest are arranged by given time window units.
2) Generating frequent episodes: A set of frequent episodes, which satisfy the minimum frequency, are extracted from the set of candidate episode.
3) Generating final episodes.

In the case of cluster miner, we implemented the modified CURE algorithm, which can cluster datasets with multi-dimensional attributes because of the characteristics of alert data. Such a clustering analysis technique improves the efficiency of the analysis of alert data, and abstracts high-level meanings through grouping data. The implemented clustering miner has four steps of process: data preprocessing, clustering alert data, analyzing the result of clusters, classifying new alert data.

5 Experiments and Evaluation

Our experiments were performed with the factors like minimum support and window width of frequent episodes. We evaluated 32,000 records of the simulated alert data.

The experiments were designed for two objectives. First, how can we decide the minimum support for the alert data. And second, we estimated of window width which could make the frequent episodes miner keep higher performance.

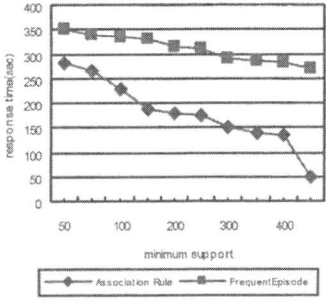 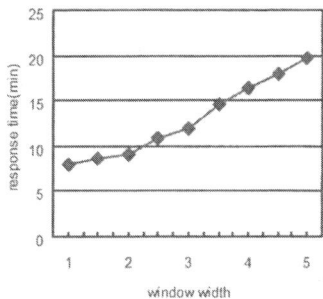

Fig. 1. Experimental Results

Figure 1 showed the time of each minimum support value. In the association rule miner, if the value of minimum support was smaller than the performance was higher .In the frequent episodes miner, the support depended on window width. Figure 1 also showed a little change in the case of the frequent episodes. The results of the frequent episode miner were affected by time variables.

For the clustering miner, two experiments were carried out. One was to test the performance of clustering of the implemented system. The other was to define the cluster previous to each cluster generated, and to determine if the sequence of clusters could be generated based on the sequence. The test data used in this experiment were the KDD Cup 1999 dataset. The test data were assigned to each cluster with relatively high accuracy for attack types such as DOS and Probing, which were distributed in a relatively large amount in the training dataset. However, the attack types such as R2L and U2R, which were rarely distributed in the training dataset, were clustered less accurately. The experiment was defining the previous cluster of each generated cluster, and determining if the sequence of clusters could be generated based on the defined previous clusters. For the experiment, real alert data were used as the input dataset, and the values derived from the experiment above were used as user-defined variables. This experiment generated the sequences of clusters by analyzing the distribution of previous alerts, which were the cause of the generation of the resulting sequences, and showed that it was possible to provide a method of forecasting the future type of alerts occurring by abstracting the sequences of clusters through integrating each sequences of clusters generated.

6 Conclusion

The major contributions of this paper are to apply data mining techniques to alert analysis for supporting security policy server in policy based network security manager. The alert analyzer with mining engine performed three main tasks. The first task was to store alert data in databases and analyze the alert data through the mining tasks. The second one was to construct black list of fault host and user by analyzing the alert data stored in databases. And the third task was to detect the dangerous hosts and users, and reported them to security manager. The alert analyzer with mining engine supports the security policy server to build the active security rules.

References

1. D. Schnackenberg, K. Djahandari, and D. Sterne, "Infrastructure for Intrusion Detection and Response", Proceedings of the DARPA Information Survivability Conference and Exposition, Hilton Head, SC, Jan. 2000
2. Lincoln Lab MIT. DARPA 2000 intrusion detection evaluation datasets. http://ideval.ll.mit.edu/2000 index.html, 2000.
3. W. Lee, S. J. Stolfo, K. W. Mok "A Data Mining Framework for Building Intrusion Detection Models*", Computer Science Department, Columbia University 500 West 120th Street, New York, NY 10027
4. KDD99Cup, ttp://kdd.ics.uci.edu/databases/kddcup99/kddcup99.html, 1999.
5. E. Lupu and M. Sloman, "Conflicts in Policy-based Distributed Systems Management", IEEE Transactions on Software Engineering", Vol. 25, No. 6, Nov. 1999.
6. A. Westerinen, J. Schnizlein, J. Strassner, M. Scherling, B. Quinn, S. Herzog, A. Huynh, M. Carlson, J. Perry, and S. Waldbusser, "Terminology for Policy-Based Management", IETF <draft-ietf-policy-terminology-04.txt>, July. 2001
7. B. Moore, E. Ellesson, J. Strassner, and A. Westerinen, "Policy Core Information Model – Ver. 1 Spec.", IETF RFC3060, Feb. 2001.
8. H. Debar and A.Wespi, "Aggregation and correlation of intrusion-detection alerts", In Recent Advances in Intrusion Detection, number 2212 in Lecture Notes in Computer Science, pages 85–103, 2001.
9. A. Valdes and K. Skinner, "Probabilistic alert correlation", In Proceedings of the 4th International Symposium on Recent Advances in Intrusion Detection (RAID 2001), pages 54–68, 2001.
10. P. Ning and Y. Cui., "An intrusion alert correlator based on prerequisites of intrusions", Technical Report TR-2002-01, Department of Computer Science, North Carolina State University
11. H. S. Moon, M. S. Shin, K. H. Ryu and J. O. Kim "Implementation of security policy server's alert analyzer", ICIS, Aug. 2002

Grid-Based Method for Ranking Images with Multiple Objects

Atul Sajjanhar

School of Information Technology
Deakin University
221 Burwood Highway
Burwood, VIC 3125
Australia
atuls@deakin.edu.au
http://www.deakin.edu.au/~atuls

Abstract. One of the content-based image retrieval techniques is the shape-based technique, which allows users to ask for objects similar in shape to a query object. Sajjanhar and Lu proposed a method for shape representation and similarity measure called the grid-based method [1]. They have shown that the method is effective for the retrieval of segmented objects based on shape. In this paper, we describe a system which uses the grid-based method for retrieval of images with multiple objects. We perform experiments on the prototype system to compare the performance of the grid-based method with the Fourier descriptors method [2]. Preliminary results have been presented.

1 Introduction

Several techniques have been proposed for shape representation and similarity measure. Some of the techniques are Fourier descriptors [2], chain-code [3], moment invariants [4] and decomposition by clustering [5].

In real life scenario, there are several objects within an image. We attempt to use a combination of shape representation techniques to index images with multiple objects. The indices thus generated are used for retrieval of images with multiple objects. In this paper, we describe a prototype system, which uses the grid-based method for indexing images with multiple objects. We use the area of the objects in images to complement the grid-based indices. The resulting indices are used for similarity measure between images with multiple objects. A comparison is performed using Fourier Descriptors based indices for similarity measure. Results of preliminary experiments have been reported.

The technique for normalisation and subsequent derivation of indices for shape representation and similarity measure for the grid-based method and the Fourier descriptors method is described in Section 2 and Section 3 respectively. The experiments are described in Section 4. We present the conclusion in Section 5.

J. Liu et al. (Eds.): IDEAL 2003, LNCS 2690, pp. 1113–1117, 2003.

2 Grid-Based Method

Sajjanhar and Lu proposed the grid-based method [1] for retrieval of objects based on shape. In this section, we discuss the implementation of the grid-based method for images with multiple non-occluded objects. We illustrate the implementation for the image in Fig. 1.

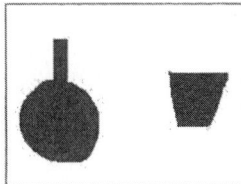

Fig. 1. An Image with Multiple Objects

In the pre-processing stage the objects are segmented based on thresholding [6]. After segmenting the objects, indexing is performed in two stages. In the first stage, we use the grid-based method to derive an index for each object. The indices thus derived represent the shape of the objects. We describe briefly, the process of normalising the objects and deriving the grid-based indices.

An object is normalised for rotation by aligning it's major-axis along the horizontal axis. Normalisation for scale is achieved by scaling each object in a fixed area. We use an area of 300x300 square pixels. The grid-based method is inherently normalised for translation, hence, it is not required to be done explicitly.

We overlay the normalised object with a 20x20 grid with each grid cell being 15x15 pixels. The grid-based index is derived, by overlaying the grid on the normalised object. The index is called the binary number. The binary number of an object is used to represent the shape of the object.

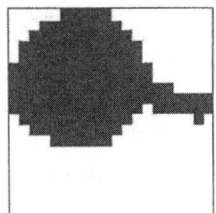 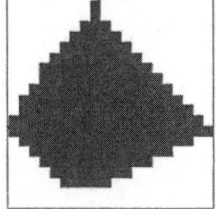

Fig. 2. Indexing by Overlaying a Grid

So far, we have described how to use the grid-based method for indexing multiple objects within images. In the second stage of indexing, we complement the binary number for each object with the size of the object. The size of an object is represented by it's area, which is the count of the internal pixels within the object. An object "*j*" will have an index of the form $(bin_j, area_j)$ comprising of the binary number and the area.

An index for an image with multiple objects will be of the form shown below.

$$IMG : [(bin_0, area_0)(bin_1, area_1)...(bin_{N-1}, area_{N-1})] \tag{1}$$

Where, the image has N *objects*. For computing the difference between images with multiple objects, the computation is done in two steps. In the first step, we compute the difference between the images based on the shapes of the comprising objects. This is obtained as the global best difference between the binary numbers of the objects in the two images. The objects in one image are mapped to the objects in the other image so that the sum of the differences between the binary numbers of the mapped objects is minimum. Equation 2 below shows the difference between two images based on the binary numbers of the comprising objects.

$$Diff_{shape}(IMG_1, IMG_2) = \min\left[\sum_{i,j=0}^{N-1} diff(bin_{1i}, bin_{2j})\right] \tag{2}$$

Where, both the images have N objects. $diff(bin_x, bin_y)$ is the difference between two binary numbers, which is implemented as shown in the Java code above.

In the second step, the difference between object sizes in the images is computed. This step is required because objects in images may be similar in shape but their relative sizes may be vastly different. As a precursor, the mapping of the shapes in one image which best-matched with the shapes in the other is recorded. This mapping is obtained from the global best match in Step 1 above.

The difference in the areas is computed for each pair of the mapped objects in the two images. The sum of the differences thus obtained gives the measure of the difference between the images based on the size of the comprising objects.

To compute the *total difference* between two images, we use a combination of the shape-based difference and size-based difference between the two images. Hence, we combine the difference obtained from Step 1 and Step 2. The combination of the shape component and the size component is done according to user defined weights. For example, we can use a weighting of 0.8 for the difference based on shapes and a weighting of 0.2 for the difference based on sizes of objects.

The weighted difference between two images based on the shapes of the objects is computed as shown in Equation 3. The shape-based difference between the two images is scaled in the range 0-100. The scaled difference is multiplied by the user assigned weight to obtain the final difference.

$$wt\_diff_{shape}(IMG_1, IMG_2) = wt_{shape} \times \left[\left(\frac{Diff_{shape}(IMG_1, IMG_2)}{\max[Diff_{shape}(IMG_1, IMG_j)]}\right) \times 100\right] \tag{3}$$

The size-based difference is computed similarly. The sum of differences obtained on the basis of shape and size gives the total difference between the images.

3 Fourier Descriptors Method

Fourier descriptors have been used for computing the similarity between objects based on shape [2]. In the Fourier descriptors method the object boundary is represented in terms of a function, which is called the shape signature. Fourier descriptors for object boundaries are derived from the Fourier transformation of the function used as the shape signature. We use the centroidal distance as the shape signature [2]. We use 64 Fourier coefficients obtained from the DFT of the shape signature to derive indices for the shapes. The Euclidean distance between the Fourier descriptors of two objects gives the measure of difference between the objects based on shape.

For images with multiple objects, each object is represented by Fourier descriptors. The shape-based difference between two images is computed as the global best difference between the sets of Fourier descriptors for the two images.

We also need to compute the difference between the sizes of objects in the images. This is done similarly to the method used in Section 2. Hence, this is computed as the sum of the difference between the areas of the best-matched shapes.

A combination of the shape-based and size-based difference is used to obtain the *total difference* between two images. The combination of the two components is done, by assigning user defined weights to each component.

4 Experimental Results

We compare the performance of the methods described in Sections 2 and 3 for retrieval of images with multiple objects.

Our database consists of 35 synthesised images. Each image in the database has two non-occluded objects. We perform 5 queries on the database. The recall and the precision for the 5 queries is obtained for the Fourier descriptors based method and the grid-based method. Fig. 3 shows the average values of recall-precision for the 5 queries. In this experiment a weighting of 0.2 was assigned to the size component of the difference between the query image and the database image.

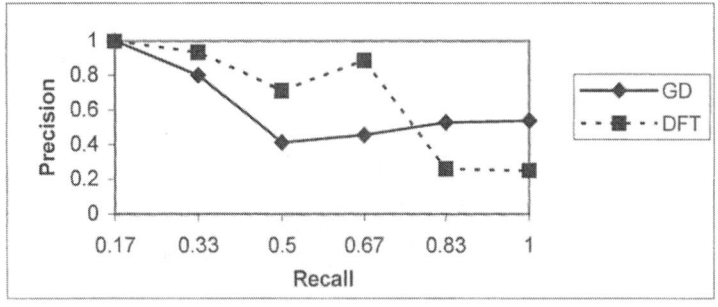

Fig. 3. Weighting of 0.2 for the Size Component

Fig. 4 shows the recall-precision for the second experiment. In this experiment, same queries were made but with a weighting of 0.5 assigned to the size component of the difference between images.

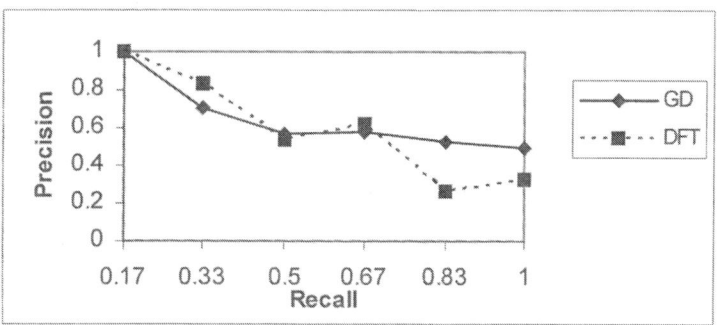

Fig. 4. Weighting of 0.5 for the Size Component

5 Conclusion

We have implemented the grid-based method and the Fourier descriptors method for the retrieval of images with multiple objects. The experiments performed show that the grid-based method and the Fourier descriptors method perform comparably.

References

1. Sajjanhar, A., Lu, G.: A Grid Based Shape Indexing and Retrieval Method, The Australian Computer Journal, Vol. 29, No. 4 (1997) 131–140
2. Kauppinen, H., Seppanen, T., Pietikainen, M.: An Experimental Comparison of Autoregressive Fourier-Based Descriptors in 2D Shape Classification, IEEE transactions on Pattern Analysis and Machine Intelligence, 17(2) (1995) 201–207
3. Freeman, H.: Computer Processing of Line-Drawing Images, Computing Surveys, 6(1) (1974) 57–97
4. Hu, M. K.: Visual pattern recognition by moment invariants, IRE transactions on Information Theory, IT-8 (1962) 179–187
5. Shapiro, L. G., Haralick, R. M.: Decomposition of two-dimensional shapes by graph theoretic clustering, IEEE transactions on Pattern Analysis and Machine Intelligence (1979) 10–20
6. Gonzalez, R., Woods, R.: Digital Image Processing, 2nd edn, Prentice Hall (2002)

Asynchronous Messaging Using
Message-Oriented-Middleware

Sushant Goel[1], Hema Sharda[1], and David Taniar[2]

[1] School of Electrical and Computer systems Engineering, Royal Melbourne Institute of
Technology, Australia
{hema.sharda}@rmit.edu.au
[2] School of Business Systems, Monash University, Australia
David.Taniar@infotech.monash.edu.au

Abstract. Different middleware technologies have been facilitating the communication between the distributed applications. RMI and CORBA are the most commonly used technology for communication between distributed components. This research work was undertaken in view of increasing e-business requirements. The *Transfer of Messages in Distributed Systems* (TMDS Architecture) proposed in this paper is based on the concept of asynchronous communication between components. The advantage of the proposed architecture is that the sender of the message can continue processing after sending the message and need not wait for the reply from other application. TMDS Architecture ensures guaranteed delivery of the message. TMDS Architecture supports two major domain of asynchronous messaging: (*i*) Publish/Subscribe and (*ii*) Point-To-Point. In addition TMDS architecture has the facility to prioritize the message, filter messages on certain conditions and also supports easy integration of new systems with the existing legacy systems.

1 Introduction

In today's scenario computers are a vital part of modern infrastructure. Type of applications has evolved rapidly from stand-alone architecture to mainframe architecture to two-tier client/server or three-tier (multi-tier) client/server architecture [3,6]. To communicate between physically separated machines, there must be a mechanism to establish the relationship between the two.

The main objective of this paper is to enhance the features of messaging-architecture in distributed environment. The concept of middleware has been into existence since late 1970. Middleware is connectivity software that consists of a set of enabling services that allow multiple processes running on one or more machines to interact across a network [3].

Different technologies have been used for implementing the middleware like Remote Procedure Call (RPC), Remote Method Invocation (RMI), Common Object Request Broker Architecture (CORBA), COM, DCOM etc. One of the important issues in the distributed systems is communication between different components of the distributed system [4]. A great deal of research is going on in this field.

J. Liu et al. (Eds.): IDEAL 2003, LNCS 2690, pp. 1118–1122, 2003.

The rest of this paper is organized as follows. Section 2 describes the background including messaging systems, middleware, JMS, and domain of messaging. Section 3 presents our proposed architecture. Section 4 gives the conclusions and explains future work.

2   Messaging Systems: Background

This section discusses various concepts of Message Oriented Middleware (MOM), including various domains of messaging like publish/subscribe and point-to-point messaging. Message is the package of business data, which contains the actual load and all the necessary routing information to travel in the network for delivery.

2.1   Enterprise Messaging and Message-Oriented-Middleware (MOM)

Messaging is a peer-to-peer communication between software applications [5]. A messaging system allows separate, uncoupled applications to reliably communicate asynchronously. Distributed applications can communicate in two ways:

Synchronous Communication: When the application sends any message to another application and waits for the reply.

Asynchronous Communication: When the application sends the message and continues processing without waiting for any reply from another application [8].

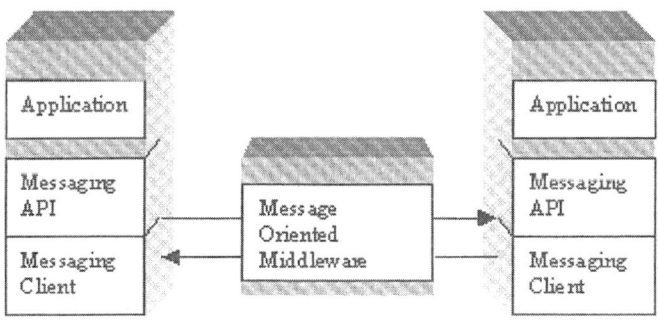

Fig. 1. Message Oriented Middleware

To open up from the tightly synchronized hardware *Messaging-Oriented-Middleware (MOM)* provides the reliable data delivery mechanisms.

Java Message Service (JMS) and Domains of Messaging Supported by JMS: The JMS API provides the way to decouple the clients. JMS is a specification, which contains interfaces and abstract classes in itself needed by the messaging clients while communicating with messaging systems.

Publish and Subscribe Domain of Messaging: Pub/sub domain of messaging is used when a group of users are to be informed about a particular event. Communication between the two is done by a central concept called 'topic' [8].

Point-To-Point Domain of Messaging: Point-to-point messaging domain communicates between clients using the concept of 'queue'.

Major components to build up the application are: (*a*) Administered Objects, (*b*) Connection Factories, (*c*) Sessions, (*d*) Message Producers, (*e*) Message consumers, and (*f*) Messages. JMS defines five types of message body [7] – Text, Object, Byte, Map and Stream messages. Components are shown in the following figure.

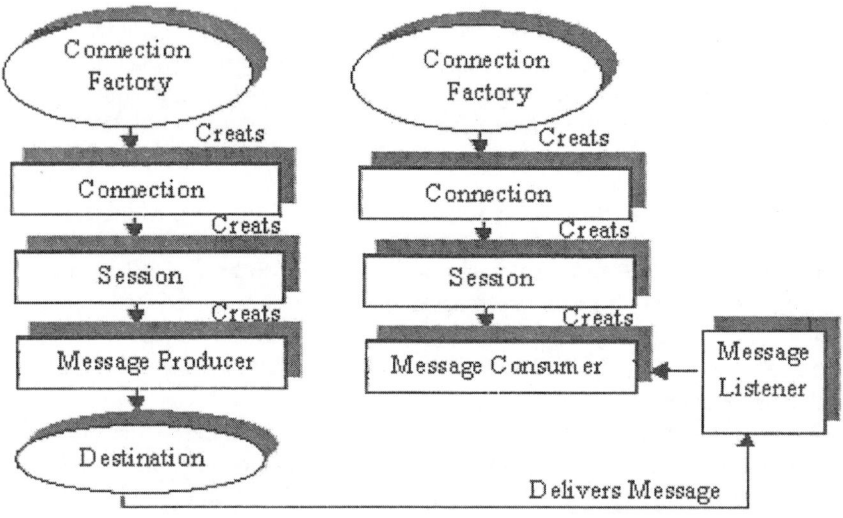

Fig. 2. Architecture of JMS application [8]

3   The Proposed Architecture: TMDS

TMDS architecture is able to handle the messages not only when the consumer of the message is disconnected, but also is able to provide the acknowledgment of the received message. TMDS architecture supports XML message formats. The benefit of using the XML message format is that, the industry has a unanimously agreed standard of communication and the messages can be shared between different vendors without any conflict. The XML data transfer between applications is shown in figure.

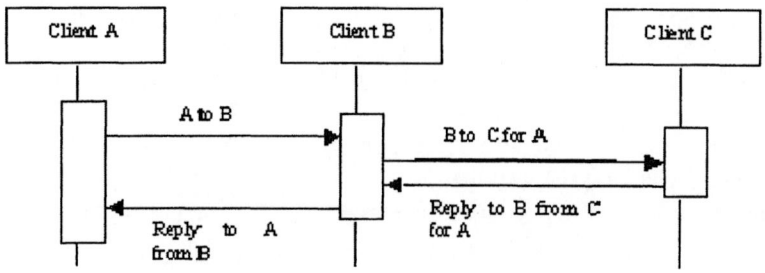

Fig. 3. XML data transfer between applications

3.1 Message Acknowledgment

Message acknowledgment protocol is most important in the guaranteed messaging domain. The successful message consumption takes place in three stages: (*i*) Message is received, (*ii*) Message is processed, and (*iii*) Message is acknowledged.

The session automatically acknowledges a client's receipt of a message when the client has successfully executed the `receive()` method for the queue or when the `messageListener()` is successfully executed for the topic.

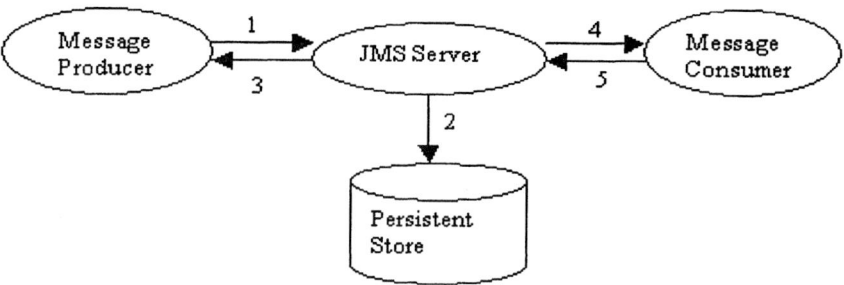

Fig. 4. Flow sequence for delivery of persistent message

3.2 Setting System Properties

Setting Message Priority and Allowing Messages to Expire: To increase the performance of the application, TMDS architecture provides the facility to expire the message after a certain amount of time and to deliver an urgent message it allows setting the priority level of the message.

Creating Durable Subscription: In pub/sub domain to make sure that the messages are delivered to the client, TMDS architecture uses the `PERSISTENT` messages and the durable subscription for the subscriber. The messaging server keeps the message in the persistent storage till the message is delivered to all the durable subscribers or the message expires.

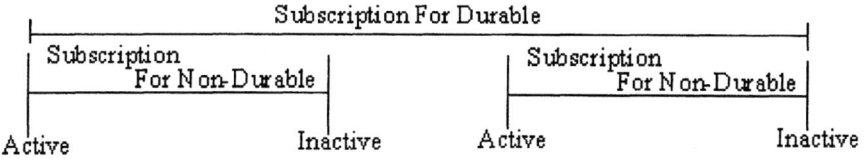

Fig. 5. Subscriber and Subscription for durable and Non-durable subscriber

3.3 Features and Advantages of TMDS Architecture

The messages are not directly delivered to the recipient but the messages are delivered to the recipient via the virtual destinations called '*topic*' or '*queue*'.

Destinations are the delivery labels in messaging rather than the place where the message is ultimately delivered. A destination is the commonly understood staging area for the message.

Because of traditional messaging system's inherent weaknesses like – limited client connections, poor performance due to lack of resource pooling, no store-and-forward mechanism or load balancing, lack of guaranteed messaging and security as well as static client and server's location dependent code, Asynchronous JMS messaging could be a better option to implement solution to distributed systems.

4 Conclusion and Future Work

TMDS messaging architecture provides a flexible way of communication between distributed systems. TMDS architecture supports pub/sub and PTP domain of messaging enhancing the features of JMS specification. The proposed architecture is scalable, ensures guaranteed delivery, supports asynchronous messaging, and extends the features of JMS specifications by transferring the data in XML format.

As discussed, TMDS architecture uses the XML data format, which is data-centric XML. Using the document-centric XML can still enhance the features of TMDS architecture. The present architecture uses the RDBMS and text files for managing the data. Using the Object Databases and XML enabled databases can still increase the performance of the application. The present architecture can very easily be extended to implement the clustering of the centralised server to ensure non-stop availability of the server.

References

1   Adler, R. M. "Distributed Coordination Models for Client/Sever Computing." *Computer 28*, 4, 14–22 April 1995.
2   Bernstein, Philip A. "Middleware: A Model for Distributed Services." *Communications of the ACM 39*, 2, 86–97, February 1996.
3   Eckerson, Wayne W., "Three Tier Client/Server Architecture: Achieving Scalability, Performance, and Efficiency in Client Server Applications", *Open Information System 95.*
4   Newell D., Jones, O., and Machura, M. "Interoperable Object Models for Large Scale Distributed Systems," *Inter. Seminar on Client/Server Computing.* Oct 95. London.
5   Rao, B.R. "Making the Most of Middleware." *Data Communications International 24*, 12, 89–96 September 1995.
6   Schill, Alexander. "DCE-The OSF Distributed Computing Environment Client/Server Model and Beyond," *International DCE Workshop.* Oct 93. Germany: Springer-Verlag.
7   Gopalan S, Grant S., Giotta P *"Professional JMS"*, 1ˢᵗ Edition, Wrox publicaton.
8   Mark Hapner, JMS Specification version 1.0.2b, Sun Microsystems, August, 2001
9   Birmen K., *"Building Secure and Reliable Network applications"* Manning Publishing and Prentice Hall, December 1996.

Improved Object Recognition – The RoboCup 4-Legged League

Vladimir Estivill-Castro[1] and Nathan Lovell[1]

School of Computing and Information Technology
Griffith University
Brisbane 4111 QLD Australia

Abstract. The RoboCup competition has brought back to attention the classification of objects in a controlled illumination environment. We present a very fast classifier to achieve image segmentation. Our methods are based on the machine literature, but adapted to robots equipped with low cost image-capture equipment. We then present new fast methods for object recognition, based on also rapid methods for blob formation. We describe how to extract the skeleton of a polygon and we use this for object recognition.

1 Introduction

RoboCup has brought back to attention the classification of objects in a controlled illumination environment. Color plays a major role since certain objects are uniquely colored [2,7,8]. For Robocup, the dynamics of the environment forces rapid analysis of images. There is no use in analyzing a frame that is not current. We describe the design of a vision system for the legged league. In this league, each robot has a camera capable of grabbing a frame of 174×144 pixels, each with 3 components of one byte, representing the YUV color space [12]. The challenge is that color segmentation and object recognition share CPU time with all other tasks on the robots. Moreover, the camera moves along with the robot, so no steady background exists. We present a very fast classifier to achieve image segmentation. In a sense, it is surprising that very little investigation has been performed on the methods available form the Machine Learning (or Data Mining) literature given that this task fits a classical classifier learning framework. We then discuss fast methods for object recognition, based on also rapid methods for blob formation. We also describe a new and fast method to extract the skeleton of a polygon and we use this for object recognition. Our experiments show we can identify opponents and their posture in each frame. This is something none of the participating research teams in the competition has reported so far.

2 Image Segmentation

The segmentation task is to identify, for each pixel, what is the corresponding environment color. This fits the classification task framework — from 3D space

J. Liu et al. (Eds.): IDEAL 2003, LNCS 2690, pp. 1123–1130, 2003.

to a set of 10 or 11 classes of colors (depending if there is interest in classifying white). Research in RoboCup has explored machine learning and statistical discrimination techniques like linear discriminants, decision trees (DT), Artificial Neural Networks (ANN) and instance-based classifiers (k-nearest neighbors and other non-parametric statistics), but the state of the art (in terms of accuracy vs speed) for this environment remains a look-up table of characteristic vectors for each of the 3 dimensions [2]. Look-up table is simply much faster. Our approach delivers a method to build a classifier of equivalent speed to the look-up table, but for which the accuracy is remarkably higher. Our method matches the accuracy levels of DT and k-nearest neighbor (k-NN) schemes.

We therefore describe first the look-up table approach and how it takes advantage of the parallelism of operations on bytes. We will represent a function $color\_class : Y \times U \times V \to Color$ that given a triplet (y, u, v) produces the color class by much simpler functions. In particular, we first focus on characteristics functions for each color. For example, $Class_{orange} : Y \times U \times V \to \{True, False\}$ returns $True$ when the pixel is in the class $orange$ and $False$ otherwise. It is clear that the target function can be represented in terms of the characteristic functions of the colors. However, each characteristic function remains hard to represent efficiently because regions where it evaluates to $True$ have irregular shapes in 3D. A direct look-up table representation would require an array of size $\|Y\| \times \|U\| \times \|V\| = 256^3$, which is over 16 Megabits and totally unfeasible for the robots' RAM capacity.

Therefore, a simplification represents the domain by rectangular boxes in 3D. The characteristic function of each color is represented by characteristic projection functions on each of the dimensions Y, U and V. For example, 3 characteristic projections Y_{orange}, U_{orange} and V_{orange} are used to approximate $Class_{orange}$. Namely, $Class_{orange}(y, u, v) \approx Y_{orange}(y) \wedge U_{orange}(u) \wedge V_{orange}(v)$. Each of the characteristic functions Y_{orange}, U_{orange} and V_{orange} has a domain of 256 values. Thus, they are represented by a look-up array that stores 1 if the projection function evaluates to $True$ and 0 if it evaluates to $False$. The approximation is a region shaped as a box because each projection function test if its input is in an interval defined by constants $Min_{projection,color}$ and $Max_{projection.color}$. That is, they are of the form

$$projection_{color}(x) = \begin{cases} 1 \text{ if } Min_{projection,color} \leq x \text{ and } x \leq Max_{projection,color} \\ 0 \text{ otherwise.} \end{cases}$$

Because the 3 look-up tables of a color only store binary values, we can take advantage of parallelism on RAM-word size. Namely, we only need 3 arrays Y, U and V of 256 bytes each to represent the classifier function of eight colors. The representation of the first color is placed in the left most bit position of the 3 arrays. The bit in the second position is used for the second color, and so on. A C/C++ bit-wise AND-operation like

$$\text{color} = \text{Y[y]\&U[u]\&V[v]};\tag{1}$$

essentially represents the classifier function $Color\_class$. The only thing left to do is to compute $\log_2$ of the value in $Color$ to obtain the id of the color class. The task then consists of finding the values of $Min_{projection,color}$ and $Max_{projection,color}$ for $projection \in \{Y, U, V\}$ and all colors.

After this explanation is not surprising that classifiers like ANN, DT, or k-NN are a significant constant factor slower for classification. These other classifiers require much more complex operations involving computation of Euclidean (or similar distances), floating point multiplications, or even comparisons that even between bytes result in an integer subtraction and test with integer representation of zero. How can one do better that the single Statement (1)?

The key observation that we make here is that after Statement (1), we still need some piece of code as follows:

```
color_id =0;
while (color & 1 == 0)  {color>>=1; color_id++; }
```

This means decision lists [13] test the clauses $(Min_{projection,color} \leq x) \wedge (x \leq Max_{projection,color})$. Thus, our approach is to build a large training set and use covering algorithms to learn decision lists that classify into the color classes. We briefly explain the generalities of these methods [13]. Given a training set T consisting of N labeled instances $(u, u, v, color\_class)$, this supervised learning technique attempts to find the best rule for some class. Once this rule has been found, the rule constitutes the next rule in the decision list. All instances in T covered by the recently produced rule are removed from T and the algorithm repeats with the instances left. This continues until no instances are left. Variations on these algorithms appear as rules are assessed. The more sophisticated measures of rule quality result in slower learning algorithms.

We experimented with three algorithms of this class. The first is PRISM [3]. This algorithm evaluates rules by their accuracy. That is, simple by the ratio p/t where p is the number of instances correctly classified by the rule and t is the total number of instances covered by the rule. The next variant degree is to evaluate rules by their information gain, namely, by $p\left[\log_2(p/t) - \log_2(P/N)\right]$ where P are the total number of examples of the class in T. However, our experiments showed that classifiers built with these algorithms are inaccurate for this application. The next innovative observation we make with respect to this environment is that we are not constrained to have only one rule for each color class. In fact, we suggest here to use the more powerful algorithms for decision lists. As long as the decision list has less rules than the RAM-word length and each rule can be encoded as a conjunction of characteristic functions in each projection, then we can represent the decision list in 3 arrays and evaluate them with Statement (1) and the code discussed before. We can use statistics to select the more frequent color classes as those whose rules will be in the right-most bits. This makes faster execution than a random ordering of the color classes. We suggest here the use of the algorithm PART as implemented in Weka [13]. We used a training set of 6,226 instances and a testing set of 1,349 instances. The data set has instances from 11 color classes. We compared PART (with the state of the art implementation of Decision Trees (DT) and k-Nearest Neighbor (k-NN) provided by Weka. Table 1 shows accuracy results from two test modes. First, 10-fold cross validation on the training set and accuracy on the un-seen instances of the testing set. Clearly PART is a competitive alternative. But in

Table 1. Accuracy Comparison.

Algorithm	10-fold accuracy	lowest accuracy per class	largest 2-class confusion	size	learning time	test set accuracy
PART	99.0%	96% (yellow goal)	10 blue dog vs gray dog	26 rules	1.15s	99.3%
k-NN	99.3%	97% (blue dog)	8 red dog vs gray dog	$k = 3$ 6,226 instances	0s	99.7%
DT	98.8%	95% (yellow goal)	10 red dog vs gray dog	34 leaves, 67 nodes	1.27s	99.6%
Look-up table	71.6%	64% (yellow goal)	45 yellow goal vs orange ball	11 rules	manual	68.2%

this application, the crucial factor is the classification time (training time is not important because it can be performed off-line). Thus, the next set of results discusses classification time.

The k-NN algorithm in Weka stores the training data set and takes no time. However, the classifier is very large and classification time is extremely slow (proportional to N). We implemented a $logN$-time classifier by using Oct-trees (Quad-trees in 3D). This achieves classification times twice slower than DT but model construction requires half the time than DT. We used a MS-Windows API accurate to $1/3579545$ of a second to compare our algorithms versus table look-up on 100 different images each consisting of over 25,000 pixels. Table 2 displays the maximum amount of time in mili-seconds that both methods take to classify a pixel, as well as the minimum and the average over all classified pixels. Our decision list approach does not use frequency of colors to order the decision rules, so it is the slowest version in our approach. The look-up table classifies only orange, so it is the fastest of the look-up table approach. We can see that the decision list approach, as implemented is less than twice slower. It should be noted that classification time of ANN and Decision Trees and Quad-Tree k-NNis much slower. We used **snns2c** and SNNS[14] to construct ANN, but these were a factor of 20,000 times slower than PART. Quad-tree k-NN and DTwere 2,000 times much slower at classification time.

Table 2. CPU time per pixel.

	DL	Look-up Table	ratio
Maximum	$2.87ms$	$2.46ms$	1.16
Average	$2.33ms$	$1.41ms$	1.65
Minimum	$2.08ms$	$1.27ms$	1.63

3   Blob Forming

We present a new approach to computing "blobs" (maximally contiguous groups of pixels of the same color class).

The most compact representation for a blob is not given by any list of the pixels that form it. A description of its boundary is much more succinct. Moreover, after color segmentation, we can only expect to perform object recognition because of the features of the boundary. We construct an intermediate data structure to concurrently construct all blobs. This data structure will rapidly merge information for each color. Then, using the segmented image, the boundary can be traced to obtain the polygonal lines that define the blob. The intermediate data structure for a blob contains (among other things) the ids of two pixels (the left-most pixel in the blob and the right-most pixel in the blob). Initially, these ids are null (for an empty blob). Blobs are computed by appending to them horizontal run-length blocks of pixels (we call this Maximal Contiguous Horizontal blocks of pixels of the same color class MCH-blocks). It takes two comparisons to update the right-most and left-most pixel ids in the intermediate data structure when a MCH-block is added to a blob.

For the construction of blobs, a row of pixels is processed with respect to "the row above" it. In the current row, from left to right, the next MCH-block is processed. An MCH-block may cause the start of a new blob, if there is no overlapping blob of the same color class in the row above. This is how the top row, which does not have a row above, is processed. The other option is that the MCH-block does overlap with blobs of the same color class in the row above. In this case, the current MCH-block has to be included into a blob that overlaps. If more than one blob overlap form the row above, the current MCH-block forces these blobs to merge. The merge operation needs to update the pixel ids by choosing, as the left-most pixel, the left-most pixel of the left-most pixels in each merging blob. Analogously for the right-most blob.

We have chosen 'overlap' to mean there is a pixel in the current MCH-block for which one of its 8 neighbors (as moves of a chess-king) is in the blob above (of course, because the blob is above, it is only 3 neighbors). However, one can chose 'overlap' to mean there are two pixels with adjacent y-coordinates and common x-coordinate. Others [11] implement UNION-FIND algorithms to update the blob's names when a merge operation occurs. However, we opt for a different solution due to the higher precision of our image segmentation. The intermediate data structure for a blob has a sorted list of the MCH-blocks that are currently exposed in the row above. The list is sorted by the x-coordinate of the left-most pixel in the MCH-block. Since good segmentation reduces the holes in color patches, this lists are typically very short. A merge operations goes though the lists of blobs being merged unifying the blob id in the row above.

Now, we are in a position to describe the data structure for the row-above. This is also a sorted list with key the x-coordinate of the left-most pixel (in the row) in a a block and each block has a blob id. The processing of a row in the image is now very similar to merging two sorted list (it does not backtrack on the row). It transforms the current-row into the new row above for the processing of next row. Moreover, we found it feasible to discard blobs that are one or two pixels in total and integrate them as part of the surrounding blob. This removes noise from color segmentation.

Because we classify all colors in our row processing, another advantage of our approach emerges. Typically a blob with color-class white crosses horizontally the entire image. This corresponds to the surrounding barriers of the field and all blobs above it can be discarded from any further processing.

Because the identification of the ball (in orange) is a crucial task for the entire behavior of the robot, we have a specialized treatment for orange blobs. The intermediate data structure not only keeps track of the 2 pixel ids (right-most and left-most), but also top-most, bottom-most and 4 pixel ids that correspond to the pixels in a bounding box with sides congruent with 45°. When adding a MCH-block to an orange blob, updating the additional pixels is slightly more costly but still requires constant time. However, these pixels guarantee that we always have at least 3 pixels in the boundary of the physical ball (irrespectively of the clipping by the camera frame). Fig. 3 illustrates this. These pixels are reasonably spread to compute a circumcircle though them. This then allows us to estimate the center of the ball, and the radius of the projected circle. From this, we can compute distance to the ball, orientation of the robot relative to the ball, and so on, without further analysis of the orange blob. This compares favorably with algorithms that trace boundaries/edges of orange blobs or the approach in the middle sized league [1]. There, the distance from the robot to the ball is estimated by finding boundary pixels of orange against green, and assuming this is the ground. Then, an expected orange blob is computed (from the physical size of the ball) and compared to the orange blob in order to decide if this orange blob is indeed the ball. Similarly, goals and post have regular shapes that are easy recognized. We now discuss recognizing opponents.

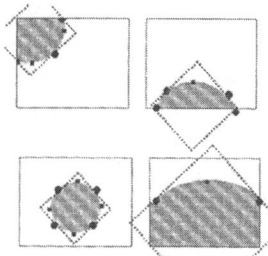

Fig. 1. Ball is identified with pixels in the boundary.

4   Shape Finding

The now classical approach to object recognition based on shape is the notion of skeleton (and the very closely related concept of medial axis [5]). Fig. 2 illustrates this concept. Several algorithms have been developed for computing the skeleton. Raster based algorithms have complexity proportional at least to the number p of pixels in the polygon. The vector-based approach computes the Voronoi Diagram of the line segments that constitute the boundary of the polygon [9]. We have chosen this approach because the input is at most the number b of pixels in the

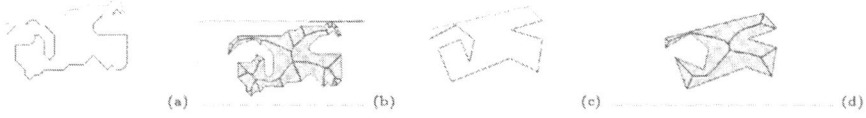

(a)   (b)   (c)   (d)

Fig. 2. Skeleton abstracts the shape in the boundary.

boundary of the polygon. For most blobs b is much less than p. The computation of the blobs above does not directly produce a vector-based representation of the boundary of the blob. Space prevents us from describing our algorithm to trace the boundary pixels in order to obtain the sequence of vertices that defines the boundary of the blob as a polyline. The algorithms is not new, but its time requirements are proportional to the number of pixels on the boundary of the blob. We could compute the skeleton directly from the boundary of the blob. However, the pixel resolution creates many artifacts that are attributable to the grid of pixels and to the segmentation rather than to the shape of the blob. As a result, the skeleton of the blob is unnecessarily complicated. For example, Fig 2 (a-b) shows the skeleton of the boundary patch of the torso of an Aibo robot (dog) and its graph has over 20 vertices. Many of the edges and vertices of this skeleton introduce large discrepancies with expected skeletons. This results in ineffective shape recognition. We propose here to use a polyline simplification algorithm. We import ideas from the Douglas-Peucker algorithm for discretizing a curve. We observe here that, after tracing the boundary of a blob, we have a polyline where every pixels in the boundary is a vertex of the polyline. We therefore simplify the polyline using less vertices but maintaining the shape. Typically, to simplify a polyline, the Douglas-Peucker [4] algorithm choses the straight line between the start and the end vertices as a simplification and halts if a satisfactory approximation is obtained. Otherwise, the vertex v_h halfway between the start vertex v_s and the end vertex v_e is chosen and the algorithms continues with two recursive calls on the polyline from v_s to v_h and on the polyline from v_h to v_e. We here asses the approximation of the polyline by the straight line of its endpoints as follows. We compute the value of the largest Manhattan distance (also known as L_1 metric) of a point in the polyline to the approximating line. This is much faster than the classic Euclidean distance computation. Not only is squaring and taking roots avoided, but we can compute parameters of the straight line once, outside the loop that iterates on the pixels of the polyline. Thus each Manhattan distance is computed with a couple of additions per boundary pixel. The halving technique of the algorithm guarantees $O(b \log b)$ time complexity where b is the number of vertices on the boundary of the blob. The effect of a simplified boundary is shown in Fig. 2 (c-d).

In order to complete the object recognition task we encode skeletons as attributed graphs. That is, we consider skeletons as graphs where each edge has a weight equal to the Euclidean distance between its endpoints. Vertices also have a weight that corresponds to the number of pixels of the blob they represent. We construct a database of graphs representing known 6 views of opponent (or friendly) robots. These include a view from the front, the back, and the side while standing as well as while laying on their bodies. We then use an heuristic for the Error-Correcting Graph Isomorphism [6,10] to identify the most similar object to the current view. We represent the attributed graph by its (symmetric) adjacency matrix. The edge from vertex v_i to vertex v_j with weight w_{ij} results in the matrix entry $a_{ij} = w_{ij}$. The weight of vertex v_i results in the diagonal entry $a_{ii} = w_i$. The heuristic that tries to find the permutation of rows and columns that minimizes the discrepancy between the matrices works as follows. If adds the values of every row in both matrices. It then pairs rows as they rank by their sum. We have found this heuristics very efficient and fast since typically our graphs have less than 10 vertices.

References

1. T Bandlow, M. Klupsch, R Hanek, and T. Schmitt. Fast image segmentation, object recognition and localization in a robocup scenario. M. M. Veloso, et al eds, *3rd RoboCup Conf.*, LNCS 1856, 174–185, 1999. Springer-Verlag.
2. J. Bruce, T. Balch, and M. Veloso. Fast and inexpensive color image segmentation for interactive robots. *2000 IEEE-RSJ Int. Conf. Intelligent Robots and Systems (IROS '00)*, 2061–2066, Robotics Society of Japan, IEEE.
3. W Cendrowska. PRISM: An algorithm for inducing modular rules. *International Journal of Man-Machine Studies*, 27(4):349–370, 1987.
4. D.H. David H. Douglas and T.K. Peucker. Algorithms for the reduction of the number of points required to represent a digitized line or its caricature. *Canadian Cartographer*, 10(2):112–122, December 1973.
5. R.O. Duda and P.E. Hart. *Pattern Classification and Scene Analysis*. John Wiley & Sons, NY, USA, 1973.
6. V. Estivill-Castro and R. Torres-Velazquez. Classical sorting embedded in genetic algorithms for improved permutation search. *2001 Congress on Evolutionary Computation CEC2001*, 941–948, , Seoul, Korea, 2001. IEEE Press.
7. R. Hanek, W. Schmitt, B. Buck, and M. Beetz. Fast image-based object localization in natural scenes. In *In Proc. of the IEEE Intl. Conf. on Intelligent Robots and Systems (submitted) (2002), IEEE/RSJ.*, 2002.
8. R. Hanek, The contracting curve density algorithm and its application to model-based image segmentation. In *Proc. Conf. Computer Vision and Pattern Recognition*, pages I:797–804, 2001.
9. Ogniewicz R.L. and O. Kübler. Hierarchic voronoi skeletons. *Pattern Recognition*, 28(3):343–359, 1995.
10. L.G. Shapiro and R.M. Haralick. Structural discriptions and inexact matching. *IEEE T. on Pattern Analysis and Machine Intelligence*, 3(5):504–519, 1981.
11. M. Veloso, S. Lenser, J. Bruce, W. Uther, and M. Hock. CMPack-01: CMU's legged robots soccer team. Report from Participnats if RoboCup 2001, October 16th.
12. M. Veloso, W. Uther, M. Fujita, M. Asada, and H. Kitano. Playing soccer with legged robots. *IROS-98, Intelligent Robots and Systems Conference*, Victoria, 1998.
13. I. Witten and E. Frank. *Data Mining — Practical Machine Learning Tools and Technologies with JAVA implementations*. Morgan Kaufmann CA, 2000.
14. A et al Zell. SNNS stuttgart neural network simulator, user manual, version 4.2.

Objectionable Image Recognition System in Compression Domain

Qixiang Ye, Wen Gao, Wei Zeng, Tao Zhang, Weiqiang Wang, and Yang Liu

Institute of Computing Technology, Chinese Academy of Sciences, Beijing 100080, China
{Qxye, Wgao, Wqw}@ict.ac.cn

Abstract. In this paper, we propose an intelligent recognition system for objectionable image in JPEG compression domain. First, the system applies robust skin color model and skin texture analysis to detect the skin regions in an input image based on its DC and ACs. Then, the color, texture, shape and statistical features are extracted from the skin regions and input into a decision-tree classifier for classification. A large image library including about 120,000 images is employed to evaluate the system's effectiveness.

1 Introduction

Internet has been brought more and more objectionable information especially objectionable images to people. There has been a strong demand for screening out these objectionable images from underage children, and this demand is also growing.

For that there are lots of limitations when using text analysis to recognize objectionable images, there has been existed some solutions for recognizing objectionable images by image content analysis. In [1], Forsyth designed and implemented an automatic system for identifying whether there are naked people presenting in an image. After skin detection, the geometric processing is used to grouping skin into human figure for human body detection. Wang et al. [2] presented a system of screening objectionable images for practical applications. Wang's method uses a combination of an icon filter, a graph-photo detector, a color histogram filter, a texture filter and a wavelet-based shape matching algorithm. Jones and Rehg developed objectionable images system based on a statistic skin color detection models and a neural network classifier [3].

By observing that most of objectionable images on the web are JPEG format images, and compressed domain processing may yield great advantages compared with spatial domain processing in the following aspects, a) smaller data volume, b) lower computation complexity since full decompression can be avoided, we develop this objectionable image recognition system for compressed images.

The entire objectionable image recognition system consists of three steps: skin detection, features extraction and objectionable image recognition. We will introduce them in the section 2 and 3. Experimental results are summarized in section 4. Section 5 gives the summary.

J. Liu et al. (Eds.): IDEAL 2003, LNCS 2690, pp. 1131–1135, 2003.

2   Skin Detection in Compressed Domain

Before introducing skin detection algorithm, we introduce the block-DCT briefly.

2.1 Block-DCT Transformation

Given a JPEG image, after the Huffman decoding, DCT information for each 8x8 block can be directly gotten by the image IDCT operation [4]. The first coefficient of a given block (DC) represents the average pixel intensity for that block (Fig.1) [4]. Then we can judge if an 8 x 8 block is or is not a skin color block just according to the DC value. We can tell if an 8×8 block is or is not a skin texture block according to the ACs and by the proposed method in Section 2.3.

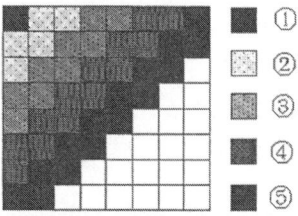

Fig. 1. DCT feature of an 8 x 8 block. ① is DC coefficient, ② ③ ④ ⑤ are the coefficients groups representing each frequency band characteristic.

2.2 Skin Color Detection

To weak the influence of illuminations, we propose a simple and efficient solution to detect the skin color under different illuminations. We pre-group the sample images into different clusters according the average image brightness and learned different color models in YCbCr color space.

In proposed approach, the pixel is represented by the color and average image brightness L. Then, the posterior probability of skin pixels is

$$P(Skin \mid YCbCr, L) = \frac{P(YCbCr, L \mid Skin)P(Skin)}{P(YCbCr, L \mid Skin)P(Skin) + P(YCbCr, L \mid \neg Skin)P(\neg Skin)} \quad (2)$$

where $P(YCbCr, L \mid Skin)$ and $P(YCbCr, L \mid \neg Skin)$ are the prior probability of skin and non-skin pixels under the average brightness L. They are formulated as

$$P(YCbCr, L \mid Skin) = \frac{P(YCbCr \mid Skin, L)P(Skin, L)}{P(Skin)} \quad (3)$$

$$P(YCbCr, L \mid \neg Skin) = \frac{P(YCbCr \mid \neg Skin, L)P(\neg Skin, L)}{P(\neg Skin)} \quad (4)$$

Then, the equation (1) can be re-written as

$$P(Skin \mid YCbCr, L) = \frac{P(YCbCr \mid Skin, L)P(Skin, L)}{P(YCbCr \mid Skin, L)P(Skin, L) + P(YCbCr \mid \neg Skin, L)P(\neg Skin, L)} \quad (5)$$

Under the equal prior probability assumption of $P(Skin, L)$ and $P(\neg Skin, L)$, we get

$$P(Skin \mid YCbCr, L) = \frac{P(YCbCr \mid Skin, L)}{P(YCbCr \mid Skin, L) + P(RGB \mid \neg Skin, L)} \qquad (6)$$

A pixel is classified as skin if $P(Skin \mid YCbCr, L) \geq \theta$ where $\theta \in [0,1]$ is the threshold.

For deciding the threshold, the receiver operating characteristic (ROC) curve is drawn from the relationship between the correct and false detections as a function of the detection threshold θ. The selection is based on the fact that optimal value for the threshold should lie near the bend of the ROC curve [5]. Fig.3 gives skin color results of an images, which show that our method is better than single model.

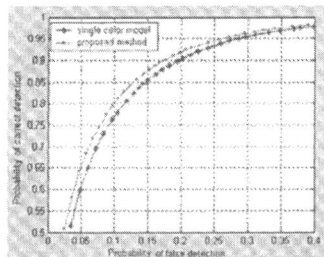

Fig. 2. The ROC curves of for skin color detection as a function of θ.

Fig. 3. Results of skin color detection. The first column is original image, the second column is the result of the single color model and the third is the result of presented method.

2.3 Skin Texture Detection

We cannot distinguish skin with other things only by color. There are too many things in nature that share same color with human skin, like desert, lion skin, yellow grass etc. Texture property should be employed to assist skin detection. In this paper, we use ACs to verify the smoothness of an 8×8 skin color block. As shown in Fig. 1, we use ② ③ ④ ⑤ to capture the skin texture information, which represent texture distribution from low frequency to high frequency [6]. Experiments show that the texture energy of the nature materials, which share color with skin like desert, yellow grass etc., mainly focuses in the middle frequencies. Therefore, in Fig.1 ③ ④ frequency bands will be assigned higher importance, and ② ⑤ will be assigned lower importance. A block will be skin texture block if the following equation holds,

$$\sum_{i=2}^{N} \left(e^{-(i-\mu)^2 / 2\sigma^2} \cdot \sqrt{s_i} \right) < T_s \qquad (7)$$

where s_i is the sum of the square of the ACs in the ith frequency band. N represents fives frequency bands as shown in Fig.1. T_s is the threshold. μ is set as 3.0 in the experiment, which represents the center frequency. σ is set as 2.0 according to Fig.1.

The threshold T_s is also determined as the method used to determine the skin color threshold in Sec.2.2. Fig. 4 shows two examples of skin texture process results.

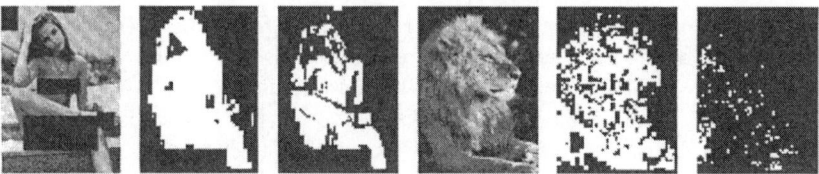

Fig. 4. Results of skin texture detection. From left to right: original image, mask by only skin color detection and mask by skin color detection and skin texture analysis.

3   Objectionable Image Recognition System

Based on the detected skin regions, we extract features to describe an image and the decision tree classifier is employed to classify it into objectionable or benign image.

3.1   Image Representation

In our work, the color feature and textures are extracted from skin mask, shape feature and statistical features are extracted from the dwindled (1/8) skin mask.
- Color features: percentage of skin color area
- Texture features: percentage of skin texture area, smoothness of the image
- Shape features: color moments, Zenike moments
- Statistical features: percentage of max connected skin area, the number of connected skin regions

3.2   Image Classification

After we obtain the trained model, the recognition system is built as

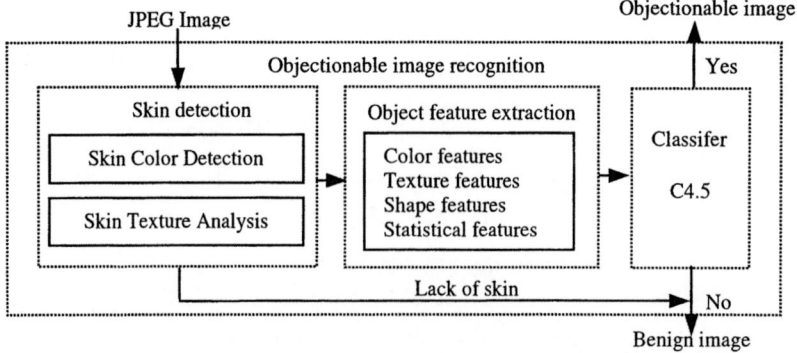

Fig. 5. Flow chart of the proposed objectionable image recognition system.

4 Experimental Result

In the field of information retrieval, the terms of precision and recall are widely used [7]. In this paper, we use accuracy instead of precision as

$$Recall = \frac{a}{c}, \; Accuracy = \frac{a+b}{c+d} \qquad (9)$$

where a is the number of truly positive case classified as positive case, b is the number of truly negative case predicted as positive case, c is the total number of truly positive case and d is the total number of truly negative case.

We build an image library that includes 117,695 images from Internet and Coredraw CDs. Images are manually divided into two categories: one is objectionable and the other is benign. Each time, 1/10 of the images are selected for training, and 9/10 of the images for test. The proportion of the objectionable images and benign images is set as 1:5. The average recall and accuracy is 79.2% and 92.2% respectively. The average processing speed is about 27 images/s on PC (Pentium IV 1.6GHZ CPU), which is much faster than that of the system [3] whose speed is about 1 image/s. For that experiments are completed on a much larger image library, the experimental result will be more robust compared with that of [3].

5 Summary and Acknowledge

A simple but robust objectionable Image recognition system in compressed domain is proposed in this paper. The recognition speed is much faster than that in spatial domain and can be easily extended to the MPEG video. This work is supported by National Hi-Tech Development Programs of China under grant No. 2001AA42140.

References

1. Margaret Fleck, David A.Forsyth, Chris Bregler.: Find Naked People. Pro. 4th European conference on Computer Vision: ECCV'96. Vol. 2. UK. (1996) 593–602
2. James Z. Wang, Jia Li, Gio Wiederhold, Oscar Firschein.: System for screening objectionable images. Computer Communications, Vol. 21, Elsevier. (1998) 1355–1360
3. Michael J. Jones and James M. Rehg.: Statistical Color Models with Application to Skin Detection. In Proceedings of CVPR. June (1999) 274–280
4. G.K. Wallace.: The JPEG Still Picture Compression Standard. Communications of the ACM, Vol. 34. April (1991) 31–44
5. Leonid Sigal, Stan Sclaroff, and Vassilis Athitsos.: Estimation and Prediction of Evolving Color Distributions for Skin Segmentation Under Varying Illumination. In Proceedings of CVPR. March (2000) 152–159
6. Hee-Jung Bae, Sung-Hwan Jung.: Image Retrieval Using texture based on DCT. ICICS'97. (1997) 1065–1068.
7. Raghavan, V., Bollmann, P., and Jung, G.: A critical investigation of recall and prcision as measures of retrieval system performance. ACM Trans. on Information Systems, vol. 7, issue 3. (1989) 205–229.

Author Index

Lecture Notes in Computer Science

For information about Vols. 1–2665
please contact your bookseller or Springer-Verlag

Vol. 2708: R. Reed, J. Reed (Eds.), SDL 2003: System Design. Proceedings, 2003. XI, 405 pages. 2003.

Vol. 2709: T. Windeatt, F. Roli (Eds.), Multiple Classifier Systems. Proceedings, 2003. X, 406 pages. 2003.

Vol. 2710: Z. Ésik, Z, Fülöp (Eds.), Developments in Language Theory. Proceedings, 2003. XI, 437 pages. 2003.

Vol. 2711: T.D. Nielsen, N.L. Zhang (Eds.), Symbolic and Quantitative Approaches to Reasoning with Uncertainty. Proceedings, 2003. XII, 608 pages. 2003. (Subseries LNAI).

Vol. 2712: A. James, B. Lings, M. Younas (Eds.), New Horizons in Information Management. Proceedings, 2003. XII, 281 pages. 2003.

Vol. 2713: C.-W. Chung, C.-K. Kim, W. Kim, T.-W. Ling, K.-H. Song (Eds.), Web and Communication Technologies and Internet-Related Social Issues – HSI 2003. Proceedings, 2003. XXII, 773 pages. 2003.

Vol. 2714: O. Kaynak, E. Alpaydin, E. Oja, L. Xu (Eds.), Artificial Neural Networks and Neural Information Processing – ICANN/ICONIP 2003. Proceedings, 2003. XXII, 1188 pages. 2003.

Vol. 2715: T. Bilgiç, B. De Baets, O. Kaynak (Eds.), Fuzzy Sets and Systems – IFSA 2003. Proceedings, 2003. XV, 735 pages. 2003. (Subseries LNAI).

Vol. 2716: M.J. Voss (Ed.), OpenMP Shared Memory Parallel Programming. Proceedings, 2003. VIII, 271 pages. 2003.

Vol. 2718: P. W. H. Chung, C. Hinde, M. Ali (Eds.), Developments in Applied Artificial Intelligence. Proceedings, 2003. XIV, 817 pages. 2003. (Subseries LNAI).

Vol. 2719: J.C.M. Baeten, J.K. Lenstra, J. Parrow, G.J. Woeginger (Eds.), Automata, Languages and Programming. Proceedings, 2003. XVIII, 1199 pages. 2003.

Vol. 2720: M. Marques Freire, P. Lorenz, M.M.-O. Lee (Eds.), High-Speed Networks and Multimedia Communications. Proceedings, 2003. XIII, 582 pages. 2003.

Vol. 2721: N.J. Mamede, J. Baptista, I. Trancoso, M. das Graças Volpe Nunes (Eds.), Computational Processing of the Portuguese Language. Proceedings, 2003. XIV, 268 pages. 2003. (Subseries LNAI).

Vol. 2722: J.M. Cueva Lovelle, B.M. González Rodríguez, L. Joyanes Aguilar, J.E. Labra Gayo, M. del Puerto Paule Ruiz (Eds.), Web Engineering. Proceedings, 2003. XIX, 554 pages. 2003.

Vol. 2723: E. Cantú-Paz, J.A. Foster, K. Deb, L.D. Davis, R. Roy, U.-M. O'Reilly, H.-G. Beyer, R. Standish, G. Kendall, S. Wilson, M. Harman, J. Wegener, D. Dasgupta, M.A. Potter, A.C. Schultz, K.A. Dowsland, N. Jonoska, J. Miller (Eds.), Genetic and Evolutionary Computation – GECCO 2003. Proceedings, Part I. 2003. XLVII, 1252 pages. 2003.

Vol. 2724: E. Cantú-Paz, J.A. Foster, K. Deb, L.D. Davis, R. Roy, U.-M. O'Reilly, H.-G. Beyer, R. Standish, G. Kendall, S. Wilson, M. Harman, J. Wegener, D. Dasgupta, M.A. Potter, A.C. Schultz, K.A. Dowsland, N. Jonoska, J. Miller (Eds.), Genetic and Evolutionary Computation – GECCO 2003. Proceedings, Part II. 2003. XLVII, 1274 pages. 2003.

Vol. 2725: W.A. Hunt, Jr., F. Somenzi (Eds.), Computer Aided Verification. Proceedings, 2003. XII, 462 pages. 2003.

Vol. 2726: E. Hancock, M. Vento (Eds.), Graph Based Representations in Pattern Recognition. Proceedings, 2003. VIII, 271 pages. 2003.

Vol. 2727: R. Safavi-Naini, J. Seberry (Eds.), Information Security and Privacy. Proceedings, 2003. XII, 534 pages. 2003.

Vol. 2728: E.M. Bakker, T.S. Huang, M.S. Lew, N. Sebe, X.S. Zhou (Eds.), Image and Video Retrieval. Proceedings, 2003. XIII, 512 pages. 2003.

Vol. 2729: D. Boneh (Ed.), Advances in Cryptology – CRYPTO 2003. Proceedings, 2003. XII, 631 pages. 2003.

Vol. 2731: C.S. Calude, M.J. Dinneen, V. Vajnovszki (Eds.), Discrete Mathematics and Theoretical Computer Science. Proceedings, 2003. VIII, 301 pages. 2003.

Vol. 2732: C. Taylor, J.A. Noble (Eds.), Information Processing in Medical Imaging. Proceedings, 2003. XVI, 698 pages. 2003.

Vol. 2733: A. Butz, A. Krüger, P. Olivier (Eds.), Smart Graphics. Proceedings, 2003. XI, 261 pages. 2003.

Vol. 2734: P. Perner, A. Rosenfeld (Eds.), Machine Learning and Data Mining in Pattern Recognition. Proceedings, 2003. XII, 440 pages. 2003. (Subseries LNAI).

Vol. 2741: F. Baader (Ed.), Automated Deduction – CADE-19. Proceedings, 2003. XII, 503 pages. 2003. (Subseries LNAI).

Vol. 2742: R. N. Wright (Ed.), Financial Cryptography. Proceedings, 2003. VIII, 321 pages. 2003.

Vol. 2743: L. Cardelli (Ed.), ECOOP 2003 – Object-Oriented Programming. Proceedings, 2003. X, 501 pages. 2003.

Vol. 2745: M. Guo, L.T. Yang (Eds.), Parallel and Distributed Processing and Applications. Proceedings, 2003. XII, 450 pages. 2003.

Vol. 2746: A. de Moor, W. Lex, B. Ganter (Eds.), Conceptual Structures for Knowledge Creation and Communication. Proceedings, 2003. XI, 405 pages. 2003. (Subseries LNAI).

Vol. 2748: F. Dehne, J.-R. Sack, M. Smid (Eds.), Algorithms and Data Structures. Proceedings, 2003. XII, 522 pages. 2003.

Vol. 2749: J. Bigun, T. Gustavsson (Eds.), Image Analysis. Proceedings, 2003. XXII, 1174 pages. 2003.

Vol. 2750: T. Hadzilacos, Y. Manolopoulos, J.F. Roddick, Y. Theodoridis (Eds.), Advances in Spatial and Temporal Databases. Proceedings, 2003. XIII, 525 pages. 2003.

Vol. 2751: A. Lingas, B.J. Nilsson (Eds.), Fundamentals of Computation Theory. Proceedings, 2003. XII, 433 pages. 2003.

Vol. 2752: G.A. Kaminka, P.U. Lima, R. Rojas (Eds.), RoboCup 2002: Robot Soccer World Cup VI. XVI, 498 pages. 2003. (Subseries LNAI).

Vol. 2753: F. Maurer, D. Wells (Eds.), Extreme Programming and Agile Methods – XP/Agile Universe 2003. Proceedings, 2003. XI, 215 pages. 2003.

Vol. 2758: D. Basin, B. Wolff (Eds.), Theorem Proving in Higher Order Logics. Proceedings, 2003. X, 367 pages. 2003.

Vol. 2759: O.H. Ibarra, Z. Dang (Eds.), Implementation and Application of Automata. Proceedings, 2003. XI, 312 pages. 2003.

Vol. 2762: G. Dong, C. Tang, W. Wang (Eds.), Advances in Web-Age Information Management. Proceedings, 2003. XIII, 512 pages. 2003.